THE OXFORD HAN

ROMAN STUDIES

The Oxford Handbook of Roman Studies is a unique collection of fifty-five articles which together explore the ways in which ancient Rome has been, is, and might be studied. It is intended less as an encyclopaedia of the well-established, and more a research tool to aid the development of the subject: a guide that does not just inform but also inspires. The emphasis is on the different ways in which evidence can be used, on the breadth and potential of Roman Studies, and on informing dialogue between its subdisciplines, with the aim of widening the perspective of readers as well as meeting their particular needs for information. The volume includes guidance on primary sources (especially useful in areas where this is complex, such as epigraphy and numismatics), and bibliographies of suggested reading.

Alessandro Barchiesi is Professor of Classics at New York University.

Walter Scheidel is Dickason Professor in the Humanities and Professor of Classics and History at Stanford University.

Praise for *The Oxford Handbook of Roman Studies*

'This volume on Roman studies certainly follows a wide and open-minded concept. Far from claiming a totalizing view on the Roman world, it offers in fact what it aims to offer: orientation, but also very much to think about what Roman studies could be, by content and form.'

Bryn Mawr Classical Review

'*The Oxford Handbook of Roman Studies* is a very important collective work . . . The volume is much more than a reference book: it can be read for its own sake with much profit and interest.'

Mikolaj Szymanski, *Eos*

THE OXFORD HANDBOOK OF

ROMAN STUDIES

Edited by
ALESSANDRO BARCHIESI
and
WALTER SCHEIDEL

OXFORD
UNIVERSITY PRESS

OXFORD
UNIVERSITY PRESS

Great Clarendon Street, Oxford, OX2 6DP,
United Kingdom

Oxford University Press is a department of the University of Oxford.
It furthers the Universitys objective of excellence in research, scholarship,
and education by publishing worldwide. Oxford is a registered trade mark of
Oxford University Press in the UK and in certain other countries

First published 2010
Reprinted 2013
First published in paperback 2019

Published in the United States of America by Oxford University Press
198 Madison Avenue, New York, NY 10016, United States of America

British Library Cataloguing in Publication Data
Data available

Library of Congress Cataloging in Publication Data
Data available

ISBN 978–0–19–921152–4 (Hbk.)
ISBN 978–0–19–885600–9 (Pbk.)

Cover illustration: Foot of the colossal statue of the Roman emperor
Constantine from the Basilica of Constantine (c.313–330 CE),
now in the Palazzo dei Conservatori, Rome. Photo: Darian Totten.

Contents

PART II APPROACHES

PART III GENRES

PART IV HISTORY

List of Illustrations

List of Contributors

Clifford Ando is David B. and Clara E. Stern Professor and Professor of Classics, History and Law at the University of Chicago. He is an historian of religion, law and government in the Roman Empire.

Roger S. Bagnall is Emeritus Professor of Ancient History and Director of the Institute for the Study of the Ancient World (Emeritus) at New York University. He is a papyrologist and historian of Hellenistic, Roman, and Late Antique Egypt.

Peter Fibiger Bang is Associate Professor of History at the University of Copenhagen. He works on the comparative economic history and political economy of early empires.

Alessandro Barchiesi is Professor of Classics at New York University. He works on Roman poetic texts and fiction, and on the impact of modern literary-critical approaches; he is general editor of a multi-authored commentary on Ovid's Metamorphoses.

Maurizio Bettini is Professor of Classical Philology (Emeritus) and Director of the Centro Antropologia e Mondo Antico (AMA) at the University of Siena. He is also Visiting Professor of Classics at the University of California, Berkeley. His main fields of research are Anthropology and the Classics, Latin Literature, Historical Linguistics, and Metrics.

John Bodel is W. Duncan MacMillan II Professor of Classics and History at Brown University. He writes about Latin epigraphy and literature, Roman social history and religion, and ancient slavery.

Keith Bradley is the Eli J. and Helen Shaheen Professor of Classics Emeritus at the University of Notre Dame and Adjunct Professor in the Department of Greek and Roman Studies at the University of Victoria. He is an ancient historian who specializes in the field of Roman social relations.

Susanna Braund is Professor of Latin Poetry and its Reception and holds a Canada Research Chair in Latin Poetry and its Reception at the University of British Columbia. Her current research interests include the translation histories of Virgil, Lucan, and Seneca's tragedies into European languages from the Renaissance to the modern day.

Kai Brodersen is Professor of Ancient Culture in, and former President of, the University of Erfurt in Germany. His research covers Greek and Roman historiography and geography, ancient inscriptions, oracles and wonder-texts, social and economic history, and reception studies (including Asterix).

Kathleen M. Coleman is James Loeb Professor of the Classics at Harvard University. She specializes in the literature and culture of the early Roman Empire, including spectacle and punishment, and has published commentaries on two volumes of Flavian poetry, Statius, Silvae IV and Martial, Liber Spectaculorum.

Joy Connolly is the President of the American Council of Learned Societies. She works on ancient rhetoric, political thought, Latin poetry, and the reception of classical thought from the seventeenth century to today, and has published about the relevance of Roman republicanism for the contemporary world.

Anthony Corbeill is Basil L. Gildersleeve Professor of Classics at the University of Virginia. He has published books on political humour and gesture in Roman society and a volume on the boundaries of sex and gender in ancient Rome.

Emma Dench is McLean Professor of Ancient and Modern History and of the Classics at Harvard University. Her work focuses on Roman cultural history.

Mario De Nonno is Professor of Latin Literature at 'Roma Tre' University in Rome. He has mainly worked on the textual tradition and significance of Latin grammarians, metricians, and scholarly authors, and on topics related to the school and the book in the Roman Empire.

Florence Dupont is Professeur de Latin at the University of Paris VII (Emerita), and member of the Centre Gernet, Recherches sur les Sociétés Anciennes. She is the author of numerous books on Roman performance culture, including theatre, oratory, politics, and daily interactions.

Jennifer Ebbeler is Associate Professor of Classics at University of Texas, Austin. Her research interests are Latin literature, epistolography, and late antique literary and cultural history.

Werner Eck is Professor Emeritus of Ancient History at the University of Cologne. He has worked especially on the political, administrative, and social history of the Roman Empire on the basis of prosopography and Greek and Latin inscriptions.

Joseph Farrell is Professor of Classical Studies at the University of Pennsylvania. His main teaching and research interest is Roman poetry of the Republican and Augustan periods.

Denis Feeney is Giger Professor of Latin at Princeton University. He has published on Roman time, on translation, and on the interaction between Roman religion and literature.

Ellen Finkelpearl is Professor of Classics at Scripps College. Her work has focused on the Roman author Apuleius and the ancient novel.

Rebecca Flemming is Senior Lecturer in Classics and Ancient History at the University of Cambridge, and a fellow of Jesus College. She is a social and cultural historian of the Roman world.

Harriet I. Flower is Andrew Fleming West Professor of Classics at Princeton University. She is a Roman historian who works on social, political, and cultural history, with a special interest in the Roman Republic. Much of her work has focused on themes of memory or of spectacle within the city of Rome.

Philip Hardie is a Senior Research Fellow at Trinity College, Cambridge, and Emeritus Honorary Professor of Latin Literature in the University of Cambridge. His interests range widely across Latin literature and its reception.

Jill Harries is Professor of Ancient History at the University of St Andrews in Scotland. She has published on the Later Roman Empire and Roman legal history.

William V. Harris taught in the History Department at Columbia for many years. His book *Roman Power: A Thousand Years of Empire* came out with Cambridge University Press in 2016.

Stephen Hinds is Professor of Classics at the University of Washington in Seattle. With Denis Feeney, he co-edited the Cambridge book series 'Roman Literature and its Contexts' (fourteen volumes between 1993 and 2016); his own research interests are in Roman poetry and its (early) modern receptions.

Henry Hurst is University Reader in Classical Archaeology (Emeritus) and Fellow of Churchill College, Cambridge. Main research interests are in Roman archaeology, particularly the archaeology of cities with special reference to Rome, Carthage, and Gloucester.

Robert A. Kaster is Professor of Classics, Emeritus, and Kennedy Foundation Professor of Latin Language and Literature, Emeritus, at Princeton University. He has taught and written mainly in the areas of Roman rhetoric, the history of ancient education, Roman ethics, the history of emotions, and has worked on the transmission and textual criticism of various Latin authors.

Joshua T. Katz is Professor of Classics and Director of the Program in Linguistics at Princeton University. He is broadly interested in the languages, literatures, and cultures of the ancient world and has recently published a number of articles on wordplay.

Paul T. Keyser's publications include work on gravitational physics, computer science, stylometry, Greek tragedy, and especially ancient science and technology. Formerly a teacher of Classics, he is currently crafting Java for IBM's Watson Research Center.

Christina Shuttleworth Kraus is the Thomas A. Thacher Professor of Classics at Yale. She has published on Latin historiography (especially Livy and Caesar) and on the classical commentary, and, with A. J. Woodman, a commentary on Tacitus' Agricola.

Andrew Laird, is John Rowe Workman Distinguished Professor of Classics and the Humanities at Brown. He has published on a number of Latin authors, including Catullus, Virgil, and Apuleius. His current interests are in Roman literary biography and the traditions of Latin humanism in Italy and colonial Spanish America.

Eugenio La Rocca is Professor of Greek and Roman Archaeology (Emeritus) at the University of Rome 'La Sapienza'. His main fields of research are Greek and Roman art and the archaeology and topography of Rome.

Richard Lim, Professor of History at Smith College, teaches the history of the ancient Mediterranean and Near East. His research focuses on the cultural and religious history of late antiquity, and he is currently finishing a book project on the reception of public spectacles during the later Roman Empire.

Michèle Lowrie, Andrew W. Mellon Professor of Classics and the College at the University of Chicago, works on Roman literature and culture, especially in the Republican and Augustan periods.

Kathleen McCarthy is Professor of Classics at the University of California at Berkeley. Her current research interests focus on the relationships between narrative, address, and audience in first-person Latin poetry.

William E. Metcalf is Professor (Adj.) of Classics at Yale, Emeritus, and Ben Lee Damsky Curator of Coins and Medals at the Yale University Art Gallery, Emeritus. He works mainly on Roman and Roman provincial coinage.

Kristina Milnor is Tow Family Foundation Associate Professor of Classics at Barnard College. Her book Gender, Domesticity, and the Age of Augustus: Inventing Private Life won the 2006 Goodwin Award of Merit from the American Philological Association.

Llewelyn Morgan is a University Lecturer in Classical Languages and Literature at Oxford University, and Tutorial Fellow at Brasenose College. He has research interests in many aspects of Latin literature.

Carlos F. Noreña is Associate Professor of History at the University of California at Berkeley. He works on the history of the Roman Empire, and has published a book on the figure of the Roman emperor as a unifying symbol for the western empire.

James J. O'Donnell is Professor of Historical, Philosophical, and Religious Studies and University Librarian at Arizona State University. His most recent books are *Pagans*, and *Caesar: The war for Gaul.*

Ellen Oliensis is Professor of Classics at University of California at Berkeley. Her research centres on late Republican and early Imperial poetry, and her latest book is *Loving Writing/Ovid's Amores.*

Nicholas Purcell is Camden Professor of Ancient History at the University of Oxford and Fellow of Brasenose College. He works on Roman social, economic, and cultural history, and is particularly interested in the long-term history of the Mediterranean world.

Beryl Rawson(†) was Professor Emerita and Adjunct Professor in Classics at the Australian National University in Canberra. Her research interests were in the social, cultural, and political history of ancient Rome and iconography and epigraphy, with special focus on the Roman family.

Andrew Riggsby is Lucy Shoe Merritt Professor in Classics and Professor of Art History at the University of Texas at Austin and is author of *Crime and Community in Ciceronian Rome and War in Words: Caesar in Gaul and Rome.* His research interests are in the cultural history of Roman political institutions and in cognitive history.

Matthew Roller is Professor and Chair of Classics at Johns Hopkins University. As a Romanist, he is engaged with the literature, history, art, philosophy, and culture generally of the ancient Roman world. He has worked in recent years on imperial ideology in the Julio-Claudian period, on various questions related to Roman dining, and on Roman exempla.

Charles Brian Rose is James B. Pritchard Professor of Mediterranean Archaeology, University of Pennsylvania. Since 1988 he has been Head of Post-Bronze Age excavations at Troy, and is English-language editor of Studia Troica, the annual journal of the Troy excavations.

Jörg Rüpke is Historian of Religion and Co-Director of the International research group 'Religious Individualization in Historical Perspective' of the Max Weber Centre of the University of Erfurt. His special research interests are ancient Roman and Mediterranean religions.

Walter Scheidel is Dickason Professor in the Humanities and Professor of Classics and History at Stanford University. His work focuses on ancient social and economic history, premodern historical demography, and comparative and transdisciplinary history.

Seth Schwartz is Lucius N. Littauer Professor of Classical Jewish Civilization, and Professor of History and Classics at Columbia University. He works on the social and cultural history of the Jews in antiquity.

David Sedley is Laurence Professor (Emeritus) of Ancient Philosophy at the University of Cambridge, where he is also a Fellow of Christ's College. His research ranges widely over Greco-Roman philosophy, including the editing of philosophical papyri.

Hagith Sivan is Professor of History (Emerita) at the University of Kansas. Her interests include late antiquity (in its broadest sense) and the Hebrew Bible.

Nicola Terrenato is Esther B. Van Deman Collegiate Professor of Classical Archaeology at the University of Michigan. He directs the excavations at Gabii and has worked on early Central Italy, Roman conquest, and field survey methodology.

Edmund Thomas is associate professor in Ancient Visual and Material Culture at Durham University. His main research interest is Roman architecture and its relation to Roman society and culture.

Alfonso Traina(†) was Professor (Emeritus) of Latin Literature at the University of Bologna. He has been a leading scholar in the study of poetic and literary style and of Roman literary history, and has done influential work on translation, literary bilingualism, sound patterns, and the psychological and ideological aspects of literary form.

Tim Whitmarsh is A. G. Leventis Professor of Greek Culture, University of Cambridge. He is a specialist in the literature and culture of Greece in the Roman period.

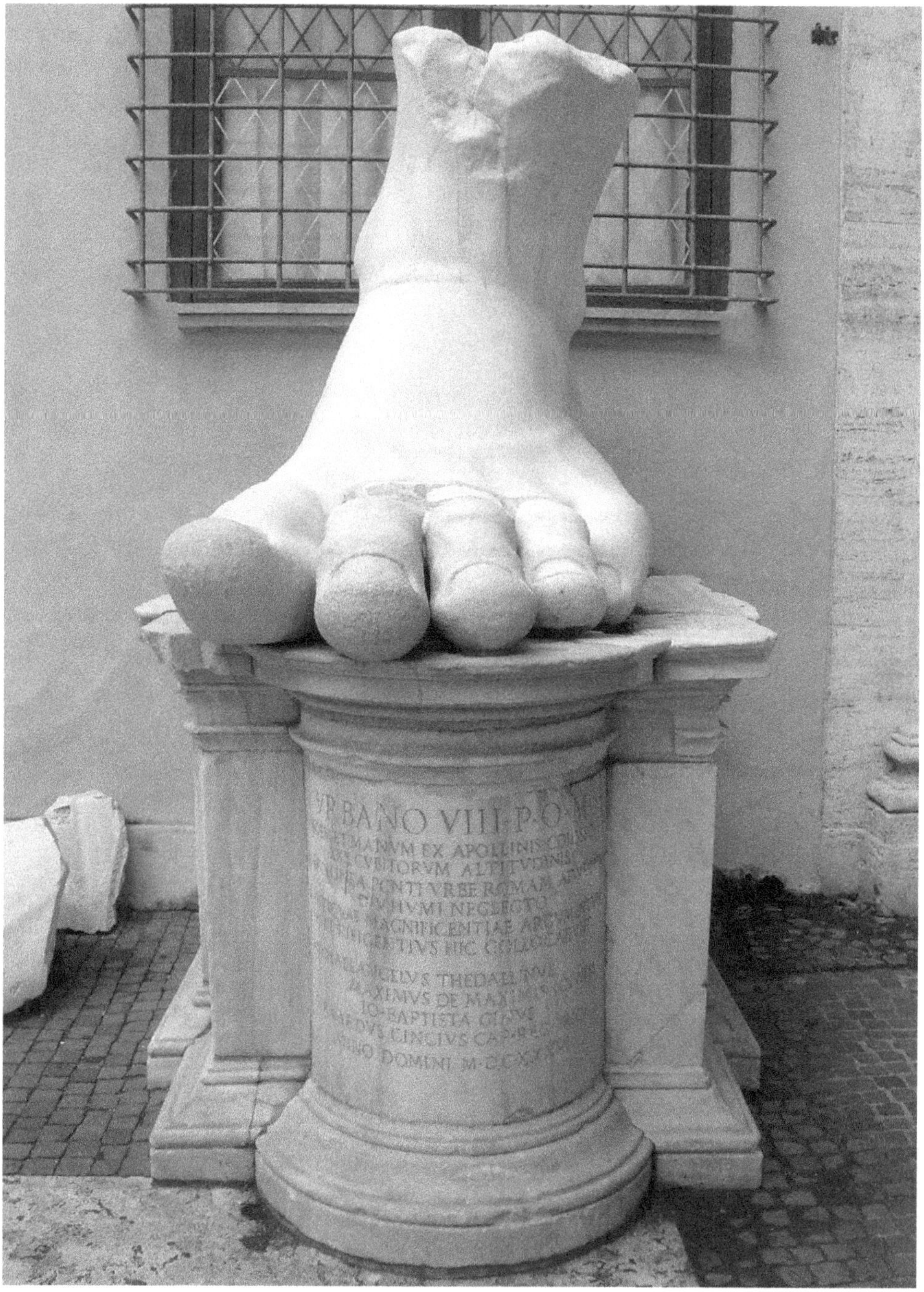

Frontispiece: Foot of the colossal statue of the Roman emperor Constantine from the Basilica of Constantine (c.313–330 CE), now in the Palazzo dei Conservatori, Rome. Photograph: Darian Totten

INTRODUCTION

ALESSANDRO BARCHIESI
WALTER SCHEIDEL

Roman Studies defies straightforward definition in large part because of the sheer size and depth of the footprint of the Roman Empire. Constantine's giant foot, pictured on the front cover and as a frontispiece, illustrates this crucial point. A marble fragment of a colossal—originally close to 10 metres tall—seated statue of the equally colossally named Imperator Constantinus, Victor, Maximus Augustus, Pontifex Maximus, Pater Patriae, Proconsul, Triumphator Omnium Gentium, Restitutor Libertatis, Restitutor Totius Orbis, Germanicus Maximus, Sarmaticus Maximus, Britannicus Maximus, Persicus Maximus, Adiabenicus Maximus, Medicus Maximus, Gothicus Maximus, Carpicus Maximus, Arabicus Maximus, Armenicus Maximus, Dacicus Maximus (r. 306–37 CE) now on display at the Palazzo dei Conservatori in Rome, it speaks loudly of the power of the largest and most durable empire ever created in Eurasia west of Russia. But at the same time the emperor's foot symbolizes the utter ruination of Roman civilization, reduced to Ozymandian rubble. It stands for the seismic shift from universal empire to the dynamic environment of polycentrism and competition that became a hallmark of medieval and modern Europe. Belonging as it does to the first Roman ruler to embrace the expanding Christian faith, Constantine's foot straddles the divide between religious pluralism and the new monotheism, and between the image of the gargantuan god-king reaching back to the days of the Pharaohs and universal subordination to a deity who suffered no earthly rivals.

As such, it foreshadowed what has arguably become the weightiest legacy of Rome, the Constantinian turn that put a particular brand of Christianity on a path to claiming some 2 billion (effective or nominal) adherents in the world today. No wonder that, in 1635, Pope Urban VIII placed the imperial foot on the massive pedestal on which it has rested ever since. Yet it was a secular movement that heaved Roman civilization as a whole onto a metaphorical pedestal. In the eighteenth century, as European powers began to dominate the globe, its intellectuals came up with a radical new theory to account for this success: European superiority was derived not from Christianity but from a cultural tradition that began in ancient Greece. The Greeks invented freedom and rationality; Rome then spread these gifts across Europe. This was why only Europe had a Scientific Revolution and an Enlightenment; and why Europe was now colonizing the other continents. Anyone who wanted to understand the world had to begin with the history, literature, and art of Greece and Rome. Even if Roman Studies has in the meantime stepped down—or may still be in the process of being brought down—from this neo-humanistic pedestal, all these manifold continuities and discontinuities highlight the richness and bewildering complexity of our relationship with the Roman past: alien and distant, as the giant marble foot; broken down and finished, as the authority and specious permanence of the Roman Empire; but at the same time still very much with us, through the many ways in which what took place in the Mediterranean fifty or a hundred generations ago continues to shape the present.

Roman Studies does not represent an established academic discipline in the way that philology, history, or archaeology have developed into discrete fields with their own departments and degrees. When the Society for the Promotion of Roman Studies was first set up in London a century ago, it sought 'to promote the study of the history, archaeology, and art of Italy and the Roman Empire, from the earliest times down to about A.D. 700'.[1] As such, Roman Studies not only cuts across conventional disciplinary boundaries but also liberally extends the notion of 'Roman-ness' across a variety of cultures from the Atlantic into the Middle East. From this perspective, Roman Studies becomes the study of everything once covered by the Roman state, nothing less than perhaps a quarter of humanity during the first few centuries CE.

In his inaugural address delivered at the first annual meeting of the newly founded Society on 11 May 1911, Francis Haverfield, the Camden Professor of Ancient History at Oxford and an expert on the Roman remains of Britain, emphasized the need for professional training to support research into all aspects of the history and material culture of the Roman Empire that had thus far been overshadowed by a preoccupation with Greek and Latin language and literature. This broadening in scope was bound to reveal more of the complexity of the Roman past and consequently required greater efforts to come to terms with it: Haverfield's judgement that, 'if the study has grown harder, the rewards for the

[1] 'Memorandum of Association of the Society for the Promotion of Roman Studies', *Journal of Roman Studies*, 1 (1911), 249.

student have become immensely more abundant', seems as true today as it was then.[2]

And yet, what are these rewards? To paraphrase a famous exchange from the 1979 comedy movie *Monty Python's Life of Brian*, what has Roman Studies ever done for us? It was tempting for Haverfield to consider it 'at the present day the most instructive of all histories'. After all, did the constitution of the Roman Republic not offer 'the one true analogy to the seeming waywardness of our own English constitution'; or did the Roman imperial system not 'light up our own Empire, for example in India, at every turn'; and did not 'the forces which laid the Roman empire low concern the modern world very nearly, more nearly indeed than do the reasons for the downfall of any other empire about which we have full knowledge'? Sweeping analogies that rediscover the past in the present and the present in the past may seem quaint today, as academic professionalization and the intellectual detachment it encourages has made the Roman world seem more remote, exotic, and thus more different than it may have appeared to previous generations of observers.[3]

At the same time, this process has by no means resulted in the creation of a single, hegemonic approach to Roman Studies. Instead, the Anglo-Saxon tradition of 'Classics'—the study of all aspects of the Greco-Roman world under the umbrella of a single academic programme or department—continues to uphold a claim for the exclusive character of this endeavour, an exclusivity that is implicit not merely in the very term 'classic(al)' but also in this field's separation from the study of more recent periods that is conventionally divided among different disciplines such as Archaeology, Art History, Comparative Literature, History, Modern Languages, Philosophy, and Religious Studies. (In this respect, Classics has long foreshadowed recent transdisciplinary trends in ever-expanding fields such as English and Cultural Studies.) The location of Roman Studies within Classics entails a notion of guardianship, of preserving and increasing our knowledge of cultures that owe their privileged status in the present to putatively unique traits or their putative influence on what is in similarly loaded terms labelled 'Western Civilization'. Alternatively, Roman Studies might be considered an early specimen of the transdisciplinary institution of 'Area Studies', devoid of preferential treatment but intellectually useful in coordinating and contextualizing the efforts of archaeologists, historians, linguists, and literary critics—and indeed anthropologists, artists, botanists, climatologists, economists, geologists, philosophers, political scientists, psychologists, sociologists, zoologists, and many

[2] F. Haverfield, 'An Inaugural Address Delivered Before the First Annual General Meeting of the Society, 11th May, 1911', *Journal of Roman Studies*, 1 (1911), pp. xi–xx.

[3] To be sure, this shift must not be exaggerated: witness the flood of recent publications likening the United States to the Roman Empire, one of them by blithely asking, *Are We Rome?* Vaclav Smil's forthcoming book *Why America is Not a New Rome* gives the right answer.

others—who share an interest in the period and territory circumscribed by the Roman Empire, in the legacy of its cultural production, and in our engagement with this legacy. Returning once more to the question of 'rewards', this approach yields benefits more diffuse than those envisaged by Haverfield, in the most general sense by adding to and refining our understanding of human behaviour through the study of the past, an objective that—amongst fellow humans—should require no further justification.

We have tried to imagine at least three specific categories of readers who will find something of interest in this collection: the first is made up, quite obviously, of students and scholars in their formative stages. A successful career often depends on a highly personal and individual approach, and people are drawn towards the study of antiquity for a wide variety of reasons; after the initial impulse they are also encouraged to specialize quickly. At some stage, during the learning process or the first research experiments, it can be helpful to glance at the entire panorama of what has been done or attempted with the past. The second category is the 'good neighbour'; fortunately for the profession of Classics, a substantial number of neighbouring disciplines maintain an interest in developments in the study of Roman civilization. This book intends to offer updated points of access for many intellectual trajectories of enquiry that are concerned with the modern world, or different 'antiquities', or even science. The third category is ourselves—not the two of us as individuals, but as scholars and teachers of Roman matters in general: in the process of editing this group of essays we have been surprised by the number and range of questions that can be asked about Roman antiquity and remain out of sight for us while we engage in our daily work or cultural practice.

This feeling of disconnectedness is particularly strong across the divide that has (quite literally) been papered over by our choice to produce a handbook of 'Roman Studies': that between the literary and the historical, between approaches to philology and material culture.[4] While most of the authors of chapters on history, society, law, and the arts would be happy, we presume, to identify themselves as 'Romanists' (on top of being 'historians', 'archaeologists', and so on), an expert on Latin texts from the Roman age is and remains a 'Latinist'. The term carries ideological baggage: it reminds us of a language that—whilst hardly counting as 'alive'—has nevertheless refused to 'die' like many other pre-modern languages. The study of Latin literature and related forms of expression remained important in medieval and early modern Europe, in literary history and in diverse areas such as religion, history of thought, science, and postcolonial studies. The evolution of 'Latin Studies' even differs in outlook from Roman antiquarian and historical studies. It is rooted in early modern Europe, not in the seventeenth and eighteenth centuries as is the case with professional history and

[4] For a Hellenic reconciliation, cf. now R. P. Martin, 'Words Alone Are Certain Good(s): Philology and Greek Material Culture', *Transactions of the American Philological Association*, 138 (2008), 313–49.

antiquarianism, and has a strong formalist and textual aspect. Of course, as so often, form is just a different name for politics. Debates on 'Latinity' in Italian Humanism, for example, were enmeshed in power structures, social distinction, and religious politics. Textual criticism began, with scholars such as Politian and Valla, at a time when disenfranchised intellectuals enjoyed growing influence. Later on the advent of national systems of education in Europe became the crucial factor: 'Latin' was turned into a massive, yet also elitist, educational practice. (We regret not having a separate chapter on modern education: this is perhaps the most glaring gap in our line-up.)

As a result, the Latinist has long been a specialist of form, grammar, and style. This tradition still loomed large when the founders of the Society for the Promotion of Roman Studies surveyed their resources back in 1911. Initially, they chose to ignore literature, and with reason. Their initiative was propelled by (at least) three driving forces, all of them of significance in the competitive environment of the early 1900s: the accelerating pace of archaeological discovery; the increasing importance of 'territorial' knowledge and national heritage; and the spectacular success of Mommsen and his German 'science of antiquity'. In many ways the study of Latin literature and philology had been lagging behind. Germany was home to the leading academic community of the late nineteenth century, and Latin studies in that country had long nurtured an inferiority complex towards Hellenists. The decisive impulse for serious 'Latin studies' at the university level came from a generation slightly later than that of the foundational scholars of ancient history, philosophy, or Greek literature: the breakthrough came too late for the 'Roman Studies' meeting of 1911, and was felt outside Germany only after World War I. The work of Friedrich Leo, Richard Heinze, Eduard Norden, and later Eduard Fraenkel was based on two principles: taking the typical Roman practices of imitation and Hellenization as a serious topic of research, and applying a rigorous historicizing model. This model was intellectually superior to other European traditions, but the decisive factor for its dissemination was the diaspora of Jewish and other German-speaking intellectuals from Nazi Germany to Britain, the United States, and other destinations.

Back in 1911, even the Roman Society felt the need to accommodate Latin letters. This task, an afterthought, fell to the Labourite politician and enlightened Classicist John William Mackail, who two years later tackled the problem of establishing the importance of Latin authors within the new project. In 'Virgil and Roman Studies' he claimed that, 'Year by year, almost day by day, we are getting more into touch with the ancient world, as something alive and solid': our appreciation of a classical author such as Virgil had to be revised accordingly. Mackail's public address was marked by enthusiasm about new archaeological discoveries: it ended with a visionary parallel between Virgil's exploring the labyrinth at Cumae and reports of a spooky Cretan night spent by Manolis Akumianakis, the foreman of Sir Arthur Evans, at Knossos.[5] Latin studies, however, were never fully harmonized with these novel concerns. The historicizing turn typical of Leo's generation had strong motivations: it was a basic requirement of a new professionalism (an unavoidable trend in the new system of research-based institutions of knowledge), and offered a clean break with centuries of dilettanti and school grammarians. Artificial grammatical study abated (at least to some extent); textual criticism was retooled; literary studies acquired a promising perspective on Rome's cultural hybridity. The only breaking-point of this tradition was the increasing need to imagine historicism as a foreclosing of modern perspectives. It was one thing to issue a clarion call towards readings of Latin literature within a Roman cultural and social context; yet another actively to discourage questions that could not be framed in 'Latinized' terms of reference. That way, historicism became its own worst enemy, and revived a recurring temptation of studies of Latinitas, that of obsessive formalism. A reopening of the literary field was necessary, and for many of us is still ongoing. But the question, then as now, remains which competing approaches to history are leading 'Roman Studies', and what kind of approach to the textual material is more suited to a dialogue between historians and literary scholars, or to a productive disagreement? It is too early for us to say whether a dialogue between 'Latinists' and 'Romanists' will continue and how, or indeed whether, such labels will retain any validity, but in the meantime we have been experimenting with cohabitation between two book covers.

For all these reasons it is hard for a handbook to do justice to the sweep and intricacies of Roman—and Latin—Studies.[6] Loosely grouped into five sections focusing on the tools needed to unlock the Roman past, on theoretical approaches, literary genres, historical change over time, and key elements of cognition, all these fifty-five chapters can hope to do is convey a taste of what this field has to offer. By combining factual information with suggestive ideas, their authors seek to shape as well as describe and interpret scholarly practice. Emphasis on one or the other varies from chapter to chapter, reflecting therein the different traditions and expectations that a diverse set of scholars has brought to this collaborative project. Reinforced by the transnational character of pertinent scholarship, this eclecticism is very much an inevitable consequence of the lack of a single 'party line', of a fully 'disciplined' academic field of Roman Studies. Often more of an ideal than established practice, Roman Studies will—and indeed ought to—continue to mean different things to different practitioners and audiences. Orientation, therefore, is our main goal.[7]

[5] J. W. Mackail, 'Virgil and Roman Studies', *Journal of Roman Studies*, 3 (1913), 1–24.

[6] For overlapping and complementary surveys, see now especially G. Boys-Stones, B. Graziosi, and P. Vasunia (eds.), *The Oxford Handbook of Hellenic Studies* (Oxford, 2009); S. A. Harvey and D. Hunter (eds.), *The Oxford Handbook of Early Christian Studies* (Oxford, 2008); and E. Jeffreys, J. Haldon, and R. Cormack (eds.), *The Oxford Handbook of Byzantine Studies* (Oxford, 2008).

[7] Abbreviations in the text are generally those used in *The Oxford Classical Dictionary*, 3rd edn., ed. S. Hornblower and A. Spawforth (Oxford, 2003).

CHAPTER 1

NEW MEDIA (AND OLD)

JAMES J. O'DONNELL

THE gnomic sages complement and contradict one another. 'You cannot step in the same river twice', said Heraclitus, but 'The content of a new medium is an older medium', said McLuhan (McLuhan 1965: 8). Every generation's innovation in the means of communication presents itself at the outset *as though* it were merely a plunge into familiar waters. To think about the fate and future of Roman Studies in an age of technological revolution, we must begin as boats against the current.

In the beginning—no, there was no beginning. 'Roman Studies' do not descend from a Big Bang of formation in crisis, much less do they come about as the result of Intelligent Design by a benign and supervising deity. Rather, they accrete like a coral reef, where the fact of beginning is only visible long after, when elaborate development has made it clear which inklings would emerge as solid foundations—or obstacles—for understanding. This chapter will attempt to situate the present moment of our practices by capturing a picture of the reef as it now stands, some sections hoary with seaweed and neglect, others offering jagged and threatening edges, others still preserving bits of flotsam and jetsam drifted in from other atolls.

The onrush of new technologies and media of communication in our time betoken far-reaching changes in the way humankind consumes, produces, and transmits knowledge—*a fortiori*, the particular kind of knowledge about our pasts that scholars create and transmit. A materialist history of classical scholarship is overdue to be written, but if it existed, it would make this chapter easier to write and read. Nepos, alas, remains the patron saint of the history of scholarship, and so to speak of the present will require some framing of the past.

But start here. An essay on the history, present, and future of classical scholarship knows how it should start. *Compositio loci*, as the old Jesuits would say: vivid imagination of scholars in their workplace. If we were determined to be conventional, the chances are good that we would have found an anecdote about Bentley or Erasmus or Photius or Cassiodorus or Varro or Callimachus to place on the first page. I might myself have preferred the story from Sandys's *History of Classical Scholarship* about the German worthy who declined an invitation in the nineteenth century to spend the winter in Italy. 'What', I would quote Lobeck to say, 'is this that I hear, my dear friend? I can hardly believe my ears. Are you *really* wanting to go to Italy? Why Italy, of all parts of the world? NO! If I cannot visit Niagara, or the Mississippi, or Hekla, I prefer sitting here beside my own warm stove, reading GREEK SCHOLIASTS—which is, after all, the true end of the life of man' (Sandys 1903–8: 104).

I have quoted that anecdote over more dinner tables than Sandys might have imagined, but I'll only come back to it after a different *compositio loci*. This chapter has been in my head for weeks, with scattered notes, but the scholarly primal scene of fertilization and creation in which I begin writing the first draft of the *actual text* is a fresh one. I wrote the first words (now long since deleted) on a laptop computer, sitting in the window seat on a railroad train entering Baltimore on a Sunday afternoon in spring, frustrated that we do not yet have wireless networking capabilities sufficient to let my laptop have full access to the riches of information of the Internet. First, the laptop itself holds a small ocean of downloaded materials, including, for example, the complete Latin works of Augustine. The formal and magisterial Augustine, who not long ago lived only in long rows of volumes on bookshelves in privileged places, now rides trains and a few months ago mailed himself around on a mini-CD sent through the post inside a greeting card. I have a primitive gadget (technology, that is, of a year ago) along with me that does have some network capability, and lets me tell how late my train will be (modestly), what the weather will be like (summery and humid), and even confirm that I told the one about the scholar by his stove in a book review in an online journal thirteen years ago. The same gadget brings me electronic mail that has nothing to do with this essay and lets me, depending how I like to think about it, productively multitask or distract myself from the business at hand. That handheld will be replaced by more and more powerful devices in the next years, or rather months, ones that be phones and cameras and music players and emailers and web browsers and GPS locators and... I also use the same laptop to write and do e-mail while lying in a hammock outside my home, and cannot decide at all whether this is better than working at my desk or worse than lying in the hammock reading Orhan Pamuk. (The *penultima manus* has been applied to these pages in November 2006 on the same laptop in a hotel lounge in Cairo, lifting my eyes every few minutes to a view of the great pyramid in the distance at sunset.)

But the devices are secondary to the reader who uses them, and it is the evolution of textual practices that this chapter will follow, not the history of electromechanical devices. Let me start with the scholiast-reader by the stove.

He embodies the main tropes of the classical age of classical scholarship to a tee. He is, first of all, German. He has countrymen who will elaborately explain that their ancestors were the essential un-Romans, the *Germani* who overthrew the Roman Empire, but from the late eighteenth century until World War II classical philology went to live in Germany. The crafts practised in those decades elsewhere in Europe, all embodying older traditions of great worth, seemed in those decades amateurish and derivative. The professionalization of American classical scholarship happily dates itself to the voyages of scholars like Gildersleeve to study in German institutions, while comic relief can be found in the wanderings of James Henry, the Irishman obsessed with Virgil, who chronicled his wanderings afoot in Germany with his daughter in diaristic verse of surpassing awfulness recounting very serious studies in the manuscript transmission of the poet. In observing that transfer of the heartland of classical scholarship to Germany, as in its arguable retransfer to the United States in the post-World War II world, we make visible the principal fact of Roman Studies as of all classical scholarship: the here and now (Germany in the nineteenth century, the United States today) take precedence over the there and then, and the media of choice of the here and now threaten to obscure and efface the media by which Rome's traces come to us. The double dislocation of time and space is accepted and normalized.

The dislocation of time and space also has the effect of privileging text over artefact—the bound volume suitable for reading by a stove in Germany over the statues with broken noses that can be visited in Italy. More precisely, we regularly read inscriptions in volumes of *CIL* or *SEG*, where the performative and ostensive character of the (often surviving original) is elided in favour of normalization, linearity, and textuality. The text is, as we say too conventionally but quite truly today, a constructed idea about reality, the supposedly consistent and persistent thing that migrates from one manuscript to another, thence into one printed edition after another. I used, when young, to boast to an art historian of my acquaintance that while he needed to go to Spain to see the real paintings he was working on, I could hold the real Virgil or Augustine in my hands. I spoke an untruth that all agree to be valid and important.

Even, or rather especially, for the literary text, the elision of the artefact in favour of the text misleads. The student of Shakespeare is in a position to confirm what we should always know and remember, that before the moment of canonizing print, the likelihood of finding two copies of the 'same' text that are alike in every detail is vanishingly small. An author or a work's title denotes a family of artefacts, not any one thing. In the ancient world, those artefacts were almost always linear in construction, trapped in the format of a papyrus roll, where one piece of the work could only be found by scrolling past all the others—VHS rather than DVD, to suggest a comparison that will make immediate sense to one generation only.

But the preference for text to artefact replicates itself indefinitely. Our self-satisfied scholar is reading not a primary text but ancient scholia—marginalia to a text—and what he himself will produce is further derivative—notes on notes on a text.

One last dislocation essential to our trade is present in that nineteenth-century worthy: he is reading Greek scholiasts and sneering at a visit to Italy. 'Roman' studies as we construe them are shaped and defined by their connectedness to 'Greek' studies, which have trumping prestige. Though we congratulate ourselves on the broadening of horizons in the last generations that takes classicists beyond golden and silver ages to a more embracing vision of Roman study from the archaic city to the late empire, we still constrain that Roman study (as does this volume) to the period of time when political hegemony was exercised from Rome *and* the adjacency and prestige of Greek culture form a constant subtext, or perhaps better a *continuo*, for the Roman account of itself. 'Greek' studies are similarly perversely constrained in most institutions to a comparable time-frame, usually defined by the adjacency and prestige of a 'Persian' threat or opportunity, but when contemporary generosity and ambition expand the chronology, the word 'Greek' can persist and embrace study of periods as late as the present. By contrast, when Roman studies extend much past 600 CE, common consent adjusts the appellation from 'Roman' to 'Latin' (Farrell 2001) and still finds it hard to push the terminal date much past the invention of printing, for all that a lively, if learned and sometimes perverse, Latin culture persisted well past that date (Binns 1990).

The achievement of modernity in classical textual studies is the creation of the printed and seemingly reliable critical edition of the ancient text, the convenient book-in-hand that appears to relegate reference to the textual history and material substrate of literature or document to merely secondary importance. It was the responsibility of senior professors to terrify the young into remembering that the printed text was a false friend, but at the same time the undeniable progress of textual studies left each year fewer and fewer pages of ancient texts unprovided with serviceably reliable printed representations. So at the moment in time, when electronic texts begin to undermine the stability we have believed in, it is possible (indeed necessary) to find priests of the new medium who profess absolute blank incomprehension in the face of the notion that it matters what edition you might use as basis for your electronic text. The text so self-authorizes itself to such readers that all the acts and interventions of scholars, copyists, and printers' helpers simply vanish from the imagination and only the eternal verity of the text remains.

In the exact same moment of digital dawn, however, scholars imagine the yet more perfect critical edition, the one that comprises images and transcriptions of every important manuscript of an ancient work, the one that allows the reader to select and attend to manuscript evidence in different ways for different purposes—though no such edition is yet more than a gleam in a scholar's eye.

So what now? Prophecy, of course, is a mug's game. I argued in a book ten years ago that the errors of prophecy that confused the first generations of critics of the printed book were all errors of limited imagination (O'Donnell 1998). The economy and the culture that the printed book would make possible were both so many orders of magnitude larger than what denizens of manuscript culture knew, that their natural habit, of taking what is known and inflating by 50 per cent in order to get a picture of the future, fell laughably short of what would happen in short historical time. Our own imaginations not only fall short by more orders of magnitude than was the case 500 years ago, but the time-frame within which we will be proven laughably wrong is to be measured in a small number of decades at most.

Consider now afresh the history of Roman Studies—of the things we study and the way we study them—not in terms of genres and authors and readers but in terms of the artefacts of culture—the media—that made them powerful in their time and gave them their chance of surviving to our own.

Henri Pirenne made a famous name for himself in the early twentieth century by arguing that the ancient world did not come to an end until the Muslim conquest of North Africa closed the Mediterranean's commercial ways and gave Christian post-Rome reason to turn in on itself and look north (1939). The decline in the trade in papyrus was one of his chief pieces of evidence, a subject over which much ink has been spilled since. Papyrus was not necessary for any given act of communication, but it was essential for the culture. Roman literature is the product of a Mediterranean-wide social order, where papyri brought out of Egypt originally by Phoenicians are the vehicle for works of literature that imitate Greek models.

Greeks and Latins relied not only on the facile, portable, and technologically advanced medium of papyrus, but on the continuing reliability and increased exploitation of what seemed to be the originary medium, carving on stone. The 'epigraphic habit' is a source of precious information for historians, but at the same time an essential part of the permeation of Hellenistic and *a fortiori* Roman society by the written word. Augustus's *Res Gestae*, for example, had several important effects: first, it spun the story of Augustus for an elite audience; second, by its many public copies, it got that spun story to a broad audience of literate elites and semi-elites throughout the Roman world; but third, and by no means least, it declared to the illiterate and the semi-literate that there was a story to be told by the god-like ruler, and that the fact of its flamboyant presentation in public places was a sign of the power of the ruler and the power of his story.

This culture of words on papyrus and stone lasted as long as the city of Rome and its cultural institutions did—that is, until the 'Roman Empire' under Justinian set out to destroy the empire in order to save it in the sixth century. The final closing of the schools of the city of Rome may as well be dated to 554 CE as to any given year, and that one is convenient because it is the year in which Justinian's

Pragmatic Sanction established the terms for the reopening of the schools and their staffing. What the distant imperial capital decrees after such regime change does not always come to pass. Until Justinian intervened, Roman gentlemen, often with names that harked back to former centuries and former glories (Henderson 1997), continued to copy the old books and write their names proudly in the colophons. Macrobius' *Saturnalia* in the mid-fifth century embodied this spirit of the culture of perpetual repetition, representing scholarly gentlemen at work comparing the virtues of Homer and Virgil, cataloguing old, bad jokes, and poking a little discreet—so discreet that it long escaped notice—fun at contemporary foibles. That Macrobius by this time had to crib much of his erudition from Aulus Gellius is a sign that repetition can be a creative and original activity (the classical Chinese mandarin would agree).

The upper classes are not the place to look for innovation. The papyrus roll, imported fetish of literary culture, was a luxury commodity, not a workaday tool. When words needed to be recorded on the run, away from the leisured study, for temporary use, they found their way into physical objects of a different shape, books in the codex form. So men used wooden boards of some thickness, made concave on one or both sides as the thickness allowed. The cavity was filled with melted wax in a smooth, flat surface. Any kind of pointed stick could serve as stylus to record words, words only slightly less evanescent than spoken ones, inasmuch as a thumb's rub could turn ordered words into *tabula rasa* in a second. Two or more of these tablets attached together by a string or thong produced a rudimentary compendium. By habit these objects were rectangular on more or less the golden section's proportions, and by habit again, they were bound together at the longer sides, depending on an aesthetic of the 'page' that descended from the papyrus roll and the stonecutter's art. (Our laptops are bound the same way but turned on their side for writing, and it is too early to tell whether we will accept 'pages' shorter than they are wide in consequence.)

From the second to fifth centuries of the common era, a collection of peoples who called themselves devotees of Christ, the godly Jewish carpenter, began to use more flexible forms of the codex book to carry their message. They were not the only ones to do so, and they can, on present evidence, make no secure claim to originality, for the moments at which the codex began to be more widely used in more literary, or at least textual, ways are at present lost to our sight. Since, for other reasons, history brought Christians forward to a leading place in Mediterranean society in the fourth century and after, an easy narratology lets us combine their success with the success of the medium.

This 'codification' of the book was voiceless. We have no witness to tell us what anybody was thinking and no originary document to see what purpose drove them to the new form. But at each stage in the adoption of the codex form Christian texts predominate, and by the fifth century the form was standard. There are papyrus codices, and the old material adapted well enough to the new form, but it is also clear that the new form adapted itself well to materials that were less suitable for making book rolls, such as animal skins. The parchment or vellum book could be produced anywhere and did not require trans-Mediterranean importation, but the medieval manuscript was far more costly to produce than the mass-market papyrus-back of antiquity.

Nothing from the rise of the codex to the introduction of printing is of comparable importance for our topic, and all has been well and faithfully explored in many standard scholarly works. Three developments of the millennium that separated Augustine from Gutenberg are worth emphasizing for our purposes.

First, the return of Greek. Antiquity meant Latinity for almost a thousand years, the Greeks known mainly by rumour and report. The recovery of Greek (aided, for the West, by the conquests of Mehmet II, one of numerous favours he performed for Greek civilization) gave Latinity and thus Roman Studies not only a competitor for the attention of scholars, but gave back to Rome itself a dominant elder sibling that it had thought itself long since to have mastered and subjugated. From the fourteenth century to the present, Rome has been put firmly in its place as the second of ancient privileged western civilizations—still distinctly ahead of anything Semitic or Germanic, to be sure, but distinctly behind the miraculous birth of the Greek genius. Modern Roman Studies have been well and truly Greeked.

The second transformation was brought about by the realization of the possibilities that print gave birth to. Though many of the scholarly aids to inquiry and memory that print would bring to fullness had begun to appear in manuscript culture, the emergence of the lexicon, the commentary, the decisively edited text, and the collection of texts began to build libraries of classical and *a fortiori* Roman authority different from anything known before. These collections differed first by virtue of their encapsulation and isolation from the rest of 'contemporary' (often theological) culture, and second by their powers of collection. Where once it had been the work of a hunter-gatherer culture of librarians and scholars to bring together disparate materials that might be of interest, now the same could be done by purchase. If we today sometimes feel a little bit like cheats when our electronic tools let us find apposite passages and quotations in a twinkle of the eye, we should remember that the early readers of, for example, Erasmus' *Adagia* must have had the same sense of guilt at the thought of erudition-by-purchase.

Third, where polite studies under a Quintilian were carried out for the formation of gentlemen, now *Bildung* has acquired a rival, a sibling, a cousin, and cannot shake it: that is to say, the spirit of study for *Wissenschaft*. (Both have acquired an even more powerful rival, of course, the spirit of study for utility, commonly—rightly?—seen by all those who admire the ancients as an enemy of our studies.) In the United States in particular, one of the central functions of the university is to be the place in which the contested relationship of *Wissenschaft* (which we call research) and *Bildung* (which we call teaching) works itself out laboriously and divisively. The main thing to be said in favour of this system is that any system in which research has decisively prevailed over teaching, the new over the old, is one in which the teaching is demonstrably inferior. We are what we argue about.

For classicists, one upshot of that long irresolution is the marginalization of material culture. The *Bildung*-culture of classics is textual—verbal/literary, with offshoots reaching into history and philosophy. The *Wissenschaft*-culture of classics embraces the material remains of antiquity and works assiduously to extend our knowledge of those material remains by excavation, but a modern classics major for undergraduates and a modern Ph.D in classics for the advanced remains a thing of words in the main. That could change, and should, as more students approach classics through courses and experiences that integrate the visual with the verbal.

The best tools created in the first, foundational digital age are intended for research. The scholarly journal—to which it is conventional to assign a seventeenth-century birthdate, though the serious classical journals are all nineteenth- or twentieth-century in initiation and elevation—is the most reliable and predictable vehicle for the advancement of Greek and Roman studies. The emergence of the standard forms of the modern classical 'book' in the nineteenth century, however, is intimately bound up with the history of the journal, inasmuch as the book looms larger (in classics than in the sciences) in prestige and durability. Research begins with the book—the reference work, the standard edition, the authoritative treatment—and then proceeds to the article. The best articles are eventually collected in book form—either the author's *opera minora* or, increasingly, anthologies of the best work on this or that topic—and book publication effectively ratifies and canonizes the journal work. (A different form of book, the translation, has a sluggish history of emergence into the light, long thought slightly embarrassing for an elite that was supposed to know its Greek and Latin, now thought to be of secondary importance for scholarly contribution, but there are signs that the balance of opinion is changing.)

The great shift of the twentieth century fell in the domain of literary studies, where a decisive transition from textual and editorial activity towards critical and theoretical activity reshaped the output of book publishers in the field. That classicists famously lagged by a generation the practices of literary scholars in other fields is a testament either to the depth of their learning or their slow learning: opinions will differ. The transition was also marked at its outset (say 1950–80) by a narrowing of authors and genres towards the canonical and the classical and the poetic, especially in American practice. That narrowing is repeated cyclically through the centuries, and is now abating somewhat.

The emergence of the great research universities of the nineteenth and twentieth centuries, in whose history the story of classical scholarship plays a diminishing part (Frank and Gabler 2006), combined with the explosion in the production of scholarly work in classics (attested by the ballooning shape of the standard annual bibliographical reference volume, *L'Année Philologique*), is a Renaissance-that-kills of its own sort. As late as the 1960s, Arnold Toynbee could marvel at the possibility of producing high-quality original scholarship (he was completing *Hannibal's Legacy*) in a small liberal-arts college in the American Midwest. But the need to have access to libraries of constantly expanding *richesse*, combined with the need to have time and leisure to devote to scholarship, has increasingly disprivileged the smaller institution (to say nothing of the secondary school and its faculty) in favour of those at the institutions which offer the broadest library facilities and the most generous teaching loads to their faculty. An ideology of democracy and equality of access among scholars and librarians only partially offsets this material concentration and privileging. The opportunity for a liberating explosion in access has been tasted in the last decade, but both policy and technology need to be shaped to achieve our ends in this regard.

All that I have said so far is familiar, or could be. To sketch the rudiments of the history of classical scholarship can help sketch the way new media will continue and disrupt old practices. The need for such a sketch is the widespread perception that all is changed, changed utterly, by the introduction of digital media. A sketch of this sort, taken in the fourteenth year of the graphical web browser, the twenty-fifth year of the personal computer, and still within the lifetime of the founding fathers of humanities and classical computing—I mean Roberto Busa, Joseph Raben, Theodore Brunner, Steven Waite, David Packard—will inevitably be as accurate as a sketch of the Irish revolution of 1916 and following made before World War II. At such a moment someone may prophesy with accuracy a De Valera, but not a Celtic Tiger, and assuredly not Bono.

What has in fact changed? The new media that influence our modes of understanding of the ancient world are, I would suggest, these:

1. Media of transportation that bring together scholars and readers into physical communities, and that bring the books and articles produced in those communities to readers and scholars around the globe, with greater ease and diversity than ever known before. That said, the communities created remain chiefly those of the speakers of Germanic and Romance languages, but it is undeniable that the Americas and Europe and that the British Isles and the continent see far more movement and communication than ever before among scholars. David Lodge is the poet of this revolution and its sexual implications.

2. Media of creation, storage, and dissemination of text. As late as the 1980s classicists would handwrite manuscripts and leave them to be typed by employees of lower social status and limited education (I hear that this is still done in one place in, of course, Oxford), but the adoption of the technology undoubtedly sped

and spread scholarly activity apace, especially when accompanied, from the early 1960s onward, by the photocopier and its power of reproducing the written and printed word rapidly, if in modest quantities at first. (By the early 1980s *Bryn Mawr Commentaries* used very limited and locally available repro shops in order to produce serviceable if cheaply bound—and very cheaply sold—runs of hundreds of copies of high-quality classroom editions.)

The digital computer represented at first an intensification of what the typewriter could do. In the late 1960s I earned tidy sums as a college student typing papers for my less dexterous peers, but joined in the general mockery of the engineering student who sought to compete with us typists by producing instead computer printouts on the university's mainframe. He boasted accuracy, though he could not boast elegance, and none of us thought him the wave of any future; and on a strict accounting, the service he provided was far too expensive, if the full costs of the computing service were recognized.

A few of the earliest worthies of the tribe well understood the value of 'machine-readable texts' (*ut nostrates tunc aiebant*) and did all those who would follow remarkable service in creating an abundant supply of mainly classical authors in both Greek and Latin. Absent a project, and a project manager, as intensely focused and well-managed as the TLG, and Ted Brunner, Latin studies lagged a bit, but by the late 1980s the Packard Humanities Institute produced a serviceable CD-ROM with a sober collection of classical texts. Where TLG had begun with the classical but laudably pressed forward with the Hellenistic and Byzantine, however, not-for-profit classical scholarship made no comparable advance in Latin, with the result that traditional boundaries of the 'classical' were mainly preserved and reinforced. For-profit European publishers, in creating the CETEDOC Library of Christian Latin Texts, the Chadwyck-Healey (now Proquest) Patrologia Latina Database, and the electronic Monumenta Germaniae Historica, as well as many enthusiastic non-professionals creating resources like the Bibliotheca Augustana and the Latin Library, have built up, however, repositories that allow study and research to go far beyond the polite confinement of golden and silver ages. It is now conventional, among some of those excited by these prospects, to belittle the pioneers, inappropriately, for their inattention to matters of apparatus and variant.

With the introduction of the 'personal computer' in the early 1980s the transformation of the working lives of individual scholars began. The ability to create, organize, manage, reproduce, revise, and reproduce again one's own academic materials, whether for teaching or for publication, offered an immense but often invisible boon to productivity. Younger scholars, for example, scarcely credit my own story of rising an hour early every day of the week for two months at the outset of my first year of full-time employment, simply to spend that hour at the typewriter creating a clean copy of the manuscript of my first book to send off to a publisher, and I do not have the heart to gaze into the endless pages of laboriously handwritten notes that I took in the 1970s for later use, notes that are now immensely less usable—because not searchable or copyable—than anything I have done since 1983.

Much attention was given by some in those early days of the PC to specialized software that would create and manage bibliographical records for the individual scholar, well mindful of the labours that had gone into creating sometimes immense files of small file cards with either notes or bibliographic entries. (That same book manuscript of mine cost my typewriter one of its keys, the numeral 6, whose upper-case character was the underscore mark—battered to an early death by endless repeated striking to provide the typewritten ersatz of italics.) Roman Studies were in the main foreign to the efforts of the *Graeculi* to find ways to represent Greek text on screen, and to the sense of liberation that came with the release of the first Macintosh computers in the mid-1980s. I have lost count of the different ways I have known and used to represent Greek text with full diacritical marks on screen, most of them now a sheer waste of effort in a world of ubiquitous Microsoft software and Unicode standards.

3. Media of communication: Electronic mail became more or less widely available among faculty at research institutions with technological ambitions in the 1980s and at all institutions in the United States and United Kingdom in the 1990s. Anglophone scholars typically welcomed the advance of communication, with its democratizing inclinations, while continental scholars have been more cautious, if also less immediately well-served institutionally. By the mid-1990s universal student access to e-mail was common, and by the late 1990s it became possible to presume that e-mail was an acceptable alternate form of communication to anything that would have been sent on paper. The transition was more obvious among scientists, who had, for example, long employed staff to manage the photocopying and mailing of 'preprints' of their articles, only to abandon that practice wholesale and quickly in the mid-1990s; they are now emulated in a start-up project shared for classicists by Princeton and Stanford.

Electronic mail has become ubiquitous among scholars, while the cellular telephone has made its societal ubiquity felt among scholars as well, though academics were scarcely leaders in that area, and indeed the United States lingered behind many European and developing countries in adopting cellularity. The other modes of immediate communication that are of intense interest and widespread use in some social sectors around the globe, notably Instant Messaging and SMS text-messaging, to say nothing of blogging, have had almost no discernible impact among working scholars of 2006. Podcasting is making slight inroads into pedagogy. (Contemporary students give an enormous amount of their often divided attention to a variety of media. So far their teachers compete mainly for a share of the time they devote to print media.) Internet discussion lists devoted to the classics have been a signal failure at engaging the time and attention of senior and serious scholars, many of whom sampled the genre and ran in fright from the democracy they discovered there, unable to stay long enough to help shape valuable communities of dialogue—an opportunity that remains open and unfulfilled. The 1960s vintage telefax technology remains in widespread use, for no good reason.

4. Media of widespread representation of text, image, and other media. Beginning in the very early 1990s, there was wide interest among technologists in means of disseminating information broadly through the Internet. 'Listserv' discussions and Usenet newsgroups, common from the late 1980s, were mainly seen to be limited to plain text and were vulnerable to abuse (O'Donnell 1994 is a period piece describing possibilities). There was a clear market for media that would allow the individual to seek out the information she or he wanted and the standard of that time, Usenet news groups, was broadly unacceptable. The early 1990s saw the emergence of 'gopher' software, coming from the University of Minnesota, that allowed a rudimentary menu of textual files for immediate access, and academic technologists spent a great deal of time debating the merits and usefulness of 'Campus-Wide Information Services'—running on specialized software and representing the institution to its stakeholders. All such inklings of the future were demolished in an eye-blink by the arrival of the World-Wide Web.

The first graphical web browser, Mosaic, was released in 1993 and over the course of the next year gradually penetrated the consciousness of an elite of early adopters, including a few classicists. The release of Netscape in October 1994, with greater ease of use and smoother function, however, dramatically changed the landscape of information presentation. Within a year, no reasonable academic institution failed to have a website of its own, and pages with links to scholarly resources multiplied apace. The fundamental transformation that the WWW offers is that it is medium-indifferent and universal. The WWW is as happy presenting video as audio as 3-D graphics as text. It creates a global space in which information can dwell and be readily accessible in what is, at least in principle, an absolutely democratic manner.

The absoluteness of that democracy is limited by what is often regretted as the 'digital divide', that which separates those with access to networked computing from those without. Three observations of the mid-2000s on that point: (i) the penetration of 'cybercafes' (first seen in Seattle in 1995) to what might reasonably be called the ends of the earth (e.g. Luang Prabang, Laos, where I saw them in 2004) and the thronging of them by young people of evidently modest means in post-Soviet Russia and beyond suggests that the divide is less than impenetrable; (ii) it may be taken as a rule that no social group of which I am told by politicians that I should be afraid will be without easy and widespread access to the WWW; (iii) the emergent convergence of cellular telephony and web browsing, combined with the broad penetration of the lower end of the socioeconomic scale of western societies by cellularity, suggest that progress does occur.

Since the introduction of the graphical browser in 1993, there has been no further indication of any fundamental technological change in the near future. It is controversial to assert, as I have done elsewhere, that we live in a technologically stagnant age, but in one important regard that is true. The fundamental paradigm of 1993, an individual full-featured information appliance connected to a global community of information and communication through an Internet connection, remains unaltered. The technological advances of the last decade and more have refined that paradigm and enriched it, to be sure, but they have not changed it. The personal appliance shrinks in size and cost and the variety of forms of information accessible via the network grows apace, but in important ways we have made a permanent mental shift already, and nothing comparable yet looms. (Any such statement is given, quite deliberately, as a hostage to fortune, in the brave hope that it will not yet be obsolete at the date of publication of this chapter.)

That we live in a moment in which the new media pose challenges to our ways of scholarship and to the future of Roman Studies cannot be denied. But in suggesting the limitations of technological change for us now, I emphasize that the work to be done is intellectual and scholarly, not technological. The tasks of the next decade and more for the renovation and extension of Roman Studies are for scholars, not geeks. I will outline a few of them by way of conclusion:

I. *E pluribus plura.* We think we understand how to locate and use high-quality scholarly information. Our model is the library, and a model of surpassing splendour that is indeed. The essential structure of the library is found in the intersection between the urge to collect and the urge to classify and evaluate. The ideal library is infinite in scope but meticulously catalogued. No such library exists, which is why the model can prevail. An infinite library, after all, could not be catalogued and could not be selective. Our poverty empowers us in the libraries we really know and use. Without fully realizing the change, we use the WWW in a different way, driven by inquiry rather than by taxonomy. Search engines use various strategies to prepare material for our quest, but formal cataloguing by intelligent beings is almost never one of them. The rise of the jargon of 'Web 2.0', which captures a sense that the content of the new medium is evolving to favour the user and her role in shaping the information space by her choices over the role of providers in defining what is possible is an important change, and as yet entirely under-theorized by academics, who inherit long traditions in which the elders define curricula and the young follow them, in which the elders construct libraries and the young explore them. We are historically certain that such authority structures are necessary to assure that quality and truth prevail over ignorance and superstition.

And can we accept materials whose quality we do not control? Among tools I regularly use today, with every consciousness that I am not applying my usual standards, are the Wikipedia encyclopedia site and Google Books—the latter resembling not so much a scholarly library as a combination of large public library with collection of materials from a decade of publishers' remainder sales. Do I trust them the way I trust my library? Of course not. Do I think I can use them cautiously and sceptically and well? Of course I do. Am I correct? Perhaps.

But search is still an imperfect strategy when assurance of quality is desired, and the more abundant the searched material becomes, the more urgent that assurance is sought. For the student of the history of cultures, the truly interesting question about our time is the extent to which we will continue to be able to master and control the dissemination of information by the assignment of markers of quality and approval, and how far we will come to accept and trust statistical probability as a market of reliability. The underlying question is how we will navigate a transition from a culture of scarcity of information to a culture of superfluity of information. Classicists are in an unusually good position to appreciate this dilemma, for we know better than most the culture of scarcity. To reconstruct the history of Roman Africa, for example, has traditionally led us to seek out with obsessive diligence every possible fragment of evidence—every inscribed stone, every fragment of an ancient wine-press or church, every allusion in a manuscript-transmitted text. Our training of younger scholars has been training in this kind of hunter-gatherer culture, and among the tragedies of our profession are those of the scholar who never quite gathers all that she or he thinks is necessary to begin the work of interpretation and synthesis.

For now, classicists may imagine that they still live in such a world. They should supplement their imagination, from time to time, by attention to their own and their colleagues' complaints about how difficult it has become to 'keep up' with work in even very narrow subfields of antiquity. I had occasion a year or so ago to revisit a familiar shelf of books in the library where I wrote my dissertation. Sentimental to a fault, I gazed on this shelf and thought, I've read these very books before! It was a quiet shelf, one unvisited by notable revolutions or insurgencies in the last thirty years, but as the mist of memory cleared from my eyes, I found that of the thirty or so volumes on that shelf, only five had been there when I last visited it. I'd found time, in the intervening thirty years, to read—actually read from one end to the other—about five more of them, I knew the titles of most of the rest, but half-a-dozen were strange to me. And there are *many* shelves in that library that I think I know as fondly as I know that one.

There is real work to be done. Classicists were, indeed, among the leaders in the creation and use of digital resources supporting our scholarship and teaching. Perseus and TLG, the Database of Classical Bibliography and Bryn Mawr Classical Review, PHI and V-Roma, Diotima and Stoa: what we already have is abundant, significant, and well used. The open question at the instant of 2006 is whether and how we will find ways both to create new resources that genuinely build on what has gone before and link together both our classical resources and others created from outside our disciplinary boundaries in ways that increase by orders of magnitude their usefulness. At the moment, navigation of the 'library' of electronic classical scholarship requires once again the skills of the hunter-gatherer or the hunter-gatherer's apotheosis, the gourmet chef—not the discipline of the library-goer. One area of particular excitement at the 2006 moment is in the assembling of textual corpora and the preparation of textual editions that such corpora can comprise. In particular, epigraphers from around the world are discovering common purpose and, better still, common technical standards for the preparation of their searchable e-corpora.

II. *Littera scripta friget.* I said above that traditional classical scholarship and culture, even into the twenty-first century, is far too commonly limited to the use of written evidence—and indeed, 'canonical' written evidence. Integrating the world of words with the world of images, and then bringing the discipline of indexing and analysis to the images is more than just creating a website. Here, along with every other academic discipline, we will face the challenges of intellectual property law and its tendency to restrict access to materials, confronted with a deep academic urge to collect and explore materials of every kind. There are image projects of various kinds, notably ArtSTOR, but there is as yet no appropriately ambitious project (to my knowledge) that offers the student of antiquity, or some part of antiquity, the ability to explore textual and visual materials of high quality with confidence in the scholarly value of the experience.

A fortiori, if we do not know the material traces of the past as well as the textual, we are far too little informed about the remains of ancient societies. The great archaeological projects of the last century have produced their precious volumes and articles, but have accumulated as well masses of information that never see the light of print. There are some inklings now of how these projects can begin to digitize, catalogue, and make available *all* that they know of their sites, but again, we are very far from the moment when the enlightened general classicist—the new graduate student, the working scholar moving into a new area—can survey, explore, and use the diverse evidence of archaeological sites from Scotland to Egypt to Ukraine to Morocco with any facility. This too can and should change, but will take concerted intellectual effort with the familiar division between the taxonomic work that the experienced scholar can provide and the brute force of computer-powered search engines.

III. *Semper fidelis.* Some challenges are not for us to solve, but for us to worry about. I am fond of telling the story of how Scipio Maffei rediscovered a trove of manuscripts in the chapter library at Verona in the eighteenth century when he looked on top of a large armoire that contained better-cared-for manuscripts. One of the triumphs of medieval technology he found was a sixth-century manuscript containing the *Complexiones in Epistulas* of Cassiodorus, which he published in 1721. That manuscript had survived what could at that point have been as much as a thousand years, and was certainly many decades to hundreds of years, of complete neglect because of the robustness of the animal skin of which it was made and the persistent standardization of the 'encoding system' on which it relied. The only tool he needed to make sense of that manuscript was the naked eye.
A floppy disk of the 1980s, discovered on top of an armoire in my home in the year 2006, is not an information source, but a curio—and possibly a great loss of time, effort, and memory. With considerable effort, I might now be able to extract information from it, if I track down the right service maintaining specialized equipment. In another decade that service will be at least very expensive, and in another century preposterously expensive if not completely impossible. Techniques for the long-term preservation of digital information are like techniques for the long-term storage of radioactive waste: non-standard, of debatable merit, and entirely unproven. Classicists, with their acute sense of the challenges of long-term preservation and the risks of loss, can and should be active participants in broader societal dialogues about techniques and priorities for assuring the survival of our culture. (Academics should indeed be working with librarians and others in their universities to find the most economical and effective ways for such preservation to become the norm of scholarly practice.)

IV. *Mens immota manet.* So has the revolution arrived? No. Classicist academics are intensely conservative people, especially those of progressive politics. We have been venturesome enough in creating tools for ourselves in digital form—as long as those tools resemble those of former generations fairly closely. But the fundamental business of creating and disseminating new scholarly work remains extraordinarily unchanged. We write articles for the same journals, indifferent to the months-to-years of delay that will impede their publication. We labour for years over books that take more years to produce and more years to review. Archaeological publication famously lags discovery by decades—think of the Derveni papyrus or the Dead Sea Scrolls—and there are as yet no institutional structures to encourage serial publication, flexible publication, or collaborative discussion of fresh materials. Classicists remain fundamentally humanistic in their insistence on working alone, not in teams; archaeologists are the only real exception, and even they are for the most part far less flexible and productive than those who work in science laboratories.

Our forms of inquiry are similarly traditional. Computing power can ask and answer questions that we do not yet know how to pose, and comparative questions across much broader fields than we usually think we know can be pursued. Those possibilities remain for the future, but can give comparative studies of, let's say, Roman and Chinese empires new point and new power to instruct.

V. *Optimates an populares?* At bottom, our challenge is social. We have built our institutions, our practices, and our forms of social capital gradually over time in environments dependent on control, scarcity, authority, and privilege. The study of the ancient Roman world has been and remains the prerogative of a small group of people marked by access to social privileges denied to all but the few. To exercise influence in the study of the Roman world has been limited to a much smaller elite, only lately and with great difficulty diversified even in the obvious matter of gender, but still confined in the main to academic institutions attended and patronized by the prosperous and the powerful. Such studies are carried out at a high level in societies that are themselves prosperous and powerful. Though the Latin language has been regularly used at various times in the past as an everyday vehicle of communication and the recording of public business in every country of Latin America, no Latin American country has stood in the first or second rank of nations exploring Roman pasts—ancient or Christian—in the last century. For as long as the relative privilege and power of 'the West' (better, 'the Northwest') has been unchallenged, the privileged place of those who study the past of 'the West' has had no reason to think itself challenged.

That privilege depends on a master narrative about the history of the world itself, a master narrative in which the rise of 'the West' offers the central armature of all history. That narrative now, suddenly, in the first years of the twenty-first century, seems to face challenges unthought-of during what some were pleased to call 'the American Century'. The domination, in particular, of the world of University learning by institutions of the American model, a domination that has at least some years left to run, has left for humanistic studies a particular place of privilege that they will not be guaranteed in 'emerging market' countries with vast populations. And if the humanities *do* thrive in China or India, the attention that will be paid there to the Roman past may reasonably be expected to be less than we would find in Italy or the United States, and quite different in form.

The forces arrayed, in short, against 'classics' and *a fortiori* Roman Studies of the traditional structure are considerable. The ability of classicists to use the new media in order to extend the conversation, extend the inquiry, and extend the discipline that animates our communities will be the touchstone for the success or failure of Roman Studies in the century to come.

Further reading: A Guide for Hunter-gatherers (in 2006)

Assume that we begin where an enlightened student would begin: Googling a topic and finding it addressed in Wikipedia. No sceptical reader of these pages should fail to try that approach with an open mind, sampling a few well-known subjects to see the strengths and limitations of the resource. (Wikipedia is produced by an entirely democratic community, it is true, but it is also edited, sometimes fiercely, by a similar community, and if that does not always bring expertise to bear, it can be surprisingly effective at bringing clarity and even-handedness.)

Where might Google take the reader that she should be glad to go?*

For texts of the ancient authors

Thesaurus Linguae Graecae: comprehensive collection of digital representations of critical editions of classical, Hellenistic, and (more as time goes on) Byzantine texts ($$).

Packard Humanities Institute CD of Latin texts: the texts are *not* available on the WWW, but the PHI website can lead to ordering information ($$).

The Latin Library: very broad collection of classical, medieval, and neo-Latin texts; comprehensive with respect to conventional authors for the classical period, highly selective thereafter. Editions are generally not indicated. A set of 'vulgate' texts, but very widely and easily used.

Bibliotheca Augustana.

Perseus: a path-breaking collection of resources for classical students, including texts, translations, and reference works. Of particular note and value are the digital editions of standard lexica and reference works, especially the lexica where references cited in word entries are 'hotlinked' to the cited primary text.

For a few samples of specialized textual resources freely available

Heidelberg Corpus of Latin Inscriptions: includes contents of *CIL*.

Monumenta Germaniae Historica: full text of MGH editions going back to the nineteenth century.

* In consultation with the editors, we have decided to omit URLs from the print edition of this essay. They are ugly, typographically difficult to represent accurately, and liable to change. We have tested and are confident that in every case a simple Google search will lead to the resource in question. The ($$) indicates that the resource is not freely available.

Less freely available and instructive

Patrologia Latina Database ($$): this commercially produced representation of the abbé Migne's nineteenth-century *Patrologia Latina* is searchable and of high quality. It has several limitations: (1) incompatibility of format with other collections of texts; (2) a price that restricts it to users associated with institutions capable of paying a regular annual fee in four figures or making a purchase in five figures (US $); (3) the obsolete nature of most of the editions contained in the set. There are other databases of some of the *PL* texts—notably the *Corpus Augustinianum Gissense* ($$) and *Cetedoc Library of Christian Latin Texts* ($$)—also too expensive for the general user and in proprietary formats.

For bibliographical guidance, compare and contrast *L'Année Philologique* online (not free, but not expensive, and widely available in academic settings) with http://print.google.com (mainly out-of-copyright books) and http://scholar.google.com (journal literature, mainly scientific) and with a simple Google search. Ask yourself how much better the latter will have to become to be a serious rival. If publishers, moreover, provided bibliographical information in more standardized formats, automated harvesting and selection would become much easier very quickly.

Also useful are GNOMON ONLINE, and two websites: RASSEGNA DEGLI STRUMENTI INFORMATICI PER LO STUDIO DELL'ANTICHITA' CLASSICA, maintained by A. Cristofori (www.rassegna.unibo.it), and KIRKE by Ulrich Schmitzer (http://www.kirke.hu-berlin.de/).

Recent and nearly-recent scholarship in good-quality collections

History E-Book Project: sponsored by the American Council of Learned Societies, good quality digitization of 'best-sellers' in recent historical scholarship. Invaluable for those who have access ($$).

E-brary: less scholarly in its selection, a broad collection of contemporary scholarly books in digital form, widely held by many libraries, haphazard in its classical coverage ($$).

JSTOR: founded by the Andrew W. Mellon Foundation, contains archival texts of major scholarly journals in major humanities and social science fields, so for classics complete runs from volume 1 to near present of *JHS*, *JRS*, *Past and Present*, *Classical Philology*, and numerous others. Bias towards the anglophone. Texts presented as page images of original publication, but with 'dirty OCR' (scanned but not fully proof-read) searchable text hiding behind the images ($$).

Muse: Johns Hopkins University Press's e-publishing arm for current scholarly journals in the humanities, including several of immediate interest to classicists ($$).

Bryn Mawr Classical Review: the oldest (1990 founding) completely open access and freely available electronic journal in classics, devoted to book reviews, and indeed limited in the main to reviews of print materials, despite several attempts by the editors over the journal's history to solicit and disseminate reviews of electronic-only publications.

Material remains and visual images

ARTStor: still nascent and highly selective attempt to establish (also with Mellon support) a broad library of images for use by humanists, with emphasis on pedagogy rather than research ($$).

Worthy but still incomplete and nascent enterprises of collaboration

Vroma; Stoa; Diotima: each of these represents a largely volunteer effort to produce high-quality teaching and research materials in traditional classics and to make them freely and universally available.

For the shape of things to come, in late 2006, the American Council of Learned Societies published 'Our Cultural Commonwealth', a report on current and prospective needs and possibilities. The two main lines that I would choose to emphasize are, first, the current mismatch between needs, the expression of needs, and the funding for those needs, which leaves too much work at the mercy of intermittent funding and volunteer labour; and second, the desirability of supporting policies and funding strategies that will support production and preservation of work that can be universally available at no cost to users ('Open Access' publishing). The economic and social challenges in both domains are substantial and real conundra remain unresolved.

Technology, of course, is always one step ahead of us. The culture of online games absorbs the time and energy of millions and suggests one form of human interaction at a distance that has still been kept outside the academy's formal pursuits. (Or almost kept outside: Jerome McGann at the University of Virginia has piloted an online 'game' environment called *Ivanhoe* that allows for collaborative critical activity around a common text structured in the fashion of a game. Whether this represents *World of Warcraft* brought to the academy or Hesse's *Glasperlenspiel* brought to life is an open question.) Beyond gaming, however, the website called *Second Life* already offers a virtual space for the interaction of computerized representations of real people that some corporations are already using for conferencing. Do we yet imagine the point at which we will find it useful to enter into such spaces (purpose-built spaces created for scholarly use, like the work of Bernard Frischer (now of the University of Virginia) and the Cultural Virtual Reality Lab at UCLA on things like a detailed VR model of the Roman Forum) and do our teaching and scholarship surrounded by new-generation images of the things we study? Stranger things have happened, and will happen.

References

J. W. Binns, *Intellectual Culture in Elizabethan and Jacobean England: The Latin Writings of the Age* (Leeds, 1990).

J. Farrell, *Latin Language and Latin Culture* (Cambridge, 2001).

D. J. Frank and J. Gabler, *Reconstructing the University* (Stanford, 2006).

J. Henderson, *Figuring Out Roman Nobility* (Exeter, 1997).

M. McLuhan, *Understanding Media* (New York, 1965).
J. J. O'Donnell, *Avatars of the Word* (Cambridge, Mass., 1998).
—— *New Tools for Teaching* (Philadelphia, 1994– ; http://www.georgetown.edu/faculty/jod/teachdemo).
H. Pirenne, *Mohammed and Charlemagne* (New York, 1939).
J. E. Sandys, *A History of Classical Scholarship* (Cambridge, 1903–8).

PART I

TOOLS

CHAPTER 2

TRANSMISSION AND TEXTUAL CRITICISM

MARIO DE NONNO *

Transmissional History and Textual Criticism

Our knowledge of Latin literature and, more generally, of any text of a non-documentary nature written in Latin after the First Punic War depends as a rule on an unbroken process of conservation, transformation, and loss that developed from antiquity to the modern age and moved through subsequent phases of aggregation and disgregation, recovery and dispersion (Norden 1998[7]). Prior to the invention of the printing-press, texts destined for circulation were disseminated through a succession of individual handwritten copies, which were chronologically discontinuous and more or less faithful to the exemplar. Such circumstances of textual transmission require that the text's surviving copies, which often contain widely differing readings, undergo a comparative evaluation—a judgement or criticism (in Greek, *krísis* means 'judgment')—that goes by the name of 'textual criticism'. The primary goal of textual criticism is to identify the oldest possible form (or forms) of a given text which we can reach through the inspection and comparison of its

* Translated by Ilaria and Simone Marchesi.

surviving witnesses. This first stage of criticism involves a series of formalized procedures, traditionally labelled *recensio*. As a rule, it is only after a sufficiently thorough *recensio* has been carried out that one may move forward with a diagnosis about the local and overall reliability of the transmitted text, and then propose particular conjectural emendations.

The task of reconstructing historically the entire process of transmission, starting from the data that can be extracted from the preserved manuscripts (in the case of texts that have reached us) or from indirect external witnesses (when they are available), belongs to the 'history of the tradition'. Unless it were to become, as Alfred Housman dismissively put it, 'a longer and nobler name than fudge' (Housman 1926: p. xiii), the history of the tradition should produce more than a simple background onto which one may project the philological reconstruction of the relationships of dependence existing between manuscript- and print-witnesses of a given author or work. Its goal should not be the often futile quest for criteria which may render the choice among diverging readings attested in the tradition 'automatic'; rather, it should aim to develop an understanding of the nature and quality of each individual text (or group of texts). It should, in short, contribute to an awareness of the limits and extent of historical and philological reliability for any textual reconstruction. As Giorgio Pasquali remarked, 'only someone who knows the centuries-long vicissitudes a work suffered in the time that passed between its publication and the oldest preserved witnesses will be able to reconstruct, by way of a comparison and evaluation of the tradition—hence, through a *recensio*—the original text' (Pasquali 1952^2: p. ix). Beyond the identification in the history of the tradition of overall trends which deserve to be investigated and studied as such, Pasquali's fundamental lesson was that each text has *its own* history and constitutes *a distinct* critical problem. The old adage, *habent sua fata libelli* ('every book has a destiny of its own'), perfectly captures the situation.

Of course, the claim to exemplarity and universality that, in the past, classical philology has advanced for *its* methods and goals of textual analysis and reconstruction has increasingly come under attack, and it should certainly be re-evaluated—from the 'Lachmann method' (Timpanaro 2005) to the system of *recensio* that Maas formalized (1958). Yet it is precisely the deeper awareness of the historical specificity inherent in the modalities of transmission of Latin classical authors (differing from those of their Greek counterparts) that should discourage us from exporting to the philological reconstruction of their texts methodologies developed in the examination of other texts and traditions. Medieval or modern texts, either in Latin or—to an even larger extent—in the vernacular, have been transmitted in different circumstances and for essentially different motivations than the Latin classics (Ferrari 1998).

The nature, modalities, and varying outcomes of the transmission process of individual texts (or groups of texts) from ancient Latin literature are the products of several intervening factors, essentially unique to their situation. First, the preservation or the loss of texts (and, in the case of preservation, the amount of entropy occurring in their transmission), depends on differences in the type or genre to which they belonged: the binary opposition, for instance, of poetry vs. prose, literary vs. technical texts, 'institutional' vs. occasional literature, and so on. Second, specific processes of historical and cultural change play a considerable part in determining a text's chances of survival: texts may be selected for preservation because they are to be adopted in the schools; they may be manipulated and epitomized when put to practical use; but most of all they are subject to the changes in taste or in the goals that different times assign to the production of literary works, with the ensuing decline in the appeal that given products or categories of products may exert. Third, the transmission and preservation of texts are dependent on the breaks—often traumatic ones—in the socio-economic context in which books are produced: some ages have been favourable, others deeply unfavourable to a widespread production of books as goods. Fourth, technical and material factors have exerted considerable influence (for example, the shift away from papyrus to the more durable parchment as support for writing, or the epoch-defining change from the scroll to the codex). Last but not least, classical Latin texts have been forced to reckon with the capricious nature of chance: there seems to be no explicable reason, for example, why the last ancient copy of Tacitus' *Histories* found safe haven in the Montecassino ruled by the Abbot Desiderius, while the only ancient codex of Sallustius' *Histories* attested in the West was left to the mercy of the blade of an early medieval binder.

Loss is the 'zero-degree' of tradition (Canfora 1974): entire eras of Latin writings, entire literary genres that were perhaps too deeply tied to particular occasions or that were no longer understood or fashionable, are now to be viewed as lost in transmission. Even in the case of centuries that may be considered relatively more fortunate, the mass of the unknown Latin literature (Bardon 1952–6) is immeasurable. In the crowded graveyard of the bulky first volume of the *Handbuch der lateinischen Literatur der Antike*, which stretches from the origins of literature in Rome to the death of Sulla (Suerbaum 2003), only three authors have more than a ghostly presence. The first is Plautus, with the *corpus* of his twenty-one genuine comedies already selected by Varro (Gellius, *Attic Nights* 3.3). He survived thanks to the fortunate recovery and transcription during the Carolingian period of a late-antique edition which haphazardly escaped from the 'dark centuries'. The witness of a different edition, incomplete and reduced to a palimpsest, was discovered in the Ambrosiana Library in Milan at the beginning of the nineteenth century—only to be wrecked by the acid used to decipher it. Then there is Terence, who enjoyed an uninterrupted favour in the schools up until the sixth century CE—a success that is attested to by several late-antique commentaries. In his case, the uneasiness with which his treatment of the spoken verse in archaic Latin drama was received (a discomfort relieved only by Bentley) seemed to matter little. Finally, the old Cato: he is present neither because of his ground-breaking historical work (*The Origins*) nor for any of the orations that Cicero and Gellius enjoyed so much, but for the para-literary reference book *On Farming*. His survival was secured by his inclusion in a thematic *corpus* of 'Writers on Farming' as the founder of the genre, an extremely popular one in Rome. The most ancient witness of this *corpus* reached the hands of Angelo Poliziano only to vanish immediately thereafter. All the rest—be it oratory before Cicero, epics before Lucretius and Virgil, historiography before Caesar and Sallust, drama before Seneca—is represented only by the dust-cloud of the 'indirect tradition'. We owe these tantalizingly fragmentary citations mostly to linguistic and antiquarian erudition and to the school. The latter, to make things even worse, followed its own conventions in quoting (De Nonno 1990), and a case like the one offered by frg. II 114 Maurenbrecher is not rare. It is a fragment from Sallustius' *Histories* that the grammarian Aelius Donatus, in his gloss of Terence's *Phormio* 171, preserved as *et poni fere adversus a. n. e. m.*—that is, by reducing the final words of the quotation to an acronym. The abbreviation conformed to a widespread habit of the schools and relied on the assumption that the immediate audience would be familiar with, or could easily locate, the abbreviated words. After all, Donatus was citing from a work as canonical as Sallust's *Catiline's Conspiracy* and *War against Jugurtha*—and, as such, indexed as late as the end of the fourth century in the collection of syntagms by the rhetorician Arusianus Messius. As incredible as it may seem, the work is now almost entirely lost: we only have tiny scraps of ancient papyri and parchment folia and a small anthology of speeches and epistles that were extracted (again, at the same time) from the *duo bella* and from the *Histories*. This collection, in turn, was compiled in late antiquity (with a rhetorical goal in mind) and is aptly rounded off by the spurious *Epistles to the Old Caesar*. Similarly, it is only from the citations gathered and ordered in Justinian's *Digest* (533 CE) that we know the vast output of centuries of Roman jurisprudence. I hope this last brief mention suffices to show the need for studies of the transmission of ancient texts to trespass artificial fences between disciplines, since they are a nuisance to a comprehensive historical understanding.

'Corpora' and (Late-)Ancient Editions: Fixation of Textual Arrangements

Let me now turn to the Latin works which have been preserved in 'direct tradition'. They are the few that successfully passed through the 'hourglass narrow middle' of manuscript transmission (Reynolds 1983: p. xiii). They too have suffered wounds, often deep ones, after their original had been published by the author or by others (such is the case with the far-from-infrequent unfinished works). A preliminary terminological caveat is in order here: in the definition of direct tradition the terms 'original' and 'published' need to be taken loosely, lest they produce anachronistic assumptions and expectations about individual textual tradition. Texts may have been released as 'in progress', a circumstance that finally produces several authorial editions of the same work. Similarly, Rome had genres (important ones) for which initial 'publication' was entirely oral and strictly tied to performance—oratory and archaic theatre, for example. In Plautus' *corpus* the dangers of practising a reconstructive fundamentalism are particularly pronounced, insofar as they promote the mirage of a global *Plautus restitutus*, beyond the textual arrangement of his plays established by the philological work of Varro's age. Finally, not every written text in Roman culture enjoyed the same degree of authorial prestige: in the eyes both of their copyists and eventual users, technical writings (such as repertoires, manuals, commentaries, *scholia*) or literature for entertainment or consumption (love- or adventure-novels, paradoxographical texts, accounts of miracles, saints' lives) were basically *res nullius* (De Nonno 1998).

It is not a coincidence, one should note, that the first of the 'formative stages' in the tradition of the Latin classics (Pecere and Reeve 1995) coincided with the most highly structuring time of textual recovery that took place in antiquity: namely, the formation of clear-cut *corpora* ('bodies'—the metaphor is at least as old as Cicero) of *books* by one or more authors that had been originally published and disseminated independently and in different times in *volumen* form (or as collections of several *volumina*, bound together in bundles or sheltered in boxes called *capsae*: Birt 1882). In several instances, the process had already been initiated in an age close to the author, but more often it was the result of editorial decisions and interventions beyond the author's control. The tendency to form these editorial *corpora* found in the *codex*—a book-form in which a high number of gatherings could be bound together—an ideal repository. Increasingly popular (beginning in the first century CE) and destined to become the dominant medium, the *codex* was perfectly suited to contain in a single and easy-to-handle physical object the large amounts of text which could only be divided among a number of rolls before. As Isidore remarked, 'the codex contains many books, the book is made of only one roll' (*Etymologies* 6.13.1). As is often the case when widespread and deep-seated habits are surrendered, several technical elements which used to mark the external appearance of the roll were transferred to the codex. A case in point is the habit of placing titles at the end of each book in the shape of *explicit* (/*incipit*): together with the textual errors caused by the simultaneous shift in script (from capital to minuscule, from cursive to bookhand: Zelzer 1995), these vestigial practices of titling act as 'guide fossils' for the philologist (Pecere 1990). The effects of the textual aggregation described above were widespread. The archaic Cato was saved because he was joined to Varro, Columella, and the 'modern' Gargilius Martialis (third century?). Pliny the Younger's *Panegyric for Trajan* escaped the shipwreck that engulfed Latin oratory before and after Cicero and until the late-antique and

Christian homiletic texts because it was placed as earliest and best example of the genre in a thematic *corpus* of panegyrics, dating from the third to fourth century and delivered by orators from Gaul, which was assembled after 389 CE. Similarly, the apologetic speech Apuleius composed to refute the accusation of having circumvented his wife Pudentilla survived in the form of *Two Books on Magic* because it was grafted on to a late-antique *corpus* of non-philosophical writings by the African sophist. Our knowledge of the *Golden Ass* and the anthological *Florida* also depends on a lone witness of this *corpus*, reread and signed by a Sallustius who was in Rome and Constantinople in 395 and 397—the thinnest of threads.

In the textual tradition of the most eminent Latin classics, the incorporation into larger bodies of texts with different natures and origins was a defining step. This phase in the tradition is crucial for textual criticism because such editorial operations were, as a rule, conducted according to the principles set by Alexandrian philology; that is, they were prudentially conservative and essentially respectful of the available documentation (Leo 1895²). On the one hand, the reorganization of their textual environment usually means that texts have shifted from an 'active' and erratic tradition to a 'dormant' and rigid one; on the other hand, this new phase in the tradition often constitutes a rigid limit for our reconstruction of the oldest coherent appearance of the preserved texts. When the textual *corpora* were the product of more ambitious and carefully planned philological and editorial undertakings, we often find ancillary material of variable extent and different levels of erudition, which, in time, will come to include long-lasting strategies for presenting the text (Questa and Raffaelli 1984). The most striking apparatus that still characterizes modern editions of Terence are the tables that preface almost every play: they contain erudite information on the Greek models, the circumstances of the original staging, and so on. These *didascaliae* are the product of an editorial operation of the kind described above that has helped to stabilize an essential feature in the textual transmission of Terence's works: its success is evident in both the ancient editions of which we have knowledge, one of which is attested to in a priceless late-antique codex held by the Vatican Library and owned by one of the leading intellectuals of the sixteenth century, the Italian Pietro Bembo. The same may be said for the standardized page layout that is applied to the plays of, again, Terence and Plautus and to Seneca's tragedies: the different indentations applied to parts of the text written in different metres; the methodical and consistent criteria for the bipartition of exceedingly long lines; the interposition in the dialogues of name- and role-tags for the characters present on stage at different times, resulting in the breakdown of the textual continuum into scenes—all are the product of ancient standardized editorial processes. (On the other hand, the modern division of Latin comedies into acts was introduced in the humanistic period.)

In the case of Virgil, the classical poet par excellence, we still can browse through several codices dating from the fifth and sixth centuries—before, that is, the massive medieval and humanistic tradition. These witnesses are copies (sometimes illustrated ones) that, even after having suffered various degrees of mutilation, preserve those Collected Genuine Works that were the constant object of attention and passionate reading inside and outside the schools (the commentary of Servius being only one of the many works of Virgilian exegesis that have reached us). Both the *Bucolics* and the *Georgics*, which were released with the author's *imprimatur*, and the *Aeneid*, which Augustus ordered to be published posthumously and conservatively (down to the point of allowing incomplete lines to stand), have come down to us only through the filter of such containers. They attest to a textual set-up (a 'paleotype', as it is sometimes referred to) essentially unitary, in spite of the random emergence of a swarm of ancient alternative readings. The ways and times in which the so-called *Appendix Vergiliana* has been preserved and transmitted are completely different, even though it too derives from an editorial work of collection aimed at satisfying the morbid curiosity of the public for the Great Poet's first steps. Both Propertius' *Monobiblos* (the 'Single-book' edition of his first book for Cynthia), which exploded on the Roman literary scene between 29 and 28 BCE, and Tibullus' 'book of Delia', which came a few years later (so the common opinion) to counterbalance it, splitting the fans of elegy into two opposed camps, have come down to us only in the framework of posthumous 'Collected Poems' editions of both poets, of which we only have very late manuscript copies. In the latter's case, the compilation added a second book, genuine but perhaps incomplete, to the first, and then rounded off the edition with a miscellaneous 'third book' of 'Scattered and Spurious Poems' (including a mediocre hexameter panegyric for Messalla Corvinus, the poet's patron). These have survived only thanks to their inclusion in the larger *corpus*. Even in the case of Horace, a poet who cultivated widely different poetic genres, the manuscript tradition goes back to two distinct late-antique editions of 'Collected Works'. Regardless of the still-lingering doubts about the relationships among the medieval manuscripts preserved to date (all more or less complete or contaminated), we know that these editions existed: they differed both in the sequencing of the texts they presented and for a group of undoubtedly old variant readings. They were united, however, by the common purpose of reuniting the whole textual *corpus* of the poet, rejecting the nonsensical fakes that Suetonius had already dismissed, with insightful discrimination, at the end of his *Life of Horace*. In the case of the *Tragedies* ascribed to Seneca, the tradition is similarly bipartite. Differences in ordering, inclusion or exclusion of the spurious *Octavia*, and a lot of macroscopic textual differences separate the two late-antique editorial redactions that have mediated the *corpus*. The rubricated medallion with the table of contents on the frontispiece of the famous *codex Etruscus* (*Laurentianus* plut. 37.13, from the eleventh century) certainly reproduces a late-antique model. The codex is the ultimate ancestor of one of the two branches of the tradition and is opposed to the basic concordance in the so-called 'vulgate' branch also of the readings found in the recently published fragments of a Michigan papyrus (inv. 4969 fr. 36). For the so-called *corpus*

Caesarianum it is clear that one of the two branches of the tradition (the other comprises the *Commentaries on the Gallic War* only) originates in an edition that gathered together the genuine *commentarii* with other commentaries of different authors, in an operation explicitly or implicitly designed to produce integration, in accordance with the ancient tradition of a historiographic continuum. This may be said regardless of the *corpus*' complex compositional issues, which are still unresolved, despite the many ancient witnesses available. Very likely dating from antiquity was also the *corpus* of the major rhetorical writings by Cicero. An early medieval copy of this edition surfaced at Lodi, around Milan in 1421 and brought back into circulation the *Brutus*, a work that had remained until then unknown. The imposing 'Leyden philosophical *corpus*' of the same Cicero (the name derives from the place in which the most important manuscripts are preserved) originated in a pre-medieval period. Owing to some material damage suffered by the only exemplar that had reached the threshold of the Middle Ages, the *corpus* shows some *lacunae* and transpositions. Nevertheless, we owe to it our knowledge of the treatises *On the Nature of Gods*, *On Divination*, *On Destiny*, the *Timaeus*, the *Topics* (which are known also from a different and more complete tradition that collects the work, in a scholastic fashion, among other writings of dialectics), the *Paradoxes of the Stoics*, the *Lucullus*, and the three books *On the Laws* (probably in a version that did not have any authorial approval). The exceptional preservation of the *Lucullus* is due precisely to its having been inserted in a *corpus*. This treatise is the second book of the first version (in two books) of the *Academic Books*, one that Cicero replaced a few months later with a second version in four books. Of the latter we only have the first book (now materially broken off at paragraph 46) that was attached as a 'sixth book' to the five books of the treatise *On the Ends of Goods and Evils* in a branch of the tradition of this work. It is certainly possible, as Leighton D. Reynolds and others proposed, that the joining of the 'sixth book' was not traditional, but rather the consequence of a medieval recovery. Thanks to the exemplary 1998 Oxford edition Reynolds produced, however, there is no way, now, of proving the hypothesis. In truth, nothing conclusive may be said about the ending of the *De Finibus* in the codex *Vaticanus Palatinus Latinus* 1513 (which alone represents half of one of the two branches of a bipartite tradition), since the last few gatherings of the manuscript have now been lost and the text breaks off mid-sentence after paragraph 16 in the fourth book. Our tradition of the so-called *Dialogues* by Seneca derives from their collection into a late-antique *corpus*. This *corpus* gathered between two covers ten, mostly short, works originally divided up between twelve rolls, and prefaced them with a table of contents now reproduced in red at the opening of the fundamental codex *Ambrosianus* C 90 inf. In addition, the tradition is marked by a significant lacuna that has swallowed up irretrievably the ending of the treatise *On the Happy Life* and a good chunk of the following *On Leisure*. None of the ancient roll-books containing Martial's *Epigrams*, which commercial booksellers published regularly in order to meet the demands of a market of habitual consumers, reached the Middle Ages. The works of Martial travelled only in late-antique complete editions in codex form, which all shared a systematic as well as chronological principle for ordering their material, and thus included the texts of the early *Xenia* and *Apophoreta* as Books 13 and 14, respectively. *Corpora* similarly organized as single-author collections brought together Statius' *Thebaid* and *Achilleid* (the latter suffering from a material loss at its end), Pliny the Younger's nine books of private correspondence along with the single-book official correspondence with Trajan, and even the two minor works ascribed in the ultimate ancestor of the whole tradition to Tacitus. Pliny's tradition offers a rather exceptional case, in which we have both descendants from the above-mentioned *corpus* (which was already available to Symmachus) and copies of an exemplar stemming from a different ancient edition that contained only Books 1–9. As a consequence, in his reconstruction of the text Sir Roger Mynors has essentially been able to dispense with conjectures. As for Tacitus, the exquisite *Dialogue on the Orators* was found in the same medieval manuscript as the *Germania* and *Agricola*, but most likely as an anonymous text and in a codicologically distinct section (where it was thematically associated with Suetonius' *On the Teachers of Grammar and Rhetoric*). Given the general framework I have sketched out this far, I must confess that I find it quite unlikely that the Collected Poems that a late and extremely corrupted tradition has handed down to us as *Liber Catulli Veronensis* actually bear the traces of an overall authorial care and a meticulous ordering (one, incidentally, in which the criterion of metrical uniformity plays such a large role). To say the least, it would be close to a miracle.

Next to single-author *corpora* that generally go back to the earliest phases of the textual transmission, other kinds of collections are developed with time: collections organized according to 'genres', such as the already-mentioned *corpora* of 'Writers on Farming' and 'Old Panegyrists'. These collections respond to that distinctively late-antique urge toward typology which inspired Cassiodorus when he organized the library in the Vivarium monastery. Some of these collections have transmitted minor grammatical texts. A similar collection, real or alleged, saved for our curiosity the spicy biographies of the so-called *Historia Augusta Writers*. Of the *corpus* of the land-surveyors, we still have an illuminated exemplar dating from late antiquity, characterized by the presence of brief anthologized complete texts together with excerpts of various origin and age. Still on the topic of anthological *corpora*, we should not pass over in silence the late (fifth–sixth century) but precious *corpora* of 'modern and contemporary poetry', gathered together in the circles of poets-*scholastici* such as Dracontius and Luxorius. They have come down to us in early-medieval miscellaneous collections of minor poets, the most organic of which is the so-called *Anthologia Salmasiana* (from the name of the seventeenth-century scholar Claude de Saumaise). Saumaise's early medieval manuscript, which had unfortunately suffered a sad mutilation in its opening, transmits the text preserving relevant traces of the late-antique sectioning and titles. It is only thanks to its inclusion in containers of this kind that the *Pervigilium Veneris* has been preserved in all its refined grace and has provided T. S. Eliot with one of the 'fragments shored against his ruins' heaped up in the envoi of *The Waste Land*. Finally, the best example of the role that late, highly miscellaneous *corpora* played in the transmission of texts is the famous codex *Vaticanus Latinus* 4929 (second half of the ninth century). In one section, the manuscript reproduces a *corpus* assembled in Ravenna in the sixth century and preserves several of its paratextual features. Thanks to it we can now read Julius Paris' epitome to Valerius Maximus (drafted perhaps in the fourth century), the three books of the treatise on geography by Pomponius Mela (in the first century), and a small lexicon of poetic place-names compiled by a certain Vibius Sequester (from the fourth–fifth century).

The works that have been preserved outside of the logic of these *corpora* are those that were each large enough to occupy a late-antique codex of varied format and extent. Here I can only mention several, somewhat randomly selected, examples of this phenomenon. Lucretius, for instance, came down to us in a six-book edition that broke down didactically the text into sections preceded by explanatory titles, sometimes even in Greek. (The same practice marked the transmission to us of another lenghty didascalic text, the difficult *Astronomics* by M. Manilius.)

Among the works of Cicero I have already mentioned the treatise *On the Ends oj Goods and Evils*, but the *Tusculan Disputations* were also transmitted independently. Vitruvius, Livy's *Decades* (of which we still have several late-antique codices, while of the fifth *Decade* only the first volume of a two-volume edition from late antiquity has survived), Ovid's *Metamorphoses*, Lucan, and Silius Italicus were all transmitted in isolation. The rather exceptional survival of tiny literary singularities may perhaps be accounted for by the fortunate salvaging of elegant booklet editions during the Middle Ages—if not even, perhaps, by the recovery of some of the increasingly rare rolls. Such is the case of the acerbic pamphlet *Emperor Claudius Becoming a God* (to be identified with the *Apokolokyntosis* by the vindictive Seneca), or of the bizarre collection of *Poems for the God Priapus* unearthed by Giovanni Boccaccio around Montecassino, or even of the first chunk of a sophisticated dialogue on the theme *Virgil: Orator or Poet?*, attributed to a certain P. Annius Florus and copied down in the twelfth century on a leaf of a Brussels manuscript along with the frustrating note: *in altero quaternione ex integro hanc scripturam habeo* ('in a different gathering I have this script in full').

In all the cases surveyed above, the essential processes that determined the initial status of the textual transmission of that part of Latin literature which has come down to us took place in antiquity or, more often, in late antiquity (Cavallo 2002: 31–47). Having introduced various degrees of modification in the 'original' authorial textual set-up, these (late-)antique alterations strongly condition our knowledge of the text. Such is the case of the anthology of portions of rhetorical exercises that the elder Seneca put together at the bequest of his studious offspring. All the manuscripts preserve the work as made up of one book of *suasoriae* and five of *controversiae*—all duly numbered from 1 to 6 in the editorial transitional formulas placed between books. It is only thanks to the chance survival of an independently transmitted set of excerpts from the *Controversiae* that we are afforded a glimpse into the original set-up of the work. A valuable Montpellier manuscript, descended from a late-antique rhetorical *corpus*, shows that the elder Seneca's work originally included, in addition to the *suasoriae*, ten full books of *controversiae*, half of which the six-book tradition has thus elided (namely, Books 3, 4, 5, 6, and 8). Only partly similar, but similarly instructive, is the case of the treatise on agriculture in twelve books by Columella. The late-antique edition, to which the medieval manuscript discovered by the humanist Poggio Bracciolini goes back, had suffered an interpolation. Between Books 2 and 3 it contained a book belonging to a different work and probably a different author: the so-called *Liber de Arboribus*. As a result, the books that had been originally numbered 3–12 were numbered 4–13. A different tradition, gravely damaged but free from the *De Arboribus*, did indeed exist and has left traces up through the fifteenth century: nonetheless, this time because of the process of contamination, all of the manuscripts that have come down to us offer a Columella in thirteen books. Conversely, the cases in which the essential textual set-up of classical works has coalesced only in the Middle Ages are extremely rare. I am not referring, of course, to the normal process of continuous alteration caused by the conscious or unconscious innovations that is inherent in any transmission of the text via a succession of handwritten copies, but to the major defining events in the formation of the tradition. The most notable case, all the more so for the exceptional artistic merit of the text, is perhaps the *Satyricon*. The text of the sole manuscript that had survived the end of antiquity and (very partially) preserved this work underwent a repeated process of dismemberment, contouring, and partial reassembly, first at the hands of scholars in the circle of Heiric of Auxerre, and then in the milieu of Orléans. These interventions in the text have deeply shaped both the content of and the relations between the various branches of the tradition, separating the 'brief excerpts' from *The Dinner of Trimalchio*, and giving birth to a collection of *sententiae* and to the compilation of the so-called 'long excerpts'. This disfigured mosaic is the starting-point of any attempt to appreciate the absolute masterpiece of the Arbiter of Elegance.

Archetypes, Lost and Preserved

A necessary outcome of the situation described above, that of the historical and cultural conditions of textual transmission, is that a great many Latin works have reached us through a tradition originating in a single archetype (Brunhölzl 1971). Single-archetype traditions descend from a physically distinct manuscript preserving a particular text that is defined (and may in some case be reconstructed) on the basis of the alterations and corruptions shared by all the witnesses in the tradition. The process through which these copies have been obtained may be more or less widespread in space, sequential in time, and articulated in the stages through which it has passed. What matters is that, directly or indirectly, all (other) copies of the work presently available have been derived from this sole manuscript. The parenthesis above indicate a real possibility: even if the archetype is often conceptualized as a 'lost' manuscript, Reeve 1986 has shown that this loss is far from being logically binding and historically mandatory. For many works it is actually possible, by way of textual comparisons and the examination of its 'external' codicological features, to isolate one manuscript from which all other witnesses of a tradition have derived: this manuscript is the archetype of *that* tradition. A study of cases like, for instance, the books from Varro's treatise *On Latin Language* that still survive today, badly battered, or like Tacitus' major works, or like Livy's Books 21–5, may also teach a valuable heuristic lesson by shedding light on the mechanisms of a tradition in the making. A whole set of phenomena that may only be postulated in the case of traditions deriving from a fully or partially lost archetype may be observed in practice. An example of the partial eclipse of the archetype is offered by the erudite lexicon *On the Meaning of Words* by Sextus Pompeus Festus: the famous *codex Farnesianus*, which was already seriously mutilated when it was rediscovered in the humanistic age, is still preserved today in Naples, having suffered additional damage with the loss of three further gatherings. These, however, are preserved in fifteenth-century copies drawn from the manuscript when it still was in the condition in which it had been found. Several cases offer clear examples of the effects that traditions suffer when they descend from a single archetype that was originally damaged and is now lost. For us today the *Histories of Alexander the Great in Ten Books* by Curtius Rufus inevitably begin with the middle of the third book, and lack the end of the fifth, the beginning of the sixth, and the ending of the tenth book. In Lucretius' poem, the material damage suffered by one leaf in the archetype has maimed lines 1068–75 of Book 1, leaving only their initial bits, and has caused the loss of eight lines (between those now numbered 1093 and 1102)—a *lacuna* that the most faithful descendant of the archetype duly notes by leaving a blank space. Finally, Seneca's 'Fürstenspiegel' *On Mercy* was joined to the seven books *On Benefits* in a small, author-based *corpus*, and now lacks its ending because of the damage suffered by the exemplar which was exhumed around Milan at the end of the eighth century and there entrusted to a small gang of clumsy 'scribes in training' as a writing exercise (as was often the case for the classics).

Dissemination and Restoration

The times, places, and circumstances in which the Middle Ages recovered late-antique manuscripts containing classical works that had weathered 'the big chill' around the seventh century vary greatly from author to author and from work to work (Reynolds 1983: pp. xiii–xliii). In many cases the recovered books were decorated with the patent of nobility conferred by 'subscriptions' recording that they had undergone a summary revision at the hands of their aristocratic owners in the age of Symmachus or Boethius (Pecere 1986). Starting generally from the middle of the eighth century, several areas emerge throughout Europe in which ancient codices resurface and manuscript traditions widen, thanks mainly to the fervent activity of the *scriptoria* associated with the schools of monasteries and cathedrals, whose ancient catalogues of books we can still in some cases browse and check up: Carolingian France, Ottonian Germany, Romanesque Italy, Papal Rome, and the Lombardic Beneventan area. The humanists, who became the protagonists of the 'rediscovery' of ancient authors (a cultural movement that had started before Petrarch, but that he certainly promoted and channelled: Billanovich 1996), were rarely able to access late-antique manuscripts, as happened at the end of the fifteenth century in the case of the remote monastery of Bobbio. What humanists usually brought back to light were early medieval copies of texts that had been marginalized after the waning of the Carolingian renaissance and 'forgotten' during the modernizing age of Scholasticism and the Universities (Sabbadini 1967^{2}). This was the destiny, for instance, of the didascalic poetry of Lucretius and Manilius, but also of Statius' *Silvae*. In other cases, what was recovered and put back into circulation were copies that had produced no offspring for centuries but that could provide readers with (relatively) more complete texts than the current ones, which had descended from damaged ancestors: such was the case not only with Columella and Petronius, but also with the vast treatise *On the Education of the Orator* by Quintilian—a text that exerted a powerful influence on the ideology of Humanism. For the most closely and frequently read authors we have to reckon, starting from the Carolingian age, with a tight interweaving of textual transmission and literary reuse, a more and more intense and wider circulation of people and books, the pervasive practice of school-annotation, and the increasing openness to 'dialogue' with the texts. All that produced precocious phenomena of textual cross-checking and contamination that interfered with the vertical transmission from exemplar to copy, though they generally stopped short of entirely obliterating its traces. Contamination is different from the uniform alteration that an epitome or the reduction to a set of excerpts produces. The two phenomena should be carefully distinguished in the critical discourse: excerpting causes a more rigid discontinuity in transmission and hinders, in the absence of other branches of the tradition, the reconstruction of the original. In a few unusual cases, the contamination process must have gone back to ancient witnesses of radically alternative redactions which have, however, disappeared in their totality. Such contamination with early textual versions may account for the random surfacing of authentically ancient textual bits (preserved in papyrus fragments and known to Augustine) in otherwise totally undistinguished manuscripts of Sallustius' works. Contamination has an additional consequence: In order to be convincing, any reconstruction of the relationship among preserved manuscripts that aims at ascertaining the earliest reading of a text should not be limited to considering only strictly philological proofs. Rather, it should combine the analysis of the shared innovations produced by 'conjunctive and disjunctive errors' (as they are labelled in Maas's systematic treatment) with the 'archeological' clues that a thorough evaluation of all codicological, paleographic, and paratextual features of the existing manuscripts may produce (Cavallo 2002: 25–9).

When the earliest reading witnessed in the tradition (the so-called *paradosis*) can be shown to be a blatant or subtle corruption in its sense, metre, or style, then it will be possible to accept or attempt a conjectural restitution of clear-cut portions of the original text. As hypotheses about such a remote stage in the history of the text, such interventions should be carried out with great methodical care, and should be openly marked off as a piece of restoration. Throughout the ages classical philologists have exercised their learning and acumen in formulating conjectural emendations. In fr. 30 Morel from the *Song on the Punic War* by Gnaeus Naevius, for instance, readers are presented with the majestic epiphany of the god of Delos: *dein pollens sagittis inclutus arquitenens / sanctus Ioue prognatus Putius Apollo*, 'and hence (comes forth,) powerful for his arrows, celebrated archer, awe-inspiring, Jupiter's offspring, Apollo the Pythian'. The reading *sanctus Ioue prognatus* is a brilliant conjecture introduced by Franz Bücheler to replace the *sanctusque Delphis prognatus* shared by all the manuscripts of the text preserving the fragment, Macrobius, *Saturnals* 6.5.8 (-QVE < IOVE, and the rejection of *Delphis* as a clear gloss incorporated into the text). In order to recover Naevius' voice, Bücheler's virtuoso emendation short-circuits the transmitted text. On the other hand, all editors of Macrobius' text are absolutely right when they print the manuscripts' text, and thus preserve the reading that Macrobius had found, already corrupted, in the learned collection of quotations from which he drew it. This having been said, however, the field in which *emendatio* is to be applied should not be programmatically limited. Claims made in this direction are both wrong and potentially misleading. Indeed, emendation may really 'allow, in some fortunate instances, the recovery of a text no less certain (sometimes more certain) than some unpersuasive readings present in the tradition, against which the textual critic has no just cause to act' (Mariotti 2000: 509). How could we dispense with such sensible and delightful conjectures as the one which an anonymous humanist made in resetting the delicate mechanism of

Catullus' dirge for Lesbia's sparrow, when he reconstructed *o factum male! o miselle passer!* ('oh! what a pity! oh poor little sparrow!') from the traditional nonsensical manuscript reading: *bonum factum male bonus ille passer*?

Further reading

In order to understand historically the transmission of the classics, one needs to gain familiarity with the manuscripts that materially transmit them. Several aids may help to once again associate a physical dimension with the dry *sigla* used in critical editions. Chatelain 1884–90 is well complemented, for the earlier periods, by Seider 1978–81 and the fundamental Lowe 1931–71. Very good is the selection of texts with limited tradition whose witnesses are reproduced by Merkelbach and van Thiel 1969. To these may be added the full reproductions of celebrated manuscripts or exhibition catalogues such as Dell'Omo 1996 or De Robertis and Resta 2004. After all, as Augusto Campana used to say, 'behind a codex there is always a man'. Excellent guides to the cultural study of medieval manuscripts are Bischoff 1990 and 1994; a stimulating array of essays is gathered in Ganz 1986 and Chavannes-Mazel and Smith 1996. Sabbadini 1967[2] remains a cornerstone for the humanistic period. Billanovich 1996 collects the seminal contributions of a ground-breaking scholar. On codicological questions in textual tradition, Birt 1882 and Clark 1918 were epoch-making, and still prove valuable; Questa and Raffaelli 1984 provide modern examples. The essays in Cavallo 2002 are notable for their methodological advancements. Trustworthy overviews of the tradition of the classics as a general phenomenon may be found in Reynolds and Wilson 1991[3] (including a chapter on the principles of textual criticism) and Pöhlmann *et al.* 2003. Zelzer 1995 and, in particular, Pecere 1990 offer more personal and thought-provoking insights. Leo 1895[2] and Norden 1998[7] still deserve an attentive rereading. By bringing together synthetic accounts from a team of experts working (often at first hand) on the tradition of all major authors (and many minor ones), Reynolds 1983 has become an absolute reference point, as may be gathered from the wide-ranging survey in its Introduction, pp. xiii–xliii. The valuable grouping of manuscripts in Munk Olsen 1982–9 (with an update in progress: Munk Olsen 1991–2007) conveys an idea of how and how far the most important works were transmitted. Valuable material on the main crossroads of transmission may be found in Pecere and Reeve 1995; on individual issues, see also Canfora 1974, De Nonno 1990 and 1998, Pecere 1986, and Brunhölzl 1971. The meditated repertoire of traditions and actual editorial case studies offered in Pasquali 1952[2] remains essential, both for the rich historical sensibility and the fruitful synthesis of philology and criticism. Only partial and tendentious readings treat his work as the manifesto of that undiscriminating textual 'anti-reconstructionism' which appears to be fashionable today. Similarly, any criticism one may want to level against the excessive abstractness of Maas 1958, however legitimate, should follow an unprejudiced and attentive study of the 'golden booklet'. On the history of classical philology as a disciplined method of textual reconstruction, see the critical contributions of Timpanaro 2005 (with the relevant discussion in Reeve 1986 and elsewhere) and Kenney 1974. Several user-friendly and accurate introductions to the practical and technical aspects of ecdotics are in Willis 1972 (which even includes exercises at the end of each chapter) and West 1973 (with a practical commentary of several model editions). More recently, see Tarrant 1995 and Delz 1997. The latter has perhaps a somewhat restricted focus (literary texts in direct tradition), but it certainly contains a flawless typology of the most frequent kinds of textual corruption, accompanied by extremely well-chosen examples. Mainly devoted to conjectural *emendatio* is Havet 1911—a rich volume, daring as it is acute. Housman 1922 remains seminal, in its sharpness, and should be read with the soothing reassessment by Nisbet 1991. With various degrees of coherence, essays on the method(s) for editing classical works are gathered in Grant 1989 and (more ambitiously) in Most 1998. On the tasks and goals of Latin ecdotics, however, the balanced account of Reeve 2000 and the sensible and experienced handling of Reynolds 2000 recommend themselves. Finally, in order to understand the patient work of textual criticism, no theorizing may replace the assiduous consultation of the introductions and masterful critical apparatuses such as those prepared by Sir Roger Mynors (for Cassiodorus, Catullus, Virgil, Pliny the Younger, and the Panegyrics), Leighton D. Reynolds (for Seneca, Sallust, and Cicero), Konrad Müller (for Curtius Rufus, Petronius, and Lucretius), or Edward J. Kenney (Ovid, and Apuleius).

References

Bardon, H. (1952–6), *La littérature latine inconnue*, I–II (Paris: Klincksieck).

Billanovich, Gius (1996), *Petrarca e il primo umanesimo* (Padoue: Antenore).

Birt, Th. (1882), *Das antike Buchwesen in seinem Verhältnis zur Literatur* (Berlin: W. Hertz).

Bischoff, B. (1990), 'The Manuscript in Cultural History', in *Latin Palaeography. Antiquity and the Middle Ages*, tr. D. Ó Cróinín and D. Ganz (Cambridge: Cambridge University Press), 179–238 (German edition: Munich 1977[1]).

—— (1994), *Manuscripts and Libraries in the Age of Charlemagne*, tr. and ed. M. Gorman (Cambridge: Cambridge University Press).

Brunhölzl, F. (1971), 'Zu den sogenannten "codices archetypi" der römischen Literatur', in J. Autenrieth and F. Brunhölzl (eds.), *Festschrift B. Bischoff* (Stuttgart: Hiersemann), 16–31.

Canfora, L. (1974), *Conservazione e perdita dei classici* (Padoue: Antenore).

Cavallo, G. (2002), *Dalla parte del libro. Storie di trasmissione dei classici* (Urbino: QuattroVenti).

Chatelain, É. (1884–1900), *La Paléographie des classiques latins*, I–II (Paris: Hachette).

Chavannes-Mazel, C. A. and Smith, M. M. (eds.) (1996), *Medieval Manuscripts of the Latin Classics: Production and Use* (Los Altos Hills and London: Anderson-Lovelace/The Red Gull Press).

Clark, A. C. (1918), *The Descent of Manuscripts* (Oxford: Clarendon Press).

Dell'Omo, M. (ed.) (1996), *Virgilio e il Chiostro* (Rome: Palombi).

Delz, J. (1997), 'Textkritik und Editionstechnik', in F. Graf (ed.), *Einleitung in die lateinische Philologie* (Stuttgart and Leipzig: Teubner), 51–73.

De Nonno, M. (1990), 'Le citazioni dei grammatici', in G. Cavallo *et al.* (eds.), *Lo spazio letterario di Roma antica* (Rome: Editrice Salerno), iii. 597–636.

—— (1998), 'Testi greci e latini in movimento: riflessi nella tradizione manoscritta e nella prassi editoriale', in Ferrari 1998: 221–39.

De Robertis, T. and Resta, G. (eds.) (2004), *Seneca: una vicenda testuale* (Florence: Mandragora).

Ferrari, A. (ed.) (1998), *Filologia classica e filologia romanza: esperienze ecdotiche a confronto* (Spoleto: Centro italiano di Studi sull'alto Medioevo).

Ganz, P. F. (ed.) (1986), *The Role of the Book in Medieval Culture*, I–II (Turnhout: Brepols).

Grant, J. N. (ed.) (1989), *Editing Greek and Latin Texts* (New York: AMS Press).

Havet, L. (1911), *Manuel de critique verbale appliquée aux textes latins* (Paris: Hachette).

Housman, A. E. (1922), 'The Application of Thought to Textual Criticism', *Proceedings of the Classical Association*, 18: 67–84 (= *The Classical Papers of A. E. Housman*, collected and ed. J. Diggle and F. R. D. Goodyear (Cambridge: Cambridge University Press, 1972), iii. 1058–69).

—— (ed.) (1926), M. Annaei Lucani *Belli civilis* libri decem, editorum in usum (Oxford: Blackwell).

Kenney, E. J. (1974), *The Classical Text: Aspects of Editing in the Age of the Printed Book* (Berkeley, Los Angeles, and London: University of California Press); revised Italian edition: *Testo e metodo. Aspetti dell'edizione dei classici latini e greci nell'età del libro a stampa*, ed. A. Lunelli (Rome: GEI, 1995).

Leo, F. (1895^2), *Plautinische Forschungen* (Berlin: Weidmann), 36–48.

Lowe, E. A. (1931–71), *Codices Latini antiquiores: A Palaeographical Guide to Latin Manuscripts Prior to the Ninth Century*, I–XI and Supplement (Oxford: Clarendon Press); II^2 (1972); *Addenda* di B. Bischoff, V. Brown e J.J. John in *Mediaeval Studies*, 47 (1985), 317–66, and 54 (1992), 286–307.

Maas, P. (1958), *Textual Criticism*, tr. B. Flower (Oxford: Clarendon Press; German edition: Leipzig 1957^3 (1927^1; 1960^4)).

Mariotti, S. (2000), *Scritti di filologia classica* (Rome: Editrice Salerno).

Merkelbach, R. and van Thiel, H. (1969), *Lateinisches Leseheft zur Einführung in Paläographie und Textkritik* (Göttingen: Vandenhoeck & Ruprecht).

Most, G. W. (ed.) (1998), *Editing Texts—Texte edieren* (Göttingen: Vandenhoeck & Ruprecht).

Munk Olsen, B. (1982–9), *L'Étude des auteurs classiques latins aux XIe et XIIe siècles*, I–II–III/1–2 (Paris: Éditions du CNRS).

—— (1991–2007), 'Chronique des manuscrits classiques latins (IXe–XIIe siècles)', *Revue d'Histoire des Textes*, 21: 37–76; 24: 199–249; 27: 29–85; 30: 123–88; 32: 73–106; NS 2: 49–106.

Nisbet, R. G. M. (1991), 'How Textual Conjectures are Made', *Materiali e discussioni per l'analisi dei testi classici*, 26: 65–91.

Norden, E. (1998^7), 'Erhaltung und Überlieferung der römischen Literatur', in *Die römische Literatur*, herausg. von B. Kytzler (Stuttgart and Leipzig: Teubner), 93–100 (= 1927^3).

Pasquali, G. (1952^2), *Storia della tradizione e critica del testo* (Florence: Le Monnier; 1934^1).

Pecere, O. (1986), 'La tradizione dei testi latini tra IV e V secolo attraverso i libri sottoscritti', in A. Giardina (ed.), *Tradizione dei classici. Trasformazioni della cultura* (Rome–Bari: Laterza), 19–81 and 210–46.

—— (1990), 'I meccanismi della tradizione testuale', in G. Cavallo *et al.* (eds.), *Lo spazio letterario di Roma antica* (Rome: Editrice Salerno), iii. 297–386.

—— and Reeve, M. D. (eds.) (1995), *Formative Stages of Classical Traditions: Latin Texts from Antiquity to the Renaissance* (Spoleto: Centro Italiano di Studi sull'alto Medioevo).

Pöhlmann, E. *et al.* (2003), *Einführung in die Überlieferungsgeschichte und in die Textkritik der antiken Literatur*, I^2–II (Darmstadt: Wissenschaftl. Buchgesellschaft).

Questa, C. and Raffaelli, R. (eds.) (1984), *Atti del Convegno internazionale 'Il Libro e il Testo'* (Urbino: Università di Urbino).
Reeve, M. D. (1986), 'Archetypes', in *Studi in onore di A. Barigazzi* (Rome: Edizioni dell'Ateneo), ii. 193–201.
—— (2000), 'Cuius in usum? Recent and Future Editing', *Journal of Roman Studies*, 90: 196–206.
Reynolds, L. D. (ed.) (1983), *Texts and Transmission: A Survey of the Latin Classics* (Oxford: Clarendon Press).
—— (2000), 'Experiences of an Editor of Latin Classical Texts', *Revue d'Histoire des Textes*, 30: 1–15.
—— and Wilson, N. G. (1991[3]), *Scribes and Scholars: A Guide to the Transmission of Greek and Latin Literature* (Oxford: Oxford University Press; 1968[1]).
Sabbadini, R. (1967[2]), *Le scoperte dei codici latini e greci ne' secoli XIV e XV.* Edizione con aggiunte e correzioni dell'autore a cura di E. Garin, I–II (Florence: Sansoni; 1905–14[1]).
Seider, R. (1978–81), *Paläographie der lateinischen Papyri*, II: *Literarische Papyri*, 1–2 (Stuttgart: Hiersemann).
Suerbaum, W. (ed.) (2003), *Die archaische Literatur von den Anfängen bis Sullas Tod* (Munich: C. H. Beck).
Tarrant, R. J. (1995), 'Classical Latin Literature', in D. C. Greetham (ed.), *Scholarly Editing: A Guide to Research* (New York: MLAA), 95–148.
Timpanaro, S. (2005), *The Genesis of Lachmann's Method*, ed. and tr. G. W. Most (Chicago: Chicago University Press; Italian edition: Padoue, 1985[3] (Florence, 1963[1])).
West, M. L. (1973), *Textual Criticism and Editorial Technique Applicable to Greek and Latin Texts* (Stuttgart: Teubner).
Willis, J. (1972), *Latin Textual Criticism* (Urbana, Chicago, and London: University of Illinois Press).
Zelzer, M. (1995), 'La tarda antichità', in G. Cavallo *et al.* (eds.), *Lo spazio letterario del medioevo*, 1. *Il medioevo latino* (Rome: Editrice Salerno), iii. 301–38.

CHAPTER 3

ICONOGRAPHY

CHARLES BRIAN ROSE

DECIPHERING the language of imagery used by the Romans requires an examination of all components of material culture, whether or not we would classify them as 'art'. We often ask 'what is "Roman" in Roman art', but a more appropriate question would be 'what is "art" in Roman art?' Ancient art historians have consistently attempted to draw a line between objects whose aesthetic qualities merit study, and those that should be assigned to the domain of the archaeologist. The Romans made such aesthetic judgements too, but most of the images whose meaning we try to explicate formed part of larger verbal and visual contexts that would have influenced their interpretation.

Focusing solely on a selection of objects within an already lacunose context makes an analysis of the broader meaning more difficult than it would already have been. If we genuinely want to understand an image, then we need to examine the entire associated assemblage, which means the loomweights and spindlewhorls next to a cult statue, the bone tools in a terracotta workshop, and the residue on the paint pots from a sanctuary dump. Such an analysis applies even to faunal and botanical remains, which can add important clues to the meaning of a monument's original spectacle: analysis of the root channels next to the Parthian arch of Augustus in the Roman Forum revealed that it was flanked by living laurel trees, sacred to the emperor, while an investigation of the bones from Troy's Sanctuary of Cybele indicated that actual skins of her holy lions decorated the altar precinct (Andreae 1957: 165–6; Rose 2006: 141).

Even at a fixed moment in time no object had a single meaning, since the intellectual, social, and political background of the viewer would have prompted a multiplicity of responses, especially in the absence of inscriptions. If one were to have queried separately the women, priests, and freedmen who viewed the Ara Pacis after its dedication in 9 BCE, one would undoubtedly have received three very different reactions. A similar variation in interpretation is evident in contemporary scholarship on the altar, and there are no signs that a consensus will ever be reached (e.g. Rehak 2001; LaRocca 2002; Rose 2005).

Within the limited scope of this chapter I review a selection of issues related to Roman self-representation, focusing primarily on political and religious imagery of the late Republic and Empire, but touching on all visual media and most geographic regions. In the process, I attempt to highlight the fundamental ambiguity of Roman iconography as well as the problems in comprehension encountered both by the Roman viewer and the modern scholar.

It seems appropriate to begin with the issue of space and time: how did the Romans indicate the extent of the empire that they controlled, and how did they express its unlimited duration? An advertisement of empire seems to emerge under Pompey in the mid-first century BCE, when text as well as image conveyed the geographic scope of Rome's conquests, from Asia to Celtiberia (Kuttner 1995). In Spain itself, Pompey's triumphal monument in the Pyrenees listed 876 defeated Spanish tribes (Pliny, *HN* 7.96; Castellvi, Nolla, and Roda 1995); other monumental inscriptions announced his subjugation of over thirty regions throughout the Mediterranean and Near East (Diodorus 40.4). Fourteen of these regions were anthropomorphized as statues and grouped together in the portico of his theatre-temple for Venus, thereby forming the first of a series of large visual assemblages that diagrammed the empire's components (Kuttner 1999*b*). The erection of colossal public maps of the empire made the same point, as evinced by those of Agrippa and Mussolini in the Saepta and on the Via dell' Impero, respectively, but this format was less common than the figural groups (Nicolet 1991: 103–31).

Similar advertising schemes celebrating the empire's scope were developed in the provinces as well by local elites anxious to win the favour of the imperial family. The most impressive of these appeared at Aphrodisias in the city's Sebasteion, where fifty life-size marble reliefs featured personifications of regions conquered by Augustus and his Julio-Claudian successors (Smith 1988; figs. 3.1, 3.2). One distinctive feature of the Sebasteion personifications is that all of them appeared with labels, which raises the issue of ambiguity in the representation of places and peoples, or *ethne*. The iconography in many cases was intended to connote the power that the region had once exercised, but since all personifications of place were female, only a limited number of martial models were available as options, primarily Minerva and the Amazons. Consequently, the costume and age of most images of Roma and Virtus (fig. 3.3) are not substantially different from those of Britannia (fig. 3.2), except for the missing helmet, nor does the personification of the Pirousti, a subjugated tribe in Yugoslavia (fig. 3.1), deviate significantly from images of Athena (Smith 1987: 115–17; 1988: 60–2; Di Filippo Balestrazzi 1997; Rose 2005: 25–7). The ancient workmen at Aphrodisias also got confused when

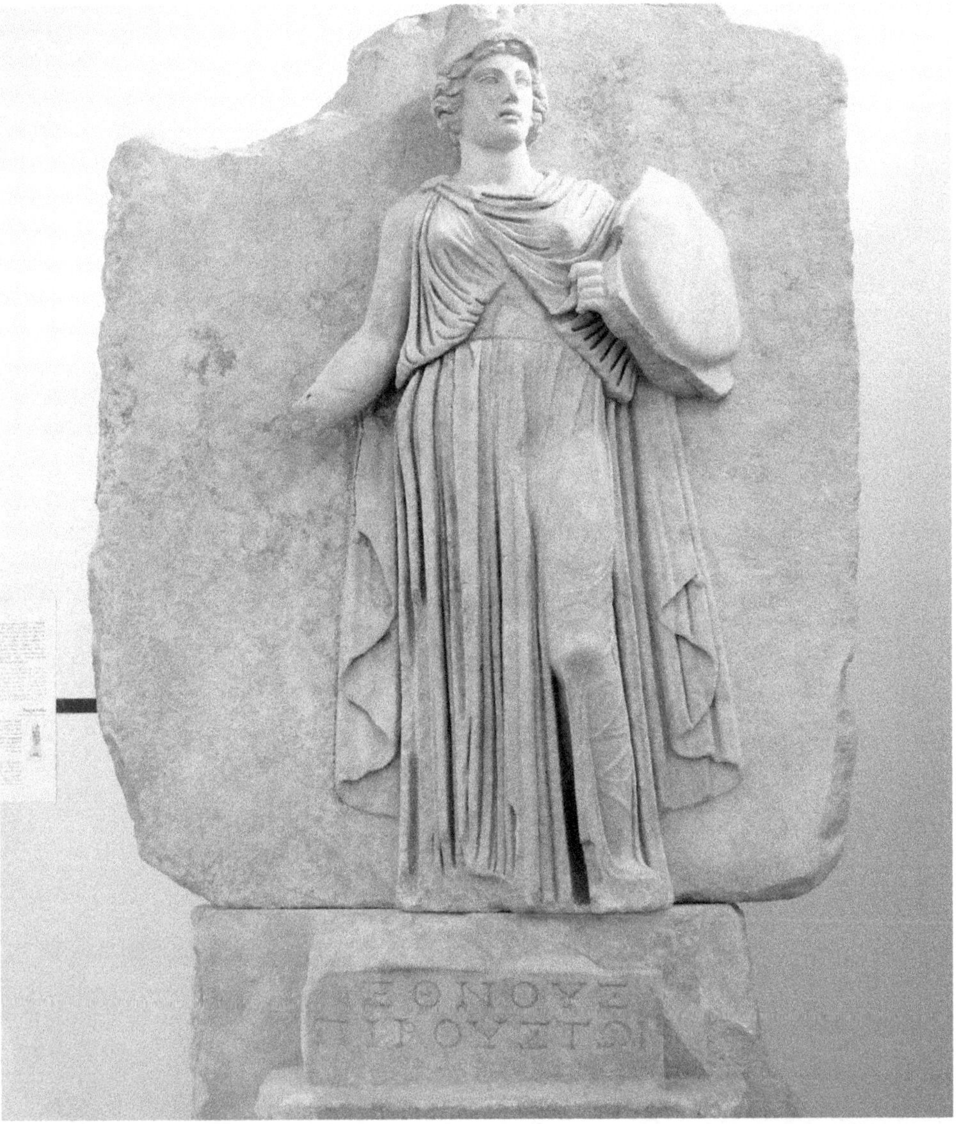

Fig. 3.1. Personification of the Pirousti, from the Sebasteion at Aphrodisias

Source: Aphrodisias Excavations.

assembling the *ethne* series, and lightly incised a graffito on the back of the Pirousti relief to ensure that the right label ended up with the right personification (Smith 1988: 61).

This ambivalence is apparent in Rome too, especially in recent discussions of the decoration of the Forum Transitorium: the sole surviving attic relief was always interpreted as one of many representations of Minerva that originally would have surrounded the entire forum (D'Ambra 1993; fig. 3.4); it is now regarded by

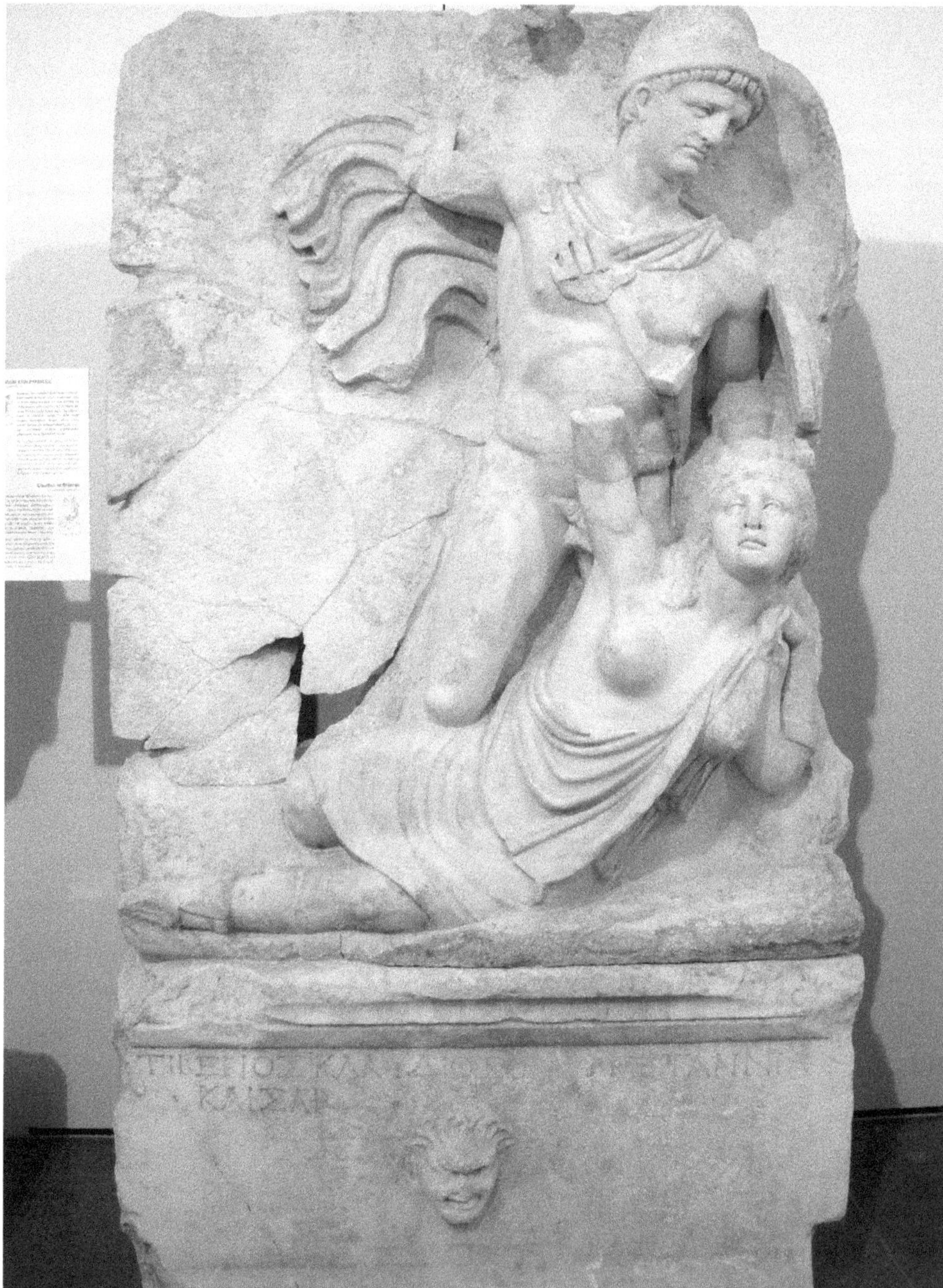

Fig. 3.2. Claudius vanquishing Britannia, from the Sebasteion at Aphrodisias

Source: Aphrodisias Excavations.

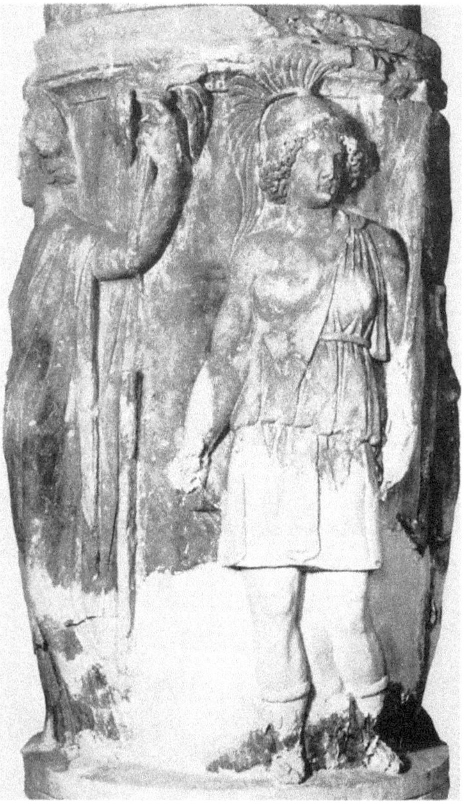

Fig. 3.3. Roma or Virtus, Jupiter column, Mainz

Source: After Bauchhenss 1984: fig. 16.

some as one of a whole series of provincial personifications, not unlike the Aphrodisias Sebasteion (Wiegartz 1996).

The representation of pacified provinces did not preclude a chronicling of the warfare that resulted in that pacification, and the Romans have left us some of the most vivid war documentaries of the ancient world (Hölscher 2003). In painting, sculpture, and the so-called minor arts, such as coinage, cameos, and pottery, Romans were typically shown vanquishing the enemy on the field of battle or displaying the defeated and chained leaders in triumphal processions (Dillon and Welch 2006). In so doing, they responded differently to the memorialization of conflict than artists in Europe and the Americas did during the twentieth century, although this is not often noted. A survey of contemporary war memorials would reveal that scenes of conflict and carnage on the battlefield are extremely rare; the composition instead features the men, women, and children allied with the group or country that has dedicated the monument (Borg 1991; Rose 2005: 21).

Images of battles dominated the landscape of Republican Rome, although many of these were paintings and survive only in ekphrastic form. From the Empire, however, we have an extensive amount of triumphal imagery, some of which, especially those on the colossal narrative columns of Trajan and Marcus

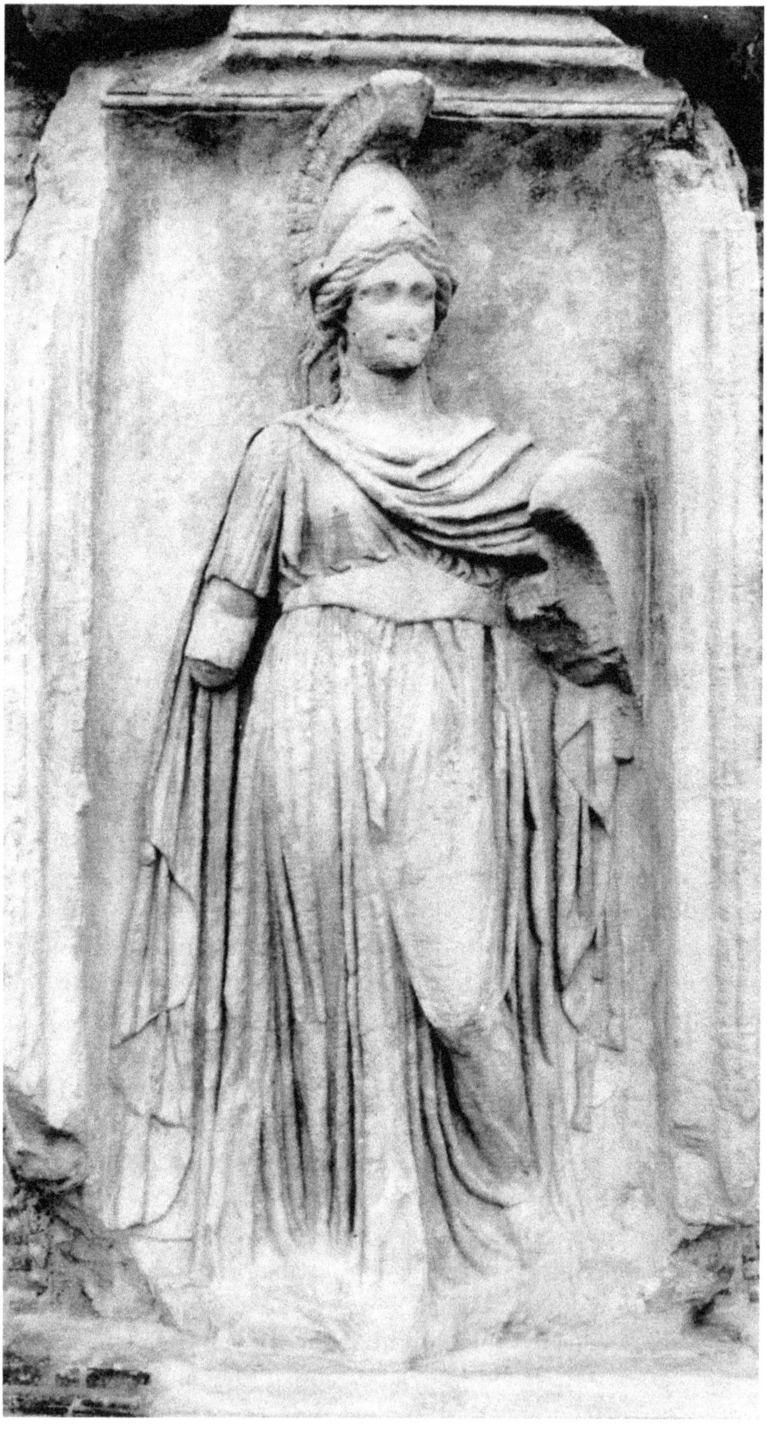

Fig. 3.4. Attic relief from the Forum Transitorium in Rome

Source: D'Ambra 1991: fig. 43.

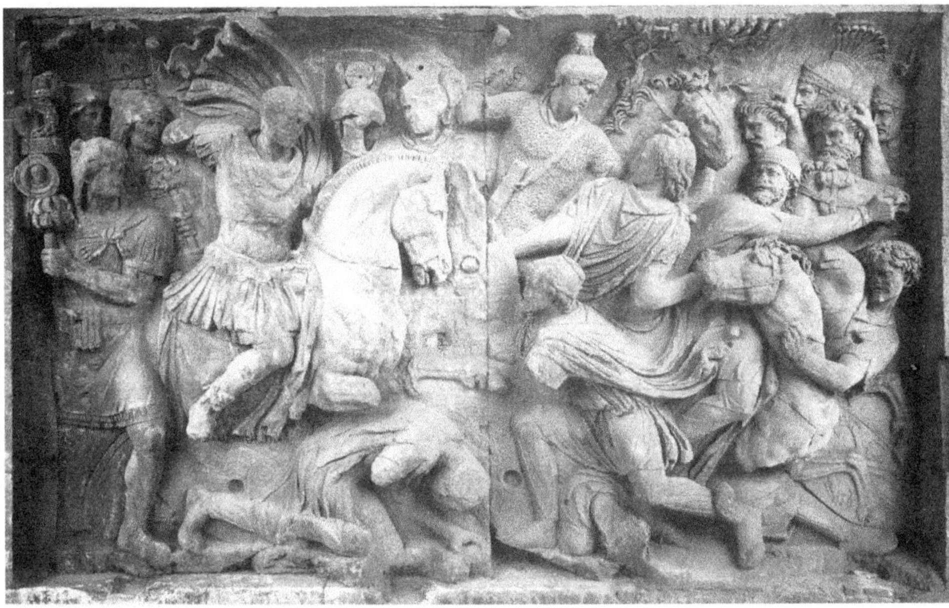

Fig. 3.5. Great Trajanic relief, Arch of Constantine

Source: After Kleiner, 1992: fig. 185.

Aurelius, are unusually graphic in their documentation: the heads of the enemies are systematically severed and carried in the mouths of the Roman conquerors; enemy women inflict torture on the bodies of the Romans or their allies, pressing torches against bare skin; and enemy chiefs, convinced of impending defeat, commit suicide *en masse*. This is not to say that the iconography of war in Rome was static from start to finish: several monuments of Augustan date show the former enemy as a contributor to peace, fully domesticated, and the same message appears in Hadrianic coinage (*RIC* II, 374–8). More common was the presentation of the enemy as already dead or pleading for mercy, not unlike Sassanian triumphal monuments in the East. In fact, a comparison of one of the 'Great Trajanic Reliefs', showing Trajan defeating the Dacians (fig. 3.5), with one of the rock-cut victory reliefs in Iranian Bishapur documenting the Sassanians' defeat of the Romans (fig. 3.6), reveals that the iconography of subjugation in both cases is fundamentally the same.

Since war with the East was a consistent theme in Roman triumphal imagery, Parthians and Sassanians consistently played a major role in the iconographic programmes formulated throughout the Mediterranean, beginning in the Augustan period. Each of Rome's enemies had a certain set of attributes that, in theory, allowed for easy identification; in fact, they were far from straightforward, as the distinctive iconography of the East can easily demonstrate. The trousers and Phrygian caps that characterized the Parthians also designated the men and boys of Troy (fig. 3.19) and

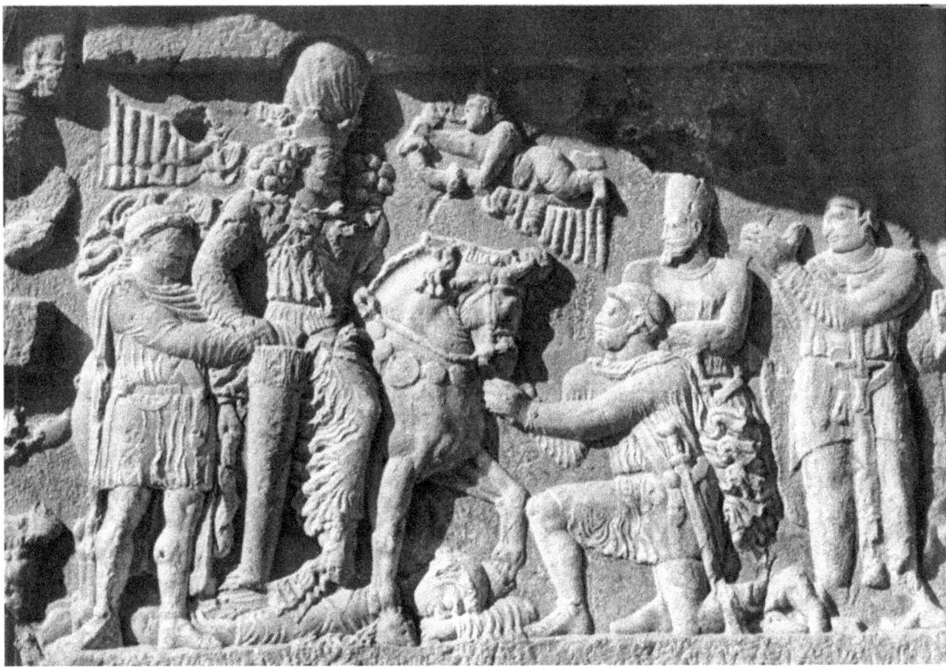

Fig. 3.6. Rock-cut relief of Shapur I from Bishapur, Iran

Source: After Ghirshman 1963: fig. 197.

Attis, the consort of Cybele, whose cult was celebrated on the Palatine hill next to the house of Augustus (Miller 1995; Vermaseren and DeBoer 1986).

From the point of view of political philosophy, this confluence of attributes is easy to understand: it was the destiny of the Romans to dominate the East, from which they had originally come, and the overlapping iconography reinforced this. From a practical point of view, however, such ambiguity was more problematic: if Rome's founders also looked like Rome's fiercest enemies, then only the context, or the associated inscriptions, could indicate whether the attributes had a positive or negative significance. Not surprisingly, Aeneas was not shown in eastern costume until the early Christian period, and images of Trojans and Parthians never occupied the same space in Imperial Rome (Rose 2005: 34–44). The distinction between the two was clearer in Latin literature of the late Republic and early Empire, in that different words were used to refer to the two types of easterners: Trojans were 'Phryges' while Parthians were 'Medes'. In other words, Asians could be bad or good.

The wearing of torques or twisted metal necklaces would have immediately distinguished Trojans from Parthians, in that the former never wore them. But torques also identified a wide range of additional characters, including the Celts, the priests of the Magna Mater, and the aristocratic youths who participated in the *lusus Troiae*. The confusion that the torque has caused is readily apparent in recent scholarship on the Ara Pacis, where the two boys wearing torques have been alternately identified as the adopted sons of Augustus, or as barbarians linked to Gaul, Cappadocia, or Parthia (Kuttner 1995: 100–23; LaRocca 2002; Rose 2005: 39–42). Usually, the context, if known, can provide the answer; yet the Ara Pacis is nearly complete, with a known context, and questions about its iconography still continue.

Consistently incorporated into all of this triumphal iconography was the element of time or perpetuity, for which a variety of iconographic formulae were devised. These included, among others, personifications of the Four Seasons, who framed portraits of the deceased on Roman sarcophagi; complementary figures of the sun and the moon on the Arch of Constantine; or the flanking letters of alpha and omega in early Christian imagery (De Maria 1988: pl. 69; Grabar 1968: figs. 128, 289). The most egregious use of a temporal frame for a triumphal monument lay in the northern Campus Martius, where the gnomon of Augustus' new horologium cast a shadow toward the centre of the Ara Pacis on his birthday, 23 September, thereby continuously linking the emperor with the establishment of peace throughout the empire (Buchner 1982). Hellenistic royal spectacles had made use of personifications of the phases of the day, such as the Morning and Evening Stars, and the same solution appears to have been devised by the designers of the Aphrodisias Sebasteion in an attempt to convey the expected eternity of the Julio-Claudian dynasty (Athenaeus 195b, 197b; Kuttner 1999*a*; Smith 1988: 51–2).

The examples listed above constitute only a fraction of the symbols developed to connote eternity—zodiac rings, the personification of time itself (Aion/Aeternitas), and the addition of the epithet 'Aeterna' to Roma could also be cited, as could iconographic schemes intended to evoke earlier periods. The early Empire, in particular, is filled with visual and verbal references to a former golden age that had allegedly returned due to the judicious guidance of the current ruler, just as later emperors used slogans like *felicitas temporum reparatio* ('I brought back the good times'). In painted landscapes, historical reliefs, and most of the minor arts, one can find well-fed and contented animals and children situated in fertile fields overseen by benevolent gods and personifications (Leach 1988: 197–260; fig. 3.12).

Style itself could, by revival, suggest temporal renewal of society: the return of the Republicanizing 'veristic' portrait type, under Vespasian and Trajan in particular, sought to persuade the viewer that the lost values of the Republic had crystallized again in the character of the new ruler (Kleiner 1992: 172, 208–9; Gowing 2005). One of the most persuasive methods of fusing heroic past and political present involved the use of the same pose and gesture for rulers and divinities on a single monument. This was employed very effectively for Augustus and Aeneas on the Ara Pacis (figs. 3.7, 3.8), for Divus Augustus and Caligula on coins struck by the latter, and for Trajan and Jupiter on the triumphal arch at Beneventum, among others, although it also had a long history in the Near East (*RIC* I: 111, no. 36; Ghirshman 1963: figs. 246, 283; Rotili 1972: figs. 77, 86, 129).

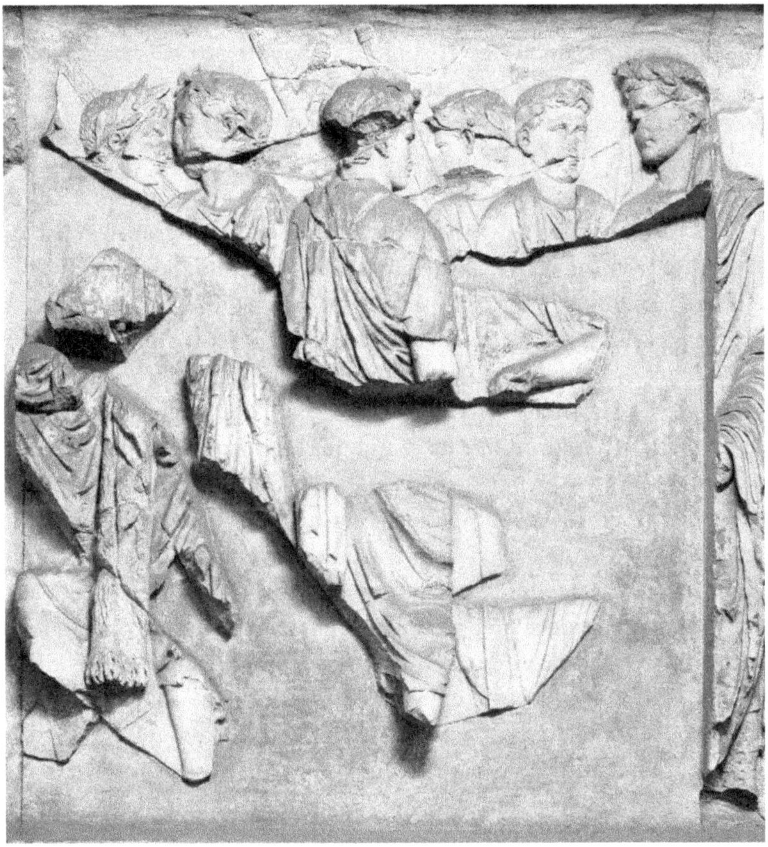

Fig. 3.7. Augustus, Ara Pacis Augustae, Rome

Source: Simon 1968: fig. 11.

Rome's military supremacy over foreign regions did not prevent the arts of the conquered from leaving an indelible stamp on the decoration of the capital city. The victories in southern Greece and Macedon during the second century BCE are a case in point, in that the conquering generals seized as many statues as they could carry back to Rome. The triumphal procession of M. Fulvius Nobilior in 187 reportedly displayed 515 of them, while two decades later Aemilius Paullus paraded 250 wagons, all filled with statues and paintings looted from Macedonia (Livy 39.5.13–16; Plutarch, *Aemilius Paullus* 32–3; Gruen 1992: 84–13; Hölscher 2004). An especially noteworthy addition to Rome at this time was a statuary group executed by Lysippus that commemorated the Macedonian victory by Alexander over the Persians at the battle of Granicus. This was transferred from Dion to Rome in 146 by one of the conquering heroes, Metellus, who set it up in his new sanctuary as his own ready-made triumphal monument over Macedon. No technical changes were necessary; the new context alone transformed what would otherwise have been

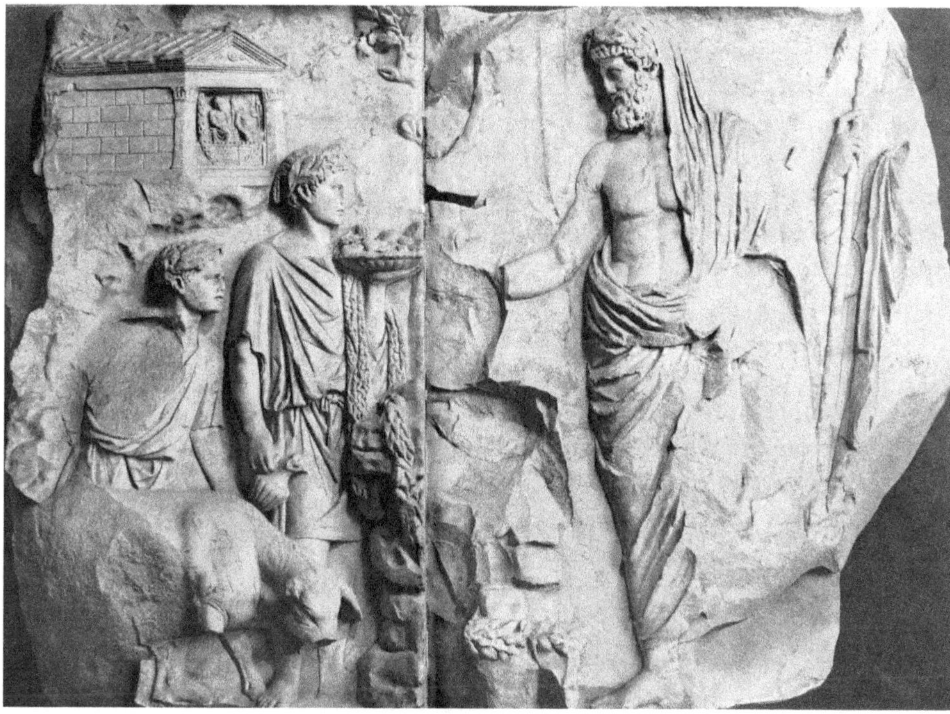

Fig. 3.8. Aeneas, Ara Pacis Augustae, Rome

Source: Simon 1968: fig. 24.

construed as a statement of Macedonian triumph into a testament to their defeat (Stewart 1994: 123–30).

Standing in the vicinity of these looted masterpieces were the statues of the men who had been responsible for the conquest. Although the iconography of their portraits is more straightforward than that of the enemy, here too one sometimes encounters difficulty in distinguishing conqueror from conquered, and human from divine. By about 200 BCE a distinctive portrait type had been developed for the Roman aristocracy (the so-called 'veristic' style); here, physiognomic individuality (aquiline noses, pointed or squared chins, thin or thick lips) were coupled with the signs of age (receding hair, lines on forehead and cheeks, crows' feet around the eyes). The basis of these portraits is usually asserted to have been the wax masks, or *imagines*, that were modelled from the face of a Roman aristocrat once he had reached the rank of aedile, typically between the age of 35 and 40. We often refer to these as death masks because they were worn during funerals, but they were made when the subject was relatively young and, in many cases, without the emphatic marks of age (Flower 1996; Tanner 2000).

The incorporation of advanced age in portraiture leads one to ask what age actually meant during the Republic, and why its physical manifestation was viewed in such a positive light. In examining the iconography of advanced age in Greek and Etruscan imagery prior to the development of the veristic type, one finds that it was used rather selectively, and primarily for teachers, seers, and philosophers—in other words, as a designation of knowledge, piety, and moral character. Veristic portraiture was probably created with this tradition very much in mind: it enabled the Romans to co-opt the moral superiority associated with the features of advanced age, while simultaneously distinguishing the portraits of the *triumphatores* from the looted idealized images of their opponents that stood nearby (Rose 2008).

Body types associated with the veristic portrait were a different matter altogether. A significant number of extant portraits represented military men who had just earned triumphs; to counterbalance the appearance of advanced age in the portraits, sculptors often supplied body types and attributes that denoted physical strength, such as a muscled torso, a cuirass, or a combination of both, as one finds on the 'General from Tivoli' (fig. 3.9). This uneasy assimilation of two very different ages was studiously avoided by the Greeks, but it allowed the Romans to achieve their goal of presenting an image of martial prowess guided by moral probity.

Individualized human physiognomies also played a role in helping Republican viewers differentiate between images of the gods and those of men, although there were usually other devices on which one could have relied: gods tended to be larger than men, often barefoot, and either nude or semi-nude, whereas the men were generally clothed (Hallett 2005). These distinctions of scale are typically maintained in votive reliefs showing humans and gods in the same zone, as well as in temple pediments such as the second-century BCE example from the Via di San Gregorio (fig. 3.10), where even a quick glance leaves no doubt as to the relative status of the participants (Ferrea 2002).

In cases where a military event was celebrated, however, such distinctions were less straightforward, because both military gods (i.e. Mars) and men wore cuirasses, helmets, and sandals. A case in point is the so-called Altar of Domitius Ahenobarbus (fig. 3.11), probably a monumental base intended to honour Marcus Antonius, grandfather of the famous triumvir, for his victory over a group of pirates in Asia Minor *c.*100 BCE (Ryberg 1955: 27–34; Kuttner 1993; Stilp 2001). Flanking the altar in the *suovetaurilia* scene are two men: one in a cuirass, one in a priestly costume. Since Mars is the intended recipient of the sacrifice, he is usually identified as the cuirassed figure at the left of the altar, on the grounds that he is larger than anyone else, divorced from the action, and stands with his foot on a globe. But cursory scrutiny of the figure shows that he is essentially the same height as the others—only his helmet makes him appear taller—and he is just as involved in the action as everyone else. The object under his foot has an unusual shape, rather like a stone, but it is certainly not a globe, nor are there any surviving images of Republican date in which human and god are the same size.

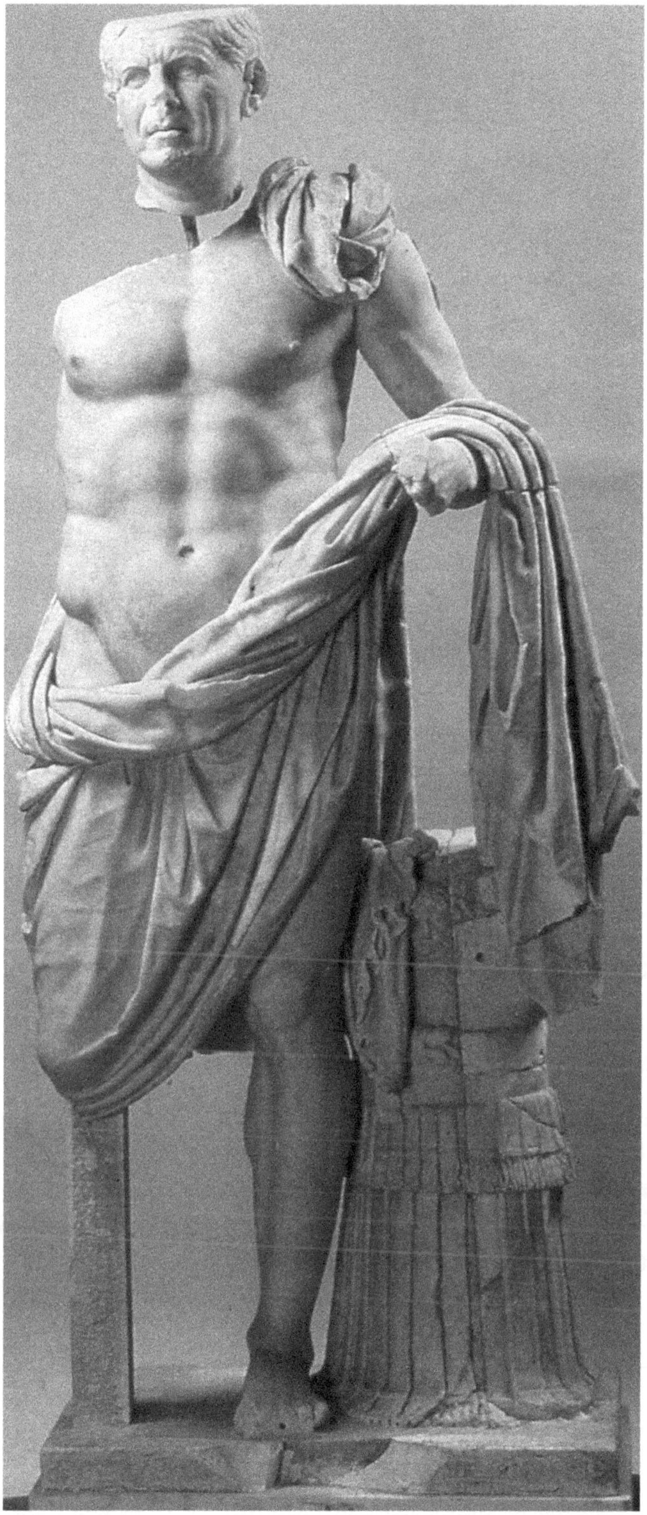

Fig. 3.9. General from Tivoli

Source: After Himmelmann 1989: 218, fig. 12*a*.

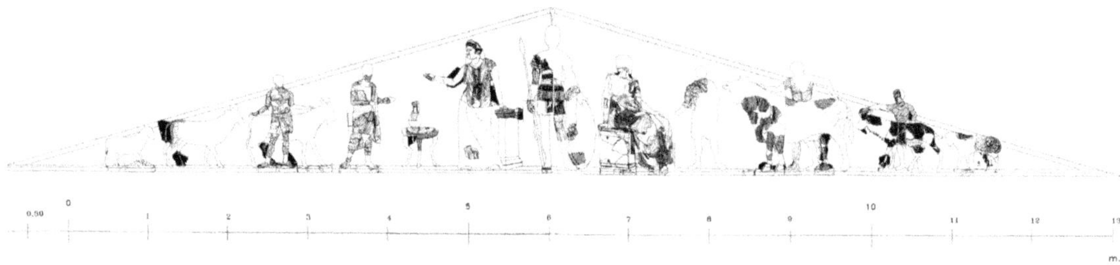

Fig. 3.10. Terracotta pediment from a temple on the Via di San Gregorio, Rome

Source: After Ferrea 2002: 142–3.

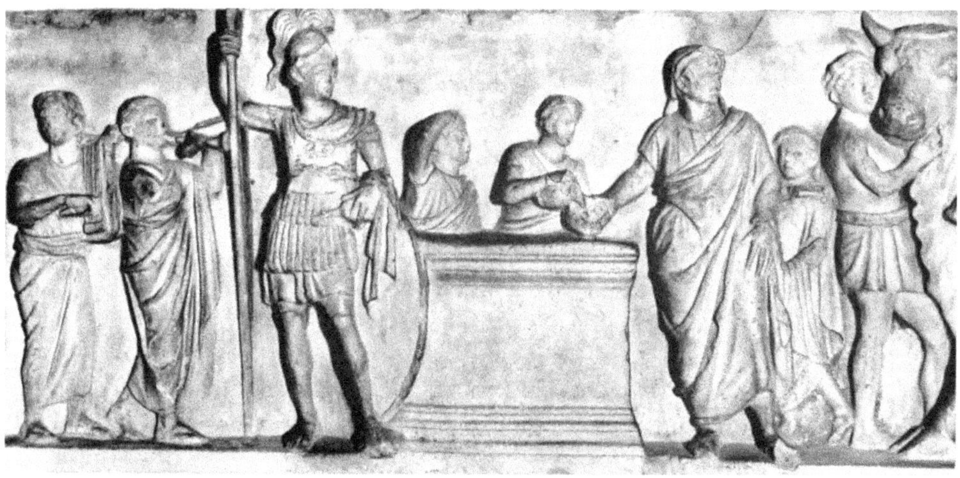

Fig. 3.11. Detail of the 'Altar of Domitius Ahenobarbus', Louvre

Source: After Kähler 1966: pl. 5.

If the figure is Mars, then the monument makes a striking statement about relationships between humans and gods at the beginning of the first century BCE, one that is very much at odds with contemporary Roman imagery. If the cuirassed man is the commander whose maritime triumph is honoured in the relief, then we have an equally striking representation of an armed commander witnessing a sacrifice. The fact that we cannot be certain of the figure's status, even though the monument is complete and its general context is known, shows us how fragile our understanding of Roman iconography actually is.

The same problem occurs when one examines domestic wall- and ceiling-decoration produced during the early Empire, as one of the stucco ceilings in the Villa Farnesina in Rome makes clear (figs. 3.12, 3.13). A rustic landscape is flanked by two identical statues of an idealized nude youth with caduceus who serves as the support for a canopy on which a sphinx sits (Brendel 1980). He is traditionally

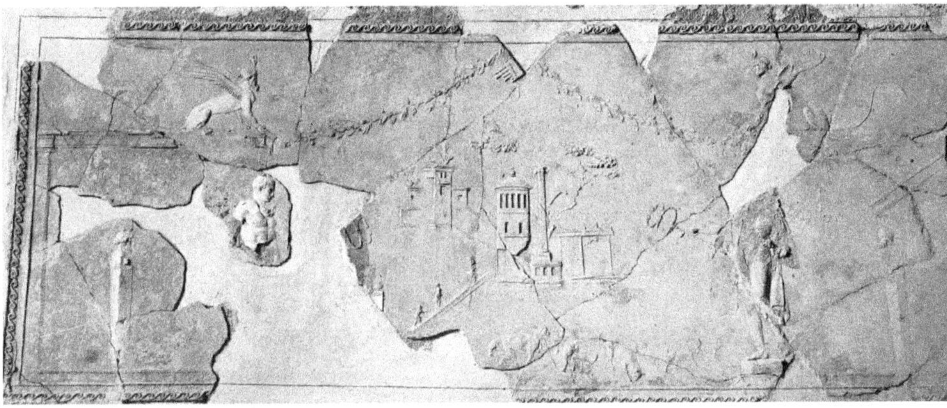

Fig. 3.12. Stucco ceiling panel from the Villa Farnesina, Rome

Source: Grabar 1968: fig. 83.

Fig. 3.13. Stucco ceiling panel from the Villa Farnesina, Rome

Source: Brendel 1980: 28, fig. 2.

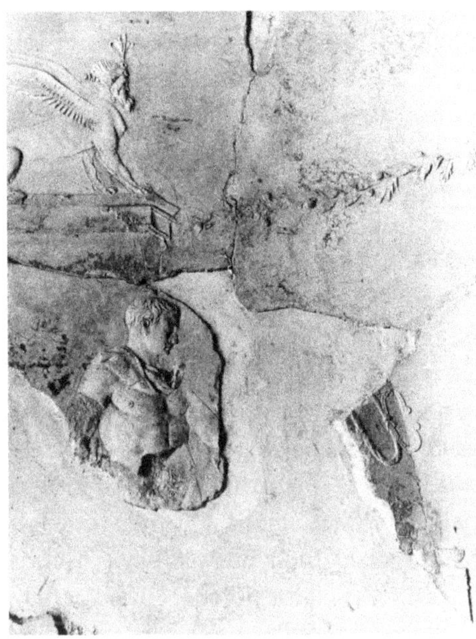

identified as Augustus in the guise of Mercury, and cited in support of the argument that a living emperor could and did appear as a divinity in interior decoration produced during his life.

We are accustomed to seeing large, detailed photographs of this figure which give us an inaccurate sense of its scale; in fact, the head is only 2 centimetres in height, positioned nearly 3 metres above the floor, and surrounded by a panoply of landscape elements. Moreover, as one scholar has noted, emperors do not serve as architectural supports; it is the architecture that supports them (Smith 1982: 199). Viewing the figure in context casts significant doubt on the Augustus identification, which also leads us to question arguments about the appearance of emperors in such idyllic landscapes.

Yet the similarity between the canopy support and Augustus is undeniable, and it captures the essence of a political trend that continually occurs, even in contemporary society. From time to time, a ruler's accession is accompanied by the creation of a new portrait type that deviates significantly from those of past rulers, quickly becoming so influential that portraits of everyone else, regardless of their status, tend to follow the same model. Americans witnessed this phenomenon in the 1960s with the accession of John F. Kennedy, whose portrait matched the youth and idealization of images of Augustus. Kennedy's type became so dominant, despite his short-lived presidency, that it even influenced the manner in which generic figures were conceived. An examination of any popular magazine produced during the early 1960s shows that nearly all of the figures in the advertisements look like Kennedys, even though none of them actually was (fig. 3.14). The same phenomenon occurred during the reigns of Augustus, Trajan, and Hadrian, in particular, which makes it difficult, at least for us, to distinguish imperial from non-imperial, as the generic figure on the Villa Farnesina ceiling demonstrates.

Another reason we have difficulty separating human from superhuman is that the same attributes were occasionally used for both, especially in the portraiture of elite women during the Empire. The beaded woolen fillet or *infula* worn by the 'Juno Ludovisi' (fig. 3.15) is often cited in support of her imperial status, although the *infula* was simply a general mark of sanctity, worn by gods, priestesses, and animals about to be sacrificed (Wood 1999: 133–6). The crescent-shaped crown or *stephane* (figs. 3.10, 3.15, 3.16) had a similar significance, although its history is more complex: in the eastern Mediterranean it was used as a badge of royalty; in Italy and the West it served as an attribute of priestesses, sacrificial animals, or the goddesses themselves. It did not figure in the iconography of imperial women, however, until they began to be deified under Caligula, at which time it became a symbol that the woman in question had reached the status of *diva*. Only subsequently did it enter the repertoire of attributes used for portraits of imperial women still living (Rose 1997*a*: 76).

Since imperial women were valued primarily for their ability to produce children who could continue the dynasty, a range of agrarian symbols were borrowed for their portraiture from the iconographic repertoire of fertility goddesses, primarily Ceres, Venus, and Fortuna (Alexandridis 2004: 25–6, 290–4). The most popular attributes, cornucopiae or stalks of wheat, were often placed in the hands or hair of women whose images were positioned near those of their husbands or sons, such as Livia on the Grand Camée or Julia Mamaea on medallions of Alexander Severus (fig. 3.16). Incorporation of words like 'karpophoros' (fruit-bearing) in the dedicatory inscription is also found, as is the insertion of women's portraits into

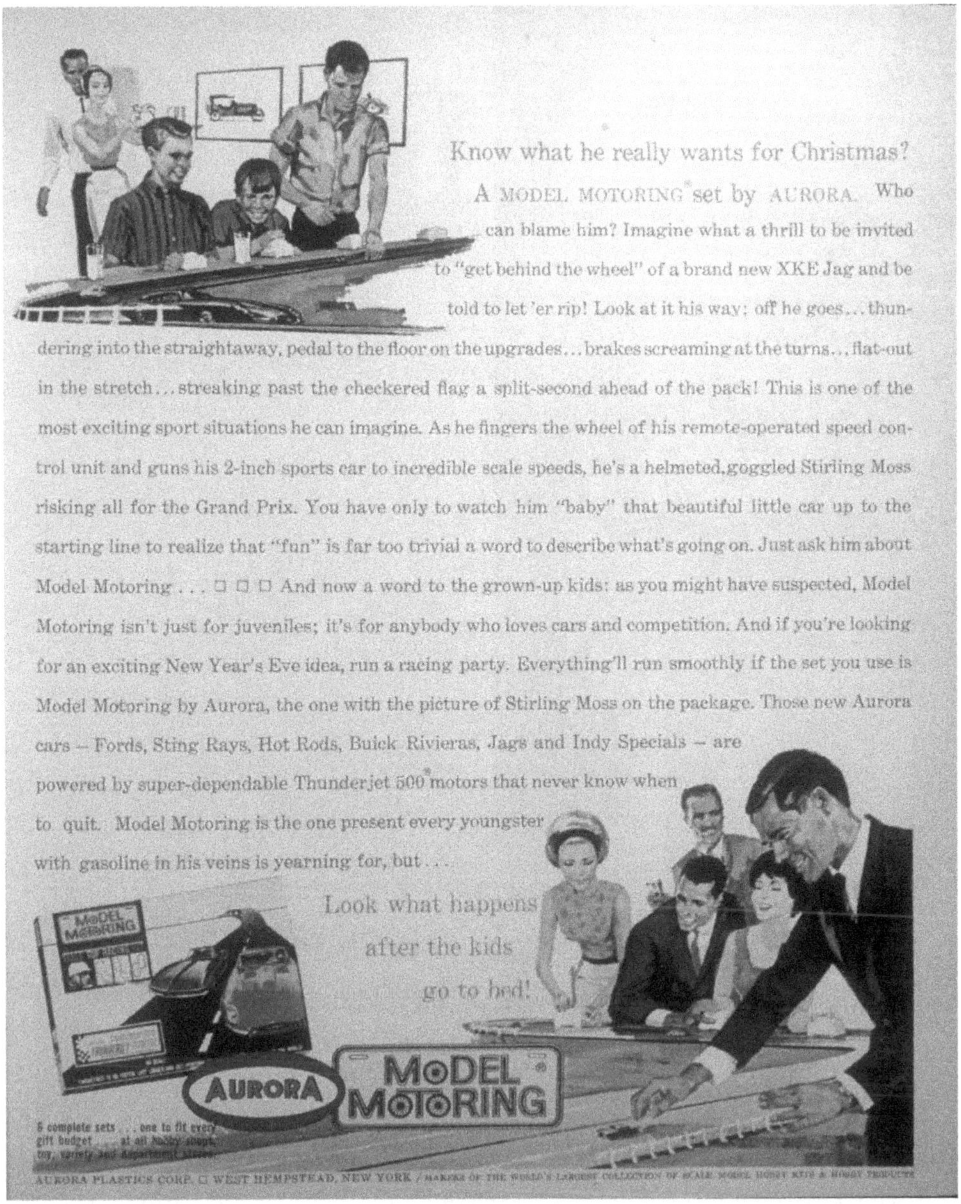

Fig. 3.14. Advertisement from *Life* Magazine, December 1963

statuary types of Venus or Ceres; the statue of Livia from Lepcis Magna, identified as 'Ceres Augusta', is a particularly noteworthy example (Rose 1997*a*: 75–6; Bartman 1999: 179–80, cat. 74; Smith 1987: 127–32 [Agrippina the Younger]).

This interweaving of political and religious iconography applies also to large public spaces in cities and sanctuaries. In the Roman Forum, the temple of Divus

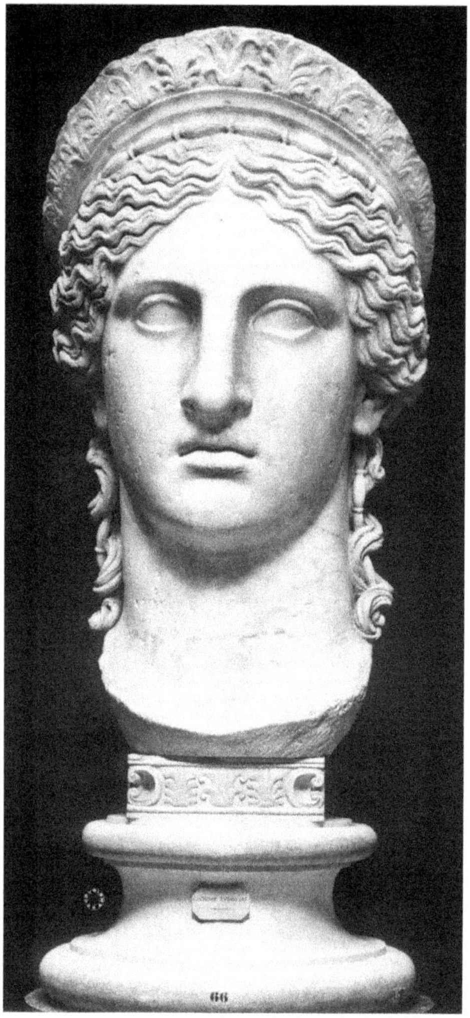

Fig. 3.15. 'Juno Ludovisi', Rome

Source: After Wood 1999: fig. 50.

Iulius shared a platform with the Regia, the former home of the *pontifex maximus*, while the stairs of the adjacent temple of Castor and Pollux opened directly into the Parthian arch of Augustus (Nielsen 1993). These links operated on a vertical level too, which we often forget due to our preference for plans over elevations. The star that filled the pediment of the temple of Divus Iulius would have complemented the stars above the Dioscuri in the pediment of their adjacent temple; centuries later, the Tetrarchic statues above columns on the Forum's opposite side would have been framed by the trophy-bearing Victoriae above the neighbouring temple of Concord (Rose 2005: 63–4).

The most prominent element that shifted between the realms of politics and religion was the arch, which had begun to serve as a symbol of triumph by the first century BCE (De Maria 1988). Although initially exploited as a symbol of

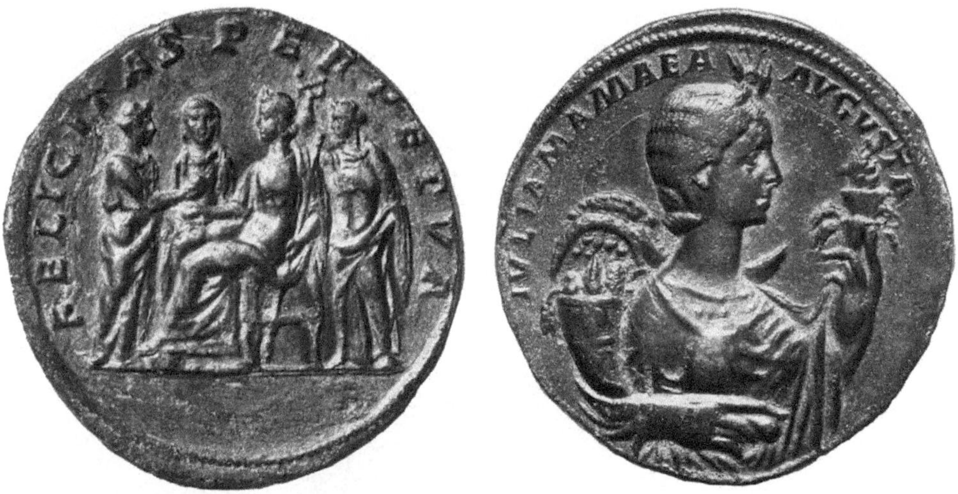

Fig. 3.16. Medallion of Julia Mamaea, 228 CE

Source: After Kent *et al.* 1973 : pl. 101.434.

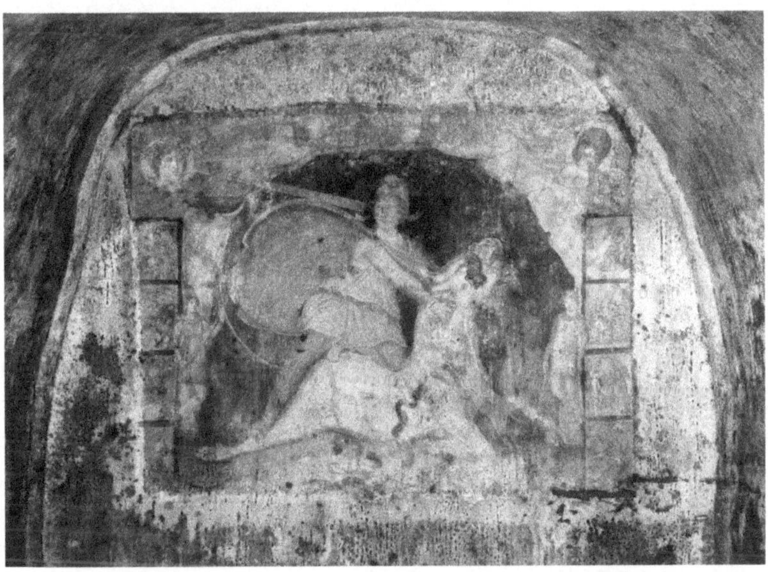

Fig. 3.17. Painting from the Mithraeum at Marino, near Rome

Source: After Vermaseren 1982: pl. III.

political victory within an exterior setting, arches were eventually incorporated into Mithraea and Christian churches as a frame for the altar where the birth or rebirth of the divine agent was celebrated (figs. 3.17, 3.18). Political arches had featured small relief panels on the supporting piers and attic that offered commentaries on the emperor's triumph and political programme; this format too

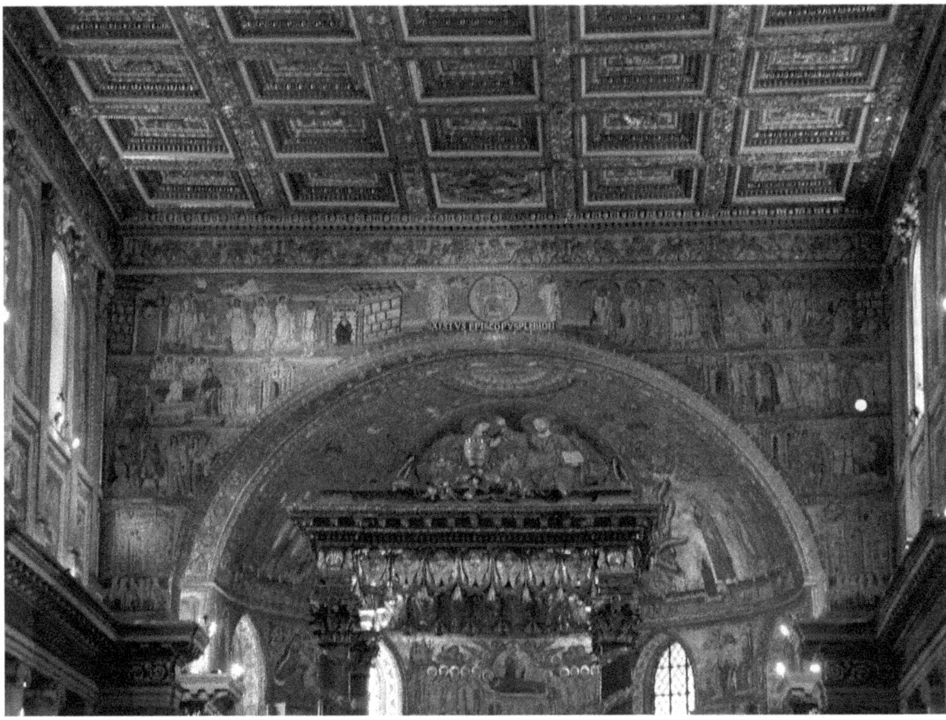

Fig. 3.18. Apse mosaics of Santa Maria Maggiore, Rome

Source: After Grabar 1968: fig. 130.

was pulled into the religious realm, with similar panels highlighting the god's exploits on earth and reinforcing the human and divine components of his identity (Grabar 1968: 102).

What we tend to forget in our analyses of these monuments are the spectacles that periodically embraced them, lifting the iconography to a new level of potency. The dedication of Augustus' Parthian arch appears to have been timed to coincide with the *ludi saeculares*, which featured purification rituals with brimstone and pitch, dramatic presentations, games and sacrifices, and choirs of women and children marching between the Capitoline and Palatine. The opening ceremony of the temple of Mars Ultor immediately followed the slaughter of thirty-six crocodiles in the Circus Flaminius, symbolizing the Roman victory over Cleopatra at Actium, and the re-enactment of the battle of Salamis, which ended the Persian Wars (Dio 55.10.7–8; *Res Gestae* 23; Ovid, *Ars. Amat.* 1.171–2). Most of the spectacles would have entailed live music, burning incense, and elaborate feasts, among other activities, which means that each of the senses would have been heightened whenever these imposing monuments were unveiled (Scullard 1981).

If one were to have walked through the Roman Forum during any of these spectacles, most of the statues on view, apart from those of the gods, would have represented members of the imperial family. Outside Rome, however, the public spaces would have been crowded with images of local benefactors as well, many of which were erected next to those of the imperial family. Here again one would have encountered the problem of distinguishing between them. Both were generally slightly over life-size (just over 2 metres), made of the same materials, and set up in the same location, usually the agora or forum (Rose 1997*b*).

During the early Empire, in particular, elite private portraits also featured the same idealized faces as the Julio-Claudian rulers, and the *corona civica*, or crown of oak-leaves, had not yet become a standard badge of imperial portraiture. As a result, the only absolute criterion for identifying an imperial statue would have been the associated inscription, making literacy, or access to a literate guide, absolutely critical. One can easily see this ambiguity in the published corpus of Roman imperial portrait statues from Asia Minor, with so many entries given a question-mark after the label 'Imperial' (Inan and Rosenbaum 1966; 1979).

Assessing imperial status during the second century CE would have been more straightforward, since the *corona civica* began to be widely used as an imperial designation, yet the same period witnessed more frequent combinations of private and imperial statues in façade architecture, such as propylons, fountain houses, and theatre *skenes*. This was especially true of cities in the East, which had placed rulers and benefactors in the same honorific categories since the Hellenistic period. If an image were colossal, of course, it would have been easier to assess its status, since colossality appears to have been used only for individuals of imperial or superhuman status, but such images were usually excluded from outdoor public spaces (Kreikenbom 1992; Burrell 2004: 104–8, 317–21). In other words, the visual ambiguity that characterized imperial and Olympian imagery extended also to the non-imperial realm.

Not all of these commanders and benefactors remained in favour after their deaths, despite the inclusion of symbols promising limitless fame, which meant that *damnationes* also became an ingredient in the iconography (Varner 2004; Flower 2006). In Pharaonic Egypt and various parts of the Near East, figures who had fallen from favour were often battered but not completely erased, so that the viewer would be aware that a *damnatio* had occurred (Bahrani 1995; Dorman 1988). Although this did happen from time to time in the Roman provinces, such admonitory mutilation in the public monuments of Republican and Imperial Italy was generally avoided: the positions occupied by Domitian, Commodus, and Geta in the Cancelleria reliefs, Aurelian panels, and Arch of the Argentarii, respectively, have been completely flattened or recut (Varner 2004: 112–47, 170–84). Their place in history had literally been erased.

So far this discussion has focused on the meaning of forms and symbols, but the materials out of which the images were constructed were often iconographic too. A number of inscriptions indicate that white marble was considered more valuable than bronze during the late Republic/late Hellenistic period, in large part because it was extremely expensive to obtain, at least in Italy, until the opening of the Carrara quarries in the mid-first century BCE (Tuchelt 1979: 70–90). The decision to use marble for an image, therefore, automatically signalled the subject's elevated status, which is undoubtedly the reason it was popular for cult statues in Republican Rome (Martin 1987).

This was true as well for architecture during the Republic, when most of Rome's buildings were constructed of limestone, tufa, or travertine. The change to marble began to occur in the second century BCE as generals who had been victorious in Greece and Asia Minor returned to Rome intent upon building large, eye-catching temples that could also symbolize the success and scope of their conquests (Rakob 1973; Gruen 1992: 86–152). The commanders began signing their temples with monumental inscriptions, and a system of aristocratic competition quickly developed wherein the marble composition of the new temple became as important as the booty it contained. Even more prominence was accorded to the name of the sponsor or dedicant once the Empire began, when gilded bronze letters, separately cast, replaced the old incised forms (Rose 2005: 29, n. 52). At the same time, gilding became the preferred finish in Italy for bronze statues, both imperial and private, as it had been for Hellenistic kings and benefactors in the eastern Mediterranean (Lahusen 2001: 505–18).

Coloured stone played as fundamental a role in iconography as white marble, especially in Rome (De Nuccio *et al.* 2002). Egyptian porphyry had been favoured by rulers since the Ptolemies, but by the time of the Tetrarchy it had emerged as an unmistakable sign of imperial status, which was maintained through the Byzantine period (Malgouyres 2003). A very different symbolism was attached to the purple-veined marble (pavonazzetto) from the Dokimeion quarries near Afyon in central Turkey, which were first exploited during the Augustan period. Since the stone came from Phrygia, it was regularly used for images of foreigners from the East, such as the Parthians in the Augustan Basilica Aemilia, the Dacians in the Forum of Trajan, or the Trojans, as demonstrated by the pavonazzetto Ganymede from Tiberian Sperlonga (fig. 3.19). In these cases, the Asian provenance of the stone signalled the eastern origins of the foreigners as much as their trousers and caps (Schneider 1986; Ungaro 2002; Sichtermann 1988: 166, no. 250).

We frequently speak of the effect that state-sponsored iconography would have had on the viewer, and of the ways in which their opinions about religion, politics, or society would have been modified as a consequence of the viewing process. What we should ask, but do not, is how many could actually have seen all of this imagery clearly. There is no reason to believe that the ancient viewer was any less myopic than we are, and if one were to travel today to a village in the Near East where literacy was low and television was essentially non-existent, one would find the same basic rate of optical diminution. Images at ground level would have been relatively easy to scrutinize, but many of these images were several metres above the head of the spectator, easily viewed by children and far-sighted adults, but a blur to

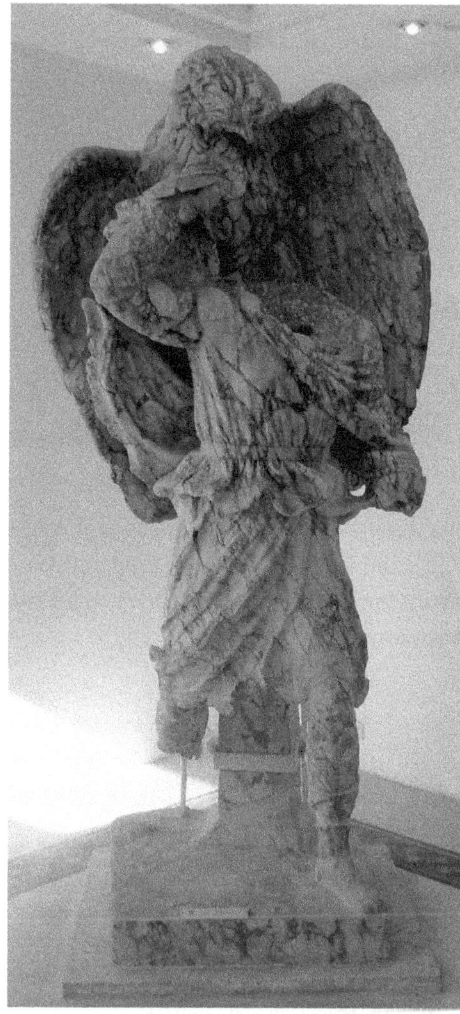

Fig. 3.19. Pavonazzetto statue of Ganymede from Sperlonga

Source: photo author.

many. The use of 'easy-to-read signs' such as gilded bronze letters on triumphal arches therefore makes a lot of sense, as do gaudily painted acroterial decoration on the roofs of public buildings.

I mentioned in the introduction that the meaning of an icon, whether political or religious, is always in flux, and subject to reinterpretation by each successive generation of scholars. Visual evocations of peace in the ancient Roman world are read differently by those who have witnessed World War II, as by those who observe daily the conflicts in Iraq and Afghanistan. And yet the fundamental issues with which the Romans grappled in their attempts to convey images of power and sanctity, victory and loss, or prosperity and desire, are not appreciably different from our own. The past continues to be reshaped by word and image to suit the needs of the present, with periodic iconoclasm; the visual line between politics and religion grows increasingly

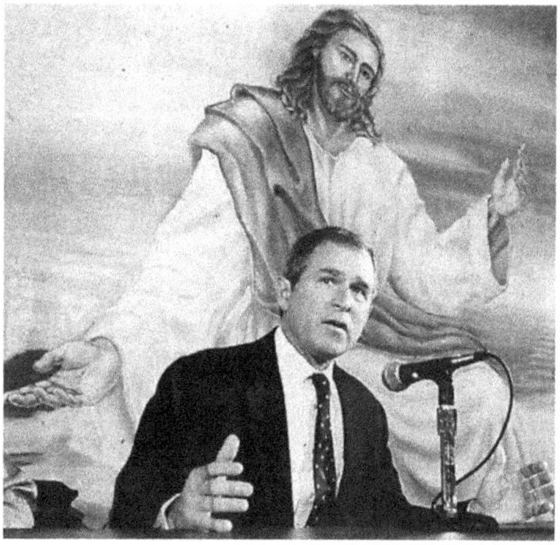

Fig. 3.20. George W. Bush presenting a speech, from the *New York Times*, 2006

less distinct, not unlike Aeneas and Augustus, as rulers rush to co-opt their gods (fig. 3.20); and the wars between East and West continue to be waged, although the current representation of military success and misfortune assumes a visual form very different from anything the Romans might have devised.

Further reading

New scholarship in Roman iconography has tended to echo contemporary political and economic changes in western societies, with a sharpened focus on the issues of gender, power politics, and ethnic identity. Recent work in the first category (D'Ambra 1993; Kampen 1995; Wood 1999; Bartman 1999; Alexandridis 2004) has devoted considerable attention to the reconstruction of women's social and political position in Roman society, with extensive use of inscriptions, coinage, and cross-cultural comparanda. Research within the domestic sphere (Bergmann 1994; Wallace-Hadrill 1994; Clarke 1998; Dunbabin 2003; Allison 2004) has provided more of a sociological framework for the iconographic analysis of villa decoration. The extended Roman family, including women and children, now receive attention, as do the themes of dining and sex, in particular. The recent rise of so many nationalist movements in Eastern Europe and the former Soviet Union has sparked a renewed interest in the ethnic diversity of the Roman world, as well as the artificial construct of Rome's enemies in triumphal imagery (Kuttner 1995; Hölscher 2003; Rose 2005; Dillon and Welch 2006). The treatment of 'the other' in the context of postcolonial theory has become a dominant theme in iconographic studies in general, from ancient to modern, as exemplified by Pinder 2002. Related to this is an awareness that no imagery of any period can have a single meaning, nor will the network of meanings remain static over time, for which see Baxandall 1985.

The historiography of Roman art, beginning with the Renaissance, is provided by Brendel 1979, to which Kampen 2003 should be added for an overview of current theoretical approaches to both style and iconography.

The most influential work in Roman iconography during the last twenty years has been that of Paul Zanker (1988), whose synthetic treatment of Roman literature and art has yielded an extremely successful portrait of early Imperial culture and society.

References

Alexandridis, Annette (2004), *Die Frauen des römischen Kaiserhauses. Eine Untersuchung ihrer bildlichen Darstellung von Livia bis Julia Domna.* Mainz: von Zabern.

Allison, Penelope (2004), *Pompeian Households: An Analysis of the Material Culture.* Los Angeles: Cotsen Institute.

Andreae, B. (1957), 'Archäologische Funde and Grabungen im Bereich der Soprintendenzen von Rom 1949–1956/7.' *Jd.I* 72: 110–358.

Bahrani, Zainab (1995), 'Assault and Abduction: The Fate of the Royal Image in the Ancient Near East', *Art History*, 18: 363–82.

Bartman, E. (1999), *Portraits of Livia: Imaging the Imperial Women in Augustan Rome.* New York: Cambridge University Press.

Bauchhenss, Gerhard (1984), *Die grosse Iuppitersäule aus Mainz.* Mainz: Römisch-Germanischen Zentralmuseums.

Baxandall, Michael (1985), *Patterns of Intention: On the Historical Explanation of Pictures.* New Haven: Yale University Press.

Bergmann, Bettina (1994), 'The Roman House as Memory Theater: The House of the Tragic Poet in Pompeii', *Art Bulletin*, 76: 225–56.

Borg, Alan (1991), *War Memorials from Antiquity to the Present.* London: Leo Cooper.

Brendel, Otto (1979), *Prolegomena to the Study of Roman Art.* New Haven: Yale University Press.

—— (1980), 'Novus Mercurius', in *The Visible Idea: Interpretations of Classical Art*, 27–48. Washington, DC.

Buchner, Edmund (1982), *Die Sonnenuhr des Augustus: Nachdruck aus RM 1976 und 1980 und Nachtrag uber die Ausgrabung 1980/1981.* Mainz am Rhein: Philipp von Zabern.

Burrell, Barbara (2004), *Neokoroi: Greek Cities and Roman Emperors.* Boston: Brill.

Castellvi, G., J. Nolla, and I. Roda (1995), 'La identificacíon de los trofeos de Pompeyo en el Pirineo', *JRA* 8: 5–18.

Clarke, John R. (1998), *Looking at Lovemaking: Constructions of Sexuality in Roman Art: 100 B.C.–A.D. 250.* Berkeley: University of California Press.

D'Ambra, Eve (1993), *Private Lives, Imperial Virtues: The Frieze of the Forum Transitorium in Rome.* Princeton: Princeton University Press.

De Maria, S. (1988), *Gli archi onorari di Roma e dell'Italia Romana.* Rome: 'L'Erma' di Bretschneider.

De Nuccio, M., L. Ungaro, P. Pensabene, and L. Lazzarini (eds.) (2002), *I marmi colorati della Roma imperiale.* Venice: Marsilio.

Di Filippo Balestrazzi, E. (1997), 'Roma.' *LIMC* Suppl.: 1048–68.

Dillon, Sheila, and Katherine Welch (eds.) (2006), *Representation of War in Ancient Rome.* Cambridge: Cambridge University Press.

Dorman, P. F. (1988), *The Monuments of Senenmut: Problems in Historical Methodology.* London and New York: Kegan Paul.
Dunbabin, Katherine (2003), *The Roman Banquet: Images of Conviviality.* Cambridge: Cambridge University Press.
Ferrea, Laura (2002), *Gli dei di terracotta. La ricomposizione del frontone da via di San Gregorio.* Rome: Electa.
Flower, Harriet (1996), *Ancestor Masks and Aristocratic Power in Roman Culture.* Oxford: Oxford University Press.
—— (2006), *The Art of Forgetting: Disgrace and Oblivion in Roman Political Culture.* Chapel Hill, NC: University of North Carolina Press.
Ghirshman, R. (1962), *Iran. Parther und Sassanid.* Munich: Beck.
Gowing, Alain (2005), *Empire and Memory: The Representation of the Roman Republic in Imperial Culture.* Cambridge: Cambridge University Press.
Grabar, André (1968), *Christian Iconography: A Study of its Origins.* Princeton: Princeton University Press.
Gruen, Erich (1992), *Culture and National Identity in Republican Rome.* Ithaca, NY: Cornell University Press.
Hallett, Christopher (2005), *The Roman Nude: Heroic Portrait Statuary 200 B.C.–A.D. 300.* Oxford: Oxford University Press.
Himmelmann, Nikolaus (1989), *Herrscher und Athlet.* Milan: Olivetti.
Hölscher, T. (2003), 'Images of War in Greece and Rome: Between Military Practice, Public Memory, and Cultural Symbolism', *JRS* 93: 1–17.
—— (2004), *The Language of Images in Roman Art.* Cambridge: Cambridge University Press.
Inan, J. and E. Rosenbaum (1966), *Roman and Early Byzantine Portrait Sculpture in Asia Minor.* London: British Academy.
—— —— (1979), *Römische und frühbyzantinische Porträt Plastik aus der Türkei. Neue Funde.* Mainz am Rhein.
Khler, Heinz (1966), *Seethiasos und Census. Die Reliefs aus dem Palazzo Santa Croce in Rom.* Berlin: Mann.
Kampen, Natalie (1995), 'Looking at Gender: The Column of Trajan and Roman Historical Relief', in Donna C. Stanton and Abigail Stewart (eds.), *Feminisms in the Academy,* 46–73. Ann Arbor, Mich.: University of Michigan Press.
—— (2003), 'On Writing Histories of Roman Art', *Art Bulletin,* 85: 371–86.
Kent, J. P. C., B. Overbeck, and A. Stylow (1973), *Die römische Münzen.* Munich: Hirmer.
Kleiner, Diana (1992), *Roman Sculpture.* New Haven: Yale University Press.
Kreikenbom, Dietmar (1992), *Griechische und römische Kolossalporträts bis zum späten ersten Jahrhundert nach Christus.* Berlin: De Gruyter.
Kuttner, Ann L. (1993), 'Some New Grounds for Narrative: Marcus Antonius's base (the Ara Domitii Ahenobarbi) and Republican Biographies', in Peter Holliday (ed.), *Narrative and Event in Ancient Art,* 198–229. Cambridge: Cambridge University Press.
—— (1995), *Dynasty and Empire in the Age of Augustus: The Case of the Boscoreale Cups.* Berkeley: University of California Press.
—— (1999*a*), 'Hellenistic Images of Spectacle, from Alexander to Augustus', in B. Bergmann and C. Kondoleon (eds.), *The Art of Ancient Spectacle,* 96–123. Washington, DC: National Gallery of Art.
—— (1999*b*), 'Culture and History at Pompey's Museum', *TAPA* 129: 343–73.

LAHUSEN, G. (2001), *Römische Bildnisse aus Bronze: Kunst und Technik.* Munich: Hirmer.

LAROCCA, EUGENIO (2002), 'Silenzio e compianto dei morti nell'Ara Pacis', *Archaia Hellenike Glyptike. Aphieroma ste mneme tou glypte Stelios Triatis*, 269–313. Athens.

LEACH, ELEANOR W. (1988), *The Rhetoric of Space: Literary and Artistic Representations of Landscape in Republican and Augustan Rome.* Princeton: Princeton University Press.

MALGOUYRES, PHILIPPE (2003), *Porphyre. La piere pourpre des Ptolemées aus Bonaparte.* Paris: Louvre.

MARTIN, HANZ GUNTHER (1987), *Römische Tempelkultbilder: eine archäologische Untersuchung zur späten Republik.* Rome: 'L'Erma' di Bretschneider.

MILLER, M. (1995), 'Priam, King of Troy', in J. Carter and S. Morris (eds.), *The Ages of Homer: A Tribute to Emily Townsend Vermeule*, 449–65. Austin: University of Texas Press.

NICOLET, C. (1991), *L'Inventaire du monde.* Paris: Fayard.

NIELSEN, I. (1993), 'Castor, Aedes, Templum', *LTUR* 1: 242–5.

PINDER, KIMBERLY (2002). *Race-ing Art History.* London: Routledge.

RAKOB, FRIEDRICH (1973), *Der Rundtempel am Tiber in Rom.* Mainz: Von Zabern.

REHAK, P. (2001), 'Aeneas or Numa? Rethinking the Meaning of the Ara Pacis Augustae', *Art Bulletin*, 83: 190–208.

RIC = *Roman Imperial Coinage*, ed. C. H. V. Sutherland and R. A. G. Carson. London: Spink, 1984–.

ROSE, C. BRIAN (1997*a*), *Dynastic Commemoration and Imperial Portraiture in the Julio-Claudian Period.* Cambridge: Cambridge University Press.

—— (1997*b*), 'The Imperial Image in the Eastern Mediterranean', in S. Alcock (ed.), *The Early Roman Empire in the East*, 108–20. Oxford: Oxbow Books.

—— (2005), 'The Parthians in Augustan Rome', *American Journal of Archaeology*, 109: 21–75.

—— (2006), 'Ilion', in Wolfgang Radt (ed.), *Stadtgrabungen und Stadtforschung im westlichen Kleinasien.* 135–58. Istanbul: Ege Yayinlari.

—— (2008), 'Forging Identity in the Roman Republic: Veristic Portraiture and Trojan Ancestry', in Sinclair Bell and Inge yse Hansen (eds.), *Role Models in the Roman world: Identity and Assimilation*, Memoirs of the American Academy in Rome. supplementary Volume 7, 97–131. Ann Arbor, Mich.: University of Michigan Press, for the American Academy in Rome.

ROTILI, M. (1972), *L'arco di Traiano a Benevento.* Rome: Istituto poligrafico dello Stato.

RYBERG, INEZ SCOTT (1955), *Rites of the State Religion in Roman Art.* Memoirs of the American Academy in Rome, 22. Rome.

SCHNEIDER, R. (1986), *Bunte Barbaren: Orientalenstatuen aus farbigem Marmor in der römischen Repräsentationskunst.* Worms: Wernersche Verlagsgesellschaft.

SCULLARD, H. H. (1981), *Festivals and Ceremonies of Roman Republic.* London: Thames & Hudson.

SICHTERMANN, H. (1988), 'Ganymedes', in *LIMC* 4: 154–69.

SIMON, ERIKA (1968), *Ara Pacis Augustae.* Tübingen: Wasmuth.

SMITH, R. R. R. (1982), Review of O. Brendel, *The Visible Idea*, *Journal of Roman Studies*, 72: 198–9.

—— (1987), 'The Imperial Reliefs from the Sebasteion at Aphrodisias', *JRS* 77: 88–138.

—— (1988), 'Simulacra Gentium: The Ethne from the Sebasteion at Aphrodisias', *JRS* 78: 50–77.

STEWART, ANDREW (1994), *Faces of Power: Alexander's Image and Hellenistic Politics.* Berkeley: University of California Press.

Stewart, Peter (2004), *Statues in Roman Society: Representation and Response.* Oxford: Oxford University Press.

Stilp, Florian (2001), *Mariage et suovetaurilia: étude sur le soi-disant 'Autel Ahenobarbus'.* Rome: Bretschneider.

Tanner, Jeremy (2000), 'Portraits, Power, and Patronage in the Late Roman Republic', *Journal of Roman Studies*, 90: 18–50.

Tuchelt, Klaus (1979), *Frühe Denkmäler Roms in Kleinasien: Beiträge zur archäologischen Überlieferung aus der Zeit der Republik und des Augustus.* Tübingen.

Ungaro, L. (2002), 'I Daci dal Foro di Traiano', in de Nuccio *et al.* (eds.), *I marmi colorati della Roma imperiale*, 129–33. Venice: Marsilio.

Varner, Eric (2004), *Mutilation and Transformation: damnatio memoriae and Roman Imperial Portraiture.* Leiden: Brill.

Vermaseren, M. (1982), *Mithriaca III: The Mithraeum at Marino.* Leiden: Brill.

—— and M. DeBoer. 1986. 'Attis', *LIMC* 3: 22–44.

Wallace-Hadrill, Andrew (1994), *Houses and Society in Pompeii and Herculaneum.* Princeton: Princeton University Press.

Wiegartz, H. (1996), 'Simulacra gentium auf dem Forum Transitorium', *Boreas*, 19: 171–9.

Wood, Susan E. (1999), *Imperial Women: A Study in Public Images, 40 B.C.–A.D. 68.* Leiden: Brill.

Zanker, Paul (1972), *Forum Romanum. Die Neugestaltung durch Augustus.* Tübingen: Wasmuth.

—— (1988), *The Power of Images in the Age of Augustus.* Ann Arbor, Mich.: University of Michigan Press.

—— (2000), 'Die Frauen und Kinder der Barbaren auf der Markussäule', in J. Scheid and V. Huet (eds.), *La Colonne aurélienne. Geste et image sur la colonne de Marc Aurèle à Rome*, 163–74. Turnhout: Brepols.

CHAPTER 4

LINGUISTICS

JOSHUA T. KATZ

THE first surviving book of the great Roman polymath Marcus Terentius Varro's *De Lingua Latina* ('On the Latin Language') opens with the statement that 'in the Latin language' (*in linguā Latīnā*, 5.1), '[i]nasmuch as each and every word has two innate features, from what thing and to what thing the name is applied..., that former part, where they examine why and whence words are, the Greeks call Etymology, that other part they call Semantics' (5.2; trans. Kent 1951: [I.]3 and 5). The techniques that Varro used in the mid-40s BCE to explain his own *lingua*—from which noun comes our word *linguistics*—are unlike those employed by linguists today, not least because there is now a different sense of what count as 'innate features', or at least important ones. Indeed, while the study of ancient etymology (which Varro found more worthwhile than semantics) is a particularly interesting branch of intellectual history (Maltby 1991 is fundamental; see also e.g. the papers in Nifadopoulos 2003), most twenty-first-century scientists of language ignore the views of those from previous millennia on the grounds that it is difficult to discern truly methodological principles in their work. It is no accident, after all, that the single best-known Latin etymological assessment, *Lūcus ā nōn lūcendō* 'A grove (*lūcus*) is so called from not being light (*lūcendō*)'—the comment, sometimes attributed to Varro, is found as such in the fourth-century CE grammarian Servius' commentary on Virgil's *Aeneid* (*ad* 1.22) but may well be earlier (see e.g. Quintilian, *Orator's Education* 1.6.34 and, for possible antecedents already in Homer, Cazzaniga 1972)—is now a catchphrase for an absurd idea, as though 'A grove is so called from not being grave'. (Curiously, modern etymologists do believe that *lūcus* is related to *lūcēre* 'shine' and *lūx* 'light'—but for quite the opposite of the old reason '*e contrario*', which loses the 'clear-ing' for the trees.) Nevertheless, Varro did get many things right (see D. J. Taylor 1974 for a sympathetic account of Varro's 'linguistic theory'), including highlighting a certain split between form and function, with the ancient idea of 'etymology' (Gk. *etymología*, a compound whose literal meaning is 'the study of true words') corresponding to a mishmash of what we would now regard as phonological and morphological issues, as well as semantic ones. My goal in this chapter, which falls under the heading of 'Tools', is to separate the mish from the mash, to show by means of just a few prominent examples—notably the words for 'Latin' and 'language' and the very idea of 'Roman-ness'—what linguistics can do and why it matters (see also Katz 2005 and 2007).

A famous dictum about language is that it is a system in which everything holds together (Meillet 1937: 475: 'un système où tout se tient'). It is the job of the linguist to explain how this works, on both a small and a large scale, by examining the make-up of individual building-blocks (the idea of a 'periodic table' of linguistic elements, though an imperfect conceit, is exploited to good effect in a popular book by Mark C. Baker from 2001) and also determining how these blocks interact. How do they change over time (diachronically) and how do they fit together at any given point (synchronically) to form ever bigger, acceptable structures? To put a whole world into a simplistic sentence: humans, including speakers of Latin, produce sounds (the study of which is called phonetics) that interact with other sounds (phonology), and the resulting meaningful sequences (morphology) are then linked to other such sequences—most prominently words—to form clauses (syntax), which in turn combine into more intricate narratives (discourse analysis and stylistics); furthermore, everything from a morpheme to a novel has in its context an overt sense (semantics) and very likely some covert ones as well (pragmatics). In other words, the linguist's purview is very broad, and any given problem of language will have something to do with one or (typically) more of these kinds of study, whether it is coming to terms with the distant origin and contemporary sense of our earliest bits of Roman sacral diction (e.g. *cozeulodorieso* in the 'Carmen Saliare' (preserved in mangled form by Varro: *De Lingua Latina* 7.26) and LIMEN SALI STA BERBER in the 'Carmen Arvale' (*CIL* I^2 2); the former remains opaque, but see on the latter Katz 1998: 214–16 and 2006*b*: 334–7, with references), figuring out the types and use of 'directive expressions' (e.g. imperatives) in Cicero's correspondence and other texts in Latin (see Risselada 1993), or understanding why *cāre* 'o dear one' has, paradoxically, greater force than *cārissime* 'o dearest one' (see Dickey 2002: 134–41). (Capital letters in citations of Latin indicate an epigraphic source; for other Indo-European languages of ancient Italy, which are known essentially only through epigraphy, capitals are used when the words in question are written in an epichoric writing system while standard italics indicate that the original is in the familiar 'Roman' alphabet.)

For example, it is possible, and of arguably unexpected interest, to examine the phonetic and phonological properties of the two *l*-initial Latin words *lingua* and

Latīna (the els would have been written the same since the contrastive use of majuscule and minuscule letters is Carolingian and was not formalized until the development of so-called 'Roman' fonts in fifteenth-century Italy). Just as in almost all varieties of modern English (though this will come as news to most readers and native speakers), Latin has two kinds ('allophones') of *l*: this is a phonetic fact with a phonological explanation (see Sihler 1995: 174). The one allophone of the phoneme /l/, usually known as *l exilis* 'thin *l*', appears only before a high front vowel ([ī̆d]) or another [l] and is probably pronounced as a denti-alveolar [l], more or less as in the English word *linger*; the other, usually known as *l pinguis* 'fat *l*', appears in all other positions and is pronounced as a velarized (or 'dark') [ɫ], as in the English word *milk*. As it happens, there is some disagreement among native grammarians and modern scholars about exactly how many els there are (according to Priscian (*Grammatici Latini* 2.29.8–12 Keil), Pliny the Elder recognized three) and what precisely governs their distribution (W. Sidney Allen's standard *Vox Latina* (1978: 33–4) and Meiser (1998: 52 and *passim*) present pictures that are slightly different from each other and from how I have represented things here). But the bottom line is that it is nearly certain that Varro and Cicero, who were contemporaries, would not have pronounced the els in *lingua* and *Latīna* in quite the same way—a synchronic fact about Latin that has a diachronic cause before the advent of the Classical form of the language and diachronic consequences afterward (e.g. some instances of *l pinguis*—but not *l exilis*—turn into a [w] on the way into French: cf. *autre* < *alt(e)r-* 'other', not unlike the conventional transcription of *milk* as '*miwk*' in Estuary English and some other dialects). For an authoritative account of Latin's els and the origins of the split between *l exilis* and *l pinguis*, see Parker 1986: 27–86, esp. 27–43.

There is more still to say about the sounds that make up these two words, including the initial els. For one thing, *lingua*—a word that, by the way, contains the rare and hence expressive sound or sequence of sounds [g^w]/[gw], which Latin phonotactics permits only after a nasal: cf. also *unguis* 'snake', *inguen* 'groin', *ninguit* 'it is snowing', etc.—used not to have an initial *l* at all: it was *dingua*, as we know from Marius Victorinus' report (*Grammatici Latini* 6.26.2 Keil) and as 'dinguists' would have figured out anyway. There is evidence from other Indo-European languages that points to a *d*-initial word: for example, the *t* of Eng. *tongue*, the cognate—a word in a related language that goes back to the same source—of *d/lingua*, comes regularly from a **d* by something known as Grimm's Law. (An asterisk before a sound or sequence of sounds indicates that it is not attested as such but has been reconstructed.) Furthermore, there is independent evidence within Latin itself for the replacement of *d* by *l* (Paulus ex Festo (60.5 Lindsay) tells us that Livius Andronicus, the 'father' of Latin literature, 'often' (*saepe*) used *dacrima* rather than the Classical form *lacrima* 'tear'; cf. e.g. Gk. *dákry* and, with Grimm's Law, Eng. *tear*) and for a sort of synchronic alternation between the two sounds (e.g. in the noun *odor* 'smell' and the related verb *olet* 'it smells'; cf.

De Lingua Latina 6.83). (These secondary els are often called 'Sabine', but the description has little to recommend it (compare Poucet 1966), for all kinds of *d* ∼ *l*-variation are found throughout the wider Mediterranean world (see Katz 2001: 216–20 for a synopsis); furthermore, the hapax KDUÍÚ in the 'Sabine' language South Picene has a *d* and, if Rix's attractive analysis (1994) is correct, means 'I am called' and corresponds to a Latin verb that preserves an inherited **l*, *clueō* 'I am known as' (< PIE **ḱlew-* 'hear'; cf. e.g. Gk. *klýō*), rather than the other way around.) When we look at other Italic languages, of which Latin is but one (though by far the most prominent, to be sure), then we see that *d/lingua* has a cognate in Oscan, where, however, the word sports a quite remarkably different look: *fangva* (it is attested twice: acc. sg. FANGVAM and nom. pl. *fancua*; see e.g. Untermann 2000: 264). Underlying these differences in Proto-Indo-European—the reconstructed source language (dated very roughly to the late-Neolithic fourth millennium BCE) of the cognates *d/lingua*, *fangva*, and *tongue*—is a preform of notorious complexity, especially phonological (*dingua* and *tongue* go back to extensions of **dn̥ǵ*^{h}*u*; *fangva* seems to reflect **d*^{h}*n̥ǵu*°; Tocharian B *kantwo* should have been something like **tankwo* but has undergone metathesis; etc.), but also morphological (see Peters 1988–90: 242) and perhaps semantic (Hilmarsson (1982) and Winter (1982) consider connections between tongues and fish, as well as giving an overview of the phonological problems). It is all but certain (compare e.g. Hock 1991: 303–5, with references on 670) that at least some of these linguistic difficulties reflect cultural taboos about dangerous speech (for *lingua* as both 'tongue' and 'language; speech', see below).

As for *Latīna*, it is only proper to admit from the start that its etymology is uncertain (Ernout and Meillet 1985: 343: 'inconnue')—even 'latent', one might say, since the Romans themselves devised various folk-explanations for how their land, *Latium*, might be associated with *latēre* 'be hidden' (cf. above all *Aeneid* 8.319–23 and see now Nelis 2006: 255–60; further literature, ancient and modern, is found in Maltby 1991: 328–9 and O'Hara 1996: 207–8). Now, 'proper' names, including places and ethnic designations, are notoriously tricky to etymologize: the 'meaning' of *Rōma* (and *Rōmulus*, literally 'Roman') is entirely unclear, for example, and it is a matter of ongoing dispute whether the name really is borrowed (the usual suspect is Etruscan; see e.g. de Simone 2006) or is instead native to Latin (see Klingenschmitt 1992: 90); and while *Italia* is often thought to have a deep connection with the native Italic word for 'calf' (e.g. Lat. *uitulus*), via a complicated route that involves Greek, this is at least questionable (see now Wojtylak 2003), and Silvestri (2001) has advanced the novel opinion that it reflects the root PIE **$h_2$ei(-)d*^{h}- 'ignite; burn' (cf. e.g. Gk. *aít*^{h}*ō* 'kindle') and has the poetic sense 'Land of Fire (and the Setting Sun)'. Still, in view of the evident socio-cultural prominence of *Latīna*, it is frankly surprising that no modern view has received terribly much support (though this has not prevented a leading scholar from making the unqualified pronouncement in the *OCD*^{3} (s.v. *Latium*) that 'the name is connected etymologically with *l*[*ā*] *tus*, "broad"', the latter with a long root vowel). There is, however, some chance that it, too, like *lingua*, once began with a dental stop: **Tlatīna*, whose initial cluster **tl* would have developed by regular phonological change into *l* (just as it certainly has in *lātus* '(having been) carried' < **tlātos* (cf. Gk. *tlētós* 'endured'), from the root PIE **telh*$_2$- 'lift', seen also in *tulī* 'I carried'). The details cannot all be pursued here and are in any case far from evident; for one thing, it is not obvious what **Tlatīna* and its corresponding noun **Tlatium* would once have meant. But despite the scorn of Walde and Hofmann (1938: 770–1), a striking reason to accept a derivation from **tlat*- (over, say, the admittedly attractive view of Steinbauer (2003: 508) that *Lat*- goes back to **wlat-i*-, the same proximate preform of OIrish *flaith* 'sovereignty; prince' and (M)Welsh *gwlad* 'country') comes from a comparative philological analysis of the Umbrian phrase *agre . tlatie . piquier . martier*, which appears in *Iguvine Tables* Vb 9.

The *Iguvine Tables*, seven large bronze tablets discovered in 1444 in the Umbrian town of Gubbio (ancient Iguvium), about 125 miles north of Rome, are the single best (quasi-)continuous source we have for early Italic ritual and religion in any ancient language (the standard, if not entirely reliable, English-language edition is Poultney 1959); they have been neglected by mainstream Latinists, who tend to lack the requisite linguistic skills, but a book in progress on *Tables* III and IV by the classical linguist Michael Weiss should help. The four words in question, *agre tlatie piquier martier*, which are translated more or less as 'from the Ager Tlatius of Picus Martius', refer to an amount of grain that certain citizens of Iguvium are required to give each year to the principal actors of the *Tables*, the priestly Atiedian Brethren. The noun phrase *agre tlatie* (here probably in the genitive case) closely resembles the Roman historian Livy's *ager Latīnus* 'Latin territory, land of the *Latīnī*' (cf. 7.23.2 *in agrō Latīnō* and 8.11.13 *Latīnus ager*, as well as Pliny, *Natural History* 3.63 *ex agrō Latīnō*)—though they seem not to designate the same area (see e.g. Poultney 1959: 225, with reference to R. S. Conway, and L. R. Taylor 1960: 39–40, with reference to K. J. Beloch; compare also now Sisani 2001: 85–98) and though some etymologize *tlatie* differently (Untermann (2000: 744, with references) prefers to compare the participle *lātus*)—and indeed it seems likely that the existence of an **agros (T)Latīnos*, as the collocation would have been pronounced until at least 500 BCE (before *-*ros* > -*er* (cf. *sacer* < SAKROS 'sacred', attested as such in the famous (mid-sixth-century?) 'Forum Inscription', *CIL* I^2 1) and long before remaining instances of *-*Cos* 'weakened' to *-*Cus*), provides the key to an interesting Greco-Latin problem in a distant source: Hesiod.

In the 'Italian section' at the very end of the *Theogony* (1008–18), the eighth/seventh-century BCE Greek poet Hesiod turns to the mysterious west and shows a number of signs of being at or past the limit of his geographical competence (compare West 1966: 432–6). He opens by mentioning the birth of Aeneas (1008–10), and while he does not sing of Aeneas' flight from Troy and fated founding of a new homeland in Latium, it is certain that his audience would have known of this.

He then goes on to sing of Odysseus and Circe (her island home, Aeaea, Homeric and Virgilian geographers have generally placed near what is now known as Monte Circeo, a peninsula some 60 miles south-east of Rome), whose union produces two sons, *Ágrio*[*s*] *ēdè Latîno*[*s*] (1013) 'Agrius and Latinus', who together (!) rule over a people known as the Tyrsenians (1015–16), probably the Etruscans. The names of the two sons in verse 1013 have given rise to considerable controversy: *Latînos* is of course King *Latīnus*, Aeneas' father-in-law, so well known from the (late first-century BCE) *Aeneid*, but in Greek sources 'the name is not heard of again... until ps.-Scylax 8 (*c*. 350 B.C.)' (West 1966: 434); and as for *Ágrios*, literally 'Wild Man', while the name itself is otherwise known (see already Homer, *Iliad* 14.117), the referent here is wholly unclear and has been subject to all manner of speculation (see West 1966: 433–4). But in fact there is, in my view, a simple explanation for both names, one that accounts, furthermore, for the obviously awkward notion of joint rule: the immediate precursor of *Ágrios ēdè Latînos* is not two Latin personal names at all; rather, the phrase reflects a small inter-lingual miscommunication, a Greek distortion (perhaps helped along by the likewise verse-initial collocation of two brothers' names in the *Iliad*, *Ágrios ēdè Mélas* 'Agrius and Melas') of the two-part Latin place-name, a combination of noun and adjective, **agros Latīnos*. It is not unlikely that a Greek would have happened upon this *terminus technicus* sometime around the proverbial founding of Rome in 753 BCE by Romulus (whose ancestry the Romans liked to trace back to Aeneas and Latinus) and that this piece of information then reached Hesiod in slightly distorted form, for we know that there was contact between Greece and *Latium Vetus* already in the eighth century. Rather extraordinarily, our earliest known inscription in alphabetic Greek, unfortunately a mere five (?) letters whose reading and interpretation have been widely debated, comes from Osteria dell'Osa (ancient Gabii), about 15 miles east of Rome, and dates from *c*.770 BCE; there has been a great deal of discussion of the object since its initial publication by La Regina (1989–90), with Watkins (1995*a*: 36–9) leading the linguistic way (and Canali De Rossi (2005: 165–8) now putting forth a radical, and in my opinion unlikely, suggestion). (Smith (1996: 233–8) gives a handy account of the epigraphic evidence—Greek, Etruscan, and Italic—from early Latium.) If I am right, then the Greek phrase *Ágrios ēdè Latînos* reflects in a curious way a real bit of 'Very Old Latin' and is our first piece of (shakily transmitted) textual evidence that the *Latīnī* were indeed in Italy in the eighth century and were known, albeit dimly, to the Greeks.

This explanation of the Hesiodic passage will stand regardless of the derivation of *Latīnus*, *-a*, *-um* from **Tlat-* and the correctness of an equation with Umb. *tlatie*. Indeed, for this link to be valid, it is probably necessary to date the loss of the initial stop in Latin extremely early since Hesiod does not have it (it is not **Ágrios ēdè Tlatînos*). Though surprising, no linguistic evidence speaks against this, and I suggest, very tentatively, that support may be found in a further comparison between *agre tlatie piquier martier* and the end of the *Theogony*.

The second Umbrian noun phrase, *piquier martier*, is probably the genitive of something that in Latin approximates *Pīcus Mārtius* 'Woodpecker of Mars', seemingly a totem of the region of the *agre tlatie* (and another region as well: *agre casiler* (Vb 14) 'of the *ager Casilus*'). (In fact, the relationship between the (genitive) adjective *piquier* and the bird names *peico* (cf. Lat. *pīcus*) and *peica* (cf. Lat. *pīca* 'magpie') is heavily disputed: Untermann (2000: 526 and 556–7) speaks in favour of the connection; the most vehement opponent is Szemerényi (1971).) That the Picus Martius is an early Italic totemic or augural bird is known from Latin sources as well (especially Pliny, *Natural History* 10.40–1 and also 25.29; note, too, Dionysius of Halicarnassus, *Roman Antiquities* 1.14.5), and if this bird is indeed a symbol of the **agros (T)Latīnos*, then any reader of Hesiod will immediately be struck by the fact that in the *Aeneid* and elsewhere, Picus is the grandfather of Latinus (see *Aeneid* 7.45–9) and, furthermore, that according to legend (best known from Book 14 of Ovid's *Metamorphoses*), Picus was turned into a woodpecker (*pīcus*) by the goddess whose advances he repeatedly spurned—none other than Circe.

All these observations have emerged from thinking about the els of *lingua* and *Latīna*, which is sufficient to show that language is very much more than sound and is intimately tied to the wider study of culture: not just literature, but also such matters as archaeology and myth (see Katz 2006*a* on 'cultural reconstruction' as part of the history of ideas). While linguistic analysis often leads to speculation rather than hard-and-fast results (though it is certainly a 'harder' methodology than most that classicists regularly employ), I hope to persuade readers that a fear of overreaching should not prevent classical linguists from grappling with bigger questions (see above all Watkins 1995*b*). But let us pursue linguistic details for a little while longer. From one point of view, Varro's work could be referred to with the equally catchy title *De Dinguad Tlatinad* (or, with the long vowels marked, *Dē Dinguād Tlatīnād*), where the final *d* of the second and third words is not just a sound, meaningless as such, but a morpheme, that is, a linguistic element with inherent sense. Originally a self-standing postposition, PIE *h_2*elod* (cf. Eng. *at*, yet again with a *t* thanks to Grimm's Law), this ending *d* is the marker of the ablative case (used after the preposition *dē*, whose primary meaning is '(away) from'), but case-forms in -*d* are not found in Classical Latin paradigms because in the middle of the third century BCE—just as Latin 'literature' was getting started, thanks to Livius Andronicus—a phonological change took hold whereby final *d* was lost after a long vowel. Furthermore (to turn to syntax), since attributive adjectives in Classical Latin tend to follow the nouns with which they agree (this is of necessity a drastic simplification of a complex matter that involves prosodic factors and the discourse context; see e.g. Pinkster 1990: 184–5, with notes on 285, and now Devine and Stephens 2006: 403–523 and *passim*), the order of the constituents in *d/linguā(d) (T)Latīnā(d)* is expected; note in addition that it is cross-linguistically more common for languages that have this order (so-called right-branching or head-first languages) to employ prepositions, like *dē*, rather than postpositions (which seem to have been the norm in Proto-Indo-European).

Finally, both *lingua* and *Latīnus* repay closer semantic study than Varro might have imagined. It is well known that *lingua*, just like Eng. *tongue*, can refer to both the organ in the mouth and—as in Varro's title—to a particular sort of noise that this body part helps produce. As far as we can tell, the metonymy long pre-dates Latin (indeed, it is cross-culturally common, witness also Heb. *lashon*, Turk. *dil*, etc.); within Latin, the double meaning underlies Lucretius' description *mōbilis*... *uerbōrum daedala lingua* (4.551) 'nimble tongue, fashioner of words' (see Holmes 2005 for an intriguing exposition of what this line tells us about Lucretius' own sense of 'linguistics') and is exploited to terrible effect in Ovid's telling in *Metamorphoses* 6 of the story of Philomela, whom Tereus, king of Thrace, rapes and then cruelly deprives of oral expression. Perhaps more interesting, though, is the meaning of the adjective *Latīnus* (Poccetti (1999: 30–40) provides an excellent picture of *Latīnus* and also *Rōmānus*). What does it mean to be (or speak or write) Latin, and how does an understanding of this affect our conception of 'Roman Studies', a phrase prominent in the title of the present volume?

In the United States, a widespread joke about Dan Quayle—the frequently ridiculed former vice-president whose political career was in part derailed by an incident in 1992 in which he told a 12-year-old New Jersey schoolboy to spell *potato* with a final *e*—is that he came to regret on a tour of Latin America that he hadn't studied Latin harder so that he would now be able to converse with the people. It seems that Quayle never said this, but what if he had? Would he have been wrong? By conventional wisdom, yes, of course. And yet things are not so simple, for the main languages of Latin America (a term popularized by Napoleon III: in French, *Amérique latine*) are Spanish and Portuguese, both descendants of Cicero's native tongue and thus, from a certain and not unreasonable perspective, both examples—indeed, dialects—of what we might call 'Very New Latin' (Portuguese began to diverge from the Galician dialect of north-western Spain only in the middle of the second millennium). It is normal these days to refer to 'Latin music', but the relationship between *lingua Latīna* and (e.g.) *la lengua española* and *a língua portuguesa* is both more intimate and far easier to trace than that between salsa and Ennius' *tuba* 'trumpet' that *terribilī sonitū taratantara dīxit* (*Annals* 451 Skutsch) 'delivered "taratantara" with terrible sound'. It may also be noted that the adjective *Latīnus* develops by regular phonological change into *ladino* in both Spanish and Portuguese—but (according to Sihler (2000: 106)) the word means 'crafty, dishonest' in Spanish (it has undergone semantic pejoration) and 'learnèd, cultured' in Portuguese (semantic amelioration). (In fact, the semantic situation is rather more ambivalent than Sihler makes it out to be. Compare Eng. *shrewd*, which is now positive with some unsavoury associations but was in Middle English times quite definitely negative.)

In general terms, the connection between Latin and its latter-day manifestations is probably familiar to readers of this chapter (see from very different perspectives Farrell 2001 and Janson 2004, though I find the former hard to understand and the latter pedestrian). A less familiar way of thinking about the situation is to regard the so-called 'Romance languages'—that is, the *linguae Rōmānicae* or 'tongues of Rome'—of which there are now some 700 million native speakers, as dialects of a very late form of a language usually said to be dead (but see now Stroh 2007). (Note that there is no linguistic means of distinguishing between languages and dialects: the differences are socio-political, which explains how it can be that 'dialects' of Italian from the Alto Adige, in the north, and Sicily, in the south, are generally said to be less mutually intelligible than are standard Italian and standard Spanish.) Most people are simply not in the habit of thinking that the relationship between the Spanish spoken in Caracas in 2000 CE and the Latin spoken in Rome in 100 BCE is in all essential respects the same as that between the ('Modern') English spoken today in Seattle and the (now-unintelligible but nevertheless like-named) English (so-called 'Old English' or 'Anglo-Saxon') spoken by the tribe of the Angles (Tacitus' *Angliī*: *Germania* 40.2), some of whose members left Schleswig-Holstein (north Germany, near Denmark) and, according to the Venerable Bede, first landed in 449 CE in the country that would come to bear their name, England ('Angle-land').

The previous paragraphs have tried to bridge linguistic continuity and linguistic mutability, invoking such concepts as 'cognates' and 'reconstruction' and such languages as Proto-Indo-European and Umbrian. These are largely alien to people engaged in classics in general and Roman Studies in particular, for the simple reason that classics, though by nature a discipline that looks backwards, tends not to look backwards beyond itself, or even too often sideways past the walls of the *urbs*. That is to say, many classicists speak—and in most countries and at most times over the past couple hundred years have spoken—of Greek and Roman texts as a more-or-less closed canon and view Greek and Roman culture as either an island or a significant peninsula. This is, of course, not unlike how the ancient Greeks and Romans saw themselves! But it gives a restricted and restrictive picture, and at least for language, this is unfortunate, for if it is easy enough to consider what Latin has become in the two millennia since Cicero, it is not so very much harder to consider what Latin was in the millennia before him, from Proto-Indo-European times onward.

To late-first-century BCE Romans like Cicero and Virgil, there was a language known as Latin, to whose grammar they had native access and whose rhetorical and poetic possibilities they explored with verve—with a particular genius that has made their words the basis of subsequent authors' and students' understanding of Latinity. Describing the subtleties of Classical Latin grammar is an important (and, in view of the complexities involved with a substantial and culturally sophisticated corpus, basically inexhaustible) linguistic task and could well have been the subject of this chapter had someone else written it (Clackson 2004 is as good a twenty-page summary as exists for the uninitiated). But there is more to Latin than grammatical notes in *Classical Quarterly* on Cicero and Virgil, and more to linguistic research, too. As Cicero and Virgil knew well, Latin had a history, and so did Rome itself, which, archaeologists tell us, was not even a town at the end of the Bronze and beginning of the Iron Age—not long after Aeneas would have arrived from Troy, if there is any truth at all to this tale—but rather a series of hilltop settlements of wattle-and-daub thatched huts, on the Palatine and elsewhere, occupied by a people whose material remains and funerary practices from as early as 1000 and especially after 900 BCE connect them with other groups in Latium. (On the beginnings of Rome, see above all Cornell 1995 and now, from a more sceptical perspective, Forsythe 2005.) The language or languages spoken by the earliest exponents of this form of Villanovan culture, the *cultura laziale* ('Latial culture'), cannot be known since our very earliest Italic inscriptions date from the seventh century BCE, but it is clear that the differences among the Italic languages already in their first attestations are sufficiently great—though far less dramatic than the differences between, say, Latin and Greek—that we can date their immediate ancestor, reconstructed Proto-Italic, to some hundreds of years earlier, probably to the last quarter of the second millennium BCE.

The two main branches of Italic are Latino-Faliscan and Sabellic (for a quick survey, see Penney 1988; a useful recent contribution is Rix 2003). The principal languages of the latter—whose name is related to 'Sabine', on which see above—are Oscan, Umbrian, and South Picene (all the texts are collected in Rix 2002, but without commentary (Buck 1928 remains useful for the first two and Marinetti 1985 is indispensable for the third); see also Untermann 2000 for etymologies and Wallace 2007 for a linguistic overview); the former group, as its designation suggests, comprises Faliscan (see Giacomelli 1963) in addition to Latin. (Some believe Venetic to be an Italic language as well, but it seems safer for now to regard it as a separate branch of the Indo-European family; see Wallace 2004 for a brief survey.) An immediately recognizable difference between Latino-Faliscan and Sabellic is that the outcome of the Proto-Indo-European labiovelar $*k^u$ is [k^w] or [kw] in the one but [p] in the other (so the Latin conjunction *quod* 'that' corresponds in Oscan to *pod*). Further differences are apparent from a comparison of one of our earliest (and certainly most infamous) Latin inscriptions, MANIOS : MED : FHE ⁝ FHAKED : NVMASIOI 'Manius made me for Numerius' (on the 'Praenestine Fibula', *CIL* I^2 3, which is probably not a forgery and may date already to the seventh century BCE; see Hartmann 2005: 67–106 and *passim* for detailed discussion), with the palaeo-Umbrian *dipinto* SETUMS : MÍOM | FACE 'Septimus made me' (on a sixth-century BCE ceramic vase from Tolfa). Particularly noteworthy are the discrepancies between the accusative pronouns MED (i.e. *mē(d)*) and MÍOM, differently extended forms of PIE **me*, and between the frankly unexpected reduplicated perfect FHE ⁝ FHAKED (cf. Gk. *tét*^{h}*ēke*) and the original aorist FACE (which itself does not look much like Class. Lat. *fēcit* (cf. Gk. *(é)t*^{h}*ēke*)).

As with the unrelated Etruscan and the more distantly related Lepontic and Messapic, the Italic languages fell by the wayside with the rise of Rome, which in 338 BCE conquered the rest of Latium, within a century thereafter had power over all of peninsular Italy, and eventually came to dominate so much of the known world, from Hadrian's Wall to the Caspian Sea. (On contact between speakers of Latin and speakers of other languages in and around Italy, see Adams 2003: 111–296 and *passim*, with 112–59 largely about inner-Italic interactions.) There is almost no inscriptional evidence for any Italian languages other than Latin after the first century BCE, just the time when Roman literature truly came into its own. If the Umbrians had won out, we would, as Alan Nussbaum has quipped, now be saying '*pe sera, sera*'; as it is, however, the linguistic consequences of the domination of the *Latīnī* and of Rome are such that it is typically not possible to tell where a writer of Latin is from on the basis of his use of the language. The supposed uniformity of Latin is a convenient simplification that Adams's study of dialectal diversity (2007) will correct, but it is nonetheless remarkable both that strikingly few major 'Roman' authors were actually born in Rome (see Watts 1971) and that (in the stirring, if evidently dated, words of Watts (1971: 100)) '[t]he widely scattered origins of Rome's writers, combined with the universality of most of her literature, is a specific and significant indication of the absorption by Rome's empire, especially the West, of the spirit of Rome, however indefinable that spirit may be'.

Those who read this chapter are likely to be interested in the first place in literature and have, I hope, picked up from it a linguistic trick or two that will allow them to better understand the Roman spirit as it is found in Latin texts. Recent years have seen fierce debates in Latin literary studies between colleagues who try to bridge the divide between pre-literary times and the Latin texts we know by appealing to a continuous (oral) tradition (see e.g. Wiseman 2004 and Habinek 2005) and those who stress the overwhelming influence of Greek literate culture as the crucial factor that allowed what Feeney (2005: 229) has called 'the contingency of Latin literature' to be realized. And yet both sides have a point: there is undoubtedly a pre-literary tradition, pieces of which we may hope to recover, not unlike as happens regularly in the study of archaic Greece; at the same time, early Roman literary production and culture do seem meaningfully different from their would-be Greek counterparts. Since all linguists are 'oralists' (see Katz 2003), I have a natural sympathy with scholars who choose to look backwards (and, for that matter, forwards), but because they tend to ignore linguistic evidence and base their claims about tradition on other, and sometimes very flimsy, grounds, I have found myself siding with those who prefer hard evidence to asterisked forms (see Feeney and Katz 2006).

Philology, it has been said (notably by Roman Jakobson and, before him, Nietzsche), is the art of reading slowly (see e.g. Watkins 1990: 25), and a fundamental technique of philology—an out-of-vogue word for a sadly maligned discipline of breadth and lasting value that is often sabotaged even by its would-be champions (see Ziolkowski 2005)—is linguistics, both synchronic and diachronic/comparative. I have in these pages pointed out a few linguistic features to watch out for as one slowly reads Latin. There are plenty more.

Further reading

Among the many introductions to linguistics in general and historical/comparative linguistics in particular, Fromkin 2000 and Campbell 2004 are especially recommendable. The best introduction to (Proto-)Indo-European language and culture is Fortson 2004. The most readable and wide-ranging English-language introduction to Latin remains Palmer 1954: the first half, 'An Outline History of the Latin Language', is particularly good; aside from the chapter on syntax (remarkably detailed for its time), the second half, 'Comparative-historical Grammar', should be avoided in favour of Sihler 1995 (equally about Latin and Greek), Baldi 1999, and (for those who read German) Meiser 1998, all of which are serviceable but idiosyncratic. Michael Weiss's forthcoming historical/comparative grammar of Latin will set a new standard. Ernout and Meillet 1985 (in French) is the outstanding etymological dictionary, endeavouring to provide a true (if generally laconic) 'history of words' and not just strings of asterisks. Much of the linguistically sophisticated work on synchronic Latin 'grammar' as that word is usually conceived (e.g. in courses on prose composition) comes from the Netherlands: the work of Harm Pinkster, who is currently preparing *The Oxford Latin Syntax*, has been very influential (see e.g. Pinkster 1990).

References

Adams, J. N. (2003), *Bilingualism and the Latin Language*, Cambridge: Cambridge University Press.

—— (2007), *The Regional Diversification of Latin 200 BC–AD 600*, Cambridge: Cambridge University Press.

Allen, W. Sidney (1978), *Vox Latina: A Guide to the Pronunciation of Classical Latin*, 2nd edn., Cambridge: Cambridge University Press.

Baker, Mark C. (2001), *The Atoms of Language*, New York: Basic Books.

Baldi, Philip (1999), *The Foundations of Latin*, Berlin: de Gruyter.

Buck, Carl Darling (1928), *A Grammar of Oscan and Umbrian with a Collection of Inscriptions and a Glossary*, rev. edn., Boston: Ginn.

Campbell, Lyle (2004), *Historical Linguistics: An Introduction*, 2nd edn., Cambridge, Mass.: MIT Press.

Canali De Rossi, Filippo (2005), *Le relazioni diplomatiche di Roma*, vol. I: *Dall'età regia alla conquista del primato in Italia (753–265 a.C.) con una appendice sulla più antica iscrizione greca del Lazio*, Rome: Herder.

Cazzaniga, Ignazio (1972), 'Lucus a non lucendo', *Studi Classici e Orientali*, 21: 27–9.

Clackson, James P. T. (2004), 'Latin', in Roger D. Woodard (ed.), *The Cambridge Encyclopedia of the World's Ancient Languages*, Cambridge: Cambridge University Press, 789–811.

Cornell, T. J. (1995), *The Beginnings of Rome: Italy and Rome from the Bronze Age to the Punic Wars (c. 1000–264 BC)*, London: Routledge.

de Simone, Carlo (2006), 'I nomi Romolo e Remo come etruschi', in Andrea Carandini (ed.), *La leggenda di Roma: Dalla nascita dei gemelli alla fondazione della città*, [Milan]: Mondadori, 455–68.

Devine, A. M. and Laurence D. Stephens (2006), *Latin Word Order: Structured Meaning and Information*, Oxford: Oxford University Press.

Dickey, Eleanor (2002), *Latin Forms of Address from Plautus to Apuleius*, Oxford: Oxford University Press.

Ernout, A. and A. Meillet (1985), *Dictionnaire étymologique de la langue latine: histoire des mots*, 4th edn., rev. by Jacques André, Paris: Klincksieck.

Farrell, Joseph (2001), *Latin Language and Latin Culture from Ancient to Modern Times*, Cambridge: Cambridge University Press.

Feeney, Denis (2005), 'The Beginnings of a Literature in Latin', *Journal of Roman Studies*, 95: 226–40.

—— and Joshua T. Katz (2006), Review of Habinek (2005), *Journal of Roman Studies*, 96: 240–2.

Forsythe, Gary (2005), *A Critical History of Early Rome: From Prehistory to the First Punic War*, Berkeley: University of California Press.

Fortson, Benjamin W. IV (2004), *Indo-European Language and Culture: An Introduction*, Malden, Mass.: Blackwell.

Fromkin, Victoria A. (ed.) (2000), *Linguistics: An Introduction to Linguistic Theory*, Malden, Mass.: Blackwell.

Giacomelli, Gabriella (1963), *La lingua falisca*, Florence: Olschki.

Habinek, Thomas (2005), *The World of Roman Song: From Ritualized Speech to Social Order*, Baltimore: Johns Hopkins University Press.

Hartmann, Markus (2005), *Die frühlateinischen Inschriften und ihre Datierung: Eine linguistisch-archäologisch-paläographische Untersuchung*, Bremen: Hempen.

Hilmarsson, J[ö]rundur (1982), 'Indo-European "Tongue"', *Journal of Indo-European Studies*, 10: 355–67.

Hock, Hans Henrich (1991), *Principles of Historical Linguistics*, 2nd edn., Berlin: de Gruyter.

Holmes, Brooke (2005), '*Daedala lingua*: Crafted Speech in *De rerum natura*', *American Journal of Philology*, 126: 527–85.

Janson, Tore (2004), *A Natural History of Latin*, tr. Merethe Damsgård Sørensen and Nigel Vincent, Oxford: Oxford University Press (revision of the 2002 Swedish original).

Katz, Joshua T. (1998), 'Testimonia ritus Italici: Male Genitalia, Solemn Declarations, and a New Latin Sound Law', *Harvard Studies in Classical Philology*, 98: 183–217.

—— (2001), 'Hittite *ta-pa-ka-li-ya-<aš>*', in Onofrio Carruba and Wolfgang Meid (eds.), *Anatolisch und Indogermanisch—Anatolico e indoeuropeo: Akten des Kolloquiums der Indogermanischen Gesellschaft, Pavia, 22.–25. September 1998*, Innsbruck: Institut für Sprachen und Literaturen der Universität Innsbruck, 205–37.

—— (2003), 'Oral Tradition in Linguistics', *Oral Tradition*, 18: 261–2.

—— (2005) 'The Indo-European Context', in John Miles Foley (ed.), *A Companion to Ancient Epic*, Malden, Mass.: Blackwell, 20–30.

—— (2006*a*) 'Reconstruction, Cultural', in Keith Brown (ed.), *Encyclopedia of Language and Linguistics*, 2nd edn., vol. X, Amsterdam: Elsevier, 389–93.

Katz, Joshua T. (2006*b*), 'The "'*Urbi et Orbi*'-Rule" Revisited', *Journal of Indo-European Studies*, 34: 319–61.

—— (2007), 'What Linguists are Good for', *Classical World*, 100: 99–112.

Kent, Roland G. (1951), *Varro, On the Latin Language*, 2 vols., rev. edn., Cambridge, Mass.: Harvard University Press (Loeb Classical Library).

Klingenschmitt, Gert (1992), 'Die lateinische Nominalflexion', in Oswald Panagl and Thomas Krisch (eds.), *Latein und Indogermanisch: Akten des Kolloquiums der Indogermanischen Gesellschaft, Salzburg, 23.–26. September 1986*, Innsbruck: Institut für Sprachwissenschaft der Universität Innsbruck, 89–135. (Reprinted in Gert Klingenschmitt, *Aufsätze zur Indogermanistik*, ed. Michael Janda *et al.*, Hamburg: Dr. Kovač (2005), 301–51.)

La Regina, Adriano (1989–90), 'Il vaso con iscrizione dalla tomba 482 di Osteria dell'Osa', pp. 83–8 of Anna Maria Bietti Sestieri, Anna De Santis, and Adriano La Regina, 'Elementi di tipo cultuale e doni personali nella necropoli laziale di Osteria dell'Osa', *Scienze dell'Antichità*, 3–4: 65–88.

Maltby, Robert (1991), *A Lexicon of Ancient Latin Etymologies*, Leeds: Cairns.

Marinetti, Anna (1985), *Le iscrizioni sudpicene*, vol. I: *Testi*, Florence: Olschki.

Meillet, A. (1937), *Introduction à l'étude comparative des langues indo-européennes*, 8th edn., Paris: Hachette.

Meiser, Gerhard (1998), *Historische Laut- und Formenlehre der lateinischen Sprache*, Darmstadt: Wissenschaftliche Buchgesellschaft.

Nelis, Damien (2006), 'Wordplay in Vergil and Claudian', *Dictynna*, 3: 255–63.

Nifadopoulos, Christos (ed.) (2003), *Etymologia: Studies in Ancient Etymology. Proceedings of the Cambridge Conference on Ancient Etymology, 25–27 September 2000*, Münster: Nodus.

O'Hara, James J. (1996), *True Names: Vergil and the Alexandrian Tradition of Etymological Wordplay*, Ann Arbor, Mich.: University of Michigan Press.

Palmer, L. R. (1954), *The Latin Language*, London: Faber & Faber (= Norman, Okla.: University of Oklahoma Press (1988).

Parker, Holt Neumon (1986), 'The Relative Chronology of some Major Latin Sound Changes', Ph.D dissertation, Yale University.

Penney, J. H. W. (1988), 'The Languages of Italy', in John Boardman *et al.* (eds.), *The Cambridge Ancient History*, 2nd edn., vol. IV: *Persia, Greece and the Western Mediterranean* c. *525 to 479 B.C.*, Cambridge: Cambridge University Press, 720–38.

Peters, Martin (1988–90 (publ. 1991)), 'Ein tocharisches Auslautproblem', *Sprache*, 34: 242–4.

Pinkster, Harm (1990), *Latin Syntax and Semantics*, tr. Hotze Mulder, Routledge: London (revision of the 1988 German translation of the 1984 Dutch original).

Poccetti, Paolo (1999), 'Identità e identificazione del latino', in Paolo Poccetti, Diego Poli, and Carlo Santini, *Una storia della lingua latina: Formazione, usi, comunicazione*, Rome: Carocci, 9–171.

Poucet, Jacques (1966), 'L'Origine sabine de la "commutatio" du -d- en -l-, un mythe linguistique?', *Antiquité Classique*, 35: 140–8.

Poultney, James Wilson (1959), *The Bronze Tables of Iguvium*, Baltimore: American Philological Association.

Risselada, Rodie (1993), *Imperatives and other Directive Expressions in Latin: A Study in the Pragmatics of a Dead Language*, Amsterdam: Gieben.

Rix, Helmut (1994), 'Südpikenisch *kduíú*', *Historische Sprachforschung*, 107: 105–22.

——(2002), *Sabellische Texte: Die Texte des Oskischen, Umbrischen und Südpikenischen*, Heidelberg: Winter.

——(2003), 'Ausgliederung und Aufgliederung der italischen Sprachen', in Alfred Bammesberger and Theo Vennemann (eds.), *Languages in Prehistoric Europe*, Heidelberg: Winter, 147–72.

Sihler, Andrew L. (1995), *New Comparative Grammar of Greek and Latin*, New York: Oxford University Press.

——(2000), *Language History: An Introduction*, Amsterdam: Benjamins.

Silvestri, Domenico (2001), 'Per una etimologia del nome *Italia*', in Maurizio Bugno and Concetta Masseria (eds.), *Il mondo enotrio tra VI e V secolo a.C.: Atti dei seminari napoletani (1996–1998)*, Naples: Loffredo, 207–38.

Sisani, Simone (2001), *Tuta Ikuvina: Sviluppo e ideologia della forma urbana a Gubbio*, Rome: Quasar.

Smith, Christopher John (1996), *Early Rome and Latium: Economy and Society* c. *1000 to 500 BC*, Oxford: Clarendon Press.

Steinbauer, Dieter H. (2003), 'Lateinische Sprachgeschichte—Histoire du latin', in Gerhard Ernst *et al.* (eds.), *Romanische Sprachgeschichte—Histoire linguistique de la Romania (Ein internationales Handbuch zur Geschichte der romanischen Sprachen—Manuel international d'histoire linguistique de la Romania)*, vol. I, Berlin: de Gruyter, 504–15.

Stroh, Wilfried (2007), *Latein ist tot, es lebe Latein! Kleine Geschichte einer großen Sprache*, Berlin: List.

Szemerényi, Oswald (1971), 'The Name of the Picentes', in Eugenio Coseriu and Wolf-Dieter Stempel (eds.), *Sprache und Geschichte: Festschrift für Harri Meier zum 65. Geburtstag*, Munich: Fink, 531–44. (Reprinted in Oswald Szemerényi, *Scripta Minora: Selected Essays in Indo-European, Greek, and Latin*, ed. P. Considine and J. T. Hooker, vol. II: *Latin*, Innsbruck: Institut für Sprachwissenschaft der Universität Innsbruck (1987), 911–24.)

Taylor, Daniel J. (1974), *Declinatio: A Study of the Linguistic Theory of Marcus Terentius Varro*, Amsterdam: Benjamins.

Taylor, Lily Ross (1960), *The Voting Districts of the Roman Republic: The Thirty-five Urban and Rural Tribes*, Rome: American Academy in Rome.

Untermann, Jürgen (2000), *Wörterbuch des Oskisch-Umbrischen*, Heidelberg: Winter.

Walde, A. and J. B. Hofmann (1938), *Lateinisches etymologisches Wörterbuch*, 3rd edn., vol. I: *A–L*, Heidelberg: Winter.

Wallace, Rex E. (2004), 'Venetic', in Roger D. Woodard (ed.), *The Cambridge Encyclopedia of the World's Ancient Languages*, Cambridge: Cambridge University Press, 840–56.

——(2007), *The Sabellic Languages of Ancient Italy*, Munich: Lincom Europa.

Watkins, Calvert (1990), 'What is Philology?', in Jan Ziolkowski (ed.), *On Philology*, University Park, Pa.: Pennsylvania State University Press (= *Comparative Literature Studies*, 27/1 (1990)), 21–5.

——(1995*a*), 'Greece in Italy Outside Rome', *Harvard Studies in Classical Philology*, 97: 35–50.

——(1995*b*), *How to Kill a Dragon: Aspects of Indo-European Poetics*, New York: Oxford University Press.

Watts, W. J. (1971), 'The Birthplaces of Latin Writers', *Greece & Rome*, 18: 91–101.

Weiss, Michael (forthcoming), *Outline of the Historical and Comparative Grammar of Latin*, Ann Arbor, Mich.: Beech Stave.

West, M. L. (1966), *Hesiod, Theogony*, Oxford: Clarendon Press.

Winter, Werner (1982), 'Indo-European Words for "Tongue" and "Fish": A Reappraisal', *Journal of Indo-European Studies*, 10: 167–86.

Wiseman, T. P. (2004), *The Myths of Rome*, Exeter: University of Exeter Press.

Wojtylak, Łukasz (2003), 'On the Etymology of the Name *Italia*', *Incontri Linguistici*, 26: 87–96.

Ziolkowski, Jan M. (2005), 'Metaphilology', *Journal of English and Germanic Philology*, 104: 239–72.

CHAPTER 5

ARCHAEOLOGY

HENRY HURST

ENTERING at once into the debating spirit of this volume, the idea of classifying archaeology as a 'tool' alongside prosopography, metre, and numismatics, while 'culture change', 'urbanism', and 'fall and transitions' are classified under 'history', is provocative to any archaeologist. The concept of history under which the classification is made will no doubt be explained elsewhere in this volume and I do not want to argue with that. But for this piece where we are talking about archaeology within a 'historic' period, working definitions of both history and archaeology are needed. History I take to be the predominantly though not exclusively document-based study of human endeavour in those periods for which contemporary written information is available; and I would follow Braudel (1975) in seeing the historical process as resulting from the interaction of three major sets of influences, which he defined as: the role of the environment; collective destinies and general trends; and events, politics, and people. Archaeology is a different study of mankind and it has evolved modes of thought appropriate to its data-set, which could be described as the material remains of human activity of any sort from the appearance of the first tool-making hominid millions of years ago to the present (Renfrew and Bahn 2000). The Roman period, as part of the short stretch of time in which human thoughts have been recorded in writing, is little more than a flick of the eyelid in that time-span. Not only that, but the consensus appears to be that in the most educated populations of the High Roman empire around 90 per cent of the population was illiterate (Harris 1989), so that even in this 'historic' period the activities of most human beings can only be reached through study of their material remains.

There is a fundamental methodological reality that when archaeology operates on evidence occurring within a historical period, if it is to yield anything of value, it has to do so on its own terms in the first instance. Even if an initial stimulus for research may come from some other field of study, as one of the many branches of history, sociology, or anthropology, archaeology cannot therefore be a 'tool' of that field of study, in the sense of being a device to throw direct light on concepts formulated in that other study. It can only directly serve concepts formulated as a result of knowledge of the nature of its own proper field of study. An additional, but lesser, point is that to call it a 'tool' even in this context would be to misrepresent it as a static device, whereas it is a form of enquiry where methods and thought about the results of applying methods are in continuous interaction with each other and thus in continuous development.

Saying that is absolutely not to imply that no synthesis is possible between 'historical' and archaeological data in an historic period, merely that this is more intellectually challenging than seems implicit in so many publications which still appear in Roman Studies. So hard, indeed, does the concept die that some form of unproblematized synthesis can be taken for granted that first it seems necessary to take up space in looking negatively, as it were, at some topics before turning the argument round to some of the positive contributions of archaeology. There are plenty of straw men on the synthesis front, like virtually any imposition of 'événementielle' history onto archaeological data ranging from emperors' names used as chronological adjectives—Augustan urbanism, Trajanic pottery, Neronian occupation, and so on—to the 'clustered' way many chronological studies are done of sites, military and urban especially, according to the haphazard survivals of literary references or the prestige of names mentioned in texts: were there really so many Agricolan forts or so much urban development under Hadrian and Septimius Severus? It is, in fact, easy enough—if one looks at the Braudelian categorization—to say that 'politics, events, and people' are that part of history least easily fitted to a synthesis with archaeological data, although a recent concern in archaeological theory with 'agency' complicates this point (to which we will return). But let us instead look at two more complex and recently studied areas of synthesis relating to the other two Braudelian historical categories—demography and Romanization.

Demography, a field in which one of the editors has made a distinguished contribution (and takes a cautious view of a 'glass ceiling' lying over the field as a whole: Scheidel 2001), might be considered a classic area where archaeology could serve as a 'tool', for, by careful studies of buildings and sites, could we not arrive at population sizes for those categories, and by study of the landscape could we not project those populations and their fluctuations through regions? From the study of human skeletal remains in cemetery sites could we not arrive at a close understanding of the composition of populations? The clear answer to all three questions, from a host of well-meaning and diligent studies, is 'no' (see Bintliff and Sbonias 1999, especially the articles by Chapman and Wilkinson on general points and by Cambi and Lo Cascio on Roman Italy). For buildings and sites, let us take the example of the best-known Roman site, Pompeii. Probably the most widely accepted estimate of the population of the urban area is that of 8,000–10,000 suggested in 1975 by Eschebach from his analysis of the plan of the city and followed by Jongman (1988: 108–12) within a discussion where the population of both the urban area and its territory is estimated at 37,500, based on the estimated carrying capacity of the land (Jongman 1988: 135). Eschebach's estimate is necessarily impressionistic, not because a third of the walled area of Pompeii remains unexcavated, but because it is virtually impossible to make more than guesses about the two-thirds which have been excavated: what was in the upper storeys of buildings, how many materially invisible or nearly-invisible inhabitants, as domestic slaves and shopkeepers sleeping on the premises were there? How much of the time did wealthier persons and their immediate entourages stay in their townhouses... and so on? Duncan-Jones (1982: 276–7) adduced modern parallels for orders of magnitude of urban density within a discussion which has a prevalently negative thrust about the use of archaeological evidence; Storey (1997) has used this approach in criticizing the conventional document-based estimate of the population of Rome as around a million (cf. Lo Cascio 2000) as being far too high; I tried a slightly different tactic on an estimate of the population of Roman Carthage, of using the analogy of sixteenth-century Tunis, as an adjacent capital city on a similar scale and at a comparable technological level, albeit within a different urban culture, to argue that that city might have had a population around the 100,000 mark (Hurst 1993), while economic historians such as Hopkins (1983: 89) and Harris (1993: 12) were suggesting that it might have been as much as five times that size. For views of fluctuating regional populations based on landscape studies, one only has to look at the (implicitly) different levels of optimism about the contribution of archaeological survey to this between Potter's *Changing Landscape of S. Etruria* (1979) and the Tiber Valley Survey volume relating to the same area (Patterson 2004). Leaving aside issues over the identification of sites, on top of any difficulty of converting sites into people is the realization of how much this type of landscape study is dominated by varying patterns of pottery production and marketing (brought out especially clearly in the Ager Tarraconensis study: Carreté, Keay, and Millett, 1995). The brutal truth is that survey archaeologists mostly find pots, not people. The most direct contribution to demography of survey archaeology has probably been to document the appearance and disappearance of human beings from marginal landscapes, however much the appropriately-named 'proxy-data' have been marshalled in support of arguments in other situations (Chapman 1999). A good sense of the vagueness we are left with on a larger scale can be obtained by reading Millett's pages (1990: 181–6) estimating the population of Roman Britain, taking into account an overview of regional survey work, and resulting in possibilities between 180,000 and 290,000 for the urban population, 50,000–200,000 for the military population and 1.8 ± 1.2 to 4.6 ± 2.9 million for the rural population. The necessarily imprecise calculations leave little confidence in the overall 'mid-range' figure of 3.7 million, and even Millett's conclusion that the total is unlikely to have been as low as the figure estimated (of around 2 million) for the eleventh century from Domesday Book or as high as the 5–6 million of some 'optimistic' Roman estimates seems not beyond question. At this point Hopkins's eulogy of the large-scale model is not a consolation: 'if we investigate the population size of a single town in Roman Britain, or of a single province, we can be wildly wrong. But if we are careful in our construction of a model on a large scale, with luck and good judgement, some of our errors, and some local or temporary fluctuations, should be self cancelling' (Hopkins 2002: 193).

Cemetery archaeology, like landscape archaeology, has in the last generation blossomed to create a world of its own, where, to the many pathological, dietary, and socio-religious indicators revealed by the condition of bones and their disposal in graves is tentatively being added the results of DNA analysis (cf. Pearce, Millett, and Struck 2000). Cemeteries tell us about individuals and about individual instances of physical conditions, and they tell us in a skewed way about the age of those buried (being accurate on the young and, though improving, still imprecise about mature adults); potentially, familial relations and endemic conditions of disease or nutrition can also be revealed. What is not revealed as a rule is the make-up of whole populations, not so much for the reason that few cemeteries can be uncovered in their entirety, though that is overwhelmingly the case, as because of the ancient social constraints determining who ended with a formal burial in the ground (Morris 1992) or, as Hodder (1980) illustrated long ago, whether populations were necessarily buried locally.

In these illustrations, then, it should be clear that while archaeology can produce demographic information of all sorts, it cannot do it to what we might call a historical demographer's order. If you want to compare, say, the documented early modern population of the Naples region with that of ancient Campania, archaeology today gives you no better an estimate for the latter than Beloch made 120 years ago (Beloch 1890: 457), nor does it show any sign of being able to. If, on the other hand, you want to know when the Molise uplands or the wadi valley sides of Tripolitania were inhabited and how, archaeology has answers, just as it can have on the incidence of *cribra orbitalia* or the likelihood of familial relationships in cemetery groups.

Romanization—a topic which has been prominent in the English-speaking literature of the last two decades—seems to involve an implicit rather than an explicit synthesis of archaeology and history. It is the label for a concept formulated in an age of archaeological and historical thinking very different from our own—in Francis Haverfield's lectures to Oxford University undergraduates of the 1890s and 1900s, though as Hingley (2000, 2005) has shown, Haverfeld drew from the earlier work of Mommsen. A lecture on this theme was published in the Proceedings of the British Academy for 1905 under the title *The Romanization of Roman Britain*, and this subsequently went through three further editions (in 1912, 1915, and 1923) as a small, but highly influential, book. In the time since, the label Romanization has remained while what it signifies has altered substantially. What Haverfield meant was the degree of Roman material culture which might be manifested in a site or area, measured by straightforward markers such as the use of Roman forms in art and architecture, the use of Roman-style technology as wheel-turned pottery, built roads, and masonry buildings, and the use of Roman coins and inscriptions in Latin. His main interest was to chart the varying degrees to which this material culture was deployed in Britain. He evidently thought that those who lived in masonry buildings of right-angled plan, bathed, and used shiny red pottery had thrown their lot in with the imperial authorities more than those who did not, and his general view, in common with the prevailing attitude of his time, was that this would be to their advantage. Without entering into the elaborations of this view made by leading Romano-British archaeologists who followed him, it seems fair to identify Peter Salway's *Oxford History of Roman Britain* (1981) as the last major work on Roman Britain offering a straightforward narrative of the march of a more advanced civilization over a lesser one, with the unstated assumption that this was, as it were, the natural order of things. A turning-point was marked by Reece's *My Roman Britain* (1988), Hingley's *Rural Settlement in Roman Britain* (1989), and Martin Millett's *The Romanization of Britain* (1990). The archaeology of Britain had to divorce itself from history and, substantially, from Rome (Reece), Romanization in material-culture terms could be and was actively resisted (Hingley), while for Millett there were options about 'becoming Roman'; local elites tended to do it in order to retain their social superiority within the colonial society, others accepted it to a lesser or greater degree; with time, 'anti-Roman' tendencies arising from the nature of pre-Roman British society showed through, as for example in the chequered history of urbanism. The changing climate of thought led to what can be categorized as the 'discrepant experience' approach most explicitly stated by Mattingly (1997, 2006) but also implicit (though used to a different end) through Woolf's *Becoming Roman* (1998): Roman material items could be deployed for different purposes, including subversive ones, according to context; everywhere there were different usages; that and the purpose of those uses is what we need to look at.

On the face of it this might seem to be a debate about interpreting material culture, and thus to fall within the framework outlined above of archaeology serving 'concepts formulated as a result of knowledge of the nature of its own proper field of study'. But, especially in Hingley's *Roman Officers and English Gentlemen* (2000) and his *Globalizing Roman Culture* (2005), or if one looks through the pages of the published proceedings of the Theoretical Roman Archaeology conference (TRAC) since 1990, it is clear that this is really a debate about imperialist and post-imperial narratives and, for the books which are Britain-centred—so excepting, for example, Woolf's *Becoming Roman* (1998) about Gaul and Terrenato's writings about Romanization in Italy (e.g. his Introduction to Keay and Terrenato 2001)—this is not about Roman imperialism so much as nineteenth- and twentieth-century British imperialism and its reception: Haverfield first made the analogy, though as Hingley says (2000: 53–6, 121–3), it was somewhat peripheral to his main line of thought. This has been less true for the 'post-imperialists'. In his 1997 edited volume on Romanization, Mattingly introduces the topic by referring explicitly to Said's well-known volume *Culture and Imperialism* (1993) on the British Empire in the East. This debate in Roman Britain evokes an earlier discussion of Roman Africa, where, in response to Broughton's *The Romanization of Africa Proconsularis* (1929), the Algerian scholar Marcel Benabou published *La Résistance à la romanisation de l'Afrique romaine* in 1974, a decade or more after the termination of the Algerian War of Independence; however, while that could be seen as a debate between colonizer and colonized, the British discussion has been between colonizers and their sons or grandsons. Although the British debate especially has widened our ways of looking at Roman material culture and in a sense put its study into a new perspective (the African argument was more on historical matters), it must be seen that archaeology here is being used as a tool in an agenda that essentially lies outside it and that, as far as this is the case—as is perhaps already evident—the debate seems unlikely to lead anywhere much further than it has reached at present. The central question in Roman material culture might be thought to be not so much about different usages in different places and times, as how it achieved the uniformity it had.

Having, then, given these two quite complex examples of archaeology being deployed, first as a tool in a field of study where its contribution is qualified, then as ammunition in a debate which cannot be resolved in purely archaeological terms, it is appropriate to ask what are the particular qualities of an archaeological contribution to our image of the Roman world. The obvious answer is that this is the only way to encounter that physical world in all its complexity, from the remarkable art it produced to its impact on the global environment, and the choice is almost infinite about which aspects we choose to focus on. Focusing specifically on the archaeology/history relationship, the most important way in which the study of the human material past gives a divergent view from any written record or account is in the degree of change: archaeology's basic unit of study is measurable change in some form, whether chronologically or simply as variety, and what it shows is that there was a huge amount more of both than is ever documented. When we look at categories for which there is both a documented and material culture manifestation, as, for example, urbanism, the documentary aspect, through the very semantics of language, as well as for legal or other reasons, de-emphasizes change. Thus, for example we have entities of very different character, as between, say Cosa, a Hellenized Italian town founded in 272 BCE for a few thousand souls engaged predominantly in managing a parcel of agricultural terrain and having an erratic existence thereafter (Fentress 2003); Carthage, refounded in 29 BCE to be the cultural and commercial metropolis of Africa, brandishing its Phoenician identity beneath a stylish imperial Roman veneer, ten or more times the size of Cosa at its moment of foundation, and growing headlong from that (Hurst 1993); and York, a civilian settlement outside the walls of a long-standing legionary fortress in the far north of the empire, which probably received a promotion in status at the beginning of the third century CE when the fortress was used as a base for the Severan campaigns into Scotland (Ottaway 1999). All of these were *coloniae*, they all had a constitution in which common elements were present, members of their leading social class were probably called *decuriones* in all three cities, and their inhabitants all probably thought of themselves as Romans; there were physical similarities too, in that all three cities had a forum, temples, and rich houses and at some stage were surrounded by a wall. There could be a narrative dwelling on the 'continuity' of urban ideas and ideals which all three cities shared, or another dwelling on their hugely divergent characters, contexts, and histories. We can appreciate those city identities and histories and be prompted to think about why they should have developed as they did only through their archaeology: rich as the documentation for Carthage is, it gives us little more than glimpses of a few peaks in a mountain range, while that for Cosa and York gives no sense of what these places amounted to. Even in Rome itself, for all the weight of ancient eyewitness comments and a crushing weight of scholarship about it, archaeology sets our understanding of the city in a completely new dimension, essentially by showing that a great deal more happened than we would guess from the written record but also—of course—in bringing us into contact with a physical reality we can hardly grasp from the written word.

An archaeology of Roman urbanism will, then, highlight the hugely varied nature of what we might class as Roman cities and bring us up against problems of functional definition, and it will document the dynamism of life in these places in all its varied forms and illuminate accompanying phenomena in vivid detail; it will give us images of living and dead city inhabitants and their lifestyles; it will tell us about both poor and rich—in an unstructured way. It will produce a great deal of information which reflects at one remove social structures and organization, while yielding little statistical information which can be converted straightforwardly into sociological data. Its challenge to any institutional account of Roman urbanism can be summed up in one word—dynamism. It reveals these social organisms in their true state of dynamic tension, never remaining the same and all different from each other.

Perhaps a more celebrated illustration of this character of archaeological data and its impact upon a field of study has been in the study of ancient economic mechanisms. As has often been remarked, neither Moses Finley's famous *The Ancient Economy* (1973) nor the influential writings of Keith Hopkins which followed and modified Finley's view (among which it will suffice to cite 'Taxes and Trade in the Roman Empire': Hopkins 1980; see also Hopkins 2002), made much use of archaeological data despite there being a welter of seemingly relevant information. One consequence of the Finley study was indeed to stimulate a certain way of processing archaeological data, particularly pottery, so as to highlight large-scale production, markets, and long-distance trade and thereby provide material for arguing with his 'primitivist' view of the relative insignificance of trade and its restriction to luxuries. One might mention particularly an Italian school of social historians/archaeologists, originally deriving from a Marxist tradition, which devoted great energy to studying pottery production and distribution (Giardina and Schiavone 1981), and, on a more purely archaeological and less social-historical level, Greene's *The Archaeology of the Roman Economy* (1986), both aiming to refute Finley. Greene has more recently (2007) expressed regrets that, instead of taking a great deal of archaeological information on board, and thereby refining their arguments, Roman economic historians mostly turned their attention away from mechanisms and towards the study of economic institutions where archaeological data had little role to play. This is not quite how it has appeared to me. First, although the historical debate was described as an academic battleground by Hopkins in his introduction to the volume of *Trade in the Ancient Economy* presented to Finley (Garnsey, Hopkins, and Whittaker 1983), it was one where by that time most of the big ideas had been deployed and many participants had entrenched themselves in well-established positions. A host of detailed historical and especially archaeological studies seemed to show variety and contradictions of the big picture and thus undermine such broad-brush terms as 'the ancient economy' or 'the Roman economy'. Within the Roman world, it appeared that there was a myriad of economic mechanisms only pulled together to a limited extent by the trading of 'a smallish surplus, say 10% of the actual gross product... The main stimuli to that trade were taxes and rents' (Hopkins 2002: 224–5). For all the superficial uniformity of a single currency from Scotland to the Sahara, it was clear from the archaeological study of lost coins that low-value coins were used in different ways in different parts of the Roman Empire and that in some, as Britain and northern Gaul in the first two centuries CE, they may not have been greatly used at all (Reece 1973). Even the favourite archaeological marker of trade movements—pottery—suffered a study crisis in which it was realized that counting pot types and provenanced fabrics might not be quite as revealing about economic mechanisms as was initially hoped, and that perhaps as large or in some cases a larger factor influencing which pots ended up where was cultural choice (cf. Woolf 1998: ch. 7)—a phenomenon which places less of a premium on precise numbers.

The effect of all this, aided in no small way by Hopkins's forceful intervention of 1995 (reprinted as Hopkins 2002), was to divorce the debate about overall economic models from the accumulation and discussion of the detailed data. Hopkins argued that in a situation where the detailed evidence is always found wanting to a greater or lesser extent while it is cumulatively impressive, the most appropriate construct is a model accounting for as many as possible of the disparate phenomena within a logical whole. If so, the only way to replace the model is to construct another with a superior logic; saying that this or that piece of detailed evidence does not agree with it was of no consequence in itself. It is a deliciously Platonic view of things, and thus might archaeology (but not only it) appear to be tamed. A limitation of this view amounting to a logical flaw in the model rhetoric would seem to lie in the low level of integration. If only 10 per cent of the gross product was available as a force for integration, then the model is largely not talking about the 90 per cent not caught up in this process. An alternative framework might seem to be offered by the distinction made between 'world economies' and 'world empires' in Wallerstein's World Systems analysis: economic integration was only optional for world empires (cf. Woolf 1990, discussing Wallerstein 1974 and 1980). At all events, debate about the ancient economy shifted decisively from the positions of the 1980s (cf. Scheidel and von Reden 2002 for an overview of many aspects over the following years). Archaeology's role in this was to show that a great deal more was going on and it was more complex than when the 'big' arguments were formulated, but also that reading the detail was not straightforward. It did not, then, determine the debate so much as require it to be conducted in a different form.

So far this account of archaeology has stayed close to a history-dominated framework, both in showing where it cannot fully respond to the demands of such a framework in the terms in which they have been set out—as in the demography and Romanization examples—and in showing where it has been able to alter the agenda, as in the urbanism and economic-history examples. What about frameworks or modes of thought generated from prehistoric archaeology and applied to Roman-period remains? As has been said, most of Roman archaeology is strictly prehistory in the sense of being about people who could not write and for the most part were not written about except at a rather schematic and distant level. Although the more historically-minded Roman archaeologists have tended to proceed in a fair degree of ignorance of the concerns of prehistoric archaeology, and there has been much criticism of Roman archaeologists for being 'untheoretical', in reality Roman archaeology has never had difficulty in following the lead of prehistory, even if it has often done so without the rhetoric and sometimes with a time-lag. Thus the quantification of pottery and other artefacts and the self-consciousness about sampling sites and landscapes developed in the 1970s and 1980s can be traced to the intellectual framework of processualism and systems analysis which held sway in 1970s prehistory (cf. Renfrew and Bahn 2000). Post-processual prehistory is a more diffuse set of intellectual influences, but some themes which have come to the fore—contextual archaeology, a focus on agency, phenomenology—have obvious homes in Roman archaeology. The problem indeed is not to be lazy about them because of recourse to the written word.

As regards the use of prehistoric archaeological theory in Roman archaeology, there has been and still is a revealing divide between the English-speaking scene, where archaeology is often taught in universities in isolation from history or other humanities studies, and the rest of western Europe, where Roman archaeology is more closely linked with history or the wider study of the Classics. Younger British academics have felt the need for an annual Theoretical Roman Archaeology conference, which has met with success each year since 1990. Although it has become a fairly broad church as regards theoretical approaches to Roman material, it was substantially born of the desire to treat Roman archaeology more like prehistory: there is indeed an amusing introduction by Hodder in 'contextual' mode in the proceedings of the first conference (Scott 1993), where he urges Roman archaeologists not to try late in the day to apply the sweeping theoretical approaches which prehistory had just liberated itself from. One could imagine a theoretical Roman archaeology conference in Germany, France, or Italy, but a great deal more of the theory would be generated from historical studies. For the reason stated above, British Roman archaeology has tended to remain more ahistorical in its terms of reference and approaches; this has been to its advantage in making it adventurous and often to the fore methodologically, but it has the disadvantage of tending to cause some of its interesting findings to be isolated from historically-linked discussion and consequently from what continues to be the mainstream of academic thought about the Roman period. An important unifier of these divergent intellectual traditions in Roman archaeology over the last twenty years has, however, been the *Journal of Roman Archaeology*, which, though having a strong Anglo-American editorial style, has proved to be a truly international journal as regards scholarly contributions; it has lessened the divide between 'anglophone' and non-anglophone Roman archaeology.

A question for the conclusion of this discussion is to what extent does or will archaeology give us a different view of the whole Roman phenomenon? Hingley's book *Globalizing Roman Culture* (2005) points towards an answer, though I would not give it quite in the same terms as him. He goes to lengths there, as in his earlier work, to show how we have, as it were, an elitist view of Roman culture, focusing in an unbalanced way on the rich and powerful and on their engagement with the most visible forms of 'Roman' culture—as towns, villas, and large monuments—and that we have developed a circular form of argumentation in labelling anything uniform and widespread in the Roman world like certain types of pottery 'Roman', even though there may be no independent justification for that. Further, we are motivated as westerners to continue to see the imposition of order by Roman civilization as far-reaching and beneficial in the way we like to believe that our recent western history is of central importance and, on balance, beneficial within the world of today. Yet when we look at the archaeology of the less powerful in the Roman world we find that towns and villas are in a distinct minority as types of site, and that the classic forms of Roman material culture, as art, coins, and those types of pottery thought to be Roman, are in a minority in the totality of what was called the Roman world. Our view is therefore unbalanced and, if we did more of this type of archaeology, and steered historical and archaeological study towards some of the more unpleasing aspects of the imposition of Roman rule, we could—in effect—end up with a less Romanocentric view of the Roman world.

While making good points about material culture in Roman times, this view seems to me to be too caught up in what might be called the postcolonial angst of the Romanization discussion. Hingley (2005: 117–18) seems too ready to be dismissive of a view he cites of Woolf, who is in effect developing Hopkins's exposition in *Conquerors and Slaves* (1978), of Rome as an organism that metabolizes other matter and is itself transformed by what it feeds on (Woolf 1997: 347, cited by Hingley 2005: 47). This, it seems to me, is the most satisfying explanation of the discrepant experience approach discussed above, since, unlike the other explanations which tend to dwell simply on difference and un- or anti-Romanness, this one explains how Roman material culture could function in a given context according to the rules of that context, yet at the same time that experience would feed back into a higher sense of Romanness. For example, Woolf shows in *Becoming Roman* (1998) that the use of terra sigillata pottery made in Gaul with a repertoire of classical imagery may have been characteristic of un-Roman peoples towards the outer edges of the empire. What motivation these peoples used the pottery with is neither here nor there; the one effect of using it about which it is possible to be confident is that familiarity with this visual imagery created a shared cultural element between these people and the inhabitants of the city of Rome. The large question is how far this percolated through the populations of the Roman world, and here one is tempted to see an analogy with Hopkins's model of the Roman economy, in which only a small proportion of Gross Product moved around as rents and taxes to establish a 'Roman economy'. One might say that only a correspondingly small proportion of the gross cultural product had to move around to establish a 'Roman culture'. Even if we can be clear in understanding that both in the socio-economic and the socio-cultural spheres these 'Roman' elements were absolute minorities of the whole, they were enough to establish the distinctive Romanness of the world to which they belonged. The development of more archaeology focused regionally will enable us to understand better both the metabolizing process in its many manifestations and its place within the world to which it belongs.

References

Beloch, J. (1890), *Campanien. Geschichte und Topographie des antiken Neapel und seine Umgebung* (2nd edn.). Breslau: Morgenstern.

Benabou, M. (1975), *La Résistance africaine à la romanisation de l'Afrique romain.* Paris: François Maspero.

Bintliff, J. and Sbonias, K. (1999), *Reconstructing Past Population Trends in Mediterranean Europe (3000 B.C.–A.D. 1800).* The Archaeology of Mediterranean Landscapes, ed. G. Barker and D. Mattingly, 1. Oxford: Oxbow.

Braudel, F. (1975), *The Mediterranean and the Mediterranean World in the Age of Philip II*, tr. S. Reynolds, 2nd edn., 2 vols. London: Fontana.

Broughton, T. R. S. (1929), *The Romanization of Africa Proconsularis.* Baltimore and London: Johns Hopkins University Press and Oxford University Press.

Cambi, F. (1999), 'Demography and Romanization in Central Italy' in Bintliff and Sbonias 1999: 115–27.

Carreté, J.-M., Keay, S. J., and Millett, M. (1995), *A Roman Provincial Capital and its Hinterland: The Survey of the Territory of Tarragona 1985–90.* Journal of Roman Archaeology Supplementary series, 15. Ann Arbor, Mich.

Chapman, J. (1999), 'Archaeological Proxy-data for Demographic Reconstructions: Facts, Factoids or Fiction', in Bintliff and Sbonias 1999: 65–76.

Coulston, J., and Dodge, H., eds. (2000), *Ancient Rome: The Archaeology of the Eternal City.* Oxford University School of Archaeology monograph 54. Oxford: Oxford School of Archaeology.

Duncan-Jones, R. (1982), *The Economy of the Roman Empire: Quantitative Studies* (2nd edn.). Cambridge : Cambridge University Press.

Eschebach, H. (1975), 'Erläuterungen zum Plan von Pompeji', in B. Andreae and H. Kyrieleis (eds.), *Neue Forschungen in Pompeji: und den anderen vom Vesuvausbruch 79 n. Chr. verschütteten Städten*, 331–38. Recklinghausen: Bongers.

Fentress, E. (2003), *Cosa V: An Intermittent Town, Excavations 1991–1997.* Ann Arbor, Mich.: University of Michigan Press for the American Academy in Rome.

Finley, M. I. (1973), *The Ancient Economy.* London: Chatto & Windus.

Garnsey, P., Hopkins, K., and Whittaker, C. R., eds. (1983), *Trade in the Ancient Economy.* London: Chatto & Windus.

Giardina, A., and Schiavone, A., eds. (1981), *Società romana e produzione schiavistica. 2, Merci, mercati e scambi nel Mediterraneo.* Rome: Laterza.

Greene, K. (1986), *The Archaeology of the Roman Economy.* London: Batsford.

—— (2007), 'Archaeological Data and Economic Interpretation', in P. F. Bang, M. Ikeguchi, and H. G. Ziche (eds.), *Ancient Economies, Modern Methodologies: Archaeology, Comparative History, Models and Institutions*, 109–36. Santo Spirito (Bari): Edipuglia.

Harris, W. V. (1989), *Ancient Literacy.* Cambridge, Mass.: Harvard University Press.

—— ed. (1993), *The Inscribed Economy: Production and Distribution in the Roman Empire in the Light of* instrumentum domesticum. *Journal of Roman Archaeology* supplementary ser. 6. Ann Arbor, Mich.: Journal of Roman Archaeology.

Haverfield, F. (1923), *The Romanization of Roman Britain* (4th edn., rev. G. Macdonald). Oxford: Clarendon Press.

Hingley, R. (1989), *Rural Settlement in Roman Britain.* London: Seaby.

—— (2000), *Roman Officers and English Gentlemen: The Imperial Origins of Roman Archaeology.* London: Routledge.

—— (2005), *Globalizing Roman Culture: Unity, Diversity and Empire.* London: Routledge.

Hodder, I. (1980), 'Social Structure and Cemeteries: A Critical Appraisal', in P. Rahtz, T. Dickinson, and L. Watts (eds.), *Anglo Saxon Cemeteries.* BAR British Series 82: 161–9.

Hopkins, K. (1978), *Conquerors and Slaves.* Cambridge: Cambridge University Press.

—— (1980), 'Taxes and Trade in the Roman Empire (200 BC–AD 400)', *Journal of Roman Studies*, 70: 101–25.

—— (1983), 'Models, Ships and Staples', in P. Garnsey and C. R. Whittaker (eds.), *Trade and Famine in Classical Antiquity.* Cambridge Philolological Society, Suppl. vol. 8: 84–109.

—— (2002), 'Rome, Taxes, Rents and Trade', in Scheidel and von Reden 2002: 190–230: repr. from *Kodai: Journal of Ancient History,* 6/7 (1995/6), 41–75.

Hurst, H. (1993), 'Cartagine, la nuova Alessandria', in A. Carandini, L. C. Ruggini, and A. Giardina (eds.), *Storia di Roma,* vol. III/2, *L'età tardoantica, I luoghi e le culture,* 327–37. Turin: Einaudi.

Jongman, W. (1988), *The Economy and Society of Pompeii.* Amsterdam: J. C. Gieben.

Keay, S., and Terrenato, N., eds. (2001), *Italy and the West: Comparative Issues in Romanization.* Oxford: Oxbow.

Lo Cascio, E. (1999), 'The Population of Roman Italy in Town and Country', in Bintliff and Sbonias 1999: 161–71.

—— ed. (2000), *Roma imperiale. Una metropoli antica.* Rome, chap. 1, 'La popolazione'. Rome: Carocci.

Mattingly, D. J. (2006), *An Imperial Possession: Britain in the Roman Empire, 54 BC–AD 409.* London: Allen Lane.

—— ed. (1997), *Dialogues in Roman Imperialism: Power, Discourse, and Discrepant Experience in the Roman Empire.* Journal of Roman Archaeology, Supplementary series, 23. Portsmouth, RI.

Millett, M. (1990), *The Romanization of Britain: An Essay in Archaeological Interpretation.* Cambridge: Cambridge University Press.

Morris, I. (1992), *Death-ritual and Social Structure in Classical Antiquity.* Cambridge: Cambridge University Press.

Ottaway, P. (1999), 'York: The Study of a Late Roman *colonia*', in H. Hurst (ed.), *The* Coloniae *of Roman Britain: New Studies and a Review.* Journal of Roman Archaeology, Supplementary series, 36: 136–50. Portsmouth, RI.

Patterson, H., ed. (2004), *Bridging the Tiber: Approaches to Regional Archaeology in the Middle Tiber Valley.* Archaeological Monographs of the British School at Rome, 13. London: British School at Rome.

Pearce, J., Millett, M., and Struck, M., eds. (2000), *Burial, Society and Context in the Roman World.* Oxford: Oxbow Books.

Potter, T. W. (1979), *The Changing Landscape of South Etruria.* London: Elek.

Reece, R. (1973), 'Roman Coinage in Britain and the Western Empire', *Britannia,* 4: 227–52.

—— (1988), *My Roman Britain.* Cirencester: Cotswold Studies at the Apple Loft.

Renfrew, C. and Bahn, P. (2000), *Archaeology: Theories, Methods and Practice,* 3rd edn. London: Thames & Hudson.

Said, E. W. (1993), *Culture and Imperialism.* London: Chatto & Windus.

Salway, P. (1981), *Roman Britain.* The Oxford History of Britain, 1A. Oxford: Clarendon Press.

Scheidel, W. (2001), *Debating Roman Demography.* Leiden: Brill.

—— and von Reden, S., eds. (2002), *The Ancient Economy.* Edinburgh: Edinburgh University Press.

Scott, E., ed. (1993), *Theoretical Roman Archaeology: First Conference Proceedings.* Aldershot: Avebury.

Steinby, E. M., ed. (1993–2000), *Lexicon topographicum urbis Romae,* 6 vols. Rome: Quasar.

Storey, G. R. (1997), 'The Population of Ancient Rome', *Antiquity,* 71: 966–78.

TRIGGER, B. G. (1989), *A History of Archaeological Thought.* Cambridge: Cambridge University Press.
WALLERSTEIN, I. (1974), *The Modern World System,* I: *Capitalist Agriculture and the Origins of the European World-economy in the Sixteenth Century.* Orlando, Fla.: Academic Press.
—— (1980), *The Modern World System,* II: *Mercantilism and the Consolidation of the European World-economy, 1600–1750.* New York: Academic Press.
WILKINSON, T. (1999), 'Demographic Trends from Archaeological Survey: Case Studies from the Levant and Near East', in Bintliff and Sbonias 1999: 45–64.
WOOLF, G. (1990), 'World-systems Analysis and the Roman Empire', *JRA* 3: 44–58.
—— (1997), 'Beyond Roman and Natives', *World Archaeology,* 28: 339–50.
—— (1998), *Becoming Roman: The Origins of Provincial Civilization in Gaul.* Cambridge: Cambridge University Press.

CHAPTER 6

EPIGRAPHY

JOHN BODEL

ABBREVIATIONS

POMPEY in 52 BCE faced a dilemma. The jewel in the crown of the theatre complex in Rome he had inaugurated with great fanfare three years previously, the temple to Victory perched at the top of the seating section, was nearing completion and required a suitably grand dedicatory text to adorn its architrave. Convention demanded a record of his office at the time, a third consulship, and Pompey was uncertain whether he ought to write *consul tertium* or *consul tertio*. Having consulted the learned men of the day and finding opinion divided, he had turned to Cicero, but Cicero, ever unwilling to offend the powerful, sought refuge in ambiguity by advising him to inscribe only the first four letters of the numeral, TERT, thus avoiding offence to any whose advice had not been followed. What made Cicero's deft evasion possible was the common Roman practice of abbreviating words in inscriptions, a convention shaped as much by architectural as by rhetorical context. Cicero's freedman Tiro recounted the anecdote in some detail a few years later, but Varro, who knew the right answer (*tertium*) and cited a verse of Ennius (*Annales* 290 Skutsch) to prove it, alluded to it only discreetly, remarking that Pompey had behaved timidly (*Disciplinae* Book 5 Popma, p. 202 Bipont.). Twenty-five years later Marcus Agrippa inscribed the full correct form onto the façade of the original Pantheon he had built a few hundred metres to the north: M. AGRIPPA.L.F.COS.TERTIVM.FECIT (*CIL* 6.31196. For the letters we see today, see Boatwright 2014: 260–61). The numeral spelled out in Agrippa's dedication appears striking beside the standard abbreviations for *consul* (COS) and the *praenomina* Marcus (M.) and Lucius (L.), the latter with the patronymic indicator *filius* (F.) in the formulaic phrase indicating paternal descent (Badian 1988: 203–4). In it we may recognize the assertive confidence of the new man, just as we remark Pompey's diffidence and Cicero's shrewdness in their responses to the epigraphic puzzle that Pompey's dedication presented, the solution of which was less a matter of grammar than of epigraphic decorum. How one expressed oneself in a public dedicatory inscription mattered to men concerned with political reputation and public image during the waning days of the Republic, and there were visual as well as verbal conventions for doing so properly that differed from those that determined literary propriety. It was not just what one said or how one said it but how it appeared that counted.

A coda to the story comes down to us at the start of the tenth book of the miscellany by Aulus Gellius known as the *Attic Nights*. Many years later, when the back wall of Pompey's stage building collapsed and was rebuilt, the number of Pompey's consulship was re-inscribed, not, as before, with the first four letters of the word but with the Roman numeral III, the form that could be read there still in Gellius' day (*Noctes Atticae* 10.1.8–9). The trend toward abbreviation and concision, not only to save space but for aesthetic effect, grew with time, as the simple combinations of two and three letters (ligatures) that characterized monumental lettering of the first two centuries CE eventually evolved into the elaborate monograms of the early medieval and Byzantine periods. By Gellius' time, around the middle of the second century CE, the mania for curtailing text was in full swing (in one famous document, a record of the regulations of a funerary society at Rome dated in 153 CE, one of nearly every four words—142 of 613—is abbreviated: Gordon 1983: 148–50 no. 66), but the phenomenon was well entrenched, especially in legal contexts, already by the early first century BCE, when a standard formula exempting existing arrangements from the new law could be registered simply by the initial letters of the fourteen words needed to write it fully:

S·S·S·E·Q·N·I·S·R·E·H·L·N·R.

The precise interpretation of the phrase was not always clear even at the end of the Republic (it remains ambiguous today; cf. Badian 1988), and by the time of the Flavian emperors grammarians such as Valerius Probus were compiling glossaries of such formulaic abbreviations to help readers work their way through publicly inscribed documents (Aistermann 1910, *De notis iuris*; for a modern version, Cagnat 1914: 407–72).

One standard clause requiring that a statute be posted publicly 'whence it can be read clearly from the ground' (*unde de plano recte legi possit*) and regularly indicated by initials alone shows that severity of abbreviation was considered no impediment to legibility, which required only that the lettering be clearly seen (cf. Crawford 1996: 1. 19–20; Williamson 2005: 310–14). Reading public notices in Latin, in the minds of Roman lawmakers and of those who implemented their decisions, meant knowing how to decipher the abbreviated formulae. The skills required were not purely linguistic but cultural. As Probus' glossary suggests, for one born in the eastern, Greek-speaking parts of the empire and therefore less accustomed to hearing Latin spoken aloud, the system could be baffling. When the same phrase appeared in Greek versions of Roman documents, it was normally written out in full (e.g. Crawford 1996: 1. 241, lines 25–6; *P. Coll. Youtie* 1.30; *P.Oxy.* 8.1100.2–3, 34.2705.10–11). To the question whether a public notice should be posted in Greek or Latin, the early third-century jurist Ulpian replied that it depended upon the locality, but that if it were written up in the open in clear letters, 'whence it can be read clearly from the ground' (the formulaic phrase), no one could claim not to know what it said (*Digest* 14.3.11.3). It was not assumed that everyone could read, only that readers of the two administrative languages of the Roman Empire (Greek and Latin) would be able to read publicly posted documents in the form in which they were normally published, provided that the letters could be clearly seen. An inability to read, in other words, was no excuse for ignorance of the law, if the law could be locally read. Implicit in the execution of the principle across the empire is the understanding that reading Latin meant deciphering its standard formulae written only in abbreviated form, whereas a similar capacity was not expected of the readers of Greek.

The same situation applies equally to other types of inscription: epitaphs, dedications, honorary texts, building inscriptions, labels, administrative documents—virtually all types of Latin inscription employed specific sets of abbreviations, quite apart from those that were embedded in onomastic formulae and were therefore endemic throughout the system (see Salomies 1987: 139–48 and Kajava 1994: 229–32 on *praenomina*). Greek usage during the Roman period, on the other hand, although it betrayed the influence of Latin practice in expanding greatly its use of abbreviations, especially in titles, never incorporated the system fully into common use and generally restricted itself to Latin loan-words and translated offices (e.g. Greek *antistr(ategos)* = *p(ro)p(raetor)*; see Mason 1974: 9, 106–8). Nor did the Romans share with their Italic neighbours the passion for abbreviation that characterized written Latin as it emerged in Latium during the third century BCE (Salomies 1987: 138–9). The phenomenon, in other words, was primarily scriptural rather than linguistic, Latin in the first instance and Roman only secondarily and by association. Inevitably, given the patterns of Latin lexical formation and syntax, certain common combinations of letters occurred repeatedly and could be resolved in multiple ways: the pair P P, for example, could stand for any of more than thirty different phrases. How one interpreted a string of initials depended upon where they appeared within a text, what type of text it was, and where the text was located. Context—linguistic, physical, and cultural—determined meaning. Correct reading, in Roman terms, meant knowing how to decode what the abbreviations signified, which was not simply a matter of knowing how to read but of being able to interpret the conventions correctly in their setting.

Letter Forms and Literacy

The significance of inscriptions for determining general levels of literacy in the ancient world is a matter of controversy (Harris 1989; Beard *et al.* 1991), but it is clear that basic literacy for the Romans meant some form of epigraphic literacy, in the sense that whatever reading ability a Roman possessed probably included the capacity to decipher public monumental lettering, and whatever writing skills he or she may have exercised were more likely to have been practiced in the forms conventionally defined as epigraphic than in any other. Epigraphy is traditionally defined as the study of inscriptions—a term, according to one authoritative opinion, that could properly be applied to any form of writing produced in a given culture with writing instruments and on surfaces other than those normally used in day-to-day life. In Roman society that would exclude, at different times and in different places, writings not only on papyrus and parchment but on thin strips of wood, broken bits of pottery (ostraka), and waxed wooden tablets (though not, perhaps, as universally as generally believed: Meyer 2004: 23–4). In practice, however, the territory conventionally covered by epigraphy includes all modes of writing that are not regularly employed for the production of literary texts (Panciera 1998: 313–14 [= 2006: 1795]).

In Roman society that territory encompasses a wide variety of uses and media and styles of script, not all of which would have been equally familiar, or even comprehensible, to all readers. Near the bottom of the scale of epigraphic literacy, for example, we might place the freedman character in Petronius' *Satyrica* who boasts of knowing *lapidariae litterae* ('letters on stone', 58.7), by which he means the type of block capitals (*litterae quadratae*, 29.1) that were used for monumental texts on stone and bronze (epitaphs, honorific inscriptions, official documents—laws, treaties, milestones, and the like—as well as dedications), and publicly posted notices on painted wood (Corbier 2006: 9–50, for the concept of monumental writing). These are the sorts of texts normally associated with epigraphy and the ones from which many of those without schooling are likely to have learned to read, but in Roman culture the field also embraces such vehicles of everyday writing as inked wooden leaves (used for routine communication, both public and private, at military outposts in Britain: Bowman 2003, Terras 2006), metal sheets (conventionally 'lead', in fact often pewter, the favoured medium for conveying written curses: Gager 1992: 3–4), the exterior wall surfaces of buildings (commonly pressed into service in Italian towns as billboards for painted election posters—Chiavia 2002; cf. Mouritsen 1999; Biundo 2003—and announcements of gladiatorial exhibitions—Sabbatini Tumolesi 1980), and the terracotta fabric of amphorae and other transport vessels (variously stamped, etched, or painted, before or after firing, with commercial administrative texts and declarations of ownership or responsibility: Rodríguez-Almeida 1993)—all of which by the time of

Augustus were normally being written in a more attentuated and informal type of capital letters called 'actuarial' or 'cursive' (Bischoff 1990: 54–61). It is difficult to know what percentage of the readers of block capitals would have had difficulty with the cursive writing of everyday correspondence and business documents, but some, at least would have reacted similarly to the slave Pseudolus in Plautus' comedy of the same name, who described the letters as mounting one another and likened the markings to chicken scratches (Plautus, *Pseudolus* 21–30) but was able to read the text of a private letter nonetheless (39–72).

A more elegant version of the same cursive capitals ('canonical' or 'rustic') was learned by the tiny minority of readers who acquired formal schooling past the elementary level and served as the standard literary bookhand until the third century. Already by then literary texts were being produced in a form of cursive minuscule that ultimately predominated for the rest of antiquity (thus establishing the basis of the dual system of lettering we have today: Bischoff 1990: 63–6), and monumental inscriptions were being carved in taller, attenuated, heavily serifed letters more similar to those drawn with a brush than those incised with a sharp instrument. Toward the end of the fourth century, at about the same time that Jerome was writing out in minuscule cursive, at the behest of his employer Pope Damasus, what would become the Vulgate version of the Bible (382/385 CE), Damasus was also commissioning his official engraver (Furius Donysius) Filocalus to carve epitaphs and other monumental texts in an elegant block-capital script distinguished by elaborate curly serifs that Filocalus had designed specifically for formal inscribed public lettering (see e.g. Gordon 1983: 176–8 no. 91 [383 CE]). Two decades later Augustine was commending to his congregation as more accessible and retainable than the holy scripture entombed in the book four verses he had inscribed in a chapel for all to read and learn (*Sermones* 319.8; Sanders 1990). By that time the palaeographic paths of epigraphic and literary writing had diverged decisively, and although they subsequently tracked certain courses in parallel, the two tracks tended to develop more independently of one another than they had done earlier during the classical period.

Latin Epigraphic Culture

Throughout the Roman era different forms of writing were appropriate to different media and different contexts. Deviation from the norm signalled specific intent. Thus two famous late-antique (late fifth- or early sixth-century) codices of Virgil written in the traditional lapidary block capitals aimed to confer monumentality on the text (Bischoff 1990: 59), just as a woman with the Punic name Beccut in third-century Mactar (Tunisia) hoped to elevate the Latin hexameters she composed for her daughter's epitaph by having them inscribed on a standard tombstone with the type of cursive capitals in which contemporary literary works were produced (*L'Année Épigraphique*, 1969–70, 658; cf. Corbier 2006: 80–1). Each made a bid for authority by transposing lettering associated with one medium to the other, in the understanding that the mode of writing would convey particular connotations derived from its normal range of uses in the different spheres.

To the socially ambitious, for whom epigraphic propriety was a matter of prestige, correct usage meant more than simply knowing what abbreviations or lettering to use where. Epigraphy, like literature, had genres, and the generic boundaries of different types of text, like those of letter forms, had to be observed: an epitaph was not an honorific inscription, although both might record similar information with similar commemorative intent; a dedication to a god differed greatly from that to patron, even if both employed the same syntax (cf. Eck 1984: 133–5, 149–52; Judge 1997). Where and how an inscription was displayed was integral to its genre and quite often also to its message, which could be subverted by displacement of the text (Chioffi 2001; Feraudi-Gruénais 2003). Accordingly, Beccut, like Agrippa a parvenu in the social ranks in which her epigraphic statement places her, while pushing the limits of acceptable experimentation with form, nonetheless, like Agrippa, knew what the text she composed ought to say and drew the line at content. Not so the wealthy freedman Trimalchio, whose anxiety about the suitability of his preposterously worded epitaph (*Satyrica* 71.12) reflects both the height of his social pretension and the depth of his insensitivity to epitaphic idiom and form: what he says is not entirely outré, only out of place in an epitaph or incorrectly placed within the normal structure of one (Bodel 1999: 42–3).

In Petronius' satiric portrait the incongruous juxtaposition of modes and cultural contexts conveys humour rather than authority, and similar epigraphic *faux pas* provoked similar reactions in the real world. The younger Pliny, in describing to a correspondent the rural sanctuary of the river-god Clitumnus near Hispellum in Umbria, characterizes the vows of thanks and praise inscribed by grateful visitors across the walls and columns of the precinct as mostly admirable but occasionally laughable (Pliny, *Letters* 8.8.7; cf. Beard 1991: 39–40). Rusticity of language was not itself a source of amusement to Pliny and his supercilious friends; rather, it was the formality of the written commemoration of a humble personal event, whether in a cursive graffito or a carved plaque, that rendered the texts incongruously inept. Banality, for the sophisticated, was worse than faulty execution. Trimalchio, as always an infallible guide, falls short in both: when accidentally bruised by a slave, he will not allow the mishap to pass 'without an inscription' but hammers out on the spot three limping verses of doggerel on the unexpected turns of Fortune of a sort one can read in numerous variations among the surviving inscribed verse epitaphs (Petronius, *Satyrica* 55.2–3; cf. Lattimore 1942: 154–8). Elsewhere Pliny waxes indignant about commemorative inscriptions inappropriately denied to (*Letters*

6.10.3–5) or bestowed upon (7.29.2, 8.6.14) recipients deserving of different epigraphic treatment (Verginius Rufus, deprived of an epitaph; the imperial freedman Pallas honoured by senatorial decree: Woolf 1996: 25–6), and Petronius, by drawing attention to his narrator's varied reception of the profusion of inscribed texts in Trimalchio's home, implicates his own reader in a hermeneutic *mise en abîme* (Nelis-Clément and Nelis 2005: 1–16). Both authors bear witness to a reading culture that recognized literary and epigraphic modes as distinct but constantly in dialogue with one another, neither being intrinsically high nor low but each with its own range of registers.

Graffiti

As Trimalchio's behaviour and Pliny's testimony further demonstrate, the Roman fascination with inscriptions extended to the production as well as the consumption of texts and influenced behaviour well below the highest levels of society. At the precinct of Clitumnus, according to Pliny, the humble dedications were inscribed 'on all the columns and all the walls' (*Letters* 8.8.7), and indeed, where evidence is well preserved, as in the Campanian towns buried by Vesuvius in 79 CE, we can see that scribblers with a variety of interests, from sex to commerce to literature to public entertainments, availed themselves of public (and private) walls and monuments to publicize their messages wherever they could (Gigante 1979; Franklin 1991). One often-cited graffito found scrawled up on the basilica, in the amphitheatre, and at the theatre at Pompeii marvels (in elegiac verse) that the wall which supports it has not collapsed under the load of writing it bears (*Carmina Latina Epigraphica* [hereafter *CLE*] 957; cf. Franklin 1991: 82–3). At another well-frequented street corner near the centre of town more than 120 texts scratched onto the walls outside a brothel regale passers-by with greetings, prostitutes' advertisements, and clients' accounts of their triumphs and disappointments (*CIL* 4.2173–2301, at VII.12.18–20; cf. Varone 2005). In the basilica one scribbler wrote up in Augustan elegiacs an Epicurean reflection on love, which another answered with an imprecation against the reader, a third with a target-reversing '(on the one) who wrote it', a fourth with confirmation ('right'), a fifth, who evidently hoped to end the discussion, with an apparently independent salutation to a Hedystus (*CIL* 4.1837 = *CLE* 949). Beneath it another versifying wag paired a famous Virgilian hexameter (*Aeneid* 6.460) with a lasciviously undercutting pentameter in a manner reminiscent of contemporary Menippean satire (e.g. Seneca, *Apocolocyntosis* 3.2–3, Petronius, *Satyrica* 111.12, 112.2–3; cf. Cugusi 1985: 233–5). Next to another door an obscene bit of doggerel is circumscribed within a perimeter drawn in the shape of a tablet to suggest a formal public notice (*CIL* 4.1517; cf. *CLE* 955).

Whether inflating or deflating, Pompeian humour tended to manifest itself in graffiti through an interplay of form and content; the ingenuity exercised was not only verbal but often visual and situational. In a room in the House of Pansa (VI.6.1), for example, a hexameter Greek palindrome written retrograde is accompanied by the same text running left to right in Roman characters (*CIL* 4.2400a; cf. Gigante 1979: 76–7); beside it a certain Curvius and his friends engaged in a series of salutations in which the words are arranged in normal sequence left to right but proper names are spelled backwards (*CIL* 4.2400d–g). One of them (Aemilius), a professional poster-painter (*scriptor*) and inveterate scribbler (he is credited with some thirty-five graffiti at Pompeii) habitually wrote his name in this fashion (Franklin 1991: 91–3). What one senses throughout is an exuberant delight in writing in its various forms and a fascination with its multiple uses—utilitarian, decorative, and performative (e.g. apotropaic). Above all, one observes an active appreciation of the graphic and visual elements of inscribed texts, which often complemented crude images etched or painted near them and sometimes incorporated visual imagery into the script itself (e.g. *CIL* 4.4716, 4755, the 'signature' of an architect Crescens, who wrote his name and title into the shape of a ship; cf. Corbier 2006: 91–128 on text in images; Langner 2001: 32, 79–84 on pictorial graffiti and rebuses). So too at Rome, in a tavern of the Augustan era discovered beneath Santa Maria Maggiore, an entire wall was decorated with 'nonsense' graffiti and epigraphic *jeux d'esprit*—alphabets, letter groups, lists of Roman numerals, palindromes (in Greek and Latin), 'magic' word squares (able to be read both vertically and horizontally), and the like (Castrén 1972; cf. Gigante 1979: 77–9). Whatever value such evidence may have for determining general levels of literacy, it unequivocally illustrates a characteristic feature of the Roman epigraphic habit, a certain *joie de scrivere* devoid of utilitarian purpose and independent of any functional use.

It is often pointed out, not incorrectly, that, unlike literary texts, which provide access only to the world of the educated elite, inscriptions open a window into the lives of ordinary Romans otherwise largely closed to us. It should be added at the same time (but often is not) that the formulaic nature of much epigraphic expression undermines the wishful thinking that we read unfiltered in the inscriptional record the thoughts and sentiments of the man in the street. We do not, as even such apparently spontaneous effusions as we find among the Pompeiian graffiti indicate. Rarely, when a text rises above mere salutation or erotic declaration of the 'x with y here' variety, do we find genuine originality of thought or expression (Gigante 1979: 203–21; Cugusi 1985: 217–19; cf. Langner 2001: 139–41). Creativity, where it is found, emerges rather in the presentation of the writing, wit in mock-heroic parody or the incongruous juxtaposition of formulaic elements. Many more quotations of well-known verses by famous Augustan authors than original compositions crowd Pompeian walls (Gigante 1979: 71–99, 142–201; cf. Corbier 2006: 73–5). When unattributed verses of more than ordinary sophistication are encountered, they find their place in literary discussions of Hellenistic epigram (e.g. Gigante 1979: 88–99). The Pompeian graffitist who signed his elegiac compositions 'Tiburtinus epoese', for example, has a substantial bibliography (Lieberg 2005; cf. Cugusi 1985: 24–37). But the observation that usually follows on such encounters—that some Pompeians were remarkably literate—gets hold of the wrong end of the stick: more noteworthy than that some residents of (or visitors to: one oft-repeated distich represents the perspective of an urban tourist longing for a return to Rome: Cugusi 1985: 217–19) a coastal town on the fashionable Bay of Naples were sufficiently cultured to write original epigrams is the fact that any who could do so would publicize their work by writing it up on public walls. The graffiti are invaluable as a source of information primarily as a cultural phenomenon, less for what they say (one hopes that Pompeians' sex lives were more imaginative than their accounts of them) than for the way they say it and the fact that it is said at all.

Text and Context

The Pompeian couplet addressed to a wall burdened with graffiti has often been invoked to suggest the pervasiveness of writing at Pompeii: a commonplace repeated four times in different hands, it no more demonstrates the truth of that supposition (though it no doubt supports it) than it does the wit of even one of the town residents. Rather, it suggests a phenomenon no less interesting: the prevalence of an impulse to share publicly and anonymously a platitude that serves no other communicative purpose than to call attention to its setting amidst numerous similarly autonomous texts and the close association of all of them with their architectural supports. The union of text and material context celebrated in a written form that participates meta-textually in the phenomenon it describes represents precisely the sort of conceptual fusion that lies at the heart of Roman epigraphic culture. Epigraphy as a discipline is sometimes celebrated (mainly by epigraphists) as the place where archaeology and philology meet, where the study of texts and objects comes together in the interest of a holistic interpretation that is sometimes more philological, sometimes more archaeological, but is always in some sense broadly historical in that it fleshes out the framework of our picture of a culture (e.g. Sanders 1984). Less often remarked is the contemporary ancient perception of inscribed writing as exploiting both realms in full awareness of its position at the intersection of the two. A variation of the same ironic tag written up in Greek in the imperial palace on the Palatine hill in Rome takes the conceit to a self-contradictory extreme and at the same time reminds us that the ultimate source of this particular form of epigraphic self-consciousness, itself an urban phenomenon, lay in Alexandria of the Hellenistic period: 'many have written many things,' the graffitist declares with pointed polyptoton: 'I alone have written nothing' (Castrén and Lilius 1970: 145).

The desire to express oneself in public writing, however, and concern with the forms it took, were characteristic particularly of Roman imperial culture, where the epigraphic impulse influenced the behaviour of Romans of high and low station alike. Pompey, Pliny, Trimalchio, and the Pompeian scribblers shared a mentality about publicly inscribed texts, whether formal or informal, that both unites them, despite the range of their social differences, and distinguishes them among the peoples of the ancient Mediterranean world as distinctively Roman. The ecumenical quality of the Roman epigraphic habit sets it apart from that of other peoples in the ancient world, even those (such as the residents of Hellenistic Asia Minor) for whom monumental public texts were a regular part of the urban fabric. Often, as Roman power spread unevenly across the western provinces, the clearest sign of an established Roman presence in an area was the emergence there of the characteristic types of Latin inscription (particularly epitaphs and honorific monuments); even in cases where native linguistic and commemorative traditions continued to thrive, the advent of Roman rule usually meant the disappearance of local scripts and a reorientation of local epigraphic behaviours along Roman lines (Woolf 1994; Beltrán Lloris 1995).

Eventually, most regions of the Western Empire shared a common epigraphic culture, based on that at Rome and centred on public honorific monuments, civil administrative texts, and epitaphs, which, despite numerous minor local variations, provided a cultural *lingua franca* for the commemorative expression of diverse populations across Europe and North Africa. Urbanized parts of the eastern Mediterranean nurtured well-established traditions of diverse epigraphic expression which, though clearly betraying the influence of the new conventions, were less fully overwhelmed by the full onslaught of Roman epigraphic practice and retained many of their own, often localized and distinctive features (Bodel 2001*a*: 13–15). Radical abbreviation never fully caught on in the eastern Mediterranean, nor did the Greek-speaking regions of the empire adopt the western practice of engraving public laws, senatorial decrees, and imperial edicts on bronze to signal their legitimacy, but instead preserved a regional preference (driven only partly by the availability of resources) for stone (Williamson 2005: 396–7; cf. Thomas 1995). There are thus two levels at which we should try to understand what has come to be known as Roman epigraphic culture, one primarily social, centring on a new or increased use of monumental inscribed writing for honorific (self-)representation as a means of articulating status relations, which manifested itself across the empire following the imposition of Roman rule; the other more narrowly scriptural, confined to the western parts of the empire and, although not purely linguistic, nonetheless closely associated with the Latin alphabet and the way it was used to represent public writing at Rome. The first may have had a wider influence on behaviour throughout the ancient Mediterranean world, but the second was more characteristic in its preoccupation with the appearance of the writing and the physicality of its supports, and thus comes closer to what made the Latin epigraphic culture of the Western Empire more essentially Roman.

Cui Bono?

Implicit in the preceding discussion has been the belief that understanding the epigraphic culture of the Romans requires bearing in mind the context in which the writing was produced, not only in the narrow and specific senses of where, when, how, and why but more broadly within a spectrum of writing cultures, each with its own distinctive hues. Doing so makes it possible to avoid many of the pitfalls of epigraphic bias that dot the minefield of historical interpretation, the treacherous territory that unwary investigators too often stumble into when they fail to account for the filter through which all inscribed information comes down to us—the epigraphic climate that influenced what was inscribed when and where (Bodel 2001*a*: 34–9, 46–7). Many, however, approach Latin inscriptions with specific interests and questions, and alert to the problem of bias. What is there for them? Ancient historians, who perhaps have more frequent recourse to epigraphic evidence than others, are the ones most frequently catered for in manuals and general introductions (e.g. Calabi Limentani 1991; Bodel 2001) and the ones most likely to know what to expect to find. What do Latin inscriptions offer to the philologist, the linguist, or the archaeologist?

For the philologist and the linguist there are the grammar of colloquial speech and the phonology of contemporary spoken Latin (e.g. Väänänen 1966; cf. Marcillet-Jaubert 1960), as well as the occasional intrusion into the classical lexicon and Latin literary texts of even the most humble epigraphic forms (Bodel 1989). Our knowledge of early Latin—indeed, our direct knowledge of any Latin before the middle of the first century BCE—is exclusively epigraphic (cf. Vine 1993; Hartmann 2005). For the archaeologist, most helpfully, there is the tell-tale function served by any inscription found *in situ* or by a group of inscriptions found together of identifying a place (a building, a street, a sanctuary, an estate, a town) or indicating a purpose (Panciera 1998: 316–22 [1797–1801]). Milestones, boundary markers, and other territorial delimiters (e.g. epitaphs declaring the size of a tomb-plot: Eck 1987: 82–3) give invaluable assistance to topographers; 'catalogue' texts listing features of a building or appurtenances to a property are a boon to architectural historians. Apart from artists' signatures and labels on paintings and sculpture, epigraphy serves the art historian by anchoring the chronology of the typologies of objects so important for understanding stylistic developments.

Students of literature may find among the *carmina epigraphica* short works of more than passing interest and occasional merit that benefit from the same kind of exegesis as literary texts (e.g. Horsfall 1985; Courtney 1995; cf. Cugusi 2004). For those interested in the reception of classical literature, the story often begins with inscriptions and the implicit and explicit testimony they bear to the contemporary reading of authors whose works have come down to us also (Hoogma 1969). Scholars of Roman law depend upon inscriptions not only for the great bronze exemplars of public statutes (Crawford 1996), decrees of the senate—in Greek (Sherk 1969) and Latin (e.g. Eck, Caballos, and Fernández 1996)—municipal charters (e.g. Lamberti 1993), and the like, but also for a large body of private law touched upon only in passing by the juristic sources (notably tomb law, virtually a field unto itself: e.g. De Visscher 1963; AA. VV. 2004). The list could go on: there are very few areas of Roman Studies that inscriptions do not somehow illuminate. If there is a general bias to the preponderance of their testimony, it is a chronological one, weighted heavily in the Imperial period and particularly in the first three centuries CE (less than 2 per cent, fewer than 4,200 of some 220,000 surviving Latin inscriptions on stone, are datable to before the death of Caesar: cf. Solin 1999: 379–91). That epigraphy seems to touch so widely throughout the territory of Roman Studies is one sign of its centrality to the culture. In the diversely multicultural Mediterranean world of the Roman Empire, setting up an inscription in one of its characteristic Roman forms not only signified being Roman, it enacted it. In that sense epigraphy has a claim to the attention not only of Romanists but of anyone interested in understanding the civilizations of the ancient world.

Further reading

The best introduction to the subject in English is Gordon 1983. Keppie 1991 offers a more accessible approach. Cooley 2012 provides a wide-ranging overview of epigraphic cultures in the Roman West. Bruun and Edmondson 2015 assemble 35 chapters by international experts on both technical and general aspects of the subject. Of the older guides, that of Sandys 1927 provides a useful introduction for general classicists. For more serious study, Cagnat 1914, though necessarily out of date in certain respects, remains fundamental. Calabi-Limentani 1991 provides the best modern equivalent. Di Stefano 1987 is a technical guide to editing texts on stone that presents much useful information of interest also to more general readers. McClean 2002 makes ignoring the Greek epigraphy of the Hellenistic and Imperial East less excusable for Romanists than it once was. Synthetic overviews are offered by Bodel 2001, on the uses of inscriptions as historical evidence, and Corbier 2006, which unites several important studies on monumental public writing in Rome, a topic for which the studies of Petrucci (1993 and 1998) provide essential orientation. Schmidt 2007 gives a concise and up-to-date history and prospectus of the standard corpus (*Corpus Inscriptionum Latinarum*), which now comprises some 180,000 inscriptions in eighteen volumes, most with multiple fascicles. Bérard *et al.* 2000, with annual supplements on the internet, is an indispensable guide to the vast bibliography.

References

AA. VV. (2004). '*Iura sepulcrorum* a Roma. Inediti e revisioni. Consuntivi tematici ragionati', in Silvio Panciera (ed.), *Libitina e dintorni* (Libitina 3), Rome: Edizioni Quasar, 177–427.

Aistermann, Josef (1910), *De M. Valerio Probo Berytio capita quattuor; accedit reliquiarum conlectio*, Bonn: F. Cohen.

Badian, Ernst (1988), 'E.H.L.N.R.', *Museum Helveticum*, 45: 203–18.

Beard, Mary (1991), 'Writing and Religion: *Ancient Literacy* and the Function of the Written Word in Roman Religion', in *Literacy in the Roman World* (Journal of Roman Archaeology Supplementary Series 3), Ann Arbor, Mich.: Journal of Roman Archaeology, 35–58.

—— Alan K. Bowman, Mireille Corbier, Tim Cornell, James L. Franklin, Jr., Ann Hanson, Keith Hopkins, and Nicholas Horsfall (1991), *Literacy in the Roman World* (Journal of Roman Archaeology Supplementary Series 3), Ann Arbor, Mich.: Journal of Roman Archaeology.

Beltrán Lloris, Francisco (1995), *Roma y el nacimento de la cultura epigráfica en occidente*, Zaragoza: Institución 'Fernando el Católico'.

Bérard, François, Denis Feissel, Pierre Petitmengin, Denis Rousset, and Michel Sève (2000), *Guide de l'épigraphiste. Bibliographie des épigraphies antiques et médiévales*, 3rd edn., Paris: Presses de l'École Normale Supérieure. For annual supplements, see http://www.antiquite.ens.fr/txt/dsa-publications-guidepigraphiste-en.htm.

Bischoff, Bernhard (1990), *Latin Palaeography: Antiquity and the Middle Ages*, tr. Dáibhí ó Cróinín and David Ganz. Cambridge: Cambridge University Press.

Biundo, Raffaella (2003), 'La propaganda elettorale a Pompei', *Athenaeum*, 81: 53–116.

Boatwright, Mary T. (2014), 'Agrippa's Building Inscriptions', *Zeitschrift für Papyrologie und Epigraphik* 189: 255–64.

Bodel, John (1989), 'Missing Links: *Thymatulum* or *Tomaculum*?', *Harvard Studies in Classical Philology*, 92: 349–66.

—— (1999), 'The *Cena Trimalchionis*', in Heinz Hofmann (ed.), *Latin Fiction: The Latin Novel in Context*, London: Routledge, 38–51.

—— (ed.) (2001), *Epigraphic Evidence: Ancient History from Inscriptions*, London: Routledge.

—— (2001*a*), 'Epigraphy and the Ancient Historian', in John Bodel ed. 2001: 1–56.

Bowman, Alan K. (2003), *Life and Letters on the Roman Frontier: Vindolanda and its People*, revised edn., London: British Museum. Cf. *Vindolanda Tablets Online*: http://vindolanda.csad.ox.ac.uk.

Bruun, Christer and Jonathan Edmondson (2015), *The Oxford Handbook of Roman Epigraphy*, Oxford and New York: Oxford University Press.

Calabi Limentani, Ida (1991), *Epigrafia latina*, 4th edn., Milan: Cisalpino–La Goliardica.
Castrén, Paavo (1972), 'I graffiti del vano XVI', *Atti della Pontificia Accademia romana di archeologia, Ser. III. Memorie*, 11.1: 67–87.
—— and Henrik Lilius (1970), *Graffiti del Palatino. 2. Domus Tiberiana* (Acta Instituti Romani Finlandiae 3), Helsinki: Institutum Romanum Finlandiae.
Chiavia, Catherine (2002), *Programmata: Manifesti elettorali nella colonia romana di Pompei*, Turin: S. Zamorani.
Chioffi, Laura (2001), '*In sacro vel publico*. Tributi d'onore a personnaggi eminenti tra Repubblica e Impero', *Rendiconti della Pontificia Accademia romana di archeologia*, 71: 241–72.
Cooley, Alison E. (2012), *The Cambridge Manual of Latin Epigraphy*, Cambridge: Cambridge University Press.
Corbier, Mireille (2006), *Donner à voir, donner à lire. Mémoire et communication dans la Rome ancienne*, Paris: CNRS Editions.
Courtney, Edward (1995), *Musa Lapidaria: A Selection of Latin Verse Inscriptions*, Atlanta, Ga.: Scholars Press.
Crawford, Michael H. (1996), *Roman Statutes*, 2 vols. (Bulletin of the Institute of Classical Studies Supplement 64), London: Institute of Classical Studies.
Cugusi, Paolo (1985), *Aspetti letterari dei Carmina Latina Epigraphica*, Bologna: Pàtron.
—— (2004), '*Carmina Latina Epigraphica* e novellismo. Cultura di centro e cultura di provincia: contenuti e metodologia di ricerca', *Materiali e Discussioni*, 53: 125–74.
De Visscher, Fernand (1963), *Le Droit des tombeaux romains*, Milan: Giuffrè Editore.
Di Stefano Manzella, Ivan (1987), *Mestiere di epigrafista. Guida alla schedatura del materiale epigrafico lapideo*, Rome: Quasar.
Eck, Werner (1984), 'Senatorial Self-Representation: Developments in the Augustan Period', in Fergus Millar and Erich Segal (eds.), *Caesar Augustus Seven Aspects*, Oxford: Clarendon Press, 129–67.
—— (1987), 'Römische Grabinschriften. Aussageabsicht und Aussagefähigkeit im funerären Kontext', in Henner von Hesberg and Paul Zanker (eds.), *Römische Gräberstrassen. Selbstdarstellung—Status—Standard* (Abh. Bayer. Akad. Wiss, Phil.-Hist. Kl. 96), Munich: C. H. Beck: 61–83.
—— Antonio Caballos, and Fernando Fernández (1996), *Das Senatus Consultum de Cn. Pisone Patre* (*Vestigia* 48), Munich: C. H. Beck.
Feraudi-Gruénais, Francisca (2003), *Inschriften und 'Selbstdarstellung' in stadtrömischen Grabbauten*, Rome: Edizioni Quasar.
Franklin, James L., Jr. (1991), 'Literacy and the Parietal Inscriptions of Pompeii', in *Literacy in the Roman World* (Journal of Roman Archaeology Supplementary Series 3), Ann Arbor, Mich.: Journal of Roman Archaeology, 77–98.
Gager, John E. (1992), *Curse Tablets and Binding Spells from the Ancient World*, Oxford: Oxford University Press.
Gigante, Marcello (1979), *Civiltà delle forme litterarie nell'antica Pompei*, Naples: Bibliopolis.
Gordon, Arthur E. (1983), *Illustrated Introduction to Latin Epigraphy*, Berkeley: University of California Press.
Harris, W. V. (1989), *Ancient Literacy*, Cambridge, Mass.: Harvard University Press.
Hartmann, Markus (2005), *Die frühlateinischen Inschriften und ihre Datierung: eine linguistisch-archäologisch-paläographisches Untersuchung*, Bremen: Hempen.

Hoogma, Robertus P. (1969), *Der Einfluss Vergils auf die Carmina latina epigraphica. Eine Studie mit besonderer Berücksichtigung der metrisch-technischen Grundsätze der Entlehnung*, Amsterdam: North-Holland.

Horsfall, Nicholas (1985), '*CIL* VI 37965 = *CLE* 1988 (Epitaph of Allia Potestas): A Commentary', *Zeitschrift für Papyrologie und Epigraphik*, 61: 251–72.

Judge, E. A. (1997), 'The Rhetoric of Inscriptions', in S. E. Porter (ed.), *Handbook of Classical Rhetoric in the Hellenistic Period 330 B.C.–A.D. 400*, Leiden: E. J. Brill: 807–28.

Kajava, Mika (1994), *Roman Female Praenomina: Studies in the Nomenclature of Roman Women* (Acta Instituti Romani Finlandiae 14), Rome: Institutum Romanium Finlandiae.

Keppie, Lawrence (1991), *Understanding Roman Inscriptions*, Baltimore and London: Johns Hopkins University Press.

Lamberti, Francesca (1993), *'Tabulae Irnitanae': Municipalità e 'Ius Romanorum'*, Naples: E. Jovene.

Langner, Martin (2001), *Antike Graffitizeichnungen. Motive, Gestaltung und Bedeutung*, Wiesbaden: Ludwig Reichert Verlag.

Lattimore, Richmond (1942), *Themes in Greek and Latin Epitaphs*, Illinois Studies in Language and Literature, 28.1–2, Urbana, Ill.: University of Illinois Press.

Lieberg, Godo (2005), '*Tiburtini versus Pompeiani. CIL* IV 4966–4973', *Museum Helveticum*, 62.1: 56–64.

Marcillet-Jaubert, M. (1960), 'Philologie et inscriptions', *Revue des Études Anciennes*, 62: 362–82.

McLean, Bradley H. (2002), *An Introduction to Greek Epigraphy of the Hellenistic and Roman Periods from Alexander the Great down to the Reign of Constantine (323 B.C.–A.D. 337)*, Ann Arbor, Mich.: University of Michigan Press.

Mason, Hugh J. (1974), *Greek Terms for Roman Institutions: A Lexicon and Analysis* (American Studies in Papyrology, 13), Toronto: Hakkert.

Meyer, Elizabeth A. (2004), *Legitimacy and Law in the Roman World: Tabulae in Roman Belief and Practice*, Cambridge: Cambridge University Press.

Mouritsen, Henrik (1999), 'Electoral Campaigning in Pompeii: A Reconsideration', *Athenaeum*, 77: 515–23.

Nelis-Clément, Jocelyne and Damien Nelis (2005), 'Petronius' Epigraphic Habit', *Dictynna*, 2: 1–27.

Panciera, Silvio (1998), 'Epigrafia. Una voce soppressa', *Archeologia Classica*, 50 (1999): 313–30 [= *Epigrafi, epigrafia, epigrafisti. Scritti vari editi e inediti (1965–2005) con note complementari e indici*, Roma: Quasar, 2006: 1794–1808].

Petrucci, Armando (1993), *Public Lettering: Script, Power, and Culture*, tr. Linda Lappin (of an updated edition of *La Scrittura. Ideologia e rappresentazione*, Rome, 1980, 1986), Chicago: University of Chicago Press.

—— (1998), *Writing the Dead: Death and Writing Strategies in the Western Tradition*, tr. Michael Sullivan (of *Le scritture ultime. Ideologia della morte e strategie dello scrivere nella tradizione occidentale*, Turin: Einaudi, 1995), Stanford: Stanford University Press.

Rodrguez-Almeida, Emilio (1993), 'Graffiti e produzione anforaria della Betica', in W. V. Harris (ed.), *The Inscribed Economy: Production and Distribution in the Roman Empire in the Light of* instrumentum domesticum (*Journal of Roman Archaeology*, Supplementary Series 6), Ann Arbor, Mich.: Journal of Roman Archaeology, 95–106.

Sabbatini Tumolesi, Patrizia (1980), *Gladiatorum Paria: Annunci di Spettacoli Gladiatorii a Pompeii* (Tituli 1), Rome: Edizioni di Storia e Letteratura.

Salomies, Olli (1987), *Die römischen Vornamen. Studien zur römischen Namengebung* (Commentationes Humanarum Litterarum 82), Helsinki: Societas Scientiarum Fennica.

Sanders, Gabriel (1979), 'L'Au-delà et les acrostiches des Carmina Latina Epigraphica', *Roczniki Humanistyczne*, Lublin, 27/3: 57–75; repr. in Sanders 1991: 183–205.

—— (1984), 'Texte et monument: l'arbitrage du musée épigraphique', in Angela Donati (ed.), *Il Museo Epigrafico. Colloquio AIEGL-Borghesi 83 (Castroarco Terme–Ferrara, 30 settembre–2 ottobre 1983)* (Epigrafia e Antichità 7), Faenza: Fratelli Lega Editori, 85–118 = Sanders 1991: 393–426.

—— (1990), 'Augustin et le message épigraphique: le tétrastique en l'honneur de saint Etienne', in B. Bruning, M. Lamberigts, and J. van Houtem (eds.), *Collectanea Augustiniana. Melanges T. J. Van Bavel*, Leuven: University Press: Uitgeverij Peeters, 95–124.

—— (1991), *Lapides Memores. Païens et Chrêtiens face à la mort: le témoignage de l'épigraphie funéraire latine*, ed. Angela Donati, Dorothy Pikhaus, and Marc van Uytfanghe (Epigrafia e Antichità 11), Faenza: Fratelli Lega Editori.

Sandys, John E. (1927), *Latin Epigraphy: An Introduction to the Study of Latin Inscriptions*, 2nd edn. revised S. G. Campbell, Cambridge: Cambridge University Press.

Schmidt, Manfred G. (2007), *Corpus Inscriptionum Latinarum*, tr. Orla Mulholland, Berlin: Berlin-Brandenburgische Akademie der Wissenschaften.

Sherk, Robert K. (1969), *Roman Documents from the Greek East: Senatus Consulta and Epistulae to the Age of Augustus*, Baltimore: Johns Hopkins University Press.

Solin, Heikki (1999), 'Epigrafia repubblicana. Bilancio, novità, prospettive', in *Atti del XI Congresso Internazionale di Epigrafia Greca e Latina (Roma, 18–24 settembre 1997)*, Rome: Edizioni Quasar, 1. 379–404.

Terras, Melissa M. (2006), *Image to Interpretation: An Intelligent System to Aid Historians in Reading the Vindolanda Texts*, Oxford and New York: Oxford University Press.

Thomas, Rosalind (1995), 'Written in Stone? Liberty, Equality, Orality and the Codification of Law', *Bulletin of the Institute of Classical Studies*, 40: 59–74.

Väänänen, Veikko (1966), *Le Latin vulgaire des inscriptions pompéiennes*, 3rd edn., Berlin: Akademie-Verlag.

Varone, Antonio (2005), 'Nella Pompei a luci rosse. Castrensis e l'organizzazione della prostituzione e dei suoi spazi', *Rivista di Studi Pompeiani*, 16: 93–109.

Vine, Brent (1993), *Studies in Archaic Latin Inscriptions* (Innsbrucker Beiträge zur Sprachwissenschaft 75), Innsbruck: Institut fur Sprachwissenschaft der Universitat Innsbruck.

Williamson, C. (2005), *The Laws of the Roman People: Public Law in the Expansion and Decline of the Roman Republic*, Ann Arbor, Mich.: University of Michigan Press.

Woolf, Greg (1994), 'Power and the Spread of Writing in the West', in Alan K. Bowman and Greg Woolf (eds.), *Literacy and Power in the Ancient World*, Cambridge: Cambridge University Press, 84–98.

—— (1996), 'Monumental Writing and the Expansion of Roman Society in the Early Empire', *Journal of Roman Studies*, 86: 22–39.

CHAPTER 7

PAPYROLOGY

ROGER S. BAGNALL

In a broad sense, papyrology is a discipline concerned with the recovery and exploitation of ancient artefacts bearing writing and of the textual material preserved on such artefacts. For the most part it focuses on what can be called the spectrum of everyday writing, rather than forms of writing intended for publicity and permanence, most of which were inscribed on stone or metal and belong to epigraphy in the scholarly division of labour. The edges of these domains, however, are fuzzy. Papyrology cannot actually be defined by the material support—potsherds can belong to epigraphy or papyrology depending on their origin and nature. Technique of writing is not an adequate discriminant, for not all epigraphical texts are incised, and some papyrological texts are. A public/private dichotomy is undermined by papyri put up as public notices, and many types of content are found in both epigraphical and papyrological texts—edicts of Roman governors, to give only one obvious example. Nor does geography divide the fields; both papyrological and epigraphical texts can be found from Britain to Afghanistan. None of this, however, is a problem unless one wants to close oneself into a discipline. For the Roman world, papyrology is pragmatically just part of a larger domain involved with these surviving witnesses to the ubiquity of writing in antiquity.

For enviromental reasons, most papyrological material does come from Egypt. The Ptolemaic kingdom was the last of the main Hellenistic states to come to an end and be taken into the Roman Empire. But papyrological evidence for matters Roman goes back to the century before Actium; a Roman senator touring Egypt got the VIP treatment (*P.Tebt.* I 33; Bagnall and Derow 2004: 118 no. 69), Rabirius Postumus gets a bad press in another papyrus ('He appointed unsuitable and desperate men...': *SB* XXII 15203, Bagnall and Derow 2004: 109 no. 62).

These and other texts give a sense of the ways in which the Roman presence in the few decades before Octavian's triumph had already begun to change Egypt. Even in public one sees the impact: an inscription confirming the right of asylum of a sanctuary has a Latin phrase ('the queen and king ordered this') so that Roman troops would know it concerned them (Bingen 2007: 71). The Arab conquest of 641 brought to an end only Roman rule, not Romanity. The Arabs took over the Roman administrative structures of the country, and the Egyptian population continued for centuries to use the legal forms of late Roman times, in both Greek and Coptic documents (Richter 2002). In this broader sense, the 'Roman' period in the papyrological documentation is at least 900 years long.

The Roman period in a narrower sense—the Principate, really—has become a kind of 'standard' or normative period for the papyrological documentation. The reason is in part archaeological. Ptolemaic papyrus finds come from only a handful of types of discoveries. Most are either family archives saved as units, and thus focused mainly on asset-defending documents like deeds of sale or litigation papers, or else waste paper used in cartonnage, the wrappings of human or crocodile mummies. This waste paper came above all from government offices or office-holders, and it informs us well about the Ptolemaic bureaucracy and bureaucrats, but poorly about many other things. The more varied kinds of papers usually left in houses or thrown away on rubbish dumps are much less well preserved for the Ptolemaic period than for the Roman, where cartonnage vanishes as a source and the excavation of habitation sites and their dumps becomes more widespread. The archaeological horizon narrows in again with late antiquity, the 'Byzantine' period of papyrologists, particularly in that villages almost disappear as sources, leaving a handful of the cities and a very skewed geographical perspective (Bagnall 1995: 26–9). It is thus for the Roman period that we have the best overall spread of documents, even if important unevennesses and gaps remain.

The 'normality' of the Roman period is probably not just a matter of survivals, however; or, to look at it from another point of view, the survival of documents is probably not only the product of archaeological contingency. Roman rule brought with it the development of a society of 'notables', the prosperous elites of both villages and cities who governed them—the cities especially after Septimius Severus granted them city councils. These groups, the property they owned, and the public duties they carried out generated an immense amount of paperwork, much of which had not been there in the Ptolemaic period, and these papyri are a large part of what gives us our impression of the 'middle-class' (but really upper-middle or lower-upper class) society to which the modern middle-class reader connects so easily. It is the village societies of the Fayyum and the bourgeoisie of Oxyrhynchos that have generated most of the stories papyrologists tell about life in Greco-Roman Egypt.

The Empire is also the period in which the geographical range of papyrological finds outside Egypt is at its greatest. From the first to early second centuries CE there are important finds from the pre-Hadrianic forts at Vindolanda in northern

Britain (*T.Vindol.* I–III), with their snapshot of frontier military life, and the fort of Masada by the Dead Sea, where, near the other end of the empire, the Roman army was engaged in putting down a rebellion (*Doc.Masada*). Second- and third-century documents from the Dead Sea (*P.Yadin*) and the Euphrates valley (*P.Euphr.*, *P.Dura*) have also helped prevent too Egyptocentric a view of the papyrological world, as the interplay of Roman, Greek, and local languages and legal norms has given more specificity, bite, and controversy to questions all too easily buried in generalizations. The ongoing debate over the legal character—how much Jewish, how much Hellenistic, how much Roman—of the archives of Babatha and Salome alias Komaise from Nahal Hever has been particularly fascinating both for provincial Roman society in the early years after the arrival of Roman rule and for fault-lines in contemporary Israeli academe. The army is documented again in third-century Libya with a large find of ostraca (*O.Bu Njem*). Later still, Petra and Nessana give us city and village documents, linked to church and military but highly revealing about private-property transactions, in the sixth and seventh centuries (*P.Petra*, *P.Ness.*). Once again, the Roman Empire dominates the papyri, because there is nothing really comparable for the Hellenistic period.

Papyri and Roman History

One straightforward approach to thinking about the papyri as a source for Roman Studies is the kind of hierarchical method characteristic of most survey articles. The *JRS* has periodically run such articles about inscriptions, but not in thirty years now about papyri; the last was Bowman 1976, explicitly limited to 'imperial history' to the exclusion of law and religion. It begins with the imperial court, surveying new information about the emperors and their immediate circles, like Augustus' funeral oration for Agrippa, data about the imperial *consilium*, and a reference to Seneca's estates in Egypt. Many points of the chronology of the emperors' reigns and magistracies normally crop up in newly published documents in any given decade, and the emperors' visits to Egypt are documented in some texts. Sometimes the points at stake are minor, sometimes important; Aurelian and Diocletian were the emperors about whom the most significant new information had recently appeared when that survey article was done. Topics relevant to imperial history in this sense tend to be highly technical, but their relevance to the larger Roman world is obvious and needs no particular emphasis.

A second level of subjects concerns Egypt as a Roman province: its status; its administrative organization; the administrators who governed it, in particular the higher ones like the prefect and procuratorial positions, but also the mid-level officials and even local liturgists; its land regime, including taxation; its economy and society. In this category also comes the Roman army, although much of what is written about the military is also of immediate and uncontested application wider than the province itself.

Another such survey article, covering the quarter-century 1956–80, was organized very differently but touched on many of the same key points (Keenan 1982). That survey, however, focused more on visible changes within the directions of papyrology itself, looking at the field's own changes rather than new data within fixed categories. One of these was the already-mentioned geographical widening of the range of find-places of papyrological documents, a trend that has only accelerated in the quarter-century since Keenan's survey (Cotton, Cockle, and Millar 1995). We shall return to the others later, but one fundamental point is still to some degree true today: the unbroken flow of papyri from the Roman period, the very fact that has helped make the Roman period the 'standard' in papyrology, has also kept papyrologists busy editing and has hindered the production of syntheses.

The papyri, in this respect very much like inscriptions, are ideally suited to a whole range of subjects in the domains that lend themselves to construction as lists of one sort or another—a category that includes much of what falls into the 'imperial history' approach. The information from the documents is in most cases highly analytic; that is, it provides discrete data about very specific questions: Who commanded a cohort of Ituraeans under Nero? Which prefects served under Hadrian? What taxes did a villager pay in the mid-second century? Gradually, as new documents appear, holes are filled in, and our lists of prefects, heads of the *idios logos*, strategoi, amphodarchs, and even centurions gradually fill out. The science of prosopography, which played such a central role in Roman history in the twentieth century, is nowhere more at home or better served than with administrative documents of the sort provided by the papyri. Now that such lists can be published electronically, even the drawback of instant obsolescence that plagued such lists in print (Keenan 1982: 23–4) is avoidable. By the same token, thematic collections of documents on particular subjects are a natural project, even if not as commonly undertaken as they might be (see Daris 1964 and Fink 1971, both on the army, for examples).

There is no reason to suppose that the papyri will not continue to make new contributions to the study of Roman political and institutional history for the foreseeable future. This is particularly true as the definition of 'Roman' encompasses later centuries to a greater degree, with late antiquity now much more firmly assimilated into the field than used to be the case. Papyrology too has engaged with the centuries from Diocletian to the Arab conquest (and even beyond) to a far greater degree than it did a generation ago. Keenan (1982: 31) called attention to the growing tendency twenty-five years ago to make the fourth century an integral part of 'Roman' Egypt, and in the following quarter-century the later centuries have come increasingly to the fore. Even Arab Egypt is starting to be not only a lively area of scholarly work but one more closely tied to its Roman past (Sijpesteijn and Sundelin eds. 2004).

To an even greater degree, papyrology has become increasingly intertwined with the study of major issues in Roman social, economic, and legal history, where the question of the relevance of the papyri to the empire outside Egypt has been more contested. From papyrology's earliest days, it was evident to those who read the documents that they could inform us about areas of life very poorly represented in the ancient authors and not easily studied even from inscriptions or the normative legal sources. Juristic papyrology was the first of these areas to blossom, with Ludwig Mitteis's contribution to the great four-volume *Grundzüge und Chrestomathie der Papyruskunde* that he and Ulrich Wilcken published in 1912. It was perhaps also the first to fade, as the progressive withdrawal of European law schools from ancient legal history in recent decades has destroyed its institutional base; but there are substantial signs of new life in recent years, with a more strongly historical character (e.g. Beaucamp 1990; Yiftach-Firanko 2003).

Social and economic history also has a long pedigree in papyrology, and Rostovtzeff (1926, 1941) used the papyri extensively in his great syntheses. Papyrology has also played a large part in more revisionist approaches in recent years, as major issues in Roman Studies like the economic activities of the elite, the possibilities of true economic growth, the status of Roman women, and social mobility have been tackled by scholars with a primarily historical rather than papyrological formation (e.g. Arjava 1996; Beaucamp 1992; Kehoe 1992; Rathbone 1991; Rowlandson ed. 1998; Tacoma 2006).

Underlying this work has been a growing conviction of the utility of the material of the papyri, even when mainly or exclusively Egyptian, for larger currents in Roman history, a point argued most fully by Rathbone (1989) for the economy and to one degree or another by others. It might be too much to say that this is a settled issue, but the results of this work have been sufficiently compelling that the need for self-justification in applying the papyri to the Roman Empire at large no longer seems so pressing. Undoubtedly the papyri from the Judaean desert and the Vindolanda tablets (with the accessible synthesis in Bowman 1994) have also helped to awaken a sense of the broader importance of everyday documents.

Asking Different Questions

'Roman Studies', however, is a different matter from Roman history, even in the extended sense described above. Because most of the papyri come from the Greek-speaking part of the empire, they may not at first glance seem like the most obvious source for a major renewal of the questions we can ask about the Roman world. Bu Njem and Vindolanda are one obvious rejoinder, but at a deeper level the question is one of our conception of the Roman world. In a number of respects the papyri give us the opportunity to look at aspects of the culture of the Roman world and think about the interconnectedness of the Greek and Latin spheres. These offer opportunities to engage a wider circle of scholars in the study of the papyri, something that can only bring yet other questions to bear and open up papyrology to further approaches. Here we will look at a few areas in which important work has been done in recent years.

Language

Papyri are full of words and sentences, and study of the language of the papyri began early in the history of papyrology. The most immediate impact of the papyri was on the question of the existence of a specifically Jewish dialect of Greek, which was already controversial more than a century ago and has remained a live issue despite attempts to lay it to rest. As one scholar has remarked: 'Possibly a certain theological predisposition has encouraged the continuing acceptance of Jewish Greek in some quarters' (Horsley 1989: 40). Apart from that debate, the papyri have been heavily mined for the study of the language of the Septuagint and the New Testament, a continuing process visible a century ago in Deissmann's famous *Licht vom Osten* and continuing still in the volumes of *New Documents Illustrating Early Christianity.* From a linguistic and cultural point of view, it is most realistic to see the Greek of early Roman Palestine as simply the pervasive *koinē* of the Hellenistic and Roman East, with some phenomena coming from bilingual interference. Such phenomena can be seen also in the Egyptian papyri of the period and no doubt would be equally visible if we had papyri from other eastern provinces.

It has taken longer for any real consciousness of the papyri to affect mainstream classical linguistics, to the point that a recent conference on the language of the papyri was called 'Buried linguistic treasure' (Evans and Obbink, forthcoming). Not entirely buried, of course. Every reader of J. N. Adams's recent book on *Bilingualism and the Latin Language* (2003) will see that it draws deeply not only on the Latin papyri, as one would expect, but on those in Greek, and not only in the 115 pages of the chapter on 'Latin in Egypt' but at many other points, as in the discussion of code-switching. The non-Egyptian papyrological texts, including of course the Vindolanda tablets, are drawn on at still other points.

More unexpectedly and still more subtly, Eleanor Dickey has pointed out in recent articles that Latin idioms start to appear in the Greek of the Egyptian papyri already in the first century BCE, in the reign of Ptolemy XII (Dickey 2003, 2004): 'As the Romans conquered the Greek world, contact with Latin led to a perceived need for a Greek address system that would allow the expression of contemporary types of politeness, and this need was met (perhaps after some experimentation with other methods, at least in Egypt), by calques of the most common Latin vocatives'

(Dickey 2004: 527). Similarly, Hélène Cuvigny (2002) has shown that the Greek epistolary use of *idios* is a calque of the Latin *suus*. It is likely that the 'Romanization of the Greek East', although hardly a new discovery, will be a lively area of research for some time to come, even at fundamental levels hardly suspected until recently.

Education and Ownership of Books

We can study language use in antiquity only when speech took written form. The last decade-and-a-half have seen a remarkable development of studies of literacy, education, and ownership of the written word, in the wake of the pessimistic views of literacy and education set out in William Harris's important book on *Ancient Literacy* (1989), which cites papyri extensively. Two stimulating collective volumes (Humphrey ed. 1991 and Bowman and Woolf eds. 1994) followed up quickly and deepened the picture of many aspects of the subject; a host of further articles has followed, in which the papyri continue to play a central role.

People acquired the capability to write and read through one sort of educational process or another, and it is here that the contribution of the papyri has been most decisive, as Raffaella Cribiore's studies (1996, 2001) of the papyri, ostraca, and wooden tablets that survive from ancient schooling have given much greater precision and depth to our understanding of this process and its role in the formation of elite culture in the Roman period. Bernard Legras's study of the formation of youth (1999) has also traced cultural formation using the papyri.

Legras has also (2002) written about what one might see as the logical extension of studies of education, the reading and book-ownership that could extend throughout adult life the participation in the literary culture inculcated in the grammarian's classes. Greater depth in our understanding of just who owned books and how they used them has also come out of study of the papyri in recent years, especially where some sense of archaeological context is possible. Peter van Minnen (1994) used the records of the excavations at Karanis to identify the owner of a particular house as a tax-collector named Socrates, who owned copies of Menander, the 'Acta Alexandrinorum', and a grammatical treatise. He is also the individual brought vividly to life years ago by Herbert Youtie (1970), who wrote nicknames for taxpayers in the margin of his tax-roll, using in one case an obscure word known only from Callimachus, an author of whom, van Minnen points out, a fragment was found in the house across the street. Van Minnen (1998) has also looked more broadly at the finds of literary texts from Fayyum villages, although the same degree of precision is hardly ever available. We may anticipate more such studies, including particularly of the ownership of both Greek and Egyptian literature by priests in Roman Tebtunis. From a later period, Jean-Luc Fournet's study of Dioskoros of Aphrodite (1999) has put on an entirely new footing our knowledge of this late-antique village notable, poet, and notary.

These and many other studies are beginning to give us a far more nuanced sense both of who could write and read and who owned books. There have been surprises, and there will be more. It is increasingly clear that it was not only the intellectual and scholarly elite of the cities who took an interest in literature. The villages of Roman Egypt housed at least some people we are not accustomed to thinking of as society's cream—tax-collectors do not make many A-lists—who had scholarly interests. How far this continued to be true after the fourth century is hard to say, as the evidence becomes much scarcer. Dioskoros is probably not a typical figure. But he was probably not unique, and in any case we may expect that an interest in reading will have taken different forms in a Christianized Egypt.

The Ubiquity of Writing

Papyrological texts thus continue to reshape our most basic notions of the cultural texture of Roman society. Although they will never tell us what percentage of people could write, they warn us not to underestimate the centrality of writing in everyday life and the complexity of individuals' relationship to the written word. Relatively few women learned to write, and yet women wrote or had written for them large numbers of personal letters in the Roman period, more than in the Hellenistic period (Bagnall and Cribiore 2006). When it became possible to write letters easily in Egyptian, with the advent of Coptic, women started to use that language more extensively in correspondence. More generally, vernacular languages gave birth to new scripts for both literary and documentary use. Greek and Latin are only part of a spectrum of languages and scripts; we find similar texts from the Mediterranean to Central Asia in languages ranging from Syriac to Bactrian.

As the example of the tax-collector Socrates showed, it is a mistake to think that the use of writing can be neatly categorized. We would expect that a career collector like Socrates could write; he needed to keep accounts. But we might have anticipated that his was a practical, business-oriented literacy. Instead, he had broader interests. So perhaps did another tax-collector whom we know well, Nemesion of Philadelphia, who copied out Claudius' letter to the Alexandrians onto the back of a tax-roll (Hanson 1991: 172, n. 46).

Our chances of understanding just how pervasive and varied writing was in Roman society are best where papyrological texts come from an archaeological context and are not isolated from 'epigraphical' types of texts or other objects found in the same context. The Dakhleh Oasis offers a particularly rich opportunity to see papyrology, archaeology, and epigraphy working together to create a picture of writing in daily life. The excavations at Kellis have brought some striking juxtapositions: a wooden codex with a schoolteacher's copy of three orations of Isocrates discovered with another such codex full of three years' accounts of rents and expenditures on a unit of a large estate, with one scribe's hand probably found in both codices (*P.Kell.* III and IV); and a trove of private letters in Greek and Coptic in one house found along with Manichaean literature on papyrus and wood, and with enough clear references to Manichaeism in the letters to show that the juxtaposition is no coincidence (*P.Kell.* I, II, and V).

Across the oasis as a whole, another phenomenon stands out: the ubiquity of Greek poetry in public and private. A recently published miniature wooden codex found at Kellis contains a Homeric parody displaying both wit and knowledge (Hope and Worp 2006). At the temple of Ain Birbiyeh, toward the eastern end of the oasis, a temple gateway excavated in 2006 has the remains of Greek poetry incised on a now-shattered and effaced block, evidently a visitor's graffito. And at Amheida, ancient Trimithis, at the opposite end of the oasis, a thick chunk of plaster found on the surface by a boy from the neighbouring village in 2005 has several fragmentary lines of Greek, in poetic vocabulary, probably from the same source as fragments published by Guy Wagner (1976). The new fragment seems to have a reference to Bousiris; across the top, in larger letters, is ΣΑΡΠ[, probably part of the name of the hero Sarpedon, who in some ancient mythographic sources is indeed connected with Egypt. But that is not all. In 2006 the excavation of a fourth-century house at Amheida found a room with multiple columns of a red painted inscription on one whitewashed wall, the remains of an ancient 'white-board' on which more washed-out text can be seen (Cribiore, Davoli and Ratzan 2008). The lines are elegiac couplets in Greek, addressed to pupils, and invoking the Muses for poetic inspiration, Hermes for rhetoric, and Herakles for hard work. The presence of all possible critical marks—accents, breathings, long marks, and caesura indicated by a high dot, as well as paragraphos between poems—shows that the pupils were learning to write rhetorical compositions in verse and had to master the rules of Greek prosody. With all of these discoveries, both papyrological and epigraphical in the same setting, we are beginning to get a sense of just how the poetry-heavy literary and rhetorical education of the Greek world in the Imperial era led to a physical environment saturated with what are probably in at least some of these cases local poetic products. At the same time, some ostraca from the same house as the rhetorical composition show that the rudiments of writing the alphabet were being practised there at the same time.

Most of what was written in the ancient world does not survive, and a host of circumstances have left us a sample that is anything but random. The papyri are part of a spectrum of surviving writing that embraces, as we have seen, many other media. It is when they are integrated with those other types of writing and placed in an archaeological context that we can recover the place of writing in Roman society most effectively. At the same time, the bringing of new questions to the papyrological documentation can enable it to play a greater role, in conjunction with other types of evidence, in broadening our vision of the everyday realities of the Roman world.

Further reading

Introductions to papyrology are Turner 1968, 1980², the succinct but recent and handy Rupprecht 1994, and the massive Montevecchi 1973, 1988² with poorly organized but extensive bibliographies. Bagnall ed. (2007) offers an introduction by twenty-seven scholars to a variety of topics. A selection of Greek texts for reading appears in Pestman 1990. For method and approaches in writing history using papyri, see Bagnall 1995. Bibliographies can be found in all of these works.

Editions of papyri are cited according to the abbreviations in Oates *et al.* 2001. Among the main digital tools for papyrology are the following:

Advanced Papyrological Information System (APIS), a union catalogue of metadata and images from many papyrus collections, at http://www.papyri.info.

Duke Data Bank of Documentary Papyri, a full text database only for Greek and Latin documents, at http://www.papyri.info.

Heidelberger Gesamtverzeichnis der griechischen Papyrusurkunden aus Ägypten; www.rzuser.uni-heidelberg.de/~gvo/gvz.html, a database (without texts) of Greek and Latin documentary papyri and ostraca.

Leuven Database of Ancient Books (LDAB), a guide to Greek, Latin, and Coptic literary texts, including school exercises, at http://www.trismegistos.org.

Leuven Homepage of Papyrus Archives and Collections, at http://www.trismegistos.org, databases with description of archives and dossiers and of modern institutional collections.

The Oxyrhynchus Papyri, at http://www.papyrology.ox.ac.uk/POxy/, metadata and images of the more recent volumes.

'Pack-Mertens, 3rd edition', a digital update of R. A. Pack, *Index of Greek and Latin Literary Texts from Greco-Roman Egypt* (2nd edn. Ann Arbor, Mich., 1965). A listing of literary papyri with full references, at http://promethee.philo.ulg.ac.be/cedopal/index.htm.

The Vindolanda Tablets, metadata, translations, and images, at http://vindolanda.csad.ox.ac.uk/.

References

Adams, J. N. (2003), *Bilingualism and the Latin Language*, Cambridge: Cambridge University Press.

Arjava, Antti (1996), *Women and Law in Late Antiquity*, Oxford: Clarendon Press.

Bagnall, Roger S. (1995), *Reading Papyri, Writing Ancient History*, London: Routledge.

—— (ed.) (2009), *The Oxford Handbook of Papyrology*, New York: Oxford University Press.

—— and Raffaella Cribiore (2006), *Women's Letters from Ancient Egypt, 300 BC–AD 800*, Ann Arbor, Mich.: University of Michigan Press.

—— and Peter S. Derow (2004), *The Hellenistic Period* (Historical Sources in Translation), Oxford: Blackwell.

Beaucamp, Joëlle (1990, 1992), *Le Statut de la femme à Byzance (4ᵉ–7ᵉ siècle)*. I, *Le Droit impérial* (1990); II, *Les Pratiques sociales* (1992), Paris: De Boccard.

Bingen, Jean (2007), *Hellenistic Egypt: Monarchy, Society, Economy, Culture*, Edinburgh: Edinburgh University Press.
Bowman, Alan K. (1976), 'Papyri and Roman Imperial History, 1960–75,' *JRS* 66: 153–73.
——(1994), *Life and Letters on the Roman Frontier*, London: British Museum Press.
——and Greg Woolf (eds.) (1994), *Literacy and Power in the Ancient World*, Cambridge: Cambridge University Press.
Cotton, Hannah M., W. E. H. Cockle, and F. G. B. Millar (1995), 'The Papyrology of the Roman Near East: A Survey', *JRS* 85: 214–35.
Cribiore, Raffaella (1996), *Writing, Teachers, and Students in Graeco-Roman Egypt*, Atlanta, Ga.: Scholars Press.
——(2001), *Gymnastics of the Mind. Greek Education in Hellenistic and Roman Egypt*, Princeton: Princeton University Press.
——Paola Davoli, and David M. Ratzan (2008), 'A Teacher's Dipinto from Trimithis (Dakleh Oasis)', *JRA* 21: 170–92.
Cuvigny, Hélène (2002), 'Remarques sur l'emploi de *idios* dans le praescriptum épistolaire', *BIFAO* 102: 143–53.
Daris, Sergio (1964), *Documenti per la storia dell'esercito romano in Egitto*, Milan: Vita e Pensiero.
Dickey, Eleanor (2003), 'Latin Influence on the Greek of Documentary Papyri: An Analysis of its Chronological Distribution', *ZPE* 145: 249–57.
——(2004), 'The Greek Address System of the Roman Period and its Relationship to Latin', *CQ* 54: 494–527.
Evans, Trevor, and Dirk Obbink (forthcoming), *Buried Linguistic Treasure.*
Fink, Robert O. (1971), *Roman Military Records on Papyrus*, Cleveland: Case Western Reserve Press.
Fournet, Jean-Luc (1999), *Hellénisme dans l'Égypte du VIe siècle*, 2 vols., Cairo: IFAO.
Hanson, Ann E. (1991), 'Ancient Illiteracy', in John H. Humphrey (ed.) (1991), *Literacy in the Roman World*, Ann Arbor, Mich.: Journal of Roman Archaeology, 159–98.
Harris, William V. (1989), *Ancient Literacy*, Cambridge, Mass.: Harvard University Press.
Hope, Colin A., and Klaas A. Worp (2006), 'Miniature Codices from Kellis', *Mnemosyne*, 59: 226–58.
Horsley, G. H. R. (1989), *New Documents Illustrating Early Christianity*, vol. 5, Sydney: Ancient History Dowmentary Research Cnetre in Macquarie University.
Humphrey, John H. (ed.) (1991), *Literacy in the Roman World*, Ann Arbor, Mich.: Journal of Roman Archaeology.
Keenan, James G. (1982), 'Papyrology and Roman History, 1956–80', *Classical World*, 76: 23–31.
Kehoe, Dennis P. (1992), *Management and Investment on Estates in Roman Egypt During the Early Empire*, Bonn: Habelt.
Legras, Bernard (1999), *Néotês: recherches sur les jeunes Grecs dans l'Egypte ptolémaïque et romaine*, Geneva: Droz.
——(2002), *Lire en Egypte, d'Alexandre à l'Islam*, Paris: Picard.
Mitteis, Ludwig, and Ulrich Wilcken (1912), *Grundzüge und Chrestomathie der Papyruskunde*, 4 vols., Leipzig and Berlin: B. G. Teubner.
Montevecchi, Orsolina (1973, 1988^2), *La papirologia*, Turin: Società Editrice Internazionale and (2nd edn.) Milan: Vita e Pensiero.

OATES, JOHN F. *et al.* (2001), *Checklist of Editions of Greek, Latin, Demotic and Coptic Papyri, Ostraca and Tablets*, 5th edn., Oakville, Conn.: David Brown Book Co.; up-to-date electronic version available at http://scriptorium.lib.duke.edu/papyrus/texts/clist.html.

PESTMAN, P. W. (1990), *The New Papyrological Primer*, Leiden: Brill.

RATHBONE, D. W. (1989), 'The Ancient Economy and Graeco-Roman Egypt', in Lucia Criscuolo and G. Geraci (eds.), *Egitto e storia antica dall'Ellenismo all'età araba. Bilancio di un confronto*, Bologna, 159–76.

—— (1991), *Economic Rationalism and Rural Society in Third-Century AD Egypt: The Heroninos Archive and the Appianus Estate*, Cambridge: Cambridge University Press.

RICHTER, TONIO SEBASTIAN (2002), *Rechtssemantik und forensische Rhetorik: Untersuchungen zu Wortschatz, Stil und Grammatik der Sprache koptischer Rechtsurkunden*, Leipzig: H. Wodtke and K. Stegbauer.

ROSTOVTZEFF, M. I. (1926), *The Social and Economic History of the Roman Empire*. Oxford: Clarendon Press.

—— (1941), *The Social and Economic History of the Hellenistic World*. Oxford: Clarendon Press.

ROWLANDSON, JANE (ed.) (1998), *Women and Society in Greek and Roman Egypt*, Cambridge: Cambridge University Press.

RUPPRECHT, HANS-ALBERT (1994), *Kleine Einführung in die Papyruskunde*, Darmstadt: Wissenschaftliche Buchgesellschaft.

SIJPESTEIJN, PETRA M. and LENNART SUNDELIN (eds.) (2004), *Papyrology and the History of Early Islamic Egypt*, Leiden: Brill.

TACOMA, LAURENS E. (2006), *Fragile Hierarchies: The Urban Elites of Third-Century Egypt*, Leiden: Brill.

TURNER, E. G. (1968, 1980²), *Greek Papyri*, Oxford: Clarendon Press.

VAN MINNEN, PETER (1994), 'House to House Enquiries: An Interdisciplinary Approach to Roman Karanis,' *ZPE*, 100: 227–51.

—— (1998), 'Boorish or Bookish? Literature in Egyptian Villages in the Fayum in the Graeco-Roman Period', *Journal of Juristic Papyrology*, 28: 99–184.

WAGNER, GUY (1976), 'Inscriptions et graffiti grecs inédits de la Grande Oasis', *BIFAO* 76: 283–8.

YIFTACH-FIRANKO, URI (2003), *Marriage and Marital Arrangement: A History of the Greek Marriage Document in Egypt. 4th century BCE–4th century CE*, Munich: C. H. Beck.

YOUTIE, HERBERT C. (1970), 'Callimachus in the Tax Rolls', in D. H. Samuel (ed.), *Proceedings of the Twelfth International Congress of Papyrology*, Toronto: A. M. Hakkert, 545–51.

CHAPTER 8

NUMISMATICS

WILLIAM E. METCALF

HISTORICAL SURVEY

NUMISMATICS is the study of coins and coin-like objects. The material of Roman numismatics has chronological range of about eight centuries. Beginning in Italy in the late fourth century BCE, coinage comes to be produced all around the Mediterranean basin, as far west as London and as far east as Alexandria.

The first Roman money was measured in *aes*, literally copper or bronze but in numismatics describing any alloy of copper. The first copper coins conformed to a libral standard (one unit = one pound), and this surprisingly cumbersome coin was still being produced into the 220s BCE at least. Silver began to be produced around the beginning of the third century BCE, and at first closely followed contemporary standards and styles of Greek coinage in Italy. The financial pressures of the Second Punic War led to a reduction of weight both in silver and in copper. The silver coin that emerged was the denarius, tariffed at ten *asses*, which at the time the denarius appeared (*c.*211 BCE) were equal by weight to the original *sextans* or 1/6-as. A measure of the emergency was the striking of gold, which had been done only once before and would hardly be done again before the triumviral period.

Until the end of the Republic silver was coined almost continuously, copper intermittently down to the 80s BCE and hardly at all thereafter, gold only in the Sullan and triumviral periods. As part of a reformed currency, a large orichalcum (copper + zinc) sestertius was introduced in 23 BCE. The denarius, the sestertius and its fractions (dupondius in orichalcum, as and occasionally semisses and quadrantes in copper), and a regularly produced gold *aureus* made up the currency of the next two-and-a-half centuries.

While the denominations remained the same, their substance declined. The gold was never actually debased to any significant degree, but Nero lightened both the gold and the silver, and the silver gradually slipped in quality to about 50 per cent under Septimius Severus. Under Caracalla the 'antoninianus' was introduced, only to be dropped under Elagabalus; it was reintroduced during the brief reign of Balbinus and Pupienus and by the end of Gordian III's reign had become the standard silver coin, with a tariff generally taken to be 2 denarii but only about 1.5 times the weight of the older coin. Under Gallienus it reached its nadir, with silver content as low as 2 per cent; reform was attempted by Aurelian but its success is unknown.

In 293 CE Diocletian set off a series of adjustments, with an attempt to restore the Neronian denarius against a gold coin of 1/60 lb. The reform began in the West and concluded three years later in Alexandria. It included a substantial argentiferous copper coin and smaller radiate and laureate fractions. The tariff of all these subsidiary denominations seems to have been doubled in 301 (Erim, Reynolds, and Crawford 1971); some connection with the Edict on Maximum Prices can be supposed, so close is the chronology.

Diocletian's initial reforms did not last, and it is impossible in a chapter of this sort to detail the repeated adjustments. The most important was the introduction of the solidus, a gold coin of 1/72 lb., which would remain the core of Mediterranean currency long after the fall of the empire itself. Through the fourth century there was abundant base-metal coinage and a scarcer silver one; in the fifth century the *nummus* becomes the only regular copper coin, tariffed at 7,200 to the solidus. It was left for Anastasius I—who, for numismatists, defines the beginning of the Byzantine period—to reform the currency within its old framework.

This rather straightforward history does not do justice to the coinage that must have filled the purses of most residents of empire, which was produced closer to home. Although denarii and (from the time of Augustus) aurei were certainly current everywhere, most coinage was produced in the provinces, and it has been the focus of renewed study since the pioneering work of Michael Grant (1946), now more fully realized in *Roman Provincial Coinage* (Burnett, Amandry, and Ripollés 1992; Burnett, Amandry, and Carradice 1999; Spoerri Butcher 2006).

As Rome conquered or absorbed territory both east and west, she sometimes found in place sophisticated systems of currency, particularly in the East; in the West many coinages were already under Roman influence, and in Spain, for example, the massive colonial enterprises of Augustus yielded a coinage that was barely distinguishable from the imperial. Gold was produced only to the imperial standard, but silver was sometimes continued along the lines of local precedent and copper was left to the devices of the locals.

The 'system' was difficult; the relationship between local currency and the silver was sometimes uncomfortable, and clearly local *trapezitai* profited from exchanging not only base-metal coin for silver and vice versa, but converting 'foreign' denominations to local ones. During the Severan period as many as 400 cities issued coin, and this no doubt provides the background to Dio Cassius' staged debate between Agrippa and Maecenas, in which Maecenas advocates the imposition of uniform coinage, weights, and standards (52.30.9).

Mainstream and provincial systems occasionally intersected, for there are clear instances of production at Rome of coins that would otherwise be taken to be provincial products. Caesarea Cappadociae from Domitian through Trajan (Metcalf 1996; Butcher and Ponting 1995), Alexandria under Severus Alexander (Burnett and Craddock 1983), and Antioch in Syria under Philip I (Baldus 1969) are conspicuous examples. Moreover provincial cities themselves shared minting facilities, as has been recognized since the pioneering work of Kraft (1972). All this—combined with the insight into local *mentalité* that these coinages provide—has made what used to be called the 'Greek imperial' coinage a fruitful area of investigation.

Numismatic Scholarship

There are two bases for the study of Roman, indeed ancient, coinage. The first to develop chronologically was based on the appearance of the objects themselves—the images and words they bear, and the messages they may thus be taken to convey. The second is the behaviour of the objects, as mirrored by their survival. We shall address these in order.

The study of Roman coinage began in the thirteenth century (Weiss 1968, 1988). The rediscovery of classical authors invigorated interest in the ruins of Rome, and coins lent personality to figures whose images were otherwise unknown. Coins were also instrumental—as they continue to be today, in an environment in which collecting is stigmatized as piracy or looting—in promoting interest in antiquity. At its extreme, this led to serious competition and to the accumulation of vast collections, some of which can still be traced.

Serious scholarship, however, would await the eighteenth century. The first systematic attempt to deal with the mass of Roman coins was that of Eckhel (1792–8), the bulk of which was concerned with Greek coins. In part Eckhel was responsible for the revival of the Eratosthenic arrangement of the Greek world, and for the definition that made a Roman coin one that bore a Latin legend, a 'Greek' one anything else from the Mediterranean, be its language Greek, Hebrew, Punic—or even Latin, if it happened to be struck at a Roman colony with a prior history. The consequences for our view of ancient coinage lasted until the closing years of the twentieth century.

Eckhel's work had attempted a sort of universality, and was based on travel to huge numbers of collections, most of them lost today. The nineteenth century was important for its insistence on description of individual collections, first in France and then in England. Chronological primacy in the Roman field belongs to Henry Cohen (1857, 1859, 1880), who had before him the model of Mionnet's catalogue of Greek coins (1806). Cohen's attempt to comprehend the imperial coinage was almost anti-historical. His arrangement, still popular today, was chronological by emperor, then alphabetical by reverse legend (or, failing a legend, type); bust and obverse legend varieties were included under the major rubric of the reverse legend. This meant that those coins whose chronology was indicated on the reverse emerged in more or less chronological order; but coins of, for example, Trajan, where the chronology was normally indicated on the obverse, were all a jumble.

The great scholar Ernst Babelon (1885) attempted to deal with the Republic, which was even more problematic. Here there were only the vaguest of chronological clues before the emergence of figures known to history in the time of Caesar; Babelon hit upon an alphabetical arrangement by family. His work is accurate but a-historical; the coins of the Caecilii Metelli, to name but one example, are a mess.

Both scholars ignored important work that was going on, or in some cases had already gone on, in Germany. Mommsen's major work, mainly devoted to the Republic (1860), was translated into French by the duc de Blacas (1865–75), and he was the author of numerous contributions to numismatic literature; in the succeeding generation and beyond the towering figure is M. von Bahrfeldt, who left only one book (1923) but whose every word (over 120 articles in the American Numismatic Society's library) shed light where others had failed.

The great catalogue of Republican coins in the British Museum was scarcely any better than its predecessors as a work of science. Lip-service was paid to hoard evidence, and it is clear from the notes that the cataloguer, H. A. Grueber (not a Romanist by trade), was shackled by a stylistic arrangement arrived at by the Count de Salis, whose untimely death prevented articulation of his views (Grueber 1910: 1. pp. xii–xiv).

If this catalogue had failed, the next effort to emerge from London would set the standard for all subsequent work of the sort. Mattingly (1923–50) and his successor Carson (1962) laid out, in six volumes with ample commentary, Imperial coins arranged by mint, chronologically. This had been anticipated by the initial volumes of *Roman Imperial Coinage* (Mattingly *et al.* 1920–), which were initially little more than a historically based rearrangement of Cohen's material as supplemented by that in the British Museum—in essence, the outline of the catalogues that followed, which were somewhat more critical in taking over material cited only by Cohen. Only when the momentum for the British Museum catalogues was lost, in the 1960s (and it was probably realized that the sheer mass of material would make later catalogues uneconomical) did *RIC* emerge as the standard handbook of later coinage. These works, which drew on expertise outside the BM, picked up where J. W. E. Pearce (1950) had left off, and provided documented arrangements, with indications of issue size, for all the later coinage. While revisions are in hand where they are badly needed (vols. 3 and 5), the whole of the Imperial coinage has now been embraced in this series.

Still, within the limits of chronology and metal, the arrangement, and in particular the selection of illustrations, is based on type (used in the numismatic sense of the images borne by the coin); and this carries over to the formation of collections themselves, which normally overemphasize rare coins at the expense of more common ones. To this extent generalizations based on imagery are compromised.

More importantly, the type remains the major feature of interest even to those who have limited interest in coins as such. For type comprehends portrait, and for art historians numismatic portraits, bearing as they do firm identification of the individual as well as an indication of chronology, are critical evidence (e.g. Fittschen 1982). The reverses too may be used in the reconstruction of monuments (e.g. Kleiner 1985), and (in ways that have not yet been satisfactorily explored) in determining the relationship between the publicity generated by the issue of coins and the erection of monuments at Rome. I shall return to another use below.

The Material and its Survival

There are two major modes in which coins come down to us. These reflect two different ancient behaviours. One consists of intentional secretion of coins for safekeeping; the other is simple loss.

The first category is represented by coin hoards. Hoards may run from as few as two coins (in theory, a hoard could consist of a single coin, but it would be difficult to distinguish from a loss) to many thousands: the famous Reka Devnia hoard (Mouchmov 1934; Depeyrot 2004) was said to have numbered over 100,000 coins, and over 80,000 are recorded. Hoarding is well attested in antiquity (to take but three examples, Jesus' parable of the three stewards (Matt. 25: 14–28); the theft of a hoard secreted in a wall (*P. Ryl.* 125 = Hunt and Edgar (1934): 259 no. 278); the chance discovery of a hoard by Pompey's troops on arrival in Africa (Plutarch, *Pomp.* 13.2)). Thousands of hoards survive from antiquity: the *Inventory of Greek Coin Hoards* (Thompson, Mørkholm, and Kraay, 1973) listed over 2,200 coins of this category; a similar inventory of Roman Republican coin hoards ran to over 500 (Crawford 1969). Regional inventories (e.g. Robertson 2000, etc.) note hundreds of others, and still more have escaped anything but the barest mention.

A hoard captures a moment in time, and there has been much theorizing about the difference between currency hoards (those that reflect the currency of the day) and savings hoards (gradual accumulations over time); in practice it is seldom possible to make this distinction. What is important from a methodological point of view is that the latest coin provides a *terminus ante quem* for all the others, which may or may not be so easily dateable. This is useful for its own sake, but hoards are even more useful when compared. As Crawford (1969: 1) has put it: 'Of two hoards which have some issues in common, that which is later will contain issues which do not occur in the other hoard and which are less worn. A relative order of issues follows automatically.' The method was used to build up a chronology for the whole Republican coinage (Crawford 1969, 1974). The only serious corrections to that chronology came from another hoard which filled a gap in the series (Hersh and Walker 1984). Finally, the discovery of a coin in a hoard context may serve to authenticate both it and previously known coins of the same type, as with the recent coin of 'Domitianus II' found in Oxfordshire (Abdy 2004; cf. Estiot and Salaun 2004).

Regrettably, the evidence of hoards is ephemeral. Because sites that draw the attention of archaeologists were not ideal hiding-places in antiquity, relatively few hoards have been recovered in excavations; most of them are uncontrolled and, especially in the poorer countries that once formed part of the Roman world, there is every incentive to release them into the trade, where lots may be broken up or even added to. Much effort has to be expended to reconstruct the contents of a hoard once its dispersal has begun, but on the whole this is worth the effort, even if the evidence is not perfect.

Finds fall into two categories of their own: excavation coins and casual finds. Only the former category can occupy us here. In contrast to hoards, these were coins whose loss was not missed and whose recovery was not worth the effort—in this context one might consider how likely one is to give chase to a dropped cent rolling about the floor of a coffee-shop—or whose recovery was impractical (the same coin dropped down a sewer grate). Archaeological finds are heavily weighted toward low denominations struck nearby: a classic study of coins of Asia Minor shows that representation of 'foreign' coin approaches zero over distances up to 150 miles (Jones 1963).

Though excavations are normally without fixed termini, two exceptions may be cited. The more important is Morgantina (Buttrey, Erim, and Holloway 1989), where discovery of the earliest denarii in a context of destructions identified with those placed by Livy in 214 and 211 BCE confirmed the pioneering work of Thomsen (1953–61). The second is the pinpointing of the great battle of the Teutoborg Forest, Rome's great military disgrace, at Kalkriese (Berger 1996).

Authority for Coinage

The Republican coinage was seen to by a board of three junior magistrates, the *tresviri aere argento auro flando feriundo*, more commonly *a.a.a.f.f.* Since Mommsen, it has been supposed that this office was elective, but this view has been questioned by Burnett (1977). The model calls for the Senate's determination of the annual need for coinage, then its execution by the magistrates; this conveniently explains instances of hiatus in the striking of one metal or another, or indeed any coinage at all. From *c.*135 BCE the moneyers, who had long signed their issues, began to employ that array of changing types that make Roman coinage so distinctive. These might make reference to family history, contemporary events, or even political affiliation, though too much is often made of the last (e.g. Frier 1967; Badian 1968; Luce 1968 on the Marians and Sullans). Caesar temporarily expanded the office to four magistrates, who may be taken as his creatures; after a long gap from about 40 BCE, the moneyers reappear, signing coins in colleges of three or four from *c.*23 to *c.*7 BCE. The office is attested later (Jones 1970), though the signatures had disappeared forever.

Who, then, was responsible for coinage? One can read as late as the British Museum catalogues of a 'diarchy' on Mommsen's model, but even he did not press this very far and most have seen the coinage as the province of the emperor, who after all controlled the financial resources of the state. An exception is Burnett (1977), who argues from a passage in Dio (60.22.3) recording a senatorial decree that ordered the melting down of Caligula's bronze coins, and from the absence of precious-metal coins from later hoards, that the Senate had such authority; but the evidence is tenuous and the hypothesis has not found broad favour.

Since one face of the Imperial coinage bears the image of an emperor or member of his family, while the other often focuses on imperial 'virtues', achievements, and events surrounding the imperial family, it is natural to look to the images on the coins as bearers of imperial 'propaganda'. But in a famous essay Jones (1956) questioned both the intent and the effectiveness of such a reading. The discussion has gone on ever since, with no real end in sight (Sutherland 1959; Levick 1982; importantly, Meadows and Williams 2001); and the issue has spawned other discussions of image and authority (Burnett 1977; Wallace-Hadrill 1986).

Modern Methods

Since its first recognition in the mid-nineteenth century, it has been recognized that coins preserve evidence for the matrices—the dies—used to produce them. Use of a common die (a 'die link') is a strong indicator of community in time and place. Often even the priority of one coin over another can be determined through deterioration of dies with time; and sometimes it is possible to put in chronological order whole series of die-linked coins (the best example in the Roman context remains Buttrey 1956).

It has also long been recognized that the counting of dies is a better indicator of initial production than counting surviving specimens, for survival can be distorted by the discovery of a single large hoard or two; nor is the use of museum collections a good guide, since museums normally focus on rarities and under-represent common coins. But a coin surviving from 100 obverse dies is likely to have been produced in greater numbers than one surviving from ten. Sample size also matters. If these same two figures were derived from a sample of, say, 200 coins, the likely number of original dies can be calculated using one of a number of formulae (Esty 1986). As has been seen since the 1970s, it is possible to think of determining how much coinage was produced in a given year, and applying this information in the broader historical context.

Die studies have long been a prominent feature of Greek numismatics, but the sheer size of the coinage is an obstacle to the application of this method to Roman issues. The number of die studies, even if provincial mints are counted, is relatively small, and often circumscribed in purpose. Given the rewards, it was almost inevitable that short-cuts would be devised, and there is no shortage of them. Crawford (1974) was the first to attempt this on a large scale. He took sample issues in which the dies had been counted, compared their occurrence in hoards with issues whose dies had not been counted, and projected die totals for the latter on the basis of the former. He wound up with year-by-year estimates of the consumption of denarius dies, and it was a relatively simple matter to convert this to expenditure by estimating coin output per die.

I have pointed out elsewhere (Metcalf 1999; and see Buttrey 1993, 1994; de Callataÿ 1995) the pitfalls of this practice. Dies do not bear a constant relationship to coins produced; no single hoard—even a massive one such as Reka Devnia (Mouchmov 1934; Depeyrot 2004)—nor any aggregation of hoards into one Ur-hoard will represent with any precision output over time; and the introduction of a simple multiplier (to convert dies used to coinage produced) has not a scintilla of contemporary evidence to support it.

Still, there is little doubt that when used carefully hoards can have relative value: an issue consistently unrepresented (e.g. the Trajanic restorations of earlier denarii) or represented in small numbers was doubtless much smaller than one that consistently constitutes a significant percentage of a ruler's output. A holistic approach to the question of reverse types, such as that attempted by Noreña (2001)—aggregating occurrences of, say, Fides in a large population of coins—is unlikely to mislead if not pressed too hard.

Because of their sheer abundance, coins invite counting, and interpretation of the answers that simple counting can suggest. But more and more the direction of study has moved back, if in more sophisticated fashion, to the interpretation of individual objects, images, or more narrowly defined classes of coins. A number of specialized studies have borne on Romanization vs. civic identity (e.g. Howgego, Heuchert, and Burnett, 2005); this is, of course, a major theme in the broader field of Classical Studies as well. This is a fine example of the integration of the discipline into the mainstream of study, where it has always belonged.

Further reading

Howgego 1995 provides a good introduction to the relationship of coins and history. There is no wholly satisfactory handbook of Roman coins: Mattingly 1960 is the only full-scale survey, and its treatment of the early Republic is now superseded and its bibliography badly out of date; Carson 1990 deals with Imperial coins but without any consideration of the provinces. Burnett 1987 is the best survey but has no bibliography at all. The introductions to Crawford 1974 and to the British Museum Catalogues (Mattingly *et al.* 1923–50; Carson 1962) provide starting-points for the early Imperial coinages, and Estiot (2004) for the coinage of Aurelian; the volumes of Roman Imperial Coinage (Mattingly *et al.* 1920–) are fundamental for the coinages from the tetrarchy on; vols. 8 and 10, by J. P. C. Kent, are particularly strong. For the social role of coins in the provinces, see Harl 1987 and Howgego, Heuchert, and Burnett 2005. On coins and archaeology Casey 1986 is fundamental.

References

Abdy, R. (2004). 'The Second Known Specimen of a Coin of Domitian II', *RN* 160: 20–221.

Babelon, E. (1885). *Description historique et chronologique des monnaies de la république romaine vulgairement appellées 'consulaires'.* Paris: Rollin et Feuardent.

—— (1901). *Traité des monnaies grecques et romaines*, I. *Théorie et doctrine.* Paris, E. Leroux.

Badian, E. (1968). 'Sulla's Augurate', *Arethusa*, 1: 26–46.

Bahrfeldt, M. von (1923). *Die römische Goldmünzenprägung während des Republik und unter Augustus.* Halle (Saale): A. Riechmann.

Baldus, H. R. (1969). *MON(eta) VRB(is) ANTIOXIA. Rom und Antiochia als Prägestätten syrischer Tetradrachmen des Philippus Arabs.* Frankfurt/Main: B. Peus.

Berger, F. (1996). *Kalkriese I. Die römischen Fundmünzen.* Römisch-Germanische Forschungen 55. Frankfurt: von Zabern.

Burnett, A. M. (1977). 'The Authority to Coin in the Late Republic and Early Empire', *NC* 7th ser. 17: 37–63.

—— (1987). *Coinage in the Roman World.* London: Spink.

—— and P. Craddock (1983), 'Rome and Alexandria: The Minting of Egyptian Tetradrachms under Severus Alexander', *ANSMN* 28: 109–18.

—— M. Amandry, and P. P. Ripollés (1992), *Roman Provincial Coinage*, I. *From the Death of Caesar to the Death of Vitellius 44 BC–AD 69.* London: British Museum Press and Paris: Bibliothèque Nationale de France.

—— —— and I. Carradice (1999). *Roman Provincial Coinage*, II. *From Vespasian to Domitian (AD 69–96).* London: British Museum Press and Paris: Bibliothèque Nationale de France.

Butcher, K. and M. Ponting (1995). 'Rome and the East: Production of Provincial Coinage for Caesarea in Cappadocia under Vespasian, A.D. 69–79', *OJA* 14: 63–77.

Buttrey, T. V. (1956). *The Triumviral Portrait Gold of the Quattuorviri Monetales of 42 B.C.* ANS Numismatic Notes and Monographs.

—— (1993). 'Calculating Ancient Coin Production: Facts and Fantasies', *NC* 153: 335–51.

—— (1994). 'Calculating Ancient Coin Production II: Why it Cannot Be Done', *NC* 154: 341–52.

Buttrey, T. V., K. T. Erim, and R. R. Holloway (1989). *Morgantina Studies*, vol. 2. *The Coins*. Princeton: Princeton University Press.
Callataÿ, F. de (1995). 'Calculating Ancient Coin Production: Seeking a Balance', *NC* 155: 289–311.
Carson, R. A. G. (1962). *Coins of the Roman Empire in the British Museum*, VI. London: The British Museum.
—— (1990). *Coins of the Roman Empire*. London and New York: Routledge.
—— and C. H. V. Sutherland (1956). *Essays in Roman Coinage presented to Harold Mattingly*. London: Oxford University Press.
Cohen, H. (1857). *Description générale des monnaies de la republique romaine communément appelées médailles consulaires*. Paris.
—— (1859). *Description générale des monnaies communément appelées médailles impériales*. Paris.
—— (1880) *Description générale des monnaies communément appelées médailles impériales.*[2] Paris.
—— (1981). 'Galba's *Aequitas*', *NC* 141: 20–39.
Casey, P. J. (1986). *Understanding Ancient Coins: An Introduction for Archaeologists and Historians*. London: Batsford and Norman: University of Oklahoma.
Crawford, M. H. (1969). *Roman Republican Coin Hoards*. RNS Special Publication 4. London: Royal Numismatic Society.
—— (1974). *Roman Republican Coinage*. Cambridge: Cambridge University Press.
Depeyrot, G. (2004). *La Propagande monétaire (64–235) et le trésor de Marcianopolis (251)*. Collection Moneta 39. Wetteren: Moneta.
Eckhel, J. (1792–8). *Doctrina Numorum Veterum*. Vienna.
Erim, K. T., J. Reynolds, and M. Crawford (1971). 'Diocletian's Currency Reform: A New Inscription', *JRS* 61: 171–7.
Estiot, S. (2004). *Bibliothèque Nationale. Catalogue des monnaies de l'empire romaine*, XII.1. *D'Aurélien à Florien (270–276 après J.-C.)*. Paris and Strasbourg.
—— and G. Salaun (2004). 'L'Usurpateur Domitianus', *RN* 160: 201–18.
Esty, W. W. (1986). 'Estimation of the Size of a Coinage: A Survey and Comparison of the Methods', *NC* 146: 185–215.
Fittschen, K. (1982). *Die Bildnistypen der Faustina Minor und die Fecunditas Augustae*. Göttingen: Vandenhoeck & Ruprecht.
Frier, B. W. (1967). 'Augural Symbolism in Sulla's Invasion of 83', *ANSMN* 13: 111–18.
Grant, M. (1946). *From Imperium to Auctoritas: A Study of the Aes Coinage of the Roman Empire*. Cambridge: Cambridge University Press.
Grueber, H. A. (1910). *Coins of the Roman Republic in the British Museum*. London: The British Museum.
Harl, K. W. (1987). *Civic Coins and Civic Politics in the Roman East A.D. 235–284*. Transformation of the Classical Heritage 12. Berkeley and London: University of Californa Press.
Hersh, C. A. and A. Walker (1984). 'The Mesagne Hoard', *ANSMN* 29: 103–34.
Howgego, C. J. (1995). *Ancient History from Coins*. London and New York: Routledge.
—— V. Heuchert, and A. Burnett (2005). *Coinage and Identity in the Roman Provinces*. Oxford: Oxford University Press.
Hunt, A. S. and C. C. Edgar (1934). *Select Papyri II: Non-Literary Papyri, Public Documents*. Cambridge, Mass.: Harvard University Press.

Jones, A. H. M. (1956). 'Numismatics and History', in Carson and Sutherland 1956: 13–33.
Jones, J. R. (1970). 'Mint Magistrates in the Early Roman Empire', *BICS* 17: 70–8.
—— (1963). 'A Numismatic Riddle—The So-called Greek Imperials', *PAPS* 107: 308–47.
Kleiner, F. S. (1985). *The Arch of Nero at Rome: A Study of the Honorary Arch at Rome Before and Under Nero.* Rome: Giorgio Brettschneider.
Kraft, K. (1972). *Das System der kaiserzeitliche Münzprägung in Kleinasien.* Istanbuler Forschungen 29. Berlin: Gebr. Mann.
Levick, B. M. (1982). 'Propaganda and the Imperial Coinage', *Antichthon*, 16: 104–16.
Luce, T. J. (1968). 'Political Propaganda on Roman Republican Coins 92–82 B.C.', *AJA* 72: 23–39.
Mattingly, H. *et al.* (1923–50). *Coins of the Roman Empire in the British Museum*, I–V. London: British Museum.
—— (1960). *Roman Coinage from the Earliest Times to the Fall of the Western Empire.*[2] Chicago: Quadrangle and London: Methuen.
—— and E. A. Sydenham *et al.* (eds.) (1920–). *Roman Imperial Coinage.* London: Spink.
Meadows, A. and J. Williams (2001), 'Moneta and the Monuments: Coinage and Politics in Republican Rome', *JRS* 91: 27–49.
Metcalf, W. E. (1996). *The Silver Coinage of Cappadocia, Vespasian–Commodus.* Numismatic Notes and Monographs 166. New York: American Numismatic Society.
—— (1999). 'Coins as Primary Evidence', in Paul and Ierardi 1999: 1–17.
Mionnet, T. E. (1806). *Description de monnaies antiques, grecques et romaines, avec leur degré de rareté et leur estimation, ouvrage servant de catalogue à une suite de plus de vingt milles empreintes en soufre, prise sur les pieces originales.* Paris: Imprimerie de Testu.
Mommsen, T. (1860). *Geschichte des römischen Münzwesens.* Berlin: Wiedmann.
—— (1865–75) *Histoire de la monnaie romaine*, tr. de l'allemande par le duc de Blacas. Paris: Rollin et Feuardent.
Mouchmov, N. A. (1934). *Le Trésor numismatique de Réka Devnia.* Sofia.
Noreña C. (2001). 'The Communication of the Emperor's Virtues', *JRS* 91: 146–68.
Paul, G. M. and M. Ierardi (1999). *Roman Coins and Public Life Under the Empire.* Ann Arbor, Mich.: University of Michigan Press.
Pearce, J. W. E. (1950). *Roman Imperial Coinage*, IX. London: Spink & Son.
Robertson, A. S. (2000). *An Inventory of Romano-British Coin Hoards*, ed. R. Hobbes and T. V. Buttrey. London: RNS Special Publication 20. London: Royal Numismatic Society.
Spoerri Butcher, M. (2006). *Roman Provincial Coinage*, VII. *De Gordien I à Gordien III. (238–244 après J.-C.)*, 1. *Province d'Asie.* London: British Museum Press and Paris: Bibliothèque Nationale de France.
Sutherland, C. H. V. (1959). 'The Intelligibility of Roman Imperial Coin Types', *JRS* 49: 46–55.
Thompson, M., O. Mørkholm, and C. M. Kraay (1973). *An Inventory of Greek Coin Hoards.* New York: International Numismatic Commission.
Thomsen, R. (1953–61). *Early Roman Coinage: A Study of the Chronology.* Copenhagen: National Museum.
Wallace-Hadrill, A. (1986). 'Image and Authority in the Coinage of Augustus', *JRS* 76: 66–87.
Weiss, R. (1968). 'The Study of Numismatics During the Renaissance', *NC* 7th ser. 8: 177–87.
—— (1988). *The Renaissance Discovery of Classical Antiquity.*[2] Oxford: Blackwell.

CHAPTER 9

PROSOPOGRAPHY

WERNER ECK*

THE word is, for someone who hears it for the first time, rather hard to pronounce: prosopography; and it is also, indeed, hardly straightforward to understand. Derived from the Greek word *prosopon*, person, it denotes a scholarly discipline which is concerned with historical personages. Prosopography is, taken literally, 'the study of persons'.

To be occupied with persons in the context of Roman history and culture is not something that has emerged only with more recent developments in scholarship. Even medieval historiography, and, to an ever greater extent, antiquarians since the time of the Renaissance have constantly been concerned with people from the age of Rome. That is something they could not by any means avoid, since before anything else, Roman historiography is to a high degree concerned with persons. Cato Censorius, in whose historical work, the *Origines*, only collective and institutional units act (without individuals being distinguished by name), is more than untypical for Roman historiography, in which, as a rule, the individual historical person, identified by name, appears as agent. The non-literary tradition too, indeed, consists almost exclusively of sources which are related to one or more persons. During the Roman Republic, mints placed the name of the mint-master on their coins, and beginning with Augustus, we see the name of the ruler. Soon afterwards, family members of the *domus Augusta* were included as well. Local coins from Asia Minor bear the names of the governors and even more frequently that of municipal magistrates or others who were involved in the process of minting coins. Almost without exception, inscriptions on durable materials

* Translated by James Kierstead.

name one or more individuals: for it was one essential goal of epigraphic monuments to preserve the memory of persons for posterity. This purpose was served above all by funerary inscriptions, the *monumenta*, which account for the bulk of the epigraphic evidence, and likewise by building inscriptions which commemorated the beneficence of a donor or official, and religious dedications which a particular worshipper offered to a deity. Finally, papyrological documents, which dominate the evidence from Roman Egypt, are almost invariably associated with particular individuals, ranging from officials such as *praefecti Aegypti*, financial procurators, *strategoi* of Egyptian nomes or village scribes, to subjects who had to pay taxes or perform liturgies and received receipts or letters of appointment in return. In this way, several million individuals from a wide range of social backgrounds are documented, from all across the Roman realm from Britain to Upper Egypt and from Gibraltar to the Euphrates.

Many of these personalities are of outstanding historical importance and have therefore been studied for a long time. This includes the likes of Fabius Maximus Cunctator, who played an important role organizing Roman resistance after the crushing defeat of Rome by Hannibal in 216 BC; and also Sulla, Pompey, and Caesar, who left deep marks on the history of the late Republic. Most of the Roman emperors belong in this group, as well as some of their wives, such as Livia, Agrippina, and Iulia Domna. It also includes Parthian kings as partners or enemies of Rome; client rulers such as Herod the Great or Iuba of Mauretania; generals of the Late Empire such as Arbogast or Stilicho; Church Fathers such as Augustine or Hieronymus (Jerome); the influential hermit Paula, who founded monasteries in Bethlehem; or Roman bishops such as Damasus or Gregory the Great, or Athanasius, the bishop of Alexandria. However, most people, from the perspective of who is to be considered as a driving force in historical develepmont, were either unimportant, or are—and this is certainly not infrequently the case—unrecognizable (any longer) to us as driving forces of this sort. Yet at the same time, everyone who was alive then was in one way or another involved in shaping history; if not—as with most of them—as individual agents, then at least as members of a particular category or group of people. This includes persons who had held certain offices and military ranks, from the republican officials—consuls, praetors, or censors—to various kinds of governors in the Roman provinces from the late third century BC until late antiquity, and likewise army commanders such as the legionary legates of the Principate or the ethnically diverse *magistri militum* of the Later Roman Empire. Individual social groups also belonged to such formative classes as, for example, the equestrian class, whose leading personalities, as tax-collectors (*publicani*), and later as controllers of the fiscal administration with the official title of *procurator*, had at their disposal enormous, though admittedly very differently structured, influence. Closely linked to the equestrian class were the decurions of the cities, the empire's units of self-government, who, assembled in the city council, determined, to a considerable degree, the lives of their municipalities; the great mass of the equestrian class was at the same time part of the elites of the countless towns. Below the high office-holders of the empire and of late antiquity a large and ever-increasing number of subalterns operated, who for the most part were taken from two social groups: slaves or freedmen of the emperor, but above all from the troops who were stationed in all the provinces but also in Rome.

What the significance of these and other groups of people was, what they did exactly, where they came from socially, how such groups changed through time—such questions are hardly ever answered directly in ancient literary sources, except in statements whose purposes are almost entirely polemical and aim to defame an entire group by attacking individual people. Thus the emperor Constantine is accused, by an indiscriminate adoption of Germans into the armed forces, of having entrusted even the leadership of the armies to enemies of the empire, made the empire dependent on Germans, and so brought it into danger. There are repeated complaints about the influence of imperial slaves, but above all freedmen, as a general phenomenon of the first century AD. But such general statements are altogether rare, and hardly ever of an objective nature.

In order to be able to answer questions such as those introduced above, as well as numerous others, or assess the historical worth of polemics like that directed at Constantine, it is generally not enough to examine individual examples; it requires a more all-encompassing approach. Only an examination of the concrete cases that have come down to us can in this instance lead to scholarly conclusions, so that what was genuinely the norm is recognized without outstanding individual examples—even those judged to be typical—distorting our vision.

Mommsen and the Beginnings of Prosopography in Ancient History

It is in such a context that prosopography acquires its particular significance, since while it primarily examines individual people and studies them from different points of view, it has above and beyond that the inclination and the capacity to make more general statements which transcend the individual cases. This so-called prosopographical method is, however, a more recent development, which—if my view is correct—in its systematic approach goes back to Theodor Mommsen.

On 31 March 1874 Mommsen submitted a proposal to the Royal Prussian Academy of Sciences in Berlin, in which he requested funding for a project whose goal was to develop 'a Proso(po)graphy of the notable persons of the Roman Empire' (Eck 2003: 21–2). Mommsen intended before anything else to produce a new type of tool to use with the *Corpus Inscriptionum Latinarum* (*CIL*), which was in the process of being created. He would accomplish in this way, on the one hand 'a relatively complete prosopography of the more notable men of this era', and the other hand 'a compilation of chronologically arranged lists of consuls, governors, and magistrates in general'. The result, which was presented to the scholarly public more than twenty years later, was the first edition of the *Prosopographia Imperii Romani*, in three volumes (1897–9). The work presented, though, only the prosopography, and not the lists of different office-holders that Mommsen had advertised in addition. The *PIR* (the abbreviation used in citations), in any case, very consciously did not represent a comprehensive dictionary of all persons known from the empire, but rather encompassed only those, as Mommsen expressed it, 'notable persons of the Empire', by which on the one hand was meant all those attested in the literary sources—indeed, almost all persons known of in this fashion, without limitations. From the other types of sources, that is, in essence from inscriptions, papyri, or coins, however, he included only persons who belonged to the Roman governing classes, in other words, all members of the senatorial class (*ordo senatorius*) as well as those from the equestrian class (*equester ordo*) who had taken on state functions in some form or other. Also included were all female members of the relevant social classes. Chronologically the dictionary was dedicated to the early and high Empire, that is, to the period roughly from the time of Augustus (27 BC–AD 14) to the beginning of Diocletian's reign in the year AD 284.

These chronological parameters alone make clear that Mommsen saw the Prosopography as primarily an auxiliary tool, in essence, for the *CIL*. For the great mass of the epigraphic material came from the first three centuries of the empire, which was likewise collected at the behest of Mommsen in the *CIL* at the Berlin Academy. The inclusion of all literarily attested persons in the *PIR* also bears witness to the intention of supporting the new body of inscriptions; for while increments to the literary tradition could hardly be expected, the people who appeared there could easily crop up again in an inscription, on a coin, or in a papyrus. It was important, though, with regard to new attestations that the material relevant to a person found in literary sources was systematically collected, and therefore directly accessible to researchers.

From the beginning, the *PIR* far exceeded in its possibilities even what Mommsen had intended, even if—according to the guidelines that had been laid down—it did so only in the form of lists of holders of high office. But soon the prosopographical dictionary became something like a general model, which quickly influenced other fields of the study of the Greco-Roman world. Only a few years after the *PIR* for the early and high Empire, Johannes Kirchner's *Prosopographia Attica* (1901–3) appeared, covering the Athenian city-state and a completely different period of ancient history. Not by chance, Kirchner's work served a historical period in which further great bodies of inscriptions, the *Corpus Inscriptionum Graecarum* and the *Inscriptiones Graecae*, had just presented copious quantities of documentary material, but which needed to be sifted before they could be utilized.

From these beginnings there developed a broad programme of research, which in the course of the twentieth century spread to all the major scholarly cultures, many different subdivisions of classical scholarship, and beyond that to broader studies of Roman history and culture, and which sought to encompass a great variety of groups of persons. For the broad spectrum of such research within the study of Roman history and culture one is referred to works such as the *Prosopography of the Later Roman Empire* (*PLRE*, 3 vols., 1971–92), or the *Prosopographie chrétienne du Bas-Empire* for Africa and Italy (2 vols. so far, 1982, 1992). The former work, in recording influential social circles, essentially followed the *PIR*, whose second edition had progressed to the letter L by 1971 (in 2009 vol. 8.1, for the letter T, was published); chronologically the *PLRE* began where the *PIR* left off, collecting the prosopographical material from the time of Diocletian to the middle of the seventh century AD. However, persons who had influence only within the Church hierarchy were excluded from the *PLRE*. In contrast, the *Prosopographie chrétienne* strove to include all persons whose adherence to Christianity between the first and the seventh centuries is attested, independent of the concrete social or functional position of the individuals. Other works took aim from the beginning at more precisely defined groups: the authors of some of these adopted a more narrowly political perspective, like T. R. S. Broughton, who set out in annalistic fashion all the magistrates of the Roman Republic, or H.-G. Pflaum, who analysed all the careers of the procurators of the empire (Pflaum 1960–1). Other authors focused rather on the social divisions of Roman society, like C. Nicolet, who dealt with the equestrian class of the Republican era (Nicolet 1966–74); or M.-T. Raespaet-Charlier, with her collection of female members of the senatorial class during the first two centuries AD (Raepsaet-Charlier 1987); or H. Devijer, who has presented a comprehensive catalogue of all equestrian officers from Augustus to Gallienus, which come down to us in inscriptions, but also partly in papyri, and only rarely in literary works (Devijver 1976–2001). Finally, numerous prosopographical catalogues were dedicated to more narrow geographical districts, above all to the greater self-governing units, like Macedonian Beroea or northern Italian Brixia; but the inhabitants of the bigger villages, like, for example, Theadelphia in the Fayyum in Egypt, here on the basis of numerous papyrus texts, were also prosopographically recorded.

Most of the works named here—as well as many others—fulfilled, then, for some time similar functions in their sub-fields as *Paulys Realenzyclopädie der Classischen Altertumswissenschaft* (*RE*), which was completed in the year 1978 and included in its aims the presentation of the prosopographical material of Greco-Roman antiquity. For the Republican period this was for the most part accomplished, above all through the contributions of Friedrich Münzer and Matthias Gelzer, a task called for by the state of the sources; for prosopographical knowledge for this period depends to a great extent on literary evidence, to which we can expect hardly any additions. For the subsequent eras, however, the source material grew—and grows still—unremittingly, through new inscriptions, papyri, and coins, because of which many articles on individual persons quickly go out of date, and not a few recently discovered persons are lacking entirely. But even more importantly, in the conception of the *RE* the classical ages of Greece and the Roman Republic had centre-stage, while the Hellenistic era, the Empire, and late antiquity were not treated with the same thoroughness; additionally, many social groups lay outside the historical field of vision of the *RE*. Because of this, this comprehensive encyclopedia for the whole of Greco-Roman antiquity could provide no general basis for prosopographical work. Into its place stepped other works, such as those mentioned above, which became the basic lexica of prosopography.

All these works, whose number could easily be increased, have a single common goal: to include in a lexicon (and therefore make more accessible) the individual groups of people from a certain time and a definite area; to document them precisely with source material; and to make as complete a catalogue of them as possible, all the time employing consistent criteria of inclusion. From which it is immediately clear that prosopography was even by then no longer concerned primarily with individual historical people, but with historical phenomena, which, due to the state of the sources that has already been described, could be discovered only through the examination of a variety of individuals. Friedrich Münzer's work is a classic example of this approach. First of all, in countless articles in the *RE*, he described all the foremost people of the Republic known from literary sources, in particular members of the Senate. On this basis, he wanted to show how these people were influenced to a great degree in their politics by their family ties, and in this way he was able to lay bare many lines of continuity in the Roman Republic (Münzer 1920). Although not many today would follow him very far in his conclusions, it was by these means that he made this supremely personal factor in the politics of the Republic, the link and connection of the individual member of the ruling class with his background, with the history of his family, into one of the fundamental insights about this period of Roman history.

Equally impressive is what Hans-Georg Pflaum has brought to light with regard to the administrative tasks of equestrian functionaries, above all the so-called procurators, in imperial service, from the time of Augustus till the late third century AD, and equally with regard to their geographical and social background and the consequences that these had for the development of a widespread imperial aristocracy. In his *Carrières équestres* Pflaum discussed each individual person who belonged in this category, their career, and their social environment. In his *Procurateurs* (which appeared some time before the former work), he integrated all that could be discovered from his data on individual people, as far as this was relevant to the equestrian functionaries (Pflaum 1950).

On these foundations laid by Pflaum it has been possible, in the last few decades, to describe more precisely the development of the administration, to the extent that it has left traces in the prosopographical record. In general, though, only the structures of the administration can be approached by this method (as far as is at all possible through the study of individual people), while execution of state functions and the general *modus operandi* must be investigated primarily by other means. Similarly, it is scarcely possible to discover motives, for example, for what reason a person was allocated a certain task by the emperor, on a purely prosopographical basis. Just consider what Tacitus' biography of his father-in-law Iulius Agricola reveals in this respect; if we had only a record of Agricola's *cursus honorum*, we would have only the fleshless skeleton of his career, and could at best make guesses as to the reasons why Agricola held these individual offices (Birley 2005: 71–95; Eck 2005: 71 f.). Still less do prosopographical sources, as a rule, reveal anything about politics and its internal workings and forces. And yet occasionally prosopography does allow us insights of this sort. One example will suffice.

Nerva and the Adoption of Trajan: A Prosopographical Case Study

After the assassination of the emperor Domitian (AD 96), the senator Cocceius Nerva, already advanced in years, was acclaimed as the new ruler. Very soon he was under considerable pressure, because the praetorian guard was still enraged about the assassination of Domitian, and also because he could die at any moment because of his age, and there was no clear successor since he had no son. On account of this Cornelius Nigrinus, the governor of Syria, the biggest military province of the East, invoking his military power, made it known that he considered himself a suitable candidate to succeed Nerva. Nerva, we are told, reacted to this in October 97 with a surprising decision. During a sacrifice on the Capitol in Rome he unexpectedly received an inspiration (so the story goes) from the highest god of the Roman state, Jupiter, to adopt the senator Marcus Ulpius Traianus as his son and so to make him his successor. Trajan was at that time the governor of Germania Superior, another big military province which bordered directly on northern Italy. The only contemporary record of Nerva's divine message is given to us by the senator Plinius Secundus in a speech which he gave a few years later in the Senate. We can be sure that he did not deviate from the official version of events that had been spread abroad in Rome.

That this version of the events of October 97 cannot have represented reality requires no demonstration. Yet how can we get any closer to what really happened? Who came to the decision to adopt Trajan? How was the official account spread abroad? Was Trajan himself unaware of what it was that Nerva was going to do in Rome? Pliny's account might suggest this, if we wanted to go along with the literal meaning of his text. But this hypothesis is ruled out even on general grounds of rational action, and still more by power-political considerations. In this case, though, it can actually be demonstrated, with the aid of prosopographical sources and their analysis, that we must imagine an entirely different scenario.

Every new emperor, shortly after coming to power, imparted special honours to those who had supported him on his path to power. Trajan could not have done any differently. One of the ways in which a leader's closest helpers were distinguished was by the bestowal of a consulship, and above all the bestowal of a second or even a third consulship. For this magistracy still represented the summit of the hierarchy of prestige in Roman society. Since Trajan was adopted by Nerva in October 97, reactions to this event can be identified at the earliest in 98. As a matter of fact, we can identify an unusually large number of consuls in 98 who held the office for the second time, as the following list shows:

1 January	Nerva IIII, Trajan II
13 January	Traian II, Cn. Domitius Tullus II
1 February	Traian II, Sex. Iulius Frontinus II
1 March	Traian II, L. Iulius Ursus II
1 April	Traian II, T. Vestricius Spurinna II
1 May	Traian II, C. Pomponius Pius

Nerva assumed the consulship together with Trajan on 1 January, but stepped down on 13 January, while Trajan held on to the office until the end of June. Four senators then appear as his colleagues until the end of April, all of whom held the office of consul for the second time. Four *consules iterum* in one year is very unusual, but no conclusions can yet be drawn from this as to whether some (or even all) of these men were involved in some way in the adoption and succession of Trajan. For Nerva too, who had not come to power until September 96, could not have honoured his four fellow senators in an appropriate way until the beginning of the year 98 without depriving other senators who had just been designated for the consulship in 97, for reasons which dated back to the year 96 and which depended on him personally. While the year 99 in the consul-lists is not a very unusual one, the year 100 reveals with greater certainty something of what had really happened in the year 97. For the list shows the following consuls for the first months of the year 100:

1 January	Traian III, Sex. Iulius Frontinus III
1 March	Traian III, L. Iulius Ursus III
1 April	M. Marcius Macer, C. Cilnius Proculus

On 1 January Trajan assumed the consulship once again, on this occasion for the third time; his colleague is Sextus Julius Frontinus, who also holds the office for the third time. He steps down at the end of February, while Trajan stays in office; at this point one Lucius Iulius Ursus appears as his colleague, he too as consul for a third time. What is highly peculiar is that Trajan himself is holding the consulship for

only the third time, while rulers normally made sure that they surpassed fellow members of the elite even in such ceremonial distinctions, and so had usually been consul on at least one more occasion than their colleagues in the office. In the year 100 this is not the case. Even more important, and more revealing politically as well, is that Frontinus and Ursus too had already held the *fasces* with Trajan in the year 98, at that point for the second time. Both senators were named consul twice, then, within the space of only two years, and both times together with Trajan. This is an absolutely exceptional occurrence. First of all, a third consulship was in any case more than rare; only thirteen other senators in total had reached such a level of honour in the 130 years or so between the reign of Augustus and the end of the first century AD. In all these cases, the men in question are the closest and most trusted accomplices of the ruler in power at the time. Only once before this occasion, however, had a senator been exalted in such a way above all his other senatorial colleagues in the space of only two years, and this was Licinius Mucianus, who secured the throne for Vespasian in 69/70 AD. Licinius Mucianus' example shows that also in the case of Frontinus and Ursus only absolutely exceptional services to the new emperor could have led to such a distinction, and that means that they were involved in Trajan's adoption by Nerva. In fact even Pliny, in the speech we have already mentioned, talks about two senators who had served Trajan 'in the toga', that is, in Rome itself and not as leaders of an army. Everyone in the Senate, where the speech was given, knew who was meant. Once we have advanced thus far in the analysis of the events of the year 97, it becomes clear through further prosopographical details how Frontinus and Ursus, together with others (and above all Trajan himself), so arranged matters that Nerva really had no choice but to adopt Trajan, if he wanted to defend himself against the praetorian guard in Rome and against Cornelius Nigrinus in the East. Trajan had deliberately obtained the governorship of Upper Germany, and so of the military province that was closest to Italy. At the same time, senators who had been initiated into the plans of the group of Trajan, Frontinus, and Ursus were placed as governors in other provinces, for instance, in the province Belgica or in Pannonia. One of these initiates, a certain Sosius Senecio, governor of the province Belgica in the year 97, was the son-in-law of Frontinus. In the same province in the same period, moreover, one Attius Suburanus was serving as financial procurator, who controlled the provision of funds to the military in Upper and Lower Germany. He therefore secured Trajan's position in Upper Germany. But Attius Suburanus was not just anyone from the great mass of procurators of equestrian rank; on the contrary, he had worked for many years as a close associate of Iulius Ursus. Personal relationships had been converted into political capital.

What reveals itself after a synthesis of the evidence as a deliberate political strategy of the year 97 is never explicitly formulated as such in our literary tradition. The evidence is composed almost exclusively of dry facts, that is, the offices held by a few senators or knights in certain years, relationships of kinship or familiarity formed from previous formal contexts, and then the exceptional honours accorded to Frontinus and Ursus. These facts are concerned primarily with individuals, but when we draw them together they reveal certain relationships and in this way even lead to the reconstruction of a certain political strategy, which for understandable reasons has not entered into the historiographical tradition. For if Nerva, who was then in power, was not involved (as seems to have been the case), then the whole affair was a sort of *coup d'état*, conceived, planned, and carried out by a small group of senators because they wanted to obstruct the adoption of Cornelius Nigrinus, who was attempting to force the issue of the succession. If we did not have these many facts concerned with individuals, then all that would remain for us to do would be to have our doubts about the official account proffered by Pliny, hardly a satisfactory situation (Eck 2002*b*).

The Methodology and Hazards of Prosopography

Nonetheless, prosopographical arguments often entail methodological risks which are not always easy to recognize. This is true in particular when the sources in question are used as direct evidence, without considering whether they are representative of past realities, or when an *argumentum e silentio* is employed as a decisive method of demonstration. In general it can be said that the higher people stood socio-politically, the more often they are named in the sources. This means in the Roman context that those who attained the consulship, and thereby achieved consular rank, are far more frequently attested than others who only made it to praetor or even lowlier offices, except when we have a complete listing of all the magistrates of a given year (as in Livy). But this is the case for only a relatively brief part of the Roman Republic, and later such listings are no longer found apart from some exceptional and short cases. Otherwise, though, this observation applies to the Republic no less than to the Empire or to late antiquity, as long as such offices were awarded. During the early and high Empire this observation is especially to the point, because most senators from these periods are known only through epigraphic evidence. But the longer a person's career lasted, and the higher the offices undertaken by him were, the greater the chances that he would be mentioned in an inscription (and this was true of senators, knights, and members of the army like tribunes, auxiliary prefects, and centurions). He would be mentioned either because he himself had commissioned an inscription, or because others had honoured him, for example, with a statue under which a text was inscribed, identifying the honorand. Once we have recognized this principle it becomes clear that we cannot simply compare numbers of holders of various offices but also have to consider the question of whether the sources are representative. This is especially important when we are comparing careers, since people who have progressed far are necessarily mentioned more often (since they have filled more offices and acquired more power) than those who have ascended less far. This would not be important, at least as regards senators, if their past socio-economic conditions did not influence the later course of people's careers. But because they did, certain offices awarded only within a socio-economic group (as, for example, senators or knights) do not appear in our sources in a representative way. This is clear in the so-called Vigintivirate, an office that served as an entry-point to the senatorial *cursus honorum*, and was divided into four different functions: three *triumviri monetales* for the minting of coins, ten *decemviri stlitibus iudicandis* for the judiciary, four *quattuorviri viarum curandarum* with responsibility for the streets of Rome, and finally three *triumviri capitales*, who were responsible for executions (at least in theory). We know about these offices almost exclusively via inscriptions in which the entire *cursus* of a senator appears. If our sources were representative, the percentages of all senators who held one of these positions would therefore be 15, 50, 20, and 15 per cent. But the percentages obtained from the sources such as we have them are *c.*19, 53, 18, and 10 per cent. The deviation is conspicuous above all in the last instance: this is a clear under-representation. That would not be so significant if we did not know from recorded instances that those who served as *triumviri capitales* were people who had been newly appointed to the senatorial class by the emperor. This shows that this group within the senate is distinctly under-represented in our sources, even in inscriptions recording a full *cursus honorum*. And as a result of this, all statements about additions to the Senate from new families (and that means to an increasing extent from provincial families) are somewhat problematic.

There are similar problems with regard to the determination of the regional provenance of recruits to the Roman army, that is, for a very different kind of socio-political group. In general it is assumed that the further provision of recruits from the first century AD onwards came increasingly from the area in which troops were stationed. This is thought to apply to units composed of Roman citizens, the legions, but still more to auxiliary units, who were drawn from the populations of subjugated peoples and tribes. These troops, however, as a rule did not yet have the rights of Roman citizenship. From the reign of the emperor Claudius at the latest (AD 41–54), Roman citizenship was granted to the soldiers of these auxiliary units, for the most part at the end of their period of service. This legal recognition was granted, or so it seems, to individual soldiers or veterans more and more through so-called military diplomas. These were documents which contained a copy of the imperial constitution, and besides the name of the recipient also included that of the city or of the tribe that the soldier came from. The number of these diplomas has sharply increased in the last two decades; today almost 1,000 such documents are known. Since they turn up for the most part on the antiquities market, we only know for sure the provenance of some of the newly discovered diplomas. Still, origin can usually be determined by other criteria, and we can usually conclude that a veteran settled down in the same region as his diploma was found in.

The numerous newly discovered diplomas can now tell us quite a different story about the recruitment of new soldiers. For the vast majority come from the eastern Balkans, the ancient provinces of Lower and Upper Moesia, Thracia, and Pannonia, and in part also from the southernmost regions of today's Turkey. And yet the auxiliary units for which the recruits were enrolled and enlisted are located in all parts of the empire. For instance, in August AD 127 three veterans were discharged who had been recruited twenty-five years earlier from the Daci and Eravisci, tribes from Pannonia and Thracia (Dacian-Thracian linguistic region); none of these men had ever served in a unit stationed in their home province. Instead, they had served in the provinces of Lower Moesia, Lower Germania, and Britannia. When thousands of recruits were needed in the year AD 133/4 for the fleet at Misenum, they were all brought in from the regions of Thracia and Moesia. Something similar occurred, to all appearances, in the year AD 128, in the recruitment of troops for Mauretania Tingetana; since of the six recipients of military diplomas who obtained Roman citizenship twenty-five years later in this province, all of them—or at least all of them whose diplomas are in a good enough state for us to tell—came from this region. In all these instances, and in many others besides, no local or regional recruitment took place at all; instead, new soldiers were brought in from distant regions, to which they returned, for the most part, after their discharge. The new documentation, then, with its prosopographical content, can be seen to correct previous research in a fundamental way. Of course, it is not to be taken as completely unassailable proof. A unique context for the transmission of these epigraphical texts in the eastern Balkans may lie behind this, which would nonetheless make necessary a revision of our assumptions about army recruitment; but even this revision would only apply to certain units in the Roman army and to certain periods of the second and third centuries AD, and would not necessarily affect the general drift of the earlier research.

Prosopography is a method of research which, perhaps more than any other, requires us to reflect on the meaning and validity of our sources, and especially on the question of how far missing sources influence our perception of historical realities. And yet it is also a method of research whose strengths we cannot do without if we want to open up broad swathes of Roman history and culture in a scientific way. The dictum of Sir Ronald Syme, the historian who more than most of his colleagues employed prosopography to the benefit of Roman history, still stands today: 'One uses what one has and there is work to be done' (Syme 1979: 711).

References and further reading

Prosopographical Dictionaries

Epigrafia e ordine senatorio, ed. S. Panciera, Rome, 1982 [1984].

Prosopographia Imperii Romani (*PIR*), ed. E. Klebs, H. Dessau, and P. von Rohden, 3 vols., Berlin, 1897–8.

Prosopographia Imperii Romani saeculi I, II et III (*PIR*²), ed. E. Groag, A. Stein, L. Petersen, K. Wachtel, M. Heil, W. Eck, and J. Heinrichs, Berlin, 1933–2009 (8 vols. so far, up to letter T).

Prosopographie chrétienne du Bas-Empire. I. *Prosopographie de l'Afrique chrétienne (303–533)*, ed. A. Mandouze, Paris, 1982.

Prosopographie chrétienne du Bas-Empire. II 1. *Prosopographie de l'Italie chrétienne, 313–604*, ed. Ch. Pietri, L. Pietri, J. Desmulliez, and Ch. Fraisse-Coué, Rome, 2000.

The Prosopography of the Later Roman Empire. I. *A.D. 260–395* ; II. *A.D. 395–527*, ed. A. H. M. Jones, J. R. Martindale, and J. Morris, Cambridge, 1971–80.

The Prosopography of the Later Roman Empire. III. *A.D. 527–641*, ed. J. R. Martindale, 2 vols., Cambridge, 1992.

Prosopographical Studies

G. Alföldy, *Fasti Hispanienses. Senatorische Reichsbeamte und Offiziere in den spanischen Provinzen des römischen Reiches von Augustus bis Diokletian*, Wiesbaden, 1969.

—— *Konsulat und Senatorenstand unter den Antoninen. Prosopographische Untersuchungen zur senatorischen Führungsschicht*, Bonn, 1977.

G. Barbieri, *L'albo senatorio da Settimio Severo a Carino (193–285)*, Rome, 1952.

A. R. Birley, *Onomasticon to the Younger Pliny: Letters and Panegyric*, Munich, 2000.

—— *The Roman Government of Britain*, Oxford, 2005.

T. R. S. Broughton, *The Magistrates of the Roman Republic*, New York, 1968–86.

A. Caballos Rufino, *Los senadores hispanorromanos y la romanización de Hispania (siglos I–III)*, Ecija, 1990.

M. Christol, *Essai sur l'évolution des carrières sénatoriales dans la seconde moitié du IIIe siècle ap. J.-C.*, Paris, 1986.

R. Delmaire, *Les responsables des finances impériales au Bas-Empire romain (IV*ᵉ*–VI*ᵉ *s.)*, Brussels, 1989.

S. Demougin, *Prosopographie des chevaliers romains julio-claudiens (43 av. J.-C.–70 ap. J.-C.)*, Rome, 1992.

H. Devijver, *Prosopographia Militiarum Equestrium quae fuerunt ab Augusto ad Gallienum*, 6 vols., Leuver, 1976–2001.

W. Eck, *Senatoren von Vespasian bis Hadrian. Prosopographische Untersuchungen mit Einschluss der Jahres- und Provinzialfasten der Statthalter*, Munich, 1970.

—— 'Imperial Administration and Epigraphy: In Defence of Prosopography', in A. K. Bowman, H. M. Cotton, M. Goodman, and S. Price (eds.), *Representations of Empire: Rome and the Mediterranean World*, Oxford, 2002 (*a*): 131–52.

—— 'An Emperor is Made: Senatorial Politics and Trajan's Adoption by Nerva in 97', in G. Clark and T. Rajak (eds.), *Philosophy and Power in the Graeco-Roman World: Essays in Honour of Miriam Griffin*, Oxford, 2002 (*b*): 211–26.

——'The Prosopographia Imperii Romani and the Prosopographical Method', in A. Cameron (ed.), *Fifty Years of Prosopography: The Later Roman Empire, Byzantium and Beyond*, Oxford, 2003, 11–22.

——'Auf der Suche nach Personen und Persönlichkeiten: *Cursus honorum* und Biographie', in K. Vössing (ed.), *Biographie und Prosopographie. Festschrift zum 65. Geburtstag von A. R. Birley*, Stuttgart, 2005: 53–72.

M. Gelzer, *Die Nobilität der römischen Republik*, Leipzig, 1912.

H. Halfmann, *Die Senatoren aus dem östlichen Teil des Imperium Romanum bis zum Ende des 2. Jh. n. Chr.*, Göttingen, 1979.

P. M. M. Leunissen, *Konsuln und Konsulare in der Zeit von Commodus bis Severus Alexander (180–235 n. Chr.)*, Amsterdam, 1989.

L'Ordre équestre. Histoire d'une aristocratie (IIe *siècle av. J.-C.–IIIe siècle ap. J.-C.*), ed. S. Demougin, H. Devijver, and M.-Th. Raepsaet-Charlier, Rome, 1999.

F. Münzer, *Römische Adelsparteien und Adelsfamilien*, Stuttgart, 1920.

C. Nicolet, *L'ordre équestre à l'époque républicaine (312–43 av. J.-C.). I. Définitions juridiques et structures sociales*; II. *Prosopographie des chevaliers romains*, 2 vols., Paris, 1966–74.

P. Petit, *Les fonctionnaires dans l'oeuvre de Libanius. Analyse prosopographique*, Paris, 1994.

H.-G. Pflaum, *Les carrières procuratoriennes équestres sous le Haut-Empire romain*, 3 vols., Paris, 1950, 1960–1; Supplément 1982.

——*Les procurateurs équestres sous le Haut-Empire romain*, Paris, 1950.

I. Piso, *Fasti Prouinciae Daciae. I. Die senatorischen Amtsträger*, Bonn, 1993.

Prosopographie und Sozialgeschichte. Studien zur Methodik und Erkenntnismöglichkeit der kaiserzeitlichen Prosopographie, ed. W. Eck, Cologne, 1993.

M.-T. Raepsaet-Charlier, *Prosopographie des femmes de l'ordre sénatorial (Ier–IIe siècles)*, 2 vols., Louvain, 1987.

J. Rüpke, *Fasti sacerdotum. Die Mitglieder der Priesterschaften und das sakrale Funktionspersonal römischer, griechischer, orientalischer und jüdisch-christlicher Kulte in der Stadt Rom von 300 v. Chr. bis 499 n. Chr.*, 3 vols., Stuttgart, 2005. Translated as *Fasti sacerdotum: A Prosopography of Pagan, Jewish, and Christian Religious Officials in the City of Rome, 300 BC to AD 499*, Oxford, 2009.

J. Scheid, *Les Frères Arvales. Recrutement et origine sociale sous les empereurs Julio-Claudiens*, Rome, 1975.

——*Le collège des Frères Arvales. Étude prosopographique du recrutement (69–304)*, Rome, 1990.

D. R. Shackleton Bailey, *Onomasticon to Cicero's Speeches*, Norman, Okla., 1988.

——*Onomasticon to Cicero's Letters*, Stuttgart, 1995.

——*Onomasticon to Cicero's Treatises*, Stuttgart, 1996.

R. Syme, *The Roman Revolution*, Oxford, 1939.

——*Tacitus*, 2 vols., Oxford, 1958.

——*Roman Papers I–VII*, Oxford, 1979–91.

B. E. Thomasson, *Fasti Africani. Senatorische und ritterliche Amtsträger in den römischen Provinzen Nordafrikas von Augustus bis Diokletian*, Stockholm, 1996.

CHAPTER 10

METRE

LLEWELYN MORGAN

'METRE is measure' is the lapidary first sentence of a recent account of Greek metre (West 1982: 1), and in Greek (as in English) it is a tautology: *metron* is 'measure' or 'rule' before it is 'metre'. As the word implies, the fundamental effect of metre on language is to organize and regulate it; and language so structured automatically rises in status, gaining a heightened, even ritualistic character purely by virtue of the artificial patterns it is obliged to obey.

What precisely is 'measured' by 'metre' varies. It may be the number of syllables, or the number of accentual stresses; it may be a combination of the two. Accentual stress had a role to play in Roman poetry, as we shall see, and there was also an element of syllable counting, seemingly inherited from the syllabic metres of the Indo-Europeans, the ancient common source of Greek, Roman, Indian, and other metrical systems (Meillet 1923; Gasparov 1996: 5–10). But Roman metres were taken over wholesale from Greece, and hence it was the fundamental principle governing Greek metrics, the length (or 'quantity') of individual syllables, that came to predominate in Latin verse as well, even though Romans continued to refer to metre as *numerus*, 'number', as if the syllabic criterion was still dominant. A useful general model is the dactylic hexameter, which Rome, in imitation of Greece, made the metre of epic, and hence the benchmark for all other metres (just as epic was for all genres). A hexameter can be analysed as six dactylic 'feet' (a dactyl is — ∪ ∪, a long syllable followed by two shorts), but in any given foot a long might take the place of the two short positions (a process known as 'contraction'), yielding a spondee (— —, long-long): a position of this kind which may be filled by a long or two shorts is known as *biceps*. The last foot of the line was always — —, even though the very final syllable might be naturally short: a short in the final position counted as long by virtue of the pause that followed the end of the line, and is often described as *brevis in longo*, that is, a short (syllable) in a long element, or a 'final *anceps*', the word *anceps*, 'doubtful', indicating a position where a long or short is equally acceptable. Further conventions, less rigid, also applied to the hexameter: there was a resistance to contraction in the penultimate foot (the last opportunity for the defining dactyl), and pauses known as 'caesuras' were observed in certain regular positions within the line.

Hexameters might be coordinated with other metrical lengths (for example, with a dactylic pentameter, to form an elegiac couplet), but in epic they were deployed in a continuous sequence. Here, for example, are the last three lines of Virgil's *Aeneid* (12.950–2):

— — — — — — — — —UU — —
hoc dicens ferr(um) aduerso sub pectore condit
With these words he buries his sword in his opponent's breast,

—UU — — — — — — —UU — —
feruidus; ast illi soluuntur frigore membra
burning with rage. Turnus' limbs grew slack with cold

—UU — UU— UU — — —U U — —
uitaque cum gemitu fugit indignata sub umbras.
and with a groan his life fled resentfully to the shades below.

A few preliminary remarks might even here be made about the interplay of the metrical structure with the poetic text. It should be immediately apparent that the third of these lines contains many more short syllables than the first two, and thus has a lighter and faster quality appropriate to the description of Turnus' insubstantial life-force fleeing his body. (There is a contrastingly languid quality to the longs of *soluuntur*, 'grew slack', in the previous line.) The placement of *indignata*, 'resentfully', in the last line represents a more subtle effect: seasoned readers of the hexameter would expect a word-break somewhere in the section of the line filled by the word, and the lack of any break stretches and swells the poetic line and underlines the word so positioned: it helps that it is also the only extended sequence of longs in the verse. In the first line the brackets around the second syllable of *ferrum*, 'sword', indicate that it has been melded with the vowel that opens the next word, a process (rather inaccurately known as 'elision') with considerable expressive power: here the (word for) sword is buried by the poet in the opponent's chest; elsewhere elision might contribute to the prosaic character of a passage (particularly in satire), since it obscures the element of definition which is of the essence of metrical order. In Virgil's text also there is a hint of the messiness attendant upon Aeneas' thrust (cf. Soubiran 1966: 630).

But if metre gives language a formal, artificial character, it is telling that the literary form which the Romans were most keen to claim as their own, the verse satire composed by Lucilius, Horace, Persius, and Juvenal, made a career out of a deliberately incompetent handling of this same metre, the dactylic hexameter—properly the metre of epic, but Lucilius in an inspired act of literary hooliganism had also claimed it for the grubby genre of satire. This is not to say that the satirists were not exceptional manipulators of metrical form: one of them in particular, Horace, celebrated as *numerosus Horatius*, 'multi-metred Horace' (Ovid, *Tr.* 4.10.29), competes with the comic playwright Plautus (whose *numeri*, 'metres', were *innumeri*, 'beyond count', according to an epigram quoted at Gellius 1.24.3) for the crown of most versatile Roman metrist: not coincidentally, Horace's satires are the subject of one of the best modern studies of a Roman author's metrical style (Nilsson 1952). But as Nilsson illustrates, Horace in his satire deploys his superlative mastery of metrical form to subvert the very claim of his compositions to the elevated status that metre bestowed. An example from a later satirist will help us to appreciate the motive for such a procedure. When Juvenal wants to spoof an epic evocation of the Muse in his attack on the (dead) emperor Domitian in Satire 4, which takes the form of a parody of an imperial panegyric by the loyal poet Statius, he makes some standard satirical moves: *incipe, Calliope. licet et considere: non est* | *cantandum, res uera agitur*, 'Begin, Calliope. And you can sit down: there's no | singing required, this is a *true* story' (4.34–5). The paraphernalia of high literature (inspiration from the Muse of Epic, standing to recite, a formal style of delivery) are debunked, and it is implied that such 'respectable' poetry is deceitful; satire, on the contrary, is concerned with the truth, and for that no such affectation will do. But this archetypically satirical exercise is taking place within a metre that is itself evocative of epic ideals, and Juvenal's parody operates on the metrical plane as much as any other. Opening with the majestic rhythm of *incipe, Calliope* (probably purloined directly from Statius), the metrical line thereafter dissolves into the *est* that signally fails to define the line ending: *est cantandum* is effectively one sense unit stretched over, and effacing, the line division, and the suppression of metrical form is reinforced both by the heavy punctuation of both lines (which implies a competitive structural principle) and by the elision in the following line (between *uera* and *agitur*) which denies the element of definition provided by the mid-line caesura. But metre *is* definition (cf. Cicero, *De Oratore* 3.186), and a line without it lacks any clear metrical identity at all. Juvenal has thus contrived to make prose of the heroic hexameter.

The critical point here is that consideration of the metrical dimension of a poetic exercise is not an optional extra. The corrupt hexameter is utterly integral to the greater argument of the satirists: fundamentally the pattern imposed on language by *metron* was Greek, and hence from the prejudiced perspective of satire metre ranked alongside such deplorable Greek imports as rhetoric, marble, and ladies' make-up as a threat to the moral integrity of Rome. This is why satire always wears its Greek metre like borrowed and ill-fitting clothes, encouraging its readers to mark the contradiction between form and subject-matter, between Greek artifice and unembellished Roman sincerity.

No other Roman poetry had quite so combative a relationship with its own metre as satire, but it could still be argued that Rome was never entirely at ease with its Greek metres. The commonsensical principle that 'a meter customary in a given language has become customary precisely because it measures the most conspicuous phonetic characteristic of that language' (Fussell 1979: 12) does not seem to apply when a language like Latin is somehow accommodated to metres developed for a language which displayed some fundamental phonetic differences. It was the lingering sense that Greek metre and Latin language made uncomfortable partners that satirical metrical practice was able to exploit: but the consequences for Roman poetry are more widespread.

Perhaps the clearest indication that there were limits to how far the Latin language could be reconciled with Greek metrics is the simple fact that Roman poets do not attempt the more complex Greek systems, and Latin metre is, as a consequence, in such technical respects, both 'simpler' and 'less interesting' than Greek (Raven 1965: 20). For its relative simplicity we may be thankful; and for any interest deficit on the technical side there is more than enough compensation in the wealth of associations that accrued to Latin metres. But the latter development may itself be related to the traumatic process of transposing Greek metres to Latin. For one unavoidable peculiarity of Roman poetry is how self-conscious it is about its metre—to a degree simply not seen in its Greek models. The general reader of Roman poetry may think here of Ovid's play on the structure of the elegiac couplet, the preferred metre for love poetry: Elegy herself sporting a limp because the pentameter that is coordinated with a hexameter in elegiacs is shorter by one metrical 'foot' (*Amores* 3.1.7–10), for example. But if I avoid any more illustrations from Ovid in this chapter it is partly because good work has already been done here (Kennedy 1993: 58–63 on the sexual implications of another metrical allusion in Ovid; Barchiesi 1997: 22–3 on the Callimachean, unwarlike King Battus, who 'expresses himself in pentameters, never hexameters'), and partly to make the point that Ovid was, in this respect at least, not so exceptional in his self-reflexivity about poetic form: Roman poetry throughout its history seems to need to comment upon—in a sense, excuse—the remarkable piece of cultural appropriation presupposed by Latin metre. It has been suggested, for example, that what is probably the opening line of Ennius' epic *Annals* (composed in the 170s BCE), and as such the very first heroic hexameter in Latin, *Musae quae pedibus magnum pulsatis Olympum*, 'Muses, who with your feet beat mighty Olympus . . .', annotates in the unusual attention it gives to the Muses' feet, *pedibus*, the revolutionary metrical departure that the line represents (Hinds 1998: 56–7).

Roman metre is thus always liable to be more than the inert form of a composition, intruding its own independent significance into the poetic artefact. I would propose as a particularly thoroughgoing example of this pervasive Roman readiness to contemplate metre in its own right, and to feed this theoretical appreciation of metre into the reading of poetry, the exquisite moment in the last poem of Horace's first collection of *Odes* where the poet proudly anticipates his survival 'as long as the Pontifex climbs the Capitol with the silent (Vestal) Virgin', *dum*

Capitolium | *scandet cum tacita uirgine pontifex* (3.30.8–9). Its metre, the 'First Asclepiad', can be understood as an unusually accessible lyric form (like epic hexameters, identical lines placed in uninterrupted sequence) appropriate to the opening and close of a collection (*Odes* 1.1 has the same form) which in its course will expose the reader to some unfamiliar and demanding forms. The beauty of the metrical structure of the second line quoted is best illustrated schematically:

— — — UU— ‖ — UU — U —
scandet cum tacita uirgine pontifex

A regular caesura or word-break is observed in the middle of the line. Here it is indicated by the symbol '‖', and it falls between the two words meaning 'silent Virgin': Horace has thus positioned the word for 'silent' before the momentary silence that the metrical scheme demands. Even left there it is a wonderful manipulation of metrical form. But I am inclined to pursue the effect a little further. The Roman literary public that I am proposing has an advanced, theoretical grasp of metrical form, necessarily so by the end of the first lyric collection of *numerosus Horatius*. Here I imagine them doing pretty much what I have just done, which is to conceptualize the asclepiadic line in its most abstract form, its regulated sequence of longs and shorts and intervening caesura. If I am right, the effect will reside not only in the silence that illustrates the sense of *tacita* so beautifully but also in the very betrayal of the line *as* a metrical artefact: Horace's metrical play necessarily evokes the high formality of the pattern of rules that constitutes its metre—and that is itself the perfect metaphor for the ceremonial scene of the Pontifex ascending to the temple of Jupiter alongside Vestals maintaining a ritual silence. Since *scandere* is a term of Roman metrical theory (the derivation of 'scansion'), furthermore, we may even be being primed to think metrically by the first word of the line.

A more extended passage of poetry can serve as an illustration of what metre can offer the reader of Roman poetry and what, conversely, the reader will gain from knowing about a poem's metre. *Silvae* 4.3, by Statius, is another poem about the emperor Domitian, but rather more complimentary than Juvenal's account. This poem celebrates a road, the Via Domitiana, constructed by the emperor along a marshy stretch of coastline south of Rome (Coleman 1988: 102–5). The major cause of the boggy conditions was the River Volturnus, and in the following passage the river himself regrets his former habit of overflowing his banks and expresses his gratitude to the emperor for the engineering works (including a magnificent new bridge) that have restored him to the circumscribed course of a 'proper' river (4.3.72–84):

camporum bone conditor meorum,
qui me, uallibus auiis refusum
et ripas habitare nescientem,
recti legibus aluei ligasti,

en nunc ille ego turbidus minaxque,
uix passus dubias prius carinas,
iam pontem fero peruiusque calcor!
qui terras rapere et rotare siluas
assueram (pudet!) amnis esse coepi.
sed grates ago seruitusque tanti est
quod sub te duce, te iubente, cessi,
quod tu maximus arbiter meaeque
uictor perpetuus legere ripae.

O gracious organizer of my fields,
you who, when I was spread out over my pathless valley
ignorant of how to live within banks,
bound me with the laws of a strict channel,
look at me, once turbulent and threatening,
hardly tolerating diffident craft:
now I carry a bridge and am crossed and trampled underfoot!
I who once would snatch up lands and roll along
forests (shame on me!) have begun to be a river.
But I offer you thanks and it is worth such servitude
because I have yielded under *your* guidance, *your* command,
and your name will be read as supreme judge
and everlasting conqueror of my banks.

The starting-point for any assessment of the metrical dimension of this passage, today or in 95 CE when it was written, has to be the established rules of the metre in which it is couched. That metre was known as the hendecasyllable, 'eleven-syllable', and the syllabic restriction in this case actually marks it out as a relic of ancient Indo-European metrical practice (Meillet 1923: 31–42). But the hendecasyllable had in addition become progressively more restrictive in respect of the *lengths* allowed for each syllable, until, by Statius' day, it was an exceptionally rigid system both syllabically and quantitatively, obeying the following invariable scheme:

— — — — ∪ ∪ — ∪ — ∪ — —

Already we have made progress. At the very least, appreciating that Statius' only scope for freedom in syllable length is the option of a short in the final long position should enhance our admiration for a poem that extends to 163 hendecasyllabic lines, a marvel of poetic virtuosity impressive enough to do justice to the remarkable engineering achievement of the emperor.

But the notion of 'rules' which I have introduced needs immediate qualification. The greatest exponent of the hendecasyllable, to Roman eyes, was Catullus, 150 years before Statius—and Catullus would certainly not have accepted my schema as an accurate account of his own practice, which was much more flexible, for example, treating each of the first two positions as *anceps* (allowing either short or long). A hint of an explanation for the hardening of the rules that occurred in the interim is to be found in Pliny the Elder's preface to his monumental encyclopedia *Natural History* (*HN praef.* 1), where Pliny quotes a line from Catullus' first poem, rewritten to correct what he considers a metrical infelicity in the Catullan original. The only difference between Catullus' *meas esse aliquid putare nugas* and Pliny's *nugas esse aliquid meas putare* (both mean '[you used to] think that my trifles were worth something') is that Pliny has replaced Catullus' iambic (short-long) opening with a spondee (long-long). Pliny's explanation of the change is that the authentic iambic opening made Catullus 'a little too rough than he wanted to be thought by his darling Veraniuses and Fabulluses'. Much might be made of this throwaway remark—the facility with which Pliny engages in technical metrical discussion, for example. But the most important thing Pliny illustrates is the degree to which the metre was identified with its most celebrated exponent, to the extent that the rules of the form mutate so as better to reflect the perceived character of the poet: for the sensitive Catullus only a smooth opening spondee will do.

The deep affinity between Catullus and this metrical form in the eyes of posterity may be illustrated by Pliny's nephew, Pliny the Younger, who quotes some self-conscious and none-too-accomplished hendecasyllables by a younger associate, 'Songs I sing in the tiny verses | that once dear Catullus and Calvus and the ancients composed'. Calvus was a friend and collaborator of Catullus, and 'ancients' may refer to other members of their circle, or conceivably even to much earlier (Greek) figures such as Sappho who also used the metre: but it is the primacy of Catullus in any discussion of the hendecasyllable that is the most important thing to appreciate about the metrical dimension of Statius' poem on the Via Domitiana. If I was right earlier to argue that no appreciation of a metrical trope on the part of a Roman reader was innocent of a higher understanding of metrical technicalities, it is also true that metres could not fail to carry along with them the history of their own usage, or at least its defining moments. The implications for Statius' celebration of the Via Domitiana of this immanent Catullan presence are as rich and diverse as the Catullan persona (Morgan 2000), but when the subject turns to a newly disciplined and civilized river boasting a bridge in the most contemporary style of architecture there are obvious analogies with the Alexandrian poetic ideals espoused by Catullus, since the turbulent river had been Callimachus' influential image for the kind of flaccid poetic practice he abjured (Smolenaars 2006). The newly acquired sophistication of the River Volturnus thus discovers a perfect accompaniment in the Catullan associations of a metre redolent of Hellenistic refinement.

Another aspect of metrical meaning relevant to this poem will take us back, momentarily, to the dactylic hexameter. This was, as I suggested earlier, 'the benchmark for all other metres', but this was particularly so in relation to the hendecasyllable, which came to be seen as the very antithesis of the hexameter, a short length where the hexameter was proverbially the *uersus longus*, and a metre suited to a light style of poetry that contrasted absolutely with the sombre gravity of epic. A poem celebrating the emperor (which is effectively what this poem is) *should*, according to ancient notions of metrical propriety, be composed in hexameters: Statius' failure to do so on its own throws attention on to the metrical form he does employ. But it has also been noted that a metre which delivers an unusually narrow text, and if extended to 163 lines a very *long* and narrow text, ensures an image on the page that itself bears more than a passing resemblance to a road. In the section I have excerpted the Via Domitiana is not in fact the centre of attention. But another narrow, circumscribed (and spatially extended) object is, and here again Statius works to establish his restrictive metre as a metaphor for the newly enchannelled Volturnus. But at this point a return to the more technical aspects of metrics is required.

The hendecasyllable also had a caesura, and it became a firm rule for later poets such as Statius and Martial that it should fall either after the fifth or sixth syllable (preferably the fifth) of the hendecasyllabic line. But the stronger a rule, the more compelling becomes any violation of it, and hence an observable tendency on Statius' part to lay a word requiring special emphasis across the positions where a caesura was expected, *stretching out* the line in a comparable way to that freighted *indignata* in the last line of the *Aeneid*. A good example earlier in this poem is line 16, *qui reddit Capitolio Tonantem*, 'who restores the Thunderer to the Capitol', a reference to Domitian's reconstruction of the most important cult place in Rome, the temple of Jupiter Optimus Maximus on the Capitol hill (also the destination of the Pontifex and Vestals in Horace's poem). In Statius' line the name of the Capitol, *Capitolio*, occupies the space between the fourth and eighth syllables of the verse, precluding any caesura, and the metrical anomaly is clearly designed to capture the magnificence of a place—simply too great to be comfortably contained within the eleven-syllable length.

In our section of *Silvae* 4.3 we can concentrate our attention on the masterpieces of meticulous construction that are lines 74–5. I set them out here with marks of scansion above them:

— — — ∪∪ — ∪ — ∪ — —
et ripas habitare nescientem
ignorant of how to live within banks

— — — ∪∪ ‖ — ∪ — ∪ — —
récti légibus áluei ligásti
(you who) bound me with the laws of a strict channel

In the first of these lines Volturnus' former ignorance and consequent failure to observe his proper limits is represented metrically by another example of an effaced caesura, achieved by the placement of *habitare*: the metrically literate reader recognizes the appropriately anomalous disposition of a line that describes a river which does not know his proper place. But when we turn to 75, where the river is firmly restored to his proper position, we not only observe the most orthodox caesura available to the poet, after the fifth syllable, but also an unusually close correlation of word accent and long positions, with the effect that the Latin stress accent seems to highlight the metrical character of the line, and the line to give the impression of a highly regimented piece of metricized language. At a quite formal level, then, metrical style is varied, like a musical accompaniment, to illustrate the meaning of the language it contains. But it is impossible also, once we have travelled this far, to fail to recognize the analogy established by the poet between metrical structures and the restrictions that hem in—or previously failed to confine—the River Volturnus. Statius is exposing the architecture of his metrical line in order to illustrate the structure which is the subject of his poetry, and metrical and engineering artefacts are identified in the process.

I have dwelt for some time on a relatively obscure poem because it provides an excellent illustration of the manifold, albeit interrelated, ways in which the metrical form of a poem might determine its meaning, and by the same token of the work that readers of Roman poetry need to do if the metre of a composition is to make the contribution it should. If this is unwelcome news, it should certainly not be surprising. In the Roman context, at least, metre was *the* defining characteristic of the mode of expression known as poetry, and it is inevitable that much of the pay-off of the poetic exercise relates to its most characteristic feature. I want to use the remainder of this chapter to establish that *Silvae* 4.3 is not an anomalous and unrepresentatively self-reflexive piece of metrical composition. A good place to start is another ode of Horace, 4.2, a thoroughly canonical text and an important model for Statius. Here in the first six sapphic stanzas of the poem (prefaced by a schema for the metre) Horace admits the utter supremacy and inimitability of the greatest of the Greek lyric poets, Pindar (*Odes* 4.2.1–24):

— U — — — U U — U — —
— U — — — U U — U — —
— U — — — U U — U — —
— U U — —

Pindarum quisquis studet aemulari,
Iulle, ceratis ope Daedalea
nititur pennis uitreo daturus
nomina ponto.

monte decurrens uelut amnis, imbres
quem super notas aluere ripas,
feruet inmensusque ruit profundo
Pindarus ore,

laurea donandus Apollinari,
seu per audacis noua dithyrambos
uerba deuoluit numerisque fertur
lege solutis,

seu deos regesque canit, deorum
sanguinem, per quos cecidere iusta
morte Centauri, cecidit tremendae
flamma Chimaerae,

siue quos Elea domum reducit
palma caelestis pugilemue equomue
dicit et centum potiore signis
munere donat,

flebili sponsae iuuenemue raptum
plorat et uiris animumque moresque
aureos educit in astra nigroque
inuidet Orco.

Whoever strives to rival Pindar, Iullus, relies on wings waxed by the craft of Daedalus, soon to give his name to the glassy sea.

Like a stream rushing down from a mountain, which rain-storms have swollen over its familiar banks, Pindar seethes and, beyond measure, rushes on with fathomless voice,

deserving to be honoured with Apollo's laurel, whether he rolls down new words in his bold dithyrambs, and is borne along by rhythms free of rule,

or sings of gods and kings, the blood of gods, at whose hands the Centaurs fell in deserved death, the fire of the terrifying Chimaera fell,

or talks of those, whether boxer or steed, whom the palm of Elis brings home divine, and honours them with a tribute greater than a hundred statues,

or laments the youth snatched from his tearful bride, and exalts to the stars his strength, his courage and his golden character, and begrudges them to black Orcus.

Metre is again absolutely central to Horace's characterization of Pindar and of himself, although I am only aware of one scholar (Steinmetz 1964) who has properly appreciated it. Once explicitly and once rather more obliquely, Pindar's supreme quality is related to his metrical practice: at 11–12, *numeris . . . | lege solutis* Pindar's (seemingly) free metrics are boldly and paradoxically described by an idiom normally reserved for prose, *oratio soluta*; but this explicit reference to metre is anticipated in the previous stanza, where *inmensus*, 'immeasurable', unmistakeably echoes Latin metrical vocabulary—and the image of overflowing riverbanks clearly suggested as much to Statius. But what should ensure that the reader's attention is directed to metrical issues is the form in which Horace has chosen to handle Pindar's transcendent flights of inspiration—a metre carefully selected as embodying the very opposite ethos.

The sapphic stanzas of 4.2 are another form with traceable links back to Indo-European practice, but they are named after the Greek love-poet Sappho, and whatever the original source of the association (ancient metricians wondered whether she had invented the form, or else was just especially fond of it), rather more than just the *name* of Sappho clung to her signature metre. As with Catullus, 'Sappho' could mean many things, but the poetry of this rarest of things, a female ancient poet, was typically intimate and personal, lacking the overtly public orientation of Pindaric verse; and 'her' verse form was bound to preserve this character to some extent. An amusing moment in recent scholarship of Horace is in a commentary on another poem, *Odes* 1.12, in which Horace uses sapphics to engage with Pindar. Horace's choice of metre does not meet with his editors' approval—'Metre: Sapphic (not altogether appropriate for the matter in hand)' (Nisbet and Hubbard 1970)—but one suspects that Horace knew his trade even better than Nisbet and Hubbard, and that his interrogation of Pindaric values, represented in his surprising choice of metre, is more searching than generally supposed.

In *Odes* 4.2, at any rate, the contrast between Pindar's expansive forms and the restrictive structures of the sapphic stanza, and hence between Pindar's limitless genius and Horace's more humble capacities, is brought out beautifully by a measured violation of metrical expectations, which (rather like Statius' disproportionate *Capitolium*) is suggestive of a Pindaric grandeur which the miniature sapphic form is quite unequal to containing. A stanzaic form like the sapphic has a somewhat different dynamic from the metres we have so far considered, insofar as the metrical period is as likely to be identified with the whole stanza as individual lines. Horace's strategy in this passage is to compromise the various structural principles operative in the sapphic stanza, although it is important to understand that it is generally Horace's own, self-imposed principles that he is violating. First, although Horace's strong preference is for a caesura after the fifth syllable of the longer sapphic line, here Horace repeatedly leaves the pause until after the sixth, after *immensusque*, for example, stretching the line out of shape. (See Rossi 1998 and the bibliography for a different kind of significance attaching to the violation of this convention in Horace's *Carmen Saeculare*.) If that might be seen as undermining the internal integrity of the line, there is a comparable effect, this time affecting the whole line, in the final stanza, where the poet allows two consecutive lines to run into each other: *moresque* elides into *aureos* and *nigroque* into *inuidet* in such a way as to undermine such definition as might be vouchsafed by the discrete verses. But the most important way in which Horace imperils the structural integrity of his verse form is by flouting a strong convention (not limited to Horace) that the sapphic stanza should be coextensive with a grammatical period (another convention that had become stronger over time: the progressive closing-up of the sapphic stanza is another example of the rules of a metre falling in line with its ethos, in this case one of feminine seclusion). Here, on the contrary, as Horace recounts the sublimity and breadth of Pindar's poetry he produces one sweeping period that runs across five stanzas: Pindar's torrential exuberance threatens to sweep away Horace's delicate sapphic structures. Quite what the sum is of Horace's self-comparison with Pindar has not met with general agreement: is Horace's humility before Pindar all it seems, or does he imply a kind of comparability with the master by encapsulating Pindar's entire oeuvre? Either way we must accept that much of Horace's formulation of the relationship between his own and Pindaric lyric is done on the metrical plane, and our experience of one of the very greatest of literary statements is impoverished if its metrical dimension does not receive our full attention.

But if I have given disproportionate emphasis to the matter of metrical character—in Fussell's formulation, '[b]ecause of its associations with certain kinds of statements and feelings, a given meter tends to maintain a portion of its meaning, whether symbolic sounds are attached to it or not' (Fussell 1979: 12)—it is because it is an area where Roman metre seems quite distinctive, but which is significantly underworked in contemporary criticism of Roman poetry, a notable exception being recent work on Horace's *Epodes*, iambic poetry in imitation of Archilochus which takes some interesting and meaningful metrical turns in its later stages (Heyworth 1993; Barchiesi 1994*a* and *b*). Yet the associations of the metre potentially constitute a crucial component of a poetic artefact, and I offer as a final example of this Catullus 17, a poem in which I would claim that metre holds nothing less than the key to its meaning.

In this poem Catullus rebukes a friend for neglecting his attractive and flirtatious young wife, and proposes to hurl him headfirst from a bridge in the hope that this will rouse him from his lethargy. As it is (14–22),

> cui cum sit uiridissimo nupta flore puella
> et puella tenellulo delicatior haedo,
> adseruanda nigerrimis diligentius uuis,
> ludere hance sinit ut lubet, nec pili facit uni,
> nec se subleuat ex sua parte; sed uelut alnus
> in fossa Liguri iacet suppernata securi,
> tantundem omnia sentiens quam si nulla sit usquam,
> talis iste meus stupor nil uidet, nihil audit,
> ipse qui sit, utrum sit an non sit—id quoque nescit.

> Although he has a girl in the very greenest flower of youth,
> and a girl more delicate than a tender little kid,
> needing to be protected more carefully than the blackest grapes,
> he allows her to frolic as she pleases, does not care a jot,
> doesn't raise a finger: but as an alder
> lies in a ditch, hamstrung by Ligurian axe,
> perceiving just as much as if it weren't there at all,
> that's what he is like, this dimwit I'm talking about: he sees nothing, hears nothing,
> and himself who he is, whether he is or not—he doesn't know that either.

The metre is the priapean, so named because there was a tradition of using it in poems addressed to the god Priapus: there is a fragment of such a poem by Catullus himself. The priapean thus evokes the spirit of Priapus as surely as the sapphic does Sappho and hendecasyllable Catullus: and a compelling figure he makes. Priapus was the tutelary deity of gardens and smallholdings: a figure of the god, with an erect and brightly painted phallus, stood in gardens to ward off intruders and malign influence. But once we allow Priapus access from the metre to the poem, his role is not hard to see (cf. Kloss 1998). Catullus' friend is the very opposite of *custos Priapus*, 'Priapus the guardian'. He neglects a girl as precious and vulnerable as an array of the kind of agricultural products—flowers, kids, grapes—protected by Priapus; and the image of the insensate block of wood evokes (by contrast) a common motif in the extensive literature that grew up around the god, the paradoxical power of a figure who was, after all, just carved from wood. The metrical framework thus offers, by way of accompaniment to Catullus' exhortation of his friend to assert himself, the model of masculine self-assertion and power represented by Priapus: a Priapus is what the friend should be. But the metre also cues the reader's response to the imagistic turns that Catullus' harangue takes, perhaps most effectively in *nec se subleuat ex sua parte*, an expression that, if the metre is allowed its full force, assumes an irresistibly priapic resonance. A familiar poem, then—but one for which the characteristically Roman self-consciousness about metrical form cannot be other than a central concern of scholarly interpretation. But metre works at many registers, and let us not forget either the simpler pleasures of metrical analysis. Catullus' poem ends with the hope that, thrown from the bridge, his friend will leave his torpor behind him in the mud, 'like a mule its iron shoe in the clingy quagmire',

— ∪ — ∪∪— ∪ — || — ∪—∪∪ — —
ferre(am) ut soleam tenac(i) in uoragine mula

I have marked a caesura in this line, but in actual fact it is effaced by the elision of the last syllable of *tenaci*: that licence in particular, but the elision also of ending of the first word, gives a wonderfully glutinous quality to the line. The antidote to Virgil's gruesome sword-thrust is thus a brilliant metrical representation of mud.

Further reading

In metrical terms Rome's debt to Greece was near-total, and Greek metre is thus a constant reference-point. The classic account remains Maas 1929. West 1982 provides detail, illustration, and a sense of historical development lacking from Maas (a masterpiece of compression), but non-experts will find Raven 1962 or West 1987 (a simplified version of West 1982) more accessible. Roman metre represents a predictably massive field in itself, but general introductions may be found in Raven 1965, Boldrini 1992, Nougaret 1948, Crusius 1997, Halporn and Ostwald 1962, and Halporn, Ostwald, and Rosenmeyer 1963 (covering both Greek and Latin). Some of the thorniest controversies cluster at the earlier end of Roman poetic history. For example, although there is reasonable consensus about the prehistory of Greek and Roman metre in Indo-European practice, as plotted by Meillet 1923 (whose conclusions are usefully summarized by Gasparov 1996: 5–10), the character of the earliest Roman metrical forms, which are mainly represented for us by the so-called Saturnians used for epic, funerary epigram, and triumphal inscriptions, remains obscure in the extreme: it is not clear if it is quantitative or accentual, a native Italian form or another Greek import. The most influential recent contribution, Cole 1969, postulates an Indo-European ancestry unmediated, for once, by Greece; but in the survey of recent scholarship in Kruschwitz 2002, a collection of inscribed epigrams which either are or have been supposed to be in Saturnians, the picture remains one of wildly divergent theories, with any consensus effectively restricted to the recognition of a regular word-break, the *caesura Korschiana*, identified 150 years ago (Korsch 1868). The very identification of inscriptions as Saturnian or not becomes more a question of poetic style than metrical form (Kruschwitz 2002, 18–23).

With the comic playwrights Plautus and Terence the inclination of recent scholarship has been to confirm a debt to Greek practice formerly doubted by many scholars. The scholarship of comic metre represents some of the most challenging material in the discipline, and there are fundamental issues at stake, including the very question of what constituted the rhythmical character of the iambo-trochaic metres most prominent in Roman comedy. Anglo-German scholarship, exemplified by Drexler 1967, has typically regarded the quantitative metrical scheme adapted from Greek drama as subordinate to, indeed swamped by, the Roman stress accent, which (it was believed) the playwrights positioned to coincide as regularly as possible with a notional verse beat: thus Roman comic metre was assimilated to the native accentual metres familiar to Anglo-German critics. But both the notion of an inherent beat in iambo-trochaic or other verse (on which topic, see also Stroh 1990) and the concomitant denial that Roman comic verse had the positive quantitative character of its Greek models have been disputed, notably by Questa 1967 (now updated as Questa 2007), Soubiran 1988, and Gratwick 1982: 86–93 and 1993: 40–62 and 248–60, all of which also offer more general guides to comic metrical practice (without necessarily agreeing on all issues). One consequence of this turn in scholarship is the restoration to Plautus of his status as metrical virtuoso and master of *numeri innumeri*, against the aspersions of Horace (*AP* 270–4), for whom admiration of Plautus' *numeri* was a mark of literary primitivism, and whose fundamentally unfair critique of comic metrical practice has exerted an influence over scholarship ever since.

The metres of the only surviving Latin tragedian, Seneca, are comparatively straightforward: the warmest controversy surrounds the colometry of anapaestic passages in his lyric sections, i.e. how the text should be divided into lines, and a lucid introduction to this and other aspects of Senecan metre is provided by Tarrant 1985: 27–33 and 245–9. More detail can be found in Fantham 1982: 104–15 and Zwierlein 1983: 182–230.

Metrical studies all too easily become dissociated from literary criticism. Readers and critics often find the technicality of metrics intimidating, and scholars of metre bear some responsibility for this, tending to treat their discipline as a discrete, abstract exercise only tangentially related to the reading of poetic texts. Special mention should thus be made of a school of French metricologists, their work exemplified by Hellegouarc'h 1964 and Soubiran 1966, who undertook demanding and often seemingly esoteric studies of metrical phenomena which have nevertheless contributed directly to our appreciation of Roman poetic technique.

Finally, one of the most suggestive recent contributions to Roman metrical studies concerns Horace's *Carmen Saeculare*, a unique example of a Roman lyric composition that was set to music. The *Carmen*, like *Odes* 4.2, was in sapphic stanzas, a form which in Sappho's day would have had musical accompaniment, but in Rome was (with this single exception) an exclusively literary form. Rossi 1998 shows how a metrical peculiarity of the *Carmen* is characteristic of verse that was sung rather than read or recited, and his conclusions have wider implications for our understanding of the form of the strictly literary metrical exercises which were the Roman norm.

References

Barchiesi, A. (1994*a*). 'Alcune difficoltà nella carriera di un poeta giambico: Giambo ed elegia nell'Epodo XI', in R. Cortès Tovar and J. C. Fernandez Corte (eds.), *Bimilenario de Horacio* (Salamanca), 127–38.

—— (1994*b*). 'Ultime difficoltà nella carriera di un poeta giambico: L'Epodo XVII', *Atti del Convegno Oraziano*, 3 (Venosa), 205–20.

—— (1997). *The Poet and the Prince: Ovid and Augustan Discourse.* Berkeley and Los Angeles.

Boldrini, S. (1992). *La prosodia e la metrica latina.* Rome. Tr. into German by B. W. Häuptli as *Prosodie und Metrik der Römer* (Stuttgart and Leipzig, 1999).

Cole, T. (1969). 'The Saturnian Verse', *YCS* 21: 1–73.

Coleman, K. M. (1988). *Statius, Silvae IV.* Oxford.

Crusius, F. (1997). *Römische Metrik. Eine Einführung*[8] (rev. H. Rubenbauer). Hildesheim.

Drexler, H. (1967). *Einführung in die römische Metrik.* Darmstadt.

Fantham, E. (1982). *Seneca, 'Troades'.* Princeton.

Friedländer, L. (1886). *M. Valerii Martialis epigrammaton libri* (2 vols.). Leipzig.

Fussell, P. (1979). *Poetic Meter and Poetic Form.* New York.

Gasparov, M. L. (1996). *A History of European Versification.* Oxford.

Gratwick, A. S. (1982). 'Drama', in E. J. Kenney and W. V. Clausen (eds.), *The Cambridge History of Classical Literature*, II: *Latin Literature.* Cambridge. 77–137.

—— (1993). *Plautus, Menaechmi.* Cambridge.

Halporn, J. W. and Ostwald, M. (1962). *Lateinische Metrik.* Göttingen.

—— —— and Rosenmeyer, T. G. (1963). *The Meters of Greek and Latin Poetry.* London.

Hellegourc'h, J. (1964). *Le Monosyllabe dans l'hexamètre latin: essai de métrique verbale.* Paris.

Heyworth, S. J. (1993). 'Horace's *Ibis*: On the Titles, Unity and Contents of the *Epodes*', *PLLS* 7: 85–96.

Hinds, S. (1998). *Allusion and Intertext: Dynamics of Appropriation in Roman Poetry.* Cambridge.

Kennedy, D. F. (1993). *The Arts of Love: Five Studies in the Discourse of Roman Love Elegy.* Cambridge.

Kloss, G. (1998). 'Catulls Brückengedicht (c.17)', *Hermes* 126: 58–79.

Korsch, T. (1868). *De versu Saturnio.* Moscow.

Kruschwitz, P. (2002). *Carmina Saturnia epigraphica.* Stuttgart.

Maas, P. (1929). *Griechische Metrik*[3]. Leipzig. Tr. H. Lloyd-Jones as *Greek Metre* (Oxford, 1962).

Meillet, A. (1923). *Les Origines indo-européennes des mètres grecs.* Paris.

Morgan, Ll. (2000). 'Metre Matters: Some Higher-level Metrical Play in Latin Poetry', *PCPS* 46: 99–120.

Nilsson, N.-A. (1952). *Metrische Stildifferenzen in den Satiren des Horaz.* Uppsala.

Nisbet, R. G. M. and Hubbard, M. (1970). *A Commentary on Horace, Odes Book I.* Oxford.

Nougaret, L. (1948). *Traité de métrique latine classique.* Paris.

Questa, C. (1967). *Introduzione alla metrica di Plauto.* Rome.

—— (2007). *La metrica di Plauto e Terenzio.* Urbino.

Raven, D. S. (1962). *Greek Metre: An Introduction.* London.

—— (1965). *Latin Metre.* London.

Rossi, L. E. (1998). 'Orazio, un lirico greco senza musica', *Seminari romani*, 1: 163–81.

Smolenaars, J. J. L. (2006). 'Ideology and Poetics Along the Via Domitiana: Statius Silv. 4.3', in R. R. Nauta, H.-J. van Dam, and J. J. L. Smolenaars (eds.), *Flavian Poetry*. Leiden. 223–44.

Soubiran, J. (1966). *L'Élision dans la poésie latine*. Paris.

—— (1988). *Essai sur la versification dramatique des Romains*. Paris.

Steinmetz, P. (1964). 'Horaz und Pindar. Hor. carm. IV 2', *Gymnasium*, 71: 1–17.

Stroh, W. (1990). 'Arsis und Thesis, oder: Wie hat man lateinische Verse gesprochen?', in M. von Albrecht and W. Schubert (eds.), *Musik und Dichtung. Neue Forschungsbeiträge, Viktor Pöschl zum 80. Geburtstag gewidmet*. Frankfurt am Main. 87–116.

Tarrant, R. J. (1985). *Seneca's 'Thyestes'*. Atlanta, Ga.

West, M. L. (1982). *Greek Metre*. Oxford.

—— (1987). *Introduction to Greek Metre*. Oxford.

Zwierlein, O. (1983). *Prolegomena zu einer kritischen Ausgabe der Tragödien Senecas*. Mainz.

CHAPTER 11

LITERARY CRITICISM

JOSEPH FARRELL

Most of the literary theorists and critics of classical antiquity who are still studied today—Plato, Aristotle, 'Longinus', and a few others—are Greeks. The Romans, who by reputation came late to literature and lacked a theoretical cast of mind, are not generally accorded a prominent place in the development of this discourse. Indeed, few surviving Roman texts address as their main topic the business of literary criticism, at least as that phrase is understood today. Nevertheless, the critical discussion of literature was a popular social activity among the Roman elite and an obligation of the intelligentsia. For professional writers, even from an early date, an explicitly critical perspective was de rigueur, and almost every genre of Latin literature reflects this fact. But because so much has been lost, we have to infer and extrapolate from fragmentary sources to understand the full range of Roman activity. In addition, since this discourse overlaps with those of grammar, rhetoric, and philosophy, all of which were more explicitly theorized and even better supported as cultural practices, we have to take into account their contributions as well—without, however, allowing them to overwhelm our subject, as they constantly threatened (and threaten) to do.

Most of what we know is told us by creative writers rather than by full-time theorists and critics. Some of this information comes in the form of explicit statements of principle or as criticism of other writers, and some of it has to be inferred from their own writerly practice. What is explicitly stated does not always agree with what can be inferred. It is fitting, then, that Horace's *Ars Poetica* is the closest thing we have to a Roman treatise on literary theory. This work undoubtedly reflects the Roman reception of Greek theory and criticism; but in places, 'refracts' might be a more accurate word. Not a straightforward handbook, but a poetic representation of one, like Vergil's *Georgics* or Ovid's *Ars Amatoria*, it is far from being the straightforward discussion that one might like to have. In some ways, Horace's satires dealing with Lucilius (*Serm.* 1.4, 1.10) and his literary epistles (*Epist.* 2.1, 2.2) offer more useful and representative perspectives. We know of other verse treatises, earlier than Horace's, on different literary subjects. These survive only in fragments, few but useful, and we shall meet them further on. Other authors who make literary criticism an important element of their work include Petronius, whose characters pronounce theoretical manifestoes and recite exemplary compositions of tragedy, epic, Milesian tale, and other genres. Obviously, the irony that permeates the *Satyricon* complicates our ability to draw definite inferences from such material, not to mention rivalries within Nero's court. It is quite possible that Seneca's tragedies are among Petronius' targets. But Seneca too shows himself an acute critic, perhaps especially in his *obiter dicta*, such as the observation that Virgil wrote the *Georgics* not so much to instruct farmers as to delight readers (*Epist.* 86.15)—a point that has been lost on many another critic, ancient and modern.

The only actual treatises on poetics after Aristotle that might be relevant to Roman literature have been found among the essays of the Greek philosopher and poet Philodemus of Gadara. Titles include 'On Poems', 'On Rhetoric', 'On the Good King according to Homer', and others. These essays fill some gaps in our knowledge of Hellenistic theory while presenting a serviceable account of Philodemus' own views. Philodemus (*c.*110–40/35 BCE), who was supported by the senator L. Calpurnius Piso Caesoninus (*cos.* 58, *cens.* 50, father-in-law to Julius Caesar), lived on close terms with Roman intellectuals, including some of the most important poets of the day (see e.g. Armstrong 1995: 44). So the trove of essays found at Herculaneum—not all of them yet published—should have a continuing influence on our understanding of the theoretical underpinnings of Roman literature.

More broadly, theory and criticism were implicated in the rather vaguely defined discourse of 'literary scholarship'. Most of the surviving material relevant to this discourse was produced under the twin banners of Grammar and Rhetoric. Robert Kaster (in this volume) points out that, for Roman scholars, 'a desire to accumulate and categorize plainly outstripped any desire to synthesize'—or, we may add, to theorize or interpret. Much of the scholarship that has survived, such as the commentaries by Donatus, Servius, *et al.*, reflects the perspective of the *grammaticus* (Kaster 1989). These works place a very high value on texts as collections of facts, or as vehicles for communicating facts, about history, mythology, language, and so on. The approach has little to do with the desire to construct a complete and coherent idea of how literature, or a work of literature, is put together or of how to interpret it. Rather, the point is to impart knowledge that might (or might not) shed light on almost any work of literature—or, conversely, knowledge to which any work of literature might provide a convenient point of access. This focus was well suited to elementary education, so that the *ars grammatica* formed a basic part of the educated Roman's conception of literature. Some aspects of grammar, such as the idea of canonical authors (on which more below), did contribute to what we would recognize as literary theory and criticism, but others, such as its remarkably doctrinaire character, are almost antithetical to a mature literary sensibility.

The *ars rhetorica* was for more advanced students, and the theory of rhetoric was both older and better developed than that of grammar. It was rhetoric that supplied much of what passes, in the surviving evidence, for literary theory by providing a rationale for producing as well as for judging actual literary performances (see Riggsby on 'Rhetoric as the Art of Discourse' in this volume). According to this rationale, all texts are in principle scripts for *viva voce* performance, and are judged accordingly. Today we must remind ourselves just how important this aspect was for Roman readers: despite a healthy book trade and a readership that extended throughout the empire, the performance of literature remained a crucial social institution, and the ability to perform oneself and to judge the performance of others was a defining mark of learning, sensibility, and taste (Johnson 2000). For this reason, passages like the one in Quintilian (*IO* 11.36–8) that explains how to deliver properly the opening lines of the *Aeneid*, are valuable, not just as pieces of a 'how-to' manual, but as identifying the qualities that make this very familiar passage an effective performance vehicle.

Still, rhetoric itself cannot account for all aspects of literary criticism that were of interest to Roman writers and readers or that are of interest to us. The point needs making because quite a few modern scholars have made the mistake of assuming that ancient rhetoric does indeed tell the modern reader all that is needed about creating and interpreting ancient literature. The importance of our grammatical and rhetorical sources is real, but they must not be allowed to obscure the ancient discourse of literary theory and criticism per se, to which we now turn.

From the beginning Roman writers took a strong interest in evaluative criticism, canon formation, philology, and literary history. The distinct outlines of a critical consciousness appear in our earliest surviving literature. For Livius Andronicus, translating Homer's *Odyssey* was an activity that required a philological approach to poetic language of the sort that thrived in the Library of Alexandria (Mariotti 1952/1985). For Naevius, a passage such as the enigmatic Gigantomachy ecphrasis (fr. 19 Morel–Buechner 1982) seems indebted to allegorical exegesis in the style of the Pergamene critics, an important critical tradition that has only recently come to be properly appreciated (Lamberton 1989; Struck 2004). Plautus identified and discussed his Greek sources in the prologues to at least six of his comedies, and Terence's prologues are a rich and sophisticated source of critical ideas and vocabulary. The tragic poet L. Accius (170–*c.*86 BCE) composed a work, probably in prose, called *Didascalica* (conventionally 'production notices', but the root meaning of 'instructional materials' may come into play) in at least nine books on (*inter alia*) the Athenian and the Roman theater (frr. in Morel and Buechner 1982). Another poem, of indeterminate length, written by one Volcacius Sedigitus (*c.*100 BCE), was entitled 'On Poets' (*De Poetis*: Gellius, *NA* 15.24). Our sources for the first 150 years of Latin literature are extremely spotty; but it is therefore remarkable how much of the material that survives has to do with literary theory, history, and criticism.

The impulses behind this activity are of course Hellenistic: the first Latin literature that is visible to us bears an unmistakably Greek stamp. For us this is a fact. For the Romans it may not have been so: they could easily have had, and probably did have, access to earlier texts that appeared to them innocent of Greek influence. But the idea that the Romans got all of their literature from Greece became received wisdom. It also became a principle to which the literary critic might appeal. Ennius staked a claim to the superiority of his *Annales* over the *Bellum Poenicum* of Naevius on the fact that Naevius composed in uncouth Italic Saturnians, while Ennius had adapted the Homeric hexameter to Latin (*Ann.* frr. 206–12 Skutsch). Ennius acted here as a highly interested critic, to be sure. Nevertheless, his criticism of Naevius reflected both theoretical and practical concerns, and it inaugurated a long tradition of critical and apologetic interventions. The idea that Latin literature derives from Greek and is to be measured against Greek became a basic element of Roman literary thought. For Horace, in fact, the idea actually appears as an injunction: 'look to your Greek models, night and day' (*AP* 268–9).

In a certain sense, it is almost as if the overriding theoretical perspective regarded Latin literature not only as deriving from Greek, but almost as a general effort to convert Greek literature, or the best of it, into Latin. A tendency, if not a rule, that informed this effort was that any Greek work needed to be latinized only once. After Livius' *Odusia* no one really needed to do the job again: in fact, a later version in hexameters survives (in a few lines) only because it came to travel under Livius' name. Terence defends himself against the charge, real or fictive, of adapting Greek plays that others had already made into Latin versions. If two contemporaries simultaneously took on similar projects, it would be for the reading public to decide between them. Cicero, writing to his brother about Lucretius' poem, contrasts it favourably with the (otherwise unknown) *Empedoclea* of one Sallustius, a text that he implies he could not finish reading (*Q. Fr.* 2.9.4). It may be that part of Cicero's evaluation concerns which poem is the better rendition of Empedocles for a Roman audience (Sedley 1998: 1–34). In his *Brutus* Cicero proceeds systematically along these lines, comparing the defining characteristics of individual Roman orators to those of specific Greek predecessors. He does not say that the Roman speakers had deliberately modelled themselves on their Greek 'counterparts', as Lucretius and Sallustius had done. Instead his comparisons, like Plutarch's *syncrises*, stand purely as acts of interpretation. It could be that an unspoken system of this sort informed the way in which the Augustan poets chose their projects, as if the various Greek authors representing the different genres were arranged on a grid consisting of cells or slots (Conte 1994: 116–17)—or, more concretely, of library shelves (Horsfall

1993)—that remained available to all comers until successfully filled by a Roman equivalent. Thus Virgil called his *Eclogues* 'Syracusan' or 'Sicilian' (= Theocritean) and his *Georgics* 'Ascraean' (= Hesiodic), Propertius called himself 'the Roman Callimachus', and Horace boasted that he was the first to have shown Parian (= Archilochean) iambs to the Latin people (*Epist.* 1.19.23–4) and that he followed this achievement in Aeolian (= Sapphic and Alcaic) lyric.

By the later Augustan period this conceit seems to have run its course. The same Horace who invokes it seriously was also capable of mocking it (*Epist.* 2.2.99–100). At about this same time we encounter claims by this or that author that he deserves to stand alongside earlier Roman as well as Greek writers. In this case there is less a question of latinizing some Greek exemplar than of enriching the genre itself by whatever means. This attitude, too, had earlier roots. In a passage quoted by Gellius (*NA* 15.24), the aforementioned Volcacius Sedigitus lists Rome's ten best comic poets in descending order according to his judgement, claiming that it is a controversial matter on which many have expressed different opinions (fr. 1 Courtney). He does not include everyone who wrote comedies: Livius Andonicus, for instance, is not named; Ennius appears in last place 'out of respect for his antiquity'. It seems obvious that Volcacius, in addition to making relative value judgements, is also making the absolute judgement of which Roman comic poets belong in the canon. He makes no comparison here between Greek and Roman poets, nor do we know whether he promulgated canons for genres other than comedy, or whether his was the first Roman exercise in canon formation. But the critical impulse behind his work, and its Hellenistic inspiration, are impressive. Volcacius followed the practice of Greek critics by ranking specific poets as the most gifted exponents of a particular genre, the ones who set the standard by which others would be judged. Poets like Horace (*Carm.* 3.30), Propertius (2.34), and Ovid (*Tr.* 4.10) would later assert that their achievements had earned them the right to be numbered with writers who excelled in their respective genres. At the end of the Flavian period Quintilian gave this sort of criticism definitive form, adding to the traditional Greek canon (*IO* 10.1.46–84) his own judgements concerning the Romans (1.85–131). All that was left was for the idea of 'classic' authors to crystallize, as it had done by the time of Marcus Aurelius. We will return to this idea below.

In Volcacius' day the process of Roman canon formation was very much in flux; by the time of Quintilian it was pretty well fixed. For Imperial poets this meant having to reckon with towering Roman as well as Greek predecessors. It was no longer possible to refer with disdain, as Ennius had done, to the insufficiently Hellenized efforts of the past, nor was it necessary to defend an updated treatment of a familiar Greek work. Instead, any new work had to vie with the most esteemed products of earlier Greek and Latin literature.

Perhaps because Roman writers and critics constantly measured their own literature against the standards first of earlier exemplars, they also had a reasonably well-developed consciousness of literary history. The second-century poet and critic Porcius Licinus (fr. 1 Courtney, *apud* Gellium *NA* 17.21.44) is the earliest writer to date the arrival of literature at Rome:

> With the Second Punic War, the Muse with winged gait
> made war against Romulus' wild tribe.

Latin literature is thus not merely a product of Hellenism, but is to be numbered among the manubial spoils taken during the conquest of a Mediterranean empire. Horace, who in one famous passage (*Epist.* 2.1.156–62) echoed Porcius' conceit, boasted in another of being first 'to have brought home in triumph' (*deduxisse*) to Italy the poetry of Sappho and Alcaeus (*Carm.* 3.30.13–14; cf. *Epist.* 1.19.26–33). The imagery of conquest is not accidental. It may allude to the original conclusion (lost but plausibly conjectured: Skutsch 1985: 6, 553–63) of Ennius' *Annales*, in which the poet may have likened his own conquest of the Greek Muses to that of his patron, the Roman general Fulvius Nobilior, who conquered Ambracia and imported from there Rome's first cult of the Muses. Porcius and Horace speak for the majority, though, in linking Rome's acquisition of Greek literary culture to the prior conquest of Carthage, Rome's only important rival as a world empire.

In any event, Roman critics traced the beginnings of their literature not to the mists of time, but to datable events with definite military and political significance. As their chronological expertise improved, so did their grasp of literary history. Cicero, again in the *Brutus*, developed explicitly the idea of periodization along with that of relativism in literary evaluation. In doing so, he admitted that, over time, the best practitioners of a given art will surpass the best of their forerunners. But he declared that it would be wrong to condemn all earlier works as lacking the polish of the contemporary. Instead, the connoisseur should understand the character of each generation and judge by that standard. The idea is not original, but is borrowed from the history of art: Cicero refers to Greek sculptors like Myron and Polyclitus, each with his own excellence and each the best of his own generation (*Brutus* 70, 75).

This is a sophisticated view of the matter and a clear advance on the prevailing tendency of Greek critics to divide literary history into 'Homer' and 'later writers'. But it is not clear how widely accepted the more advanced view was. Livy, in one of the most frustrating passages of his history (27.37.1), informs us of Livius Andronicus' commission to compose a hymn to Juno during a crisis in the Second Punic War, but he explicitly refuses to quote the text because of its stylistic crudity. Cicero, at least, upheld his relativistic theory in his practical criticism, declaring his admiration for Ennius against the opinion of the literary avant garde (*Tusc.* 3.45), even though his own poetry has on the whole more in common with the avant garde than with Ennius (Townend 1965). Horace occupies a kind of middle ground: he dismisses his predecessor Lucilius as merely a facile but careless versifier (*Serm.* 1.4.6–14), but admits that, had he lived in Horace's own day, Lucilius would have observed a much higher standard (*Serm.* 1.10.64–74).

The notion of periodization appears in other guises as well. In Tacitus' *Dialogus de Oratoribus* the dividing-line is the beginning of the Principate, and the great question is whether oratory has maintained the social importance and the artistic standard that it had achieved by the end of the Republic. Until then, important issues were decided by the power of oratory in a climate of free speech; afterwards, with no scope for meaningful action, oratory went into severe decline. Less pessimistically, Tacitus hails Trajan's accession as the dawn of a new era in political and cultural life (*Agr.* 1–3). Tacitus' own literary career and that of his friend Pliny do in fact begin at this time, and the following century witnesses a distinctive literary culture, especially in prose but to a lesser extent in poetry as well, before the dislocations of the third century have their effect. What is perhaps most characteristic about second-century literature is precisely its literary-critical and historical consciousness, which is characterized by a strong component of archaizing and anti-classical revisionism (Holford-Strevens 2003: 193–225).

Roman criticism, then, regarded Roman literature as deriving from Greek, and judged works of Roman literature largely on their success in adapting specific Greek models. It borrowed the Hellenistic idea of the canon (Nicolai 1991) and fashioned a Roman canon on the model of the Greek one (Citroni 2005). But on what criteria did Roman critics base their judgements that a specific effort was successful or not?

It is possible to distinguish between formalist and ethical criteria in Roman criticism, even if ultimately the distinction is artificial, because the two strands are so thoroughly intertwined. The grammatical and rhetorical category of 'style' is a basic formal characteristic; and yet, it is notable that the stylistic choices of writers like Sallust and Tacitus go closely with a distinct ethical persona, that of the highly judgemental, disappointed idealist. By the same token, when Horace criticizes Lucilius' style he makes the ethical or even moral observation that Lucilius simply shrank from the sheer effort involved in writing well (*Serm.* 1.4.32–3). Nevertheless, formal and ethical categories correspond approximately to two dominant concerns of modern theory and criticism, which makes them, for us, useful heuristic categories.

From everything that has been said so far, it is clear that formal categories meant a lot to Roman critics. Probably the most imposing of these categories was that of genre; and it is also one of the most instructive. We cannot even name an ancient work that is likely to have contained a well-developed theory of genres. Nevertheless, genres were used constantly to categorize and evaluate literature—as we have already seen in the case of canon formation. There as elsewhere, the simplest marker of any genre is metrical. Epic poems were composed as a succession of dactylic hexameter lines (each of them called *epos* in Greek), and epic poets composed such poems. Sub-genres were recognized as well, and these might differ sharply from one another. Horace tells us that Varius was the unrivalled master of epic in the 'powerful' (*forte, acer*) mode, while Virgil excelled in the 'gentle' (*molle atque facetum*) mode (*Serm.* 1.10.43–5, written after the *Eclogues* had appeared but before the *Georgics* had been made public or the *Aeneid* had begun to take shape). To modern readers, the phrase 'pastoral epic' seems oxymoronic, because to us epic means heroic, and pastoral and heroic poetry seem like entirely different genres. We recognize the fact that both happen to be written in the 'epic' metre as technically true, but relatively unimportant. To Roman critics, though, pastoral and heroic epic were kindred sub-genres, distinguished by style and content, but related by a common metre. Horace's hexameter poetry represents a third style, distinct from those of pastoral or heroic epic and veering in the directions of conversation and epistolography. But Horace begs the question of whether his hexameter compositions are really poetry at all (*Serm.* 1.4.39–65), muddying the waters still further.

At any rate, metre and subject-matter were in theory interrelated, constitutive elements of genre, and genres remained true to themselves. Horace, again, states as much with great clarity in the *Ars Poetica* (73–85), and the principle is echoed over and over by the poets. This, however, is where prescriptive statements come into conflict with actual practice. It is not surprising that Roman poets transgress the boundaries of genre, because no literary work of art can be permanently and exclusively assigned to any single genre (e.g. Morson 1988). Roman literature is no different from any other in this respect. What is perhaps different is that Roman writers, in their self-reflexive moments, embrace the prescriptions of theorists and the strictures of critics, and suppose that their own works ought to behave as perfect specimens of one single genre. But despite their guilty consciences, they constantly flout these rules to produce works that are, from a generic point of view, not merely hybrid but brilliantly and provocatively so.

Ovid is the champion of this schizophrenic pose. He constantly 'worries' (when he is not actually boasting) about forcing his elegies to do what they were never meant to do. This is amusing in itself, since elegy was to begin with a highly malleable genre without the definite pedigree of genres like epic, tragedy, and comedy, so that it had always done unprecedented things. But Ovid took this process to great lengths, and his expressions of concern that he is transgressing the boundaries of genre seem intended to advertise the fact (Farrell 2003). Feigned generic concern shows up in epic as well, where a succession of poets fret over their decisions to introduce prominent female characters into this most masculine of genres—in spite of the fact that women like Helen and Penelope had been indispensible 'elements' of the genre since its Homeric beginnings (Hinds 2000). In both these cases, poets acting as critics espouse a theory of genre that is widely at variance with their usual practice, advancing this theory in a spirit of apparent self-reprehension, and they do it with straight faces. These are passages of creative and critical sophistication, and they force us to acknowledge the existence of an implied theoretical discourse on genre more advanced than anything found in any surviving ancient treatise.

It is difficult to say what if any influence these sophistications had on those who actually determined the Roman literary canon. It could be meaningful that Quintilian, when evaluating Ovid as an elegist, ranks him (and Cornelius Gallus, who 'founded' the genre) behind Tibullus and Propertius, finding him 'too frivolous' (just as he finds Gallus 'too dour', *IO* 10.1.93). Whether Quintilian is thinking only of the *Amores*, which are comparable to the elegies of Tibullus and Propertius, or whether Ovid's frivolity encompasses the generic experimentation embodied in the *Ars Amatoria*, the *Heroides*, the *Fasti*, the exile poetry, and other works, we cannot say. It could also be meaningful that the Ovidian work that Quintilian most admires is his generically unambiguous tragedy, the *Medea*, and that he speaks only in passing of Ovid's masterpiece, the unclassifiable *Metamorphoses*.

Quintilian's judgement on Ovid's elegies takes us from formal to ethical concerns: the critic ranks the elegist as he does not because his poems were formally imperfect, but because they were too silly. This is as if to say, they are definitely elegies (their metre tells us that much), but they are not sufficiently respectful of generic decorum. Just as in Horace's judgement on Lucilius, ethical concerns are hard to separate from formal ones. Many of the ideas involved could be represented in terms of dichotomies that pose problems rather then stating simple truths. These include the ideas of the pleasing and the useful (*dulce*, *utile*: Horace, *AP* 343) and the competing roles of genius and artistry (*ingenium*, *ars*: Cicero, *Q. Fr.* 2.9.4; Ovid, *Am.* 1.15.13–14, 19; cf. *Tr.* 2.424) in producing literature. Such concerns had of course been an important part of the earliest Greek literary theory and criticism. They are rooted in the idea that a writer's work is a faithful reflection of his character. For Plato and Aristotle this point is so fundamental that they cannot imagine the same writer being successful in both tragedy and comedy. By Hellenistic times versatile poets like Callimachus had disproved this theory many times over, and Roman poets from Livius onward followed their lead (Farrell 2002). Here especially theory failed to keep pace with practice: Quintilian remembers Callimachus simply as an elegist (*IO* 10.1.58), and the biographies of Roman poets, like those of the Greeks, tend to treat a writer's life and his work as two sides of the same coin. A number of poets, in different ways, insist that the work is not an accurate reflection of the life. Catullus chides Furius and Aurelius for supposing that his risqué themes bespeak a debauched life (poem 16). Racy Martial (*Epigr.* 1.35) and prudish Pliny (*Epist.* 4.14.4) both cite this poem to ward off criticism, as does Apuleius when defending himself in court (*Apol.* 11). To a casual reader, these passages outline a simple commonplace; but in the broader context of Roman literature and social life, they take on a more pointed significance. And, in fact, with a lot at stake Ovid makes the ethical and moral gap between his earlier work and the life that he has actually lived into a major theme of his exile poetry.

In recent years literary criticism has increasingly abandoned the notion that the critic's job is to distinguish better literature from worse and to explain the difference between the two. In contrast, ancient criticism always involved value judgements and was seldom if ever a matter of disinterested description. Nevertheless, the judgements that went into producing the canonical literature of antiquity were deeply implicated in a powerful social system, the workings of which have left a far clearer mark on the classical literature that has survived, than have any abstract principles of literary excellence.

Traditionally, the very idea of 'classical literature' assumed that all works so labelled met certain standards of excellence. But it is always worth remembering that this idea is in origin a metaphor based on the Roman imperial tax code, and that the classic authors are, by the terms of the metaphor, those who find themselves in a high bracket (M. Cornelius Fronto, *apud* Gellium, *NA* 19.8.5; Curtius 1948, tr. 1953: 249–50; Citroni 2006: 204–11). The socio-political nature of this metaphor is the point. In antiquity no less than today, a writer's reputation depended on many factors that had nothing to do with literary criticism as such. In the first place, Roman writers of all periods depended on networks of social relations to find an audience (Starr 1987; White 1993). For most of the Republic, poets tended to be men of lower social status who depended heavily on the sponsorship of the socially powerful. In the late Republic, when men of more secure position began devoting themselves to poetry, they generally continued attaching themselves more or less closely to this or that patron. Writers of prose tended to be members of the elite; therefore, instead of looking to patrons, they carefully adopted distinctive positions with respect to other elite writers, for instance, in choosing the addressees of individual works, in a way that mirrors the alliances that they were constantly forming and then either nurturing or dissolving in their wider social and political lives (Habinek 1998: 34–68). With the rise of the Principate, all writers found themselves in a position of undeniable inferiority to one all-powerful patron, and state sponsorship became the dominant factor in establishing a writer's reputation. It is true that Rome was full of declaimers and reciters who might attract a following, and Martial, for instance, could boastfully name specific bookshops that carried his own best-sellers (*Epigr.* 1.2, 4.72, 5.16, 11.3). Moreover, Ovid, even though he complains in his exile poems of being excluded from the Palatine Library (e.g. *Tr.* 3.1), nevertheless enjoyed popularity in his lifetime and a spectacular *Nachleben.* But neither Martial nor any other author earned money from the sale of his works, and Martial's success really derives from being sponsored by the Flavian dynasty, just as his eclipse dates from the succession of Nerva. As for Ovid, having been the most celebrated poet in Rome for most of his life was a historical fact that his fall from grace could not undo. In reality, his career is an easily explained exception to an iron rule, and the literate public, even if it played a role in bringing a writer to the notice of the powerful, played a larger one in following the lead and broadcasting the decisions of the patron class.

The question, then, is how literary patrons decided which writers to sponsor and which to leave in eternal obscurity. Some, like Maecenas, were no doubt men of taste and discernment, but we know little about the principles by which he and others discerned good poets from bad. Indeed, Horace, who tells us most of what we know about this process (*Serm.* 1.6), says practically nothing about aesthetic criteria. Instead, he speaks of social and, again, ethical and even moral categories as the foundation of Maecenas' little sodality. Horace does represent his powerful friend as relying on the advice of others—in his own case, of Virgil and Varius—who would presumably be well qualified to recommend a man on the basis of his talent as well as his character. But while Horace does have something to say about his own literary ideals, he does not explicitly ascribe them to Maecenas or to anyone else, preferring to characterize his relationship with his patron and with these other men of letters as purely social and personal, rather than essentially literary.

Further reading

There exist several surveys of ancient literary criticism. Inevitably and understandably, these tend to concentrate on surviving prose treatises, most of which were written in Greek (even if, like the treatise 'On the Sublime' wrongly ascribed to Longinus, they were addressed to a Roman audience) and concern themselves mainly with grammatical and rhetorical categories. These surveys remain helpful resources for students who wish to situate the field of literary theory and criticism within the broader discourses of 'literary scholarship'. They include Grube 1965, Russell 1972, and Kennedy 1989. Russell 1996 is also useful and compendious. Russell and Winterbottom 1972 contains a selection of sources in English translation. Laird 2006 gives a different selection in new translations and relates Greek and Roman criticism and theory to later developments. For the evidence and interpretation of the theoretical foundations that are implied by the imaginative and the critical work of Roman poets, see Schwindt *et al.* 2001.

References

Armstrong, D. (1995). 'The Impossibility of Metathesis: Philodemus and Lucretius on Form and Content in Poetry', in D. Obbink (ed.), *Philodemus on Poetry: Poetic Theory in Lucretius, Philodemus, and Horace.* Oxford.

Citroni, M. (2005). 'The Concept of the Classical and the Canons of Model Authors in Roman Literature', in J. Porter (ed.), *Classical Pasts: The Classical Traditions of Greece and Rome.* Princeton. 204–34.

Conte, G. B. (1994). *Genres and Readers: Lucretius, Love Elegy, Pliny's Encyclopedia*, tr. J. Solodow, rev. D. Fowler and G. W. Most. Baltimore.

Courtney, E. (1993), *The Fragmentary Latin Poets.* Oxford. Repr. with corrections, Oxford, 2003.

Curtius, E. R. (1948; tr. 1953). *European Literature in the Latin Middle Ages*, tr. W. Trask. New York.

Farrell, J. (2002). 'Greek Lives and Roman Careers', in F. de Armas and P. Cheney (eds.), *Literary and Artistic Careers from Antiquity to the Renaissance*. Toronto. 24–46.

—— (2003). 'Classical Genre in Theory and Practice', in R. Cohen and H. White (eds.), *Theorizing Genres II, New Literary History*, 34/3: 383–408.

Grube, G. M. A. (1965). *The Greek and Roman Critics*. Toronto.

Habinek, T. (1998). *The Politics of Latin Literature: Writing, Identity, and Empire in Ancient Rome*. Princeton.

Hinds, S. (2000). 'Essential Epic: Genre and Gender from Macer to Statius', in M. Depew and D. Obbink (eds.), *Matrices of Genre: Authors, Canons, and Society*. Cambridge, Mass. 221–44.

Holford-Strevens, L. (2003). *Aulus Gellius: An Antonine Scholar and his Achievement*. Rev. edn. Oxford.

Horsfall, N. (2003). 'Empty Shelves on the Palatine?', *Greece & Rome*, 40: 58–67.

Johnson, W. (2000). 'Toward a Sociology of Reading in Classical Antiquity', *AJP* 121: 593–627.

Kaster, R. (1989). *Guardians of Language: The Grammarian and Society in Late Antiquity*. Berkeley.

Kennedy, G. A. (ed.) (1989). 'Classical Criticism', in *The Cambridge History of Literary Criticism*, vol. 1. Cambridge.

Laird, A. (ed.) (2006). *Ancient Literary Criticism*. Oxford.

Lamberton, R. (1989). *Homer the Theologian: Neoplatonist Allegorical Reading and the Growth of the Epic Tradition*. Berkeley.

Mariotti, S. (1952). *Livio Andronico e la traduzione artistica. Saggio critico ed edizione dei frammenti dell'* Odyssea. Urbino. Repr. 1985.

Morel, W. and Buechner, C. (1982). *Fragmenta Poetarum Latinorum*. Leipzig.

Morson, G. S. (1988). *The Boundaries of Genre*. Chicago.

Nicolai, R. (1991). *La storiografia nell'educazione antica*. Pisa.

Russell, D. A. (1972). *Criticism in Antiquity*. Oxford.

—— (1996). 'Literary Criticism in Antiquity', in S. Hornblower and A. Spawforth (eds.), *The Oxford Classical Dictionary*.[3] Oxford.

—— and Winterbottom, M. (1972). *Ancient Literary Criticism*. Oxford.

Schwindt, J. *et al.* (2003). *L'Histoire littéraire immanente dans la poésie latine. Huit exposés suivis de discussions*. Introduction by E. A. Schmidt. Fondations Hardt Entretiens 49. Geneva.

Sedley, D. (1998). *Lucretius and the Transformation of Greek Wisdom*. Cambridge.

Skutsch, O. (1985). *The Annals of Quintus Ennius*. Oxford.

Starr, R. (1987). 'The Circulation of Literary Texts in the Roman World', *CQ* 37: 213–23.

Struck, P. (2004). *The Birth of the Symbol: Ancient Readers at the Limits of their Texts*. Princeton.

Townend, G. (1965). 'The Poems', in T. A. Dorey (ed.), *Cicero*. New York.

White, P. (1993). *Promised Verse: Poets in the Society of Augustan Rome*. Cambridge, Mass.

CHAPTER 12

TRANSLATION

SUSANNA BRAUND

TRANSLATION has a crucial role in the democratization of knowledge. Systems of thought and belief ranging from science to religion have often depended on translation for their effective transmission. For students of Roman antiquity, translation figures in two arenas. First, it was a Roman cultural activity from the third century BCE onwards, when a Romanized Greek called Livius Andronicus, probably enslaved by the Romans and then freed, 'turned' (the Latin verb is *uortere*) Greek epic and drama into Latin and thus inaugurated Latin literature with his versions of Homer's *Odyssey* and Greek drama. Livius' respectful imitation soon modulates into imperialistic appropriation of Greek culture when in the 50s BCE Catullus translates poems by Sappho (Poem 51) and Callimachus (Poem 66) and when the Hellenistic poet Aratus' didactic poem on astronomy and meteorology is translated into Latin by Varro Atacinus and Cicero in the late Republic, by Germanicus, nephew and heir to the emperor Tiberius, in the early Principate, and by Avienus in the mid-fourth century CE. Secondly, translation from Latin has extended the influence of Latin literature throughout Europe and beyond. My chapter will deal with the second manifestation of translation—translation from Latin into various vernaculars. I shall suggest that the importance of translation extends beyond the aesthetic sphere into the social, political, moral, and even economic spheres.

The complexities of translation often go under-appreciated from both directions. People with little knowledge of foreign languages often assume that translation operates on a word-for-word basis—at least until their hand-held automatic translation gadget lets them down in a crisis by translating 'he is losing blood' as 'il est sang perdant' (source: http://babelfish.altavista.digital.com/cgi-bin/).

Similarly skewed is the Pepsi slogan 'Come alive with the Pepsi Generation', which in Taiwan becomes 'Pepsi will bring your ancestors back from the dead' (source: http://www.ojohaven.com/fun/translation.funnies.html). In the world of scholarship, at least from the time of Matthew Arnold on, translation has often been dismissed as a second-class activity by elitists, who would doubtless style themselves purists. It is only ten years ago, in fact, that the British Academy, the major funding agency for the humanities in the United Kingdom, altered its rule that no funding could be awarded to projects involving translation. This essay will advocate appreciation of translation from Latin as just one manifestation of a wider phenomenon that could be a huge force for good. In a world in which the exponential increase in acts of communication is by no means matched by an increase in mutual understanding, I view it as a moral imperative that we all try better to understand one another's cultures and ideologies. Translation can be the first step in that direction.

The story of translation from Latin is long and complex. In my highly selective study I shall explore explicit and implicit attitudes revealed by the process of translating from Latin and towards the activity of translating from Latin. Though these attitudes actually operate along a spectrum, they are often conceived by theorists as polarities between, for example, servility and freedom (thus Alexander Tytler in his 1791 *Essay on the Principles of Translation* (London), 50–7), between moving the reader towards the writer or vice versa (Friedrich Schleiermacher, 'On the Different Methods of Translating', tr. Waltraud Bartscht in *Theories of Translation*, ed. R. Schulte and J. Biguenet (Chicago, 1992), 36–54); between formal and dynamic equivalence (Eugene Nida, 'Toward a Science of Translating' (Leiden, 1964), 156–71), and between domestication and foreignizing (Lawrence Venuti, *The Translator's Invisibility* (London, 1995), 17–39). I shall start by using a diachronic framework to explore the formation and re-formation of the canon of Latin texts along with shifting patterns in translation activity, and I shall then examine the emergence during the nineteenth and twentieth centuries of comprehensive series of translations from Latin and Greek aimed at a growing 'middlebrow' audience. I shall use three specific case studies to confront the challenges of translating from Latin. Finally, in the interactive spirit of our times, I shall consider a challenge that I here pose to the reader, namely, how you would turn the English concept 'culture' into Latin. That question takes us to a final, crucial question: what, exactly, is 'culture' and how does translation relate to culture?

The patterns of translation of Latin texts into European vernaculars immediately challenge any preconceptions we might have about the canonical status of particular authors and works. We are fortunate that several scholars have investigated the translation histories of Latin texts into Italian, Spanish, English, French, German, and other European languages. In what follows I am especially indebted to the catalogue of translations prior to 1600 in Robert Bolgar's *The Classical Heritage and its Beneficiaries* (Cambridge, 1954). The Latin prose texts translated before the advent of printing in the mid-fifteenth century barely match our contemporary lists of important items. Cicero's three Caesarian speeches (*Pro Marcello*, *Pro Ligario*, and *Pro Deiotaro*) were translated into Italian around 1290; Vegetius' *De Re Militari* was translated into French around 1300; Valerius Maximus' *Memorabilia* into German in 1369 (and printed in 1489); and Suetonius' *Vitae* into French around 1381. There were fourteenth-century translations of part of Cicero's *De Inventione* into Italian and of *Rhetorica ad Herennium* and *De Inventione* into Spanish. Some of Seneca's prose works were translated into French in 1408 by the aptly named pioneering humanist Laurent de Premierfait. Palladius' *De Re Rustica* was translated into English around 1420 and Curtius' *De Rebus Gestis Alexandri* into Italian in 1438 (and printed forty years later). Around 1430 Christine de Pisan translated Frontinus' *Strategemata*, Vegetius, and parts of Valerius Maximus into French, in her *Le Livre des fais d'armes et de chevalerie*, and this was the source of William Caxton's English translation of Frontinus, printed in 1489.

The most notable item in Bolgar's catalogue is Boethius' *De Consolatione Philosophiae*, which is perhaps not surprising, given its enormous popularity during the Middle Ages. This philosophical dialogue between the personification of Philosophy and Boethius himself, written in prison, was translated into English by Alfred the Great around 900, into German by Notker Labeo around 1000, into French by Jean de Meun around 1300, into Italian by Alberto of Florence in 1332, into English by Geoffrey Chaucer around 1380, into Catalan around 1360, and into English by Queen Elizabeth I in 1593. It is said to have been translated into more European languages than any other book except the Bible.

These patterns of translation imply a positive valuation of the works selected, whether for practical purposes, in the case of the military and rhetorical treatises, or for moral purposes, in the case of the philosophical and poetic works. At the same time, it is striking that the enduring staples of the school curriculum, such as Terence and Virgil, were translated more rarely, and not until after the advent of printing. For example, the first complete translation of the *Aeneid* into English was Gavin Douglas's 1513 translation into Scots, published 1553; the first English translation of the complete works of Terence, by Richard Bernard, dates from 1598. There may have been a presumption that anyone who needed to could read these works in Latin. But in the case of the works that were made more widely available through translations, it is worth pondering the reasons for the selection. Spanish translators of Seneca were presumably at least partly inspired by national pride. In France, Christine de Pisan translated to make a living after she was widowed; it will have been crucial for her to choose texts for which there was a market. In the case of Caxton's Frontinus, we know he worked at the instruction of King Henry VII, who lent Caxton the manuscript from which the translation was done. While the reasons and audiences for translators' efforts and activities must vary, the selection of particular Latin texts for translation at any era always opens a fascinating window onto intellectual, moral, religious, social, or political history. We should ask ourselves who was translating what, when, why, how, and for whom.

A glance at some of the landmarks of translation from Latin into English during the sixteenth to twentieth centuries provides an economical way of indicating diachronic shifts in taste and judgement. One of the earliest published translations from Latin into English is William Adlington's lively 1566 version of Apuleius, *The Golden Asse*. The year 1567 was highly signifiant for the reception of Ovid's poetry, with the publication of Arthur Golding's *Metamorphosis* and of George Turbervile's *Heroycall Epistles*, swiftly followed by *Ibis* (1569) and *Tristia* (1572), all in fourteeners. Another landmark was Thomas Newton's collected publication in 1581 of Seneca's *Tenne Tragedies*, also in fourteeners. In the 1590s Christopher Marlowe initiated deployment of the more versatile heroic couplet, with versions of Ovid's *Amores* and his translation of the first book of Lucan, written in 1593, the year of his death, and published in 1600. George Sandys updated Ovid's *Metamorphoses* into heroic couplets in 1626. Thomas Creech's translation of Lucretius appeared in 1682 to a warm reception, and John Milton turned his attention to Horace's *Odes* in the 1650s. But the translation event of the seventeenth century was John Dryden's *Aeneis*, which appeared in 1697 and which remains the dominant translation in English, despite competition from C. D. Lewis (1952), Mandelbaum (1971), Fitzgerald (1983), Lombardo (2005), and now Ahl (2007) and Ruden (2008). The impact of Nicholas Rowe's translation of Lucan, published in 1719 and much admired by Samuel Johnson, seems to have deterred others from attempting the task, until Robert Graves's disdainful effort for Penguin Classics in 1956 (of which more below). Highlights of the eighteenth century are Alexander Pope's *Imitations of Horace*, composed during the 1730s, and Samuel Johnson's transmutations of Juvenal's *Satires*, 3 and 10, 'London' (1738) and 'The Vanity of Human Wishes' (1748). From the nineteenth century the stand-out is John Conington's 1863 translation of Horace's *Odes*; of the many Victorian translations of Tacitus my personal favourite is that of Church and Brodribb, published by Macmillan in London in a series of editions between 1864 and 1877. The twentieth century saw an explosion of translation activity by scholars as well as poets; from the latter group I select for mention Ezra Pound's *Homage to Sextus Propertius* (1919), Janet Lembke's translations of the fragments of early Latin literature in her *Bronze and Iron* (Berkeley, 1973), Ted Hughes's *Tales from Ovid* (London, 1997); from the former, Peter Green's lively 1967 Juvenal (better than his more academic 1998 revision) stands out, as do Guy Lee's translations of *Eclogues* (1980) and especially his *Amores* (1968). Very welcome is the 2000 Loeb Classical Library edition of Valerius Maximus' *Facta et Dicta Memorabilia* by D. R. Shackleton Bailey; despite the work's popularity at earlier periods, attested by the huge number of early manuscripts and by trecento translations into French, Italian, Sicilian, Castilian, and Catalan (see *Texts and Transmission: A Survey of the Latin Classics*, ed. L. D. Reynolds (Oxford, 1983), 430), this is the first complete translation into English. Although it is too soon to see what the special contribution of the early twenty-first century is, Amy Richlin's rap versions of Plautus, whereby *Persa* becomes *Iran*

Man—in *Rome and the Mysterious Orient* (Berkeley, 2005)—seem to me to take translation of comedy to an altogether higher plane.

To offer this list of greatest hits highlights different priorities from our own—for example, Ovid's *Heroides* are currently little read—but obscures the diachronic shifts in interest in particular authors, which form patterns that may be scrutinized for their cultural significance. Take as an example the translation histories of Seneca's tragedies and Lucan's epic poem. The first English translations of Seneca's tragedies appeared from 1559 onwards and there was a huge amount of activity during the seventeenth century. (Eloquent is the fact that a good deal more than half of the Penguin Classics volume *Seneca in English*, edited by Don Share (London, 1998), is devoted to 'Renaissance Seneca'.) But this came to a halt in the early eighteenth century, and in fact there was only one full translation into English verse of any of Seneca's plays between 1702 and 1904. The second half of the twentieth century saw a revival with Ted Hughes's *Oedipus* (1968), memorable for its stark, Anglo-Saxon monosyllables, and Caryl Churchill's *Thyestes* (1995), both of them performable and indeed performed, as well as John Fitch's fine new Loeb Classical Library translation (2002 and 2004). In the case of Lucan, after a period of energetic activity from 1600 to 1719 there is a striking gap until the late nineteenth century, followed by sporadic interest during the twentieth century until a torrent of four new translations published between 1988 and 1993. To what can we attribute this revival of interest in the macabre horrors of Seneca and Lucan at the end of the twentieth century? I suggest that it is connected with our awareness of the atrocities that human beings can perpetrate on one another, such as genocide, the Holocaust, torture, and ethnic cleansing, as well as an increased tolerance for the representation of horror in cinema, such as that of Greenaway and Tarantino. Since Seneca and Lucan deal with horror unflinchingly, I suggest that these texts have a special appeal for us at this cultural moment; and since Seneca and Lucan both enjoyed palpable popularity in England during the seventeenth century, we might also ask if the late twentieth century reprises socio-political aspects of that earlier period. At any rate, it suggests variability in the capacity of audiences of literature to stomach barbaric content.

Translations from Latin may not only reflect cultural trends but also affect the development of literature and the formation of canons. For example, Golding's translation of Ovid's *Metamorphoses* not only opened up the world of classical mythology to a wider audience but may have influenced Shakespeare and Marlowe in the conception of short mythical narrative poems such as *Venus and Adonis*, *The Rape of Lucrece*, and *Hero and Leander*; and it clearly affected the tone and specific details in *A Midsummer Night's Dream*. In the case of Seneca's tragedies, translation brought revenge tragedy—'Tragedy of Blood', to use the phrase of the Victorian scholar John Addington Symonds—to England, with lasting cultural impact. The first English translations appeared from 1559 onwards—for example, Jasper Heywood's *Troas* (1559), *Thyestes* (1560), and *Hercules Furens* (1560)—in Thomas

Newton's project that was fulfilled with the publication of *Tenne Tragedies* (including *Hercules Oetaeus* and *Octavia*) in 1581. Here we stumble over issues of cause and effect: this coincided with—and may have facilitated—the zenith of Seneca's influence, as T. S. Eliot discusses in his famous 1927 essay 'Seneca in Elizabethan Translation' (in *Selected Essays*, 3rd edn. (London, 1951), 65–105). At any rate, it is impossible to imagine the emergence of plays such as Kyd's *The Spanish Tragedy* (1582/1592), Shakespeare's *Titus Andronicus* (*c.*1590), Jonson's *Sejanus* (1605) and *Catiline* (1611), Webster's *The White Devil* (1612) and *The Duchess of Malfi* (1613), and Massinger's superb *The Roman Actor* (1626) without the influence of Seneca.

In an era when we can take it for granted that translations of Latin authors are readily available, in the library and increasingly on the internet, most obviously at the Perseus site (http://www.perseus.tufts.edu/), it takes an effort of the imagination to envisage a world in which many Latin texts were the exclusive province of those who read Latin. A world without translations was a world in which education and culture were in the hands of the elite. This stark division between the haves and the have-nots, which prevailed into the nineteenth century in England and the United States (see information in *The Oxford History of Literary Translation in English* (details in 'Further reading', below) and discussions by Sheets, Stray, and Winterer: Kevin B. Sheets, 'Antiquity Bound: The Loeb Classical Library as Middlebrow Culture in the Early Twentieth Century', *Journal of the Gilded Age and Progressive Era*, 4: 2, (1995) presented online: http://www.historycooperative.org/journals/jga/4.2/sheets.html; Christopher Stray, *Classics Transformed: Schools, Universities, and Society in England, 1830–1960* (Oxford, 1998); Caroline Winterer, *The Culture of Classicism: Ancient Greece and Rome in American Intellectual Life, 1780–1910* (Baltimore, 2002)) generated interlinear translations such as Locke's Classical System, published from 1827 onwards (though there was a precedent for this as early as 1756, in Christopher Smart's parallel Latin–English Horace), and provided the context for efforts by wealthy philanthropists to make the Greek and Latin classics available to individuals committed to self-improvement. This coincided with the foundation of the Chautauqua movement in the United States (a development of antebellum literary societies and mechanics' institutes) and the establishment of the Workers Education Association in the United Kingdom in 1903.

One of the pioneers, in a background provided by multi-volume series such as The Works of the Greek and Roman Poets (1809–12) and Valpy's Family Classical Library (1830–4), was Henry Bohn (1796–1884), a British publisher who from 1846 onwards inaugurated a series of libraries of standard works and translations, which together comprised some 776 volumes. They included Bohn's Antiquarian Library (1847), Bohn's Scientific Library (1847), Bohn's Classical Library (1848), Bohn's Ecclesiastical Library (1851), Bohn's Philological Library (1852), Bohn's French Memoirs (1865), and Bohn's Economic Library (1882). Bohn's Classical Library editions contain translations in English prose, without the Latin or Greek. Similar were the translations in the Everyman's Library, the conception in 1905 of the

London publisher Joseph Dent (1849–1926). His goal was to create a 1,000-volume library of world literature, in categories such as Contemporary Classics, Victorian Literature, Non-Western Classics, and Ancient Classics, 'to appeal to every kind of reader: the worker, the student, the cultured man, the child, the man and the woman', so that 'for a few shillings the reader may have a whole bookshelf of the immortals; for five pounds (which will procure him with a hundred volumes) a man may be intellectually rich for life' (as quoted on the Everyman's Library website). The series was launched in 1906 with fifty titles, had published 500 titles within five years, attained the 1,000-volume goal in 1956, and has just celebrated its 100th anniversary. The first 1,000 titles included at least thirty-eight Greco-Roman classics.

The success of these series may lie behind the foundation of a different kind of book, which presented the original text alongside the translation. I refer, of course, to the Loeb Classical Library and to its French counterpart, Les Belles Lettres series, commonly known as the Budé collection, which were conceived virtually simultaneously, immediately before the outbreak of World War I. Both series had ambitious aims: to translate all of Greek and Latin literature from Homer to late antiquity, both famous and obscure. Both set out to engage scholars of the highest calibre to produce authoritative critical texts alongside literary but precise translations. And both series were self-consciously aimed at an audience consisting of both specialist and amateur readers. James Loeb's mission statement, printed in the first LCL volumes, expresses this passionately:

> To make the beauty and learning, the philosophy and wit of the great writers of ancient Greece and Rome once more accessible by means of translations that are in themselves real pieces of literature, a thing to be read for the pure joy of it, and not dull transcripts of ideas that suggest in every line the existence of a finer original form from which the average reader is shut out, and to place side by side with these translations the best critical texts of the original works, is the task I have set myself.

James Loeb (1867–1933), who studied Classics at school in New York City and then at Harvard, was a philanthropist who used his banking fortune to support projects that included medical research, health-care, art, and music as well as classical philology; his was the money that founded what later became the Juilliard School in New York City. The Loeb Classical Library was launched in 1912 with fifteen volumes and maintained production through World War I; by the time of Loeb's death in 1933 there were nearly 300 volumes, and there are now 508 and counting. In France, Les Belles Lettres series was the result of French awareness of the lack of critical editions and resentment of the dominance of the German Teubner editions. L'Association Guillaume Budé, named for the sixteenth-century classical scholar, was founded in 1914, and in 1919, thanks to funding supplied by industrialists who viewed the project as 'utile à notre pays' (in the words of Paul Mazon, translator of Homer and Aeschylus, and first President of L'Association), it founded 'la société Les Belles Lettres pour le développement de la culture classique'. The first volume, Plato's *Hippias Minor*, appeared in 1920, and seems to have been viewed almost as 'la deuxième défaite de l'Allemagne'. This was followed in 1921 by editions of *Hippias Maior*, Theophrastus' *Characters*, Persius' *Satires*, and the insane edition of Seneca's *De Clementia* by Préchac. (One wonders why the first Budé editions constitute such peripheral texts: the result of commissioning policy, or what?) There are now well over 800 volumes in the Budé edition.

James Loeb has been described as a 'purveyor of middlebrow culture' who 'thought of literature as ennobling', saw 'a connection between virtue and culture', and had 'faith in the power of the classics to transform an individual' (Sheets (1995): paragraphs 1, 2, 15, 16). His particular goal was to help those who had studied some classical texts at high school and at college—he was probably thinking of business acquaintances from his days as a banker—renew their acquaintance with Latin and Greek. Although Virginia Woolf was hardly the audience Loeb was thinking of—as revealed by references to pocket-sized books, since it is a well-known fact that women's clothes do not have book-capacity pockets if they have pockets at all—her acclamation in 1917 in the *Times Literary Supplement* of the arrival of the Loeb Classical Library conveys the sense of breakthrough: she declares that this amounts to recognition of the existence of the amateur and she celebrates the Library as 'a gift of freedom'.

The Loeb Classical Library and the Budé Library continue to fulfil their mission by producing editions that make available obscure or fragmentary texts and that reflect the latest scholarship, often by commissioning revisions or totally new editions. Meanwhile, other series of translations have sprung up based on the conventional canon, most notably the Penguin Classics and the Oxford World's Classics, both of which include on their lists a fair number of classical classics as well as Jane Austen and Leo Tolstoy. E. V. Rieu's prose translation of the *Odyssey* launched the Penguin Greek and Latin Classics series in 1946 and went on to sell more than 3 million copies—in fact, for fifteen years it was the best-selling Penguin book until it was displaced by *Lady Chatterley's Lover*—thus vindicating this bold step by Allen Lane, the founder of Penguin Books. It worked because (if one accepts Penguin's self-fanfare) 'Penguin books were liked and trusted; they had been among the closest companions of many thousands throughout the war, guiding and helping them, assuming . . . a deep interest and thirst for knowledge. What this new Penguin edition of the *Odyssey* proclaimed was that this was a book that anyone—everyone—could, and should, read. The classics were no longer the exclusive province of the privileged few.' In other words, translation was a means of the democratization of knowledge and culture—and this precisely fit the mood in post-World War II Britain, with the election of the Labour Party in 1945 and the founding of the National Health Service in 1948.

Accordingly, Rieu, the editor of the Penguin Classics series, declared his intention 'to commission translators who can emulate his own example and present the general reader with readable and attractive versions of the great writers' books in modern English, shorn of the unnecessary difficulties and erudition, the archaic flavour and the foreign idiom that renders so many existing translations repellent to modern taste'. Initially he invited scholars to contribute, but (he told his son) on finding that very few of them could write decent English and that most were enslaved by the idiom of the original language, he turned to professional writers such as Robert Graves (Apuleius, Lucan, Suetonius), Rex Warner (Xenophon, Thucydides, Plutarch), and Dorothy L. Sayers (Dante, *The Song of Roland*). (Source: Penguin Classics website.)

This policy produced very uneven results, with some terrible mismatches between translator and author. A startling example is Robert Graves, who obviously conceived an intense dislike for what he calls 'Lucan's Neronian modernism'. In his Penguin Classics version (I cannot dignify it with the label 'translation'), published in 1956, he depicts Lucan as an unprincipled reporter ('the father of yellow journalism', p. 13) devoted to sensation, and he takes it upon himself to unpack the tensions of Lucan's Latin poetry by incorporating historical footnotes into a dull and flaccid prose rendition. His introduction reveals his aversion: linking Lucan with the modernist poets of the early twentieth century, above all Eliot and Pound, Graves condemns his 'impatience with craftsmanship, digressive irrelevances, emphasis on the macabre, lack of religious conviction, turgid hyperbole, inconsistency, appeal to violence', and concludes his Introduction by revealing his sense of superiority to his readership as well as his author. Categorizing Lucan in markedly Freudian terms as one of those 'prodigiously vital writers with hysterical tendencies', he explains that he has undertaken the obviously distasteful task of translating him 'for the admiration... of the great majority whose tastes differ from mine' (pp. 23–4).

Such an arrogant attitude was not, however, typical of Penguin translators. It was Rieu's successor as general editor of Penguin Classics, Betty Radice, who had the vision to understand that the series had a role to play in teaching. She saw that changes in classical teaching offered a great opportunity for new titles with line-references, notes, indices, bibliographies, and fuller introductions, designed for use in the classroom. Consequently, the series moved towards accommodating the needs of teachers and their students, although perhaps not as much as the recent translations in the Oxford World's Classics series.

Translations have probably never been so important as now, when the reception of classical literature is possibly the fastest-growing area in the field of Classics. Study of translations of Latin literature is just one element in this new awareness that our readings of ancient texts may be affected by earlier readings in a complex process of mediation and interpenetration and superimposition; it is now possible to pose the question: how does its modern reception change our perception of an ancient text? Interest in contemporary translations of classical literature was pioneered by the journal *Arion* (now at Boston University) from its inception in

1962; earlier translations are the subject of the Toronto-based *Catalogus translationum et commentariorum: medieval and Renaissance Latin translations and commentaries; annotated lists and guides*, begun in 1960. The journal *Translation and Literature*, published by Edinburgh University Press, was founded in 1992 by Stuart Gillespie, who with Peter France is also one of General Editors of the new *Oxford History of Literary Translation into English* (vol. 3: 2005; vol. 4: 2006; vol. 1: 2009; vols. 2, and 5 forthcoming). It seems likely that activity in this area will continue to grow, at least while publishers understand the economic benefits that can accrue. As Andrew Laird observes in his essay on 'Reception' in this volume, classicists have always been engaged in reception; what is new is our heightened awareness of this phenomenon and of its potential to offer new illumination of classical antiquity as well as to make significant contributions to intellectual and cultural history. It is certainly very exciting to explore the perceptions of ancient texts as revealed through later translations in a kind of triangulation between antiquity, and later receptions, and our own reception(s) of ancient texts.

I now move from the historical patterns and cultural weight of translations of Latin texts to explore some specific and typical challenges of translating from Latin into English. I shall offer three examples. My first is the challenge of technical or scientific language as represented by the concept of 'atom' in Lucretius' *De Rerum Natura*. As Lucretius sets out to offer the first explanation of Epicurean atomism in Latin, he has to devise a terminology to express the unfamiliar central concepts, a task he describes as difficult—at *DRN* 1.136–9 he mentions the 'poverty of language' (*egestas linguae*) and 'novelty of the subject-matter' (*rerum nouitas*). He does not invent a Latin neologism equivalent to Epicurus' Greek term *atomoi*, which literally means 'uncut' or 'uncuttable', but instead deploys several terms, including *corpora* (1.58), *semina* (1.59), and *elementa* (2.93), and his favourite, *primordia* (1.55). Just as Lucretius faced a challenge in translating from Greek, so translators of Lucretius into English have faced a challenge, especially since our concept of 'atom' is not any longer of something 'uncuttable'. Most translators assiduously avoid the term 'atom'. In the earliest published translation of the complete poem (1682), Thomas Creech translates 'Seeds or Principles', explaining in a note (p. 8): 'He means the Atoms. And let it suffice to give notice once for all, that he calls them by several other Names likewise: as, Corpuscles, Elements, first Matter, first Causes, first Bodies, little Bodies, etc.' Lucy Hutchinson's translation, which certainly precedes that of Creech although it was not published until 1996 (in the Duckworth edition by Hugh de Quehen), privileges 'bodies' and sometimes uses 'seeds' too. W. H. D. Rouse, who produced the Loeb Classical Library edition in 1924, and Cyril Bailey, whose monumental edition appeared in 1947, both use 'first-beginnings', 'bodies', and 'seeds'. In his 1951 Penguin Classics edition R. E. Latham defends his translation of *primordia* as 'atoms' or in some contexts 'elements' (p. 17). Which of these is the best choice? There is no right answer.

My second example is from the world of politics, and it raises issues of anachronism: the word *princeps*, which is usually translated as 'emperor'. Anyone who studies the Principate has to find some strategy for dealing with this term. It was used in this way as early as the early 20s BCE in Horace's *Odes* (e.g. 1.2.50, 'you like to be hailed as Father and Prince', *ames dici pater atque princeps*), a usage consolidated by Augustus who three times calls himself *princeps* in his *Res Gestae* (13, 30.1, 32.3). The problem is that the word's etymology (*Oxford Latin Dictionary*: *primus* + *ceps*) clearly indicates 'first'-ness; so, used as a noun it can mean 'initiator', 'founder', 'leader' or 'leading citizen', as in the title *princeps senatus*, denoting the senior member of the Roman Senate. English has no word that captures this idea of 'first'-ness. In Italian, *principe* seems to be fine, as deployed in the original title of Alessandro Barchiesi's book about Ovid's *Fasti*, *Il Poeta e Il Principe* (Rome, 1994; translated as *The Poet and The Prince*: Berkeley, 1997). But in English 'prince' misses the mark, because it denotes not the ruler but a son of the ruling king or queen—unless we hear the term through Machiavellian ears, in the knowledge that for Machiavelli *il principe* denoted an absolute ruler. Should we then resort to 'emperor' or to 'ruler'? Neither makes the kind of political claim (a claim whose fiction was exposed by the historian Tacitus; see too R. Syme, *The Roman Revolution* (Oxford, 1939), 311–12) that the ruler of the Roman world was simply 'the leading citizen'.

My third example enters the realm of the abstract: the vocabulary of moral quality, words such as *uirtus* and *pietas* and *honor*. How can we find adequate translations of Latin words and Roman concepts that have no exact equivalent in modern English culture? As so often, John Dryden pinpointed this when, in his long Dedication to his *Aeneis*, he remarked on the difficulties posed by the term *pietas* for all modern languages (*Works of John Dryden*, vol. 5, ed. William Frost and Vinton A. Dearing (Berkeley, 1987), 286): 'the word in *Latin* is more full than it can possibly be exprest in any Modern Language.' Usually the worst solution is to use the Latinate derivative. To praise Aeneas' 'piety' makes him sound like an Anglican priest rather than a heroic warrior; to laud his 'sense of duty' is even more dull; 'devotion' might just do, but requires explanation of the objects of his devotion—his father, his son, his fatherland, his gods, his destiny.

To close, let us return to the challenge I posed earlier: how to turn 'culture' into Latin. There is, of course, a whole range of possibilities. Suppose we wanted to say: 'as students of Roman culture, our project is to understand the value-system of Roman society', the Latin word *mores* might do. Suppose it were: 'the Romans saw it as their mission to civilize the world by acquainting the conquered with their culture'; the phrase *artes liberales* is adequate but *humanitas* is probably better. In a third possibility, 'people at Rome commonly viewed new arrivals from distant lands as totally lacking in culture', the Latin word that leaps to mind is *urbanitas*. But of course all these Latin concepts, none of which is readily translated by a single English word, overlap with or flow into one another.

My challenge is designed to indicate problems involved in translating and at the same time to raise large questions about the relationship between translation and culture. We need to confront the role of translation: is it a vehicle of culture, or a betrayal of culture? Should translation aim at assimilation or dissimilation, at 'domesticating' the 'source' language, or 'foreignizing' the 'target' language, to use metaphors found in contemporary translation studies theory? These questions—and the vocabulary in which they are framed—entail issues of cultural superiority and inferiority that seem impossible to separate from the phenomenon of translation.

'Western Europe owes its civilization to its translators': so wrote L. G. Kelly in *The True Interpreter: A History of Translation Theory and Practice in the West* (Oxford, 1979; quoted in the *Oxford Classical Dictionary*[3] entry 'Translation'). Others have viewed the original texts as in need of being civilized through the process of translation, for example, when Christian translators grappled with the threateningly heathen elements in Lucretius' poetic exposition of the Epicurean philosophy. Yet others have treated translation virtually as a manifestation of decadence and decline, with academics criticizing translations as 'mere cribs to be consulted furtively under the desk by weaklings unable to construe' (Betty Radice's words as reported on the Penguin Classics website).

The myriad metaphors used for the activity of translation reveal a bias, one way or the other. Positive metaphors, which include the idea of recovering buried treasure, are far outnumbered by ambivalent metaphors, for example, of alchemy, grafting, refinement, conversion, transfusion, boundary-crossing, and the banyan-tree theory of translation (rooted shoots in the shadow of the big tree), and by negative metaphors that represent translation as bastard offspring, as supplanting, as violence, as guerilla warfare, as cannibalism, as the profanation of the dead. The spectrum extends from 'true translation is metempsychosis' (the classical scholar Ulrich von Wilamowitz-Moellendorff) to murder: 'What is translation? On a platter a poet's pale and glaring head' (Vladimir Nabokov). The preponderance of negative images suggests an attitude of suspicion, if not of outright hostility.

Yet contemporary society is clearly fascinated by translation—if the evidence of a recent novel and a recent movie is anything to go by: John Crowley's *The Translator* (2002), about the Cuban missile crisis, and Sydney Pollack's 2005 movie *The Interpreter*, about a simultaneous translator at the United Nations, starring Nicole Kidman). Thinking globally, translation has the potential to expand our individually limited perspectives by opening up other cultures—whether those of the Arab world or the Far East or the Indian subcontinent. Reading other literatures in translation can be the first step towards understanding and tolerating difference. Translations of Latin texts have a part to play in this process: they give access to the Romans' alien value-system and cultural priorities. And just occasionally, a truly wonderful translation emerges, that stands as a work of literature in its own right, like Dryden's *Aeneis*. There can be no doubt that translation is a tool essential to the survival of our profession—and that while translation is itself an aesthetic act it is also a social, political, and moral act.

Further reading

George Steiner's *After Babel: Aspects of Language and Translation* (Oxford, 1975; 3rd revised edn. 1998) remains essential reading on the broad issues of translation theory and practice. Susan Bassnett-McGuire's 1980 volume *Translation Studies* has remained in print and is now in its third edition (London, 2002). There already exist several sourcebooks and readers of differing emphases: *Translation/History/Culture: A Sourcebook*, edited by André Lefevere (London and New York, 1992); Douglas Robinson's *Western Translation Theory from Herodotus to Nietzsche* (Manchester, 1997), which includes excerpts from ancient authors; *The Translation Studies Reader* edited by Lawrence Venuti (London and New York, 2000), where the focus is on modern approaches, starting with Walter Benjamin's 'The Task of the Translator'. Another compilation, *Translation—Theory and Practice: A Historical Reader*, edited by Daniel Weissbort and Astradur Eysteinsson (Oxford, 2006), contains material especially germane to the study of translation from the classical languages, taking as its starting-point a quotation from Cicero.

Classicists might turn immediately to L. G. Kelly's *The True Interpreter: A History of Translation Theory and Practice in the West* (Oxford, 1979) and then to C. A. Martindale's *Redeeming the Text: Latin Poetry and the Hermeneutics of Reception* (Cambridge, 1993), ch. 4, 'Translation as rereading: Symphony in three movements'. The real pioneer within classical studies has been Lorna Hardwick: an excellent starting-point to some of the central issues is provided by her *Translating Words, Translating Cultures* (London, 2000) and by her overview of *Reception Studies* for the Greece & Rome New Surveys in the Classics (Oxford, 2003).

For Latinists, the first destination might well be the study of translations of Latin poetry into English in the *Oxford Guide to Literature in English Translation*, edited by Peter France (2000), and the new *Oxford History of Literary Translation into English* in five volumes (vol. 3: 2005; vol. 4: 2006; vol. 1: 2009; vols. 2, and 5 forthcoming), edited by Peter France and Stuart Gillespie. Gillespie's pioneering role is also reflected in his 1992 founding of the journal *Translation and Literature* (Edinburgh University Press), which regularly publishes papers of relevance to the classicist. A fine blend of theory and practice is provided by the Penguin Classics series of anthologies of translations of Latin authors (Horace, Martial, Ovid, Virgil, Seneca, and Catullus, as well as Homer), which enjoyed a short existence during the 1990s under the editorship of Christopher Ricks before Penguin aborted the project, to the chagrin of everyone involved. Penguin's misjudgement leaves a gap which will surely be filled before long, given the enthusiasm for translation studies among classicists.

PART II

APPROACHES

CHAPTER 13

STYLE

ALFONSO TRAINA*

> The difference among languages is not about sounds and signs: it is a difference in terms of vision of the world.
>
> (Humboldt)

> If they want to write the history of dead languages, they have to palpate and auscultate at every moment some literary works which are definitely alive.
>
> (Valery-Larbaud)

I

The *History of the Latin Language* by Friedrich Stolz (Stolz 1911; Stolz–Debrunner–Schmid 1966) remains a solid product of historical-comparative linguistics. It has two blind spots, both dependent on its method: it privileges the evolution of Latin over its characteristics, and sacrifices literary language to the advantage of aspects such as the rustic, the vulgar, and dialects.

* Translated by Alessandro Barchiesi. This is an abridged version of Traina's introductory paper ('Riflessioni sulla storia della lingua latina') in Stolz–Debrunner–Schmid 1993, repr. 2007 (the Italian original has a rich and useful bibliography and many more references to the work of Friedrich Stolz and of J. M. Tronskij, whose chapter 5, translated into Italian from Tronskij 1953, was included as an appendix); it was written, a first version already in 1968, as a preface to an Italian volume on the history of Latin, which included Italian versions from the German and Russian originals, with updates, and in the 1993 revision it was enriched with an insightful paper by Edoardo Vineis on the state of research on spoken Latin.

There are problems today in accepting a purely diachronic vision of Latin as an 'intermediate stage' between the Indo-European and the Romance languages (Stolz–Debrunner–Schmid 1993: 128). Understanding language as a system forces us to attempt a description of those master-structures, phonetical, morphological and syntactical, that identify Latin in isolation from and contrast with the other IE languages and the Romance languages. Those structures persist and are unchanged, poised in a dynamic balance, throughout the history of Latin, starting with its fixation into literature, even if recurring aftershocks and peripheral collapses gradually alter the system of relationships until it is destroyed. This perspective is a way of vindicating the true historicity of a language against the mere temporal succession of diachrony, if it is true that a difference of structure (as Humboldt already perceived) is a difference in 'vision of the world', which means the result of a different historical experience. In fact, for us it is perfectly justified to think, as Trager for example does (cf. Mounin 1963: 60), that linguistic structures are just as defining of a given society as social, juridical, religious structures are. The problem is, of course, that there are dangers in attempts to prove this societal connection. Even Meillet in his sketch of the evolution of Latin (Meillet 1966: 164) did not manage to avoid those dangers completely. Before we run into the same difficulties, two short clarifications are needed. First of all, we should remove the phantom of race. There is no reason to fear that an attempt towards a linguistic characterization of speakers of Latin might implicitly evoke racial and biological factors. It is enough to answer with the clear words of a specialist, M. F. A. Montagu (1966: 225): civilizations differ from one another insofar there was differentiation in the history and the experience of every group, through a process of reciprocal influence. Language is one of the patterns which organize the data of those experiences. In turn, those patterns generate models of behaviour, and affect the interpretation of reality. On this tack, some have progressed so far that they claim for language the power to condition our perception of reality and shape our image of the world. This is the so-called Sapir–Whorf theory (although more Whorf than Sapir: Sapir 1929: 206–14, esp. p. 219 = Sapir 1949: 169; Whorf 1956), a very interesting area for linguists and psychologists, although not for pure structuralists, who disregard all non-linguistic elements. The theory has the advantage of stating that linguistic structures and image of the world are connected. Like Schaff (1965: 316), we choose to understand the connection as interaction: reality moulds language, language in turn moulds our image of reality.

We thank Alfonso Traina and Pàtron Editore (Bologna) for permissions to translate and adapt. It is unusual for an *Oxford Handbook* to include already published material, and our choice has more than one justification: the difficulty of finding a suitable contribution on the interface between studies of Latin style and historical linguistics, and on the relationship between literature and language; the importance and breadth of the methodological ideas in such a short space; a homage to a scholar whose inspiring work has been accessible for a long time only to readers with a working knowledge of Italian.

II

'It is a Roman principle to have unity as the contrary of multiplicity and love of variation; simplicity as opposed to complication; the process of streamlining, a reduction to a few ideas whose expression is clear.' This is Fritz Schulz about the principles of Roman law (Schulz 1946: 60), and the same could be said about the Latin language. If it is true (the concept was important to Meillet) that the evolution of IE languages tends to a gradual simplification, it is also true that this simplification does not occur in all of the languages with the same degree and in identical ways. We can use as a term of reference (as Bally does, 1963: 49) the other IE language that was coupled with Latin by historical accidents as a vector of Western culture, Greek. To me, one observation stands out: in all fields of grammar, although with different intensity (since characteristic tendencies of a language will not emerge in a uniform way in all different parts of a system), Latin displays structures that are simpler and more orderly than Greek: in particular, it tends to match binary oppositions versus the ternary oppositions of Greek (after writing this, I noticed with some satisfaction that Momigliano 1988: 64–6, while discussing the well-known theories of Dumézil, argues that, to describe Roman *mentalité*, a binary opposition would serve us better than Dumézilian tripartition).

This is, to repeat, only a tendency, and those generalizations always require immediate caution. In any case, the consequences of this preference for the binary have been very visible. We may begin with a quick glance at phonetics. Not much is yielded by consonantism, yet one feature is evident. While IE tripartition of mute consonants according to the place of articulation (labial, dental, guttural) has been preserved in Greek as in Latin (with Latin additionally preserving the voiceless labiovelar *kw*, not extant in Greek although still featured by Mycenaean), the fourfold division according to places of articulation has been stripped down to a tripartite division in Greek (voiceless, voiced, aspirated), to twofold in Latin after the loss of aspirated (which were reintroduced into Latin in more recent times, only in Graecisms, true or imaginary; the legitimate successors to IE aspirated, *h* and *f*, are out of the picture here, since they only matter in a diachronic perspective). For instance, the sequence *lego lektos elekthen* corresponds to *lego lectus*. More original, therefore more representative, is the evolution of Latin vocalism. I am not thinking in particular of the repertory of phonemes, where Greek and Latin diverge, especially in the treatment of diphthongs, which are preserved in Greek in two tripartite sequences (*ai oi ei*; *au ou eu*), and reduced to two in Latin, *ai* (*ae*) and *au* (with sporadic survival of *oe*): the point here is about the working of alternation. There is a crucial point here, one that defines Latin vocalism in its entirety.

The semantic function of IE apophony has been preserved in Greek, especially in tripartite sequences: *leipo leloipa elipon*; *egenomen gegona gignomai*; *phemi phatis phone*, etc. In Latin the sequences, where surviving, have been reduced to binary:

the series of *leipo* corresponds to *lĭ(n)quo līqui* < **loiquai*, the series of *gignomai* corresponds to *genus gigno*, the series of *phemi* corresponds to *făteri fāri*. Cases such as *fīdo* < *feido*, *foedus* < *foidus fĭdes*, or *precor procus posco* < **porcsco* < **presco* are exceptional and masked as secondary alterations. The apophony is only really functional in the opposition infectum/perfectum, to be discussed later: *făcio fēci*, *vĕnio vēni*, *fŏdio fōdi*. More importantly, true Latin apophony results from the alteration of short internal vowels. This apophony plays simple against compositum: *făcio afficio*, *factus affectus*, *medius dimidius*, *annus biennium*, etc.; simple against derivation: *nouos nouitas*, *tempus temperi*, *manus manica*, *exul exilium*, etc.; nominative against oblique cases: *flumen fluminis*, *caput capitis*, *cinis cineris*, etc.; infectum against perfectum: *pario peperi*, *pello pepuli*, *cado cecidi*, *caedo cecīdi*, etc.

Finally, Greek accent operates on three syllables; Latin accent—we do not need to enter the debate on the nature of this accent—on two: series such as *thýgater thygáter thygatrós*, *lábete labéto labé* are impossible in Latin, where we only have *eligo elegi*, *legito legunto*, *domini dominorum*, and where oxytony is secondary and limited to cases of apocope (*illíc*, *addúc*) or syncope (*nostrás*, *Samnís*). The result is the disappearance of the distinctive value of IE accent, still an active force in the typology *tróchos trochós*; *tómos tomós*, etc.

III

In the system of morphology and syntax the bipolarity of Latin is evident especially in the verb. As far as nouns are concerned, and this is also relevant as we shall see, Greek is more modern. The eight cases of IE are reduced to five, while Latin continues the ablative and significant traces of locative. Yet even here one is able to discern signs of a binary opposition in Latin. The fact is that Greek, which reduces the number of cases, has been forced to extend to each of them—with the exception of nominative and vocative which are not strictly speaking 'cases', *ptoseis*, the use of prepositions. Latin, however, where the remains of locative are frozen into adverbial forms (*domi*, but *in pulchra domo*; *Romae*, but *in urbe Roma*), has regrouped the four remaining cases into two couples: concrete cases with preposition (the accusative and ablative) and abstract cases without a preposition (the genitive and dative). In fact the real peculiarity of Latin is its verbal flexion, with huge effects on syntax. Here binary structure dominates, with a degree of coherence that cannot be accidental. The three IE numbers—a category implicated by person, hence shared between noun and verb—are reduced to two, with exclusion of the dual; note also that a residual archaism such as the coupling of neuter plural—an ancient collective expression—with a singular verb, *ta zoa trechei*, has vanished in Latin. In correspondence to three Greek diatheses, active middle passive (with a prevalence of the older middle diathesis over passive), Latin develops, building on the impersonal, the couple active/passive: a couple that contrasts, with a legal kind of clarity, at the level of grammatical subject, the agent and the one who is affected by an action: *et is qui adoptat... et is qui adoptatur* (Gaius 1.99). As for the middle, it is quarantined in the archaic category of deponents, one already on its way towards disappearance in the earliest literary texts, or it has been distributed between intransitive and middle-passive (*uerto/uertor, muto/mutor*); the true substitute for the middle in Latin is the reflexive, in which the circularity of action is made more explicit in the separation of subject and object (*me uerto*), while the action of the middle was contained in the sphere of the subject. The outcome is a secondary opposition between middle-passive, whose morphology was designed for the expression of a passive, mechanical character, and reflexive, a sign of intention and awareness: one might contrast the self-victimization of Catullus 85.2: *nescio, sed fieri sentio, et excrucior*, with the more active desire of Plautus, *Curc.* 170: *ipsus se excruciat qui homo quod amat uidet nec potitur.*

Even more momentous as innovations have been the syncretism of perfect and aorist, and of subjunctive and optative. With this change, both aspect and mode were transformed by radical, binary oppositions: infectum/perfectum, indicative/subjunctive, while moving away from the IE ternary system, faithfully mirrored in Greek. 'The structure developed by the verb in the Latin of Rome is an original one' (Meillet 1966: 147).

IV

The noun, as a symbol of an object, is static: the verb is the sign of a process unfolding in time. If we focus on the different directions taken by the system of nouns and the system of verbs in Greek and in Latin, an antithesis in terms of vision of the world manifests itself: Greek *theoria* and Latin temporality. 'Romans looked at reality less in terms of its essence than in temporal terms' (Altheim 1955: 63; Dupont 1990: 81 asserts that the Romans 'live and think according to space more than time', but what she says on religion at p. 83 confirms our take on religious practice and time). This temporality, so opposite to Greek *theoria*, influences all aspects of Latin civilization. In art, it takes on the form of a continuous narrative style, the one of Trajan's Column. A manifestation of this tendency can be found in the ecphrasis of art objects by Latin poets. The Homeric shield of Achilles has a purely spatial organization, a series of vignettes framed by the Ocean. In the shield of Aeneas the succession of episodes is in chronological order, as if on the film of a moving picture (*Aen.* 8.626–9):

> Illic res Italas Romanorumque triumphos
> haud uatum ignarus uenturique inscius aeui
> fecerat Ignipotens, illic genus omne futurae
> stirpis ab Ascanio pugnataque in ordine bella.

There the Lord of Fire, in his knowledge of prophets and the future, had fashioned Italian history and the triumphs of the Romans, there the entire race of the future progeny of Ascanius, and the wars, in their sequence.

The same adverbial construct, with the idea of order and sequence, recurs in another Virgilian ecphrasis, that of the temple doors in Carthage (*Aen.* 1.456): *uidet Iliacas ex ordine pugnas*, 'he sees the Trojan battles, in sequence'; a little later, in line 483, the temporal adverb *ter* gives away that narrative has supplanted representation: *ter circum Iliacos raptauerat Hectora muros*, 'he had dragged Hector around the walls of Troy for three times'. Before Virgil, Catullus had described his abandoned Ariadne in successive tableaux, thus frustrating scholarly attempts to identify one or more Greek models in sculpture or painting. In fact, the whole episode in Poem 64 is an ecphrasis translated into narrative: 'Catullus narrates what took place in time, instead of representing what is visible through space' (Pasquali 1920: 19). After Virgil, the most plastic of Latin poets, Ovid, will know how to extend into motion the tortured postures of his sculptural groups. As late as Ausonius, in his description of the statue of Occasio (*Epigr.* 33, p. 323 Peip.), inspired by an epigram of Posidippus (*AP* 16.275), the dominant mode is 'temporality turning the Greek forms, contained in a fixed space, into fluidity and movement' (Traina 1989: 175). We have much to learn from new studies of poetic ecphraseis in Latin.

No less than art, Roman religion is soaked in time. The characteristic Roman divinities are divinities of the instant, 'Augenblicksgötter': devoid of shape and myth, they are revealed in action, whether they punctuate the rhythms of life and human work (more than 100 divine powers are known from the Indigitamenta), or divinize one unrepeatable historical moment (Aius Locutius, a voice that warned the Romans about Gauls approaching; Tutanus Rediculus, the power that stopped Hannibal in front of the Capena Gate; on gods as manifested only through time and action, cf. Altheim 1955: 66; Bayet 1969: 63). Even the principal god, of Indo-European background, Jupiter, is represented, as Altheim showed, *sub specie temporis*, in the person of the *flamen Dialis*, whose entire existence is one continuous cultic action. In parallel, myth is historicized (cf. Altheim 1955: 79, 'all Roman myths were historical'; Dumézil 1949: 117 and 170; Dumézil 1966: 86–7), drawing its paradigmatic value not any more from 'sacred time', to be continuously renewed through ritual, but from the past of the civic community. The heroes are *uiri*, the protagonists of *res Romanae*. In this approach we find a convergence even among very different approaches, such as the ones of Dumézil and Altheim.

Nor is the most original Roman achievement, the law, exempt from this sense of time. Law will find its systemic fixation only very late, in the East, when the cycle of Latin civilization was extinct. Latin law is asystematic and dynamic, exactly because it avoids every a priori formulation and sticks to the continuous mutations of life, in a continuous work of regeneration: the 'edictum perpetuum' (De Sanctis 1957: 7; Schulz 1946: 42 and 57). The same adaptation, progressive and continuous, is found in political institutions: they are strikingly flexible in combining tradition and innovation (one thinks about the Augustan Principate). There is awareness of this aspect in Cato, when he contrasts the constitutions of Greek city-states, the works of individual legislators, with the continuous collective creation of the Roman constitution: 'he was wont to say that the superiority of our constitution over the other polities is that they regularly had individuals, who shaped their own state according to their own legislation and institutions; while our republic was the product of many people's mind, not of one, and was shaped over the course of many generations and eras, not just of a single human life' (Cic. *Rep.* 2.2).

What changes in Rome is a sense of time. Greek time is cosmic time, measured on celestial revolutions, and tends to close itself in a circle, as a mirror of eternity: 'time (*chronos*)... imitating *aion* and moving in a rhythmic cycle' (Plato, *Tim.* 38a). Thus Aristotle: 'time in itself seems to be a *kyklos*' (*Phys.* 223b). It appears to be, but not always is: because the circle is a symbol of divine unchangeability. Its mythical projection in time is eternal return, such an entrenched idea in Hellenic cosmologies, from Pythagoras to the Stoics. In contrast, history, human time, is the realm of contingency and particularity (*ta kath'hekastou*, Aristotle, *Poet.* 1451b). Having chosen being, Greeks involve history in the devaluation of change. Yet, in its imperfection, even historical time mimics the circle: it is the Herodotean '*kyklos* of human affairs' (1.207), alternating human vicissitudes; its desecration in Hellenistic culture will become the 'wheel' (*trochos*) of Fortune. Thucydides writes for those 'who will want to know both past events and future events, who will repeat, analogue or identical, according to the dynamics of human actions' (1.22.5). Polybius will offer the theory of *anakyklosis* of political constitutions; but Cicero will retort that eternity is the achievement of a well-constituted state: *debet enim constituta sic esse ciuitas, ut aeterna sit*, 'the constitution of a state must aim at eternity' (*Rep.* 3.34; cf. 1.69). Naturally, this is the condition of Rome, whose historical example was contrasted, again by Cicero in another context of *De Re Publica* (2.3), with the ideal model of Plato's *Republic.*

In Rome time is historical time, fundamentally a linear one. It is hard to adduce theoretical evidence, since the Romans, when they theorize, follow the Greeks. But we have indirect clues. Virgil's Fourth Eclogue would seem to be a variation on the theme of eternal return. However, the backwards succession of the Ages, when we return from Iron Age to Golden through Bronze and Silver (gold–silver–bronze–iron–bronze–silver–gold), allows us to block the cyclic movement of history. As a solution, it is utopian and metahistorical. Not that the *Aeneid* will end up with a different solution: the Golden Age is historicized in Augustan Rome, to whose rule Jupiter has granted a time without limits: *imperium sine fine dedi*, 'I have granted an empire without limits' (1.279). Rome's eternity is a dogma for the Latins, even the ones who contemplate the nadir: *Quae restant nullis obnoxia tempora metis,* | *dum stabunt terrae, dum polus astra feret*, 'Times that are lasting and exempt from any boundary, as long as lands will be there, as long as the sky will carry the stars' (Rutilius Namatianus 1.137–8). Even more significant as a dogma if it is true that it had to overcome (as Hubaux 1945 asserts) a millenaristic ideology, linked to the omen of the twelve vultures. So we have Roman cosmic space remaining, as the Greek cosmos, a limited one—and this is the way it will remain through the Middle Ages—while time opens up towards an unlimited vista: *urbs in aeternum condita*, 'a city founded for eternity' (Livy 4.4.4). This way history is redeemed, because it is Roman time. 'From its origins to its fall, Roman historiography is, and only intends to be, the history of the Roman people' (De Sanctis 1931: 280): basically, the continuation of *Annales pontificum*. The foundation is one unrepeatable event, splitting history in two straight half-lines: *ante* and *post urbem conditam*. It is difficult not to think about the linearity of Christian time, since Christian time too is bisected by the historical and unrepeatable event of the incarnation of Christ. Augustine will in fact use the death of Jesus as proof of the absurdity of eternal return: *absit ut nos ista credamus. Semel enim Christus mortuus est*, 'This belief must be far from us: Christ died only once' (*CD* 12.13.2). 'Christocentric' history is in fact modelled on 'Romanocentric' history. We are all used to saying that Christian time owes its linearity to biblical time, and this must be true, but it looks as if this change has been anticipated and prepared by the Latin sense of time and temporality (note especially Mazzarino 1966: II/1. 85: 'a "Romanocentric" history, as it had been from the very start of this tradition... has a tendency to be, so to speak, rectilinear; the entire storyline is measured on a single, ascending parameter, that of the Roman city state'; 426: 'when during the Middle Ages and the modern era the reckoning of years *ab incarnatione* has become common and almost mandatory, only at this stage can we see a linear conception of time—and this idea, one should notice, is grafted on the Roman idea of an era *post Romam conditam*').

V

I should apologize for straying away from my area of research, repeating well-known and necessarily generic ideas. My aim has been to stress the possibility of linking the language with other Roman structures of meaning. Now let me go back to the main line of this discussion. The reduction of three IE aspects to two Latin aspects is not just a matter of quantity, although it matters greatly to the orderly distribution of verbal flexion into two main themes, as opposed to the variety of IE themes. From the beginning, the opposition we have is clearly based on aspect: infectum, the action as it unfolds (unbroken line)—perfectum, the action when it has reached completion (line followed by full stop). We all know the example of Plautus, *Bacch.* 151: *uixisse* (having finished one's life) *nimio satiust quam uiuere* (to keep living), and I would add Seneca, *Ep.* 9.7: *artifici iucundius est pingere quam pinxisse*, indicating that the opposition was never far from the linguistic sensibility of speakers of Latin. Yet while the durative value of infectum was always alive and perceived, from the closural value of perfectum we have, very early on, two distinct developments, and they are a function of time, not of verbal aspect: the absolute value of past tense (in the indicative perfect, with a gradual fading of 'logical' perfect in favour of 'historical' perfect), and the relative value of anteriority (especially in subordinate clauses), balanced by the relative value of contemporaneity in the infectum. In Martial 6.40.4: *hanc uolo, te uolui*, the perfect indicates the past (I used to want); in Ouid, *Met.* 15.412: *adsimulat, tetigit quoscumque colores*, 'it simulates whatever colour it has touched', it denotes anteriority; in both examples, then, the perfectum expresses time. The fact is, the main morphological opposition in Latin verbs is infectum/perfectum, a distinction based on aspect, and yet the main opposition on a semantic level (Ronconi 1959: 46) tends to shift towards the temporal level, be it absolute (present past future) or relative (contemporaneity, anteriority, posteriority): this on the one hand confirms that the Latin verb is more modern than the Greek one, because the aspect, a category of duration, is less abstract and more primitive than the category of segmented time (cf. Meillet 1926: 186, on Latin as transition between IE languages dominated by aspect, and Romance languages, dominated by tense; Pagliaro-Belardi 1963: 98 and 105). The formation of the future is, as is well known, a relatively late phenomenon in IE evolution. On the other hand, the system of relative tenses is what allows that typical, solid structuring of temporal subordination (*consecutio temporum*), a tool that reflects, as we shall see, one of the great laws of Latin syntax.

Just as the Latin language has substituted IE apophony with its own apophony, so it happened to verbal aspect. The real opposition, in terms of aspect, which operates in historically attested Latin, is the one between durative and momentary action, as represented by the couple of simplex and compositum: *facio conficio*, another binary pair of opposites. While aoristic survival is blocked in fixed and unproductive formulas (*ne feceris, aliquis dixerit*, perhaps *fecisse uelim*), the punctual aspect of actions is expressed in prevalence through preverbs, especially *com-*: *lacrimo collacrimo* (burst into tears), *clamo conclamo* (start screaming), *labor collabor* (collapse), etc. (cf. Meillet 1897: 81–90). There is not a page in Latin without this kind of opposition, explicit or implicit: it is so vital, so rooted in the language, that when Seneca needs to express through a compositum the idea of 'falling down together' he must forge the neologism *concado*, because in *concido* the preverb was totally empty of semantic autonomy, and so *concido* can only mean 'to fall down', not 'to fall down in someone's company': *cum magno comitatu populorum concadentium*, 'accompanied by a great multitude of those who fell down with him' (*Nat.* 6.1.9).

VI

Infinitive, participle, gerundium, and supine are—a well-known fact—not so much modes as verbal nouns. Even the imperative, whose second-person singular coincides with the basic theme (*amā, fer*, etc.), is not a true 'mode', meaning 'a mental approach of the speaker', *diathesis*, and its position in verbal flexion is an analogue to that of vocatives in the nominal flexion. Therefore there are three modes in Greek, indicative, subjunctive, and optative, and two in Latin, as a result of fusion between subjunctive and optative. This way the Latin subjunctive was inheriting all of the values of subjectivity: will and potentiality from subjunctive, desire and possibility from optative, and has polarized the opposition between objective (indicative)/subjective (subjunctive). This opposition is a dominant of Latin syntax. It regulates the choice of a mode in relative clauses, in *quod* causal sentences, in temporal sentences with *antequam*, in suppositive sentences (with a subjective and an objective type), and the choice of concessive (*quamquam/quamvis*), disjunctive (*aut/vel*) or conclusive (*itaque/igitur*) conjunctions, of pronoun (anaphoric/reflexive), of negatives (*non/nē*), and more. This importance assigned to the linguistic expression of subjectivity suits people about whose legal culture it was stated that 'its active center is subjectivity, the active will to be translated and affirmed through objective reality' (De Ruggiero 1967: 20), and whose poets have been regarded (Rostagni 1939: 119) as 'more personal, more subjective, more lyrical' than the Greeks.

The subjunctive is not only a vector of subjectivity; as a mode of indirect expression, it has easily become the mode of subordination. The transition from the former value to the latter is still caught in action through the establishment of indirect questions in the age of Plautus. The polarity indicative/subjunctive contributed, therefore, to endowing with clarity and profile the hypotactic structure through which Latin syntax realizes its centripetal character. The subordinate clause gravitates towards the main clause, and can be affected by it in mode, tense, and pronoun. *Flumina senserunt ipsa quid esset amor* (Ouid, *Am.* 3.6.24): Greek, Italian, and English, all languages with a centrifugal character, respect the autonomy of the subordinate clause, as if a statement with its own claim to truth: 'what love is'. In Latin, this truth only exists in the sphere of experience of the subject of the main clause, so that mode and tense are affected. This centripetal character, the foundation of modal attraction (to the extent that it is legitimate to recognize it: Ghiselli 1966) and of *consecutio temporum*, often operates in the same direction as subjectivity, as in the case of indirect style; at times, it explains its apparent exceptions, as in the case of consecutives, where you would expect the indicative of objectivity: but in fact the consequence is being viewed from the vantage-point of its cause, that is, of the main sentence. This is the other great law in Latin syntax. Hierarchic organization is no less perceived at the level of language than it is perceived at the level of society and politics (Meillet 1966: 154). A language for empire-builders: *totum sub legibus mitteret orbem*, 'in order to subject the whole world to laws' (Virgil, *Aen.* 4.231).

VII

The lexicon has a special status in a language, being the most open and least structured area. For this reason, it is more apt to highlight the various phases of a civilization and its contacts with neighbouring or contemporaneous civilizations: in the specific situation of Latin, with Italic languages, with Etruscan, and Greek, and all those contacts are well documented in Stolz (who strangely disregards the documentation of agricultural and commercial strata in the Latin lexicon). Yet even the lexicon responds to certain rules of formation (derivation, composition, and the like), and those rules affect its evolution. In addition, the distribution of a same semantic value in different lexical and syntactic categories results in functional balances and compensations, visible only to those who focus on the totality of the linguistic system. If a quick example is needed, we may reflect on the different fortunes of abstract and composita. Latin offers resistance to both abstraction (cf. Schulz 1946: 35, discussing legal culture; Vossler 1948: 116–17 on a language without articles) and nominal compounds. Abstracts for qualities, derived from adjectives, are (in spite of what is often claimed) commonly used, but abstracts for actions, or derived from verbs, are substituted by preference with syntagms based on verbal nouns, on infinitives (*credo deos esse*, 'I believe in the existence of the gods'; *claudi tabernas iubet*, 'orders the closure of shops'), participles (*mors nuntiata*, 'the announcement of death'; *ab urbe condita*, 'after the foundation of Rome'), gerundives (*in urbe capienda*, 'in the conquest of the town'; *ad frumentum emendum*, 'for grain purchase'). In spite of that, the need for a vocabulary more synthetic and syntactically handy encouraged the proliferation of the -tiōn- suffix, with a head-start in technical languages, such as the legal, the agricultural, and the military. This kind of derivation has been inherited by the Romance languages and triumphs in modern nominal style. On the other hand, the resistance of Latin against nominal composition (for orientation on compounds see Oniga 1988), a phenomenon already noticed by the ancients (*nobis minus succedit*, Quint. 1.5.70; cf. Quint. 8.3.30; Livy 27.11.5), was insurmountable. There is preservation of ancient compounds with nouns in technical expressions (*agricola*, *gallicinium*, *pontifex*, *suouetaurilia*, *iudex*, etc.; theonyms such as Domidūca, Viriplāca, Noctilūca, etc., with a verbal second element). New adjectival compounds on a Greek matrix (even if it is a mistake to look for systematic one-on-one match between every Latin innovation and an individual Greek model) enter poetic language as early as Naevius (*arquitenens*, *bicorpores*). But in general, the compound is replaced by verbal syntagms (*trilinguis* = *cui tres sunt linguae*, Lygd. 4.88) or by associations of nouns (*terrigenae* = *filii Terras*, Naeuius, *Bell. Poen.* 19 Mor.; *multibibus* = *multi meri*, Horace, *Carm.* 1.36.13; *trisaeclisenex* = *ter canus*, *In Maec.* 137, *PLM* 1. 133). This weakness, already a feature of Latin when compared to the majority of IE languages, has been transmitted to the Romance languages, and differentiates them from the Germanic languages, constituting a barrier (cf. Devoto 1946: 22) towards the development of a shared European vocabulary.

VIII

There is so little space for literary language in Stolz's volume that the latest editor has felt the need to offer a motivation, one that really looks like an excuse (Stolz 1993: 128). In fact, the undervaluation of the 'artificial' language of literature as opposed to the 'spontaneous' popular language is a distant echo of Romantic prejudice, one that it was not easy to remove or modify without profoundly altering the structure of the work. Today we cannot accept this relegation of the literary, and a history of Latin language without a serious interest for the language of the classical authors is for us something truncated and incomplete (cf. Devoto 1951: 77). First of all, the great artists of the word, and especially poets, are major sources for linguistic innovation, because they react to deep tendencies of a language and explore its latent resources. As Dámaso Alonso noticed, 'only in poetry do we have a full realization of language' (1965: 69; cf. Spitzer 1959: 15). Second, the cultural and societal prestige of a literary language results in a continuous source of linguistic models for the lower levels of a society. Literary language gives back at least as much as it receives, if not more. Imagine what a history of the Italian language would be with Dante as someone barely mentioned. Virgil did not enjoy the chronological positioning of Dante, but his influence on the language of the Imperial era was no less decisive, in particular through the medium of schooling: already the walls at Pompeii are full of Virgilian graffiti. This is even more important since Latin is a dead language anyway, therefore out of reach if not through written texts, all of them composed in a literary language or at least influenced by it (see e.g. the introduction to Norden 1958).

It is wrong to sacrifice documents to monuments, but equally wrong to do the opposite. To compensate at least partly for this lacuna, one could meditate on chapter 5, on the formation of literary language, from J. M. Tronskij's *Outlines of a History of the Latin Language.* Tronskij was a Marxist, of course; but his Marxist approach, if we discount the emphasis on slave-owning societies and some polemics against bourgeois linguistics, is cautious and refrains from imposing preconceived ideological patterns on the ancient data. Tronskij has contributed much to a complete analysis of literary language at every level, phonetics, morphology, syntax, and lexicon. There are unusually subtle observations on the semantic enrichment of Latin through the last two centuries of the Republic. Tronskij well evaluates the importance of literary language, 'an apt instrument for the most various aspects of literature about art, science and philosophy, and helpful both for the expression of complex thought processes in conceptual areas, and for the delicate nuances of spiritual emotions' (Tronskij, in Stolz–Debrunner–Schmid 1993: 129).

IX

However, one substantial problem remains unfortunately hidden. We do not have a literary language in Greek: what we have is as many literary languages as are the dialects enshrined in the various genres and forms. In Rome, on the contrary, *urbanitas* has produced the extinction of dialects, and enforced, as a consequence, a relative unity of the language of letters. Again, in this respect too, Hellenic particularism conflicts with Roman centralism: 'In Greek territory, a variety of idioms and a multiplicity of literary languages; almost no writer whose language overlaps with another's; in Rome, one single spoken language in circulation, and a unified literary language remains fundamentally unchanged from the beginning of a tradition to the end of the Empire' (Meillet 1966: 2). But since Latin literature was born already under the sign of Alexandrianism, and its first poets are 'grammarians' and bilingual, the problem of the formation of a Latin literary language coexists with that of differentiation, not only from spoken language, but also according to the literary genres. So the first poets of Rome had to confront and to solve the problem of multilingualism, a problem theorized and exemplified by the Greek models. In spite of the paucity of preserved fragments, we have some idea of how Livius Andronicus made the breakthrough (Leo 1913: 59; Mariotti 1986): a solemn and archaistic language, for epic; a precious and Hellenizing language, open both to calques and to imported words, for tragedy; *Umgangssprache*, the language of daily communication, for comedy.

This distinction will remain a canonical one for his successors, but already in Naevius we notice a trend towards eliding the distinction between the epic and the tragic tradition. Direct Graecisms are still not viable in the *Bellum Poenicum*, but compounds based on Greek models, not attested in Livy's *Odusia*, begin to surface (Barchiesi 1963). Finally, with Ennius, Graecism will enter epic in the form of Homerisms. This results, once more, in some stylistic dichotomy, opposing the highbrow epic-tragic style to the humble style of comedy, and later, of satire: in the meantime comedy has reached full maturity and autonomy with the three great specialists of Palliata, Plautus, Caecilius, and Terence. In spite of this polarization, the two levels still have points of contact. Ennius does have some colloquial expressions in the *Annales* and in tragedies, whose *sermo* Cicero thought—rather oddly for us—to be not very far from *Umgangssprache* (*Or.* 36), and *sermo comicus* occasionally rises to tragic arias for the purpose of parody (Plautus) or of pathos (Terence). Yet the antithesis is and remains a tight one, and even increases towards the age of the archaic period, when the two styles are pushed to opposite extremes by Accius and by the genre of Atellana.

Archaic lyric had been, as far as we know, essentially choral: it was made for liturgy, or for the stage. Subjective lyric emerges with the so-called circle of Lutatius Catulus: the problem, of course, was to fashion a new medium for expression. Those poets solved the problem, under the influence of Hellenistic epigrams, by combining elements of the two styles in one *poikilia*, with the intention to endow personal, daily experience with a refined literary hue. But these were not great poets, and it was more of a juxtaposition than a fusion. The one who will create, in this direction, the lasting style for subjective lyric, with an astute mix of the two styles, and a dose of elegance and freshness, will be Catullus. Much more than Lucretius, whose style is backwards-looking (although in his epic of atoms we perceive the same rebel individualism opposed to the *mos maiorum* that Catullus cultivates), Catullan poetry is a crucible of linguistic experiences loaded with future. His absence in a history of the Latin language is untenable.

X

Another node of the Latin language of literature, this time in prose, is Seneca, who falls beyond the chronological limits of Tronskij's chapter, and is ignored in the rest of the book, just as he is not discussed by Stolz. A *rhetor*, he is usually labelled.

Concetto Marchesi (1944: 217) had seen the real picture: 'Seneca has subjugated Latin literature to the revolution initiated half a century before him.' Senecan style, in opposition to Ciceronianism, will be in permanence a stylistic resource of European culture. It is the least Classical among Classical styles. The basic cell is the clause, the *sententia* of declaimers, while the cell of 'Classical' style had been the period, and the cell of Frontonian archaism will be the single word, the *insperatum atque inopinatum uerbum* (Front. p. 57 V. Den Hout). Seneca substitutes the logical sinews that support Ciceronian and Caesarian discourse with a parataxis which has as many centres and pauses as its clauses. Anaphora and assonance create a sonic texture that re-enacts the *carmina* tradition, and it is to its psychagogic impact, much more than to the aloof evidence of reasoning, that Seneca entrusts the effect of his moral preaching: *facilius... singula insidunt circumscripta et carminis modo inclusa*, 'individual ideas are easier to remember if they are defined through a form similar to poetry' (*Ep.* 33.6; Traina 1987, with bibliography). In parallel, Tacitean history deconstructs the temporal and causal scaffolding of Caesarian prose, while refusing the epic majesty of Livian narrative. In a world of chaotic and unrelated events (*ludibria rerum mortalium, Ann.* 3.18), the *abruptae* sentences of this historian cast sinister flashlights on the abyss of souls, where the motives of human actions are a tangle. This is the existential anxiety that destroys, after the conquest of empire, the lucid Classical mastery of logos, and heralds the end of a culture. 'Hellenism has foundered because it was not able to give its place to human suffering—pride of place.' Christianity will exorcize suffering through deification. The great Christian writers will then be able to recuperate the architecture of Latin prose, and conciliate it with the semantic density and the rhythmic fabric of Senecan *sententia*-style. But every time, in European culture, the ancestral angst of loneliness resurfaces, it will always be through Seneca's style. The century when the shock of cosmic infinity was felt was the most Senecan century ever in European letters.

XI

The history of the Latin language is not over with the end of the Empire. Uprooted from its historical humus, Latin survives as a superstrate, in a tiresome compromise between the rigidity of original structures and the pressure of new cultural experiences. The Middle Age has contributed the abstract power and dialectic finesse of scholasticism, and was able to disclose, through the literature of mysticism, uncharted areas of the human mind. Great poetry, in compensation, turned towards a brand-new linguistic expression, Romance languages. The Latin of Humanism, freed from the excesses of medieval logicism, celebrates the enthusiasm for a rediscovery of man, of a new spiritual dynamism, under the sign of 'studia humanitatis': *ibi Romanum imperium est, ubicunque Romana lingua dominatur*, 'the place of the Roman Empire is the dominance of the Latin language' (Lorenzo Valla, *El. praef.*, p. 9 ed. 1545). It was a short-lived springtime: Humanism soon is limited by its belaboured philological origins. In poetry, enthusiasm yields to *ludus*, the rediscovery of the ancients declines into *imitatio*. In prose authors, too, *imitatio* ends up creating rigidity and sterility at the level of language. It is true that Erasmus opposes Ciceronianism in the name of the necessity that the Latin language *personis et rebus praesentibus congruat*, 'should be consistent with subjects and topics of the present' (*Cicer.* 1696 Gambaro), but precisely in the name of this principle Martin Luther will shatter the Erasmian compromise, the ideology of a 'modern Latin', and support national languages instead. As the Reformation moves on, the second unity of Europe, the religious unification, is now fractured. Yet Latin is still the vehicle for a third kind of universalism: science. Until the eighteenth century Latin is the prevailing language of science. The announcement of the new dimensions of the universe, a message bound to revolutionize human sense of space, had been encoded in Latin. This is the final service of Latin to modern culture.

This history does not continue beyond Romanticism. The space of human interiority is now wider and muddied: Latin, a language mirroring historical experiences across a distance of twenty centuries, lacks adequate resources to express those new dimensions. There is still, however, an influence on European languages via loanwords, semantic and syntactic calques, modes of derivation: 'the European sign, is the Latin language' (De Maistre 1821: 203). Today the process of cultural unification on a planetary scale is not moving, as far as we can see, in the direction of Latin; even the conservatism of the Roman Catholic Church has necessarily taken this shift into account. Yet before all is said and done, a great work of lyric poetry, the *Carmina* by Giovanni Pascoli, through the force of a bilingualism based not on separation (as in early modern Humanism) but on simultaneous presence and on the osmosis of the two linguistic systems of Italian and of Latin, perceived through their genetic unity (Traina 1971: 270), had offered the final testimony of the 'iron immortality' (G. K. Chesterton) of this dead language.

References

D. Alonso (1965), *Saggio di metodi e limiti stilistici*, Bologna.

F. Altheim (1955), *La Religion romaine antique*, Paris.

C. H. Bally (1963), *Linguistica generale e linguistica francese*, ed. by C. Segre, Milan.

J. Bayet (ed.) (1969), *Histoire politique et psychologique de la religion romaine*, II.

M. Barchiesi (1963), *Nevio epico*, Padua.

J. De Maistre (1821), *Du pape*, Paris.

G. De Ruggiero (1967), *La filosofia del Cristianesimo*, Bari.
G. De Sanctis (1931), 'Livio e la storia della storiografia romana', *Pégaso*, p. 280.
—— (1957), *Storia dei Romani*, IV, II, 1, Florence.
G. Devoto (1946), *Dizionari di ieri e di domani*, Florence.
—— (1951), *I fondamenti della storia linguistica*, Florence.
G. Dumézil (1949), *L'Heritage indoeuropéen à Rome*, Paris.
—— (1966), *La Religion romaine archaique*, Paris.
F. Dupont (1990), *La vita quotidiana nella Roma repubblicana*, Rome–Bari.
A. Ghiselli (1966), *L'attrazione modale in latino*, Bologna.
J. Hubaux (1945), *Les Grands Mythes de Rome*, Paris.
C. Kerényi (1951), *La religione antica*, Rome.
F. Leo (1913; repr. 1958), *Geschichte der römischen Literatur*, I, Berlin.
S. Mariotti (1986), *Livio Andronico e la traduzione artistica*,[2] Urbino.
C. Marchesi (1944), *Seneca*,[3] Milan.
S. Mazzarino (1966), *Il pensiero storico classico*, 2 vols., Bari.
A. Meillet (1897), 'De l'expression de l'aoriste en latin', *Rev. Philol.* 21: 81–90.
—— (1926), *Linguistique historique et linguistique générale*, Paris.
—— (1966), *Esquisse d'une histoire de la langue latine*,[7] Paris.
A. Momigliano (1988), *Saggi di storia della religione romana*, Rome.
A. Montagu (1966), *La razza. Analisi di un mito*, Turin.
G. Mounin (1963), *Les Problèmes théoriques de la traduction*, Paris.
E. Norden (1958), *Antike Kunstprosa*,[3] Darmstadt.
R. Oniga (1988), *I composti nominali latini*, Bologna.
A. Pagliaro and W. Belardi (1963), *Linee di storia linguistica dell'Europa*, Rome.
G. Pasquali (1920), 'Il carme 64 di Catullo', *Stud. Ital. Fil. Class.*, NS 1: 1–23.
A. Ronconi (1959), *Il verbo latino*,[2] Florence.
A. Rostagni (1939), *Classicità e spirito moderno*, Turin.
E. Sapir (1929), 'The Status of Linguistics as a Science', *Language*, 5: 206–14.
—— (1949), *Selected Writings*, ed. D. G. Mandelbaum, Berkeley and Los Angeles.
A. Schaff (1965), *Introduzione alla semantica*, Rome.
F. Schulz (1946), *Principii del diritto romano*, Florence.
L. Spitzer (1959), *Marcel Proust e altri saggi di letteratura francese*, Turin.
F. Stolz (1911), *Geschichte der lateinischen Sprache*, Leipzig.
—— A. Debrunner, and W. P. Schmid (1966), *Geschichte der lateinischen Sprache*,[4] Berlin.
—— —— —— (1968), *Storia della lingua latina (Appendice: La formazione della lingua letteraria latina, di J. M. Tronskij)*. Introduzione e note di A. Traina, Bologna.
—— —— —— (1993), *Storia della lingua latina (Appendice: La formazione della lingua letteraria latina, di J. M. Tronskij)*,[4] rev. E. Vineis, Bologna.
A. Traina (1971), *Saggio sul latino del Pascoli*,[2] Florence.
—— (1987), *Lo stile 'drammatico' del filosofo Seneca*, Bologna.
—— (1989), *Poeti latini (e neolatini)*, III, Bologna.
J. M. Tronskij (1953), *Ocerki iz istorii latinskogo yazyka*, Moskow and Leningrad.
K. Vossler (1948), *Civiltà e lingua di Francia*, Bari.
B. L. Whorf (1956), *Language, Thought and Reality*, Cambridge, New York, and London.

CHAPTER 14

GENDER STUDIES

ANTHONY CORBEILL

Ancient Romans Examine Gender

Writers in ancient Rome devoted considerable energy to the investigation of gender, revealing a deep interest in the nature of the masculine and feminine as well as of a third category that they labelled with the characteristically non-committal term *neutrum* ('neither'). These writers are not particularly heavily studied today since the sexual characteristics that we see continually queried and catalogued by them belong not to human beings, but to the grammatical gender of nouns. And yet the time they spend considering grammatical gender is remarkable: Nonius Marcellus devotes in modern editions seventy pages of his treatise on Latin grammar and vocabulary to the subject, with terse entries such as the following: *GREGES, ut saepe, generis masculini sunt. Feminini. Lucretius lib. II: 'lanigerae pecudes et equorum duellica proles | buceriaeque greges'* ('GREGES is often masculine; Lucretius uses it in the feminine in book 2'; Non. p. 208.22–3). In the sixth century Priscian devotes a book of his highly influential *Institutiones* to the topic, and this scholarly activity culminates in the early twentieth century with a full compendium of 130 tightly packed pages offering the rules and exceptions for Latin gender discussed in these ancient texts (Neue 1902: 1. 889–1019). As un-sexy as these philological investigations may sound to modern scholars interested in sexual practice and blurred anatomies, they are in fact implicated in what ancient scholars hypothesized to be the very origins of sex and gender.

A single Latin word, *genus*, is used to describe both biological sex and grammatical gender (the less common *sexus* has a similar semantic range). The research produced in this area commonly appears under the title 'On Indeterminate Genders' (*De indiscretis generibus*), covering those nouns that have a standard, usually invariable, gender in Latin prose but that, particularly in poetic texts, a writer could vary according to context (and, it would seem, to whim). It is in such investigations that Roman grammarians are found speculating about their culture with the tools that they had available. One particularly productive approach was the use of etymology as a means of tracing cultural origins through observable linguistic phenomena. In a statement that reverberates throughout the lexicographical and grammatical tradition, in the first century BCE Varro derives *genus* from the verb *generare*, 'to beget', since grammatical gender, he says, is 'born from' the explicitly male or female aspect of the word it describes (Varro fr. 245 Funaioli). Words themselves participate in a biology of sexual reproduction. Any distinction between 'gender' and 'sex', if in fact one ever exists for these writers, vanishes. In conjunction with this etymology seems to have arisen a common story of origins, whereby the Latin language, 'born together with human beings', contains minor inconsistencies that, over time, specialists in the language are expected to explain and regularize (Charisius, *Ars Grammatica* p. 62.2–14 Barwick, apparently following Varro). It is here that these grammatical catalogues from antiquity become relevant to contemporary scholars of gender: the combination of anomaly and regularity that the Roman grammarians faced in the assignment of grammatical gender—words describing males and females tend to be (but are not always) masculine and feminine respectively, while inanimate objects could receive a range of genders that poetic texts felt free to assign in accordance with context (Renehan 1998)—finds its echo in the concerns of much of what nowadays falls under the rubric of 'Gender Studies'. In giving genders to Latin, the earliest Romans inevitably had to sex the world into explicit categories that anyone who uses the language is bound to follow. Men are men, women are women, but in between falls a range of sexualities that are continually the subject of negotiation.

Modern Scholars Examine Gender

'Gender Studies' among contemporary classicists has decidedly different origins and approaches from its ancient counterpart. As in other fields of the humanities, this area of study arises not so much from a repertory of discrete texts and facts as from attitudes that must be excavated out of the extant visual and textual evidence. Historically, the sub-discipline developed from an amalgamation of other areas of interest such as the study of sexual behaviours (particularly homoerotic behaviours) and masculinity, but the ultimate impetus arises from early feminist investigations,

investigations whose initial impulse was to recover the lived experience of women in Greek and Roman antiquity (Dixon 2001: 3–15 offers a concise history of work on the Roman material; see too Milnor in this volume). Feminist classicists have rightly observed that more recent scholarship on gender does not always acknowledge sufficiently its debt to this earlier work, particularly that done in the area of Roman Studies (Richlin 1991), and debate continues over whether this shift from the study of women to that of gender more generally will encourage a marginalization, rather than assimilation, of feminist approaches (see, for example, the panel 'Changing Lenses: The Politics and Discourse of Feminism in Classics', from the fourth conference on 'Feminism & Classics' [Skinner 2004]). Regardless of the repercussions of this shift, the changes in titles of some of the standard textbooks alone tell the story: from the still-essential sourcebook on *Women's Life in Greece and Rome*, first issued in 1982 (Lefkowitz and Fant 2005), to the new millennium's sourcebook *Sexuality and Gender in the Classical World* (McClure 2002) and narrative text *Sexuality in Greek and Roman Culture* (Skinner 2005). The shift in emphasis from women to gender and sexuality is reflected in what is taught: an on-line perusal clearly reveals the growing number of college-level courses on Greek and Roman gender and sexuality. In accordance with this shift, I shall be making only passing reference to classic feminist studies of Roman antiquity in the following remarks. In so doing, I am attempting neither to elide differences between studies of women and of gender, nor to minimize the importance of the former, but instead to concentrate on the new areas of research that have come open as a result of this hybridization. The permeability of disciplinary boundaries suggested by these origins involves a range of topics as broad as the field of Classics itself, from conceptions of Latin grammar to the effeminization of male poets to everyday tableware that depicts explicit sexual activity. In the few thousand words allotted, I hope to convey the excitement of this field, alternating my discussion (with inevitable idiosyncrasy) between seminal works and recent studies that seem to portend future trends. Citation does not imply agreement, nor does omission preclude endorsement.

Split

The grammarians' analysis of the Latin noun provides a convenient paradigm for analysing gender in Roman culture: masculine and feminine each normally describes a category requiring little negotiation, but uncertainty necessitates the creation of the third category of a true other, where status is defined negatively as not-masculine, not-feminine (*neutrum*). Analogous combinations of masculine, feminine, and neither recur outside the realm of Latin grammar. For example, a clear-cut dichotomy of the sexes is exemplified in the city of Rome's principal presiding deities, Venus and Mars, but these paradigms of the masculine and feminine share company with the city's *Genius*, over whose sex ancient scholars registered uncertainty (Servius Auctus, *Aeneid* 2.351). Another clear differentiation of the male from the female was on display during ancient festivals of Liber. At Lavinium, a disembodied phallus is paraded around the territory until coming to rest in the city's forum, where it is crowned by the most respected woman in the town (Varro in Augustine, *City of God* 7.21). This powerful image, delineating a difference between the sexes that concludes with their union, contrasts with depictions given by another source, where celebrations of this same deity imported from the East blur the sexuality of worshippers. Men, the historian Livy tells us, participate in ritual activity involving Bacchus that causes them to resemble women (*simillimi feminis mares*; Livy 39.13–17). The threat of this deviant religious activity caused the Senate to take steps to control worship. It is in border areas such as these, where biological sex contends with constructions of gender, that much recent scholarship has tended to concentrate. And in a pragmatic fashion that is truly Roman, much of the scholarship centres on the concrete, on the ways that gender is described as manifesting itself in bodily dispositions. In surveying the areas that follow, therefore, the human body will emerge repeatedly as the starting-point of investigation.

Men and Non-men (Women)

The Latin language has two sets of words to designate the biological distinction between 'man' and 'woman'. The designation chosen in any particular case carried ideological impact in Latin prose works, with *vir/femina* tending to connote members of the elite in contrast with the non-elite *homo/mulier* (Santoro L'Hoir 1992). As one might expect in the contentious world of Roman society, the definition of 'elite' in this discourse depends not simply on birth or political office, but carries over into behaviours and attitudes. As a result, any member of the elite who poses a political threat or can be shown to be morally dubious may be labelled by an opponent with the derogatory pair *homo/mulier*. Among scholars of the last few decades, the element of this lexical distinction that has received the most attention is how these terms play out in the realm of sexuality. Attracting particular interest are the many ways in which the activities ascribed to the Roman *vir* receive meaning by contrast with the behaviours that are considered appropriate for a Roman woman. The political, in other words, coalesces with the sexual as the man who does not live up to being a *vir* comes to have his alleged immorality written on his body for all to see—or, more frequently, for all to be taught to see by an opponent (Edwards 1993: 63–97).

In her landmark study of Roman sexual humour, Richlin uses the figure of the god Priapus, ithyphallic protector of gardens, as a paradigm for the often violent forms of aggression expressed in Roman treatments of sexual matters (Richlin [1983] 1992). Her observations were to anticipate the so-called 'penetration model' of Roman sexuality, according to which the Roman man is envisioned as always playing the insertive role in sexual acts—vaginal, oral, anal—with the receptive, or passive, role identified with the woman or effeminate male (Parker 1997; Williams 1999: 160–224). Such a rigid model of man as penetrator and woman as penetrated requires that any deviation signal deviance. Two types of sexual inverts referred to in invective texts of prose and poetry illustrate well the model in action. *Tribades*, the dominant women in a homoerotic relationship, take a role that in Roman texts can be envisioned only as analogous with the phallic role of the male (Hallett [1989] 1997; Ormand 2005). The male deviant, the receiving counterpart to the person penetrating sexually, is commonly designated by the Greek loan word *cinaedus*. Among the scholarly controversies aroused by this figure is the issue of whether the *cinaedi* that are frequently derided in extant texts had correspondence with identifiable figures in the real world and, if so, whether they constituted a recognizable 'sub-culture' (Richlin 1993; Williams 1999: 172–229). Habinek has recently discussed this figure within the historical context of song in early Rome. By emphasizing that the term *cinaedus* properly describes a dancer, he argues that developing suspicions about a man's relationship with the body in Rome came to associate overly expressive movements of cinaedic song and dance with sexually effeminate decadence (Habinek 2005: 177–219). An important outcome of these analyses is that most modern scholars acknowledge that these categories of female *tribades* and male *cinaedi*, since they normally involve non-reciprocal homoerotic acts, do not correspond to the standard modern conception of female and male homosexuality.

Public Life

Recent studies of Roman rhetoric and oratory demonstrate some of the repercussions of the underlying principle that 'speaking style mirrors life style' (Seneca, *Epistulae Morales* 114.1: *talis... oratio qualis vita*). During the Republic, rhetoric offered a public site for contesting the definition of maleness, with the political opponent being consistently stigmatized as effeminate, a charge that involves him in a host of vices associated with lack of control over the body (Corbeill 1997: 99–128). The correlation of the physical and the moral seems implicated in ancient views that external appearance can supply to the attentive observer valuable indications regarding internal moral character (Gleason 1995). Indeed, both theory and oratorical practice appear to isolate rhetorical virility not simply as a function of gender, but of political orientation and social class as well (Corbeill 2004: 107–39; Connolly 2007). As would be expected, this rhetoric also intrudes upon formal discussions of style during the Republic, when the literary-critical terminology of the Atticist/Asianist debate involves men describing the speaking styles of their opponents using words that denote effeminacy and lack of self-control (Dugan 2001). The identification of oratorical style with life style was eventually to become a motif that characterized the biography of prominent speakers, Julius Caesar and Maecenas being notable examples (Kraus 2005; Graver 1998). During the empire, the ever-precarious nature of masculinity continued to dominate the declamatory schools, which come to legislate not just words but gendered types of movement (Richlin 1997*b*). These same texts complement Quintilian's account of the education of the orator, as he details that the steps involved in training boys to be effective orators include exploiting existing prejudice against the speech and appearance of women (Connolly 1998). Aspiring orators were not simply allowed to grow into manhood; they had to learn precisely how to become men (Gunderson 2000). Indeed, it has recently been suggested that not simply the modes of speaking Latin properly but the Latin language itself is gendered as masculine, a situation that by definition compels the speech of women to be viewed as degenerate or substandard unless they adopt characteristics of the dominant, male form of discourse (Farrell 2001: 52–83). The notion that the very language is masculine provides an interesting lens through which to view gender criticism in Latin poetry, since a key controversy of recent studies in this area has been whether Roman poets (almost exclusively male) can offer an exception to the dominant tropes of male speech that pervade the oratorical texts and rhetorical treatises.

Poetry

Anxieties about masculinity determine the approach of much recent work on Roman poetry. I can give only a few representative examples, organized by author. In the poetry of Catullus, the castration of Attis in Poem 63, which results in his grammatical transformation into a woman, has been read as expressive of male anxieties over the state of masculinity in the late Republic, with the poet displacing feelings of political impotence onto his feminized persona (Skinner [1993] 1997). A reading inspired by anthropological parallels and postmodern theory has taken a similar view of Catullus' invective poetry, reading it as a self-conscious performance of Roman manhood that makes manifest the homosocial interactions prevailing among the male elite, even in the case of the poems that overtly deal with erotic attraction to women (Wray 2001). This reading Romanizes the often Romanticized poet by placing the fiercely aggressive language and posings of his erotic life into the well-known context of male political rivalry. In so doing, it resists the popular tendency to see Catullus as some kind of ironic advocate of social reform. In opposition to this rivalry of aggression stands the erotics of male bonding. Oliensis has demonstrated ways in which Horace, Tibullus, and Propertius construct friendship in their poetry in resistance to the phallic model of domination and submission so that both parties in a friendship play each role alternately rather than one doing so to the exclusion of the other (Oliensis 1997).

Latin love elegy has proven to be a particularly rich area for exploring issues of gender: do these poems represent a male-dominated view of society, as would seem a priori likely, or is there gender subversion taking place? The suggestion of Hallett (1973) that elegy may present us with a 'counter-cultural feminism' competes with alternative views that the women of these poetic texts are gendered, textual constructions of the male poet that serve to illustrate the male poet's alienation from political life, an alienation that he marks, or that Roman society forces him to mark, as 'effeminate' (Wyke 2002: esp. 11–45, 155–91). Informing this latter interpretation is once again the assumed equivalence of an engagement in politics with true masculinity.

It is hardly surprising that the pre-eminently male genre of epic assists in reproducing gender hierarchies at Rome. The tales of martial heroism found in these texts function analogously to the heroic exempla from Roman history that form such an essential part of a young Roman boy's education. A recent analysis of gender in epic has noted this resemblance and, accordingly, has focused not only upon the poetic texts themselves, but also upon how their reception in exegetical and pedagogical texts helps teach (primarily) young men of the elite the true nature of Roman masculinity (Keith 2000: 8–35).

Violence

As some of the studies already mentioned show, the relationships of dominance and submission observable in poetic and prose texts are often accompanied by both verbal and physical violence. Several literary examinations have paid explicit attention to how the violence that permeates Roman society informs our understanding of gender roles. The many accounts of female rape in Ovid's poetry are examined by Richlin, who analyses ways that these narratives reflect Roman attitudes regarding violence toward women and suggests critical approaches that can be adopted in reading and teaching them (1992: 158–79). Rape in fact underlies two well-known events from Roman history, events that would have provided moral exempla to Roman children concerning proper behaviour for the virtuous woman. In Livy's depictions of Lucretia and Verginia (sixth and fifth centuries BCE), the survival of an ideal of female chastity after sexual violation necessitates that each woman die. These particular tales, taking place at critical junctures in the development of the Roman Republic, reveal the reciprocal relationship of masculine honour and female sexuality, and the importance of both in the creation and development of Roman political ideology (Joshel 1992: 112–30; see a similar analysis of women in epic at Keith 2000: 101–31).

Ironically, the Roman soldier has been held up as an exception to the strict model of masculine/penetrator and feminine/penetrated. Although possessing hypermasculine qualities, the soldier is nevertheless subject to penetration from both enemy weapons and the punishment meted out by his superiors (Walters 1997). Analogously, one way that the elegiac poet has been conceived as stepping outside the trap of effeminacy is through descriptions of his own violence as acted out upon the feminine beloved, a violence that, like that against the soldier, allows the poet to act as penetrator (Fredrick 1997). Studies such as these are beginning to nuance the oppressive pervasiveness of the phallic model, both in Roman culture and scholarship.

Art and Archaeology

Extant visual material from ancient Rome reaffirms the dichotomies of active men and passive women that are found in the textual evidence. The ways in which seated figures are portrayed, for example, reflect the division dictated by treatises that treat bodily etiquette (e.g. Cicero's *On Duties*, Quintilian's *Institutio*): male figures tend to sit with a wide, open posture of the arms and legs, while women adopt a pose that is more reserved and focused inward (Davies 2005). And yet, just as powerful women can be described in texts as slipping into the behaviour that Roman society has marked as male (Santoro L'Hoir 1994), so too do the visual representations of women such as the empress Livia adopt postures more in keeping with the masculine. This trend toward masculine iconography becomes particularly prevalent in the depiction of women known to wield a degree of power unusual for their sex (Varner 2008). The meaning of a representation can also change over time; a clear example can be found in depictions of Omphale, the Lydian queen who enslaved the hypermasculine Hercules and forced him to adopt the clothing and to perform the domestic labour of a woman. Although this mythical episode constituted a problematic source for artistic representations during the early empire, by the second and third centuries Omphale appears on funerary and honorific sculpture as her ability to destabilize gender boundaries becomes a desideratum, promising the possibility of transcending the boundaries between life and death as well (Kampen 1996). In an analysis of architectural remains, Kellum has offered an engaging analysis of the gendering of the Forum of Augustus in Rome. Depictions of captive women alternate with statues of Rome's 'greatest men' (*summi viri*) in a space whose ground-plan, she suggests, resembles a phallus (Kellum 1996). Much further work could be done on the ways in which the very physical spaces of the Roman Empire were gendered. At the same time as it seems to support the phallic model, however, art also offers up the occasional deviations from what male elite texts would anticipate, such as the scenes of lovemaking between adult males depicted on the finely carved Warren Cup, or the imaginative sexual scenarios recently discovered in the Suburban Baths at Pompeii (Clarke 1998: 61–78, 212–40).

While pre-dating what would traditionally be termed 'Roman Studies', Whitehouse 2001, by moving beyond the simple cataloguing of grave goods as either 'male' or 'female', provides a fascinating, while inevitably speculative, survey of the kinds of information that the silent archaeological remains can offer concerning the construction of sexuality in pre-literate Italy. Koloski-Ostrow and Lyons 1997 contain a further sampling of the sorts of investigations of the material evidence that can provide comparison or contrast with the written record, and includes consideration of breast-feeding, hermaphrodites, and the ways in which the design of the Imperial Roman house reflects the control of the male *patronus*.

Law, Ritual, and Medicine

Studies of Roman law have concentrated on reconstructing the legal position of women, particularly in relation to marriage and the family (Herrmann-Otto 2002 summarizes the literature; see too Milnor in this volume). Here too a broader analysis of gender can open new avenues of investigation. Dixon, for example, has analysed both legal and other prose texts over the course of Roman history that refer to the guardianship (*tutela*) of adult women, a system originally designed to safeguard a family's claim on its property in the event of marriage. This convenient form of supervision, however, becomes misrecognized over time as invective texts come to attribute its establishment to a woman's inherent mental and intellectual deficiencies regarding matters of business (Dixon 2001: 73–88). An analogous claim has been made concerning a woman's inability to have legal *postestas* in Roman law: most likely enacted because of the constraints felt by women from childbirth and child-rearing, this responsibility too became construed by jurists as a lack stemming from a deficiency inherent in the female sex (Gardner 1993: 85–109). These attempts to read against the extant written sources offer ways of reconstructing woman's lived experience in the absence of testimony written by women themselves. Outside the legal sphere, such a methodology has been applied to the female role in mourning the dead; rather than representing an inherent weakness in the face of grief, as male-authored texts unanimously depict it, the elements of funerary ritual performed by women can be interpreted to show them actively participating in the welfare of the deceased in a way that frees them from the notion that they are unwilling, polluted agents for disposing of the dead (Corbeill 2004: 67–106).

Other rituals that communicate with the more-than-human have received attention for the information that they provide about Roman gender categories. The hermaphrodite, a figure offering a true 'third sex', is recorded by Pliny as moving from being the object of religious awe under the Republic to being a plaything of the rich in the Empire (*Natural History* 7.34). This transition from the mystical to the entertaining is echoed in modern studies. Closer analysis of the texts and myths that treat the hermaphrodite reveal that its dual sexuality was in fact thought to embody within itself the state of mysterious indistinction from which the universe originates, while at the same time the living creature of the hermaphrodite, along with its artistic representation, provides pleasure and entertainment for human beings (Ajootian 1997; Brisson [1997] 2002).

Investigations into Greek and Roman love magic reveal that the social construction of gender also appears in these non-elite texts, but in such a way that gender-types become a reflection of class and not biological sex. Men of subordinate social status, such as freedmen, perform the types of magic traditionally associated with women, while the aggressive love charms typically deployed by men to arouse the women that they desire are also found in use by powerful female figures such as courtesans and prostitutes (Faraone 1999: 132–72). Types of behaviour that seem a peculiarity for the sex of the person involved in fact accord with what we should expect of their particularly Roman gender.

The practice of Roman medicine, as inherited from the Greek tradition, has recently been the subject of a thorough analysis that attempts to locate the many ways in which women's roles are shaped by this male-dominated practice and discourse (Flemming 2000). The more difficult to recover world of folk medicine, in which women frequently appear as both sites of pollution and agents of cure, offers possible insight into how women viewed the potential of their own bodies, divorced from the elite male discourses of medicine and philosophy (Richlin 1997*a*).

Final Remarks

Much recent work that falls under the rubric of 'Gender Studies' has moved from attempting to recover the real, lived experience of a 'Roman woman' or 'Roman man' to analysing the discourses that shape these categories (and their transgressions). One area of future growth, instances of which I have already referred to above, would involve the attempt to find areas in which individuals or groups can be shown to work outside the dichotomous model into which I have placed (in some cases perhaps unfairly) the majority of the previous studies. Fredrick has outlined this kind of approach by incorporating modern scholarly insights regarding Roman gender—in particular the penetration model—into an analysis of the various social hierarchies that one finds in the late Republic and Empire to show 'how Roman space reflects and encodes degrees of immersion in the body that vary with social class and gender' (Fredrick ed. 2002: 237). Emphasis on the impact of sexual behaviours on masculinity has also caused scholars to ignore the influence of the feminine on social behaviours and political ideology. Milnor 2005 examines a range of textual evidence to show how the articulation of female presence in both domestic contexts and public spaces serves to reinforce Augustan views of the relationship between each citizen's home and the state. Such readings promise to add nuance to the strictly bipolar society that I have outlined above (for other examples from recent scholarship, see the survey in Corbeill 2006: 451–4). Many areas remain to be explored; the application of Gender Studies to Rome is limited by neither genres nor periods, but only by imagination.

Further reading

To suggest bibliography in such a vibrant and growing field is to invite disagreement, and to ensure obsolescence upon publication. I concentrate on general and recent work where interested readers can find good bibliography on particular points. For a full bibliography, along with teaching materials, images, and more, see the essential website *Diotima: Materials for the Study of Women and Gender in the Ancient World* (www.stoa.org/diotima). An excellent survey of Roman sexuality and gender, with up-to-date bibliography, appears in Skinner 2005. Among recent collections, those devoted to exclusively Roman issues include Hallett and Skinner 1997, Fredrick 2002, and Ancona and Greene 2005. The impression from the preceding that Gender Studies in the scholarship on ancient Rome is largely an Anglo-American concern is being corrected by a series founded in 2002 entitled *Iphis: Beiträge zur altertumswissenschaftlichen Genderforschung*, which explicitly aims to promote the study of gender in antiquity among German-speaking scholars. Three volumes have appeared to date (Feichtinger and Wöhrle 2002; Fuhrer and Zinsli 2003; Harich-Schwarzbauer and Späth 2005).

References

Ajootian, A. (1997), 'The Only Happy Couple. Hermaphrodites and Gender', in Koloski-Ostrow and Lyons eds.: 220–42.

Ancona, R., and E. Greene, eds. (2005), *Gendered Dynamics in Latin Love Poetry*, Baltimore: Johns Hopkins University Press.

Brisson, L. (2002), *Sexual Ambivalence: Androgyny and Hermaphroditism in Graeco-Roman Antiquity*, Berkeley and Los Angeles: University of California Press. Tr. J. Lloyd of *Le Sexe incertain*, Paris 1997.

Clarke, J. R. (1998), *Looking at Lovemaking: Constructions of Sexuality in Roman Art, 100 B.C.–A.D. 250*, Berkeley and Los Angeles: University of California Press.

Connolly, J. (1998), 'Mastering Corruption: Constructions of Identity in Roman Oratory', in S. Joshel and S. Murnaghan (eds.), *Women and Slaves in Greco-Roman Culture: Differential Equations*, London and New York: Routledge, 130–51.

—— (2007), 'Virile Tongues: Rhetoric and Masculinity', in W. J. Dominik and J. Hall (eds.), *A Companion to Roman Rhetoric*, Oxford: Blackwell Publishing, 83–97.

Corbeill, A. (1997), 'Dining Deviants in Roman Political Invective', in Hallett and Skinner eds.: 99–128.

—— (2004), *Nature Embodied. Gesture in Ancient Rome*, Princeton: Princeton University Press.

—— (2006), 'The Republican Body', in R. Morstein-Marx and N. Rosenstein (eds.), *A Companion to the Roman Republic*, Oxford: Blackwell Publishing, 439–56.

Davies, G. (2005), 'On Being Seated: Gender and Body Language in Hellenistic and Roman Art', in D. Cairns (ed.), *Body Language in the Greek and Roman Worlds*, Swansea, 215–38.

Dixon, S. (2001), *Reading Roman Women: Sources, Genres and Real Life*, London: Duckworth.

Dugan, J. (2001), 'Preventing Ciceronianism: C. Licinius Calvus' Regimens for Sexual and Oratorical Self-Mastery', *Classical Philology*, 96: 400–28.

Edwards, C. (1993), *The Politics of Immorality in Ancient Rome*, Cambridge: Cambridge University Press.

Faraone, C. (1999), *Ancient Greek Love Magic*, Cambridge, Mass.: Harvard University Press.

Farrell, J. (2001), *Latin Language and Latin Culture from Ancient to Modern Times*, Cambridge: Cambridge University Press.

Feichtinger, B., and G. Wöhrle, eds. (2002), *Gender Studies in den Altertumswissenschaften: Möglichkeiten und Grenzen*, Trier: Wissenschaftlicher Verlag Trier. Iphis: Beiträge zur altertumswissenschaftlichen Genderforschung 1.

Flemming, R. (2000), *Medicine and the Making of Roman Women: Gender, Nature, and Authority from Celsus to Galen*, Oxford: Oxford University Press.

Fredrick, D. (1997), 'Reading Broken Skin: Violence in Roman Elegy', in Hallett and Skinner eds.: 172–93.

—— (2002), 'Mapping Penetrability in Late Republican and Early Imperial Rome', in Fredrick ed.: 236–64.

—— ed. (2002), *The Roman Gaze: Vision, Power, and the Body*, Baltimore: Johns Hopkins University Press.

Fuhrer, T., and S. Zinsli, eds. (2003), *Gender Studies in den Altertumswissenschaften: Rollenkonstrukte in antiken Texten*, Trier: Wissenschaftlicher Verlag Trier. Iphis: Beiträge zur altertumswissenschaftlichen Genderforschung 2.

Gardner, J. (1993), *Being a Roman Citizen*, London and New York: Routledge.

Gleason, M. (1995), *Making Men: Sophists and Self-Presentation in Ancient Rome*, Princeton: Princeton University Press.

Graver, M. (1998), 'The Manhandling of Maecenas: Senecan Abstractions of Masculinity', *American Journal of Philology*, 119: 607–32.

Gunderson, E. (2000), *Staging Masculinity: The Rhetoric of Performance in the Roman World*, Ann Arbor, Mich.: University of Michigan Press.

Habinek, T. (2005), *The World of Roman Song: From Ritualized Speech to Social Order*, Baltimore: Johns Hopkins University Press.

Hallett, J. (1973), 'The Role of Women in Roman Elegy: Countercultural Feminism', *Arethusa*, 6: 103–24.

——(1997), 'Female Homoeroticism and the Denial of Reality in Latin Literature', in Hallett and Skinner eds.: 255–73. Orig. publ. *Yale Journal of Criticism*, 3 (1989), 209–27.

——and M. Skinner, eds. (1997), *Roman Sexualities*. Princeton: Princeton University Press.

Harich-Schwarzbauer, H., and T. Späth, eds. (2005), *Gender Studies in den Altertumswissenschaften: Räume und Geschlechter in der Antike*, Trier: Wissenschaftlicher Verlag Trier. Iphis: Beiträge zur altertumswissenschaftlichen Genderforschung 3.

Herrmann-Otto, E. (2002), 'Frauen im römischen Recht mit einem Ausblick auf Gender Studies in der Alten Geschichte und der antiken Rechtsgeschichte', in Feichtinger and Wöhrle eds.: 25–40.

Joshel, S. (1992), 'The Body Female and the Body Politic: Livy's Lucretia and Verginia', in Richlin ed.: 112–30.

Kampen, N. (1996), 'Omphale and the Instability of Gender', in Kampen ed.: 233–46.

——ed. (1996), *Sexuality in Ancient Art*, Cambridge: Cambridge University Press.

Keith, A. M. (2000), *Engendering Rome: Women in Latin Epic*, Cambridge: Cambridge University Press.

Kellum, B. (1996), 'The Phallus as Signifier: The Forum of Augustus and Rituals of Masculinity', in Kampen ed.: 170–83.

Koloski-Ostrow, A. O., and C. Lyons, eds. (1997), *Naked Truths: Women, Sexuality, and Gender in Classical Art and Archaeology*, London and New York: Routledge.

Kraus, C. S. (2005), 'Hair, Hegemony, and Historiography: Caesar's Style and its Earliest Critics', in T. Reinhardt, M. Lapidge, and J. N. Adams (eds.), *Aspects of the Language oj Latin Prose*, Oxford: Oxford University Press, 97–115.

Lefkowitz, M., and M. Fant, eds. (2005), *Women's Life in Greece and Rome: A Source Book in Translation*, 3rd edn., Baltimore: Johns Hopkins University Press.

McClure, L., ed. (2002), *Sexuality and Gender in the Classical World: Readings and Sources*, Malden, Mass.: Blackwell Publishing.

Milnor, K. (2005), *Gender, Domesticity, and the Age of Augustus: Inventing Private Life*, Oxford: Oxford University Press.

Neue, F. (1902), *Formenlehre der lateinischen Sprache. Erster Band: Das Substantivum*, 3d edn. C. Wagener, Leipzig: O. R. Reisland.

Oliensis, E. (1997), 'The Erotics of *amicitia*: Readings in Tibullus, Propertius, and Horace', in Hallett and Skinner eds.: 151–71.

Ormand, K. (2005), 'Impossible Lesbians in Ovid's *Metamorphoses*', in Ancona and Greene eds.: 79–110.

Parker, H. (1997), 'The Teratogenic Grid', in Hallett and Skinner eds.: 47–65.

Renehan, R. (1998), 'On Gender Switching as a Literary Device in Latin Poetry', in P. Knox and C. Foss (eds.), *Style and Tradition: Studies in Honor of Wendell Clausen*, Stuttgart and Leipzig: Teubner, 212–29.

Richlin, A. (1991), 'Zeus and Metis: Foucault, Feminism, Classics', *Helios*, 18: 160–80.

—— ([1983] 1992), *The Garden of Priapus: Sexuality and Aggression in Roman Humor*, Oxford: Oxford University Press.

—— (1992), 'Reading Ovid's Rapes', in Richlin ed., 158–79.

—— ed. (1992), *Pornography and Representation in Greece and Rome*, Oxford: Oxford University Press.

—— (1993), 'Not Before Homosexuality: The Materiality of the *Cinaedus* and the Roman Law Against Love Between Men', *Journal of the History of Sexuality*, 3: 523–73.

—— (1997*a*), 'Pliny's Brassiere', in Hallett and Skinner eds.: 197–220.

—— (1997*b*), 'Gender and Rhetoric: Producing Manhood in the Schools', in W. Dominik (ed.), *Roman Eloquence: Rhetoric in Society and Literature*, London and New York: Routledge, 90–110.

Santoro L'Hoir, F. (1992), *The Rhetoric of Gender Terms: 'Man', 'Woman', and the Portrayal of Character in Latin Prose*, Leiden: E. J. Brill.

—— (1994), 'Tacitus and Women's Usurpation of Power', *Classical World*, 88: 5–25.

Skinner, M. (1997), '*Ego mulier*: The Construction of Male Sexuality in Catullus', in Hallett and Skinner eds.: 129–50. Orig. published in *Helios*, 20 (1993), 107–30.

—— (2005), *Sexuality in Greek and Roman culture*, Malden, Mass.: Blackwell.

—— ed. (2004), 'Gender and Diversity in Place: Proceedings of the Fourth Conference on Feminism and Classics', http://www.stoa.org/diotima/essays/fc04/.

Varner, E. (2008), 'Transcending Gender: Assimilation, Identity, and Roman Imperial Portraits', in S. Bell and I. L. Hansen (eds.), *Role Models in the Roman World: Identity and Assimilation*, Ann Arbor, Mich.: University of Michigan Press, 185–206. Supplements to the Memoirs of the American Academy in Rome 7.

Walters, J. (1997), 'Invading the Roman Body: Manliness and Impenetrability in Roman Thought', in Hallett and Skinner eds.: 29–46.

Whitehouse, R. (2001), 'Exploring Gender in Prehistoric Italy', *Papers of the British School at Rome*, 69: 49–96.

Williams, C. (1999), *Roman Homosexuality: Ideologies of Masculinity in Classical Antiquity*, New York and Oxford: Oxford University Press.

Wray, D. (2001), *Catullus and the Poetics of Roman Manhood*, Cambridge: Cambridge University Press.

Wyke, M. (2002), *The Roman Mistress*, Oxford: Oxford University Press.

CHAPTER 15

CULTURE-BASED APPROACHES

MATTHEW ROLLER

Over the past generation, 'culture' has been a key analytical category across virtually all disciplines within the humanities and social sciences. The enormous range of ideas and values that has been associated with the term 'culture' makes it—along with its yokemate 'nature'—among the most complex and internally contradictory of all contemporary critical concepts. Various theorists have offered histories and interpretations of 'culture' in its multifarious deployments (e.g. Eagleton 2000), which I will not attempt to summarize, let alone replicate, here. Rather, my aim is to examine some of the ways this concept has been deployed in Roman Studies, and in classical scholarship more generally. In so doing, I hope to show what kinds of critical work this concept can be made to do; to make explicit some of the intellectual commitments that accompany the various uses of this term; to illustrate how these commitments are manifested in scholarly works that seem (to me) to represent useful points of reference in our ever-shifting understandings of what 'Roman culture' is; and to relate these manifestations in Roman Studies to those found in other disciplines of the humanities and social sciences. Many scholarly works discussed or cited below contain the word 'culture' in the title, or otherwise explicitly thematize the concept. Others do not, yet make assumptions about 'culture' that are the more revealing for being entirely implicit. When discussing my own work, I do not imagine it is the best or only work of a particular sort: it is merely familiar, hence a ready source of examples of the broader scholarly tendencies I seek to describe.

I begin with a usage of 'culture' as a category that encompasses various kinds of aesthetic activity. This usage derives ultimately from eighteenth- and nineteenth-century aesthetic theory. For Matthew Arnold, for example, culture marks a domain of endeavour—art, literature, music, and the like—that aids in the construction of the bourgeois citizen of the (nineteenth-century) nation-state, and is separated from but privileged over the sphere of sordid, practical activities like politics and economics. Hence cultural activities, being both elevated and elevating, are particularly appropriate to those who are, or aspire to become, bourgeois (Lloyd and Thomas 1998: 1–8). This concept of 'culture' remains current in everyday speech: 'cultural institutions' and 'cultured people' are those concerned with music, art, literature, and so on. Moreover, this concept has long been widespread in Roman Studies and Classics generally. The 'new critical' approach to literature that was current in Classics in the 1950s and 1960s, and somewhat earlier in other disciplines, presupposed something like this view of culture—treating the literary text as an autonomous object with no connections (of critical interest, at least) to the wider world. While few classical scholars nowadays would accept the idea of a completely autonomous, transcendent aesthetic sphere (due perhaps to the impact of Marxism or other materialist theories of society), nor would most scholars now restrict 'culture' to the socially elevated, the term continues to be used by classicists as an umbrella category whose contents are 'art plus literature plus philosophy (plus perhaps religion) . . .', which are collectively distinguished, if not held completely apart, from economics and politics.

Consider two instances from recent scholarship in Roman studies. Garnsey and Saller's survey, *The Roman Empire: Economy, Society, and Culture* (1987), contains chapters on imperialism, government, economy, land and agriculture, trade, status, family, and religion—traditional concerns of economic and social history. The 'culture' of the title is picked up only in the final chapter (ch. 10), where the authors examine how 'values and cultural life in Rome gradually adjusted to the monarchy' (p. 178); the specific areas in which they observe such adjustment taking place are philosophy, literature, rhetoric, art and architecture, law, and language, both in the city of Rome and in the provinces. Karl Galinsky's *Augustan Culture: An Interpretive Introduction* (1996) supposes a similar conception of culture. Despite the term's prominence in his title, Galinsky does not explicitly discuss or define it, nor is it found in his index. In his 'Introduction', however, he clearly distinguishes 'culture' from politics, and associates it with literature and art (pp. 4–5). Indeed, the book's heart is a series of chapters on 'Ideas, Ideals, and Values', art and architecture, literature, and religion. He asks what is distinctively 'Augustan' about such activities and products in this era, and how Augustanism makes its mark upon them. Thus both Galinsky and Garnsey/Saller implicitly embrace the aesthetic conception of culture as being the domain of art, literature, and the like, and as being separate (or separable) from politics and economics, albeit imprinted with political and economic concerns.

The aesthetic conception of culture is probably easy for classical scholars to adopt because it both reflects and reproduces the field's long-standing subdisciplinary structure. The objects that literary critics, art historians, and historians of philosophy study are neatly assigned to the category of 'culture', while historians of the social, economic, and political stripes preside over everything else. Thus a materialist/idealist dichotomy is built into the structure of the field—indeed, this dichotomy may have originated in Arnoldian-style aesthetic theory. It seems fair to say that this is the default conception of culture for many classical scholars, and can be deployed 'untheorized' without special justification or explanation (as Garnsey/Saller and Galinsky do), notwithstanding the edifice of Romantic aesthetic theory that underpins it. This conception, however, is not what the editors of this volume had in mind when they asked me to discuss 'culture-based approaches'. Being congruent with the traditional demarcation of subdisciplines, this conception offers no distinctive 'approach'—no critical purchase that is not already implied or suggested by that pre-existing subdisciplinary structure. Nevertheless, since this conception of culture is widespread among classicists, it is important to have its characteristics clearly in mind as we turn to other conceptions, including (eventually) the one intended by the editors.

An alternative way of conceptualizing culture derives from anthropological ideas about how to characterize the distinctive way of life of any particular group of people, and how to relate different ways of life to one another. An early articulation of this conception comes from E. B. Tylor's *Primitive Culture* (1871: 1): 'Culture or civilization, taken in its wide ethnographic sense, is that complex whole which includes knowledge, belief, art, morals, law, custom, and any other capabilities and habits acquired by man as a member of society.' Leaving aside the equation of 'culture' with 'civilization' (which probably no modern scholar would accept), we find here a definition of culture that differs strikingly from those discussed above. Far from restricting culture to specific products such as literature and art, and to the socially elevated activity of producing and consuming them, culture here embraces virtually every product and practice, implicitly including economics and politics, that could be attributed to *any* member of a society; yet it also casts the net still wider to capture beliefs, knowledge, and other mental states.

This definition, and others like it, have been criticized for being so broad as to exclude nothing except perhaps genetic inheritance, thus making 'culture' coextensive with society itself and depriving the concept of any critical edge (Eagleton 2000: 34). Yet the goal of such a definition is, more or less explicitly, to establish grounds for differentiation and comparison among the ways of life of different groups, which in turn presupposes that each group's way of life has a distinctive, specifiable coherence and systematicity. Accordingly, scholars impose limits in practice that enable the concept of 'culture' to perform these functions of differentiation and specification. Consider how the concept was inflected by anthropologists of the early-to-mid twentieth century who studied non-western, pre-industrial, non- or proto-commercialized societies of the sort they characterized as 'primitive'. These anthropologists tended to select a particular range of objects for investigation—notably kinship systems, rites and rituals, and regimes of exchange. Though these objects may have been constituted arbitrarily (others might have been constituted instead, or in addition), what matters is that they provided a usable, because sufficiently concrete and limited, basis for analysing any given group's way of life and for comparison among groups. Ancient societies were readily included in such analysis. For instance, Marcel Mauss's *Essai sur le don* (French 1924; English as *The Gift*, 1990) begins with an analysis of exchange in Polynesia, which is then extended to aspects of archaic Roman (and other ancient) law. Likewise Hendrik Wagenvoort, in his *Roman Dynamism* (English 1947, Dutch 1941), deploys the Austronesian category of *mana* as an umbrella category by which to encompass a number of seemingly divergent Roman concepts and practices relating to power, sanctity, and authority. On the basis of the *mana*-comparison, he argues for deep connections and regularities and among the Roman concepts. The overtly comparative method that characterizes these studies has modern counterparts in the current work of the Hellenist Marcel Detienne and the Romanist Maurizio Bettini. The latter's *Anthropology and Roman Culture*, for instance (English 1990, Italian 1987), contains essays on Roman kinship terminology, understandings of temporal relations, and images of the soul; the title itself announces the disciplinary affiliation of the concept of 'culture' deployed therein. Yet, this overtly comparative approach to ancient societies is typically labelled 'anthropological' rather than 'cultural', not least by Detienne and Bettini themselves.

This idea of 'culture' as encompassing a group's particular products, practices, and values potentially allows such groups to be defined almost at will on the basis of shared characteristics, and so distinguished as different 'cultures'. On what bases, and to what ends, such cultures should be defined is a live question in Roman Studies, as elsewhere. For example, the old idea of 'Romanization'—that is, that Roman imperialism resulted in the transference, by force or cooperatively, of Roman culture onto subjected peoples like Gauls, Britons, and Illyrians (but not Greeks!)—is currently being rethought; in question are both the utility of ascribing 'culture' on ethnic or geographic bases (i.e. at what level of analysis the very ideas of 'Roman culture', 'Gallic culture', etc. make sense and are helpful), and the dynamics and mechanisms by which these different groups exchanged their products and practices (e.g. Woolf 1998: 1–23, Barrett 1997). Moreover, one can seek to identify 'subcultures' within a notionally larger, more encompassing culture (e.g. Eagleton 2000: 36–44, Kurke and Dougherty 2003). Thus the non-elites of urban Rome have recently received intensive study, especially regarding how their products and practices relate to those of urban elites (e.g. Clarke 2003; Demaine and Taylor 1999). Among this work, Nicholas Horsfall's *The Culture of the Roman Plebs* (2003) offers a hybrid conception. In ascribing a distinctive form of 'culture' to urban non-elites, he hews to the anthropologically inflected conception of culture just described. Yet he is primarily interested in how people with little formal schooling and minimal literacy can nevertheless learn history and encounter literature. Thus the particular practices and products he considers are those associated with the aesthetic conception of culture.

What the editors of this volume are interested in is a conceptualization of culture that also has anthropological roots, but is not overtly comparative, and admits of other intellectual influences as well. The conceptualization in question was most compellingly articulated and widely disseminated, at least for North American scholars, through the work of Clifford Geertz. In his classic collection of essays *The Interpretation of Cultures* (1973), Geertz outlined an 'interpretive' anthropology that was fundamentally semiotic. Culture, he asserted, is 'an interworked system of construable signs' that forms the context in which social processes, practices, and concepts take on meaning and may be described (pp. 14, 24). For him, culture is ontologically much the same as what Tylor took it to be—a system of concepts, products, and practices. Yet Geertz gives it an epistemology as well: it has an observable symbolic character that makes it available to all, and potentially knowable to anyone who can interpret or construe that sign-system. Culture is less *what* a group thinks, feels, and makes, than the symbolic *medium* by, through, or with which it does these things (Ortner 1997: 6–7; Sewell 1997: 39). The paradigmatic symbolic system, for Geertz, is writing, and it is by analogy with literary-critical techniques that he imagines the interpretation of other cultural 'scripts' to proceed. While Geertz's formulations have probably been most influential among Anglophone scholars, continental theorists have expressed a similar conceptualization of culture employing the Foucauldian category of 'discourse' in place of Geertz's 'symbols'. Under this formulation, 'discursive formations' are the domain of cultural analysis; culture is then broadly understood as those social products and practices (or particular dimensions thereof) that are constructed discursively (e.g. Chartier 1994).

Just what are the concepts, products, and practices that count as 'cultural' on this understanding? Literature and texts in general, being the symbolic/discursive activity and product par excellence, still fall within the ambit of 'culture'. But so also does much of the 'political' sphere, since (for instance) governmental regimes and their opponents engage in symbolic activity that is supposed to be meaningful and interpretable to citizens/subjects, external enemies, and other interested observers. Likewise for many other dimensions of public or civic life: all kinds of performance and ritual practice, exchange, games, and so on involve symbolic activity that takes its meaning in relation to overarching symbolic structures. Thus culture resides in the symbolic or discursive *dimension* of social practices and products—the place where specific, socially situated deployments of signs intersect with the symbolic structures that give these deployments meaning. Some practitioners have held that symbolic structures actually determine human thought and practice, reducing the latter to mere 'expressions' of the former and thereby sweeping away agency. Other theorists argue, more plausibly, that structures organize and regulate practice but without determining it, hence that persons actively *make* meaning as they manipulate the symbolic resources that the structure puts at their disposal in any given social situation. On this view symbolic structures provide, as it were, the rules of a game and the equipment with which to play it, while practice involves the players' strategic, tactical, situationally conditioned interpretations of those rules and deployments of that equipment, as they play in quest of social advantage (Chartier 1988: 14; Ortner 1997: 10; Sewell 1999: 44–7; Kurke and Dougherty 1993: 3–5; Spiegel 2005: 11–18).

The cultural (in the sense of symbolic/discursive) dimensions of specific social practices may not, however, exhaust the interest and significance of these practices. The Roman practice of enslaving defeated enemies en masse, for instance, created new forms of symbolic capital, along with new modes of aristocratic display, in the last two centuries BCE. It also changed rural settlement and cultivation patterns, as well as the social status and identity of the people working the land. On the understanding of culture under discussion here, only the former, symbolic aspects of the practice admit of 'cultural' analysis, while the latter, non-symbolic aspects do not, notwithstanding their great interest to social historians. However, the questions of where exactly the boundaries of symbolic construability lie in specific cases or in general, how non-discursive or non-symbolic practices or processes can be recognized, and even whether all systems of signification should *ipso facto* be deemed 'cultural' systems, are much debated (e.g. Chartier 1994; Stedman Jones 1996: 26–8; Morris 2000: 14–17; Spiegel 1997: 28; Sewell 1999: 48–9; Eagleton 2000: 33–4). There remains, moreover, a wide range of opinion about whether, and to what extent, 'cultural' activity is dependent on more 'basic', material social processes (as orthodox Marxism would have it), or instead is autonomous enough to affect other processes and drive social change itself.

This semiotic conception of culture has had important theoretical and methodological consequences for students of past societies. Consider first the relationship between texts and the social situations in which they were produced. Insofar as texts and other social practices and products are regarded as discursively constructed and therefore amenable to similar interpretive techniques, any notional boundary between text and context, between literary product and the historical circumstances of its production, is dissolved into a single continuum of interpretable signs. Confronted with this, the famous 'linguistic turn', some literary critics—whose *métier* is the analysis of discourse—have been enticed to undertake semiotic analyses of cultural systems other than literary texts, which might formerly have been deemed 'context' and reserved for historians. Conversely, some historians have been spurred to develop their skills as interpreters of signs and discourses, the traditional domain of literary critics. Out of this mixing, the interdisciplinary categories of 'new historicism', 'cultural poetics', and '(new) cultural history' (a long-standing subcategory of social history, now reconfigured in light of the semiotic conception of culture) emerged in the 1980s—different flavours, essentially, of the semiotic analysis of 'culture' understood as an undifferentiated amalgam of text-and-context (Spiegel 1997: 12–18; Chartier 1988: 13–14). This convergence of literary and historical concerns and methods has had the salutary effect of reminding both literary critics and historians how complex the other's interpretive activity is; for instance, neither can provide full, true, clear knowledge to serve as a 'stable term' against which the other's complexities and enigmas can be tested (Kraemer 1989: 115–16, 126–8; Spiegel 1997: 19–23; Morris 2000: 27–8). In Roman Studies, early hints of this *rapprochement* between literary and historical studies may perhaps be seen in the 1980s vogue for projects entitled *Literature and Politics*..., or the like (e.g. Woodman and West 1984; Sullivan 1985; Powell 1992). While none of these studies are overtly semiotic, they do work on the assumption that literary discourses encode or project political discourses, and that the task of understanding how, why, and to what effect this encoding occurs requires the expertise of historians and literary scholars alike. To my knowledge, classicists began to articulate such questions in terms of the cultural theory under discussion only in the 1990s. Kurke and Dougherty (1993: 1–6) explain why the idea of culture as a 'text' constituted from writing, art, ritual practices, and so on—and whose interpretation therefore requires the expertise of historians, literary critics, art historians, and archaeologists together—offers an especially fruitful approach to the study of archaic Greece. And in Roman Studies, Thomas Habinek's *Politics of Latin Literature* (1998: 1–9) explicitly positions itself with respect to contemporary critical debates about the textuality of culture, the relation of text to context, and the social function of literature as an arena for competition among elites and the discourses they produce.

Such interdisciplinarity is a welcome consequence of the semiotic theory of culture. Yet the collapsing of text and context entails further complications. A familiar conundrum for classicists is that, when we seek to place an ancient text into some kind of context, we must often construct this context from assertions, hints, and silences within that very text. Thus we have long realized the necessity of considering to what extent the worlds our texts project as existing outside themselves may be objectively 'real', and to what extent such worlds are subject to fabrication, distortion, the imposition of characteristics convenient for the literary genre, and so on. To this extent, we have always understood that contexts themselves are (in the terms of cultural theory) discursive constructs. In its strongest poststructuralist form, however, the semiotic theory of culture finds here not a problem of insufficient evidence, but a fundamental epistemological limit. Drawing on Saussurean linguistics, according to which the signs that constitute the system of language (*langue*) take their meanings not through reference to an objective, external reality, but only through their differential relations to other signs, poststructuralism asserts that there is no unmediated access to an independently existing, objectively external 'context'. Rather, it holds that texts can give access only to 'circumambient discourses' projected from within themselves, discourses that are but further varieties of the same essential textuality as the text itself (e.g. Spiegel 1997: 14–15, 19). On this view we are in an inescapable abyss of textuality, with no access to pre- or extra-discursive reality—a view famously crystallized in Derrida's lapidary pronouncement: 'il n y'a pas de hors-texte.' Classicists (and others) are thereby relieved of the task of teasing apart the 'real' from the (purely) 'constructed' in our texts, though social historians have been nonplussed to have their entire field of enquiry bracketed off as inaccessible.

For several reasons, the strongest form of this claim—always controversial—does not now seem to command significant assent. Increasingly careful consideration of how texts and other discursive formations relate to the material practices that condition their production has led some scholars to conclude that the post-structuralist denial of *all* referentiality and instrumentality to language is indefensible (see Spiegel 1997: 24–8, 48–56; Morris 2000: 16). Moreover, non-discursive or non-symbolic aspects of social practice (discussed above), even if knowable only through discourse—that is, by talking or writing about them—nevertheless may operate according to different rules from discourse, and so cannot be fully encompassed by discourse; these necessarily form some kind of 'outside' with relation to textuality (Chartier 1994). Finally, methods that reject the Saussurean premise of non-referentiality have become more widely known and accepted among humanists. Cognitive scientists, for example, have argued that all human language is subtended by conceptual categories and schemata that are rooted in the human body and its modes of interacting with its environment, and indeed are hard-wired into the human brain. On this view, language does derive its meaning referentially, though that reference is ultimately to internal cognitive schemata rather than to things in an external world (e.g. Lakoff 1987: 269–303 and *passim*).

While Romanists have assuredly become more aware of the presence and character of discursive formations in ancient representational forms and of the difficulties of inferring 'real life' from them, I know of no significant Roman scholarship that has followed the poststructuralist move of denying referentiality on principle. On the contrary, some areas of Roman Studies are noteworthy for their efforts to strike a balance—to acknowledge that discursive construction is pervasive and poses an epistemological challenge, yet without abandoning 'reality'. Scholars who study Roman women, for example, have demonstrated that the moralizing, normative discourses about women that are commonly found in our (male-authored) texts cannot be taken to present historical realities (e.g. Maria Wyke's 1980s work on the elegiac 'mistress', now collected and updated in Wyke 2002). Yet in their desire to recover the 'hard surfaces' of ancient women's lives, these scholars have been reluctant to accept that *all* we can know securely about ancient women are the various discourses of which they are constructions. Let me present an instance from my own work on Roman dining. Certain texts assert that the ancestral, 'modest' practice of Roman women was to dine seated and abstain from wine. Other texts, meanwhile, represent women reclining and drinking wine, thus sharing with men the characteristic practices of leisured elite dining. Assuredly these are contradictory discourses about women's commensality projected by, and circumambient to, our texts. But must we stop there? If we attend to the rhetoric of these two modes of representation, we find that the first mode appears in very few texts, yet is always thematized and rhetorically elaborated. It makes an ideologically potent, normative claim about proper female comportment, whose retrojection into the past frames it as a compelling model for behaviour in the present. These texts project specific social anxieties about gender, sexuality, and intoxication. The second representation, conversely, tends to appear unthematized in many texts widely diffused over time and genre, texts that have entirely other focuses and themes. To me, the conclusion seems inescapable that the latter representations are textual reflexes of an actual contemporary social practice, apprehended as such by various authors in a range of contexts. These authors deploy such representations to construct a veristic background against which to pose their thematized representations, which often have nothing to do with gender or dining practices. The former representations, in fact, make little sense as behavioural norms unless actual social practice were exactly the opposite, that is, as the second discourse represents it (Roller 2006: 116–18, 153–6; see also Morris 2000: 16; Spiegel 1997: 24–8). Close attention to the rhetoric of such representations, then, may enable us to discern respects in which literary language functions referentially—indeed, to see that referentiality can itself participate in the construction of the discourses that constitute and mediate our perceptions of the world. Thus it seems possible to retain a semiotic view of culture as the symbolic/discursive medium through which human practices and products become meaningful, and to exploit the considerable power of semiotic analysis for interpreting ancient societies, without plunging into the poststructuralist abyss of non-referential textuality.

There is a second key way—beside its manner of articulating text with context—in which the semiotic conception of culture has impacted the study of past societies: namely, by promoting the formulation of 'synchronic' objects of analysis. This propensity follows from the conception of culture as (in part) a *system* of signs, or as a discursive *formation*. The structural aspect is thus presented as static, with all constituent signs existing simultaneously. This is not quite a 'snapshot' of a particular moment: it is the analytic suspension of time within a particular epoch so that signs actually deployed sequentially appear to coexist. The resulting analysis tends to elucidate the relationships among signs within a given system, hence explain what various moves and counter-moves within that system might mean and do, rather than illuminating the diachronic process of how and why the structure came into being and undergoes transformation (on these matters see Sewell 1997: 39–42; Spiegel 1997: 20–1). To be sure, synchronic analysis—identifying patterns, regularities, and consistencies that supposedly characterize the whole of a given time period—has always been an indispensable tool in the historian's kit, and there is nothing inherently semiotic about it. Indeed, synchrony is characteristic of much sociological theory, which generally seeks to explain particular states of society rather than social transformation. In Roman studies, certain time-spans have traditionally been constituted as synchronic epochs, for example, the 'age of Augustus' (Galinsky 1996; Zanker 1990) and the 'age of Nero' (Sullivan 1985). In these cases, the justification for constituting such a synchronic epoch appears to be that one person's mind, policies, and ideas subtend the period's cultural production in a consistent, regular manner. In fact this assumption is dubious, and a semiotic cultural analysis could as easily stress incoherence and disunity as coherence and systematicity. The larger point, however, is that any time-span might potentially be constituted as a synchronic epoch, depending on what one wishes to analyse. And semiotic cultural analyses are particularly prone to being framed synchronically.

A few examples of recent work in Roman Studies illustrate the capabilities of synchronic cultural analysis, as well as its limitations. Consider first Harriet Flower's *Ancestor Masks and Aristocratic Power in Roman Culture* (1995). As in certain studies mentioned earlier, Flower does not explicitly discuss or define the term 'culture', despite deploying it prominently in the title. Her argument, however, is unmistakably a synchronically framed semiotic analysis of a particular social product (the *imago* or ancestor mask) and the practices that involve it. Several chapters describe a discrete discourse or symbolic system within which the *imago* has meaning: the funeral, the *laudatio*, the atrium of the aristocratic house, the electoral assembly. The representations assembled for analysis are textual (literary or inscriptional), visual, architectural, and topographical, and for the most part date from or refer to the middle to late Republic. This, implicitly, is the synchronic epoch within which the systems of symbols and practices examined in these chapters are presented as coexisting. What justifies constituting this synchronic epoch, presumably, is the persistence of an oligarchic political system and a range of strategies by which aristocrats competed for prominence and power within this system. Flower pays a modicum of attention to change over time, with two chapters on imperial manifestations of the *imagines* and an appendix on putative Etruscan origins. But the book's heart is in the analysis of *imagines* deployed as symbols that create meaning in key arenas of competitive elite display, during an epoch in which a particular political system made such display both possible and advantageous.

A different epoch, with different justification, appears in Robert Kaster's *Emotion, Restraint, and Community in Ancient Rome* (2005). Here the author examines a group of Roman emotions that involve specific sequences of perception, evaluation, and response by persons experiencing them. Kaster calls these sequences 'scripts', a term in this case derived from cognitive studies of emotion. From cognitive science, too, comes his conception of how emotions instantiate and map onto psychological states. He also argues, however, that the emotions in question relate to one another and to social values in predictable ways; he thus considers how a set of practices—the 'scripts' that enact the emotions—relate to a structure of values that give them meaning. In this respect, the analysis of how signs in practice relate to signs as structure, his study is 'cultural' in our sense. The structure, moreover, is extremely durable: Kaster contends that the scripts he analyses barely change between about 100 BCE and 100 CE.

My own article entitled 'Exemplarity in Roman Culture' (2004) discusses what I call the discourse of exemplarity. I contend that a certain structure of values and practices, involving action, evaluation, commemoration, and imitation, remains essentially unchanged from the second century BCE (the age of Polybius) into the high empire. After describing this structure (pp. 4–7), I examine in detail how two specific exemplary figures are invoked and deployed in texts from this period, considering how each invocation both derives meaning from the structure and inflects elements of that structure to the advantage of the person deploying the exemplum.

Finally, consider Paul Zanker's celebrated study *The Power of Images in the Age of Augustus* (1990). Zanker's use of the term 'culture' in this study is purely aesthetic, referring always to art and literature. Yet the project itself, as the title suggests (equally in the original 1987 German edition: *Augustus und die Macht der Bilder*), insists on understanding visual representation in the context of 'power'—as a medium, indeed, through which the regime exercised its power. Thus the notionally unifying aims of Augustus himself—or rather, according to Zanker, the two quite different faces Augustus showed before and after Actium—provide the structures within which artworks of this era take on their individual and collective meaning. This book's warm reception and wide readership among literary critics and historians is largely attributable, I think, to its approach, which may have seemed familiar and comprehensible to scholars who themselves embraced a similar conception of culture. In short, Zanker's book made other scholars aware that the analysis of art could employ methods, and address problems, shared across subdisciplines.

Yet most students of past societies would probably agree that synchronic modes of analysis, no matter how powerful, cannot by themselves provide a fully satisfactory account of the past: equally essential are diachronic analyses that address how and why change occurs. Explaining change over time within a semiotic conception of culture involves explaining how one synchronically constituted system of signs turns into another that is significantly different. Such a project, one might reckon, entails more than twice the work of simply analysing a given cultural system synchronically. For one must undertake two such analyses of different synchronic stages, and then additionally account for how and why signs and their relations are transformed from the first stage to the second.

How might such transformation be understood, and what might an analysis of it look like? In any given situation, an individual actor combines and deploys available signs in a unique, individually and contextually determined way (Sahlins 2000). Thus the pre-constituted structural relations among signs are always being jostled, as it were, by the countless everyday cultural transactions of innumerable individual agents. The overall structural impact of such 'everyday' jostling is probably small. Significant structural shifts would seem to require special conditions: for instance, if many actors, through their everyday transactions, consistently press the pre-constituted relationships among signs in the same direction. Such pressure might be spurred by the appearance of unfamiliar or unprecedented situations that cannot be assimilated within the current symbolic structure. Marshall Sahlins's study *Historical Metaphors and Mythical Realities* (1981) is frequently praised for showing how such change was spurred in Hawaii by contact with European culture. Sahlins combines synchronic analyses of particular symbolic orders with diachronic accounts of how each order was transformed into the next, as the local culture assimilated European products and practices (see also Biersack 1989: 84–96; Kurke and Dougherty 1993: 3–4; Sewell 1997: 46–8, 1999: 51; Stedman Jones 1996: 30). I know few attempts at such diachronic symbolic analysis in Roman Studies. However, two studies seem worth mentioning. Consider first Habinek and Schiesaro's 1997 collection *The Roman Cultural Revolution*. Despite the titular nod to Ronald Syme's classic study *The Roman Revolution* (1939), the editors contend, *contra* Syme, that cultural change is central to whatever 'revolutionary' character the Augustan age and preceding decades may be thought to have. While the contributors embrace diverse conceptions of culture, one contribution—Andrew Wallace-Hadrill's '*Mutatio morum*: The Idea of a Cultural Revolution'—employs the semiotic conception in order to identify practices and structures that changed over this period. Wallace-Hadrill contends that the authoritative discourses of tradition, time, law, and language, which had long been embedded in a network of traditional aristocratic discourses and practices, were isolated and transformed under Augustus into specialist discourses. These were ordered according to 'scientific' principles derived from Hellenism, and controlled by specialized practitioners (antiquarians, astronomers, jurists, grammarians) who were new to the aristocracy and patronized by the Augustan regime. For Wallace-Hadrill, then, the signs and relations among signs that characterize these discursive formations in the late Republic (implicitly the first of two synchronic epochs) are reordered according to principles extrinsic to this system, and thus are transformed into their 'Augustan' configurations (the later of the two synchronic epochs). The second pertinent study is my own *Constructing Autocracy: Aristocrats and Emperors in Julio-Claudian Rome* (2001). In chapter 4 (pp. 213–87) I contend that a particular pair of metaphors played a central role in the evolution of the emperor's authority during the Julio-Claudian period: namely, the understanding of his relationship to other aristocrats as that of master to slave, or as father to son. Other models were also in play: the patron in relation to his clients, and the Republican magistrate in relation to fellow citizens. But when contemporary aristocrats applied these domestic models of authority—'father' and 'master' being contrasting faces of the *paterfamilias*—to their relationship with the *princeps*, they were not simply seeking to comprehend changes that had already occurred, but were also proactively imposing normative expectations about what the relationship of emperor to aristocrat *ought* to be like, and of how these parties should regard and treat one another. Julio-Claudian aristocrats thus seized the initiative in shaping the evolution of the Principate by transferring cultural symbols from one social domain to another, thereby establishing new meanings—new structural relations among symbols—that were advantageous to themselves.

I conclude with a prospect, and some desiderata. First, if the semiotic conception of culture is to achieve its full potential as a tool for analysing the ancient Roman world, diachronic modes of analysis must be further developed and more widely practised, to supplement the impressive results already gained from synchronic modes of analysis. Second, and more fundamentally, the interdisciplinarity that the semiotic conception of culture makes both possible and necessary must be pursued more aggressively. Much of the theoretical discussion surrounding 'cultural approaches' has focused on the relationship thereby forged between literary criticism and history. Yet art is also implicated in this rapprochement of subdisciplines. No critical technique is more semiotic by nature than iconography, and the most impressive examples of this approach to date in Classics—the work of Flower and Zanker, for example—have integrated iconography with textual and historical analysis. I myself attempt something similar in *Dining Posture in Ancient Rome* (2006), which combines literary, historical, and iconographic methods to interpret the meanings associated with different bodily dispositions in the Roman *convivium*. To be sure, the template for interdisciplinary work that the semiotic approach to culture provides—that many disciplines allow for the analysis of signifying structures and practices, and that knowledge so generated, being all on the same (semiotic) epistemological footing, becomes intelligible and commensurate across disciplines—is but one of many possible templates for interdisciplinary work. All forms of interdisciplinarity, though, require that the materials and techniques of more than one discipline be present simultaneously in a single scholar's mind.

Appropriate multidisciplinary training can best be supplied by graduate programmes. Graduate students trained in iconographical, historical, and literary methods alike will turn into scholars capable of articulating broad, new, fundamental questions at the points where these forms of representation intersect and cross-illuminate (Morris 2000: 27–8). Indeed, the Classics Ph.D programme at Johns Hopkins University aims to achieve exactly this, with all students required to take a range of seminars and a battery of examinations in Greek and Roman history, Greek and Latin language and literature, and classical art and archaeology. Naturally, compromises among the demands of the subdisciplines are necessary lest the programme expand to unreasonable length. For instance, rather than attending eight or ten graduate seminars in a single, 'major' subdiscipline (as I did in graduate school), our students attend three or four seminars in each subdiscipline; thus they gain representative, though not comprehensive, training in each subdiscipline prior to beginning dissertation work. Language training is in no way compromised, however, since cultural semiotics requires the fullest possible access to the sign systems of the cultures being studied: hence our students must develop fully professional Greek and Latin skills, no less than students in traditional philological programmes. By such means we hope to overcome Balkanization by subdiscipline, which remains the biggest barrier to the sort of interdisciplinarity that the semiotic approach to culture requires of its practitioners (Greenblatt 1995: 230).

Further reading

Gabrielle Spiegel provides lucid, brief narratives of the emergence and development of the semiotic approach to culture (from an historian's perspective) in ch. 1 of *The Past as Text* (1997), and in her 'Introduction' to the edited collection *Practicing History* (2005). Clifford Geertz's 1973 collection *The Interpretation of Cultures* is foundational for this approach, especially ch. 1, 'Thick Description: Toward an Interpretive Theory of Culture', and ch. 15, 'Deep Play: Notes on the Balinese Cockfight'. A special issue of *Representations* (59, 1997), edited by Sherry Ortner, provides a valuable retrospective and assessment of Geertz's impact. Stimulating discussions of the state of play at particular moments in the development of this approach are found in L. Hunt (ed.), *The New Cultural History* (1989), and V. Bonnell and L. Hunt (eds.), *Beyond the Cultural Turn* (1999).

References

Barrett, J. C. (1997). 'Romanization: A Critical Comment', in D. J. Mattingly (ed.), *Dialogues in Roman Imperialism: Power, Discourse, and Discrepant Experience in the Roman Empire*. Portsmouth, RI: Journal of Roman Archaeology, 51–64.

Bettini, Maurizio (1990 [1987]). *Anthropology and Roman Culture: Kinship, Time, Images of the Soul*. Baltimore: Johns Hopkins University Press.

Biersack, Aletta (1989). 'Local Knowledge, Local History: Geertz and Beyond', in Hunt 1989: 72–96.

Bonnell, V. and Hunt, L. (eds.) (1999). *Beyond the Cultural Turn*. Berkeley: University of California Press.

Chartier, Roger (1988). *Cultural History: Between Practices and Representations*, ed. L. Cochrane. Ithaca, NY: Cornell University Press.

—— (1994). 'The Chimera of the Origin: Archaeology, Cultural History, and the French Revolution', in J. Goldstein (ed.), *Foucault and the Writing of History*. Malden, Mass.: Blackwell, 167–86.

Clarke, John (2003). *Art in the Lives of Ordinary Romans: Visual Representation and Non-elite Viewers in Italy, 100 B.C.–A.D. 315.* Berkeley: University of California Press.

Demaine, Mary, and Taylor, Rabun (eds.) (1999). *Life of the Average Roman: A Symposium.* White Bear Lake, Minn.: PZA Publishing.

Eagleton, Terry (2000). *The Idea of Culture.* Malden, Mass.: Blackwell.

Flower, Harriet (1995). *Ancestor Masks and Aristocratic Power in Roman Culture.* Oxford: Oxford University Press.

Galinsky, Karl (1996). *Augustan Culture: An Interpretive Introduction.* Princeton: Princeton University Press.

Garnsey, Peter, and Saller, Richard (1987). *The Roman Empire: Economy, Society, and Culture.* Berkeley: University of California Press.

Geertz, Clifford (1973). *The Interpretation of Cultures: Selected Essays.* New York: Basic Books.

Greenblatt, Stephen (1995). 'Culture', in F. Lentricchia and T. McLaughlin (eds.), *Critical Terms for Literary Study.* Chicago: University of Chicago Press, 225–32.

Habinek, Thomas (1998). *The Politics of Latin Literature.* Princeton: Princeton University Press.

—— and Schiesaro, Alessandro (eds.) (1997). *The Roman Cultural Revolution.* Cambridge: Cambridge University Press.

Horsfall, Nicholas (2003). *The Culture of the Roman Plebs.* London: Duckworth.

Hunt, L. (ed.) (1989). *The New Cultural History.* Berkeley: University of California Press.

Kaster, Robert (2005). *Emotion, Restraint, and Community in Ancient Rome.* Oxford: Oxford University Press.

Kraemer, Lloyd S. (1989). 'Literature, Criticism, and the Historical Imagination: The Literary Challenge of Hayden White and Dominick LaCapra', in L. Hunt (ed.), *The New Cultural History.* Berkeley: University of California Press, 97–128.

Kurke, Leslie, and Dougherty, Carol (1993). *Cultural Poetics in Archaic Greece: Cult, Performance, Politics.* Cambridge: Cambridge University Press.

—— —— (2003). *The Cultures within Ancient Greek Culture: Contact, Conflict, Collaboration.* Cambridge: Cambridge University Press.

Lakoff, George (1987). *Women, Fire, and Dangerous Things: What Categories Reveal About the Mind.* Chicago: University of Chicago Press.

Lloyd, David, and Thomas, Paul (1998). *Culture and the State.* New York: Routledge.

Mauss, Marcel (1990 [1924]). *The Gift*, tr. W. D. Halls. London: Routledge.

Morris, Ian (2000). *Archaeology as Cultural History: Words and Things in Iron Age Greece.* Malden, Mass.: Blackwell.

Ortner, Sherry (1997). 'Introduction'. *Representations*, 59: 1–13.

Powell, Anton (ed.) (1992). *Roman Poetry and Propaganda in the Age of Augustus.* Worcester: Bristol Classical Press.

Roller, Matthew B. (2001). *Constructing Autocracy: Aristocrats and Emperors in Julio-Claudian Rome.* Princeton: Princeton University Press.

—— (2004). 'Exemplarity in Roman Culture: The Cases of Horatius Cocles and Cloelia'. *Classical Philology*, 99: 1–56.

—— (2006). *Dining Posture in Ancient Rome: Bodies, Values, and Status.* Princeton: Princeton University Press.

Sahlins, Marshall (1981). *Historical Metaphors and Mythical Realities: Structure in the Early History of the Sandwich Islands Kingdom.* Ann Arbor, Mich.: University of Michigan Press.

——(2000 [1982]). 'Individual Experience and Cultural Order', in *Culture in Practice: Selected Essays.* New York: Zone Books, 277–91.

Sewell, William H. (1997). 'Geertz, Cultural Systems, and History: From Synchrony to Transformation'. *Representations,* 59: 35–55.

——(1999). 'The Concepts(s) of Culture', in Bonnell and Hunt 1999: 35–61.

Spiegel, Gabrielle (1997). *The Past as Text: The Theory and Practice of Medieval Historiography.* Baltimore: Johns Hopkins University Press.

——(2005). 'Introduction', in G. Spiegel (ed.), *Practicing History: New Directions in Historical Writing After the Linguistic Turn.* New York: Routledge, 1–31.

Stedman Jones, Gareth (1996). 'The Determinist Fix: Some Obstacles to the Further Development of the Linguistic Approach to History in the 1990s'. *History Workshop Journal,* 42: 19–35.

Sullivan, J. P. (1985). *Literature and Politics in the Age of Nero.* Ithaca, NY: Cornell University Press.

Tylor, Edward (1871). *Primitive Culture: Researches into the Development of Mythology, Philosophy, Religion, Language, Art, and Custom.* New York: Holt.

Wagenvoort, Hendrik (1947 [1941]). *Roman Dynamism: Studies in Ancient Roman Thought, Language, and Custom.* Westport, Conn.: Greenwood Press.

Wallace-Hadrill, Andrew (1997). '*Mutatio morum:* The Idea of a Cultural Revolution', in Habinek and Schiesaro 1997: 3–22.

Woodman, Tony, and West, David (eds.) (1984). *Poetry and Politics in the Age of Augustus.* Cambridge: Cambridge University Press.

Woolf, Greg (1998). *Becoming Roman: The Origins of Provincial Civilization in Gaul.* Cambridge: Cambridge University Press.

Wyke, Maria (2002). *The Roman Mistress: Ancient and Modern Representations.* Oxford: Oxford University Press.

Zanker, Paul (1990 [1987]). *The Power of Images in the Age of Augustus,* tr. Alan Shapiro. Ann Arbor, Mich.: University of Michigan Press.

CHAPTER 16

ANTHROPOLOGY

MAURIZIO BETTINI

In 1908 Robert R. Marett published a collection of six articles under the promising title of *Anthropology and the Classics*. The papers, all written by prestigious scholars of the time—A. J. Evans, A. Lang, G. Murray, F. B. Jevons, J. L. Myres, and W. Warde Fowler—had been delivered previously before an audience at Oxford University and explored a fascinating range of topics, from 'primitive' pictography to Homer, from Herodotus to Greco-Italic magic. The Roman world was also well represented: William Warde Fowler closed the volume with thirty pages dedicated to the ceremony of the *lustratio*.

Initially, at least, Marett was able to present this marriage between Anthropology and the Humanities as a natural union: 'On verbal grounds one might suppose them coextensive', he declared (Marett 1908: 3). Etymology certainly has its entitlements: *homo*/*humanus* and *anthropos* designate the same object. Does this mean that the editor wished to place the 'humanizing studies' on the same level as research on 'the *mobbish* character of primitive religion', as he once expressed himself in a letter to J. G. Frazer (Ackerman 1987: 227 ff.; on Marett, cf. 224 ff.)? No, of course not—let the reader be assured! In fact, not a moment later, Marett corrected his initial statement, clarifying that Anthropology and the Humanities actually address two very different forms of human culture. The first, Marett explained, deals with that 'of the simpler or lower kind', while the Humanities—which have 'their parent source in the literatures of Greece and Rome'—focus 'on whatever is most constitutive and characteristic of the higher life of society' (Marett 1908: 3).

Anthropology and the Humanities, then, both deal with *Man*: but they deal with utterly different *kinds* of man. If the Humanities concern themselves with *homo* as a member of 'higher culture', Anthropology refers instead to an *anthropos* 'of the simpler or lower kind'. To put them together was a difficult task, therefore: it was not a simple question of reconciling two disciplines (which our own academic experience teaches us is a tricky undertaking), but of reconciling two different types of human being: the Romans and the 'savages', 'classical' and 'primitive' man (cf. Fowler, in Marett 1908: 185). And yet Marett and his illustrious colleagues had every intention of celebrating the happy marriage of these two worlds. But how?

The solution that Marett hit upon in his Preface was twofold. On the one hand, he appealed to a category of 'phenomena of transition' in which 'high' and 'low' cultures could meet halfway: in this case, 'Anthropology must cast forward, the Humanities cast back' (Marett 1908: 3). On the other hand, he relied upon the unique (not to say peculiar) characteristics of the individual scholars who participated in that endeavour: 'Indeed,' he affirmed, 'how can there be conflict [between the two disciplines], when, as in the case of each contributor to the present volume, the two interests in question, Anthropology on this side, and Classical Archaeology and Scholarship on that, are the joint concern of one and the same man?' Upon this followed a panegyric of each contributor on the basis of his humanistic as well as anthropological merits. Needless to say, neither of these two solutions would satisfy our modern methodological demands, even if the first might still be able to offer some interesting material for reflection. But the question that we must address is very much another.

Since the publication of Marett's volume nearly a century has passed. Are we now able to say that, in all these years, scholars have continued to cast an anthropological gaze upon the Roman world? The answer to that question is substantially affirmative, even if such attention has been both sporadic and varied in perspective. Leaving aside the inheritors of *The Golden Bough* who were active in the first half of the last century, as well as the singular (Jungian) enterprise of William F. Jackson Knight (1967), since at least the 1970s it has been possible to identify a developing interest in 'Roman anthropology' among not only historians but also students of Roman literature and Roman culture.

The fact remains, however, that in the field of Classics the anthropological perspective continues to be a limited (if not entirely circumscribed) phenomenon. Rarer still are studies that take a truly comparative approach to Roman culture, following the model of that 'comparative sociology' which represented the very essence of anthropology for Alfred R. Radcliffe-Brown (1958 and 1951; cf. Evans-Pritchard 1965), and of which those broad cultural comparisons undertaken by Claude Lévi-Strauss in many of his studies have given us such fascinating examples (above all the works on American Indian mythology in *Mythologiques*). In other words, the more comparative the anthropology of Rome demonstrates itself to be—proposing a comparison of Roman culture with the culture of *others*, with non-Romans in the broadest sense of the term—the more it is perceived to be distinct from the rest of Classical Studies.

Of course, we cannot rule out that some may still find it troubling that 'the parent source of the humanizing studies', as Marett defined classical culture, can be considered just one culture among many and, as such, comparable with so many others. This transformation in the image of the Classics dates back at least a century now, and certainly James George Frazer—introducing anthropological data into his commentaries on classical works and making extensive use of Greek and Roman parallels in his interpretations of 'primitive' customs—made an important contribution in this respect. It may be that the consternation provoked by the classical world's demotion of status has not yet waned (cf. Ackerman 1987: 129 ff. and Dei 1998: 320 ff.). On the other hand, it is precisely the limitations of the Frazerian method, based on a 'savage' form of comparatism and on an unbreakable faith in the doctrine of survivals (Dei 1998: 36 ff. and *passim*; see also the papers in Clemente 1984), that have influenced the reputation of anthropology in the field of Roman Studies so negatively. For a contemporary Latinist, the notes of the great Sir James to Ovid's *Fasti*, for example—with all those tattooed Arundas mixing with honest Italic beekeepers—are hardly acceptable. What most careful scholars of the *Fasti* declare nowadays is their intention to clear Ovid's text from the 'collective codes' imposed upon it by anthropologists and historians of religion, in order to restore the dignity or substance of the text as such (cf. Barchiesi 1997: 40–1). Naturally, this attitude cannot conceal the fact that 1,900 years before *The Golden Bough*, Ovid was actually doing something very much like Frazer. Both, in fact, tried to transform the rather 'dry' subjects of scholarship and folklore into *literature*. Both scratched beneath the surface of an extremely advanced and refined civilization—their own contemporary societies—in order to uncover its origins and to reveal its savage and unsettling traditions (Kezich 1984: 63–6; Dei 1998: 107 ff. On the notoriously 'literary' approach of Frazer's anthropology, see Dei 1998: 304 ff. and 393 ff.; on his comments to the *Fasti*, see Ackerman 1987: 300).

Furthermore, a widespread awareness in the field of anthropological scholarship, as well as in popular perception, that each culture should be examined first and foremost according to its own parameters and principles, and that its books should be read for their content, rather than being rearranged and used as brochures for cultural tourists, is a commanding invitation to concentrate our attention on Roman culture *in itself*, instead of on its external projections. This even if we realize that the most current anthropology invites us to change perspective once again—at least in the sense that the practice for which modernists greatly rebuked Frazer (that of extracting data and evidence from its original context) is that now dear to postmodernists, precisely because it permits one to broaden and play with contexts, leaving the reader to find his own way through the maze of different opinions and different voices. This may actually be an invitation to read the interminable 'collages' created by the author of *The Golden Bough* in a rather more polyphonic and intertextual way (Strathern 1987, cited by Dei 1998: 405, articulating this position).

Traditionalism and an honest reaction against 'savage' comparatism are not the only ways to explain the resistance encountered by Roman anthropology, however. In fact, if we want to make real progress towards solving our problem, at least for the time being it may be better to shift own attention away from the subject in question—Rome—in order to place it upon the observer: that is, upon ourselves. And so, as might happen in a debate between Jesuits, to the question scholars generally ask when they read the works of Livy or Virgil—'Who are the Romans for us?'—I would like to respond with another: 'Who exactly are we for the Romans?'

Nos Sumus Romani, Qui Fuimus Ante Romani

Let us try to imagine what would happen if a Roman were to observe us, the participants in modern Western society, as anthropological objects. In other words, what would happen if a Roman questioned himself about *our* cultural identity? Here is a brief list of the field-notes that he might take down.

First, languages. The Roman anthropologist would definitely find that some (such as Spanish, Italian, and French) are similar to his own. In fact, they might appear to him as simple dialects or ungrammatical versions of his own Latin language. A writer (not a linguist) has already perfectly described this situation: 'those French words which we are so proud of pronouncing accurately are themselves only "howlers" made by Gaulish lips which mispronounced Latin ... our language being merely a defective pronunciation of several others' (Proust 1993: 184). But even if the syntax, pronunciation, and lexicon of those languages might sound quite foreign to someone *latine loquens*, the Roman would nevertheless be able to identify a number of lexemes that were absolutely comprehensible: 'monitor', 'visual', 'extreme', 'index', 'participation', 'authority', and so on—a remarkable mishmash of Latin ingredients in barbarian dishes, so to speak!

Furthermore, let us suppose that our Roman friend started to speak with us and, like a good anthropologist, to ask us for some information about our society. He would discover that we have private Institutions called 'marriage' and 'divorce'—'but aren't *we*', he would say, 'aren't *we*, the Romans, supposed to have invented these?'—and public Institutions such as 'the Republic', 'the Senate', 'tribunals', and so on. Quite disconcerted, he might think: 'These foreigners are incredibly similar to us; these foreigners are actually Romans!' We could interrupt our anthropological flight of fancy at this point to conclude that the distance between our culture and that of the Romans is actually quite small. As the poet Ennius said, '*nos sumus Romani*'—with the only difference that, while he went on '*qui fuimus ante*

Rudini', we instead might add (rather tautologically) '*qui fuimus ante Romani*'. But apart from our direct historical and cultural descent from the Romans, there is an additional element of identification in the relationship between 'us' and 'them' that is even more determinant—a link so present to us that we are often not even aware of it.

Across the centuries, Europeans and westerners have continued to read the same books as the Romans—Cicero, Livy, Virgil, and so forth—and to study, usually very intensely and for many years, the Latin language. Browsing through the pages written by Françoise Waquet, we realize for just how long and with what an iron grip the Empire of Latin (supported by the Church, the *fortresse du latin* as Brunot (1967: 67) called it) has been able to keep the West under its control (Waquet 2001: esp. 41 ff.). From Italy to the Russia of Peter III, from Holland to Germany, from Spain to Poland, even to the missions and schools of the New World, young students aspiring to receive a proper education all had to start from the 'rules' of the Latin language. Often in different European countries the same primers were adopted, and Latin grammar could even be the subject of royal legislation. In fact, in 1540 Henry VIII established by decree which text should be adopted in England as the 'Common' or 'Royal Grammar': in that case, it was the book composed by William Lilly (Waquet 2001: 20). So there have been long periods in our history when—at school—Latin has been studied even more than our own native languages. This phenomenon may help explain the similarities between the different European languages, even those that do not derive directly from Latin.

But it is not only a question of language. By reading Latin texts, Europe and the West have assimilated visions of the world, of society, of politics, and of personal relations that come from Rome. If we really reflect on the fact that in the West the study of the Latin classics has continued practically uninterrupted from the golden years of the Empire until the 1900s, perhaps we would have a better idea of what 'our' culture—the culture of Western society—is. The question is one of those that send shivers of pleasure down the spine of anyone keen on identitarian taxonomies (and nowadays, unfortunately, there are quite a few enthusiasts of this kind). When we have read the books of a certain population over the centuries and we have studied its language as though it surpassed our own in importance, we might well then ask: *what are we?* From this point of view, ours is obviously a Roman culture.

By all this I mean to say that it is exceptionally difficult for us to observe the Romans with that 'gaze from afar' necessary for any anthropological approach, when we are so deeply immersed in *their* culture. Rome is almost *too* familiar to us, and this fact, especially when we are not aware of it, creates insurmountable difficulties for comparing Roman culture to another. It is almost as if we were comparing ourselves, almost as if we were decontextualizing ourselves. And we know how difficult *that* is.

Let us suppose for a moment that Benjamin Lee Whorf (1956) was right (though, after Chomsky's generativism, we cannot be so certain) in stating that every language possesses its own 'hidden metaphysics'. If we start rummaging about for a hidden Roman metaphysics, scrounging through *their* representations of *their* world manifested in *their* language, we are constantly afraid of running into *our own*. We have been studying Latin for so long that there can hardly be any doubt that we have absorbed some of the 'hidden metaphysics' of the Latin language. In this respect, there might even be some hope that the growing ignorance of the ancient world afflicting our society can actually foster the possibility of regarding Rome—finally!—as 'another' culture. But that would really be quite bitter optimism.

Romans, Etics, and Emics

I think that the reasons that we have given so far *do* help account for why we are so resistant to the idea of viewing Rome as an anthropological object, even before resorting to categories such as classicism, traditionalism, Eurocentrism, and so forth. These are actually a more or less unwelcome consequence of our primary identification with (or, as it were, prolonged contamination by) the culture of the Romans. In the end, this reflection may explain the curious paradox affecting the studies of certain Latinists and Romanists.

As I have already said, many of us would no doubt prefer to dedicate ourselves to a description of Roman culture classifiable according to Pike's categories as not 'etic', but 'emic' (Pike 1954: 8–15). More precisely, most Latinists would prefer an in-depth study of the internal mechanisms of Roman culture (the contexts, the details, the historical consistencies) to one of its possible external or cross-cultural projections. However, this does not prevent such 'emic' descriptions of Roman society and culture from being 'etic' as well: at least in the sense that when we carry out individual studies, we often employ concepts and categories introduced into the culture under examination from our own models as analysts. When we are speaking about Rome, we often use modern concepts such as 'democracy', 'freedom', 'capitalism', 'imperialism' (not to mention 'literature'), without asking ourselves whether and how the Romans would have used similar expressions to speak about the same things.

The question is: why is there so much emic attention for details and their related historical aspects, but so much etic freedom in using concepts linked to the culture of the observer? This contradiction is actually quite easy to explain. The conflict between the emic and the etic level is not perceived for the simple reason that when we speak of the Romans we are speaking about *ourselves*—or, at least, that's what we think we're doing—and therefore we can speak in a general and particular manner at the same time. When someone believes that he is dealing with his own *ethnos*, he can allow himself to be ethnocentric. But is the *reader* (meaning the consumer of our 'narratives' on the Roman world, whether they are historical, historico-literary, or historico-cultural) really satisfied by the images provided to him?

The answer to this question, at least in the opinion of Paul Veyne, is decidedly negative. In fact, in his inaugural lecture before the Collège de France, the celebrated historian underscored that in such cases 'the reader is a bit confused, because he sees clearly that Roman law or Roman imperialism are not the same as the Napoleonic Code or Athenian imperialism... The reader feels obscurely that the Roman conquest... is something which is strange and which resembles nothing else... The reader feels no less obscurely that the attitude of the Roman jurist interpreting law resembles only externally that of a modern jurist doing the same thing' (Veyne 1986). The examples chosen by Veyne are historical, as is only natural. But the same also holds true in regard to literary and cultural analysis in general. Take, for example, the case of Propertius' *Elegies*, where the poet's love for Cynthia is *not* the same thing as Petrarch's love for Laura; or that of Plautus' *Amphitruo*, in which Sosia and Amphitryon's loss of identity is *not* perceived in the same way as in Dostoevsky's *The Double*. This means that, despite the mechanism of primary identification between 'us' and 'them' that I have tried to describe above, at least in some instances Roman culture inspires in us a feeling of *difference*. Thus, we realize that the infusion of Roman into Western culture over the last 2,000 years does not at all exhaust that culture: in fact, there remains in it a strong component of *otherness*, which it is precisely the job of Roman anthropology to point out.

But how? In order to discover the best path along which to proceed—and we know that this is always a difficult task—the thing to do is to take the Romans themselves as our example.

Eccentricities and Oddities

When faced with the necessity of making a complicated choice, the Romans followed an infallible practice: they turned to their *maiores*. 'How would our ancestors behave in such a situation?', they would ask. 'Which path would they have taken in our place?' I am going to employ the very same method: I am going to turn to the *maiores* of anthropology and—just as was taught by the oracle of Delphi to the Roman ambassadors—I am going to take the liberty of choosing from among them whoever seems to me to be 'the best' (Cicero, *De Legibus* 2.16.40; cf. Xenophon, *Memorabilia* 4.3.15).

In this case, I am going to choose Clyde Kluckhohn as our 'best' anthropological ancestor. Kluckhohn insisted several times in his work on the indissoluble connection between anthropology, on the one hand, and an interest for what we could define as 'oddities', on the other. According to him, the anthropologist is someone who sets out along the path of 'oddities' ('Queer Customs, Potsherds, and Skulls' is the title of the first chapter of Kluckhohn 1987) and takes the longest route home—only to discover of course that *that* was really the shortest route to reach man. And it is actually by passing through these 'oddities' that—still according to Kluckhohn—we can free ourselves from local or particular forms of conditioning, to reach an image of humanity that is not spoilt by the preconceptions typical of our own culture. As Francesco Remotti (1987: 12) remarked, Kluckhohn's approach practically leads right into that of Clifford Geertz, who has often stressed the importance of oddities or peculiarities in anthropological investigation. With his usual elegance, Geertz writes: 'The comment that Cromwell was the most typical Englishman of his time precisely in that he was the *oddest*, may be relevant in this connection too: it may be in the cultural peculiarities of people—in their *oddities*—that are to be found some of the most instructive revelations of what it is to be generically human' (Geertz 2000: 84). Oddities are not there to be ignored in the name of emphasizing the common traits of man, nor are they there to be exploited by 'merchants of astonishment' (Geertz 1984: 275). Oddities arouse in us the feeling of *difference*. If I perceive a custom or a type of behaviour as strange, bizarre, or unusual, this is because I recognize implicitly that such a custom or behaviour is *different* from that which is familiar to 'us' or to 'me'. Inevitably, therefore, oddity presumes or inspires questions which have to do with comparison. If in considering another culture's customs I ask myself, 'Why do they do *that*?', then I am already on the right track to ask the next question: 'Why do *we* not do that as well?', or 'Why do *others* not do it?'

When dealing with 'oddities', we recognize that comparison and interpretation work together in a way that Plutarch would certainly have approved, at least from the methodological position that he took in the *Roman Questions*. In this work—which, together with Cornelius Nepos' *Praefatio*, can be considered the first anthropological and comparative reflection on Roman culture (cf. Piazzini 2004; Bettini 2000)—Plutarch put to himself questions like this (*Roman Questions* 6): 'Why do Roman women kiss their kinsmen on their mouths?' 'How strange! There must be an explanation for this.'

But to return to where we left off. In order to get a Roman anthropology off the ground, we must focus on the most unusual and remarkable aspects of that culture.

But above all we must estrange ourselves from it and break the bonds of that 'primary identification' discussed above. We must emphasize both what we *do not* and what the Romans *do* do; both what we *do* and what the Romans *do not* do. To do this, we do not need to make comparisons, as Frazer or Warde Fowler did, with the 'savages', only to discover that the Romans were (both unfailingly and surprisingly) really 'like them' after all. On the contrary: the kind of comparatism that should appeal to the Roman anthropologist should involve juxtaposing modern society and ancient culture, Roman culture and Greek culture, with the possibility then of comparing Rome with cultures yet farther afield. But above all, this comparatism should play more on differences than on analogies, more on what is present and what is absent in particular cultures than on coincidences between peoples that are geographically and chronologically remote from each other. If Frazer (e.g. 1931) based his method exclusively on the *similarities* between cultures (cf. Evans-Pritchard 1965), today's research should be oriented rather towards their *differences*, offering an experimental and constructive comparatism that does not predetermine the 'meaning' of any specific cultural representation after meticulously combing through ethnographic catalogues in search of some analogous representation. Instead, it should actively construct this meaning through juxtapositions and comparisons of what is different. (Here, Detienne 2000 and 2005 come to mind.)

Take, for example, the case of the Roman woman who kisses all her male relatives on the mouth, up to the sixth degree inclusive. When considering this custom, the reader is forced to reflect upon the fact (already implicitly emphasized by Plutarch) that this does not occur in his own culture. The very opposite practice may hold there, in fact; and there are certain cultures in which it is absolutely forbidden for a woman to behave in this way, at least if she wishes to retain some shred of respectability (whereas at Rome, *not* kissing a female relative on the lips indicated that she was disreputable). But why was this? Asking questions in this way, zigzagging across cultures, inevitably forces us to highlight *other* cultural differences as well, all related to the position of women in the two societies: the functions imposed by family relationships, the matrimonial rules that are in use, and so on. In looking at the differences between two cultures, step-by-step we assemble a repertoire of 'comparables'.

Plutarch had, of course, already hit upon an explanation for this peculiarity in the behaviour of Roman women—an explanation which can be confirmed with other internal data. At Rome during the archaic period marriage was prohibited up to the sixth degree of kinship, the same degree for which the *osculum* was, on the other hand, prescribed. Kissing a female relative on the mouth meant, therefore, the exact opposite of what we might expect: it did not indicate any kind of openness to endogamic relationships within these degrees, but functioned instead as an explicit and public demonstration of their closure.

The *osculum* was a way to call attention to the network of kinship relationships and the consequences of matrimonial exchanges (Bettini 1990: 27–49 and 1991: 21 ff.).

Textualities

Let us now shift our attention from things 'as the Romans did' (but as we, or others, *do not* do), to what the Romans *say* (but that we, or others, *do not* say). The time has come to focus on the world of Roman speech: that is to say, on their texts and on their words.

Roman culture is characteristically textual, not only because (to borrow one of Geertz's metaphors) 'the culture of a people is an ensemble of texts... which the anthropologist strains to read over the shoulders of those to whom they properly belong' (Geertz 2000: 452), but because for us it is, in fact, a collection of books written in Latin. There are, of course, conspicuous material remains, but no student of ancient Rome can ignore the fact that Roman culture has been textually codified. Even the most zealous practitioner of Roman archaeology and material culture would often be at a loss to give names to the objects he has dug up if he were without the corpus of Latin texts. For example, at Pompey or at Pozzuoli the visitor can see a number of large millstones. They are very impressive indeed. Our guides tell us that they were called *molae* and that the places where they were used were called *pistrina*—but only because Plautus' comedies tell us that this is so.

First and foremost, the Roman world for us is a collection of textual places in which the 'natives' have left representations of themselves in linguistic, stylistic, and rhetorical codes that are (already by themselves) capable of communicating important characteristics of their culture. In this respect, classicists who apply their own philological and literary-critical knowledge to Latin texts find themselves spontaneously involved in an undertaking like that of Geertz's anthropologist, for whom 'doing ethnography is like trying to read (in the sense of "construct a reading of") a manuscript...' (Geertz 2000: 10; cf. 448 ff.). Even so, we should not forget that reading ancient Rome's cultural texts with an anthropological eye can be a useful opportunity for the Latinist to reflect upon *his own* practices of rewriting the Roman world—something that we have long known to be indispensable in the construction of anthropological knowledge (Geertz 1988; cf. Remotti 1987: 25 ff. and Dei 1998: 393 ff.).

The textuality of Roman culture has a very special feature, however: its 'closure'. Unlike the situation obtaining in other cultures, the cultural texts that the Romans have left us cannot be renewed, nor their number increased (since, of course, we do not count towards this the philologist's interpretive mediation). The corpus of Roman texts has long been fixed, just as has long been fixed the language in which they were written, filtering every aspect of our knowledge about Roman culture. That is why I think it is essential to approach the *lexicon* of this language in particular with our eyes wide open: so that we may get hold of whatever it is that this lexicon may offer us in terms of the diverse, the strange, and the unusual.

Proceeding in this way, we observe that the Romans frequently express notions that we possess and that are in common use among us, but that they follow a semantic course that is profoundly different from ours and, for that matter, that of the Greeks. Beginning from the 'oddities' of their lexicon, bringing under discussion a particular 'meaning' and observing the categories that are at play between Roman culture and our own, between Roman culture and that of the Greeks, between Roman culture and that of 'others': this seems to me a constructive way of doing anthropology 'with' the Romans (as suggested by Detienne 2005: 9 ff., for the Greeks).

In this way, we will at least be able to catalogue all of those cases in which the hidden metaphysics of the Latin language (supposing that it exists, of course) has *not* been infused into our culture. Let us look at the Romans, for instance, when they present us with something 'freakish', with something 'monstrous'—something that they would define as 'reminding of, warning about' (*monstrum* coming from *moneo*). Let us ask: 'Would we ever say that?' We conceive what is 'monstrous' as something with terrible, horrible, and surprising features—what on earth could it be warning us about? 'Monstrous' for the Greeks meant something that was surprising—a *thauma*—or something excessive in size—a *pelōrion* or *tēras*. For the Romans, on the other hand, what is monstrous is what immediately conveys (*monet*) a divine message or gives warning or demands our attention. For the Romans, something 'monstrous'—something that warns or reminds us—exists expressly for that purpose; it is a kind of natural palimpsest that communicates the language of the gods.

'Der liebe Gott steckt im Detail', Aby Warburg used to say: 'The good God is in the details.' Yes—in words, actually, and in some cases suffixes, too. Indeed, the meticulous, exacting study of a suffix—asking what kinds and classes of roots it combines with, exploring the constellation of meanings that bind these elements together—can provide us with invaluable information about the ways in which the Romans constructed certain cultural representations. I admit, it is not always easy to find a suffix 'strange' in Kluckhohn's or in Geertz's sense of the word. But I can guarantee the reader that his trouble will be repaid in interesting surprises.

Take, for example, the rare suffix *-bula* that appears in a term of exceptional importance for Roman culture: *fabula*, derived from the verb *fari*, 'to say'. The same suffix recurs in *su-bula*, 'awl' (an instrument used by cobblers, from *su-ere*, 'to stitch'), in *fi(g)-bula*, 'fastener' (from *fig-ere*, 'to fasten'), in *mandi-bula*, 'mandible' (literally, 'instrument for chewing', from *mand-ere*, 'to chew'), and *tri-bula* (*tri-bulum*), 'harrow for beating grain' (from *tri-* of *ter-o*, 'to beat, trample, wear down'). From this we deduce that in Latin the suffix *-bula* designates the 'instrument' that serves to complete the action indicated by the verb. But not only this. In fact, we note that the suffix regularly recurs in words indicating instruments that have the ability to work deeply upon some material, gouging it with 'points' (*subula*, *fibula*) or 'teeth' (*mandibula*, *tribula*). In this case, then, the suffix's *liebe Gott* functions as what linguists call a 'submorphemic differential' (Jakobson and Waugh 1979: 198–9)—that is, as a phonemic unit that, precisely because it shared among many words, suggests a *semantic* affinity between them. The awl, the fastener, the mandible, and the harrow are all instruments that have 'points' or 'teeth', used for forcefully incising some object—and they are all substantives in -*bula*. Finally, then, *fabula*—the Roman 'fable'—appears to be an 'instrument' that works deeply upon the material of an act of *fari*, an act of 'saying', and that is capable of profoundly modifying its object. From here we could depart on an interesting reflection upon what *fabula* truly is for the Romans, and then upon their way of representing what we define as 'discourse' or 'story' (as, e.g., Ferro 2005 has done; Bettini 2009*a*, on *fabula* and *fari* expressing powerful speech). This is why lexical 'oddities' must occupy a place of honour in the Roman anthropologist's *carnet*.

Further reading

The anthropological approach to Roman culture and Roman literature should be considered less an established itinerary to follow than a route that still needs to be drawn, by tracing various lines of thought and interest (see Bettini 2009*a*). In particular, it is interesting to take in new, specifically Roman directions the themes and interpretive models developed for the study of the Greek world by J.-P. Vernant, M. Detienne, F. Frontisi, N. Loraux, and the entire 'French School' of historical anthropology. But there are different ways to start on the path of Roman anthropology:

1. Through texts. Valuable and stimulating evidence about Roman culture may be found just about anywhere in literature, but in particular:
   (a) in the first five books of Livy's *Histories*, which can be read with the help of Liou-Gille 1998;
   (b) in Plutarch's *Quaestiones Romanae*, to be read in parallel with the *Quaestiones Graecae*. For the former, Rose 1924 can be used; for the latter, Halliday 1928;
   (c) in Ovid's *Fasti* (with Frazer's monumental commentary);
   (d) in the *Aeneid*—above all Books 6 (Norden), 7, 8 and 12 (Fowler 1916, 1917, and 1919)—which already once served as a great reservoir of 'anthropological' knowledge

for the ancient commentators Servius and Macrobius, who then left behind a wealth of additional information for us.

We must, of course, remember that the brand of Roman anthropology undertaken by Rose, Halliday, Fowler, and Frazer was still based on the principle of 'savage comparativism' (see above). This, though, does not mean we cannot find many interesting things in the works of these scholars—merely that we should regard them from an informed, contemporary perspective.

2. Through texts and themes. Some texts are particularly relevant for thematic anthropological studies:
   (a) Divination: Cicero's *De Divinatione* (to be read with the help of Pease and Timpanaro) is a veritable storehouse of information on this peculiar 'science' (there is also a useful comparative sketch in Vernant 1974);
   (b) Roman 'folklore' (proverbs, beliefs, customs, etc.): themes of this kind can be found in Petronius' *Cena Trimalchionis* and in some chapters of Book 28 of Pliny the Elder's *Naturalis Historia* (Deonna and Renard 1961; Wolters 1935; Halliday 1927 and 1928; Riess 1896; Bettini 2000);
   (c) Roman magic is well represented in some of Horace's *Epodes*, in the *Cena Trimalchionis*, in Pliny's Book 28, and in Apuleius' *Metamorphoses* and *De Magia* (Luck 1985; Tupet 1986; Graf 1997);
   (d) Beliefs about animals: Pliny the Elder, *Naturalis Historia* 8–10 (Bettini 1998; Franco 2003; Shepard 1996; Li Causi 2003).

3. Themes;
   (a) Kinship: a good introduction to the 'otherness' of the Romans is to study their kinship system, which we learn about from certain 'myths' of origin and other literary evidence (see Benveniste 1973 for the terminology; Bettini 1991 and 2009*b*; Guastella 1985; Moreau 2003; Flower 1996; Beltrami 1998; Mencacci 1996; Lentano 1996). Moreover, kinship has the advantage of being one of the most fully developed themes within anthropological studies (Lévi-Strauss 1949);
   (b) Otherness and cultural interaction (above all with the Greek world): Feeney 1998; Dupont and Valette-Cagnac 2005;
   (c) The theatre. The anthropology of representation at Rome, with particular reference to the 'presence' of the actor (or orator), has been developed above all by Florence Dupont 1986 and 2000 (cf. Moreau 2002);
   (d) Images (situating artistic representation in its literary and cultural context). Here, too, it is interesting to take Vernant 1965 and 1990, in a Roman direction (Bettini 1998; C. Auvray-Assayas 1998);
   (e) Writing. Of the innumerable works dedicated to this topic in the last decade, see in particular Valette-Cagnac 1997.

Finally, an interesting way of picking up some of the ancient anthropological strands that connected anthropology and classical antiquity could be to reread E. De Martino, *The Land of Remorse* (London, 2005); *Primitive Magic* (Bridport, 1998); and *Morte e pianto rituale nel mondo antico* (Turin, 1958).

References

Ackerman, R. (1987), *J. G. Frazer: His Life and Work*, Cambridge.

Auvray-Assayas, C. (1998), *Images romaines*, Paris.

Barchiesi, A. (1997), *The Poet and the Prince*, Berkeley.

Beltrami, L. (1998), *Il sangue degli antenati*, Bari.

Benveniste, E. (1973), *Indo-European Language and Society*, London.

Bettini, M. (1990), 'Il divieto fino al "sesto grado" incluso nel matrimonio romano', in J. Andreau and H. Bruhns (eds.), *Parenté et stratégies familiales dans l'antiquité Romaine*, École Française de Rome, 1990: 27–49.

—— (1991), *Anthropology and Roman Culture*, tr. J. Van Sickle, Baltimore.

—— (1998), *Nascere. Storie di donne, donnole, madri ed eroi*, Turin.

—— (2000), *Le orecchie di Hermes*, Turin.

—— (2008), 'Weighty Words, Suspect Speech: fari in Roman culture', *Arethusa*, 41: 313–75.

—— (2009*a*), 'Comparare i Romani. Un'antropologia del mondo antico', *Studi Italiani di jilologia classica*, Supplemento al fasc. 1/2009, 'La stella sta compiendo il suo giro', Atti del Convegno Internazionale di Siracusa 21–23 maggio 2007, 1–47.

—— (2009*b*), *Affari di jamiglia. La parentela nella cultura e nella letteratura antica*, Bologna, Il Muline.

—— (forthcoming), *Birth: Stories of Women, Weasels, Mothers and Heroes*, tr. E. Eisenach, Chicago.

Clemente, P., ed. (1984), 'I Frutti del ramo d'oro. James. G. Frazer e le eredità dell'antropologia', *La ricerca folklorica*, 10.

Dei, F. (1998), *La discesa agli Inferi. James G. Frazer e la cultura del novecento*, Lecce.

Deonna, W. and Renard, M. (1961), *Croyances et superstitions de table dans la Rome antique*, Latomus 46, Brussels.

Detienne, M. (2000), *Comparer l'incomparable*, Paris.

—— (2005), *Les Grecs et nous*, Paris.

Dupont, F. (1986), *L'Acteur roi ou le theatre dans la rome antique*, Paris.

—— (2000), *L'Orateur sans visage*, Paris.

—— and Valette-Cagnac, E. (2005), *Façons de parler grec à Rome*, Belin.

Evans-Pritchard, E. E. (1965), 'The Comparative Method in Social Anthropology', in *The Position of Women in Primitive Society and Other Essays in Social Anthropology*, London.

Feeney, D. (1998), *Literature and Religion at Rome*, Cambridge.

Ferro, L. (2005), 'Intorno a fabula. Ricerca sull'efficacia di una parola screditata', doctoral dissertation, University of Siena.

Flower, H. I. (1996), *Ancestor Masks and Aristocratic Power in Roman Culture*, Oxford.

Fowler, W. W. (1916), *Virgil's 'Gathering of the Clans', Being Observations on Aeneid VII.601–817*, Oxford.

—— (1917), *Aeneas at the Site of Rome*, Oxford.

—— (1919), *The Death of Turnus*, Oxford.

—— (1920), *Roman Essays and Interpretations*, Oxford.

Franco, C. (2003), *Senza ritegno: il cane e la donna nell'immaginario della Grecia antica*, Bologna.

Frazer, J. G. (1922), *The Golden Bough*, London.

—— (1929), *Publii Ovidii Nasonis Fastorum Libri Sex*, London.

Frazer, J. G. (1931), 'The Scope and Method of Mental Anthropology', in *Garnered Sheaves*, London.

Geertz, C. (1984), 'Anti Anti-Relativism', *American Anthropologist*, 86.

—— (1988), *Works and Lives: The Anthropologist as Author*, Palo Alto, Calif.

—— (2000), *The Interpretation of Cultures*, New York.

Graf, F. (1997), *Magic in the Ancient World*, Cambridge.

Guastella, G. (1985), 'La rete del sangue', *Materiali e discussioni per l'analisi dei testi classici*, 15: 49–123.

Halliday, W. R. (1927), *Greek and Roman Folklore*, London.

—— (1928), *Greek Questions of Plutarch*, Oxford.

Jackson Knight, W. F. (1967), *Vergil: Epic and Anthropology*, London.

Jakobson, R. and Waugh, L. (1979), *The Sound Shape of Language*, Bloomington, Ind.

Kezich, G. (1984), 'Frazer e Ovidio. Classicismo e romanticismo in etnologia', *La ricerca folklorica*, 10.

Kluckhohn, C. (1949), *Mirror For Man*, New York.

Lentano, M. (1996), *Le relazioni difficili. Parentela e matrimonio nella letteratura latina*, Loffredo.

Lévi-Strauss, C. (1949), *The Elementary Structures of Kinship*, Boston.

Li Causi, P. (2003), *Sulle tracce del manticora*, Palermo.

Liou-Gille, B. (1998), *Une lecture 'religieuse' de Tite-Live I: cultes, rites, croyances de la Rome archaique*, Paris.

Luck, G. (1985), *Arcana Mundi: Magic and the Occult in the Greek and Roman Worlds*, Baltimore.

Marett, R. R., ed. (1908), *Anthropology and the Classics*, Oxford.

Mencacci, F. (1996), *I fratelli amici: La rappresentazione dei gemelli nella cultura romana*, Venice.

Moreau, P., ed. (2002), *Corps romaine*, Grenoble.

Moreau, P. (2003), *Incestus et prohibitae nuptiae*, Paris.

Pease, A. S. (1920–3), *Ciceronis, De divinatione*, 2 vols., Urbana = Darmstadt, 1963.

Piazzini, C. (2004), 'Plutarco "antropologo": le *Questiones Romanae*', doctoral dissertation, University of Siena.

Pike, K. L. (1967), *Language in Relation to a Unified Theory of the Structure of Human Behaviour*, Glendale.

Proust, M. (1993), *Sodom and Gomorrah*, in *In Search of Lost Time*, IV tr. C. K. Scott Moncrieff and T. Kilmartin, New York.

Radcliffe-Brown, A. R. (1951), 'The Comparative Method in Social Anthropology, *Journal of the Royal Anthropological Institute*, 81.

—— (1958), *Method in Social Anthropology*, Chicago.

Remotti, F. (1987), *Introduzione*, in C. Geertz, *Interpretazione di culture*, It. tr. Bologna.

Riess, E. (1896), 'Pliny and Magic', *American Journal of Philology*, 17/1: 77–83.

—— (1893–1988), 'Aberglaube', in A. Pauly and G. Wissowa (eds.), *Paulys Realencyclopädie der Classischen Altertumswissenschaft*, Stuttgart: 1. 29–93.

Rose, H. J. (1924), *The Roman Questions of Plutarch*, Oxford.

Shepard, P. (1996), *The Others: How the Animals Made Us Human*, Washington, DC.

Strathern, M. (1987), 'Out of Context: The Persuasive Fiction in Anthropology', *Current Anthropology*, 28: 251–81.

Timpanaro, S. (1991), *Cicerone, Della divinazione*, Milan.

Tupet, A. (1986), 'Rites magiques dans l'antiquité romaine', in *Aufstieg und Niedergang der römischen Welt*, Berlin.

Valette-Cagnac, E. (1997), *La Lecture à Rome: rites et pratiques*, Paris.

Vernant, J.-P. (1965), 'La Catégorie du double', in *Mythe et pensée chez les Grecs* II, Paris.

—— (1974), *Divination et rationalité*, Paris.

—— (1985), *La Mort dans les yeux: figures de l'Autre en Grèce ancienne*, Paris.

—— (1990), *Figures, idoles, masques*, Paris.

Veyne, P. (1986), 'The Inventory of Differences', *Economy and Society*, 11: 173–96.

Waquet, F. (2001), *Latin: Or, The Empire of a Sign*, tr. John Howe, London.

Whorf, B. L. (1956), *Language, Thought and Reality*, ed. J. B. Carroll, Cambridge, Mass.

Wolters, X. F. M. G. (1935), *Notes on Antique Folklore*, Amsterdam.

CHAPTER 17

ROMAN IDENTITY

EMMA DENCH

Introduction

> In addition to the blessings of their land, gentleness and civility have come to the Turdetani.... The Turdetani, especially those who live about the Baetis, have utterly changed over to the Romans' way of life, not even remembering their own language any more. Most of them have become Latins, and received Roman colonists, so that they are not very far from being all Romans. The cities that are currently jointly settled... demonstrate the change in lifestyles that I have mentioned. All the Iberians who take this form are called 'Toga-wearers'. Amongst these are the Celtiberians, who formerly were considered the most savage of all.
>
> (Strabo, *Geography* 3.2.15 = 151C)

The geographer Strabo, depicting a world progressively centred on Rome and newly brought together under the 'fatherhood' of Augustus and his successors, writes of Spanish peoples within well-established Greek ethnographical and geographical traditions but with distinctively new world slants on questions of identity. We can track theories of the interconnections of environment and custom, of conquest and behavioural change, of barbarism and lack of civilization that are familiar patterns of classical Greek thought. But there is a particular emphasis here on the idea of becoming Roman, with a range of manifestations of this process, crossing our categories of cultural, institutional, and political change: when the Iberians don togas, their action suggests all three categories of change all at once (Clarke 1997;

1999). This passage is a useful place to start thinking about some of the peculiarities of Roman identity, and some of the preoccupations of recent scholarship.

Modern Terminology

'Identity' and 'ethnicity' are terms that overlap considerably in modern scholarship, as in the use of the phrase 'ethnic identity'. Both terms are decidedly recent within scholarly discourse, and no ancient equivalent exists, although the word 'ethnicity' is rooted in the Greek noun *ethnos*, meaning 'people' or 'group' (Jones 1996; Just 1989). It is perhaps the comfortable mixture of 'authenticity' and dispassionate sociological usage that has encouraged scholars of antiquity to believe that the concept of ethnicity is both precise and less subject to anachronistic overtones than a term such as 'race'. Classical scholars have found appealing and helpful sociologists' emphasis on the subjective nature of ethnicity, that is, people's own understanding of who they are, rather than the supposedly objective and empirical categories of race, not least because of a sometimes compromising relationship between classical studies and racial 'science' of the later nineteenth and earlier twentieth centuries. Beyond this, there is considerable disagreement about what 'ethnicity' might mean in ancient contexts: it may be restricted to criteria of descent, whether 'fictive' or actual (Hall 1997, 2002), or used much more broadly to refer to perceptions of common identity based primarily on culture (Hall 1989; Malkin ed. 2001). While there is an increasingly extensive theoretical discussion of the term 'identity', its very looseness, particularly in everyday usage, is perhaps useful when we are trying to open discussions of the ways in which ancient peoples perceived selves and others (Lieu 2004: 11–21).

More broadly, it is important also to recognize the danger of using modern sociological definitions prescriptively, importing conditions peculiar to the modern nation-state, or maintaining rigid categories that would exclude 'social', 'religious', or 'political' identity from one's enquiry. It is also perhaps the case that we interpret the 'subjective' quality of ethnicity in modern liberal terms, overestimating the degree to which people's identities in ancient societies might be a matter of 'choice', with the result that we can be more interested in complex self-scrutiny exercised in literature than in legal and tax categories. On the other hand, we should be receptive to ideas in antiquity that will sound a little like thoroughly modern concepts such as nationhood or race, without expecting these ideas to work in the same way. Thus, recent scholarship has emphasized that ancient people's own understanding of who they are can be expressed in apparently essentialist terms, such as blood purity, language that coexists with more fluid ideas of change (Buell 2005; Dench 2005; cf. Walbank 1951, 1972).

My concern in this chapter is with ancient ways of expressing what it was for themselves and/or other peoples, things, and behaviour to be 'Roman', and, since juxtaposed, contrasted, or hyphenated identities are a striking feature of the Roman world, the relationship between being 'Roman' and being 'Athenian', 'Jewish', or 'Etruscan'. Modern scholars have tended not to categorize the state of being or becoming Roman in 'ethnic' or in 'cultural' terms, but more frequently as a 'political', 'national', or 'legal' status. In comparison with classical Greek identity, being or becoming Roman has been assumed to be shallower and less meaningful, 'just' a matter of citizenship (Hall 2002: 22–3). However, the relative significance of blood (and occasionally blood purity), descent, language, and clothing is actively debated in the rich ancient discourses of what it was to be Roman, and the 'meaning' of the Roman citizenship itself expressed in such terms.

Approaches

Assumptions about the primacy of Greek thought and culture and its reception as the foundation of 'western civilization' have encouraged decades of heated debate about both the 'real' racial identity of the Greeks and their culture and the more or less 'ethnocentric' ways in which Greek peoples constructed their identities and those of 'barbarians' (Bernal 1987, 1991, 2001; Peradotto and Levine eds. 1989; Lefkowitz and Rogers eds. 1996; van Binsbergen ed. 1997; E. Hall 1989; J. Hall 1997, 2002). Rome and her empire have been received in very different ways, with profound effects on the bibliography of Roman identities. The idea of Rome as an imperial power has historically encouraged lines of enquiry that push comparison with modern imperial situations. In the earlier twentieth century preoccupation with 'race-mixture' in Roman society and even as a factor in the 'decline' of Rome occasioned anxious comparisons with European and American models, while a strand of British scholarship embraced the status of Rome as 'racially mixed' (Duff 1928: 206; Frank 1920: 128; Grose-Hodge 1944: 98). Recently, attention has focused on the Roman provinces, reconstructing the perspectives and self-perceptions of Rome's subjects, sometimes invoking the vocabulary of postcolonial studies or globalization (Mattingly ed. 1997; Webster and Cooper eds. 1996; Hingley 2005).

In addition to her status as an imperial power, Rome's major contributions to 'western civilization' have traditionally been perceived to be law and civil institutions, and thus it is no surprise to see scholarship on Roman identity cluster around technical aspects of the citizenship, both in its geographical and social extensions (Sherwin-White 1973; Gardner 1993). There are, however, more creative possibilities here, such as the question of how far Roman law constitutes a socio-specific kind of philosophy, both reflecting and enabling complex thinking about the freedpersons who constitute a middle ground between slaves and free people (Schiavone 2005).

Perhaps the most vexed question in ancient identity studies is that of the relative contribution of texts and material culture to our understanding of ancient self-perceptions. Do texts distort our vision and understanding of ancient identity, because they are Romanocentric, centralizing, and elitist? How can we use material culture to understand peoples' sense of themselves, without appeal to a more 'discursive' narrative of the kind articulated in literature? Scholars are increasingly challenging the idea that texts and material culture are antithetical, in the sense that texts give us an elite, male, Roman perspective, while material culture will allow us to construct independently more authentic versions of local and 'ordinary' perspectives, evidence for the ways in which lives were lived rather than merely talked about. Challenges to this antithesis are made in terms of emphasis on cultural forms that cross categories of text and object, such as inscriptions; on Roman literature itself as a feature of the relative permeability of Roman culture; and on methods of 'reading' material culture and reconstructing its logics to create alternative narratives (Jones 1996, 1997; Alcock 2001; Laurence 2001; Clarke 2003). It has to be said, however, that a great deal of lip-service to these ideals is apparent right now, and that the study of Roman identity is characterized by a series of parallel conversations largely separated in terms of both ancient geographical region and modern disciplinary leanings. In the remainder of this chapter I take a thematic approach to articulations of Roman identity, seeking to cut across different cultural forms.

Greeks, Barbarians, and Beyond

The 'Greek–barbarian' antithesis, alongside the more subtle conventions of classical ethnographical thought and socio-specific interpretations of 'Greekness', was appropriated creatively by peoples of the Hellenistic and Roman worlds to articulate distinctive identities. Thus, the Romans could portray themselves or be portrayed as particularly suited to protect and promote traditional 'Greek' values and interests, such as 'freedom' and civilization. Assuming the role of 'Greeks' was also an important feature of Roman imperial thought, certain subjects being relegated in both literature and iconography to the role of flamboyant, excessive, or uncivilized barbarians (Schneider 1986; Ferrary 1988; Smith 1988; Gruen 1993,

1998). Alternatively, the Romans could embrace their own distinctively non-Greek identity as Trojans, or alternatively as morally upright and austere avoiders of luxury (Momigliano 1975, 1984; Erskine 2001; Dench 1995, 2003, 2005). From Greek perspectives, Romans could be very hard to place in the scheme of things: Polybius' assessment of Roman domination of 'almost the entire world' positions their character with some subtlety between Greeks and barbarians (Walbank 1985; Millar 1987; Erskine 2000).

Perceptions of 'Greek' culture and tradition more generally are also important in Roman self-positioning. These too are specific to particular cultural and social contexts. One example is the concept of *Graeco ritu*, 'according to Greek ritual', that emerges at the end of the third century BCE, a wholly Roman notion characterized above all by sacrificing with the head uncovered, in contrast with the standard 'Roman' practice. *Graeco ritu* became very much part of the available repertoire of Roman religious practice and is a socio-specific interpretation of what 'Greek' ritual was all about, one that bore a tenuous relationship with the multiple varieties of local practice within the Greek world (Scheid 1995). Broader studies of Roman self-positioning have sought to trace the dynamics of Roman appropriation and co-option of ideas of Greekness in public and less-public space, and also challenge the idea that this appropriation in some way compromises Roman identity (Zanker 1988; Wallace-Hadrill 1989, 1998; Woolf 1994).

Most recently, the imagined entities of 'Greek' and 'Roman' have themselves been increasingly questioned: the subtlety of the self-positioning of authors such as Polybius, Strabo, Dionysius of Halicarnassus, and Plutarch between and beyond monolithic 'Greek' and 'Roman' identities has been emphasized, with attention also to the specifics of smaller local identities within the Roman world (Clarke 1997, 1999; Whitmarsh 2001). The idea of Greekness has proved an absorbing and engaging focus in studies of Roman self-definition, but this is by no means the only significant cultural interface, a point that is illustrated by recent work on Italy, Egypt, and Gaul (Giardina 1997; Williams 2001*a*; Riggs 2005).

'Race'

In the self-consciously multi-ethnic and mobile Roman world, it is initially surprising to see the language of 'race' invoked, whether in the form of a descent group, the idea of 'pure' or 'mixed' blood, or the interpretation of 'meanings' of skin colour and physiognomy. Recently scholars have tended to protest, arguably too much, that the Romans were not 'racist', emphasizing the permeability of citizenship, the apparently eclectic character of 'Roman' culture or the strictly social dynamics of chauvinism (Snowden 1970, 1983; Thompson 1989; Galinsky 1992). We should certainly not expect Roman ideas of 'race' to work in the same ways as those of the modern Western world. On the other hand, we should also practise what we preach about the subjective nature of ethnicity and its discourses rather than falling into the assumption that the essentialist language of descent and blood cannot have been taken seriously because of the 'objectively' 'multicultural' and mobile nature of Roman society. One of the most enlightening discussions in recent years has been Denise Kimber Buell's work on perceptions and self-perceptions of Christians as a 'race', and particularly as a 'new race': this formula suggests neatly the paradox of juxtaposed ideas of fixity and ideas of change that is a familiar aspect of ancient discourses of identity in general (2005).

Within ancient Mediterranean and Near Eastern thought, genealogical thinking is one of the fundamental bases for understanding and organizing the past. 'Fictive' descent groups trace the roots of individuals, communities, or larger imagined groupings, such as 'Hellenes' or 'Latins', and of relationships between them. Aspirational genealogies link individual Roman and Italian families with mythological heroes. The most notorious of these is the Julian family's claims of descent from Aeneas, linking them to the foundation of Rome itself. Roman articulations of their collective ancestry are characterized by the multiple available possibilities, each of which could clearly make sense and be convincing within individual contexts, while the tension between different elements, notably Trojan, Greek and Italian, is creatively exploited in the literature of the late Republic and early Imperial period, such as Virgil's *Aeneid* (Bickermann 1952; Wiseman 1974, 1983; Jones 1999).

Given the dynamics of Rome's interface with 'Greekness', and the potency of relationships with the Hellenistic kingdoms around the beginning of the second century BCE, it is unsurprising to find that Rome's first prose writer, Fabius Pictor, writing in Greek for an international audience, traced her ancestry ultimately to Herakles. Rome's descent from a Greek hero was surely rendered plausible, with neat irony, by the particular ethnocentric character of traditional Greek thought and its tendency to people the Mediterranean with familiar mythological figures. The Augustan antiquarian writer Dionysius of Halicarnassus could invoke such versions in a thesis that set out to prove that the Romans really were a Greek *genos*, 'race'. He exhaustively catalogues the Greek origins of the 'aborigines' living on the future site of Rome, as well as citing aspects of historical and contemporary Roman culture that best prove 'memory' of the Romans' truly Greek origins. Significantly, here as elsewhere, a connection is made between descent and culture. While in other contexts culture or clothing can be valued above descent as a marker of who people 'really' are, in Dionysius' formula culture is a symptom, a more or less persistent sign, of descent (*Ant. Rom.* 1.89; Gruen 1990; Schultze 1986; Luraghi 2003).

The Trojan identity of Rome is best seen within the broader Mediterranean context of the appeal of a non-Greek status rooted securely and venerably within Greek culture. Trojan identity has a particular appeal in the perception and self-perception of peoples at a dynamic cultural and political interface with Greek culture. Rome's Trojan origins via Aeneas were demonstrably emphasized from the end of the fourth century BCE, and both her internal and external relations were brokered with appeal to her Trojan identity (Gruen 1993; Erskine 2001; Dench 2005: 252–3). 'Latin' identity in the later Republic is generally discussed as a matter of legal status alone. After 338 BCE, when Rome definitively achieved hegemony over the Latin League, Latin status was granted by the Roman state both to the majority of colonies founded by Rome, where those who had been Romans, 'ethnic' Latins, and locals made up the civic population, and to certain of the original Latin communities. By the early Imperial period Latin status, by extension, had begun to be extended to communities well beyond Italy, and had also become a means of designating ex-slaves who had not yet qualified for Roman citizenship, but who could yet do so if they passed certain tests ('Junian' Latins). Thus, Latin status was indeed reconfigured by Rome. Nevertheless, rich mythological and ritual 'memories' of common Latin descent continued to be invoked in myth and ritual, such as the *feriae Latinae*, the 'Latin festival', well into the early Imperial period, and should make us hesitate before characterizing 'Latinity' as a 'purely' juridical matter (Thomas 1990; Dench 2005: 201–3).

Alongside descent myths that invoke heroic genealogies that could be claimed by individual illustrious families, other important Roman traditions reflect more anonymously on the collective descent of Rome. The myths of the asylum opened up by Romulus to welcome newcomers and the rape of the Sabine women are stories that, from the later Republic to late antiquity, reflect in various forms Rome's capacity to incorporate other peoples, ranging from her enemies to former slaves. By the early Imperial period these stories can contain very juridical language and function effectively as myths of the Roman citizenship. The versions we have suggest active and fraught debate about the social mobility, inter-ethnic 'mingling', and violence of imperialism that are part of Rome's very essence. Much later, the 'natural' association between citizenship and ideas of descent will be invoked in the idea of a Roman *gens*—'race' or 'descent group'—on a global scale, brought about by the emperor Caracalla's edict of (nearly) universal citizenship in 212 CE (Guastella 1985; Moatti 1997; Dench 2005: 11–25, 101–3).

The language of descent is thus very much part of the vocabulary of Roman identity. We can also see interest in the idea of exclusivity of blood or kin in the dynamic ancient debates about Roman identity, in the second- and first-century BCE arguments surrounding popular sovereignty and about Italian membership of the Roman citizen-body. Notoriously, Suetonius attributes to Augustus a 'policy' of keeping 'the Roman people pure and unsullied by any mixing in of foreign and servile blood' by infrequently granting the Roman citizenship and setting a limit to manumission (*Aug.* 40.3). This probably belongs alongside other well-advertised measures to stop the spiralling societal and even cosmic breakdown that was perceived to accompany the civil wars of the end of the Republic, such as adultery legislation. Suggestively, however, the 'purity' of the Roman citizenship body is to be maintained by limiting manumission and admissions to the citizenship rather than stopping them altogether: this rhetoric functions in very different ways from pseudo-biological nineteenth- and twentieth-century versions of 'blood purity'. Some of the other well-known expressions of 'blood purity', such as Tacitus' attribution to the Germans of 'pure blood', are examples of curiosity and ambivalence concerning peoples who are 'not us' (Tacitus, *Germ.* 4.1; Thompson 1981; Dench 2005: 257–9).

In contrast with popular modern Western assumptions, ancient thought does not closely associate physiognomy and skin colour with rhetorics of descent, 'race', and blood purity. Although the *Aethiops* exists as a type of extreme and alarming blackness, a whole range of ethnographical names, such as 'Moor', Gaetulian, and Egyptian is used to signify (in ancient language) 'dark', 'black', or 'dusky' peoples. The problem of finding any close correspondence between ancient and modern depictions of 'black people' is immediately apparent. The Aethiops is proverbially unchangeable, but it is far from clear that his status is automatically inherited: his child will only be described as an Aethiops if he looks like an Aethiops, while a whole range of defences is available for 'a [non-Aethiops] woman who gives birth to an Aethiops', including atavism (an Aethiops in the family past) and maternal impression (the mother seeing a black animal, person, or thing while pregnant). While an Aethiops, Moor, Gaetulian, or Egyptian at Rome might be assumed to be a slave, the corollary is not true: it was notoriously difficult to detect slaves by their appearance. None of this is to say that Rome was a 'tolerant' or 'non-racist' society. The Aethiops was regularly classed as a physical freak, and the defences for 'a woman who gives birth to an Aethiops' played with the fear and surprise of offspring born from adulterous liaisons, most probably with slaves (Snowden 1970; Thompson 1989; Dench 2005: 292–7).

Changing and Multiple Identities

Rome's expansion of her citizen-body both socially, by enfranchising former slaves, and geographically, by annexation and extension way beyond the normal expectations of ancient city-states and empires, was accompanied by an exceptional interest in the phenomena of changing and juxtaposed identities. Legislation concerning the manumission of slaves and the status of freedmen can be seen within the archaic law-code of Rome, the 'Twelve Tables', and the Roman conquest of Italy in the mid-Republic was accompanied by the assignment of differential statuses, occasionally including annexation of peoples and their lands and incorporation within the Roman citizenship. The uprising of some of Rome's Italian allies in the Social War of 91–89 BCE was eventually followed by the mass enfranchisement of the free peoples of Italy south of the River Po. As the citizenship came to be seen as a gift bestowed by the over-prominent individuals of the late Republic and their successors, the emperors of Rome, individuals and communities of veterans and other friends beyond the Po, the Alps, and across the Mediterranean Sea were enfranchised, and finally a near-universal grant was made through the edict of Caracalla. The pun on the similar-sounding Latin words *urbs*, 'city' and *orbis*, 'world', surviving in the modern world through the papal formula *urbi et orbi*, 'to the city and the world', is attested from the late Republic. This pun illustrates ancient consciousness of the extraordinary status of the city of Rome, the community of which included increasingly far-flung Roman citizens as nominal members, with profound consequences for the ways in which they perceived themselves (Sherwin-White 1973; Edwards 1996; Edwards and Woolf 2003).

The merits and problems of Rome's mobile and multi-ethnic nature were hotly debated at the end of the Republic and in the early Imperial period, and the Roman social vocabulary of 'outsiders within' is correspondingly rich. *Novi homines*, 'new men', who made it into Roman political life without illustrious senatorial ancestors, may be both disparaged for their lack of urbanity and seek to make a virtue of this 'newness' and its supposed moral advantages. Cicero, perhaps the most famous 'new man', regularly turned the 'newness' of his clients and juries to forensic advantage, but was himself asked by the blue-blooded tribune of the people, P. Clodius Pulcher, what a man from Arpinum wanted with the hot springs of Baiae (Wiseman 1971; Dench 2005: 179–87). The 'transitional' status of freedmen, enfranchised ex-slaves subject to some legal limitations for the duration of their lives, is marked by their portrayal in literature and by their self-representation in monumental ways (Zanker 1975, 1979; Kleiner 1977, 1987; Bradley 1997; Fitzgerald 2000). At the slave market we can observe a more brutal economy of ethnic origins: sellers were legally required to state the birthplace of slaves, some being more desirable than others. Tombstones of immigrants in Rome sometimes give a place of origins, and the choices made of 'tribal' names or those of towns and cities hint at the cultural and geographical imagination of their adoptive home. In other cases of slaves and freedmen in particular, the place of origin is lost altogether, and the individual is distinguished by his or her profession, another quintessentially 'Roman' means of identifying oneself (Joshel 1992; Noy 2000: 37, 205–84).

In the last decades of the Republic Cicero formulated an ideal relationship between an individual's two 'fatherlands': the local fatherland is the place of one's native cults, and the place where one's ancestors are buried, but the Roman fatherland is the one 'for which we give our lives when necessary' (*Laws* 2.2.5).

Cicero's response here to the effects of enfranchisement on a massive scale after the Social War is to relegate somewhat the local fatherland. Although his response cannot be imagined to be typical, it should be understood within the context of a huge change in the potential scale of 'Roman' politics, exemplified by the entry of considerable numbers of Italians to the Roman Senate by the Augustan period. Cicero's formulation is nevertheless strikingly Romanocentric, and can be compared with the centripetal tendency of ancient and modern histories of the extension of the Roman citizenship (Mouritsen 1998). Evidence for the value of the Roman citizenship within strictly local contexts is similarly rich. Inscriptions and letters include suggestive examples of claims made for the avoidance of local civic obligations and for preferential treatment on the basis of the citizenship. While it is a fantasy to imagine that male Roman citizens were clad permanently in togas, portraiture of the Imperial period suggests some of its local symbolism: as a 'best dress' and thus suitable for funerary portraits, as one of the markers of newly free status, or as one of a number of illustrated costumes, denoting the several 'ethnic', social, or political roles that the subject could assume (Vout 1996; Hallett 2005). The spectacular funerary monument of Philopappos, Roman consul of 109 CE, which overlooks Athens and commemorates his tripartite identity in choices of dress and language, as heir of the Commagene kingdom, Athenian archon, and Roman consul, is an excellent example of this phenomenon (Kleiner 1986; Miles 2000).

In comparison with other ancient imperial powers, the Romans imagined their impact on other peoples and cultures to be interventionist to a peculiar degree. By the late Republic and early Imperial period there is considerable interest in the idea of cultural tests for worthiness of citizenship, including knowledge of Latin, while Strabo is not alone in his fascination with the processes of change at the interface of Roman and local cultures. Notoriously, in his *Agricola*, Tacitus implicated his father-in-law in the morally ambivalent 'civilization' of the Britons, encouraging them in the pleasures of porticoes and baths, in toga-wearing and in competitive displays of their new-found facility with Latin (*Agr.* 21; Dauge 1981; Veyne 1993; Clarke 2001; Dench 2005: 80–91). The extent to which changes to the material culture of the provinces should be interpreted in accordance with such narratives is currently one of the most vexed issues in Roman Studies. Should we imagine the impetus for change as primarily directed by the Romans, or with the locals, and how should we characterize the motivations behind this? When we see patterns of profound cultural change, should we interpret this as primarily an indication of the will to become Roman rather than as part of a generalized 'cultural revolution'? How far should we emphasize the 'unifying' or 'globalizing' significance of shared culture within the Roman empire, as opposed to the specificities of local usages and meanings, and of enhanced social and economic divisions within individual societies? (See on this Millett 1990; Woolf 1992, 1998, 2001; Williams 2001*b*.)

If much modern research emphasizes the permeability and hybridity of identities within the Roman world, the most serious exceptions might seem to be Jews and Christians, whose identities are generally imagined to be less 'negotiable' than those of other peoples, and to be of a different quality altogether. The argument has been made that Jewish identity shifts from being an 'ethnic' identity to a 'religious' identity partly in connection with the destruction of the Temple of Jerusalem in the Jewish War fought by Vespasian and Titus in 66–70 CE. Similarly, Christianity is generally considered to be a distinctively 'religious' identity, as opposed to an 'ethnic' or 'geographical' identity. This shift has been depicted as both a matter of self-perception and as a matter of how 'Jews' and 'Christians' were perceived by others. The notorious anecdote of Domitian having an elderly man stripped to find out whether he was circumcised and thus eligible for the special tax on Jews is an unpleasant illustration of the impulse to look for ('cultural'/'ethnic'?) markers of identity, and the 'test' apparently became a matter of self-declaration under Nerva (Suet. *Dom.* 12.2). Connections have been made with the emphasis on 'profession', the declaration 'I am a Christian' in the literature of persecution. There are, however, problems with these schemes, which are perhaps partly survivals of more traditional teleological patterning of Roman history that places undue emphasis on the 'rise of Christianity'. It may be that we have been seduced by the rhetoric of self-styled 'Jewish' and 'Christian' writers who seek to mark their distance from other peoples even as they appropriate traditional modes of representing identity, including the vocabularies of race, and even as members of their audiences live in infinitely more culturally complicated ways than rhetorics of separatism might suggest (Goodman 1989; North 1992; Cohen 1993; Schwartz 1995; Lieu 2004).

References

ALCOCK, S. (2001). 'Vulgar Romanization and the Dominance of Elites', in S. Keay and N. Terrenato (eds.), *Italy and the West: Comparative Issues in Romanization* (Oxford), 227–30.

BERNAL, M. (1987). *Black Athena: The Afroasiatic Roots of Classical Civilization*, vol. 1: *The Fabrication of Ancient Greece 1785–1985* (New Brunswick, NJ); vol. 2: *The Archaeological and Documentary Evidence* (London).

—— (2001). *Black Athena Writes Back: Martin Bernal Responds to his Critics*, ed. D. C. Moore (Durham, NC).

BICKERMANN, E. (1952). 'Origines gentium', *CP* 47: 65 ff.

BINSBERGEN, W. VAN (ed.) (1997). *Black Athena: Ten Years After* (Hoofdoorp).

BRADLEY, K. (1997). *Slaves and Masters in the Roman Empire: A Study in Social Control* (New York).

BUELL, D. KIMBER (2005). *Why this New Race? Ethnic Reasoning in Early Christianity* (New York).

Clarke, J. R. (2003). *Art in the Lives of Ordinary Romans: Visual Representation and Non-Elite Viewers in Italy, 100 BC–AD 315* (Berkeley, Los Angeles, and London).
Clarke, K. (1997). 'In Search of the Author of Strabo's Geography', *JRS* 87: 92–110.
——(1999). *Between Geography and History: Hellenistic Constructions of the Roman World* (Oxford).
——(2001). 'An Island Nation', *JRS* 91: 94–112.
Cohen, S. D. (1993). '"Those who say they are Jews and are not": How Do You Know a Jew in Antiquity When You See One?', in S. D. Cohen and E. Frerichs (eds.), *Diasporas in Antiquity* (Atlanta, Ga.), 1–45.
Dauge, Y. (1981). *Le Barbare: recherches sur la conception romaine de la barbarie et de la civilisation* (Brussels).
Dench, E. (1995). *From Barbarians to New Men: Greek, Roman, and Modern Perceptions of Peoples from the Central Apennines* (Oxford).
——(2003). 'Beyond Greeks and Barbarians: Italy and Sicily in the Hellenistic Age', in A. Erskine (ed.), *A Companion to the Hellenistic World* (Oxford).
——(2005). *Romulus' Asylum: Roman Identities from the Age of Alexander to the Age of Hadrian* (Oxford).
Duff, A. M. (1928). *Freedmen in the Early Roman Empire* (Oxford).
Edwards, C. (1996). *Writing Rome: Textual Approaches to the City* (Cambridge).
——and Woolf, G. (eds.) (2003). *Rome the Cosmopolis* (Cambridge).
Erskine, A. (2000). 'Polybios and Barbarian Rome', *Mediterraneo antico: economie, società, culture*, 3/1: 165–82.
——(2001). *Troy Between Greece and Rome: Local Tradition and Imperial Power* (Oxford).
Ferrary, J.-L. (1988). *Philhellénisme et impérialisme: aspects idéologiques de la conquête romaine du monde hellénistique, de la seconde guerre de Macédoine à la guerre contre Mithridate* (Rome).
Fitzgerald, W. (2000). *Slavery and the Roman Literary Imagination* (Cambridge).
Frank, T. (1920). *An Economic History of Rome to the End of the Republic* (Baltimore).
Galinsky, K. (1992). *Classical and Modern Interactions: Postmodern Architecture, Multiculturalism, Decline and Other Issues* (Austin, Tex.).
Gardner, J. (1993). *Being a Roman Citizen* (London).
Giardina, A. (1997). *L'Italia romana: storie di un'identità incompiuta* (Rome).
Goodman, M. (1989). 'Nerva, the fiscus Judaicus, and Jewish Identity', *JRS* 79: 40–3.
Grose-Hodge, H. (1944). *Roman Panorama: A Background for Today* (Cambridge).
Gruen, E. S. (1990). *Studies in Greek Culture and Roman Policy* (Leiden).
——(1993). *Culture and National Identity in Republican Rome* (London).
——(1998). *Heritage and Hellenism: The Reinvention of Jewish Tradition* (Berkeley, Los Angeles, and London).
Guastella, G. (1985). 'La rete del sangue: simbologia delle relazioni e modelli dell'identità nella cultura romana', *MD* 15: 49–123.
Hall, E. (1989). *Inventing the Barbarian: Greek Self-Definition Through Tragedy* (Oxford).
Hall, J. (1997). *Ethnic Identity in Greek Antiquity* (Cambridge).
——(2002). *Hellenicity: Between Ethnicity and Culture* (Chicago).
Hallett, C. (2005). *The Roman Nude: Heroic Portrait Statuary 200 BC–AD 300* (Oxford).
Hingley, R. (2005). *Globalizing Roman Culture: Unity, Diversity and Empire* (London).
Jones, C. P. (1996). 'Ethnos and genos in Herodotus', *CQ* NS 46/1: 315–20.
——(1999). *Kinship Diplomacy in the Ancient World* (Cambridge, Mass.).

JONES, S. (1996). 'Discourses of Identity in the Interpretation of the Past', in P. Graves-Brown, S. Jones, and C. Gamble (eds.), *Cultural Identity and Archaeology* (London), 62–80.

—— (1997). *The Archaeology of Ethnicity: Constructing Identities in the Past and Present* (London).

JOSHEL, S. (1992). *Work, Identity and Legal Status at Rome: A Study of the Occupational Inscriptions* (Norman, Okla.).

JUST, R. (1989). 'Triumph of the Ethnos', in E. Tonkin, M. McDonald, and M. Chapman (eds.), *History and Ethnicity*, ASA Monograph 27 (London).

KEAY, S. and TERRENATO, N. (eds.) (2001). *Italy and the West: Comparative Issues in Romanization* (Oxford).

KLEINER, D. C. E. (1977). *Roman Group Portraiture: The Funerary Reliefs of the Late Republic and Early Empire* (New York).

—— (1986). 'Athens Under the Romans: The Patronage of Emperors and Kings', in C. B. McClendon (ed.), *Rome and the Provinces: The Transformation of Art in the Mediterranean* (New Haven), 8–20.

—— (1987). *Roman Imperial Funerary Altars with Portraits*, Archaeologica 62 (Rome).

LAURENCE, R. (2001). 'Roman Narratives: The Writing of Archaeological Discourse—A View from Britain?', *Archaeological Dialogues*, 8: 90–101.

LEFKOWITZ, M. and ROGERS, G. M. (eds.) (1996). *Black Athena Revisited* (Chapel Hill, NC).

LIEU, J. (2004). *Christian Identity in the Jewish and Graeco-Roman World* (Oxford).

LURAGHI, N. (2003). 'Dionysios von Halikarnassos zwischen Griechen und Römern', in U. Eigler *et al.* (eds.), *Formen römischer Geschichtsschreibung von den Anfängen bis Livius* (Darmstadt), 268–86.

MALKIN, I. (ed.) (2001). *Ancient Perceptions of Greek Ethnicity* (Cambridge, Mass.).

MATTINGLY, D. (ed.) (1997). *Dialogues in Roman Imperialism: Power, Discourse and Discrepant Experience in the Roman Empire* (JRA suppl. 23).

MILES, R. (2000). 'Communicating Culture, Identity and Power', in J. Huskinson (ed.), *Experiencing Rome: Culture, Identity and Power in the Roman Empire* (London), 29–62, esp. 29–36.

MILLAR, F. G. B. (1987). 'Polybius Between Greece and Rome', in J. Koumoulides (ed.), *Greek Connections: Essays on Culture and Diplomacy* (Notre Dame, Ind.), 1 ff.

MILLETT, M. (1990). *The Romanization of Britain: An Essay in Archaeological Interpretation* (Cambridge).

MOATTI, C. (1997). *La Raison de Rome: naissance de l'esprit critique à la fin de la République (IIe–Ier siècle avant Jésus-Christ)* (Paris).

MOMIGLIANO, A. D. (1975). *Alien Wisdom: The Limits of Hellenization* (Cambridge).

—— (1984). 'How to Reconcile Greeks and Trojans', *Settimo Contributo*, 437–62.

MOURITSEN, H. (1998). *Italian Unification: A Study in Ancient and Modern Historiography* (London).

NORTH, J. (1992). 'The Development of Religious Pluralism', in J. Lieu, J. North, and T. Rajak (eds.), *The Jews Among Pagans and Christians in the Roman Empire* (London and New York), 174–93.

NOY, D. (2000). *Foreigners at Rome: Citizens and Strangers* (London).

PERADOTTO, J. and LEVINE, M. (eds.) (1989). *The Challenge of Black Athena* (Buffalo, NY).

RIGGS, C. (2005). *The Beautiful Burial in Roman Egypt: Art, Identity and Funerary Religion* (Oxford).

SCHEID, J. (1995). 'Graeco ritu: A Typically Roman Way of Honouring the Gods', *HSCP* 98: 15–31.

SCHIAVONE, A. (2005). *Ius: l'invenzione del diritto in Occidente* (Turin).

SCHNEIDER, R. (1986). *Bunte Barbaren: Orientalstatuen aus farbigem Marmor in der römischen Repräsentationskunst* (Worms).

SCHULTZE, C. (1986). 'Dionysius of Halicarnassus and his Audience', in I. Moxon, J. Smart, and A. Woodman (eds.), *Past Perspectives: Studies in Greek and Roman Historical Writing* (Cambridge), 121–41.

SCHWARTZ, S. (1995). 'Language, Power and Identity in Ancient Palestine', *Past and Present*, 148: 3–47.

SHERWIN-WHITE, A. N. (1973). *The Roman Citizenship* (2nd edn., Oxford).

SMITH, R. R. R. (1988). 'Simulacra Gentium: The ethne from the Sebasteion at Aphrodisias', *JRS* 78: 50–77.

SNOWDEN, F. (1970). *Blacks in Antiquity: Ethiopians in the Greco-Roman Experience* (Cambridge, Mass.).

—— (1983). *Before Color Prejudice: The Ancient View of Blacks* (Cambridge, Mass.).

THOMAS, Y. (1990). 'L'Institution de l'origine. Sacra principiorum populi Romani', in M. Detienne (ed.), *Tracés de fondation* (Paris), 143–70.

THOMPSON, L. A. (1981). 'The Concept of Purity of Blood in Suetonius' Life of Augustus', *Mus. Afr.* 7: 35–46.

—— (1989). *Romans and Blacks* (London).

VEYNE, P. (1993). 'Humanitas: Romans and non-Romans', in A. Giardina (ed.), *The Romans* (Eng. tr. Chicago), 342–69.

VOUT, C. (1996). 'The Myth of the Toga: Understanding the History of Roman Dress', *Greece & Rome*, NS 43/2: 204–20.

WALBANK, F. W. (1951). 'The Problem of Greek Nationality', *Phoenix*, 5: 41–60.

—— (1972). 'Nationality as a Factor in Roman History', *HSCP* 76: 145–68.

—— (1985). 'Polybius Between Greece and Rome', in *Selected Papers: Studies in Greek and Roman History and Historiography* (Cambridge) 280–97; first publ. in *Polybe: neuf exposés suivis de discussions* (Vandoeuvres and Geneva, 1974), 1–31.

WALLACE-HADRILL, A. (1989). 'Rome's Cultural Revolution', *JRS* 79: 157–64.

—— (1998). 'To be Roman, go Greek', in M. Austin, *et al.* (eds.), *Modus Operandi: Essays in Honour of Geoffrey Rickman, BICS Supplement 71 (London), 79–91.*

WEBSTER, J. and Cooper, N. (eds.) (1996). *Roman Imperialism: Post-colonial Perspectives* (Leicester Archaeological Monographs 3).

WHITMARSH, T. (2001). *Greek Literature and the Roman Empire: The Politics of Imitation* (Oxford).

WILLIAMS, J. (2001*a*). *Beyond the Rubicon: Romans and Gauls in Republican Italy* (Oxford).

—— (2001*b*). 'Roman Intentions and Romanization: Republican Northern Italy', in Keay and Terrenato eds.: 91–101.

WISEMAN, T. P. (1971). *New Men in the Roman Senate* (Oxford).

—— (1974). 'Legendary Genealogies in Late Republican Rome', *Greece & Rome*, 21: 153 ff.

—— (1983). '*Domi nobiles* and the Roman cultural élite', in *Les Bourgeoisies municipales italiennes aux II et I siècles av. J.C.: Centre Jean-Bérard, Institut français de Naples, 7–10 décembre 1981* (Paris), 299–307.

WOOLF, G. (1992). 'The Unity and Diversity of Romanisation', *JRA* 5: 349–52.

Woolf, G. (1994). 'Becoming Roman, Staying Greek: Culture, Identity and the Civilizing Process in the Roman East', *PCPS* 40: 116–43.
—— (1998). *Becoming Roman: The Origins of Provincial Civilization in Gaul* (Cambridge).
—— (2001). 'The Roman Cultural Revolution in Gaul', in Keay and Terrenato eds.: 173–86.
Zanker, P. (1975). 'Grabreliefs römischer Freigelassener', *JDAI* 90: 267–315.
—— (1979). 'Die Villa als Vorbild des späten pompejanischen Wohngeschmacks', *JDAI* 94: 460–523.
—— (1988). *The Power of Images in the Age of Augustus*, tr. A. Shapiro (Ann Arbor, Mich.).

CHAPTER 18

PERFORMANCE

MICHÈLE LOWRIE

THE ancients did not have the word 'performance'. The modern one has many resonances (Barchiesi 2001*a*), ranging from acting a drama on stage, to less formal production modes, to reading aloud, to playing a role—understood as an act of imitation and consequently false—to bringing things into being, as in performative discourse. Is the performance of a play more or less socially embedded than the text? Is playing a social role putting on an act, or creating a reality? Despite the lack of a corresponding Latin word, Roman literature is preoccupied by performativity. References to production and reception media abound from the earliest times, and these are linked to poetic power. Roman poetry represents itself both as incapable of effecting political change, and as having the power to create reality through representation. Different authors put this dynamic together in different ways according to genre, their purported access to god, and political circumstance. Particularly in the Augustan age, political and social change constitute a crisis for literature. The Republican independence of Lucilius, Catullus, and Lucretius has been compromised, but new avenues for literary production open in relation to the new shape of the state. Literature's ability to form reality is figured in this period through its representations of the media, specifically in the interaction each work sets up between writing and literal performance modes.

Although early Latin literature is self-conscious about media of production and distribution, the density of references to writing and song for both composition and reception becomes thicker with the Augustans. The main transition in the institutions supporting literature came in the late Republic, when libraries began to be made public, booksellers made book circulation more than an elite activity, and recitation began as a regular practice. Goldberg (2005) locates this moment in the second half of the second century BCE, when, in his words, literature was constructed, namely, texts began to be received as literary by scholars. As Kaster points out in this volume, scholarship was not a professional activity done to the exclusion of public life. Asinius Pollio was an important politician who wrote history and tragedy, and intervened decisively in literary distribution in both written and performance modes. He helped to establish the library at the Atrium Libertatis and his name is associated with publicizing recitation (Goldberg 2005: 190–2, 46–7). The mechanics of representation are a major preoccupation among the Augustans, and by their time the literary institutions had stabilized, though their patina remained new. Horace's (*Epistles* 2.1.214–18) and Ovid's (*Tristia* 3.1) concerns about inclusion (or not) in the library are fresh, modern, and unimaginable for Catullus, who locates poetic success in the longevity of the paper transmitting the poetry (68.45–6) and the distance of its circulation (95), rather than the approbation granted by inclusion in a library.

During the period of solidification in the literary institutions, the political situation was in transition. The poets channel their concerns about social stability by questioning poetry's effectiveness. Although Virgil's Tityrus recovers his farm (*Eclogues* 1), Menalcas' song has not met the same success, and the social vulnerability sparked by the land confiscations engenders a crisis in poetic memory—further song is postponed to the uncertain future (*Ecl.* 9.10–13, 55–67). An index of insecurity is the difference between Catullus' confident invective against leading men (e.g. sexual slurs against Caesar) and Horace's unwillingness to satirize anyone of consequence. The pervasive failure of speech acts in Horace's *Epodes* conveys a sense of powerlessness (Barchiesi 2001*c*: 147–9). Along with greater confidence in the potential for literary longevity came decreasing space for political accomplishment. Horace's biography is indicative. As a military tribune on the losing side at Philippi, his potential public career was curtailed. Few had the resources and family clout of Pollio, which were needed despite Augustus' vaunted clemency. Horace took a day job as a scribe in the quaestor's office and devoted his creative energies to poetry. The climate was sufficiently open that he later turned down an offer from Augustus to be his letter-writer. He could also consistently question his own and poetry's social role throughout his career. The combined strengthening of literary institutions and changing possibilities for public expression resulted in the so-called Golden Age of Latin Poetry—an intensely creative period conjoining a heightened self-consciousness about the technicalities of representation with an exploration of what poets could hope to achieve in society.

Scholarship in the late twentieth and early twenty-first centuries has taken a turn toward performance because of the intersection this concept affords between actual media of representation and performativity in the pragmatic sense. Not much reflection, however, has clarified what links these topics (attempted in Lowrie 2009). There has been an explosion of interest in the book, its production and metaphorics (Don Fowler's work was tragically cut short, but Joseph Farrell and others are carrying on; Williams 1992), actual reading practices (Starr 1990–1; Horsfall 1995*b*; Johnson 2000; Markus 2000), and the history and sociology of song (Zorzetti 1990 and 1990–1; Habinek 2005). Social performance has also become a dominant interest, as a reality (Lendon 1997; Gleason 1995; Gunderson 2000; Wray 2001) or topic of literature (Oliensis 1998; Krostenko 2001). This work responds to the collapse of the New Criticism and the turn toward the social that has been the past generation's dominant paradigm, and Classics has, as usual, followed wider literary critical trends. What the concept of performance allows is the pragmatic link between art and society, whether performance is conceptualized literally as an event before an audience, distanced through reading, or regarded even more abstractly as the development, playing out, and reflection about a role over a lifetime. Suetonius reports that Augustus himself asked on his deathbed whether he had played well in the mime of life (*Aug.* 99). This anecdote neatly demonstrates the intersection between public discourses of power, the media, and self-awareness.

The transition out of formalism has been bumpy for Roman Studies. Because Hellenists have long focused on orality and Latinists began to hunger for the social fabric formal (epic, tragedy) and informal (sympotic) performance allegedly support, there was initially a tendency among sociologically oriented historians to set the oral, 'warm' culture of Greece against the written, 'cold' culture of Rome (Dupont 1994), and a desire to find literal performance at Rome as a partial solution to that dichotomy (Zorzetti 1990 and 1990–1; Habinek 1998: 35; Rüpke 2001). These issues are part of the debate about Hellenization at Rome. Questions are: what exactly happened at a dinner party; was there a separate symposium *à la grecque*; was poetry performed, and if so, was it sung or recited, and by whom; and when did this start? These questions have no secure answers, and the frame for approaching them has recently shifted. Emphasis now falls equally on the individuality of Roman culture and Rome's participation in Greek acculturation since its prehistory (Habinek 1998: ch. 1). Although this idea dates at least to Momigliano (1957), it is currently receiving a new formulation: Greece stands as Rome's 'included alterity' (Dupont 2005; Dupont and Valette-Cagnac 2005). Similarly, it has been recognized that writing is constitutive of (transmitted) Greek literature to some degree from the beginning (Edmunds 2001: 79) and has as dynamic a social function as orality (Feeney 2000). Furthermore, attention is focusing on the pragmatics of the written word outside literature, for instance, in documents (Meyer 2004), and on the complex relation to literature of other discourse systems, such as the law (Lowrie 2005 and 2006). These areas of research will produce a more nuanced understanding of how the Romans understood the relation between the form of a particular discourse and its role in society.

The Poetic Speech Act: Vocabulary

No word in the vocabulary of poetic composition exists to perform the poetic speech act literally. Virgil's *cano* ('I sing', *Aeneid* 1.1) calques the Greek αειδο ('I sing') without corresponding to a native tradition. Volk (2002: 13) calls 'the illusion that the poem is really only coming into being as it evolves before the readers' eyes' 'poetic simultaneity'. This at Rome required a catachresis in the language of song. *Canere* is a figurative word for authoritative utterance. It does not occur in writing contexts, such as letters, where authoritative utterance is also at issue. Although *carmen* ('song'), a related word, goes back to the Twelve Tables, there it means not poetry, but spells or incantation. Even in historical times, song at Rome covers a broader range than poetry (Habinek 2005). Its oldest meanings are religious (*carmen Aruale*, *carmen Saliare*) and juridical ('law of an awful song', Livy 1.26.6) (Ernout–Meillet 1939: at *carmen*), and it only comes to mean poetry via song, which pertained as much to tunes as to words (Ennius, *Annales* 519 Skutsch, of trumpets), and this apparently relatively late. The *carmina conuiualia* are mired in controversy, but even if our late Republican sources preserve the traces of a lost practice, references to them present contemporary ideas about what archaic song was in contemporary vocabulary (Sciarrino 2004*a*; Goldberg 2005: 8–16). The word *carmen* becomes standard for poetry before *canere* regularly denotes the poetic speech act. The former becomes common in Lucretius, but the latter seems to colour poetry with the brush of the Alexandrian style, even when he uses it of himself (Newman 1965; Volk 2002: 84). It is absent in a meaning that a poet could adopt for his own utterance before this time. In Ennius *canere* refers to poetry he disavows (207 Skutsch), and it similarly has negative connotations in Pacuvius (336–7 W = 337–8 Ribbeck). Although the Romans distinguish between *canere*, poetic utterance, and *cantare*, poetic performance or vocalized song (Markus 2000: 141–4; Habinek 2005: 67), the latter can be appropriated metaphorically for the poetic act (Horace, *Odes* 2.9.19). When a poet claims to sing, *canere* does not necessarily correspond to the poetry's performance medium, but rather makes a claim to authoritative utterance. The language of song in Roman poetry is consequently ideological rather than denotative.

Writing is commonly used of poetic composition, but in Republican and Augustan times describes a practice (e.g. Horace's 'writing verses', *Epist.* 2.1.111) and is not an explicit performative (Austin 1962: 32). Horace's 'I write' (*Epist.* 2.2.103) denotes an activity. Lucretius describes his late-night lucubrations (1.142–4) without the vocabulary of writing, but nevertheless implies the medium. In Ovid's *Heroides*, the various explicit performatives are verbs of utterance (7.4, 14.45, 19.108) and of sending (1.1, 13.1), but writing is an explicit performative in the first person only when accompanied by clear signs of visual description (ecphrasis: 7.183–4, 15.96) and vividness (*enargeia*: 20.33). The verb that comes closest to the

Greek ποιειν ('to make') is *fingere* ('to fashion'), though this requires some specification when the made object is poetry. *Poema*, *poiesis*, and *poeta* are brought over from Greek. In Ennius and Lucretius the most common word for the poetic act is *pangere* ('to give forth'), which can be used in the first person (Lucretius 1.933) and is neutral in terms of production medium. It acquires 'an archaizing or mock-heroic ring' by Augustan times (Skutsch at Ennius, *Annales* 293), leaving no neutral vocabulary for poetic production.

The vocabulary chosen for poetic composition depends greatly on generic orientation. This depends partly on the genre's historical production medium: epigram, satire, and epistles tend to present themselves as writing, while epic and lyric tend toward song. More decisive, however, is the extent a genre offers a realistic or idealized view of the world. Realism attaches to writing, elevation to song. Neither criterion, however, is absolute. The self-presentation of some genres, like elegy, depends partially on their development over time (lyric exercises a strong pull on elegy toward song away from its imagined written origins), partially on context (realism versus elevation), and partially without particular emphasis. To a great extent, however, the figuration of poetry with one or another production medium grants it different kinds of power. Catullus' consistent representation of his poetic activity as writing in the polymetrics (Wiseman 1982: 38) is one technique by which he creates his vivid and famous realism. Horace, whose lyric is thoroughly imbued with the language of song and music, demurs when it comes to depicting himself actually singing to a lyre (Heinze 1972: 187; Barchiesi 2007: 148, 155–7). This stance accompanies his ambivalence about adopting the role of spokesman for the Augustan programme. The musical instruments at *Odes* 1.1.29–36 serve less to suggest performance than the genre in which Horace aspires to achieve canonicity. The canon is a literary institution implying the codification arising through libraries. The single instance of the language of song for Horace's own utterance is at *Odes* 3.1.4 ('I, the priest of the Muses, sing a previously unheard song to maidens and boys'), where the elevation introduces the Roman Odes to great fanfare. Conversely, Ovid, whose *Amores* largely present their means of production realistically as writing, spoofs his erotic failure—and Horace's pretentious stance—by deflating the singing *uates* shut out by his mistress: 'I, that pure priest of the Muses and Phoebus, sing an empty song at stiff doors' (*Amores* 3.8.23–4).

This dynamic is picked up in later Imperial poetry, regardless of whether the poetry is actually performed. Statius' *Siluae* present themselves as performed more formally than warranted by their recitation medium, and these claims are linked to the poet's construction of his social role and his anxiety about it (Newlands 2002: 27–36).

The vocabulary of poetic production, far from being indifferent (as suggested by Wilamowitz-Moellendorff 1924: 1. 180–1), affords a rich palette for poetic definition of oneself and others. The media of composition map onto the different degrees of power offered by realism and elevation. Writing and song each entails a different kind of authority.

The Poetic Speech Act: What Is It?

A primary task of reading is to determine a poem's ostensible speech situation. Lyric poetry is often said to imitate real-life speech acts such as invitation, leave-taking, requesting, ordering, warning, encouragement, praise, and blame (Heinze 1972: 180–1; Cairns 1972). Actual poems, however, rarely line up exactly with a situation that can be imagined to be as real even as those in drama. Catullus' epithalamia (61 and 62) conflate into short compass aspects of a ceremony requiring a greater amount of time. In *Odes* 1.5 Horace is not actually addressing Pyrrha while she lies in amorous embrace (Nauta 2004: 375). Rather, he reflects on her new love to himself. We overhear his musings (Oliensis 1998: 6–7), not a spoken utterance. Even more dramatized utterances, such as Catullus 42, frequently fail of their professed speech act (Selden 1992). The *flagitatio* Catullus sets in motion is a social institution ostensibly designed to retrieve his tablets, but the invective on the girl who has stolen them precludes any pragmatic success. Another effect is achieved: the insult. The distance between the actual and the represented speech act is figured by Catullus' address of his poetry (42.1) instead of the girl.

The conundrum of the poetic speech act has long exercised criticism. Heinze famously called Horace's lyric utterances fiction (1972: 188), but resistance has followed several lines. Some emphasize the real social relation between Latin poets and their addressees (Citroni 1995), others the meditative or conceptual act of lyric discourse, which distances poetry from its social context (Payne 2006). These apparently antithetical approaches can, however, be combined. Although a poem's represented utterance may be made up, some displaced communication is still transmitted to the addressee as well as the reader of posterity. Horace's invitation to Maecenas in *Odes* 1.20 may not invite him to a party, but to the celebration that is poetry itself (Commager 1962: 326). The poem's force is to commemorate rather than invite, and this canonical poetic function is received equally by reader and addressee. The contingency of any historical party makes it unnecessary for the poem's interpretation. Horace reflects on the distance between the represented and actual speech act: the ostensible invitation is infelicitous as it lacks essential indicators such as time and place, while the praise which is only mentioned (1.20.7) carries the poem's true performative weight. Similarly, *Odes* 1.5 communicates to Pyrrha that Horace has moved on from his infatuation with her enough to reflect on his raw emotions in tranquillity. Therefore, the speech situation may be fictitious while the communication is nevertheless real, so that the poetic speech act is a 'partial fiction' (Nauta 2002: 366–7). The votive tablet Horace offers in return for recovering from love's shipwreck figures the poem's own written status (*Odes* 1.5.13–16). Latin poetry typically indicates awareness of the distance between represented and actual poetic speech acts by an indirect nod to the poem's medium.

The reality of represented speech acts, however, must be understood differently where there is no contemporary addressee. Lucretius may honour Memmius with his dedication, but the didactic addressee separates from the historical as the poem attempts to convert all posterity to Epicureanism. Since this cannot be accomplished, the didactic addressee never learns anything and the poem's task remains in process (Mitsis 1993).

Virgil's *cano* offers a different problematic. It communicates the poem's inception as an epic and conveys authoritative utterance. Virgil forges the role of bard for himself through the utterance, which, being actually written, enters into a complex dynamic with the poem's figuration of speech modes. In one gesture, Virgil indirectly aligns his speech with the Sibyl's. Helenus tells Aeneas how she writes her prophecies on leaves, which fly around and become uninterpretable when anyone enters the cave where she stores them, and advises him consequently to make her sing. When she does, she is divinely possessed. Although Virgil never intimates such violence of his own poetic inspiration, his adoption of song links him with god over against unreliable writing. Nevertheless, the poet's utterance meets the recurring metaphor of the book of fate (e.g. Jupiter's 'unrolling the secrets of the fates', *Aen.* 1.262), which has a complex relation to the plot (Barchiesi 2001*b*: 130–2). 'Fate', derived etymologically from a verb for 'speaking', is both handed down and made up in the telling. The result is a book, whether Jupiter's or Virgil's, and a hint of realism tinges even the sung *Aeneid.*

Actual Reception Media

Little evidence remains for the full-fledged performance of elite literature outside drama, though a rich culture of popular song existed at Rome (Horsfall 2003). Plautus and Terence were staged and new plays continued to be composed and performed into the Augustan period, when revivals became more prevalent, plays began to be composed for recitation, and theatre took a turn toward entertainment (Boyle 2006: ch. 6). Cicero attests to political expression in the theatre, where phrases were taken by the audience to have contemporary relevance (Gruen 1992: 184–5). Varius' *Thyestes* was likely performed at Augustus' triple triumph in 29 BCE (Goldberg 2005: 210 n. 13), but the performance of Seneca's plays remains mired in controversy (Harrison 2000). Other texts circulated among friends, reading was done mostly orally alone or in groups, and, from the late Republic on, recitation became a regular public event (Goldberg 2005: 38, 46–8), often skewered by the satirists as occasions to be avoided (Horace, *Epist.*

1.19; Juvenal 1.1). The publication and circulation of late third- and early second-century literature is controversial. Rüpke (2001) has reasonably suggested, though without evidence, that early Roman epic was performed at aristocratic banquets. The various Lives depict Virgil reading the *Georgics* and selections from the *Aeneid* to Augustus and his family, but these stories' authenticity is tenuous (Horsfall 1995*a*: 2, 15–24). The adoption of elite literature by mime is attested for Virgil (*Vita Donatiana* 26; *Vita Donati Aucti* 41; *Vita Philargyriana* 1, Brugnoli and Stok 181, 1–3), and performances of Ovid were also probably mime (*Tr.* 2.519 and 5.7.25; Horsfall 2003: 15, 56). These performance media, however, appear informal and sporadic (Markus 2000) compared to the great Hellenic festivals.

It remains an open question whether Horace performed his *Odes* in sympotic contexts. Many attempts to argue he did interpret the lyric apparatus of song over-literally (Bonavia-Hunt 1972; Lefèvre 1993). Horace's utterances cohere imperfectly with dramatic situations—some slight distance inhabits such scenes. Ovid's depiction of Horace at the lyre (*Tr.* 4.10.49–50) is no independent witness, since his vocabulary of song suits the lyric genre. Du Quesnay (1995) argues that *Odes* 4.5 was performed during the festivities welcoming Augustus on his return from Gaul, but the leap from the poem's occasion to actual performance remains an act of faith. We know Horace sent presentation copies of his poetry to Augustus, although the poetry in question cannot be proved to be lyric (*Epistles* 1.13), and a letter of Augustus preserved in Suetonius' Life of Horace jocularly contrasts the girth of the poet's belly to his slim book. If Horace did recite to the emperor (*Epistles* 1.19.41–4), he also presented a text.

The great exception for the Augustan period is Horace's *Carmen Saeculare*, which was performed twice during the *Ludi saeculares*, on the Palatine and Capitoline hills, by a chorus of twenty-seven boys and twenty-seven girls. Its uniqueness makes it an interpretive challenge, as a poem and an occasion (Barchiesi 2002). The complex relationship between its role in the festival and its status as a literary work has been contested since the appearance of the *Acta* of the *Ludi saeculares* in 1890, with some emphasizing the former (Habinek 2005: 150–7), some the latter (Fraenkel 1958: 365–82), and some aiming for balance (Feeney 1998: 28–38). Festival and poem are both innovations working within traditional contexts (Schnegg-Köhler 2002: ch. 14). Horace's pride in referring to it (*Odes* 4.6.35–44; implicitly at *Epistles* 2.1.119–38) attests to this anomaly's importance. It furthermore contains a remarkable representation of its own performative power: at lines 70–2 the present indicative indicates the prayer is already coming true (Putnam 2000: 94–5). The link between actual performance and the utterance's power to create realities is symptomatic of the Augustan age's preoccupation with the relation between poetic media and verbal power.

Social Performance

Recent criticism of Latin poetry has turned toward the social. The aesthetic creates symbolic capital for its creator in a world governed by elite competition. Manhood is the ever-elusive goal of self-fashioning (Gleason 1995; Gunderson 2000). Krostenko (2001) shows how the language of literary criticism in Cicero and Catullus overlaps with the language of social positioning. The problem is that writing poetry does not necessarily make you a man, or at least, not a very manly one. Elegists typically define themselves as *mollis* ('soft'). Satire after Lucilius complains of its inability to bite (Freudenburg 2001). Horace has trouble in the first collection of *Odes* rising to the heights of the praise poetry he presents as expected of him. When he finally composes the *Carmen Saeculare*, his adoption of the public mantle entails the absorption of his personal identity into a collective. In *Odes* 4, *ego* is gradually replaced by *nos* (Putnam 1986: 28–9; Lowrie 1997: 347). Virgil's genres, none of which has a strong authorial 'I', are still fraught with the question of individual authority. From the land-confiscations in the *Eclogues* to the trauma of civil war in the *Georgics* and *Aeneid*, the political subject confronts obstacles to the successful performance of his social role. Aeneas eventually fulfils his destined role, though the violence of his act of foundation compromises his basic values.

These Augustan instances entail a shift from the empowering and aggressive poetry of the late Republic. Lucilius' fragmentary state makes it difficult to ascertain the accuracy of later representatives of his freedom to engage in invective, but much of the Catullan polymetrics aims to wound (Wray 2001). Even Lucretius, whose protreptic is well-meant, deploys verbal coercion against his didactic addressee. Aggression returns in the empire, whether in the more bitter strain of satire of Persius, Martial, and Juvenal, or the desperation of Lucan's desire for a healthy state.

It is easier to discuss self-fashioning in poets with a strong first-person 'ego', but this approach should be fruitful even for poets without it. The value of epic as a vehicle for ideology gains symbolic capital for the poet capable of the medium, yet this topic has not been framed in authorial terms for Virgil or Ennius. Much of early Latin poetry is less concerned with individual self-definition than cultural. The substitution of Roman institutions for Greek in Livius Andronicus' translation of the *Odyssey* and Ennius' adoption of Greek metres raise questions of national identity (Gruen 1992: ch. 6; Dupont and Valette-Cagnac 2005: 33). The *primus* ('first') motif in Latin literature is an overt expression of pride for bringing a previously un- or slightly practised genre to Rome. Even when this is not expressed, as in the Catullan long poems, the author performs a socially recognized function.

The danger inherent in the topic of self-fashioning is to lend transparency to the poets' manipulation of their social roles within their poetry. Again, we should be alert to displacements between reality and representation and ask why, if the ability to control the aesthetic field is in fact empowering, the poets so consistently depict themselves as disempowered. Just as poetic speech acts achieve their effects indirectly, so do poets create a limited social power for themselves through the rhetoric of inability. This rhetoric acknowledges the dominant ideology which lends the full achievement of manhood only to those who control politics. Nevertheless, intervention in the social sphere through poetry allows for an alternative, more lasting domain of social power than the transient sphere of the forum—at least, in the poets' representations.

Competing for Power

Roman poetry has a fascination with rival spheres of discourse, particularly with areas where decisions and the speech that conveys them have consequences. Catullus teases Cicero and Calvus about their oratorical prowess (49 and 54), and Horace appropriates the voice of an orator in *Epodes* 7 and 16 in an attempt to address—however ironically—the current national crisis, civil war. Asinius Pollio's history-writing seems dangerous in Horace, *Odes* 2.1. Talking about civil war was fraught with danger, and while Pollio had enough political clout to risk it, Horace himself approaches the topic gingerly (Lowrie 1997: ch. 5).

In the Augustan period the law is figured occasionally, but consistently, as a rival sphere. Poets impute to the law a greater degree of power than poetry can aspire to, though in some way or other poetry usually ends up asserting its superiority, often through the topos of longevity versus transient worldly success. Horace's dialogue with Trebatius Testa in *Sermones* 2.1 at first presents the libel laws as inhibiting to satire, though by the poem's end Horace emerges as having Augustus' ear—a power transcending any legal constraint. A formal analogy between their shared medium links satire and the law: both are written on tablets (*tabella*, 33; *tabulae*, 86). But while law is sometimes elsewhere referred to as *carmen* (Cicero, *Leg.* 2.59), Horace's satire results in its target's being sung all over town (46; Lowrie 2005).

Another rival sphere is the military. Here too poetic media contribute to the figuration of poetic power, though again not in a one-on-one correspondence between power and any medium to the exclusion of others. Elegy's 'warfare of love' (*militia amoris*) appropriates for itself metaphorically the power it knows well it does not have. Propertius' claim that he will 'sing of wars, once his girl has been written' (2.10.8) gives a greater impression of an alignment of high-style song with (declined) military themes and of writing with elegy than is borne out consistently elsewhere, but the language of mediality tends to contribute to the debate. This dynamic continues into the empire. Statius depicts Lucan's song in a contradictory way as part of his own poetic self-definition: he unsheathes it, though it is clad in the civic toga (*carmen*... *exseres togatum*, *Siluae* 2.7.53; Newlands 2002). Poetry can do no harm, yet it is a potent weapon.

Poetry's ability to persist after the poet's death is a conceit enabling poetry to trump more present power centres. Ovid, *Amores* 1.15.7–8, contrasts the mortality of the world of law and the forum (*mortale*... *opus*) with poetry's 'lasting fame' (*fama perennis*). His youthful resistance to his father's preferred career path becomes in exile a more mature reflection on the difference between Augustus' control of the law versus his own ability to create lasting representations (Lowrie 2006). Although Augustus' speech has the power to exile him, and Ovid's nine books of pleadings cannot effect his return, still, Ovid controls a representation of the emperor, who chose not to be clement, that circulates to this day.

Immortality Through Reception

Latin poetry is preoccupied with immortality, and the persistence of the text after the poet's death is figured sometimes as oral performance, sometimes as writing. Although Ennius' epitaph ('I fly alive through the mouths of men', *Epigrams* 18V) was widely imitated, signally by Virgil ('to fly victorious through the mouths of men', *Georg.* 3.9), we often forget that another epigram, cited by Cicero in the same context (*Tusc. Disp.* 1.15.34), sets in motion an alternative and equally influential metaphor for poetic immortality, the monument: 'O citizens, look at the form of the image of old Ennius. He divulged the greatest deeds of your fathers', Ennius, *Epigrams* 15–16V).

Oral performance and monumental writing are brought together for purposes that must be determined individually. Horace's famous monument in *Odes* 3.30 implies the metaphor of writing: it surpasses bronze, a medium of both statuary and inscription. Its longevity, however, is not due to writing's materiality but to the author's continuing to be spoken of after death (*dicar*, 10). The priority Horace gives orality corresponds to lyric's self-identification with song, while the prevalent writing metaphors attest to his unwillingness to deny his actual medium (Barchiesi 2000 and 2007). Ovid's boast ('I will be read in the mouth of the people', *Met.* 15.378) makes explicit the implied writing metaphor in Horace's *dicar* and Ennius' epigraph. At *Amores* 1.15 he asserts his immortality with both *canar* (8) and *legar* (38), but it is another generation before a poet combines these in a boast about his present reception. Martial takes this step ('I am sung and read all over the world', 8.61.3; Williams 2002), but the context—jockeying for social position symbolized by country villas—trivializes the socio-political concerns expressed when the Augustans boast about immortality.

Conclusion

Roman poets conceptualized various aspects of the modern word 'performance' not abstractly, but by a complex interplay between their awareness of the media of production and reception and their playing out the different degrees they could aspire to have an effect on the world. Although a poet could make a good living for himself under a generous patron, true independence emerged only with the continued circulation of his work after death, regardless of the medium of its reception.

References

Austin, J. L. (1962), *How to Do Things with Words*. Cambridge, Mass.
Barchiesi, A. (2000), 'Rituals in Ink: Horace on the Greek Lyric Tradition', in Depew and Obbink 2000: 167–82.
—— (2001*a*), review of Stephen Wheeler, *Discourse of Wonders* (Philadelphia, 1999), *CW* 94: 287–8.
—— (2001*b*), *Speaking Volumes*. London.
—— (2001*c*), 'Horace and Iambos: The Poet as Literary Historian', in Cavarzere, Aloni, and Barchiesi 2001: 141–64.
—— (2002), 'The Uniqueness of the *Carmen saeculare* and its Tradition', in Woodman and Feeney 2002: 107–23, 229–35.
—— (2007), '*Carmina*: *Odes* and *Carmen Saeculare*' in *The Cambridge Companion to Horace*, ed. S. J. Harrison. Cambridge, 144–61.
—— Rüpke, J., and Stephens, S. (eds.) (1994), *Rituals in Ink*. Stuttgart.
Bonavia-Hunt, N. (1969), *Horace the Minstrel*. Kineton.
Boyle, A. J. (2006), *An Introduction to Roman Tragedy*. London.
Cairns, F. (1972), *Generic Composition in Greek and Roman Poetry*. Edinburgh.
Cavarzere, A., Aloni, A., and Barchiesi, A. (2001), *Iambic Ideas*. Lanham, Md.
Citroni, M. (1995), *Poesia e lettori in Roma antica*. Rome.
Commager, S. (1962), *The Odes of Horace*. New Haven.
Depew, M. and Obbink, D. (2000), *Matrices of Genre*. Cambridge, Mass.
Dupont, F. (1994), *L'Invention de la littérature*. Paris. English translation 1999.
—— (2005), 'Les Mots grecs au banquet romain', *Métis*, 3: 35-56.
—— and Valette-Cagnac, E. (2005), *Façons de parler grec à Rome*. Paris.
Du Quesnay, I. M. Le M. (1995), 'Horace, *Odes* 4.5: *Pro Reditu Imperatoris Caesaris Divi Filii Augusti*', in Harrison 1995: 128–87.
Feeney, D. C. (1998), *Literature and Religion at Rome*. Cambridge.
Edmunds, L. (2001), 'Callimachus *Iamb* 4: From Performance to Writing', in Cavarzere, Aloni, and Barchiesi 2001: 77–98.
Ernout, A. and Meillet, A. (1939), *Dictionnaire étymologique de la langue latine*. Paris.
Feeney, D. C. (1998), *Literature and Religion at Rome*. Cambridge.

—— (2000), review of Dupont (1994), tr. J. Lloyd (Baltimore 1999), *TLS* 28 April: 9.

Fowler, D. P. (unpublished), 'Unrolling the Text'.

Fraenkel, E. (1957), *Horace*. Oxford.

Freudenburg, K. (2001), *Satires of Rome*. Cambridge.

Galinsky, G. K. (1988). 'The Anger of Aeneas', *American Journal of Philology*, 109: 321–48.

Gleason, M. (1995), *Making Men*. Princeton.

Gold, B. K. (ed.) (1982), *Literary and Artistic Patronage in Ancient Rome*. Austin, Tex.

Goldberg, S. M. (2005), *Constructing Literature in the Roman Republic*. Cambridge.

Gruen, E. (1992), *Culture and National Identity in Republican Rome*. Ithaca, NY.

Gunderson, E. (2000), *Staging Masculinity*. Ann Arbor, Mich.

Habinek, T. (1998), *The Politics of Latin Literature*. Princeton.

—— (2005), *The World of Roman Song*. Baltimore.

Harrison, G. W. M. (ed.) (2000), *Seneca in Performance*. London.

Harrison, S. J. (1995), *Homage to Horace*. Oxford.

Heinze, R. (1972), 'Die Horazische Ode', in *Vom Geist des Römertums*. Darmstadt: 172–89.

Horsfall, N. (1995*a*), *A Companion to the Study of Virgil*. Leiden.

—— (1995*b*), 'Rome Without Spectacles', *G&R* 42: 49–56.

—— (2003), *The Culture of the Roman Plebs*. London.

Johnson, W. A. (2000), 'Toward a Sociology of Reading in Classical Antiquity', *AJP* 121: 593–627.

Krostenko, B. A. (2001), *Cicero, Catullus, and the Language of Social Performance*. Chicago.

Lefèvre, E. (1993), 'Waren horazische Gedichte zum "öffentlichen" Vortrag bestimmt?', in Vogt-Spira 1993: 143–57.

Lendon, J. (1997), *Empire of Honour*. Oxford.

Lowrie, M. (1997), *Horace's Narrative Odes*. Oxford.

—— (2005), 'Slander and Horse Law in Horace, *Sermones* 2.1', *Law and Literature*, 17: 405–31.

—— (2006), 'Reading and the Law in Ovid', in E. Horn, B. Menke, and Ch. Menke (eds.), *Literatur als Philosophie—Philosophie als Literatur*. Munich.

—— (2009), *Writing, Performance, and Authority in Augustan Rome*. Oxford.

Markus, D. (2000), 'Performing the Book: The Recital of Epic in First-Century C.E. Rome', *CA* 19: 138–79.

Meyer, E. A. (2004), *Legitimacy and Law in the Roman World*. Cambridge.

Mitsis, P. T. (1993), 'Committing Philosophy on the Reader: Didactic Coercion and Reader Autonomy in the De Rerum Natura', *MD* 31: 111–28.

Momigliano, A. (1957), 'Perizonius, Niebuhr and the Character of Early Roman Tradition', *JRS* 47: 104–14.

Murray, O. ed. (1990), *Sympotica*. Oxford.

Nauta, R. (2002), '"Lyrisch ik" en *persona* in de bestudering van de Romeinse poëzie', *Lampas*, 35: 363–86.

Newman, J. K. (1965), 'De verbis *canere* et *dicere* eorumque apud poetas latinos ab Ennio usque ad aetatem Augusti usu', *Latinitas*, 13: 86–106; tr. and rev. in Newman 1990: 422–34.

—— (1990), *Roman Catullus and the Modification of the Alexandrian Sensibility*. Hildesheim.

Oliensis, E. (1998), *Horace and the Rhetoric of Authority*. Cambridge.

Payne, M. (2006), 'On Being Vatic: Pindar, Pragmatism, and Historicism', *AJP* 127: 159–84.

Putnam, M. C. J. (1986), *Artifices of Eternity*. Ithaca, NY.

PUTNAM, M. C. J. (2000), *Horace's Carmen Saeculare.* New Haven.

RÜPKE, J. (2001), 'Kulturtransfer als Rekodierung: Zum literaturgeschichtlichen und sozialen Ort der frühen römischen Epik', in J. Rüpke (ed.), *Von Göttern und Menschen erzählen.* Stuttgart.

SCHNEGG-KÖHLER, B. (2002), *Die augusteischen Säkularspiele.* Archiv für Religionsgeschichte 4. Munich.

SCIARRINO, E. (2004*a*), 'Putting Cato the Censor's *Origines* in its Place', *CA* 23: 323–57.

—— (2004*b*), 'A Temple for the Professional Muse: The *Aedes Herculis Musarum* and Cultural Shifts in Second-Century B.C. Rome', in Barchiesi, Rüpke, and Stephens 2004: 45–56.

SELDEN, D. (1992), '*Ceveat lector*: Catullus and the Rhetoric of Performance', in R. Hexter and D. Selden (eds.), *Innovations of Antiquity.* New York, 461–512.

STARR, R. J. (1990–1), 'Reading Aloud: *Lectores* and Roman Reading', *CJ* 86: 337–43.

VOGT-SPIRA, G. (1993), *Beiträge zur mündlichen Kultur der Römer.* Tübingen.

VOLK, K. (2002), *The Poetics of Latin Didactic.* Oxford.

WILAMOWITZ-MOELLENDORFF, U. von (1924), *Hellenistische Dichtung in der Zeit des Kallimachos.* Berlin.

WILLIAMS, C. (2002), 'Ovid, Martial, and Poetic Immortality: Traces of *Amores* 1.15 in the *Epigrams*', *Arethusa*, 34: 417–33.

WILLIAMS, G. (1992), 'Representations of the Book-Roll in Latin Poetry: Ovid, *Tr.* 1,1,3–14 and Related Texts', *Mnemosyne*, 45: 178–89.

WISEMAN, T. P. (1982), '*Pete nobiles amicos*: Poets and Patrons in Late Republican Rome', in Gold 1982: 28–49.

WOODMAN, T. and FEENEY, D. (2002), *Traditions and Contexts in the Poetry of Horace.* Cambridge.

WRAY, D. (2001), *Catullus and the Poetics of Roman Manhood.* Cambridge.

ZORZETTI, N. (1990), 'The *Carmina Convivalia*', in Murray 1990: 289–307.

—— (1990–1), 'Poetry and the Ancient City: The Case of Rome', *CJ* 86: 311–29.

CHAPTER 19

PSYCHOANALYSIS AND THE ROMAN IMAGINARY

ELLEN OLIENSIS

> By passing under [the letter's] shadow, they become its reflection.
>
> (Lacan 2005: 21)

In those vertiginous years after the midpoint of the last century, when so many new forms of criticism were making their way into classical studies, many Latinists were probably relieved that Freud had made so much more of Sophocles' Oedipus than (say) Ovid's Narcissus, thereby largely sparing them the labour of refutation. It is true that the psychoanalytic Oedipus always retained something of his Sophoclean identity, whereas Narcissus was almost entirely displaced, and from the very first, by his lower-case derivatives. All the same, Narcissus had his part to play in the development of psychoanalysis. It was thinking about narcissism that made Freud discard the dualism of sexual and self-preservative ('ego-') drives and that launched his most far-ranging speculations on the dynamics of identification and introjection (Freud 1957). It is Narcissus who stars in Lacan's mirror stage and who embodies the suicidal fascination of his imaginary order (e.g. Lacan 2005: 152–3). And it is Narcissus—indeed, the Ovidian Narcissus, hanging motionless over the glassy pool, admiring his image as it admires him—who provides the model for Jean Laplanche's portrait of the ego, a 'love object' that is 'capable of passing itself off, in a more or less deceptive and usurpatory manner, as a desiring and wishing subject' (Laplanche 1976: 74, 66). For Freud, the ego is not born but made (it 'has to be developed', Freud 1957: 77). For Lacan and Laplanche, by contrast, the ego is less made than made up, a dangerously persuasive fiction. But whatever its ontological status, it is through and with Narcissus that the ego comes into being. Narcissism is not just a particular 'perversion' but the originary libidinal turn that founds the unity of the ego. There could be no Oedipus if Narcissus were not there first.

The question that matters for this chapter, however, is less what Narcissus may have done for psychoanalysis than what psychoanalysis can do for Narcissus, and for Roman Studies at large. In the ever-widening temperate zone between the scoffer's 'nothing' and the convert's 'everything!' is to be found an invigorating array of productive answers; psychoanalysis is flourishing, these days, as never before. Two tendencies are worth identifying at the outset. First, as my epigraph attests, one especially prominent figure in the landscape is Jacques Lacan; it is to the absorption of his multifarious writings that the current efflorescence of psychoanalytic work is above all to be traced. And secondly, this efflorescence has been accompanied and fostered by a shift of interest from individual authors and characters toward the impersonal (or interpersonal, transpersonal) psychic formations of texts, genres, and culture. My goal in the readings that follow is to represent these tendencies while working out my own answer, an inevitably idiosyncratic one, to the question of the value of the psychoanalytic approach.

Narcissus

Let me begin by remarking that the priority of Narcissus is not just a psychoanalytic but an Ovidian theme. Indeed, as recent scholarship has stressed (see e.g. Hardie 2002: 165–6), for Ovid's purposes, Narcissus effectively *is* Oedipus. A relatively minor mythological character without royal or Olympian credentials, Narcissus seems out of place in *Metamorphoses* 3, a book devoted to the legendary history of Thebes and featuring such mythological heavyweights as Cadmus, Bacchus, Tiresias, and Pentheus. What justifies his inclusion here (but the justification is ostentatiously thin) is the role he plays in another story: his tragic fate is brought in 'merely' by way of confirming the newly acquired powers of Tiresias, who warns at the outset that the beautiful boy will live into old age only 'if he doesn't come to know himself' (*Metamorphoses* 3.347). Who will not be put in mind of Oedipus? It is as if Narcissus had stolen into a picture-frame designed for that vastly more eminent Theban hero, likewise warned by Tiresias, likewise undone by self-knowledge, whose story we might have expected to find, but don't find, somewhere in Ovid's Theban chronicle.

To replace a famous king with a little-known lover, affairs of state with affairs of the heart, is very much in Ovid's manner. The use of an Oedipus-surrogate also enables Ovid (with the help of the conveniently long-lived Tiresias) to finesse the chronological gap between Cadmus and Oedipus, thereby maximizing the thematic coherence of his Theban material, with its reiterated episodes of transgressive sightings triggering deadly reversals (e.g. Actaeon). Yet the translated Oedipus has left his mark on the episode, and not only in its Apollonian thematics of self-knowledge. One of the few things we know about Narcissus is that he is the product of a watery union, his cerulean nymph of a mother, the 'exceedingly beautiful' Liriope (344), having been ravished by the river Cephisus, 'enfolded in his curving stream and enclosed within his waves' (342–3). The tragedy of the son unfolds when he reaches the age of 16—in Roman terms, the perilous season of downy cheeks, when a boy, teetering on the verge of sexual maturity, begins to attract girls while remaining an object of desire for men. This is just the condition of the fair Narcissus, who 'could be seen as both boy and youth' (*poteratque puer iuvenisque videri*, 352), and who kindles the ardour of youths and girls alike—chief among these the nymph Echo (already reduced to 'echoing' by a vindictive Juno, but still possessed of a body). What thwarts Narcissus' passage into adulthood is not some Hippolytus-style refusal of desire but his simultaneous occupation of the two positions on either side of the threshold: the girlish boy seen (and seeing), the virile youth seeing (and seen). (In the preceding episode Tiresias likewise inhabits two sexual roles, but in comic sequence rather than tragic simultaneity.)

It is the Roman habit of viewing the boy as a desirable object (a 'little woman', so to put it; contrast Freud's view of the girl as an actively desiring 'little man') that gives Narcissus a look of Oedipus. The boy trapped in the spring mirrors not only the boy bending over it but also the mother locked within the father's watery embrace—though Narcissus' desire (blocked by the paternal medium: *exigua prohibemur aqua*, 450) will yield no fruit, of course, neither pleasure nor offspring. I am not proposing that 'deep down' Narcissus is 'really' in love with his mother but that the episode's opening cameo of the ravished water-nymph gives the reflective 'source' (*fons*, 407) a maternal sheen. Yet if the episode supports an oedipal reading, it also invalidates it by turning it inside-out. It is not that Narcissus desires his image because it represents his mother, but that the mother is desirable just (only) insofar as she bears the image of the son. The progress of Narcissus' brief infatuation with the nymph Echo, or rather with the reflection she supplies of his own amorous pleading (*veni!, quid me fugis?, huc coeamus!*), makes the same disclosure; he is drawn by her likeness before he is repulsed by her difference. The narcissism of Narcissus is thus not derived from but a model for the oedipal desire of Oedipus—as if what Oedipus desired in his mother were likewise only a return to himself.

In Lacan's abstraction of the oedipal triangle, the child's desire for the mother is rewritten as the imaginary order, which dangles the fantasy of untrammelled agency and unbroken coherence before the child's dazzled eyes; this dyadic trance is broken not by any actual father but by the 'name of the father', representative of all the differential structures into which the child finds himself inserted, and by which he is saved. (This is but one way, but it is one way, to take hold of the imaginary and the symbolic, notoriously protean concepts.) The Narcissus episode, turning as it does on the polarity of the seen and the heard, fascinating reflections and authoritative injunctions, has the feel of a Lacanian fable. On the side of the imaginary, we would range the fair image in the pool as well as the *imago* (Latin has no distinct term for the acoustic reflection) supplied by Echo; on the side of the symbolic, the sightless Tiresias, whose prophetic authority frames the entire episode, along with the unseen narrator, who reiterates the seer's warning in a famous apostrophe to his heedless character: 'Gullible boy, why chase after a fleeting image? What you seek exists nowhere; what you love—turn away, and you'll destroy it! That (*ista*) which you see before you is but the shadow of a reflected image; that shadow of yours (*ista*) has nothing of its own', etc. (432–6; more on *ista* below). Deaf to the paternalistic interventions of the third party, Narcissus remains trapped in communion with the imaginary second person.

I have lodged Echo in the imaginary. Yet the 'vocal nymph' (*vocalis nymphe*, 357, her first appearance; contrast Narcissus' entrance, beside his mother-nymph, *infantem nymphe*, 345) is not only image but language. While the luring reflection she holds out aligns her with the image in the pool, her automatic responsivity makes her the twin of the oracular Tiresias, who is likewise in the business of providing 'responses' (340, 380, 387) to all comers. The relation between these two figures of voice is evident in the curious intertwining of their fates. Though Echo enters the episode as 'body, not [mere] voice' (*corpus adhuc Echo, non vox erat*, 359), her grief at being spurned by Narcissus precipitates her desubstantiation into mere voice without body (cf. *corporis*, *vox*, 396–9)—the echo we know, echo with a small 'e'. At the very same time, and via the same set of events, Tiresias' apparently vacuous prophecy—literally, his 'empty voice' (*vana... vox*, 349)—is working its way toward the preordained fulfilment that will not just make his name, but make it 'huge' (*nomenque erat auguris ingens*, 512). The narrative chiasmus that produces echo and Tiresias goes a long way toward stabilizing the opposition between empty imaginary speech and the full speech of the symbolic—what we might term echoic self-consciousness and the prophetic unconscious (see Lacan 2005: 206–20). And yet the narrator who arranges this denouement is himself a creature of divided allegiances, though he (I mean the narrator, not Ovid) doesn't seem to know it. After all, as many readers have remarked, his anomalously extended apostrophe discloses him to be a victim of the very narcissistic error he is rebuking: it is his own creation he fondly addresses across the mirroring surface of the page—as if Narcissus had independent life, and could hear and respond!

The episode is thus less a cautionary tale about the failure to pass from the imaginary to the symbolic than an illustration of the inevitable implication of the one order in the other. In poetry at least, there is no state before language. If there is a psychoanalytic term that comprehends everybody in this episode, it is castration, that quintessentially symbolic operation. In this irrational math problem, one is always less than one and requires a complement to make up the sum. It is the verbal tally supplied by Echo in response to Narcisssus' initial call, 'Is there anybody there?' (*ecquis adest?* 380), that entices him with a promise of fulfilment; it is only when he sees Echo and discovers the image to be defective that he turns from her in disgust. Conversely, it is the absence of response in his beautiful reflection that reveals that this image is likewise castrated: 'as I guess from the movements of that beautiful mouth, you're answering me, though with words that don't reach my ears' (461–2). What Narcissus comes to realize, at this instant, is that the boy is not just muted by the pool but mute, maimed, forever incapable of responding. And so he recognizes the image for what it is: 'that [boy] of yours am I, I have sensed it, my image doesn't play me false' (*iste ego sum, sensi, nec me mea fallit imago*, 463).

The riddle of Oedipus' identity has a solution, however terrifying. But at this moment Narcissus has moved far beyond the self-reflexive paradoxes of incest. It is not just that the imaginary coherence of his *ego* has been interrupted by the structural, impersonal (or third-personal) symbolic; Narcissus has not stopped at what Lacan terms 'the ecstatic limit of the "*Thou art that*"' (Lacan 2005: 81). The untranslatable *iste*, 'that (of yours)', ties the second person to a third person or thing at some distance from the first person of the speaker, often with a contrastive force ('yours' but not 'mine'). In the narrator's apostrophe it conveys the overdetermined intimacy of Narcisssus and his reflection as well as the gap between knowing speaker and deluded addressee ('that shadow of yours [which casts no spell over *me*]'). But in Narcissus' formula of self-recognition, it hardly makes sense at all. The force of *iste* is to pry apart the three grammatical persons: the speaker of the sentence (Narcissus), its subject (Narcissus), and 'you' over there (again, Narcissus) who own the subject: 'that boy of yours (no boy of mine!) am I.' Thus it is in the act of putting himself together that Narcissus really falls to pieces; the conjunction of grammatical persons in *is–te–ego*, far from fixing his identity, fractures it by locating him in too many places at once. It is at this moment of vertigo that Narcissus grasps, however momentarily, the answer to his original question, *ecquis adest?*: there is no one there. No wonder, then, that Narcissus relapses so quickly into his delusion ('Stay, cruel boy, don't abandon your lover!', 477–8). He will die in it, but he can't live outside of it.

Amphitruo

If there was ever a drama of the imaginary, Plautus' *Amphitruo*, with its fantastically elaborated exploration of the theme of the double, would seem to be it. Bringing on stage doubles who are more inclined to hate than to love, the play offers a fine aggressive complement to Ovid's Narcissus episode. Yet *Amphitruo* is also a comedy of paternity. Whereas the Narcissus episode begins with the hero's conception and seems thereafter to dispense with the services of the father, *Amphitruo* culminates with the titular hero's wife giving birth to twin boys. These twins have different fathers: one was planted by Amphitruo before he set out on the campaign from which he is returning victorious as the play begins, the other by that most renowned and successful of Roman womanizers, Jupiter, who gained access to Alcumena's bed by impersonating her husband in his absence (with the help of Mercury, himself impersonating Sosia, Amphitruo's faithful slave). These newborns are hardly in a position to take part in the standard (blandly oedipal) comic scenario of father–son conflict. Yet even in the absence of a rebellious adolescent, the play works, and works indeed all the more effectively, to eviscerate the authority of the father—even Jupiter's, at least so long as he is operating on the mortal stage.

Though I will return to the imaginary, it is the play's engagement with the symbolic order that will preoccupy me here. For the purposes of this play, the symbolic is projected by the three interlocking positions of husband, father, and victorious general; Amphitruo will be ejected from all three simultaneously. As Mary Beard has pointed out, the generative invention of the comedy is its inversion of the Roman triumph ceremony. The general to whom the Senate had awarded this supreme honour would parade through the city, preceded by his prisoners and his booty, and followed by his thronging soldiers, to the Capitoline temple of Jupiter Best and Greatest—the god whom he was costumed, it seems, to resemble, with rouged cheeks, and a purple robe worn over a toga emblazoned with stars. Plautus' Amphitruo, however, returns home victorious only to find that Jupiter has donned *his* costume and usurped *his* role—stolen his welcome and impregnated his wife (Beard 2003). The super-virile, quasi-divine spectacle of the triumph is converted into something worse even than defeat. The point is driven home by Sosia in an aside that punctuates the quarrel of the befuddled husband and wife. When Alcumena appeals to her husband (*mi vir, Amphitruo* 812) for an explanation of his suspicions (aroused by the cool reception she has accorded him), Amphitruo replies by repudiating the relation: 'I'm "your husband," am I? Don't call me, false woman, by a false name' (*vir ego tuos sim? ne me appella, falsa, falso nomine*, 813). This cues Sosia to misconstrue *vir* as not 'husband' but 'man': 'We're stuck, if he's really been turned now from a man into a woman' (*si quidem haec iam mulier facta est ex viro*, 814). The joke communicates an old 'truth', that the woman who is false to her man thereby falsifies his manhood.

It is the adulterous Jupiter, the false Amphitruo, who generates these deceptions. Yet Alcumena plays her part, however unwittingly, in cutting Amphitruo down to size. When Amphitruo reaches home, he expects his wife to welcome him with open arms, not knowing that she has already welcomed 'him' (Jupiter) the night before; Alcumena, who has just seen 'him' off again, is naturally annoyed by his bizarre behaviour on his seemingly premature return. Their quarrel reaches a climax in connection with a stage prop: the golden goblet, presented by 'Amphitruo' to his wife just two scenes earlier, and now adduced by Alcumena as evidence of her husband's mendacity: 'will you deny this too, that you presented me with a golden goblet today, which you said had been presented to you there?' (760–1). A worried Amphitruo, baffled by her foreknowledge of his intended gift, is reassured by Sosia, who points out that the goblet must still be in the box he is toting—Amphitruo's seal is unbroken (774). At this point a slave, in response to Alcumena's orders, fetches the goblet from the house. Amphitruo is flabbergasted, but Sosia takes it in stride: 'You've given birth to another Amphitruo, I to another Sosia; now if the goblet has given birth to another goblet, we'll all have gotten ourselves twinned!' (784–6). Alas, Sosia has the plot wrong. There may be two masters and two slaves, but there is only one Alcumena—and only one goblet. As we learn from Mercury's prologue, this one was stolen by Jupiter ('my father finds it easy to do what he wants', Mercury comments smugly, 139), and when Sosia breaks the seal, he discovers the box is empty.

The treasure inside the box, sealed with the husband's seal, figures the chastity of the wife, who preserves the household and herself for her husband's exclusive use. This conventional equivalence is indirectly registered by Mercury-as-Sosia, revising Alcumena's gracious observation, that the gift is as worthy as the giver (537): 'No no,' corrects Mercury, 'say rather, it is as worthy as the one to whom it is given' (538). The theft of the goblet thus not only confirms but represents the adultery of Alcumena: if the box is empty, then Alcumena is false. Yet the equivalence Alcumena proposes is also in play. Deployed as a tribute to her wifely virtue, the treasure was originally awarded to Amphitruo in token of his manly excellence, and it is cloaked from the first in an aura of heroic potency. As we are told no fewer than three times, first by Sosia (practising the report of the battle he will deliver to his mistress), then by Mercury (quizzed by his baffled double), and finally by Jupiter (presenting the gift to Alcumena in parting), the goblet was the property of the enemy king (*rex*, 261, 419, 535) whom Amphitruo slew in single combat (*ipsus... sua obtruncavit manu*, 252; *ipsus... obtruncavit*, 415; *ego mea occidi manu*, 535); it was thereafter awarded to the victor *ob virtutem* (260, 534). Martial heroism, victory, and kingship are mixed together in the goblet, a heady brew for the triumphant general, but one that he will not be permitted to quaff. Thus the disappearance of the goblet figures not only the loss of the wife's chastity but also the evacuation of the husband's heroic identity.

The box may be empty, but Alcumena, as a series of jokes underscores, is exceedingly full: doubly pregnant (and with a costume padded accordingly). This hypermaternal presence draws attention to the other, complementary meaning of the goblet. I call it a goblet, because so much emphasis is laid on its use for drinking. But this object, named no fewer than nineteen times in the course of the comedy, is not quite a goblet but the kind of shallow bowl, used mostly for pouring libations, known as a *patera*. When the box, opened in the presence of the overstuffed mother, is discovered to be empty of the *patera*, it is difficult not to hear the paternal pun, especially as amplified by the syllables of the tippling king with whom the purloined *patera* is repeatedly associated: *qui **Pterela potitare** rex est solitus* (261); ***Pterela** rex qui **potitare*** (419); ***Pterela** rex qui **potitavit*** (536). The contest between full wife and empty husband is reiterated in Sosia's fantasy of the (feminine!) *patera* 'giving birth' to its double (*si patera pateram peperit*, 786)—as if his paternity had been altogether absorbed and displaced by her parturient maternity.

Of course, there is another *pater* on the scene of whom we never cease to hear. A leitmotif of Mercury's marvellously meandering prologue, and of his conversation throughout (Mercury pretty well owns the expression), is the moniker *pater*, usually *meus pater*. Mercury cannot too often, it seems, remind us that Jupiter is his father, and that it is his father's bidding he is so eagerly engaged in carrying out, both in addressing the audience and in facilitating the affair with Alcumena (forms of *meus pater* appear nine times in lines 104–44). At the end of the prologue Mercury helpfully gives us a way of distinguishing the pairs of doubles. His hat will sport his characteristic mini-wings, and as for Jupiter: 'my father will have a golden tassel under his hat—Amphitruo won't have this sign' (*id signum Amphitruoni non erit*, 143–4). The distinction anticipates the empty box with its useless seal (*Amphitruonis obsignata signo*, 421, *tuo signo obsignata*, 774). That 'my father' Jupiter will have, and Amphitruo won't, the only other golden object in the play already points to the disproportionate paternity that will be realized at its conclusion.

The disproportion that matters is not to be found in the difference either between Jupiter and Amphitruo or between the sons they respectively father, however. It subsists rather in the contrast between the two sons of Jupiter this comedy presents. As scholars have well noted, Jupiter's pliant son Mercury models the most extreme imaginable version of filial subjection. Playing Sosia to his father's Amphitruo, this son is, precisely, his father's slave. A slave-son as perfectly unrebellious, moreover, as any master-parent could wish: a most willing tool, whose greatest pleasure it is to further the pleasures of his father (*si quid patri volup est, voluptas ea mihi multo maximast*, 994). The other son of Jupiter will sustain a radically different relation to his father—not the immortal father who planted him, but the mortal father whose name he will bear. Amphitruo is ultimately upstaged less by the cuckolding Jupiter and the overstuffed Alcumena than by the son of their union: the baby who is born at the end of the play and who leaps from his cradle, as the slave who witnessed these events excitedly reports, to perform his first exploit (strangling a pair of fearful snakes). Many other exploits are to follow, of course. Though the baby remains unnamed (even by Jupiter in his final *deus ex machina* intervention), everyone knows that this is the infant Hercules, destined to be the greatest of heroes, as befits the son of Jupiter Best and Greatest, and to be honoured at Rome with cult and an altar (the *ara maxima* or 'greatest altar', in fact), from the earliest days of the city.

The title of the comedy thus itself encapsulates an aggressive joke. For despite its elevation, the name of Amphitruo has, it emerges, nothing in it; like Narcissus' reflection, it has no substance of its own. It is entirely eclipsed, before the play even begins, by that other name, the name of the son who is not his son, but to whom nonetheless he will owe whatever renown will be his share. So Jupiter can solemnly congratulate Amphitruo on the valour of his (Jupiter's) son, who 'by his heroic deeds will supply you with immortal glory' (*suis factis te immortali adficiet gloria*, 1140). And it is true that the name of Amphitruo will be preserved in the resonant patronymic that subsequent poets will apply, however illegitimately, to Hercules: *Amphitryoniades*, 'son of Amphitruo' (thus Catullus, Virgil, Ovid). Yet the name has currency only and precisely because Hercules is *not* Amphitruo's but Jupiter's son.

The promotion of the father's name and suppression of the son's takes us to the comic core of *Amphitruo*. I say 'suppression' to mark that fact that Hercules could easily have been named, if not by the mortal players (who cannot know the full significance of the impending birth), then by one or both of the knowledgeable and chatty gods who dominate the play. No one in Plautus' audience needs to hear the name of Hercules pronounced, of course. Still, this loud silence draws attention to a complementary effect: the inaudible sounding of the name, pronounced no fewer than seven times in the course of the play. That no one hears it is due to its absorption into general discourse. It surfaces not as a name but as an expostulation or exclamation, the familiar *hercle*, a syncopated vocative akin to such expressions as *ecastor* ('by Castor') and *pol* ('by Pollux'). It is Sosia who provides the first four instances in the course of his first encounter with Mercury, with Amphitruo and Mercury supplying the remaining three. (Other plays positively abound in *hercle*s, and the small number found here suggests that Plautus was alive to the word's anachronistic value.) The first pops out when Sosia arrives home at night to report Amphitruo's victory and spots Mercury posted outside the door: 'I'm totally dead. Egad, what a great strong fellow he is!' (*obsecro hercle, quantus et quam validus est*, 299). The joke is that Sosia is cowering before an exact image of himself. But the exclamation also communicates Sosia's sense of the intimidatingly 'Herculean' look of this son of Jove—as if Mercury shadowed forth Jupiter's other, mightier son, the one yet to be born.

The crucial point for my argument, however, is that Hercules is already part of the world before Amphitruo even comes on stage. In this case, it is the father who finds himself inserted within a symbolic order that is organized around the name of the son. This symbolic castration has all the more weight in that it is loaded on top of the generational displacement (a figurative castration, the 'passing of the sceptre') to which all fathers are conventionally subject (in the usual compensatory formula, it is the son who suffers symbolic castration en route to getting use of the phallus). This displacement is violently enacted near the end of the play, when the desperate Amphitruo, having failed to prove his identity, resolves to break into his own house, into which Jupiter (noting that Alcumena is on the point of giving birth) has just withdrawn. As he charges, there is a clap of thunder, and he drops down as if dead. There now appears from the house a slave appropriately named Bromia ('Thunderetta'), who announces the miraculously swift birth that has just occurred before noticing that she has company on stage: 'But what's this? Who is this old man who is stretched out like this in front of our house?' (1072). 'Old man', *senex*, comes as a bolt from the blue. (The single prior reference to Amphitruo's 'old age' by Mercury, *senecta aetate*, 1032, is meant as an insult and does not carry the same weight as Bromia's casual identification.) Can it be that the great warrior Amphitruo is past his virile prime? It is true that Plautine comedy has no category between the stock characters of *adulescens* and *senex*, and that the *paterfamilias* will inevitably have been costumed as a *senex* (Christenson 2000: 308). Up till now, though, the audience will have processed this costume as an approximation, the best available, of unmarked manhood. It is only at the end of the play that it is activated, as it were: made visible, brought into focus.

The trigger for this transformation can be identified: it is the moment of Hercules' birth. This birth brings in its train the symbolic death from which Amphitruo returns, not as the *vir* he was, but as the *senex* he now is. Thus Jupiter's aside, 'Alcumena is giving birth', has as its immediate complement Amphitruo's exclamation, 'I'm dead!' (IU. *Alcumena parturit.* AM. *perii miser*, 1039; Amphitruo is not responding to Jupiter's comment, which it is clear he has not heard). And it is likewise directly after reporting the birth that Bromia spots the man she identifies as a *senex*: 'And then I see that she's given birth (*peperisse*) to twin boys; but none of us were aware of it, when she gave birth (*parturit*), or saw it coming. But what's this? Who is this old man...?' (1070–2). Normally it takes an *adulescens* to contest the authority of his *senex* father. But in this accelerated version of the story, the infant son instantly renders the father obsolete. The hyper-servility of Mercury to his father is finally answered by the hyper-dominance of Hercules in relation to his. Hercules is the other panel of the compression machine that squeezes the authority out of Amphitruo: an unspeakably potent son, who is the closest thing Rome knows—closer certainly than the approximations of the triumphal charade—to Jove on earth. Or better, not to Jove on earth (a puppet authority at best) but to the symbolic Jupiter lodged permanently elsewhere. The ultimate triumph belongs to the son precisely by virtue of his pervasive absence from the stage.

I began by filing Narcissus in the imaginary, Amphitruo in the symbolic. But if this opposition has any value, that value does not derive from their engagement (or lack of engagement) with father-figures. As Maurizio Bettini has done so much to show, the Roman imaginary is haunted by the image of the image: twins, doubles, actors, ghosts, statues (*simulacra*), reflections (*imagines*), ancestral masks (likewise *imagines*)—and also sons, ideally figured as reproductions in miniature of their fathers (see e.g. Bettini 2000). The thematics of paternity in *Amphitruo* is thus not a departure from but an extension of Plautus' exhaustive exploration of the double. And conversely, the symbolic father has his niche in Ovid's fantasia on the image: it is his name that is impressed upon the son at the very moment he turns 16 ('son of Cephisus', *Cephisius*, 351)—as if summoning him, albeit ineffectually (Narcissus never heeds the discourse of the narratorial unconscious), into the symbolic order. But in the (non)confrontation of Amphitruo with Hercules, we have to do with something more radical than failure. Here the father is not just displaced by his son, but forfeits his claim to the status of original originator, and not only because he has been cuckolded by Jupiter. By the end of the play that bears his name, Amphitruo has turned into the shadow that he always was: the shadow not of himself, but of his brilliant son.

Like most methodologies, psychoanalysis is a protean discourse which means different things to different people. If anything can be said to unite its adherents, it is not their common commitment to some subset of myths (Narcissus, Moses, Electra) or even to some distinctive selection of themes and terms (incest, identity, desire, trauma, castration, *objet a*, etc.). For most of us at least, psychoanalysis is in the end less a set of contents than a mode of interpretation, one that retains a strong family resemblance to other forms of reading (close, structuralist, deconstructive, etc.). What Freud did, chiefly through his work on the unconscious artistry of dreams, jokes, and parapraxes, was to expand the range of what counts as interpretable. Psychoanalysis lets in phenomena that tend to be missed or ruled out by other modes of reading: missed, because they are too slight or marginal to be readily noticed; ruled out, because they are not readily noticed (for reader-oriented theorists) or not obviously intended—not (or beside) 'the point' (for author-oriented theorists). For psychoanalysis, it is precisely the character of being missed or ruled out that gives these phenomena their interpretive value; it is this that authenticates them as communications of the unconscious. Erich Segal once prefaced a discussion of *Amphitruo* with the trenchant proclamation (responding to the misplaced emphasis, as he saw it, of some prior interpretations) that the play 'is *not* about the birth of Hercules' (1987: 173), and he was right; more aftermath than climax, the birth falls outside the core action of the comedy. This does not mean that the Hercules of *Amphitruo* is off-limits for interpretation, and scholars have had much of interest to say, and from the most various perspectives, about his value in the comedy (see e.g. Bettini 2000: 204–8; O'Neill 2003). What differentiates the psychoanalytic reading is that it takes Hercules up not despite but *by way of* Segal's observation. It takes him up, that is, just insofar as he is, so to put it, (not quite) repressed—displaced from the centre to which he has so much greater a claim than the father who gives his name to the comedy.

Psychoanalytic criticism is thus programmatically literal-minded: attentive above all to the wayward communications of the textual surface. This attention can take many forms: so, for example, Charles Segal focuses on the figurative density of Seneca's language (Segal 1986), Micaela Janan on the gaps and contradictions in Catullus' erotic narrative (Janan 1994), Ellen O'Gorman on stray details (e.g. the African fig) in the Roman discourse about Carthage (O'Gorman 2004). As this chapter will have demonstrated, my own readings often foreground what is usually termed 'wordplay'. This a traditional topic of literary criticism, of course, but the effects that interest me (following Shoptaw 2000) do not quite qualify as displays of authorial wit. No one in *Amphitruo* speaks the name of Hercules, not even Plautus; *hercle* is not a pun but a parapraxis, an open secret let slip by the text. And 'text' here is not just an evasion of the problem of intention but the proper name for the structured set of possibilities from which effects such as these emerge, with or without the knowing collaboration of the author.

A final generalization I will venture is that psychoanalytic criticism works best when it doesn't feel obliged to make the text conform to predetermined theoretical paradigms. Quite to the contrary, as Mark Buchan has urged, the mission of psychoanalysis is to keep us 'focusing on what the text says rather than reducing it to what we think it should mean' (Buchan 2005: 202). What good is theory, after all, if it only forestalls reading by taking its place? Though it may hold out the reassuring (imaginary) promise of coherence, solidity, permanence, theory is only frozen reading; concepts such as the ego ideal, the symbolic, and so on, are states of reading, provisional congelations that are likely to change shape when they are thrown back into the stream. Of course, psychoanalysis can lend itself to authoritative solutions and definitive diagnoses. But as the abundance of recent work amply demonstrates, it can open texts up as well as shut them down, surprising us with the pleasure of something new.

Further reading

A useful overview of the varieties of psychoanalytic criticism (without particular reference to classics) is provided by Wright 1998. An especially compelling and influential work (omitted by Wright) is Orlando 1978, taking Freud's rhetorical works (chiefly *Jokes and their Relation to the Unconscious* and 'On Negation') as models for how literature works, both locally and transhistorically (the theory is backed up by a dazzling exemplary reading of Racine's *Phèdre*).

Within Roman Studies, despite sporadic early ventures (the most rewarding remains Segal 1987, originally published 1968), psychoanalysis did not really 'take' until the appearance of Janan 1994. This programmatically Lacanian exploration of Catullus' love poetry remains valuable both as an influential example of Lacanian literary-critical practice and as a primer (designed specifically for classicists) of Lacanian theory. Much subsequent work has carried forward Janan's focus on love poetry along with her commitment to Lacan; see especially Miller 2004, an ambitious Lacanian analysis of the short-lived genre of love elegy in its Augustan setting. The set of genres and topics of interest to Lacanian critics is rapidly expanding, however; some rewarding examples include Gunderson 2003 (on declamation), O'Gorman 2004 (on Roman representations of Carthage), Porter 2004 (on Virgil). While Lacan has been the dominant inspiration, there remain those, typically of a more literary and formalist bent, who take their bearings more from Freud; see e.g. Segal 1986 and Schiesaro 2003 (both on Senecan tragedy, and both informed by Orlando 1978). My own thoughts on psychoanalysis and Latin poetry are further developed in Oliensis 2009. I would like to thank Alessandro Barchiesi for his incisive editorial interventions, and John Shoptaw for his patient scrutiny of successive drafts.

References

Beard, Mary (2003), 'The Triumph of the Absurd', in Catherine Edwards and Greg Woolf (eds.), *Rome the Cosmopolis*, Cambridge: Cambridge University Press, 21–43.

Bettini, Maurizio (2000), *Le orecchie di Hermes*, Turin: Einaudi.

Buchan, Mark (2005), review of Miller 2004, *CP* 100: 198–202.

Christenson, David M. (2000), *Plautus: Amphitruo*, Cambridge: Cambridge University Press.

Freud, Sigmund (1957), 'On Narcissism' (1914), *The Standard Edition of the Complete Psychologial Works* (James Strachey, ed.), vol. 14, London: Hogarth Press, 73–81.

Gunderson, Erik (2003), *Declamation, Paternity, and Roman Identity*, Cambridge: Cambridge University Press.

Hardie, Philip (2002), *Ovid's Poetics of Illusion*, Cambridge: Cambridge University Press.

Janan, Micaela (1994), *'When the Lamp is Shattered': Desire and Narrative in Catullus*, Carbondale, Ill.: Southern Illinois University Press.

Lacan, Jacques (2005), *Écrits*, tr. Bruce Fink, New York: Norton & Co.

Laplanche, Jean (1976), *Life and Death in Psychoanalyis*, tr. Jeffrey Mehlman, Baltimore: Johns Hopkins University Press.

Miller, Paul Allen (2004), *Subjecting Verses*, Princeton: Princeton University Press.

O'Gorman, Ellen (2004), 'Cato the Elder and the Destruction of Carthage', *Helios*, 31: 99–125.

O'Neill, Peter (2003), 'Triumph Songs, Reversal, and Plautus' Amphitruo', *Ramus*, 32: 1–38.

Oliensis, Ellen (2009), *Freud's Rome: Psychoanalysis and Latin Poetry*, Cambridge: Cambridge University Press.

Orlando, Francesco (1978), *Toward a Freudian Theory of Literature*, tr. Charmaine Lee, Baltimore: Johns Hopkins University Press.

Porter, James I. (2004), 'Vergil's Voids', *Helios*, 31: 127–56.

Schiesaro, Alessandro (2003), *The Passions in Play*, Cambridge: Cambridge University Press.

Segal, Charles (1986), *Language and Desire in Seneca's* Phaedra, Princeton: Princeton University Press.

Segal, Erich (1987), *Roman Laughter*, New York: Oxford University Press.

Shoptaw, John (2000), 'Lyric Cryptography', *Poetics Today*, 21: 221–62.

Wright, Elizabeth (1998), *Psychoanalytic Criticism: A Reappraisal*, Cambridge: Polity Press.

CHAPTER 20

ART AND REPRESENTATION

EUGENIO LA ROCCA*

When we recommend the introduction of art history into the syllabus, because works of art so perfectly reflect their age, we should also add that like mirrors they will reflect different facts about the age according to the way we turn them, or the standpoint we adopt, not to mention the tiresome tendency of mirrors to throw back our own image.

(E. H. Gombrich, *Ideals and Idols: Essays on Values in History and in Art* (Oxford, 1979), 134)

Classical Art as Mimesis and the 'Anxious Objects' in Contemporary Art

In the *Vocabolario della lingua italiana* published by the Istituto della Enciclopedia Treccani (1986), the entry 'art' reads: '... as a rule, the term art is used to designate particular cultural products, commonly classified as painting, sculpture, architecture, music, poetry and so on; the cultural associations with the term are various,

* Translated by Ilaria and Simone Marchesi.

depending on the different ages and critical attitudes.' An on-line resource extremely popular with American undergraduates (Wikipedia) provides the following definition of art: 'Art is commonly understood as the act of making material works (or *artworks*) which, from concept to creation, hold a fidelity to the *creative impulse*... As such, art may be taken to include forms as diverse as prose writing, poetry, dance, acting or drama, music, sculpture, architecture, and painting.' With its emphasis on the 'cultural product', the definition recovers the semantic value of the etymological antecedent *ars* and of its Greek equivalent *technē*, two terms which are strongly connected to the production of objects via a manual process. While the definition tends to obscure the qualitative difference between art and craft (within the limits in which differentiation is legitimate), it also eschews the opposite risk of classifying as art only the work of the greatest artists. Within the parameters of the definition, both the so-called 'minor' works and objects of serial production are art.

In recent years the question of what constitutes art has often been asked. The question arose quite naturally from the dismissal of the traditional concept of art as imitation of the real—a notion that, though variously inflected, has held sway up until the dawn of the twentieth century. In order to understand the role it played in Roman art, the following pages explore this notion, tracing it back to the origin of Greek art. In the ancient world images were intended as a representation of the real, as 'mimesis', and they were perceived accordingly. By now it is common knowledge that the mimetic theory of art does not correspond to the actual practices of artists, even if they earnestly believed they were representing humans and objects as they really were. Just as it is possible that, in the age in which they were produced, 'Daedalic' works might have been considered absolutely faithful to the real, Plato might also have preferred works that departed from pure naturalism and thus allowed the essence of the divine to transpire more: his rejection of art as mimesis of the sensible world, in turn a mimesis of the idea, suggests this corollary. In reality, however, artists have always worked inside schools and artistic traditions from which they would depart only advisedly and in limited ways. More than an actual imitation of the real, it was their apprenticeship in the workshop of established sculptors and their acquisition of traditional techniques that determined how ancient artists worked. The sculptors who produced the *kouroi* and *korai* between the end of the seventh and the late sixth century BCE (fig. 20.1) believed they had produced *agalmata*, that is, surrogates *sub specie aeternitatis* of the mortal bodies belonging to the young donors. They were also working under the conviction that they had reproduced the human body with utter naturalism. Anecdotes evidencing Daedalus' ability to emulate natural reality are widely known: the following generations indulged in fantastic accounts of his statues that 'were quite like their living models; they could see, they said, and walk and, in a word, preserved so well the characteristics of the entire body that the beholder

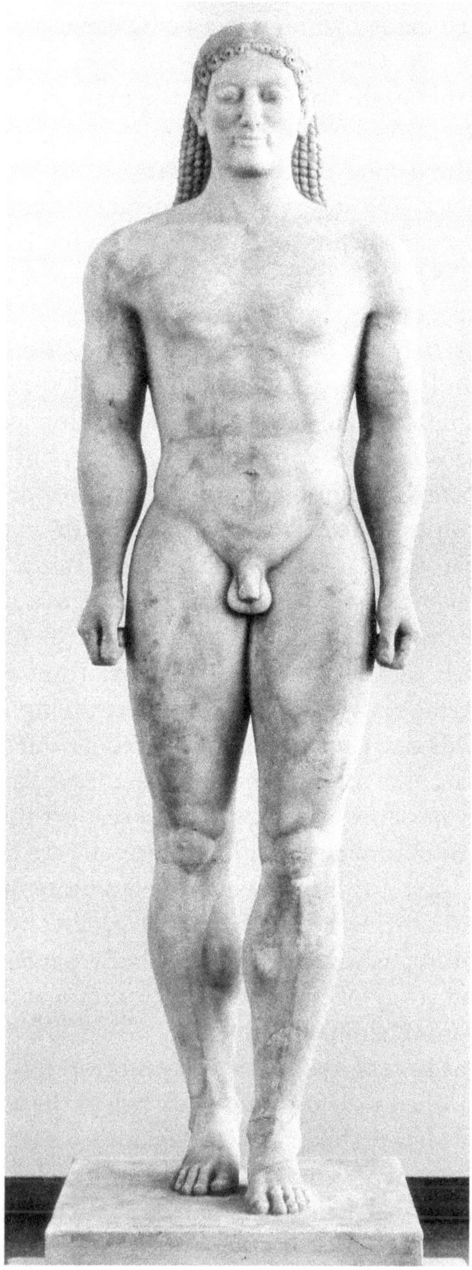

Fig. 20.1. Anavysos Kouros (Kroisos). National Archaeological Museum, Athens. © Hellenic Ministry of Culture/Archaeological Receipts Fund

thought that the image made by him was a being endowed with life' (Diodorus Siculus 4.76.2 f., tr. C. H. Oldfather, Loeb edn. 1952). These accounts, which were probably elaborated quite late, grant to the masters of the ancient past the ability to model their works on the real. Even in the absence of retrospective anecdotes, however, the defiant dedications attached to works from the archaic age speak for themselves. The *agalma*, which originally could be a sculpture or any other artefact, is deemed *perikalles*, 'of remarkable beauty', and produced with *sophia* (which is the virtue of the excellent craftsman—be he a charioteer, a musician, or a ship's captain). Often the patron goes so far as to identify himself with the work that represents him, as in the case of one of the statues portraying the Branchidae in the temple of Didyma: 'I am Chares, son of Keisis, lord (*archos*) of Teichiussa.' The rest of the inscription posits the distinction again, by marking the object as 'Votive gift to Apollo', but the force of the first statement remains. More commonly, it is the work of art itself that is given voice. A funerary sculpture, labeled as *sēma* (sign or marker), says of itself: 'I, *sēma* of Phrasikleia, will forever be called a girl, *kourē*, since from the gods I have received this name instead of marriage.' The statue of Phrasikleia, the work of Aristion of Paros, is certainly remarkable for its quality, but it also fits the well-known models of archaic *korai*. It departs from the paradigm mainly on account of the well-preserved inscription identifying statue and deceased with one another. In his day Giotto was considered an outstanding realist and a good portraitist on account of similar circumstances. Vasari reports that 'he became such a versed imitator of nature that he cast off the clumsy style of the Greeks [*scil.* the late-Byzantine painting] and brought the modern and good art of painting back to life, by introducing the accurate portraiture of living people'. Clearly, artistic forms have evolved by progressively approaching the real according to nature; when this too has been perceived as unsatisfying, artists moved into the study of the optical deformations that allowed them to make objects appear more similar to the real.

The rules of the game have worked effortlessly more or less until the threshold of the twentieth century, when the slow but steady rise of the so-called 'readymades' (a coinage we owe to Marcel Duchamp) or 'anxious objects' (as they have been labelled by Harold Rosenberg) changed the rules of the game. These everyday objects, organic structures, or living beings are subtracted from and deprived of their original context and exposed in galleries or museums with labels or titles or descriptors that invite the viewer to interpret them metaphorically (fig. 20.2). Apparently, the art historian is at an impasse: she no longer has suitable criteria to provide a definition of art or to adjudicate the actual value of the work of art. This is why, in a recent essay, Nigel Warburton proposed to focus on the individual works and on what constitutes their 'visual philosophy' rather than waste time pondering a question that always seems to require different answers, depending on when it is posed.

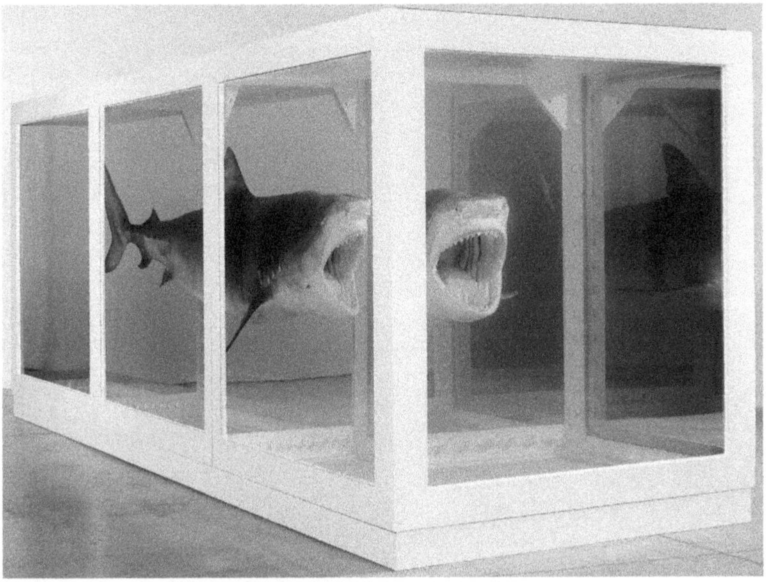

Fig. 20.2. Damien Hirst, *The Physical Impossibility of Death in the Mind of Someone Living*, 1991. © Damien Hirst. All rights reserved, DACS, 2009

Art as a Means of Communication and Medium of Expression

A good deal of twentieth-century art criticism has focused on the relation between form and content in a work of art, since many artists have polemically rejected the imitation of the real and apparently disregarded the theme and potential message of the work of art. In reality, even in a contemporary work of art content has not been eliminated: as the artist's intended message, it is only conveyed in new ways and according to a grammar independent from codified tradition. One may even go as far as to say that its actual message is the vindication of the absence of any message. And yet, inevitably there is a message: it emerges from the fabric of even the most abstract forms such as Pollock's or Burri's works (fig. 20.3). It consists of the intense, often overwhelmingly dark impact that the sombre colours, the swift and broken brushstrokes, or the scarring and wrinkling of fire on plastic sacks and bags have on the viewer.

Unlike what happens in contemporary art, in the classical world form was perhaps less important than content. The beauty of a work of art was, in a way, taken for granted—not because people could not appreciate the differences in the quality of individual artists' work, but because the high level of craftsmanship

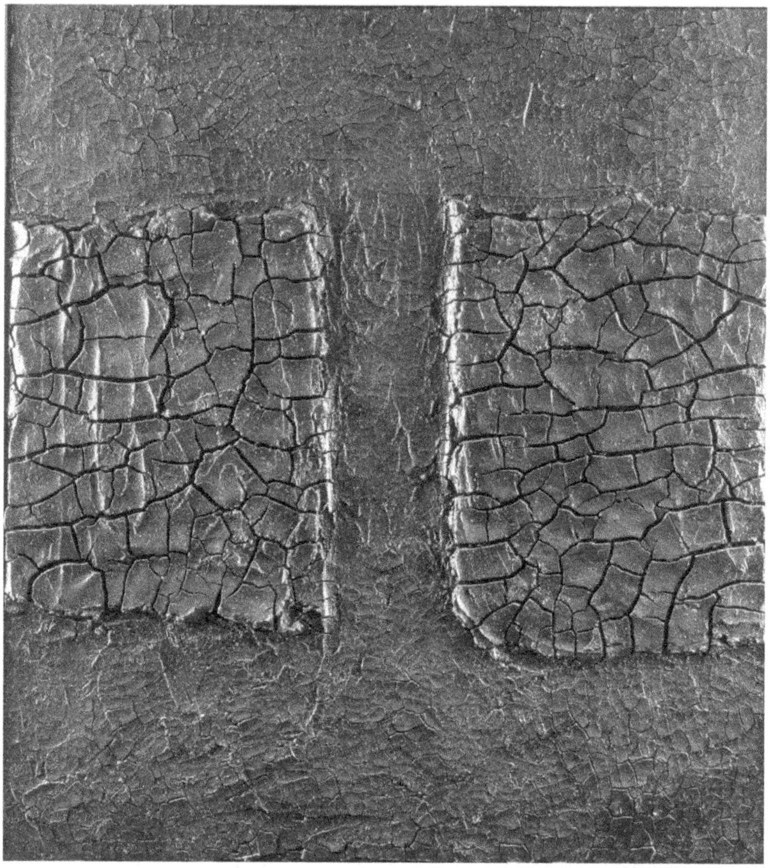

Fig. 20.3. Alberto Burri, *Cretto Nero*, 1974. Reggio Emilia, Collezione Maramotti. © Estate of Alberto Burri. DACS 2009

made up for any lack of originality and inventiveness. The work of art was expected to carry out a primary, specific duty: to convey a meaning. The patron—whether the *polis* itself, the Roman Senate, associations, individual magistrates, or even private citizens—did not pick one among many works of art in the artist's workshop. They picked the subject, worked out the costs, chose the material and the size, and most likely followed the progress of the work as well. The artists' freedom was restrained both by the techniques they had acquired in their training and by the will of their customers. The latter was a form of control no less strict and taxing than the former, as evidenced by the in-progress decrees of payment to artists and craftsmen working on monumental buildings in Athens—projects in which sculptures played a fundamental role. This is why today we prefer not to evaluate a work of art exclusively from a formal point of view: we recognize the inherent danger of measuring the work according to aesthetic specifications that it was not designed to meet. At this point, the privileged approach is to study the work of art as a social phenomenon: not unlike language, art is a distinctive means of communication among different social groups. Even notions such as 'form', 'style', and 'structure' are not ahistorical, pure concepts of art; rather, they are essential categories which frame the perception of the environment in which we live and work.

However, once we conceptualize the work of art as a means of communication, we need to establish what kind of communication this is, and in what way it differs from other forms of communication—in particular, spoken and written language. This step is particularly difficult. The danger of turning art into a secondary by-product of the word (art as 'figured word') is always lurking. To counteract it, we should thoroughly analyse the reasons of its genesis, and the total independence and non-equivalence of these two forms of communication. Artistic forms bear a witness to social history and cannot be replaced by any other medium.

Not unlike writing, art is a language of signs. By the term 'sign' one should not merely mean a pure convention, but a cultural construct with a complex and articulated history. In semiotics a sign designates an abstract or concrete object: it shapes a theme which may be read semantically or iconographically. But, less immediately, a sign is also the signifier of values that transcend the sign itself and cannot be correctly interpreted without careful consideration of its historical context. Evidently, signs tend to form systems, and it is imperative that one understand their syntax, that is, the combinations of signs, considered regardless of their specific meanings, individual properties, and any other syntactic relations (as those determined by syntactical rules, studied by Charles Morris under the rubric of 'syntactics'). Such combinations rely on more than a pure stylistic and formal analysis; they require a familiarity with the entire cultural apparatus of a given age—that is, with the way it collectively conceptualizes and perceives phenomena. Unless they are evaluated in connection with their interpretation and their meaning, stylistic forms alone have little to tell. That little is, furthermore, not enough; unless one adds an analysis of the relations the users establish with the signs (the section of semiotics Morris defines as 'pragmatics'). It is not enough, therefore, that we examine the sign either in itself or in its relation with other signs: first, we have to advance our understanding of the mentality of a given age, bridging the distance that separates us from a remote past by conceptually reconstructing its psychological and mental processes—and them alone. A semiotic study of art can only take place if it is situated in the frame of the life and the psychology of an age and requires that its practitioners identify with the original spectators. It is not an easy task. Whether consciously or not, the mentality of our age influences us, and we read the past through the biased lens of our contemporary parameters, without fathoming the cultural abyss that separates us from the ancient world and the specific ways in which it perceived reality.

Roman Art in the Frame of 'Lebenswelt'

When the work of art is examined as part and parcel of its coeval 'Lebenswelt'—that is, of what we may call (albeit imprecisely) the 'sphere of life' in which it was produced—the shortcomings of the formal approach are avoided. In addition to being often criticized in itself, this method of analysis is—as we have seen—incapable of providing insights into the mentality of the age in which the work of art was produced. On the contrary, the unitary approach brings into focus not only what may be defined, strictly speaking, as 'works of art', but also the world in which humans live and by which their identity is defined. Every era creates a particular world-view, and art is one of its representations: in its language, art mirrors an era's way of life, customs, and habits. It conforms to its social dynamics, its moral and religious convictions, its governing fashions and etiquette. In what remains a fundamental work on the relationship between Gothic architecture and Scholastic thought, Erwin Panofsky served as precursor this important strand of criticism when he downplayed the 'Kunstwollen' (or 'artistic volition': a notion inherited from the idealistic Vienna School) in favour of the 'habitus-forming force' of tradition. In his analyses, habitus is featured as the factor that controlled the connections linking the structure of society and its ways of thinking to art, seemingly through unconscious mechanisms but with overwhelmingly rapid diffusion. So conceptualized, habitus is much more than a simple parallel configuration of ideas determined by the influence that individuals or groups of individuals exerted on others; rather, it is the tight web of relations constituting the mental habitus of those living in a particular epoch. Ideally, the 'Lebenswelt' is the development of this notion—one that has, however, extended the web of relations to the whole system of social life.

In the frame of Roman art, this approach proves fruitful in several areas. One may look, for instance, at the art of portrait-painting, a genre in which the interplay of image and social life is most evident. This connection controls various aspects: fashion, behaviour, etiquette, attitudes in the public or private sphere, forms of self-representation all leave traces in the portraits. Some relatively recurrent features in the portraits of late-Republican magistrates may be read in this light: taking as their model portraits of Hellenistic monarchs, they emphasize the dramatic mobility of the surface in their countenance, the torsion of the neck, the deep and frowning gaze. In this way, through their images they presented themselves as embodying both the heirs to the conquered empires (according to the commonplace that made a senator the equal of a sovereign) and men of action, capable of making executive decisions, often painful but always necessary for the common good. This was a solution that was successfully adopted in (and adapted to) a different age: Michelangelo reused it in the bust of Brutus and in the funerary statue of Giuliano de' Medici, duke of Nemours, and

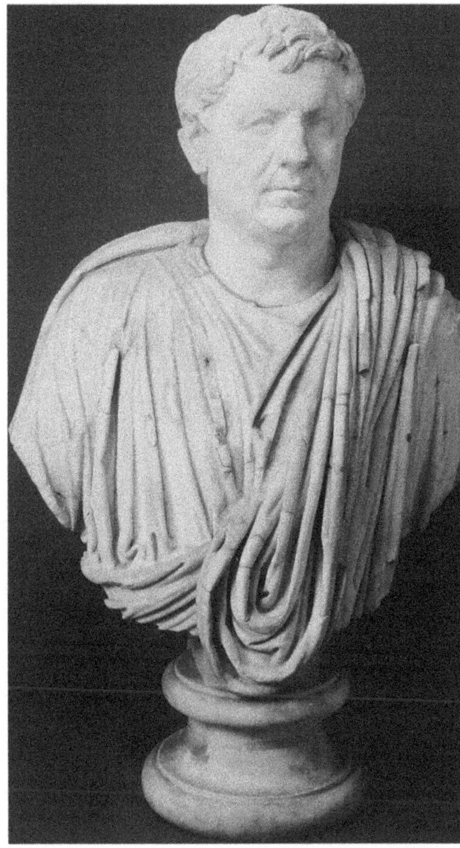

Fig. 20.4. Male portrait. © National Museums Liverpool, Ince Blundell Collection of Classical Sculpture

established a model destined to great success in the Renaissance. Other magistrates from the same period (fig. 20.4) opted for a different model; namely, the one offered by the portraits of the early Hellenistic Greek poets, in particular that of Menander by the Younger Kephisodotos, son of Praxiteles (fig. 20.5). Though still relatively unexplored, this choice is telling. Late-Republican artists appear interested in retrieving from those portraits the model of a human being who has suffered, meditated, and now knows the value of human life: among the duties of the magistrates, they chose to underscore the grave burden of the decisions that a true statesman need to make for the common good. The portraits of the young Augustus, with their significant downplaying of the strongest physiognomic traits (inspired by the models of the Greek heroes from the classical age) and their calming gaze, convey yet another message—that of peace and reconciliation after the havoc wreaked by the civil wars.

The literary sources do not depart from these images in their description of the men of the late Republic and early Empire. Indeed, it is even possible to say that some men adopted similar paradigms in their public appearances and thus confirmed the strong bond between artistic forms and forms of (self-)presentation

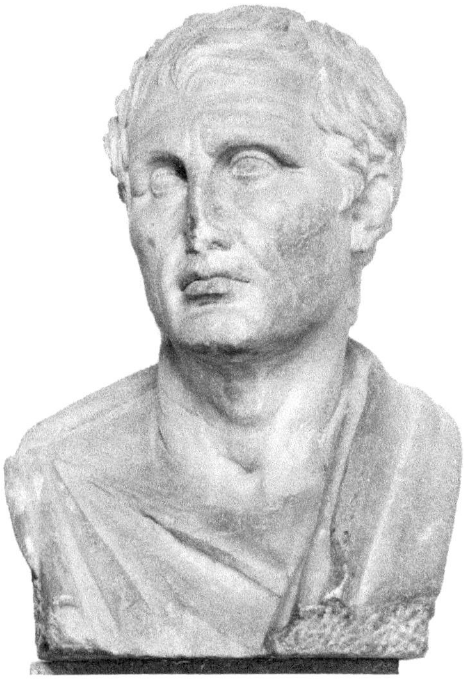

Fig. 20.5. Portrait of Menander. Venice, Seminario Arcivescovile

in public. In the consciousness of the Greeks, any senator was the equivalent of a Greek sovereign. One case is emblematic. When in 167 BCE, after Perseus was defeated, Prusias II, king of Bithynia, went to Rome to claim some lands from the Galatians (or, perhaps, from Eumenes II, king of Pergamon), he entered the Curia wearing a *pilleum* on his shaven head like a manumitted slave and addressed all the senators present as *theoi sōteres*—a title that had thus far been reserved for the dynastic cults of Greek sovereigns (Polybius 30.18; Livy 45.44; Diod. 31.15.2). In the sources there is no hint of any scandalized reaction on the part of the senators. Only a few decades before they would have despised a form of homage that turned them into the equals of Alexander the Great or Ptolemaeus I. Starting from the second century BCE, when they were abroad many individual magistrates behaved as sovereigns. At the end of the war against Perseus, in Macedonia, Aemilius Paulus found several royal hunting-grounds teeming with game, since for the last four years the Macedonian kings, who had been dedicated hunters, had deserted them:

> Aemilius, thinking that hunting was the best training and amusement for the young men, placed the royal huntsmen at Scipio's disposal, and gave him complete control over the preserves. Scipio, availing himself of this and regarding himself as being nearly in the position of king, spent the whole time that the army remained in Macedonia after the battle of Pydna in this pursuit, and, as he became a very enthusiastic sportsman, being of the right age and physique for such an exercise, like a well-bred dog, this taste of his for hunting became permanent. (Polybius 31.29.5–6, tr. W. R. Paton, Loeb edn. 1927)

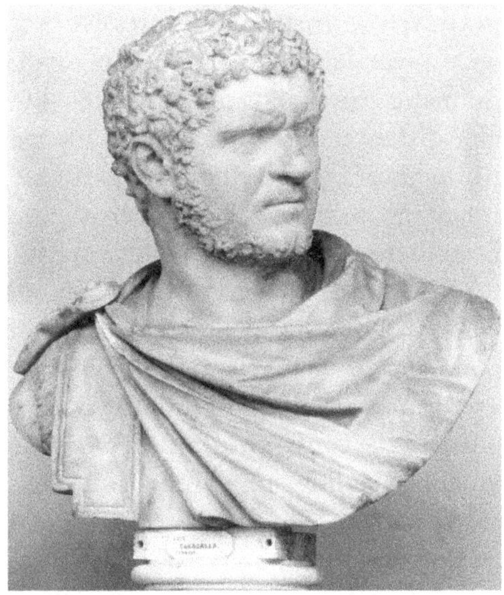

Fig. 20.6. Portrait of Caracalla. Naples, Museo Nazionale

Metellus Pius made a display of *luxuria* and *libido* while in Spain, fighting against Sertorius (Valerius Maximus 9.1.5): the brazen extravagance of his excesses was unheard of in the West, but it was symptomatic of an increasingly open imitation of eastern customs and habits that had been long since adopted by Greek rulers. In the smear campaign launched against Marc Antony, he was depicted as living in kingly luxury and in a soft, womanish manner (Cassius Dio 50.27.4). Augustus' moderation, on the contrary, was proverbial, just as was his habit of stopping on the streets to talk—a true *civis inter cives.*

For quite some time Roman art was a pendulum swinging between these main forms of representation. Emperors and members of their family, as well as private citizens who imitated imperial portraits to the last iconographic details (thus conforming to a well-known process of cultural assimilation: the 'period face', *Zeitgesicht*), all modelled their images either on the Augustan portraits or on those of the energetic magistrates of the late Republic. Sometimes, as in the emblematic case of Caracalla (fig. 20.6), they also refer to the portraits of Hellenistic rulers or to those of contemporary, more pensive magistrates. For instance, Caracalla's effigy, which features the emperor with his head turned impetuously to the side and a menacing gaze, responds to what Herodian narrates of his behaviour in public at a climactic moment. After having killed his brother, the Emperor went to the Curia and gave a speech to the senators justifying his actions: 'With these words delivered at the top of his voice he gave a piercing stare at the friends of Geta, full of anger. Then leaving them trembling and pale, he hurried back to the palace' (Herodian, IV 5, 7, trans. C. R. Whittaker, Loeb 1996). It is only in the second half of the third century CE that the image tends to become increasingly abstract and stately, representing less and less concretely individual features. Emperors were then portrayed with strongly expressive features, as men of action—in tune with the widespread label of 'soldier emperors'. Imperial portraits initially emphasized the dramatic expressions of the visage—big, menacing eyes, absorbed in an unbridgeable distance. In later exemplars the face is more relaxed: the gaze, which remains the locus of intense emotions, is turned away, to an 'elsewhere' untouched by any mundane concern. The emperor's image tends to become an intangible icon, beyond the reach of daily reality. Artists preserve, however, the traditional reference to the dramatic power of the harsh and inexorable gaze, typical of third-century emperors. It is present in the portraits of Magnentius and in those of some members of the Valentinian dynasty; it even reaches as far down as its last exceptional manifestation in the Barletta Colossus. Theodosius I and his descendants, on the contrary, appeal to the more sedate, typically Constantinian, model of an always young emperor, with increasingly fine and delicate features, manneristically softened, and rendered independently from his real physiognomic features. In this case too, literary sources lead us to think that this form of representation was the dominant one in the etiquette of the court. In the *Panegyric* that Claudius Mamertinus wrote for Maximianus' birthday in the year 290 CE we read that entry into the imperial palace was forbidden to the majority of the public: those who entered it, like initiated members of a cult into a temple, did so only to worship a

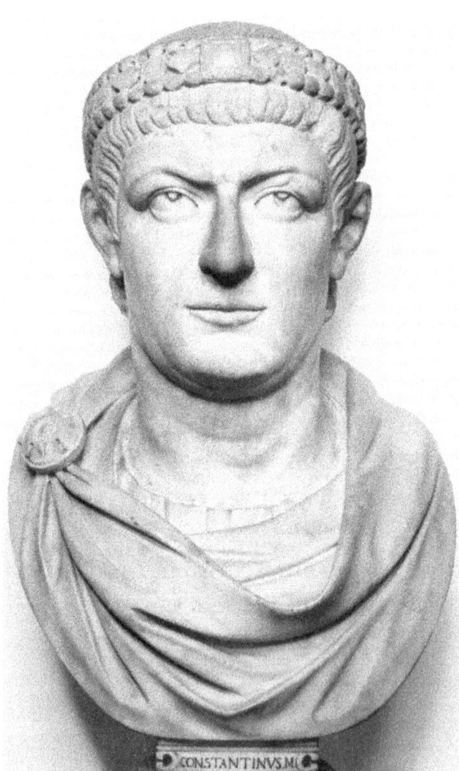

Fig. 20.7. Portrait of Valentinianus I (?). Florence, Museo Archeologico

deity: *sacros vultus adorare*. In Justinian's *Codex* imperial images on coins are called *aeternales vultus* (*Cod. Iust.* 11.11.3); in the *Codex Theodosianus* the emperor himself proclaims *aeternitas nostra* (*Cod. Theod.* 10.22.3) and *numen nostrum* (1.9.2; 5.5.2; 8.1.3.5.40; 12.12.7; *Cod. Iust.* 12.50.9).

Against this vast background several variants stand out. Ammianus Marcellinus attests that Valentinian's gaze was constantly 'oblique and stern' and his impulsive nature was easily drawn to cruelty; often, when he fell prey to wrath, his voice, features, gait, and colour would change. It is a description that suits the coin portraits of Magnentius and Valentinian I (fig. 20.7), in particular those from coinage issued in explicit opposition to the peaceful and youthful image chosen by Constantine and his sons. The Vienne portrait attributed to Magnentius as well as those in the Uffizi and Rome, which plausibly portray Valentinian I (fig. 20.7), have the same characteristics. Of the Spaniard Theodosius, people said that he resembled Trajan, both in physiognomy and character (*Epit. de Caes.* 48.8 s.), but his coins do not bear a resemblance to Trajan's portraits. Rather, they go back to the features of the Constantinian emperors. The *missorium* of Madrid (fig. 20. 8), in turn, offers a more delicate and almost fragile image of Theodosius, whom Cedrenus describes as elegant, with blond hair and an aquiline nose (1.552.7). The portrait corresponds to the model of a

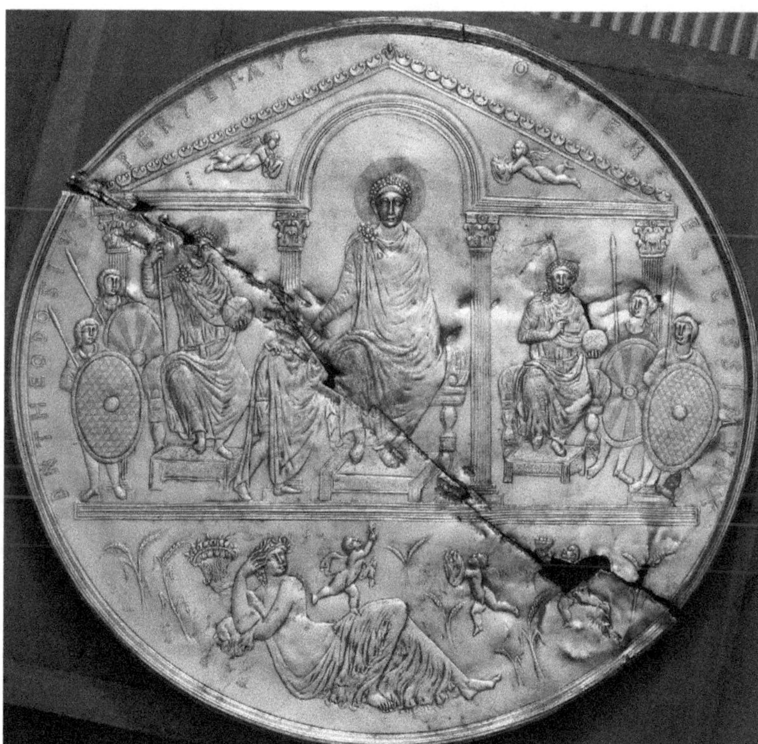

Fig. 20.8. *Missorium* of Theodosius. Madrid, Archaeological Museum

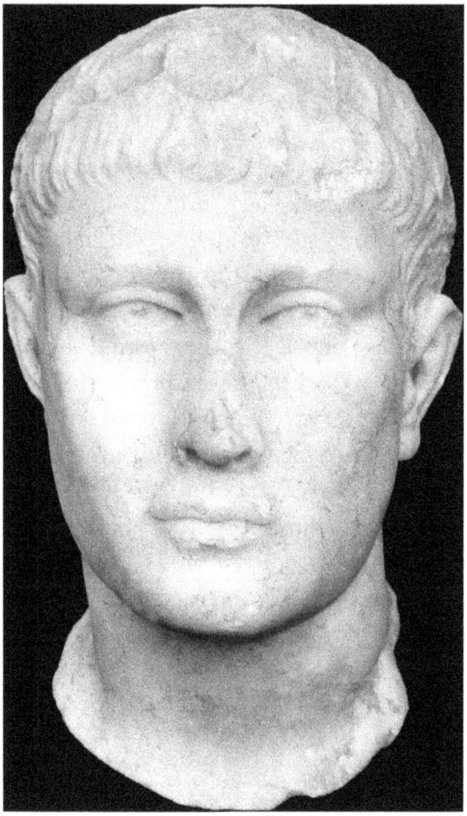

Fig. 20.9. Portrait of Theodosius I (or II). Aphrodisias, Museum

sovereign who appeared affable (Zos. 4.27.1) and whose continence, modesty (*Epit. de Caes.* 48.9 f.), meekness, *pietas*, and *humilitas* (Ambrose, *De Ob. Theod.* 5, 12 s., 28, 34 s.; Augustine, *De Civ. Dei* 5.26; Theodoret, Eccl. hist. 5, spec. 5 s., 15, 18, 24 s.) were frequently praised: a monarch who cared more about the condition of the Church than his own health, even as death was approaching (Ambrose, *De Ob. Theod.* 35). There is only one portrait statue that with some measure of certainty may be assigned to him (there remains a margin of doubt whether the subject is actually Theodosius I or his grandson Theodosius II), and it may be said to conform to this model. In his exceptional work of reconstruction, conducted on the remnants of a statue found in the western portico of the Tetrastoon behind the theatre at Aphrodisia, R. R. R. Smith was able to see through the features of the statue's head, which had been contaminated by, and reworked along the lines of a Julio-Claudian portrait (fig. 20.9). That the statue embodies a specific mode of official self-representation rather than a 'realistic' trait of his personality is confirmed by the widespread accounts of the emperor's irascible nature (Ambrose, *Epist. extr. coll.* 11.4–5; *De Obit. Theod.* 34; Paulinus, *Vita S. Ambros.* 24; Augustine, *De Civ. Dei*, 5.26; Rufinus, *Eccl. Hist.* 11.18; John Chrysostom, *Hom.* 21.4; Sozomen, *Eccl. Hist.* 7.25; Theodoret, *Eccl. Hist.* 5.17). The brutality he showed in quelling the rebellion of the Thessalonians against Roman military presence was a sign

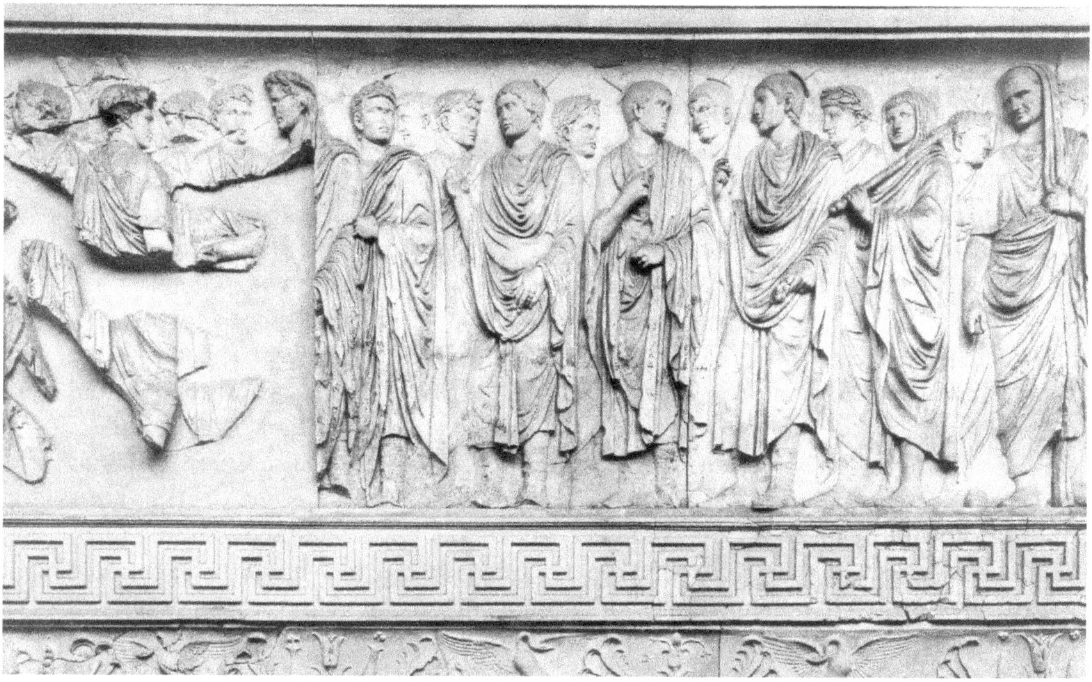

Fig. 20.10. A detail of the procession on the south side, featuring the images of Augustus, the *flamines* and Agrippa. Rome, Ara Pacis

of his well-known propensity to wrath: this specific act won him a severe censure on the part of the bishop, Ambrose, to which he responded by publicly and theatrically performing an act of penance in Milan, before a populace weeping 'for the spectacle of the sublime imperial power so prostrate' (Aug. *De Civ. Dei* 5.26.1).

Responding to a similar impulse, in the reliefs designed to honour the emperor as symbol of Roman power and of Rome's eternal greatness, the image of the imperial dignity is progressively isolated and abstracted from the surrounding figures. At first, as in the Ara Pacis, the figure of the emperor is portrayed as equal in size to the magistrates and as engaged in dialogue with them (fig. 20.10). In later examples, the figure progressively acquires pre-eminence: its size increases, the posture becomes more frontal, the gestures are more measured, and the space isolating the emperor and the members of his household from the surrounding characters widens. As a result of this almost irresistible iconographic tendency, the figure of the emperor becomes an unapproachable icon (fig. 20.8), hieratically positioned in isolation—an object of full-fledged veneration rather than respect—against the background of a progressively indistinct crowd, whose characters grow increasingly smaller in size and are gradually deprived of any distinctive symbolic feature. That such an iconographic and programmatic choice responded to real-life behaviours is suggested by other examples. Julian, for instance, grew a long beard, in a gesture clearly antagonizing the model set by the Constantinian dynasty (to whose bloodline he belonged). By incorporating this feature in his portraits, including those on coins, he polemically refused the traditional, strongly Christianized images of the emperors: he favoured, as Luisa Musso has demonstrated, the iconography of some Greek philosophers and also of Numa Pompilius, the king who was at the root of traditional Roman religion and whose features included a long beard both on late Republican coins and in late antique medals (contorniate coins). Eugenius, Theodosius' rival, imitated his iconographic choices in order to emphasize his non-Christian stance against the Christian emperor of the East.

Despite the radical changes that the general perception of space and environment underwent, even urban landscape may be read in the light of 'Lebenswelt'. In Roman bas-reliefs both the actual arrangement of public spaces and their spatial composition are subjected to a similar iconographic translation. Architecture is tied to the social environment and to the modalities in which political activities unfold more strongly than any other visual art. Actually, architecture depends most directly on the successive political systems that are in force and the resulting shifts in the general mentality. If this is true in modern architecture and urban planning, it is just as true in the Roman world. We know that the modern eye commonly errs in reading ancient urban planning according to the laws of Renaissance linear perspective; namely, by organizing space around a single vanishing-point, as in the famous oil paintings of cities now in Urbino, Baltimore, or Berlin. These are all works of Central Italian artists who created marvellous cityscapes in the vein of Leon Battista Alberti. The mistake is particularly dangerous for Roman urban architecture: imperial Rome was a cluster of individual monumental buildings, each surrounded by porticoes or walls, isolated from and unrelated to one another. They could only be read individually and, in most cases, only partially. The harmonious play of space created by the exedrae in Augustus' and Trajan's Forum—always eclipsed by the shining of the various qualities of marble—could be perceived, for instance, only once the intervening impediment of the porticoes was ideally removed. Only then could the semicircular rooms be seen from the great central courts. Similarly, ancient viewers perceived the Basilica Ulpia as a large four-sided bowl, from the centre of which one could not intuit the presence either of the exedras, barred from view by a double row of high colonnades, or of the side aisles. Today we may well enjoy a great view from Via Biberatica in Trajan's markets toward Trajan's Forum, and the Capitoline and the Palatine hills, but the viewers had their sight blocked by high walls (fig. 20.11). There might have been windows looking out onto Trajan's Forum, but from them one could only see an uneven surface of anonymous roofs. Furthermore, the widespread presence of porticoes reduced the internal courts of the houses (in most cases as wide as a modern city square) to a predictable element of the city decor: the only variation was the rich ornamentation of the architectural elements, but even that did not prevent viewers from perceiving the complex as two-dimensional. In poetic

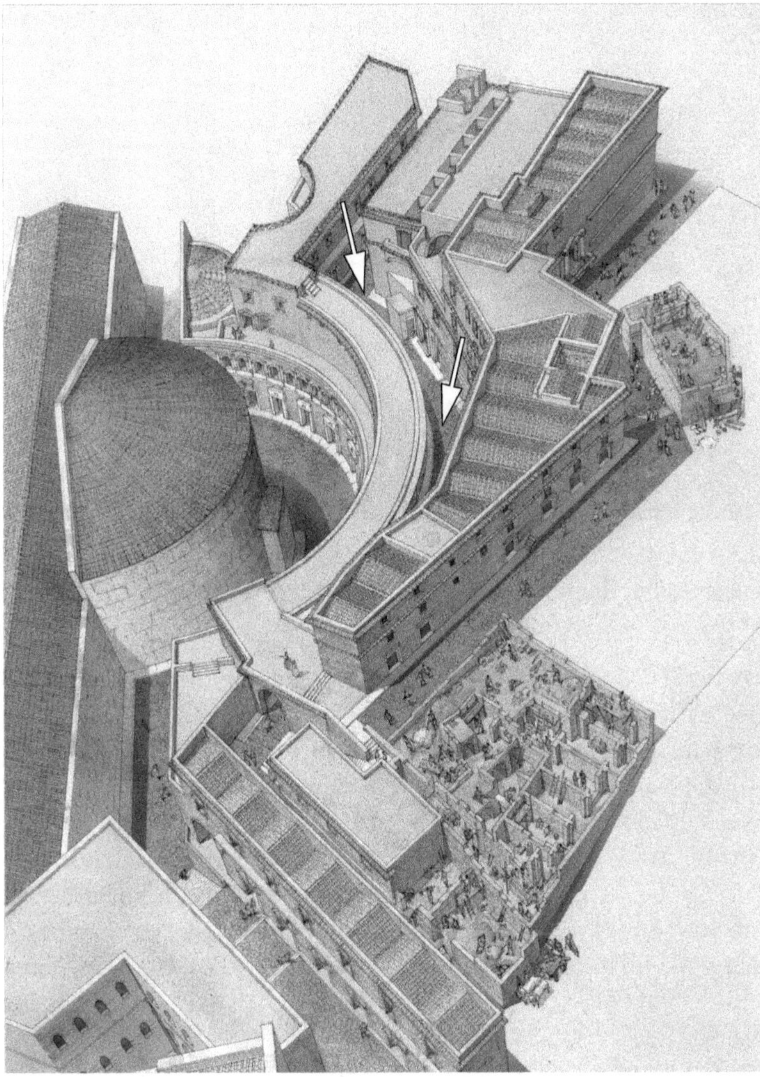

Fig. 20.11. Axonometric reconstructive view of the Markets of Trajan facing Trajan's Forum. The arrows indicate the s.c. via Biberatica (drawing: Inklink)

descriptions of Roman luxury *domus*, the quality of the building and the architectural originality are always eclipsed by the shining of the various qualities of marble:

Here is Lybian stone and Phrygian, here hard Laconian rock shows green, here are versatile alabaster and the vein that matches the deep sea, here marble oft envied by Oebalian purple and the blender of the Tyrian cauldron. Airy gables rest on countless columns, beams glitter allied with Dalmatian ore. Cool descends from ancient trees, shutting out the sunshine, translucent fountains live in marble. (Statius, *Silvae* 1.2.148–55, tr. D. R. Shackleton Bailey, Loeb edn., 2003)

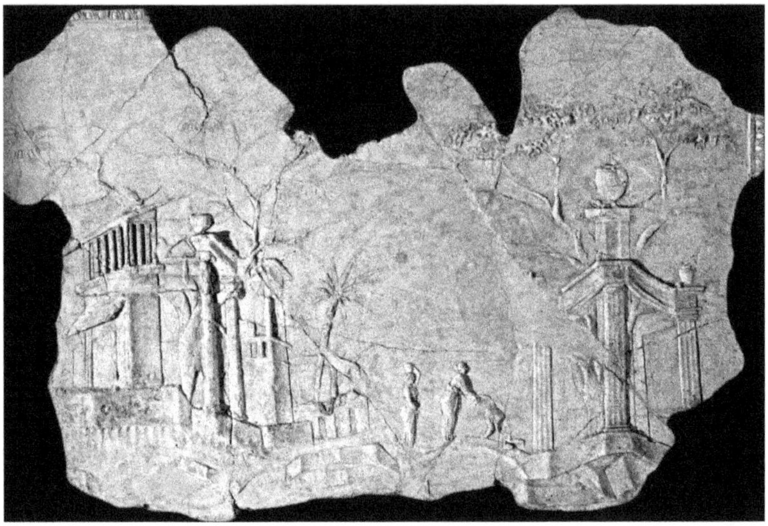

Fig. 20.12. A detail of the stucco decoration from the vault of Cubicolo B from the Villa della Farnesina. Rome, Museo Nazionale Romano, Palazzo Massimo

Likewise, nature is never perceived with a Romantic eye, but as circumscribed and transformed by the hand of man. It is a space that human work has shaped with astonishing artifice. In the Tiburtine villa of Vopiscus, the River Anio is forced to conform to the iron laws of architecture: 'Anio himself, wondrous to tell, full of rocks above and below, here rests his swollen rage and foamy din, as though loath to disturb Vopiscus' Pierian days and songfilled slumbers. Either shore is at home, nor does the gentle river divide you. Stately mansions keep either bank, no strangers to each other, nor complain that the river blocks them' (ibid. 1.3.20–6, tr. Shackleton Bailey). Nature yields, conquered, to the work of man even in Sorrento, in the villa of Pollio Felix:

> Some spots Nature has favoured, in others she has been overcome and yielded to the developer, letting herself be taught new and gentler ways. Where you see level ground, there used to be a hill; the building you now enter was wilderness; where now you see lofty woods, there was not even land. The occupant has tamed it all; the soil rejoices as he shapes rocks or expels them, following his lead. Now behold the cliffs as they learn the yoke, and the dwellings as they enter, and the mountain bidden to withdraw. (ibid. 2.52–9, tr. Shackleton Bailey)

In the reliefs, spatial perception is reduced to its bare minimum. The monuments portrayed there are two-dimensional, and flattened against the background (fig. 20.12). They appear totally deprived of the attributes of depth-representation typical of the Renaissance. The artists seem to have little or no interest in establishing spatial relationships between monuments and characters, which are usually arranged in dense rows parallel to the background. Illusionistic effects are mainly reserved for indoor spaces, where they are amplified through the lavish use of colourful marble, frescos, or floor- and wall-mosaics (we now have full documentation, thanks to the important discoveries on the Oppian hill). Both large monumental courts and interior rooms are affected by this kind of ornamentation. Though lacking any realistic intention, the decorative motifs illusorily open up the interior spaces onto the external world: theatre backdrops, gardens, and views of land- or cityscapes crowded with characters busy with daily activities construct the illusion of the real world—an effect which is immediately defused by non-perspectival representation. The representational system flattens objects and people on an impenetrable backdrop plane.

It should be clear that the hermeneutic paradigm informed by the 'Lebenswelt' goes beyond a mere analysis of the content of a work of art. It also investigates the ways in which representational schemes and, in part, artistic forms harmoniously develop with changes in society and mentality.

Roman Art and the Greek Canon

It is known that for a long time (at least until the late Hellenism) Roman art used artistic forms and representational schemes elaborated by the Greeks. They constituted a vast inventory of different models available for emulation, a wide range of examples from which to choose depending on varying representational needs. In Roman art one perceives a conscious desire to conform to precise models derived from Greek artistic culture on the basis of ideological paradigms dictated not only (or not primarily) by the taste of the patron, but also (or rather) by the social and political role the work of art was called to play. Forms and schemes were not neutral: they acquired a symbolic value that controlled the relation between the subject of representation and the form it took. It was such a cohesive and comprehensive system that it became part and parcel of the mental *habitus* of the Romans—seeping undetected into the repertoire of formulas of all artists, whether in literature, oratory, or the visual arts. How and why this happened will most likely be a matter of dispute for some time. It is certain, however, that at a precise point in the evolution of Greek art the works of the great artists of the past appeared to embody eternal and perpetual ethical norms in their purest form. This conviction led to the creation of canons of artists who were considered unmatched in specific fields—whether as technical, formal, or moral paradigms—and whose works became the standard of judgement for the subsequent artistic production in different genres. Canons were allowed some measure of flexibility, according to changing social habits and needs; however, canonical works were generally used as both an occasion for inspiration and an object of emulation. For the artisanal production of large quantities of artefacts, the canon was beneficial in setting and keeping a high standard. Yet it could also serve as a thwarting system of rules that piloted the work of the artists and compelled them to remain within predetermined boundaries, so as not to break the rigid norms of ethics or genre.

In the case of oratory, for instance, Cicero was adamant in rejecting the pathos formulas typical of Asian rhetoric in favour of a more measured style, fuelled by the examples of the classical tradition and more befitting, in his view, to a Roman magistrate. Even the 'classical tradition', however, was far from monochord: it offered a variety of styles that could combine with the alluring oratorical modes of the Hellenistic age at the roots of Asianism, just as well as they could be made to clash with them. In truth, the classical tradition was defined more in terms of themes than of style: it was considered to symbolically embody the highest moral qualities of a Roman magistrate—namely, his *auctoritas* and *gravitas*. In general, even individual models could be disassembled, according to a logic that had very little in common with the original. Once recombined in new and innovative arrangements, the original components of the model could, in their turn, act as models for future practitioners of the genre. This is the case, for example, in Virgil's use of Homer: the *Aeneid* takes the Homeric tradition as a *code-model*, adapts it to the taste of his age by reworking its text in an Alexandrian vein, and thus establishes itself as a code-model for the future.

In the field of the visual arts, Romans showed a predilection for the thick and dramatic compositions of the Hellenistic age in their treatment of battle scenes, an analogue of the style of Asianism. Instead, for the treatment of idylls, they went back to more relaxed and sedate models (again from the Hellenistic tradition), in which the characters move in a symbolic space, strongly connotated as non-urban. However, when the work's goal was the definition of the moral virtues characterizing Roman mores, models were adopted from the classical age: only these, it was felt, could most aptly express the values Rome claimed for itself, such as *sanctitas*, *auctoritas*, and so on. This is the reason why the Ara Pacis appears as a melting-pot of different representational formulas. While it shows a strong dependence on fourth-century BCE models for the procession (figs. 20.10, 13), it also appears to rely on fully Hellenistic schemes for the short panels that include background landscapes (which are balanced, however, by the presence of classically inspired figures portrayed in a calm and authoritative posture). Similarly, the beautiful acanthus volutes branching out across the lower panels (fig. 20.14) depend on the Hellenistic tradition (fig. 20.15), but they are organized according to strongly measured partitions inspired by the decorative tradition of the classical age.

Roman artists are caught as in a double bind. On the one side they are hard pressed by the canon that has progressively formed (as 'sacralized' corpus) and

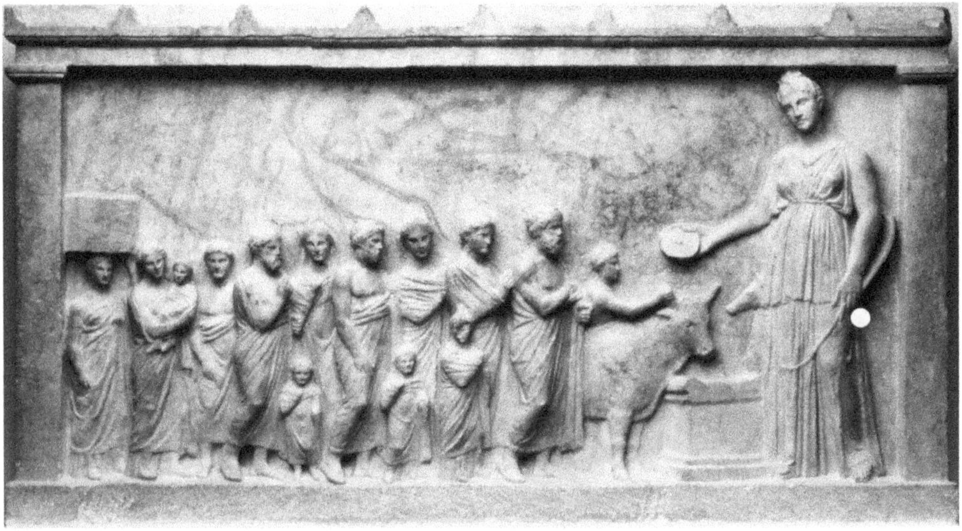

Fig. 20.13. Votive relief dedicated to Artemis Brauronia. Brauron, Museum

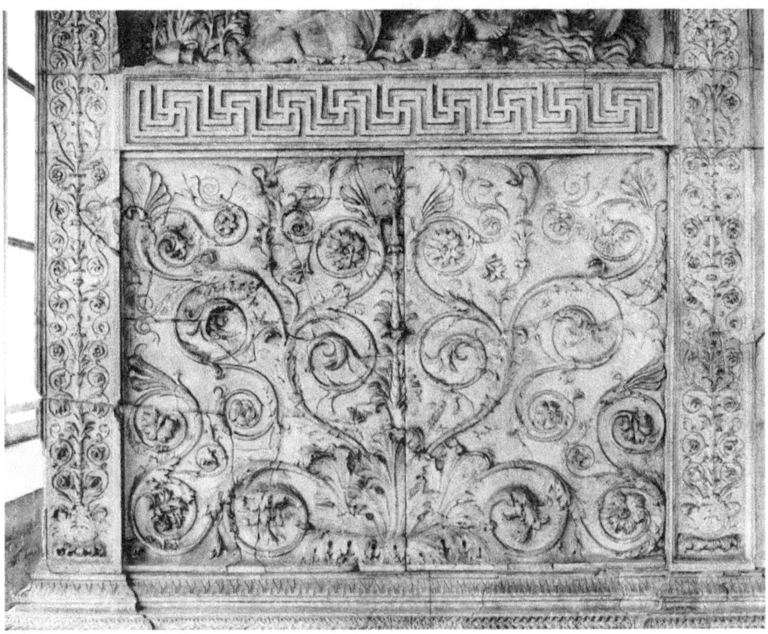

Fig. 20.14. Vegetal frieze belonging to the left wall of the east side. Rome, Ara Pacis

includes works which shape a way of life, embody what is deemed eternally valid, and act as paragon for future artistic production. On the other side they are influenced by Greek art (the whole of its evolution), from which they draw key elements for their representations, as lemmas from a dictionary. To be sure, this

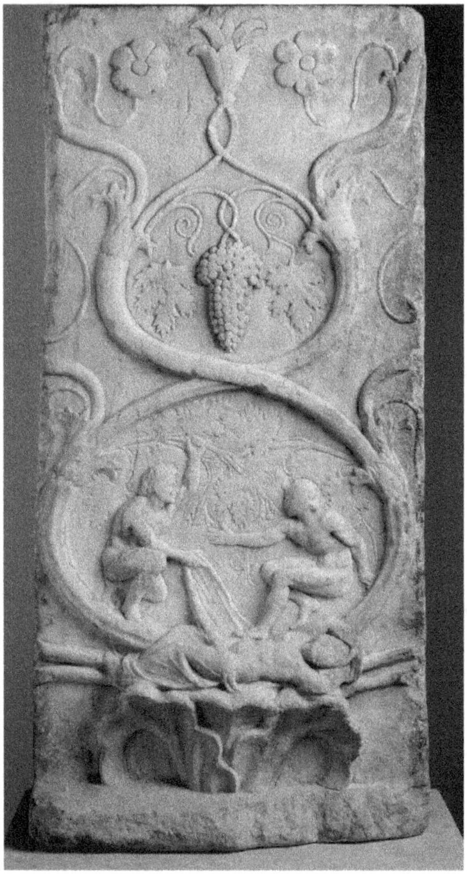

Fig. 20.15. Stele with vine scrolls, two Satyrs, and a sleeping Maenad, from Pergamum. Berlin, Staatsmuseum

system of redeployment does away with the real essence of Greek art. In particular, it severs its ties with the social dynamics from which it had originated. Every drawn element takes on a metaphoric import. As Bruno Snell remarks, 'what is received from Greek culture becomes allegory, and art an empire of symbols'. In truth, the very idea of canon that Romans used had been born in Greece, under different circumstances. Alexander the Great's conquests forced Greece to reckon with the rapid expansion of its cultural and then political borders: feeling that its ancestral traditions were thus endangered, Greek society decided to construct a clear-cut system of rules and canons that could be considered universally valid. This effort did not ultimately produce the congealing of Greek cultural complexity that might be expected; actually, its effect was a strong thrust towards innovation rather than tradition. For artists, the canon represented a movement towards what was grand, exacting, and categorical. It pointed in the direction of a pinnacle of absolute perfection and worked as the ideal measure and point of reference to overcome one's own limitations. However one may want to interpret it, the canon—especially in architecture, understood as the ideal model for building—is intended as the source of stable relational schemes; it provides equality, precision, and cohesiveness, and it counteracts capricious, arbitrary, and random individual deviations. The canon is also an innovative form of cultural cohesion, departing from the traditional, unqualified reliance on 'the past'; it is the obvious by-product of the process of Hellenization that affected the whole Mediterranean, apparently wiping out the rigid hierarchies of *poleis* and surrounding territories that were typical of its ancient social system and hence of the Greek identity itself.

Further study will be needed to understand why the Romans felt the urge to invoke the Greek canon, taking up its sacral nature, but subjecting it to different cultural needs that had little to do with its original meaning. The question is partly specific to the Roman situation and partly interwoven with the recurrence of the same choice of going back to the Greek model that we may observe in different ages. It is not by chance that the Renaissance canons did not curb artistic production, but acted as an authoritative (and authority-enhancing) point of reference. Far from limiting artists, canons led them to the elaboration of new forms and languages, which were only apparently bound to the observance of models from Greek and Roman antiquity.

The Symbolic Language of Roman Art

Despite its (at least apparent) connection with, and dependence on Greek art, which are based on the common 'naturalistic' understanding of images, Roman art departs from its antecedent thanks to a different conceptual attitude. Often improperly classified as 'utilitarian', this mind-set is actually functional to the prevailing political ideology. This does not mean that Greek art is indifferent to the political message it is designed to convey; more than the initial motives for acting, what differentiates Roman and Greek art are the diverging intentions and the eventual results.

In portraying an event, visual arts provide a certain number of information elements, but not all. The intrinsic limitations of their techniques dictate their inability to convey the complexity of abstract notions. In order to be decoded, a work of art needs the input of external information: aesthetic and formal analyses alone cannot account for the complexity of the image. Every visual document intends to convey a message, one that artists receive from their patrons. In the Greco-Roman world, patrons are mainly (but not exclusively) the political bodies of the *polis* or of the state, acting either for themselves or in the name of the highest magistrates who intend to commemorate particularly meaningful historical events.

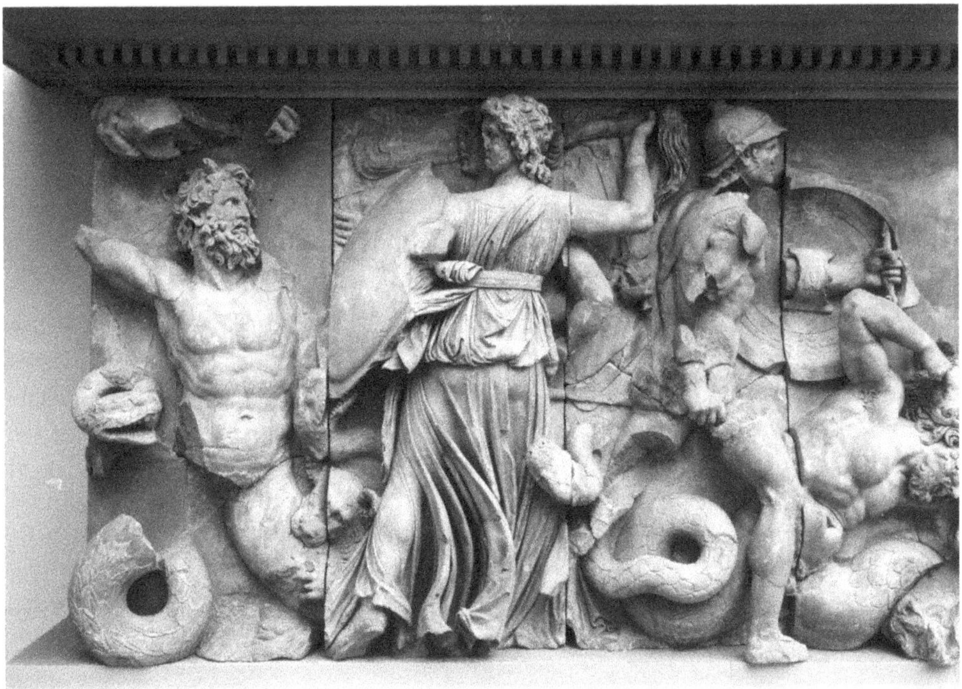

Fig. 20.16. A detail from the Gigantomachy of the Great Altar at Pergamum. Berlin, Staatsmuseum

While Romans tend to depict historical events as examples of *virtus* according to fixed and crystallized iconographic schemes, however, Greeks prefer to construct analogical connections with myth. On the Pergamon Altar, for example, the victories of Eumenes II are portrayed as a grand gigantomachy that contains only minimal hints to the present (fig. 20.16). On the contrary, the long and solemn procession on the Ara Pacis depicts Augustus' actual return to Rome (on 4 July of the year 13 BCE) as a timeless event. Even better, the frieze depicts Augustus' return as an event that may and will be repeated through time according to a similar format (fig. 20.10). The bas-relief crystallizes an event that took place in history (even if not in exactly the same way) and turns it into a model: the *reditus Augusti*, that is, the homecoming of the *princeps* who brings back peace, happiness, and prosperity. No less symbolical than Greek art, Roman art was designed to represent abstract notions as timeless (*sub specie aeternitatis*). Once formalized in an artistic depiction, the individual historical event becomes an *exemplum*, a moment in history that manifests all the *virtutes* which have made Rome great and her mission in the world eternal. Even when, towards the end of the Republic, personal and familial ambitions became the driving factor behind the artistic patronage of individual magistrates, the iconographic schemes did not cease to be repeated: Roman *virtus* appeared formally stilted and regimented in conceptually abstract forms.

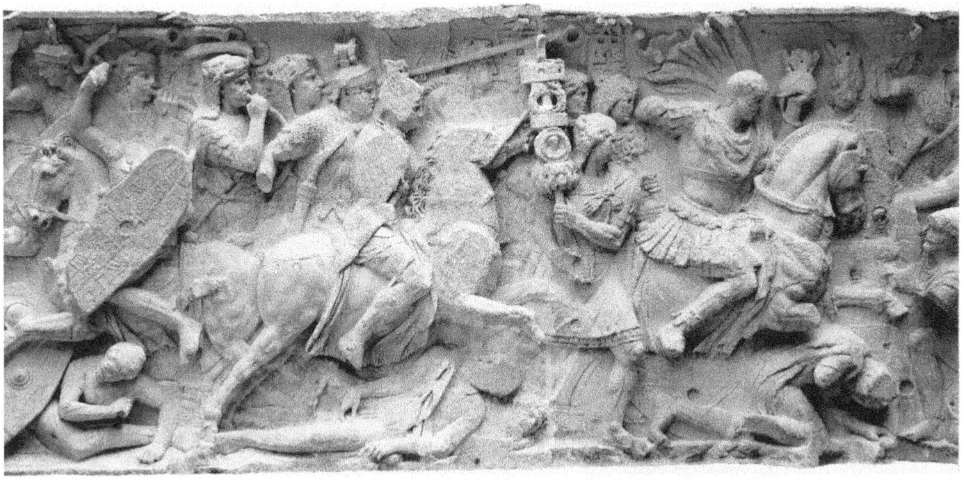

Fig. 20.17. A detail from the Great Frieze of Trajan. Rome, Arch of Constantine

Trajan's Column provides a characteristic example. Its ornamentation apparently chronicles in great detail the deeds that the Roman army performed during the two Dacian campaigns, starting with its departure from the city and ending on its final victory. Actually, each vignette corresponds to precise representational schemes that only a superficial reading could mistake for a real depiction of events. Each of them embodies and manifests a *virtus* or a strongly charged political, religious, and ritual action: the departure of the army (*profectio exercitus*) is followed by the *consilium principis*, then by a *lustratio* with *suovetaurilia*, intended as a figurative representation of Rome's *pietas erga deos*. A barbarian who falls from his steed is a good omen—translating the gods' *providentia* for the emperor. *Adlocutiones*, which are strictly connected to the notion of the army's *fides*, are followed by scenes in which the army's *labor* is presented as a reason for glory and success: the setting of camps, the harvesting of wood, the building of roads. In no case do individual scenes depict concrete events; rather, they are narrative representations of ideologically charged notions.

Similarly, the military *virtue* of the Roman emperor (or of a general) is often portrayed as caught in the thick of an apparently chaotic warring frenzy. Roman and barbarian foot-soldiers pile up, in a composition strongly marked by lights and shadows: from the central, overbearing figure of the general on horse radiates a circular wave of energy that seems to engulf the surrounding bodies and overwhelm them. In all its variants, the scheme presents a formulaic and purely symbolic description of specific historical events in works both for Trajan (as in the Great Trajanic Frieze, fig. 20.17) and for other generals, such as those portrayed on the Portonaccio (fig. 20.18) or the Ludovisi sarcophagi. The reuse of Trajan's Frieze on the Arch of Constantine (achieved by simply replacing Trajan's features with those of Constantine) shows that the same typology still maintained its

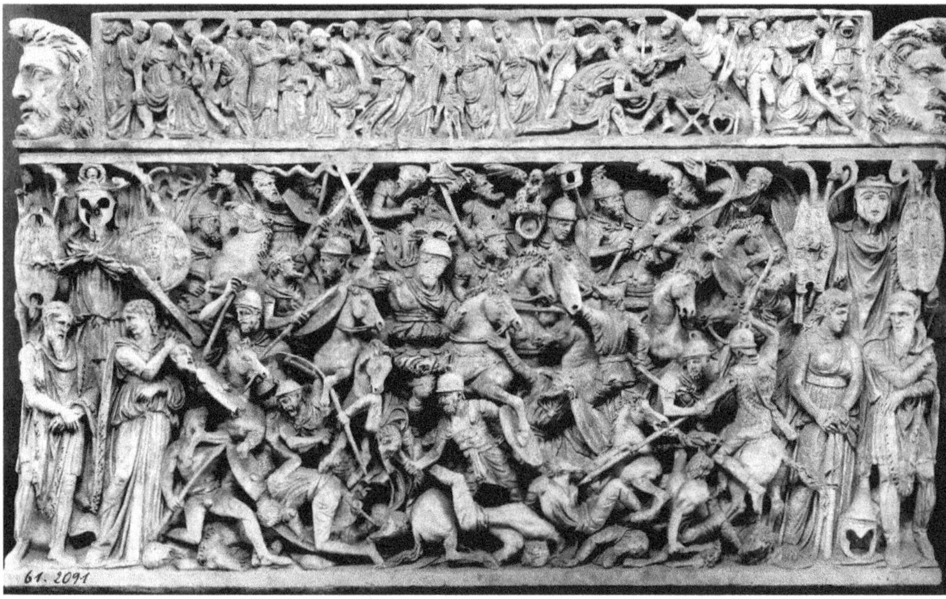

Fig. 20.18. Portonaccio Sarcophagus. Rome, Museo Nazionale Romano

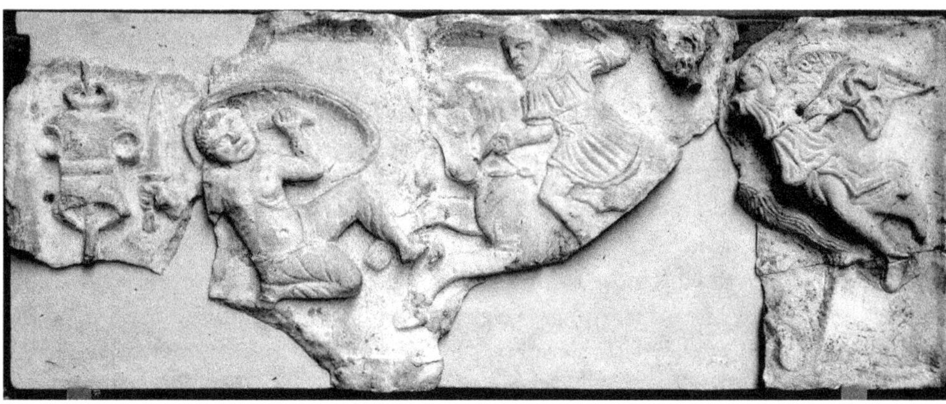

Fig. 20.19. Relief: the emperor Constantine (I or II) on horseback, crowned by a Victory, subdues a barbarian. Merida, National Archaeological Museum

original symbolic function even after two centuries. The same basic elements of this representational pattern, though brutally simplified, may be found also in an important bas-relief in the theatre of Mérida, which apparently portrayed Constantine II (fig. 20.19). After his death the relief was reworked so as to represent the image of an anonymous Roman emperor as *semper victor*.

The solution adopted in Greece is, as a rule, different. When the object of representation was an event which had actually taken place, as in the mosaic in

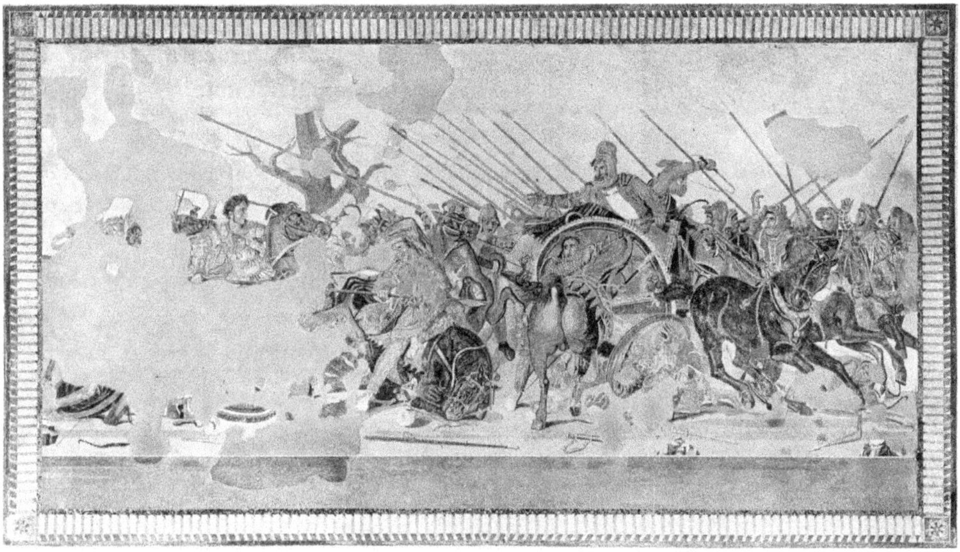

Fig. 20.20. Alexander Mosaic, from the House of the Faun at Pompeii. Naples, Museo Nazionale

Pompeii depicting the battles between Alexander and Darius, the *Iliad* was the adopted paradigm, with an implicit identification of Alexander with Achilles and Darius with Priam (fig. 20.20). In the House of the Faun mosaic, the irresistible onslaught of Alexander/Achilles is paired with the tragic figure of Darius/Priam who watches, helpless, the death of a Persian cavalryman (perhaps one of his sons), as his charioteer frantically whips the horses to put the king out of harm's way. The scene offers neither an *exemplum virtutis* nor a sufficiently coalesced scheme that may be repeated through time in order to convey the same notion; rather, it establishes a singular connection with the vast mythical repertoire merely adding an atemporal aura to the composition.

Roman Art and Stylistic Dissonance

For its constant change and manifold local varieties, style is what neither the 'Lebenswelt' (as mental habit) nor symbolic readings may decode. When interpreting a work of art, it is not enough for the critic to declare what representational scheme has been chosen over any other, nor does the literature of a specific time shed sufficient light on artistic forms. The example of the correlation existing between Gothic architecture and Scholastic thought may be used again. Such a relation certainly offers insight into the meaning of that architecture and illuminates

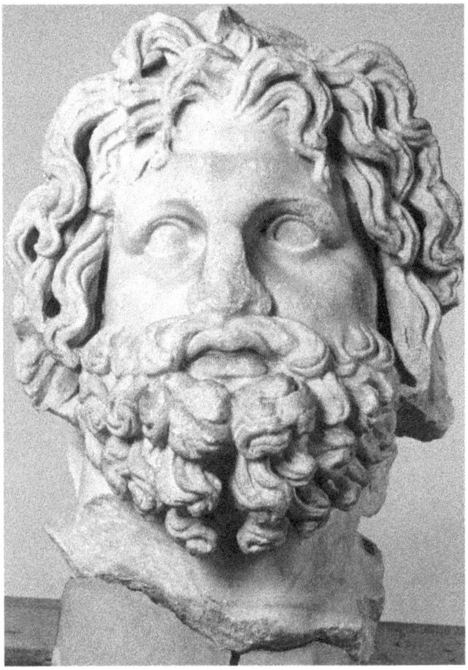

Fig. 20.21. Colossal head of a bearded god (Asclepius?). Siracusa, Museo Archeologico Regionale

the connections between individual elements and structural whole. However, the conceptual frame is powerless when it comes to adjudicating the value of the work in itself, its style, the dissonant artistic languages adopted at the centre of a culture and in its periphery, and, most of all, the different formal choices operated by individual, often apparently competing, architects. A clear demarcation-line separates written and oral language from figurative language: they do not share the same medium of communication.

A comparison between the head of a mature male deity (perhaps Asclepius) from Syracuse (fig. 20.21)—an original or, more likely, a copy from an original dating back to the third century BCE—and a head of Jupiter from Sabratha (fig. 20.22), late Antoine or early Severan, may provide a rough sense of the stylistic changes that have taken place in Greco-Roman art in the span of a few centuries. The comparison may also help to interpret the modalities of this change. Simplifying the question, but not misrepresenting its essential terms, one may observe the shift from an organic phase, in which the attention paid to the truth in nature is predominant, to a phase in which the natural and the organic has ceased to satisfy the artist's desire for new forms of representation. It is this shift that, more or less consciously, eventually undermines the strong bond with natural and organic truth established by Greek art—its greatest, most dangerous, and longest-lasting achievement in the western world (until the last decades of the nineteenth century). But what are the essential elements of such disintegration? The first radical change may be observed in how the hair on the head is sculpted. Upon careful inspection, the

Fig. 20.22. Head of Jupiter. Sabratha, Museum

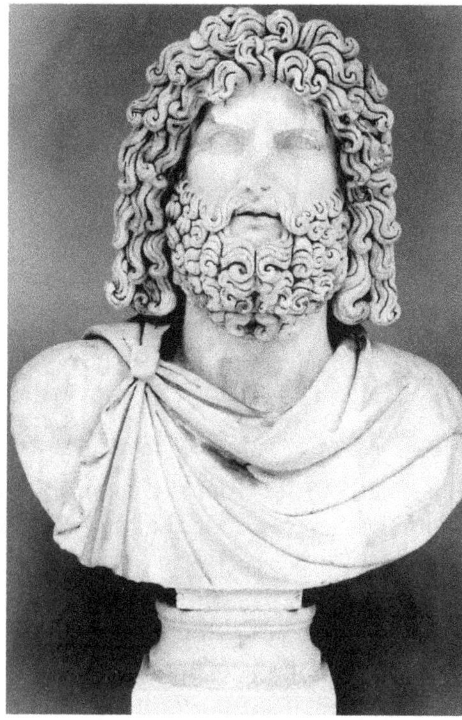

head from Sabratha shows that the hair, which from afar may still seem to having been conceived organically, is but a thin lace in chiaroscuro, realized with the help of a drill and almost deprived of any tri-dimensional depth effect. It is as if the artist had arranged the hair on a single backdrop plane, thus refusing—whether consciously or not is beside the point—to let the image acquire any plastic quality. The schematic arrangement of the locks in both the beard and the hair contributes to the strong decorative quality of the technique: the symmetrical pattern in which the tufts are arranged finds no correspondence in nature. Contrasting with the laced surface of the hair, the visage, although plastically expressed through a long tradition, becomes fluid and almost dissolves between luminous and levigated surfaces. Even if the character's features are sculpted according to ancient models of plastic representation, what seems to interest the artist is the surface. The skeletal structure plays a secondary role, if it plays one at all. And yet, taken together, the sculpture still meets the essential requirement of Greco-Roman artistic culture: it can still be perceived as true to nature.

A further element of interest emerges from the comparison. When considered more closely, not even the head from Syracuse may be said to be fully organic and natural, in a classical sense. The expressiveness of its features are achieved only through a radical alteration of several anatomical details—of the kind that, in nature, would be considered the product of a bone disease worth a specific medical study. The basic correspondence to nature, however, is not affected: the animated

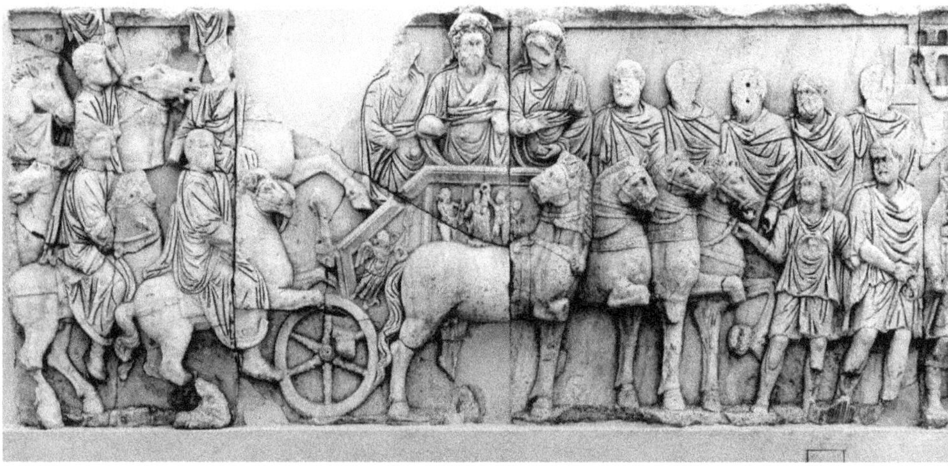

Fig. 20.23. Relief from the honorary arch of Septimius Severus at Lepcis Magna: Septimius Severus on a quadriga with Caracalla and Geta. Tripoli, Archaeological Museum

and somewhat unnatural treatment of the surfaces in the visage does not conceal the massive bone structure, and, unlike the head from Sabratha, it allows the skin to collect the shadows within heavy and hardly natural grooves.

Stylistic differences may not be understood by simply referring to different mental habits distinguishing the man of middle-Hellenistic age from the man of the age of Commodus or Septimius Severus. The style in which the head of the Sabratha Jupiter has been sculpted shows notable formal affinities with the reliefs of the arch in Lepcis Magna, dating from the Severan age (fig. 20.23). Since documentation is lacking, it is impossible to assign both artefacts to the same workshop—one that we know only from few examples that have barely left trace in the subsequent artistic output in the area of Tripoli. In Rome, the artistic language of that same age is based on different formulas. There is no stylistic unity underlying both the reliefs of Septimius Severus' arch (fig. 20.24) (or the Argentari arch, fig. 20.25) and the reliefs on the Severan arch in Leptis Magna (fig. 20.23). There are several points of contact: characters are increasingly arranged in a frontal composition, their figures are flattened onto the background, and the members of the imperial family are isolated. More generally, the two compositions seem to respond to similar requirements: their composition is utterly paratactic, the forms are simplified (with the darker, shadowy contours of the bodies standing out from a background), and the details in the drapings are likewise simplified and schematic (their strong chiaroscuro is produced using a drill). Several, if not all, of these themes may be understood through a detailed analysis of the period's history—approached in light of its 'Lebenswelt'. But even this does not fully account for the novelty of the artistic idiom used both in the arch of Leptis Magna and in the head of Jupiter from Sabratha. Their bold innovations compel some of the common representational schemes of

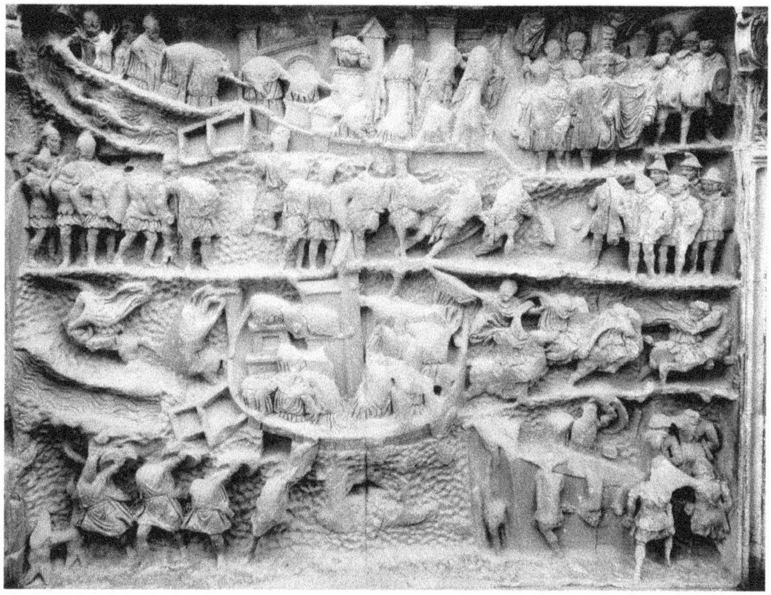

Fig. 20.24. Left panel of the Capitol side: the conquest of Babylon and of Seleucia. Rome, Arch of Septimius Severus (Fototeca Unione Askew Coll.)

the age to alter: a foreshadowing of what will happen several decades later, once the cultural environment and social structure had been permanently altered.

At the end of the day, there is no such a thing as a homogeneous style in any given historical period, not even within the limits of a single artist's works, and sometimes not even within a single work of art. If 'historical periods' are 'segments of history that may be isolated', as Panofsky notes, in order for them to be isolated they need to offer a certain degree of cohesion. The task of historians is to look for analogies that may exist among apparently unrelated phenomena, such as the arts, literature, philosophy, social and political movements, and so on. It is a task that requires intellectual honesty: consisting in a deep familiarity that goes beyond misleading summative schemes and partial or second-hand information, the complete knowledge of an entire historical period is perhaps beyond the reach of an individual researcher. Even in the single field of figural arts, there are too many variants that a generic appeal to the often misused and exceedingly abstract concept of a 'Kunstwollen' leaves all too often unaccounted for. The notion that a 'style of an age' (that is, an artistic common denominator independent of the will of individual artists) may exist is perhaps appealing, but it is also intrinsically problematic.

Equally problematic is any talk of either a 'style of a genre' or of a 'bi- (or multi-) polarism'. In the first case, the difficult assumption to make is that the style of a work is in direct correlation with its medium and theme. In the other case, the presupposition is that distinctions such as the one postulated between 'Hofkunst' and 'Volkskunst' may actually hold: one would really be hard pressed in defending

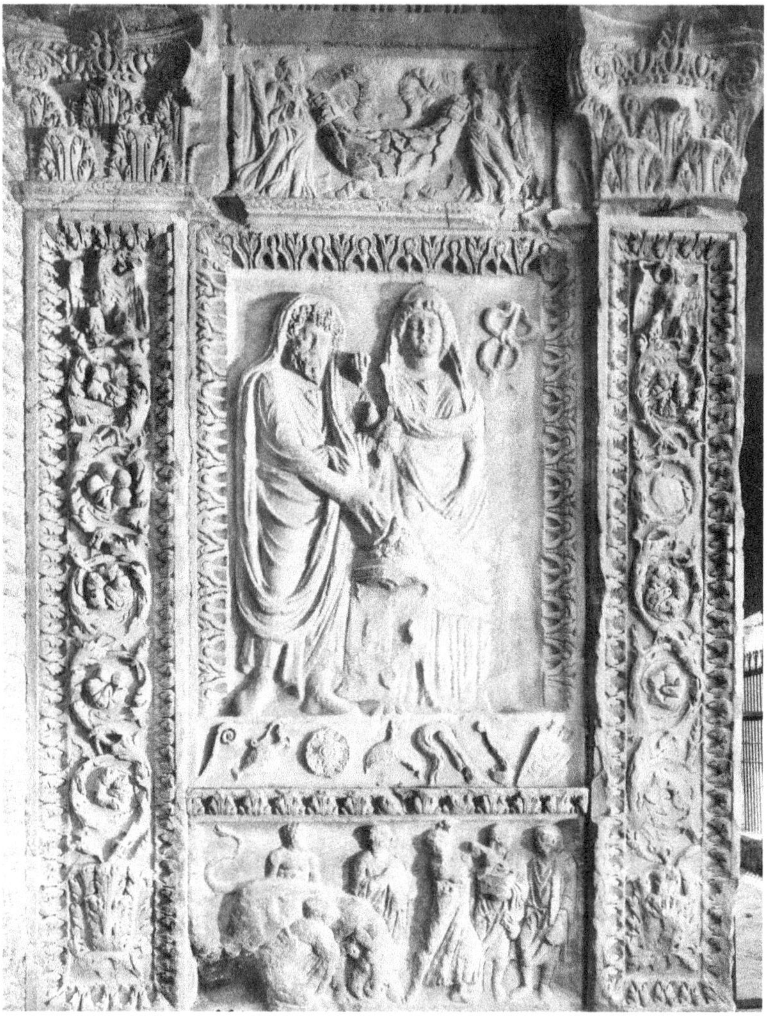

Fig. 20.25. Reliefs internal to the right pillar: above, sacrifice by Septimius Severus and Iulia Domna in front of a foculus (the image of Geta has been erased); below, representation of blood sacrifice. Rome, Arch of the Argentari

a typology that would simply oppose 'court art' and 'popular art' (or even, as Ranuccio Bianchi Bandinelli suggested, emphasizing social factors in the definition, 'plebeian art'). Artists are caught in a field of tensions between the constraints of their training and environment, of the patron's taste, and of the specifications that the work of art commissioned to them has to meet. In short, they are influenced by their own culture and by that of the environment where they live. Sketch albums and fully fledged catalogues of decorative formulas, specific technical teachings and apprenticeship in different artistic schools, and the close interaction with individual patrons (who may have different social backgrounds) or cities (run by different political regimes)—these are the factors that determine the alleged 'style of an age'. Even all these factors may not be enough to account for the myriad of variants, consisting of heterogenous elements in their diverse stages of formal development, which are grafted on a stylistic trunk that may only appear unitary. The 'style of an age' is a critical construct that historians and art historians assemble *a posteriori*, after the fact, by desperately seeking a stylistic common denominator for all the works produced in a given age. It is an abstraction, one that depends in the first place on the depth of our knowledge (actually, often on its superficiality). It is neither unitary nor, in a way, coherent, since it is the result of a process of addition in which formal motifs—sometimes insufficiently or incompletely understood in their historical importance by the contemporaries—emerge and interact according to no clear pattern and in no particular order. These casual interactions not only escape prompt critical analysis, but also fail to exert an immediate formative effect. We know how difficult it is today to predict, in the unbelievably large plethora of elements that constitute contemporary art, what formal motifs will last and thus exert an influence on future generations. Likewise, from our vantage-point it is impossible to tell if our posterity will make the right choices or the most innovative ones; just as the reasons for their eventual preference are unfathomable. We also know that often the serendipitous discovery of a new work of art may come to correct retrospectively an established critical framework and the depending corollaries. The formal elements of a given historical period are many, but they are allowed to coalesce only within precise ranges that are distinctive of that phase and alien to other ones. Discerning the main thread in the complex and tangled web of forms is not always easy or possible. A contribution by George Kubler emphasizes the technical problems that artists tackle in order to bring their works to fruition. His focus on the problem-technique dynamics allows him to isolate and study 'formal classes' and 'series of solutions relating to the same problem'. The 'formal sequence' is, in his own words, 'an historical network of gradually altered repetitions of the same trait' (*The Shape of Time* (New Haven and London, 1972), 37), repeated until the problem that had initiated the sequence will have been solved. Even when different artistic problems seem to follow similar development cycles, they never reach the same results—nor may they be repeated—because they are fully dependent on the programme inherent to their sequence: when the artistic problem changes, a new sequence is generated. Kubler's approach provides a remarkably effective interpretive tool. It most efficiently accounts for the functional modes of the genres in Roman art and for the presence of more than one sequence at a given historical moment, each marked by different formal problems and undergoing a different evolution.

A further comparison may help clarify this concept. Only a few years separate the procession reliefs of the Ara Pacis (fig. 20.10) from the large panel belonging to Gaius Caesar's cenotaph in Limyra, depicting what is most likely a *transvectio equitum* (fig. 20.26). In the Ara Pacis the composition is harmonious and responds to a

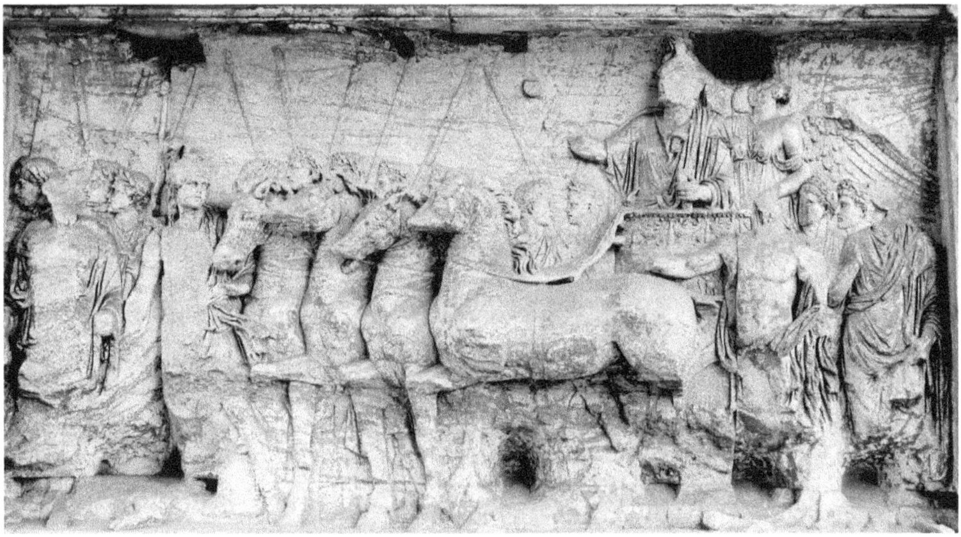

Fig. 20.26. Relief with representation of the triumph of Titus over the Judaeans. Rome, Arch of Titus

classicizing logic: no figures are superimposed (the ones in the background are reduced to a silhouette) and they move with a dignified gaze, flattened against a blocked and indistinct background. Composure and calm dominate the scene: the gestures are solemn and poised—as befits the representatives of Roman power. In the bas-reliefs of Limyra, on the contrary, *pathos* is the dominant note. To be sure, the background is still used as a neutral and impassable threshold, but the figures stand out from it in a plurality of layers that is unprecedented in the early Imperial age. The effect of frenzy in their movements is achieved less by any compositional technique than by the chiaroscuro effects of the surfaces, but the general effect is radically different from the new Augustan classicism embodied in the Ara Pacis. Gaius Caesar's cenotaph rejects the classicizing language and recuperates the Hellenistic tradition in its purest form: it transcribes its modes in a new and eventually influential key—one that offers several points of contact with the artistic modes of certain workshops in the Flavian age (cf. the reliefs in the Arch of Titus, fig. 20.27). In spite of their chronological proximity, the two works surveyed above belong to two different formal sequences: the former is consistent with a sequence of 'classical' descent, the latter with one deriving from the so-called 'Hellenistic baroque'. The different solutions offered by each sequence may be compared stylistically only with some difficulty and only when the manifold variants that the Augustan figurative culture produced are taken into account. As has become clear, during the first years of the Principate Augustan culture laid down the groundwork for the construction of a new classical era that was modelled as much on fourth- and fifth-century Greek art as on the most intensely Hellenistic products of their time. This idea may be easily confirmed by examining the ornamentation of the porticoes in the Forum of Augustus: here the

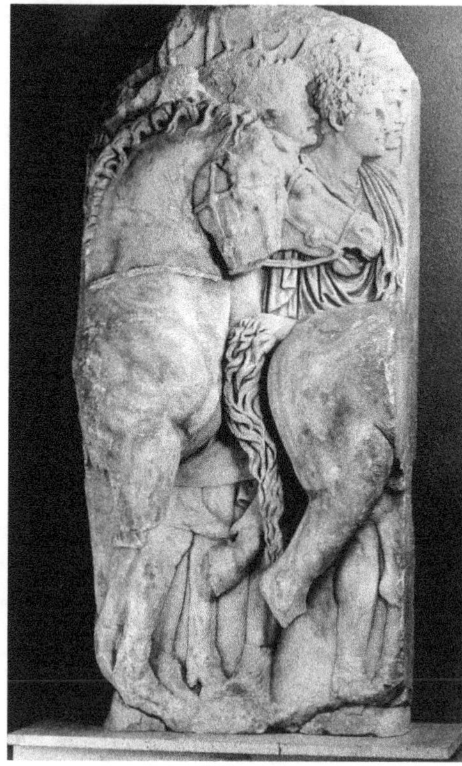

Fig. 20.27. Fragment of relief from the cenotaph of Gaius Caesar at Limyra. Antalya, Archeological Museum

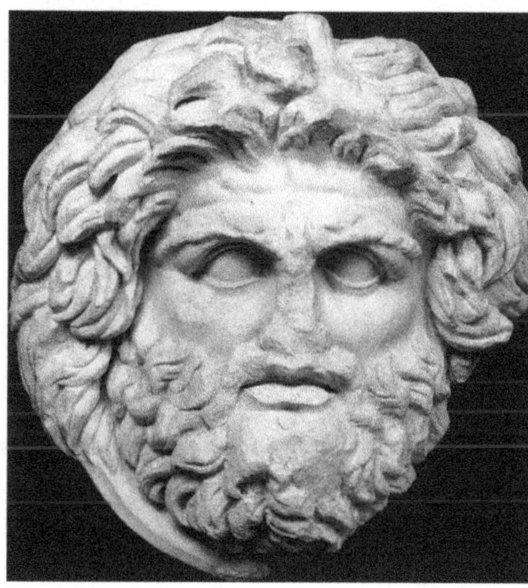

Fig. 20.28. Head of Jupiter Ammon. Rome, Museo dei Fori Imperiali nei Mercati di Traiano (photo: Museo)

noble and sedate *korai*, copied from the ones in the Erechtheion, are joined by the sombre and pathos-filled head of Jupiter Ammon (fig. 20.28), which seems to issue from the same artistic climate that produced the Laocoon (fig. 20.29) or the Pasquino group (a work that depends, in turn, on the great tradition of Pergamon).

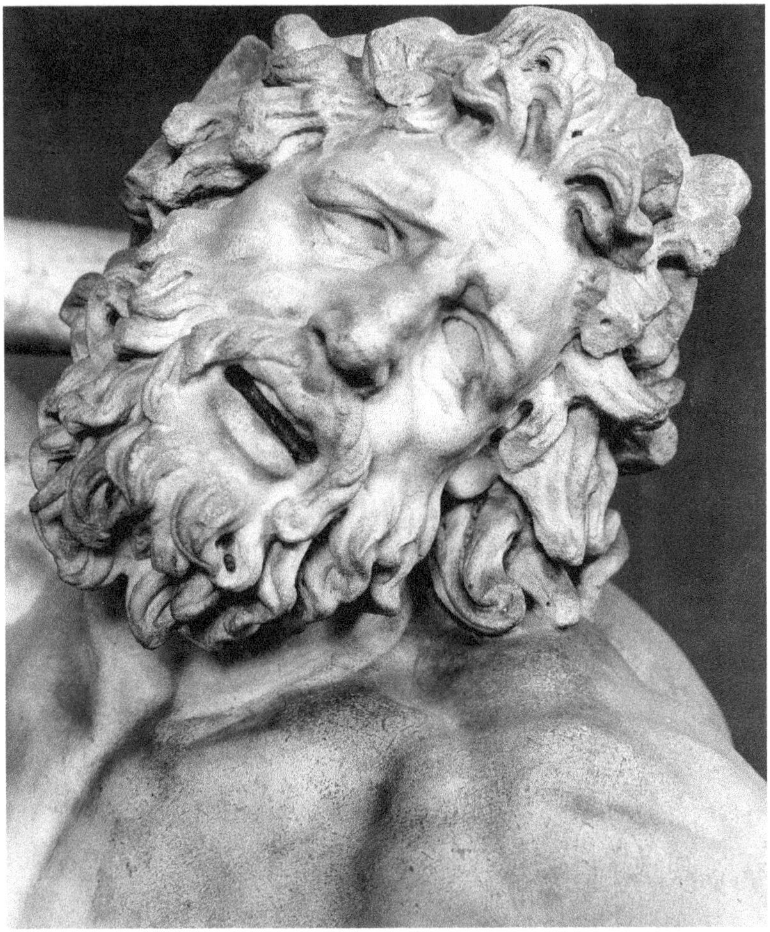

Fig. 20.29. Head of Laocoon. Rome, Musei Vaticani

Conclusion

The brief notes laid down in these pages cannot account for the rich and complex variety of tones present in Roman art. For a long time there has been talk of the supremacy of Greek art, and even today there are some who cannot conceive abandoning that ranking. In their view, three elements militate against recognizing originality to Roman artistic culture: first, Roman art seems—at least at first sight—to have derived from its Greek counterpart forms and schemes; second, it apparently lacks any coherent line of evolution; third, by spreading throughout the vast territories of the Roman Empire and absorbing formal elements which originated in other countries and cultures, Roman art has progressively developed a language marked by strong geographic inflection that has, in several cases, fallen short of becoming a fully fledged, autonomous artistic language. In light of especially this last bias, it may be appropriate to conclude with Claude Lévi-Strauss's comments on cultural diversity and on the value of their collaboration in the forming of new cultures, characterized by a more 'cumulative' history. They capture, in fact, the innovative quality of Roman art and its openness to the advancement of many fields in the sciences and art:

> These most extreme forms [of cultures that have enjoyed more markedly cumulative histories] have never been produced by isolated cultures. Rather, they have arisen in cultures that—willingly or not—have matched their respective games and implemented by way of migrations, influence, trade, and wars those *coalitions* the model of which we have imagined. It is cultures as these that render obsolete and absurd the notion that a culture is 'superior' to another: insofar as a given culture were alone, it could never be superior.... No culture, however, is alone: every culture exists only in coalition with other cultures—and this is what allows it to build cumulative series. ('Race and History', in *Structural Anthropology*, vol. 2 (Chicago, 1976), 354)

There is little doubt that Roman culture was a 'cumulative culture'. It certainly was capable being infused with the new blood of surrounding cultures, and certainly it did so in no systematic way, along non-linear patterns of progress. Some elements deriving from these cultures are assimilated; others are left to their destiny; 'progress' does not happen in orderly and continuous series, but in leaps and bounces—or, in Lévi-Strauss's own words, borrowed from the lexicon of biology, by 'mutations'. From the point of view of art, the result of cumulative progress is absolutely unique for both the high quality and the rich variety of formal solutions it may produce. The language of Roman art is first the product and then the source of such a dynamics: with all its borrowings from the idiom of Greek art and its contaminations with the artistic habits of Middle Eastern cultures, it will remain a vital organism. It will eventually engender both the Byzantine and Islamic artistic languages and, having passed the reefs of the Middle Ages, it will contribute to the creation of yet another great 'cumulative culture', the European Renaissance.

Further reading and references

On art criticism in the ancient world: E. Grassi, *Die Theorie des Schönen in der Antike* (Cologne, 1962); F. Preisshofen and P. Zanker, 'Reflex einer eklektischen Kunstanschauung beim Auctor *ad Herennium*', in *Dialoghi di Archeologia* 4: 1 (1970/1), 100–19; J. J. Pollitt, *The Ancient View of Greek Art: Criticism, History, and Terminology* (New Haven and London, 1974); F. Preisshofen, 'Kunsttheorie und Kunstbetrachtung', in H. Flashar (ed.), *Le Classicisme à Rome aux prémiers siècles avant et après J.-C* (Entretiens sur l'antiquité classique, Vandoeuvres–Genève 1978) (Geneva, 1979), 263–77; J. P. Small, *The Parallel Worlds of Classical Art and Text* (Cambridge, 2003).

On Greek archaic art and votive dedications: Ch. I. Karusos 'Perikalles agalma—Exepoies ouk adaes, Empfindungen und Gedanken der archaischen Griechen um die Kunst', in *Epitymbion Christos Tsuntas* (Athens, 1941), 535–78; M. L. Lazzarini, 'Le formule delle dediche votive nella Grecia arcaica', *Mem.Linc.* ser. VIII, vol. XIX, 2 (1976), p. 315, n. 952 (esp. pp. 95 ff., for a discussion of the term 'agalma'); J. Svenbro, *Phrasikleia. Anthropologie de la lecture en Grèce ancienne* (Paris, 1988); N. Kaltsas, 'Die Kore und der Kuros aus Myrrhinous', *Ant.Pl.* 28 (2002), 7 ff., figs. 1–12, pls. 1–7, 10, 11.

The meaning and value of modern art: N. Warburton, *The Art Question* (New York, 2002).

On semiology: C. Morris, *Foundations of the Theory of Signs* (Chicago, 1938); *Signs, Language, and Behavior* (New York, 1946); U. Eco, *Trattato di semiotica generale* (Milan, 1975; tr. *A Theory of Semiotics*, Bloomington, Ind., 1976).

On the notion of 'Lebenswelt': A. Schütz and Th. Luckmann, *Strukturen der Lebenswelt*, I (Frankfurt am Main, 1984); T. Hölscher, 'Formen der Kunst und Formen des Lebens', in T. Hölscher and T. Lauter (eds.), *Positionen zur Gegenwartskunst, Formen der Kunst und Formes des Lebens* (Ostfildern-Ruit, 1995).

On the notion of *habitus*: E. Panofsky, *Gothic Architecture and Scholasticism* (New York, 1952); P. Bourdieu, Postface to E. Panofsky, *Architecture gothique et pensée scholastique* (Paris, 1967), 135–67.

On imperial forms of representation: A. Alföldi, *Die monarchische Repräsentation im römischen Kaiserreiche* (Darmstadt, 1970), which collects two essays originally published in 1934 and 1935; A. Grabar, *L'Empereur dans l'art byzantin* (Paris, 1936).

On the 'period face' in portraiture: P. Zanker, 'Herrscherbild und Zeitgesicht', *Wiss. ZBerl.* XXXI (1982), 307–12; P. Zanker and Kl. Fittschen, 'Herrscherbild und Zeitgesicht. Probleme mit der Forschung in der klassischen Archäologie', in *Forschung in der Bundesrepublik Deutschland. Beispiele, Kritik, Vorschläge* (Weinheim, 1983), 23–30; P. Zanker, 'Herrscherbild und Beamteporträt', in *Ritratto ufficiale e ritratto privato. Atti della II Conferenza internazionale sul ritratto romano*, Roma 1984 (Rome, 1988), 105–9; E. La Rocca, 'Divina ispirazione', in: S. Ensoli and E. La Rocca (eds.), *Aurea Roma. Dalla città pagana alla città cristiana*, exhibition catalogue (Rome, 2000), 1 ff.

On the portrait of Theodosius in Aphrodisias: R. R. R. Smith, 'A Portrait Monument for Julian and Theodosius at Aphrodisias', in Ch. Reusser (ed.), *Griechenland in der Kaiserzeit, Neue Funde und Forschungen zu Skulptur, Architektur und Topographie, Kolloquium zum sechzigsten Geburtstag von Prof. Dietrich Willers* (Bern, 2001), 125 ff., fig. 33, 1; 34.

On the portrait of Julian: L. Musso, 'La barba di Giuliano', forthcoming.

On Renaissance perspectives in painting: R. Krautheimer, 'Le tavole di Urbino, Berlino e Baltimora riesaminate', in: H. Millon and V. Magnano Lampugnani (eds.), *Rinascimento. Da Brunelleschi a Michelangelo. La rappresentazione dell'architettura*, exhibition catalogue (Venice, 1994), 233 ff.

On the perception of architectural space in Rome: E. La Rocca, 'Passeggiando intorno ai Fori Imperiali', in L. Haselberger and J. Humphrey (eds.), *Imaging Rome: Documentation, Visualization, Imagination*, JRA Suppl. 61 (2006), 120 ff.

On the perception of pictorial space in Greek and Roman art: E. La Rocca, *Lo spazio negato. La pittura di paesaggio nella cultura artistica greca e romana* (Milan, 2008).

On literary genres and code-models: G. B. Conte, *The Rhetoric of Imitation: Genre and Poetic Memory in Virgil and Other Latin Poets* (Ithaca, NY, 1986).

On the notion of canon: J. Assmann, *Das kulturelle Gedächtnis. Schrift, Erinnerung und politische Identität in frühen Hochkulturen* (Munich, 1992).

On symbolic language in Roman art: P. G. Hamberg, *Studies in Roman Imperial Art* (Uppsala, 1945); T. Hölscher, *Monumenti statali e pubblico* (Rome, 1994).

On the Ara Pacis: M. Torelli, *Typology and Structure of Roman Historical Reliefs* (Ann Arbor, Mich., 1982), 27 ff., figs. II.2–II.32; D. Castriota, *The Ara Pacis Augustae and the Imagery of Abundance in Later Greek and Early Roman Imperial Art* (Princeton, 1995); D. A. Conlin, *The Artists of the Ara Pacis: The Process of Hellenization in Roman Relief Sculpture* (Chapel Hill, NC, 1997); E. La Rocca, 'Silenzio e compianto dei morti nell'Ara Pacis', in *Archaía elleniké gluptiké. Aphiéroma ste mnéme tou glúpte Stéliou Triánte* (Athens, 2002), 269 ff.; O. Rossini, *Ara Pacis* (Milan, 2006).

On Trajan's Column: S. Settis, A. La Regina, G. Agosti, and V. Farinella, *La Colonna Traiana*, ed. S. Settis (Turin, 1988); L. E. Baumer, T. Hölscher, and L. Winkler, 'Narrative Systematik und politisches Konzept in den Reliefs der Traianssäule. Drei Fallstudien', *Jd.I* 106 (1991), 261 ff.

On Trajan's Frieze: A.-M. Leander Touati, *The Great Trajanic Frieze* (Stockholm, 1987).

On battle-scene sarcophagi: B. Andreae, *Motivgeschichtliche Untersuchungen zu den römischen Schlachtsarkophagen* (Berlin, 1956).

On the relief in the theatre of Mérida: J. Arce, S. Ensoli, and E. La Rocca (eds.), *Hispania Romana. Da terra di conquista a provincia dell'impero* (Rome, 1997), 443, n. 284 (W. Trillmich).

On the Alexander mosaic in the House of the Faun at Pompeii: B. Andreae, *Antike Bildmosaiken* (Mainz am Rhein, 2003), 63 ff., figs. 62–77.

On the notion of style and on the critical tendencies in art history: M. Shapiro, 'Style', in: A. Kroeber (ed.), *Anthropology Today* (Chicago, 1953); A. Hauser, *Philosophie der Kunstgeschichte* (Munich, 1958); G. Kubler, *The Shape of Time* (New Haven and London, 1972); E. H. Gombrich, *Ideals and Idols* (Oxford, 1979).

On the problems specific to Roman art: P. H. von Blanckenhagen, 'Elemente der römischen Kunst am Beispiel des flavischen Stil', in: H. Berve (ed.), *Das neue Bild der Antike*, II Band: *Rom* (Leipzig, 1942), 310 ff.; N. Himmelmann, 'Der Entwicklungsbegriff der modernen Archäologie', *Marb.WPr.* (1960), 13–40; O. J. Brendel, *Prolegomena to the Study of Roman Art*, foreword by J. J. Pollitt (New Haven and London, 1979); S. Settis, '"Ineguaglianze" e continuità: un'immagine dell'arte romana', in O. Brendel, *Introduzione all'arte romana* (Turin, 1982), 161 ff.; T. Hölscher, *Römische Bildsprache als semantisches System*, Abhandlungen der Heidelberger Akademie der Wissenschaften, phil.-hist. Klasse (1987), no. 2; S. Settis, 'Un'arte al plurale. L'impero romano, i Greci e i posteri', in *Storia di Roma Einaudi*, 4, *Caratteri e morfologie* (Turin, 1989) 827 ff.; A. Leibundgut, *Künstlerische Form und konservative Tendenzen nach Perikles. Ein Stilpluralismus im 5. Jahrhundert v. Chr.*, 10. Trierer Winckelmannsprogramm 1989 (1991); A. H. Borbein, T. Hölscher, and P. Zanker (eds.), *Klassische Archäologie, Eine Einführung* (Berlin, 2009)—for artistic questions, see the essays by A. H. Borbein, pp. 109–28, W.-D. Heilmeyer, pp. 129–46, T. Hölscher, pp. 147–65, M. Bergmann, pp. 166–88, N. Boymel Kampen, pp. 189–204, and P. Zanker, pp. 205–26.

On the head of Asclepius from Syracuse: B. Andreae, 'Der Asklepios des Phyromachos', in B. Andreae (ed.), *Phyromachos-Probleme* (Mainz am Rhein, 1990), pp. 45 ff., figs. 20–3, 25–35.

On the head of Jupiter from Sabratha: Ch. Landwehr, 'Die Sitzstatue eines bärtigen Gottes in Cherchel. Zur Originalität römischer Vatergottdarstellungen', in B. Andreae (ed.), *Phyromachos-Probleme* (Mainz am Rhein, 1990), pp. 105 n. 4, 116, fig. 59.

On the arch of Septimius Severus in Rome: R. Brilliant, 'The Arch of Septimius Severus in the Roman Forum', *Mem.Am.Ac.Rome*, 29 (1967).

On the arch of Septimius Severus in Leptis Magna: V. M. Strocka, 'Beobachtungen an den Attikareliefs des severischen Quadrifrons von Lepcis Magna', *Ant.Af.r* 6 (1972), 147–72.

On the Argentari arch in Rome: M. Pallottino, *L'Arco degli Argentari* (Rome, 1946).

On the Cenotaph of Gaius Caesar in Limyra: J. Borchhardt, G. Forstenpointner, and R. Heinz, *Der Fries vom Kenotaph für Gaius Caesar in Limyra* (Vienna, 2002).

On the notion of 'classic' in Augustan artistic culture: P. Zanker, *The Power of Images in the Age of Augustus* (Ann Arbor, Mich., 1989); E. La Rocca, 'La fragile misura del classico. L'arte augustea e la formazione di una nuova classicità', in M. Barbanera (ed.), *Storie dell'arte antica*, Atti del Convegno 'Storia dell'arte antica nell'ultima generazione: tendenze e prospettive' [Roma 2001] (Rome, 2004), 67–116.

On 'cumulative' cultures: Claude Lévi-Strauss, *Race et histoire, Race et culture* (Paris, 2000). The two papers, published separately for the first time in 1952 and 1971, have appeared also in English translation: 'Race and History', in *Structural Anthropology*, vol. 2 (Chicago, 1976), 323 ff.; 'Race and Culture', in *The View from Afar* (Chicago, 1985), 3 ff.

CHAPTER 21

RECEPTION

ANDREW LAIRD

Rome's azure sky,
Flowers, ruins, statues, music, words, are weak
The glory they transfuse with fitting truth to speak.
(Shelley, *Adonais* (1821), 52.7–9)

I

Henri Matisse once remarked that a spectator who responds to an artwork by trying to identify with those who lived at the time it was created is impoverishing himself, 'a bit like the man who searches, with retrospective jealousy, the past of the woman he loves' (Flam 1973: 135). Something similar could be said of anyone whose interest in Roman culture excludes the richness of its reception. The importance of Rome consists in the enormity and dynamism of its legacy:

(i) The Roman alphabet is the most widely used in the world, either serving languages which had no logographic systems of their own or supplanting earlier scripts: its use in some Balkan nations, Turkey, and Azerbaijan remains a matter of controversy.

(ii) The Roman language of Latin continued to function from the Middle Ages well into the Enlightenment—not merely for humanist scholars, *belle-lettristes*, and theologians, but as a routine vehicle of education and a vital *lingua franca* for progressive thought and scientific knowledge. The imprints of both Classical and Vulgar Latin are also very evident in most European languages, including English and Spanish which, after Chinese, have the greatest number of native speakers in the world.

(iii) The language of Greece no less than Latin—along with Greek literature and thought—was primarily diffused and transmitted to posterity by the Romans and their descendants.

(iv) Roman forms of knowledge, which incorporated Greek accomplishments including grammar, rhetoric, philosophy, historiography, and natural science, as well as practical arts like medicine, architecture, and warfare, provided the foundations for most areas of learning in medieval and early modern Europe.

(v) Roman law, the codification of which rested on legislation and enactments by statute, underpins most contemporary legal systems; many other modern patterns of social organization, including political and fiscal practices, roads, and urban planning, find their origin in the infrastructures of ancient Rome.

(vi) Roman religion, though it was polytheistic and non-Abrahamic, helped to provide a vocabulary, an institutional structure and—in the city of Rome itself—a spiritual centre for the Catholic Church, still the world's largest religious denomination.

(vii) The Roman Empire, reinvoked by Charlemagne (who was crowned as *Imperator Augustus* in 800) and later by the more enduring institution of the 'Holy Roman Empire', offered a model for Spanish, Portuguese, French, and British imperialism, through which Rome's influence was conveyed beyond Europe and the Near East to Asia, Africa, the Americas, and Australasia. The world's greatest military power today is governed by a 'Senate' from a building which is called the 'Capitol' and which was designed to resemble the Roman Pantheon (Kennon and Somma 2004).

The immensity of this influence shows at once that Rome's reception involves something far broader and much more open-ended than the monolithic and self-conscious inheritance once connoted by the term 'classical tradition' (cf. Budelmann and Haubold 2008). Yet studies of both Greek and Roman *reception* have now come to focus almost exclusively on literature and art (Martindale 1993; Hardwick 2003; Martindale and Thomas 2006). That narrowing focus is illustrated by comparison of an original volume entitled *The Legacy of Rome* (Bailey 1923), which had only one chapter on literature, with its recent successor (Jenkyns 1992). Jenkyns's 'new appraisal' of Rome's legacy, produced in 1992, devotes five out of fifteen chapters to poetry and a further chapter to rhetoric: it contains no specific treatments of historiography or science. It is also significant that the *Oxford Classical Dictionary* defines reception in terms of 'the specialized sense used within *literary* theory': 'Reception theory thus dissolves the distinctions between texts in their initial contexts, read "in their own terms" and the afterlife of those texts in a way which threatens traditional positivistic attempts to reconstitute "original" meanings as the only true meanings' (*OCD*[3] 1294–5; cf. Iser 1978; Jauss 1982; Maclean 1986).

The routine use of terms like 'text', 'hermeneutics', 'mimesis', and 'persona' in modern aesthetic and literary theory show that this is another area in which classical terms and categories are ubiquitous (Laird 1999, 2006*a*: 1–37). And the central role of the 'text' in accounts of classical reception can be practically justified: absolutely everything apprehended about Greco-Roman antiquity and its inheritance can be conceived as a range of *texts* (Bakhtin 1986). Material artefacts and buildings, no less than brief inscriptions or lengthy written works, can be regarded as 'texts' in a broad sense—along with scholarly discussions and commentaries. The question of how all these texts are to be interpreted in relation to each other is the essential business of reception.

So although reception is commonly regarded as a range of possible *objects* of investigation, it is classified in this volume as an *approach* to Roman Studies. Its potential has yet to be fully exploited. Reception is only peripheral to Roman Studies if those studies are conceived narrowly—as the scrutiny of discourses and artefacts *only* in their constructed contexts in ancient Rome. But in fact interpretation of those discourses and interpretations in their original Roman provenance depends on the meanings and contextualizations they have been acquiring over time. That dynamic function of reception will be illustrated at length in section II below. Though this illustration mostly involves literary examples, it will serve to highlight reception's central characteristics (section III). Finally, some comments on the singular and special pertinence of reception to Roman studies (section IV) will precede a brief concluding section (V).

II

In the early 90s CE the Neapolitan poet Publius Papinius Statius wrote, in his collection entitled *Silvae* ('Forests'), a consolation to a Flavius Ursus for the death of his favourite slave. In order to justify Flavius' depth of feeling for someone outside his family who was not a free man, Statius pointed out that even animals can be mourned (*Silvae* 2.6.18–20):

> gemit inter bella peremptum
> Parthus equum fidosque canes flevere Molossi;
> et volucres habuere rogum cervusque Maronis.

> For his horse snatched away amidst wars
> groans the Parthian, and Molossians have wept for their loyal dogs;
> birds too have had a pyre as well as Maro's [Virgil's] deer.

In his Latin commentary on Statius' *Silvae* the Renaissance scholar Angelo Poliziano explained this puzzling reference to the funeral pyre of a deer belonging to Virgil (Martinelli 1978: 496):

CERVUSQUE MARONIS. Virgilius in VII:

> *Cervus erat forma praestanti et cornibus ingens,*
> *Tyrrhidae pueri quem matris ub ubere raptum*
> *nutribant* etc.

Quamvis apud Virgilium non legatur habuisse hunc cervum rogum, sed verisimile, quippe in quo tantum fuerit momenti ut bellum illud inter Latinos et Troianos concitarit.

MARO'S DEER. Virgil in [*Aeneid*] 7 [483–5]:

> *There was a deer of outstanding appearance with huge horns,*
> *which, after it had been snatched from its mother's breast, the Tyrrhenian boys*
> *used to feed* etc.

Although it may not be read in Virgil that this deer had a funeral pyre, this is effectively true, in that the matter was of so much consequence that it incited the actual war between the Latins and the Trojans.

The conflict triggered by the Trojan Ascanius' inadvertent killing of a pet cherished by the Rutulian princess, *Silvia*, dominates the latter part of the *Aeneid* and leads to funeral fires aplenty. In Virgil's own words, the animal's death 'inflamed the conflict and was the cause of toils' (*Aeneid* 7.481–2). Statius' economical conceit of the pyre of Maro's deer was thereby justified to Poliziano as he was writing in the 1400s. Andrew Marvell's poem 'The Nymph Complaining for the Death of her Fawn' makes a similar association. Composed in the 1650s, Marvell's poem refers allegorically to the English Civil War: the deer lamented by the Nymph was the gift of her admirer who is named *Sylvio* (Muir 1951; Sandstroem 1990). While Marvell's style exhibits a general debt to Statius' *Silvae*, his historical allegory renders more prominent the *Aeneid*'s implicit references to the social and civil wars of Rome—which now preoccupy more recent studies of Virgil.

The capacity of such post-classical readings to illuminate our understanding of ancient sources can be taken further, in quite a specific way, by Poliziano's interpretation of the Statius passage quoted above. His comment does much to justify the reading of *Silvae* 2.6.20 in Q, an important Renaissance manuscript which has been disregarded by modern editors. Without exception those editors present *Silvae* 2.6.20 as follows:

et volucres habuere rogum **cervusque Maronem**
birds too have had a funeral pyre **and the deer [has had] Maro**

a reading first proposed in the nineteenth century by Peter Hofmann Peerlkamp. The sense that the deer had none other than Virgil to commemorate him, 'an unexpectedly pointed semantic variation' (Van Dam 1984: 404), may be appealing, but it is incongruous with the other *exempla* of grief aroused by the animal deaths which Statius assembled to comfort his bereaved addressee: Virgil could commemorate the deer, but he could hardly *mourn* for his own literary creation; the animal's death was more for lamentation by Silvia and the Rutulians in the *Aeneid.*

Poliziano was a shrewd textual critic (he restored the aitches which Catullus had used to comic effect in his poem on Arrius: Haig Gaisser 1993: 67–9). Having collated all the available manuscripts of Statius, Poliziano had seen no need to change *Silvae* 2.6.20 as it stood in Q:

birds too have had a funeral pyre **as well as Maro's deer**

and his remark quoted earlier shows he had already anticipated and dismissed as too literal-minded the objection that there is no actual funeral pyre for the deer in the *Aeneid.* Poliziano's view of the deer's pyre as something 'effectively true' in *Aeneid* 7 foregrounds the link—absent from Peerlkamp's emendation—Virgil had forged between the animal's death and the escalation of war. That was made again by Statius in an epic of his own. In Book 7 of the *Thebaid*, Aconteus' slaughter of Bacchus' tigers by the walls of Thebes infuriates the Thebans, causing them to renew the war with greater force. Similarly, the death of a doe is a harbinger of conflict in the *Punica* (13.115–37), an epic by Statius' contemporary, Silius Italicus.

Artistic engagement with classical culture from more recent centuries inspires broader interpretations of ancient texts, images, and artefacts in ways which go well beyond the confines of textual criticism. Even a patently literary text like 'The Nymph Complaining' has implications for the scholarly reading of Virgil. Marvell's critics have yet to note that his poem alludes to *another* passage from the *Aeneid* involving a deer-hunter, at the point when the Nymph's grief for her fawn gives way to a lament for the false lover who first presented it to her:

But **Sylvio** soon had me **beguiled**
This waxèd tame, while he grew wild,
And quite **regardless** of my smart,
Left me his **fawn** but took his heart.

Silvio the huntsman turns out to have been a seducer who then abandoned and injured his quarry. Although the Nymph's 'smart' is not fatal, her words recall the way Dido was also taken by surprise in Virgil's prefiguration of her blighted love (*Aeneid* 4.69–72):

> . . . qualis coniecta **cerva** sagitta,
> quam procul **incautam** nemora inter Cresia fixit
> **pastor** agens telis **liquit**que volatile ferrum
> **nescius**

like a **deer** struck by an arrow, which a **shepherd** hunting in the Cretan woods with darts pierced from far off as she was **unawares**, and quite **regardless**, **left** in her the winged iron.

As well as Virgil's *Silvia*, the name of Marvell's hunter, *Sylvio*, evokes the *pastor* in Virgil's simile here. What is more, the eponymous 'loyal shepherd' of *Il Pastor Fido* (1590), a popular play by Guarini, was named 'Silvio', as was one of the loyalist shepherds in *A Pastoral Sung to the King* (1600) by Robert Herrick. By so naming the negligent lover, Marvell seems to discern, within Virgil's original simile, an identification of the *pastor* with Aeneas, the lover who won and rejected Dido. Marvell's conjunction of two separate deer-hunting vignettes from the *Aeneid* demonstrates recognition of the recurrent use of this motif in Virgil. Such observations were not made by seventeenth-century commentators any more than they had been in antiquity: early modern scholars instead used comparanda from *other* classical authors to elucidate particular passages of Virgil (Laird 2002). The accumulation of hunting and wounding imagery *within* the *Aeneid* has only recently led to consideration of Medea's injury by Eros' arrow in Apollonius' *Argonautica* epic as a key model for Virgil (Nelis 2001: 125–85; Anderson 2006).

Beyond anticipating the current practice of interpreting the *Aeneid* in the light of its pervasive motifs, Marvell's poem offers two further potential insights on the Roman epic. First, the fawn in 'The Nymph Complaining', which has been identified with both Christ and Charles I, invites consideration of the possibility that Virgil's deer might too be invested with religious and historical significance. A taboo from the Greek Iphigenia myth, in which Agamemnon angered the goddess Artemis by hunting a hind, passed into Roman tradition: before the battle of Sentinum in 295 BCE a soldier in the Roman front-line declared that victory over the Gauls was assured because they had unwisely slaughtered a hind 'sacred to Diana' (Livy 10.27). Secondly, the lighter erotic dimension of 'The Nymph Complaining' could excavate some sentimental, even humorous, aspects of the *Aeneid* which are ignored by modern specialists (with some exceptions: Lloyd 1976–7; Anderson 1980, 1981). A short seventeenth-century English composition can thus extend the range of our responses to the *Aeneid* itself—responses that are relevant to our construction of the climate in which it was first produced.

III

As well as showing how more recent cultural and political history can intersect with the history of scholarship to deepen or correct the reading of an ancient Roman text, the illustrative cluster of authors surveyed above also helps to highlight some central properties of reception:

(i) *Connections between authors, texts, and ideas in reception are infinite.* The exemplary treatment of the hunted deer has involved not only Virgil, Statius, Poliziano, and Marvell, but also Apollonius, Livy, Silius Italicus, Guarini, and Herrick. And this treatment has not been comprehensive: for instance, the reception of the motif could ramify into the legend of Cyparissus:

> This was the one subdued by your halter, Cyparissus.
> Or rather, Silvia, was it that deer of yours?
> (Martial, *Epigrams* 13.96)

Cyparissus, having accidentally killed a deer given to him by Apollo, was transformed by the god into a weeping cypress tree (Ovid, *Met.* 10.106 f.; cf. Connors 1992). The presence of Ovid as well as Virgil may be discerned in *Adonais*, Shelley's homage to Keats, which pictures Adonais as both hunter and victim in the same stanza: 'A herd-abandon'd deer struck by the hunter's dart' grasps a spear 'topped with a cypress cone' (*Adonais* 33). One could go on tracking Virgil's deer, through literature, political discourse, opera (Lotti and Mozart took up the theme of Ascanius and Silvia), visual art (ranging from late antique manuscript illumination to Claude Lorraine's 1682 painting of Ascanius shooting the stag), and cinema (the game-shooting in Michael Cimino's 1978 film *The Deer Hunter* mirrors the trauma of combat in Vietnam). The tangled strings of reception are as potentially endless as etymologies which run through different languages and tie them together.

(ii) *Reception, just like intertextuality, is constituted by the horizons or 'competence' of readers, audiences and spectators.* Reception does not consist of stable and incontestable objects of study. Instead it reflects the inclinations of given 'interpretive communities' (Fish 1980)—inclinations which often amount to prevailing academic protocols. Thus, how far reception actually involves a principle of historical causation is debatable. Virgil's *Aeneid* may be no more historically responsible for engendering the image of the deer in *Adonais* than it is for the lyrics of the Sex Pistols' punk rock-pastoral *Who Killed Bambi?* (1978), which declare war on hippies after the murder of 'the gentle pretty thing who only had one spring'. It is liberating and unsettling to realize that no one instance of reception has any more authority than any other: 'classics can include writing about *Paradise Lost*, or the mythological *poesie* of Titian, or the film *Gladiator*, or the iconography of fascism' (Martindale 2006: 2). And as this statement suggests, conceptions of 'classics' or 'Roman Studies' themselves depend on operations of reception.

(iii) *The current of influence between an ancient text (or artefact) and its evocation in a later time flows in more than one direction.* Like an intertextual relation, interaction between a text and its reappearace in another place and time involves a dynamic two-way movement (cf. Laird 2003: 19; Hardwick 2003: 4). It is also important to realize that this interaction, like intertextuality, is in the eye of the beholder. By presupposing this, current notions of reception differ from that of *Nachleben* ('survival'). The theory of *Nachleben*, developed by the art historian Aby Warburg (1866–1929), offered a *temporal* model for studying motifs and images (Didi-Huberman 2003; Michaud 2004). *Nachleben* represented an advance on previous artistic and literary history which had been grounded in aesthetics. But Warburg's stress on 'survival' presupposed that the ancient text or artefact exerting influence on the cultures of later times itself remained the same. No text or artefact can ever retain a continuous identity through the ages—irrespective of its physical durability and issues of transmission.

That is because the content and significance of a text or artefact are constituted by interpretation. The *Venus de Milo* notoriously changed from being a classical work (hastily attributed to Praxiteles at its discovery in 1820) into a Hellenistic statue (Kousser 2005; Prettjohn 2006). As for the way a Roman text can mutate over time, Virgil's Fourth Eclogue is a striking example. Universally regarded by readers in the Middle Ages as a prophecy of Christ's nativity, this bucolic poem is now believed to hint at the birth of a child of Antony and Octavia (Clausen 1994: 121–2), if not of Octavian and Scribonia. Even so, the long-lasting consensus on the poem's Christian meaning must still have inspired a classicist as sober as Eduard Norden to hold that the Eclogue expressed something analogous to the Messianism of eastern religions (Norden 1924). Norden's view in turn prompted the hypothesis that Virgil drew on Jewish 'Sibylline' oracles (Nisbet 1978). The scholarship on the Fourth Eclogue alone suffices to show how the frantic traffic between antiquity and later phases of reception runs along a dual carriageway.

Investigation of Roman culture in terms of its ancient provenance, its 'original' historical context, cannot be isolated from the study of Rome's later legacies. Any purportedly scientific scrutiny of ancient sources is governed by the effects of modern reception. These effects, which may not be immediately visible, lead to certain emphases and partialities—even in the apparently empirical business of identifying known Greek models for a work of Roman poetry. For example, modern accounts of Greek influences on the *Aeneid* analyse in detail the poem's debt to Homer, to Greek tragedy, and nowadays to Apollonius of Rhodes' *Argonautica*—whilst they largely neglect consideration of pertinent authors in other genres like Pindar, Herodotus, Plato, and the Hellenistic poet Lycophron (cf. Horsfall 1991: 205–6; 2006). A predilection for epic and tragic poetry in the source-criticism of Virgil and other Roman epic poets reflects and further reinforces the confines of recent and contemporary curricula.

As well as biases, there are exclusions in the institutional study of ancient Roman civilization—of subjects (ancient linguistic and metrical theory); of certain kinds of discourse (Latin philosophical dialogue and imperial oratory), historical periods (phases of later antiquity), and of certain authors (Cornelius Nepos, the Augustan didactic poet Manilius, Valerius Maximus) whose contemporaries are subject to far more intensive, and often repetitive, study. It is widely assumed that these exclusions have been made on the basis of informed aesthetic or historical judgements. Yet judgements of either kind are rarely incontrovertible. When they are probed, it becomes very clear that the operation of reception is ultimately responsible for what is or is not visible in today's vistas on Roman culture.

The long history of Classics as a discipline shows the role of reception at its most potent. There was a firmly utilitarian agenda to the gradual formation of what might now be called 'Roman Studies', more than a millenium ago. Classical Latin sources then offered vital practical knowledge which was not otherwise available. Partly in consequence of this, symbolic value was attached to familiarity with Rome's legacies. Thus Latin and the learning which accompanied it functioned as both an emblem and an instrument of power for medieval elites. In a rather more progressive spirit, Renaissance humanists sought to apply insights gained from ancient texts to the art of government and education. Though Greek was certainly championed, humanist political thinking was actually directed by Latin authors, especially Cicero: 'civic humanism' was 'not Florentine, but [ancient] Roman' (Hankins 1995: 329). Classical republicanism has had a long and important legacy, although a more general esteem for Latin and Roman culture turned out to be more pervasive and enduring (Waquet 2000). For example, from the 1880s Indians who passed examinations in Latin could reach higher ranks in the civil service of the British Raj (Majeed 1992, 1999).

These patterns of reception indicate that Roman Studies have never been just about recovering the actuality of the Roman past. Even now, the learning of Latin is promoted by appeals to its general utility and intrinsic value rather than to its indispensability for a better understanding of antiquity, let alone medieval and early modern Europe. The aspiration to emulate and appropriate Roman models did not fizzle out in the Enlightenment: it helped fire patriots in North and South America to secure independence from Europe (Cole, forthcoming; Earle 2002; Laird 2010*b*). The same aspiration was a notorious facet of twentieth-century totalitarianism (Stone 1999; Losemann 1999), and it will never be completely eschewed by those who study the Romans either. Textual criticism has always required its practitioners, however unconscious of this they may be, to *imitate* an ancient author by reconstructing his words. Conjecture, rather than evidence, underlies this purest of scholarly practices. Whatever one makes of W. F. Jackson Knight's decision to seek—through a psychic medium—Virgil's personal advice on his 1956 Penguin translation of the *Aeneid*, it is clear that for this accomplished commentator and historical anthropologist research into Roman antiquity involved something more personal than historical method (Wilson Knight 1975; Wiseman 1992: 209).

The study of Roman antiquity has never been exclusively antiquarian and its methods were sometimes markedly unhistorical—long before the advent of postmodern thinking. However, the debates generated by such recent theory, though valuable, have tended to focus on specific epistemological and methodological questions, without bringing the broader perspective of reception to bear on 'cultural historical' approaches to Roman studies (Fowler 2000; De Jong and Sullivan 1994). Cultural history is supposed to focus on popular traditions: yet the recurrent emphasis laid on canonical literary sources like Virgil, Livy, and Ovid by self-professed Roman cultural historians reveals more about their pedagogical formation in Classics than the reality of their professed domain. It can be conceded that historiography, myth, poetry, and drama, all well reflected in today's curricula, did enjoy popularity in the Roman world (artistic and architectural achievements were prominent too). But legal, oratorical, and astrological discourses exemplify forms of knowledge prevalent in ancient Rome which are under-explored at the present time. And material evidence from archaeology provides much to indicate that Ovid's report of his father's admonishment reflects the real social priorities of the first century BCE: 'Why are you attempting the useless pursuit [of poetry]? | Homer himself left no wealth' (Tristia 4.10.21–2). Fortunately the classical tradition has been more concerned with the poet than his parent.

To regard reception as irrelevant to our apprehension of Roman antiquity is nothing less than a categorical misunderstanding. Conversely, it is unhelpful to see the study of reception as something that has to be opposed to the 'conservative' or 'positivistic' practices of contemporary classical scholarship (*pace* Martindale 2006). Quite simply, reception amounts to interpretation by means of contextualization. Reception is thus something quite different from the technical 'tools' like epigraphy, papyrology, and linguistic analysis surveyed earlier in this volume. And reception is in play—inevitably—before the broader methods or paradigms (e.g. performance, gender, anthropology) outlined in previous chapters can be consciously applied to any area of the field: it is reception which has already determined the *nature* and *selection* of texts, artefacts, and discourses to which apparently empirical approaches may be applied. Reception is thus at the very core of Roman Studies and forces us to interrogate our presuppositions about what they might involve.

IV

Although there had been important precedents in Renaissance Latin humanism, it was *Altertumswissenschaft*, the 'science of antiquity' founded by Friedrich August Wolf (1759–1824), which most definitively systematized the study of the ancient past. How that systematizing should be done, what fields should be prioritized, needless to say, continue to remain difficult questions. Nonetheless, the fundamental position that the principal purpose of classical studies was to uncover and understand the world of antiquity has become orthodoxy, even if it is not always adopted wholesale in practice.

Barring onslaughts from the aporetic perspective of deconstruction (e.g. Kennedy 1992) and, more convincingly, on the basis of Rortian neo-pragmatism (Fowler 2000), the view that classical studies involves recovering knowledge of antiquity can accommodate a wide range of contemporary theories and methodologies. However, there is no room for *reception* in a model for classical studies which posits the historical reality of the Greco-Roman world as its primary object. That is unfortunate because the study of reception exposes a long-standing flaw in that model: the exclusion of Jews, Egyptians, Persians, and other civilized peoples from the domain of *Altertumswissenschaft* as it was originally defined by Wolf (Grafton 1999). This exclusion is something subsequent scholarly and educational practice has done little to rectify. Wolf's definition also led to the unchecked growth of a fundamental misconception about the place of Roman culture in relation to that of Greece and to the ancient world as a whole.

The artificial priority given to Greece and Rome in nineteenth-century Germany has given an exaggerated impression of an essential parallelism between the two civilizations, compounded by the Plutarchan Greek-to-Roman correspondence which is a standard feature of syllabuses and programmes in Classics. That impression has been further reinforced by the fact that far fewer humanities students nowadays have the acquaintance with the Judaic tradition that was not so long ago afforded by a Christian theological training. Although Egypt, Persia, and Arabia never loomed large in western education, at least there used to be three ancient Mediterranean cultures in play—now there are only two. So when the Greek and Roman civilizations are thus set side by side, isolated from their broader context in the region's history and from their respective receptions in later cultures, cold comparison between them is almost bound to be injurious to Rome. That contrived pairing plays into all the clichés of German and English Romantic Hellenism: the superiority of Homer to Virgil, Plato to Cicero, democracy to empire, Greek sculpture to Roman statuary, inspired originality to unimaginative imitation. In short, 'the glory that was Greece' comes to surpass 'the grandeur that was Rome' (Poe 1831).

But once reception comes into play things change drastically. The languages and ideas of Rome and Greece were more in constant interaction than in parallel. Even now Homer would count for very little without the mediation of a colossal figure like Virgil and his Roman imperial imitators (not to mention later European poets like Dante, Petrarch, Camoens, and Milton). Cicero did more than import philosophical and rhetorical categories into Italy: no Greek source offers so full and systematic a picture of the diversity of Hellenic thought as the one afforded by Cicero's scepticism. And Rome's absorption of Stoic 'cosmopolitanism' in tandem with the short-lived democracy of the early Republic offers a possibly more credible and palpably influential set of connections beween philosophical ideals and political practice than the Athenian system (Hankins 1995, 2000). The fundamental, underlying point here is that in one crucial respect Romans showed more profound originality than the Greeks, Persians, and Egyptians—by *deliberately* accommodating the languages and ideas of other peoples from the very beginning of their civilization. The Romans invented and thrived on this process. The first reception of Greek culture was Roman, and in effect Greek culture itself, very early on, became Roman. And, as our view of the Empire extends past the Julio-Claudian dynasty to the Second Sophistic period and beyond, it is very clear indeed that Greek culture remained Roman (Bowersock 1969; Swain 1996; Adams, Janse, and Swain 2002; Reynolds and Wilson 1991).

Yet Rome's considerable interference in Greek history has been invisible to modern eyes for a long time. Johann Joachim Winckelmann (1717–68), a champion of Neoclassical Hellenism, was led by Roman copies of Greek statues to discern the aesthetic ideal in Greek sculpture (Potts 1994). Mainstream Hellenic Studies still present the Greeks 'in a vat', much in the way Evans-Pritchard sought to describe the Azande—and a variety of anthropological approaches applied by Dodds, Burkert, Vernant, and others to ancient Greek culture may have unintentionally contributed to a specious sense of its uniqueness and independence. Whilst interest in the later influence of Greece continues to grow, with some exceptions (e.g. Silk 2000), it is rarely used to interpret ancient texts directly. Moreover the study of Greek reception is very selective: it is seldom acknowledged that the ancient Greek text which has had most diffusion after antiquity was not Homer but the translated books of the Greek Old Testament known as the Septuagint.

Roman studies are different. Cross-cultural comparisons, the inclusion of Greek material, and accommodation of periods after antiquity do not threaten the field, but constitute it. There is another reason why reception might be germane to the study of Roman literature in particular. Latin poetry and drama regularly showed a reflexivity and self-consciousness about its dynamic appropriations (*aemulatio*) of Greek models, amounting to a theory of reception (Jaeger 1939; Hardwick 2003: 12–31). This Roman 'theory' was recurrently articulated in terms of identification with *individuals*: following a cue from the Alexandrian Callimachus, the poet Ennius dreamt that Homer's soul was reborn as his own; Catullus (poem 51) puts his own name to a Latinized expression of Sappho's intense desire; Virgil becomes a Hesiod singing through 'Roman towns' of Cisalpine Gaul (*Georgics* 2.176); Propertius (3.1) invokes Callimachus' own spirit... To this day the study of Latin literature remains author-centred and overall Roman studies are markedly more prosopographical in nature than Greek. Ovid, however, addresses the anxiety of *imitatio* in another way by remarking that the two-headed deity of new transitions and new beginnings, simultaneously looking forward to the future and back to the past, is exclusively Roman (*Fasti* 1.89–90):

> Which god shall I say you are, Janus, with your double shape?
> For Greece has no divinity like you.

Such intimations from the Romans themselves—along with the extraordinary longevity and complexity of Rome's metahistory after antiquity (Greece appeared only later after all)—explain why classical Latinists and Roman historians instinctively involve the traffic of reception to and from Rome in their work.

V

The aim of this chapter has been to show that reception is far more than something ancillary to Roman Studies: it is a central precondition for their existence. To affirm that reception *is* Roman Studies is no exaggeration. At the same time, reception is not limited to certain periods and places, nor confined to the arts and literature (let alone to high culture). Reception is bound to involve controversy at a fundamental level: should the era known as 'late antiquity', for example, be regarded as the tail-end of classical Rome or as the period in which Rome's afterlife begins? (see e.g. Rees 2003). Whichever answer one gives will provoke further debate (cf. Horace, *Epistles* 2.1.19–49).

And reception never involves unmediated interaction with antiquity. The classical allusions in *The Emperor's Babe* (1997), Bernadine Evaristo's verse romance about a Sudanese 'It-girl' in Roman London, are probably less significant than the precedent of Evelyn Waugh's *Helena* (1950), a novella about the emperor Constantine's British-born mother. But it may be much less obvious that our impressions of an ancient source—even one freshly discovered—cannot be unmediated either. Our own traditions of knowledge are what render the words of a familiar ancient author visible in the sparsest of papyrus fragments (see e.g. Obbink 2007: 34–7). Reception can never be divorced from the history of scholarship—and both these examples again confirm that every field of reception is constituted by the eye of the beholder.

Connections between selected ancient sources and selected target texts can always be demonstrated. A thorough study of Astérix in relation to the *Gallic Wars* or of Marguerite Yourcenar's *Les Mémoires d'Hadrien* may be dutifully offered as evidence of the abiding influence of Rome and its Caesars, even if such evidence is not really necessary or interesting (*pace* Hardwick 2003: 113). Far more significant—and far more in need of scrutiny in the future—is the basis for selecting a given field of reception in the first place. That selection will of course reveal, more than it reveals anything else, a lot about the priorities (if not the capabilities!) of an individual student or scholar. These priorities are hardly ever just personal. Educational, institutional, linguistic, even national determinations and constraints all play a part. Hence it is no surprise to find that a current Oxford University course on 'The Reception of Greece and Rome in Twentieth-Century Poetry' makes reference only to twentieth-century poetry in *English.* But it has always been possible to break the mould of inherited traditions. An Aztec relative of Montezuma, in the hope of regaining the title to his ancestral property, wrote a series of letters in elegant classical Latin to the king of Spain in the mid-1500s, quoting Ovid and Justinian and alluding to Horace and Lucan (Laird 2010*a*). These documents showed that Roman civilization had advanced into a startlingly new domain, and no doubt they were suppressed partly for that reason. Even now, in an academic climate which affects to champion ethnic diversity, such texts offer a powerful challenge to the way Roman Studies are currently conceived.

Of course, British people will justify laying emphasis on Roman reception in Britain on the basis that it is natural to concentrate on one's own heritage. Similar justifications will be employed, *mutatis mutandis*, for France, Germany, and Italy—and indeed for Europe as a whole (although important interactions with Rome in, for example, Ireland, Catalonia, and Portugal are overlooked: Coroleu 2007; Harris and Sidwell 2009; Quint 1993: 99–131). At the same time, the more one affirms the centrality of one's own tradition, the more one risks becoming parochial, if not chauvinistic, in a multicultural world. Britain, France, Germany, and Italy all have sizeable Arabic-speaking populations, yet few classicists in those countries are aware that a Latin translation of the Koran commissioned in 1142 enjoyed diffusion all over Europe, and fewer still realize that Roman as well as Greek studies played a prominent part in the Arab *Naḍha* or 'cultural awakening' during the past century (Pym 2000; Pormann 2006–7).

Given that the daunting range of Rome's influence—in the western world at least—appears to be almost as large as life itself, reception can go anywhere. Is it possible to identify the directions it *should* take in the future? That is not a methodological question but a moral one. The contradictions of globalization invite us to interrogate the significance, value, and centrality of Rome's ever-growing and ever-changing legacy. This can partly be done by recognizing the depth and sophistication of dialogues with Rome that have taken place in ages, places, and languages (including later Latin) other than our own. It may now be time to look outside the anglophone world and the Mediterranean in order to follow Virgil's stag beyond the Pillars of Hercules.

Further reading

Maclean 1986 introduces reception and reader-response theory (cf. Schmitz 2007: 86–97); Machor and Goldstein 2001 offers fuller coverage. For theory of *classical* reception, Hardwick 2003, Hardwick and Stray 2008, and Martindale and Thomas 2006 are orientations; Fowler 2000 and Martindale 1993 and 2005 are polemical discussions grounded in Latin literature. Edwards 1999, Bailey 1923, and Jenkyns 1992 treat Rome's reception, as do 'Cambridge Companion' volumes on Roman authors or subjects. Bolgar 1954, Highet 1953, and Kallendorf 2006 survey the 'classical tradition': *CML*, *IJCT*, *JWCI*, and *Traditio* are relevant journals. Conte 1994 has thirty articles by Glenn Most on reception of individual Latin authors—see further Carver 2008, Gaisser 2008 on Apuleius; Gaisser 1993 on Catullus; Vickers 1989 and Kraye 1996 on Cicero; Martindale and Hopkins 1993 on Horace; Norbrook 1994 and 1999 on Lucan, Bergson 1959 on Lucretius; Martindale 1990, Hardie, Hinds, and Barchiesi 1999 and Coroleu and Taylor 2008 on Ovid; Comber 1998 on Propertius; Miola 1992 on Seneca; Skoie 2002 on Sulpicia; Luce and Woodman 1993 and Rubiés 1994 on Tacitus. For Virgil: the *Enciclopedia Virgiliana*, *PVS*, *Vergilius*, Comparetti 1997, Zabughin 1921–3, Chevallier 1978, Farrell and Putnam 2010, Kallendorf 1989, Martindale 1984, Rees 2003, Thomas 2001; Putnam and Ziolkowski 2008. Godman 1987 treats the Carolingian Renaissance; Curtius 1953 surveys medieval and later literary history; Baxandall 1986, Caruso and Laird (forthcoming), Hankins 2000, Kraye 1996, and McLaughlin 1995 treat aspects of Rome's pervasive influence in the Italian Renaissance. Cole (forthcoming), Haase and Reinhold 1993, Lupher 2003, and MacCormack 2007 offer perspectives on the colonial Americas. Goff 2005, Edwards 1999, and Stephens and Vasunia (2010) appraise the nineteenth and twentieth centuries. On film: Winkler 2001, Wyke 1997. Godman and Murray 1990, Ijsewijn 1990, Haskell and Ruys 2007, Laird 2006*b*, and *Humanistica Lovaniensia* convey the wide range and reach of Latin after Rome.

References

Adams, J. N., Janse, M., and Swain, S. (eds.) (2002), *Bilingualism in Ancient Society: Language Contact and the Written Text* (Oxford).

Anderson, W. (1980), 'Vergil, the best in the world for the tragical-comical-historical-pastoral', *Vergilius*, 26: 10–17.

—— (1981), 'Servius and the Comic Style of the *Aeneid*', *Arethusa*, 14: 115–25.

—— (2006), 'The Hunts of Books 4 and 7', *Classical World*, 99/2: 157–65.

Bailey, C. (ed.) (1923), *The Legacy of Rome* (Oxford).

Bakhtin, M. M. (1986), 'The Problem of the Text in Linguistics, Philology, and the Human Sciences: An Experiment in Philosophical Analysis', in *Speech Genres and Other Late Essays* (Austin, Tex.), 103–31.

Baron, H. (1955), *The Crisis of the Early Italian Renaissance: Civic Humanism and Republican Liberty in an Age of Classicism and Tyranny* (Princeton).

Baxandall, M. (1986), *Giotto and the Orators: Humanist Observers of Painting in Italy and the Discovery of Pictorial Composition 1350–1450* (Oxford).

Bergson, H. (1959), *Philosophy of Poetry: The Genius of Lucretius*, tr. W. Baskin (New York).

Bolgar, R. R. (1954), *The Classical Heritage and its Beneficiaries* (Cambridge).

Bowersock, G. (1969), *Greek Sophists in the Roman Empire* (Oxford).

Budelmann, F. and Haubold, J. (2008), 'Reception and Tradition', in Hardwick and Stray 2008: 13–25.

Caruso, C. and Laird, A. (eds.) (2009), *Italy and the Classical Tradition: Language, Thought, and Poetry* (London).

Carver, R. (2008), *The Protean Ass: The Metamorphoses of Apuleius from Antiquity to the Renaissance* (Oxford).

Chevallier, R. (ed.) (1978), *Présence de Virgile: actes du colloque des 9, 11 et 12 décembere 1976 (Paris ENS, Tours)* (Paris).

Clausen, W. (1994), *A Commentary on Virgil, Eclogues* (Oxford).

Cole, N. (forthcoming), *The Ancient World in Thomas Jefferson's America* (Oxford).

Comber, M. (1998), 'A Book Made New: Reading Propertius Reading Pound. A Study in Reception', *JRS* 88: 37–55.

Comparetti, D. (1997), *Virgil in the Middle Ages* (Princeton) (Italian original 1885).

Connors, C. (1992), 'Seeing Cypresses in Virgil', *Classical Journal*, 88/1 (Oct.–Nov.): 1–17.

Conte, G. B. (1994), *Latin Literature: A History*, tr. J. B. Solodow (Baltimore and London).

Coroleu, A. (2007), 'Classical Scholarship, Cultural Prestige and National Identity in Modern Catalonia', review of J. Malé, R. Cabré, and M. Jufresa (eds.), *Del Romanticisme al Noucentisme: els grans mestres de la Filologia Catalana i la Filologia Clàsica a la Universitat de Barcelona*, Barcelona, 2004, *International Journal of the Classical Tradition*, 13/4 (Spring): 608–12.

—— and Taylor, B. (eds.) (2008), *Ovid in Renaissance Spain: Latin and Vernacular in Renaissance Spain III* (Manchester).

Curtius, E. R. (1953), *European Literature and the Latin Middle Ages*, tr. W. R. Trask (London; German orig. 1948).

De Jong, I. J. F. and Sullivan, J. P. (eds.) (1994), *Modern Critical Theory and Classical Literature* (*Mnemosyne* Supplement 130) (Leiden).

Didi-Huberman, G. (2003), 'Artistic Survival: Panofsky vs. Warburg and the Exorcism of Impure Time', *Common Knowledge*, 9/2 (Spring): 273–85.

Earle, R. (2002), '"Padres de la Patria" and the Ancestral Past: Commemorations of Independence in Nineteenth-Century Spanish America', *Journal of Latin American Studies*, 34: 775–805.

Edwards, C. (1999), *Roman Presences: Receptions of Rome in European Culture, 1789–1945* (Cambridge and New York).

Evaristo, B. (1997), *The Emperor's Babe* (London).

Farrell, J. and Putnam, M. C. J. (eds.) (2010), *A Companion to Vergil's Aeneid and It's Tradition* (Oxford).

Fish, S. (1980), *Is There a Text in This Class? The Authority of Interpretive Communities* (Cambridge, Mass.).

Flam, J. D. (ed.) (1973), *Matisse on Art* (New York).

Fowler, D. P. (2000), *Roman Constructions: Readings in Postmodern Latin* (Oxford).

Gaisser, J. H. (1993), *Catullus and his Renaissance Readers* (Oxford).

—— (2008), *The Fortunes of Apuleius and the Golden Ass: A Study in Transmission and Reception* (Princeton).

Godman, P. (1987), *Poets and Emperors: Frankish politics and Carolingian Poetry* (Oxford).

—— and Murray, O. (eds.) (1990), *Latin Poetry and the Classical Tradition: Essays in Medieval and Renaissance Literature* (Oxford).

Goff, B. (ed.) (2005), *Classics and Colonialism* (London).

Grafton, A. (1999), 'Juden und Griechen bei Friedrich August Wolf', in R. Markner and G. Veltri, *Friedrich August Wolf: Studien, Dokumente, Bibliographie, Palingenesia*, 67 (Stuttgart), 9–31.

Haase, W. and Reinhold, M. (eds.) (1993), *The Classical Tradition and the Americas: European Images of the Americas and the Classical Tradition*, Part 1 (Berlin).

Hankins, J. (1995), 'The "Baron Thesis" after Forty Years and Some Recent Studies of Leonardo Bruni', *Journal of the History of Ideas*, 56/2 (April): 309–38.

—— (ed.) (2000), *Renaissance Civic Humanism: Reappraisals and Reflections* (Cambridge).

Hardie, P., Hinds, S., and Barchiesi, A. (eds.) (1999), *Ovidian Transformations: Essays on Ovid's Metamorphoses and its Reception*, Cambridge Philological Society Supplementary vol. 23 (Cambridge).

Hardwick, L. (2003), *Reception Studies*, New Surveys in the Classics 33, *Greece & Rome* (Oxford).

—— and Stray, C. (eds.) (2008), *A Companion to Classical Receptions* (Oxford).

Harris, J. and Sidwell, K. (2009), *Making Ireland Rome: Irish Neo-Latin Writers and the Republic of Letters* (University of Cork Press).

Haskell, Y. and Ruys, J. (eds.) (2010), *Latin and Alterity in the Early Modern Period* (*Medieval and Renaissance Texts and Studies*) (Tempe, Ariz.).

Highet, G. (1953), *The Classical Tradition: Greek and Roman Influences on Western Literature* (Oxford).

Horsfall, N. (1991), 'Virgil and the Poetry of Explanations', *Greece & Rome*, 38/2 (Oct.): 203–11.

—— (2006), 'Lycophron and the *Aeneid*, Again', *Ancient World and Archeology* (Saratov), 12: 436–9 [in Russian, summary in English].

IJsewijn, J. (ed.) (1990), *Companion to Neo-Latin Studies*, 2 vols. (Louvain).

Iser, W. (1978), *The Act of Reading: A Theory of Aesthetic Response* (Baltimore).

Jaeger, W. (1939), *Paideia: The Ideals of Greek Culture* (New York).

Jauss, H. R. (1982), *Toward an Aesthetic of Reception*, tr. T. Bahti (Minneapolis).

Jenkyns, R. (ed.) (1992), *The Legacy of Rome* (Oxford).

Kallendorf, C. (1989), *In Praise of Aeneas: Virgil and Epideictic Rhetoric in the Early Italian Renaissance* (Hanover and London).

—— (ed.) (2006), *The Blackwell Companion to the Classical Tradition* (Oxford).

Kennedy, D. (1992), '"Augustan" and "Anti-Augustan": Reflections on Terms of Reference', in A. Powell (ed.), *Roman Poetry and Propaganda in the Age of Augustus* (Bristol), 26–58.

Kennon, D. R. and Somma, T. P. (ed.) (2004), *American Pantheon: Sculptural and Artistic Decoration of the United States Capitol* (Athens, Ohio).

Kousser, R. (2005), 'Creating the Past: The Vénus de Milo and the Hellenistic Reception of Classical Greece', *American Journal of Archeology*, 109/2: 227–50.
Kraye, J. (1996), *Cambridge Companion to Renaissance Humanism* (Cambridge).
Laird, A. (1999), *Powers of Expression, Expressions of Power* (Oxford).
—— (2002), 'Virgil, Juan Luis de La Cerda and the Predicament of Commentary', in C. Kraus and R. Gibson (eds.), *The Classical Commentary* (Leiden), 171–204.
—— (2003), 'Roman Epic Theatre? Reception, Performance and the Poet in Virgil's *Aeneid*', *Proceedings of the Cambridge Philological Society*, 49: 19–39.
—— (2006*a*), 'The Value of Ancient Literary Criticism', in A. Laird (ed.), *Ancient Literary Criticism* (Oxford), 1–36.
—— (2006*b*), *The Epic of America: An Introduction to Rafeal Landívar and the Rusticatio Mexicana* (London).
—— (2010*a*), 'Latin in Cuauhtémoc's Shadow', in Haskell and Ruys 2010.
—— (2010*b*), 'The Cosmic Race and a Heap of Broken Images', in Stephens and Vasunia (2010).
Lloyd, R. B. (1976–7), 'Humor in the *Aeneid*', *Classical Journal*, 72: 250–7.
Losemann, V. (1999), 'The Nazi Concept of Rome', in Edwards 1999: 221–35.
Luce, T. J. and Woodman, A. J. (ed.) (1993), *Tacitus and the Tacitean Tradition* (Princeton).
Lupher, D. (2003), *Romans in a New World: Classical Models in Sixteenth-century Spanish America* (Ann Arbor, Mich.).
MacCormack, S. (2007), *On the Wings of Time: Rome, the Incas, Spain, and Peru* (Princeton).
Machor, L. and Goldstein, P. (eds.) (2001), *Reception Study: From Literary Theory to Cultural Studies* (London and New York).
McLaughlin, M. L. (1995), *Literary Imitation in the Italian Renaissance* (Oxford).
Maclean, I. (1986), 'Reading and Interpretation', in A. Jefferson and D. Robey (eds.), *Modern Literary Theory: A Comparative Introduction* (London), 122–44.
Majeed, J. (1992), *Ungoverned Imaginings: James Mill's 'The History of British India' and Orientalism* (Oxford).
—— (1999), 'Comparativism and References to Rome in British Imperial Attitudes to India', in Edwards 1999: 88–109.
Martindale, C. (1993), *Redeeming the Text: Latin Poetry and the Hermeneutics of Reception* (Cambridge).
—— (1996), 'Reception', in *Oxford Classical Dictionary*[3] (Oxford), 1294.
—— (2005), *Latin Poetry and the Judgement of Taste* (Oxford).
—— (2006), 'Introduction: Thinking Through Reception', in Martindale and Thomas 2006: 1–13.
—— (ed.) (1984), *Virgil and his Influence* (Bristol).
—— (ed.) (1990), *Ovid Renewed* (Cambridge).
—— and Hopkins, D. (ed.) (1993), *Horace Made New: Horatian Influences on British Writing from the Renaissance to the Twentieth Century* (Cambridge).
—— and Thomas, R. (ed.) (2006), *Classics and the Uses of Reception* (Oxford).
Martinelli, L. (ed.) (1978), *Angelo Poliziano. Commento inedito alle Selve di Stazio* (Florence).
Michaud, P. (2004), *Aby Warburg and the Image in Motion* (New York).
Miola, R. S. (1992), *Shakespeare and Classical Tragedy: The Influence of Seneca* (Oxford).
Muir, K (1951), 'A Virgilian Echo in Marvell', *Notes and Queries*, 196: 115.

Nelis, D. (2001), *Vergil's Aeneid and the Argonautica of Apollonius Rhodius* (Leeds).

Nisbet, R. G. M. (1978), 'Virgil's Fourth Eclogue: Easterners and Westerners', *BICS* 25: 59–78.

Norbrook, D. (1994), 'Lucan, Thomas May, and the Creation of a Republican Literary Culture', in K. Sharpe and P. Lake (eds.), *Culture and Politics in Early Stuart England* (London), 45–66.

—— (1999), *Writing the English Republic: Poetry, Rhetoric and Politics, 1627–1660* (Cambridge).

Norden, E. (1924), *Die Geburt des Kindes* (Leipzig).

Obbink, D. (2007), 'Lucretius and the Herculaneum Library', in S. Gillespie and P. Hardie (eds.), *The Cambridge Companion to Lucretius* (Cambridge), 33–40.

Poe, E. A. (1986), 'To Helen' (1831), in *The Fall of of the House of Usher and Other Writings* (Harmondsworth), 68.

Pormann, P. (2006–7), 'The Arab "Cultural Awakening (Naḍha)", 1870–1950, and the Classical Tradition', *International Journal of the Classical Tradition*, 13: 3–20.

Potts, A. (1994), *Flesh and the Ideal: Winckelmann and the Origins of Art History* (New Haven).

Prettjohn, E. (2006), 'Reception and Ancient Art: The Case of the Venus de Milo', in Martindale and Thomas 2006: 227–49.

Putnam, M., and Ziolkowski, I. (2008), *The Virgilian Tradition: The First Fifteen Hundred Years* (New Haven and London).

Pym, A. (2000), *Negotiating the Frontier: Translators and Intercultures in Hispanic History* (Manchester).

Quint, D. (1993), *Epic and Empire: Politics and Generic Form from Virgil to Milton* (Princeton).

Rees, R. (2003), *Romane Memento: Vergil in the Fourth Century* (London).

Reynolds, L. D. and Wilson, N. G. (1991), *Scribes and Scholars: A Guide to the Transmission of Greek and Latin Literature* (Oxford).

Rubies, J.-P. (1994), 'Nero in Tacitus and Nero in Tacitism: The Historian's Craft', in J. Elsner and J. Masters (eds.), *Reflections of Nero: Culture, History and Representation* (London), 29–47.

Sandstroem, Y. (1990), 'Marvell's "Nymph Complaining" as Historical Allegory', *Studies in English Literature* (Winter), 30/1: 93–114.

Schmitz, T. (2007), *Modern Literary Theory and Ancient Texts* (Oxford).

Silk, M. S. (2000), *Aristophanes and the Definition of Comedy* (Oxford).

Skoie, M. (2002), *Reading Sulpicia: Commentaries 1475–1990* (Oxford).

Stephens, S. and Vasunia, P. (eds.) (2010), *Classics and National Cultures* (Oxford).

Stone, M. (1999), 'A Flexible Rome: Fascism and the Cult of *Romanità*', in Edwards 1999: 205–20.

Swain, S. (1996), *Hellenism and Empire: Language, Classicism, and Power in the Greek World AD 50–250* (Oxford).

Thomas, R. F. (2001), *Virgil and the Augustan Reception* (Cambridge).

Van Dam, H.-J. (1984), *Statius, Silvae Book II: A Commentary* (Leiden).

Vickers, B. (1989), *In Defence of Rhetoric* (Oxford).

Visser, R. (1992), 'Fascist Doctrine and the Cult of the *Romanità*', *Journal of Contemporary History*, 27/1 (Jan.): 5–22.

Waquet, F. (2001), *Latin or the Empire of a Sign* (London).

Waugh, E. (1950), *Helena* (London).
Wilson Knight, G. (1975), *Jackson Knight—A Biography* (Oxford).
Winkler, M. (2001), *Classical Myth and Culture in the Cinema* (Oxford).
Wiseman, T. P. (1992), *Talking to Virgil: A Miscellany* (Exeter).
Wyke, M. (1997), *Projecting the Past: Ancient Rome, Cinema and History* (New York).
Yourcenar, M. (1951), *Mémoires d'Hadrien* (Paris).
Zabughin, V. (1921–3), *Vergilio nel rinascimento italiano da Dante a Torquato Tasso*, 2 vols. (Bologna).

CHAPTER 22

BETWEEN FORMALISM AND HISTORICISM

STEPHEN HINDS[1]

O Attic shape! Fair attitude! with brede
  Of marble men and maidens overwrought,
With forest branches and the trodden weed;
  Thou, silent form, dost tease us out of thought
As doth eternity: Cold Pastoral!
  When old age shall this generation waste,
    Thou shalt remain, in midst of other woe
  Than ours, a friend to man, to whom thou say'st,
Beauty is truth, truth beauty,—that is all
    Ye know on earth, and all ye need to know.

(Keats, 'Ode on a Grecian Urn', st. 5)

Conflicts between formal or stylistic analysis and historical scholarship are a traditional problem in literary studies.

(Jerome McGann, 'Keats and the Historical Method in Literary Criticism', 988)

[1] The author owes a debt of gratitude to the graduate student organizers of and participants in an April 2008 conference on Historicisms and Formalisms in the Department of Classics, Princeton University, in the collaborative context of which many of the ideas in this chapter took shape.

Unpacking the Urn

Certain canonical texts can become programmatically associated with certain issues in literary criticism. My first epigraph invokes not just the 'Grecian Urn' of Keats (1820) but *The Well Wrought Urn* of Cleanth Brooks (1947), an icon of the so-called 'new criticism', and a manifesto for an influential Anglo-American version of formalism associated with the practice of 'close reading'. Brooks's title-phrase is drawn not in the first instance from Keats but from Donne (*The Canonization*): his book's plot ('the urn... is the poem itself', 1947: 20–1) mobilizes a series of readings tightly focused upon formal and artistic structure to bring together poems and poetic urns from Shakespeare to Donne to Keats and beyond. My second epigraph, the opening sentence of a 1979 essay by Jerome McGann, points to the enduring tendency (reductive of any actual critical position, including that of Brooks, but still useful to think with) for historicism to be identified as the natural opposite of formalism; the essay's title illustrates the persistence of Keatsian terms in the discussion.

In the context of a sketch for a handbook (and not a handbook of modern literary studies, at that), and with some consequent diminishment of the responsibility to acknowledge all the intellectual-historical currents which might betray such a narrative as a simplification, a little follow-up quotation may be allowed to suggest a generational oscillation in perceptions of critical imbalance in this area—from the beleaguered formalist of the late 1940s, 'We have had impressed upon us the necessity for reading a poem in terms of its historical context, and that kind of reading has been carried on so successfully that some of us have been tempted to feel that it is the only kind of reading possible' (Brooks 1947: p. x), to the beleaguered historicist of the late 1970s: 'A text-only approach has been so vigorously promoted during the last thirty-five years that most historical critics have been driven from the field...' (McGann 1979: 988).

In the set-up of *The Well Wrought Urn*, the use of the word 'merely' is perhaps even more of a provocation to the critical and institutional sensibilities of our time than it was in 1947: 'If poetry exists as poetry in any meaningful sense, the attempt [to view it *sub specie aeternitatis*] must be made. Otherwise the poetry of the past becomes significant merely as cultural anthropology, and the poetry of the present, merely as a political or religious, or moral instrument' (Brooks 1947: pp. x–xi). Contrast the opposite but equally non-negotiable bottom line in 1979 (after one of critical theory's longest and busiest generations): 'The historical method—and specifically a sociological poetics—must be recognized not only as relevant... but in fact as central to... the study of the so called "purely poetic" or "intrinsic" aspects of literature' (McGann 1979: 1025). And now? After another long generation, in which the sociological tendency has arguably carried the day in many visible arenas of literary studies, it would be easy to continue this simplified doxography by tuning into new cries of oppression from the other side: in response to a period of institutional dominance by various and genealogically distinct versions of 'new historicism' and 'cultural materialism', the stage is set for various kinds of 'text-only' formalism to (re)assert their claims.

So do we keep coming back to the same point in the argument? Well, no. The risk of schematizing the opposition between formalism and historicism as I have just done (even, or especially, as a caricature of critical practice in another field) is that it may lend aid and comfort to a post-theoretical position ready to see these and other critical '-isms' as mutually self-cancelling. Rather, the schematization should be treated as heuristic: the fact is that movements of critical thinking *between* formalism and historicism, along with the ceaseless interrogation of the two polar terms themselves, may fairly be said to define the range of possibility within which all literary reading occurs; a way of thinking hardly foreign to Keats's 'Ode on a Grecian Urn' itself, with its richly self-reflexive meditations on history, aesthetics, and the memorialization of human experience. Thus, in the particular nexus under discussion here, if McGann's capsule treatment of the 'Ode' (1979: 1008–11) opens with a provocative feint towards rehabilitation of the old-style historicist quest for the urn's 'original' in the actual antiquarian collections of early nineteenth-century Europe (a quest long derided in formalist interpretations), it soon moves to a more subtle and more textually implicated version of historicism, in which the connoisseurship question is reformulated in terms of a more tangible historical context, namely the decision by Keats to publish the poem first in the *Annals of the Fine Arts*.

Now, despite its use of the Keatsian introduction, this essay is a rough guide not to formalism and historicism *tout court*, but to formalism and historicism as categories for use by readers of Roman texts. Part of my aim below is to test the relationship between these terms in the particular disciplinary context of Classics; and this may turn out to yield an oblique *intradisciplinary* justification (if one is needed) for my opening citation.

For the fact is that Keats's 'Grecian Urn' has never felt so much like one of *our* texts. The students of the Greco-Roman world addressed in the present volume will regard eighteenth- and nineteenth-century versions of Hellenism and classicism as legitimate objects of study both in themselves and as part of a chain of receptions which constructs *us* as readers of our ancient texts: so that (as we mine Keats's 'Ode' for our disciplinary purposes) our sense of—say—the Greek lyric voice, of ancient pastoral, of the Platonic Forms, of Homeric and post-Homeric ecphrasis, may all not only find reflection in Keats's poem, but be partly *constituted*, for a post-Romantic reader of the Classics, *by* Keats's poem.

And meanwhile, as it enters our critical discussions, a case can be made that, in the English departments down the corridor from us, the Urn's long-standing claim to centrality is under some threat. In a reinvented discipline of English, in which not just the poetic canon but the literary text itself is increasingly displaced from the centre of critical activity, the question may seem to be not so much *how* to inflect the latest '-ism' in Keatsian terms as *whether* it is helpful to inflect it in Keatsian terms at all. In other words, it is no longer clear that in a discussion of formalisms and historicisms Keats would have a guaranteed seat at the table—save in his own sub-field of English Romanticism. Is a comparable shift in the critical canon imaginable in our field? I think not: but the point at issue is an interesting one, and may bear on what follows.

Perusia: History as Text

It is customary to remark on the proliferation of unanswered questions in 'Ode on a Grecian Urn'. In Stanza 1:

> What leaf-fringed legend . . . ?
> What men or gods . . . ? What maidens loth?
> What mad pursuit? What struggle to escape?
> What pipes and timbrels? What wild ecstasy?

Except for some special pleading in the case of the first question (McGann 1979: 1010), no answers supplied. Or in Stanza 4:

> Who are these coming to the sacrifice?
> To what green altar, O mysterious priest,
> Lead'st thou that heifer . . . ?
> What little town by river or sea shore . . . ?

Again (and despite the arguable image of the Elgin Marbles behind the heifer: Beard 2003: 17), no answers supplied. One of the effects of the strongly advertised timelessness and placelessness of Keats's 'Ode' is simultaneously to attract and to frustrate those readers who *want* to adduce some historical specifics, whether in terms of the times and places described on the urn, or in terms of the times and places of the poem's production and reception. The fact that the 'Ode' ends in the penultimate line with an answer, but not (on the face of it) an answer to any of the questions asked, and an answer which is then said (whether in the voice of the poet or of the urn itself) to disallow any and all preceding questions, adds to the poem's teasing refusal of inquiry—*historia*—and indeed of historicism:

> Beauty is truth, truth beauty,—that is all
> Ye know on earth, and all ye need to know.

The poem ends on a note of formalism, even of upper-case Platonic Form-alism, so that a historicist reading will in some sense be a reading against the grain.

Now, conversely (to leave Keats behind at last), Propertius 1.21 looks at first sight like a poem hospitable to a reading attuned to historical specifics—all the more so in its contrast with the normal expectations of the sometimes dehistoricized genre of Augustan erotic elegy (Veyne 1988, tendentiously; cf. Kennedy 1993: 90–100):

tu, qui consortem properas evadere casum,
  miles ab Etruscis saucius aggeribus,
quid nostro gemitu turgentia lumina torques?
  pars ego sum vestrae proxima militiae.
sic te servato possint gaudere parentes,
  haec soror acta tuis sentiat e lacrimis:
Gallum per medios ereptum Caesaris enses
  effugere ignotas non potuisse manus;
et quaecumque super dispersa invenerit ossa
  montibus Etruscis, haec sciat esse mea.

Soldier, wounded on the Tuscan ramparts, who hasten to avoid your comrade's doom, why at my groan do you turn your bulging eyes? I am the closest to you among your fellow soldiers. On this condition may your parents rejoice at your safe return: from your tears let your sister learn the news that Gallus, though he passed unscathed through the midst of the swords of Caesar, yet was not able to escape unknown hands; and, whatsoever bones she finds scattered on the Tuscan hills, let her know that these are mine. (Propertius 1.21, in text of Goold 1990; trans. slightly modified)

In this ten-line vignette we have a battle, we have Etruscan ramparts, a Caesarian army (blockading), and a dead man called Gallus. Even before reading the pair-poem which combines with this to end Propertius' *Monobiblos* (published in the early 20s BCE), we may well have identified the bloody siege of Perusia (modern Perugia) in 41–40, with Mark Antony's brother Lucius and his wife Fulvia under siege, and Octavian, the future Augustus, in command of the force which is destined to inflict such slaughter.

qualis et unde genus, qui sint mihi, Tulle, Penates,
  quaeris pro nostra semper amicitia.
si Perusina tibi patriae sunt nota sepulcra,
  Italiae duris funera temporibus,
cum Romana suos egit discordia cives—
  sic mihi praecipue, pulvis Etrusca, dolor,
tu proiecta mei perpessa's membra propinqui,
  tu nullo miseri contegis ossa solo—
proxima suppositos contingens Umbria campos
  me genuit terris fertilis uberibus.

What is my rank, whence my lineage, and who my ancestral gods, Tullus, you ask in our eternal friendship's name. If you know Perusia, grave of our countrymen who fell in the days of Italy's agony, when discord at Rome took hold of her citizens—Tuscan soil, especially to me do you bring grief, for you have borne the abandoned limbs of my kinsman with not a handful of earth to cover his poor bones—there neighbouring Umbria, bordering on the plains below, a country rich in fertile fields, gave me birth. (Propertius 1.22, in text of Goold 1990; trans. slightly modified)

But even as they welcome in the historicizing reader, the two short elegies frustrate that reader too. Poem 22 tells us that the poet Propertius lost a kinsman in the Perusine struggle, whose unburied bones still lie on Tuscan ground. This seems to invite the identification of Propertius' kinsman with the Gallus of poem 21, . . . and thus to tell us that the unnamed 'tu' of poem 21 did not in fact bury the corpse who addressed him there. Why not? (A plea for burial is surely generically implicit in such an address.) The more narrow kinds of historicist reading (i.e. the ones which believe that an actual factual scenario is retrievable from the poems) can overreach amusingly at this point. Maybe Gallus is still just hanging on to life when he addresses the 'tu' in 21 (hence his ability to talk); and then *subsequently*, at some point *after* giving his addressee the message for the sister, he dies—at a point when the addressee is no longer around to bury him.

Why such an elaborate scenario of exculpation? For this reason. Evidently (the reasoning goes), the 'tu' of 21, despite having eyes 'bulging' with fear or horror, did not simply ignore his dead or dying interlocutor (though there is a subsidiary argument about the sense of *torques*). He must have taken the news of Gallus' death, as requested, to the 'sister' of 21.6; otherwise Propertius, over a decade later, would lack the information which he uses in these two little elegies. So if the *miles* was altruistic enough to take responsibility for the message, he would have been altruistic enough to perform the minimal burial rites too . . . unless Gallus wasn't quite dead yet. An alternative attempt to retrieve factual sense *switches the personnel* in the correlation of 21 with 22. This reading points out that the 'tu' of poem 21 is himself *saucius*: so maybe *he*, not Gallus, is the unburied relative mentioned by Propertius in poem 22; that is, maybe after his encounter with Gallus (who can on this reconstruction be allowed to be buried by him) he himself dies and fails to secure burial.

To contemplate the above scenarios is to wonder at what point such literal historicism will fall into an egregious case of the documentary fallacy. Well, perhaps at some point before the commentators make the case (and it is a surprisingly strong case) that things will work out best if *both* Gallus *and* the unnamed 'tu' of poem 21 are related to Propertius. This involves fastening upon the *soror* of 21.6, who, on any normal reading of the generic conventions of epitaph, should be the dead man's sister (as in 'go tell my sister that I'm dead'), and instead making her the surviving soldier's sister (as in 'go tell *your* sister that I'm dead'); a bizarre thing to say unless the surviving man's sister were also the dead man's wife or fiancée. And that, oddly enough, is exactly the historical reconstruction preferred in several modern interpretations—as in the Loeb-influenced translation used here (Goold 1990, with note ad loc.: 'The poet imaginatively dramatizes the epitaph so as to represent the dead Gallus as uttering it to the brother of his betrothed; the poem which follows reveals that both were kinsmen of Propertius'; cf. the further prosopographical elaboration in DuQuesnay 1992).

With this as an alternative, it is no surprise that one dissentient commentary should retreat to the minimalist position that the corpse in poem 22 has no connection at all with the corpse in poem 21—beyond death in the same battle (Richardson 1977 on 1.21, introductory note). More subtly, Nicholson 1998–9 resists the perceived historicist overreach by arguing for a kind of stylized refusal of prosopographical specificity in the poems.

So what in turn can a formalist approach (and specifically, perhaps, a genre-driven formalism) contribute to the interpretation of these two little elegies, which have been so hospitable—perhaps too hospitable—to the (re)constructions of historicism? It will not have escaped notice that one or two appeals have already been made to genre and form, since, in practice, no poem is readable without *some* sense of form. More emphatically, a formalist approach can begin by simply ruling out the option of treating the two Perusine corpses in poem 21 and 22 as completely irrelevant to one another. When two poems like these are juxtaposed at the end of a poetry book like this, not to relate them would be a basic failure of reading.

Slightly more controversially, for any form- or genre-driven critic there is an elephant in the room when we talk about prosopography and poem 21; and that elephant is called Gallus. No fewer than five poems in the *Monobiblos* address or treat a man called Gallus (Cairns 1983: esp. 83–8). The commentators are not slow to make the obvious prosopographer's point that the Gallus of poem 21 cannot be the Gallus of poems 5, 10, 13, or 20, since that Gallus (or those Galli) is (or are) alive and interacting with the poet in the 'present' of his book in the early 20s BCE, whereas the Gallus of poem 21 dies at Perusia in 41–40.

But here again it can be argued that a fundamental error in reading (and, in a sense, an error in prosopography) is committed by the many critics of Propertius who speculate about the identity of Gallus in these five poems without paying sufficient attention to the fact that Propertius' immediate predecessor in the genre of love elegy, and the *founder* of the genre, was... a poet called Gallus. That is not to say that all (or any) of the Galli of the *Monobiblos* must in a literal sense be the poet Cornelius Gallus (the biographical obstacle at Prop. 1.5.23–4 is well known); it is not to say that these other potential Galli do not merit prosopographical investigation in their own terms; but it *is* to say that the intertextual availability of the poet Gallus constitutes one important reason for all five Galli being there. To treat the poetic Gallus as irrelevant to the naming of a Gallus in a book of early Augustan elegy, or indeed in any early Augustan book of poetry (think of the *Eclogues*) is not, or should not be, an option.

Now, at what point does a formalist reading strategy go out of control and risk becoming a caricature of itself? Perhaps at the point where it is insisted that the Gallus of poem 21 must represent the poet Gallus *and no other*—despite the death-date of 41–40 BCE dictated by a minimal acknowledgement of history in this poem and its pair. No argument there: but we do still need to ask what kind of interpretative work can arise from a less literal shadowing of the prosopographically various Galli by their poetological namesake. (I assume here (*pace* Heyworth 2007: 99) that the Gallan elephant is not to be emended out of the text entirely at 21.7; but it is worth emphasizing that, at every turn in this poem, the constitution of the text is part of the interpretative problematic.) If the name Gallus is allowed to carry its genre-specific weight, it becomes significant that the *Monobiblos* ends with an elegiac *sphragis* spoken by Propertius (22) preceded and balanced by a kind of epitaph spoken by a man called Gallus (21): given that the Ur-form of elegy, to the Romans, is funereal and epitaphic lament, this adds up to a kind of metapoetic doubling of elegiac closure. More tentatively, the approach through genre offers a novel way of short-circuiting the prosopographer's question about how the poet Propertius comes to be related (through cross-reference between poems 22 and 21) to a dead man called Gallus: Propertius is related to this Gallus because he is related, through *literary filiation*, with the poet Gallus.

A different way of tampering with the prosopographer's rules of engagement may point towards another extreme of 'text-only' reading. (I borrow this idea, with kind permission, from Mark Buchan, who will develop it in a larger context; for an allied thought cf. Heyworth 2007: 100–1.) Poem 22, as just noted, is a *sphragis* or 'signature'-poem, which sets out Propertius' autobiographical details without actually naming him. Poem 21 begins by addressing a nameless addressee with the words *tu qui . . . properas*. Etymologically speaking, what would one call a man who is defined by his 'hastening', *a properando*? Perhaps *Prop*ertius? (Cf. 4.1.71 *quo ruis imprudens . . . Properti?* 'Whither heedless do you rush . . . *Prop*ertius?') Or in poem 22 itself, when line 7 refers to the poet's dead relative as *mei . . . propinqui*, does an alternative etymology again sound out, sphragistically, the name *Prop*ertius?

To a reader predisposed toward the etymological habit (cf. Hinds 2006), this is a brilliant *aperçu*: but others will undoubtedly feel nervous about such a close-up commitment to textuality. It is time to stand back and offer an overview. One of the principles of the new criticism, first established in Brooks's *Well Wrought Urn*, was 'the heresy of paraphrase'. When a poem, or a book of poems, is fetishized as a carefully constructed artefact, with every juxtaposition of verses, of words, of syllables having a contribution to make to its meaning, it follows that much of that sense will be lost if the meaning of the poem is taken to amount to no more than an extractable paraphrase. An apparently intended consequence of many recent moves towards culturalism has been a de-fetishizing of the poem as a transcendent object of study. A perhaps *un*intended consequence of this 'loss of religion' has been a loss of appetite for close analysis of verbal construction even *within* the poem, so that, despite the paradigm-shifting work of the deconstructionists and the new critics before them, a poetic text is again often treated, by a kind of shorthand (competing as it now is with so many other objects of study), as equivalent to its paraphrase.

This is by no means to exhaust the available talking-points in Propertius 1.21 and 22. To do no more than to pose a parting question about early reception history: how differently does poem 21 read when, a couple of years after its publication, the elegist Gallus himself (like his namesake in the Propertian elegy) meets a violent death associated with the 'swords of Caesar', in his case a forced suicide after his conduct as prefect of Egypt incurs official imperial displeasure? But it is time to broaden the terms of the discussion.

Perusia: Contexts and Bullet-points

What other text about the siege of Perusia can add some context, for a historicizing reader, to the indirections and involutions of Propertius' pair of epigrams? A reader in search of a narrative treatment in the extant historiographical record will turn first to Appian's second-century CE Roman History (*Civil Wars* 5.33–49, probably based on Pollio). But other ways of contextualizing the Perusine elegies are available too. In approaches influenced by the generation-old new historicism of Stephen Greenblatt (to some, not so much an '–ism' as a rhetorical strategy defined by one critic's flair), one shock-tactic for cutting loose from the aestheticist involutions of canonical literary texts has been to juxtapose them with aggressively non-literary texts, or indeed with material objects and cultural practices readable as texts. So what kind of 'text' might offer a suitable provocation in the Perusine instance?

Perhaps one of the lead *glandes* or sling-bullets shot from besiegers to besieged, and from besieged to besiegers, during the extended confrontation of 41–40 BCE. Remarkably, such bullets came to light in and around Perugia and have been available in the archaeological archive since the nineteenth century; even more remarkably, they come inscribed with actual texts: *CIL* 11.6721; cf. Hallett 1977. Among the contexts for Propertius 1.21–2, then, is one materially embodied text-message which reads *peto landicam Fulviae* ('my target is the clitoris of Fulvia'), and another which reads *peto Octaviai culum* ('my target is the arse of Octavian'—or, better, 'of she-Octavian': Hallett 1977: 152).

Though space forbids extended discussion, the small methodological observation which I want to advance here is that for us to adduce this kind of evidence in a discussion of Propertius 1.21 and 22 is less of a surprise tactic than the equivalent move would be for an early new historicist working on, say, Shakespeare. What in Greenblattian terms would be an unexpected turn in 'the circulation of social energy' (the subtitle of Greenblatt 1988) is for a classicist business as usual. A typical learned commentary in our field is a kitchen-sink operation, which adduces anything and everything conceivably relevant to the business at hand. The centre of a department of Classics is its seminar room, a space in which we are programmed to pull down texts and commentaries, lexica and concordances, *corpora* of inscriptions and papyri, iconographic repertoires, archaeological reports, and more, and to make them all talk to one another. (We have never, institutionally, inhabited a space restricted to 'the literary'.) The Perusine bullets, since their discovery, have been catalogued and displayed as objects of study, edited and re-edited, cited and re-cited; in a sense they are not just random bullets but for us as classicists, always and already, *well-wrought bullets.*

Another swirl in the circulation of social energy will juxtapose the bullets with an epigram written at or around the time of the siege by the young Octavian himself—preserved *verbatim* in a poem by Martial over a century later:

> quod futuit Glaphyran Antonius, hanc mihi poenam
> Fulvia constituit, se quoque uti futuam.
> Fulviam ego ut futuam? quid si me Manius oret
> pedicem? faciam? non puto, si sapiam.
> 'aut futue, aut pugnemus' ait. quid, quod mihi vita
> carior est ipsa mentula? signa canant!

Because Antony fucks Glaphyra, Fulvia determined to punish *me* by making me fuck her in turn. I fuck Fulvia? What if Manius begged me to bugger him? Would I do it? I think not, if I were in my right mind. 'Either fuck me or let us fight', says she. Ah, but my cock is dearer to me than life itself. Let the trumpets sound! (Octavian *apud* Mart. 11.20.3–8, in text of Shackleton Bailey 1993)

In 1977 Judith Hallett could juxtapose this epigrammatic text with the Perusine bullets, and give to the readers of the *American Journal of Ancient History* an early *practicum* in gender criticism—pointing out, *inter alia*, the profound difference (in Roman cultural terms) between envisaging Octavian as receiving a penile *glans* in his *culus* (via the hostile bullet) and as administering a penile thrust to someone else's *culus* (in this case the despised Manius). This material points, indeed, in many directions: it can make us think about *positionality* within a war narrative; it can make us think about sexual aggression, about male constructions of female agency, about overlap between the vocabularies of war and the vocabularies of sexual activity. Potentially, some of these insights can impinge upon Propertius 1.21, and thence, via the rest of the *Monobiblos*, upon a conversation about the poetological and ideological entailments of the Gallo-Propertian *topos* of *militia amoris* ('love's warfare')—which are already open to correlation with the poet Gallus' own parallel career as a soldier of some consequence. The new-historicist example, like the gender-critical example, can help us to make and to pursue such connections; but for us as classicists the move will not have required a paradigm shift *in our sense of what counts as evidence* (just some encouragement, of a kind vital to the continuing dynamism of the discipline, to use our evidence more nimbly). This question of transferability of method will be picked up at the end of my remaining case study.

Terentia's Intertextual Habit

As already noted, shifts in emphasis between formalism and historicism are sometimes bound up with decisions to privilege, or not to privilege, canonical literary texts. Historicist initiatives are perhaps especially likely to de-centre the canon, to enlarge it, or to propose new kinds of canon. Partly with this in mind, consider the following text, quoted (with minor modification of the translation) from Edward Courtney's 1995 anthology of Latin inscriptions in verse (a volume whose preface declares an explicit aim to encourage new thinking about such epigraphic material):

vidi pyramidas sine te, dulcissime frater,
et tibi, quod potui, lacrimas hic moesta profudi
et nostri memorem luctus hanc sculpo querelam.
sic nomen Decimi Gentiani pyramide alta
pontificis comitisque tuis, Traiane, triumphis
lustra<que> sex intra censoris consulis exstet.

I have seen the pyramids without you, most sweet brother, and in sorrow I have here shed tears for you, all I could do, and inscribe this lament in record of my grief. So may the name of Decimus Gentianus, pontifex and participant in the triumphs of Trajan, censor and consul before his thirtieth birthday, survive on the lofty pyramid. (Courtney *Musa Lapidaria* 74 = *CLE* 270 = *CIL* 3.21 = *ILS* 1046a)

We owe our knowledge of these hexameters to two Holy Land pilgrims, one in the 1330s and one in the 1480s, who saw them (along with other, non-Latin texts) inscribed upon one of the pyramids of Giza (Friedlaender 1913: 4. 137–8); the actual inscription is now of course lost, along with the pyramid's outer coating. Decimus Terentius Gentianus, whose name and career can be fleshed out from other sources, was a prominent figure in Trajanic and Hadrianic Rome (he is even mentioned at *Scriptores Historiae Augustae* 1.23.5 as a potential successor to Hadrian); the author of these verses was, then, his sister, whom we can call Terentia.

To come to this after Propertius 1.21 is to move from a text which is at one level a high-concept literary 'riff' on the idea of inscribed commemoration to an actual commemorative inscription. The information about the personnel involved is correspondingly more direct. But that does not necessarily mean that we have moved from literary form to non-literary formlessness, or indeed from a heavy stylization of history to a transparent record of unadorned fact. 'The sister introduces a number of literary references' (Courtney 1995: 296). Indeed she does; let us flag the patterns of verbal resemblance, with Courtney, and proceed from there.

Line 2, *et tibi, quod potui*: cf. Catullus 68.149, *hoc tibi, quod potui, confectum carmine munus*, 'this gift achieved in song for you, all I could do...' The text which invites comparison is not an address to Catullus' dead brother but (as

Courtney notes) a verse in a poem 'much concerned with the death of Catullus' brother, though not in the immediate context' (68.19–26 and 89–100). Catullus' dedication in 68.149 is to his friend and benefactor Allius; but what underlies *quod potui* here is, explicitly, the fraternal bereavement (*ei misero frater adempte mihi*), lamented both in this poem (68.20, 92) and in the celebrated short elegy which renders Catullus' own commemoration quasi-epigraphic and quasi-epitaphic (101.1–2):

multas per gentes et multa per aequora vectus
advenio has miseras, frater, ad inferias...

Travelling through many nations and through many seas I have come, brother, for these sad funeral rites...

Line 3, *et nostri memorem luctus hanc sculpo querelam*: cf. Horace, *Odes* 3.11.51–2, *et nostri memorem sepulcro | scalpe querelam*, '... and carve on my tomb a lament in record of my person'. The startlingly close verbal correspondence is with the final *envoi* of Horace's Hypermestra Ode (in sapphics); after having defied the order to murder her bridegroom Lynceus, the heroine bids him to flee far away (*i pedes quo te rapiunt et aurae*), asking only for an appropriate memorial when she herself dies. Two moments, then, of epigraphic commemoration; the Horatian situation is in other respects quite unlike Terentia's, but the classic Horatian wording could hardly be more minutely tracked.

What are we to make of these two lines of textual detail in Terentia's second-century pyramidal memorial to her brother? Are these and related literary references noted by Courtney just generally appropriate tags, verbal furniture in the mind of a well-educated elite Roman? Or—a question to exercise the formalist critic—should we interpret them with some of the same protocols as if Terentia's inscription were a canonical poem (cf. e.g. Hinds 1998)? (The question will persist even if we allow ourselves to acknowledge an element of clunkiness in these undeniably *ad hoc* verses.)

In other words, would it be a category mistake to unpack as *artful, post-Alexandrian obliquity* (rather than as semi-random reuse) the echo in line 2 of a verse of Catullus which is not in itself a lament dedicated to his dead brother but is contiguous with and in some ways a surrogate for his lament for his dead brother? In the hexametricization of the closing words of the Hypermestra Ode in line 3, do we interpret the acoustic morphing of Horace's *sepulcro/scalpe* into Terentia's *sculpo* as a subconscious (mis)remembering of the original verb, or as a high-end learned wordplay (*sculpo sepulcro*), near-anagrammatic and possibly etymologizing? Is it relevant to Terentia's replay of this motif that the great Horatian speech, like her own verse inscription, is female-voiced and that, even though not addressed by a sister to a brother but by a bride to a groom, it is addressed by one of a band of sisters to one of a band of brothers? And is some enhanced idea of the reciprocity of commemoration to be drawn from the fact that in Terentia's case the memorial is inscribed to the man, in Horace's to the female speaker herself?

Finally, and most teasingly, if allusion to Horace *Odes* 3 is in play here, what about another intertext from that same poetic book, unmentioned by Courtney? Terentia has inscribed a memorializing poem *upon* one of the pyramids of Egypt (*sic nomen ... pyramide alta ... exstet*). How can we not think of that famous poem which seals the end of Horace's third book (*Odes* 3.30.1–2)?

> exegi monumentum aere perennius
> regalique situ pyramidum altius

I have completed a monument more enduring than bronze, more lofty than the regal site [but also 'decay'] of the pyramids...

So what is going on here? It is probably uncontroversial to allow that these intertextual entailments are at *some* level relevant to the production and reception of Terentia's epigraphic poem. What will concern the well-wrought-urn formalist is whether this is *attentive* or *inattentive* intertextuality; that entails a question of value. (One pertinent question here is whether the intertexts become more insistent, or less so, as they proliferate in the narrow compass of Terentia's inscription.) If, on the other hand, we identify with historicists (old or new), wary of overly fetishizing the aesthetic detail of our texts, we are likely to stand back from the correspondences and to content ourselves with a broader point about how Roman elite self-positioning in the early second century of the empire involves identification with and processing of experience through canonical texts. In other words, we will not dwell upon the *specifics* of the apparent allusions, but we will be interested in them as symptoms *of social practice*.

But it is perhaps more interesting to try to bring the two approaches together into a thicker description (involving a historicization of form? a formalization of history?). As noted earlier, a recurrent blind-spot in some otherwise excellent manifestos for a new culturalism is a habit of perfunctoriness in dealing *in detail* with literature as social production. What does identification with the literary canon mean *in detail* for an educated Roman?

One of the advantages of this way of framing things is that (to revisit the formalist concern above) the contrast between attentive and inattentive intertextuality can be rehabilitated, but with the difference that the latter will now be just as interesting in its way as the former, as a window on to the practices of writers and readers. In the present case, what happens if, pursuing a more specifically textualized version of the historicist approach, we find in Terentia's words no more than the Pavlovian reaction of a well-educated Roman verse-composer to a given set of associations—dead loved one in a distant land, brother, pyramid? Even (or especially) if 'inattentive'—if composed, as it were, on autopilot—does this epigraphic poem show that no educated Roman could look at an Egyptian pyramid after

23 BCE without thinking of Horace *Odes* 3.30? For an elite Roman, are all pyramids now Horatian pyramids? And so too, are all deaths on foreign service now retextualizations of the death of Catullus' brother? More broadly, in the circles in which these people move, are all dead brothers now Catullan dead brothers?

Not that these rhetorical questions should foreclose the possibility that Terentia really *is* an attentive intertextualist. It is easy, while admitting Terentia's allusion to *exegi monumentum*, to dismiss her poem-on-a-pyramid as a mere trivialization of a Horatian original whose point, after all, involves the *transcendence* of pyramidal by poetic immortality. But what if her manoeuvre is self-conscious and ironic? If Horace's poem is a monument more enduring and more lofty than a royal pyramid, does Terentia's poem, inscribed *upon* the *pyramide alta*, self-consciously reject the Horatian sublime, and allow itself to be—by this standard—an amateur or subaltern production? ('Horace's words add meaning to mine: but really, for this public yet private memorial, the pyramids themselves are a sufficient guarantee of enduring fame.')

There does seem to be good reason to allow to the author of this poem a more than minimally 'literary' sensibility. (And I make the fair assumption that this aristocratic woman composed the verses herself, rather than merely commissioning them: Stevenson 2005: 57.) If Terentia's commemorative words do lend encouragement to analysis along such lines, this may suggest something about the sociology of the early second-century Roman elite: that is, that in their everyday belletrism they sustain a level of conversation with literary culture, and a level of commitment to literary display, that makes such texts more individually responsive to aesthetically informed reading than we are wont to allow.

On the other hand, if we find ourselves upgrading one epigraphic *carmen* after another to a status of functional indistinguishability from the 'classic' poems on which they draw, we need to be on the lookout for formalist overreach. If it turns out to be *hard to decide* how far to press the intertextual correspondences in the case of a sub-canonical production like this, should that perhaps lead us to interrogate our own expectations of canonicity, our own formal criteria for evaluation, our own disciplinary baggage as readers who are wont to treat intertextual complexity as a touchstone of *something*...?

And now, one more methodological context (already sketched at the end of the previous section). With a few adjustments, the present discussion could have been worked out as a test-case of new-historicist anecdote: that is, take a canonical poetic text about death, about commemoration, about elite foreign service (say Catullus 101), and 'ambush' it with a non-literary or at least non-canonical text associated with an overlapping set of cultural practices. Why, aside from differences in the ordering and weighting of the texts involved, did it not quite come out this way?

In part because the surprise tactic was out of the question. Terentia's inscription is not an unknown text, but one which has been repeatedly edited and anthologized in standard epigraphic collections in the course of the past 150-odd years, as well as (more recently) finding a new frame in the feminist context of a major survey of women's writing in Latin (Stevenson 2005: 56–8, 561–2). The key consideration, then (as earlier for the Perusine bullets), is that, in our disciplinary perspective, the majority of 'stuff' (textual and material) which can be brought anecdotally to bear upon the literary canon is already well established within our critical ambit. Which is to ask the question: does this epigraphic poem have its apparatus of learned commentary, including commentary (like Courtney's) which relates it to canonical literature, because *it is so close to that literature*, or is it more that, in our world of *Altertumswissenschaft, everything is so close to everything*? The surviving textual and material archive from classical antiquity is so finite in comparison with the archives of most modern periods and cultures, and the discourse of classicism, so often reified, reinforced, and reinvented over the centuries, is so powerful an actant upon that body of material, that what we have in Classics, perhaps, is a *well-wrought discipline*—in which everything is always already described, always already aestheticized, and, more than that, in a sense, always already canonized.

The procedures of new-historicist anecdote show some correspondence with ours, then, but with the difference that the anecdotes available to us are limited enough in number to pre-empt or to change some of the usual questions about arbitrariness in the choice of evidence. New historicists are often put on the defensive about their trademark 'attempt to isolate significant or "interpreting" detail from the mass of traces that have survived in the archive' (Gallagher and Greenblatt 2000: 15). In Classics, the corresponding move is rendered easier (but also harder) by the fact that a comprehensive approach and an anecdote-driven 'interpreting detail' approach will in many cases end up with the same finite set of traces. Through a mixture of necessity and choice, we Romanists do undeniably spend a great deal of time on the 'interpreting detail' (often because it is the only detail we have), asking it to tell us stories about a larger whole. Our characteristic *modus operandi* (it can hardly be otherwise) is synecdoche: this it is that informs (and in-forms) most of our receptions of Roman culture.

I Began with the Desire to Speak with the Dead (and so did the Dead)

A lingering reason for invoking Greenblattian historicism as a point of reference (although it be just one more episode, already receding from view, in the unending negotiation between this essay's titular terms) is the intuitive affinity which we cannot but feel (especially when faced with a dominant 'presentism' in the Humanities) with its programmatic starting-point: 'I began with the desire to speak with the dead.' Greenblatt (1988: 1) is writing about the Renaissance; as classicists and Romanists, we are inheritors of a tradition which is *constituted* by the repetition and reenactment of that desire across time and space.

Terentia speaks with her dead brother, and with those to whom a career like his will speak, in a conversation complicated by dialogue with dead poets, and by supplementation of the memorializing function of an age-old Egyptian monument. Her words are preserved for the classical tradition because of a fourteenth-century pilgrim who saw her inscription and thought it worth recording in his journal. Here is another conversation with the dead, one (indeed) which can speak anachronistically down the centuries to us in the voice of Romantic classicism ('I met a traveller from an antique land...'). And how, in its own time, did the discourse of late medieval pilgrimage assimilate this pagan text? As a mere parenthesis, or as an experience which fed into the totality of the project of pilgrimage, and hence part of a sort of a *paganisme moralisé*? This chain of receptions now extends to readers like us, for whom any monument to a dead Roman official is at some level, synecdochically, a way of speaking about the pastness of Rome itself; and for whom Terentia's particular commemoration seems to gain some kind of added value from the fragile processes which give us access to her words long after their inscribed record has crumbled from the face of the pyramid. Fragile processes; but (with a nod to Porter 2006) an enduring sense of classicism.

References

Beard, Mary (2003). *The Parthenon.* Cambridge, Mass.: Harvard UP.

Brooks, Cleanth (1947). *The Well Wrought Urn: Studies in the Structure of Poetry.* New York: Harcourt Brace.

Cairns, Francis (1983). 'Propertius 1.4 and 1.5 and the Gallus of the Monobiblos.' *Papers of the Liverpool Latin Seminar,* 4: 61–103.

Courtney, E. (1995). *Musa Lapidaria: A Selection of Latin Verse Inscriptions.* American Classical Studies 36. Atlanta, Ga.: Scholars Press.

DuQuesnay, Ian M. Le M. (1992). '*In memoriam Galli*: Propertius 1.21.' In T. Woodman and J. Powell (eds.), *Author and Audience in Latin Literature,* 52–83. Cambridge: CUP.

Friedlaender, Ludwig (1913). *Roman Life and Manners Under the Early Empire,* 4 vols. Tr. from German, 7th edn. London: Routledge.

Gallagher, Catherine and Greenblatt, Stephen (2000). *Practicing New Historicism.* Chicago: University of Chicago Press.

Goold, G. P. (ed.) (1990), *Propertius: Elegies.* Loeb Classical Library. Cambridge Mass.: Harvard UP.

Greenblatt, Stephen (1988). *Shakespearean Negotiations: The Circulation of Social Energy in Renaissance England.* Berkeley and Los Angeles: University of California Press.

Hallett, Judith P. (1977). '*Perusinae glandes* and the Changing Image of Augustus.' *American Journal of Ancient History,* 2: 151–71.

Heyworth, S. J. (2007). *Cynthia: A Companion to the Text of Propertius*. Oxford: OUP.
Hinds, Stephen (1998). *Allusion and Intertext: Dynamics of Appropriation in Roman Poetry*. Roman Literature and its Contexts. Cambridge: CUP.
——(2006). 'Venus, Varro and the *vates*: Toward the Limits of Etymologizing Interpretation.' *Dictynna*, 3: 173–208. http://dictynna.revue.univ-lille3.fr/dictynnanumero3.html.
Kennedy, Duncan F. (1993). *The Arts of Love: Five Studies in the Discourse of Roman Love Elegy*. Roman Literature and its Contexts. Cambridge: CUP.
McGann, Jerome (1979). 'Keats and the Historical Method in Literary Criticism.' *Modern Language Notes*, 94: 988–1032.
Nicholson, Nigel (1998–9). 'Bodies Without Names, Names Without Bodies: Propertius 1.21–22.' *Classical Journal*, 94: 143–61.
Porter, James I. (2006). 'What is "Classical" about Classical Antiquity?' In James I. Porter (ed.), *Classical Pasts*, 1–65. Princeton: Princeton UP.
Richardson, L., Jr. (ed.) (1977), *Propertius: Elegies I–IV*. Norman, Okla.: University of Oklahoma Press.
Shackleton Bailey, D. R. (ed.) (1993), *Martial: Epigrams*, 3 vols. Loeb Classical Library. Cambridge Mass.: Harvard UP.
Stevenson, Jane (2005). *Women Latin Poets: Language, Gender and Authority from Antiquity to the Eighteenth Century*. Oxford: OUP.
Veyne, Paul (1988). *Roman Erotic Elegy: Love, Poetry, and the West*. Tr. from French. Chicago: University of Chicago Press.

Abbreviations

CIL: *Corpus Inscriptionum Latinarum*, ed. T. Mommsen *et al.* (1863–1995).
CLE: *Carmina Latina Epigraphica*, ed. F. Bücheler and E. Lommatzsch (1895–1926).
ILS: *Inscriptiones Latinae Selectae*, ed. H. Dessau (1892–1916).

PART III

GENRES

CHAPTER 23

RHETORIC

ANDREW RIGGSBY

What is Rhetoric?

The term can be profitably approached in somewhat different ways depending on whether one adopts a classical or modern frame of reference. As for the former frame, the formal definition of rhetoric was highly contested in antiquity. The problems, however, have mostly to do with attempts to write into those definitions positions on issues that are not clearly definitional (e.g. the ethics or the learnability of persuasive speech). With such debates left behind, I use 'rhetoric' in contrast to 'oratory'. Oratory is the practice of public speaking; rhetoric comprises the various theories—instructional, evaluative, taxonomic, and so on—overtly devised to direct, evaluate, and/or shape oratory (though, as we shall see, the actual importance of rhetoric extends beyond the world of oratory). Rhetoric in this sense demands the attention of any student of the Roman world for at least four reasons. First, and even if this fact were more arbitrary than it is, rhetoric is simply one of the areas of life about which we are best informed. We have a variety of complete texts by a number of authors over a span of centuries, as well as a host of testimonial evidence. There are few other areas of which that can be said. Second, public speaking was of crucial importance to Rome's pre-print culture. Though other means of communication (gossip, monuments) were not negligible in the political world, it is generally agreed that none were as important as deliberative oratory before the people or within the Senate. Legal proceedings, though they came increasingly to hinge on written documents, always remained oral in conception, and the training for this venue was in the schools of rhetoric.

Third, rhetoric provided training not just for the law-courts and politics, but the whole life of the elite. Rhetoric was in fact the sole component of what amounted to standard higher education. So, for instance, the one thing nearly every known author of surviving Latin texts can be counted on to have shared was knowledge of the same rhetoric that has been passed down to us. Finally, rhetoric seems to have had a considerable 'spill-over' effect beyond the worlds of oratory or even of verbal production in general. As we will see, it was what made many Romans the men they were.

If only as a matter of convenience we may divide most of the ancient texts into two categories: manuals of instruction and works that include a meta-rhetorical component, touching on the philosophy and/or sociology of rhetoric and oratory. The manuals share a common style (also used in related disciplines such as grammar and more distant ones like agriculture or law), which is stipulative, normative, and taxonomic. They are stipulative in that propositions are simply asserted; they are rarely backed up either by argument or by external evidence. The subject-matter is nearly always how speeches *ought* to be given, not how they might be or in fact are (except to warn of potential errors). The normative approach is even more striking since the norms are often specific to a single context: the Roman courts, and especially the civil courts. How far this is a matter of universalizing the norms of that venue and how far simply of ignoring other possibilities is perhaps an open question. The taxonomic tendency is characteristic of much of the intellectual production of antiquity. Writers of rhetorics (or grammars, etc.) name and define categories and their subdivisions (and their subdivisions . . .). Below I will give a number of examples as a way of giving some of the flavour of these works.

A fourth characteristic, however, and one not shared by the other technical genres, is generativity. Rather than providing rules to assess or analyse speeches, the manuals give a set of procedures to follow in composing speeches for various occasions. Those procedures determine both the content and the style of the speech. A further aspect of the generative approach to persuasion, and one presumably applicable outside the composition of speeches, was to provide a framework to facilitate brain-storming (*inventio*, 'finding' in the technical jargon). In matters of substance, the orator was told to consider, for instance, arguments based on actions prior to, coincident with, and following the event in question or motive, opportunity, and hope of escape. Now none of these categories is individually very surprising, nor do they automatically generate arguments of any particular power. No rhetorical training is necessarily needed, for instance, to associate flight (action after the fact) with consciousness of guilt. It is rather the comprehensiveness and multi-dimensionality of the whole array that gives the method its power. Talented speakers would likely intuit most arguments that could be generated in this way. The power of the cultural capital embedded in *inventio*-theory is to give the merely practised a leg up in finding the same moves.

Similarly, in matters of style, rules do not actually give you forms or cut down the many possibilities. Still, they give you the basic tools of composition.

The earliest surviving handbooks are Cicero's juvenile *On Brain-storming* and an anonymous *Rhetoric for Herennius*. (Manuscripts assign this work to Cicero, but this is universally understood to be an error. A series of references by Quintilian to the work of one Cornificius could well be speaking of the *Rhetoric*.) Both date to the early first century BCE (the order is unclear), and substantial overlap in phrasing suggests there was a close connection between Cicero's work and the corresponding section of the *Rhetoric*, perhaps a common source. We also have a variety of similar treatises dating from the early part of the first century CE to beyond the end of antiquity, some treating all of rhetoric and others focusing on a particular aspect (notably several lists of figures of speech).

The works of meta-rhetoric follow not this handbook pedagogical tradition, but the more 'philosophical' form of the dialogue. The first and greatest of these is Cicero's *On the Orator* (55 BCE), in which statesmen of the recent past are made to discuss, among other things, the roles of art and nature, theory and practice, in the proper shaping of the oratory. The form adopted makes the work more clearly continuous with Cicero's political philosophy than with the more technical *On Brain-storming* (see further below). Cicero also used a similar form to write a history of oratory (*Brutus*, 46 BCE) and, slightly later, a more general work with an emphasis on style (*The Orator*). In a relatively early work, the historian Tacitus took up a very similar dialogue form to write *On Orators*. This work asserts, questions, and analyses the decline of oratory reputed to have taken place after the fall of the Republic. In addition to the difficulties inherent in the subject-matter of these works of meta-rhetoric, their polyphonic form has made consensus in interpretation rare.

One work really transcends the distinction between the manuals and the meta-rhetoric: Quintilian's *Training in Oratory* from the very end of the first century CE. In form, most of this massive work (over 750 pages in the standard modern edition) is a blown-up handbook, re-creating the standard taxonomies in a fairly conventional order. However, there are several differences. The first, tenth, and last of the twelve books are devoted to the educational formation of the would-be orator before and after his formal rhetorical training. Also, Quintilian's versions of rhetorical theory are not simply asserted. He often reviews varying opinions of specific questions; he answers potential objections he foresees; he appeals not just to logic but to his own substantial experience as a courtroom advocate.

Finally, we have several collections of declamations. These are speeches on set topics (primarily mock trial cases) originally given as school exercises, though later also practised recreationally by adults. There are several books of these by the Elder Seneca (early first century CE), as well as briefer collections by Calpurnius Flaccus and (purportedly) Quintilian.

It would be impossible to summarize the content of classical rhetoric in this chapter, much less in a single section. Instead, I offer a more focused view of a few fragments of the taxonomies. There are innumerable variations, many of them fairly small, in terminology and structure. While one cannot speak of a real consensus, I offer an 'averaged' or synthetic view of the field. I note the range of variation only when there is a specific point to make.

Divisions of the whole subject-matter (these operate independently of each other):

- The duties of the orator are: to instruct, to entertain, to move [the emotions].
- The virtues of speech are: clarity, [correct] Latinity, ornament, propriety.
- The tasks of the orator are: brain-storming, organization, style, memory, delivery.
- The kinds of speeches are: forensic, deliberative, epideictic. (NB only the first of these receives much actual attention.)

Much of the typology provides a flow-chart for composition, in part:

- Parts of a speech are: (a) introduction, (b) narration, (c) proof of the case, (d) refutation of the opposition, (e) conclusion.
- The introduction (a) should make the audience: (1) attentive, (2) teachable, and (3) well-disposed to your side.
- Sources of being well-disposed (a3) are: (a) the character of the advocate, (b) the character of the client, (g) the nature of the opposing side, (d) the audience's character, (e) the circumstances of the case (at this level, but not at the higher ones, many of the possibilities will not come in to play in any given case).

Some elements of argument and style:

- Bases of argument. A speech derived focus from identifying the 'status' of the case. The theory of status set up a checklist of questions which helped the speakers identify the fundamental point of disagreement between the two sides:

  questions of fact (did he do it?)
  questions of definition (did the act fit a formal, legal definition?)
  questions of 'quality' (was the act really wrong?)
  procedural questions (does the court have jurisdiction?)

- Figures of speech, i.e. ways of speaking that are unnatural and 'ornamented' without changing propositional content (a few examples):

  rhetorical question;
  dubitatio (feigning hesitation over some point);
  apostrophe (addressing a person [or other entity] not actually present);
  asyndeton (running together a list of items without conjunctions to join them).

- Tropes, i.e. ways of speaking that are meant to indicate something other than what they literally say (a few examples):

  metaphor (a word 'transferred' from its 'proper' signification to another; many of the tropes are special cases of metaphor);

hyperbole;
allegory (a systematic set of metaphors, such as the 'ship' of state tossed by political 'storms');
antonomasia (the replacement of a proper name with a title, patronymic, or other epithet).

It would be a lengthy and probably unfair project to list possible critiques of Roman rhetoric as a general system of persuasion, but it may be worth noting that it had certain weaknesses even as an attempt to capture the range of Roman oratorical practice. At this point, I would like to move slightly beyond the (ancient) notion I have invoked to define the scope of my inquiry, and employ a more modern notion that will add to the substantive analysis. In particular, I look at rhetoric as a member of a family of classificatory schemes, of ways of knowing (and so exercising influence on) the world. Since no rhetoric (and no such scheme more generally) is infinite in scope, each particular one simultaneously enables and limits its users. Moatti has pointed out a growing interest in classification at Rome in and around the first century BCE (drawing heavily on Hellenistic Greek precedents), and at the expense of competing modes (like the deductive form of geometry). She puts formal rhetoric at the head of this parade. If rhetoric represents the cutting-edge of Roman information technology, we will do well then to ask what limits it sets on what can and cannot, on what must and must not, be said, for these will form meaningful limits on human action.

In some cases the rhetoricians themselves note that their rules cannot capture various subtleties of practical speaking (Quintilian is particularly sensitive to the problem). So, for instance, there are rarely rules to fix the value of scalar quantities, for example, how many similar arguments to run together on the same topic, what density of figures of speech is appropriate in a given context. The variousness of context (see below on *decorum*) is also at issue. It is impossible for the rhetorician to list all the potentially salient social contexts of speaking, much less all their possible combinations. Finally, the problem often lies in the relevance of information that is never articulated anywhere in the society. Posture and gait were closely tied to class and upbringing in ways that were never fully explained and often deliberately mystified. As in broader social life, so in oratory; even Quintilian, who offers an elaborate catalogue of useful gestures, despairs of canvassing all possibilities (11.3.12). (On the possibility that the 'failure' of rhetoric to capture fully such features was an advantage for its authors, see below.)

Other gaps in rhetorical theory seem to have existed precisely because they were not seen as such by the rhetoricians. I will discuss the most important and general of these in the last section of this chapter, but a few other examples here may be useful. The generative patterns of rhetoric are highly sequential, both in terms of working through the stages of composition in order (brain-storming, then organization of the results, then putting the resulting outline into specific words) and working through the individual speech linearly. Thus it is hard for classical rhetoric to recognize global strategies, such as 'resonance' (the repetition of an assertion or suggestion so as to persuade by sheer familiarity), the exploitation of admissions by the other side (which falls between 'proof' and 'refutation'), or the structuring of a speech around key thematic terms (since 'style' is supposed to come after 'organization').

The formalization of rhetoric produced these entirely internal constraints on speaking, but it also lead to canonization of pre-existing audience expectations (though these were then presumably reinforced by hearing speakers trained in this fashion). For instance, it is hardly a natural fact of persuasion that proof of one's own case should *follow* refutation of the other side, that a speaker's grammar should always be formally correct, that sentences should not end in rhythms like those of certain poetic metres, or that one should commonly be expected to touch one's middle finger and thumb while extending the other fingers (Quint. 11.3.91). Now, at Rome the situation is somewhat confused by the importation and adaptation of Greek rhetorics underlain by potentially different traditional expectations. Advocates, for instance, were hardly unknown in Athens, but were not used there as a matter of course as they were in the Roman courts. In practice this allowed Roman advocates to admit weakness or make naked appeals to authority (in supposedly fact-based proceedings), but it took a long time for the writers of rhetoric to catch up. Conversely, writers like Quintilian (5.10.14) or the author of the *Rhetoric to Herennius* (2.27–45) expend considerable effort working out the typology of syllogisms and their kin, derived from Greek tradition, despite Roman audiences' apparent distaste for such overtly formal reasoning.

Rhetoric as the Art of Decorum

Although, as noted above, the classical rhetorical tradition was much more narrowly normative than any modern version is, it was not merely formulaic. In addition to specific forms, audiences also expected a certain amount and type of variety, and rhetoric had in these cases to provide multiple options for speakers to combine. In some respects the choice is essentially free (at least as far as is specified by theory). Most of the figures of speech, for instance, seem more or less interchangeable. In other cases, the choice is made by very specific facts of the case. One authority, for instance, says the formal introduction of the speech may be skipped if the audience is already exhausted by a wordy opponent. Most important, however, is the broad principle of *decorum*, 'appropriateness'. In Roman thinking this was an important notion far beyond its application to oratory, and I will discuss some consequences of this at the end of this chapter, but even within rhetoric its applications are multiple. One adjusts the general stylistic level of the speech to fit the gravity and character of the subject-matter: whether, for example, the case deals with violence or just with money or (in the latter case) the amount of money in question, or whether individuals, the state, or the gods have been injured. Choosing the basis (*status*) of definition or of quality might be appropriate to one defendant (say, a young or obscure man), but another might require a defence of straight denial (say, a moralistic politician like Cato the Younger). In what follows, I will touch on three contexts in which the notion of decorum is activated: genre, gender, and the nature of language itself.

A 'genre' may be defined roughly as a stabilized pattern of association between features of style, content, and context. Such standardization of forms of speaking probably exists in all societies (and need not, as Bakhtin pointed out, be a matter of literary or even explicit theorizing), but it takes on particular importance at Rome, for a variety of reasons. First of these is the Roman commitment to tradition, the *mos maiorum*. While the specific content of this tradition (as with most so-called traditions) may be variable and strategically flexible, what nearly all our surviving evidence points to is a shared view that there were traditional, and so correct, ways to act in most situations. *A fortiori*, there were correct styles of expressing particular content in particular contexts. Second, genre's connection to context created, in at least some contexts, a connection to social status. Oratory, for instance, was a job for aristocrats, poetry for slaves and foreigners, and history somewhere in between. (Again, what I've just stated as fixed rules were in fact subject both to change over time and to ad hoc strategic manipulation. Nonetheless, none of that would be necessary or even meaningful if the underlying association of genre and status did not exist at all.) Third, the taxonomic character of ancient scholarly discourse (discussed above) tends to reinforce the tendency to categorize—here into genres—as a means of analysis. On the one hand, the rules of rhetoric are often phrased in terms of generic appropriateness. On the other, we will see that rhetoric sometimes also tries to colonize genres other than oratory, becoming at times a theory of discourse in general. After all, there was no overt competition for this role except perhaps with philosophy, and philosophy as would-be master discourse would perhaps replace rather than direct other forms of speech. Manuals for letter-writing and poetry are late, scattered, and limited in scope to their named subject-matter.

Orators are not to be poets; on this point there is both agreement and emphasis. Now one might suspect that there is some 'protest[ing] too much' here, and I will suggest below that there is something to that suspicion. At the very least, this is one of those areas of style in which, as the theorists worry, virtues and vices are especially close to each other (see also below). Presently, however, I will note that the rule apparently does not keep *rhetoricians* away from the poets. For instance, while Cicero is Quintilian's number-one source for examples, Virgil is the next most common (and closer to first than third). Horace comes up about as often as Aristotle. Contrast the marginality of such poets in the modern literature on rhetoric and oratory. Poetry is included both for its (qualified) difference and for its sameness. It is different enough to provide ornament to prose (Quint. 10.1.27, 10.5.4; though see below on the apparent need for oratory to be different from itself to succeed). In other respects, however, such as vocabulary, there is more difference within prose and within poetry than between the two categories (10.1.9). A different kind of connection is apparent in the *Rhetoric for Herennius.* While the author does appeal to poetic examples, most of his are prose because the examples in his discussion of style (by far the greatest part of the total) are, unusually, self-authored. His defence of the practice is the one extended meta-rhetorical passage in the whole work, and it incidentally illustrates a general attitude near to Quintilian's. For instance, all references to orators/orations as potential sources of examples are paired with a reference to poets or poems. Now, this might be taken to imply a particular closeness or similarity of oratory and poetry, but I think the point is actually the opposite. Poetry is the opposite of oratory. The combination is therefore a merism, and it stands in for the whole universe of (formal) verbal production, as we see from the lack of distinctions within poetry and the casual inclusion of history with the standard pair at one point (see also below on Quintilian's explicit partition of prose and verse). Moreover, we can see direct influence flowing out from rhetoric. Its terms (most notably its stylistic terms) become the vocabulary of poetic criticism.

Another salient distinction is noted and collapsed in the discussions just cited. Oratory is, at least in the first instance, an oral practice, but Herennius' instructor is very much caught up with written texts. (This distinction is not central to classical genre theory, but it fits well with the definition offered above. Moreover, the relationship between written text and oral performance was the subject of intense contestation in late Republican and early Imperial Rome.) The authorities cited in this discussion (and earlier in the work) were mostly already deceased 'classics' at the time of writing. The universe in which the author is operating is one of written texts. Moreover, what he is producing himself is a written text. This is true in two senses. The text itself was literally written down, whatever other instructional practices it might have related to. But it also seems to be the case that the examples are set in the past. Many of them explicitly interact with the same cast of (dead) characters on whom he does not draw directly, or are set even further back in the Greek past. The practice of composing examples blurs the line between rhetoric and oratory, and its specifics blur the line between written and oral in general. Transforming performance (in the narrow sense) and occasion into iterable text neutralizes genre and makes possible a generalized 'discourse'.

Narducci and Dugan have stressed Cicero's exploitation of this fact, and we can find further discussion in Quintilian again.

First, we should note the relationship between reading and writing in his training programme. Reading, writing, and speaking are mutually dependent to the point that failure in one leads to failure in the others (10.1.1–2), and contrary to the views of some unnamed others, the same criteria define success in spoken and written discourse (12.10.51). The performance context that had traditionally defined oratory (and continued to do so elsewhere in Quintilian) has been cut entirely out of the loop. Second, the one part of Quintilian's treatise well known even to those who otherwise shun rhetoric is the 'reading list'. He lists Greek and Latin authors of every literary genre and evaluates their worth for the practising orator. In many respects Quintilian's approach is congenial to a very literary world-view. The grand divisions are between Greek and Latin and then between prose and poetry. Conventional genre distinctions are the main structuring principle. Below that, the individual judgements, at least in kind, seem fairly ordinary. Homer is both first and best. Yet all of this is subordinated to rhetoric's project. Homer is best because he provides first-rate examples of all different styles, genres, and parts of speaking.

A traditional society such as that of ancient Rome is relatively compartmentalized. It would be difficult for rhetoric to expand its authority 'horizontally' into genres other than oratory. It might actually have been easier to expand 'vertically' by creating a (would-be) master discourse. This strategy could in turn be executed in different ways. The figure of Homer invoked by Quintilian had a pre-existing cultural authority which could suppress doubts, at least momentarily. More generally, the increasing abstractions of rhetoric's schemata (see above and Moatti) concealed what might previously have seemed mismatches between domains and therefore violations of decorum.

To turn to gender, the principle of decorum meant that normatively male orators had to speak in 'manly' ways. Moreover, this 'normal' speech was really only normal for the *vir*, a term usually translated just 'man', but tending to shade over into 'aristocratic adult male'. From a modern point of view, rhetoric would then be interesting as a particular arena in which Roman politics of gender, class, and status played out, but the issues are perhaps more involved than that. Rhetoric provided a nearly unique technology for micro-management of the self to the men of the ruling class—habits of voice, posture, dress, and the like. Thus it had a special primacy of place in the making of men into *viri*. (Military training, about which we know much less, is the only plausible competitor.)

But, as many commentators have noted, rhetoric was an exercise in controlled transgression. Oratory was the marked speech of certain special occasions. The stylistic virtue of 'ornament' (*ornatus*) implies by definition deviation from normal speech (Quint. 8.3.1; *Her.* 4.18; *De Or.* 3.33). The 'abundance' (*copia*) that the oratory was expected to develop would have meant redundancy in other contexts.

But there was a problem here. These kinds of deviation from 'normal' speech were elsewhere associated with a variety of negative social stereotypes. Speaking more or differently than was necessary was made to be the mark of women, eunuchs, slaves, and foreigners (Quint. 8.3.6). Hence, while decorum may have required *orators* to be manly, it pushed *oratory* to be at least a little deviant. Hence virtues of style, as noted above, are near to vices (Quint. 8.3.7; *De Or.* 3.100).

As a result, the rhetorical texts are haunted by the various others to the proper *vir.* Normally this is in the form of warnings not to be like them, but the very repetition of those warnings signals the impossibility of exorcizing the problems entirely, since some similarity is actually required, as in Quintilian's famous characterization of declamation by the figure of the eunuch (quoted below). Actors, who were typically slaves and at the least legally 'infamous', generated a similar problem, though Cicero could himself be a little more ambivalent: sometimes actors merely imitated what oratory did for real, but at other times, their tasks seem parallel, and occasionally the orators even have reason for jealousy.

Concerns of this sort manifested themselves primarily within rhetoric, but in a pair of famous instances the consequences bubbled up into state regulation of teachers of speaking. In 161 BCE one of the praetors asked for and received from the Senate a commission to see to the departure from the city of Rome of philosophers and rhetoricians. Then in 92 the censors announced that they were displeased by the establishment of schools by self-styled 'Latin rhetors'. Now, it is easy to overstate the scope of these actions. Even if both were enforced systematically and beyond the terms of the respective officials (there is no known mechanism for either), their effect was limited to the city of Rome, and they would only have interfered with the establishment of 'public' schools (in the English sense of that term). Private tutelage, presumably involving travel or instruction in the houses of the very wealthy who could hire or simply buy teachers, would not be affected, nor would apprenticeship (*tirocinium*) to older practitioners. Similarly, when Latin instruction was attacked in 92, that still left Greek teachers, probably the more prestigious ones, in place. This is all to say that the state was not really trying to stop formal instruction in rhetoric; it was not even acting out of hostility to rhetoric as such (despite the opinion of our centuries-later main sources for the decrees). Rather, it was trying to make access to that instruction more exclusive, and so to maintain its value as a scarce resource. If rhetoric was a means of making *viri,* not just teaching a technical skill, then this approach makes sense. As a practical matter it helps preserve elite privilege. As a side benefit, by hiding rhetorical education it helps maintain the illusion that that distinction was a fact of nature, not of differential access to resources.

While we might today regard categories such as gender and class as involving considerable social construction, the Roman rhetoricians (and most other Romans, for that matter) were generally emphatic about their naturalness. Hence, their supposed stylistic correlates were not mere matters of individual (or even collective) taste, but were themselves taken as natural facts. As the case of state action against the rhetoric schools suggests, however, it must be noted that the naturalization works in both directions. That is, the purported naturalness of social roles justifies certain styles of speaking, but at the same time the whole rhetoric of decorum presupposes the naturalness of the various social categories. A student (or teacher) focusing on precisely how to achieve a 'manly' style of speaking is likely to take the category 'man' for granted.

Up to this point I have been primarily discussing attempts to naturalize terms that are important for certain modern modes of analysis: gender, class, nationality, and so on. The issue, however, is broader still. The rhetoricians share the view (hardly unique to them) that there are such things as natural descriptions of the world in general. This applies both at the level of the events in question and of the rhetorical conflict as a whole. That is, speeches could be measured by their fit both with the truth of the subject-matter and with the circumstances of speaking. Moreover, the two levels interconnect. Whether to describe an opponent as a gladiator involves calibration of metaphor (i.e. relationship to the facts). It also involves calibration of one's gendered and status-dependent persona (i.e. relationship to the situation). This constant reference to specific circumstances gives rhetoric flexibility and power. At the same time, however, it involves a commitment to an ultimate criterion of truth that also limited what rhetoric could do. Let me illustrate by pointing to two difficulties the rhetoricians seemed constantly to run into without ever being able to extricate themselves.

Most overt discussion of rhetoric and oratory, at least in what survives, was carried out in texts wholly devoted to that topic. One striking exception is controversy over the practice of declamation—mock trial speeches and exercises in persuading historical figures at decisive moments in the past. The world discussed by the declaimers often resembles second-rate fiction. It is full of pirates, tyrants, and disabled war-heroes. The laws involved are largely fictional. Moreover, so few facts are stipulated in any given case that the only practice is in verbal fluency, rather than 'real' argument. Seneca himself (as well as Quintilian, Asinius Pollio, and Cassius Severus) objects to the 'abuse' of declamation. It is at best a 'mere show' and at worst effeminate and morally corrupting (Quint. 5.12.19; cf. Seneca, *Controversiae* 1.pr.10). But not only were these exercises a matter of some dispute within the world of rhetoric, they were also ridiculed for their unreality by writers like Persius, Petronius, Tacitus, Martial, and Juvenal. Why retain such a controversial, if not simply unpopular, practice? Let me suggest that there was another irresolvable tension here, that there was no way declamation could have been 'fixed'. The practice of declamation is clearly one of what Habinek has described as the 'ludic' activities of Roman culture. That is, it represented a preparation/substitution for a real/serious activity (in this case oratory), and involved the submission of the body to formalized external patterning (as in the many rules of *actio*, 'delivery'). But this breaks down the whole logic of decorum.

Practice speeches will necessarily be inappropriate to their real situation or to the notional one (or quite possibly both). Reformist attempts to make declamation more 'realistic' do not really solve the problem; they just specify how decorum will be violated.

This comes through most clearly in their discussions of 'figured' language, and in particular of metaphor (*Her.* 4.42 ff., esp. 45; *De Or.* 3.155). Thus Quintilian devotes most of a book to the many forms of 'trope', that is, to the 'beneficial shift of a word or expression from its proper signification to another' (8.6.1, cf. 9.1.4 where he describes the original signification as 'natural and principal'). The definition stipulates that such a usage may be a good thing, as when it avoids repetition, euphemizes, or simply adds grace. It may even be necessary, for some things apparently have no true name of their own. Still, the principle of correspondence is clear and nearness is taken to be an inherent good. Whatever its usage, any given word by nature *means* some specific thing. This view, combined with the division of the tasks of rhetoric, creates a double blindness to one of the fundamental meta-strategies recognized by modern rhetoric and, it would seem, by ancient oratory.

Linguists like George Lakoff and Geoff Nunberg have recently argued for the importance of 'framing' and overarching 'narrative' to modern American political discourse. The party that can set the metaphorical terms of debate—whether the defence of *libertas* or the modern 'death tax'—is most of the way to winning. Lakoff's terminology derives from his work on metaphor in cognitive linguistics, but similar insights about setting the terms of debate have been expressed in various contexts. As for the Roman world, Axer has sketched a more specialized version of this method in Cicero's speeches, and I have noted it in Caesar, so the orators had already caught on by the late Republic (and conceivably much earlier). What is missing in the rhetorical tradition is any account like Lakoff's (or, for that matter, Axer's or mine). In part, this is because of the division of labour described above. Arguments are collected first, then put into actual words only later, so it is hard to find an opportunity to build strategy around framing choices. But even beyond that problem, the whole idea of framing is difficult. The presumption of the rhetoricians is that (nearly) everything has a 'proper' description. Metaphor is an optional extra. Even if we sometimes choose deviant language, that choice is always marked. On more modern views, however, there are often multiple correct descriptions of a state of affairs, or perhaps often none. So, for instance, it is central to Chaim Perelman's (1979) 'new rhetoric' to operate in areas in which there is no 'unicity of truth'. Metaphor may be the only way to address many situations. It may still be possible to discriminate objectively between choices of metaphor, but decorum is not the tool for the task. Then, given this view of things, there is perhaps an ethical problem. Metaphor is deviation from truth, and so systematic metaphor is systematic lying (if perhaps not always deception). Truth-telling was already a touchy issue for rhetoric; had a theory of framing been proposed, it might have seemed a trick to license gross misbehaviour.

Further reading

There are a variety of general works on Roman (or classical) rhetoric which take on the whole subject from a variety of different points of view. Lausberg 1998 offers a synthesis of the substance of ancient theory, and forms something like a culmination of the handbook tradition. Kennedy 1972 gives a more historical perspective, summarizing the sources for both rhetoric and oratory. (Kennedy 1969 amounts to an [extremely valuable] extended index to Quintilian's treatise.) Habinek 2005 offers a still broader and more theoretical perspective, particularly from the point of view of political theory. On the special importance and complications of Cicero as rhetorician, see Fantham 2004, Narducci 1997, and the articles by him and others in May 2002. There is a massive commentary on *On the Orator* by Pinkster *et al.* (1981–), and a more accessible version in the translation by May and Wisse 2001 (the latter one of the editors of the previous item). On the evolving relationship between text and performance, see Habinek 1998, Moatti 1997, and Dugan 2005. On the gendering of rhetoric, see Gunderson 2000 and 2003, Gleason 1995, and Dugan 2005. For the expansion of this line of argument beyond the conventional limits of gender, see Connolly 2007.

Bonner 1949 does an excellent job of collecting the evidence for the practice and contexts of declamation. More modern analyses of the questions surrounding declamation (though still relying on most of the same data) can be found in Bloomer 1997 and Gunderson 2003. Winterbottom's Loeb edition of Seneca's declamation collection and Sussman's of Calpurnius Flaccus also contain much useful information.

References

Bloomer, M. (1997). 'Schooling in Persona: Imagination and Subordination in Roman Education', *CA* 16: 57–78.

Bonner, S. (1949), *Roman Declamation in the Late Republic and Early Empire* (Liverpool: University Press of Liverpool).

Connolly, J. (2007), *The State of Speech: Rhetoric and Political Thought in Ancient Rome* (Princeton: Princeton University Press).

Dugan, J. (2005), *Making a New Man: Ciceronian Self-fashioning in the Rhetorical Works* (New York: Oxford University Press).

Fantham, E. (2004), *The Roman World of Cicero's 'De oratore'* (Oxford and New York: Oxford University Press).

Gleason, M. (1995), *Making Men: Sophists and Self-presentation in Ancient Rome* (Princeton: Princeton University Press).

Gunderson, E. (2000), *Staging Masculinity: The Rhetoric of Performance in the Roman World* (Ann Arbor, Mich.: University of Michigan Press).

Gunderson, E. (2003), *Declamation, Paternity, and Roman Identity: Authority and the Rhetorical Self* (Cambridge and New York: Cambridge University Press).

Habinek, T. (1998), *The Politics of Latin Literature: Writing, Identity, and Empire in Ancient Rome* (Princeton: Princeton University Press).

—— (2005), *Ancient Rhetoric and Oratory* (Chichester: John Wiley & Sons).

Kennedy, G. (1969), *Quintilian* (New York, Twayne Publishers).
——(1972), *The Art of Rhetoric in the Roman World, 300 B.C.–A.D. 300* (Princeton: Princeton University Press).
Lausberg, H. (1998), *Handbook of Literary Rhetoric: A Foundation for Literary Study* (Leiden and Boston: Brill).
May, J. (ed.) (2002), *Brill's Companion to Cicero: Oratory and Rhetoric* (Leiden and Boston: Brill).
——and J. Wisse (2001), *Cicero on the Ideal Orator* (New York: Oxford University Press).
Moatti, C. (1997), *La Raison de Rome* (Paris: Seuil).
Narducci, E. (1997), *Cicerone e l'eloquenza romana: retorica e progetto culturale* (Rome: Laterza).
Perelman, C. (1979), *The New Rhetoric and the Humanities* (Dordrecht: D. Reidel).
Pinkster, H. *et al.* (1981–), *De oratore libri III: M. Tullius Cicero* (Heidelberg: Winter).

CHAPTER 24

HISTORIOGRAPHY AND BIOGRAPHY

CHRISTINA SHUTTLEWORTH KRAUS

> how men lived, what their moral principles were, under what leaders and by what measures at home and abroad our empire was won and extended...
>
> (Livy, Preface 9)

A Roman coin typically has a head on the obverse and a scene depicting or suggesting action on the reverse. The two images work together. In the most explicit cases, as on the Neronian issue illustrated here (fig. 24.1), the subject of the verb on the reverse (*clusit*, 'he closed') is understood to be the emperor whose representation graces the obverse, making a complete sentence.

The ablative absolute (*pace p(opulo) R(omano) terra mari(que) parta*, 'now that peace has been achieved for the Roman people on land and sea') suggests historiographical narrative, in which strings of ablatives absolute are regularly deployed to sum up action—a stylistic mannerism perhaps originally derived from the 'telegraphic style' of reports on their deeds from generals in the field to the Senate (Fraenkel 1956). On Republican coins the head more often represents an anthropomorphized symbol, as on the silver denarius in Figure 24.2, an Augustan issue thinly disguised as a Republican type (see Metcalf, this volume).

The head—with features recalling Augustus'—is that of *Honos*, 'Distinction' accruing from, and perhaps also envisioned as producing, the so-called submission

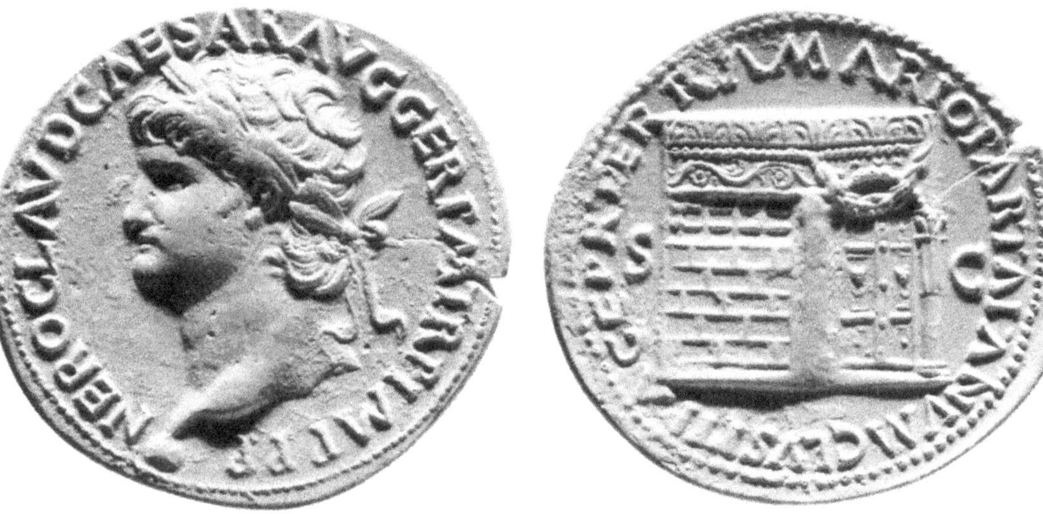

Fig. 24.1. Coin of Nero, 66–8 CE. Obverse: bust of Nero, *Imp Nero Caesar Aug Pont Max Tr Pot P P*; reverse, temple of Janus, *pace p R terra mariq(ue) parta ianum clusit / S - C.* Ex Numismatik Lanz 128, 22 May 2006, 284

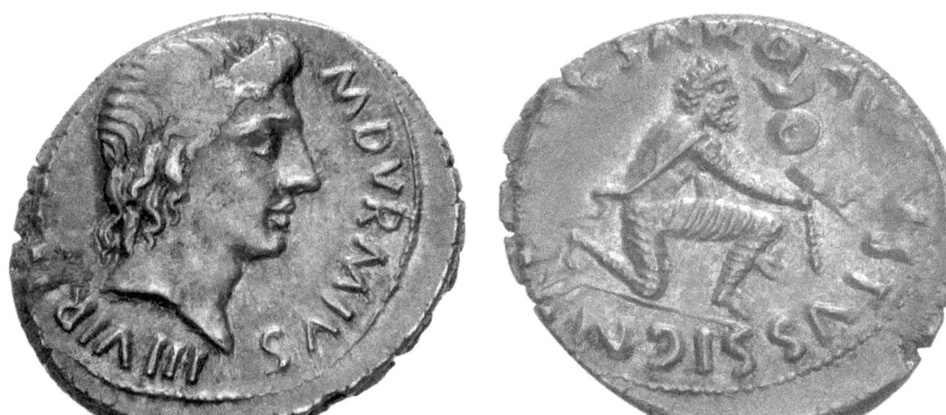

Fig. 24.2. Silver denarius of Augustus, Rome, 19 BCE. Obverse, head of Honos; reverse, kneeling Parthian with standard. Yale University Art Gallery 2001.87.991

of Parthia upon its return of the standards captured at Carrhae (reverse). Here too, there is no mistaking the inextricable combination of character (*mores*, or *uita*, 'life') and deeds (*res gestae*)—and no resisting the impulse to explore the connection by turning the coin over.

Like other genres in antiquity, the various prose forms of Roman historiographical narrative had certain formal attributes and aroused certain expectations. But just as it is impossible to get a full sense of its function and meaning by considering only one side of a coin, so it is a mistake to separate too rigorously 'historiography' from 'biography'. For, though ancient authors were conscious of, and sometimes indeed formulated, distinctions between *historia* and *uita*, those distinctions—like other generic and sub-generic boundaries—were more honoured in the breach (or the 'Kreuzung') than the observance (on sub-genres see Fowler 1982: 111–18). This chapter seeks, through the analogy of the coin, to explore the similarities as well as the differences in these two literary modes with which the Romans preserved their cultural memory.

Form

Scholars used to claim that the primary formal distinction between *historia* and *uita* lay in the choice of how to organize the material, with topic-based organization typically found in biography, linear chronological narrative in historiography. Organization *kata genos* or *per species* ('by type', or 'by rubric') is characteristic of antiquarian writing in general; it is also regularly found in literary biography (e.g. Nepos, *Atticus*), and—to a lesser extent—in political lives, especially those in the Suetonian tradition (a subset of 'scholarship': Wallace-Hadrill 1983: 50–73; see Edwards and Swain 1997: 30 on the 'grammatical-exegetical tradition'). It can be seen, for example, in the Suetonian biography of Claudius (chapter outline based on Hurley 2001):

1: family;
2–9: life before Principate;
10–25: the public face of the emperor;
26–42: the private face of the emperor (topics include Claudius' wives and children, his freedmen, their influence on him, his appearance, health, and habits, his character, and literary accomplishment).

The narrative of history proper, on the other hand, whether monographic (e.g. Sallust, *Bellum Iugurthinum*), outline (e.g. Florus), or annalistic (e.g. Ammianus Marcellinus), while capable of accommodating extensive digressions on topics such as morals (Tacitus, *Annals* 3.55), ethnography (Livy 5.33–5), and literary development (Velleius 1.16–18), tends to proceed in a straighter line. The linearity follows the sequence of time, usually organized by years or by combinations of years into periods, such as reigns. The sequence de-emphasizes the boundaries of individual human lives, though these may be used as punctuating devices—so, for instance, Livy and Tacitus regularly put deaths at the end of their textual years (Martin and Woodman 1989: 19). In Roman *historia* the state is by definition not commensurate with the body of a single man:

There was no heart or vigour in the old man's tactics. Camillus has had enough of life and glory; but why should the state, which ought to be immortal, age and decline in strength along with the mortal body of a single man? (Livy 6.23, tr. Radice: the speaker, a young commander, echoes Cicero's words to Caesar in 46 BCE: 'In fact, when I think of you night and day—as I ought—I am frightened by the accidents that befall humans, and the uncertain outcome of illnesses, and the fragility of our common nature; and I grieve that, though the state ought to be immortal, it is comprised of the spirit of a single mortal man' (*Pro Marcello* 22).)

Those who sing [Alexander's] praises on the grounds that the Romans have been defeated in many battles, even if they have never lost a war, whereas Alexander's good fortune never failed him in a single battle, do not understand that they are comparing one man's achievements—and those of a young man too—with the exploits of a nation now in its eighth century of warfare... Indeed, Alexander would have run greater risks than [the Romans] would, seeing that the Macedonians had only a single Alexander, who was not only exposed to many dangers but also placed himself in their way, while there would have been many Romans who could have been his match in glory or in the magnitude of their exploits, each one of whom could have lived and died as his own destiny ruled, without endangering the State. (Livy 9.18, tr. Radice: again, a Ciceronian parallel shows that the idea goes back well before Livy: Cato, the character Scipio claims, praised the Roman state because it 'was not the possession of one man's *ingenium* but of many, nor was it established for the length of one lifetime but for epochs and ages': *Republic* 2.2.)

Sequences of biographies could create a sense of continuation (e.g. Diogenes Laertius' *Lives of the Sophists*, Suetonius' *Vita Caesarum*), but they were separable the way individual books of *historia* were not.

Historians recognized the artificiality of such a linear system, which could easily separate parts of a complex event that would perhaps be better treated as a unity; still, organization by year—following 'time's arrow'—dominated in Roman historiography, which was as teleological, in its way, as is epic (e.g. Henderson 1989). Time is not only relative, of course, but a cultural product; in Latin historical works the change of years is almost always marked by the change of consuls, the principle of annuity that characterizes the time and the record of the time (Feeney 2007). For example, in the unusually brief year 332 BCE (Livy 8.17.5–12), all the military affairs are causally linked in a chronological chain:

a. consuls appointed by *interrex*, but
b. rumour of Gallic uprising causes appointment of dictator; though that rumour proves false
c. rumour of Samnite war causes him to leave the army in the field, but Samnites instead fight Alexander of Epirus, who then makes peace with Romans;
d. census held in Rome;
e. tribes added;
f. new consuls elected.

The major appearance in *historia* of organization by '*species*' was in the capacious categories 'home' and 'abroad': the split between events outside Rome (generally military) and those inside (generally political). So this Livian year ends, *haec eo anno domi militiaeque gesta* (17.12, 'these were the deeds in this year, at home and abroad').

This distinction between the formal shapes of *historia* and *uita*, while sometimes useful, is a very blunt instrument. Political biography, in particular, can tend strongly toward the linear. As for *historia*, the 'founder' of Latin (as opposed to Roman) historiography, Cato the Elder (234–149 BCE), wrote a seven-book work that—as far as we can tell from the fragments—began with an organization by (geographical) rubric, telling the foundations (= biographies ?) of Italian cities one by one. Once he settled on his *telos*, Rome, the *Origines* shifted to a more linear narrative. An even more famous seven-book narrative, Caesar's *Bellum Gallicum* (capped with an eighth book by his lieutenant, Aulus Hirtius), is organized annalistically, but in a Thucydidean spirit: it largely eschews mention of the elections that typically punctuate extended Roman historical narratives, instead using the campaign season as a structuring device. The *Bellum Gallicum* is monographic in its focus on a single (extended) campaign; an easy parallel is Sallust's *Bellum Iugurthinum*, which narrates the military campaign in North Africa of 118–104 BCE. But Caesar's persistent exclusion of political events at Rome (with which one can contrast the frequent Roman 'reaction narratives' in Sallust), while still maintaining the book year = real year *fable convenue* of annalistic history, focuses our attention on his literary experimentation. The work's generic status, which shares elements of annals, monograph, and (auto)biography, is appropriately blurred, given its position at the end of the Republic—when the body of the dynasts, and eventually of the *princeps*, begins to engross attention.

Content

On the level of content, the idea that biography treats the *minutiae* of a man's life, historiography the big picture, is an ancient distinction. So Plutarch, in the famous preface to the *Life of Alexander* (1.1–3, tr. Perrin):

It is the life (*bion*) of Alexander the king, and of Caesar, who overthrew Pompey, that I am writing in this book, and the multitude of the deeds (*praxeon*) to be treated is so great that I shall make no other preface than to entreat my readers, in case I do not tell of all the famous actions (*ton periboeton*) of these men, nor even speak exhaustively at all in each particular case, but in epitome for the most part (*epitemnontes ta pleista*), not to complain. For it is not *Histories* (*historias*) that I am writing, but *Lives* (*bious*); and in the most illustrious deeds there is not always a manifestation of virtue or vice (*delosis aretes e kakias*), nay, a slight thing (*pragma brachu*) like a phrase or a jest often makes a greater revelation of character (*ethous*) than battles where thousands fall, or the greatest armaments, or sieges of cities. Accordingly, just as painters get the likenesses in their portraits from the face and the expression of the eyes, wherein the character (*to ethos*) shows itself, but make very little account of the other parts of the body, so I must be permitted to devote myself rather to the signs of the soul in men, and by means of these to portray the life of each, leaving to others the description of their great contests (*ta megethē kai tous agonas*).

This distinction between life and deeds (here envisioned exclusively as military deeds) is characteristic enough of ancient thought about the two kinds of historiographical record that D. R. Stuart could refer to 'the law of biographical relevance' (quoted, and nuanced, by Pelling 2002: 53–8). His declaration of intent does not keep Plutarch from writing up those 'great contests' (e.g. the 'great battle', *megalen machen*, of Gaugamela, *Alexander* 31–3; the war against Vercingetorix, *Caesar* 25–7). But the presence of this disclaimer at the start of the *Life of Alexander* is particularly telling: it is Alexander's combination of larger-than-life personality and memorable *res gestae* that make him such a diverse subject. There is only hypothetical room for him in Livy, who uses him as the textbook case of a single individual facing off against the centuries of Roman *annales* (quoted above); when a historian does let him in—for example, Curtius Rufus—he pulls the narrative irresistibly toward the biographic. And Plutarch's *Alexander–Caesar* pairing stands well on the historical end of Plutarch's biographical–historical continuum (Pelling 2006). Plutarch's pre-emptive strike here in *Alexander* 1 demonstrates the fuzziness between the two sub-genres, even as it asserts their differences.

In emphasizing the differences in content between *historia* and *bios*, Plutarch in fact integrates them through his chosen metaphor. Eyes and the 'other parts' all work together to form the whole body (two sides of the coin, again). And indeed, 'character', 'virtue', and 'vice' are the main interest of many historians, whose works focus intently on the *uita* and *mores* that made great Romans tick. This could tip into virtual biography, especially in the Imperial period, in which 'the biographic' comes into its own. One ancient reader refers to Tacitus' combined *Annals* and *Histories* as *uita Caesarum* (Jerome, *Comm. ad Zach.* 3.14); a century on from Tacitus, Dio stands out as a 'semi-biographer' when writing about emperors (Pelling 1997: 137). As Simon Swain points out, the marked increase in 'the portraiture of the individual in writing and art' over the course of the empire is accompanied (especially with the rise of Christianity) by a growth in the importance of the individual body as a status marker and as a subject of self-control (Edwards and Swain 1997: 22–36). Livy and Cicero's insistence that the *res publica* is bigger than the body of a single man looks increasingly antiquated in the world of the Principate, where all aspects of the Roman state home in on the body of the emperor. Military honours, coinage, the law, art, and literature all converge on the super-sized *princeps*, whose body becomes a metonymical representation of Rome: so, for example, Ovid can claim that 'the state is Caesar' (*Tristia* 4.4.15). Conversely, some biographies include rich quantities of *res gestae*. Aside from the Alexander story (above), Tacitus' *Agricola*, from 98 CE, is the most obviously mixed-genre *uita* (Marincola 1999). But already near the start of the biographical flood, in the very early Imperial period, Cornelius Nepos was 'wrestling with the problem of how to organize his material both by chronological sequence and by topic without excessive duplication' (Horsfall 1988: 9)—a problem that derives, ultimately, from the biographer's desire to marry the linear tendency of *historia* with the antiquarian's categories.

In the *Alexander* preface Plutarch opposes small to great, in a Callimachean contrast between the broad canvas—the battles that kill thousands (*machai murionekroi*)—as opposed to the sharply focused detail, the playful *bon mot* (*rhēma kai paidia*). These are understood to be representative, highly selective items that will allow a better view of a man's interior (his *psuchē*) than the exhaustive (*kat' hekaston exeirgasmenos*), every-detail-in-place working-through of the hero's famous actions. This contrast takes us back to the beginnings of the genre. Biography, it can be argued, was an invention of the Hellenistic period (though like other Hellenistic works it had its earliest roots in Isocrates and Xenophon), and Rome's first experiments in 'high' literature stand firmly in the Hellenistic aesthetic. Here too, we can see a blurring of lines between the biographic and *historia*: Cato the Elder put voguish *ktisis* literature, a darling of Hellenistic scholars (Cairns 1976: 168–70), at the heart of his experimental prose history. And when biography did get a start at Rome, in the second century BCE, its attraction to the exemplary anecdote so common in political and military rhetoric—that is, oratory and (often partisan) history—brought Latin political *uita* close to *historia* (see Roller 2009; Bernard 2000: 163–5, 280). Cato is said to have refused to name commanders in his *Origines*, making all Rome's deeds—at least up to the author himself—the *res gestae rei publicae*: it makes sense that, in the heated atmosphere of competition that was the mid-Republic, biography and autobiography derived one spur from the historian's pointed avoidance of the prominent individual.

PURPOSE

Plutarch claims that narratives of great conquests cannot as easily look into a man's soul as can the biographic. He is looking for a 'showing' (*delosis*) of virtue and vice. For him—the greatest ancient exponent of 'moral' biography—the portrait not only represents a single unique individual, the original subject, but judges it; and in judging, makes it exemplary. Yet it is biography's very pull toward singularity that puts its chief exemplary function—that of being a guide to conduct (Chaplin 2000: 3)—at risk. In this last section I want to explore the practical uses of exemplarity, and to consider how the Roman obsession with *aemulatio* plays itself out in the two historiographical sub-genres under discussion.

A conventional distillation of a (male, aristocratic) Roman life might look something like this epitaph of Scipio Barbatus from the early second century BCE (the man himself was consul in 298, but the poem is later, from perhaps 185 BCE: Courtney 1995: 216–19):

Cornelius Lucius Scipio Barbatus,
Gnaeuod patre | prognatus, fortis uir sapiensque,
quoius forma uirtutei parisuma | fuit,
consol, censor, aedilis quei fuit apud uos,
Taurasia(m) Cisauna(m) | Samnio cepit,
subigit omne(m) Loucanam opsidesque abdoucit.

Lucius Cornelius Scipio Barbatus, begotten of his father Gnaeus, a brave and sapient man, whose handsome form was fully a match for his courage, who was consul, censor, aedile among you, captured Taurasia, Cisauna, Samnium, reduced all Lucania and took hostages from there. (tr. Courtney)

This, and the other Scipionic epitaphs (*CIL* 1.6–11, 15), have been seen as miniature exemplary lives. By a process akin to that by which Roman historiography has been imagined to be a narrativized version of the early priestly chronicles (Frier 1999: 83–105), or military *res gestae* an expansion of reports to the Senate (above), so exemplary stories such as those found in Sallust, Livy, or Ammianus can be analysed as narrative elaborations of the elements of these *elogia*. Barbatus' epitaph begins with the man's father and his birth, then moves to his outer and inner character. It then situates him within the state, with the asyndetic *cursus honorum* of line 4, and the explicit incorporation of 'you'—the readers, the citizens. The *cursus* is formally echoed by the asyndetic list of the three places conquered (line 5), itself capped (line 6) with 'all' of Lucania and with the centripetal result of that conquest, the hostages brought back to Rome. By rubric, then: family, personal appearance and inner character, political offices, military deeds.

Similar traits are brought out in epitaphs for women, as on this mid-second-century BCE verse *elogium* for a *matrona* from the *gens Claudia* (*CIL* 1.1211):

Stranger, what I have to say is brief, halt and read it. This is the unlovely tomb of a lovely woman. Her parents gave her the name Claudia. She loved her husband with all her heart. She gave birth to two sons; one of them she leaves on earth, the other she places [placed?] beneath it. She was charming in conversation and modest in gait. She kept to the house and made wool. That is all I have to say; be on your way. (tr. Courtney)

If war is to a man what childbirth is to a woman, then here we see an analogous commemoration of public and private accomplishments, together with a similar combination of inner and outer qualities: this woman was lovely, accomplished, and carried herself well (on walking, see Corbeill 2004: 107–39); she performed within the house what was expected, and gave birth to sons who—one assumes—were meant to grow and perform deeds outside the house. The importance of genealogical continuity alluded to in the Scipionic epitaphs, where the dead man is named son of his father, is here emphasized by the three generations of those connected to Claudia: the parents who named her, the husband whom she loves, and the sons whom she creates and buries.

Exemplarity resides especially not in the elaboration of description, whether of character or of actions, but in harnessing the power of an audience and the judgement of author and community. In Scipio Barbatus' epitaph one notes especially the twice-repeated face-off of qualities external and internal, in which line 3 spells out the implications of line 2's folding of *fortis* and *sapiens* around the noun which they both qualify, *uir*. The echo of *uir* in *uirtuti* 'proves' that this *uirtus* in line 3 is not just '[inner] excellence'—though we might have thought so, given the unmistakable philosophical overtones of *sapiens*, 'wise man/philosopher'. (Clear early examples of *sapien-* having a philosophical flavour include Ennius, *Annals* 211–12 Skutsch, *nec quisquam sophiam sapientia quae perhibetur* | *in somnis uidit prius quam eam discere coepit*; Terence, *Adelphoe* 425–8, *sedulo* | *moneo, quae possum pro mea sapientia:* | *postremo tamquam in speculum in patinas, Demea,* | *inspicere iubeo et moneo quid facto usus sit*; 951–3, *postremo nunc meum illud uerbum facio, quod tu, Micio,* | *bene et sapienter dixti dudum: 'uitium commune omniumst,* | *quod nimium ad rem in senecta attenti sumus'.*) Conversely, that *forma* picks up the first syllable of *fortis* should not distract us from the fact that 'handsome form' is often opposed to 'courage', though the echo also suggests that courage is both an internal and an external quality—as, indeed, *uirtus* may be. Scipio's outside and inside, the *elogium* suggests, are not easily separable: rather, these intertwining echoes reinforce the statement that his outer shape was 'fully a match' (*parisuma*) for his inner man. One might compare Figure 2, where the inner quality of *Honos* is in constant play with the Parthian subjugation to Roman military might, represented on the reverse.

In inviting us to compare inner with outer, the adjective *parisuma* introduces the idea of judgement. Who claims, who counts, this precise equality? And who deems this equality 'superlative': who rejects the others against whom Scipio's *forma, uirtus, sapientia*, and *fortitudo* are compared? Line 4 has the answer: *uos*. This epitaph, like its companions from the same family, emphasizes the judging Roman citizenry, who elect these men leaders (consul, censor, and aedile are, after all, elected magistracies in a republic) and for whom these men perform their deeds. The reciprocal arrangement, and the need for an evaluative audience to set the Great Man in perspective, are apparent in the epitaph of Barbatus' son, consul in 259 BCE:

honc oino(m) ploirume(i) cosentiont R[omai
duonoro(m) optumo(m) fuise uiro(m),
Luciom Scipione(m) filio(m) Barbati.

consol, censor, aidilis hic fuet a[pud uos,
hec cepit Corsica(m) Aleria(m)que urbe(m),
dedet Tempestatebus aide(m) mereto[d.

Most people agree that this man, Lucius Scipio, son of Barbatus, was uniquely best among the good men at Rome. He was consul, censor, aedile among you, he captured Corsica and the city of Aleria, he gave to the Storm-deities a temple, as they deserved. (tr. Courtney)

As Andrew Riggsby cogently puts it, 'Roman traditions of evaluation... constitute a normative theory of the *personne*: these traditions emphasize evaluation of individuals by the community and in terms of their effects on that community. Obligations are both based on the social role of the individual and defined in terms of the interaction of that role with other roles and with the society as a whole' (Riggsby 1998: 77). In the second Scipionic epitaph considered here, the locality of that audience is specified as being in some way Roman (the reading of the end of line 1 is conjectural); in both, *apud uos* ('among you') brings the point home, while at the same time expanding its relevance to include referents unimagined by the composer: here lies a member of the community being addressed each and every time the inscription is read. And though in these cases the 'you' certainly includes the conventional 'passer-by' addressed in epitaphs (cf. the 'stranger' in the Claudia inscription, above), in the Preface to Livy's history matters are less simple: 'The special and salutary benefit of the study of history is to behold evidence of every sort of behaviour set forth as on a splendid memorial; from it you may select for yourself and for your country what to emulate, from it what to avoid, whether basely begun or basely concluded' (Preface 10, tr. Luce). This elaboration of the 'generalizing second-person singular' is so unusual that some scholars have in desperation argued that this *tu* is Augustus. But failing any evidence to support this—and given that Livy probably wrote the Preface in the 30s—we have to assume that it denotes the reader—any reader, in any commonwealth—who desires the ameliorative power of exemplary history.

The twin notions of a judging community and competition/comparison between/among Great Figures are fundamental to the Roman *exemplum*. Normally, those *exempla* are seen in a much expanded narrative form, but they need not be (for them in a small compass see Roller 2004). As a coin places back-to-back a man and his deeds in the most compressed form imaginable—inviting (challenging?) us to make sense of their symbolism by filling in the narrative gaps, so in their short compass the Scipionic epitaphs adumbrate the narrative genres of Roman history. *Vita* will expand on all the topics sketched there—family, personal appearance and inner character, philosophical and literary accomplishments, political offices, military deeds—with a proprietary interest in the first four; *historia* expands primarily on the political offices and military deeds, illustrating character through action *domi militiaeque*.

Greco-Roman biography, with its roots in encomium (Momigliano 1993: 49–52), has generic expectations built in to focus our attention—as external audience—on the central figure: the authorial voice, which points to the subject either in praise or blame (cf. Plutarch, *Alexander* 1, quoted above); the deictic devices of didaxis, which direct us from one theme to another (e.g. Nepos, *Atticus* 19.1, 'up to this point'; Suetonius, *Caligula* 22); prominent transitional headings at the beginnings of sections (e.g. Suetonius, *Diuus Augustus* 16, *Magistratus atque honores*...; 27, *Triumuiratum*...; 29, *Publica opera*, etc.); and the comparative device of syncrisis, whether explicit (as in most of Plutarch's *Lives*, with their paired Greek and Roman subjects) or relatively implicit (Nepos, *Miltiades* 1, 'Miltiades... alone flourished above all others on account of the antiquity of his family and of the glory of his ancestors and of his own restraint').

Though *historia* can and does employ such techniques (e.g. Velleius' vocative addresses to his dedicatee, or Livy's headings: Luce 1977: 285–7), it is more likely to work through the construction of internal audiences, which—like the inward-gesturing, outward-gazing figures in many Renaissance paintings—invite us to look with them at the event under description. These internal audiences—the Senate or people listening to a speech, peers or clients judging a man's deeds, family approving or disapproving an action, military peers or subordinates reacting to a decision—demonstrate one consensus, whether of approval or opposition, about a given historical character. The mechanism of the internal audience can be relatively simple, as in Thucydides' spectators at the battle in Syracuse harbour, whose emotions track the winning or losing of their sides, as if at an athletic event. Or, it can involve layers of interpretation and hermeneutic design, as in Livy's story of Horatius, where the historian allows the different audience assessments of the central figure to remain unresolved (Solodow 1979). Sometimes our eyes are deliberately drawn to a character whose precise function in the narrative remains a matter of varied interpretation, such as Agrippina the Elder in Tacitus, *Annals* 1–3, whom the historian deploys as a statuesque metaphor for fecundity and power. And sometimes a character takes charge of her own exemplarity, only to find that the text goes on to use her differently. Lucretia, at her death, tells her despairing male relatives that she chooses suicide, 'lest any unchaste woman hereafter continue to live because of the precedent of Lucretia' (Livy 1.58). When, two Livian books later, she does appear as a parallel, it is as a helpless woman whose power of action has been shifted to her male relatives. This is the story of Verginia, whose father kills her to keep her from the hands of the lecherous Appius Claudius Decemvir (3.44.1): 'A second outrage took place in the city, originating in sexual passion and ending as ignobly as that which drove the Tarquins from the city and their throne, when Lucretia was raped and died: *the same fate* befell the decemvirs as the kings and *the same cause* precipitated their fall from power' (tr. Luce; emphasis added). Lucretia begins this later narrative as structuring-point (this episode, too, will cause great upheaval in the structure of the state) and as *comparandum* (*finis*... *idem*... *causa*... *eadem*); the historian thereby shows us that the meaning and utility of *exempla* is not confined to or controlled by their authors.

One final thing about exemplarity—and this will take us back to biography. Despite their interest in *exempla* and the symbolic representation these make possible, biographers such as Suetonius and Plutarch are also generically inclined to provide us with the kind of circumstantial detail that historians omit, whether for reasons of interest, decorum, or space. As Quintilian reminds us in his criticism of Servilius Nonianus (10.1.102), who is 'less compressed' than a historian's authority demands, the *historiae auctoritas* should be concise. This was also Sallust's praise of Cato: 'he, most skilled in speaking of the Roman race, summed up [his topic] in few words' (*Histories* 1.4 Maurenbrecher). That concision depends not only on stylistic brevity, but especially on the ability to present individuals and their deeds in such a way that an audience can make sense of them: that is, by building them out of familiar models both of character and action that allow the historian to communicate a wealth of information powerfully and telegraphically. The technique is akin to that of intertextuality, which brings in whole layers of nuance and meaning through a single gesture. When Tarquinius Superbus cuts off the heads of his poppies, he not only imitates the Herodotean Periander, but Livy also thereby activates the stereotype of the tyrant. When Tacitus' Livia behaves like Livy's Tanaquil while Augustus is dying, the nascent Principate is mapped onto that long-ago monarchy—with consequences for our understanding of both character and causation. The subjects of *uita* are by definition less universal—though here, too, Plutarch and others work hard against what I've been calling the antiquarian pressures of the scholarly mode, to relate their specific phenomena to wider patterns.

Aristotle makes a famous distinction between history, which is 'what Alcibiades did or what he suffered', and poetry, which 'tends to speak of universals . . . the sort of thing that a certain kind of person may well say or do in accordance with probability or necessity' (*Poetics* 1451b6–9, tr. Janko). In narrative *historia*, however, it is precisely the generalizable quality appropriate to poetry that enables both communication and didaxis. *Topoi*, the conventional building-blocks of literary *historia*, are to the representation of past events as analogies are to Lucretian science: they bridge between the single, unique, inimitable, and random occurrences of 'reality' and the mental world of the reader, who processes 'reality' as patterns. It is in the 'manipulation of shared vocabularies' (Stewart 2003: 13) that exemplary narrative makes contact with the understanding and expectations of its consumers.

As a—paradoxical—consequence, *uita*, which can become overloaded with specifics, in theory runs a greater risk than *historia* of failing to provide exemplary models, despite its greater concentration on the memorable individual. To learn what unparalleled shape or colour of underwear a star favours may satisfy the antiquarian in us: but to understand the star—the emperor, the philosopher, or the general—as an actor in society, we need that central subject to be in some sense familiar. So Pelling (1997: 143–4) remarks of the third-century CE historian Dio Cassius: 'this taste for generalizability is a feature of Dio the historian, not Dio the biographer . . . the man who is interested in the way imperial history as a whole ticks; the man who consequently finds factors which might well come back in the same way under different emperors, rather than explanations which are specific to a determinate quirky individual in a determinate historical context.' Too many *minutiae*—too many anecdotes and *bons mots*—destroy one of the main purposes of ancient history.

If that is the case, we might well ask what ancient historiography offers us in the way of truth—that is, of a reconstruction of the past that transparently shows us 'how it actually was'? On the one hand, over the last twenty years modern historiographers have shown that ancient historians worked by conventions and with expectations that are alien to us, who tend to regard history more as a social science than as a literary art. Ancient historians constructed their works with techniques that were as much at home in oratory or the novel as with what we might call 'historical research'. On the other hand, it is clear that some ancients were concerned with what we call 'facts', and even with getting them straight: narratives about the world were expected to refer to that world, and were in that sense 'representative' rather than 'imaginative' discourse (see Cohn 1999, with White 1974). But it is short-sighted and superficial to ignore the medium for the message. Nor is it contradictory to claim, at the same time, that a history can be 'rhetorical and didactic' (Kraus 1994: 9, n. 39) and that there is a 'hard core' of facts that is preserved in our ancient narratives (ibid. 28; I would now be even more sceptical about the fifth-century BCE, but it would be quixotic to deny such a 'hard core' to Tacitus or Velleius). But how can we say how far that hard core should extend? It's probably safe to say, on the authority of the ancient narratives, that Tiberius lived from what we call 42 BCE to 37 CE, or that the Palatine hill became the residence of the emperors in the first century CE. But was Tiberius difficult to reach and jealous of competitors? Was Germanicus a rival for imperial power? Was he a drama queen? Was he dominated by his wife? The ancient historians claim each of these things; and it is possible to understand these claims as part of their effort to interpret Tiberius and Germanicus as (complex) examples of certain basic 'folk models of character' (Riggsby 2004: 166), a sort of interpretative stereotyping well known in ancient narrative genres. What we cannot do, however—any more than anthropologists can keep their own perspective and expectations out of their observations and the questions they ask—is to separate the hard core either from its ancient narrative web or, indeed, from the new one in which we propose to enmesh it.

Hayden White showed long ago that the movement from a list of dates (or, we might also say, a hard core) to a narrative about those dates *necessarily* involves both moralizing judgements and fictionalized plots: the 'value attached to narrativity in the representation of real events arises out of a desire to have real events display the coherence, integrity, fullness, and closure of an image of life that is and can only be imaginary' (White 1980: 23). Narrative is a cognitive instrument: it makes things understandable. But the converse is also true. Without narrative, there are no events; there are only isolated, nonsensical, *unrelated* pieces of stuff. They have no function, no temporality, no chronological or causal connection; they are neither good nor bad, neither useful nor harmful. Narrative—whether our own or that of the ancient historians and biographers—provides those judgements, and those shapes.

Modern historians know this. They also know that any given narrative may connect the dots either partly or wholly erroneously; and they cite with glee David Macaulay's brilliant account (1979) of the archaeologists from the future who, without the help of contemporary written sources, reconstruct a twentieth-century hotel bathroom as a religious shrine. But what many contemporary historians of antiquity seem to resist is the idea that one cannot separate narrative from hard core *and retain meaning*. We may re-narrativize the stuff (e.g. Tiberius distrusted Germanicus because the young man was a bad commander, not because he was an actual rival for the purple), but we cannot return to a pristine state of 'hard core' facts without a story to make some sense of them. We choose the story we want to tell based as much on our own notions of probability as on those of truth. In Britain the current dominant view of Augustus is that he was not such a bad emperor; but when in 1939 Ronald Syme interpreted Augustus' reign by analogy to the Nazi regime, it was a strong interpretation that convinced for decades. Whatever Augustus actually was, *at no point* was he, or is he now, comprehensible without interpretation. And no interpretation is possible without the constructions, texture, biases, and rhetoric of human storytelling: 'from the moment that language is involved... the fact can only be defined in a tautological fashion.... We thus arrive at the paradox that governs the entire question of the distinctiveness of historical discourse.... The fact can have only a linguistic existence, as a term in a discourse, and yet it is exactly as if this existence were merely the "copy", purely and simply, of another existence situated in the extra-structural domain of the "real"' (Barthes 1981: 19).

The way a writer, or a culture, connects the dots of experience is of as much interest and importance as the dots themselves. Without the connective tissue, in fact, the dots make no picture at all. Productive work has been done, and is being done, on studying the ancient historical narratives, and we increasingly understand the role *topoi*, intertextuality, rhetorical moves, audience involvement, and audience expectations play in the constructions of reality we call ancient history. The more we can see that rhetoric, in Peter Gay's words, is a 'part of meaning', the more we can understand the usable past that the Romans created for themselves (Gay 1974: 206, 216–17). And the more we accept that inventing a discourse always means inventing 'a form of social life' (Saussy 2005: 128), and that 'narration is itself always a social act' (Henderson 1993: 216), the more we can profit from looking not through, but at, the discourses of historiography.

Further reading

On biography and the biographic, see also Richard A. Burridge, *What are the Gospels? A Comparison with Graeco-Roman Biography* (Grand Rapids, Mich.: Eerdmans, 2004) and W. W. Ehlers (ed.), *La Biographie antique* (Vandoeuvres: Fondation Hardt, 1998). Challenging the idea of any meaningful division between prose genres is J. Geiger, *Cornelius Nepos and Ancient Political Biography* (Wiesbaden: Franz Steiner Verlag), ch. 1. On the organization of thought see E. Rawson, 'The Introduction of Logical Organisation in Roman Prose Literature', *PBSR* 46 (1978), 12–34. For the fragmentary historians see E. Badian, 'The Early Historians', in T. A. Dorey (ed.), *Latin Historians* (London: Routledge), 1–38, with A. E. Astin, *Cato the Censor* (Oxford: Clarendon Press, 1978), 211–39 on the *Origines*; on the *Bellum Gallicum* see A. M. Riggsby, *Caesar in Gaul and Rome: War in Words* (Austin, Tex.: University of Texas Press, 2006). On Livy's 'Alexander digression' see R. Morello, 'Livy's Alexander Digression (9.17–19): Counterfactuals and Apologetics', *JRS* 92 (2002), 62–85. On the body in historiography see Elizabeth C. Evans, 'Roman Descriptions of Personal Appearance in History and Biography', *HSCP* 46 (1935), 43–84. On the relationship of history to anecdotes see Richard Saller, 'Anecdotes as Historical Evidence for the Principate', *G&R* 27 (1980), 69–83, Claude Mossé, 'Temps de l'histoire et temps de la biographie: les *Vies* de Démosthène et de Phocion de Plutarque', *Métis*, 12 (1997), 9–17, and John Henderson, 'On Getting Rid of Kings: Horace, *Satires* 1.7', *CQ* 44 (1994), 146–70 (repr. in *Fighting for Rome* (Cambridge: Cambridge University Press, 1998), 73–107). On *ktisis*-literature see esp. Elias J. Bickerman, '*Origines gentium*', *CP* 47 (1952), 65–81. On Plutarch's moralism and *exempla* see Tim Duff, *Plutarch's Lives: Exploring Virtue and Vice* (Oxford: Oxford University Press, 2000), and on character in ancient literature, start with the essays collected in Christopher Pelling (ed.), *Characterization and Individuality in Greek Literature* (Oxford: Clarendon Press, 1990). The Scipionic epitaphs are well analysed by John van Sickle, 'The Elogia of the Cornelii Scipiones and the Origin of the Epigram at Rome', *AJP* 108 (1987), 41–55; on social virtues and values see also Robert A. Kaster, *Emotion, Restraint, and Community in Ancient Rome* (New York: Oxford University Press, 2005) and Shadi Bartsch, *The Mirror of the Self: Sexuality, Self-Knowledge, and the Gaze in the Early Roman Empire* (Chicago: Chicago University Press, 2006). On audiences and *exempla* see A. M. Feldherr, *Spectacle and Society in Livy's History* (Berkeley: University of California Press, 1988); on historiographical second persons see K. Gilmartin, 'A Rhetorical Figure in Latin Historical Style: The Imaginary Second Person Singular', *TAPhA* 105 (1975), 99–121, and John Moles, 'Livy's *Preface*', *PCPhS* 39 (1993), 141–68. On narrative in historiography see the essays collected in Geoffrey Roberts (ed.), *The History and Narrative Reader* (London: Routledge, 2001), and for a recent challenge to the narrative–meaning relationship see Galen Strawson, 'Against Narrativity', *Ratio*, 17 (2004), 428–52. On the different nature of ancient historiography start with T. P. Wiseman, *Clio's Cosmetics* (Leicester: Leicester University Press, 1979) and A. J. Woodman, *Rhetoric in Classical Historiography* (London: Croom Helm, 1988); add John Marincola (ed.), *A Companion to Greek and Roman Historiography* (Oxford: Blackwell Publishing, 2007). On truth, theory, and ancient history see Elizabeth Clark, *History, Theory, Text* (Cambridge, Mass.: Harvard University Press, 2004) and W. W. Batstone, 'Postmodern Historiographical Theory and the Roman Historians', in Andrew Feldherr (ed.), *The Cambridge Companion to Roman Historiography* (Cambridge: Cambridge University Press, 2009). On complex stereotyping in Tacitus see B. Walker, *The Annals of*

Tacitus: A Study in the Writing of History (Manchester: Manchester University Press, 1952) and Christopher Pelling, 'Tacitus and Germanicus', in T. J. Luce and A. J. Woodman (eds.), *Tacitus and the Tacitean Tradition* (Princeton: Princeton University Press, 1993), 59–85. On history and memory in Livy see Gary Miles, *Livy: Reconstructing Early Rome* (Ithaca, NY: Cornell University Press, 1995), ch. 1; for a splendid example of a study of the social nature of language see Brian Krostenko's *Cicero, Catullus, and the Language of Social Performance* (Chicago: University of Chicago Press, 2001).

References

Barthes, Roland (1981), 'The Discourse of History', tr. Stephen Bann, *Comparative Criticism*, 3: 7–20.

Bernard, Jacques-Emmanuel (2000), *Le Portrait chez Tite-Live*, Brussels: Latomus.

Cairns, Francis (1976), *Tibullus: A Hellenistic Poet at Rome*, Cambridge: Cambridge University Press.

Chaplin, J. D. (2000), *Livy's Exemplary History*, Oxford: Oxford University Press.

Cohn, Dorrit (1999), *The Distinction of Fiction*, Baltimore: Johns Hopkins University Press.

Corbeill, Antony (2004), *Nature Embodied: Gesture in Ancient Rome*, Princeton: Princeton University Press.

Courtney, E. (1995), *Musa Lapidaria: A Selection of Latin Verse Inscriptions*, Atlanta, Ga.: Scholars Press.

Edwards, Mark, and Swain, Simon (eds.) (1997), *Portraits: Biographical Representation in the Greek and Latin Literature of the Roman Empire*, Oxford: Clarendon Press.

Feeney, Denis (2007), *Caesar's Calendar: Ancient Time and the Beginnings of History*, Berkeley: University of California Press.

Fowler, Alistair (1982), *Kinds of Literature: An Introduction to the Theory of Genres and Modes*, Oxford: Oxford University Press.

Fraenkel, Eduard (1956), 'Eine Form römischer Kriegs-bulletins', *Eranos*, 34: 189–94 (repr. in *Kleine Beiträge zur klassischen Philologie*, Bd. 2 (Rome, 1964), 69–73).

Frier, Bruce W. (1999; 1st edn. 1979), *Libri annales pontificum maximorum: The Origins of the Annalistic Tradition*, Ann Arbor, Mich.: University of Michigan Press.

Gay, Peter (1974), *Style in History*, New York: W. W. Norton & Co.

Henderson, John (1989), 'Livy and the Invention of History', in A. Cameron (ed.), *History as Text: The Writing of Ancient History*, London: Duckworth, 64–85 (repr. in *Fighting for Rome* (Cambridge: Cambridge University Press, 1998), 301–19).

Horsfall, Nicholas (ed. and tr.) (1988), *Cornelius Nepos: A Selection, Including the Lives of Cato and Atticus*, Oxford: Clarendon Press.

Hurley, Donna (ed.) (2001), *Suetonius: Divus Claudius*. Cambridge: Cambridge University Press.

Kraus, Christina Shuttleworth (ed.) (1994), *Livy Ab Vrbe Condita Book VI*, Cambridge, Cambridge University Press.

Luce, T. J. (1977), *Livy: The Composition of his History*, Princeton: Princeton University Press.

Macaulay, David (1979), *Motel of the Mysteries*, Boston: Houghton Mifflin Co.

Marincola, John (1999), 'Genre, Convention, and Innovation in Greco-Roman Historiography', in C. S. Kraus (ed.), *The Limits of Historiography*, Leiden: Brill, 281–324.

Martin, R. H. and Woodman, A. J. (eds.) (1989 and frequently reprinted), *Tacitus Annals Book IV*, Cambridge: Cambridge University Press.

Momigliano, Arnaldo (1993), *The Development of Greek Biography*. Expanded edition. Cambridge, Mass.: Harvard University Press.

Pelling, Christopher (1997), 'Biographical History? Cassius Dio on the Early Principate', in Edwards and Swain 1997: 117–44.

—— (2002), *Plutarch and History*, London: Duckworth.

—— (2006), 'Breaking the Bounds: Writing About Julius Caesar', in Brian McGing and Judith Mossman (eds.), *The Limits of Ancient Biography*, Swansea: Classical Press of Wales, 255–80.

Riggsby, Andrew M. (1998), 'Self and Community in the Younger Pliny', *Arethusa*, 31: 75–97.

—— (2004), 'The Rhetoric of Character in the Roman Courts', in Jonathan Powell and Jeremy Paterson (eds). *Cicero the Advocate*, Oxford: Oxford University Press, 165–85.

Roller, Matthew (2004), 'Exemplarity in Roman Culture: The Cases of Horatius Cocles and Cloelia', *CP* 99: 1–56.

—— (2009), 'The Exemplary Past in Roman Historiography and Culture', in Andrew Feldherr (ed.), *The Cambridge Companion to Roman Historiography*, Cambridge: Cambridge University Press.

Saussy, Haun (2005), 'Seventeenth-Century Language Technologies', in W. Martin Bloomer (ed.), *The Contest of Language: Before and Beyond Nationalism*, Notre Dame, Ind.: University of Notre Dame Press, 111–33.

Solodow, J. B. (1979), 'Livy and the Story of Horatius, 1.24–26', *TAPhA* 109: 251–68.

Stewart, Peter (2003), *Statues in Roman Society: Representation and Response*, Oxford: Oxford University Press.

Syme, Ronald (1939), *The Roman Revolution*, Oxford: Oxford University Press.

Wallace-Hadrill, Andrew (1983), *Suetonius: The Scholar and his Caesars*. London: Duckworth.

White, Hayden (1974), 'The Fictions of Factual Representation', in Angus Fletcher (ed.), *The Literature of Fact*, New York: Columbia University Press, 21–44.

—— (1980), 'The Value of Narrativity in the Representation of Reality', *Critical Inquiry*, 7: 5–27.

CHAPTER 25

EPIC

PHILIP HARDIE

> O sacred and great labour of the poets. You snatch all things from death and give eternal life to mortal men. Do not feel jealous, Caesar, of sacred fame: for, if the Latin Muses are allowed to make a promise, for as long as the honours paid to the bard of Smyrna last, coming generations will read you and me; our Pharsalia will live, and no age will condemn us to the shadows.
>
> (Lucan, *Civil War* 9.980–6)

LUCAN's bitterly ironic address to the anti-hero of his epic on the Roman civil war acknowledges the traditional collusion between Roman epic and the power structures of the Roman state. Through his achievements the statesman and general, Caesar, gives the poet his subject-matter. Through his own heroic efforts (*labor*) the epic poet ensures that the fame of Caesar's deeds will be perpetuated in a lasting memorial. This is the gift of the Latin Muses, whose power over the destructive forces of time vies with that of the Greek Homer. Roman epic defines Roman identity, but never forgets that it transplants a Greek poetic form onto Italian soil. Lucan chooses as the moment to address Caesar the occasion of Caesar's visit, after his defeat of Pompey at the battle of Pharsalus, to the ruins of Troy, whence according to Roman legend bloodlines and gods were transplanted to Italy in order to found the city of Rome. Roman epic is much occupied with beginnings and endings, foundation and destruction: Lucan narrates both the destruction of the Roman Republic as the end of a story that began with the narrative of Trojan foundation in Virgil's *Aeneid*, and the foundation at the battle of Pharsalus of a new order, the Roman Principate stretching forwards in a line of Caesars.

A National Epic

The history of Roman epic begins for us with the translation into Latin of Homer's *Odyssey* by Livius Andronicus in the later third century BCE. Both author and text display a hybridity typical of the origins of Latin literature: the author was probably Greek by birth, from the Greek city Tarentum in the south of Italy (Andronicus is a Greek name), brought to Rome as a slave and later freedman of a Livius (hence his other name). The translation seems to have kept fairly close to the Greek, but the metre was the Saturnian, believed, at least, by some in antiquity to be a native Italian form. In the first line, *Virum mihi, Camena, insece uersutum*, the Greek 'Muse' of *Odyssey* 1.1, 'Tell me, Muse, of the man of many shifts', is replaced by a native goddess of fountains and song, a Camena.

However, the main line of Roman epic, retrospectively at least, down to the central achievement of Virgil's *Aeneid*, takes for its theme Roman history. In the late third century Naevius, of Campanian origin, wrote the *Bellum Poenicum*, also in Saturnians, on the First Punic War between Rome and Carthage. The decisive work for the future of Roman epic was the *Annals* of Quintus Ennius (239–169 BCE), a southern Italian from Rudiae in Calabria who claimed to have 'three hearts', because he spoke Greek, Oscan, and Latin. The *Annals*, in fifteen books later extended to eighteen, told of the whole history of Rome, 'annalistically' (in year-by-year sequence), from its origins in Aeneas' flight from Troy down to the military campaigns of Ennius' own day. In a revolutionary move Ennius substituted for the older Saturnians the Greek hexameter, and opened the poem with an invocation to the Greek 'Muses' (Hinds 1998: 52–63). This highly innovative epic established itself as the monument and literary storehouse of Roman tradition until it was superseded one-and-a-half centuries later by Virgil's epic on Rome's Trojan origins, the *Aeneid*, whose authority as the canonical text of the Latin epic tradition and as the defining literary statement of Roman national identity was never contested.

Although Greek epics in plenty had been written on the foundation and local history of individual cities, this line of a Roman national epic was something new. It helped that, whereas the supreme god of the Homeric pantheon, Zeus (Jupiter) had been a Panhellenic divinity for the Greeks, for the Romans Jupiter was the state god, housed in his temple on the Capitol (Feeney 1991: 113–15). The two-and-a-bit centuries from Livius Andronicus to Virgil also coincided with Rome's rise from being the dominant state in the Italian peninsula to hegemony in the Mediterranean after the defeat of Hannibal, and then to empire with the conquest of the kingdoms of the Greek east. The first edition of Ennius' *Annals* culminated with the dedication by his patron M. Fulvius Nobilior of the temple of Hercules of the Muses, which housed statues of the Muses plundered on Fulvius' campaign in Aetolia. Finally the *Aeneid* provides the charter myth for the conversion of a military and economic empire into the Roman Empire of the Augustan Principate.

Social and Institutional Contexts

The Homeric epics arose out of an oral tradition to become the foundation of the literary and educational system of a literate and increasingly professionalized Greek culture. Roman epic developed as part of a Hellenistic culture adopted with a high degree of self-consciousness by a nation anxious to define itself within an international community of Greek and Italian states. It was by no means the sole, and perhaps not at first even the most important, Greek literary form to be adopted in Rome (on the place of epic in Ennius' overall output see Zetzel 2007). Livius, Naevius, and Ennius all wrote in a range of other genres, and in particular were prolific in writing comedies and tragedies for the stage. All three were part of an advanced Hellenistic cultural system. Livius and Ennius both gave grammatical instruction to the children of Roman noblemen. Ennius' *Annals* is alert to the grammatical and scholastic apparatus that had grown up around the Homeric poems; it has been argued that the first line of Livius' translation of the *Odyssey* already shows awareness of etymological and exegetical scholarship on Homer (Goldberg 1995: 64–73, 86–108, Hinds 1998: 52–63). There is a direct line to the *Aeneid*'s demonstrable and intensive engagement with Greek literary scholarship: Virgil is as much a scholar-poet as is the Alexandrian Callimachus (Schmit-Neuerburg 1999).

The epics themselves quickly became the staple of Roman education (Keith 2000: ch. 2) as well as the object of higher-level scholarly attention. Still in his day Horace remembers having the poems of Livius beaten into him at school (*Epistles* 2.1.70–1); but it was Ennius' *Annals* that formed the staple of late Republican education. Scholarship on the *Annals* probably started in the second century BCE. The *Aeneid* became a school-book from the moment of its publication, and the object of a large-scale scholiastic industry, some of whose fruits are deposited in the surviving late-antique commentary of Servius.

More controversial are the conditions of patronage, performance, and original reception of the earlier Roman epics. The Romans themselves believed in the existence of an earlier tradition of songs in praise of great men sung at banquets (Macaulay's *Lays of Ancient Rome* are an imaginative reconstruction of this tradition), and it has recently been argued that the epics of Livius, Naevius, and Ennius were written for performance at upper-class symposiastic occasions (Rüpke 2001). On the other hand, Ennius draws attention to the writtenness of his poem, alluding to the unrolling of the book-scroll (*Ann.* Skutsch 164) and elaborated a claim, later famously taken up by Horace, for the greater endurance of his literary monument as compared with the statues and tombs of kings (ibid. 404–6). The title *Annals* (*Annales*) aligns the poem with the official annual records of the Roman priests, with their bare lists of magistrates and short notices of religious and other events. Thereby Ennius, an outsider and of low social status in Rome, boldly lays claim both to the permanence and to the authority of the priestly records. It is likely that Ennius' poetic annals were decisive for the annalistic form taken by the mainstream of Roman Republican historiography in prose; the connection between epic and history, always close, becomes closer still in the Roman tradition. Ennius may well have had an active part in the devising of another monument to Roman time, the innovatory *fasti* (religious calendar) erected by his patron Fulvius in the temple of Hercules of the Muses, which included, probably for the first time notices of temple dedications that commemorated military victories, thus celebrating the individual Roman generals who won them, as the *Annals* proceeds in part as a record of the achievements of great Romans (Rüpke 1995: ch. 9). Ecphrases in Virgil's *Georgics* and *Aeneid* imply an equivalence between literary and architectural or sculptural forms of memorialization and an ambition on the part of the epic poet to rival the great artistic monuments with which Augustus was transforming the face of Rome (Barchiesi 1997: 272–3).

Disputed also is the relationship between epic poet and patron (Goldberg 1995: ch. 5 for the earlier poets; for the Augustan period see White 1993). Some have seen Ennius as a dependent client writing to praise his patron of the moment, in the way that the Greek epic poet Archias, whose claim to Roman citizenship was defended by Cicero in the *Pro Archia* (62 BCE), wrote poems in praise of the victories of Marius and Lucullus. More prevalent now is the view of a more independent Ennius, whose epic celebrates the contribution of great Roman heroes to the collective interest of Rome (on Ennius' self-presentation as an epic poet see Gildenhard 2003). Similar questions bedevil the interpretation of Virgil's relationship to his patron Augustus. There can be no doubt that the primary medium for the lasting circulation of the *Aeneid*, as for the other later epics, was the book-scroll, but we have reliable evidence, both for the *Aeneid* and later epics, of publication (or pre-publication) through the institution of the *recitatio* (public reading to an invited audience); we have perhaps less reliable reports of Virgil reading out portions of the *Aeneid* to members of the imperial family. Nor should we doubt that Virgil received very material benefits from the patronage of Augustus and his 'minister of culture', Maecenas. The question of whether the *Aeneid* celebrates primarily the patron (Augustus) or the Roman state and its history becomes qualitatively different in an age when, in the words of Ovid (*Tristia* 4.4.15), 'the state is Caesar'. What kind of distance, if any, Virgil sets between the narrative of the *Aeneid* and the promotion of the *princeps* has been an obsession of twentieth-century criticism.

Praising or Problematizing?

A traditional view of the function of epic is that it perpetuates the praises of the great men whose deeds it narrates. Homer sings of the 'famous deeds' (*klea*) of his heroes. The commentator Servius gives as the 'intention' of the *Aeneid*, 'to imitate Homer and to praise Augustus through his ancestors'. In Roman historical epic, as in prose history, the heroes of the past are set before the reader as *exempla*, examples or paradigms of virtuous behaviour to be imitated in the future. The parade of future Roman heroes which Aeneas views during his visit to the Underworld in *Aeneid* 6 is a gallery of such 'examples'; it is largely made up of figures who will have featured prominently in Ennius' *Annals*, so that what is a vision of the future for Aeneas is for Virgil's reader a survey of the national epic that dominated Roman culture for the past 150 years. Epic continues to function as praise poetry to the end of antiquity: a late and splendid flowering comes with the hexameter panegyrics of Claudian (born *c.*370 CE), which deploy the full machinery of early imperial epic to magnify the emperor Honorius and his minister Stilicho.

Yet Aeneas is also given a preview of great men whose achievements are more questionable, notably Julius Caesar and Pompey the Great, harmoniously together in the darkness of the Underworld but headed towards the inevitable civil war once they surface into the light of the world of the living. It is hard to judge from the surviving fragments how straightforwardly laudatory might have been Ennius' *Annals* (written before the social turmoil of the later second and first centuries BCE that led to full-scale civil war), but one of the most famous lines (*Ann.* 156 Skutsch), 'the Roman state is founded on the morality and men of old', almost a definition of Roman *mos maiorum*, traditional values, was spoken by T. Manlius Torquatus Imperiosus to justify his notoriously harsh decision to execute his son, who had led a successful attack on the enemy but in disobedience to his father's order not to engage in battle.

Modern criticism of the Homeric epics has focused not so much on the element of praise as on the way in which the narratives interrogate the nature and goals of heroic behaviour, with particular reference to the possibility of balancing the ambitions of an individualist hero striving for pre-eminence with the need for stability and security within the group, and to the competing demands of an active and outward-going heroism and the quieter virtues of the family within a household.

The *Aeneid* tells the story of one man, Aeneas, charged with the task of transporting the remnants of Troy to the promised land of Italy, there to found a city from which eventually will be founded the city of Rome. Aeneas plays the roles of both the Homeric Odysseus and Achilles, but, in his often lonely position at the top, he also grows into the cares and responsibilities that characterize the image of the good emperor in the ideology of the Principate. Since he succeeds in bringing with him to their new home a nuclear band of Trojan survivors he is more successful than Odysseus, who survived to reach home but after losing all his companions. Yet Aeneas' marriage alliance with an Italian royal family has all the allure of an arranged wedding when compared with the full restoration of domestic order and affective ties in Odysseus' reunion on Ithaca with his wife, father, and son. There had earlier in the *Aeneid* been a relationship—Dido would even call it a marriage—between a man and a woman who understood each other perfectly, and who might have enjoyed domestic bliss and presided over a prosperous society, but the happiness of Dido and Aeneas had to be sacrificed to the future interests of the Roman state. In the *Odyssey* reunion of man and wife is only achieved after the violent killing of the suitors, but they are fairy-tale villains compared with the alliance of Italians prompted by a variety of motives both honourable and dishonourable to oppose Aeneas' destined marriage. The war in Italy is all the more disturbing in that it is in the image of later civil wars on Italian soil. The hero Aeneas is as much given to excessive outbursts of emotion as his chief opponent, Turnus. Aeneas' most violent loss of self-control comes at the end of the poem, when he kills Turnus in a repetition of the Homeric Achilles' killing of Hector. The death of Turnus removes the major obstacle to the future success of the new society of Trojans and Italians, and hence of the future city of Rome, but the killing itself is a solipsistic act of vengeance on Aeneas' part. In this instance the individual hero's anger and violence serves the interests of the group, but will it always?

In the later Roman Republic the problem of the individual had become acute, as dynasts pre-eminent in wealth, influence, or military power threatened the cohesion of the commonwealth, and ultimately involved it in the meltdown of civil war, for which the solution would be the emergence of a single and unchallenged man of power, the emperor. But the Principate itself is inherently unstable: the emperor may turn into a tyrant, and opposition from the upper class may threaten a return to civil war, a threat realized in the year of the four emperors, 68–9 CE, after the death of Nero.

The Virgilian Line of Epic

This is the social and political background against which to read the six surviving epics of the first 120 or 130 years of the Principate (leaving aside Ovid's *Metamorphoses* for now): Virgil's *Aeneid* (published in a not-quite finished state on the poet's death in 19 BCE); Lucan's *Civil War* (left incomplete on the poet's forced suicide in 65 CE after his involvement in Piso's conspiracy against Nero); Valerius Flaccus' *Argonautica* (of Flavian date, probably unfinished); Statius' *Thebaid* (the only certainly finished surviving Latin epic, published 91/2 CE), and his *Achilleid* (only one-and-a-bit books, left at his death in 96); and Silius Italicus' *Punica* (perhaps left unrevised at his death in 102 CE). The major reorientation in studies of Latin epic over the past few decades has been the recognition that these poems form a dynamic and vigorous tradition, creatively engaged with the wider social and literary contexts in Rome, replacing a view that the Neronian and Flavian epics are failed responses to the overpowering presence of the instantly canonical *Aeneid* (although for some the jury is still out on Silius).

The five post-Virgilian epics divide into two groups of (i) poems on Greek mythological subjects, and (ii) poems on Roman historical themes. But attention to this divide, an old one in the history of Greco-Roman epic, can distract from the important features that unite the two groups. The obvious shared feature from which to start is 'response to the *Aeneid*', an epic which combines the mythological and historical: Virgil breaks with the epics of Naevius and Ennius in taking as his primary subject-matter characters and events from the legendary world of Homer, but at the same time Roman history is incorporated through inset episodes of various kinds, and, as importantly, through devices of allusion and foreshadowing in the primary narrative of the adventures of Aeneas.

At the beginning of his first satire Juvenal complains indignantly that he has to endure endless recitations of epics on Greek mythological subjects (with perhaps specific reference to Valerius Flaccus' *Argonautica*). Juvenal too will take up his pen, but on the endless subject of the vices of contemporary Rome. The implication is that this is more relevant to the modern world than the Greek romances of the epic poets. The satirist is as partial in this as he is in all his judgements. The mythological epics of Valerius Flaccus and Statius transport the reader into remote and glamorous—and Greek—worlds, and this should not be underestimated. At the same time, and as had always been the case in Roman culture, the alternative Greek world offers a mirror to Roman concerns. Statius himself came from one of the major contact zones between Rome and Greece, Naples, a Greek city in the bay area where many upper-class Romans had their villas, taking their relaxation in an atmosphere of Greek culture away from the business of public life in Rome.

Greek and Roman are joined in more violent ways in Statius' *Thebaid*, an epic on the war of the Seven against Thebes who supported Polynices' attempt to win back Thebes from his brother Eteocles' usurpation of sole kingship in the city. Strife between the brothers is fuelled by the mythological machinery of outbursts of Hellish fury, modelled on Juno's mobilization of the Fury Allecto to provoke the war in Italy in the second half of the *Aeneid* (a passage of which the early imperial epicists were especially fond—Hardie 1993: ch. 3). What had been figurative civil war in the *Aeneid* becomes a literal civil war between brothers in the *Thebaid*. Romans had not been slow to see a parallel between Theban fratricide and the fratricide on which Rome had been founded, Romulus' killing of Remus. The *Thebaid* is stocked with stage tyrants (Eteocles and Creon) and a good king (the Athenian Theseus) in whom might be recognized types of the good and bad emperor (as seen in the opposing portraits of Trajan and Domitian in the slightly later *Panegyricus* of the younger Pliny). The temptation to make identifications with specific figures in recent Roman history should perhaps be resisted, but this is certainly mythology with a contemporary resonance.

A major innovation in Valerius Flaccus' version of the voyage of the *Argo* in his *Argonautica* is the inclusion of a full-scale civil war between the ruler of Colchis, Aeetes, and his brother Perses, so engineering the inclusion in the second half of the epic of a war to correspond to that in the second half of the *Aeneid*, after the narrative of wanderings by sea in the first half of the *Argonautica*. A rewriting of the *Aeneid* through the myth of the Argonauts also recognizes Virgil's prior incorporation in his poem of extended allusion to the *Argonautica* of the Hellenistic poet Apollonius of Rhodes (Nelis 2001). As well as retracing the homeward journey of Odysseus, Aeneas is also questing for a Golden Fleece, the prize of Rome's glorious future. Virgil, in the complex exploration of Roman culture and history conducted through all three of his major works, tests both the idea that Rome now lives in a fallen Iron Age and the hope that a political saviour may lead it to a new Golden Age. Valerius, unlike Apollonius, emphasizes the role of the *Argo* as the first ship ushering in a new age, here not so much the end of the Golden Age with the advent of seafaring (as often), but a new epoch of civilization, in a cycle of ages that will lead ultimately to the Roman Empire. Mythical and historical voyages of discovery are set in parallel in the prologue, praising Vespasian's yet greater voyage out into the open Ocean as far as Caledonia.

The two surviving historical epics respond to the *Aeneid* in different ways. Lucan's *Civil War* tells of the war between Caesar and Pompey that Anchises foresees in the Underworld in *Aeneid* 6, but which for Virgil was to be redeemed two decades later by Augustus' new order, born out of the ashes of the Republic. Lucan tells a different story in an epic that celebrates the funeral, not the triumph, of Rome: the civil war is the death of the Republic and of Roman liberty, to be followed only by unending servitude to the line of Caesars. Lucan's account of the death of Pompey in Book 8 alludes to Virgil's account of the death of Priam (*Aeneid* 2.554–7), and acknowledges that in that passage Virgil already foreshadows the historical event of the death of Pompey. The end of Priam is the starting-point for Aeneas; the end of Pompey is the end of everything for Lucan. As part of his unmasking of the pretences of Virgil's providential plot Lucan strips his epic of much of the traditional poetic ornament, including the whole machinery of the Olympian gods. The unstoppable energy of the anti-hero Caesar in his relentless course of destruction needs no helping hand from a mythological Fury. Lucan's historical epic drew largely on the prose histories of Livy and Caesar, yet the result is far from a historiographical realism, marked by a use of paradox, hyperbole, and emotionalism whose seeds are already visible in Virgil, but taken to an extreme that matches the monstrosity and horror of what it is that Lucan has to tell. Part of the poem's unrealism can be attributed to the fact that it is not so much a record of historical events as a response to a poetic text, Virgil's *Aeneid*: despite its anti-poetic tendencies, the *Civil War* is continuously engaged with the *Aeneid* (Narducci 1979). Lucan's 'anti-*Aeneid*' exercised an irresistible fascination on later writers of epic and forms a part of their Virgilianism.

Like Lucan, Silius Italicus drew on Livy for his narrative of the war against Hannibal in his *Punica*, at seventeen books the longest of all Latin epics. Unlike Lucan, he practised a religious devotion to the memory of Virgil, even owning the poet's tomb, and he restored to his historical poem the full panoply of traditional Virgilian epic. His anti-hero Hannibal swears at the shrine of Dido in Carthage that he will fulfil her curse of eternal enmity against the descendants of Aeneas. The *Punica* is thus faithful to Virgil in writing that sequel to the *Aeneid* for which the *Aeneid* had itself provided when it inscribed the living hatred of Dido into the Latin epic tradition. Silius' subject is a critical moment in the history of Rome, that time of greatest danger when the steady growth to which Virgil's *Aeneid* looks forward came closest to being abruptly cut off by the Carthaginian threat, and also the time when, in response to that danger, Rome reached its peak of moral greatness. The external threat to Rome is matched by the internal threat to political cohesion, in the temptations to policy dissensions between different parties in Rome, which come to a head when consul is set against consul in another version of fraternal harmony turned into strife. The last books of the poem chart the rise and success of the single great war-leader, Scipio Africanus—yet another model for the good emperor. But Silius can surprise by breaking out of the mould of a safe and diligent purveyor of traditional Roman messages about history and morality, for example in the infuriated mutual suicide of the inhabitants of the Spanish city of Saguntum in the face of a Carthaginian siege, a supreme example of virtue but also disturbingly excessive—in a city that is presented as an image of both Troy and Rome.

Literary Authority and Literary Systems

A genre that tells stories about national origins and military power is also self-conscious about its own history and authority. The post-Virgilian epicists' self-positioning in relation to the *Aeneid* in varying combinations of deference and defiance is the expression of a literary rivalry that is practised with greater intensity in epic than in other ancient genres, an intensity ultimately to be traced to the almost godlike authority of the founder of the genre, Homer. To rival Homer is to aim high indeed. Ennius, with a breathtaking insouciance that perhaps no Greek epic poet could have dared, asserts himself to be the Roman Homer when, in the proem to the *Annals*, he reports a dream in which the phantom of Homer announced to Ennius that the true soul of Homer has been reincarnated in him. Ennius is not just inspired by Homer; the breath of Homer gives him life. Unassailable in this confidence, in the proem to a later book (Book 7) he dismisses the earlier Latin epic poets such as Naevius as 'Fauns and bards', unsophisticated and provincial practitioners who did not succeed in scaling the heights of the (Greek) Muses; only Ennius had the courage and ability to unlock the gates (or perhaps fountains) of Homeric epic (*Ann.* 206–10 Skutsch). Virgil, in this pointedly faithful to Homer's own practice, does not explicily state his poetic ambitions. However, his choice of a subject contemporary with those of the *Iliad* and *Odyssey*, his skilful inclusion of the plots of both Homeric epics within the compass of the twelve books of the *Aeneid*, and the almost incredible density and continuity of his detailed allusion to Homer (Knauer 1968), implicitly assert that Virgil, not Ennius, is the true Roman Homer; perhaps greater than Homer to the extent that the matter of Rome is greater than the relatively small world of the Homeric heroes. 'Something greater than the *Iliad* is coming to birth', had announced the elegiac poet Propertius (2.34.66) while Virgil was at work on the *Aeneid*. Within his epic Virgil includes versions of an annalistic Roman history, in the parade of heroes in Book 6 and the scenes of Roman history on the Shield of Aeneas in Book 8, both of them by way of homage to his predecessor Ennius, but both miniaturizations of the *Annals*, dwarfed by the greater, in both senses, poem that frames them. In the proem to the third *Georgic*, an allusive programme for a future epic, Virgil had made an equally bold claim for the power of the epic poet of the new age in developing a parallel between his own prospective achievement and the triple triumph of Octavian in 29 BCE (with possible precedent in an Ennian equivalence of poetic and military achievement in the celebration of his patron Fulvius' triumph in *Annals* 15). Lucan, in the passage quoted at the start of this chapter, twins his own poetic power with the world-shattering victory of Caesar: 'future generations will read *you and me*', with no precedence assigned as between the two pronouns; this in an epic that smashes the cosmos so carefully crafted by the collaboration of Virgil and Augustus. Statius, in the epilogue to the *Thebaid*, instructs his epic to follow the 'divine *Aeneid*' at a respectful distance, like Creusa following behind her husband Aeneas as they left Troy; modern readers detect some dissimulation here of Statius' true ambitions, for which a more adequate figure might be the overreaching and blasphemous Capaneus in *Thebaid* 10, who in his assault on Thebes challenges the supreme god Jupiter, to be hurled down by a thunderbolt: a sublime but failed venture (Leigh 2006).

In addition to the obsession of epic poets with their standing within the succession to Homer and Virgil, epic as a genre also stands on its dignity as occupying the summit of the hierarchy of genres. Roman poets, especially from the Augustan period on, are more self-conscious about their choice of genre and about generic boundaries than are their Greek predecessors (Conte 1994: 115–17). Those writing in humbler genres like pastoral, elegy, or lyric use the convention of the *recusatio* ('refusal') to justify or apologize for their decision not to aspire to the higher genre of epic (or sometimes tragedy), using for their own purposes Callimachus' defence in the prologue to his *Aitia* of his preference for small-scale, finely crafted, poetry over large-scale thunderings or brayings. Virgil's career ascended from the lesser genres of pastoral and didactic to the heights of epic, but the *Aeneid* plays skilfully on the whole system of literary genres to set in relief the central epic action. For example, in delaying in Carthage to indulge in a love-affair with Dido Aeneas strays into the softer world of the Latin love elegist, from which he must be sternly recalled to the hyper-masculine world of epic endeavour. Dido, who hitherto has been successful as an epic leader of men, despite her gender, is doomed to bring her life to an end in a tragic plot (and in general the *Aeneid*'s power owes much to a renewed attention to the old links between the genres of epic and tragedy—Hardie 1997). The war in Italy in the second half of the poem rudely introduces new epic violence to a land that had become used to the peaceful pursuits of pastoral and georgic.

Ovid's *Metamorphoses* tests the generic system to the point of deconstruction, so successfully that critics cannot agree whether the poem is or is not itself to be classified as epic. It is a very long poem (fifteen books, three books longer than the *Aeneid*), which undertakes the grandest of subjects, a history of the world from its beginning to the poet's own day. It contains lofty episodes of cosmogony, apotheoses of heroes, hyperbolical battle scenes. From another point of view it falls into a loosely connected series of short narratives, many of them on erotic subjects that would be more at home in elegy than epic, at the same time as it persistently questions the boundaries by which we define epic and elegy (Hinds 1987: chs. 5 and 6). One thing is certain, that it belongs with the more conventional early imperial epics as a sustained and intensive response, the first such, to the *Aeneid*. One answer to the question of definition is to see in it an attempt to establish an alternative tradition of epic, one taken up by Statius in his unfinished *Achilleid* (Heslin 2005: 69–70, ch. 7).

Epos of Knowledge: Roman Didactic Poetry

One of the longest passages in the *Metamorphoses* is the Speech of Pythagoras in the last book, a 400-line specimen of didactic poetry on metempsychosis and mutability. The link between narrative epic and didactic poetry had always been close: Hesiod, the first didactic poet, is paired with Homer at the beginning of Greek literature, both using the hexameter. In antiquity didactic was often classified with epic under the shared label of 'epos' (hexameter poetry). Ovid's Speech of Pythagoras comments on the ways in which that link had become closer in Roman literature (Hardie 1995): its allusivity reaches back to the Speech of Homer in

Ennius' dream at the beginning of the *Annals*, a passage of Pythagorean didaxis. In the *Annals* Ennius also drew on Empedocles' didactic poem *On Nature*, a key model for the first surviving Latin didactic poem, Lucretius' *On the Nature of Things*, a presentation in verse of Epicurean physics as a project of enlightenment whose ambition is nothing less than a revolution in the belief structures and social practices of its Roman readers. Symbolic of that revolution is the presentation of the master Epicurus as an epic hero of the mind, rendering superfluous and misguided traditional models of epic achievement, and relegating to the dustbin of history the national epic of Ennius, whose manner and language are diverted to Lucretius' philosophical ends. Virgil's didactic poem, massively indebted to Lucretius, the *Georgics*, takes the farm and the natural world as a stage on which to explore Roman history and identity at a critical moment, as Octavian, victorious in the civil war, is faced with the question of how to reorder Rome in what will become the new Augustan dispensation. In a more relaxed time of settled peace Ovid's *Art of Love*, gently parodic of the *Georgics*, offers the male and female inhabitants of Venus' city, Rome, instructions in how to use the arts of civilization to achieve erotic success. Conversely, Virgil's great epic of national identity continues Ennius' incorporation in a narrative epic of natural-philosophical didactic material: the *Aeneid* is permeated by a sense that Rome's destiny is part of a larger cosmic order, that Roman history is written into the 'nature of things' (but a very un-Lucretian nature—Hardie 1986). The later Augustan didactic poem by Manilius on astronomy and astrology also views Rome's imperial power as part of the natural order. Science and philosophy are an especially strong presence in Lucan's epic, but here to show how the collapse of the political structure coincides with the dissolution of the natural cosmos (Lapidge 1979).

In Latin hexameter poetry power and knowledge, traditionally the separate preserves of narrative epic and didactic, become mutually reinforcing, as they do in other areas of Rome's imperial project. For example, recent work has brought out the connections between the power of the Roman Empire and the encyclopedic scope of Pliny the Elder's *Natural History*.

Conclusion

When Juvenal contrasts epic with satire, he perhaps knowingly draws attention to what they have in common as much as to what separates them. Sander Goldberg has argued that the Romans invented satire in order to have a genre capable of a more direct criticism of Roman social reality than was possible for any of the genres inherited from Greece (Goldberg 2005). But at another level it is Latin epic, in both its Roman historical and Greek mythological strands, that most extensively explores what it is to have become Roman over the centuries, and what it is to be a Roman in the later Republic or early Empire.

Further reading

Boyle 1993 contains essays on the whole Roman epic tradition. There is much of value, not just on the gods, in Feeney 1991. On pre-Virgilian epic see Goldberg 1995; for Ennius use the monumental edition by Skutsch (1985). **Virgil, *Aeneid*:** General books: Heinze 1993 (first pub. 1902) marks the beginning of modern criticism, and is of lasting value. Later landmarks include Pöschl 1962, Otis 1964, and Putnam 1988. Hardie 1986 and Cairns 1989 explore the politics and ideology of the poem; Johnson 1976 and Lyne 1987 develop pessimistic, 'Harvard' readings. On Virgil's imitation of Homer, see Knauer 1964; of Apollonius of Rhodes, see Nelis 2001. Collections of articles: Harrison 1990, with good introduction on the history of Virgilian criticism; Hardie 1999; Thomas 1999. Martindale 1997 contains a wide range of essays. On the response of post-Virgilian epic to the *Aeneid*, see Hardie 1993. **Ovid, *Metamorphoses*:** General books: Otis 1970, Due 1974, Galinsky 1975, Holzberg 2002, Fantham 2004. Hinds 1987 is seminal for recent work on Ovid's generic play. **Lucan, *Civil War*:** Ahl 1976 is still a good general introduction; Masters 1992 studies the metapoetics of the poem; Leigh 1997 and Bartsch 1997 offer different approaches to Lucan. **Statius, *Thebaid*:** Vessey 1973 is still a useful introduction; the new wave of criticism was largely kick-started by Henderson 1998. On the poem's Roman relevance, see Dominik 1994. **Statius, *Achilleid*:** Heslin 2005. **Valerius Flaccus, *Argonautica*:** Hershkowitz 1998. **Silius Italicus, *Punica*:** von Albrecht 1964, Ahl *et al.* 1986. **Didactic poetry:** Toohey 1996; on Lucretius and Virgil, see Gale 2000.

References

Ahl, F. (1976), *Lucan: An Introduction*, Ithaca, NY: Cornell University Press.

—— Davis, M., and Pomeroy, A. (1986), *Silius Italicus*, *ANRW* II.32.4: 2492–561.

Barchiesi, A. (1997), 'Ecphrasis', in Martindale 1997: 271–81.

Bartsch, S. (1997), *Ideology in Cold Blood: A Reading of Lucan's Civil War*, Cambridge, Mass.: Harvard University Press.

Boyle, A. J. (ed.) (1993), *Roman Epic*, London and New York: Routledge.

Cairns, F. (1989), *Virgil's Augustan Epic*, Cambridge: Cambridge University Press.

Conte, G. (1994), *Genres and Readers: Lucretius, Love Elegy, Pliny's Encyclopedia*, tr. G. W. Most, Baltimore and London: Johns Hopkins University Press.

Dominik, W. J. (1994), *The Mythic Voice of Statius: Power and Politics in the Thebaid*, Leiden and New York: Brill.

Due, O. S. (1974), *Changing Forms: Studies in the Metamorphoses of Ovid*, Copenhagen: Gyldendal.

Fantham, E. (2004), *Ovid's Metamorphoses*, Oxford: Oxford University Press.

Feeney, D. C. (1991), *The Gods in Epic*, Oxford: Oxford University Press.

Gale, M. R. (2000), *Virgil on the Nature of Things: The Georgics, Lucretius and the Didactic Tradition*, Cambridge: Cambridge University Press.

Galinsky, K. (1975), *Ovid's Metamorphoses: An Introduction to the Basic Aspects*, Oxford: Blackwell.

Gildenhard, I. (2003), 'The "Annalist" Before the Annalists; Ennius and his *Annales*', in U. Eigler *et al.* (eds), *Formen römischer Geschichtsschreibung von den Anfängen bis Livius*, Darmstadt: Wissenschaftliche Buchgesellschaft, 93–114.

Goldberg, S. M. (1995), *Epic in Republican Rome*, Oxford: Oxford University Press.

—— (2005), *Constructing Literature in the Roman Republic*, Cambridge: Cambridge University Press.

Hardie, P. (1986), *Virgil's Aeneid: Cosmos and Imperium*, Oxford: Oxford University Press.

—— (1993), *The Epic Successors of Virgil: A Study in the Dynamics of a Tradition*, Cambridge: Cambridge University Press.

—— (1995), 'The Speech of Pythagoras in Ovid *Metamorphoses* 15: Empedoclean Epos', *Classical Quarterly*, 45: 204–14.

—— (1997), 'Virgil and Tragedy', in Martindale 1997: 312–26.

—— (ed.) (1999), *Virgil: Critical Assessments of Classical Authors*, London: Routledge.

Harrison, S. J. (ed.) (1990), *Oxford Readings in Vergil's Aeneid*, Oxford and New York; Oxford University Press.

Heinze, R. (1993), *Virgil's Epic Technique*, tr. H. and D. Harvey and F. Robertson, Bristol: Bristol Classical Press.

Henderson, J. (1998), 'Statius' Thebaid/Form Premade', in *Fighting for Rome: Poets and Caesars, History, and Civil War*, Cambridge: Cambridge University Press, 212–54.

Hershkowitz, D. (1998), *Valerius Flaccus' Argonautica: Abbreviated Voyages in Silver Latin Epic*, Oxford: Oxford University Press.

Heslin, P. J. (2005), *The Transvestite Achilles: Gender and Genre in Statius' Achilleid*, Cambridge: Cambridge University Press.

Hinds, S. (1987), *The Metamorphosis of Persephone: Ovid and the Self-conscious Muse*, Cambridge: Cambridge University Press.

—— (1998), *Allusion and Intertext: Dynamics of Appropriation in Roman Poetry*, Cambridge: Cambridge University Press.

Holzberg, N. (2002), *Ovid: The Poet and His Work*, tr. G. M. Goshgarian, Ithaca and London: Cornell University Press.

Johnson, W. R. (1976), *Darkness Visible: A Study of Vergil's Aeneid*, Berkeley, Los Angeles, London: University of California Press.

Keith, A. M. (2000), *Engendering Rome: Women in Latin Epic*, Cambridge: Cambridge University Press.

Knauer, G. N. (1964), *Die Aeneis und Homer*, Göttingen: Vandenhoeck & Ruprecht.

Lapidge, M. (1979), 'Lucan's Imagery of Cosmic Dissolution', *Hermes*, 107: 344–70.

Leigh, M. (1997), *Lucan: Spectacle and Engagement*, Oxford: Oxford University Press.

Leigh, M. (2006), 'Statius and the Sublimity of Capaneus', in M. J. Clarke, B. G. F. Currie, and R. O. A. M. Lyne (eds.), *Epic Interactions: Perspectives on Homer, Virgil, and the Epic Tradition Presented to Jasper Griffin by Former Pupils*, Oxford: Oxford University Press, 217–41.

Lyne, R. O. A. M. (1987), *Further Voices in Vergil's Aeneid*, Oxford: Oxford University Press.

Martindale, C. (ed.) (1997), *The Cambridge Companion to Virgil*, Cambridge: Cambridge University Press.

Masters, J. (1992), *Poetry and Civil War in Lucan*, Cambridge: Cambridge University Press.

Narducci, E. (1979), *La provvidenza crudele. Lucano e la distruzione dei miti augustei*, Pisa: Giardini.

Nelis, D. (2001), *Vergil's Aeneid and the Argonautica of Apollonius Rhodius*, Leeds: Francis Cairns.

Otis, B. (1964), *Virgil: A Study in Civilized Poetry*, Oxford: Oxford University Press.

Pöschl, V. (1962), *Virgil's Poetic Art*, tr. M. Seligson, Ann Arbor, Mich.: University of Michigan Press.

Putnam, M. C. J. (1988), *The Poetry of the Aeneid*,[2] Ithaca and London: Cornell University Press.

Rüpke, J. (1995), *Kalendar und Öffentlichkeit. Die Geschichte der Repräsentation und religiösen Qualifikation von Zeit in Rom*, Berlin: Walter de Gruyter.

—— (2001), 'Kulturtransfer als Rekodierung: Zum literargeschichtlichen und sozialen Ort der frühen römischen Epik', in J. Rüpke (ed.), *Von Göttern und Menschen erzählen. Formkonstanzen und Funktionswandel vormoderner Epik*, Stuttgart: F. Steiner, 42–64.

Schmit-Neuerburg, T. (1999), *Vergils Aeneis und die antike Homerexegese. Untersuchungen zum Einfluß ethischer un kritischer Homerrezeption auf imitatio und aemulatio Vergils*, Berlin and New York: Walter de Gruyter.

Skutsch, O. (1985), *The Annals of Quintus Ennius*, Oxford: Oxford University Press.

Thomas, R. F. (1999), *Reading Virgil and his Texts: Studies in Intertextuality*, Ann Arbor, Mich.: University of Michigan Press.

Toohey, P. (1996), *Epic Lessons: An Introduction to Ancient Didactic Poetry*, London: Routledge.

Vessey, D. W. T. C. (1973), *Statius and the Thebaid*, Cambridge: Cambridge University Press.

von Albrecht, M. (1964), *Silius Italicus: Freiheit und Gebundenheit römischer Epik*, Amsterdam: P. Schippers.

White, P. (1993), *Promised Verse: Poets in the Society of Augustan Rome*, Cambridge, Mass., and London: Harvard University Press.

Zetzel, J. (2007), 'Cicero's Influence on Ennius', in William Fitzgerald and Emily Gowers (eds.), *Ennius Perennis*. Proceedings of the Cambridge Philological Society Supplementary vol. 31, Cambridge: Cambridge University Press, 1–16.

CHAPTER 26

FIRST-PERSON POETRY

KATHLEEN McCARTHY

For modern readers 'first-person poetry' is a term that not only needs no explaining, but even risks redundancy, since first-person, non-narrative poetry has come almost to coincide with the category of poetry itself. Roman readers, on the other hand, would have seen such poetry as part of a broader and much more well-populated poetic domain and, more importantly, would have found this term a strange kind of description, since it cuts across the inherited generic categories organized by metre, diction, and topoi. Roman first-person poetry is thus likely to seem more familiar to modern readers than, say, epic or verse drama, and yet this very familiarity may make it hard for us to gauge how this poetry operated within its own literary environment. Although the persistence of the first-person voice as an organizing frame of short poems offers a form of continuity across historical periods from archaic Greece into the modern day, the meaning of this continuity is not self-evident and its explanatory power has proven equally easy to over- and under-value.

Beneath the apparent continuity of the first-person form are two very different conceptions of how that voice operates. One conception accents the representational aspect of the poem, seeing it as a mimesis of a moment of social speech. The limiting case for this form would be dramatic monologue, which fully fleshes out a character and a situation through a first-person speech; because this conception of first-person poetry comes so close to the speech of a character in drama it lends itself readily to a reading practice that assumes that the poetic speaker is a character produced as part of a scene, not the voice of the poet him/herself. The other conception understands the poem not as representing some speech imagined as spoken in a certain situation, but as an utterance that exists in and of the poem itself. The limiting case here would be meditative lyric, which communicates with the reader precisely by seeming to forgo communication at all (as John Stuart Mill put it, 'feeling confessing itself to itself in moments of solitude'). This latter conception understands the language of the poem, its ideas and images, to be issuing from the poet, not from a character created by the poet.

In any given poem there are cues as to which of these two governing conceptions is operative, but the dividing-line between them is not as obvious as we might imagine. Roman first-person poetry, like its Greek predecessors, is much more likely than modern western poetry to exhibit a robust and well-defined 'context of utterance' (that is, the scene which the poem implies as a setting in which it could be imagined as spoken); not every poem with a first-person speaker in Latin has an addressee and a scenic context, but this formula accurately describes the norm of the three major genres of Latin first-person poetry (elegy, lyric, and satire). Such a context of utterance, however, can be ambiguous: does it close the gap between the communication that happens in poetry and that which occurs in social life, as the poetry gains traction from having speakers addressing, not themselves or a skylark, but a friend or rival or lover, as they do in social life? Or does it strengthen the fictionality and even figurality of the poetry, since the scene of speech is so obviously a poetic construction? As an example of the first view, we might note W. R. Johnson's influential formulation of a few decades ago: 'Again and again, the You to whom Horace's poem is spoken serves as a metaphor for the readers of the poem.... Horace is present to us because he makes sure, through his metaphoric second-person pronouns, that we are present to him' (1982: 127). The second view can be represented by Lowell Edmunds's recent forceful objections to the way that speech-act theory has been applied to poetry, for example: 'While poems may represent or dramatize speech acts that have illocutionary or perlocutionary force (prayers, entreaties, warnings, etc.) they are not speech acts on the part of an empirical poet in relation to an empirical addressee' (2001: 27). Neither Johnson nor Edmunds is confused about the actual status of the poem as a literary creation rather than an act of social speech, but while Edmunds maintains that a speech act cannot be both an object of representation in the poem and the poem itself, for Johnson the represented speech act is a conduit through which a quasi-social speech act between author and reader takes place.

Although this debate may seem to involve only formal and structural aspects of the poetry, it involves historical questions as well, since the context of utterance is the most obvious feature of Rome's inheritance from the Greek literary tradition. This Roman literary practice preserves within a corpus of poetry which will be circulated primarily in books the structure of a face-to-face encounter, thus, depending on one's view, either mimicking (representing a speech act) or re-creating (constituting a speech act) the performative aspect of early Greek poetry. The perspectives cited here offer specific examples, then, of the general problem I noted at the outset of how to assess first-person poetry's long history: Edmunds stresses the decisive break that comes with writing—'it is, in general, only for as long as poetry is oral and performed that poems can be considered speech acts' (2001: 29)—thus severing the apparent continuity offered by the first-person form, while for Johnson the Roman poets successfully inhabit and revivify this archaic practice, producing 'a constant, unified impression of living speech, of intimacy, exchange, and discourse' (1982: 4). Underpinning Johnson's belief in the sleight-of-hand by which, for example, Horace's address to Postumus becomes Horace's address to ourselves is the knowledge that there was a time when the poetry that later ended up in books was in fact a stylized act of communication, addressed by a real speaker to a real addressee in a setting that was itself represented in the poem.

Because Edmunds strictly preserves the boundary between the represented speech act and the poem itself, he also preserves the boundary between the poetic speaker and the historical poet, while Johnson's way of reading lends itself to hearing the voice of the historical poet as that of the speaker in the text (note that while he claims the poetic addressee is metaphorical, he makes no similar claim for the speaker). The rubric under which these questions have usually been handled by scholars is the concept of *persona*. Strictly speaking, *persona* designates the poetic speaker, and using this label implies that we are recognizing that this speaker is a textual feature, not a person in the world; most often, however, this bare demarcation has been overshadowed by the larger claim that the poetic speaker is not one particular person in the world, that is, the author. As the term has been used in the scholarship on Latin poetry it meets several different needs and, in doing so, tends to obscure the differences between them. The context in which the term appeared earliest and has had the greatest influence is in the criticism of satire; beginning with W. S. Anderson's ground-breaking analyses in the 1950s and 1960s, the concept of *persona* became a potent way of articulating the poet's artistic control in texts which featured a first-person voice that seemed ranting and uncontrolled. But a slightly different understanding of *persona* has also been important in the recent scholarship on elegy, a genre which, unlike satire, builds up an implicit narrative thread among the poems in the corpus, linking them by means of repeated characters and situations; thus the central elegiac speaker is more like a character in a novel than like the dramatic 'mask' worn by the speaker of satiric tirades. Finally, the most minimal use of *persona* tends to be found in the scholarship on lyric, especially Horace's *Odes*. For example, Davis (1991: 6) writes: 'My purpose in maintaining such analytical discrimination [between the historical author and the textual speaker] is... to separate biographical experience... from its representation in art', thus assimilating lyric to autobiography.

Since the issue of *persona* is linked to the double-edged quality of the context of utterance, looking at these two concepts together can help us to reformulate in larger terms some persistent interpretive debates. Both interpreting the context of utterance and determining the poet's relation to the speaker turn on how and to what extent the poem orients its audience toward the scene represented or toward the action of the poem itself, which is not wholly exhausted by its function as a medium of representation. Roman first-person poetry is hardly unique in offering a range of forms situated at different points on this spectrum, but it is unusually useful for examining these issues, for two reasons: first, its historical position (which it shares with Hellenistic Greek poetry) between the performance culture of archaic and classical Greece and the textual culture which came to dominate western literature of later times; second, its well-defined system of genres which offers several different forms of first-person poetry, each with its own configuration of key elements. What follows here is a description of the three major genres of first-person poetry in light of the way they deploy the context of utterance. I hope to demonstrate that the characteristic effects of each genre, including the distinctive way it positions its speaker in relation to the poet, are generated by the genre's deployment of the three primary features that together make up the context of utterance: speaker, addressee, and setting.

Of these three elements, satire invests itself most fully in the first; compared to the overpowering voice of the satiric speaker, addressee and setting contribute relatively little to the genre's effects. The relative weights given to the speaker, the addressee, and the setting can be seen in Persius' arresting image for the production of satire: alluding to the wiles by which Midas' barber both kept and told the secret of the king's asinine ears, he compares his book to a pit into which he can speak what he has seen of human folly (1.119–222). Nor is this the only programmatic opening poem of a satiric collection that self-consciously presents the genre as focused both on a dominating speaker and on the 'unspeakable' quality of his speech. We see this also in Juvenal's introduction of himself as a listener first and a satirist only once he has given up struggling not to be (1.1, 30), and in Horace's self-silencing close to his opening salvo (*Satires* 1.1.121, *verbum non amplius addam*, 'I won't add another word'; echoed at 2.1.5–7).

Satire's persistent image of itself as speech which should not be spoken has usually been understood as part of the genre's claim to transgressive power, but it is important to note that, unlike the invective poetry we find in such collections as Catullus' polymetrics, Martial's epigrams, or Horace's *Epodes*, satire rarely depicts itself as transgressive in a social context by having the speaker aggressively attack a specific person whom he is pictured as addressing at that very moment. Satire tends not to specify its addressee and setting strongly, and in the cases where it does, the addressee is not the one being abused (as would be the case in invective), nor are the particular characteristics of addressee and setting crucially relevant to the development of the poem. For example, Persius 2, addressed to Macrinus and set in the context of celebrating his birthday (including such cues as *funde merum Genio* (line 3), 'make a libation to your genius'), is focused not on the friendship between speaker and addressee or on anything unique to either of them, but on the irrationality and impiety revealed by the way most people pray. Rather than representing itself as an instance of socially transgressive speech, satire is transgressive in the degree to which it arrogates to its speaker a power to observe and judge his fellow citizens and motivates his speech without reference to a specific moment.

Satire was famously a genre that Romans invented without a pre-existing generic pattern inherited from the Greeks (Quintilian 10.1.93–5), but that is not to say that it has no meaningful relation to other literary forms. Two particular forms are often used as analogies to the specific kind of speaking voice offered by satire: drama, in general, has been cited as a way of describing the mask-like character of the speaker (e.g. Braund 1988; 1996), and diatribe—the form of street-corner harangue associated especially with Cynic philosophers—provides a model for satire's larger-than-life speaker and his equally outsize appetite for moral indignation (e.g. Ferri 1993). These two forms can give us an idea of why *persona* theory took root first in satire and has been most productive there. Drama offers a model for direct speech which is taken to be the speech of a character, rather than that of the author; diatribe offers a model of speech which is not fictionalized, like that in drama, but operates outside the frame of social speech, commenting on social life rather than participating in it. Thus, while the character's voice in drama is set in context it is that of a fictional character, and while the speaker's voice in diatribe is associated with that of the philosopher himself it is placed on the margins of social life.

We might say that Juvenal gives full play to the diatribic potential in satire, while the other two poets explore more intensely the dramatic potential, especially through the mechanism of dialogue, where satire departs from the category of first-person poetry. Juvenal's poetry features long tirades voiced by a speaker who is virtually an embodiment of indignation; although he makes frequent use of other voices as brief interjections and, in one case (*Satire* 3) as a central speaker, there is very little scene-setting and very clear characterization of the main speaker. Significantly, satires that do clearly establish setting and addressee tend to be those which make use of dialogue. The majority of poems in Horace's second book of *Satires* do in fact have relatively strong contexts of utterance, but these are also the poems which use as speaker not an alter ego of the poet but a more obviously fictional character; in some of these poems the character 'Horace' participates as a secondary speaker (almost like an interviewer who asks the main speaker leading questions), while in *Satire* 2.5 both speakers are fictional characters (Odysseus and Tiresias). It is conventional to place Horace at one, genial and approachable, end of the satiric spectrum and Juvenal at the other, more rebarbative, end; this comparison, based on the implied mildness of the satiric speaker, also holds if we consider the degree of engagement with an addressee, since Horace is much more likely to evoke the presence of an addressee and to attempt to engage such a listener in the speaker's moral programme (Muecke 1990), while Juvenal's speaker is more focused on his own speech than on any reception of it. Persius' twist on this pattern is to offer poems that use that structure of dialogue but without clearly defining the two participants, so that it is possible to read them not as exchanges between two distinct characters, but as self-interrogation (Henderson 1999). There are also monologue poems spoken in the voice of a fictional character, either filling the whole frame of the poem (as Priapus does in Horace, *Sat.* 1.8) or introduced by a narrative in a voice consistent with that of the main speaker of the corpus (Juvenal 3; Persius 4).

Satire focuses intently on the twin acts of social observation and the artful expression of those observations, and thus on the speaker as agent of these powerful acts. In its emphatic descriptions of social life satire clearly throws in its lot with the representational powers of language, and derives much of its memorable force from its searing critique of bad behaviour; but the odd, 'unsociable' position of its speaker—who implicitly has a stronger connection to the reader than to anyone in his own context—also brings to the fore questions of how poetry communicates, in parallel with or at a tangent to everyday social communication.

Like the speaker of satire, the speaker of elegy is highly characterized, but there is an important difference in the way that the elegiac voice is positioned and presented. If the satiric speaker is reluctantly prodded into speech by the accumulation of folly he has witnessed, the elegiac speaker generally bursts into speech in an attempt to make something happen in his immediate social situation—to overcome his lover's indifference, to apologize for (or acquit himself of) a failure in his own behaviour, to rebuke a potential rival (in amatory or poetic endeavour). As this description implies, setting plays a much more important role for elegy than it does for satire. Where satire tends toward the descriptive, elegy re-enacts a moment of social speech, with each poem offering a fragment of poeticized speech, orienting itself strongly toward the imagined world in which it takes place. In keeping with this orientation, the addressee tends to have an important influence on the development of the poem: since the poem itself is figured as intervening in social intercourse, the motivations and intentions of the addressee become a prime force in shaping the poem.

Although first-person elegy is often referred to as 'love poetry' this is by no means the only theme it treats, and one could argue that its amatory content is not the driving force behind this genre, but rather a privileged expression of the genre's focus on representing speech as a means by which individuals struggle to make their will felt in the world. As a case in point for the role that love and desire plays in elegy, Propertius' first book is unmistakably centred on the figure of the magnetic Cynthia, the Ego's beloved, but pursues the expression of this unrequited love by addressing almost all of its poems to men who are pictured as peers of the speaker and who bear the brunt of his anger, frustration, or shared suffering (Sharrock 2000). But we might also consider Ovid's exile poetry (*Tristia* and *Letters from Pontus*), written in elegiac couplets (as is all of Ovid's extant corpus with the exception of the *Metamorphoses*); in the starkest terms the speaker deploys his language to express his suffering and try to change his situation and, in the *Letters*, uses the structure of address to apply pressure on individuals as allies in his cause. Like the more familiar amatory poetry in elegiac couplets, this poetry written in exile focuses on the speaker as beleaguered and disempowered, but just as clearly marks the poetry itself as a realm of (potential) power which stands in contrast to the trammels the speaker confronts in the represented social world.

But even if it is true that the focus on an unhappy devotion to a faithless lover is the result rather than the cause of elegy's generic goals, it is important to consider this most foregrounded theme. Within the obvious coherence provided by intensely mining a small number of recurring topoi (such as the plaint before the locked door or the half-hearted renunciation of the faithless lover), each of the elegiac poets pursues a distinctive approach to the genre and its constitutive structure of speaker, addressee, and setting. Propertius, the author whose work forms the largest bulk of canonical 'love elegy', most closely fits the pattern I described above, in which each poem focuses on a moment of social friction represented through the speaker's energetic attempt to use his speech to change something in the situation. (Even for Propertius, this pattern loses some of its importance in his third book, and his fourth book of poems takes a completely new direction toward avowedly fictional voices and narrative.) The poetry of the other elegists conforms to this pattern, but each in his or her own way unsettles the underlying assumptions that shape it. Tibullus' poetry is striking for its unwillingness to stabilize its context of utterance; although he maintains the central conception of the poem as a fragment of social speech, the situation in which this speech is imagined to take place shifts, sometimes quite abruptly, within a given poem and is rarely drawn with very sharp lines or rich colours. In contrast to Propertius, for whose work the triad of speaker–addressee–setting forms a coherent and almost realist mode, Tibullus' poetry is structured heavily on the characterization of the speaker and uses setting (and sometimes addressee as well) almost as an anti-realist device, to destabilize the implied realism of the social context (Kennedy 1993; Lee-Stecum 1998; Edmunds 2001). Ovid's *Amores* also take a step away from the realism courted by Propertius' poems. Ovid keeps all the key features of speaker, addressee, and setting prominent as they were for Propertius and continues to use these features to produce stable contexts of utterance; the difference is that the represented world produced by this procedure is now to be recognized not as the social world of contemporary Rome, but as the world of the elegiac genre itself. This generic reflexivity has prompted earlier generations of critics either to decry Ovid as facile or to see him as sounding the death-knell of the genre, but more recent critics have imagined in broader scope the effects of this self-reflexive form of literary imagination (most recently Hardie 2002). Finally, Sulpicia perhaps is closest in procedure to the norm represented by Propertius' first and second books, but she too differentiates herself from her peers. Just by making the speaker female, her poetry heightens the paradoxical power relationship which shapes the genre; while the male speakers invented by the other poets use metaphors such as slavery to depict their abasement, Sulpicia's poetry uses a literal representation of the life of an elite woman to show the speaker as under the control of others. Further, her small corpus (only six poems) intriguingly accents the possibility of speaking across a physical distance which separates the lovers, and her first (perhaps programmatic) poem thematizes the role of writing in the complex act of revealing and concealing which it claims this poetry is performing (Milnor 2002; Flaschenriem 1999). Thus Sulpicia displaces the conversational energy between speaker and addressee into writing, a form of social language which activates new possibilities for communication and which makes the speaker's communication within the poem parallel the poet's communication to readers.

Elegy not only privileges the speech of social life as its model, it deepens this effect by using recurring names and characterizations, so that each poet's corpus reads as if the individual poems were snapshots from a lively, complex life, in which a series of people and relationships cross and influence one another as they develop; in short, elegy has a quasi-narrative quality which differentiates it from both satire and lyric. It is almost impossible to read the poems of an elegiac corpus without applying to each poem what we have 'learned' about the characters and situation from the others. For much of elegy's reception history this quality was taken at face value, that is, the poems were read with the assumption that they were generated by events (or at least impressions) from the poet's own life. This manner of reading always had its sceptics (e.g. Allen 1950), but since Paul Veyne's charismatic description of elegy's play with the illusion of sincerity (published in French in 1983 and in English in 1988) the scholarly consensus has turned decisively away from autobiographical readings. Veyne's designation for the first-person speaker, the Ego, has become normative, thus stressing the fact that this genre offers us a view of the world through the eyes of one of its participants, while satire's use of the term *persona* for a parallel phenomenon stresses instead the quasi-dramatic quality of its speaker's rants. Unlike the *persona* of satire, who functions as an alibi for the poetry's excesses (because he, like the historical author, speaks from the margins of the represented world, but unlike the author is overtly characterized), the persona in elegy is distinguished from the author by being embedded in the represented world. In other words, elegy promotes something like the reading practice we bring to a novel narrated in the first person, taking the first-person point of view as a literary structure rather than as the speech of the author. This effect is made possible by the highly developed world in which the characters interact and from which they speak; the speech presented in elegy rarely acknowledges a reader as the recipient, and more often the speaker turns his back on the reader to address the co-inhabitants of his fictional world.

Lyric is perhaps the most difficult genre to generalize about, both because of the complex historical continuities and discontinuities between Greek, Latin, and post-classical lyric and because the two primary practitioners at Rome—Horace in his *Odes* and Catullus—have very little in common (though see now Putnam 2006). Like all ancient genres, lyric is defined at least in part by metre, in this case, a set of metrical patterns adapted from Greek and known collectively as Aeolic verse. The strictest definition would include only the strophic patterns used in Horace's *Odes*, a small number of Catullus' poems (11, 34, 51), and some other scattered examples (e.g. Statius 4.5, 4.7), while a slightly broader definition would include also the stichic Aeolic patterns, including the phalaecean hendecasyllable, which is the most common metre in Catullus' polymetric collection. Some would argue that polymetry itself is an index of the lyric and thus would include all of Catullus' polymetric collection (poems 1–60) and even Horace's *Epodes*, which are not written in Aeolic verse at all but mostly in couplets based on iambic and dactylic metres.

Although the differences among these collections are salient, it is important to note one quality which they share: the relative independence of each poem, especially in contrast to satire and elegy. Certainly there are patterns that draw together each collection, but where elegy uses a narrative thread to link the poems and satire uses the highly characterized speaker to provide a kind of coherence, lyric plays on the possibilities of variation as a patterning device. This is most obvious at the level of metre, which can change from poem to poem, but the topics and formats of the poems differ as well. So, for example, although Horace's *Odes* offer a single unitary voice, they also show more freedom in topic and approach than the label 'lyric' might lead us to expect, including examples of character speech (1.28) and narrative with character speech (1.15), along with a range of roles for the first-person voice, from bard to sympotic gossip. Another way in which the *Odes* are notably varied is that anything that could point to a sequence of events is disrupted; this is especially obvious in the *Odes*' treatment of erotic themes, in which they contrast strongly with elegy by changing the name of the beloved from poem to poem and thus making each poem a mini-narrative of the charms and disappointments of love rather than, as elegy does, make the collection as a whole a narrative. Catullus' polymetric collection is perhaps a less obvious instance of this principle, since there we do have recurring characters (especially Lesbia, but also Furius and Aurelius, Calvus, Fabullus, etc.); but when we compare this to the elegiac collections, which train every poem into the implicit narrative of the love affair, even Catullus' poems can be seen to claim for themselves some independence from one another.

It is possible to see this separateness of the poems as an inheritance from Greek lyric, which was born and flourished in oral performance and was only later collected by scholars into books. As I noted above, one of the treacherous aspects of describing lyric is the question of historical continuity. In this case, the fact that

Horace's *Odes* are both the lyric collection which most obviously references its descent from archaic Greek lyric and the most 'bookish' lyric collection (in the sense that it uses the spatial arrangement made possible by the book to generate its effects) shows that would be naive to see Roman lyric as either a simple continuation of Greek lyric or a wholesale break with that tradition.

Catullus and Horace make use of their relation to earlier Greek poetry in significantly different ways. Catullus' practice is closer to, though not identical with, that of the elegists. When elegy signals its relation to Greek poetry, it is more likely to be the Alexandrian milieu of Callimachus and Philetas than the traditions of classical or archaic Greece. Since the Alexandrians were themselves the founders of a textual literary culture—that is, one that saw books as a natural home for poems, not as an archive of previously performed texts—the tension between performance and textuality is less activated. (On this aspect of Alexandrian literary culture see e.g. Bing 1988, Gutzwiller 1998; for the effects in Latin poetry, Barchiesi 2000.) Catullus is like the elegists in openly declaring his allegiance to an Alexandrian aesthetic, with its distinctive taste for the library as a source of creative energy and the related recognition of one's own production as a book (his collection opens with a memorable description of itself as a 'polished little book'); however, the greater variety his collection offers (compared to those of the elegists) includes a wide range of Greek models, including prominent exemplars of performed archaic poetry, especially Sappho but also the iambic tradition (Heyworth 2001). Horace's *Odes*, on the other hand, consistently refuse to acknowledge their status as written texts (e.g. Lowrie 1997) and emphatically align themselves with the song culture of archaic Greece, with the great tradition of Alcaeus, Sappho, Pindar, Anacreon, and others.

These four features of lyric noted so far—variation within the corpus, relative independence of each poem, self-conscious reflection on one's status as late-comer in the poetic tradition, and (to differing degrees) a preference for the performative quality of early Greek poetry—have important implications for the operation of first-person voice in this genre. Most obviously, these features point to a more palpable presence of the poet alongside the presence of poetic speakers who ask for our attention in their own ways. The co-presence of the persona and the poet is part of a broader lyric phenomenon, the genre's ability to enact its discourse while simultaneously pointing beyond itself to the forces that produce that discourse, especially the poet and the literary tradition. Our two major collections of Latin lyric accomplish this in different ways; I have shown above how the variety represented by Catullus' corpus achieves this doubleness, so I will pursue in more detail here how Horace's *Odes* do this by playing on the idea of performance and re-performance which is built into the ancient lyric tradition.

Scholarship on archaic Greek poetry in the last few decades has revised some long-held assumptions, and in doing so made progress toward dismantling what had been an overly simplistic division between performed Greek lyric and its textual Roman descendant. Recent scholarship (e.g. Nagy 1985, Miralles and Portulas 1983, Kurke 2007) has stressed that even the apparently concrete touchstone of performance does not require that the poet of archaic first-person poetry spoke in his or her own voice; rather, the characteristics of the speaker in the poetry are determined by generic forces, so that an iambic speaker, like Archilochos, takes on the aggressive stance distinctive to that genre, while an elegiac speaker, like Theognis or (differently) Tyrtaeus, embodies a certain kind of advice-giving or exhortation. In a sense, then, even performed Greek poetry was a representation of a speech act, not a speech act itself; further, because of the oral (and later written) circulation of poetry in the archaic and classical periods, most of the occasions when these poems were performed were in fact re-performances, which—like written Latin lyric—displayed more or less self-consciously their relation to an originary performance, from which all others descended.

This quality of re-creation or re-performance that is fundamental to lyric helps us to understand how Horace's *Odes* can acknowledge their distinctiveness from archaic Greek lyric while simultaneously claiming to replicate it—the structure of the genre allows each poem to be new (and renewed on every reading) and also to be a return of the/an original. As Jonathan Culler famously posited for post-classical apostrophic lyric (1981: 135–54), wc might say that lyric—to a degree unknown to the other genres—is above all an event, not a story. This claim has important implications, as it reorders the relationship between literary language's discursive power and referential power: the representation of anything in lyric—the speaker, the addressee, the setting—is not an end in itself but is instrumental in producing lyric's unfolding event. Some might object that the 'figuration of voice' that Culler finds in Romantic lyric relies precisely on its difference from ancient lyric, not its similarity, especially the later form's adoption of unreal addressees and contexts of utterance in contrast to the strongly grounded social settings of ancient lyric. But if we focus on the element of re-performance—in which the pronouns that originally referred to a specific singer and a specific audience open up to allow for new referents while insisting that each new moment is a re-creation of a previous one—the specificity which is so characteristic of ancient lyric is not a referential specificity (referring to some specific persons) but is a discursive specificity, linked to the poem as an event. Later lyric uses unreal address as a way of pointing the reader away from referential, naturalizing readings and toward the discursive event the poem enacts, while for ancient readers the tension created by the knowledge that performance was always both unique and the echo of another performance engendered a similar effect.

If lyric's effects are situated in discourse, while elegy's and satire's depend more heavily on reference, this also can explain the ways that the concept of *persona* has been deployed in the study of the three genres. While satire and elegy represent speech which is thought of as having some prior, non-poetic existence (this illusion that the scene represented exists prior to the discourse that represents it is what narrative theory refers to as 'story'), the speech that a lyric poem represents is itself already a poem, thus diminishing the distance between the poet as 'maker' of an artefact and poet as speaker within the poem. It is not surprising, then, that the kind of effort that has gone into theorizing the fictionality of speakers in satire and elegy has left lyric more or less untouched; this is not to say that readers of lyric are naive about the status of the poem as a complex artistic product, but that they are (justifiably) more comfortable in assuming that a blending together between the voice within the poem and the act of making of the poem is a goal of the genre (cf. Barchiesi 2000 on 'folding').

The expectations our reading in modern poetry tempts us to bring to ancient poetry tend to make the dividing-line between fictional and non-fictional, or between 'true' first-person and invented first-person speakers, seem both more clean than it really is and, I would argue, more important for interpretation than it really is. Recognizing the differences between the way ancient and modern poetry deploys a first-person voice is not as simple as girding ourselves to avoid the 'naive' mistake of the biographical fallacy; it requires not a rule by which we would tell these regimes apart but a layered and sensitive appreciation of the ways that the act of publishing poetry constitutes an act of communication that is neither simply co-extensive with the acts of communication represented in the poetry nor rigidly dissevered from those represented acts. A vibrant approach to the study of first-person poetry would also take into account the fact that the forms of fictionalization that seem so obvious in some poems are not restricted to literary texts, since self-presentation in daily life also involves a degree of artfulness and representation. (See e.g. Ellen Oliensis' (1998) use of the concept of 'face', a concept that originated as a sociological description of self-presentation rather than a poetic one, as a refinement over the term *persona*. Also to be noted here is Wray's (2001) critique of the apparent solidity and self-identity with which *persona* criticism implicitly endows the social self of the author, who is imagined to be immune from the kind of manipulations and falsifications the poetic speaker is vulnerable to.) The relation of the poetic speaker to the poet whose bidding s/he performs is not a question to be solved with a yes-or-no answer, but a dynamic confluence of multiple forces—genre, the poetic tradition, language's representational and discursive powers, the poet's artistic and social goals, the reader's reception.

Further reading

Since almost all criticism on Latin first-person poetry since roughly the 1960s includes an explicit or (more usually) implicit argument about persona, it might be more useful here to point to a few works which have important implications for this discussion but are not to be found in the bibliography on specific authors: Edmunds 2001 is perhaps the fullest and most direct recent discussion; Fowler 2000 gets at some of the underlying issues; and Laird 1999 considers the presentation of speech in literature in ways that could be useful for the study of first-person poetry, even though it focuses on other genres.

For useful treatments of the genres considered here: on satire, see Anderson 1982, Bramble 1974, Braund 1988 and 1996 (the latter is aimed at young students, but is still a surprisingly good overview of the representation of the satiric speaker), Ferri 1993, Freudenburg 2005, Gowers 1993, Henderson 1999, Muecke 1990, Zetzel 1980; on elegy: Conte 1994, Kennedy 1993, Sharrock 1991, Veyne 1988, Wyke 2002; on lyric: Johnson 1982, Miller 1994, Fitzgerald 1995.

On Ovid's exile poetry: Hinds 1985, Williams 1994, and the rich set of papers in Williams and Walker 1997.

In recent decades gender studies has made important contributions to all of the genres discussed here and to the consideration of how the authorial persona operates, even when not explicitly theorizing that question; in addition to works already cited above, see e.g. Skinner 1993, Richlin 1992, Wray 2001.

References

Allen, A. W. (1950), '"Sincerity" and the Roman Elegists', *Classical Philology*, 45: 145–60.

Anderson, William S. (1982), *Essays on Roman Satire*, Princeton: Princeton University Press.

Barchiesi, Alessandro (2000), 'Rituals in Ink: Horace and the Greek Lyric Tradition', in Mary Depew and Dirk Obbink (eds.), *Matrices of Genre: Authors, Canons and Society*, Cambridge, Mass.: Harvard University Press.

Bing, Peter (1988), *The Well-Read Muse: Present and Past in Callimachus and the Hellenistic Poets*, Göttingen: Vandenhoeck & Ruprecht (Hypomnemata 90).

Bramble, J. C. (1974), *Persius and the Programmatic Satire*, Cambridge: Cambridge University Press.

Braund, S. H. (1988), *Beyond Anger: A Study of Juvenal's Third Book of Satires*, Cambridge: Cambridge University Press.

Braund, Susanna Morton (1996), *The Roman Satirists and their Masks*, Bristol Classical Press.

Conte, Gian Biagio (1994), *Genres and Readers: Lucretius, Love Elegy, Pliny's Encyclopedia*, tr. Glenn W. Most, Baltimore: Johns Hopkins University Press; originally published as *Generi e lettori: Lucrezio, l'elegia d'amore, l'enciclopedia di Plinio*, Milan: Arnaldo Mondadori, 1991.

Culler, Jonathan (1981), *The Pursuit of Signs: Semiotics, Literature, Deconstruction*, Ithaca, NY: Cornell University Press.

Davis, Gregson (1991), *Polyhymnia: The Rhetoric of Horatian Lyric Discourse*, Berkeley: University of California Press.

Edmunds, Lowell (2001), *Intertextuality and the Reading of Roman Poetry*, Baltimore: Johns Hopkins University Press.

Ferri, Rolando (1993), *I dispiaceri di un epicureo: uno studio sulla poetica oraziana delle Epistole (con un capitolo su Persio)*, Pisa: Giardini.

Fitzgerald, William (1995), *Catullan Provocations: Lyric Poetry and the Drama of Position*, Berkeley: University of California Press.

Flaschenriem, B. L. (1999), 'Sulpicia and the Rhetoric of Disclosure', *Classical Philology*, 94: 36–54.

Fowler, Don (2000), 'Postmodernism, Romantic Irony and Classical Closure', in *Roman Constructions: Readings in Postmodern Latin*, Oxford: Oxford University Press.

Freudenburg, Kirk, ed. (2005), *The Cambridge Companion to Roman Satire*, Cambridge: Cambridge University Press.

Gowers, Emily (1993), *The Loaded Table: Representations of Food in Roman Literature*, Oxford: Clarendon Press.

Gutzwiller, Kathryn J. (1998), *Poetic Garlands: Hellenistic Epigrams in Context*, Berkeley: University of California Press.

Hardie, Philip (2002), *Ovid's Poetics of Illusion*, Cambridge: Cambridge University Press.

Henderson, John (1999), *Writing Down Rome: Satire, Comedy and Other Offences in Latin Poetry*, Oxford: Clarendon Press.

Heyworth, Stephen J. (2001), 'Catullian Iambics, Catullian *Iambi*', in Alberto Cavarzere, Antonio Aloni and Alessandro Barchiesi (eds.), *Iambic Ideas: Essays on a Poetic Tradition from Archaic Greece to the Late Roman Empire*, Lanham, Md.: Rowman & Littlefield.

Hinds, Stephen (1985), 'Booking the Return Trip: Ovid and Tristia I', *PCPS*, ns 31: 13–32.

Johnson, W. R. (1982), *The Idea of Lyric: Lyric Modes in Ancient and Modern Poetry*, Berkeley: University of California Press.

Kennedy, Duncan F. (1993), *The Arts of Love: Five Studies in the Discourse of Roman Love Elegy*, Cambridge: Cambridge University Press.

Kurke, Leslie V. (2007), 'Archaic Greek Poetry', in H. A. Shapiro (ed.), *The Cambridge Companion to Archaic Greece*, Cambridge: Cambridge University Press.

Laird, Andrew (1999), *Powers of Expression, Expressions of Power*, Oxford: Oxford University Press.

Lee-Stecum, Parshia (1998), *Powerplay in Tibullus: Reading 'Elegies' Book One*, Cambridge: Cambridge University Press.

Lowrie, Michèle (1997), *Horace's Narrative Odes*, Oxford: Clarendon Press.

Miller, Paul Allen (1994), *Lyric Texts and Lyric Consciousness: The Birth of a Genre from Archaic Greece to Augustan Rome*, London: Routledge, 1994.

Milnor, Kristina (2002), 'Sulpicia's (Corpo)reality: Elegy, Authorship, and the Body in [Tibullus] 3.13', *Classical Antiquity*, 21: 259–82.

Miralles, Carles and Jaume Pòrtulas (1983), *Archilochus and the Iambic Poetry*, Rome: Edizioni dell'Ateneo.

Muecke, Frances (1990), 'The Audience in/of Horace's Satires', *AUMLA* 74: 34–47.

Nagy, Gregory (1985), 'Theognis and Megara: A Poet's Vision of his City', in Thomas J. Figueira and Gregory Nagy (eds.), *Theognis of Megara: Poetry and the Polis*, Baltimore: Johns Hopkins University Press.

Oliensis, Ellen (1998), *Horace and the Rhetoric of Authority*, Cambridge: Cambridge University Press.

Putnam, Michael C. J. (2006), *Poetic Interplay: Catullus and Horace*, Princeton: Princeton University Press.

Richlin, Amy (1992), *The Garden of Priapus: Sexuality and Aggression in Roman Humor*, rev. edn., Oxford: Oxford University Press.

Sharrock, Alison (2000), 'Constructing Characters in Propertius', *Arethusa*, 33: 263–84.

—— (1991), 'Womanufacture', *Journal of Roman Studies*, 81: 36–49.

Skinner, Marilyn B. (1993), '*Ego Mulier*: The Construction of Male Sexuality in Catullus', *Helios*, 20: 107–30.

Veyne, Paul (1988), *Roman Erotic Elegy: Love, Poetry and the West*, tr. David Pellauer, Chicago: University of Chicago Press, 1988; originally published as *L'Élégie érotique romaine: l'amour, la poésie et l'Occident*, Paris: Editions du Seuil, 1983.

Williams, Gareth (1994), *Banished Voices: Readings in Ovid's Exile Poetry*, Cambridge: Cambridge University Press.

—— and Andrew Walker, eds. (1997), *Ovid and Exile* (I and II), special issues of *Ramus*, 26.1 and 26.2.

Wray, David (2001), *Catullus and the Poetics of Roman Manhood*, Cambridge: Cambridge University Press.

Wyke, Maria (2002), *The Roman Mistress: Ancient and Modern Representations*, Oxford: Oxford University Press.

Zetzel, J. E. G. (1980), 'Horace's *Liber Sermonum*: The Structure of Ambiguity', *Arethusa*, 13: 59–77.

CHAPTER 27

THEATRE

FLORENCE DUPONT*

What could be more false (*fictum*) than verse, a stage (*scaena*), and plays (*fabulae*)?

(Cicero, *De Oratore* 2.193)

Latin Verse and Greek Games

The theatre is a nodal point in the culture of Roman bilingualism. It acts as interface, first between Hellenistic tradition and the affirmation of a distinctly Roman identity—realized through *litterae Latinae* among other means—second between the ritual of the games and the literary conservation of the texts that enabled ludic performance. This ambiguity means that while the Romans designate plays as 'tragedy', 'comedy', or 'mime', that is, with Greek terms, they speak solely of scenic games (*ludi scenici*) for general theatrical practice. They indicate thereby that the ritual is strictly Roman, even if qualified as 'Greek': the *ludi scenici* are also called *ludi Graeci*.

* Translated by Michèle Lowrie.

Every theatrical performance at Rome is integrated into the ritual that is the games, where it coexists with circus spectacles. The games are dedicated to a divinity and, according to the god's rites, include or not a scenic spectacle qualified as 'Greek'. Thus Apollo, the Great Mother, Florus, and Jupiter receive 'Greek games'. The theatre is therefore a variety of game categorized under the name 'scenic games', since the spectacle takes place before a backdrop on stage (*scena*).

The Romans consequently do not use a generic term that could designate the theatre simultaneously as spectacle and as text. The text is called *uersus* and the spectacle *scenica*. In practice, however, they always distinguish between kinds of spectacle: comedy, tragedy, or mime. Thus Cicero: 'The Romans accept the *Andria* and the *Synepheboi*, as well as the *Andromache*, *Antiope*, and *Epigonoi*. Why then don't they like speeches translated from Greek, when it's not that way for verse?' (*De Optimo Genere Oratorum* 18). Individual tragedies and comedies go by their Greek titles, with the epithet 'Latin'. They are presented as 'translations'. These are in practice equivalent to the Greek original, as Plautus says:

> I would like to begin by citing Aristarchus' *Achilles*
> and to borrow from this tragedy:
> 'Be quiet, shut up, and pay attention.
> The general gives the order to listen.'
>
> (*Poenulus* 1–4)

Aristarchus' *Achilles* is quoted in Latin, doubtless from Ennius' 'translation'.

But can we speak of translation in the modern sense? Roman theatre is Greek theatre in Latin. The Romans take Roman tragedy and comedy as Latin doublets of Greek plays. These texts are therefore not translations but the result of a transfer from one cultural and religious context to another, from Greek Dionysiac ritual to the Roman ritual of 'Greek games'.

Why do the Romans qualify scenic games as 'Greek'? All games, inasmuch as they belong to the sphere of *otium publicum*, are 'Greek'. As the collective entertainment of the Roman populace, they lie outside any political framework. Public or private *otium* (banquets, spectacles, poetry, philosophy) is the Greek side of Roman culture and affords the Romans the pleasure and luxury essential to cultivated life. But the scenic games are Greek to a higher degree, since the plays that are put on are Greek and the theatre is a more refined source of leisure than circus races; that is, they are more Greek.

As a result, scenic games were not meant to be entirely 'Latinized'—they would have lost their sweetness, their charm, and hence, paradoxically, their Roman nature. If their text is in Latin and their context is a Roman ritual, the rest is all Greek: characters, places, plots, and metre.

Theatrical Texts: Traces of Ludic Performance

Is Roman drama literary? A theatrical text, written for particular games, would not ordinarily be re-performed in other games. A play does not belong to the national patrimony. The public wants novelty, and therefore most of Roman tragedy and comedy has been lost. These texts have nevertheless won a literary afterlife. Some were preserved in Roman libraries among Roman letters as models meant to furnish examples and citations for oratory alongside Greek drama.

Is Roman drama for this reason a 'literary genre'? Yes, if we consider library catalogues. No, if we consider its mode of production. Roman poets were not disciples of Aristotle.

In the *Poetics*, Aristotle attaches tragedy and comedy to what we call literature. He defines tragedy as a self-sufficient text. Neither tragedy nor comedy needs performance to exist. A text need not be written to serve any other purpose: the ritual of the Dionysia, the practice of the mask, the duality of song and utterance, or the agonistic context. Did the *Poetics* have any impact on theatrical practice in Greek city-states? The librarians at Alexandria devoted a shelf to plays they thought worthy of preservation. This editorial activity doubtless took place on the margins of the living theatre that prospered in the Hellenistic period but went in another direction, toward musical accompaniment, song, and acting.

The texts of the Greek dramas the Romans 'translated' come from the Hellenistic libraries, but that does not mean that the Latin theatre inherits Aristotle's literary conception. In essence, Roman theatre is first and foremost a ritual practice whose composition and evaluation are completely subordinate to the religious spectacle for which the text was written: the games—*ludi*. The Greek text is employed only as a means to celebrate the Greek games.

The idea of genre implicit in the appellation theatrical performance is both literary and pragmatic. What we mean by tragedy and comedy refers to the generic classification of Alexandrian philologists, and the plays the Romans 'translated' were already classified in libraries under the Muses' heading. But when it comes to the games' spectacular aspect, comedy, tragedy, and mime are defined according not to their poetic but their pragmatic function. Tragedy should move the soul and make the audience feel emotion with extraordinary force and quality; comedy's playfulness should elicit laughter; mime is erotic. Each genre has its specific type of actor, music, techniques of spectacle, gesture, and voice, but also, among other elements, its own mode of composition.

The theatre's place at Rome is consequently singular and complex. Letters cannot contain it, although it participates in them. Drama is not a poetic genre. Rather, four types of performance constitute it: comedy, tragedy, mime, and pantomime. The first three have left texts; the librettos of the fourth were not judged worthy of preservation even when written by famous authors like Statius and Lucan. Once performed, its text will not serve for other games nor be read like a story, but certain verses or short phrases will re-emerge through quotation in other discourses: oratory, philosophy, or epistolary essay. They become cultural commonplaces, sometimes with a totally different meaning from their original context in the games. A famous example is *homo sum, humani nihil a me alienum puto* ('I am a man, I think nothing human alien to me', Terence, *Heautontinoroumenos* 77). This dictum never had in Terence the serious humanist tone lent to it by Cicero (*De Officiis* 1.9.30; *De Legibus* 1.12.33; *De Finibus* 3.19.63), Seneca (*Epistulae Morales* 95.53), and Augustine (*De Vera Religione* 39; *Epistle* 51). The same goes for tragic citations that acquire political overtones after the fact, like the famous reply of Atreus, *oderint, | dum metuant* ('Let them hate, provided they fear', Accius TF 203–4 Ribbeck).

Roman plays had two kinds of reception. Outside the ritual context, the text fragments into aphorisms (*sententiae*) and the *exempla* of characters and situations. By contrast, to understand a play's meaning in its ritual context, that is, its pragmatic effect, we need to reconstruct the context of enunciation of scenic games.

Theatrical vocabulary based on the root **lud-* gives us access to the games' context: *lusus* (verbal play), *ludicrum* (spectacle), *ludius* (ritual dancer or actor), *ludere* (act, dance, mock), *illudere* and *deludere* (deceive, give the illusion of), *ludificare* (mock, celebrate games). These nouns, verbs, and adjectives place Roman drama in a framework signifying that nothing over the course of the games is to be taken seriously, that everything is game, dance, and make-believe, everything is a joke. The root **lud-* signifies the rejection of the serious. I call this ludism.

Orator and Actor: An Inseparable Couple

Outside the texts of Plautus, Terence, Seneca, and a few fragments of Ennius, all we know about the living theatre comes basically from rhetorical treatises, particularly the chapters devoted to *actio*, namely, the oral performance of speeches, and that treat the voice, body, and gestures of the orator. The actor is an anti-orator. Covered in infamy and therefore excluded from political rights, the actor is not a citizen. By contrast, the orator is the ideal of Roman nobility, and Cicero, the great orator who at his apogee achieved the consulship, is the exact opposite of a great actor like Roscius. The star actor is rather the idol of the masses and favourite of the greats; his perfect *mollitia* (softness) condemns him to prostitution just as it endows him on stage with a dancer's grace and incomparable seductive power. Even if this infamy takes different forms in the provinces and colonies, the law always imposes some sort of civic exclusion that corresponds to the actor's general social marginalization. An actor's infamy is proportional to his talent, as revealed by Cicero's *sententia* (saying) when defending Roscius before the tribunal. Attempting to affirm his morality without detracting from his success, Cicero formulates an oxymoron: he deserves at the same time most and least to be a senator (*Pro Roscio Comoedo* 17). This opposition between eloquent senator and seductive actor, ubiquitous in the Roman imaginary, is one of numerous variations on the central opposition between truth and artifice, social loyalty and hypocrisy, between seduction (effeminate, servile, and aphrodisiac), and persuasion (free, masculine, and stern). It places the theatre and politics at opposite ends of the spectrum.

The breaking-point between them is their mode of utterance. Even if he prepares at length, the Roman orator always improvises his speech according to the audience's identity and state of mind (*animus*) during his performance. His speech is the extension and instantiation of his person, his rank (*dignitas*), and his personal worth (*virtus*). Every speech puts the self on display.

In contrast, the actor recites a text already written by a poet. He never improvises. His words are therefore not an extension of his self; he lends his voice to another's words so that they shift onto a *persona* that is literally his mask and figuratively his role. His participation in the event is only via his talent for playing this role without any contribution of his individual self. Unlike contemporary actors, the Roman actor plays without accessing his feelings or lived experience; he does not incarnate his role and is comparable in this way to actors in the East Asian theatrical traditions. This is why he is an *artifex* (craftsman) and his art an *artificium* (craft): it serves the poet's word and the spectators' pleasure.

Actors and orators do, however, share the art of voice and gesture—called *actio* for oratory. This is why they can sometimes train together or even take the same classes in song and dance. But woe to the orator who seems an actor (Quintilian 6.40)!

The actor's status is therefore tied to the 'written' nature of the script at Rome; the recitation of writing implies a certain relation to the public. Why writing? Because the text is necessarily a translation from Greek. Drama, called too often vulgar and easy, whose scripts veer to farce or grandiloquence depending on the situation, actually displays complexity of composition. Its poetics, however, must be analysed according to a pragmatics different for each genre and without relation to ours today. The poet writes so the actor can play a role that pre-exists the text.

Fundamentally then, the Roman theatre audience is neither in the position of a reader, nor of a judge at court, nor of a citizen in an assembly. The actor—called in Latin *histrio* or *ludius*—is the vehicle for establishing a relation between the public and the spectacle. This relation is specific and can only be understood via the ritual of the games and the ludic expectations it imposes. The actor creates a fictitious image by joining his utterance to a written text and to a role (*persona*) that pre-exists the text. The purpose of this link is not to create illusion, but rather to raise a laugh or arouse strong emotion as appropriate.

Ludic theatre is neither illusionistic nor is it a theatre of representation (*mimesis*). Nor is it, as we will see, dramatic in the sense of being organized by a story.

Tragedy, Pantomime: Unheard-of Emotions

Tragedy under the Republic saw enormous development as a genre, but of this extensive production only a few fragments remain. Besides these, we have nine Senecan tragedies: *Agamemnon*, *Hercules Furens*, *Hercules Oetaeus*, *Medea*, *Oedipus*, *Phaedra*, *The Phoenician Women* (fragments), *Thyestes*, and *The Trojan Women*. Their value as *exempla* is by no means undercut by their being written by the richest and most powerful senator of the first century CE, an adherent of Stoic philosophy, or by the fact that they may not have been performed—on the contrary. They were probably designed for public recitation; since their author would need to display his mastery of the genre, they would have been written as tragic models. We must reconstruct Roman tragedy essentially on the basis of these plays and the ludic utterance proper to Roman theatre.

If we restrict ourselves to Seneca, his Greek sources belong to the three greats of the Alexandrian canon: Aeschylus, Sophocles, and Euripides. But if we examine the rare indications in the literature, we see that the sources are spread between the classical and Alexandrian periods, with a marked preference for two subjects: *Medea* and *Thyestes*.

If we compare Seneca's tragedies, along with the fragments and *testimonia*, and study their vocabulary in detail, we see that these plays' integration into the games has created a common structure of spectacle. The linking thread is the transformation of the heroes into superhuman monsters, whose theatrical epiphany provides the spectacle's climax and final image: Medea, having killed her children, cackles and flies off on the chariot of the Sun over a Jason racked by despair; Atreus exalts in the spectacle of his brother Thyestes, who feels his son churning in his stomach and howls from grief; Jocasta describes her suicide blow by blow to Oedipus, who, blind and bloody, begs for silence.

The texts call *nefas* the crime that has so transformed these characters. This is a religious crime that no penalty can redeem—even death. The heroes will always be marked by the memory of their crime as they enter into the black eternity that is Greek myth. Every tragedy reproduces the trajectory that leads each hero to his memorable crime, one he reinvents each time, although it already dwells in everyone's memory. Myth is the reference-point for tragic heroes. Its world is immobile and glorious, peopled with criminals who are their parents and models they aspire to surpass. This mythic society of monsters is bound by inverted values: hate replaces love, parricide or worse occurs, incest or cannibalism replace piety (*pietas*), betrayal takes the place of loyalty, cruelty of justice. The hero's trajectory ends up at this point of inversion.

His progress to *nefas* passes through two stages, designated *dolor* and *furor* in the texts. They help him leave humanity behind. Every hero begins at the mercy of *dolor*. He has lost his prestige (*honos*), that is, his glory or social status, and he has outlived his life. He has no traffic any longer with men. To recover the glory of his name, he looks for a model of *nefas* among the mythic monsters of his family. Thus does Atreus, by imitating and surpassing Pelops, offer his brother his sons' flesh in a sacrificial banquet; thus does Phaedra, doubling her mother's savage love of the bull, love the wild Hippolytus with the incestuous passion of savage beasts. But to achieve the inverted values of myth, the hero must pass through *furor*. This notion, which will be taken up by the Italian Renaissance and Baroque drama, does not categorize madness as pathology. Madness is rather an ethical notion that implies the forgetting of all human reference, all internalized social norms. In tragedy, the raging hero is ethically empty. He willingly appropriates the inverted values of *nefas* and thus invents his crime as *nefas*.

If there is indeed a narrative, it serves only as the scaffolding of the tragic trajectory, which is always the same. Every subject does no more than vary the modality of this epiphany of monsters. This is why Roman tragedy is not dramatic in the sense of being organized around an action or particular *drama*. Audience attention is not focused on the story's outcome—they know it already—nor on its course or moral or philosophical interpretation. The hero's relation to self and others is already fixed in advance in terms outside human probability. *Furor* in particular is a tragic category that has no equivalent in the world outside the theatre.

Roman tragedy is in fact constructed like opera. Every role, identified by its mask (*persona*), has its own *motus animi* (spiritual drive), which is attached to its name like an epithet: *iratus Atreus* (angry Atreus) or *ferox Medea* (fierce Medea) (Horace, *Ars Poetica* 119–37; Quintilian 11.73–4).

Each *persona*'s spiritual drive entails a particular *uox*, that is, a vocal music and specific discourse that accompany the role throughout the play. If the tragic epithet corresponds to the hero's mythic figure from time immemorial, accomplishing his *nefas* will allow the character to coincide perfectly with his mask. The hero's trajectory is a musical construction all the way up to the final 'aria' that celebrates his epiphany as a monster. The different stages and tests along this trajectory can be heard in the actor's voice and become visible through his play with the mask. In this way, Seneca's Oedipus has two masks: he wears fear from the prologue to his blinding, which gives him, as he says, 'his real face', a second mask. Up to this point his text has spoken his fear and anguish with variations in rhythm and intensity. In the last scene, blind, he remains fixed in place, subject to a final terror: the fear of stepping on the corpse of Jocasta who has just killed herself on stage.

A tragedian's *uox* is the essence of the role; it has song's force and quality even if he does not sing. Diction magnifies the text's emotional impact, itself written as a variant of a *motus animi*. The tragic voice emerges from the liberation of oratorical performance from the constraints of eloquence, veracity, and persuasion; it is emotion in its pure state. At the theatre all is fiction but the voice and the audience's emotion.

The ritual of the *ludi*, by creating a temporary space for play, where nothing is serious, allows the symbolic systems of Roman civilization to function without pragmatic consequence. In its emotive materiality, tragedy makes a trial of effective discourse.

Pantomime is a variety of tragedy with the addition of dance and song, and succeeds it beginning with the Empire. A pantomime is a tragic ballet (Lucian, *De Saltatione*). Thc famous pantomime Tiberius Julius (Slater 1995) of the second century CE called himself 'an actor of rhythmic tragic dance'. The terminology 'tragedy' and 'tragic' are quickly transferred to pantomime. Although the subjects are the same, the spectacle is divided between a narrator and actors, who dance and mime with a mask to the accompaniment of a chorus and an orchestra. In this way, tragedy goes over entirely to music and spectacle and leaves the realm of *litterae latinae*. The text is a libretto, and even if the poet is famous, like Lucan or Statius, it is not preserved (Juvenal 7.92).

Comedy: The Triumph of the *Ludus*

If the tragic actor is a voice trained and used like a musical instrument, the comic actor is a body, just as artificial and virtuoso. Like tragedy, Roman comedy is Greek comedy in Latin, taken from the authors of New Comedy such as Menander. The ritual function of scenic games is inscribed explicitly into comedy at the moment of the prologue and the final suite of applause.

In Roman comedy, the *prologus* is a character who addresses the audience and does not generally belong to the plot. He therefore does not have a role, that is, a costume, but is recognizable because of his Phrygian hat. The *prologus* calls on the public in the second-person plural to ask for silence. All Roman ritual requires this silence. At a sacrifice it is solicited with the famous formula *fauete lingua* ('be favourable with your tongue'). In the theatre the aim is to transform the public into an audience of spectators so that the ritual may proceed. The prologue also asks the public to remain seated during the play and not to get up or leave (*Poenulus* 5; *Trinummus* 22). If the ritual is interrupted it will have to be started all over again, and a new play performed. (This happened during the first and second performances of Terence's *Hecyra.*)

To stay seated and be silent is not a sign of politeness, nor a question of personal taste or aesthetic choice; it is to accept the ritual celebration of the games with the play that has been presented; it is to assent to the appropriateness of the spectacle. To listen ritually in the theatre is to alter one's state of mind in accord with the festival; the spectator should forget his fatigue and life's cares, stop being serious, and give himself over to the show and to laughter:

> Chase care from your heart, forget your debts.
> Let no one fear his creditor.
> It's time for the games (*ludi*) and it's play time (*ludus*) even for bankers.
> There is tranquility in the forum, an oiled sea . . .
> If your ears are free and ready, lend your attention to me.
>
> (Plautus, *Casina* 24–30)

Passive silence is not enough. By forgetting its cares, the present crowd must transform into an attentive and ludic public. This attention that is open to laughter—*hilaritas*—constitutes the Romans' true participation in ritual celebration. The prologue already sets the mood by joking about serious life's irritations. At the same time as the *prologus*, a herald (*praeco*), accompanied by lictors, intervenes in the stands, officially asking the public to be quiet. In fact, the herald is the only one who can legitimately demand silence. This is why the *prologus* often does not himself demand silence from the beginning and, when he does, jokes around and mocks the herald. His job supplements the herald's: the one orders ritual silence, the *prologus* transforms the silence into ludic attention. Audience applause is a ritual manifestation of closure corresponding to the ritual opening of the prologue. A singer or character addresses the public as the prologue did at the play's beginning: 'Spectators, the play has been acted (*acta est*). Now, you applaud!' (Plautus, *Mostellaria* 1181).

All possible tricks are used to make the public laugh one last time and to elicit 'a clear burst of applause' (*Asinaria* 947, *Casina* 1017, *Menaechmi* 1162, *Mercator* 1026, *Rudens* 1421). The ruckus of applause answers to the attentive silence of the prologue and, once the performance is over, the spectators may stand (*Truculentus* 967–8).

Generally, a comedy's end, like its beginning, recalls the ritual context of the performance and reactivates the spectators' participation by interpellation and by making them laugh. As in the prologue, the ritual itself is often the object of mockery. Making fun (*ludere*) of the ritual is itself part of the ritual. And the games they play with the games are not limited to wordplay, but introduce the only real suspense in the spectacle. Will the comedy take place? Will the ritual be celebrated correctly? Will the poet go too far in his play?

Such play with the ritual and more generally with the theatrical code is repeated throughout the comedy: the spectacle takes place on the basis of metatheatricality. In this way, Roman comedy keeps reiterating that the story and the show do not coincide. The show may start or stop before the story does. Sometimes the spectacle begins even before the prologue (*Miles Gloriosus*), or stops before the denouement. The plot will finish in the halls:

> Don't wait, spectators, for them to come back before you.
> No one is coming out. They will all go resolve the plot inside.
> When it's done, they'll take off their costumes.
>
> (Plautus, *Cistellaria* 782–4; same procedure in *Casina* 1011–13)

Inversely, the spectacle can extend beyond the denouement, as at the end of the *Pseudolus*: once the plot is resolved, Pseudolus comes back out on stage to execute an oriental dance.

Therefore, a comedic spectacle is not the representation of a story, a *muthos* in the Aristotelian sense, one that coheres from beginning to end. It is rather a ritual procedure opened by the silence the prologue imposes and closed by the applause at the end. This is why the public's attention is not captivated by the story but by the process and success of the ritual, which is endlessly threatened by the games the poet plays with various comic codes: story, roles, gesture, costume, blocking, the alternation between spoken scenes (*diuerbium*) and those with song and dance (*canticum*), ceremonial entrances, meetings, and exits.

These codes are known to the public, as to the actors and the poet. They allow the spectators to participate in the making of the ludic spectacle and hence to maintain throughout the play the ritual interactivity we have seen in operation in the play's opening and close. The poet 'plays' endlessly on expectation, breaking it only to re-establish it again. The public is continually surprised and worries about the spectacle's progress: a character loses his costume, enters by the wrong door, speaks when he should not, sings when he should speak, is suddenly overwhelmed by paralysis, has to change roles to stay on stage—all this independent of the story!

As in tragedy, the spectacle depends entirely on actors, a singer, and a *tibia* player. The comic actor does not incarnate his character any more than the tragic actor. Today we call a character by the name attributed to a series of replies in the script, that is, the unique subject of utterance as defined by the text and an agent in the story. In Roman comedy the characters unite three speaking subjects under one name: the agent (hardly necessary), the role, and the actor. The role is a *persona*, that is, a mask, costume, and comic function independent of the story and similar in all comedies: the cranky old man, the debauched youth, and the pimp.

The catalogue of roles is limited to a dozen, with more or less fine distinctions. For instance, there are two types of old men, the choleric and the indulgent; two types of youths, the dissolute and the good boy; but only one type of cook or soldier. The role or *persona* exists before any plot or play. As in Asian theatre conventions, such as the *vesham* of Kathakali, the role consists of a certain costume, make-up or mask, repertory of gesture, vocal tonality, a set relation with other roles, and a profile either sympathetic or repellent. Therefore the pimp has a bloated stomach, a white wig balding at the front, big ears sticking out, twisted knees making him limp, a gaudy tunic, and a straight cane. He is repellent and the public will be thrilled at his final discomfiture. Finally, the actor, as we saw for the prologue, is himself also a character in the play who celebrates the games and so on.

Each agent necessarily acquires a role from the catalogue. Therefore, in the *Comedy of the Pot* Euclion is the cranky old man, Megador the indulgent, and Anthrax is the cook. Each role has its own unique costume, wig, body, and style. Hence play is possible with the code of characters. One type of play is to attribute the same role to two different agents. This produces the *Amphitruo* or the *Menaechmi*, where twins are the subject; or isolated scenes as in the *Pseudolus*, when Pseudolus the clever slave meets his double in a slave as clever as he, Monkey; or again the two cooks in the *Pot.* A character is not a role, then; it is not a *persona* with particularizing traits arising from the story or its function as agent.

Another way to play with the code is to uncouple the agent and the role. One example is Pistoclerus in the *Bacchides.* To advance the plot, an agent needs a role or *persona.* Concretely, he needs a costume with a mask to slip on over his actor's costume. Sometimes an agent may arrive on stage without his role and hence without his costume. This happens to young Pistoclerus in the *Bacchides.* He is an agent with an essential function for the plot, because he is to watch over the interests of his absent friend Mnesilochus who is in love with one of two courtesans, the sisters Bacchides. The beloved Bacchis is on the verge of being sold off to a soldier. When Pistoclerus enters on stage he does not yet have a role, since he does not answer to either of the possible young men roles, the courtesan's dissolute lover or the nice lover of his future wife. Since he does not yet have a role, he has no costume. Therefore he enters 'naked', that is, dressed as an actor. The whole first scene of the *Bacchides* is devoted to finding him a role: he is seduced by the other Bacchis and becomes a debauched young man. This is why he exits at the end of the scene to return wearing the evening garb of the young dissolute. The poet takes advantage of the constraints of spectacle—here, the code governing comic roles—to substitute a ludic rationale for the narrative reason that doubtless organized the Greek original. The seduction of Pistoclerus is not an event of the plot illustrative of his character, but rather a metatheatrical dramatization of a character's creation during the course of the play. The dramatic code is not purely enacted; it is exhibited and turned so as to play interactively with the audience.

From one moment to the next each character may cease to be an agent or play his role to become merely an actor and intervene as a celebrant of the games. Then he addresses the audience as in the prologue, or his partner to remind him of the rules of the game, or the flutist to make him slow the rhythm down or change the accompaniment.

This triple division of the character allows much metatheatrical play, since the character is fundamentally unstable and varies according to the type of scene he plays. The character does not exist outside the performance of the actor in his role: his labile and changing reality belongs only to the show. We can identify him sometimes with a role, sometimes with a plot function, now with both, now with neither: he is nothing but an actor trying to find a reason to stay on stage. The character can be a mere text without a body (*diuerbium*), or again a body dancing without a text, or he can divide between a body dancing a role and a singer singing a text (*canticum*).

The generalized ludism that makes for Roman comedy corresponds in Latin to the verb *ludificare*, which means to 'transform through play' as well as 'deceive, mock', or 'joke', or 'put on a play'. To 'transform through play' always consists of running a code 'on empty', whether the code is linguistic, gestural, or theatrical. In this last case, it is a question of a ritual metatheatricality that links the audience with their co-celebrants. To make a display of the code is not to denounce artifice, as has sometimes been suggested, but rather to solicit public participation in the celebration of the games. It is not an aesthetic gesture, a theatrical style, or even social satire, but the very stuff of Roman comedy.

The *Eclogues*: An Unexpected Mime

Mime is well attested for the stage at Rome. We know that mimes were played by actors and actresses at least once a year at the Floralia (Cordier 2005: 216–22). The nature of the texts is less easy to determine. This problem derives from the status of Greek mime (Moretti 2001: 101–4). Greek mimes were not produced at contests and no canonical text was preserved in the Hellenistic libraries. The only ones we possess are those by Herodas and Theocritus.

The Romans integrated mime into the Greek games very early (as of 173 BCE) and gave them a status comparable to other scenic performances (in the Floralia, from 28 April to 3 May). The reason may have been the particular nature of the Floralia, which was supposed to include female prostitutes; mime was the only dramatic spectacle in Greece where women acted. We have no texts from this period.

In the later Augustan period the aim of cultural politics was to re-Hellenize poetry. Vergil takes his inspiration from Theocritus and writes scripts for mime, which were in fact played in theatres (Servius, on *Ecl.* 6.11). If they have been preserved, it is because of their ambiguous character. The *Eclogues* were written for preservation in the libraries as the founding example of Roman bucolic, but were composed at the same time for the theatre. The only other trace of a mime text is the collection of *sententiae* pulled, as was customary, from the mimes of Publius Syrus, a writer of mimes in the time of Caesar (Seneca, *Epistulae Morales* 8.8–9).

The interest of Roman theatre today is to offer within the western tradition an example of non-dramatic theatre where the text is no more than the fabric of spectacle. It is a theatre of the actor and of play that provides good material for contemporary re-performance, as evidenced by the success before a real public—not just universities—of numerous productions of Seneca and of Plautus in France.

References

Roman Theatre

Bieber, Margaret, *The History of the Greek and Roman Theatre*,[2] Princeton, 1961.

Beare, William, *The Roman Stage: A Short History of Latin Drama in the Time of the Republic*, London, 1964.

Beacham, R. C., *The Roman Theatre and its Audience*, London, 1991.

Slater, W. J. (ed.), *Roman Theatre and Society*, Ann Arbor, Mich., 1996.

The Actor

Wiles, David, *The Masks of Menander*,[2] Cambridge, 1993.

Dupont, Florence, *L'Orateur sans visage, essai sur l'acteur romain et son masque*, Paris, 2000.

Ludism

Nutti, Andrea, Ludus *e* iocus. *Percorsi di ludicità nella lingua latina*, Rome, 1998.

Metre

Questa, Cesare, *Introduzione alla metrica di Plauto*, Bologna, 1967; 2nd edn., Urbino, 2007.

Bettini, Maurizio, 'La poesia romana arcaica al lavoro', *Mat.disc.an.test.class.*, 14 (1985), 13–43.

Roman Comedy

Barchiesi, Marino, 'Plauto e il "metateatro" antico', *Il Verri*, 31 (1969), 113–30.

Slater, Niall, *Plautus in Performance: The Theatre of the Mind*, Princeton, 1985.

Bettini, Maurizio, *Verso un'antropologia dell' intreccio e altri studi su Plauto*, Urbino, 1991.

Questa, Cesare, *Il ratto dal serraglio, Euripide, Plauto, Mozart, Rossini*, Urbino, 1997.

Moore, Timothy, *The Theatre of Plautus*, Austin, Tex., 1998.
Goldberg, Sandor, 'Plautus on the Palatine', *Journ.Rom.Stud.* 78 (1998), 1–20.
Traina, Alfonso, *Comoedia. Antologia della palliata*,[4] Padua, 2000.
Leigh, Matthew, *Comedy and the Rise of Rome*, Oxford, 2005.
Questa, Cesare, *Sei letture plautine*, Urbino, 2005.
Marshall, Christopher W., *The Stagecraft and Performance of Roman Comedy*, Cambridge, 2006.

Greek Models

Fraenkel, Eduard, *Plautine Elements in Plautus* (1922), tr. New York, 2007.
Lefevre, Eckard, *Maccus Vortit Barbare. Vom tragischen Amphitryon zum tragikomischen Amphitruo*, Mainz, 1982.
—— *Diphilos und Plautus. Der* Rudens *und sein Original*, Mainz, 1984.
—— *Der* Phormio *des Terenz und der* Epidikazomenos *des Apollodor von Karystos*, Munich, 1996.
—— *Maccus barbarus. Sechs Kapitel zur Originalität der 'Captivi' des Plautus*, Mainz, 1998.
Dupont, Florence, 'Plaute le fils du bouffeur de bouillie—*Pultiphagonides*', in Florence Dupont and Emanuelle Valette-Cagnac, *Façons de parler grec à Rome*, Paris, 2005.

Atellan Farce

Frassinetti P., *Atellanae fabulae*, Rome, 1967.

Senecan Tragedy

Petrone, Gianna, *La scrittura tragica dell'irrazionale*, Palermo, 1984.
Picone, Giusto, *La fabula e il regno. Studi sul Thyestes di Seneca*, Palermo, 1989.
Sutton, D. F., *Seneca on the Stage*, Leiden, 1986.
Auvray-Assayas, Clara, *Folie et douleur dans l'Hercule furieux et Hercule sur l'Oeta. Recherches sur l'expression esthétique de l'ascèse stoïcienne chez Sénèque*, Frankfurt, 1989.
Dupont, Florence, *Les Monstres de Sénèque*, Paris, 1999.
Guastella, Gianni, *L'ira e l'onore. Forme della vendetta nel teatro senecano e nella sua tradizione.* Palermo, 2001.
Aricò, G., 'L'Atreus di Accio e il mito del tiranno. Osservazioni in margine a uno studio di Italo Lana', 19–34, in F. Bessone and E. Malaspina (eds.), *Politica e cultura in Roma antica. Atti dell'incontro di studio in ricordo di Italo Lana, Torino 16–17 ottobre 2003*. Bologna, 2005.
Schiesaro, Alessandro, *The Passions in Play: Thyestes and the Dynamics of Senecan Drama*, Cambridge, 2003.
Littlewood, C. A. J., *Self-Representation and Illusion in Senecan Tragedy*, Oxford, 2004.
Boyle, A. J., *Roman Tragedy*, London, 2006.

Mime and Pantomime

Bonaria, Mario, *Mimi Romani*,[2] Rome, 1965.
Fantham, Elaine, *Mime: The Missing Link in Roman Literary History*, *CW* 82 (1988), 156–63.
Slater, W. J., 'The Pantomimus Tiberius Iulius', *GRBS* 36 (1995), 263–92.
Moretti, Jean Charles, *Théâtre et société dans la Grèce antique*, Paris, 2001.
Cordier, Pierre, *Nudités romaines*, Paris, 2005.
Lada-Richards, Irene, *Silent Eloquence*, London, 2007.

CHAPTER 28

LETTERS

JENNIFER EBBELER

It is a sign of changing times and evolving literary sensibilities that this volume includes a chapter devoted to the genre of the letter. Already in antiquity letters were treated as the *Rohstoff* of personal and cultural history, for use in the composition of biography or historiography. In recent decades, however, it has become increasingly clear that these texts, especially in their role as objects of exchange between correspondents (or, in late antiquity, entire communities), very often did more than preserve useful details for later generations of biographers, historians, and prosopographers. Perhaps the most consequential result of recent scholarly activity is the recognition of a distinction between letter-writing as a quotidian activity available to any semi-literate Roman with access to a scrap of papyrus or a wooden tablet, and the letter that is preserved, incorporated into a collection, and transmitted to posterity with the aim of advertising its author's literary talent and social network.

I am not suggesting that the historically fascinating Vindolanda tablets, the many extant papyrus letters, or even the countless ephemeral letters that Pliny chose not to publish in his collection are not letters; but rather, that they must be treated as categorically different from the letters that we know from the collections of Cicero, Horace, Seneca, and their successors. Cicero's collection, which preserves many letters that are no more rhetorically sophisticated or literary than a papyrus letter from a soldier to his mother, complicates this easy distinction. Yet we must keep in mind that the editorial process which created Cicero's letter collections was haphazard at best (Nicholson 1998: 63–105). Had Cicero lived long enough to publish a collection of his letters, it would have been far more selective. By his own report, he planned to gather together a small selection of notable letters from his own and his correspondents' archives (Cicero, *Letters to Atticus* 16.5).

When it comes to ancient letters, the categories 'historical' and 'literary' have significant overlap. It is increasingly clear that historical prose letters, whose content is derived from real events, have much in common with their fictional counterparts. If at one time letters, especially prose letters, were treated as unmediated snapshots of their author's cultural milieu, closer study has revealed that they are sophisticated texts on a par with any other Latin literary genre. Letters—whether prose or metric, overtly fictional or apparently historical—should be understood, first and foremost, as self-conscious textual constructions (Rosenmeyer 2001: 5).

But what are the precise characteristics of this *genus epistulare*? In other words, what are the specific generic codes that distinguish a letter from other textual forms? Up to this point I have taken it for granted that we know what is meant by the label 'letter' (the words *epistula* and *litterae* appear to have been used interchangeably). In fact, as Trapp has acknowledged, the boundary between a letter and other types of literary activity can be murky (2003: 1). Derrida drew attention to the problem when, with characteristically provocative élan, he declared that 'mixture is the letter, the epistle, which is not a genre but all genres, literature itself' (1987: 48).

It is certainly the case that, like the dialogue or pastoral poetry, letters are resistant to formal modes of generic analysis. Letters can be composed in prose or a variety of metres (or, occasionally, a mixture of both); they can handle an enormous range of themes; authorship was not limited to any class of people; letters can range in length from one sentence to dozens of pages; they can be written on a variety of materials, including waxen tablets, wood, metal, papyrus, pottery, and animal skins. Whereas an epic poem can be identified with (relative) ease because it is composed in dactylic hexameter, is comparatively long, handles a limited range of themes relating to warfare and the quest for home or a homeland, generally includes gods, and so on, the form and content of a letter is far less predictable. It is indeed tempting to conclude together with Derrida that the generic labels *epistula* and *litterae* were meaningless.

We should nonetheless observe that Derrida's denial of a distinctive epistolary genre is derived from the realm of theory rather than practice; it takes no account of actual epistolary practice and, in fact, ignores the extent to which letter-writers themselves did understand and manipulate distinctions between the letter and other forms of writing. A careful look at Augustine's *Retractationes* ('Reconsiderations') reminds us that, in the eyes of letter-writers, *epistula* could be a meaningful generic label. In the final years of his life Augustine began the tedious process of cataloguing and correcting all of his writings, organized into the categories of *libri* ('books'), *sermones* ('sermons'), and *epistulae* ('letters'). He died before he got to his letters; but among his *libri* he lists a handful of texts that were originally sent as letters and are transmitted together with his other letters. For instance, he categorized two letters that he sent to Jerome in 415 CE, one on the origin of the soul (*Letters* 166) and the other on James (*Letters* 167), as *libri* (*Reconsiderations* 71).

All of these one-time letters are lengthy and focused on the explication of some scriptural knot or point of doctrinal disagreement. It seems that, after the fact, Augustine wished to elevate a small selection of his 'exegetical' letters (of which there were many others that did not make the cut) to the more elevated, transparently public, and less ephemeral status of the *liber*.

If genre is 'a conceptual orienting device that suggests to a hearer [or reader] the sort of receptorial conditions in which a fictive [or real] discourse might have been delivered', then it is safe to say that the letter, like other performance-based literary forms, was a unique genre (Depew and Obbink 2000: 6). Its 'codes' were constantly being re-negotiated and innovated upon to suit the specific demands of its time and place. In spite of these diachronic variations, however, there persisted throughout antiquity an operative sensibility that the act of letter-writing and exchange was governed by a specific, albeit adaptable, set of conventions and expectations. Certainly, the examples just discussed offer compelling evidence that Augustine and his contemporaries viewed the letter as a distinct literary genre (even if they would not have ventured to circumscribe its features).

Did their predecessors, including Cicero and Ovid, Horace and Pliny, also conceive of the letter (and letter collection) as a distinctive literary act? Does it matter that Seneca chose to cast his philosophical discourses in the form of letters addressed to Lucilius (Inwood 2007: 133–48)? More importantly, does it add to our understanding of the texts to take into account their epistolary form? One critic of the *Heroides* has lamented, 'the choice of the epistolary form for what are really tragic soliloquies was not entirely happy' (Wilkinson 1955: 86). Yet such a swift dismissal of the poems' epistolary status ignores the extent to which Ovid playfully manipulates epistolary conventions (see Kirfel 1969 and Jacobson 1974). As Duncan Kennedy has pointed out, the savvy reader of Penelope's letter will realize that she is about to hand over her letter to Ulysses, disguised as a Cretan beggar, thereby fulfilling her distinctly un-epistolary command that he not write back, but return home (*Heroides* 1.1). Whether he is portraying his heroines as readers of one another's letters (Fulkerson 2005), or highlighting their apparent failure to follow the first rule of successful letter exchange, that is, to ask for a letter in return, Ovid invokes time and again his readers' familiarity with the conventions of letter-writing and their identification of his *Heroides* as letters.

The earliest known Latin letters appear as citations in the historical narratives of the Augustan historians Livy and Dionysius of Halicarnassus. It is not clear that the historians had seen copies of the letters and no actual letters survive (Cugusi 1970*a* collects the fragments and *testimonia*). More than likely, these letters were nothing more than tersely written reports designed for the basic purpose of communication *in absentia*. Cugusi has speculated that Scipio Africanus was the author of a first-person epistolary narrative of his military exploits (1970*b*: 11). This suggestion is intriguing, and implies that the letter could function very much like a *commentarius* (see Riggsby 2006: 133–55 on the functional overlap of the letter and ancient commentary).

Still, as the case of the pre-neoteric poet/general Catulus emphasizes, the generic status of such military reports was a point of disagreement among readers (Cugusi 1970*b*: 33). Cicero characterized Catulus' report as a book, *liber*, even though it was sent (*misit*) and had an explicit addressee/dedicatee (*Brutus* 132, 'Catulus sent to the poet Furius, his close friend, this book which treated the details of his consulship and military accomplishments and was composed in the gentle style of Xenophon'). Two centuries later, however, Fronto described this same text as a letter (*Epistles* 120.3, 'Catulus' letters (*Catuli litterae*) are extant, in which, like a historian, he described his acts, both his successes and failures, but worthy of the laurel wreath').

Apart from second-hand reports of autobiographical, *commentarius*-like letters that detailed their author's *res gestae*, the sorts of letters attested before the final decades of the Republic—love letters, letters home while travelling or in exile, letters from a parent to a child, letters to the Senate, letters to opposing generals, and the like—seem not to have been composed with an eye to circulation beyond the named addressee. When letters were written for a broader audience (the Senate, a hostile government), they were not letters between individuals so much as letters between functionaries (the general, the king, the consul). More importantly, there is no evidence to suggest that these letters were intended to have a literary afterlife as part of a larger collection of their author's letters.

At the risk of implying that the generation of Caesar and Cicero invented the letter collection as a literary genre, it appears that the practice of collecting and publishing a selection of one's personal letters first emerged during the late Roman Republic. We should nevertheless keep in mind that the letters of Plato, Isocrates, and others were compiled by Hellenistic admirers who probably also incorporated contemporary forgeries into the collections. Similarly, certain pseudonymous, obviously fictional collections of letters may date to the Hellenistic period or earlier (Rosenmeyer 2001: 193–233). Still, we can conclude with some confidence that this 'last generation' of the Republic was the first to compose and collect their personal letters with the aim of eventual publication. Caesar may have prepared his letters for public circulation (Ebbeler 2003: 12). Cicero's plan to publish a selection of his letters was cut short by his untimely death, but his letters were known in the years after his death (Nicholson 1988: 63–105). Horace published a collection of hexameter letter poems, the *Epistulae*, and, in the generation after Cicero, Ovid could claim that his *Heroides* was a novel generic experiment that combined the letter and the elegiac poem (*Ars Amatoria* 3.345–6).

By the middle of the first century CE letter-writing had emerged as a favourite aristocratic pastime; and the letter collection had become an established literary genre. Both the younger Seneca and the younger Pliny published collections of their letters as part of their literary oeuvre. If Seneca's collection of philosophical letters looked back to the collections of Plato's, Aristotle's, and Epicurus' letters, Pliny's carefully crafted prose letter collection was intended to rival the sophisticated poetic *libri* of Catullus and his successors (Ludolph 1997; Gunderson 1997: 201–31; Marchesi 2008). The range of correspondents attested in Pliny's published letters indicates that letter exchange was widely practised by imperial elites, yet few traces of this activity remain. Only a fragmentary collection of letters from the correspondence of Fronto and Marcus Aurelius survives as a witness to the continued popularity of literary letter exchange between elite Romans.

Our most extensive evidence for Latin epistolary practice is late antique. It is not an overstatement to characterize the period between 200 and 600 CE as the golden age of Latin (and Greek) letter-writing (Vessey 2005: 74–5). A significant number of letters survive from a wide variety of late antique Latin writers, including Cyprian, Ambrose, Ausonius, Symmachus, Paulinus, Jerome, and Augustine. The letters of Sidonius, Ruricius, Avitus, Gregory the Great, Cassiodorus, and Ennodius, together with scattered letters from assorted bishops, scholars, emperors, and government bureaucrats, remind us of the letter's continued use both as a pragmatic means of communication and as a literary artefact throughout late antiquity. In some cases authors published a selection of their own letters (e.g. Ambrose, Jerome, Sidonius); at other times authors preserved copies of their letters in an archive, intending to publish some portion as a collection but leaving the laborious editorial work to others (e.g. Augustine).

Cicero could observe that the epistolary genre was invented to 'inform those at a distance' (Cicero, *Letters to his Friends* 2.4.1); but this was not the only or even the fundamental function of a letter. In the most basic terms, the letter was thought to be one half of a 'written dialogue' (with particular emphasis on the 'written'); it was invented to facilitate conversation *in absentia* and, it was suggested, its style should reflect its colloquial origins (Seneca, *Letters to Lucilius* 75.1–2; Gregory of Nazianzus, *Letters* 51; Julius Victor, *Ars Rhetorica* 27). Both classical and late-antique letter writers regularly described the letter exchange as a useful but imperfect substitute for face-to-face conversation (Cicero, *Letters to his Friends* 12.30.1, 'what could be more pleasing to me than to write to you or to read your letters when I am unable to speak with you in person?'; see also Symmachus, *Letters* 5.20). Seneca has a similarly optimistic view of the letter's capacity to substitute for an absent friend. He observes that whenever he receives a letter from Lucilius, it is as if he is immediately in Lucilius' presence (*Letters to Lucilius* 40.1). Letters are far superior to portraits, in that they contain traces (*vestigia, verae notae*) of the absent friend in the form of his handwriting.

The traditional view that the letter was a temporary substitute for face-to-face conversation until presence could be restored was challenged in the late fourth century by Paulinus of Nola. Contrary to classical practice, Paulinus advocated an explicitly Christian theory of the letter in which absence is preferable to presence. Specifically, he figured the letter exchange between two Christians as a sacramental act; their absence from one another was thought to be a re-enactment of their absence from the Christian god (Conybeare 2000: 41–59). While Paulinus' innovative theory had its acolytes, including Augustine, it never replaced the predominant 'classical' model. So, for instance, we see the prolific sixth-century letter-writer Ennodius pleading for a response from his correspondent. Absence, says Ennodius, is made tolerable only by the constant presence of a friend's letters (*Letters* 6.11).

Ancient epistolary theory was the domain of rhetoricians and letter-writers. Both classes of critics emphasized function over form. One exception is Demetrius. Demetrius included a brief treatment of epistolary style in his *De Elocutione*, a treatise which seems to date to sometime between 100 BCE and 100 CE (Malherbe 1988: 17–19). He offered a variety of stylistic tidbits: avoid frequent breaks in sentences, write in a way that reveals your true character, keep to a reasonable length, avoid complicated periods, keep proverbs to a minimum, adopt a tone appropriate to the addressee, and so on. Remarkably, Demetrius argued that certain topics, such as those involving logical subtleties or questions of natural history, were not appropriate to the letter. He was particularly opposed to the treatment of serious philosophical topics in letters. Demetrius' discussion is fascinating, not least because it appears to have exercised no discernible influence on actual letter-writers. Indeed, Seneca could devote an entire letter collection to the very sorts of philosophical problems that Demetrius claimed were unsuited to a letter.

In Cicero we see the origins of a more pragmatic approach to letter-writing and exchange. A letter whose function is to communicate information should be serious (*Letters to his Friends* 2.4.1, *severum et grave*), while a letter meant to entertain could be intimate and humorous (*familiare et iocosum*). At times, said Cicero to Atticus, it was the act of exchange itself rather than the communication of information that mattered most (e.g. *Letters to Atticus* 9.10.1, 'I have begun to write to you something or other without any definite subject, that I may have a sort of conversation with you'; see Conybeare 2000: 19–40 for discussion of letter exchange as an intricate 'historical event'). These sorts of 'empty' letters were particularly useful during times of political crisis, when a correspondent could not risk the possibility of his letter's contents becoming public (*Letters to Atticus* 9.4.1).

Ps.-Demetrius, whose date is wildly insecure (2nd cent. BCE–3rd cent. CE) but whose typological approach to the letter suggests that he was writing later rather than earlier, divides the letter genre into twenty-one 'types'. These types are functional, and each has an accompanying set of stylistic characteristics (Malherbe 1988: 30–41). For example, the commendation letter ought to be a mixture of praise and a demonstration of familiarity with the *commendatus* (but cf. Julius Victor, *Ars Rhetorica* 27, where he argues that a letter of recommendation should be written truthfully or not at all). Ps.-Libanius (4th cent.–6th cent. CE) nearly doubled the list of letter types to forty-one (Malherbe 1988: 67–81). There was, it seems, a letter for all occasions: censorious, encouraging, counter-accusing, erotic, even enigmatic.

In less organized fashion, the fourth-century rhetorician Julius Victor reminded his reader to adhere to specific rules, depending on the type of letter he is writing

(Malherbe 1988: 62–5). We can imagine that these typologies were useful not only to writers but also to addressees, who were often required to decode the highly stylized language of a letter to get at its message (see Chartier 1997: 1–23, who suggests that medieval letter-writing manuals functioned simultaneously to inculcate etiquette and to allow 'outsiders' to impersonate the ruling class). In an environment of circumscribed epistolary etiquette, violations of convention were just as significant as obedience to the rules.

In recent years scholars have heeded the call for 'a less atomistic and more functional approach to letters' (Stowers 1986: 23). The ill-conceived quest to distinguish between 'public' and 'private' letters or between 'literary' and 'real' letters has been replaced by a more holistic approach (Rosenmeyer 2001: 5–12 summarizes and comments on earlier approaches to the letter genre). The emphasis on classification favoured especially by New Testament scholars has given way to analyses of how letters worked to initiate and manage relationships at a distance. Although letter-writers insistently figured their texts as *colloquia in absentia*, the letter's dialogic character has only recently been recognized as an integral feature of the epistolary genre (see Hall 1998: 308–21 and Hall 2009 for the benefits of paying attention to a letter's dialogic character). Given the fact that ancient letter collections, beginning with Cicero's letters, published only the author's half of the correspondence, this lapse is understandable. There seems to have been some sense that an author's letters belonged to him and were his to publish or not. We catch fleeting glimpses of the original dialogue in Cicero's and Fronto's letters; but our only instances of surviving letter dialogues are late antique (e.g. Augustine and Jerome; Paulinus and Augustine; Ausonius and Paulinus).

An essential difference between the letter *qua* letter and the letter as part of an author's collected letters is precisely this act of erasure that accompanied its incorporation into the collection. Once it became part of a collection, the letter demanded to be read vis-à-vis the author's other letters and no longer as part of a conversation with a correspondent. De-historicized, the letters could be arranged to create a literary portrait of their author for his contemporaries and posterity. Certainly, one of the fascinating features of the few extended letter exchanges is the degree to which the correspondences were marred by miscommunication, struggles for authority, and adversarial rhetoric (Wilcox 2005: 237–55; Ebbeler 2007: 301–23). We are reminded that the letter exchange was about status management, whether between the correspondents or as a performance before a broader audience.

Governing these textual performances was a sophisticated rhetoric of epistolography, that is, an assortment of established conventions designed to ensure a letter exchange that was efficient and free of misunderstandings. Given the vagaries of the delivery process (it could take anywhere from a few hours to several years for a letter to arrive to its addressee; some letters never arrived) and the lack of opportunity to clarify confusion on the spot, it was essential that the correspondents observed the rules of engagement. Any attempt at innovation, whether in style or content, could undermine the correspondence (Van Dam 2003: 138). A timely response was essential to the success of a letter exchange. The letter is consistently figured as a 'solace' (*solacium*) and 'remedy' (*remedium*) for absence; and the performance of letter exchange as a 'duty' (*officium*) of friendship. Among our extant letters are numerous examples in which an author reproaches his correspondent for his failure to respond (Cain 2006: 500–25).

Because letters had a tendency to get lost en route, an author could never be sure whether blame lay with the correspondent's neglect of his epistolary *officia* or his messenger's incompetence. For this very reason, it was the author's responsibility to entrust his letters to reliable messengers who would ensure their safe and timely arrival while ensuring the security of the contents (Nicholson 1994: 33–63). A recipient should not pass his correspondent's letter on to a third party without the author's permission. At the same time, the author of a letter should always write with the awareness that his letter's contents could become public; for this reason, his letters should avoid rebuke or anything else that might prove embarrassing if made public. Likewise, an author should employ appropriate deference when writing to a correspondent of higher status. This is just a sampling of the spoken and tacit rules that governed letter exchange. One of the key tasks for students of ancient letters is the identification of additional 'epistolary duties' that shaped the expectations and behaviours of both author and addressee. Once we know what the normative rules were, we can begin to understand authors' often cunning manipulation of them.

The failure to reciprocate within a correspondence was considered a particularly grave offence. It was a serious violation of epistolary etiquette and demanded an explanation. Having committed this very transgression, Jerome defended himself to one correspondent with a familiar strategy—blame the messenger: 'Please don't think that, once I received your letters, I was silent; and don't blame me for the faithlessness and negligence of others. Why would I, stimulated by your letter, remain silent and push away your friendship with silence?' (*Letters* 76.1). Jerome reassures his correspondent that he did, in fact, write back; his failure was his choice of a 'faithless and negligent' messenger. So long as both correspondents were willing partners, the obligation to write back was unproblematic and, indeed, necessary. But this assumes that all letter exchanges were friendly. Symmachus helpfully reminds us that this is a dangerous assumption (*Letters* 9.26, 'very often among those who are absent, the alternating epistolary battle leads to enmity').

Some letter exchanges were, in fact, carefully orchestrated manipulations of the conventions of friendship letters. By casting a hostile confrontation in the form of a supposedly private letter of friendship, an author could pressure his resistant correspondent into a written debate that could then be circulated in public, generally to the addressee's disadvantage. If the addressee ignored the letter, he risked appearing to be an inept correspondent who had neglected the primary duty of letter-writing. If he responded, he was forced to engage with an issue as it had been framed by his correspondent. He could write back but refuse to engage with the contents of an unwanted letter, but he remained vulnerable to accusations of unresponsiveness.

We see this epistolary strategy at play in Augustine's correspondence with Maximinus, a Donatist bishop (*Letters* 23). While still a priest, Augustine boldly confronted a bishop in the rival Donatist faction (then the majority faction in most African towns) who had rebaptized a Catholic clergyman. He demanded that Maximinus respond with a confession of his own views on rebaptism, which could be read aloud to Augustine's fellow Christians (23.3). He was honest about his intention to make the letter's contents public, says Augustine, because he hoped to avoid offence (and, presumably, charges of improper epistolary behaviour). Should his correspondent ignore this confrontational letter, threatens Augustine, he will be forced to read his own letter aloud to the Catholics in Hippo. The absence of a response will be conspicuous; as a result, the Catholics in Hippo will understand that a great Donatist bishop could not defend the practice of rebaptism even to a lowly priest (23.6). At several points in the letter Augustine repeats his desire to engage in peaceful and productive discussion with his correspondent, as if this were a typical letter of friendship. We might imagine, however, that such apparently friendly rhetoric was seriously undermined by Augustine's ultimatum: if his correspondent does not engage on Augustine's terms, Augustine will publicize his silence as evidence of cowardice.

We see a similar dynamic at play in the correspondence of Cicero and Caesar in the aftermath of Caesar's victory at Pharsalia. Cicero, who had supported Pompey, was living in exile in southern Italy and desperate for permission to return to Rome. By sending letters not only to Caesar himself, but also to Caesar's agents Balbus and Oppius as well as Atticus, Cicero kept his cause in the public eye (White 2003: 75). Cicero confessed his epistolary manipulations in a letter to Atticus, and requested that Atticus solicit other supporters to pressure Caesar with letters (*Letters to Atticus* 11.6.3). He reiterated to Atticus the unique power of the letter to force Caesar's hand (11.7.5, 'it is crucial that Balbus and Oppius stay strong and that Caesar's good will toward me be reinforced by frequent letters from them'). Caesar could ignore Cicero's letters, but not the letters of Balbus, Oppius, and his other supporters. Furthermore, as Caesar undoubtedly realized, whether Cicero was in Rome or not, he would continue to be a virtual presence in the city through his letters to Atticus and his other supporters.

The practice of letter exchange, as well as the letter itself, was governed by identifiable conventions that shaped behaviour and expectations on the parts of authors and readers. The letter was something more than words on a page read in the absence of their author (i.e. Derrida's 'literature'). Those words on a page became a letter when they invoked what I have here termed 'the rhetoric of epistolography'. The obviously fictional status of Latin verse letters has meant that their 'literary' status has not been challenged; but their engagement with and manipulation of epistolary codes has yet to be explored in detail (as Rosenmeyer 2001 does for Greek fictional letters). Likewise, Latin prose letters are a treasure-trove for the adventurous student eager to look beyond the details of their content to think about what work letters did in Roman culture and how they did it. Far from being transparent windows onto particular moments in the historical past, letters were implicated in both the creation and representation of that past.

Further reading

The best general introduction to Latin letters is Stowers 1986. Morello and Morrison 2007 adds substantially to Stowers' author-centred overview. Peter 1901 remains fundamental, supplemented by Zelzer 1997 and Cugusi 1989. Thraede 1970 offers a reliable discussion of key epistolary topoi and has the added advantage of covering both Pauline and late antique letters. Altman 1982 is a non-classical but stimulating discussion of epistolarity. Likewise, Rosenmeyer 2001 (a study of Greek fictional letters) has much to inspire the student of Latin letters. Jenkins 2006 is a thoughtful study of the perils of epistolary (mis) communication in antiquity. Klauck 1998 provides a suggestive discussion of the intersection of classical and New Testament letters. Oliensis 1998: 154–97 and Lowell Bowditch 2001: 161–210 offer valuable comments on the epistolarity of Horace's *Epistulae*. White 2003: 68–95 is an exemplary study of epistolary strategy in Caesar's letters (see Ebbeler 2003: 3–20 for the reception of Caesar's letters). Hutchinson 1998 is a reliable introduction to the literary character of Cicero's letters. Beard 2002: 103–44 (on the Ciceronian letter collection) and Wilcox 2005: 237–55 (on Cicero and consolation) and Hall 2009 (on Cicero's treatment of the dialogic aspect of the correspondence) should not be missed. Kennedy 1984: 413–22, Rosenmeyer 1997: 29–56, and Farrell 1998: 307–38 offer good starting-points for thinking about the epistolary aspects of Ovid's letter poems. Edwards 1997: 23–38 is an important contribution to the growing body of work on letters and self-fashioning. Any study of Pliny's letters should begin with Gibson and Morello 2003. Similarly indispensable are Ludolph 1997, Hoffer 1999, and Marchesi 2008, together with Leach 1990: 14–39, Riggsby 1995: 123–35, and Gunderson 1997: 201–31. The venturesome reader will find many useful provocations in Henderson 2002 and 2004. Richlin 2007 and 2005: 111–29, part of a longer book in progress on the reception of the Fronto–Marcus Aurelius correspondence, offers a compelling reading of the possibly homoerotic rhetoric in the letters of Fronto. On Symmachus' letters, Brugisser 1993 is essential (see also Sogno 2006, Salzman 2004: 81–94, Matthews 1974: 58–99). Conybeare 2000 is an exemplary study of Paulinus' epistolary innovation. See also her 'dialogue' with Vessey (2005: 57–71, 73–96) on the topic of Augustine's letters to women. On Jerome's epistolary self-fashioning, Cain 2009 is indispensable. Zelzer 1989: 203–8 analyses Ambrose's literary debt to Pliny's model (see also Liebeschuetz 2004: 95–107). Mathisen 1981: 95–109 and 2001: 101–15 offer valuable insights on the role of letter-writing in fifth-century Gaul. Shanzer and Wood 2002: 58–85 is similarly illuminating. On Ennodius' letters, see now Schröder 2007.

References

ALTMAN, J. (1982), *Epistolarity: Approaches to a Form*, Columbus: Ohio State University Press.

BEARD, M. (2002), 'Ciceronian Correspondence: Making a Book Out of Letters', in T. P. Wiseman (ed.), *Classics in Progress: Essays on Ancient Greece and Rome*, Oxford: Oxford University Press, 103–44.

BOWDITCH, P. L. (2001), *Horace and the Gift Economy of Patronage*, Los Angeles and Berkeley: University of California Press.

BRUGISSER, P. (1993), *Symmaque ou le rituel épistolaire de l'amitié littéraire*, Fribourg: Editions Universitaires Fribourg Suisse.

CAIN, A. (2006), '*Vox Clamantis in Deserto*: Rhetoric, Reproach, and the Forging of Ascetic Authority in Jerome's Letters from the Syrian Desert', *JTS* NS 57: 500–25.

—— (2009), *The Letters of Jerome: Asceticism, Biblical Exegesis, and the Construction of Christian Authority in Late Antiquity*, Oxford: Oxford University Press.

CHARTIER, R. *et al.* (1997), *Correspondence: Models of Letter-Writing from the Middle Ages to the Nineteenth Century*, tr. Christopher Woodall, Princeton: Princeton University Press.

CONYBEARE, C. (2005), 'Spaces Between Letters: Augustine's Correspondence with Women', in Linda Olson and Kathryn Kerby-Fulton (eds.), *Voices in Dialogue: Reading Women in the Middle Ages*, Notre Dame, Ind.: University of Notre Dame Press, 57–71.

—— (2000), *Paulinus Noster: Self and Symbols in the Letters of Paulinus of Nola*, Oxford: Oxford University Press.

CUGUSI, P. (1989), 'L'epistolografia: modelli e tipologie di communicazione', in *Lo spazio letterario di Roma antica*, vol. 2 Rome, 379–419.

—— (1983), *Evoluzione e forme dell'epistolografia Latina nella tarda repubblica e nei primi due secoli del impero*, Rome.

—— (1970*a*), *Epistolographi Latini Minores*, vol. I, fascs. 1 and 2, Aug. Taurinorum.

—— (1970*b*), *Studi sull'epistolographia Latina: l'età preciceroniana*, Cagliari.

DEISSMANN, A. (1907), *New Light on the New Testament, from the Records of the Greco-Roman Period*, tr. Lionel R. M. Strachan, Edinburgh: T. & T. Clark.

DEPEW, M. and OBBINK, D. (2000), *Matrices of Genre: Authors, Canons, and Society*, Cambridge, Mass.: Harvard University Press.

DERRIDA, J. (1987), *The Post Card: From Socrates to Freud and Beyond*, tr. Alan Bass, Chicago: University of Chicago Press.

EBBELER, J. (2007), 'Mixed Messages: The Play of Epistolary Codes in Two Late Antique Latin Correspondences', in Ruth Morello and Andrew Morrison (eds.), *Ancient Letters*, Oxford: Oxford University Press, 301–23.

—— (2003), 'Caesar's Letters and the Ideology of Literary History', *Helios*, 30/1: 3–19.

EDWARDS, C. (1997), 'Self Scrutiny and Self-Transformation in Seneca's Letters', *G&R* 44/1: 23–38.

FARRELL, J. (1998), 'Reading and Writing the *Heroides*', *HSCP* 98: 307–38.

FULKERSON, L. (2005), *The Ovidian Heroine as Author: Reading, Writing, and Community in the Heroides*, Cambridge: Cambridge University Press.

GIBSON, R. and Morello, R. (eds.) (2003), 'Re-Imagining Pliny the Elder', *Arethusa*, 36/2.

GUNDERSON, E. (1997), 'Catullus, Pliny, and Love-Letters', *TAPA* 127: 201–31.

HALL, J. (1998), 'Cicero to Lucceius (*Fam.* 5.12) in its Social Context: *Valde Bella*?', *CP* 93: 308–21.

—— (2009), *Politeness and Politics in Cicero's Letters*, Oxford: Oxford University Press.

Henderson, J. (2004), *Morals and Villas in Seneca's Letters: Places to Dwell*, Cambridge: Cambridge University Press.

—— (2002), *Pliny's Statue: The Letters, Self-Portraiture and Classical Art*, Exeter: University of Exeter Press.

Hoffer, S. (1999), *The Anxieties of Pliny the Younger*, Atlanta, Ga.: Scholars Press.

Hutchinson, G. O. (1998), *Cicero's Correspondence: A Literary Study*, Oxford: Clarendon Press.

Inwood, B. (2007), 'The Importance of Form in Seneca', in Morello and Morrison 2007: 133–48.

Jacobson, H. (1974), *Ovid's Heroides*, Princeton: Princeton University Press.

Jenkins, T. (1996), *Intercepted Letters: Epistolary and Narrative in Greek and Roman Literature*, Lanham, Md.: Lexington Books.

Kennedy, D. (1984), 'The Epistolary Mode and the First of Ovid's *Heroides*', *CQ* 34: 413–22.

Kirfel, E. A. (1969), *Untersuchungen zur Briefform der Heroides Ovids*, Bern and Stuttgart: Noctes Romanae 11.

Klauck, H.-J. (1998), *Die antike Briefliteratur und das Neue Testament*, Paderborn: Schöningh Press.

Leach, E. W. (1990), 'The Politics of Self-Presentation: Pliny's Letters and Roman Portrait Sculpture', *CA* 9: 14–39.

Liebeschuetz, J. H. W. G. (2004), 'The Collected Letters of Ambrose of Milan: Correspondence with Contemporaries and with the Future', in Linda Ellis and Frank L. Kidner (eds.), *Travel, Communication and Geography in Late Antiquity*, Aldershot: Ashgate, 95–107.

Ludolph, M. (1997), *Epistolographie und Selbstdarstellung: Untersuchungen zu den 'Paradebriefen' Plinius des Jüngeren*, Tübingen: Gunter Narr.

Malherbe, A. (1988), *Ancient Epistolary Theorists*, Atlanta, Ga.: Scholars Press.

Marchesi, I. (2008), *The Art of Pliny's Letters: A Poetics of Allusion in the Private Correspondence*, Cambridge: Cambridge University Press.

Mathisen, R. (2001), 'The Letters of Ruricius of Limoges and the Passage from Roman to Frankish Gaul', in *Society and Culture in Late Antique Gaul*, Aldershot: Ashgate, 101–15.

—— (1981), 'Epistolography, Literary Circles and Family Ties in Late Roman Gaul', *AJP* 111: 95–109

Matthews, J. F. (1974), 'The Letters of Symmachus', in J. W. Binns (ed.), *Latin Literature of the Fourth Century*, London: Routledge, 58–99.

Morello, R. and Morrison, A. (eds.) (2007), *Ancient Letters*, Oxford: Oxford University Press.

Nicholson, J. (1998), 'The Survival of Cicero's Letters', *Latomus*, 9: 63–105.

—— (1994), 'The Delivery and Confidentiality of Cicero's Letters', *CJ* 90: 33–63.

Oliensis, E. (1998), *Horace and the Rhetoric of Authority*, Cambridge: Cambridge University Press.

Peter, H. (1901), *Der Brief in der römischen Litteratur*, Leipzig: Teubner.

Richlin, A. (2007), *Marcus Aurelius in Love*, Chicago: University of Chicago Press.

—— (2005), 'Fronto + Marcus', in Mathew Kuefler (ed.), *History, Homosexuality, and John Boswell*, Chicago: University of Chicago Press, 111–29.

Riggsby, A. (2006), *Caesar in Gaul and Rome: War in Words*, Austin, Tex.: University of Texas Press.

Riggsby, A. (1995), 'Pliny on Cicero and Oratory: Self-fashioning in the Public Eye', *AJP* 116/1: 123–35.
Rosenmeyer, P. (2001), *Ancient Epistolary Fictions: The Letter in Greek Literature*, Cambridge: Cambridge University Press.
—— (1997), 'Ovid's *Heroides* and *Tristia*: Voices from Exile', *Ramus*, 26: 29–56.
Salzman, M. R. (2004), 'Travel and Communication in *The Letters of Symmachus*', in Linda Ellis and Frank L. Kidner (eds.), *Travel, Communication and Geography in Late Antiquity*, Aldershot: Ashgate, 81–94.
Schröder, B.-J. (2007), *Bildung und Briefe im 6. Jahrhundert*, Berlin: Walter de Gruyter.
Shanzer, D. and Wood, I. (2002), *Avitus of Vienne: Letters and Selected Prose*, Liverpool: Liverpool University Press.
Sogno, C. (2006), *Symmachus: A Political Biography*, Ann Arbor, Mich.: University of Michigan Press.
Stowers, S. K. (1986), *Letter Writing in Greco-Roman Antiquity*, Philadelphia: Westminster Press.
Thraede, K. (1970), *Grundzüge griechisch-römischer Brieftopik*, Munich: C. H. Beck.
Trapp, M. (2003), *Greek and Latin Letters: An Anthology with Translation*, Cambridge: Cambridge University Press.
Van Dam, R. (2003), *Families and Friends in Late Roman Cappadocia*, Philadelphia: University of Pennsylvania Press.
Vessey, M. (2005), 'Response to Catherine Conybeare: Women of Letters?', in Linda Olson and Kathryn Kerby-Fulton (eds.), *Voices in Dialogue: Reading Women in the Middle Ages*, Notre Dame, Ind.: University of Notre Dame Press, 73–96.
White, P. (2003), 'Tactics in Caesar's Correspondence with Cicero', *Papers of the Liverpool Latin Seminar*, 11: 68–95.
Wilcox, A. (2005), 'Sympathetic Rivals: Consolation in Cicero's Letters', *AJP* 126: 237–55.
Wilkinson, L. P. (1955), *Ovid Recalled*, Cambridge: Cambridge University Press.
Zelzer, M. (1997), 'Die Briefliteratur', in L. J. Engels and Heinz Hofman (eds.), *Neues Handbuch der Literaturwissenschaft*, vol. 4, Wiesbaden: AULA Verlag.
—— (1989), 'Plinius Christianus: Ambrosius als Epistolograph', *SP* 23: 203–8.

CHAPTER 29

NOVELS

ELLEN FINKELPEARL

'NOVEL' is a highly contested term, particularly when coupled with the word 'ancient': no ancient attestation of the category, a problematic relationship to the modern term, a motley collection of texts that fits into no other generic category, uncertainty about direct filiation from antiquity to the present, insistent rejection of categorization by the works themselves. The field once known as 'ancient novel' evolved into 'prose fiction' and thence to 'ancient narrative', in part as a step toward inclusiveness, but also a retreat from the anachronism of 'novel'.

What are these texts? The *Satyricon* of Petronius and the *Metamorphoses* of Apuleius have conventionally been considered the prime, if not only, Roman novels, and felt to be of sufficient length and complexity to qualify for the name 'novel'. Some would also add the *History of Apollonius King of Tyre*, though for others it is too late, Greek, Christian, and a romance rather than novel. Other works, Latin translations or recensions of the fictional-historical *Alexander Romance* or of the comic biography of Aesop, the prose 'eyewitness' accounts of the Trojan War by Dictys and Dares, Christian saints' lives and Apocryphal Acts, are relegated to the 'fringe' conveying a sense of generic, religious, and chronological tenuousness as full relatives of the (very few) insider texts.

Certainly, the term 'ancient novel' is a convention with no satisfactory parameters, but for those who persist, the least *un*satisfactory definitions are those that define it in terms of non-genre or (differently) anti-genre or in opposition to formally recognized and restricted forms, as such definitions recognize and celebrate both its hybridity and potentially oppositional nature. Bakhtin's work on the novel and its prehistory, though of an earlier era and somewhat overused, is still the place to begin, if only because it has shaped our current thinking. 'Novel' is defined largely by its opposition to epic: epic is antiquated, fixed, and authoritative, while the novel is new, developing, dialogized, polyphonic, and heteroglot, in contact with contemporary evolving reality and associated with dethroning laughter, with the profane and everyday speech. One may add the ability of the novel to shift across cultural categories and canonical configurations of the world such as gender, class, the Christian–pagan divide, and East vs. West (and I would add animal–human) and to avoid conforming to any one logic or set of expectations (Selden), even to erase the very boundaries between those categories. The once-maligned novel, marked with contempt even in antiquity by Macrobius, who disapprovingly refers to 'fictional adventures of lovers', and Julian, 'fiction in the shape of history', is triumphantly redeemed, though the definition is still open and vague.

Can we distinguish a Roman form of the novel? For once, the Roman genre does not labour under the weight of a venerable Greek forerunner; Greek and Roman prose fiction develop simultaneously and many Greek works are later than the Roman, though the Greek romance has the appearance of the originary form. What may be an accident of survival leaves the Latin novels looking just as puzzlingly anomalous as the extant Greek romances are predictably similar. The *Satyricon* baffles readers with its prosimetric form, episodic structure, and scholarly yet naive ego-narrator (not to mention the accident of its fragmentary state), while the *Metamorphoses* eludes interpretation for some of the same reasons, as well as its unexpected religious ending with the accompanying revelation of the narrator's identity. Even the relatively simple *Historia Apollonii* begins with a story of incest peripheral to the main narrative, dethrones the romance's central focus on separated lovers, and devotes a long section to riddles. Further, the two major Latin novels share the then-unusual feature of a first-person narrator protagonist, a picaro presenting a confessional narrative from which the author maintains an ironic distance. The extant Latin novels spend more time in the world of 'slum-realism' than do the extant Greek novels/romances, and feature an inverted world in which libidinous women, slaves, freedmen, eunuchs, and robbers wield power. Where the ethos of the typical Greek novel/romance is essentially bourgeois, with a return after perilous adventures to a quiet married life amid the elite of one of the cities of the Roman Empire (though without explicit mention of Rome), scandalous adventures in Roman novels either do not end or lead to a spiritual life outside society.

Still, even these distinctions between Greek and Roman should be tempered by what, as usual, we do not know: fragments from *Iolaus*, *Tinuphis*, and other lost novels reveal that some unpreserved Greek examples lacked the decorum of the five romances we know and were possibly prosimetric (Barchiesi); what looks like the epitome of Apuleius' source (the pseudo-Lucianic *Onos*) was also narrated in the first person, irreverent and sexually explicit, and set in the real world of second-century Greece under Roman rule. Many speculate that the *Satyricon*, too, was based on a Greek original (Jensson). What surely does distinguish the Latin novel from the Greek, however, is the former's characteristically Latin engagement with Greek and especially Latin intertexts—Virgil, Ovid, Lucan, Seneca, and others.

Those who believe the creationist notion that the novel was conceived 'on a Tuesday afternoon in July' (Perry), even in its sensible form—a new genre for a new set of social circumstances, the world of the Empire with its political disengagement, its multiculturalism, and its social upheavals—do not take enough account of the hybridity and 'impurity' of prose fiction, particularly the Roman variety, its graftings and its dynamic relationship to the texts it alters and incorporates on the way to becoming itself and evolving. Two straightforward ways of looking at the novel's incorporation of other voices, parody and ornament, both have validity, but are static. Reading Petronius and Apuleius, one can move imperceptibly from an epic intertext to a scene of sub-literary mime, both of which have contributed to the genre's making. The novel does not merely parody epic, but novelizes characters like Dido, borrows the stucture of a hero's travels, creates characters who misunderstand and misrepresent their own status in relation to mythic heroes. The novel is theatrical, not merely linguistically, but in its polyphony, its presentation of dialogue, interchange, and a theatricalization of everyday life. The novel is satiric, not only in the sense that it parodies books and life, but in a literary sense—its chaos is held together by the single point of view of a first person narrator. The genre absorbs and transforms all these other genres, often self-consciously, like Seneca's bee who flits about from flower to flower (in July?) and spews out a completely different metamorphic substance: honey.

Petronius and Apuleius: Disunity

While the novels of Petronius and Apuleius differ in significant ways, they also present many of the same interpretive enigmas and debates. In the following section they will be treated together. The most prominent feature of these works is surely their episodic and fragmented structure: in both, the central first-person narrative is punctuated by 'embedded' tales narrated by others. While sub-narratives are common to ancient prose fiction in general, Petronius and Apuleius outdo the Greek novels with the sheer volume of tales and poems *extraneous* to the main plot. The fact that Petronius' book is now fragmentary (perhaps one-tenth of the original?) should not obscure its otherwise disjointed state. Disposing of earlier notions about sloppiness of composition or the frame narratives as a flimsy pretext to tell a string of merely entertaining stories (Perry), we should consider this disjunctiveness a sophisticated narrative strategy expressive of, variously, the disordered state of Rome under the Empire (Zeitlin), the psychological state of the pre-convert (Shumate), a challenge to the notion of any authorized meaning in the text (Winkler), and a play on the pretended orality of a written text.

Thematic approaches to disjunctiveness were and are still popular for both works. Critics in the 1970s and 1980s argued for the unity and consistent seriousness of the *Metamorphoses* by tracing thematic continuity (of *curiositas* or *Fortuna* in particular) running through both the tales and Lucius' adventures; the Actaeon sculptural group in Byrrhaena's atrium (2.4) represents a cautionary tale to Lucius about gazing on what is forbidden; tales of adultery in the later books represent the moral vacuum of a world without Isis. Analyses of recurring and intertwined motifs of death, food, sex, excess, and rhetoric in Petronius, like Arrowsmith's classic 'Luxury and Death in the Satiricon', offer the prospect of interpretation minimally affected by the fragmentary state of the text, though interpretation becomes somewhat subjective. Arrowsmith sees the work's obsession with death as an expression of the death of the spirit under the weight of excess and unbridled luxury in the early Empire. Others have read the book's focus on death differently: these characters, but not the society, are dead; or more recently, Trimalchio's obsession with death reflects his own vision of the transition from slavery to freedom as an apotheosis; or the freedman's existence occurs in a social underworld (Bodel).

Most of these thematic readings, fruitful as they are, still take it as a given that a literary text must cohere, rather than that fragmentation is the key to meaning. Zeitlin's 1971 essay 'Petronius as Paradox' proposes that the *Satyricon* is radically anti-classical, intentionally breaks the rules of classical genre theory, and, through its paradoxes, absurdities, and incongruities, 'expresses a consistent vision of disintegration' (Zeitlin 1971: 632). The mixing of genres both performs a rejection of traditional institutions along with canonical forms of literature and presents disorder as a vehicle to express the realities of his age. Apuleian criticism was slower to reach such conclusions, but more recent approaches to the unity of the *Metamorphoses* tend to emphasize the way that fragmentation, narratological games, and the capricious nature of the depicted world are expressive of a reality that has lost its coherence and meaning. Shumate's comparative examination of conversion ancient and modern and the 'epistemic rupture' and reintegration involved in shifting one's world-view somewhat similarly interprets the disorder as expressive. Lucius' bewildered state at 2.1, in which everything appears to be something other than what it is, magically transformed, depicts a pre-conversion disintegration of the system of values and ways of knowing. Shumate explains the sudden shift in Book 11 as the convert's radical shift in world-view. Winkler, more post-structurally, makes the multiplicity of perspectives offered by the many narrators and the mystery of the identity of the narrator an argument for the *Metamorphoses* as 'unauthorized text', a text about the process of interpretation whose ultimate meaning is undecipherable. Slater, with more orientation to the linear process of reading and more focused on reader-response theory than narratology, arrives at some of the same conclusions about Petronius.

Another aspect of this fragmentation is that both of these texts paradoxically insist on the orality of what is inscribed in writing. Minor characters enter the frame of narrative and tell stories (*Cupid and Psyche*), conversation poses as a realistic facsimile of what was said (the freedmen at the *Cena*). Apuleius, in his very first words, plays on the paradox that Lucius (or he?) as narrator is soothing our ears with delightful tales—but we must *read* his papyrus to achieve this effect (*At ego tibi... aures tuas permulceam... si papyrum... non spreueris inspicere*, 1.1), creating a disruption between the 'pretended' and 'actual' modes of reception (Fowler). Petronius adds the oral elements of poetic performance and declamation, presenting an equally polyphonic text, dominated by the live voice. The parallel orality of eating is a dominant one in Petronius. Images of eating literature or the poet, or being devoured by it (Rimell), bring an immediacy that takes the reader beyond the silent and passive words on the page. The refusal to stick to fewer narrators is a recognition of the novel's roots in humble storytelling, a bid for closer intimacy with the reader who is imagined as a present listener. But the narrative strategy also tests the boundaries between the spoken and written word when (ironically?) this polyphonic oral production is validated in *Metamorphoses* 11 by Isis, goddess of writing (Finkelpearl).

Interlude on Menippea

Much has been written about 'Menippean satire', defined loosely as a prose text generously interspersed with poetry, and whether the *Satyricon*'s anomalous form can be attributed to a set genre of this sort. Its refusal to stick to a single form Relihan links with a more generally renegade relationship to traditional literature; an 'indecorous mix of disparate elements', parodic, with no moral or aesthetic purpose. In form and spirit Petronius' work fits, yet it lacks several of the essential qualities of the genre as written by Lucian and Varro. Menippean satire chooses a precise target of attack and is self-conscious about the oddity of its form, while Petronius favours ambiguity and flows seamlessly from prose to poetry and back without reflection (Conte). The *Satyricon* appears to deviate even from this deviant form, a picaresque novel onto which this genre has been grafted. Rather than combing through scant evidence to find a category in which to place the work, another approach is to observe how the poetry and prose interact in the text, how they explore the same themes via their 'rival structures' (Connors). The abundance of epic poetry allows for a fragmenting and reshaping of epic into fiction, (Connors) in ways not dissimilar to Apuleius' dynamic incorporation of epic and other genres as a way to explore the novel's process of coming into being (Finkelpearl). Viewed in this way, verse is not *simply* fragmenting, but also cohesive.

Narrators

The disjunctive texts are held together by unreadable narrators. As the extant portion of the *Satyricon* begins, Encolpius is declaiming on the disassociation of rhetoric from reality; all the youth can speak about is pirates dangling chains standing on the beach and oracles advising that three or more virgins be immolated (1). How do we read this attack on the lifeless formulaic quality of rhetoric and its deleterious effect on the youth? Presumably, although we are invited to endorse the truth of the tirade, we must also recognize that the narrator is mocked for parroting ideas already stale in Neronian literature. This position of the narrator as a critiqued critic is visible throughout the book. Further, the narrator is an impotent conman whose social status is mysterious, a drama queen with delusions of grandeur, what Conte calls a 'mythomaniac narrator', who constantly draws ridiculous analogies between his own life and that of great tragic heroes. Yet he is an elegant storyteller and stylist, and at several points even voices sentiments that some critics see as interferences by the author, particularly the 'Catones' poem (see below). Some argue that the inconsistencies and the disparity between the debased Encolpius-*actor* and the sophisticated narration can be explained by assuming that an older, wiser Encolpius is looking back on his younger foolish days, that he is responsible for moral judgements not heeded by the *actor* and for the artistic success of the book (Beck, Stöcker). Yet, like Lucius, he never explicitly looks back on his life to condemn his experiencing character.

The nature of the narrator of Apuleius' *Metamorphoses* is just as elusive from the beginning; does author or narrator speak the prologue? One of the central interpretive problems of the *Metamorphoses* is that Lucius does not signal his ultimate identity, a problem Winkler made the centre of his reading, distinguishing between the experiencing I (*actor*) and narrating I (*auctor*). We are not told until almost the end of the work that the narrator became an Isiac priest and do not know whether he still is at the moment of narration—quite unlike the relentlessly self-revealing narrative strategy in Augustine's *Confessions*. Is Book 11 devout or parodic? Does the rereader who finally knows the narrator's identity then necessarily imagine that an Isiac convert narrates his past adventures with critical distance and disapproval?

Those readers who wish to come to some larger interpretation of the works are at a loss. If the narrator does not guide us, perhaps the author lurks behind him, and what does he want us to make of all the immoral goings-on? One hopes that 'moralist' readings are a thing of the past: Petronius shows immorality and expects the reader to condemn it (Highet); Apuleius' tales and Lucius' life are negative exempla which show bad people coming to bad ends (Tatum, Schlam). Conte's 'hidden author' is a subtler approach, but motivated by the same impulse to find an overall meaning. Conte argues that both the narrator and the 'hidden author' yearn for the great old texts and for the sublime, but the narrator is a 'scholasticus' imprisoned in the artificial schemes he condemns, hopelessly out of touch with the old classics he degrades. The work is thus read in part as a satire on *scholastici* and a lament by the hidden author for the great age lost.

Many are also eager to read authorial judgement in the *Metamorphoses* as a way of skirting the problem of uninterpretability. Though the novel can, of course, be read as the voyage of a lost soul toward religious salvation, Winkler suggested a parodic interpretation, drawing attention to the closural image of Lucius as a 'bald clown', dupe to the machinations of avaricious priests. While Winkler had argued for two equally possible readings existing simultaneously, the more recent trend (problematic, in my view) is to view the mockery of Lucius as unambiguous, perhaps even a mockery by Lucius' older wiser self of the dupe he was then (Kenney; cf. Beck on Petronius) or an exposure by the author of the absurdity of religious fanatics (Harrison).

It may simply be preferable to consider other aspects of these two works: impossibility of interpretation is not the end of reading and interpreting. Petronius presents us with a model of multiple receptions after Eumolpus narrates the Widow of Ephesus story: the sailors laugh uproariously, Tryphaena blushes, Lichas declares that the wife should be put up on the cross, the townspeople within the story are perplexed—The End. The subjectivity of interpretive responses is thematized, but not presented as a problem. Elsewhere in both texts the process of interpretation, both by the reader (Winkler on Apuleius) and the characters (Schmeling on Petronius, in *Ramus*) is made visible just as it is at the centre of that other great ancient novel, Heliodorus' *Aithiopika*.

Novel and the Social World

Another response is to look outside the text. Something is known about Apuleius and perhaps Petronius, and hence also about the social, material, and historical world around them. Rather than using what is known about them to say, for example, that Apuleius turned into an ass (as St Augustine did) and/or had a life-changing spiritual experience, or that Petronius is depicting his own life of debauchery, we may consider what social realities in Rome, Madauros, or Carthage might be reflected in the texts.

The thematic approach to the unity of the *Satyricon* was discussed above; it is also possible to root Petronius' recurring themes in the political realities of Rome under the Empire. Imposture, *dissimulatio*, and artificiality are at least as pervasive as death in the imagery and plot of the *Satyricon*. Food, sex, and language have all been deprived of their natural functions, the world is unreal and theatrical, a wooden hen sits over her pastry peacock eggs (33), the protagonists are impostors and conmen. These images may be read as critical reflections by an oppositional Petronius of the debased state of political existence under Nero, where fear prevents citizens from speaking the truth and where dissent must be covert (Rudich). Even if one questions the Neronian dating of the *Satyricon* (Laird), which perhaps too few do, seduced by the appropriateness of Tacitus' Gaius Petronius (*Annals* 16.17–20) Nero's 'arbiter elegantiae', as author of our text, *dissimulatio* is a virus at many periods under the Empire. Petronius' novel may still be read in political and social terms, a partially symbolic portrait of the strangle-hold of flattery and covertness in a once-free society.

In Apuleius' case, the Isiac priest's designation of Lucius as a man from Madauros (Apuleius', not Lucius', hometown) at 11.27 has encouraged interpretations of the novel as autobiographical symbolic voyage, either psychological (von Franz) or spiritual (Merkelbach, others). I suggest that Lucius' journey is a reflection of the life (not necessarily Apuleius' own) of the Roman colonial. In his *Apology* and *Florida* Apuleius speaks clearly and polemically about his ties to Carthage, and anchors himself in a specific set of African geographical and cultural markers. Most of these are absent from the *Metamorphoses* because Apuleius has adapted a Greek original and sets the story in Greece under Roman rule. Yet Apuleius' parallel experience of living in a Roman province may surface in the novel when, for example, the *Metamorphoses* preserves and expands a scene in the source which portrays a Roman soldier badly mistreating a poor farmer, speaking Latin incomprehensible to the Greek subject and attempting to steal his donkey (9.39–42; Graverini).

Also noteworthy is Lucius' hybrid identity, revealed first in the Prologue, where he speaks of himself as coming from Athens–Sparta–Corinth and yet descended from Plutarch. He is both man and ass, called a 'Madauran' and becomes Roman at the end, yet with an overlay of Egyptian, and he tells 'Milesian' tales (Yun Lee Too). Salman Rushdie calls him 'Lucius Apuleius, Moroccan priest, colonial of the old Roman Empire', evoking our era's discourse of post-colonialism, but an argument can be made that Lucius' tale is in part that of the subject of Roman rule, unsure of his identity, a hybrid, descended into silence only to emerge and find a place in a community of the spirit rather than of place or nation. Many of the Greek novels, too, are the products of authors at the edge of the empire and the outskirts of Hellenism. At least in Heliodorus' case, his hybrid identity and ambiguous relation to the shifting centre are consciously reflected in the portrayal of characters with confused and multiple identities. Even within Italy, Petronius depicts, with a much different sensibility from Juvenal, immigrants with shifting identities. The travel and adventure of the novel occurs in an expanded ancient world of multiculturalism, an element sometimes exploited to increase the sense of alienation and fragmentation, sometimes perhaps a casual and realistic backdrop.

Part of the same instinct to see social history in the novels are readings of the *Metamorphoses* which interpret Lucius' experience as ass in terms of the sufferings of the Roman slave (Bradley, Annequin, Fitzgerald). In fable, where animals represent different classes of humans, the donkey stands for the slave. Lucius-ass who, like the slave, is human and yet perceived as an animal, constantly abused, beaten, and overworked, voiceless, present yet erased, resembles a slave in many respects. Referring to his own state often as *servitium*, at 9.12–13 Lucius describes with vivid pity the human slaves in the mill where he works. Psyche's story can also be read as that of an overworked and abused *ancilla* who finally is freed (the formula 'Psyche, immortalis esto' echoes the Roman formula of emancipation) and marries her master, a wishful slave's tale which, like the story of Lucius' abuse, relates *from the inside* the vicissitudes of enslavement.

This novel (as well as the *Life of Aesop*) provides a perspective rare in Latin literature into the plight of victims and marginal members of society. This is true also of Petronius, and his *Cena Trimalchionis* sets freedmen at centre-stage, not primarily as an object of derision. Bradley cautions us that Apuleius himself owned many slaves and was of the provincial aristocracy; this is not an emancipation tract. Yet despite the anarchic and debauched atmosphere of the Roman novel, privileging alternative voices, breaking down boundaries, and close observation of details of everyday life, though not necessarily dissent or resistance, is some form of social awareness startling in antiquity.

In part, these texts invite scrutiny by social historians because of their apparent 'realism'. Auerbach's well-known discussion of Petronius makes the claim that the *Cena* 'marks the ultimate limit to which realism attained in antiquity', because it is precisely fixed in a particular social milieu, and the guests speak the language of the freedmen of that milieu 'almost without literary stylization' (Auerbach 30). It is not the convention in classical epic and tragedy to distinguish lower-class speech, so Petronius' largely unprecedented imitation of the colloquial Latin of uneducated and sometimes foreign speakers who confuse declensions and utter Greek expletives sets the work apart. Yet social historians reveal how much this is a fictional construction, how different are the casual scribblings of Pompei graffiti (Bodel, and see Boyce). Apuleius' brand of 'realism' springs more from his foregrounding of tales told by common men and women in flea-bitten inns and flour-mills. His language is expressive of social levels, but consists of what Callebat calls a 'realisme atemporel'; Jupiter speaks in formal, legal style and Psyche's language is filled with archaisms and diminutives, language that is 'realistic' only in a literary sense, atemporally colloquial, often Plautine.

These two somewhat different sorts of realism characterize the novel as a genre in search of the illusion that it depicts life with accuracy. Yet this masquerade is set in fantastical worlds of dream-like logic; in Apuleius we hear about bed-wetting in a cheap inn, but the presence of witches demands that we rethink 'realism'; in Petronius impotence is treated by the witch Oenothea in an episode configured with the *Odyssey* as intertext. The realism is also created in both cases by unreliable narrators (Conte) and further completely deconstructs what is real, making the unbelievable believable (Apuleius), the real surreal through detailed description of the monstrous (Petronius).

(A few words on Encolpius and impotence: this is not atypical of the way both novels treat sexuality—openly and lavishly displayed, not puritanically hidden, something shared with Greek romance to an extent—Achilles Tatius, anyway. Yet none of it closely conforms to Encolpius' misleading poetic pronouncement aimed at imagined censors (Catones) that he is narrating simply and straightforwardly the joys of love and what the common people do: 'quodque facit populus, candida lingua refert'(132). Sexual practices in both books are non-normative: Lucius exploits the slave-girl Fotis and later engages in inter-species sex; Encolpius, Ascyltus, and Giton are engaged in a destructive triangle, Encolpius is habitually impotent. While this depiction of what is normally private and hidden announces a kind of realism, both authors constantly overlay such scenes with literary parallels, as if to fictionalize and advertise their status as literary creation at the very moment when the novel is most setting itself apart from other genres.)

THE *TALE OF CUPID AND PSYCHE*

Cupid and Psyche is a complete folk-tale romance set within the *Metamorphoses* which emphasizes the distance between the work as a whole and Greek romance. The question most often posed about the tale is its relationship to the frame narrative: is it a mirror or antitype? Lucius and Psyche both look upon forbidden things, fall through 'curiosity', wander about oppressed by a goddess, and finally are brought closer to the divine, though neither has unequivocally deserved redemption. Yet Psyche's story, though mythical and situated in the realms of the gods, has a much more bourgeois outcome: she is raised to her husband's social level and settles down to take care of their child, whereas the denouement of Lucius' adventures is his spiritual enlightenment. It is as if a Greek romance about separated lovers, their trials and eventual nuptial union and reintegration into society, narrated without the complications of embedded tales, is inserted into the middle of a *Roman* novel showing off how much more complex that project is.

The surrounding narrative suggests that Apuleius was playing with variations, mostly disastrous, on the romance form. The robbers' cook narrates this tale to the abducted girl, Charite, ostensibly as consolation and encouragement, and although initially the maiden is rescued by her betrothed, a jilted suitor soon brings about the deaths of the couple and himself. The romance ending is not allowed to stand, a pattern repeated in several stories in Book 10 (James). Romance is relegated to the heavens, on earth *saeva Fortuna* intervenes, and Apuleius' book dwells on the earth, a reflection of the depths ordinary humans suffer, unsentimentally told. Apuleius also gives weight to the romance form by transforming the tale into a Platonic allegory about love and the soul.

It is worth noting, too, how much this is a female story, a story told by an old woman to a young woman about a young woman; the story's labours are all concerned with women's tasks—food, water-carrying, wool-gathering, and cosmetics; the oppressing deity is a female, and the child born to the couple is a girl. This female orientation and its internal female audience raises questions about the gender of the ancient novel's audience more generally—or perhaps it is the romance that is the female form.

The *History of Apollonius King of Tyre*

The *History of Apollonius King of Tyre* differs from the texts so far discussed by virtue of being a composition constantly reworked at different periods, characterized by Konstan, Panayotakis, and others as 'fluid' and 'open', not only because the text exists in two significantly different recensions, but because these recensions cannot be reduced to a single prototype and are subject to even more change by copyists. In this sense, the *History* has as much in common with productions of oral-formulaic composition as with the set literary texts of Apuleius and Petronius, which only play with the idea of orality. Because of its fluid nature, the *History*, over the course of its development from the third to sixth centuries CE, retains its earlier monetary units, its pagan deities, and literary allusions to Virgil and Homer, but also accretes a Christian layer (Panayotakis).

Advocates of a Greek origin for the *History* tend to focus on those elements kindred with the Greek romantic novel—travel, love, pirates, *Scheintod*—and on the dissimilarities with the Roman novel—its third-person narrative and serious-romantic plot as opposed to the comic 'realism' of Apuleius and Petronius. Yet, as S. Panayotakis notes, the opening scene of incest announces 'the text's violent relation with the novelistic agenda and its representation as a transgressive narrative' (in Rimmell 2007: 302), one that fixes attention on proper father–daughter relations and presents the males, Apollonius and Athenagoras, as strangely removed or uncommitted in courtship. The famed 'sexual symmetry' of the Greek romances gives way to a portrait of women who choose their destinies and demonstrate their wisdom and accomplishments, rather than cleverly and chastely finding their way back to a beloved. It is also a riddling narrative, not only by virtue of the inclusion of numerous riddles of Symphosius; riddles advance the narrative and are a form of communication as well as a mark, oddly, of the liberal and philosophical education of one able to solve them. Like the popular and equally fluid *Vita Aesopi* and the *Alexander Romance*, the *History of Apollonius* seems thus to advance a common man's vision of the nature and uses of education.

Like the *Tale of Cupid and Psyche*, the length and unironic tone of the *History* have more the quality of Greek romance, yet in both cases the authors have self-consciously reacted against the standard romance form either within the work itself or in the frame.

The 'Fringe', Novel-like Narratives

Given the already inclusive definition of the novel, it seems irrational to marginalize 'novel-like narratives', particularly since 'novel' is an anachronistic category (Keulen). The 'fringe' is so defined partly because the texts do not seem to be 'novels' in a modern sense, and partly because of the practice in Classical Studies which walls off pagan from Christian and Classical from 'Late'—though the novel, extending unambiguously into the fourth century CE with Heliodorus, is already a bit anomalous. The arbitrariness of this practice is clear when we see the story-lines and narrative techniques directly evolve from Greek romance into Christian fiction like *Paul and Thekla* of the Acts.

In this chapter it is space rather than ideology that curtails discussion, but there are a few justifications. Once the fringe is limited to *Latin*, the texts in question are few. Whereas the Greek anonymous *Life of Aesop*, with its populist philosophical bent, comic dethroning of the pretensions of the educated elite, inserted fables, and episodic structure conforms well to many of the observations above, the Latin version is a translation or a poor recension of what is still essentially Greek. The same can be said of the Latin *Life of Alexander*. Most Christian fiction is written in Greek, though the argument can be made that 'Roman' is not coextensive with

'Latin', and that many works written in Greek under the Roman Empire might be called 'Roman', but that is an argument for another day. The case has been made as well that Christian (or Jewish) fiction is not part of the novel tradition proper, but already part of its reception, a new exploitation of the motifs and structures that make up Greek romance—and note that it is *Greek* romance that Christian fiction emulates—that it belongs to a different social and cultural milieu. Dictys' and Dares' 'eyewitness' accounts of the Trojan War do present 'fiction in the form of history', and, like Apuleius and Petronius in their different ways, these histories transform Homer into Latin prose, but they have at their centre not the life of an individual, but the events of the Trojan War, without embellishment of comic anecdotes and *mirabilia* (Merkle).

Concluding Comments

This survey has been more exploratory than exhaustive, and has circled around questions of definition rather than settling on one. The focus has been on what the extant novels have in common, with the result that several core topics have been passed over: philosophy, rhetoric, the Second Sophistic, mystery cults, Apuleius' lost novel *Hermagoras*; or given insufficient space: theatre, laughter, the continuity of the ancient novel into the present—for all of which, see the Further Reading section below. Very likely also, these comic texts have not been presented as comic enough, surreal, ironic, incongruous, playful, and full of life-force.

Further reading

General: G. Anderson, *Ancient Fiction: The Novel in the Greco-Roman World*, London, 1984; L. Graverini, W. Keulen, and A. Barchiesi, *Il Romanzo Antico*, Rome, 2006; S. J. Harrison (ed.), *Oxford Readings in the Roman Novel*, Oxford, 1999; H. Hofmann (ed.), *Latin Fiction*, London, 1999; B. E. Perry, *The Ancient Romances*, Berkeley, 1967; G. Schmeling (ed.), *The Novel in the Ancient World*, Leiden, 1996; J. Tatum, *The Search for the Ancient Novel*, Baltimore and London, 1994; P. G. Walsh, *The Roman Novel*, Cambridge, 1970; T. Whitmarsh (ed.), *The Cambridge Companion to the Greek and Roman Novel*, Cambridge 2008.

Definition of novel genre (and romance) and its reputation in antiquity: M. M. Bakhtin, *The Dialogic Imagination*, tr. C. Emerson and M. Holquist, Austin, Tex., 1981; L. Callebat, 'Le *Satyricon* de Pétrone et *L'Âne d'or* d'Apulée sont-ils des romans?', *Euphrosyne*, 20 (1992), 149–64; M. A. Doody, *The True Story of the Novel*, New Brunswick, 1996; H. Hofmann, 'Introduction' to *Latin Fiction* (above), 1–19; B. P. Reardon, *The Form of Greek Romance*, Princeton, 1991; G. Schmeling, 'Quid attinet veritatem per interpretem quaerere?

Interpreters and the Satyricon', *Ramus*, 23 (1994), 144–68; A. Scobie, *Aspects of the Ancient Romance and its Heritage*, Meisenheim am Glan, 1969: 9–29; D. Selden, 'Genre of Genre', in Tatum, *Search* (above), 39–64.

Menippean Satire *et al.*: A. Barchiesi, 'Tracce di narrativa greca e romanzo latino: una rassegna', in *Semiotica della novella latina*, Rome, 1986; G. B. Conte, *The Hidden Author*, Berkeley, 1996, ch. 5, 'Some Skeptical Thoughts on Menippean Satire'; J. Relihan, *Ancient Menippean Satire*, Baltimore, 1993.

Milesian Tale: S. J. Harrison, 'The Milesian Tale and the Roman Novel', in *GCN* 9 (1997), 61–73.

Petronius: *Bibliography*: G. Schmeling and J. Stuckey, *A Bibliography of Petronius*, Leiden, 1977; M. Smith, 'A Bibliography of Petronius (1945–1982)', *ANRW* II.32.3, 1628–65; *Survey of criticism*: M. Plaza, *Laughter and Derision in Petronius' Satyrica*, Stockholm, 2000, ch. 1; R. Bracht Branham and D. Kinney, 'Introduction' to *Petronius Satyrica*, Berkeley, 1996. ***Satyricon**, size, date*: H. J. Rose, *The Date and Author of the Satyricon*, Leiden, 1971; Schmeling, in *Novel in the Ancient World* (above), 460–1, for a putative reconstruction; A. Laird, 'The True Nature of the *Satyricon*?', in *The Greek and Roman Novel: Parallel Readings*, Groningen, 2007: 151–67. *Petronius, miscellaneous*: W. Arrowsmith, 'Luxury and Death in the *Satyricon*,' *Arion*, 5 (1966), 304–31; E. Auerbach, *Mimesis*, Garden City, 1957; R. Beck, 'Some Observations on the Narrative Technique of Petronius', *Phoenix*, 27 (1973), 42–61; J. Bodel, 'Trimalchio's Underworld', in Tatum, *Search* (above); id., 'The Cena Trimalchionis', in Hofmann, *Latin Fiction* (above); B. Boyce, *The Language of Freedmen in Petronius' Cena Trimalchionis* (Mnemosyne Suppl. 117), Leiden, 1991; C. Connors, *Petronius the Poet*, Cambridge, 1998; Conte, *The Hidden Author* (above); G. Jensson, *The Recollections of Encolpius*, Ancient Narrative Supplement 2 (2004); V. Rimell, *Petronius and the Anatomy of Fiction*, Cambridge, 2002; N. Slater, *Reading Petronius*, Baltimore, 1990; J. P. Sullivan, *The Satyricon of Petronius: A Literary Study*, London, 1968; F. Zeitlin, 'Petronius as Paradox', *TAPA* 102 (1971), 631–84.

Apuleius: *Bibliography through 1998*: C. Schlam and E. Finkelpearl, 'A Review of Scholarship on Apuleius' *Metamorphoses* 1970–1998', *Lustrum*, 42 (2001). *General/introduction*: S. J. Harrison, *Apuleius: A Latin Sophist*, Oxford, 2000; J. Tatum, *Apuleius and the Golden Ass*, Ithaca, NY, 1979. *Miscellaneous*: J. Annequin, 'Lucius "Asinus," Psyche "Ancilla": Esclavage et structures de l'imaginaire dans les Métamorphoses d'Apulée', *DHA* 24 (1998), 89–128; K. Bradley, 'Animalizing the Slave: The Truth of Fiction', *JRS* 90 (2000), 110–25; id., 'Apuleius and Carthage', *AN* 4 (2005), 1–29; L. Callebat, *Sermo Cotidianus*, Caen, 1968; E. Finkelpearl, *Metamorphosis of Language in Apuleius: A Study of Allusion in the Novel*, Ann Arbor, Mich., 1998; W. Fitzgerald, *Slavery and the Roman Literary Imagination*, Cambridge, 2000; D. Fowler, 'Writing with Style: The Prologue to Apuleius' *Metamorphoses* between *Fingierte Mundlichkeit* and Textuality', in Kahane and Laird, *Companion* (below), 225–30; L. Graverini, 'Corinth, Rome and Africa: A Cultural Background for the Tale of the Ass', in M. Paschalis and S. Frangoulidis (eds.), *Space in the Ancient Novel*, Groningen, 2002, 58–77; A. Kahane and A. J. W. Laird (eds.), *A Companion to the Prologue of Apuleius' Metamorphoses*, Oxford, 2001; E. J. Kenney, 'In the Mill with Slaves: Lucius Looks Back in Gratitude', *TAPA* 133 (2003), 159–92; R. May, *Apuleius and Drama: The Ass on Stage*, Oxford, 2006; F. Millar, 'The World of the *Golden Ass*', *JRS* 71 (1981), 63–75; M. O'Brien, *Apuleius' Debt to Plato in the Metamorphoses*, Lewiston, NY, 2002; C. Schlam, 'The Curiosity of the *Golden Ass*', *CJ* 64 (1968), 120–5; N. Shumate, *Crisis and Conversion in Apuleius' Metamorphoses*, Ann Arbor, Mich., 1996; Y. L. Too, 'Losing the Author's Voice: Cultural and Personal Identities in the *Metamorphoses* Prologue', in Kahane and Laird, *Companion* (above), 201–12;

D. van Mal-Maeder, '*Lector, intende: laetaberis*: The Enigma of the Last Book of Apuleius' *Metamorphoses*', in *GCN* 8 (1997), 87–118; G. Sandy, *The Greek World of Apuleius*, Leiden, 1997; J. J. Winkler, *Auctor and Actor: A Narratological Reading of Apuleius's Golden Ass*, Berkeley, 1985; M. Zimmerman, 'Echoes of Roman Satire in Apuleius' *Metamorphoses*', in R. R Nauta (ed.), *Desultoria Scientia: Genre in Apuleius' Metamorphoses and Related Texts* (*Caeculus*, Papers in Mediterranean Archaeology and Greek and Roman Studies 5), Leuven, 2006; L. Graverini, *Le Metamorfosi di Apuleio: Letteratura e identità*, Pisa, 2007.

Apollonius of Tyre: E. Archibald, *Apollonius of Tyre, Medieval and Renaissance Themes and Variations* (with text and translation), Cambridge, 1991; D. Konstan, *Apollonius of Tyre and the Greek Novel*, in Tatum, *Search* (above), 173–82; G. A. A. Kortekaas, *Commentary on the Historia Apollonii regis Tyri*, Leiden, 2007; id., *The Story of Apollonius, King of Tyre: A Study of its Greek Origin and an Edition of the two Oldest Latin Recensions*, Leiden, 2004; D. Lateiner, review of Kortekaas 2007, *BMCR* (June, 2007), 44 (good overview); S. Panayotakis, 'Fixity and Fluidity in *Apollonius of Tyre*', in Victoria Rimell (ed.), *Seeing Tongues, Hearing Scripts: Orality and Representation in the Ancient Novel*, Ancient Narrative Supplementum 7 (2007); G. Schmeling, 'Historia Apollonii regis Tyri', in Schmeling, *Novel* (above), 517–51.

The Fringe: G. Bowersock, *Fiction as History*, Berkeley, 1994; R. Hock, 'Why New Testament Scholars Should Read Ancient Novels', in R. Hock, J. Bradley Chance, and J. Perkins (eds.), *Ancient Fiction and Early Christian Narrative*, Atlanta, Ga., 1998; N. Holzberg, 'The Genre: Novels Proper and the Fringe', and 'Novel-like Works of Extended Prose Fiction II', in Schmeling, *Novel* (above), 11–28 and 621–54; G. Huber-Rebenich, 'Hagiographic Fiction as Entertainment', in Hofmann, *Latin Fiction* (above); S. Merkle, 'The Truth and Nothing But the Truth: Dictys and Dares', in Schmeling, *Novel* (above), 563–80 (and similarly in Hofmann, *Latin Fiction* and much else by Merkle); R. Pervo, 'The Ancient Novel Becomes Christian', in Schmeling, *Novel* (above), 685–709; R. Stoneman, 'The Latin Alexander', in Hofmann, *Latin Fiction* (above), 167–86.

CHAPTER 30

SCHOLARSHIP

ROBERT A. KASTER

THE word appears odd up there in the centre of the page, at the end of a section on Roman literary genres, and the oddities are plural. Most examples of what we consider Roman scholarship could no more claim 'literary' status than their modern counterparts: 'sub-literary' or (more neutrally) 'non-literary' is the label most aptly applied to both. More to the point, the works we take to constitute Roman scholarship we take that way because, however contested the entity's essential traits might be, we have 'scholarship' as a cultural category ready at hand to provide the label. The Romans had no such discrete category, hence no such label: where they could speak comfortably of *historia* or *fabula palliata* or *satura*, they had no generic term for the phenomenon under consideration; and of the several familiar terms that could be promoted as candidates—*studia*, *doctrina*, *eruditio* chief among them—none simply or regularly denoted what we call scholarship. Similarly, whereas we can say that scholarship just is what scholars do—and be confident that we will be understood to refer to persons who typically occupy a small number of institutional niches (above all colleges and universities, and the institutes and think-tanks that mimic them)—the phenomenon and the Romans who perpetrated it had no such clearly differentiated place in their culture. They could appear just about anywhere, in many guises, and what they did defied generic definition in simple, formal terms.

But this chapter must be about something, and that something can be given a working definition: the scholarship that will concern us comprises writings meant to preserve or elucidate Roman cultural memory in non-narrative, non-mimetic form, with a commitment to the truth. The first part of that definition, which hinges on the very broad phrase 'cultural memory', glances at both the variousness of the works in question and their essentially backward-looking character, a feature that will be stressed at the chapter's end. The second part of the definition simply distinguishes the writings eligible for consideration here from those already considered in the immediately preceding chapters. It is not the only definition that could be proposed, and it is no doubt rough around the edges. (It does not quite embrace, for example, the greatest Roman example of obsessive scholarship, the elder Pliny's *Natural History*; still less does it cover the technical writings of a Celsus, on medicine, or a Vitruvius, on architecture.) But it will serve for the purpose at hand: to grasp the range of writings that answer to the definition and the different sorts of men who produced them, and to consider a few of the cultural consequences.

In sketching the origins of Roman *grammatica*—the scholarly study, and teaching, of language and literature—the biographer Suetonius famously delivers some hard-and-fast judgements (*On Teachers of Grammar and Rhetoric* 1–3). The first stages, at the end of the third and first half of the second century BCE, were undistinguished (he says), since the practitioners—the 'half-Greek' poets Livius Andronicus and Quintus Ennius—did no more than 'interpret' Greek authors and give readings from their own works. At the next stage, in the second half of the second century, a prolonged visit by the Pergamene scholar and critic Crates of Mallos provided a model and an impetus for (on Suetonius' view) more sophisticated study, but even then the Roman response was limited: one man, a certain Gaius Octavius Lampadio, is said to have introduced book divisions (probably an Alexandrian innovation, first imitated in Latin by Ennius) into the poem that began Rome's epic tradition, Naevius' *Punic War*, and others began to hold public or private readings of poems (Ennius' *Annals*, Lucilius' satires) that had not enjoyed wide circulation. It was really not until the end of the second century and first part of the next (Suetonius concludes) that 'order and enrichment were brought to every aspect' of these studies by Lucius Aelius (*c.*150–*c.*85? BCE) and his son-in-law Servius Clodius, who were as far superior to their predecessors in their scholarship as they were in social status (both were Roman knights).

These judgements are neither wholly reliable (especially where the direct influence of Crates is concerned) nor entirely fair; in particular, they rather understate the skill and literary sophistication that both Livius Andronicus and Ennius brought to their own work (cf. Goldberg 1995: 64–73, 86–108, Hinds 1998: 52–63). But Suetonius was nothing if not conscientious in gathering the data he used to compile his accounts: if he found little or nothing to speak of before the work of Lucius Aelius, there was probably little or nothing to find. By contrast, there was a virtual flood of work in the century that followed, as the first century BCE witnessed the construction of Roman scholarship, just as it witnessed the construction of Roman literature (cf. Goldberg 2005). Here in tabular form is a survey of the kinds of work produced in the first century BCE, or just after the start of the common era, by the men who people Suetonius' *On Teachers of Grammar and Rhetoric.* The categories indicated are merely rubrics useful for a rough sorting, and some works could plainly be sorted under more than one rubric (numbers in parentheses denote the chapter in Suetonius' text where the person is mentioned, though Suetonius himself does not cite all the works associated with each person; for details, see Kaster 1995 ad locc.):

Antiquarian research (for present purposes 'antiquarian research' can be defined as any inquiry into the origin or nature of past practices, beliefs, or institutions that does not place the inquiry's result in a narrative or other larger explanatory context: the inquiry's answer to the question 'What did the ancients do about X?' or 'How did the practice of Y come about?' is regarded as satisfactory in itself. Cf. Momigliano 1966: 3): Cornelius Epicadus, on Latin *cognomina* and on the statuettes (*sigillaria*) associated with the Saturnalia (12); Verrius Flaccus, on the calendar, on Saturn, and on Etruscan matters (17); Iulius Hyginus, on families who traced their origin back to Troy, on Italian cities, on the Penates, and on the specific attributes of gods (*de proprietatibus deorum*) (20); Iulius Modestus, on holidays (20).

Textual interpretation: Lucius Aelius, on the *ius civile*, pontifical books, Twelve Tables, and *carmen Saliare* (3); Antonius Gnipho, a commentary on Ennius (?: 7); Pompilius Andronicus, a critique (*elenchus*) of Ennius (8); Ateius Philologus, an essay 'Did Aeneas Love Dido?' (10; probably written with reference to Naevius' *Punic War*, see Horsfall 1973–4); Curtius Nicias, on Lucilius (14); Crassicius Pansa, a commentary on the poet Cinna's *Zmyrna* (18); Iulius Hyginus, a commentary on Cinna's *propempticon* to Pollio and books (perhaps commentaries) on Vergil (20).

Linguistic inquiry: Lucius Aelius, on semantics and etymology, especially of legal and sacral language (3); Servius Clodius, etymological glosses on Plautus (3); Cornelius Nepos, on apparent synonyms (?: 4); Messalla Corvinus, on the letter s (4); Antonius Gnipho, 'on Latin discourse' (7); Orbilius Pupillus, on apparent synonyms (?: 9); Ateius Philologus, a book on unusual words (*glossemata*: 10); Staberius Eros, on grammatical analogy (13); Santra, on 'ancient' usage (*de antiquitate verborum*: 14); Verrius Flaccus, books on spelling (*de orthographia*), on obscure usages of the elder Cato, and a Latin lexicon (*On the Meaning of Words*) in twenty-six volumes (17); Scribonius Aphrodisius, a polemical response to the latter on spelling (19).

Catalogues and lists: Lucius Aelius, a list of the genuine plays of Plautus, similarly Servius Clodius (3); Aurelius Opillus, a literary catalog (*pinax*: 6).

Compilations (of miscellaneous learning, edifying anecdotes, and the like): Cornelius Nepos, *Exempla* (4); Furius Bibaculus, *Lucubrationes* (4); Aurelius Opillus, *Musae* (6); Verrius Flaccus, on 'memorable matters' (*res dignae memoria*: 17); Iulius Hyginus, *Exempla* (20); Maecenas Melissus, collections of amusing anecdotes and sayings (21).

Other: Lucius Aelius, notes on Stoic dialectic (3); Ateius Philologus, an abridged account (*breviarium*) of Roman history (for Sallust), a handbook on style (for Asinius Pollio), *epistulae* with scholarly content (10); Valerius Cato, pamphlets on unspecified literary or linguistic subjects (*grammatici libelli*: 11); Cornelius Epicadus, on meter (12); Pompeius

Lenaeus, translations of Greek writings on medicinal plants (15); Verrius Flaccus, *epistulae* with scholarly content (17); Iulius Hyginus, on agriculture and apiculture (20).

And all this is to say nothing of important figures whom Suetonius—mainly concerned as he is with men who happened to teach—does not mention: so, for example, Julius Caesar tackled the subject of grammatical analogy and the morphological regularity of language; the senator Nigidius Figulus wrote on grammar also, as well as science and theology; Cicero's friend the wealthy equestrian Atticus composed a chronological summary of the history of Rome, and 'the world' more generally (the *Liber Annalis*); and the prodigious Varro wrote, almost literally, on everything, in perhaps as many as seventy-five different works ranging from a survey of the 'liberal arts' (*Disciplinae*, in nine books) through 'divine and human antiquities' (*Antiquitates rerum humanarum et divinarum*, in forty-one books) to the Latin language (see below) and beyond.

None of the works catalogued above survives intact. Most are known only by title or from some very general characterization of their content, while for the rest we must mainly content ourselves with isolated nuggets preserved by later writers (see the relevant entries in Funaioli 1907). In two cases only do we have a tolerably clear view of the whole. The twenty-six-volume dictionary of Verrius Flaccus was abridged by Pompeius Festus in the second century CE, and that abridgement was in turn abridged in the eighth century by Paul the Deacon: taken together the two epitomes—the former partially, the latter entirely extant—allow us to form reasonably firm judgements of Flaccus' working methods. Much the same can be said of Varro's *On the Latin Language*, the first work to attempt a systematic account of that subject and as such an ancestor (though not a direct ancestor) of the countless grammatical handbooks (*artes*) that were to follow. Though of the original twenty-five books only two survive completely (5–6), and 4 others in part (7–10), we have enough to know the plan and proportions of the work as a whole: after an introductory book Varro addressed, in turn, the topics of etymology and the relations between words and things (Books 2–7), inflectional morphology (Books 8–13, including the conflict between regularity and irregularity in grammar, or 'analogy' vs. 'anomaly'), and the formation of propositions (Books 14–25, a species of syntax previously addressed by Lucius Aelius).

Yet even the generally wretched state of preservation allows us to identify some important shared characteristics of all these works, which in themselves established the norms for Roman scholarship in the centuries to come. To start with the most obvious trait: a desire to accumulate and categorize plainly outstripped any desire to synthesize. Knowledge was organized in various closely related forms—especially in lists, catalogues, and miscellanies—by a process of accretion, bit by bit. Any given bit would be grouped with other bits according to one or another a priori criterion—by having a topic or letter of the alphabet in common, say, or by occupying a given place in a chronological or (in a commentary) textual sequence, or simply in virtue of being 'memorable'—but the bits did not cohere, and were not meant to cohere, so as to provide a synoptic view or sustain a thesis. In this respect, Varro's systematic approach to Latin was much the exception, whereas Verrius Flaccus' dictionary was more the norm; and even within Varro's massive oeuvre, *On the Latin Language* was rather different from the one work of his whose loss any Romanist must most regret, the encyclopedic *Account of Ancient Things Human and Divine.* Divided unevenly into twenty-five books on 'things human' (which is to say, Roman) and sixteen on 'things divine', the work was a grand *catalogue raisonné* of the culture. Thanks in no small part to Saint Augustine, who pillaged it enthusiastically for his *City of God*, the books on *res divinae* are better represented among the fragments (Cardauns 1976): organized, after an introductory book, in triads—on priestly functionaries (Books 2–4), sacred places (Books 5–7), religious celebrations (Books 8–10), private and public rites (Books 11–13), and the gods (Books 14–16)—the collection must in its original state have comprised an elaborate, and by no means unsceptical, collection of categories, definitions, and carefully catalogued attributes, accompanied by the lore of what 'people say'. As H. D. Jocelyn put it (1982: 198–9): 'Varro intended a certain unity in [Books 14–16, on gods]. This unity, however, should be distinguished from the sort of philosophical work [*On Gods*] which Varro himself refers to [elsewhere].... His model was rather of the grammatical kind exemplified by Apollodorus' [*On Gods*], a work which attempted to explain the names and descriptive epithets of the deities of the *Iliad* and the *Odyssey*.' (Compare the observation, regarding the fragments of Varro's *On the Way of Life of the Roman People*, that 'a substantial part of these are definitions of the dazzling array of jugs available to Romans of the Republic' (J. McAlhany, *Bryn Mawr Classical Review*, 12 (2004), 27.)

When Cicero praised Varro's writings for making his fellow Romans feel at home in their own city (*Academica* 1. 9), he surely meant, not that Varro had explained the city and its culture in a comprehensive or novel way, but that he had made over to them a treasure-house of lovingly organized *facts.*

Such facts attached themselves, especially, to individual words: for example, as explanations or illustrations of given lexical items, as data gathered together under certain rubrics, or as explanations attached to the words that stood as the lemmata in commentaries on literary texts. (Even less than their modern counterpart did ancient commentators lift their eyes from the lemma immediately before them to contemplate the text as a whole, and the results, when they do, usually do not make us wish that they did it more often: the late antique Virgilian commentator Servius has many useful and intelligent things to say on matters of detail but is at his least helpful when telling us that 'all' of *Aeneid* 4 is 'transferred from' Apollonius of Rhodes' *Argonautica*, Book 3 (Thilo-Hagen 1878–81: 1. 459) or that Virgil's 'aim' in the *Aeneid* is, simply, 'to imitate Homer and praise Augustus through his ancestors' (ibid. 1. 4).) Whether viewed as a linguistic phenomenon inviting description or definition, as a label for an institution, or a person, or as a component of a text, a word was the smallest unit to which meaning could be given, hence the smallest unit to which useful knowledge could be attached. Roman scholars were in this respect miniaturists, producing small, gem-like bits of learning: others might assemble these bits to tell larger stories, but the scholars generally eschewed such stories of their own. Described in these terms, the scholarly enterprise sounds rather pinched and lacking in scope, and no doubt from some points of view it was: unlike rhetoric, for example, literary and antiquarian scholarship did not claim to prepare men directly to participate in public affairs—a form of modesty plainly related to the fact that the reception and practice of formal rhetorical study at Rome were contested in ways that the study of literature and antiquities never was. (On the reception of rhetoric, and other controversies concerning rhetorical education at Rome, see Andrew Riggsby's discussion in Chapter 23.)

But the umbratile nature of the study need not imply that its practitioners thought it idle or useless. Scholars from a later period whose works survive—Aulus Gellius, for example, from the mid-second century CE—commonly stress the edifying, even ennobling, utility that they think their efforts will provide, and there is no reason to suppose that this view was not found in the earlier works of scholarship, now lost, on which Gellius certainly drew:

> I for my part... have taken on board [*sc.* from my extensive reading] only those elements that would either quickly and easily lead the eager and able to a desire for honourable learning and a contemplation of useful skills or free people hemmed in by life's other occupations from an ignorance of words and facts that is surely shameful and peasantish.
> (*Attic Nights*, preface 12)

The kind of confidence visible on the surface here seems implied in works of Roman scholarship more generally: the confidence that there are those 'out there' who will benefit, perhaps by putting the scholar's work to some use still unimagined, as a brick fired today might be used in a building not yet designed. And in fact we know that such confidence was not misplaced, that the bricks were used well: without Atticus' *Liber Annalis* to clarify many chronological details, Cicero could not have achieved the synthesis of Roman oratorical history offered up in the *Brutus*; without the antiquarian investigations of Varro, the calendrical researches of Verrius Flaccus, and other works like them, Virgil's *Aeneid* and Ovid's *Fasti* would look very different indeed. Organizing knowledge in ways that will ultimately benefit someone other than oneself requires a cultural confidence and a generosity that are the opposite of pinched.

The open-handed men who gave their learning away for the benefit of others clustered, at the outset, at the opposite ends of the social spectrum, as men who were either completely self-sufficient or completely dependent—in short, aristocrats and slaves. On the one hand, as already noted, the men who in Suetonius' estimation first put literary scholarship on a sound footing, Lucius Aelius and Servius Clodius, were Roman knights and therefore wealthy men of leisure, and they were by no means the men of highest rank to gain a reputation for scholarship. Caesar had already held the consulship by the time he wrote his work on grammatical analogy while on campaign in Gaul, and Nigidius Figulus and Varro were both men of praetorian rank; Messalla Corvinus, author of a monograph on the letter *s*, was a prominent military man, public figure, and literary patron. In a later generation, the emperor Tiberius enjoyed the company of scholars, and enjoyed testing them with particularly challenging questions (Suetonius, *Life of Tiberius* 70.3); Claudius took matters a step farther, not only writing a monograph on the need for additional letters of the alphabet but also using his authority to see that the letters were actually used in imperial documents and inscriptions (Suetonius, *Life of Claudius* 41.3, Tacitus, *Annals* 11.13.3, 11.14.5).

On the other hand, most of the men whose lives Suetonius recounts as teachers and scholars passed through slavery, a fact that significantly distinguishes the figures we meet at Rome from their counterparts in Greek culture. The ripples stirred by Rome's imperial expansion brought some such men to Italy from the eastern Mediterranean, where—if they were reduced to slavery as adults—they might already have been important actors in their own communities, carrying with them habits of Greek learning that could be adapted and cultivated in their new circumstances (see e.g. Suetonius, *On Teachers of Grammar and Rhetoric* 10, on Ateius Philologus). Still others, finding themselves enslaved by one mischance or another, came from Gaul, Spain, Illyria, and even parts of Italy itself (see, respectively, ibid. 7, 20, 12, 18, 23). Whatever their origins, and whether they were educated before being enslaved or educated in the households that enslaved them, their learning was in the first instance put at the service of their masters, teaching their children, serving as literary advisors, and in general enhancing their cultural capital. Often, they were rewarded with their freedom in return, leaving them at liberty to serve others with their learning and seek their patronage: so, for example, Ateius Philologus, who very likely came to Rome from Athens as a slave in the household of the jurist Ateius Capito's family, later cultivated the Claudii Pulchri (as tutor and travelling companion), the historian and former senator Sallust (whom he provided with a summary of Roman history), and the historian, general, and statesman Asinius Pollio (for whom he wrote a handbook on style: ibid. 10). In this respect, the story of scholarship's first three generations at Rome, from the late second century to the end of the Republic, could in good measure be told in terms of a relatively small number of great households whose members, dependants, and connections formed especially dense centres of gravity, from Sulla through Pompey to the palace of Augustus (see, respectively, ibid. 12, 14–15, and 17, 20–2).

As scholarship and *studia* came to be 'naturalized' over the course of the first century BCE, they also came to play a role as a medium of social exchange and interaction within the elite, another form of the connoisseurship through which men acquired and displayed the cultural capital that solidified their standing. The acquisition of and access to books provides one example among many. At his villa in Tusculum Lucius Lucullus painstakingly assembled a fabulous library, which he opened to the free use of friends (Plutarch, *Lucullus* 42.1–2); it became a magnet for both Greek and Roman intellectuals, and remained such even after Lucullus' death, when Cicero visited the place to use some of the books and found Cato seated amid a heap of Stoic texts (*On the Ends of Goods and Evils* 3. 7). Cicero's own acquisition and disposition of libraries reveals a similar nexus of intellectual and social relations. In 60 BCE, through the good offices of his friend Papirius Paetus, Cicero acquired the library of one of Paetus' relatives, who happened to be the Servius Clodius whom Suetonius ranks as one of the two founders of Roman literary scholarship. Because the library was in Greece (Clodius had left Rome under a cloud, after plagiarizing from his father-in-law, Lucius Aelius, who responded by dissolving Clodius' marriage), Cicero had to engage the help of yet another friend, Atticus, to ensure that the books were transmitted safely to Rome (*Letters to Atticus* 1.20.7, 2.1.12); and a few years later, when Cicero wanted to organize the library in his villa at Antium, he was able to call in Tyrannio, a Greek scholar and friend of Atticus, as well as some of Atticus' trained slaves to help with the labelling (ibid. 4.41.1, 4.8.2).

The conventions of learning also became the currency of ordinary conversation and correspondence. When he is speaking with the scholar and teacher Curtius Nicias, Cicero's conversation of course turns to matters of literary scholarship (*de philologis*: ibid. 13.28.4, cf. 7.3.10), as it does also when he is speaking about the same scholar. Reporting to his son-in-law Dolabella a financial dispute involving Nicias and another man that the former asked Cicero to arbitrate, Cicero turns the report into an elaborate joke in which he casts himself in the role of Aristarchus—the great Alexandrian scholar renowned for his ability to assess the authenticity of texts—and recounts how he had 'obelized' (condemned as spurious) the document that appeared to put Nicias in the wrong (*Letters to his Friends* 9.10.1, cf. Suetonius, *On Teachers of Grammar and Rhetoric* 14.2: to put the matter in perspective, Cicero allows himself this highly embroidered *jeu d'esprit* only because, as he says, there is nothing really important to report from Rome). The sort of conversation *de philologis* that Cicero enjoyed with Nicias surely became, for many of the elite, a staple of the refined soirees that were an increasingly important element in their self-fashioning. We have already noted the table-talk of Tiberius, which so tested the experts that one scholar tried to find out what the emperor had lately been reading, the better to 'cram' when it came time to be his guest (the scholar allegedly paid with his life: Suetonius, *Tiberius* 56). And by the time we come to the world conjured up in Aulus Gellius' *Attic Nights*, in the middle of the second century CE, such learned testing and probing are all-pervasive elements of the environment: not just a conversation at a friend's table (2.22) but a stroll through the Field of Agrippa near the Campus Martius (14.5) or a chat struck up by gentlemen standing about the vestibule of the imperial palace (19.13)—any of these occasions, and diverse others, might spark discussion, sometimes heated, of a proper grammatical form or the correct terms to denote various winds, or midgets. Though it would probably be imprudent to believe the literal truth of Gellius' vignettes (he does love to tell a good story), it would be equally imprudent to suppose that he intended to represent the culture of the day in a way that readers would find implausible and unfamiliar.

The apparent diffusion of *studia* as an ornament of the elite was accompanied by a broadening of the social base on which such pursuits were supported. Scholarship and *studia* themselves gradually came to provide a way into the elite for those who otherwise would not have enjoyed it, a shift from clientage to independence epitomized by the men whose careers are recounted in Suetonius' *On Teachers of Grammar and Rhetoric* (for what follows, cf. Kaster 1995: pp. xliv–xlv; numbers in parentheses refer to the sections of Suetonius' text). At the very start of the first century BCE we see the freedman Aurelius Opillus, whose scholarship ran to a literary catalogue and a miscellany, close up his school and accompany the Roman statesman Publius Rutilius Rufus into exile in Asia Minor (6.2), a gesture best read as an act of loyalty to a singularly important patron. From that point on each successive generation gives evidence of a change from this steeply hierarchical model. By the middle of the century we find the first attested freeborn teacher, Orbilius of Beneventum (9), establishing himself in Rome, where his pupils included Horace. A generation later another freedman, Verrius Flaccus, made a name both as the most important Roman scholar after Varro and as the most innovative and successful teacher of his day, a position that gave him a certain leverage to negotiate when the emperor Augustus sought to engage him as a tutor to his grandsons (10). Under Tiberius another grammarian, Pomponius Porcellus, did not scruple to criticize the emperor's diction to his face (22.2); not long after, the louche and arrogant Remmius Palaemon (23), another freedman and the author of a very influential grammatical handbook, defied Tiberius and Claudius, both of whom denounced him for immorality and warned fathers to keep their sons from his school—warnings that did not prevent him from becoming very rich indeed. (It is impossible to imagine Palaemon following anyone into exile.) Under the Flavians, finally, we see the lionization of Valerius Probus (24), probably a descendant of a Roman legionary settled in Beirut under Augustus, who became a taste-maker and one of the forerunners of the archaizing fashion that came to maturity under the Antonines. By the end of the first century CE learned expertise clearly provided a stable basis on which one could establish a respectable social identity. The movement that we can trace, while far from representing a 'democratization' of culture, certainly represented a distribution of cultural capital beyond the relatively few aristocratic families who were the centres of *studia* in the first century BCE.

This broadening of the base tended to stabilize the shared culture, and thereby to stabilize society at a certain level, as a literary education and with it at least a tincture of literary scholarship became one of the identifying marks of an elite that extended across the empire (Kaster 1988: 11–70). This shared culture was remarkably homogeneous despite its great geographical spread, as much the same texts were read, and in much the same ways, in whatever corners of the empire literate Latin culture extended. The homogeneity, moreover, tended to take on a temporal dimension as well: the point can be illustrated, to draw this survey to a close, if we consider the 'moving horizon' of Latin textual scholarship in the first century BCE.

The man whom Suetonius identified as the Roman founder of such scholarship, Lucius Aelius, gave particular attention to studying the language of Rome's pre-literary texts—especially the Twelve Tables (still memorized by schoolboys when Cicero was a child: *On the Laws* 2.59)—and to establishing a list of the genuine plays of Plautus. Roughly two decades later we find interest in Plautus' younger contemporary, Ennius, in the work of Antonius Gnipho and Pompilius Andronicus, both active from the 80s to the 60s BCE (Suetonius, *On Teachers of Grammar and Rhetoric* 7–8); by the 50s the horizon has reached the satires of Lucilius, from the latter part of the second century BCE, in the *libri* of Curtius Nicias (ibid. 14.4). At that point the movement accelerates: a commentary on the *Zmyrna* of Cinna, a 'new poet' in the circle of Catullus, was produced before the late 30s, not much more than a decade after the poet's death (ibid. 18.2, with Kaster 1995: 200); and while the earliest attested scholarly writings on Virgil's poetry, by Iulius Hyginus (Suetonius, *On Teachers*... 20; Funaioli 1907: 528–33), probably post-date the poet's death, they were certainly produced under Augustus, beginning a tradition of scholarly attention that continued unbroken for another five centuries.

But that is where the 'moving horizon' effectively stops. Though the poetry of another Augustan, Horace, appears to have enjoyed a more or less continuous tradition of commentary down through late antiquity, that can be said of no other contemporary or later Latin author. Indeed, when scholarly fashion next changed, it was not to take up neglected authors of the early Empire but to move in precisely the opposite direction: the 'archaizing' interests that are most fully on display in the pages of Aulus Gellius represent a turning back of the clock, to authors of (predominantly) the second century BCE. The body of commentary eventually built up around some early Imperial authors—Lucan, Statius, Juvenal—is entirely the creation of late antiquity, after those authors were introduced into the school curricula in the late fourth and early fifth centuries CE.

The early Imperial formation of a 'classical canon' in the schools—with Virgil and Terence dominating the poetry side, Sallust and Cicero the prose—had broad and obvious consequences. The language that was described in the scholarly handbooks, taught in the schools, and passed down from generation to generation allowed the educated classes to speak with one voice, the voice of 'Received Standard Imperial Latin' (Löfstedt 1959: 48), which remained immune from the changes that affected the language of the market and the countryside. In ethics, too, the stock of edifying examples—of virtuous or patriotic behaviour (or their reverse), like those collected in Valerius Maximus' *Memorable Deeds and Sayings*—remained very heavily weighted toward the Republican past rather than the Imperial present. In these and many other ways, Roman scholarship excelled at its job of 'preserving and elucidating Roman cultural memory', to the extent that much of that memory remained fixed in a golden, late Republican/mid-Augustan noon.

Further reading

Anyone seeking an overview of Roman scholarship in the late Republic must begin with Rawson 1985, which should be read with her important essay on the development of logical organization in Latin prose (Rawson 1978 = Rawson 1991: 324–51). For the earliest phase, down to 78 BCE, Suerbaum 2002: 539 ff. is useful; Della Corte 1981 brings much material together, but his synthesis is often wilful; for a broader chronological survey emphasizing the transmission of texts, Reynolds and Wilson 1991: 18–43. Varro, who is everywhere in Rawson's learned book without ever quite being its focus, still wants a comprehensive modern treatment to place him in his time and culture: pending that, Cardauns 2001 is a reliable introduction. On the scholars themselves, beyond the works referred to in the text above, see Christes 1979 and, for Aulus Gellius and his milieu, Holford-Strevens 2003 and Holford-Strevens and Vardi 2004; for later antiquity, Kaster 1988; P. L. Schmidt, in Herzog 1989: 101–58; P. L. Schmidt and K. Sallmann, in Sallmann 1997: 67–82, 218–61. On commentaries and commentators, Most 1999 and Gibson and Kraus 2002 are good places to start; on Latin scholia and textual criticism in antiquity, Zetzel 1975, 1980, 1981*a*, 1981*b*, 2005; on the history of Latin grammatical thought, Barwick 1922, Taylor 1974, Holtz 1981, Hovdhaugen 1982, Kaster 1988; on mythography in the Roman era, Cameron 2004; on the emergence of Lucan, Statius, and Juvenal as 'suitable authors' in late antiquity, Kaster 1978.

References

Barwick, K. (1922), *Remmius Palaemon und die römische Ars Grammatica*, Leipzig: B. G. Teubner.

Cameron, A. (2004), *Greek Mythography in the Roman World*, New York: Oxford University Press.

Cardauns, B. (1976), *Antiquitates rerum divinarum*, Mainz: Akademie der Wissenschaften und der Literatur.

—— (2001), *Marcus Terentius Varro: Einführung in sein Werk*, Heidelberg: C. Winter.

Christes, J. (1979), *Sklaven und Freigelassene als Grammatiker und Philologen im antiken Rom*, Wiesbaden: Steiner.

Della Corte, F. (1981), *La filologia Latina dale origini a Varrone*[2], Florence: La Nuova Italia Editrice.

Funaioli, G. (1907), *Grammaticae Romanae fragmenta*, Leipzig: B. G. Teubner.

Gibson, R. K. and Kraus, C. S. (eds.) (2002), *The Classical Commentary: Histories, Practices, Theory*, Leiden: Brill.

Goldberg, S. M. (1995), *Epic in Republican Rome*, New York: Oxford University Press.

—— (2005), *Constructing Literature in Republican Rome: Poetry and Its Reception*, Cambridge: Cambridge University Press.

Herzog, R. (ed.) (1989), *Handbuch der lateinischen Literature der Antike*, vol. 5: *Restauration und Erneuerung: Die lateinische Literature von 284 bis 374 n. Chr.*, Munich: C. H. Beck.

Hinds, S. (1998), *Allusion and Intertext: Dynamics of Appropriation in Roman Poetry*, Cambridge: Cambridge University Press.

Holford-Strevens, L. (2003), *Aulus Gellius: An Antonine Scholar and his Achievement*, rev. edn., Oxford: Oxford University Press.

—— and Vardi, A. (eds.) (2004), *The Worlds of Aulus Gellius*, Oxford: Oxford University Press.

Holtz, L. (1981), *Donat et la tradition de l'enseignement grammatical*, Paris: Centre National de la Recherche Scientifique.

Horsfall, N. M. (1973–4), 'Dido in the Light of History', *Proceedings of the Virgilian Society*, 13: 1–13.

Hovdhaugen, E. (1982), *Foundations of Western Linguistics: From the Beginning to the End of the First Millenium A.D.*, New York: Columbia University Press.

Jocelyn, H. D. (1982), 'Varro's *Antiquitates rerum divinarum* and Religious Affairs in the Late Roman Republic', *Bulletin of the John Rylands University Library of Manchester*, 65: 148–205.

Kaster, R. A. (1978), 'Servius and *idonei auctores*', *American Journal of Philology*, 99: 181–209.

—— (1988), *Guardians of Language: The Grammarian and Society in Late Antiquity*, Berkeley and Los Angeles: University of California Press.

—— (ed.) (1995), *Suetonius: 'De Grammticis et Rhetoribus'*, Oxford: Oxford University Press.

Löfstedt, E. (1959), *Late Latin*, Cambridge, Mass.: Harvard University Press.

Momigliano, A. (1966). *Studies in Historiography*. New York: Harper & Row.

Most, G. W. (1999), *Commentaries/Kommentare*, Göttingen: Vandenhoeck & Ruprecht.

Rawson, E. (1978), 'The Introduction of Logical Organization into Roman Prose Literature', *Papers of the British School at Rome*, 46: 12–34.

—— (1985), *Intellectual Life in the Late Roman Republic*, Baltimore: Johns Hopkins University Press.

—— (1991), *Roman Culture and Society: Collected Papers*, ed. Fergus Millar, Oxford: Oxford University Press.

Reynolds, L. D. and Wilson, N. G. (1991), *Scribes and Scholars: A Guide to the Transmission of Greek and Latin Literature*[3], Oxford: Oxford University Press.

Sallmann, K. (ed.) (1997), *Handbuch der lateinischen Literature der Antike*, vol. 4: *Die Literature des Umbruchs: Von der römischen zur christlichen Literatur, 117 bis 284 n. Chr.*, Munich: C. H. Beck.

Suerbaum, W. (ed.) (2002), *Handbuch der lateinischen Literature der Antike*, vol. 1: *Die archaische Literature von den Anfängen bis Sullas Tod*, Munich: C. H. Beck.

Taylor, D. J. (1974), *Declinatio: A Study of the Linguistic Theory of Marcus Terentius Varro*, Amsterdam: John Benjamins, 1974.

Thilo, G. and Hagen, H. (1878–81), *Servii Grammatici qui feruntvr in Vergilii carmina commentarii*, vol. 1: *Aeneidos librorum I–V commentarii*, Leipzig: B. G. Teubner.
Zetzel, J. E. G. (1975), 'On the History of Latin Scholia', *Harvard Studies in Classical Philology*, 79: 335–54.
—— (1980), 'The Subscriptions in the Manuscripts of Livy and Fronto and the Meaning of *Emendatio*', *Classical Philology*, 75: 38–59.
—— (1981*a*), 'On the History of Latin Scholia II: The *Commentum Cornuti* in the Ninth Century', *Mediaevalia et Humanistica*, 10: 19–31.
—— (1981*b*), *Latin Textual Criticism in Antiquity*, New York: Arno Press.
—— (2005), *Marginal Scholarship and Textual Deviance: The* Commentum Cornuti *and the Early Scholia on Persius*, Bulletin of the Institute of Classical Studies 84, London: Institute of Classical Studies.

PART IV

HISTORY

CHAPTER 31

EARLY ROME

NICOLA TERRENATO

ALMOST upon its awakening, modern historical criticism directed an unflinchingly sceptical gaze at the Regal and early Republican periods. Age-of-Reason scholars like de Beaufort or de Pouilly probably saw their chance to chalk one up for the *modernes* over the *anciennes* when they programmatically set out to expose the inherent contradiction and unreliability of the sources for the first half-millennium of Rome's development (Raskolnikoff 1992). The shadow of that primordial withering judgement is still with us, shaping for better or worse the discourse to the extent that even the most revisionist among the scholars of our times cannot avoid engaging in lengthy apologies for their alternative readings of key texts like the first decade of Livy. At various times between the 1880s and the 1950s scientific excavations in and around Rome impacted the debate in many ways, but without essentially changing the general perceptions of generations of ancient historians. Most, in fact, went on regarding early Rome as a scholarly quagmire, in which it was nearly impossible to find an unchallenged, solid point of departure that would support reliable inferences and conjectures. The archaeologists of this period, from Giacomo Boni to Ejnar Gjerstad and Frank Brown, have at times entertained hopes of a turnaround which would reclaim that elusive segment of human history, only to see a vast portion of their efforts crumble again under the two-pronged attack of sharper source criticism and more stringent analyses of archaeological data.

Another spate of discoveries, in the last decade or two, has once more rekindled dormant yearnings for new syntheses that might be brilliantly persuasive, or perhaps even only less controversial. A remarkable number of such works has actually appeared, ranging from sober historical attempts to the boldest (and even sometimes the wildest) archaeological reconstructions (Cornell 1995; Forsythe

2005; Holloway 1994; Smith 1996; Carandini 1997, 2006). It is too soon to evaluate the permanent mark that this new wave will leave, but it is hard to escape the feeling that there is a more or less silent majority of scholars who are still far from being willing to regard early Roman history as even coming close to meeting the same standards of proof that are possible for contemporary Greece, for instance. And in fairness, when it comes to early Rome there is maddeningly not enough evidence to reach widely acceptable conclusions, and yet just too much to dismiss the problem altogether as unsolvable, especially when it comes to matching archaeological findings with textual references. Even in the best cases, such as those of the Servian walls or the temple of Jupiter on the Capitoline hill, it is not easy to combine the evidence in really robust ways, finding an adequate broader historical contextualization for the undeniable archaeological evidence.

An interesting intellectual trend, perhaps arising from the frustration of most attempts at creating an absolute order, has recently prompted some, both in the historical and in the archaeological camp, to take a different tack. They have tended to sidestep altogether thorny specific problems, such as how much to believe of the complex narratives about the Tarquin kings (to name just one issue about which diametrically opposed views can and have been respectably held, e.g. Cornell 1995; Fox 1996; Poucet 2000). Instead, they have essentially tried to create alternative levels of discourse that could exist without having to untie or cut open impossible historiographic Gordian knots. One such level is the reflexive analysis of modern scholarship on the subject. But, taking a leaf from Momigliano's many books (Momigliano 1963, 1989; critique in Ampolo 1988; Cornell 2006), they craftily embedded in this form of intellectual history actual inferences about early Rome, from the vantage-point of a much more defensible epistemological position (Grandazzi 1991 is perhaps the cleverest example). In a similar way, works that dealt with the perceptions that later Romans had of their own primordial past could also, somewhat surreptitiously, make perceptive points about the original character of the community (Dench 2005).

What is remarkable in many of these important contributions, besides the obvious postmodern slant, is a marked shift away from the *histoire événementielle* as well as from the uncompromising formulations of pure materialism. It is as if the historian were squinting just enough to blur out the many unsolvable factual questions, to get instead a comprehensive glimpse of the essential nature of the phenomenon. An appropriate epistemological stance is adopted, one that embraces rather the fuzziness of the available information instead of rejecting it and also constantly weaves in and out between perception and reality, producing in the end a sophisticated, multi-level narrative that neither tells tall stories nor is entirely irrelevant to our understanding of what in fact happened during the early centuries of Rome.

In parallel, archaeologists have been following their own brand of critical thinking, namely post-processualism. Indeed, the Iron Age and archaic periods (roughly 1000–500 BCE) in Central Italy have recently become the premier testing ground for new theoretical approaches (review in Cuozzo 1996). A few examples will be sufficient here. Torelli's recent work on the role of rituals, and ancestor cult in particular, in the emergence of plastic art (Torelli 1997) is a theoretically aware exercise in cognitive archaeology, streets ahead of the simplified models that characterized the social art history of the previous generation (e.g. Bianchi Bandinelli and Giuliano 1973). Its value in providing a profound insight into the archaic mentality will always go far beyond the exegesis of any specific piece (which can always be disputed). At a different level, Coarelli's wholesale revision of the topography of pre-Imperial Rome has been founded, among other things, on a much greater reliance on archaic elements, and in particular early cults (e.g. Coarelli 1983, 1988, 1997). While many of his specific attributions have been radically challenged (Ziolkowski 2005), the greater lasting value and innovation in his work is arguably to be found in the pages that reconstruct the character of an urban district in the archaic city in terms that are essentially those of perceptive geography. His masterful re-evocation of the liminal nature of the Velabrum, for instance, would be inspired and revealing even for those who wanted to question the precise location of every single specific cult. Even in Carandini's extremely controversial formulations there is an interesting emphasis on the role of myth in shaping current events and their historical memory. Here, the specific inspiration from the later production of Sahlins (1985), with its postmodern approach to Tahitian history, would imply a world-view that is very different from his earlier explicitly Marxist stances.

There are two general conclusions that can be drawn from this cursory overview. A first striking trend is that, while century-old materialist and idealist frameworks still largely predominate in the archaeology and the history of later Roman periods, a freer theoretical rein can apparently be enjoyed when discussing the time before the expansion. It is as if these dangerous relativist forays were only deemed appropriate for those periods that have contributed less to the powerful icon of late Republican and Imperial Rome in modern western culture (cf. the full argument in Terrenato 2005*b*). The other connected phenomenon is that this intellectual liberty seems to be slowly taking early Roman specialists towards the kind of discourse that can often be found in historical anthropology. There indeed is much to be said for a move of this kind. It could open alternative avenues to the traditional erudite philological search for micro-connections (which is in any case very often not appropriate, given the quality of the available data), towards wider vistas that do not necessarily revolve around a specific set of conjectures. Such big pictures, however, do not have to be brought together at the expense of the role of individuals and small groups, as was the case with some of the syntheses of the 1970s and 1980s (e.g. the papers in *La formazione* 1980; Ampolo 1983).

The first brush with social anthropology actually dates to that period, when some experts of late prehistory were adopting the classic neo-evolutionist frameworks of Childe and Service to understand state formation and urbanization in Rome (Guidi 1982). The view of a unilinear progression through the stages of chiefdom and state which would be hailed by clear, incontrovertible indicators, however, could hardly be widely accepted as a solution to the complex problem of early Rome, plagued by insufficient archaeological data and contradictory sources. On top of that, the traditional scepticism of classical scholarship towards comparative frameworks made it hard to accept that Rome might have been moving along a well-trodden path, rather than a unique one (Colonna 1983).

The following generation of anthropological thought may have better luck at informing the current discourse on early Rome. Concepts such as agency theory or factionalism (Brumfiel and Fox 1994; Dobres and Robb 2000), for instance, can offer a useful handle for the role that the actions of individuals and groups play within the developing community. And, indeed, some recent work seems to be moving in this direction, if only implicitly. In Pacciarelli's reconstruction of the phases of the urbanization process in South Etruscan centres, what is envisaged are discrete small communities resettling to the same plateau and only later coalescing together (Pacciarelli 2000). Similarly, the Roman *curiae* are seen as pre-dating the foundation, and in many ways shaping its nature and topography (Carandini 1997: 395–429). In other words, the process (together with its actors and components) is finally coming to the fore, after decades in which the scene was stolen by an endless (and somewhat fruitless) debate over the precise date at which Rome could be called a city (review in Motta and Terrenato 2006). Other components that are enjoying new interest are *gentes* and other social groups. These long-lived clan-like entities characterize the society of early Rome just as much as that of most other contemporary Italian polities. Recent works have been extensively re-analysing the evidence and appropriately stressing the fluid and context-dependent nature of these formations (Smith 2006). This, however, does not imply that they have no political and social relevance, which is instead tantalizingly suggested by various lines of evidence.

Some legal historians had long emphasized the role of *gentes* in the administration of communal lands or the regulation of elite marriage (Capogrossi Colognesi 1994; Franciosi 1999). Even more momentous, from the political point of view, is the military role of these groups, as attested by inscriptions like the *lapis Satricanus* (Stibbe 1980) or the Vetulonia helmets, as well as by the memory of private wars such as the one waged by the Fabii against Veii (Rawlings 1999). The discourse of conspicuous self-representation developed over time by these groups is indirectly attested early on by clustered burials (Bietti Sestieri 1992), and later by the emergence of quasi-palatial structures at the end of the sixth century BCE (Terrenato 2001*a*). While it would be very dangerous to impose fixed and normative paradigms on these complex phenomena, it may be possible to suggest at this point that groups that are larger than the nuclear family (and of course smaller than the whole community) profoundly shape the landscape of power. Their competition and strife, combined with their traditional prerogatives vastly impinging upon the public monopoly on violence and upon the autonomy of law, can result in highly factionalized polities which are much more precarious than generally assumed (Terrenato, forthcoming).

It is in a context of this kind, with substantial extra-state forces that can be aggregated on grounds of kinship (real or imagined), social dependence, religious affiliation, and so on, that the importance of individual agency can be brought out without falling into the idealist myth of the Great Man. This is of particular relevance for the late Regal–early Republican period, long recognized as being characterized by violent factional clashes, even through the mist of unlikely facts and characters (e.g. Mazzarino 1945). And yet, the scholarship especially on the fifth and fourth centuries BCE has not been nearly as intellectually daring as it had been the case for previous periods, and also much more limited in quantity. Aside from a few important collections of papers (e.g. Eder and Ampolo 1990; Raaflaub and Cornell 1986), there has been comparatively little attempt at redefining this important and fascinating period, when Rome undergoes the genetic mutation that turns it from a city-state into a global empire. Paradoxically, it may be precisely because Rome now begins its expansionist move that these crucial centuries have not attracted more innovative speculation. Roman imperialism and militarism are still largely unquestioned central icons of western culture. Supposedly revolutionary materialist interpretations in the 1970s and 1980s have only essentially reversed the polarity of the idealist and nationalist ethical judgement, casting Romans as greedy imperialists, but leaving the basic historiographic structure unchanged (full argument in Terrenato 2005*a*).

It is telling that the debate on Roman imperialism has not progressed much in the last decades, in sharp contrast with what has happened for other instances of territorial expansion. The classic theories of defensive, aggressive, and economic imperialism, in part actually going back to the nineteenth century, are essentially still the only mainstream options (cf. Champion 2004*b*; critique in Woolf 1993), as if postmodern deconstruction did not dare to touch the bold actions and pristine virtues of early Republicans. Even in recent narratives (e.g. David 1994), the only historical actors are Romans, and the only truly important decisions are those taken in the Senate. Not only is there virtually no political agency but that of elite senators and generals, but they are also often implicitly assumed to move with a single mind, so that the protagonist is almost always the political abstraction called Rome. As a result of these underpinning beliefs, this is often seen as a time of transition, in which quaint archaic traits, such as the pre-eminence of the patriciate, progressively leave room to that well-balanced citizen state later admired by Polybius (Champion 2004*a*). In terms of source criticism, much more is taken at face value for this period, even if it is not at all certain that later historians understood it much better than the regal one. Even the culture and mentality have been described in fairly simplified terms. War, for instance, is of course seen as a crucial component of Roman society, but often without distinction between raids, armed suasion, and all-out conflicts (Harris 1979). Warlikeness as an explanation for expansion also fails to account for the existence of very similar cultures in neighbouring states, which were, however, defeated. Even materialist explanations for the early phases of the Roman conquest ring a bit hollow in view of the extreme scarcity of archaeological evidence for Roman exploitation. Recent work on the human landscapes of Central Italy, for instance, is showing that the emergence of large agricultural productive facilities takes place much later than previously thought. The earliest villas date to the late second century BCE, and the vast majority of them is built in or after the Caesarian period (Lafon 2001; Terrenato and Becker 2009), thus creating serious problems for those who saw the spread of *ager publicus* and villas as a direct consequence of the Roman conquest (e.g. Carandini 1988).

In short, established historical paradigms dealing with the first two centuries of the Roman expansion have been showing their shortcoming in accommodating new evidence and in keeping abreast of theoretical developments. There seems to be a need for innovative approaches that may revitalize a discourse that has been rather stagnant. One possibility is to build upon the new ideas that are being applied to the archaic period, bringing back to the fore the chronological and conceptual proximity of these two ages. Just as the role of component parts of the communities is being emphasized in the urban formation process, the same tack can be taken for the formation of the empire, breaking down the monolithic view of expanding Rome. A previous attempt in this direction took place in the 1960s and 1970s, in works that tried to interpret the political life in Rome in terms of party politics (Càssola 1962, ultimately inspired by Münzer 1920). There has been a strong (and understandable) reaction to the modernist analogy (e.g. Develin 1985), but it remains hard to dispute the coexistence of different political agendas in fourth- and third-century BCE Rome. Unlike modern parties, they are not informed by abstract creeds as much as by competing faction and clan interests. These are pursued through the creation of networks of elite alliances jockeying for eminent position in the expanding state. Old Roman clans such as the Claudii or the Fabii activate these connections to influence key issues, such as electoral results and foreign policies (Massa-Pairault 2001). But, even more interestingly, some non-Roman clans too can pursue their own peculiar interests in the same way. The Plautii from Praeneste are a good example of a group that partially relocates to Rome, reaches the consulship seven times in the second half of the fourth century, and clearly exploits its political success by implementing policies primarily concerned with their own region of provenance, such as the hostilities against Privernum (Licordari 1982). At least as far as Central Italy is concerned, non-Romans apparently have ample opportunities of making a difference in the expansion process, either by joining the bandwagon and nudging it in a direction that is favourable to them, or by resisting it to favour instead other alternative networks.

In a perspective of this kind, the ethnic polarization that has always characterized modern views of the conquest may be less useful in explaining it than a framework of factionalism. In other words, it is not so much a simple matter of Romans versus Etruscans or Samnites (which made perfect sense to Romantic historians), but rather a complex tangle of 'horizontal' groups expanding their influence and composed by aristocrats of heterogeneous backgrounds. The bonds that keep these formations together can take a variety of forms, from *hospitium* and intermarriage (just to stay with the same example, a Plautia was buried in the tomb of the Reliefs at Caere), to patronage and other forms of social dependence, but also religious and traditional affiliation (Cosi 2002). Roman expansion is clearly shaped by the presence of these structures and, to a certain extent, happens *through* them, often incorporating and integrating power networks that already linked the city to its peers in Central Italy. But even in the case of communities further away that had less well established connections with Rome than, say, Tarquinia or Capua, the conquest was far from a one-way imposition of military force. Diplomacy was the other tool that the Romans could use (Auliard 2006), benefiting from their traditional ability to find ad hoc solutions and to integrate different peoples (Dench 2005). Even if we are, of course, not well informed on the actual negotiations, if we look at the fate of the incorporated communities, it is clear that they must have wielded a measure of bargaining power. For instance, the continuity of local elite families and customs, as well as the relative ease with which some municipal aristocrats gain access to the Senate (after receiving Roman citizenship), can only be explained as the implied result of peace agreements that are not entirely slanted towards Rome (Panciera 1982).

A radical redefinition of the very nature of the early Roman conquest along new lines may be in the cards. It may be too soon to see what the next paradigm will involve, but it should certainly not have the original Roman elites as the only empowered agents in this global transformation. It is also worth observing that the debate on the later phases of the expansion, particularly in the case of western Europe, has been moving along similar directions, emphasizing the active role of non-Romans in the integration process (e.g. the papers in James and Millett 2001; Mattingly 1997). Another important lesson that can be learned from these more peripheral cases of study is the significant difference that archaeological data of good quality can make. It is not simply that they can fill in gaps in those situations, like Britain, where the textual material is not nearly as rich. But they can, even more importantly, provide an alternative insight even in supposedly better known contexts (Terrenato 2001*b*). To give just an example, the substantial continuity of traditional local elite burial practices, at least down to the early first century BCE, has now been attested at a number of central Italian sites. This can only be explained with the persistence in power of families that are representing themselves in the local traditional forms, even centuries after the conquest and even after very traumatic events (for instance at Falerii and Volsinii after the relocation,

Oleson 1982). Another interesting counterpoint to the classic narratives about the creation of Roman landscapes has been offered by recent field surveys. They seem to show that the spread of small farms that characterizes the Hellenistic period in many areas of the central Mediterranean is not as tightly correlated with the Roman conquest and the confiscation of land (as in they were for instance in Potter 1979). The farms instead appear everywhere at the same time, regardless of when each region is incorporated, which for instance in northern Etruria means hundreds of years before the conquest (Terrenato 2007), disproving the commonly held notion that they were built by new settlers on colonial lots or rented parcels of *ager publicus*.

Compared to the archaic period, the interaction between textual and archaeological material seems to be, at least potentially, much more robust, allowing the combination of these different sources of evidence in a more coherent picture. It is not uncommon to find epigraphic attestation of a character known from the sources, and the physical appearance of new cities can be more or less matched with the historical memory of their foundation. At the same time, however, the archeological record for the fourth and third centuries BCE in central Italy is much less rich than it is generally imagined, especially when it comes to public buildings (Becker 2007). In Rome itself, there is relatively little that can be safely dated to this period, other than a number of temples, the remake of the Servian walls, and a few isolated walls (Cornell 2000). While, as we have seen, the city of the Tarquins is beginning to emerge in its grandeur and complexity, that of the Manlii and Ogulnii is still rather mysterious for us. And given that the archaic levels have now been reached and shown to be very substantial, it is not easy to dismiss the scarce mid-Republican record merely as a result of insufficient explorations or accidents of preservation.

More negative evidence is coming together in a number of other cultural areas, from the aforementioned villas to the spread of Latin or of Roman law. The trend seems to be that the emergence of a great number of those traits that were generally identified with Roman culture itself actually date to a fairly late stage of the Republican period (Terrenato 2008). If this is really the case, wide-reaching implications follow for even the most basic understanding of how Roman Italy came about. At the socio-political level, the conquest can be described as a two-way process that enables groups of Roman as well as non-Roman families to create and extend their long-range power networks. As a matter of fact, given the ease with which a wide range of elites can jump on the new bandwagon, it is even doubtful that conceptualizing the issue primarily in terms of ethnic dominance and subordination is at all appropriate for this period. And indeed, at the cultural level, breaking down the false dichotomy between Romans and other Italians is a crucial first step to restore the original context and mentality of the early conquest, together with the deconstruction of a monolithic and pre-eminent Roman agency advocated above. In many important areas, from architecture and art to social and economic developments, it is extremely hard to substantiate the kind of Roman primacy that is implicit in many traditional models for the so-called Romanization of Italy. Many of the peoples of the peninsula appear instead to be moving along similar lines, reacting to the same stimuli and constantly playing off each other's responses to them. They are all negotiating their way through a new cultural phase, in which often local traditional norms are eroded and questioned by those global trends and fashions, that are often summarily referred to as Hellenization (e.g. Curti, Dench, and Patterson 1996). The resulting changes are not necessarily to be seen as an immediate consequence of the changing political conjunctures, much as it was the case with previous autonomous cultural waves such as the Orientalizing one. In this perspective, elite self-representation is clearly better explained as an active statement that redefines the identity of its authors vis-à-vis an evolving broader discourse, especially in sight of its contemporaneous adoption by peoples in radically different positions of power. This appears to be a safer and more economic hypothesis, if contrasted with the common materialist assumption that cultural change is a direct product of a discourse of social dominance.

Another interesting implication of an historical reconstruction of this kind is that the early history of Rome, from the origins at least down to the First Punic War (if not even the Gracchi) appears as a much more coherent and self-consistent entity than generally maintained, especially in comparison with the political, cultural, economic and material convulsions that characterize the century of the civil wars (Flower 2009). More specifically, there are some elements that seem to be acquiring a growing explanatory value for the time of the first creation of both the city and the empire. The mentioned role of non- (and even anti-) state groups, such as *gentes*, *sodalitates*, and other factional units as powerful actors in both political transitions may open new and revolutionary interpretative avenues. The deconstruction of state and empire as abstract, impersonal and collective political agents becomes even more subversive when combined with the parallel deconstruction of traditional views of ethnicity, which are ultimately informed by nineteenth-century nationalism. Realizing the full implication of the intense elite horizontal mobility may result in a radically different conceptualization of inter-city competition in the archaic period and even more of city-state expansion in the Hellenistic period. 'Foreign' kings, senators, and consuls are only explainable if we see Rome as a vehicle commandeered in turns by different supra-ethnic aristocratic networks, rather than as an *ante litteram* expanding little homogenous Prussia. The ultimate irony here is that while the first five centuries have always been regarded with extreme scepticism and are enormously under-represented (even in this very volume), in comparison with the later, more conspicuous half of Rome's trajectory, they may actually allow the observation of processes that could prove to be crucial to a new understanding of the quintessential nature of the Roman Empire. As the embryology of living things teaches us, the formative stages can reveal much more than the simple anatomy of the complete organism.

References

Ampolo, C. (ed.) (1983), *Sulla formazione della città di Roma* (Opus 2).

—— (1988), 'Il contributo di Arnaldo Momigliano alla comprensione di Roma arcaica. Appunti su un itinerario storiografico', *Rivista Storica Italiana*, 100: 283–96.

Auliard, C. (2006), *La Diplomatie romaine de la fondation à la fin des guerres samnites (753–290 av. J-C): l'autre instrument de la conquête* (Rennes).

Becker, J. A. (2007), 'The Building Blocks of Empire: Civic Architecture, Central Italy, and the Roman Middle Republic' (Ph.D. diss. Chapel Hill).

Bianchi Bandinelli, R. and Giuliano, A. (1973), *Etruschi e italici prima del dominio di Roma* (Milan).

Bietti Sestieri, A. M. (1992), *The Iron Age Community of Osteria dell'Osa* (Cambridge).

Brumfiel, E. B. and Fox, J. W. (eds.) (1994), *Factional Competition and Political Development in the New World* (Cambridge).

Capogrossi Colognesi, L. (1994), *Proprietà e signoria in Roma antica I* (Rome).

Carandini, A. (1988), *Schiavi in Italia* (Rome).

—— (1997), *La Nascita di Roma* (Turin).

—— (2006), *Remo e Romolo: dai rioni dei Quiriti alla città dei Romani: 775/750–700/675 a. C. circa* (Turin).

Càssola, F. (1962), *I gruppi politici romani nel III secolo A.C.* (Trieste).

Champion, C. B. (2004*a*), *Cultural Politics in Polybius's Histories* (Berkeley).

—— (ed.) (2004*b*), *Roman Imperialism: Readings and Sources* (London).

Coarelli, F. (1983), *Il foro romano. Periodo arcaico* (Rome).

—— (1988), *Il Foro Boario: dalle origini alla fine della repubblica* (Rome).

—— (1997), *Il Campo Marzio: dalle origini alla fine della repubblica* (Rome).

Colonna, G. (1983), 'Risposta a Guidi', *Opus*, 2: 425–48.

Cornell, T. J. (1995), *The Beginnings of Rome* (London).

—— (2000), 'The City of Rome in the Middle Republic (*c*.400–100 BC)', in J. C. Coulston and H. Dodge (eds.), *Ancient Rome: The Archaeology of the Eternal City* (Oxford), 42–56.

—— (2006), 'Momigliano and Archaic Rome', in L. Polverini (ed.) *Arnaldo Momigliano nella storiografia del Novecento* (Rome).

Cosi, R. (2002), *Le solidarietà politiche nella Repubblica romana* (Bari).

Cuozzo, M. (1996), 'Prospettive teoriche e metodologiche nell'interpretazione delle necropoli: la Post-Processual Archaeology', *Annali dell'Istituto Orientale di Napoli*, 3: 1–37.

Curti, E., Dench, E., and Patterson, J. (1996), 'The Archaeology of Central and Southern Roman Italy: Recent Trends and Approaches', *Journal of Roman Studies*, 86: 170–89.

David, J.-M. (1994), *La Romanisation de l'Italie* (Paris).

Dench, E. (2005), *Romulus' Asylum: Roman Identities from the Age of Alexander to the Age of Hadrian* (Oxford and New York).

Develin, R. (1985), *The Practice of Politics at Rome, 366–167 B.C.* (Brussels).

Dobres, M.-A. and Robb, J. E. (eds.) (2000), *Agency in Archaeology* (London).

Eder, W. and Ampolo, C. (eds.) (1990), *Staat und Staatlichkeit in der frühen römischen Republik* (Stuttgart).

Flower, H. I. (2009), *Roman Republics* (Princeton).

Forsythe, G. (2005), *A Critical History of Early Rome: From Prehistory to the First Punic War* (Berkeley).

Fox, M. (1996), *Roman Historical Myths: The Regal Period in Augustan Literature* (Oxford).
Franciosi, G. (1999), *Clan gentilizio e strutture monogamiche: contributo alla storia della famiglia romana* (Naples).
Grandazzi, A. (1991), *La Fondation de Rome* (Paris).
Guidi, A. (1982), 'Sulle prime fasi dell'urbanizzazione nel Lazio protostorico', *Opus*, 1: 279–88.
Harris, W. V. (1979), *War and Imperialism in Republican Rome, 327–70 B.C.* (Oxford).
Holloway, R. R. (1994), *Archaeology of Early Rome and Latium* (London and New York).
James, S. and Millett, M. (eds.) (2001), *Britons and Romans: Advancing an Archaeological Agenda* (York).
La formazione della città nel Lazio (1980), *Dialoghi di Archeologia*, 2.
Lafon, X. (2001), *Villa maritima: recherches sur les villas littorales de l'Italie romaine (IIIe siècle av. J.-C./IIIe* siècle ap. J.-C.) (Rome).
Licordari, A. (1982), 'Italia: Regio I (Latium)', in *Epigrafia e ordine senatorio* (Rome), 9–57.
Massa-Pairault, F.-H. (2001), 'Relations d'Appius Claudius Caecus avec l'Étrurie et la Campanie', in D. Briquel and J.-P. Thuillier (eds.), *Le Censeur et les Samnites: sur Tite-Live, livre IX* (Paris), 97–116.
Mattingly, D. J. (ed.) (1997), *Dialogues in Roman Imperialism* (Portsmouth).
Mazzarino, S. (1945), *Dalla monarchia allo stato repubblicano: ricerche di storia romana arcaica* (Catania).
Momigliano, A. (1963), 'An Interim Report on the Origins of Rome', *Journal of Roman Studies*, 53: 95–121.
—— (1989), 'The Origins of Rome', in *Cambridge Ancient History*, vol. 8 (Cambridge), 52–112.
Motta, L. and Terrenato, N. (2006), 'The Origins of the State *par excellence*: Power and Society in Iron Age Rome', in C. C. Haselgrove (ed.), *Celtes et Gaulois, l'archéologie face à l'histoire, 4: les mutations de la fin de l'âge du Fer* (Glux-en-Glenne), 225–34.
Münzer, F. (1920), *Römische Adelsparteien und Adelsfamilien* (Stuttgart).
Oleson, J. P. (1982), *The Sources of Innovation in Later Etruscan Tomb Design (ca. 350–100 B.C.)* (Rome).
Pacciarelli, M. (2000), *Dal villaggio alla città: la svolta protourbana del 1000 a.C. nell'Italia tirrenica* (Florence).
Panciera, S. (ed.) (1982), *Epigrafia e ordine senatorio* (Rome).
Potter, T. W. (1979), *The Changing Landscape of South Etruria* (London).
Poucet, J. (2000), *Les Rois de Rome. Tradition et histoire* (Brussels).
Raaflaub, K. A. and Cornell, T. (eds.) (1986), *Social Struggles in Archaic Rome: New Perspectives on the Conflict of the Orders* (Berkeley).
Raskolnikoff, M. (1992), *Histoire romaine et critique historique dans l'Europe des lumières: la naissance de l'hypercritique dans l'historiographie de la Rome antique* (Strasbourg).
Rawlings, L. (1999), 'Condottieri and Clansmen: Early Italian Raiding, Warfare and the State', in R. Alston and K. Hopwood (eds.), *Organised Crime in Antiquity* (London), 97–127.
Sahlins, M. D. (1985), *Islands of History* (Chicago).
Smith, C. J. (1996), *Early Rome and Latium* (Oxford).
—— (2006), *The Roman Clan* (Cambridge).
Stibbe, C. M. (ed.) (1980), *Lapis Satricanus: Archaeological, Epigraphical, Linguistic, and Historical Aspects of the New Inscription from Satricum* ('s-Gravenhage).
Terrenato, N. (2001*a*), 'The Auditorium Site and the Origins of the Roman Villa', *Journal of Roman Archaeology*, 14: 5–32.

Terrenato, N. (2001*b*), 'A Tale of Three Cities', in S. J. Keay and N. Terrenato (eds.), *Italy and the West: Comparative Issues in Romanization* (Oxford), 54–67.
—— (2005*a*), 'The Deceptive Archetype: Roman Colonialism and Post-colonial Thought', in H. Hurst and S. Owen (eds.), *Ancient Colonizations: Analogy, Similarity and Difference* (London), 59–72.
—— (2005*b*), '"Start the Revolution without me": Recent Debates in Italian Classical Archaeology', in P. A. J. Attema, A. Nijboer, and A. Zifferero (eds.), *Papers in Italian Archaeology*, VI: *Communities and Settlements from the Neolithic to the Early Medieval Period* (Oxford), 2, 39–43.
—— (2007), 'The Essential Countryside: Farms, Villages, Sanctuaries, Tombs', in S. A. Alcock and R. Osborne (eds.), *Classical Archaeology* (London), 139–61.
—— (2008), 'The Cultural Implications of the Roman Conquest', in E. Bispham (ed.), *Roman Europe* (Oxford), 234–64.
—— (forthcoming), 'The Versatile Clans: The Nature of Power in Early Rome', in D. C. Haggis and N. Terrenato (eds.), *Current Issues in State Formation in the Mediterranean* (Oxford).
—— and Becker, J. A. (2009), 'Il sito del Monte delle Grotte sulla via Flaminia e lo sviluppo della villa nel suburbio di Roma', in V. Jolivet *et al.* (eds.), *Suburbium II: Il Suburbio di Roma dalla fine dell'età monarchica alla nascita del sistema delle ville (V–II sec. a.C.)* (Rome), 393–401.
Torelli, M. (1997), *Il rango, il rito e l'immagine* (Milan).
Woolf, G. (1993), 'European Social Development and Roman Imperialism', in P. Brun, S. E. v. d. Leeuw, and C. R. Whittaker (eds.), *Frontières d'empire: nature et signification des frontières romaines* (Nemours), 13–20.
Ziolkowski, A. (2005), *Sacra Via: Twenty Years After* (Warsaw).

CHAPTER 32

THE IMPERIAL REPUBLIC

HARRIET I. FLOWER

ROME did not begin as a republic, nor as a small town any different from many others in Central Italy. In early times her language, material culture, religion, political system, and most other aspects of her life marked her as part of a cultural and ethnic continuum of peoples, rather than as an innovator or leader in any field (Cornell 1995). It was only subsequently, after the emergence of a government based on elected magistrates and its gradual development into a characteristically Roman type of political system, that Rome became the Mediterranean capital, a city of around a million people whose size and complexity would not be seen again in Europe until late eighteenth-century London. All subsequent Roman history grows out of the achievements of the Roman Republic, in its developed form. Rome's overseas empire was already vast by the time of Augustus, the first emperor. Similarly, genres of Latin literature, concepts of law and the system of the courts, the Latin language itself, and many aspects of material culture were also products of the Republic. It was this Republic that fascinated ancient writers ever since its decay. It was also this Republic that provided inspiration to European Enlightenment intellectuals and to the American Founding Fathers, as they turned away from monarchy to found a new society based on civil rights, shared political deliberation, and a concept of the common interests of a body of citizens, who were equal before the law (Sellers 2004).

Throughout their history the Romans referred to their political system as *res publica*, something like 'the public matter' or 'public business'. This term designated both the government or constitution in the abstract *and* the type of political system that emerged after the monarchy. This lack of distinction between form and content in political vocabulary is characteristic of Roman thinking and can be seen as both a strength and a weakness. The Latin language does make it difficult to discuss nuances of political change using Roman terms, since there were so few. For the Romans, the essence of their city government that was conceived as an enterprise shared by all citizens, both in terms of practicalities in political life and in terms of purpose. Politics belonged to the citizens now, and did not depend on the dictates of a king or tyrant. Republican politics was, therefore, continually shaped by two principal factors: its origins in a rejection of one man rule, which was always seen as a potential threat to the community, and its gradual development into a system that was more rather than less based on compromise and practices of inclusion and debate. Meanwhile, any appreciation of the republican system needs to take into account that it was by nature a dynamic, not a static, political culture. This chapter will address ways in which we can approach and understand the Republic between about 300 BCE, after it had developed many of its most characteristic formal features, and its decay into a new system of one-man rule with the rise of Augustus, who styled himself *princeps* ('first citizen' or 'leading man').

Modern discussions of the Roman Republic have tended almost without exception to follow ancient terminology and to speak of a republic from *c.*509 until its fall, variously dated either to 49 when Julius Caesar invaded Italy and set himself up as dictator, or to the Ides of March 44 when Caesar was assassinated, or to the defeat of Brutus and Cassius at the battle of Philippi in 42, or to the time when Augustus became undisputed ruler of Rome and her empire (either in 31 after the battle of Actium or, more plausibly, in 27 when he took the name Augustus and started to regularize his position as a civil leader rather than a warlord: Syme 1939). Yet it is easy to see that this periodization is problematic.* Modern historians use the term 'republic' to describe both an historical period and the system of government, as if there had been no changes in patterns of political behaviour over several centuries.

Furthermore, a single historical period that covers almost 500 years will inevitably be imprecise and of limited value. It may reflect ancient sentiments, particularly the nostalgia felt after the fall or the desire to stress continuity in a traditional society, but it does not help the modern student of history to offer any kind of critical analysis. It was precisely because their society and situation in the world changed so radically, especially after 300, that the Romans habitually stressed tradition and the customs of the ancestors (*mos maiorum*) as their constant concern. Similarly, their rhetoric of empire was based on self-defence: they claimed that all their wars had been fought purely as matters of self-defence. During the Republic they did not discuss, in a theoretical way, questions of hegemony or how it differed from empire and the direct annexation of overseas territory or the taxation of provincials. Without discarding it completely, we must transcend

* All dates are BCE.

their rhetoric if we aim to understand either the dynamics of individual events or the underlying patterns of political and social development (Badian 1968; Gruen 1984; Kallett-Marx 1995).

This chapter will outline the following three criteria for articulating and distinguishing different phases of the republican community: internal politics, religion, and empire. Many previous discussions focus on one or two areas. My argument is that each area needs to be considered, as well as the ways in which they overlap and complement each other. Each area could be used to create a more detailed and individualized division of the Republic into discrete periods that would better define the essence of its history. To the extent that history is the story of change, this project seems worthwhile (Flower 2009).

At the same time, it is also important to notice that in the context of Roman culture and thinking these categories were not as separate as they can seem to us now. Certainly, Republican politics was inseparable from the state system of cult and ritual. Every political act took place in the framework of religious auspices: political or military success could only be understood and represented in terms of a correct relationship with the gods (*pax deorum*) (Beard, North, and Price 1998). Similarly, politics in the city of Rome was clearly affected by military concerns, which evolved into an imperialistic pattern at a surprisingly early date (Keppie 1998). Rome was constantly at war, either by choice or by necessity, so that war became a way of life for male citizens of all social classes (Harris 1979; McDonnell 2006). Success in those wars, together with Rome's growing dominance throughout the known world, changed Romans' self-perceptions and the realities of their lives (Hölkeskamp 1993; David 1996).

One may also note the categories of literature and material culture. These areas have their own history and periodization that are important in shedding light on life in the city. The development of the Latin language and a sophisticated literary culture cannot be divorced from Rome's political and imperial pretensions. Similarly, material culture reflects everyday life in the city and the transforming effects of the wealth of empire (Claridge 1998). The societal impact of politics, religion, and war are best reflected in literature and material culture (Rawson 1985). Rome would not be much of an object for study without her development of a sophisticated and distinctive urban and literary culture in the atmosphere and under the conditions of Republican society (Gruen 1990, 1992). These latter two subjects are more fully addressed in other chapters in this volume.

In addition, recent scholarship has started to explore topics that the Romans themselves were not in a good position to evaluate, especially in the areas of the economy and of demography. The combined use of evidence from literary sources, tombstones, ancient census figures, archaeology, field surveys, paleontology, and comparative modelling based on other pre-modern societies have revealed answers to questions such as average age of marriage for Roman women, life-expectancy, seasonal mortality, and many other patterns of family life (Rosenstein 2004).

Meanwhile, there is hot debate about the overall size of Italy's population (Scheidel 2001). Related to this central demographic question is the issue of the number of slaves (and how many of them were manumitted) and of inhabitants in the whole Roman Empire. For Italy's population by the end of the Republic estimates range between 4 million (the traditional view) and 12 million inhabitants (a newer hypothesis). The answer is clearly central to our understanding of Rome's manpower and her agricultural needs and potential.

The ancient sources present their themes in terms of the experiences of adult male citizens, especially those of the elites. The same social conditions and events shaped the lives of women, children, and slaves, all of whom are of obvious interest to the modern historian. To cite one example, the development of the legal rights and social freedoms of Roman women, who could own property and lead independent lives, were shaped by the needs of a community in which so many men were away from home for increasing stretches of time. Under these circumstances women had to be active members of society who could maintain families and property while their husbands were away. In this way, the Republic created the typical Roman patterns of independence for women in a society of easy divorce and social mobility, as well as the habit of frequent manumission of slaves, which made new citizens at a rate much faster than almost any other method.

Politics

Republican political culture was sophisticated and subject to continuing change in a society that faced constant pressure from the outside and that did not have a written constitution to serve as a road-map (Lintott 1999). At the same time, Roman politics did not simply follow a pattern of reaction dictated by outside pressure. Initiatives could also come from within. The lack of formal political parties or even semi-formal alliances led to constant debate and realignment on the political issues of the day. It may appear that the rules of the game had been agreed on at an early date but, in fact, these rules were also subject to continual adjustments, often not commented on in any detail by ancient sources. As examples one may cite the introduction of more formalized rules for political careers (*lex Villia annalis*) in 180 or, even more strikingly, the change to a system of voting by secret ballot during the 130s. In a different society, these reforms would have been hailed as watershed moments in the history of the constitution; in Rome they have left hardly a trace of a comment.

Meanwhile, the heart of Republican politics was deliberative decision-making based on an idealized image of consensus, which was created by compromise and a strong desire for the (re)creation of a single community (Nicolet 1980). This political game emerged during the fourth century BCE from the period known as the Conflict of the Orders, which was a time of instability and internal political dissension between a hereditary political and religious elite (the patricians) and everyone else in society (the plebeians: Hölkeskamp 1987). Hence we can see that the history of the early Republic was one of a weak system that fought for survival with its local neighbours and was riven by discontent and continual demands for political power-sharing even at the price of a possible dissolution of the community. Repeated attempts at political dialogue over several generations produced a new system based on compromise, in which political and religious leadership was shared amongst the wealthier citizens on the basis of merit and achievement, as recognized by the community. Hence Republican politics was shaped by the conscious and continual avoidance of two extremes: one-man rule by a single leader *or* a society strongly divided into defined and opposed political groups (factions or parties). Changes in political habits nearly all seem to have aimed at maintaining a version of this balance of powers.

The citizen body, organized according to tribal or military units, would vote to confer political offices, arranged in an increasingly formalized hierarchical career pattern, on elite candidates (Broughton 1951–2; Brennan 2000). Candidates were required to meet property qualifications but did then face competitive election races against other qualified candidates. Merit and achievement were continually measured and accumulated according to societal norms in recognized spheres of competition, particularly in military contexts. The display and recognition of achievement, and its associated rank, became increasingly important. Hence the awarding of a triumph by the Senate represented the peak of a man's career and was memorialized by buildings, monuments, and artwork in the city. The badges of office and symbols of rank were enhanced by ceremonies at funerals of magistrates, which recalled the achievements of the deceased and of all his office-holding relatives in word, ritual, and spectacle. The new office-holding elite aimed to keep status and power in their families through displays of their heritage and celebrations of their own achievements in oratory, ritual, inscriptions, and monuments (Flower 2004).

This system of clearly defined rules and ranks in society could, therefore, tolerate fierce competition between elite individuals without the risk of political instability (Gelzer 1975). In fact, in a characteristically Roman way, it was the element of genuine competition that maintained the viability and integrity of the system itself. In other words, competition could work towards consensus, as more recent research has tended to demonstrate (Rosenstein 1990; Hölkeskamp 2004*a*, *b*). Yet, the categorization of the Roman Republic as a consensus system does pose the question of what 'consensus' actually meant in this cultural context (taking into account the gaps and imperfections of our sources). Certainly, it is important to note elements of consensus-building that tended to represent decisions as being those of all citizens. Elections for the highest offices provide notable examples as only the winners were announced, as soon as they had received a majority of votes, and no one ever really knew how many had voted for other candidates.

The concept of compromise can appear, in many ways, as complementary to, and perhaps even more important than, theories or representations of societal consensus. There was political capital to be had by compromising and yielding to another's viewpoint on a political issue. This fact is demonstrated by many situations in which personal appeals to yield were made to leading Romans. These appeals to civic-minded behaviour only make sense if fellow-senators and voters were expected to remember and admire the politician who compromised. By comparison, the man who always insisted on having his own way might not appear as the most statesmanlike or civic-minded. These were important personal qualities and patterns of behaviour in a society in which election candidates ran on the basis of their character, rather than on specific platforms with regard to issues of the day.

Discussions of Republican politics over the last twenty years or more have tended to return repeatedly to the question of how 'democratic' the Roman Republic was (Jehne 1995; Millar 1998, 2002). Depending on how this question is phrased, it has produced some apparently sharp divisions between scholars who actually have much to agree upon. Part of the problem is that most evidence comes from the last generation of the Republic when various pressures had produced a political situation that is not typical of what came before. In fact, answers to questions about the role of the people and the balance of influence in Roman politics would surely have varied according to the circumstances of the day. Magistrates in office had huge powers, but only for a year at a time and always with at least one colleague who had equal sway. The possibility of a veto, although apparently rarely used, did encourage collaboration and debate amongst fellow magistrates in any one year. Similarly, the advisory role of the Senate, where Roman politicians spent most of their political careers, was always vital (Ryan 1998). It symbolized the proper functioning of elite politics, but did so without many formal requirements or executive powers. In the end the role of debate and deliberation leading to some kind of agreement within a peer group (whether termed consensus or not) lay at the heart of much in Roman culture, both in politics and in individual or family decision-making (Morstein-Marx 2004). Deliberation and affirmation could take place in small groups of friends (*consilium*), in the Senate, amongst the staff of a general on campaign, or in a voting assembly that treated all citizens as members of a group.

Meanwhile, it is important to note that there was never a principle of one-man, one vote in politics. Rather, voting was always by units, which tended to favour the wealthy over the poor and those who lived in or near Rome over those who were further away. The magistrate who presided over the voting assembly also had an opportunity for influence. The composition and representative character of

Roman voting assemblies, like much else in political life, changed radically with the extension of citizenship to all free males in Italy in the early 80s as a result of the Social War. Similarly, Sulla's reforms, which created a Senate twice the traditional size and a system of law-courts to police political behaviour, introduced a new political game that relied less on deliberation and more on rules within a stricter social hierarchy.

Consequently, there were many features of Roman political life that did not look at all like Athenian democracy or like a modern democratic system. However, a picture of Rome as a strict oligarchy is also misleading. A degree of popular support was essential and expected in order to move forward with any initiative. Widespread bribery of voters in the late Republic, as well as frequent incidents of violence and anarchy, indicate limits on elite control of the masses without the direct use of soldiers (Yakobson 1999). Meanwhile, the grass-roots political culture of the individual neighbourhoods in the city (*vici*) also had a role to play, which has not been studied in much detail for the Republic.

Religion

As suggested above, religion was closely intertwined with and essentially inseparable from war and politics (Beard, North, and Price 1998; Scheid 2003; Rüpke 2007*a*, *b*). If political action was based on a degree of consensus in the Senate and amongst citizens, then it was equally based on the acquiescence and support of the gods, with whom all high-ranking magistrates communicated before undertaking any action or vote. Setbacks and military defeats were often interpreted as signs of divine displeasure or flaws in religious rituals rather than being analysed in terms of human error, especially when it came to the leadership of the general. Religious solutions were routinely sought for practical problems in all aspects of official business. Communication with the gods through augury, taking the auspices and other forms of divination, as well as scrupulous observance of traditional rituals, was central to the process of political decision-making. All levels of society came together in supporting state cults and in seeking a harmonious relationship with the gods, both traditional deities and new ones imported as Romans came across a variety of religious experience in the places they conquered.

Priests of traditional state cults were senators who, with very few exceptions, pursued political and military careers like those of their colleagues who had no special religious functions. All senators had to be able and willing to fulfil the religious duties required of each magisterial office they were elected to. Hence every senior magistrate had to be able to communicate with the gods on behalf of the community and to do so successfully in the eyes of his fellow citizens. Meanwhile, personal beliefs were not questioned or investigated. Even if many senators of the late Republic may have been personally agnostic, observance of and debate about religious matters were as central to political life as the rituals of voting or of the public speech before the citizens (*contio*). Moreover, manipulation and modification of religious practices in the late Republic should not be read as a sign of a system in decline. Rather, they confirm both the gravity of the crisis in Roman culture and the enduring role of religion in Roman political life.

In light of these considerations, it is important to recognize that challenges or setbacks experienced by the Roman community could be described and understood in terms of a religious problem, rather than an economic, social, or political issue. A modern historian may have a different view and want to use different tools of analysis. But the Romans' own way of reading a situation has clear relevance to their construction of their world and especially to the kinds of solutions they found satisfactory. Consequently, much can be revealed by a religious reading of various situations and conflicts in Roman history.

For example, the assassination of the tribune of the plebs Tiberius Gracchus in 133 is a recognized watershed in Roman political history. But a consideration of religious overtones can change the conventional picture (Linderski 2002). The murder of Tiberius, who was sacrosanct because of his political office, was undertaken by his cousin Scipio Nasica, the *pontifex maximus*. It seems to have taken place in the context of declaring Tiberius to be *sacer* or a person subject to summary execution at the behest of the gods for a serious offence, probably a charge of trying to make himself a tyrant and overthrowing the political order. Both the violence of the lynching and the aftermath are much harder to understand without taking the religious meaning into account. As it turned out, ordinary Romans felt Nasica's actions had been unjustified and he soon had to leave Rome because of being shunned as a man subject to religious pollution. Subsequently, the ultimate solution was sought by the Senate through a consultation of the Sibylline Books in Jupiter's temple on the Capitol, near where Tiberius had been killed, and an elaborate propitiation of the goddess Ceres at her ancient shrine at Henna in Sicily. It is only by studying such religious actions, in tandem with contemporary political situations, that we can gain a fuller picture of debate and policy-making in Roman society.

Empire

The politics of the developed Republic was practised in a space defined by hegemony and empire, either as it already existed or according to the ambitions of Romans to acquire more. War was constant and could be seen as a money-making proposition. The Greek historian Polybius (1.11) records the critical vote by the popular assembly in 264 to take Roman troops over to Sicily and engage in a conflict that involved the Carthaginians. This first overseas expedition was undertaken against the advice of the Senate but apparently on the promise of rich booty from Sicily and at the urgings of an ambitious consul. After the long war that ensued with Carthage, Sicily would become Rome's first overseas province in 241, soon followed by the islands of Sardinia and Corsica.

The success and resilience of the political system, based on elective offices shared by patricians and plebeians, can be measured in terms of Rome's victories in war (Hölkeskamp 1993). Any description of Republican history is inevitably articulated by war and conquest. Many scholars would say that this articulation should serve as the basic tool for periodization. Within this framework the most important conflicts after 300 were the following: the Third Samnite War; the war with Pyrrhus, king of Epirus; the three wars with Carthage between 264 and 146; Rome's wars in the eastern Mediterranean that led to her dominance in the world of the Hellenistic kingdoms; the clash with Mithridates VI of Pontus; the defeat of the Cimbri and Teutones, newly nomadic tribes who apparently wanted to settle in Italy; and lastly Caesar's conquest of Gaul in the 50s. One may note the repeated decisions to send armies ever further afield rather than to retrench or seek a compromise abroad. Meanwhile, the Roman people were mostly remarkably tolerant of long wars and regular casualties. There can be no doubt that Rome was vastly enriched by these wars, in terms of material goods, slave labour, and ideas, both practical and cultural (Shatzman 1975). At the same time, repeated defeats of various monarchs and oligarchies also confirmed the sense that their republican system of government was superior to any other and that Rome's power must reflect the will of the gods. Out of fears for survival and struggles for self-defence there gradually grew a confident sense of manifest destiny and world empire (Nicolet 1978/9; Gruen 1984).

The relationship between events abroad, especially military operations, and politics at home was always a complex and delicate one. The Senate, which really came into its own after Rome's decisive victory over Hannibal at the end of the third century, may often seem to be reacting to external pressures rather than designing and implementing a coherent foreign policy. Nevertheless, repeated military success and its enormous material rewards made the Romans see their city as the Mediterranean superpower. Their ambition is demonstrated by the decision in 146 to destroy Carthage and Corinth, both cities that claimed to be older than Rome.

Yet within less than a decade continued success and restless expansion produced fatigue and social discontent. The pressures of wars against Jugurtha in Numidia and the Cimbri and Teutones in the north caused a crisis by the end of the second century when, according to Sallust, ordinary people seemed to lose faith in their traditional political leaders. The self-made Marius (who had already been consul in 107) was elected to a string of consecutive consulships for five years from 104 to 100, in complete defiance of republican norms and precedents. It is a characteristic pattern in Roman imperialism that severe outside pressures could seem to strengthen and build the republican political system during the third century but cause stress and disruptions by the late second century. At the same time, it is important to keep in mind that the conflict between Caesar, Pompey, and various senators, which brought the end of republican government, did not play out against the background of any direct threat from a foreign enemy.

The End of the Republic

Montesquieu already suggested that it was the size of the empire that led to the fall of the Republic, which had not changed its basic governmental structures from those of a city-state. Most since have agreed with this argument, which can provide the background for individual events (Beard and Crawford 1999). Yet, however one reads the final century, it should not be allowed to overshadow the rest of the story. What has struck many is how long the Republic lasted, the culture that it built, and the overwhelming nostalgia felt for it by later Romans who had never known it (Gowing 2005). Later Romans believed that a republican system of government had made Rome great and that republicanism was in many ways still synonymous with Roman culture itself. Nor is it at all evident that any of the players in the 50s were consciously aiming to replace a republic with another system of government. The view that the late Republic faced a crisis, or rather a series of crises, to which contemporaries did not propose or conceive of an alternative political solution has been very influential (Meier 1980).

By the same token, the final collapse of a republican form of government cannot be ignored and has weighed on later politicians proposing a republican constitution, notably the American Founding Fathers who aimed to establish a republic that would not eventually disintegrate into an autocracy. The reasons for the Republic's fall have also been probably the most hotly debated aspects for modern scholars (Brunt 1988). Romans themselves, including Cicero, had trouble defining the nature of the multiple challenges they faced, whether political or economic, or in formulating an analysis of why these problems were not being addressed by their system of government (Taylor 1949). Indeed, their solutions were often couched in typically Roman terms of a return to a previous, usually idealized, time in their history, rather than a reasoned response to new challenges and changed conditions.

The argument that a republic could have continued and need not have ended has also been persuasively put and has found recent followers (Gruen 1974).

Meanwhile, the actions and motives of Caesar and Pompey and Cato pose the inevitable question of the role of the individual in history. There is no clear agreement even about the exact date at which the Republic ended, whether with Caesar becoming a dictator, or with the failure of republicans after his assassination, or with the establishment of a principate by Caesar's heir, now called Augustus. It depends on the definition of a republic and the willingness to consider whether or not there was a hiatus between what is often called the 'end of the Republic' and the establishment of the principate by Augustus in 27. Meanwhile, few historians have ventured into the no-man's-land in between, which is usually termed the triumviral period (Syme 1939; Osgood 2006).

A middle way needs to be found between a mechanistic reconstruction of an inevitable, almost biologically determined, decay and the simple assertions that it was not over until it was over or that things could have turned out differently. The following factors clearly contributed in significant ways to the disintegration of republican political culture: economic hardship and land-hunger in the countryside (Gargola 1995); continuous military campaigns; the consequent creation of large client armies of landless soldiers who were forced to rely on the patronage of their generals for veterans' benefits; repeated military and economic issues that were not addressed within the existing governmental structure; the consequent rise of several generals who were given vast powers beyond those described in the constitution; extreme political polarization and bitter personal enmities that made compromise increasingly remote; the repeated denial of civil rights to Roman citizens; the use of violence in the city even to the point of open civil war; the need to supply reliable and affordable food for the city's huge population; the inability of the Senate, over several generations, to address society's problems or to come up with viable political solutions; the willingness to suspend the republican constitution and turn to the violence of martial law; and the very belief that there would be no cost incurred by the lack of concern for the consequences of political stalemate and unconstitutional behaviour. It is notable that, despite the detailed information we have about most of these issues, the picture still remains complex and disputed. What is clear, however, is that the sense of a shared 'commonweal', a *res publica*, had been lost somewhere along the way and no one seemed to realize until it was too late.

References

Alföldy, G. (1988), *The Social History of Rome*, Baltimore: Johns Hopkins University Press.

Astin, A., Walbank, F., Fredericksen, M., and Ogilvie, R. (eds.) (1989), *Rome and the Mediterranean to 133 B.C., Cambridge Ancient History*^{2}, vol. 8, Cambridge: Cambridge University Press.

Badian, E. (1968), *Roman Imperialism in the Late Republic*^{2}, Ithaca, NY: Cornell University Press.

Beard, M. and Crawford, M. (1999), *Rome in the Late Republic: Problems and Interpretations*², London: Duckworth.

—— J. North, and Price, S. (1998), *Religions of Rome*, 2 vols., Cambridge: Cambridge University Press.

Boardman, J., Griffin, J., and Murray, O. (eds.), (1991), *The Oxford History of the Roman World*, Oxford: Oxford University Press.

Brennan, T. C. (2000), *The Praetorship in the Roman Republic*, 2 vols., Oxford: Oxford University Press.

Broughton, T. R. S. (1951–2), *The Magistrates of the Roman Republic*, 3 vols., New York: American Philological Association.

Brunt, P. A. (1988), *The Fall of the Roman Republic and Related Essays*, Oxford: Oxford University Press.

Claridge, A. (1998), *Rome: An Oxford Archaeological Guide*, Oxford: Oxford University Press.

Cornell, T. J. (1995), *The Beginnings of Rome: Italy and Rome from the Bronze Age to the Punic Wars (c. 1000–264 B.C.)*, London: Routledge.

—— and Matthews, J. (1982), *Atlas of the Roman World*, Oxford: Phaidon.

Crawford, M. (1974), *Roman Republican Coinage*, 2 vols., Cambridge: Cambridge University Press.

—— (1993), *The Roman Republic*², Cambridge, Mass.: Harvard University Press.

—— (1996), *Roman Statutes*, 2 vols., London: Institute of Classical Studies.

Crook, J. A., Lintott, A., and Rawson, E. (eds.) (1994), *The Last Age of the Roman Republic 146–43 B.C., Cambridge Ancient History*², vol. 9, Cambridge: Cambridge University Press.

Cunliffe, B. (1978), *Rome and her Empire*, New York: McGraw-Hill.

David, J.-M. (1996), *The Roman Conquest of Italy*, Oxford: Blackwell Publishers.

Degrassi, A. (1957), *Inscriptiones Latinae Liberae Rei Publicae*, Florence: La Nuova Italia.

Flower, H. I. (2004), 'Spectacle and Political Culture in the Roman Republic', in Harriet I. Flower (ed.), *The Cambridge Companion to the Roman Republic*, 322–43, Cambridge: Cambridge University Press.

—— (2009), *Roman Republics*, Princeton: Princeton University Press.

Gabba, E. (1976), *Republican Rome: The Army and the Allies*, Berkeley: University of California Press.

Gargola, D. J. (1995), *Lands, Laws, and Gods: Magistrates and Ceremony in the Regulation of Public Lands in Republican Rome*, Chapel Hill, NC: University of North Carolina Press.

Gelzer, M. (1975), *The Roman Nobility*, Oxford: Oxford University Press.

Gowing, A. M. (2005), *Empire and Memory: The Representation of the Roman Republic in Imperial Culture*, Cambridge: Cambridge University Press.

Gruen, E. S. (1974), *The Last Generation of the Roman Republic*, Berkeley: University of California Press.

—— (1984), *The Hellenistic World and the Coming of Rome*, Berkeley: University of California Press.

—— (1990), *Studies in Greek Culture and Roman Policy*, Leiden: Brill.

—— (1992), *Culture and National Identity in Republican Rome*, Ithaca, NY: Cornell University Press.

Harris, W. V. (1979), *War and Imperialism in Republican Rome 327–70 B.C.*, Oxford: Oxford University Press.

Hölkeskamp, K.-J. (1987), *Die Entstehung der Nobilität. Studien zur sozialen und politischen Geschichte der römischen Republik im 4. Jhdt. v. Chr.*, Stuttgart: Steiner.

—— (1993), 'Conquest, Competition, and Consensus: Roman Expansion in Italy and the Rise of the *Nobilitas*', *Historia*, 42: 12–39.

—— (2004*a*), *Senatus populusque romanus. Die politische Kultur der Republik: Dimensionen und Deutungen*, Wiesbaden: Steiner.

—— (2004*b*), *Rekonstruktionen einer Republik. Die politische Kultur des antiken Rom und die Forschung der letzten Jahrzehnte*, Munich: Oldenbourg.

Hornblower, S. and Spawforth, A. (eds.) (1996), *The Oxford Classical Dictionary*^{3}, Oxford: Oxford University Press.

Jehne, M. (ed.) (1995), *Demokratie in Rom? Die Rolle des Volkes in der römischen Republik*, Stuttgart: Steiner.

Kallett-Marx, R. M. (1995), *Hegemony to Empire: The Development of the Roman* imperium *in the East from 148 to 62 B.C.*, Berkeley: University of California Press.

Keppie, L. (1991), *Understanding Roman Inscriptions*, Baltimore: Johns Hopkins University Press.

—— (1998), *The Making of the Roman Army: From Republic to Empire*, Norman, Okla.: University of Oklahoma Press.

Linderski, J. (2002), 'The Pontiff and the Tribune: The Death of Tiberius Gracchus', *Athenaeum*, 90/2: 339–66.

Lintott, A. W. (1999), *The Constitution of the Roman Republic*, Oxford: Oxford University Press.

McDonnell, M. (2006), *Roman Manliness:* Virtus *and the Roman Republic*, Cambridge: Cambridge University Press.

Malcovati, H. (1976), *Oratorum Romanorum Fragmenta Liberae Rei Publicae*^{4}, Turin: Paravia.

Meier, C. (1980), *Res publica amissa. Eine Studie zu Verfassung und Geschichte der späten römischen Republik*^{2}, Frankfurt am Main: Suhrkamp.

Millar, F. (1998), *The Crowd in the Late Roman Republic*, Ann Arbor, Mich.: University of Michigan Press.

—— (2002), *Rome, the Greek World, and the East: The Roman Republic and the Augustan Revolution 1*, Chapel Hill, NC: University of North Carolina Press.

Morstein-Marx, R. (2004), *Mass Oratory and Political Power in the Late Roman Republic*, Cambridge: Cambridge University Press.

Nicolet, C. (ed.) (1978–9), *Rome et la conquête du monde mediterranéen 264–27 av. J.-C.*^{2} 2 vols., Paris: PUF.

—— (1980), *The World of the Citizen in Republican Rome*, Berkeley: University of California Press.

Osgood, J. (2006), *Caesar's Legacy: Civil War and the Emergence of the Roman Empire*, Cambridge: Cambridge University Press.

Rawson, E. (1985), *Intellectual Life in the Late Roman Republic*, Baltimore: Johns Hopkins University Press.

—— (1991), *Roman Culture and Society*, Oxford: Oxford University Press.

Rosenstein, N. (1990), *Imperatores Victi. Military Defeat and Aristocratic Competition in the Middle and Late Republic*, Berkeley: University of California Press.

—— (2004), *Rome at War: Farms, Families and Death in the Middle Republic*, Chapel Hill, NC: University of North Carolina Press.

—— and R. Morstein-Marx (2006), *A Companion to the Roman Republic*, Oxford: Oxford University Press.

RÜPKE, J. (2007*a*), *The Religion of the Romans*, Cambridge: Polity Press.
—— (2007*b*), *A Companion to Roman Religion*, Malden, Mass.: Blackwells.
RYAN, F. X. (1998), *Rank and Participation in the Republican Senate*, Stuttgart: Steiner.
SCHEID, J. (2003), *An Introduction to Roman Religion*, Edinburgh: Edinburgh University Press.
SCHEIDEL, W. (ed.) (2001), *Debating Roman Demography*, Leiden: Brill.
SCULLARD, H. H. (1980), *A History of the Roman World 753–146 B.C.*, London: Methuen.
SELLERS, M. N. S. (2004), 'The Roman Republic and the French and American Revolutions', in Harriet I. Flower (ed.), *The Cambridge Companion to the Roman Republic*, 347–64, Cambridge: Cambridge University Press.
SHATZMAN, I. (1975), *Senatorial Wealth and Roman Politics*, Brussels: Latomus.
SYME, R. (1939), *The Roman Revolution*, Oxford: Oxford University Press.
TAYLOR, L. R. (1949), *Party Politics in the Age of Caesar*, Berkeley: University of California Press.
WALBANK, F. W., ASTIN, A. E., FREDERICKSEN, M. W., OGILVIE, R. M., and DRUMMOND, A. (eds.) (1989), *The Rise of Rome to 220 B.C., Cambridge Ancient History*[2], vol. 7.2, Cambridge: Cambridge University Press.
YAKOBSON, A. (1999), *Elections and Electioneering in Rome: A Study in the Political System of the Late Republic*, Stuttgart: Steiner.

CHAPTER 33

THE EARLY IMPERIAL MONARCHY

CARLOS F. NOREÑA

THE most significant and distinctive features of the period covered in this chapter, roughly the first two centuries CE, were the political stability of the Roman state and the territorial stability of the Roman Empire. The last century BCE, by contrast, was largely defined by acute internal violence, political volatility, and an explosive extension of Rome's overseas empire, while violent political conflict, military defeat, and territorial disintegration were all characteristic of the mid-third century CE and the period from the 370s on. The early empire did not, of course, have an unblemished record in these respects. Internal tranquility was marred by two civil wars, in 69 and again from 193 to 197, while the Jewish revolt of 132–5 (and, to a lesser extent, that of 66–70), together with the large-scale invasions along the northern frontier in the late 160s and 170s, represented serious threats to the integrity of the empire. But in comparative terms our period is notable for the relative absence of the sorts of structural problems that plagued most pre-industrial empires. Indeed, on the broader canvas of world history, early Imperial Rome stands out among pre-modern states for its size and stability—only the imperial systems of ancient China bear comparison.

Political and territorial stability went together. For the last decades of the first century BCE witnessed both a political shift from an unsteady republic to a stable monarchy, a transformation in which the sovereignty of the *populus Romanus*

(Roman people) and the governing authority of the Senate were ultimately replaced by the dictates of an emperor and his inner circle, and an end to major imperial expansion, an equally momentous transformation in which aggressive conquest and the haphazard extraction of human and material resources gave way to systematic provincial administration and a more stable tributary regime. Broadly coincident with these fundamental changes in the structures of state and empire was an unprecedented intensification in the cultural and economic integration of the Mediterranean basin, and this, too, reinforced political and territorial stability. The Mediterranean world of the first two centuries CE, then, may be seen as a particular configuration of power in which interconnected networks of political, military, economic, and cultural/ideological power converged to produce what we call 'the early Roman Empire'. The aim of this chapter is to examine how this configuration of power worked in practice. The first part surveys the formal apparatus of state and empire during this period, and the second explores some of the dynamic links between different sectors of this vast and complex realm.

Monarchy and Empire

Stretching from the Atlantic to the Euphrates and from the North Sea to the Sahara, the Roman Empire in the first two centuries compelled the obedience of some 50 million subjects. Imperial control over this territory, its inhabitants, and its material resources depended ultimately upon armed force. The Roman army, which had a fighting strength of *c.*350,000 legionary and auxiliary soldiers in the second century, was occasionally utilized for imperial expansion, but its main military functions were to defend the empire's frontiers and, where possible, to provide internal security. The distribution of the legions, about thirty in number, produced concentrations on the eastern frontier, opposite the Parthian Empire, and along the northern frontier, opposite sometimes aggressive tribal groups, with a gradual shift in manpower from the Rhine to the Danube. Though simultaneous attacks on multiple points of the perimeter could stretch these forces to the breaking-point, the army successfully maintained the defence of the whole empire until the mid-third century. Its capacity to secure the submission of the empire's subjects was more tenuous. The largest cities had military garrisons, and there is scattered evidence for soldiers in small groups performing policing functions (e.g. Pliny, *Letters* 10.19–20, 27–8, 77–8), but the enormity of the empire made total military surveillance impossible. Aelius Aristides, for example, can celebrate the invisibility of the Roman army in provincial life (*To Rome* 67), and Apuleius' *Golden Ass* depicts an unruly countryside largely devoid of central authority, a credible picture consistent with other evidence. Large, organized uprisings against imperial rule were nevertheless uncommon, and whenever such revolts did arise they were crushed with exemplary ferocity (cf. Josephus, *The Jewish War* 7.37–40 on the public execution of thousands of Jewish captives in 70). In accounting for the comparative quiescence of Rome's subjects, the role of fear should not be underestimated.

The army was expensive. Total expenditure is impossible to quantify precisely, but army costs may have consumed as much as three-quarters of the state's budget (Duncan-Jones 1994: 33–46). Revenues were generated mainly through taxation. Taxes were both regular, in the form of poll tax and land tax outside Italy, both made possible by the provincial census (Lo Cascio 2000: 205–19), and irregular, in the form of taxes on manumission, inheritance, and goods in transit (cf. *SEG* 39.1180 for Asia). Taxes were paid both in coin and in kind (Brunt 1990: 324–46, 531–40; Duncan-Jones 1990: 187–98). Some were collected by imperial procurators and other officials, and some by private corporations, but most, it seems, were collected by individual cities and their local magistrates (Corbier 1991; cf. *IG* 5.1.1432–3 for procedures in first-century Messene). The bulk of these revenues came from the inner provinces of the empire's Mediterranean core, but most state expenditure went to the armies located throughout the periphery (Hopkins 1980), an inversion of the inward flow of resources characteristic of most empires.

In the basic anatomy of the Roman Empire, then, the two vital organs were the army and the tax revenues required to support it. But this 'military-tributary complex', while clearly necessary to sustain the empire, was not by itself sufficient to do so. After all, most empires are built upon the twin foundations of armed force and the extraction of material resources, but none enjoyed Rome's combination of size, stability, and longevity. The first step in understanding the long-term maintenance of this configuration of power is to recognize that the majority of the empire's inhabitants simply did not matter. In complex agrarian societies, the markedly unequal distribution of wealth and power and the technological constraints on mass communication and collective action gave rise to a steep social hierarchy in which only the uppermost strata could control resources and shape political institutions (Crone 2003: esp. 35–80). In Roman imperial society a two-tiered aristocracy fulfilled these functions. The upper tier, which included the emperor, the senatorial order, and the equestrian order, though highly stratified, nevertheless formed an empire-wide ruling class that performed the military and administrative duties of the central state. The lower tier was composed of local ruling classes, some tribal but most urbanized, that governed the many individual peoples and municipalities of the empire. The collaboration of these two aristocratic strata, facilitated by numerous channels of upward mobility, brought about the fusion of the central state and local governments in the management of the empire. This marriage of central and local power was the key to the political stability of the Roman Empire in the first two centuries CE. Many empires, of course, have relied on similar arrangements (Kautsky 1982: esp. 132–43), but the integration of local aristocracies into the political and social structures of the Roman imperial state was unparalleled in extent, depth, and effectiveness.

At the apex of this social and political hierarchy was the Roman emperor. Emperors commanded armies and determined foreign policy and military strategy (such as it was: Mattern 1999; Millar 2004: 160–94). They possessed incomparable personal wealth, and in practice controlled the state's finances (Millar 1977: 133–201; Brunt 1990: 134–62, 347–53; Lo Cascio 2000: 97–149). And their official pronouncements, whether edicts, judicial decisions, responses to petitions and queries, or instructions to officials, had the force of law (Ulpian, *Digest* 1.4.1.pr.–1). Regardless of the critical role played by the Senate in the imperial regime, the emperor's 50 million subjects realized that they lived in a monarchy (Millar 2002: 292–313), and it was to this monarch that provincial communities swore their oaths of allegiance.

What was the basis of this overwhelming power? Emperors, of course, wielded supreme legal authority. A clause of the statute that conferred imperial powers on Vespasian (*ILS* 244), for example, probably standard for all emperors, granted him 'the right and power to do or bring about whatever things divine, human, public, or private he considered best for the state', and in more prosaic terms the emperor's *imperium* (executive power) was carefully defined as being superior to that of any other official who also held it (Dio 53.32.5; *CIL* 2^2.5.900, ll. 34–6). But a narrowly constitutionalist interpretation of the emperor's authority cannot explain the acquiescence of 50 million persons in the rule of one. Nor can imperial 'propaganda' about the emperor's character, achievements, and divine support account by itself for his dominant position. It is more illuminating to analyse the emperor's relationship with those segments of the population that were capable of collective action, and which therefore stood as potential counterweights to imperial authority. In the Roman Empire of the first two centuries those groups were the army, the Senate, and the urban plebs of Rome. If the emperor could control these three collectivities, he could retain his personal power indefinitely.

How, precisely, the emperor controlled these key groups is a matter of ongoing debate. Materialist approaches emphasize the emperor's role in the allocation of resources, whether through appointments to high-ranking office, benefactions to the urban populace of Rome, or payments to soldiers, all of which, in their different ways, cemented dependence on the emperor. Idealist approaches stress cultural factors and the psychology of the actors involved. Major studies in this vein have argued that stereotyped forms of public interaction and communication between the emperor and these key groups produced specific 'modalities of obedience' (Veyne 1976: 539–730); that the new visual language that emerged in the Augustan age not only reflected, but also helped to constitute, imperial power (Zanker 1989); that the deeply ingrained sense of honour in the Greco-Roman world can account for why the emperor was obeyed (Lendon 1997); and that the emperor was the beneficiary of the charismatic power with which the imperial office was imbued

(Ando 2000). None of these studies focuses exclusively on either material or ideological factors, but uniting them even more fully is a priority for future work on the power of the Roman emperor.

The political transformation that brought the advent of monarchy at Rome also brought the advent of dynasty. For it was not only the emperor, but the imperial family as a whole, that stood as a decisive new presence in public life. Princes, in particular, were especially important under Augustus and Tiberius as highly visible political successors and as resonant symbols towards which different collectivities within the state could express their loyalty (Hurlet 1997; Rowe 2002). And the imposition of a dynastic structure on the succession of imperial power, whether through genealogical descent (Julio-Claudians, Flavians) or adoption (Nerva through Marcus Aurelius), brought political stability. The root of that stability lay in the unique capacity of the emperor to act as the ultimate arbiter between still fiercely competitive senators. Imperial power suppressed the aristocratic competition that had destroyed the Republic and harnessed this energy towards the larger goals of the imperial state. The result was far greater coordination and efficiency than had ever existed under the Republic in the military-tributary complex outlined above. In this respect, the monarchy was the institutional hub of this imperial order during the first two centuries CE. But it is important to distinguish between the monarchy, as an institution, and individual emperors, whose personal power could be quite precarious. There were, in fact, serious constraints on even the most secure emperors' capacity to assert their wills in the management of their realm, including the size of the empire, the rudimentary nature of communications within it, and the potential threat posed by aristocratic rivals.

It also goes without saying that no emperor could run the empire by himself. He depended in the first instance on his own household and on a select group of senatorial and equestrian advisors and functionaries, an inner circle analogous to those formed by the royal courts of early modern Europe (Winterling 1999). Especially important for imperial decision-making was the emperor's *consilium* (council), an informal body of aristocratic advisors that the emperor could consult on all matters great and small (Eck 2006). The Senate, as a corporate body, performed a wide range of administrative tasks, especially in the areas of provincial administration, legislation, and diplomacy (Talbert 1984: 341–487). Individual senators served as provincial governors, whose primary duties were the administration of justice and the resolution of territorial disputes, and as commanders of legions. Equestrians also served in the imperial administration, and in large numbers (Brunt 1983). Most began in the army as junior officers, but it was primarily in mid-range civilian posts that equestrians served, mainly as procurators involved in financial matters (cf. *ILS* 1348–1460 for a sample of 'career' paths). Some, however, advanced to the secretarial positions attached to the imperial court, and the most successful ascended all the way up to one of the four grand prefectures (cf. *ILS* 1321–47). Finally, at the bottom of the administrative hierarchy, the emperor's slaves and freedmen fulfilled a number of duties, especially in the financial sphere and in the management of the emperor's estates (cf. *ILS* 1473–1850).

The distinctive features of imperial government under the early monarchy were the dramatic increase in the number of administrative posts and the emergence of a proto-bureaucratic administrative structure. Scholars continue to debate the methods of appointment to the various administrative posts, however, some emphasizing the application of rational, rule-based procedures, others the role of personal patronage, but there is an emerging consensus that bureaucratic and patrimonial modes operated together: personal contacts and the economy of favours were indispensable, but the stakes involved for aristocratic writers of recommendations and the increasing specialization of many positions both put a premium on the basic competence of the officials who held these posts—even if the criteria used to judge competence were not always consistent with modern norms (Leunissen 1993; Eck 2001). This view also bears on the nature of imperial government in general. The dominant picture of the last generation has been that of an imperial state minimalist in its aims and passive in its operations (cf. Garnsey and Saller 1987: 20–40), but the pendulum of opinion now seems to be swinging in the opposite direction in the wake of detailed studies on the collection and use of official information (Haensch 1992; Moatti 1993; Demougin 1994), on administrative specialization and technical knowledge (Eck 1995–8; Lo Cascio 2000: 13–79), and on the implementation of rational-purposive policies in the administration of the empire (Burton 2002; cf. Kolb 2006 for various perspectives).

Whatever its ambitions, the central state during our period was clearly incapable of ruling the empire directly, since the number of officials scattered throughout the provinces was so strikingly small. Whereas the empire of the early sixth century was administered by some 30,000 centrally appointed bureaucrats, the imperial state of the first two centuries got by every year with just a few hundred high-ranking, salaried officials. The inevitable result was indirect rule through the devolution of key administrative tasks onto semi-autonomous local governments (Reynolds 1988). Cities, and especially the local elites who ran them, were therefore the critical intermediaries between the imperial state and the mass of its subjects. The most important duties undertaken by cities were the collection of taxes and the maintenance of order. In addition, cities were expected to bear the costs of the *vehiculatio* (imperial 'postal service'), and to maintain the roads that ran through their territories (cf. *ILS* 5864). In return for these vital services, without which the empire could not have functioned, local aristocrats were rewarded with markers of status, especially Roman citizenship, and with a greater share in the administration of the empire, and were supported, in principle, by the coercive apparatus of the central state (Brunt 1990: 267–81, 515–17; Shaw 2000: 362–73). This systematic collaboration between local aristocrats and the central state, which reinforced local hierarchies, was the foundation of imperial stability in the first two centuries CE.

Similar links had existed under the Republic, but they were less numerous, less regular, and contributed less to the imperial order as a whole. And the slow erosion of this relationship in the third and fourth centuries, the result of increasing centralization of political and administrative authority and attendant decline in local autonomy and vitality, was a root cause of the empire's deterioration in that period.

Centres, Peripheries, Networks, Hierarchies

The epicentre of this imperial universe was the city of Rome. Its centrality was not geographic, but rather symbolic and functional. As the location of the emperor's primary residence, Rome was the backdrop for a series of highly charged imperial ceremonies and rituals, especially arrivals (*adventus*), departures (*profectiones*), funerals, and, most spectacular of all, triumphs (Benoist 2005). Our period also witnessed a transformation of Rome's urban fabric, as emperors directed substantial resources to the erection of new structures and the restoration of old ones (for individual structures, Steinby 1993–2000). The result was a cityscape that corresponded visually to Rome's status as imperial metropolis, which helped to define Rome, symbolically, as the centre (cf. Strabo 5.3.8 and Pliny, *Natural History* 36.101 ff. for contemporary celebrations of Imperial Rome's monumental grandeur). In addition, the city functioned as the main hub of an empire-wide network of material and human movement. It was a magnet both for the accumulated wealth of the Mediterranean basin, especially grain, precious metals, and marble, and for immigrants and slaves. But it also served to channel and redistribute these things and persons back out to strategic nodes within this network. Bullion brought to Rome, for example, was exported in the form of coin, mainly to pay soldiers on the frontiers, and imports of marble were (it seems) shipped out as necessary to provincial workshops. And many immigrants to the city of Rome, whether slave or free, eventually moved away from this megalopolis, some settling in Rome's extensive hinterland, where they diversified the economy, and others outside Italy, where they brought with them parts of the Roman/Italic cultural package. Rome's functional centrality, then, was dynamic and productive.

Even more resonant than the city of Rome as an expression of centrality was the figure of the Roman emperor. The emperor was not only a second locus of centrality, but a highly mobile one. Imperial travels, in fact, articulated the relationship between centre and periphery, mainly because an imperial visit created a rare opportunity for provincial subjects to interact with their emperor and benefit from his largesse. But only the tiniest fraction of the empire's inhabitants ever saw the emperor in person. More important for disseminating the idea of monarchy were visual and symbolic representations of the emperor. Especially pervasive were epigraphic texts, flooding the public sphere with the emperor's names and titles; statues, rapidly replicating the imperial image in the empire's public spaces; and coins, produced on a massive scale and bearing imperial ideals and values to every corner of the Roman world. From the cumulative impact of these and other official media, the figure of the Roman emperor must have made a deep impression on the collective consciousness of the empire's inhabitants.

The principal framework for incorporating the idea of the emperor into local contexts was the set of practices and objects referred to collectively as 'the imperial cult' (Price 1984; Fishwick 1987–2005). Throughout the Roman world, from the largest urban agglomerations to the smallest towns, and in military camps as well (Stäcker 2003: 308–67), the whole apparatus of Greco-Roman religious practice (temples, altars, priests, processions, sacrifices) was employed to offer divine honours to the emperor and to other members of the imperial family. In the East, which had a long tradition of ruler worship before the Roman conquest, the emergence of imperial cult was largely spontaneous (cf. Dio 51.20.6–8 for the initial offer of cult to Octavian); in the West, by contrast, where no such traditions existed, the central state took a more active role in establishing the practice of emperor worship, especially in recently conquered areas. Throughout the empire the imperial cult was administered mainly by local aristocrats who served as priests, both at the provincial and municipal levels. In the Western Empire upwardly mobile freedpersons (*Augustales*) also helped to run the cult at the municipal level. The institutions of the imperial cult therefore served to bind important sectors of provincial society to the imperial regime. In considering the imperial cult as an empire-wide phenomenon, it is important to recognize its regional and local diversity, but there was sufficient coherence of practice for the imperial cult to have served as a powerful mechanism for binding the inhabitants of the empire into something like a single, imagined community.

The emperor, in fact, was the core unifying symbol for the empire as a whole. Indeed, the chronological coincidence between the formation of provincial cultures along Roman/Italic lines, especially in the Western Empire, and the advent of monarchy at Rome, suggests a strong relationship between political and cultural change (cf. Wallace-Hadrill 2008). But the figure of the emperor was only one element in the much broader process of cultural change during our period. Multiple indices are now employed by historians in order to describe and measure cultural change under the early Imperial monarchy, including degree of urbanization; architecture, public space, and monumentalization; the use of Latin in writing and speaking; Roman nomenclature; religious practice; epigraphic practice; artistic styles; consumption of material goods; and dietary patterns. Though there is broad consensus that the Mediterranean world, especially in the West, underwent a significant cultural transformation during the first two centuries CE, as gauged by these indices, and that at least some of the empire's inhabitants became more 'Roman' over time, debates about the mechanisms, meanings, and social patterning of these changes are far from settled (cf. Hingley 2005 for an overview). Especially urgent are debates about agency. At one end of the spectrum, it has been argued that the central state actively implemented a policy of 'Romanizing' its subjects; at the other, that Roman culture was willingly adopted because of its intrinsic attractiveness. Most scholars adopt intermediate positions, some emphasizing the initiative of the central state, others the emulation of local elites who embraced elements of Roman culture for their own purposes. Everyone can agree on the composite nature of 'Roman' culture and on the persistence of pre-Roman cultures. Perhaps the most promising approach for the historian of empire is to locate cultural change in the context of power relations, both institutional and personal, and to examine how cultural choices and expressions of identity shaped the exercise and experience of imperial power (cf. Woolf 1998; Mattingly 2006).

The intersection of culture and power under the early Imperial monarchy brings us back to cities and their ruling classes. For just as cities were the critical cogs in the administration of the empire, so too were they the main vehicles for cultural change. Nowhere is this more clear than in the monumentalization of cities throughout the empire. During the first two centuries CE older cities in the East and newer ones in the West were systematically enhanced by a more or less standard set of new or restored structures and complexes: paved central squares, temples, basilicas, porticoes, baths, circuses, theatres, and amphitheatres. The result was an empire-wide network of urban spaces linked together conceptually by their adherence to a flexible but clearly recognizable model. Some of this building was financed by local revenues (cf. Pliny, *Letters* 10.23–4, 90–1), and some by imperial munificence, but most was paid for by local benefactors. This private expenditure, which could be considerable, was not charitable in the modern sense, but belonged to a tradition that went back to the classical Greek world of 'doing good deeds' ('euergetism') in exchange for civic honours, especially commemorative decrees and statues, which reinforced the social superiority of those so honoured (Veyne 1976 is still basic). The cumulative effects of this system of civic euergetism and local commemoration were profound. It not only intensified the cultural integration of the Roman world, through the empire-wide replication of a basic urban model and its attendant practices and values, but it also served the interests of both the imperial state and local aristocrats, by idealizing and legitimating a political and social order in which the distribution of wealth and power was so conspicuously unequal.

This world of cities was a product of empire. In the West in particular, imperialism and urbanization developed in tandem. Urbanization in the Western Empire arose through veteran colonization (MacMullen 2000: 30–5, 51–5, 93–9), direct imperial intervention (cf. Florus 2.33), and local initiative. The reward of municipal status for towns deemed sufficiently civilized, which included Roman citizenship for the leading families, must have provided an incentive for the expenditure of personal resources on the building of cities (cf. Tacitus, *Agricola* 21). In addition, the municipal charters from the Western Empire reveal the extent to which these favoured communities were integrated in administrative and cultural terms into the empire's urban system. The integration of the empire's cities was also physical, as the development of primary roads and the creation of numerous secondary roads linked these cities to one another and gave rise to an empire-wide communications network that was both axial, centred on the city of Rome, and cellular, with the empire's larger urban agglomerations functioning as regional hubs. Road-building was often accompanied by other forms of imperial intervention, too, especially land survey, centuriation, and census-taking (Nicolet 1991). Together with colonization and urbanization, these processes, which peaked in intensity during our period, transformed the Mediterranean basin into a Roman imperial landscape.

Despite the capacity of the Roman state to impose order on the landscape in this way, the empire itself was fundamentally shaped by the ecology of the Mediterranean world. That ecology was characterized by a sea conducive to communications and a densely fragmented continental perimeter of diverse micro-regions; by an agrarian economy with low levels of agricultural surplus and always susceptible to environmental adversity; and by a characteristic type of 'connectivity' forged between micro-regions in order to minimize environmental and economic risk (Horden and Purcell 2000). When viewed from the perspective of the *longue durée*, in fact, the world of the early Imperial monarchy may be seen simply as the product of an especially dramatic intensification in the enduring forms of Mediterranean-wide local and regional connectivity. This intensification is certainly visible in the archaeological record from the first two centuries CE, which provides more and more evidence for the short- and long-distance movement of various material goods through trade (Harris 2000). But the role played by the Roman imperial state in generating this intensification should not be overlooked (Shaw 2001). In particular, it was Roman imperialism that (i) produced the large urban centres which provided the necessary markets for large-scale production of oil and wine, and (ii) created the necessary infrastructure for the efficient movement of these and other products, both of which in turn generated the concentrations of wealth necessary for the social and economic differentiation upon which the empire's political order was based. One way forward is to begin with the premise that the state and the ecological environment in which it was embedded developed together in a dialectical process, and then to examine how this process produced different economic, social, cultural, and political patterns in different parts of the Mediterranean basin (Shaw 2006).

The world of the early Imperial monarchy, then, was a fluid one. The movements that gave it vitality and dynamism were not limited to ideas and material goods, however, but included human beings as well (Moatti 2006: esp. 117–26). An excellent illustration is provided by the ever-expanding 'catchment area' upon which the upper tier of the Roman imperial aristocracy drew. We can trace this process for the equestrian order, which already by the mid-first century was functioning as a bridge between municipal aristocracies in the provinces and the imperial elite (Demougin 1999); for the senatorial order, which drew its membership increasingly from the provinces until, by the early third century, Italians were in the minority (Hopkins 1983: 200); and for emperors, whose families originated in the first century from the aristocracies of Rome (Julio-Claudians) and Italy (Flavians), and in the second from the municipal aristocracies of the western provinces as well (Trajan, Septimius Severus). This changing profile of the Roman imperial elite has both a demographic component, as the inability of the senatorial aristocracy to reproduce itself fully created regular openings for opportunistic social climbers (Hopkins 1983: 120–200), and an economic one, as the concentrations of wealth created by empire enabled supra-provincial promotion to the equestrian civil service and the senatorial order (Shaw 2001: 432–3). The major vehicle for human movement at a lower level in the social hierarchy was the Roman army. The legions, like the Senate, depended more and more on provincial recruits, which by the early second century outnumbered their Italian counterparts. The find-spots of auxiliary *diplomata* (discharge certificates) also provide evidence for geographical patterns in recruitment, service, and retirement, but the fast pace of discovery and publication in recent years makes generalization hazardous. And finally, there were regular movements among the rural masses of the Roman world, but these were normally limited to half-day trips to the nearest town and were regulated by the cycle of market days (*nundinae*) by which the sale and purchase of local produce was organized.

Conclusions

We return, in conclusion, to the Mediterranean world of the first two centuries CE as a particular configuration of power, one in which discrete but overlapping networks of military, political, cultural/ideological, and economic power converged in a spectacular fashion (for this approach, see Mann 1986–93). It is precisely the degree of convergence between these four networks, in fact, that distinguishes the early Imperial monarchy from both the late Republic and the later Empire. Military power was effectively organized for the maintenance of territorial stability. Political power was effectively unified by the institution of monarchy and by the collaboration between the central state and local aristocracies. Cultural/ideological power was expressed by the shared values, practices, and objects of Roman imperial civilization, and firmly located in its principal exponents, the urban elites. Economic power, based on the control of material resources, created the structures of personal dependence that legitimated a steep social hierarchy. And all four networks of power worked, for the most part, in harmony. Under the late Republic, by contrast, the conflict of political and military power prevented this type of convergence, and under the later Empire these four networks splintered in various ways, an unravelling in which the rise of Christianity as a largely autonomous source of power is only the most conspicuous example. Understanding in greater detail how these types of power worked together under the early Imperial monarchy, and how, precisely, they served to perpetuate the forms of exploitation, institutional and personal, upon which this imperial order was ultimately based, is a central task for the current generation of Roman historians.

Further reading

For a basic political narrative of the first two centuries CE, see the relevant chapters of volumes 10 (1996) and 11 (2000) of the revised *Cambridge Ancient History*. Potter 2006 offers a recent and clear overview of many different aspects of the period covered in this chapter and is equipped with an excellent bibliography. The collected articles of three giants in the field of Roman imperial history, Brunt (1990), MacMullen (1990), and Millar (2002–6), provide a convenient and incisive way into 'the state of the question' at the dawn of the twenty-first century. Translations of all the relevant literary sources can be found in the Loeb Classical Library series. Major advances in our knowledge of the Roman Empire come not from literary texts, however, but from the material record. Keeping abreast of new finds is a constant challenge. For recent epigraphic publications, the (roughly) quinquennial surveys in the *Journal of Roman Studies* are a good resource, and for archaeological discoveries and publications in general, the annual issues of the *Journal of Roman Archaeology* are invaluable.

References

Ando, C. (2000), *Imperial Ideology and Provincial Loyalty in the Roman Empire*, Berkeley: University of California Press.

Benoist, S. (2005), *Rome, le prince et la Cité*, Paris: PUF.

Brunt, P. A. (1983), 'Princeps and Equites', *Journal of Roman Studies*, 73: 42–75.

—— (1990), *Roman Imperial Themes*, Oxford: Clarendon Press.

Burton, G. (2002), 'The Roman Imperial State (AD 14–235): Evidence and Reality', *Chiron*, 32: 249–80.

Corbier, M. (1991), 'City, Territory, and Taxation', in J. Rich and A. Wallace-Hadrill (eds.), *City and Country in the Ancient World*, New York: Routledge, 211–39.

Crone, P. (2003), *Pre-industrial Societies*,[2] Oxford: Oneworld Publications.
Demougin, S. (ed.) (1994), *La Mémoire perdue*, Paris: Publications de la Sorbonne.
—— (ed.) (1999), *L'Ordre équestre: histoire d'une aristocratie*, Rome: École Française de Rome.
Duncan-Jones, R. P. (1990), *Structure and Scale in the Roman Economy*, Cambridge: Cambridge University Press.
—— (1994), *Money and Government in the Roman Empire*, Cambridge: Cambridge University Press.
Eck, W. (1995–8), *Die Verwaltung des römischen Reiches in der Hohen Kaiserzeit*, 2 vols., Basel: F. Reinhardt.
—— (2001), 'Spezialisierung in de staatlichen Adminstration des römischen Reiches in der hohen Kaiserzeit', in L. de Blois (ed.), *Administration, Prosopography and Appointment Policies in the Roman Empire*, Amsterdam: J. C. Gieben, 1–23.
—— (2006), 'Der Kaiser und seine Ratgeber', in Kolb 2006: 64–73.
Fishwick, D. (1987–2005), *The Roman Imperial Cult in the Latin West*, I–III, 6 vols., Leiden: Brill.
Garnsey, P. and Saller, R. (1987), *The Roman Empire*, Berkeley: University of California Press.
Haensch, R. (1992), 'Das Statthalterarchiv', *ZPG* 109: 209–317.
Harris, W. V. (2000), 'Trade', in A. K. Bowman *et al.* (eds.), *The Cambridge Ancient History*, vol. 11^2, 710–40.
Hingley, R. (2005), *Globalizing Roman Culture*, New York: Routledge.
Hopkins, K. (1980), 'Taxes and Trade in the Roman Empire (200 BC–AD 400)', *Journal of Roman Studies*, 70: 101–25.
—— (1983), *Death and Renewal*, Cambridge: Cambridge University Press.
Horden, P. and Purcell, N. (2000), *The Corrupting Sea*, Oxford: Blackwell.
Hurlet, F. (1997), *Les Collègues du prince sous Auguste et Tibère*, Rome: École Française de Rome.
Kautsky, J. (1982), *The Politics of Aristocratic Empires*, Chapel Hill, NC: University of North Carolina Press.
Kolb, A. (ed.) (2006), *Herrschaftsstrukturen und Herrschaftspraxis*, Berlin: Akademie Verlag.
Lendon, J. E. (1997), *Empire of Honour*, Oxford: Clarendon Press.
Leunissen, P. M. M. (1993), 'Conventions of Patronage in Senatorial Careers under the Principate', *Chiron*, 23: 101–20.
Lo Cascio, E. (2000), *Il princeps e il suo impero*, Bari: Epiduglia.
MacMullen, R. (1990), *Changes in the Roman Empire*, Princeton: Princeton University Press.
—— (2000), *Romanization in the Time of Augustus*, New Haven: Yale University Press.
Mann, M. (1986–93), *The Sources of Social Power*, 2 vols., Cambridge: Cambridge University Press.
Mattern, S. (1999), *Rome and the Enemy*, Berkeley: University of California Press.
Mattingly, D. J. (2006), *An Imperial Possession: Britain in the Roman Empire, 54 BC–AD 409*, London: Penguin.
Millar, F. (1977), *The Emperor in the Roman World*, Ithaca, NY: Cornell University Press.
—— (2002–6), *Rome, The Greek World, and the East*, 3 vols., Chapel Hill, NC: University of North Carolina Press.
Moatti, C. (1993), *Archives et partage de la terre dans le monde romain*, Rome: École Française de Rome.

MOATTI, C. (2006), 'Translation, Migration, and Communication in the Roman Empire', *Classical Antiquity*, 25: 109–40.

NICOLET, C. (1991), *Space, Geography and Politics in the Early Roman Empire*, Ann Arbor, Mich.: University of Michigan Press.

POTTER, D. S. (ed.) (2006), *A Companion to the Roman Empire*, Oxford: Blackwell.

PRICE, S. (1984), *Rituals and Power. The Roman Imperial Cult in Asia Minor*, Cambridge: Cambridge University Press.

REYNOLDS, J. (1988), 'Cities', in D. Braund (ed.), *The Administration of the Roman Empire*, Exeter: University of Exeter Press, 15–51.

ROWE, G. (2002), *Princes and Political Cultures*, Ann Arbor, Mich.: University of Michigan Press.

SHAW, B. D. (2000), 'Rebels and Outsiders', ch. 11 in A. K. Bowman *et al.* (eds.), *The Cambridge Ancient History*, vol. 11^2, 361–403.

—— (2001), 'Challenging Braudel: A New Vision of the Mediterranean', *Journal of Roman Archaeology*, 14: 419–53.

—— (2006), *At the Edge of the Corrupting Sea*, Oxford: Clarendon Press.

STÄCKER, J. (2003), *Princeps und Miles*, Hildesheim: Georg Olms.

STEINBY, E. M. (ed.) (1993–2000), *Lexicon Topographicum Urbis Romae*, 6 vols., Rome: Quasar.

TALBERT, R. (1984), *The Senate of Imperial Rome*, Princeton: Princeton University Press.

VEYNE, P. (1976), *Le Pain et le cirque*, Paris: Seuil.

WALLACE-HADRILL, A. (2008), *Rome's Cultural Revolution*, Cambridge: Cambridge University Press.

WINTERLING, A. (1999), *Aula Caesaris*, Munich: R. Oldenbourg.

WOOLF, G. (1998), *Becoming Roman*, Cambridge: Cambridge University Press.

ZANKER, P. (1989), *The Power of Images in the Age of Augustus*, Ann Arbor, Mich.: University of Michigan Press.

CHAPTER 34

THE LATER ROMAN EMPIRE

RICHARD LIM

FROM the passing of Marcus Aurelius (d. 180 CE) to the reign of Justinian (527–65) and beyond, the Roman imperial state underwent changes that were as profound and full of interest as those that had transpired between the late Republic and the Antonine age. Just as the vicissitudes of the Roman conquest state occasioned Augustus' institution of the Principate, those of the Third-Century Crisis gave rise to the reforms of Diocletian and Constantine that entailed similarly weighty implications. The period saw the further entrenchment of imperial autocracy as the ruling principle of the political and social order and the story of this further evolution of the Roman state continues to underpin most modern narratives of the Later Roman Empire.

Of what did the Later Roman Empire comprise and what were its geographical and temporal parameters? There are no simple answers to these fundamental questions. It did not exist as a single consistent political entity nor were its shifting boundaries easily sketched out on a map. Even as to when it finally drew to a close there exists no common agreement among scholars: one recent historical survey (Potter 2004) ends in 395, the year of the death of Theodosius I, while another (Mitchell 2006) takes the story to 641 when Heraclius died and Alexandria fell to Arab Muslims. Still others locate the terminus at the reign of Justinian in the mid-sixth century, whereas those who approach late antiquity through western medieval history may be inclined to favour Charlemagne's coronation in 800 as a turning-point. When scholars choose to draw this period to a close is just as likely to be determined by their own individual academic training and background as by the historical themes they regard as most salient and worthy of treatment.

Many historians continue to adopt the Roman imperial state as the main protagonist of their narratives on account of its overall impact and also because this choice allows them to address the topic of 'decline and fall' *à la* Edward Gibbon (see Ando below, Ch. 43). But even as they focus on politico-military institutions and events, an approach termed *l'histoire des événements*, others increasingly emphasize social and cultural themes that a 'national' historical narrative based on the examination of 'turning-points' inevitably relegates to the margins. Peter Brown's seminal *The World of Late Antiquity, 150–750* (Brown 1971; 2nd edn. 1989) has eloquently demonstrated how a cultural history *à la longue durée* might be written and the recent Harvard *Late Antiquity: A Guide to the Postclassical World* (Bowersock, Brown, and Grabar, 1999) is animated by the same spirit. And just as modern historians have generally forsaken national historical narratives for trans-national and/or thematic ones, the approach of cultural history, which is often expressed in this field through the concept of 'late antiquity,' has steadily gained adherents and intellectual currency. Indeed 'late antiquity' embodies a broader thematic, chronological and geographical scope than the Later Roman Empire; and by accepting, in principle at least, non-Roman peoples as central objects of study as much as the Romans themselves, it addresses the latter's Romano-centricity and allows comparisons and connections to be made more easily than would have been the case under a paradigm of 'Rome and its neighbours'.

The world of antiquity is generally taken to stretch roughly from the early third century to *c*.800 or even 1000. In geographical terms, it extends eastwards beyond the Roman imperial *limes* to Sassanian Iran and Central Asia, northwards to the North and Baltic seas, and southward to the African littoral of the Indian Ocean, '[f]or, in this period, societies as far apart as Scandinavia and the Hadramawt, Saharan Africa and western China were touched by events along that great arc of imperially governed societies and interacted decisively, at crucial moments, with those societies' (Bowersock, Brown, and Grabar 1999: p. x).

Making a Late Roman/Late Antique World

The Roman world empire has been notable for its success in imposing political coherence and a façade of Greco-Roman cultural homogeneity over a vast and varied Mediterranean landscape. Yet Rome's transformation from a particularistic conquest state to a territorial empire that accommodated the interests and aspirations of provincials in the Antonine period was closely followed by the apparent collapse of the *pax romana*. The ensuing century witnessed contested imperial successions, civil wars among rival army groups, rampant currency inflation and economic ruination, social and demographic dislocations, the recurring impact of a debilitating pandemic (to which historians have given the name of the Antonine plague), and repeated humiliation at the hands of the newly arisen Sassanian Persian Empire. This litany of woes is given the shorthand of 'the Crisis of the Third Century', a seemingly apt label for a tumultuous time. E. R. Dodds has additionally argued that the events precipitated a 'failure of nerve' and, as such, caused the Romans to enter an 'Age of Anxiety', a factor he regards as key to the rise of Christianity (Dodds 1965). His intriguing thesis has engendered a fruitful debate among scholars over the relationship between 'external' events and 'spiritual' culture; the consensus that has since emerged is that, while the troubles that the Romans faced were no doubt both real and serious, they need not directly translate into a damaged collective psyche.

Students of Imperial Rome have long been accustomed to narratives couched in terms of dynastic history even though recent scholarship has departed significantly from this traditional paradigm. In the late second to third centuries the rapid succession of emperors, together with their characteristically brief reigns, render the narratives so well suited for describing the achievements of the Julio-Claudians, Flavians, and Antonines well-nigh impossible. This problem is further compounded by the unreliability of the *Historia Augusta*, the period's major historical source. So it has become fashionable to gloss over this time as one that is too chaotic and obscure to be studied by all but the most intrepid researchers. In contrast, periods of relative political stability are eagerly grasped upon. The success of Septimius Severus (193–211), the 'African emperor' from Lepcis Magna (modern Libya), in maintaining a semblance of unity and stability allows his dynasty—one notable for its buildings and the extension of Roman citizenship to all the free inhabitants of the Roman Empire through a law called the Antonine Constitution—to be approached in the usual manner.

After the Severan dynasty came to an end in 235 the Roman world was once again engulfed in protracted civil wars. As the power at the centre noticeably weakened, political authority devolved to local regions as well as to the army groups on the frontiers. Vulnerable communities rallied around military leaders who promised them effective protection. For brief periods, Gaul and Britain successfully asserted autonomy under Postumus (258–73) and Carausius (286–93) respectively. Even former allies such as Palmyra, a caravan city in modern Syria, invaded Egypt and secure large swathes of what had been the Roman Near East at this time. These rather striking episodes foreshadow later scenarios when the imperial government became too weak to hold on to all the Roman lands and local peoples sought to safeguard their own interests through whatever means available to them.

The rise of soldier emperors was one response to these perceived weaknesses in the imperial system. Aurelian (270–5) displayed firm leadership and retook Egypt in 271, sacking Palmyra two years later, ending the reign of its remarkable queen Zenobia. With Aurelian also ended the admittedly long-fading tendency for imperial power to be worn with its Augustan mask. No longer would emperors see fit to maintain a semblance of parity with the aristocracy; they more or less stopped presenting themselves as *civiles principes*. The image of the strong man was instead coupled with that of a semi-divine ruler through the adoption of increasingly intricate imperial rituals. With the emperor styling himself *deus et dominus*, god and master, the Principate finally gave way to the Dominate.

Warfare between Rome and Iran was to remain a persistent theme throughout this time. The Parthian kingdom, long Rome's main rival in the East, was replaced by another Iranian state in the mid-third century. The Sassanian Empire (241–651) fought against the Romans with great energy, both militarily and diplomatically (Lieu 2000; Greatrex and Lieu 2002). Their recurrent and costly wars were moderated only by the annual rhythm of the seasons, and the constraints of geography and imperial finances. It was also a match of near equals. Rome and Persia were both organized, bureaucratic states with sophisticated revenue-extracting institutions and cultural foundations that integrated local native traditions with the values of an assertive imperial civilization. Both also faced challenges in combating their own tendency towards fragmentation and in dealing with tribal ethnic communities, including steppe nomadic peoples, on their borders. Aside from their strategic stand-off in Mesopotamia and Armenia, the Romans concentrated their resources on the Rhine–Danubian *limes* while the Persians kept a close watch over the open expanses of the steppe-lands to their north. The overriding need to prevent civil war and to guard their frontiers consumed the bulk of state resources and set the political agenda for these two imperial societies up to the time of the Arab conquest in the mid-seventh century.

The Fourth Century: Creating a New Order

The 'long fourth century' from the reign of Diocletian (284–305) to that of Theodosius I (d. 395) represents a critically formative period in Roman history. Many characteristically 'late antique' developments in the areas of politics and administration, relations between the state and religious communities, and the challenges of accommodating non-Roman *foederati* within imperial territories were crystallized following interactions that took place during this time. Ancient and modern narratives tend to credit Diocletian with re-establishing stability in the Roman world, even though the pattern of recurring civil and foreign wars continued well into the fourth century and beyond. What Diocletian did achieve was to introduce far-reaching administrative changes that would in time produce a distinctively 'late Roman' state and society. While claiming to restore the *mos maiorum*, he in fact sought to reinvent administrative and socio-economic structures in imaginative and radical ways. The creation of a college of four emperors, comprising two Augustuses, or senior emperors, and two Caesars, or junior emperors, lent the name of Tetrarchy or 'Rule of Four' to this period. The emperor also reorganized provincial governance, separating out military and civil functions, so as to achieve greater administrative efficiency. The augmented bureaucracy and military establishment had the unintended consequence of claiming an increased proportion of state revenues and, by extension, the total wealth produced in the empire, leading to a weaker foundation for economic growth in the future. To combat inflation, Diocletian issued mostly ineffectual edicts that placed caps on local prices and wages. To prevent economic pressures from driving peasants off the land, artisans out of their professions, and city councillors from their municipal obligations, he limited the mobility of groups whose social functions he deemed vital to state interests. Overall, the fixing of the status quo by imperial fiat was seen as the panacea to the empire's woes. The resulting loss in social mobility can be seen in peasants who were tied to the land in a way that prefigures the later medieval land-tenure system, and in vital workers, such as armourers, mint-workers, bread-makers, and public entertainers, who were locked into professions that became essentially hereditary not only in practice but also *in iure*.

The new predilection for greater centralization and conformity also turned the state into the persecutor of religious nonconformists, establishing a pattern for future rulers to follow. Manichaeans were Diocletian's first target; ironically he attacked them as Persian, and hence enemy, fifth-columnists even though the founder of their religion was himself but a few years earlier (277) executed by the Persian king-of-kings. Christians came next, as they were deemed atheists and bad Romans who, in violating the *pax deorum* by their abandonment of the worship of the gods, brought calamitous suffering to the Roman people as a whole. But if official persecution was meant to create a greater consensus in Roman society, it fell wide of its mark. Christian martyrs who resisted to the death became inspirational heroes and everyday Christians increased in numbers.

Diocletian's 'empire of the Tetrarchs' was formally ended after Constantine defeated his imperial colleagues and reintroduced the principle of dynastic rule. Yet in important respects Constantine completed and even extended Diocletian's administrative reforms, so that both emperors should be credited with being the founders of the late Roman state. The latter also embraced Christianity in 312 and followed up with generous gifts of lands and income-generating estates to local churches. With the emperor as its patron, Christianity began to enter the public (even civic) sphere in a meaningful way. Imperial largesse brought about to the creation of the first Christian public buildings in the form of basilicas, an architectural design originally used for civil law-courts but which became the standard imperial Christian building in Roman cities after the fourth century.

The affairs of state and church became increasingly entwined through the fourth century, culminating in the establishment of orthodox Christianity as the religion of the empire under Theodosius I. The emperor would become a key player in arbitrating Christian disputes, as Constantine famously dealt with the Donatist and Arian controversies, convening the first universal Christian council at Nicaea in 325 to address the latter. Through the fourth century and beyond, emperors lent their prestige and power to those bishops whose theological views were consonant with their own, and sought to ensure that divisions among Christians were ameliorated if not abolished (Barnes 1981; Drake 2000). But to no avail; instead, the imperial state became increasingly enmeshed in intra-Christian rivalry and disputes (Bowersock, Brown, and Grabar 1999: 196–218). Still, given the nature of the state's involvement and preference for harmony and a stable social order, Christian leaders such as bishops increasingly styled themselves as urban patrons, at times by claiming to be the champions of 'the poor', a group not previously conceptualized within the ancient city (Brown 2002). In terms of its social organization, patterns of authority and leadership, and relationship between centres and peripheries, Christianity would develop in ways that resemble Greco-Roman civic communities. Yet the classical city was not so easily supplanted; civic institutions and ideals continued to thrive in most places even as Christian polities, virtually cities within cities, became more prominent by the day (Lepelley 1979–81).

The rise of Christianity meant that the fourth century was one that involved appreciable cultural adaptations and even conflicts. The religion's successful expansion in demographic and ideological terms generated tensions and critical responses. The brief and colourful reign of Julian the Apostate (361–3) offers a notable instantiation of the profound and complex impact of Christianity two generations after Constantine embraced the religion (Lieu and Montserrat 1998). The emperor, who converted from Christianity to a Neoplatonizing form of polytheism, introduced reforms that sought to re-establish the worship of the gods that amounted to the wholesale invention of 'Paganism' based on a Christian model. A similar dynamic may be seen with the rise of rabbinic Judaism, which some scholars argue came about in no small measure as a response to the impact of Christianization (Schwartz 2001).

It has been traditional to regard the religious conflict between paganism and Christianity as a fundamental theme of the later fourth century (Momigliano 1963; Lee 2000). This unfolding drama, especially when set in the city of Rome, allows for late-antique religious transformations to be presented in a clear-cut series of acts: Constantine's imperial acceptance of Christianity brought about a backlash in

Julian's aborted reforms which, in turn, gave rise to a Neoplatonizing pagan revival among the 'last pagans', Roman senators who made their last throw at the battle of Frigidus in 394, after which the aristocracy converted to Christianity and submitted to the authority of the bishop of Rome or the pope. Herbert Bloch (Bloch 1963) and others have underscored this pagan senatorial resistance to Christianity, while more recently other scholars, notably Alan Cameron, have called the intensity and concerted nature of this supposed pagan reaction into question. In any event, the conversion of the Roman aristocracy from the worship of the gods to Christianity remains a central research theme (Salzman 2002), both on account of the wealth and influence of the group and also because of the richness of the surviving sources that bear on the topic.

While the theme of cultural and religious transformation would feature heavily in the history of the 'long fourth century', the challenge of holding the empire together and managing its frontiers remained a foremost imperial concern. The return to dynastic rule did not put an end to endemic warfare nor avert the trend of a mixed record of Roman military success. In the last quarter of the fourth century the westward migration of Eurasian steppe nomads whom the Romans would call the Huns pressured semi-sedentary Germanic peoples living north of the Black Sea to seek refuge at the empire's Danubian frontier. The Goths appealed to the Romans as supplicants but, savagely provoked by the abuse they received, rose up and destroyed the eastern field army, slaying the emperor Valens, at the so-called battle of Adrianople in 378. This signal defeat of Roman arms opened the imperial frontiers to the influx of newly arriving peoples who would come to be progressively diverted away from Constantinople, then the seat of empire, and into the Latin West. These Germanic peoples eventually settled in and assumed control over most regions of the Western Mediterranean while crystallizing distinctive cultural identities as Ostrogoths, Visigoths, Vandals, and so on.

The Fifth Century: Changes and Continuities

The fifth century is often mentioned in standard texts as the time when the Roman Empire fell. Such an assessment gains credence from the enumeration of events such as the ten-day sack of Rome by Visigoths in 410, the Vandal sack of Rome in 455, and the barbarian warlord Odoacer's deposition of Romulus Augustulus, the last emperor of the West, in 476. But not only is the stark vision of 'decline and fall' out of fashion among many—though by no means all—scholars; the idea that these events ushered in catastrophic ruptures with the past fails to survive close scrutiny. In the West, where barbarian kingdoms were established on former Roman soil, the conquerors often pragmatically coexisted with the Roman population and retained many aspects of Roman cultural and socio-economic life (Mathisen 1993; Pohl 1997; Pohl and Reimitz 1998). How Germanic peoples and Romans interacted in each of the distinct post-Roman societies—Visigothic Spain, Ostrogothic Italy, Merovingian Gaul, and Vandal North Africa—remains a lively topic of scholarly discussion. Historians who work in this field have need of using the full range of textual and non-textual (archaeological and visual) sources. As a general historical problem the topic also benefits from the broader perspective that is open to socio-anthropological and other modes of enquiry.

In the East, emperors and empresses from the houses of Theodosius and Valentinian continued to reign in Constantinople through the first half of the fifth century. The imperial state pursued its usual occupations: taxation and administration, diplomacy and wars (especially with the Hunnic confederation based in the Hungarian Plains and with Sassanian Persia), and managing the rifts among Christian groups in the empire. A number of church histories, such as those by Socrates and Sozomen, provide the basic historical narrative for imperial and ecclesiastical affairs during this time. They highlight the Christian piety of the emperors as the foundation of Roman peace and offer fascinating insight into how Roman Christians conceived of their own roles in history. Such works call attention to the growing trenchancy of religious disputes and to continuing pressures exerted by foreign peoples on the empire's embattled frontiers. Also central to our appreciation of this time are two sets of documents that illustrate interactions between the emperors and their subjects and how the rising importance of Christianity shaped those interactions. The first is an important codification of imperial law, the so-called *Theodosian Code*; the other is the set of conciliar proceedings produced for the Council of Chacedon in 451, convened by Theodosius' successor Marcian (Millar 2006). But it must be remembered that still more sources are available, often in languages other than Greek and Latin. Our appreciation of the history of the fifth century depends largely on what we choose to read and focus upon, with choices ranging from the works that speak about the deeds of the imperial court and ecclesiastical leaders to textual and non-textual sources that reveal the workings and aspirations of a plethora of local communities.

The Sixth Century and Beyond

The sixth century has long been approached as the century of Justinian (527–65) both on account of the centrality of his reign and the abundance of sources.

The writings of Procopius of Caesarea, a contemporary whose *History of the Wars* provides an overarching politico-military narrative as well as a set of key questions regarding the impact of the emperor's deeds, continue to shape modern discussions of this period (Maas 2005). In the first part of his reign Justinian showed himself to be an energetic and ambitious ruler. His generals brought about the reconquest of the lost western territories in North Africa, Italy, and Spain. His quaestor Tribonian presided over the codification of Roman law: the *Code of Justinian*, the *Digest* or *Pandects* and the *Institutes*, became monuments in Roman jurisprudence that later gave rise to much of modern European law. In ecclesiastical affairs, the emperor at first favoured the reconciliation of Christians who held different beliefs regarding the connection between Christ's human and divine natures. But soon Justinian became an active champion of a 'Chalcedonian' position (named after the Council of Chalcedon in 451), which he accepted as the imperial orthodoxy, and persecuted 'Monophysite' Christians. Justinian's earnest but heavy-handed approach in enforcing religious conformity succeeded in alienating sizeable segments of the Roman population, so that many Monophysite Christians in Egypt and Syria as well as Jews began to look for help against the oppression of the imperial state even to the point of welcoming first Sassanian and later Arab Muslim intervention.

A great bubonic plague devastated the Mediterranean world and the Near East in 541–3 and recurred through the seventh (and even the eighth) centuries; this pandemic effected a notable demographic shift and accelerated the ongoing process of de-urbanization in many of the coastal cities (Little 2007). The wars between Rome and Persia continued to occupy centre-stage from the reign of Justinian to the early seventh century. Antioch was taken and sacked in 540. Oscillating between peace and war, but mostly on a war-footing, the two empires tested each other's strength across the length of their common border. By and large the Romans remained on the defensive and even paid tribute to the Persians. In the early seventh century a spectacular set of Persian victories briefly won them virtually the entire Roman Near East. Heraclius (d. 641), the Roman emperor at the time, allied himself with nomadic Turkic-speaking peoples and struck deep into Persian territory. By this feat of arms, which brought on a Sassanian civil war, the balance of power was briefly restored.

These costly and damaging wars greatly exhausted both imperial states. Their mutual obsession with each other created a ripe opportunity for Arab nomadic tribesmen who, rallying to the teachings of Muhammad of Medina (d. 632), set aside their traditions of feuding to unite in a religious and national campaign of conquest. After their defeat at the battle of Yarmuk in 636 the Romans became powerless to halt the progress of Arab armies, which then proceeded to occupy imperial provinces in the Near East and North Africa. These territories and their predominantly Christian populations left imperial control for the last time. To the east, the Arabs defeated the Sassanians and took over the entirety of their empire and, after extending their reach to Central Asia, further defeated a Tang Chinese army at the battle of Talas in 751, a victory that effectively checked the westward ambitions of one of the most successful Chinese imperial dynasties. Sassanian refugees, including members of the royal house, fled to Chang'an, bringing the 'Far East' closer still to the world of late antiquity.

With the arrival of Islam the late antique world yet again shifted ground. The Roman Empire, shorn of its possessions in the Levant and along the coast of Africa, endured in its Balkan and Anatolian enclaves surrounding Constantinople. Meanwhile the western barbarian kingdoms continued to develop cultures that blended Germanic traditions, Roman civilization, and Christianity. Spain, North Africa, Egypt, Iraq, and Iran all came under the rule of Islam and began to look to Damascus under the Umayyad dynasty (660–750) and later to Baghdad (founded 762) during the Abbasid Caliphate (750–1258). These three main political blocs, which formed the tripartite world of the early Middle Ages, may be further distinguished by their different religious outlook: the Romans of the Byzantine state professed Greek Orthodox Christianity, the Germanic kingdoms a Latin Christianity based on communion with the bishop of Rome, while the Islamic lands revered God's revelation to the Prophet Muhammad in Arabia as a sacred touchstone (Herrin 1987).

Key Themes and Sources

Perhaps the most critical theme for the study of the Later Roman Empire or late antiquity remains that of civilizational decline. Edward Gibbon's *Decline and Fall of the Roman Empire* (1776–88) exemplifies the historiography of nostalgia and loss that regards the second century CE as the apex of Roman imperial civilization and its aftermath as the beginning of an inexorable slide into the Dark Ages. A similar value-judgement is implicit in the terms that scholars use to label the period, be it the post-classical age, the Later Roman Empire, or late antiquity. There can be little question that rather profound changes took place from the late second to the sixth century; the ongoing disagreement among scholars has to do with whether these changes, singly and in the aggregate, amount to decline as opposed to change. Several notable historians have recently reasserted the 'decline thesis', pointing to archaeological and material evidence for the erosion of civic culture and socio-economic activities (Liebeschuetz 2001; Ward-Perkins 2005). Still others may contend that the idea of decline as opposed to transformation rests in the domain of subjective judgement and is, moreover, one that is suggested by the (tragedic) genre of ancient and modern historical narratives (White 1973). The intellectual sparring between the 'declinists' and 'transformationalists' continues to this very day and lies behind much of the recent scholarship around the topic of the 'fall of Rome'.

Another key theme is that of the religious transformation of society. Christianization is therefore another central topic of research (MacMullen 1984). The concept itself is capable of several definitions, and in any event was an ongoing process; there was no point in time at which the Later Roman Empire became fully Christianized. Theodosius I famously declared Orthodox Christianity the official religion of the empire, but changes in social mores and institutions did not happen overnight by fiat; the triumphal narratives describing Christianity's progressive victory over paganism in Christian writings do not always offer an accurate understanding of what took place on the ground. How the growing Christian majority population adapted the classical heritage remains an important part of the story of Christianization; it became generally accepted that much of Greco-Roman culture was worthy of salvage once the most obvious forms of polytheistic worship, such as sacrifice, were abolished. But Christianization also involved the reinvention of public symbols and rituals, conceptions of time and space, notions of authority and sacrality, and sense of past, present, and future (Brown 1995; Salzman 1990). Thus Christianization tells a much richer tale than just how Christians reacted to and appropriated classical literary and artistic traditions.

Christianization involved the emergence of new elites, especially the bishops of cities and towns, and new cultural heroes, such as the martyrs at the time when Christians were persecuted, and ascetics and monks afterwards. The cult of the saints that grew up around the martyrs, whose deaths were annually celebrated on their 'birthdays' at their shrines, gave Christians a new model of the human community and source of semi-divine patronage (Brown 1981; Van Dam 1993; Howard-Johnston and Hayward 1999). Likewise, living saints—ascetics and monks—who notionally inhabited deserted landscapes on the fringes of human communities but were indeed found in even the largest cities, became the new cultural heroes of the day. Even emperors and bishops were seen as seeking the help and advice of these usually unlearned, even illiterate, men and women of God. Both dead martyrs and living ascetics had the ability to form communities around themselves and confer a sacral aura on a landscape. Urban bishops, an increasingly important group in society (Rapp 2005), began to take advantage of the charisma that these heroic Christians projected and co-opted their spiritual power to increase their own authority within the Christian community. Religion and authority were now closely conjoined in a way rather different from what had existed before.

'Iranicization', the corresponding process in the Sassanian Empire, drew on Zoroastrian religion to enhance cultural coherence in the Iranian state's far-flung domains. Indeed, the growing alliance between the state and an official religion took place even sooner in the Sassanian realm than in Rome, for already in the mid-third century Zoroastrianism was installed as Persia's state religion, and the magi, priests who tended the fire-temples that came to be built throughout the land, were highly honoured throughout the empire. Thus, in the growing alliance between state and established religion Rome and Persia, the ancient world's two great multi-ethnic empires, seemed to have marched along converging paths.

It is useful to ask whether the religious transformations that characterized late antiquity were *sui generis*. In some respects these transformations resembled aspects of the complex processes of Hellenization and Romanization that over time created the Hellenistic and Roman worlds. Seen against the longer-term transformations that had been taking place in the Mediterranean and the Near East, the erosion of the power of a centralizing state and the classicizing culture it helped promote appears more as modulations of a long-running theme than a catastrophic turn. The preceding historical projects of Hellenization and Romanization had provided challenging new ways for regional societies and communities to construct their own cultural identities in relation to various notional 'centres', and many, led by local elites, chose to join in the experiment of fashioning themselves accordingly (Woolf 1998; Ando 2000). The varied responses to Greco-Roman (civic) ideals and rapprochement with the culture of the imperial centre became a manifest feature of the Roman peace. Yet this process was neither inevitable nor teleological. The availability of yet other seemingly new ways for fashioning communal identities following the third century broadened the menu of choices that might in turn have undercut the monolithic image of empire that was so carefully cultivated before (and since). Seen against the backdrop of the dynamic and ongoing process that determined each society's interpretation of what it meant to be Roman, the transformations in late antiquity, including the challenge of maintaining Roman identity under a Germanic (barbarian) rule in the West, suggest dialogue with the past rather than rupture. The recent orientation of Roman historical studies to the question of cultural identity, which includes works on Greek responses to Roman rule, allows for seeing Christianization not as a radically new phenomenon that implemented an agenda set by the imperial centre or ecclesiastical hierarchy but, in a meaningful way, as the aggregate of local responses to available choices and challenges. Such an approach offers exciting possibilities for integrating various 'histories', including those of the various Jewish and Christian communities in the Roman Mediterranean and Sassanian Near East, as well as tying the history of late antiquity itself to the histories of the preceding Hellenistic and Roman periods.

The same types of evidence that exist for the study of Hellenistic and Roman history exist for the study of the Later Roman Empire/late antiquity. Literary sources in Greek and Latin remain abundant, and include works in all the traditional genres as well as new ones that came to the fore in this time. Histories and chronicles, biographies, panegyrics, philosophical treatises, novels, and letter collections abounded. Moderns who judge a civilization by the quality of its literary works have in the past been led to conclude that late antiquity was a period of decline on account of its 'post-classical' literary style. But historians have no cause to resort to such criteria and, in any event, late antique writers continued to produce classicizing Greek and Latin works of note.

Students of social, cultural, and economic history can also access important bodies of documentary and non-written sources. Papyri continue to come down in quantity from late Roman Egypt together with some from Palestine and Italy. On this basis, late Roman Egypt could be studied with an unmatched degree of attentiveness to the details of everyday life and the functioning of all levels of administration (Bagnall 1993). We have the important law-codes of Theodosius II and Justinian that enable the study of formal Roman institutions and practices of rule (Matthews 2000). The archaeology of late antique sites all throughout the Mediterranean and Near East has given historians a keener sense of the strong regional characteristics of communities that gravitated around emerging local or regional centres, even those that did not leave behind a discernible literary or written documentary tradition. Mosaic decorations from houses enliven our understanding of the perception of everyday life as well as the self-representations of elite villa-owners. And even those villa sites that do not yield mosaics can be studied through improved archaeological survey and remote sensing techniques to determine the nature of human settlement and activities in the surrounding countryside.

While the quantity of public inscriptions appearing on stone seems to have declined after the third century (caused by a so-called decline of the 'epigraphic habit'), the practice of self-representation on the part of the elites did not disappear. Thus decorations from churches and synagogues reveal the outlooks of the religious communities that built them. In this period, new elites and conceptions of the community were arising on account of the growing importance of Christianity. Christian bishops and priests not only helped transform the visible landscape through their church-building activities, they also put out large bodies of written works in genres both old and new. Scholars who examine the works of important 'patristic' authors have increasingly sought to situate their careers and writings in the overall social and cultural context of the time. Approaches range from single-author studies such as Peter Brown's *Augustine of Hippo: A Biography* (rev. edn. 2000) to those that try to extrapolate from an author's work the culture of a Christian community. The sermon mediates the world of theology and lay beliefs and practice and therefore affords one of the most promising resources for social reconstruction. Recent studies that focus on select homiletic corpuses take the dialectical exchanges between 'the preacher and his audience' as a fruitful starting-point for inquiring into the nature of Christian communal values and culture (Klingshirn 1994; Maxwell 2006). Among other 'new' genres is that of hagiography, those praiseful biographies of holy men and saintly bishops that became central texts that helped define the identities and ethos of local communities. Together these works allow us to take a closer look at the non-elite strata of ancient society as never before. Used in combination with the epigraphic, archaeological, and visual material, such Christian sources even make possible the re-creation of 'total histories' for regions or cities over a fairly long period of time. However, some alert scholars caution that all these Christian texts must be understood first and foremost as 'texts' that reveal mostly narrative realities and strategies and can only with difficulty and after much reflection be used as 'socio-historical documents' (Clark 2000).

Further, students of late antique Christian sources have to engage not only with works written in the two 'classical' languages but also with ones that were rendered in 'regional' languages such as Coptic, Ethiopic, Syriac, Armenian, and Old Church Slavonic on account of the rise of Christianity. The ability to engage with Coptic and Syriac texts and, by extension, the local communities that produced and used them, has greatly expanded the cultural horizons of scholars of late antiquity.

Further reading

Several fine overall treatments are available for this period: see Brown 1989 (rev. edn.), Cameron 1993, Potter 2004, and Mitchell 2006. For those who wish to study the late Roman state, Jones 1964 remains an indispensable starting-point. Surveys of the state of the field are to be found in Garnsey and Cameron 1997 and Bowersock, Brown, and Grabar 1999. Mitchell 2006: 425–9 contains a fine list of sources in translation. For a sourcebook that treats the late Roman East especially, see Maas 2000; for a collection of sources on the post-Roman West, see Mathisen 2003. Research articles are to be found not only in the usual classics and ancient history serials but also in *Antiquité Tardive*, the *Journal of Early Christian Studies*, and the new *Journal of Late Antiquity*, scholarly journals that are specifically dedicated to the study of late antiquity.

References

Ando, Clifford (2000). *Imperial Ideology and Provincial Loyalty in the Roman Empire*, Berkeley and Los Angeles: University of California Press.

Bagnall, Roger S. (1993). *Egypt in Late Antiquity*, Princeton: Princeton University Press.

Barnes, Timothy D. (1981). *Constantine and Eusebius*, Cambridge, Mass.: Harvard University Press.

Bloch, Herbert (1963). 'The Pagan Revival in the West at the End of the Fourth Century', in Momigliano 1963: 193–218.

Bowersock, Glen W., Brown, Peter, and Grabar, Oleg, eds. (1999). *Late Antiquity: A Guide to the Postclassical World*, Cambridge, Mass.: Harvard University Press.

Brown, Peter (1981). *The Cult of the Saints: Its Rise and Function in Latin Christianity*, Chicago: University of Chicago Press.

——(1989 rev. edn.; orig. 1971). *The World of Late Antiquity, A.D. 150–750*, New York: Norton.

——(1995). *Authority and the Sacred: Aspects of the Christianization of the Roman World*, Cambridge: Cambridge University Press.

——(2000 rev. edn.). *Augustine of Hippo. A Biography*, Berkeley and Los Angeles: University of California Press.

——(2002). *Poverty and Leadership in the Later Roman Empire*, Hanover, NH: University Press of New England.

Cameron, Averil (1993). *The Later Roman Empire: A.D. 284–430*, Cambridge, Mass.: Harvard University Press.

——(1993). *The Mediterranean World in Late Antiquity: A.D. 395–600*, London and New York: Routledge.

Clark, Elizabeth A. (2004). *History Theory Text: Historians and the Linguistic Turn*, Cambridge, Mass.: Harvard University Press.

Dodds, E. R. (1965). *Pagan and Christian in an Age of Anxiety: Some Aspects of Religious Experience from Marcus Aurelius to Constantine*, Cambridge: Cambridge University Press.

Drake, Harold (2000). *Constantine and the Bishops: The Politics of Intolerance*, Baltimore: Johns Hopkins University Press.

Garnsey, Peter, and Cameron, Averil, eds. (1998). *Cambridge Ancient History*, vol. 13. *The Late Empire, A.D. 337–425*, Cambridge: Cambridge University Press.

——and Humphress, Caroline (2001). *The Evolution of the Late Antique World*, Cambridge: Cambridge University Press.

Greatrex, Geoffrey, and Lieu, Samuel N. C. (2002). *The Roman Eastern Frontier and the Persians Wars.* Part II: *A.D. 363–630. A Narrative Sourcebook*, London and New York: Routledge.

Heather, Peter (2005). *The Fall of the Roman Empire: A New History of Rome and the Barbarians*, Oxford: Oxford University Press.

Herrin, Judith (1987). *The Formation of Christendom*, Princeton: Princeton University Press.

Howard-Johnston, James and Hayward, Paul A. (1999). *The Cult of the Saints in Late Antiquity and the Middle Ages: Essays on the Contribution of Peter Brown*, Oxford and New York: Oxford University Press.

Jones, A. H. M. (1964). *The Later Roman Empire, A.D. 284–602: A Social, Economic, and Administrative Survey*, Norman, Okla.: University of Oklahoma Press.

Kelly, Christopher (2004), *Ruling the Later Roman Empire.* Cambridge, Mass.: Harvard University Press.

Klingshirn, William E. (1994). *Caesarius of Arles: The Making of a Christian Community in Late Antique Gaul*, Cambridge: Cambridge University Press.

Kulikowski, Michael (2004). *Late Roman Spain and its Cities*, Baltimore: Johns Hopkins University Press.

Lee, A. D. (2000). *Pagans and Christians in Late Antiquity*, London and New York: Routledge.

Lenski, Noel (2006). *Cambridge Companion to the Age of Constantine*, Cambridge and New York: Cambridge University Press.

Lepelley, Claude (1979–81). *Les Cités de l'Afrique romaine au Bas-Empire*, 2 vols., Paris: Études Augustiniennes.

Liebeschuetz, J. H. W. G. (2001). *Decline and Fall of the Roman City*, Oxford: Oxford University Press.

Lieu, Samuel N. (2000). *The Roman Eastern Frontier and the Persian Wars*, London and New York: Routledge.

—— and Montserrat, Dominic (1998). *Constantine: History, Historiography, and Legend*, London and New York: Routledge.

Little, Lester K., ed. (2007). *Plague and the End of Antiquity: The Pandemic of 541–750*, Cambridge: Cambridge University Press/American Academy in Rome.

Maas, Michael R. (2000). *Readings in Late Antiquity: A Sourcebook*, London: Routledge.

—— (2005). *The Cambridge Companion to the Age of Justinian*, Cambridge and New York: Cambridge University Press.

MacMullen, Ramsay (1984), *Christianizing the Roman Empire (A.D. 100–400)*, New Haven: Yale University Press.

Mathisen, Ralph (2003). *People, Personal Express, and Social Relations in Late Antiquity*, 2 vols., Ann Arbor, Mich.: University of Michigan Press.

—— (1993). *Roman Aristocrats in Barbarian Gaul: Strategies for Survival in an Age of Transition*, Austin, Tex.: University of Texas Press.

Matthews, John F. (2000). *Laying Down the Law: A Study of the Theodosian Code*, New Haven and London: Yale University Press.

Maxwell, Jaclyn (2006). *Christianization and Communication in Late Antiquity: John Chrysostom and his Congregation in Antioch*, Cambridge: Cambridge University Press.

Millar, Fergus (2006). *A Greek Roman Empire: Power and Belief under Theodosius II (408–450)*, Berkeley and Los Angeles: University of California Press.

Mitchell, Stephen (2006). *A History of the Later Roman Empire, AD 284–641*, Oxford: Blackwell.

Momigliano, Arnaldo, ed. (1963). *The Conflict Between Paganism and Christianity in the Fourth Century*, Oxford: Clarendon Press, 1963.

Pohl, Walter, and Reimitz, Helmut, eds. (1998). *Strategies of Distinction: the Construction of Ethnic Communities, 300–800*, *TRW* 2, Leiden: Brill.

—— ed. (1997). *Kingdoms of Empire: The Integration of Barbarians in Late Antiquity*, *TRW* 1, Leiden: Brill.

Potter, David (2004). *The Roman Empire at Bay, AD 180–395*, London: Routledge.

Rapp, Claudia (2005). *Holy Bishops in Late Antiquity*, Berkeley and Los Angeles: University of California Press.

Rousseau, Philip, ed. (2009). *A Companion to Late Antiquity*, Oxford: Blackwell.

Salzman, Michele Renee (1990). *On Roman Time: The Codex-Calendar of 354 and the Rhythms of Urban Life in Late Antiquity*, Berkeley: University of California Press.

—— (2002), *The Making of a Christian Aristocracy: Social and Religious Change in the Western Roman Empire*, Cambridge, Mass.: Harvard University Press.

Schwartz, Seth (2001). *Imperialism and Jewish society, 200 B.C.E. to 640 C.E.*, Princeton: Princeton University Press.

Straw, Carole, and Lim, Richard, eds. (2004). *The Past Before Us: The Challenge of Historiographies of Late Antiquity*, Bibliothèque de l'*Antiquité Tardive* 6/Smith College Studies in History 53, Turnhout: Brepols.

Swain, Simon, and Edwards, Mark (2006). *Approaching Late Antiquity: The Transformation from Early to Late Empire*, Oxford: Oxford University Press.

Van Dam, Raymond (1993). *Saints and their Miracles in Late Antique Gaul*, Princeton: Princeton University Press.

Ward-Perkins, Bryan (2005). *The Fall of Rome and the End of Civilization*, Oxford: Oxford University Press.

White, Hayden V. (1973). *Metahistory: The Historical Imagination in Nineteenth Century Europe*, Baltimore: Johns Hopkins University Press.

Woolf, Greg (1998). *Becoming Roman: The Origins of Provincial Civilization in Gaul*, Cambridge: Cambridge University Press.

CHAPTER 35

POWER

WILLIAM V. HARRIS

INTRODUCTION

THE idea of Rome and the idea of power are inextricably linked. Rome's empire lasted longer than any except China's, and we may wonder what human being ever exercised more power than the more effective kind of Roman emperor—Augustus, say, or Trajan. But what is power, and what are the best ways of analysing its workings in a historical society? These questions were never easy, and since Foucault made such 'promiscuous' use of the term (Green 1999: section 1), the complexities have increased still further. An added difficulty is that historians of Rome seem to be especially liable to power-*worship*.

Any worthwhile analysis of power in the Roman world, however brief, has to be three-dimensional. It has to capture the dimension of national power, the domination by the gradually expanding group of those who called themselves Romans over the rest of the empire's inhabitants, together with their power along the empire's edges and beyond them. It must also capture the dimension of social differentiation or social class, without underestimating the importance of the political structures or of slavery or of gender power. And it must take full account of time and of the discontinuities as well as the continuities to be encountered in the 800 or 900 years of more or less accessible Roman history. And finally all of this will be much more valuable if it is done within a large comparison with other empires: it can, for instance, be safely assumed that most empires maintain their power with the help of co-opted local elites—so what was specific or exceptional about the ways the Romans did that? A number of empires have structured power relations by means of complex systems of law, so why is it that we look upon the Roman Empire as the great historical example of this phenomenon?

A system of law is an abstraction, and that will remind us that abstractions as well as people and groups of people exercise power: the Roman Empire itself is an abstraction, the Roman state is an abstraction, so is any given social class, so is religious belief. The ideas conveyed by images and buildings can have power (so that it has become natural to speak of the power of the images themselves). Traditions can have power. Emotions—anger, for instance—can have power, as historians have increasingly come to recognize. Stoicism, arguably the most powerful ideology of the high Roman Empire, is another abstraction. Slogans can exercise power too, especially perhaps if their meaning is highly unstable—*libertas* is the extreme Roman example (cf. Mouritsen 2001: 9–13). It is widely held, on the other hand, that ideas exercised relatively little power in the Roman world. So part of our task is to decide which abstractions are important.

To ward off excessive abstraction, however, I intend to illustrate the big historical processes, as much as possible in this very limited space, with the behaviour of individuals. And not all of these individuals will be emperors or senators, for it is a characteristic of power that even in the most centralized state it is extremely diffuse: the village policemen and the petty tax-gatherers of the Roman Empire exercised a sort of power as well as mighty dignitaries, and even within a system of brutal slavery, power of various kinds could in certain circumstances come into the hands of the unfree. One historian says that Christian visionaries had power in the high Roman Empire (Lane Fox 1994: 130), and in a limited sense that is clearly true.

Here is an illustration: a third-century CE mosaic floor from Smirat in coastal Tunisia commemorates a *venatio*, a massacre of wild animals, a favourite Roman sport. There is text as well as pictures, and the cries of the spectators are imagined: 'when was there ever such a show (*munus*)? . . . Magerius pays. That's what it is to be rich, that's what it is to have power (*hoc est posse*) . . .' (Beschaouch 1966). Magerius has wealth and local power (he is otherwise unknown). Everything here seems Roman—Rome had controlled this territory for 400 years. But others have power at Smirat too, the spectators to some extent, and also the 'hunters', the Telegenii, who provided the leopards and killed them.

How then did the Romans themselves, at various periods, think of the workings of power? We shall see *andando avanti*. But two questions are worth posing immediately.

(1) Was Roman thinking about power exceptionally legalistic? The natural answer seems to be yes: the Republic expressed many of the major changes in its own evolution in the form of laws, and there was a strong strain of legal pedantry in its public life. Technically proficient and politically influential experts on law were a constant feature from the first century BCE onwards. But it may be that the intense attention given to the delimitation of *potestas* (legally or constitutionally established

power) and *imperium* (the right of certain high officials to get their orders obeyed) was a result not simply of an especially legalistic mentality, but of the particular nature of the Roman social-political system itself. Under the Republic this system was aristocratic—the inner circle of power was indeed hard to enter—and even under the Principate it was socially exclusive; but at the same time the ordinary citizens had specific rights (see among others Wirszubski 1950: 24–30), and for centuries these were jealously guarded. Definitions were necessary.

(2) What was the relationship between ideology and reality? A considerable amount of what Romans said and wrote about power consisted of myth-making, and we ought to identify the prevailing myths. One is illustrated by a passage of Cicero, *On Laws*: speaking of the relationship between the citizens and the magistrates, he wrote that 'he who obeys ought to hope that one day he will command (*imperaturum*)'—which for most Romans would have been the wildest delusion. Two centuries later Aelius Aristides (*To Rome*) could solemnly tell the Romans that their political system was, under the rule of one man, a 'perfect democracy'. Presumably such fantasies mattered.

A final introductory comment. We are not pledged to obey any theoretical master, and theoreticians will be kept in the background. By the end, however, it should be clear which of them have turned out to be most illuminating. It may be said at once that a historian of empire and slavery is unlikely to be very satisfied by a Parsons-like model of power resting on accepted legitimacy, as distinct from, say, force or coercion, even if, as in the case of Rome, authority was less contested than in some other empires.

The Romans Against Outsiders, Down to Tiberius

Rome's power over its neighbours came in the first place from the sharp end of its soldiers' spears, but even in the first stages of Rome's historically known expansion, in the fourth century BCE, matters were much more complex. What was most remarkable of all was not the Romans' extraordinary ability to win battles so often, but their propensity for establishing enduring power over the peoples they defeated, so that the territory under Roman control expanded by about 3,000 per cent between 400 and 280 BCE, until it stretched from the Arno valley to the Italian peninsula's heel and toe.

The Romans were able to achieve this because of a combination of advantages, including their geographical position (which translated into demographic strength). Rome's war- and honour-oriented landowning elite, as its wealth increased, had more and more time to think about military expansion and carry it out, and furthermore, it could rely on a disciplined citizen population which was evidently convinced that it benefited from this same expansion. But the most important factor of all—what distinguished Rome from any number of other embryonic empires—was 'the invention of new organizational techniques that greatly enhanced the capacity to control peoples and territories' (Mann 1986: 3).

Which techniques were actually new in the crucial period between 340 and 280 is clear only in part: oppressive treaties may not have been new, while on the other hand Roman-style colonization and long-distance road-building undoubtedly were. The bilateral treaties Rome imposed on most of the states in peninsular Italy commonly included forced expropriation of land on a large scale, and a system of virtual conscription; Rome also on occasion disrupted local religious life, and Roman power also tended to marginalize and later eliminate local languages. Yet this system would not have worked in the long run if there had not been a persistent effort to accommodate those Italians who collaborated, above all the members of local ruling elites. The latter exercised a high degree of local autonomy, while the Romans, unencumbered by any wish to administer local affairs, concentrated on their own military and material interests. By the time Hannibal invaded Italy in 218, Roman power was imposing enough, and also acceptable enough, to ensure—though by a quite narrow margin—that the many Italians who welcomed the invader were balanced by many others who stayed loyal (on Hannibal's reception in Italy, see Salmon 1982: 78–89).

A Mediterranean state demonstrated its military power by its ability to dispatch substantial forces by sea. Rome owned warships by the late fourth century BCE, but became a great naval power quite abruptly once it decided, from 264 onwards, to challenge Carthage. The two states committed no fewer than 680 warships to the battle of Ecnomus (256), and Rome conquered the Mediterranean world because it possessed, in addition to the advantages mentioned above, the resources to dominate the sea. Between the first war against Carthage (264–241) and the battle of Pydna (168), which put an end to the Macedonian monarchy, Rome effectively eliminated as naval rivals all four of the other leading Mediterranean powers. Polybius was right to say that Pydna gave Rome command over the (Mediterranean) world, in the sense that no one could afterwards afford to disobey. A famous incident that took place in Egypt later that same year illustrated the new reality: when King Antiochus IV of Syria, invading, had reached Pelusium, he was met by an ex-consul, C. Popillius Laenas, the practically unarmed emissary of the Senate; Popillius ordered the king to withdraw, and when the latter asked for time to consult his advisers, the Roman drew a circle round him in the dust and bluntly told him to consent before he stepped out of the circle. Antiochus had to comply.

This is not the place to give even a summary account of the phenomenal growth of Roman power outside Italy which continued from 264 BCE until the emperor Tiberius called a halt to the war in Germany in 16 CE (this turned out to be a major turning-point). Except on the rarest of occasions, Rome made war every year throughout that period (Harris 1985: 9–10), which made it an extreme case of belligerence (cf. Finley 1983: 129). I will attempt instead to answer four cardinal questions.

(1) What caused Rome to behave, in general, so aggressively? What drove the Romans forward? There was a huge evolution. In 264 BCE Roman life was to a great extent centred on warfare, and there were dangerous enemies within a few days' travel. The senatorial order was dominated by a military ethos, a highly functional ethos that promoted the Senate's own political power (not least by selecting the younger men who would receive promotion) and its economic well-being. Meanwhile the ordinary citizens, brought up in military traditions, could still expect to do well from successful military campaigns. The strength of these factors appeared very clearly during the first two, very long and painful, wars against Carthage (264–241, 218–202). But there is more: after Hannibal's surprise invasion of Italy it might have seemed obvious that all Roman troops were needed in the peninsula, but instead Rome kept an army in Spain throughout the war, and sent another to Greece well before Hannibal had been driven out—in other words, there was a risk-taking strategic boldness about Rome that finds few parallels, especially in non-monarchical states.

After the defeat of Carthage at Zama (202) there was no power anywhere in the Mediterranean that could stand up to a prolonged Roman onslaught, and in short order the battles of Cynoscephalae (197), Myonnesus (190), and Magnesia (190) demonstrated Rome's superiority over the Macedonian and Seleucid monarchies. Rome's characteristic behaviour did not change at first, though in the years 151–146 we can probably see Roman citizens becoming more reluctant to fight tough and unprofitable wars, while the last war against Carthage (149–146) and the destruction of both Carthage and Corinth in 146 suggest a still more ruthless Rome. By the 120s participation in war, previously a requirement for members of the senatorial elite, had begun to be optional. Still, all the 'great men' of the late Republic built their careers on military victories, which brought spectacular wealth and still conferred prestige. Nowhere is this last truth more evident than in the campaigns of both Octavian and M. Antonius in the 30s, when a 'rational' modern calculation would have led them to concentrate on each other rather than on largely unnecessary foreign wars. With Octavian's victory at Actium the whole nature of Rome's decision-making changed for ever. But it was not simply 'path-dependance' that made Augustus engage in nearly forty years of military expansion: it was expected of him and it added to his authority (see *Res Gestae* 26–7, 30); there can be little doubt that it was also intended to add to Rome's revenues (cf. Strabo 4.200–1). Yet Augustus, at the end of his life, advised his successor to 'maintain the empire within its existing boundaries', and most—not by any means all—later emperors followed this advice.

(2) What were the organizational techniques by which these conquests outside Italy became permanent dominions? Rome adapted its city-state institutions extremely well to the ruling of empire. The major initial innovations were the creation of territorial provinces and of extra senatorial magistracies in order to provide them with continuous supervision. But that is only the most obvious part of the story: equally important was a level of diplomatic activity that was already quite intense by 200 BCE, involving communication with cities and peoples in the provinces, and the maintenance of an informal empire of vassal states outside. Tax-gathering and law-enforcement were largely left in local hands, until during the late Republic private contractors based in Rome itself (the *publicani*) got their hands on much of the work of taxation. The system allowed ample room for private Roman profiteering, and Tacitus can easily be believed when he writes that the provincials were pleased when Augustus replaced it. The new system was more centralized and much better supervised; it also integrated more provincials into the Roman state, by, among other things, recruiting legionaries in select provinces and spreading Roman citizenship (and with it the Roman legal system) much more rapidly.

The written word was also in a sense an organizational technique, and empires depend on it. The beginnings of this technology of domination can easily be seen in mid-Republican Rome: the census kept track of military manpower, and the army already made extensive use of written documents (Harris 1989: 166).

(3) What did Roman power overseas mean in practice? After the initial death and destruction, it of course meant taxes (impossible to judge how onerous they really were under the Republic), and—usually more onerous still—the private enterprise of senatorial officials and their associates. The classic texts illustrating this type of exploitation (Cicero on Verres and Cicero on the town of Salamis on Cyprus) are *ex parte*, but no one doubts that it was generally ruthless, with a tendency towards violence. The best that could be said for Roman rule in this era was that, until the civil wars began in earnest in 49 BCE, it usually prevented war; and also that it sometimes encouraged the resolution of disputes between local communities (the case of Contrebia in the valley of the Ebro provides an example: Richardson 1983). Caesar and Augustus, however, brought about significant changes by, among other measures, settling numerous colonists from one end of the empire to the other. Under the first emperor provincial communities were more often called upon to protest their loyalty (to 'Rome and Augustus'), but the financial burdens probably decreased. How much thought this ruler gave to anything we might call 'Romanization' is open to dispute.

(4) What successful imperialism did to the Romans themselves is another complex story. Power had effects far more interesting than mere corruption or economic opportunity, though there was a good deal of both. It led to the Hellenization of the Roman elite, which, whatever it may have amounted to in the second century, was by the time of Sulla, Pompey, and Cicero much more than

a surface veneer (if only we knew what exactly Cicero meant when he wrote that the Epicureans had 'conquered Italy'). Most historians reject the notion that Greek ideas seriously weakened the republican system of government, but believe that empire somehow undid the governmental system of the rulers. The conventional view is that a large empire from time to time necessitated huge military commands, which had the effect of putting strong, personally loyal armies into the hands of men such as Sulla and Caesar who could not resist the temptation to use them. Empire undoubtedly had two effects of huge political significance: it necessitated the recruitment of impoverished soldiers who had little reason to support the political status quo; and it created an enormous (by ancient standards) capital city—incomparably wealthy and grand, and also well endowed with slums—that by the 60s (indeed two generations earlier) was no longer willing to acquiesce in conservative aristocratic control. One-man rule was the logical outcome.

The Romans Against Each Other, from Republic to Monarchy

Republican Rome was ruled by an aristocracy: in each of its last three years, 51–49, one of the consulships was held by a Claudius Marcellus, members of a family that had held twelve other consulships as well as innumerable other offices since 331. Political, religious, social, and economic power remained until the late Republic within the same social stratum, and even when there were fortunes outside it, they were closely linked to the old ruling families. But this was an aristocracy of a peculiar kind that coexisted with a degree of citizen power, not in any circumstances to be confused with democracy (though in the late Republic the masses too could make themselves heard). No one held executive office for more than a year, except the censors, who lasted for eighteen months. Rather than recounting in detail how this system worked (see Lintott 1999), I shall outline the main political and other means by which the elite held on to power, how it came to be threatened from the 130s onwards, and why in the end it was replaced by a somewhat different kind of elite (the battles of Pharsalus and Actium were important, but the reign of Tiberius was once again a major turning-point).

Foucault maintained that:

> relations of power... necessarily extend beyond the limits of the State... first of all because the State... is far from being able to occupy the whole field of actual power relations, and further because the State can only operate on the basis of other, already existing power relations. The State is superstructural in relation to a whole series of power networks that

invest the body, sexuality, the family, kinship, knowledge, technology and so forth. (1980/1977: 122).

The terminological reminiscence of Marx requires us to consider what in this case is superstructural and what is basic. A full account of Roman power under the Republic and Augustus would have to take into account, among many other things, the interference of the censors in what we would consider private life, the real meaning of *patria potestas* (it taught that a citizen must even be willing to sacrifice the life of his own son for the sake of Rome: Harris 1986), and the stern discipline of the legions (Phang 2008, esp. 243–8). Members of the senatorial elite kept to themselves certain vital kinds of knowledge, especially religious knowledge. And we should not neglect gladiatorial games—fights to the death, mostly it seems between prisoners-of-war—organized by magistrates and already popular in the second century BCE. But what was most basic of all was the effective possession of land.

As Rome's external power grew during the fourth century BCE, the patrician caste struggled unsuccessfully to exclude well-to-do plebeians from public office, and the more durable plebeian families gradually became the other half of the aristocracy. In the same period the ordinary citizens struggled, successfully, to abolish enslavement for debt (*nexum*) (the Poetelian Law, probably of 313). This was much assisted by the influx of chattel slaves that resulted from successful warfare. Over the next century-and-a-half this influx made Rome into the classic Mediterranean slave state. Three events can illustrate the scale: when Rome enslaved 150,000 Epirots in 167 BCE its own official citizen numbers were only 313,000 (adult males); when Caesar conquered the Gauls we are told that he enslaved more than 400,000 of them. When Augustus conquered Pannonia in 12 BCE his commander 'sold most of the men of military age into slavery outside the province'. The economic and other effects of this slave system were pervasive.

The formal powers of the magistrates over the citizens were restrictive but not unlimited. Citizens could be compelled to undertake military service and were forbidden to address meetings on political subjects unless invited to do so by a magistrate or by a tribune of the people. It is significant that the *ius provocationis* ('right of appeal') was considered a major right, even though it *only* gave protection against condemnation to death or flogging by a single magistrate (like many topics raised in this chapter, *provocatio* is controversial: Cloud 1998).

In practice the senatorial elite was able, under the middle Republic, to maintain control of both electoral and legislative assemblies, partly thanks to rules that favoured the men of property, especially in the most important elections, partly thanks to inherited loyalties and other forms of informal power. The most interesting office is undoubtedly the tribunate of the *plebs*, much the most powerful one under the control of the tribal assembly; when a determined reformer such as Tiberius Gracchus made use of the tribune's right to propose legislation, the political climate began to change. The Senate had been in power, unchallenged, since time immemorial, helped by the confidentiality of its proceedings and by an aura of prestige. But when its power at last met some opposition, it had no solution beyond violent repression.

The history of political power in the late Republic is a highly contested affair, partly because the struggles of that time prefigure modern ones. The first sign of trouble comes in 151 when the tribunes, in a dispute with the consuls over the draft, imprisoned them; the same happened again in 138. From 139 onwards a series of four ballot laws increased the *libertas* of those Roman citizens who were able to make use of them (Harris 1989: 167–70). (But apropos of *libertas*, we must not forget Syme's formulation (1939: 155): 'the *libertas* of the Roman aristocrat meant the power of a class and the perpetuation of privilege'.)

When a threat to the actual property of the well-to-do emerged, with Gracchus' agrarian law in 133, the conservative senatorial majority resorted to murder, led by a former consul. The same fate overtook the younger Gracchus twelve years later; this time the Senate considered that the slaughter of the tribune and his followers was legalized by a decree of its own, 'that the consuls should see that the state suffered no harm' (the notorious 'final decree of the Senate'). Troublesome tribunes were then slaughtered one after another, Saturninus, Livius Drusus, Sulpicius Rufus, Clodius—Catiline too (an ex-praetor in the Senate). What historians like to call the mob—in other words, ordinary people—had many causes for discontent; it must be significant that some of them supported the slave rebellion led by Spartacus (73–71 BCE). Finally they found a leader who was too astute to be assassinated—Caesar, who brought down the republican system with wide popular support but then, in spite of some radical measures, showed that he was mostly on the side of hierarchy and property after all.

Over a period of about eighty years, starting when Caesar invaded peninsular Italy in 49 and concluding when his nominal grandson Tiberius turned to (the almost inevitable) treason-trials, Rome's political system changed from a kind of aristocracy to a near-absolute monarchy. Syme (1939: 7) asserted that this change was superficial, for power, he said, belonged to an oligarchy both before and afterwards. But this judgement may have understated an important change, for while oligarchy may abide, the recruitment methods of oligarchies vary enormously; see below.

We should also consider the power of Rome's rulers in more sociological terms. It would take an entire volume to weigh the relative importance of legitimate authority, surveillance, and the distribution of rewards through systems of patronage and otherwise (see Matheson 1987 for some conceptual tools; and see Lendon 2006 for a provocative discussion). We might conclude that all three factors were at work in the Roman world, both under the Republic and under the emperors. Under the Republic what was distinctive perhaps was that Rome's fearsome reputation often allowed it to employ the threat of force without much actual surveillance in Italy or the pacified provinces. Whether Rome's always draconian penology (see Robinson 2006) had similar effects on the domestic population is a question still to be investigated fully.

Augustus attempted of course to maximize his legitimate authority. His power was genuinely imperial, but it was not, strictly speaking, absolute: he put his personal enemies to death (the Fannius conspirators), but not in great numbers. It was Tiberius who 'broke the back of the Roman aristocracy' (Yavetz 1996: 121).

The Romans Against Outsiders, First to Fifth Centuries CE

Who is inside, who is outside? The Romans sometimes seem confused to us because they often said that the whole world was under Roman control (Brunt 1990: 433–4; the practice continued in the fourth century: Ando 2000: 333–4) even though the governing class knew that this was false, and indeed often indicated that the outsiders were there to be conquered (cf. Tacitus, *Annals* 4.32 end).

Attitudes towards those who had already been conquered gradually evolved. In Tiberius' time, in spite of the changes we have already itemized, Rome perceived the empire as existing for the benefit of Rome and perhaps Italy (Tiberius said that he wanted his sheep to be 'shorn, not flayed alive', but in any case the provinces were the sheep). By the time of Diocletian's Price Edict (301), the emperors spoke of 'our provincials'—and taxed them all, including the Italians (as to how much the provincials had really taken on a Roman identity by this time, that is a separate question).

Meanwhile, starting with Tiberius, imperial expansion had decelerated. Roman power spread to new areas such as Britain and Dacia, but relatively slowly. The reasons for this change can be debated (the best account is given by Cornell 1993); notwithstanding the prestige that a conquering emperor could still claim, most rulers of Rome no longer thought that wars of conquest were worthwhile, not least because successful generals made them nervous. When Septimius Severus, Caracalla, and later Julian revived the tradition of conquest, they had to take command themselves.

The Roman army had never been invincible, and its deplorable failure to protect the Danube frontier in 170–1 CE has many possible causes. In the third century, however, Rome's power along the frontiers was in decline for a period of a good forty years. How much this was attributable to internal weaknesses other than frequent strife between rival contenders for the purple is disputed (Drinkwater 2005, for example, stresses other factors, but argues for the view that the Roman Empire still possessed 'immense internal strength', 62).

The Romans Against Each Other: From Empire to Nation?

So the ground shifts again to the structures of power within the Roman Empire. The spread of Roman identity over many centuries made an oceanic difference to who exercised power in the Roman world and who it was exercised upon. Every student knows this, and we scarcely need to rehearse how the composition of the Roman governing class (the Severan emperors were of North African and Syrian descent) and of the Roman military (even in the mid-first century CE the majority of Roman soldiers were no longer Italians, let alone city-Romans) changed from the first to the fifth century CE. It is important to note how the recruitment of the ruling elite evolved: Hopkins and Burton were able to show that 'during the first three centuries AD membership of the Roman senate was to a large extent *not* hereditary' (1983: 194, my italics). It is likely that the main reason was that a relatively rapid turnover suited the interests of the emperor.

The Edict of Caracalla (212) gave Roman citizenship to all free inhabitants of the empire, which meant in particular the further gradual spread of Roman law. Local cultures, including languages, survived in most regions, but self-identification with Rome, at least on a superficial level, was by the fourth century very widespread.

Let us look at these structures of power from as many angles of vision as possible. First of all, from a woman's point of view. No political rights of course, only the possibility of influencing the male. On the other hand, women had extensive property rights, limited more or less by the institution of guardianship; and they could be merchants or doctors. In Roman law they could initiate divorce, in theory, and they could sue (on all this see Gardner 1986). But a vast amount depended on class and status: rich ladies could put their slaves to death if they felt like it, while female slaves could literally not call their bodies their own.

So let us face this matter of class. It should be clear that social classes existed in the Roman Empire (Finley 1983: 3; Harris 1988), but it is certainly not clear how to define them or whether it makes sense, or illuminates Roman history, to say that one class exercised power over another. Three distinct groups were: (i) well-to-do persons who, while they might pay careful attention to their investments, had access to all the amenities that existed and had no need to work; the political class in the capital was of course recruited exclusively from this group. (ii) Those who in practice or in law had very few assets, who worked for others for wages or as slaves. (iii) Those in between who possessed enough land to make their physical existence more or less secure, or a skill and a shop that would have the same effect. Our concern here is whether the first and last of these groups exercised power *as classes*, and we can at least say that the social elite, inside and outside the government, loyally defended the rights of property; from Augustus onwards, expressions of popular discontent were fragmented and usually suppressed without difficulty. The men of property successfully operated the whole system of civil law for their own benefit (Kelly 1966).

The most combustible confrontations may have concerned lower-ranking officials. One has the impression of fairly arbitrary exercises of power by police and tax-gatherers, but that may be inevitable in a society that was neither democratic nor (by modern or even by traditional Chinese standards) bureaucratic (on the last point, see Miles 1990: 640, using work by Richard Saller). 'Recently a certain collector of taxes was appointed in our area. When some of the men who were apparently in arrears because of poverty fled in fear of unbearable punishment, he laid violent hands on their wives, children, parents, and other relatives, beating and trampling them and visiting every outrage on them ... he racked their bodies with twistings and tortures, and killed them off with newly contrived modes of death': that is Philo, writing about Egypt under Tiberius. How typical was this?

Higher officials, civil and military, paid attention to precedent and administered a system of laws and regulations. More perhaps than in most empires, ordinary people in the Roman Empire seem commonly to have believed that they could obtain redress for their grievances from the emperor or the governor or their subordinates. And down to the Severan period at least, the governmental powers did sometimes respond (see e.g. Potter 2004: 5, on Africa Proconsularis under Commodus), thereby making use of one of the instruments of power that could serve as an alternative to coercion. Connections and financial resources naturally helped a person to gain official attention.

It was, of course, a sign of the near-absolute power of the ruler that the emperor's anger was a constant preoccupation, at least in court circles (Harris 2002: 249–63): if the emperor did not realize the value of self-restraint and behave accordingly, there was no other safeguard. Those in danger were primarily the members of the political class, for ancient conditions made it hard for a ruler to produce widespread misery on purpose.

How close did the state come to monopolizing force (a trickier concept than is sometimes recognized)? In the countryside—where the majority of the population lived—it is reasonably plain that men of property could get away with violence. The Roman government did not consider it necessary to disarm its subjects (see Brunt 1975/90). 'Self-help', by means of force, was to some extent permitted to the wealthy, and more so in the fourth century (Hopwood 2002: 73–4).

Into one enormous set of often violent power relations the state scarcely entered, at least until the Antonine age: the relationship between slaveholder and slave. There were admittedly palliatives, including a significant amount of manumission, but ill-treatment, including frequent corporal punishment, was taken for granted (see Harris 2002: ch. 13, for the dynamic).

A last angle of vision: the power of ideas. There is in fact a huge study to be undertaken here, for it can be argued that certain ideas had limited but defining effects, the civilizing mission of *humanitas* that gained ground in the second half of the first century CE (Pliny, *Natural History* 3.39), ideas loosely associated with Stoicism that led to legislation in favour of slaves, an ideal of *paideia* that for better and for worse shaped the way that the men of property educated their sons and occasionally their daughters. How strongly religious ideas affected the social elite is something of an open question. Its individual and collective behaviour is for the most part readily explicable without reference to religion, but it can be argued that that was because, at Rome even more than in other empires, the transcendental was integrated into the political (see Runciman 2005). As to popular religiosity—how can we measure it? Priestly power, except in a few atypical provinces, was minimal. But both magic and *outré* cults (Christianity being the most *outré* of all) continued to offer access to alternative universes where the emperor and his horrid agents were replaced by quite other powers.

The Decline of Roman Power

This is another immense topic, of course. Why in the first place did the Roman state lose so much of its power in the face of Germanic invasions over two generations between the 370s and the 430s? The debate started as soon as the event took place, and started again during the Enlightenment. I will simply make a proposal, not especially original (for other perspectives, see Ward-Perkins 2005 and also MacMullen 2006). Rather as the Republican political system lacked the firm support of numerous Roman citizens during its last decades, so the population of the Roman Empire failed to react adequately to serious external dangers to the western half of the empire. The government did little for its citizens, whom it was unable to defend from enemies, soldiers, or bandits. Their most basic freedoms had been further eroded, above all by Constantine, and they were now sharply split—as never before—in fundamental matters of religion. The citizen militia that had resisted Hannibal was very remote indeed. This kind of explanation is best set out, with some exaggeration, by de Ste. Croix (1981).

Whether the Late Roman Empire became much more bureaucratic, as is widely believed (for a recent statement see Kelly 2004), might be questioned. The nature of our sources changes. It is not, in any case, especially difficult to identify the new power-holders of the fourth- and fifth-century empire: they are primarily episcopal. Men such as Ambrose, Synesius, and Sidonius Apollinaris—very different from each other—exercised real political power as well as shepherding their own flocks.

But what is most remarkable perhaps is the ongoing power of the large landowners. We can end as we began, with mosaics, but this time the scale is incomparably grander: the famous mosaics of Piazza Armerina (Wilson 1983), a Blenheim-like residence in Sicily datable to about 325 CE, cover a full hectare-and-a-half, and are now generally agreed to have belonged to someone *outside* the imperial family, perhaps L. Aradius Valerius Proculus, a protégé of Constantine's, whose father when urban prefect at Rome had rapidly joined the winning side after the battle of Saxa Rubra. Now when Piazza Armerina was built the western Roman Empire still stood; the point is that when, a century later, it no longer did so, there were still men such as Sidonius Apollinaris who lived in a grand style and wielded great personal power.

References

Ando, C., *Imperial Ideology and Provincial Loyalty in the Roman Empire* (Berkeley, 2000).

Beschaouch, A., 'La Mosaïque de chasse à l'amphithéâtre découverte à Smirat en Tunisie', *CRAI* (1966), 134–57.

Brunt, P. A., 'Did Imperial Rome Disarm her Subects?', *Phoenix*, 29 (1975), 260–70, repr. in Brunt 1990: 255–66.

—— *Roman Imperial Themes* (Oxford, 1990).

Cloud, D., 'The Origin of *provocatio*', *Revue de Philologie*, 72 (1998), 25–48.

Cornell, T., 'The End of Roman Imperial Expansion', in J. Rich and G. Shipley (eds.), *War and Society in the Roman World* (London, 1993), 139–70.

de Ste. Croix, G. E. M., *The Class Struggle in the Ancient Greek World* (London, 1981).

Drinkwater, J. F., 'Maximinus to Diocletian and the "Crisis"', in *Cambridge Ancient History²*, vol. 12 (Cambridge, 2005), 28–66.

Finley, M. I., *Politics in the Ancient World* (Cambridge, 1983).

Foucault, M., 'Truth and Power', in *Power/Knowledge: Selected Interviews and Other Writings 1972–1977*, ed. C. Gordon (New York, 1980), 109–33; the original appeared in Foucault's *Microfisica del potere* (Turin, 1977).

Gardner, J. F., *Women in Roman Law and Society* (London, 1986).

Green, L., 'Power' [1999], in E. Craig (ed.), *Routledge Encyclopedia of Philosophy*, www.rep.routledge.com/article/5046/ (seen 4.ix.06).

Harris, W. V., *War and Imperialism in Republican Rome, 327–70 BC* (rev. edn., Oxford, 1985).

—— 'The Roman Father's Power of Life and Death', in *Studies in Roman Law in Memory of A. Arthur Schiller* (Leiden, 1986), 81–95.

—— 'On the Applicability of the Concept of Class in Roman History', in T. Yuge and M. Doi (eds.), *Forms of Control and Subordination in Antiquity* (Tokyo and Leiden, 1988), 598–610 (repr. in *Rome's Imperial Economy* (Oxford, forthcoming)).

—— *Ancient Literacy* (Cambridge, Mass., 1989).

—— *Restraining Rage: The Ideology of Anger Control in Classical Antiquity* (Cambridge, Mass., 2002).

Hopkins, K., *Death and Renewal* (Cambridge, 1983).

Hopwood, K., 'Aspects of Violent Crime in the Roman Empire', in *Thinking Like a Lawyer: Essays on Legal History and General History for John Crook on his Eightieth Birthday* (Leiden, 2002), 63–80.

Kelly, C., *Ruling the Later Roman Empire* (Cambridge, Mass., 2004).

Kelly, J. M., *Roman Litigation* (Oxford, 1966).

Lane Fox, R., 'Literacy and Power in Early Christianity', in A. K. Bowman and G. Woolf (eds.), *Literacy and Power in the Ancient World* (Cambridge, 1994), 126–48.

Lendon, J. E., 'The Legitimacy of the Roman Emperor: Against Weberian Legitimacy and Imperial "Strategies of Legitimation"', in A. Kolb (ed.), *Herrschaftstrukturen und Herrschaftspraxis* (Berlin, 2006), 53–63.

Lintott, A. W., *The Constitution of the Roman Republic* (Oxford, 1999).

MacMullen, R., 'The Power of the Roman Empire', *Historia*, 55 (2006), 471–81.

Mann, M., *The Sources of Social Power*, I (Cambridge, 1986).

Matheson, C., 'Weber and the Classification of Forms of Legitimacy', *British Journal of Sociology*, 38 (1987), 199–215.

Miles, G. B., 'Roman and Modern Imperialism: A Reassessment', *Comparative Studies in Society and History*, 32 (1990), 629–59.

Mouritsen, H., *Plebs and Politics in the Late Roman Republic* (Cambridge, 2001).

Phang, S. E., *Roman Military Service: Ideologies of Discipline in the Late Republic and Early Empire* (Cambridge, 2008).

Potter, D. S., *The Roman Empire at Bay, AD 180–395* (London, 2004).

Price, S. R. F., Rituals and Power: The Roman Imperial Cult in Asia Minor (Cambridge, 1984).

Richardson, J. S., 'The Tabula Contrebiensis: Roman Law in Spain in the Early First Century B.C.', *Journal of Roman Studies*, 73 (1983), 33–41.

Robinson, O. F., *Penal Practice and Penal Policy in Ancient Rome* (London, 2006).

Runciman, W. G., 'The Exception that Proves the Rule? Rome in the Axial Age', in E. Ben-Rafael and Y. Sternberg (eds.), *Comparing Modernities: Pluralism versus Homogeneity: Essays in Homage to Shmuel N. Eisenstadt* (Leiden, 2005), 125–40.

Salmon, E. T., *The Making of Roman Italy* (London, 1982).

Syme, R., *The Roman Revolution* (Oxford, 1939).

Ward-Perkins, B., *The Fall of Rome and the End of Civilization* (Oxford, 2005).

Wilson, R. J. A., *Piazza Armerina* (Austin, Tex., 1983).

Wirszubski, C., *Libertas as a Political Idea at Rome During the Late Republic and Early Principate* (Cambridge, 1950).

Yavetz, Z., 'Caligula, Imperial Madness and Modern Historiography', *Klio*, 78 (1996), 105–29.

CHAPTER 36

URBANISM

NICHOLAS PURCELL

ROMAN cities were just like Greek cities. Talking about urbanism from Homer to Procopius, from the first age of writing in Greek to the Mediterranean of late antiquity, it is perfectly sensible to speak of 'the ancient city', or even 'the Greek city'. We can readily distinguish such an urban category from—for instance—Egyptian or Mesopotamian urbanism, from the new settlement patterns in the Iron Age cultures with which Greeks and Romans interacted, and from medieval Islamic and Christian cities. In many ways, across 1,500 years of urban history, common qualities unite the 'ancient city' more than historical change splits it up.

The case could be made in several ways. It could be economic. The 'ancient city' represented a distinctive pattern of control of a productive landscape, and of the disposal of the fruits of that control. It could be social. These cities based a distinctive order of statuses, obligations, and rights upon those economic relations. It could be cultural. That distinctive order maintained its legitimacy through wielding a common and complex tradition of self-expression and community identity, in which the city itself played a central role. Or it could be physical. Economic, social, cultural forms were all expressed in a traditional set of manipulations of urban and rural landscapes and of the built environment, which made the ancient city a coherent set of urban architectonic and spatial forms to look at or to be in.

In all those respects, from the first urban age of Rome in the sixth century BCE to 410 CE, when Alaric sacked it, Roman cities—Rome and the dozens of cities founded as part of Roman political projects—closely resembled Greek ones.

Let us take the resemblances one by one in the same order.

That system of statuses, based on variable access to the product of land and labour, was made visible in ways which were consciously drawn from the traditional expressions of a similar hierarchy in Greek communities since the seventh century BCE. The wealth-elite displayed what it owned in elaborate conspicuous consumption, including devouring time through showy leisure. But the rest of the entitled citizenry also had to be included, albeit in a subordinate way, through a carefully modulated share in the privileges and rewards of the elite, dispensed through private patronage, benefaction, and administrative decision by the elite acting politically. The ways in which the whole citizen body was supposed to participate, in Rome and its cities—shared religious rites, cultural entertainments, military and sub-military training, and civic institutions—closely resembled Greek norms. The system was expressed, maintained, and enriched by traditional literature, access to which was itself a hallmark of elite status, and by the public deployment of the written word in inscriptions on wood, bronze, or stone, a feature of Greek public life in which many Roman cities came to specialize.

Other physical expressions of the status system were also common to Greek and Roman cities. The layout of the territory and the domestic space of the city were shaped by the regime of property. The status system and the culture which underpinned it were visible in the repertoire of buildings and open spaces—temples, political structures, city walls, commemorative displays, amenities, buildings and spaces for leisure activities—which expressed the depth and weight and authority of tradition and custom, and through which local differences of social and political ideology could be underlined.

In all of this, then, Roman cities can hardly be distinguished from Corinth in the sixth century, Athens in the fifth, Rhodes in the fourth century, Priene in the third, or Alexandria in the second. The distinctiveness of the Roman city does not lie in the local characteristics of the city, but in how it fitted into the bigger picture—networks of social and economic movement, frameworks of power.

Rome's own early urban development is a fascinating example of how new urban forms reflect social and economic change in the Iron Age Mediterranean world. Communications were vital: in this Rome was like Corinth, Carthage, or Miletus. Here, the River Tiber was the key element. Its valley gave a wide and important territory in west-central Italy access to the sea by boat or valley road, and, from lagoons in the river delta, river and road carried an important trade in salt, the indispensable wherewithal of the pastoral economy of the interior. Other early settlements in the Mediterranean prospered on river-valley communications (in Italy, the later town at Capua has a similar site, though in a far more fertile territory) but none to anything like the extent of Rome.

About 25 km from the sea, the land-route crossed the river by a cluster of low hills, and archaeology has shown how a substantial urban nucleus developed here before the end of the seventh century BCE. During the sixth century the community adapted the site with an elaborate urban infrastructure (in Greece, the modifications of the site of seventh-century Eretria are a parallel). Controlling water was especially important beside a flood-plain in an area of relatively high rainfall, and the earliest of Rome's massive stone-lined 'sewers', which became a famous monument of the city, were correctly dated by the later tradition to this epoch. Substantial defensive works were built. On the Tiber a river-harbour quarter acquired monumental sanctuaries in the style which was becoming canonical for temples in the Greek Mediterranean. The finds of this period demonstrate Rome's close links with many parts of that world, especially Corinth.

By 500 BCE the city had a levelled, planned market-place, the Forum Romanum, and a truly ambitious monumental focus in the sanctuary of Jupiter, Juno, and Minerva on the summit of the Capitoline hill, dominating both the Forum and the harbour. Building this sanctuary entailed massive landscaping of the hill, including making a roadway of moderate gradient down to the Forum to serve for festival processions. The temple itself was built on an enormous platform, to proportions which rivalled the largest shrines of archaic Greek cities, Samos, Ephesus, and Selinous. The obvious parallel for this project is the reworking of the Athenian Acropolis in the mid-sixth century, and the creation there too of conspicuous temples linked with the urban centre beneath by a processional way. At Rome, as at Athens, the reconfiguration of the central public and religious spaces of the city formulated a new identity for the community, and challenged outsiders.

Rome also shared with Greek contemporaries the setting aside of space for competitive spectacles—the valley of the Circus Maximus, where games in honour of the Capitoline cult were held. The Romans believed that religious games had been an essential part of their urban life from a very early date. Beside the Forum, the political elite responsible for the transformation of the urban landscape built a regular quarter of very large town-houses, which resemble Etruscan domestic architecture more than anything yet known in the Greek world; what appears to be a wealthy farmstead of the same period has been excavated recently on the edge of the Tiber flood-plain 3 km to the north of the urban nucleus. Both the physical extent of the early city and the (admittedly hazy) Roman tradition suggest a substantial population. The complex urban fabric could not have been created or maintained without considerable manpower, and a developed artisan base.

By 500 BCE Rome was already among the most complex and substantial urban centres of the Mediterranean, in a small group including Corinth, Athens, Miletus, Syracuse, and not many more. This success cannot be explained by the agrarian resources of Rome's immediate hinterland, which was generally cultivable, but had no special productive advantages. The gateway-function provided by the navigable Tiber helped to insert early Rome in the network of exchange which included the Etruscan coastal cities, the Greek overseas settlements, and Corinth. Among other early Mediterranean cities, essentially economic success maintained Corinth, Miletus, and Carthage and was also important at Athens and Syracuse. These last communities grew further, however, by aggressive political self-promotion, and this is likely to have been true also of Rome. High population promoted economic complexity and, above all, boosted military potential, which in turn supported further growth, especially through immigration, forced or voluntary. Rome in 500 BCE already depended more than any other urbanized Mediterranean community on an essentially aggressive dynamic which was expressed in unmissable material and ideological form in the cult-centre of the Capitoline hill.

The sixth century BCE is the key to the distinctive shape of later Roman urbanism. From then on, Rome pinned an aggressive identity, which it would carry far from home, on the characteristically urban pride with which that home had been elevated into a great Mediterranean city. Paradoxically, Roman aggression soon made Rome a state far larger than a *polis*, but one which was always highly conscious of the city which lay at its centre.

That we can call cities other than Rome 'Roman' at all marks a departure: 'Roman' is an adjective derived from one community, 'Greek' the name of a whole cultural and social complex. The Roman state began founding subsidiary daughter settlements in Italy in the fifth and fourth centuries BCE, and pioneered an urban practice which transformed Italy over the next 400 years and provided a template for an urban policy which had profound effects across the whole Roman Empire.

Later Roman tradition tended—in the face of complex and inconsistent record—to recount a master-narrative of the foundation of such cities down to the end of the Republic. We need to beware of two things. First, such a story is oversimplified, and makes Rome's ad hoc behaviour seem too regular and concerted; and later attitudes and forms are retrojected to earlier periods. Second, the Roman term for these settlements, *colonia*, is the origin of English 'colony', but that should not lead us to see Roman city-foundation as colonialism in any recognizable modern sense.

The word *colonia* strongly suggests an agrarian purpose, but the earliest settlements—such as Ostia, which controlled the mouth of the Tiber—had a clearly strategic function. They served, between their different roles, to extend coercive political authority over a territory which was soon much larger than that of most *poleis*. No doubt many of the inhabitants of such new centres were thought of as Roman. But it is important to recognize how little we know about being Roman in the fifth and fourth centuries. Roman tradition saw this as the period when the institutions which regulated citizenship and access to it for outsiders formed piecemeal. Each new city allied with the Roman state, or under direct Roman rule, involved a new set of relationships to membership of the Roman community as a whole. It was the recognition of this fact, and the evolution of responses to it, that made Roman towns different from Greek ones. One example of the complexity is especially important. Though we usually (reasonably enough) call the cities in Rome's hegemony 'Roman', the confused tradition regarding the urban history of the middle Republic also calls some of Rome's new cities after 338 BCE 'Latin', a term derived from the communities of the region south and south-east of Rome, which also spoke Latin, had their own culture, and were more or less reluctantly tied to Rome through a complex network of treaties and federations.

It helpfully enriched Rome's institutional portfolio that some Roman towns were Roman, whereas some were 'Latin'. Variety meant suppleness and flexibility.

New settlements for cultivators, strategic strong-points, control of the coasts, part-citizenship, and the idea of 'Latin' Romans were all to leave an important legacy for later practice: together with important changes to the Roman territory which they protected, which foreshadow the long history of Roman land-allotment.

Cities in antiquity were territories as well as urban nuclei. Founding a city usually meant reworking the landscape of property, expelling or downgrading previous occupiers, entitling favoured new residents with a base of landed property. The reorganization could involve the re-surveying of huge tracts of land, and their meticulous subdivision into regular plots, with a network of grid-line roads and paths giving uniform access across the whole managed landscape. The idea of the allotment, the *klēros*, was basic to Greek thinking about the citizen's stake in townscape and territory, and settlers in new communities were often assigned lands in this way, but such communities usually kept little connection with the motherland. The grids of Roman rural allotments patterned extensive landscapes all over Italy and the western provinces (where they are often fossilized within later property boundaries), and the citizen-lot remained a lively political conception at Rome until the second century CE.

Rome's early urban territory was organized in segments, the inhabitants of which made up a unit in the polity, like the *phylai* of Greek cities (the Romans called them *tribus*). Unusually big Greek cities (such as Athens) used their *phylai* to organize extensive tracts of territory (as much as 30 km away from the nucleus, in the Athenian case) and Rome's old *tribus* did likewise. In the second half of the fourth century, though, the Romans took the decisive step of creating new *tribus* as a way of organizing conquered territory. Neither the Athenians nor the Romans had surveyed and formally allotted their original homelands. But in these new, expansionist *tribus* extensive geometric grids (which we usually call by the Roman term 'centuriation') were laid out in several parts of west-central Italy, first in the plain south of the Latin cities, and then in the productive piedmont of north Campania (*tribus Falerna*). The settlers in the latter, from 318 BCE, then, were fully entitled citizens of Rome, occupying part of the urban territory of Rome, but they also lived some 140 km away from the Forum and the Capitol.

The problem of distance was resolved to an extent by another Roman speciality, the road. The building of the Via Appia, Rome's first purpose-built long-distance road, had the settlers of these new *tribus* specifically in mind. Both centuriation of the landscape and the building of the roads involved the aggressive use of technology, and advertised manpower, logistics, and organizational efficiency.

As Rome's military ascendancy increased, it became clear that simply expanding the city-state was no longer practical (thirty-five *tribus* already far exceeded any other ancient city's). At a distance from Rome, self-organizing but dependent towns were more effective; hence the many new *coloniae* founded during the late fourth and third centuries. Tied as closely to Rome as the earlier expansionist settlements, they inherited other features from them—allotted landscapes, and links with Rome via a growing network of roads. Roman urbanism, to repeat, is distinctive in its relationship to larger structures—and, above all, those of the Roman state, which meant the state's centre—the city of Rome itself.

So, between 340 and 180 BCE Rome became a single state with numerous urban centres. The level of integration was unique. Greek leagues had many component cities, but far weaker governance. In the Hellenistic kingdoms cities were effectively subject to the king, and could lack self-determination in military matters; but their idiosyncrasies were never threatened by uniformity imposed from above, even when they were new foundations bearing frequently repeated dynastic names. Rome's settlements, of different types, were all intended to be seen as offshoots of the Roman state. All their citizens had some form of citizen relations with Rome itself. Their new cities were set up precisely as allotments, by a conquering power, of the land at its disposal. Some were very small, amounting to little more than garrisons, and never developed much; others rapidly acquired a city-life of their own, such as Puteoli, which became one of Italy's principal ports. They resembled other cities of the Mediterranean world in their layout and organization. But crucially, they had no independence whatsoever in military decisions, for which they were parts of the Roman state, and it was war and diplomacy rather than some more general urban policy which led the Romans to develop this network of urban centres in the first place.

The new cities acted as strong-points in Rome's ever-more aggressive military policies in Italy, but performed a more subtle role too, for which their capillary ties with the capital were essential. It became increasingly clear to the Romans that the control of manpower, in which Italy seems to have been relatively abundant, was the secret of military success, and the new towns represented, displayed, and operated a citizenship policy which subordinated increasing quantities of Italian manpower to Roman command. At the same time, the shared experience of recruitment, victory (usually), and discharge provided important vectors of cultural convergence. Roman control could not always ensure loyalty, especially from 'Latin' *coloniae*; but the Roman urban network helped ensure the precarious survival of the Roman state in Italy during the war against Hannibal.

Victory in that war gave Rome the opportunity for Mediterranean hegemony, through which Italian cities were transformed through further convergence with Greek norms. Soldiers and traders from Roman and Italian towns opportunistically profited from military and diplomatic success. City-elites began to aspire to lavish town-houses in the Hellenistic manner, seen most vividly at Pompeii, and to provide their communities with the latest urban amenities. In the small and remote town Aletrium, a benefactor of the later second century BCE gave a water-supply, a market-building, a sundial, a gymnasium-style bath-house, and paved the streets (*CIL* I^2 1529). Their remains show that these exotic embellishments were constructed in traditional Italian style. An Italian version of the latest Hellenstic landscape architecture developed, based on spectacular works of terracing and substructions, facilitated by new concrete technology.

Neither Pompeii nor Aletrium was Roman in the strong sense until the Social War, but Rome and its cities naturally experienced these changes too. The second century saw major transformations in Rome's own urban infrastructure, with improvements to road and river communications, investment in commercial and naval harbour works, and a major aqueduct. Rome, as economic and political centre, also started to be known for the visibility of a large population, accommodated in a distinctive urban landscape of high-rise rental properties, from building and letting which the elite came to draw major revenues. Alongside the utilitarian projects, the status symbols of the Hellenistic East appeared, notably Rome's first colonnaded porticoes and marble temples. But only a few kilometres away the elite of independent Praeneste, enriched by their share in Roman imperial profits, developed their monumental sanctuary to First-born Fortune, goddess of good luck, on a scale which outdid anything in Rome, using concrete vaulting on a massive scale and terracing a whole mountainside. The urban changes of the last 150 years of the Republic are thus to be predicated of the Roman network in Italy, and not of Roman cities, or even of Rome, first. The system could not have come into being without the victory of Rome, and elites of Italian towns constantly looked at the capital which was their ultimate political goal, but it would be wrong to perceive Rome either as the architect of a cultural policy imposed on the dependent cities, or as the normal subject of their admiring imitation. At the same time, their institutions and their laws did gradually converge with Rome's. Through the influence of Roman cities, whose institutions, religion, and architecture alluded to the metropolis, spread many new ideas and institutions, ranging from the Latin language to forms of inexpensive material culture, or economic and social structures, such as the villa-agriculture whose produce was sold on, for elite consumption, in market-buildings like the one acquired by Aletrium. At cities such as Paestum, Cosa, and Alba Fucens we see, once again, cities which resemble the contemporary Greek world, but which are distinguished by being part of the Roman polity.

During the second century BCE Roman leaders became more conscious of their power over the world of cities. Like Hellenistic kings, Roman generals arbitrated between Greek cities, and, in the theatres of warfare in Spain, tried their hand at informal city-foundation. In 146 BCE two victorious generals saw fit to stage parallel abolitions of historic Mediterranean urban landmarks, Carthage and Corinth. Romans were now bidding for a place in (Greek) history, which meant city-history, and that dealt in foundations as well as sacks. Only twenty-five years after the epic siege and ritual destruction of Carthage some Romans were ready to take the equally symbolic step of establishing a Roman *colonia* for the first time outside Italy—and, of all places, on the site of Carthage.

Political opposition destroyed the controversial new Roman Carthage before it could take root, but only five years later, in 118 BCE, we see the momentous first successful transplantation outside Italy of the practice of allotment—the foundation of Narbo of the God Mars (now Narbonne). The allotment of provincial land to Roman citizens increased in importance, as the generals of the late Republic sought to reward increasingly demanding soldiers. At the same time, the aftermath of the Social War provided more opportunities for the expropriation of land and the creation of new veteran *coloniae*, and made it desirable to regularize further Italian city-statuses. The final Roman urbanization of Italy, at the expense of many of its former inhabitants, was the product of the age of violence and uncertainty, from the dictatorship of Sulla to the ascendancy of Augustus: at Pompeii and Praeneste, for instance, the old elites were largely replaced by the imposition of communities of Sulla's veterans. This, ironically, is the age in which Cicero coined the phrase that is most often quoted about *coloniae*—that they were little Romes—the time when Romans really began to think of Rome as template and original for formal imitation by all its daughter settlements.

Cicero's aspirational claim became unmistakeably true with the reign of Augustus. Through a judicious mix of innovation with the appropriation of ancient tradition, Rome was transformed into a stage for the magnificent benevolence of the emperor and his family, who needed to monopolize the instruments of prestige in the interests of their political survival. Themes long familiar at Rome—the city's antiquity, its eternal destiny, its singularity, its sanctity, and its pre-eminence in the world were elaborated as never before. The image of Rome the eternal city, which was to underpin the authority of emperors and popes for centuries, and which is part of the common cultural inheritance of today, was essentially Augustan. No one thought of the canonical Seven Hills before then.

'Father of cities' was an important royal accolade, and Augustus followed his predecessors and rivals in sponsoring new Roman daughter settlements. Julius Caesar had made a grand gesture of refounding both Carthage and Corinth—as *coloniae*—precisely a century after their destruction, and he made city-founding in Spain an ideological showcase, giving towns titles which proclaimed his unique position in Roman history. Now Augustus' stature dotted the empire with dozens of cities named from his dynasty, from Tiberias in Judaea, a Greco-Jewish town founded by King Herod, to Caesaraugusta in Spain, a Roman *colonia*. Roman power was still expressed alike in Roman and non-Roman towns. One of Augustus' most successful foundations, Nicopolis in Epirus, monument to the battle of Actium, was a Greek city. In other great Greek cities such as Ephesus, rich Roman citizen-residents transformed the urban landscape by benefactions which expressed their awareness of Augustan political messages.

Starting with Julius Caesar's conquest of Gaul, Roman provinces had increased in size and number. Augustan and later governors oversaw the widespread extension of Greco-Roman urban form. Component 'peoples' in each region were selected (according to their record of loyalty to Rome) to form the building-blocks of Roman fiscal, political, military, and ideological control, and so each was reconfigured as a territory with a city at its heart, called by historians today 'cantonal capitals' or '*civitas*-capitals'. Much of north-western Europe had experienced proto-urbanization before the Roman conquest, sometimes (Spain is a striking example) spontaneously adopting elements of Mediterranean city-form, but usually in well-defended locations. New provincial cities often kept the names of such settlements, in a titulature including also the people whose centre it was to be: as Lutetia Parisiorum or Venta Icenorum. But Rome applied a doctrine by which the town had to move down into a plain, where the new Roman roads ran. The towns gradually acquired the architectural signs of Roman government and society: forum, law-courts, theatre, baths. It is less clear how quickly or completely local society adapted to the ways of life presumed by the architecture.

Augustus and his successors made much ideological play with a revived Roman historical tradition. The achievements of the Republican past were evoked by the self-conscious development of stylized forms of distinctively Roman urbanism alongside the general encouragement of urban civilization. Two kinds of city, with distinctive sets of institutions, which are often referred to as 'chartered towns', were especially important: the *colonia* and—descended from the allied and 'Latin' cities of the Republic—the *municipium*. These cities, modelled on the now largely regular institutions of Italy itself, were Roman primarily in that they were showcases for Roman citizens functioning as citizens, registered participants in their Collective Business—which was the literal meaning of the Latin for the state, the *res publica*. This Business included civilian duties such as the maintenance of civil order, the supervision of financial concerns, and the provision of honourable service to the community in proportion to your means; and, perhaps, the duty to fight on behalf of the larger collectivity of Roman citizens everywhere (though recruitment was voluntary, and more common from some cities than others—certain *coloniae*, like Timgad in Africa, developed close links with legionary bases, providing their new soldiers and housing them after discharge). These requirements impinged variously on different subdivisions of the citizen body—only men of military age fought, freedmen were excluded from most civic office, and the role of women was limited to the spheres of public religion and community benefaction.

Relationships between such communities and with Romans who were prominent in the greater Roman state—grand senators, or later the emperors and their families—were shaped by the notion that all shared common institutions and laws. Representatives of the elites of *coloniae* and *municipia* travelled to Rome to further such relationships and to use them to win honorific or pecuniary favours. The status-hierarchy was another aspect of Roman life which was faithfully replicated in the towns. The elite also expected to provide the town council and the principal city officers, organized by analogy with the Senate and public magistrates of Rome. The citizenry outside the elite, however, retained at least some practical political function longer than the *plebs* of the city of Rome did, as we see from the election slogans for city magistracies painted on house-walls in the *colonia* Pompeii. However few citizens actually participated, nothing like this had happened at Rome since the reign of Augustus.

Since the settlement after the Social War all cities in Italy had been *coloniae* or *municipia*. Within two generations there were substantial numbers in the provinces too, especially Africa, Spain, and southern Gaul, but with some in the eastern Mediterranean as well. In the early empire the number greatly increased. Sometimes there was a province-wide upgrading of towns to the status of *municipium*, the best known of which was carried out in Spain under Vespasian. Here even tiny towns received charters, which spelled out the legal and institutional shape the community was to adopt: fragments of several such survive (the best-known is that of an insignificant place in southern Spain called Irni). The full Roman citizen franchise in *municipia* was reserved for the topmost segment of society. The idea was that if someone from the lower orders reached a magistracy they would become full citizens. Others were Roman of a different and lesser kind, the bearers of the 'Latin right'. Nevertheless, they were incorporated in a social and legal matrix which bound them palpably to often very distant Rome.

Connections with the centre were also expressed in the cities' physical structure. The elite's links with other towns, with governors, and with Italy made them highly imitative in their practice of civic benefaction. So these towns were equipped with theatre, bath-houses, and forum, with its standard appurtenances, council chamber, record-office, law-court, and temples—most often to definitely Roman deities, though sometimes tellingly incorporating local religious priorities. The architectural language of all these, moreover, was as formulaic and standardized as the phraseology of the charter or the titulature of the public institutions which it established. The striking archaeological similarity of Roman towns does reflect a common culture, but it was neither simply imposed from above by political authority nor mediated through free cultural choice. It was a by-product of a very powerful and unusual institutional milieu.

In the provinces, *coloniae* always had higher status than *municipia*. Their citizens were full Roman citizens, and in origin they were very often founded to house and reward discharged Roman citizen-soldiers, thereby allotted a symbolic political stake in the province their arms had 'pacified'. Such cities found the patronage of emperors and governors easier to win, and acquired a somewhat different, and rather grander, repertoire of monuments, but always in the same artistic idiom. One was usually the base of the governor, which provided another boost to civic fortunes. The monuments of *coloniae* tended to be more explicit than those of *municipia* in advertising the central messages of Roman power, or the particular programmes of an individual emperor.

Gaul is a good example. Julius Caesar, the conqueror of the region, founded a *colonia* of his veterans at Lugdunum (now Lyon) in 44 BCE, at a hub in the road and river network. Augustus incorporated one of the loyalest Gallic communities, the Aedui, as a *municipium*, and it took the interestingly hybrid name Augustodunum (Augustus' name combined with the Celtic for a fortress). The old hilltop centre was abandoned in favour of a location in the plain beneath, on the new Roman road-network. Over the next centuries the city (now Autun) acquired a rich repertoire of monuments; but Lyon, the base of the governor, did even better. It was equipped with a great sanctuary in honour of Rome and Augustus, at the confluence of the rivers, at which representatives of all the other communities of Gaul had to foregather annually for a festival of loyalty to Rome. The games which marked this festival were held in an amphitheatre, most distinctively Roman of spectacle-buildings, built under Tiberius at the expense of one of the Gallic leaders.

In the *coloniae* of the Augustan period the claim of Cicero about 'little Romes' was made to come true. Local notables who understood their duty to express loyalty and gratitude to the emperor and his family eagerly modelled the amenities of their towns on what the emperor had done in Rome. The patrons of Emerita Augusta, the *colonia* which is now Mérida in Spain, provided unmistakeable allusions to the architecture of the great Forum which Augustus had dedicated in Rome in 2 BCE. Such imitation became common outside the world of *coloniae* too. Vespasian's temple of Peace was the model for Hadrian's library in Athens. Hadrian's Pantheon was echoed in a temple in the sanctuary of Asklepios at Pergamon. The Colosseum was the model for rival amphitheatres in the richer cities of Italy, at Capua, Puteoli, or Pola. Real ambition was shown by building bath-complexes on the lavish scale of the great Thermae at Rome, with the showy symmetrical plan—where the magnanimity of the donor, often the emperor himself, simply doubled an already magnificent layout. Such complexes could be found at Ephesus, at Carthage, at Lepcis Magna, and at Augusta Treverorum (Trier) in northern Gaul (which briefly became an imperial capital). Circuses, evoking the Circus Maximus in Rome, were a similar component: one has recently been discovered in the principal *colonia* of Roman Britain, Camulodunum (Colchester).

It is a real question how far the outward forms and pomp of urbanism, which did credit to the local elite and their loyalty to Rome, were matched by the developed social and economic forms of the more successful Mediterranean urban tradition. Much of the evidence reflects the way cities formed bases for the local upper classes. Towns were where the produce of the territory was reallocated; consumed or traded by the rich, stored against profitable shortage, or collected to be set against the tax burden of the community, either directly or through the product of sale. Even when we see complex artisan functions, we are looking at the workshops which provided the hardware for the life of luxury.

Roman state-sponsored urbanism under the empire is often seen as a great success. But it had a mixed impact. Disruptive of existing social and economic patterns, it only in part succeeded in shaping new networks. Some foundations declined or failed. And alongside the formal expressions of Roman urban power there were many spontaneous settlements, small towns, large villages, market-centres, trading posts, some of which flourished more than official creations. Londinium (London) and Burdigala (Bordeaux) both grew from accidents of this kind. Such communities were usually in the end recognized by the Roman state and equipped with formal status, but this shows how the tradition of Roman urbanism became largely symbolic. Eventually *colonia* became a simple honorific title. Roman urbanism, which had always coexisted with and been shaped by Greek urbanism, eventually dissolved into a common urban milieu in the Late Empire. In the East the urban policy of the emperors, balancing the statuses of cities against each other, permitting large villages to become cities, refounding centres through relocating populations, wielded Greek and Roman precedents simultaneously.

I began by observing that Roman cities were not in most respects very different from Greek ones. In concluding, it is tempting to make the even stronger claim that they were actually distillations, concentrations, of Greek urbanism, constantly reinforced by new applications of Greek urban theory according to the cultural and political needs of each generation. Dionysius of Halicarnassus, a Greek literary theorist and antiquarian who wrote under Augustus, argued that Rome, intrinsically traditionalist as it was, preserved more of the ancient spirit of Hellenism than could be found anywhere in the Greek world of his time. The argument was tendentious and self-serving, but not ridiculous. There was an archaism about Roman urban form, with its religious and institutional proprieties and its carefully expressed affiliations to historical precedent. As late as the foundation of Constantinople, this idea of keeping faith with the past was spectacularly on show in the shape of cities and the messages conveyed by their institutions. It was only thereafter, with the addition of new Christian and Islamic idioms (themselves, of course, by no means devoid of classical precursors) that urban form substantially changed in the territories that had been the Roman Empire.

Further reading

The idea that ancient urbanism should be taken as a single phenomenon was developed by F. Kolb (1984), *Die Stadt in Altertum* (Munich: C. H. Beck). It is familiar to archaeologists, but has not been popular among ancient historians: see, however, the volume edited by B. Cunliffe and R. G. Osborne (2006), *Mediterranean Urbanisation* (Oxford: British Academy).

The urban history and archaeology of ancient Rome were among the first objects of Renaissance enquiry into the past, and have had a separate scholarly identity for 600 years. But modern archaeology has revolutionized knowledge of the beginnings of the city: a useful survey in C. Smith (1996), *Early Rome and Latium, 1000 BC–ca. 500 BC* (Oxford: OUP). Recent work has attempted to situate this study in a wider historical frame: C. Edwards and G. Woolf, eds. (2003), *Rome the Cosmopolis* (Cambridge: CUP); N. Morley (1996), *Metropolis and Hinterland: the City of Rome and the Italian economy* (Cambridge: CUP); N. Purcell (1994), 'The City of Rome and the *Plebs Urbana* in the Late Republic', in *Cambridge Ancient History*, 2nd edn., vol. 9 (Cambridge: CUP), 644–88; (1996), 'Rome and its Development under Augustus and his Successors', in *Cambridge Ancient History*, 2nd edn., vol. 10 (Cambridge: CUP), 782–811.

The Roman city in Italy has been studied in a similar way, but official inscriptions offer a somewhat different perspective on urban ideology in the Imperial period. A major problem is the assimilation of the Vesuvian cities. The evidence is abundant, but defies synthesis with what is known from other sites. In general, see T. J. Cornell and K. Lomas, eds. (1995), *Urban Society in Roman Italy* (London: UCL Press); a still rare attempt to see Pompeii in general historical light is W. Jongman (1991), *The Economy and Society of Pompeii* (Amsterdam: J. C. Gieben). For urban culture in Republican Italy, essential now is A. Wallace-Hadrill (2008), *Rome's Cultural Revolution* (Cambridge: CUP); for changes in the urban network after the Social War, E. Bispham (2008), *From Asculum to Actium: The Municipalization of Italy from the Social War to Augustus* (Oxford: OUP). Also N. Morley, 'Cities in Context: Urban Systems in Roman Italy', in H. Parkins, ed. (1997), *Roman Urbanism: Beyond the Consumer City* (London: Routledge); J. R. Patterson (2006) *Landscapes and Cities: Rural Settlement and Civic Transformation in Early Imperial Italy* (Cambridge: CUP).

For the wider world, there are excellent studies on the built environment of cities in the Roman Imperial period, making very clear how intertwined Greek and Roman themes were: J. B. Ward-Perkins (1994), *Roman Imperial Architecture* (2nd edn. New Haven: Yale UP); W. L. MacDonald (1986), *The Architecture of the Roman Empire*, vol. II, *An Urban Appraisal* (New Haven: Yale UP); E.V. Thomas (2007), *Monumentality and the Roman Empire: Architecture in the Antonine Age* (Oxford: OUP). On the theory of this urbanism, see R. Bedon, ed. (2002), Amoenitas urbium: *les agréments de la vie urbaine en Gaule romaine et dans les régions voisines* (Limoges: PU de Limoges), and on its politics, A. Bell (2004), *Spectacular Power in the Greek and Roman City* (Oxford: OUP). Urban society is studied through the archaeology of the house in R. Laurence and A. Wallace-Hadrill, eds. (1997), *Domestic Space in the Roman World: Pompeii and Beyond* (*JRA* suppl. 22, Portsmouth, RI).

For levels of urbanization and the spread of city-forms, see G. Woolf, 'The Roman Urbanization of the East', in S. E. Alcock, ed. (1997), *The Early Roman Empire in the East* (Oxford: Oxbow Books), 1–14. The cultural impact of cities is interestingly discussed by the studies in S. Alcock and E. Fentress, eds. (2000), *Romanization and the City: Creation, Dynamics and Failures* (*JRA* suppl. 38, Portsmouth, RI). On urban countrysides, M. Millett, 'Roman Towns and their Territories: An Archaeological Perspective', in J. Rich and A. Wallace-Hadrill, eds. (1991), *City and Country in the Ancient World* (London: Routledge), 169–90.

On the place of cities in economic networks in antiquity, K. Hopkins, 'Economic Growth and Towns in Classical Antiquity', in P. Abrams and E. A. Wrigley, eds. (1978), *Towns in Societies: Essays in Economic History and Historical Sociology* (Cambridge: CUP, 1978), 35–78, is still classic. For the vital fiscal dimension, see M. Corbier, 'City, Territory and Taxation', in Rich and Wallace-Hadrill, eds. *City and Country in the Ancient World*, 211–39. Also the collections H. Parkins and C. Smith, eds. (1998), *Trade, Traders and the Ancient City* (London: Routledge); H. Parkins, ed. (1997), *Roman Urbanism: Beyond the Consumer City* (London: Routledge).

For the late antique transformation of the classical urban paradigm, see N. Christie and S. T. Loseby, *Towns in Transition: Urban Evolution in Late Antiquity and the Early Middle Ages* (Aldershot: Scolar Press).

CHAPTER 37

ECONOMY AND QUALITY OF LIFE

WALTER SCHEIDEL

Approaching the Roman Economy

Modern debates about the nature of ancient economies have traditionally revolved around the twin problems of performance and structure. Whereas over a century ago German 'primitivists' and 'modernists' focused on the capacity of an ancient economy that was alternately envisioned as a backward conglomerate of cellular households or the equivalent of late medieval and early modern European economies (Finley ed. 1979), later generations of 'substantivists' and 'formalists' argued over structural characteristics, most notably the extent to which considerations of status shaped economic activity: according to what belatedly emerged as the most influential school of thought (Weber 1988; Finley 1999), pervasive conservative value systems constrained economic development and favoured rent-taking over market exchange as the principal source of wealth, a model framed in explicit contrast to later western developments (Morris and Manning 2005; Morris, Saller, and Scheidel 2007). Among Roman historians, the resultant picture of a highly localized, fragmented, and largely agrarian economy that sustained a thin veneer of coerced transfers and trade in luxuries and a network of towns that were dominated by landowning elites (Jones 1974; cf. also Duncan-Jones 1990) was most effectively challenged by Keith Hopkins, who put greater emphasis on dynamic processes and the probable scale of exchange (esp. Hopkins 1983*a* and *b*, 1995/6 = 2002). This has coincided with a revival of empiricist critiques of what one might call the 'low-equilibrium' model of the Roman economy, marshalling data thought to be indicative of economic diversification or growth but often lacking in theoretical conceptualization. Most recently, a growing awareness of the key issues involved in the historical study of economic growth (Saller 2002 = 2005; Scheidel, Morris, and Saller eds. 2007; Silver 2007; Scheidel 2009*b*) and a push for systematic quantification (Bowman and Wilson, in progress) have opened up promising new perspectives on the Roman economy.

The Purpose of Roman Economic History

What does economic history do, and what is it good for? In a classic definition, students of past economies seek to 'explain the structure and performance of economies through time' (North 1981: 1): performance, which represents the scale of output and the distribution of costs and benefits, is in itself determined by structure, created by institutions, technology, demography, and belief systems. Economic performance, in turn, is one—though by no means the only—critical determinant of human well-being or the quality of life. All these issues—economic performance, structure, and its contribution to overall human development—need to be approached within a comparative context: they cannot be assessed at all except in relation to other times and places. The Roman economy, therefore, cannot be studied in splendid isolation but only as a phase in the economic development of western Eurasia in particular and the pre-industrial world in general. This perspective not only permits us to situate the Roman case within a broader narrative but also encourages us to apply questions and theories we encounter in the economic history of other periods. More specifically, the Roman Imperial economy is of interest far beyond the confines of Roman Studies: the only time in history when the entire Mediterranean and much of its European hinterland was contained within a single state, it affords us a rare opportunity to address the question of whether large-scale political unity was conducive to economic growth and/or human development.

This agenda invites us to compare Roman conditions with the antecedent Mediterranean phenomenon of significant economic development in the Greek *poleis* at a time of exceptionally intense political fragmentation (Morris 2004); with the economic history of Europe from 1500 to 1800, a period of intensifying competition between emerging states when slow baseline per-capita growth and soaring inequality enriched elites and certain groups of metropolitan skilled workers but caused real incomes to decline for much of the population (Allen

2001; Hoffman *et al.* 2005); and the cyclical development of China, where political unity gradually became the norm but particular periods of imperial stability were associated with varying economic outcomes (Elvin 1973). What economists, historical sociologists, and political scientists would like to know is whether, or rather under what circumstances, a super-state tends to provide a framework that promotes economic growth. In different scenarios, Roman expansion may have fostered growth that came to be widely shared, or instead merely boosted the fortunes of the ruling class; it may have caused average incomes to rise, or resources to be more unequally distributed than before; it may have made everyone richer but the elite even more so, or may have benefited Italians relative to provincials, or city-dwellers relative to farmers. And how did these consequences change over time? We cannot hope to understand the Roman economy or its contribution to human welfare, or to tie it in with the economic history of other periods, unless we attempt to address these issues.

Assessing Roman Economic Development

Qualitative and Quantitative Approaches

How do we assess Roman economic development? The 'substantivist' camp used to rely in the first instance on impressions derived from putatively representative statements in ancient textual sources to reconstruct economic structure and to infer actual conduct from professed sentiments. This method raises serious epistemological questions: even 'true' statements need not be representative in a quantitative sense, and the rhetorical character of elite discourse necessarily undermines any attempts to link ancient texts to economic behaviour. While elite preferences may indeed have constrained actions, they may also have accommodated more divergent realities. At times, however, the mere attestation of a certain practice (for instance, in finance) may allow us to glimpse levels of development even if we cannot hope to ascertain the extent of its actual dissemination. Quantitative study, on the other hand, requires time-series of reliable as well as representative data on fundamentals such as yields, prices, wages, taxes, and rents, or at the very least bodies of relevant non-textual evidence that are susceptible to standardized measurement. The former, concentrated among the papyrus documents that survive from Roman Egypt, are rarely sufficient for diachronic or translocal analysis, while the latter range from an abundance of measurable items such as coins or ceramic remains (e.g. Duncan-Jones 1994; *Amphores* 1986) to more complex configurations such as the distribution of shipwrecks or the economic and demographic significance of surface scatter detected by field surveys (e.g. Parker 1992; Osborne 2004). Quantification is essential if we ever hope to address key questions about economic growth and compare the Roman experience with other historical cases.

Extensive and Intensive Growth

Economic growth is the single most important factor. Extensive growth—the accumulation of more output—was a simple function of population growth and must have occurred on a considerable scale as settlement densities increased in many parts of the Roman Empire, especially in the West. However, the scale of intensive growth—increases in per-capita output—is both more important and more difficult to pin down. Archaeological visibility governs and potentially distorts any modern assessment. For example, we might be inclined to interpret a proliferation of monumental infrastructure or a surge in the number of recorded shipwrecks as indicative of growing consumption per person: however, shifts in the allocation of surplus (say, from competitive feasting or war-making to civilian construction and shipping) or worsening inequality that boosted elite spending on buildings and marketed goods while many others' real incomes declined might arguably have caused the same observed features. Biased distributional arrangements make it (even) more difficult to estimate the extent of intensive growth from material remains. For this reason, we need to identify robust growth indicators that are not easily distorted by class-specific consumption patterns. Without such indicators we cannot tell when and why intensive growth arose, and when and why it ceased: whether it was gradually choked off by the very population growth it engendered (a 'Malthusian scenario'), or whether it succumbed to exogenous shocks such as epidemics or invasions (Scheidel 2009*b*).

Proxy Evidence for Economic Performance

Existing data are completely inadequate for a reconstruction of absolute levels of output and consumption. Roman per-capita or aggregate GDP is therefore unknown. Conjectures based on probabilistic assumptions about the share of total income spent on food (Temin 2006) or on the ratio of the imperial budget to the imperial population (both empirically unknown; Hopkins 1995/6 = 2002) converge in positing low average per-capita output but take as a given what would need to be empirically verified: that average GDP did not exceed subsistence levels by a very wide margin (cf. now Scheidel and Friesen 2009, for GDP approximating twice minimum subsistence). While this starting assumption, grounded in comparative evidence, must necessarily be true in the most general terms (and especially when we compare the Romans to more advanced economies), it also fails to allow for less dramatic but significant deviations from putative pre-modern norms, or indeed for change over time (cf. Maddison 2007: ch. 1 for conjectures).

Evidence for real incomes—the amount of goods and services that can be purchased at the same cost at different times—would provide insight into changes in per-capita consumption but is only available for certain parts of Roman Egypt and of uneven quality (Scheidel, forthcoming). As a result, modern estimates of household budgets in different periods (Drexhage 1991: 440–54) rest on very shaky ground, and attempts to relate apparent changes in real wages to changes in population number (Scheidel 2002; forthcoming) likewise remain open to criticism. In the near-absence of direct evidence, we must fall back on proxy data that may arguably shed some light on trends in average per-capita output and consumption levels. Due to space constraints, this section can touch only briefly on a few relevant categories.

The ratio of agricultural to non-agricultural workers is strongly predictive of per-capita output. Since we are unable to track changes in this relationship directly through occupational statistics, we are forced to rely on observable changes in the rate of urbanization, that is, the share of the population residing in urban settlements. But to what extent is it justifiable to interpret the considerable increase in the size and number of cities during the last few centuries BCE and the first few centuries CE as a shift away from farming? Urbanization is commonly considered a correlate of economic development, associated with growing division of labour and per-capita incomes, and it is hard to imagine that Roman towns failed to generate similar outcomes. At the same time, urban residence need not always denote non-agricultural labour: in an environment where cities and their hinterlands were fused together as *poleis* or *civitates* and urban elite spending and euergetism attracted immigration, many city-dwellers may have continued to be involved in rural production (cf. Hansen 2006 on Greece). The economic benefits of urbanization were also mediated by the nature of the revenue streams that sustained this process: an urban economy ultimately based on rent-taking (Erdkamp 2001) may have provided lesser economic stimuli than a market-exchange system. The growth of mega-cities such as Rome itself, moreover, is best seen as a function of the coercive and redistributive capacity of the state. On balance, however, an expansion of urban residence ought to have encouraged trade and occupational specialization, creating a more complex economy and, ultimately, some measure of intensive growth (cf. Wrigley 1978). Recent comparativist work on the provisioning of Roman cities (Erdkamp 2005), urban labour (Jongman 2003*b*), and urban trades and retailing (Hawkins 2006; Holleran, forthcoming) sheds new light on the economic consequences of urbanization.

Monetization provides a more straightforward measure of economic development. In as much as increasing liquidity facilitated investment and exchange, a great expansion of the money supply without concurrent price inflation is likely to have coincided with intensive economic growth. Recent work has reconfirmed that the volume of Roman coinage increased hugely in the late Republic (Lockyear 1999), and that the subsequent spread of gold issues greatly boosted the total value of the imperial money stock (Duncan-Jones 1994; Banaji 2007). This expansion was paralleled by a striking increase in air pollution in the northern hemisphere: lead deposits in ice cores from Greenland and in peat bogs or lake sediments from various parts of Europe are suggestive of massive lead-smelting and cupellation to extract silver and copper in the last few centuries BCE and the first few centuries CE (Wilson 2002; de Callataÿ 2005; Hopkins 2009). If, however, a conjectural estimate of the aggregate value of Roman imperial coinage based on die studies implies that the Roman Empire as a whole enjoyed greater liquidity than the eighteenth-century Netherlands (Jongman 2003*a*: 187, on Duncan-Jones 1994: 168–70), this finding will primarily cast doubt on the validity of the estimate itself. Yet even if we were eventually to arrive at a more moderate assessment of Roman monetization levels, new research on the importance of credit money (Harris 2006; 2008) and the relative sophistication of Roman financial arrangements (Temin 2004; Malmendier 2005) would nevertheless place the Roman monetary economy in close proximity to much later periods of European history. While elites would have disproportionately benefited from these advances, the sheer scale of the monetary expansion necessarily implies a rise in the volume of exchange that could hardly have been confined to a narrow circle. Once again, intensive growth is the most likely explanation.

The notion of growing exchange is, of course, also consistent with archaeological data: although a sharp upturn in the number of shipwrecks in the late Republican period (Parker 1992) may to some extent be an optical illusion created by the unusual durability of their cargo (above all amphoras, later also marble) that facilitates discovery (Wilson 2009), ample evidence for the extensive dissemination of ceramic containers and especially of low-key ceramic consumer products such as tableware and lamps documents mass-production and trade that catered to sub-elite consumers. The scale of these improvements in consumption is cast into sharp relief by the conspicuous decline in the volume and quality of attested consumer goods and infrastructural provisions after the end of the Imperial period (e.g. McCormick 2001: 25–119; Ward-Perkins 2005: 85–187; Wickham 2005).

In any pre-modern economy food consumption accounted for a large share of the average household budget: thus, certain dietary changes (for example, from husked grains to bread wheat or from cereals to meat) are likely to reflect improvements in real incomes. According to 'Engel's Law', with a given set of tastes and preferences, as income rises the proportion of income spent on food falls, even if actual expenditure on food rises. A better diet is therefore logically associated with increased consumption of non-food items as well, reinforcing the probability of intensive economic growth. In the Roman case, the growing presence of animal bones at sites of the late Republican and early Imperial periods has begun to attract attention (Ikeguchi 2007 and Jongman 2007*a*, based on King 1999 and MacKinnon 2004), and invites us to modify the conventional notion of a pervasively vegetarian diet. This perspective converges with new optimistic assessments of the capacity of Roman animal husbandry (Kron 2002).

Consumption levels are also reflected, however imperfectly, in physiological properties such as average body height: very broadly speaking, material prosperity tends to boost stature. While the study of body height has a long pedigree in more recent economic history, systematic surveys of the Roman evidence have only just begun to appear and have thus far yielded somewhat contradictory impressions (Kron 2005*a*; Koepke and Baten 2005; Jongman 2007*b*; Giannecchini and Moggi-Cecchi 2008). Moreover, economic interpretations of stature are complicated by the fact that disease affected physical growth independently of diet. Osteological studies that cumulatively allow us to relate features such as body height, diet, and disease consequently offer the most promising way forward (for recent examples from the heartland of the empire, see Manzi *et al.* 1999; Salvadei, Ricci, and Manzi 2001; Facchini, Rastelli, and Brasili 2004; Cucina *et al.* 2006; Buccellato *et al.* 2008).

Structural Determinants of Economic Performance

A variety of contextual factors influenced economic performance, most notably ecological conditions, demographic structure, legal and informal institutions, gender roles, and the stock of knowledge and resultant technological capabilities (Scheidel, Morris, and Saller eds. 2007: chs. 2–6). It is true that analysis of these features tells us more about their potential impact than about actual outcomes. At the same time, thanks to the nature of the evidence, most of them are much more readily susceptible to empirical investigation than more straightforward indicators of economic growth: we do—and always will—know much more about Roman crops or law or family relations or machinery than about real incomes or GDP. For this reason alone, these physical and cultural determinants merit careful consideration.

Climate-change is a critical variable because changes in temperature and precipitation affect food production, population size, and ultimately socio-economic complexity. In the present case, a Roman 'warm period' in the first few centuries CE must have had different repercussions in different parts of the empire (Sallares 2007; cf. Haas 2006). The gradual spread of viticulture and oleiculture—driven by a combination of warming, trade, and migration—and the shift from barley to wheat and from hulled to free-threshing wheats (ibid.) is suggestive of changing tastes associated with improving living standards.

Institutions can be defined as the 'rules of the game' that constrain economic activity, encompassing both formal, explicit rules enshrined in laws and rights as well as informal, implicit norms and conventions that tend to be established in the context of enterprises, markets, and government. The 'New Institutional Economics' school of thought in particular accords these rules a considerable role in determining economic performance. Under the influence of substantivist perspectives (see above), ancient historians have traditionally focused their attention on the informal end of the spectrum, whereas appraisals of the probable impact of formal laws and property rights on Roman economic development have only just begun to appear (Frier and Kehoe 2007; Kehoe 2007; De Ligt 2007). Once again, the relatively abundant evidence concerning these features invites more extensive study.

Recent work on technological advances in the Roman world calls for renewed attention to the interplay between increases in the stock of knowledge and economic development (Greene 2000; Wilson 2002). Roman universal rule was associated with the application of improved technology on an ever-larger scale (most famously in mining and milling), as well as with the inter-regional transfer of technologies, both of which may be considered conducive to productivity growth and economic progress (Oleson ed. 2008). In this area, the biggest challenge lies in ascertaining the ways in which economic processes were altered through technological development, and in assessing the extent of such changes in comparative terms (Schneider 2007; Lo Cascio ed. 2006).

Variation in Economic Development

Geographical divergence likewise requires careful consideration: the experience of pre-modern Europe and China shows that even under the fundamental constraints that inevitably rein in 'organic' economies, some regions (such as the Netherlands or the Yangzi Delta region) may pull well ahead of all their neighbours. Similar imbalances may have arisen in the Roman world: in this case, the spatial concentration of state power and concurrent innovations in the organization of labour represent the most likely agents of regional differentiation. Thus, recent models informed by comparative evidence and economic theory suggest that accelerating non-reciprocal inflows of plunder, taxes, and rents into the Italian heartland may temporarily have raised living standards at the political core (Scheidel 2007*b*) but ultimately undermined its economic performance (Freyberg 1989). The expansion of chattel slavery (Bradley and Cartledge eds. 2010) in the same area is logically associated with rising real wages (Scheidel 2008*a*) and may also be indicative of productivity growth. Beyond the economic differentiation of core and periphery, regional trends were shaped by the different growth potentials in the eastern and western halves of the mature empire, by the stimulation of economic activity and specialization through state extraction, and by the sustained net transfer of surplus to the military frontier zones (Hopkins 1995/6 = 2002; Bang 2007; Scheidel, Morris, and Saller eds. 2007: chs. 24–7).

The emergent 'globalization' model of Roman rule (e.g. Hitchner, forthcoming) is consistent with the notion that while large elements of the population stood to benefit economically, elites gained much more than most others, exacerbating overall inequality (Jongman 2006). For evidentiary reasons, formal measurements of inequality as expressed in patterns of land-ownership are largely confined to Roman Egypt (Bowman 1985; Bagnall 1992) and only rarely possible in other regions (Duncan-Jones 1990: 129–42). In principle, however, class-, age-, and gender-specific differences in consumption levels are amenable to archaeological inquiry (e.g. Prowse *et al.* 2005), and even textual evidence affords an occasional glimpse (Matthews 2006). Distributional issues matter not as much for estimates of average economic growth as for our understanding of how economic performance related to the quality of life, the topic of the remainder of this chapter.

From Economic Development to Human Development

Economic output is a powerful, yet ultimately insufficient, indicator of human well-being. Other variables that tend to be correlated with economic performance but at the same also vary autonomously need to be taken into account, most notably health and longevity, literacy and education, political participation, security, gender equality, and human rights. For the present, the *Human Development Index* of the United Nations documents the—generally limited—extent to which these factors diverge from economic capacity around the world. In more archaic societies, however, we may expect greater elasticity: at a time when wealth could not buy longer lives and high attrition from organized violence often coincided with real income growth, non-economic conditions would have played a greater role in determining overall well-being.

Demography

Longevity is probably the best example. In as much as we can tell, mean life expectancy at birth was low, mostly from twenty to thirty-five years or so (Scheidel 2001*b*). Unlike today, wealth and status did not normally translate to greater longevity (Scheidel 1999): instead, population density, altitude, and the consequent level of exposure to infections were the principal determinants of morbidity and mortality. In this area, it is not at all clear that economic real growth generated demographic benefits: if anything, wealth-driven urbanization may have placed an additional burden on vulnerable immigrants from lower-exposure backgrounds (e.g. Scheidel 2003), causing material and physiological well-being to diverge (as happened most recently during the Industrial Revolution). Recent research on urban seasonal mortality profiles from Roman Italy and Egypt has revealed conditions that appear to have been much more severe than in more recent periods (Scheidel 2001*b*). Imperial unification also seems to have facilitated the spread of both endemic and epidemic disease, from malaria and leprosy to smallpox (Sallares 2002; Zelener 2003). High mortality, in turn, necessitated high fertility. There is currently no compelling evidence that would lead us to believe that Roman populations were generally inclined or able to parlay productivity gains into lasting improvements in living standards by deliberately limiting family size (Frier 1994). Many basic incentives for such a move were missing in any case (Scheidel 2007*a*). Under these circumstances, some measure of family planning in elite circles would merely have served to increase inequality (Caldwell 2004). At the same time, attrition caused by war or urbanization may well have constrained demographic growth, thereby ensuring at least temporary advances in real incomes (cf. Wrigley 1978).

In the most basic sense, under a given regime of reproductive practices and normative living standards, population size is a function of economic performance. For that reason, solid evidence for Roman population numbers would give us a better idea of overall productive capacity. Recent notions of a Roman Italian or Mediterranean population that was very large by pre-modern standards (Kron 2005*b*; Lo Cascio and Malanima 2005; but cf. Scheidel 2008*b*) logically imply correspondingly high agricultural output (e.g. Kron 2000) but make it harder to envision substantial improvements in living standards. By contrast, traditionally dominant more-moderate estimates of Roman population size (Frier 2000; Scheidel 2004) are more readily consistent with intensive economic growth. Compromise scenarios (Hin 2008) may help to establish a middle ground between these competing options.

The relationship between economic and demographic development is highly complex and encompasses a whole network of interconnected variables that Roman historians will find easier to model in the abstract than to explore in practice (Scheidel 2007*a*). A surfeit of 'known unknowns'—from population number to productivity—forestalls detailed empirical analysis. Nonetheless, proper appreciation of the significance of demographic factors in shaping economic development already represents considerable progress over the longstanding neglect of this linkage: existing models of the ancient or Roman economy that pay scant if any attention to population are unfit to frame our research agenda.

Quality of Life

Health, even more so than income, is a critical factor in human well-being and overall development: disease and premature death curb productivity, thereby impeding intensive economic growth. They burden women with numerous pregnancies and childbirths, limiting their net contribution to the economy and hence their social standing and entitlements: modern surveys show a clear correlation between fertility decline and female well-being. Likewise, an unpredictable mortality regime discourages investment in education, curtailing human capital formation, and exacts a heavy toll on economic activity by destabilizing businesses and disrupting the trust networks that underpinned financing and trade. As modern development economics stresses the role of human capital and the stock of knowledge in fostering economic development, the debate over the extent of Roman literacy (e.g. Harris 1989) assumes special importance. Besides, literacy and education can be regarded as valuable in and of themselves, in as much as they enhance the quality of life. Much the same is true of political rights or freedom of worship. As I have argued elsewhere (Scheidel 2006), ancient historians stand to gain new insights into overall well-being by modelling their inquiries on modern human-development indices. For example, a simple comparison of the quality of life in classical Athens, Republican Italy, and Roman Egypt would yield a complex matrix of features: each of these cases would score quite differently on each of a variety of factors, from income growth, health, and literacy to safety, political participation, and gender equality. Each of these societies would lead in some areas but lag in others. A better understanding of human development in the Roman world requires careful consideration of the configurations of contributing factors that could be highly specific to a particular time and place.

The Road Ahead

This brief survey has taken us a long way from traditional perspectives on Roman economic and population history, and towards a more comprehensive approach to the pivotal issue of human well-being. At the end of the day, there is little point in studying the Roman economy unless doing so gives us some idea of how it benefited, or failed to benefit, the inhabitants of the ancient Mediterranean world. As I have repeatedly emphasized above, this requires explicitly comparative contextualization of the Roman experience: relative to the Greeks (Morris 2004), relative to later Europe (e.g. Allen 2001; Maddison 2007), relative to other premodern empires (e.g. Deng 2000; Bang 2008). Comparing and theorizing also help us decide which questions are more fruitful than others, how to go about addressing them, and how to interpret our findings. In converging with the preoccupations of the economic history of more recent periods, the study of the Roman economy and human development will still face the same old problems of inadequate data but will overcome its growing self-imposed conceptual isolation: while we may never be able to give the right answers, we should at least ask the right questions.

Further reading

Chapters 18 to 28 of the *Cambridge Economic History of the Greco-Roman World* (Scheidel, Morris, and Saller eds. 2007) provide the latest analytical survey of the Roman economy. Scheidel ed., forthcoming will revisit the most salient issues. General syntheses are in short supply: Finley 1999, first published in 1973 and still a classic unsurpassed for the elegant coherence of its model of 'the ancient economy', deals with Rome as well as Greece but is stronger on the latter. Hopkins 1995/6 = 2002 and 2009 are among the most accessible and stimulating shorter pieces on Roman economic development, while Harris 1993 gives a useful survey. For brief summary overviews of Roman demography, see Frier 2000 and Scheidel 2009*a*; for critiques of the field, Parkin 1992 and Scheidel 2001*a*; for a pioneering case study, Bagnall and Frier 1994. Scheidel, in preparation, will provide a systematic introduction. MacKinnon 2007 surveys material evidence of physiological well-being.

References

Allen, R. C. (2001), 'The great divergence: wages and prices from the Middle Ages to the First World War', *Explorations in Economic History*, 38: 411–47.

Amphores (1986), *Amphores romaines et histoire économique: dix ans de recherche (Actes du colloque de Sienne, 1986)*. Rome.

Bagnall, R. S. (1992), 'Landholding in late Roman Egypt: the distribution of wealth', *Journal of Roman Studies*, 82: 128–49.

—— and Frier, B. W. (1994), *The demography of Roman Egypt*. Cambridge.

Banaji, J. (2007), *Agrarian change in late antiquity: gold, labour and aristocratic dominance*. Updated edn. Oxford.

Bang, P. F. (2007), 'Trade and empire: in search of organizing concepts for the Roman economy', *Past and Present*, 195: 3–54.

—— (2008), *Roman bazaar: a comparative study of trade and markets in a tributary empire*. Cambridge.

Bowman, A. K. (1985), 'Landholding in the Hermopolite Nome in the fourth century A.D.', *Journal of Roman Studies*, 75: 137–63.

—— and Wilson, A. (in progress), 'The Oxford Roman Economy Project'.

Bradley, K. and Cartledge, P. (eds.) (2010), *The Cambridge world history of slavery*, I: *The ancient Mediterranean*. Cambridge.

Buccellato, A. *et al.* (2008), 'La Nécropole de Collatina', *Dossiers d'Archéologie*, 330: 22–31.

Caldwell, J. C. (2004), 'Fertility control in the classical world: was there an ancient fertility transition?', *Journal of Population Research*, 21: 1–17.

Cucina, A. *et al.* (2006), 'The necropolis of Vallerano (Rome, 2nd–3rd century AD): an anthropological perspective on the ancient Romans in the *suburbium*', *International Journal of Osteoarchaeology*, 16: 104–17.

De Callataÿ, F. (2005), 'The Graeco-Roman economy in the super-long run: lead, copper, and shipwrecks', *Journal of Roman Archaeology*, 18: 361–72.

De Ligt, L. (2007), 'Roman law and the Roman economy: three case studies', *Latomus*, 66: 10–25.

—— and Northwood, S. J. (eds.) (2008), *People, land, and politics: demographic developments and the transformation of Roman Italy, 300 BC–AD 14*. Leiden.

Deng, K. G. (2000), 'A critical survey of recent research in Chinese economic history', *Economic History Review*, 53: 1–28.

Drexhage, H.-J. (1991), *Preise, Miete/Pachten, Kosten und Löhne im römischen Ägypten bis zum Regierungsantritt Diokletians*. St Katharinen.

Duncan-Jones, R. (1990), *Structure and scale in the Roman economy*. Cambridge.

—— (1994), *Money and government in the Roman empire*. Cambridge.

Edwards, C. and Woolf, G. (eds.) (2003), *Rome the cosmopolis*. Cambridge.

Elvin, M. (1973), *The pattern of the Chinese past: a social and economic interpretation*. Stanford.

Erdkamp, P. (2001), 'Beyond the limits of the "consumer city": a model of the urban and rural economy in the Roman world', *Historia*, 50: 332–56.

—— (2005), *The grain market in the Roman empire: a social, political and economic study*. Cambridge.

Facchini, F., Rastelli, E., and Brasili, P. (2004), 'Cribra orbitalia and cribra cranii in Roman skeletal remains from the Ravenna area and Rimini (I–IV century AD)', *International Journal of Osteoarchaeology*, 14: 126–36.

Finley, M. I. (ed.) (1979), *The Bücher–Meyer controversy*. New York.

—— (1999), *The ancient economy*. Updated edn. I. Morris (ed). Berkeley.

Freyberg, H.-U. von (1989), *Kapitalverkehr und Handel im römischen Kaiserreich (27 v. Chr.-235 n. Chr.)*. Freiburg.

Frier, B. W. (1994), 'Natural fertility and family limitation in the Roman family', *Classical Philology*, 89: 318–33.

—— (2000), 'The demography of the Early Roman Empire', in *The Cambridge ancient history*², vol. 11, 787–816. Cambridge.

—— and Kehoe, D. P. (2007), 'Law and economic institutions', in Scheidel, Morris, and Saller eds. 2007: 113–43.

Giannecchini, M. and Moggi-Cecchi, J. (2008), 'Stature in archaeological samples from Central Italy: methodological issues and diachronic changes', *American Journal of Physical Anthropology*, 135: 284–92.

Greene, K. (2000), 'Technological innovation and economic progress in the ancient world: M. I. Finley re-considered', *Economic History Review*, 53: 29–59.

Haas, J. (2006), *Die Umweltkrise des 3. Jahrhunderts n.Chr. im Nordwesten des Imperium Romanum*. Stuttgart.

Hansen, M. H. (2006), *The shotgun method: the demography of the ancient Greek city-state culture*. Columbia and London.

HARRIS, W. V. (1989), *Ancient literacy.* Cambridge, Mass., and London.
—— (1993), 'Between archaic and modern: some current problems in the history of the Roman economy', in W. V. Harris (ed.), *The inscribed economy: production and distribution in the Roman empire in the light of* instrumentum domesticum, 11–29. Ann Arbor, Mich.
—— (2006), 'A revisionist view of Roman money', *Journal of Roman Studies*, 96: 1–24.
—— (2008), 'The nature of Roman money', in W. V. Harris (ed.), *The monetary systems of the Greeks and Romans*, 174–207. Oxford.
HAWKINS, C. (2006), 'Work in the city: Roman artisans and the urban economy'. Unpub. Ph.D thesis, University of Chicago.
HIN, S. (2008), 'Counting Romans', in De Ligt and Northwood eds. 2008: 187–238.
HITCHNER, R. B. (forthcoming), *The first globalization: the Roman Empire and its legacy.*
HOFFMAN, P. T. *et al.* (2005), 'Sketching the rise of inequality in early modern Europe', in R. C. Allen, T. Bengtsson, and M. Dribe (eds.), *Living standards in the past: new perspectives on well-being in Asia and Europe*, 131–72. Oxford.
HOLLERAN, C. (forthcoming), *Shopping in ancient Rome.* Oxford.
HOPKINS, K. (1983*a*), 'Models, ships, and staples', in P. Garnsey and C. R. Whittaker (eds.), *Trade and famine in classical antiquity*, 84–109. Cambridge.
—— (1983*b*), 'Introduction', in P. Garnsey, K. Hopkins, and C. R. Whittaker (eds.), *Trade in the ancient economy*, pp. ix–xxv. London.
—— (1995/6), 'Rome, taxes, rents, and trade', *Kodai*, 6/7: 41–75; repr. in Scheidel and von Reden eds. 2002: 190–230.
—— (2009), 'The political economy of the Roman empire', in I. Morris and W. Scheidel (eds.), *The dynamics of ancient empires: state power from Assyria to Byzantium*, 178–204. New York.
IKEGUCHI, M. (2007), 'The dynamics of agricultural locations in Roman Italy'. Unpub. Ph.D thesis, Cambridge University.
JONES, A. H. M. (1974), *The Roman economy.* London.
JONGMAN, W. (2003*a*), 'A golden age: death, money supply and social succession in the Roman Empire', in E. Lo Cascio (ed.), *Credito e moneta nel mondo romano*, 181–96. Bari.
—— (2003*b*), 'Slavery and the growth of Rome: the transformation of Italy in the second and first centuries B.C.E.', in Edwards and Woolf eds. 2003: 100–22.
—— (2006), 'The rise and fall of the Roman economy: population, rents and entitlement', in P. F. Bang, M. Ikeguchi, and H. G. Ziche (eds.), *Ancient economies, modern methodologies: archaeology, comparative history, models and institutions*, 237–54. Bari.
—— (2007*a*), 'The early Roman Empire: consumption', in Scheidel, Morris, and Saller eds. 2007: 592–618.
—— (2007*b*), 'Gibbon was right: the decline and fall of the Roman economy', in O. Hekster, G. de Kleijn, and D. Slootjes (eds.), *Crises and the Roman Empire*, 183–99. Leiden.
KEHOE, D. P. (2007), *Law and the rural economy in the Roman Empire.* Ann Arbor, Mich.
KING, A. (1999), 'Diet in the Roman world: a regional inter-site comparison of the mammal bones', *Journal of Roman Archaeology*, 12: 168–202.
KOEPKE, N. and BATEN, J. (2005), 'The biological standard of living in Europe during the last two millennia', *European Review of Economic History*, 9: 61–95.
KRON, G. (2000), 'Roman ley-farming', *Journal of Roman Archaeology*, 13: 277–87.
—— (2002), 'Archaeozoological evidence for the productivity of Roman livestock farming', *Münstersche Beiträge zur Antiken Handelsgeschichte*, 21/2: 53–73.

—— (2005*a*), 'Anthropometry, physical anthropology, and the reconstruction of ancient health, nutrition, and living standards', *Historia*, 54: 68–83.

—— (2005*b*), 'The Augustan census figures and the population of Italy', *Athenaeum*, 93: 441–95.

Lo Cascio, E. (ed.) (2006), *Innovazione tecnica e progresso economico nel mondo romano.* Bari.

—— and Malanima, P. (2005), 'Cycles and stability: Italian population before the Demographic Transition (225 B.C.–A.D. 1900)', *Rivista di Storia Economica*, 21: 197–232.

Lockyear, K. (1999), 'Hoard structure and coin production in antiquity—an empirical investigation', *Numismatic Chronicle*, 159: 215–43.

McCormick, M. (2001), *Origins of the European economy: communications and commerce, AD 300–900.* Cambridge.

MacKinnon, M. (2004), *Production and consumption of animals in Roman Italy.* Portsmouth, RI.

—— (2007), 'Osteological research in classical archaeology', *American Journal of Archaeology*, 111: 473–504.

Maddison, A. (2007), *Contours of the world economy, 1–2030 AD: essays in macro-economic history.* Cambridge.

Malmendier, U. (2005), 'Roman shares', in W. N. Goetzmann and K. G. Rouwenhorst (eds.), *The origins of value*, 31–42. Oxford.

Manzi, G. *et al.* (1999), 'Discontinuity of life conditions at the transition from the Roman Imperial age to the early Middle Ages: example from Central Italy evaluated by pathological dento-alveolar lesions', *American Journal of Human Biology*, 11: 327–41.

Matthews, J. (2006), *The journey of Theophanes: travel, business, and daily life in the Roman East.* New Haven and London.

Morris, I. (2004), 'Economic growth in ancient Greece', *Journal of Institutional and Theoretical Economics*, 160: 709–42.

—— and Manning, J. G. (2005), 'The economic sociology of the ancient Mediterranean world', in N. J. Smelser and R. Swedberg (eds.), *The handbook of economic sociology*[2], 131–59. Princeton.

—— Saller, R., and Scheidel, W. (2007), 'Introduction', in Scheidel, Morris, and Saller eds. 2007: 1–12.

North, D. C. (1981), *Structure and change in economic history.* New York and London.

Oleson, J. P. (ed.) (2008), *The Oxford handbook of engineering and technology in the classical world.* New York.

Osborne, R. (2004), 'Demography and survey', in S. E. Alcock and J. F. Cherry (eds.), *Side-by-side survey: comparative regional studies in the Mediterranean world*, 163–72. Oxford.

Parker, A. J. (1992), *Ancient shipwrecks of the Mediterranean and the Roman provinces.* Oxford.

Parkin, T. G. (1992), *Demography and Roman society.* Baltimore and London.

Prowse, T. L. *et al.* (2005), 'Isotopic evidence for age-related variation in diet from Isola Sacra, Italy', *American Journal of Physical Anthropology*, 128: 2–13.

Sallares, R. (2002), *Malaria and Rome: a history of malaria in ancient Italy.* Oxford.

—— (2007), 'Ecology', in Scheidel, Morris, and Saller eds. 2007: 15–37.

Saller, R. (2002), 'Framing the debate over growth in the ancient economy', in Scheidel and von Reden eds. 2002: 251–69, and in J. G. Manning and I. Morris (eds.) (2005), *The ancient economy: evidence and models*, 223–38. Stanford.

SALVADEI, L, RICCI, F. and MANZI, G. (2001), 'Porotic hyperostosis as a marker of health and nutritional conditions during childhood: studies at the transition between imperial Rome and the early Middle Ages', *American Journal of Human Biology*, 13: 709–17.

SCHEIDEL, W. (1999), 'Emperors, aristocrats, and the grim reaper: towards a demographic profile of the Roman élite', *Classical Quarterly*, 49: 254–81.

—— (2001*a*), 'Progress and problems in Roman demography', in W. Scheidel (ed.), *Debating Roman demography*, 1–81. Leiden.

—— (2001*b*), 'Roman age structure: evidence and models', *Journal of Roman Studies*, 91: 1–26.

—— (2002), 'A model of demographic and economic change in Roman Egypt after the Antonine plague', *Journal of Roman Archaeology*, 15: 97–114.

—— (2003), 'Germs for Rome', in Edwards and Woolf eds. 2003: 158–76.

—— (2004), 'Human mobility in Roman Italy, I: the free population', *Journal of Roman Studies*, 94: 1–26.

—— (2006), 'Stratification, deprivation and quality of life', in M. Atkins and R. Osborne (eds.), *Poverty in the Roman world*, 40–59. Cambridge.

—— (2007*a*), 'Demography', in Scheidel, Morris, and Saller eds. 2007: 38–86.

—— (2007*b*), 'A model of real income growth in Roman Italy', *Historia*, 56: 322–46.

—— (2008*a*), 'The comparative economics of slavery in the Greco-Roman world', in E. Dal Lago and C. Katsari (eds.), *Slave systems, ancient and modern*, 105–26. Cambridge.

—— (2008*b*), 'Roman population size: the logic of the debate', in De Ligt and Northwood eds. 2008: 17–70.

—— (2009*a*), 'Population and demography', in A. Erskine (ed.), *A companion to ancient history*, 134–45. Malden and Oxford.

—— (2009*b*), 'In search of Roman economic growth', *Journal of Roman Archaeology, 22: 46–70.*

—— (forthcoming), 'Real wages in early economies: evidence for living standards from 1800 BCE to 1300 CE', *Journal of the Economic and Social History of the Orient.*

—— (in preparation), *The demography of the Greco-Roman world.* Cambridge.

—— (ed.) (forthcoming), *The Cambridge companion to the Roman economy.* Cambridge.

—— and FRIESEN, S. (2009), 'The size of the economy and the distribution of income in the Roman Empire', *Journal of Roman Studies*, 99: 61–91.

—— and VON REDEN, S. (eds.) (2002), *The ancient economy.* Edinburgh.

—— MORRIS, I., and SALLER, R. (eds.) (2007), *The Cambridge economic history of the Greco-Roman world.* Cambridge.

SCHNEIDER, H. (2007), 'Technology', in Scheidel, Morris, and Saller eds. 2007: 144–72.

SILVER, M. (2007), 'Roman economic growth and living standards: perception versus evidence', *Ancient Society*, 37: 191–252.

TEMIN, P. (2004), 'Financial intermediation in the Early Roman Empire', *Journal of Economic History*, 64: 705–33.

—— (2006), 'Estimating GDP in the early Roman Empire', in Lo Cascio ed. 2006: 31–54.

WARD-PERKINS, B. (2005), *The fall of Rome and the end of civilization.* Oxford.

WEBER, M. (1988), *The agrarian sociology of ancient civilizations*, tr. R. I. Frank. London and New York.

WICKHAM, C. (2005), *Framing the early Middle Ages: Europe and the Mediterranean 400–800.* Oxford.

WILSON, A. (2002), 'Machines, power, and the ancient economy', *Journal of Roman Studies*, 92: 1–32.

—— (2009), 'Approaches to quantifying Roman trade', in A. Bowman and A. Wilson (eds.), *Quantifying the Roman economy*, 213–49. Oxford.

WRIGLEY, E. A. (1978), 'Parasite or stimulus: the town in a pre-industrial economy', in P. Abrams and E. A. Wrigley (eds.), *Towns in societies: essays in economic history and historical sociology*, 295–309. Cambridge.

ZELENER, Y. (2003), 'Smallpox and the disintegration of the Roman economy after 165 A.D.'. Unpub. Ph.D thesis, Columbia University.

CHAPTER 38

FAMILY AND SOCIETY

BERYL RAWSON

> The primary bond (in human society) is between spouses, because of the natural instinct for procreation; then with children; then there is the communality of the one household (*domus*). This is the basic principle of the city, the seed of the state.
>
> (Cicero, *De Officiis* (*On Duties*) 1.54)

THAT 'the family' is a basic unit, perhaps *the* basic unit, of society is often claimed. Cicero (above) enunciated this for the Romans. Aristotle, writing in fourth-century BCE Greece, had already expressed a similar principle: at the beginning of Book 1 of his *Politics* he identified the union of male and female for the continuation of the species as the primary association of human beings. The household (the *oikos*) thus became the fundamental unit of the city-state (the *polis*). In modern times the principle has continued to be expressed or taken for granted.

Once we begin to examine this more closely, however, we realize that there is not a single form of 'the family' at any one time in any society. For Roman society, the definition of 'the family' is now one of the most hotly debated topics. So let us think of 'Families in Roman Society'. But then the term 'Roman' will not stay still and solid: it resolves itself into a kaleidoscope of moving colours and patterns. We must therefore try to define and limit the Roman world of which we are going to speak—that vast geographical area which by the early second century CE included diverse cultures, societies, and political forms north, south, and east of the Mediterranean under the general hegemony of government centred in Rome. The forces of acculturation did 'Romanize' many aspects of this empire, just as they changed aspects of the society of Rome and Italy. To generalize about the common features, however, would give a superficial picture, and we must avoid the tendency of older work which conflated pieces of evidence from widespread areas and sometimes different periods to make generalized statements about 'the family' which were misleading and which obscured the regional diversity of the 'Roman' world (see Rawson 1986: ch. 1, esp. 1–6). To analyse the many differences would require a discussion much longer than this one. So we will focus discussion on the society of Rome and Italy, but also include the Western Empire, which became more recognizably 'Roman' than did the East during the best-documented period from the last century BCE into the third century CE. One force originating in the East, however, must be taken into account: that of early Christianity and its concept of 'the family' and its intersection with wider society. These boundaries of time and space are imposed here in order to produce a reasonably coherent study. But regional variation is perhaps one of the most promising directions to pursue for the future. Such studies could enhance our understanding not only of what 'the family' can be, but also of the multifaceted society of the ancient Roman world more generally.

The recognition that 'the family' is a central institution in society implies that it has value not only for its own sake but also for its interaction with wider society. In the past, this has often been seen in moralistic terms. For instance, the political disintegration of the Julio-Claudian dynasty in the mid-first century CE has been linked to the alleged moral degeneration of members of that family. This perception was due partly to the reliance on literary sources, especially Tacitus and Suetonius, although neither of these was a primary source (being nearly a century later than the period they wrote about) and neither had much to say about Roman society beyond the imperial family and a small elite. Modern writers, however, have sometimes applied these moral criticisms to Roman society at large. (See e.g. Zimmerman 1947: 395–6.)

In recent decades a much greater range of evidence has been used, new methodologies have been applied to help us understand and interpret the evidence better, and we have learnt much from other disciplines and areas of study. We have learnt useful approaches from sociology, demography, anthropology, art history, and archaeology, as well as from the literary study of representations, 'readings', and subtexts. We can now draw on not only literary sources but also inscriptions, the law, art, architecture, artefacts, and other kinds of archaeological evidence. There had been specialized work done previously on all these areas, but we have more recently begun to see how fruitful it can be to bring together and use in combination the great diversity of source material. This has encouraged an extension of the period studied beyond the Julio-Claudian period. Even this extended range of evidence still leaves silences. For instance, we still know little about rural society, as so much of our evidence comes from and deals with urban society.

Some of the areas in which family and society interacted in the Roman world, to be discussed below, are the influence of elite families as role models and preservers of memory and tradition; values; educational ideals and practices; legal principles and family practice; the demographic structure of the population; the role of slaves and ex-slaves; and public life, rituals, and religion. These will help highlight some of the current lively debates.

One particular way in which the Romans saw the interrelationship of family and society was in the role of a comparatively small number of elite families in the Republican period (up until at least the early first century BCE), to whom political leadership was regularly entrusted. The study of such family histories and alliances is known as 'prosopography'. As a method of analysis of Roman political life, it was developed by the German scholar Friedrich Münzer (1920) and dominated the study of Roman Republican history for at least the first half of the twentieth century. It has been subject to criticism because of the rigid and almost automatic way it has sometimes been applied. Nevertheless, when applied flexibly and sensitively it has been a productive approach, highlighting the respect and primacy which Romans were prepared to grant to a small number of families whose political or military achievements had earned their trust. More recent work has extended our understanding of how leading citizens and their families won and maintained their reputations. In 1939 Ronald Syme's *Roman Revolution* extended previous studies of patronage into a powerful study of propaganda, an approach which dominated the next half-century of scholarship. In 1988 Paul Zanker deepened understanding of the power of Augustus' family, exploring the 'power of images' in his sophisticated study of material evidence. More recently, integration of archaeological evidence, art, and material culture into Roman history more widely has shown not only how highly visible some leading families were in public life but also how other families experienced the life of the city in which they lived.

The cult of ancestors underlay much private and public ritual (see Flower 1996). From the mid-second century BCE Roman magistrates commemorated the achievements of family ancestors on official Roman coins—artefacts whose images changed constantly and which were probably more closely scrutinized than our own coins, when media of public communication were much more limited than today. Julius Caesar was the first who dared (at the end of his life) to put his own individual image onto Roman coins, but he too made use of his much-vaunted family lineage, the Julians, their association with the goddess Venus, and their ancestors Aeneas, Anchises, and Ascanius/Iulus. The names of eminent citizens, some repeated over successive generations, were commemorated in the *fasti* on permanent display in the Forum: the official lists of consuls, triumphing generals, and priests. Funeral processions of high-ranking families paraded personifications of earlier generations, and in processions for military triumphs generals fortunate enough to have one or more sons had these sons ride with them, establishing early popularity for the next generation. Although these are aspects of elite families, it is arguable that this sense of family tradition, this cult of commemoration, also underpins the widespread funerary commemoration of families of much more modest status. These latter families, however, many emerging from slave status, had little to record of themselves except their family relationships, which makes their epitaphs, in public places, such a valuable source for families at lower levels of society.

The study of public art and architecture and material culture has enabled us to see the impact of the family name on every aspect of public life. Roadways had long commemorated the family name of the magistrate responsible for their construction: the fourth-century BCE Via Appia is one of the best-known. Temples, statues, and buildings which were vowed and built at the expense of successful citizens were associated in public memory with these family names, and as building activity (especially in Rome) became more frenetic towards the end of the Republic the urban landscape displayed monuments such as the Basilica Aemilia, the Theatre of Pompey, the Basilica Iulia, and the Forum Iulium. The entertainments given in some of these places also advertised family names—the name of the magistrate giving the show, and often the name of the ancestor whose memory was being honoured by the show. At the theatre, the front rows were reserved for senators, the small elite who were eye-catching not only in these prominent positions but also in their official regalia, purple in various forms embellishing the standard white toga. Women of distinguished family, such as the priesthood of the Vestals and wives of consuls, shared in this public visibility, and other groups also had specially allocated sections. We shall return to this striking hierarchy of seating. Family records preserved in private houses probably influenced public histories. Family genealogies sometimes were linked to foundation legends of Italian towns. The connection of the Julian family with Troy and Rome became best known, but it was not the only such family connection in the late Republic. There was a whole industry of genealogy construction for ambitious families. Cicero's friend Atticus was but one practitioner.

When Augustus acquired sole political power (from 31 BCE), he still drew on elite families for public office and advisory roles. But he also extended the range of participating families, giving an increased role to leading families from many Italian towns. Really significant power was gradually drawn into the hands of Augustus' own family, but many aspects of his rule affected families more widely. His legislation of 18–17 BCE (the *lex Iulia de maritandis ordinibus*), supplemented by senatorial legislation of 9 CE (the *lex Papia Poppaea*), took the connection between family and society explicitly into the public arena (Treggiari 1991). Rewards (political and financial) were provided for those who married and produced children, with corresponding penalties against those who did not. These would not directly impact much on the lower classes, for whom inheritance and public office were largely irrelevant, but the ideology of family was being publicly proclaimed. Marriages between citizens of different status (such as senators and ex-slaves) were restricted, further promoting the social hierarchy visible in seating arrangements in the theatre. It is noteworthy that much writing on Augustus today focuses on 'family' from one perspective or another (e.g. Severy 2003; Milnor 2005).

With hindsight, we might be tempted to describe Augustus' emphasis on 'the family' as a paradigm shift. All succeeding emperors gave prominence to the imperial family and devised various policies to support and encourage families. Representations of families became frequent on public and private monuments. But this does not support claims that 'the family' had become more important or more cherished in the Roman mentality, nor that the new autocratic political system encouraged citizen men to withdraw into domesticity as a kind of refuge (claims made by P. Veyne and M. Foucault but rebutted by Cohen and Saller 1994). The increased affluence and peace may have made it easier for many to enjoy and commemorate family life, but the sentiments cannot be said to be new. In this, as in so much else, Augustus had the instinct for identifying and building on existing sentiment and values, for giving these a more public profile, and for claiming them as his own. Various discussions of Augustus' success point to his understanding of the perceived or self-proclaimed municipal morality of Italian towns, a morality harnessed by him for his own support and programme. The emphasis on the imperial family for the first hundred years after Augustus gained supreme power was aimed primarily at shoring up and legitimizing the Julio-Claudian dynasty. Various strategies of marriage and adoption ensured the continuation of the Julian family name for seventy years, and then Claudius and Nero drew on female family members such as Antonia the Younger and Agrippina the Younger for links back to the Julians.

The dynastic aim continued to be important for all future regimes, but it broadened out into policies and symbolism encompassing a large part of Roman society. Images of children were used more widely on imperial monuments and artefacts, and the emperor was presented as extending his care and generosity to all as the universal father (*pater patriae*, 'father of his country'). Programmes such as the *alimenta*, whereby the emperor made loans available to farmers who paid interest into a fund to support children in local areas, and the *congiaria* (handouts of food or money which increasingly took account of family size by including children as recipients) reached out to a wide range of citizens, and there were many visual representations of emperors in this role with fathers and children. Leading citizens in their home towns replicated such policies. The ideal of 'euergetism' ('good works') was strong in Greek and Roman societies, and for the Romans the family became a central symbol of this. Pliny the Younger contributed to a fund to provide teachers for the children of Comum and endowed a library and a child-support scheme there (see his *Letters* 1.8 and 4.13). As the first and second centuries CE progressed there was a greater density of social activity reflecting a concern with family affairs. Even after allowing for the accidents of survival of evidence, it is hard not to acknowledge an increased use of funerary epitaphs to commemorate family relationships, more sculpture of ordinary people in domestic rather than public roles, more legal activity (legislation, court cases, commentaries) focused on family matters. Underpinning this activity were values significant to family and society.

One of the values most deeply embedded in Roman society was that of *pietas*, which encompassed both public and private qualities: loyalty to gods, country, and family (Saller 1994). It was the dominant quality of Aeneas in Roman legend, especially as portrayed in the great epic of the Augustan period, Virgil's *Aeneid*. *Pietas* often focused on the reciprocal relationship between parents and children: they owed each other affection and duty. Aeneas personified this, in his relationships with father Anchises and son Ascanius. (The lateral relationship with his wife Creusa does not intervene to complicate the ascending–descending bond, as she was lost in the chaos of the burning city of Troy as Aeneas and others escaped.) Images of the threesome were ubiquitous from the early Empire, not only in literature, but on Roman coinage, in public art, and on countless artefacts. A more generalized representation of Pietas, with family implications, came to be associated with women of the imperial family from the latter half of the first century CE. The presence of a child or children with Pietas was a reminder of the importance of child-bearing in the imperial family to give continuity and stability to dynasties. The importance of the family in Roman emperors' ideology and programmes led to the use of the image by even the childless Sabina, wife of Hadrian. On the reverse of one of the coins bearing Sabina's head (about 134–8 CE), Pietas stands with her hands outstretched over the heads of two small children. Later in that century, when the emperor Marcus Aurelius and his wife Faustina the Younger could boast many children of their own, there was diverse imagery of the children and of family ideals, including coinage with representations of Pietas accompanied by many children. The 'duty' aspect of *pietas* came to be imposed by Roman law if it did not flow naturally from affection. These principles were retained in the sixth-century collection of Roman law produced under Justinian (e.g. *Codex Iustinianus* 5.25).

The varied forms of 'family' in many modern societies are due partly to personal choice, but occasionally the state takes a stand on whether some relationships can be defined as a family, for instance single-sex couples. The state has a particular interest in this in matters such as property rights and adoption of children. In Roman society governments took a similar interest in such matters. The law defined what constituted marriage, legitimacy of children, and proper succession of property. This was as much through a concern for orderliness and stability as for morality or religious scruple. The state saw that family stability, and regularity of behaviour, underpinned the stability of the wider society. Morality did play its part in principles such as that of a *testamentum inofficiosum*, 'an undutiful will'. Although Romans had considerable freedom to dispose of property to a wide range of friends, institutions, and family relatives, they could not deprive their closest relatives of a certain minimum percentage without good cause. (The rules are summarized at some length in *Digest* 5.2.) Both parents and children were bound by this duty, reflecting the same mutuality as involved in *pietas*. The fact that a stepmother was sometimes seen as a factor in seducing a father away from his proper duty to his children reflects realignments of family relationships and obligations after disruptions to marriage caused by death or divorce. Families were constantly being reconstituted. We thus cannot conceptualize 'the family' as only the unit of father and mother and their own children. Step-parents, step-siblings, half-siblings, single parents, and sometimes grandparents have to be taken into account. These changing relationships have led some (e.g. Bradley 1991) to speak of 'dislocation' in the Roman family, positing instability in emotional bonds. Nevertheless, studies of other societies show how resilient and adaptive children can be as family and social situations change. A large study of Latin epitaphs by Saller and Shaw (1984) showed that the commemorations were overwhelmingly between husband and wife or between parents and children. These were surely the core group of affective relationships. But they were not necessarily the whole household or the complete family network. The Roman term *familia* was closer to 'household' than to our term 'family'. It could comprise not only the conjugal family but also various dependants, especially slaves. It did not normally include more remote relatives and was not equivalent to 'extended' or 'joint' family.

Demographic factors combined with the institution of slavery to define the family more widely. Some basic probabilities about the demographic dynamics of the population in the Roman West have become clear in recent years, with work drawing on family-reconstitution studies of pre-modern societies in Western Europe in later periods. Richard Saller (1994) has worked with demographers to do a computer simulation which produced a plausible profile of the Roman family over its life-cycle. This reveals that by early adulthood a majority of men and women had probably lost their father because of mortality rates. This helps mitigate the picture of a severe male head of household (the *paterfamilias*) dominating the whole lives of his descendants. The law did originally allow the *pater* almost complete power (the *patria potestas*) over offspring, but this was continually being modified as the Imperial period progressed and the law intervened in family matters, probably in line with public opinion. Computer projections for other stages of childhood show that many children were deprived of a close relationship with a parent by a parent's early death. That men were usually about ten years older than women when they married has implications for relationships between spouses and between fathers and children.

The frequent loss of children at young ages helps explain the willingness of parents to raise non-kin children (often slaves) as companions to a sole surviving son or daughter or even as a substitute when all children had died or when a couple had been unable to produce any children of their own. Romans did not use adoption for this purpose. (See Corbier's collection, 1999.) The formal processes of adoption (*adrogatio* and *adoptio*) were prescribed in some detail by Roman law, and adoptees were normally young adult males (although we know of a few adopted adult females). The purpose of adoption was to create a legal heir, one who would take on the family name of his new father, continue the family line, protect and pass on family property. Useful family networks were strengthened in this way. The chances of survival for an adult adoptee were greater than for an infant, and another family might be more likely to give up a grown son at an age when they knew that they had another surviving. Most of the emperors of the first two-and-a-half centuries of the Principate had to rely on adoption: only Vespasian and Marcus Aurelius were succeeded by natural sons. Women were not able to adopt, as they did not have *potestas*, the legal power to head a household and thus take in a new member, although for everyday purposes many women did have to take on responsibility for a household when a husband was absent or dead.

Because of the strict rules for adoption, and the financial and political motives for it, it was likely to be of interest mainly to a small, upper-class section of the population. There was a less formal relationship between fosterers and surrogate children such as *uernae* (slave children raised from birth or infancy in an owner's house) and *alumni* (foster-children who may sometimes have been kin, perhaps orphans, and were more likely to be of free status). Other children who did not have a full formal relationship with parents were those deemed 'illegitimates' (*spurii*) in that they were born of a de facto union, one which did not qualify as a full Roman marriage. Augustus' status limits on eligibility for marriage, or the slave status of one parent at the time of a child's birth, made many children illegitimate in a formal sense. But *spurii* were not subject to the moral stigma which illegitimates have been subject to in modern, Christian societies. Those who are recorded were the result of a status deficiency in their parents' union, not of moral irresponsibility. They had no legal link to their father and his family, but if the mother was of free, citizen status so were her children.

Families, poor or wealthy, involved carers in addition to parents to help bring up children. This sometimes arose from necessity, but there was also a concept of shared parenting which is alien to the common assumption, in modern western societies, that all parenting functions should be vested in the one pair of biological parents. For poorer families, the extra carer might be only a wetnurse, hired or borrowed to release the mother to return to work. Slave mothers could have this imposed on them by their owner. The health of mothers of all classes will sometimes have made them unable to provide their own milk for their infants. But in wealthier families the use of extra carers was also a matter of choice, being seen as a way to release the mother from chores and to give the child the benefit of a variety of services and influences, such as those of nurse (female or male), tutor, companion, or escort on the way to school. These carers were often slaves. Modern commentators sometimes see this array of carers as weakening close family bonds; but others see it as an enrichment of a child's experience, with the *familia* providing a diverse family environment. Roman society must have been of this latter view, for its law rewarded these relationships. Normally the owner of slaves had to be at least 20 years of age to have the right to give freedom to one of the slaves of the household (to 'manumit' the slave), but under-age owners could manumit a slave who had some close relationship with the owner. Such relationships included those of the carers mentioned above. (And slaves in those carer roles could be manumitted under the normal age of 30.)

The family environment and public life both contributed to the social, intellectual, and moral formation of children. Values and ideals were absorbed by children through formal and informal education, in schools and in the home. In their early years they heard stories, legends, and myths from parents, nurses, and other carers. Such stories often had a moral basis, providing examples of behaviour to be emulated or avoided, and they provided elements of Roman history based on exploits of Roman heroes (and, occasionally, heroines). A literary collection of these was made by Valerius Maximus in the early first century CE, in his *Memorable Sayings and Doings* (*Facta et Dicta Memorabilia*). *Pietas* was one of the qualities such stories illustrated, as in the story of the daughter who suckled her imprisoned mother to keep her alive (5.4). Valerius acknowledged the moral value of these stories, and their contribution to present society, in the preface to Book 2 of his collection: 'We need to learn the origins of this fortunate life which we now lead, under the best of emperors [Tiberius], so that a backward look at them can be of some benefit to our present behaviour (*moribus*).' Stories such as these were reinforced by the monuments and physical context of the towns in which children moved, amongst temples, statues, honorific inscriptions, and (along the roads leading out of town) tombs and epitaphs, commemorating families and individuals. Religious ceremonies underlined the role of the gods in Rome's destiny; triumphs celebrated military glory and the wealth associated with conquest; speeches in law-courts and from the *rostra* helped mould opinion.

For upper-class young males, education was vital for their personal formation and public success. In their teens they embarked on the study of rhetoric, a wide-ranging training in skills necessary for public life—politics, the law-courts, military commands, senior levels of administration. Although there was not, in general, a curriculum prescribed and enforced by the state, the efforts of the Republican Senate and censors (in 161 and 92 BCE) to try to control the kind of rhetoric teachers and teaching available in Rome reflects their recognition of the public importance of that stage of education. By the Imperial period, the rhetorical exercises of *declamationes* and *controuersiae* (monologues and debating speeches) were firmly established as the basis of higher education, although philosophy and other subjects also had a role. These exercises, which usually addressed a moral dilemma, and in which family relationships dominated, have been much criticized in antiquity and modern times for their artificiality and lack of relevance to 'real life'. It is true that the situations and characters discussed are often lurid, and the laws cited are fictional, but themes such as father–son conflict, loyalty and rivalry between brothers, 'wicked' stepmothers, and rape were not necessarily remote from young men's experience, even if presented in extreme forms in rhetorical exercises. Recent analysis has suggested that the very choice of remote or taboo subjects tapped into contemporary concerns, and gave adolescents the freedom to address them and the means to work out rational solutions. The system continued for centuries. Rhetoric continued to be seen to be useful, the necessary pathway to success and standing. It was a process of learning how to 'be Roman' in private and public life. Family values and ideals intersected with those of public life.

In less established ranks of society, families identified education as the path to success and upward mobility. Some brought their sons to Rome from country towns to get access to the best of this kind of education. Ex-slave fathers were particularly conscious of the opportunities opened up by the study of rhetoric. Part of Petronius' satire on this level of society on the Bay of Naples (in his *Satyricon*) is aimed at the rhetorical education of sons who had ambitions but lacked common sense and practical knowledge. Many slaves and ex-slaves, however, acquired skills which gave them good careers in private homes and in public life. The rapidly expanding bureaucracy under the emperors was drawn largely from the emperors' own households: we refer to it now as the *Familia Caesaris*. At senior levels, freedmen such as the Secretary for Petitions, the Secretary for Correspondence, and the Treasury Secretary (*a libellis, ab epistulis, a rationibus*) were very powerful, and large numbers at lower levels provided useful services to emperor and society.

There was no formal role for most women in public life, so they did not attend rhetorical schools, but society recognized other roles for them. As mothers they shared responsibility for the early education of their children; as successful business-women they were able to donate funds and commission public works for their towns; and within ambitious families daughters might acquire educational and cultural attainments which would facilitate desirable marriages and made them more effective citizens.

How did the masses, who had no access to the various processes which might be termed 'education', become connected with their city and its values? There were wider socializing processes inherent in the life, ritual, and physical environment of towns and city. The city provided an education in what was Roman and what members of Roman society might admire and perhaps aspire to achieve. For most Romans, the city was an integral part of their lives. Many lived in cramped and crowded dwellings, and most of their activities were out-of-doors. Did they participate in public activities as families or as discrete individuals? Images of the emperor's distributions (*congiaria*) usually show a father with child or children as recipients. When thanksgivings had been decreed for the exposure of Catiline's plot to seize power in Rome in 63 BCE, the consul Cicero called on the men of Rome to come into the streets with wives and children to celebrate together. But in the theatres, from at least Augustus' time, women were separated from men, boys had their own block of seats, and their slave attendants sat in a nearby block.

The seating which provided separately and hierarchically for married men and (male) children may have advertised publicly the value placed on marriage and children, but it ensured that festivals and entertainments were experienced in groups other than the family. Roman society drew strength not only from the family unit but also from other groups bound by their own special links and experiences.

Public rituals were the vehicle for public memory. Funerals of important citizens fulfilled such a purpose for family and for society, parading ancestors of high public office. The histories written for their families had a public focus, linking family glory with public achievement and honour, and family memory was linked to public memory in the public monuments which celebrated the names of prominent families and fostered a strong sense of history. Family *gloria* and national *gloria* were intertwined.

Religion was integral to all public performance. In private rituals (such as those of birth, marriage, death, coming-of-age), families called on the gods for individual blessings and aid. In the public sphere these habits were easily applied to the common cause of the Roman people, and the emperor as *pater patriae* replicated and magnified the role of the father in the domestic setting. As emperors became increasingly identified or associated with specific gods the religious base for society was reinforced. Many different religions coexisted in this multicultural society, and there was general participation in Rome's traditional religious festivals. Only the Christians had difficulty with the worship of the emperor. This conflict surfaced publicly on a few occasions in the first two centuries, drawing the retribution of the state, but in most respects early Christians accommodated to the societies in which they resided. In the Western Mediterranean, at least, they were a subset of Roman society, living (and worshipping) in housing similar to that of others in their towns, sharing the same streets, attending the same entertainments. There was later Christian criticism of Roman festivals, and houses were specially adapted for the purposes of House Churches, but we should not retroject such evidence, from the fourth century and later, to the behaviour of Christians in Roman towns in earlier periods. It is sometimes thought that Christianity transformed attitudes to family life, but close studies of early Christian writings and legislation indicate that continuity is more obvious than change. Augustus' family legislation had continued for centuries, with details often elaborated or clarified but without dilution of the basic concept and purpose of marriage. The monogamous nature of Roman marriage and its basic purpose of raising children continued. From the fourth century on, asceticism provided new roles, outside marriage, for Christian men and women, but it did not supplant marriage. Constantine modified some aspects of the Augustan family legislation, removing disincentives to non-marriage, restricting (but not prohibiting) divorce, restricting the legal roles of wives, and being more punitive about mixed-status unions. This was more likely due to increasing conservatism than to the direct influence of Christianity, but it will have laid the basis for more restrictive Christian legislation later.

Christian commemorations of the dead which we can date to comparatively early periods do show some variation from those of non-Christians. There is less emphasis on family relationships and more on the concept of a common bond as children of God. And the imagery moves away from the representations of everyday life to biblical scenes and hopes for a future life with God. Does this indicate some disengagement from the secular life, from the city in which they lived? This is a question little explored from this point of view, but should find its place in the growing dialogue between Romanists and historians of early Christianity (as in Balch and Osiek 2003).

How did members of the large and diverse society under Roman rule learn to be Romans? Were there shared values and ideals? We have seen the effects of shared physical space and monuments and rituals, the role of formal and informal education, the interest of Roman law in family behaviour, and the ideals embodied in the public image of leading families. A list of qualities extracted from all of these would certainly include *pietas*. Augustus' shield (recorded in his *Res Gestae* 34) proclaimed *pietas*, *uirtus* (untranslatable, but perhaps 'physical and moral quality'), *clementia* ('clemency'), and *iustitia* ('justice'). Rome's world mission, advertised in Virgil's *Aeneid* (6.851–3), was to provide humane and peaceful government but to use military might to achieve this if necessary. Elaborate military parades continued, even under the Roman Peace (*pax Romana*). Monuments commemorating Rome's victories reflect a duality in Rome's treatment of families. The 'Roman family' might be valued in Roman culture and ideology, but the disintegration of families of 'the other', the enemy, was a key element in the aftermath of Rome's victories. Separation of parents and humiliation of women and children were symbolic of the loss of national identity of foreign enemies. In other areas, however, where foreigners came to an accommodation with Rome, they could aspire to be part of Roman culture, and families could hope to see their sons become magistrates and officials in the Roman system of government, just as some slave families could look to upwards mobility through the higher status of their children.

Further reading

The primary reference for marriage law and practice is S. Treggiari, *Roman Marriage*: iusti coniuges *from the Time of Cicero to the Time of Ulpian* (Oxford: Clarendon Press, 1991). B. Rawson, *Children and Childhood in Roman Italy* (Oxford: Oxford University Press, 2003), has references to the preceding series of Roman Family books, including her *The Family in Ancient Rome: New Perspectives* (London and Sydney: Croom Helm, 1986). R. Saller and B. Shaw did a large study of Latin epitaphs in the Roman West, illustrating the centrality of the conjugal group in these commemorations. Saller built on this and his own further work in his *Patriarchy, Property and Death in the Roman Family* (Cambridge: Cambridge University Press, 1994). For demography, see T. Parkin, *Demography in Roman Society*

(Baltimore and London: Johns Hopkins Press, 1992), and W. Scheidel (ed.), *Debating Roman Demography* (Leiden: Brill, 2001). The elderly are discussed by Parkin in *Old Age in the Roman World* (Baltimore: Johns Hopkins Press, 2003). In *Discovering the Roman Family* (Oxford: Oxford University Press, 1991), K. Bradley discusses many aspects of the family, upper and lower classes. He presents the argument for 'dislocation'.

Current areas of study which bear on family studies include socialization, values, sexuality, and formation of the individual. For ideals of female sexuality and behaviour, see R. Langlands, *Sexual Morality in Ancient Rome* (Cambridge: Cambridge University Press, 2006). For male ideals, see M. McDonnell, *Roman Manliness:* Virtus *and the Roman Republic* (Cambridge: Cambridge University Press, 2006). S. Dixon discusses sexuality and other methodological problems in *Reading Roman Women: Sources, Genres and Real Life* (London: Duckworth, 2001). S. Treggari, *Terentia, Tullia and Publilia: The Women of Cicero's Family* (London: Routledge, 2007), puts women of a prominent family into their private and public settings at a time of turmoil. Values are discussed by R. Kaster in *Emotion, Restraint, and Community in Ancient Rome* (New York: Oxford University Press, 2005), and by T. Morgan in *Popular Morality in the Early Roman Empire* (Cambridge: Cambridge University Press, 2007).

Law and property continue to be important topics. A useful resource is B. Frier, *A Casebook on Roman Family Law* (New York: Oxford University Press, 2004). See also E. Champlin, *Final Judgments: Duty and Emotion in Roman Wills 200 B.C.–A.D. 250* (Berkeley: University of California Press, 1991), and J. Gardner, *Family and* Familia *in Roman Law and Life* (Oxford: Clarendon Press, 1998). J. Evans Grubbs, *Law and Family in Late Antiquity: The Emperor Constantine's Marriage Legislation* (New York: Oxford University Press, 1995), takes the topic into the fourth century, joining others interested in the family in late antiquity and early Christianity, e.g. G. Nathan, *The Family in Late Antiquity: The Rise of Christianity and the Endurance of Tradition* (London: Routledge, 2000), and Balch and Osiek 2003.

The family in rural society is still difficult to reconstruct, but see N. Rosenstein, *Rome at War: Farms, Families, and Death in the Middle Republic* (Chapel Hill: University of North Carolina Press, 2004). For the context for families beyond Italy, see G. Woolf, *Becoming Roman: The Origins of Provincial Civilization in Gaul* (Cambridge: Cambridge University Press, 1998), and M. George (ed.), *The Roman Family in the Empire: Rome, Italy, and Beyond* (Oxford: Oxford University Press, 2005).

References

Balch, D. and Osiek, C. (2003). *Early Christian Families in Context.* Grand Rapids, Mich.: Eerdmans.

Cohen, D. and Saller, R. (1994). 'Foucault on Sexuality in Greco-Roman Antiquity', in J. Goldstein (ed.), *Foucault and the Writing of History.* Maldon, Mass.: Blackwell, 35–69.

Corbier, M. (ed.) (1999). *Adoption et fosterage.* Paris: De Boccard.

Flower, H. (1996). *Ancestor Masks and Aristocratic Power in Roman Culture.* Oxford: Clarendon Press.

Milnor, K. (2005). *Gender, Domesticity, and the Age of Augustus.* Oxford: Oxford University Press.

MÜNZER, F. (1920). *Römische Adelsparteien und Adelsfamilien.* Stuttgart: J. B. Metzler, tr. T. Ridley (1999). Baltimore and London: Johns Hopkins University Press.

RAWSON, B. (1986). *The Family in Ancient Rome.* London: Croom Helm.

SALLER, R. and SHAW, B. (1984). 'Tombstones and Roman Family Relations in the Principate: Civilians, Soldiers and Slaves', *Journal of Roman Studies,* 74: 124–56.

SEVERY, B. (2003). *Augustus and the Family at the Birth of the Roman Empire.* London and New York: Routledge.

SYME, R. (1939). *The Roman Revolution.* Oxford: Clarendon Press.

ZANKER, P. (1988). *The Power of Images in the Age of Augustus.* Ann Arbor, Mich.: University of Michigan Press.

ZIMMERMAN, C. (1947). *Family and Civilization.* New York: Harper.

CHAPTER 39

FREEDOM AND SLAVERY

KEITH BRADLEY

Tacitus famously opens his account of the Julii and Claudii with a disquisition on the history at Rome of freedom and monarchy (*Annals* 1.1). The rapid survey from the kings to the foundation of the Principate prepares for the work's major theme, the demise of political freedom under a sinister system of government established and maintained by a dynasty of repressive autocrats. The body of the work reveals that those who dared to speak out against the regime were silenced—the victim of imperial oppression is a stock character in Tacitus' narrative (Walker 1952)—and that freedom of speech, *libertas*, especially among the ruling elite, to all intents and purposes disappeared: freedom as the old Republic knew it was swept away and Rome's Senate, which for centuries had shaped policy and presided over the growth of Mediterranean empire, was reduced to a state of servitude—as even emperors complained (*Ann.* 3.65).

Tacitus' indictment of the Augustan system is open to dispute. The victimization of opponents was never as extreme as his artistry suggests, and claims of justification might in any case be made. The truth is that in the mission of empire most Roman senators were eager to support the Julio-Claudian emperors: personal advancement depended on the emperor's favour and there were few unwilling to seek it. Tacitus himself received the support of the Flavian emperors (*Histories* 1.1), rising to the summit of the senatorial career with a consulship, in 97, and the proconsulship of Asia some years later (Birley 2000). Tacitus was to stigmatize Domitian, the last of the Flavians, who was assassinated in 96, as a tyrant. But his consulship could scarcely have been awarded without Domitian's approval, and compliance in his rule on Tacitus' part. Hence a histrionic display of inner turmoil in an early composition in reference to monstrous assaults on senators who had risked opposition (*Agricola* 45.1–2), and a strong residue of guilt even in the more mature history. A historian celebrated for his psychological perceptiveness had a complex psychology of his own, palpably discernible in the pages of the *Annals*. Tacitus in his own person is a paradoxical symbol of the intimate bond in Roman culture between freedom and slavery.

The language of servitude that Tacitus uses to convey his concern for the loss of liberty is rhetorical and metaphorical. But the point I want to emphasize in this chapter is that the import of his language, and of the anxiety that underlies it, can be fully appreciated only when the language is set in the context of the contemporary and traditional realities of Roman slavery. My object, therefore, is to outline what I take to be some key features of the institution of slavery at Rome, and to stress in so doing that freedom and slavery for Romans were indissociable entities.

Rome was a genuine slave society. What does this mean? Terminology is all-important but problematical. First, the factors of time and place. 'Rome' can mean either the capital of empire, Rome the city, or the capital together with peninsular Italy and Sicily that formed the core of empire, or the empire at large, or, more diffusely, the culture of *Romanitas* that developed wherever Roman imperial rule established itself. Secondly, 'slave society': how is this phrase to be understood? Numbers come immediately to mind. You cannot have a slave society without a significant servile presence, and so one way to proceed is to look to numerical significance, to stipulate, for instance, that a fixed fraction of the total population, a quarter perhaps or a third, must be made up of slaves in order for a society, any society, to qualify as a genuine slave society. As a corollary it might be assumed that a significant slave population must be economically productive, engaged as were the slave populations of the Caribbean and the Americas in more recent periods of history in the production for export and sale on world markets of bulk crops such as sugar, coffee, cotton, tobacco, or indigo. The definitional weight falls on quantitative and economic factors.

In Rome's case, it is generally agreed that the numbers of slaves varied from place to place and from time to time (cf. Jones 1956). There were probably more slaves in the city of Rome in Tacitus' day than in the era of, say, the elder Cato, both absolutely and proportionally, but the number of slaves in Roman Egypt was probably smaller, both absolutely and proportionally, than in Roman Italy. On this basis 'Rome' was a slave society only in certain times and places: peninsular Italy of the central historical period, from *c.*200 BCE to *c.*200 CE, would probably qualify, but not Roman Egypt, whose slave population was only about one-tenth of the whole—though there is an irony here, because Roman Egypt with its uniquely abundant documentary evidence supplies some of the most detailed information on slavery in antiquity as a whole. Knowledge about numbers is, of course, imperfect because Romans did not express themselves in ways, or in ways still easily accessible, that permit secure statistical knowledge to emerge. In the last generation the Italian slave population in the time of Augustus has been calculated as more than a third, or about 30 per cent, or, most recently, as between 15 to 25 per cent of the total; and while slaves have traditionally been viewed overwhelmingly as primary producers living and working in rural districts, occupied especially in agriculture, a consequence of the last estimate is the proposition that more slaves were to be found in cities than in rural areas and that they were less engaged in agriculture than in the provision of services (Scheidel 2004, 2005; cf. Jongmann 2003). For the central period as a whole this notably goes against all the assumptions of the Roman writers on farming, Cato, Varro, and Columella, who evidently expected their readers, wherever they were, to have had plentiful access to slaves as a form of labour for both arable and pastoral farming. My point, however, is simply to highlight the problems of definition using conventional regional, numerical, and economic criteria, or even the related test of identifying the principal owners of slaves (Finley 1980: ch. 2). The situation becomes more problematical still once specific items of evidence are observed in which the slave presence is assumed but ill-defined, such as the body of rules that regulated operations in the mining district of Vipasca in Lusitania (Smallwood 1966: no. 439). The rules prescribed penalties for slaves who stole or caused damage that were different from (and harsher than) the penalties stipulated for free criminals, and they imply the presence, and perhaps the considerable presence, of slaves in the mines when the document was composed, probably in the early second century CE. But does it follow that Lusitania as a whole was then a slave society? How would contemporaries indeed have distinguished between a local area with a heavy concentration of slaves and one with a low concentration? What difference did it make?

The importance can hardly be overstated of determining how many slaves there were in different regions of the Roman world at different periods of history, how the development of slavery was affected by the basic economic principle of demand and supply, and how slave labour functioned in relation to free labour. Was one more efficient or preferred than the other, and if so under what conditions? But because of the difficulties involved all answers are necessarily provisional. I imagine that Roman slave-owners were as capable as owners in later ages of thinking about the economic practicalities involved in slave-owning and of the overall profitability of the labour regimes at their disposal: there is evidence in Columella, for example, of an ability to calculate, even if, as some historians suggest, mistakenly (Duncan-Jones 1974: ch. 1). But if you were to ask whether Roman civilization was based on slave labour—many take for granted that it was (Davis 2006; cf. Schiavone 2000)—no incontestably positive answer can in my view be given. In the central period some slaves were used to produce staple crops (grain, vines, olives), and others were used to manufacture finished goods and to build the theatres, amphitheatres, circuses and other buildings characteristic of Roman cities. But they were not used exclusively, either in place or in time. Slave labour and free labour were not rival economic categories but compatible options open to those with exploitative ambitions whose choices depended on a variety of local factors: the kind of work to be done, the availability of particular types of labour, their relative efficiency, reliability, and suitability for the purpose at hand.

Tacitus' preoccupation with liberty and servitude serves as a reminder that freedom at Rome, however 'Rome' is understood, was not a general right but a select privilege. It was available to some but not to all. The law stated that all men were either free or slaves (Gaius, *Inst.* 1.9), and it assumed in so doing that both categories were elemental in the construction of society. One could not exist without the other. There were, of course, different grades of freedom and different grades of unfreedom (Finley 1964). But there was no thought that one could prevail over the other, no concept that freedom was a right available to everyone as that right is presented and expressed in, for instance, the American Declaration of Independence (1776) or the French Declaration of the Rights of Man (1789). (Both these documents, incidentally, were created by slave-owning regimes.) The Saturnalia, a period of carnival celebrated close to the winter solstice during which Rome relaxed its fixation with social boundaries and allowed slaves forms of licence ordinarily disallowed, recalled for a few days each year a distant mythical age when all men had once been equal and slavery did not exist (Justin 43.1.3–4; Lucian, *Sat.* 7; Tacitus knew the connection between *libertas* and *licentia*). But once the holiday was over the 'normal' division of slave and free was quickly restored. The reality was that, in the highly status-conscious world of historical Rome, no one could imagine a society without the unfree, and for all the gifts of jellied figs in a Libyan jar and other holiday delights (Mart. 4.46), the Saturnalia was no more than a momentary diversion that never inspired a vision of social change or improvement. Slavery at Rome was not regarded as a moral evil that had to be suppressed, and it produced no abolitionist advocates of the sort prominent in the modern history of slavery: no Sharp or Wilberforce, no Stephen or Clarkson. Legend had it that slavery had entered the world when Jupiter overthrew Saturn and the powerful came to control wealth they refused to share with the less fortunate (Lactantius, *Div. Inst.* 5.5.1–5.6.13). In the event, and long into the Imperial age, it was Jupiter who remained ascendant.

The consequence was that freedom and slavery coexisted in historical Rome as mutually necessary and reinforcing social categories. Whatever the gradations on either side, freedom and slavery formed two sides of an indivisible coin each essential to the other, and it is in this ideological sense—the sense that the freedom of some depended on and was guaranteed by the enslavement of others—that Rome can be reasonably defined as a slave society. It is a definition that emphasizes cultural disposition and structure on the one hand and the bias of the historical record on the other, and it maintains validity across time and space, recognizing that slaves were a 'normal' and predictable component of society at large, as any number of familiar documents might suggest—Claudius' letter to the Alexandrians (*P. Lond.* 1912), for example, in which claims of citizenship made by people born of slave mothers are specifically and tellingly disallowed (some allowance for slavery has to be made); or the customs tariff from mid-second century Palmyra (Matthews 1984), which includes details on the tolls to be levied on slaves transported in and out of the city (the document implies a steady but essentially immeasurable trade in slaves on the far eastern edge of the Roman Empire). In a different medium, a calendar mosaic from third-century El Djem showing the month of December with a group of holidaying slaves as a matter of generally understood course allows the same kind of inference about the essentiality of slavery to be made (Parrish 1984: 158; cf. Dunbabin 1978: 111–12). As a fundamental constituent of society slavery is never in doubt, which means that its economic development followed from, and was subsidiary to, the ideological starting-point of the socially normative.

Formally slaves did not exist except as the property of their owners. Devoid of legal personality and human individuality, they were unable to own property themselves or to establish family ties. As degraded, rightless beings, they were conceptually akin to other forms of property, the only difference being that slaves were understood to be articulate (Varro, *Rust.* 1.17.1). Conventionally, therefore, historians classify slaves as marginal beings barred from participation in the affairs of the civic community. Slaves were 'outsiders' (Lévy-Bruhl 1934). This view, however, obscures in my judgement what I will call the all-pervasive ideological weight of slavery in Roman culture, some examples of which have just been seen, and the high functional visibility of slaves engaged in work and services of innumerable sorts across time and place. In the central and most characteristic era of Roman history the presence of the slave, whether actual or symbolic, was as far as I can tell everywhere inescapable. Two particular aspects of social practice make this clear.

First, the spectacular display of individual merit that Roman culture, especially elite culture, prized so heavily. One purpose of Roman slave-owning was to advertise through the possession of human property the power and prestige of the slave-owner. This is reflected in the convention of the grand entourage of slave attendants—'the splendid brigade of slaves', in Seneca's phrase (*Epistles* 110.17)—with which upper-class Romans surrounded themselves when they appeared in public. The entourage heralded the appearance of greatness and had to be appropriately noticeable, as it must have been, for instance, on 1 May 165, when the governor of Macedonia, P. Antius Orestes, entered the Sanctuary of the Great Gods in Samothrace escorted by his advisors (*amici*), his assistants (*apparitores*), and a military guard—and fifteen personal slaves who bore such names as Dionysius, Zelotus, Moschus, Lydus, and Zoticus (Oliver 1966). A small retinue of three or four slaves could be taken as a mark of personal restraint, perhaps prompted by a philosophically inspired taste for the ascetic. But a small retinue was repeatedly noted as exceptional. Size mattered. And fifteen slaves could put you in mind of a chain-gang (Valerius Maximus 4.3.11–12, 4.4.11; Apuleius, *Apol.* 17.9; Athenaeus 627e; Apuleius, *Apol.* 47.6).

Concern for the display of power is similarly evident in the way slave-owners adorned their urban residences and rural villas with elaborately rendered paintings, mosaics and statues which, incongruously it seems at first, depicted slaves and the servile at work in time- and energy-demanding menial jobs, both agricultural and domestic, that owners themselves would never have done: trampling out the vintage and gathering in the olive harvest, the multifarious tasks involved in securing the riches of the sea, serving at table or otherwise ministering to personal needs (Parrish 1984; Dunbabin 1978: ch. 7). Such images romanticized labour and concealed the drudgery the jobs demanded; but they expressed as well the capacity to own and command and to extract symbolic value from it, permitting visiting peers to witness the extent of their resources—it was impressive for a slave-owner in Baetica to have a bronze statuette of a young African in use as a lamp-stand: it implied his ability to import slaves from beyond the Sahara—and providing the slaves who saw them with reminders of their own inferiority and powerlessness. To some extent the slaves in these images were indistinguishable from the free, not marked out by race as were the slaves of the Americas, but this was evidently not an issue for Romans themselves.

Secondly, Roman religion. It was important to Romans to maintain harmony between the human world and the divine world. Roman culture was a religious culture, as Vigellius Saturninus famously reminded the Christians on trial before him in Carthage in the late second century (*Pass. Sanct. Scill.* 3). Because they were considered a defiling influence, slaves were excluded from some civic cults, and perhaps there is nothing better to substantiate the notion that slaves were outsiders than this. On the other hand, within the Roman household the *paterfamilias* was expected to conduct religious rites on behalf of everyone for whom he was responsible, and slaves might well be present when he did so as members of the *familia* on whom divine favour could fall (cf. Horace, *Epod.* 2.65–6). Cato, in his farm manual, produced specimens of prayers that a Roman farmer might offer for the well-being of his household, his slaves included, and a prayer to Mars called directly for the protection of *pastores* (*Ag.* 141.3).

Some slaves, moreover, were visibly prominent in the performance of public rituals. The *victimarii* who led to the slaughter the oxen, pigs, and sheep sacrificed by Roman magistrates and emperors on behalf of the Roman community were sometimes public slaves (Weiss 2004: 139–41; cf. Gordon 1990: 203), their physical and practical presence significant enough to find lasting commemoration in numerous well-known sculptural records such as the Ara Pacis, Trajan's Arch at Beneventum, and the Arch of Septimius Severus at Lepcis. Their incorporation in ritual was notable enough for the strange belief to develop that it was a bad sign if a kite stole food from them at the moment of immolation (Pliny, *HN* 10.28).

Slaves are also detectable as participants in the mystery cults that were so prominent a feature of Roman religious life in the central era. The great Dionysiac inscription from second-century Italy now in New York (*IGUR* 160; cf. Scheid 1986) gives the names of some 420 members of a Dionysiac *thiasos* who were probably all members of the households of the priestess Pompeia Agrippinilla and her aristocratic relatives. Originally it accompanied a statue set up to Agrippinilla by the members of the cult group. The inscription gives the names of Agrippinilla's husband, a senator, and of other elite members of their family; but it is also rich in slave names—Eutyches, Carpus, Rufa, Fortunatus—which implies that in conducting their Dionysiac rites social or juridical status made no appreciable difference to the worshippers. Distinctions between master and slave cannot have been altogether obliterated—complete social levelling is not an issue—but the cult evidently integrated its worshippers into a coherent, unified body. No constraint at least was felt as far as publicly disclosing its membership was concerned.

The Christian cult, whose origins were known to Tacitus (*Ann.* 15.44), offers another illustration. Early in its history, in order to demonstrate its unsavoury and intellectually banal character, critical charges were brought that the cult looked to slaves as potential recruits (Origen, *C. Cels.* 3.48–50). By the fourth century, however, Jerome is found (*Epistles* 22.29) exhorting his correspondent Eustochium to interact with her slave women, especially to eat with them, as a way of reinforcing their common Christian commitment to chastity.

Almost paradoxically, it emerges, slaves were outsiders and insiders simultaneously. If formally rightless, disposable commodities, they were at the same time human agents of some capacity, and recognized as such, never fully reducible to the level of the animals with which they were habitually equated (Tertullian, for instance (*Apol.* 14.1), thought the same poor cuts of sacrificial meat were as suitable for slaves as for dogs). Above all, they were always there, 'inside' in one form or another, often indispensably so, providing among other things the most intimate of services: bringing the piss-pot at the snap of the fingers (Mart. 6.89, 14.119), or standing guard in the bedroom (Val. Max. 1.7.7), even watching as their owners had sex. Slaves were everywhere, visible and essential—though you did not always talk to them (Col. *RR* 1.8.15).

More paradoxically still, for all the slave's value to the owner as an investment, and no matter how well this slave or that was treated, slavery as an institution was based ultimately on the violent subjection of one person to another that arose from the dominating power claimed when life was spared upon defeat in warfare (e.g. Dionysius of Halicarnassus 1.65.2, 1.72.4, 2.3.6). So slaves were always at war with their owners (cf. Seneca, *Ep.* 18.4). It is sometimes said that Roman slavery became more humane over time, especially in the high Imperial age because there are indications in law that excessively cruel treatment was discouraged. Tacitus might have been aware of this. In practice, however, the slave remained at the disposal of the owner, and whatever restrictions were introduced were difficult to enforce. When, in the late third century, Flavia Politta put her Christian slave Sabina in bonds and drove her out into the hills near Smyrna to rid her household of Christian contagion, her actions were questioned by neither the local temple-warden nor the proconsul of Asia who later interrogated Sabina at the trial of her Christian companion Pionius (*Mart. Pion.* 9). Christians themselves understood that the violent connection between slavery and subjection was normative and in no need of change. Lactantius (*Div. Inst.* 4.3.14–17, 4.4.1–2, 4.4.11) expected the owner to have the power of life and death over the slave and the slave to stand in fear of the owner; Jerome (*Ep.* 22.40) raised no objection to the brutalizing of slaves for trivial reasons; and while Ambrose (*De Off.* 2.70–1; cf. Cicero, *De Off.* 2.63) thought it a mark of Christian liberality to ransom enslaved prisoners—he knew of recent episodes of capture in Illyricum and Thrace—he did not question the practice of enslavement in warfare itself: rather, he said, like Joseph the slave was to endure servitude in humble submission whatever the desire for freedom (1.112, 2.20, 2.86).

Rome ruled the Mediterranean by force. Its culture was deeply militaristic and its leading citizens saw it as their destiny to build a limitless empire. Through images that glorified enslavement and validated the bending of others to their will, Romans of every generation learned that the shackled captive was a fixed element in their world (cf. Bradley 2004). Sarcophagi from Tacitus' era and beyond graphically portray scenes of battle that Romans routinely enjoyed and regarded as suitably symbolic for commemorative purposes. The Portonaccio and Ludovisi sarcophagi are supreme examples: Roman generals and troops viciously strike down barbarian enemies, and prisoners not already in the throes of death are bound in chains, their faces filled with panic and desperation, their bodies writhing in pain, in preparation for sale at the slave-market. Much earlier Cicero (*De Off.* 2.45) had pointed to warfare as the arena in which his son should seek glory. At a significantly later date Lactantius (again) said that warfare and the destruction or enslavement of the defeated remained the 'only path to immortality' (*Div. Inst.* 1.18.8). There was little scope in all this for the humane, and it is no surprise that the former slave who himself became a slave-owner should be expected, on the example of the kingly Trimalchio, to see the physical pain he had once experienced himself as an appropriate instrument of control to use on others (cf. Petronius, *Satyricon* 28.7, 34.2, 49.1–50.1). The violence inherent in slavery was part of an unchanging social order, with the odd but understandable result that you could even find the origin of the Caryatid in the shamefulness of brutal enslavement consequent on warfare (Vitruvius 1.1.5).

Intellectually, of course, slavery could be categorized as an unnatural condition (cf. *Dig.* 1.5.4; Garnsey 1996), and it is in its contrary-to-nature character that the source of its paradoxical features lies. Except in rare and untypical situations slaves did not choose to become slaves. Because slavery was unnatural, however, slave-owners consciously had to manage their human property to ensure the smooth functioning of their households and estates (Bradley 1987). In their several treatises the writers on farming make practical recommendations on slave management, giving chapter and verse on the types of slaves to use, what to feed them, how to clothe them, how to motivate them; and debts to earlier Greek works notwithstanding, their remarks remain an incontestably important expression of how urgent the need for regulation was. They display an intense concern with coercing slaves along divide-and-conquer lines, providing models in the process for slave-owners in later slave societies.

The greatest incentive owners could offer was the prospect of freedom. Manumission was a device that Rome instituted early in its history, and slave-owners used it to their advantage for centuries. By definition it assumed that slavery was an inherently undesirable condition. How many slaves in particular periods of Roman history were set free is unknown. In conventional literary and epigraphical sources former slaves are ubiquitous, and the inference that most slaves were freed sooner or later is comprehensible, though in my view erroneous. Less controversial is the underlying function of manumission. The divide-and-conquer principle of extending its power by incorporating enemies within the Roman body politic through selective grants of citizenship was a strategy of empire from the outset (Sherwin-White 1939). The legend of the Sabine chieftain Attus Clausus, who was admitted to the Roman community and subsequently became the founder of the distinctly 'Roman' Claudii—a legend known to Tacitus (*Ann.* 11.24; cf. 4.9, 12.25)—gives the paradigmatic illustration. In private relations piecemeal grants of freedom had the effect of dividing and weakening the slave population, as anticipation of manumission induced devotion to duty and promoted individualistic rather than corporate concerns (cf. Dion. Hal. 4.23). Rome was an unusual slave society in that it allowed manumitted slaves to become citizens (after Augustus this was not automatic but often the final reality), and over time the suspicion grew that there were few free Romans who did not have servile antecedents, once more as Tacitus himself was aware (*Ann.* 13.27). But if the grant of citizenship was distinctive, manumission was not an act of generosity for its own sake. Slaves regularly paid for their freedom—hope went hand in hand with good management of the *peculium*, though there were no guarantees (Virgil, *Ecl.* 1.32; Suetonius, *Vesp.* 16.3)—and this allowed owners to buy replacements for those they set free. Manumitting slaves was a way of refuelling the Roman slavery system (cf. Hopkins 1978: ch. 1).

The success of manumission as a means of social manipulation is evident in the way that some slaves internalized the values of established society and integrated themselves within it. Roman sculpture provides compelling testimony. In the last century of the Republic the habit developed among prosperous former slaves of representing themselves and their family members in commemorative reliefs, often in funerary contexts, in which through details of portraiture and clothing their arrival as new members of the Roman citizen community was marked (Kleiner 1977). Typically husbands and wives appear in the toga and *palla*, the quintessential items of Roman dress, their purpose being to show the attainment of citizen respectability and marital harmony, and, through their sternly presented facial features, their claims to traditional upper-class *gravitas* and *dignitas* as well. They show no concern with setting up memorials of life in slavery, not even with portraying what must have been for many the climactic moment of the ceremony when they were set free. Instead they emphasize accommodation and assimilation into the mainstream of society. A speculative view holds that images of ex-slaves in works of art and elaborate funerary monuments encouraged slave viewers to aspire to freedom and to work dutifully to that end (Clarke 2003). The transforming effect of manumission for those fortunate enough to experience it is more certain: with freedom non-persons instantly became real persons, stability in family relations at once replaced instability, social death gave way to social life (cf. Pliny, *HN* 35.77). The change was radical. Contingency, of course, was everything. An extreme indication of how slave-owners understood the attractions of freedom can be found in the record of offers of freedom made in return for physical aid in times of political crisis. During Rome's civil wars such offers were frequent, as they were in similar circumstances in later slave societies. The capacity of slaves to think for themselves, however, and to judge what was in their best interests can be presumed from the way that these offers were sometimes rejected. Manumission was pointless if it could not be guaranteed; but as a manipulable device it had many benefits for the slavery system.

The capacity of slaves to think for themselves can also be deduced from the record of how slaves actively struggled against servitude, either in full-scale rebellion (the enterprise of Spartacus is the classic example), or, more commonly, through trickery and deception—running away, working slowly, sabotaging property, the universal tactics, that is, of petty slave resistance (Bradley 1994: ch. 6). The Roman slave population was a far from passive body, and slave-owners were sensitive to the dangers of insurrection and obstructionism it contained. Hence their fixation with servile loyalty and obedience. Because evidence of life in slavery from slaves themselves is lacking it is sometimes said that the psychology of Rome's slaves—their motives for doing what they did—is impossible to recover (Schiavone 2000: 123–4). Yet, despite deficiencies of evidence, ancient historians have never shied away from commenting on the psychology of non-slaves and this may be too defeatist an attitude. Resistance prompted by the desire for freedom follows consistent patterns over time and place, even up to the present day, as the case of the Mauritanian fugitive Moctar Teyeb confirms. They are patterns that demand recognition of the determination shown by Roman slaves to withstand the rigours of victimization and exploitation that flowed from the contest of minds to which slave-owning naturally gave rise. In that contest slaves were at a disadvantage, but they were not impotent. Martial tells (11.58) of a slave barber who, when shaving his master, his razor at his owner's throat, demands his freedom and a small fortune besides. What is the master to do? In fear for his life he yields to the slave and saves himself from death; but once the razor is out of the way he can immediately take his revenge and have the man's arms and legs broken as the 'normal' balance of power is restored. Whether anything like this ever happened is irrelevant. It is what the story expresses that is important: unequivocal acknowledgement that the slave was an active threat to the slave-owner which somehow had to be forestalled. (The conqueror of Britain, Aulus Plautius, who probably had first-hand experience of a slave revolt, might have had this thought when he met his real-life barber: *ILS* 961, 7414.) Cunning was always matched against cunning.

The immanence of chattel slavery at Rome and the mutuality of freedom and slavery in Roman life to which I have drawn attention enrich, I think, any reading of Tacitus and heighten the force of his rhetorical and metaphorical language. Freedom and slavery are terms he often conjoins: freedom is the corollary of military victory, servitude of defeat (*Ann.* 3.45), the boldness of one senator who dares to speak freely to the emperor exposes the enslavement of the rest (*Ann.* 14.49), a courtier on the point of death claims always to have demonstrated independence rather than subservience (*Ann.* 15.61), a former consul animated by the spirit of freedom chooses to avoid servility by not naming the emperor in his will (*Ann.* 16.11). Servitude, as seen at the outset, is Tacitus' term for the state to which the Roman elite had been reduced by the Augustan dispensation (e.g. *Ann.* 1.2, 1.7; cf. *Hist.* 2.71). It is a state tantamount to death (*Ann.* 2.15), to be expected as habitual among senators even as a particular emperor fostered an image of liberty (*Ann.* 1.81). And it is a condition Tacitus claims to have known himself (*Agr.* 3.3). In a society where slavery was an all-pervasive reality and which, legend apart, knew nothing of the egalitarian or the commonality of privilege, the interplay of liberty and slavery was not a matter of rhetoric and metaphor alone. In the early second century the slave remained a living symbol of everything that was base and degraded, inescapably present and everywhere unmistakably visible. To explain the impact of monarchy through this idiom was, it follows, to pass the most condemning historical judgement possible. It was not all hopeless, of course. In the way that slave-owners allowed some slaves to cross the divide between slavery and freedom, so the beneficent *princeps* advanced his meritorious and faithful servants. The assertion could even be made that *libertas* and *principatus* had finally reached a reconciliation (*Agr.* 3.1; *Hist.* 1.1). Which may or may not be true. In pondering Tacitus' preoccupation with liberty, however, profit may accrue from investing thought in the lives of those his incomparable modern successor took to comprise one element of 'the silent and the submerged'. In a society ideologically and unwaveringly committed to slavery, the dilemma constantly before slaves, to resist or to accommodate, was a dilemma Tacitus knew at first hand.

Further reading

All contemporary studies of Tacitus begin with Syme 1958 (note before the consulship the praetorship of 88 and appointment as *quindecimvir sacris faciundis*). The essential works on *libertas* are Wirszubski 1950 and Brunt 1988: 281–350; Patterson 1991: chs. 12–15 is over-confident in my view on the development of freedom at Rome. The preoccupation is not, of course, unique to Tacitus: Lucan offers another significant illustration from the early Imperial age. For the most recent studies of Roman demography see Scheidel 2004 and 2005, stressing concentration of slaves in Italian cities. Hasegawa 2005 offers a new study of slave occupations in elite households at Rome. On the Saturnalia, see Salzman 1990: 74–6 for its vitality at a late date (fourth century) and cf. Gowers 1993 for observations on Saturnalian food. Given the dangers slavery represented, I wonder whether the festival was ever an occasion for alarm: was Pliny, for instance (*Ep.* 2.17), as secure in seclusion in his Laurentine villa as he wanted his reader to believe? And what did former slaves think and feel in the moments of merriment, especially when slave-owners themselves? In the central era reflective Romans could presumably recall that their ancestors had once abolished debt bondage, but (again paradoxically) this provided no precedent for any further change. For a riveting account of the British abolitionists, see Hochschild 2005, and for a sobering history of resistance to change in the Catholic Church ('first categorical condemnation' in 1965), see Noonan 2005. On scenes of labour much is available in Rostovtzeff 1957. The lamp-stand mentioned is in the Museu Nacional Arqueològic de Tarragona. For other objects and monuments (including the sarcophagi), see variously Ryberg 1955 and Kleiner 1992, and note on freedmen in Roman art the discussion of Petersen 2006. On slaves as witnesses of sexual intimacy, see Clarke 1998. George Orwell was distressed that few slaves are individually known: 'When I think of antiquity, the detail that frightens me is that those hundreds of millions of slaves on whose backs civilisation rested generation after generation have left behind them no record whatever. We do not even know their names': 'Looking Back on the Spanish War' (1942). More are identifiable than he realized (on slave names, see Solin 1996) but his remarks remain forceful. My thanks are due to Katy Schlegel for valuable discussion of this topic.

References

Birley, A. R., 2000. 'The Life and Death of Cornelius Tacitus', *Historia*, 49: 230–47.

Bradley, K. R., 1987. *Slaves and Masters in the Roman Empire*. New York.

—— 1994. *Slavery and Society at Rome*. Cambridge.

—— 2004. 'On Captives Under the Principate', *Phoenix*, 58: 298–318.

Brunt, P. A., 1988. *The Fall of the Roman Republic*. Oxford.

Clarke, J. R., 1998. *Looking at Lovemaking*. Berkeley.

—— 2003. *Art in the Lives of Ordinary Romans*. Berkeley.

Davis, D. B., 2006. *Inhuman Bondage*. New York.

Dunbabin, K. M. D., 1978. *The Mosaics of Roman North Africa*. Oxford.

Duncan-Jones, R. P., 1974. *The Economy of the Roman Empire*. Cambridge (2nd edn. 1982).

Finley, M. I., 1964. 'Between Slavery and Freedom', *Comparative Studies in Society and History*, 6: 233–49; repr. in R. P. Saller and B. D. Shaw (eds.), *Economy and Society in Ancient Greece* (London, 1981), ch. 7.

—— 1980. *Ancient Slavery and Modern Ideology*. New York; expanded version ed. B. D. Shaw (Princeton, 1998).

Garnsey, P. D. A., 1996. *Ideas of Slavery from Aristotle to Augustine*. Cambridge.

GORDON, R., 1990. 'The Veil of Power: Emperors, Sacrificers and Benefactors', in M. Beard and J. North (eds.), *Pagan Priests.* Ithaca, NY, 199–231.
GOWERS, E., 1993. *The Loaded Table.* Oxford.
HASEGAWA, K., 2005. *The* Familia Urbana *During the Early Empire.* Oxford.
HOCHSCHILD, A., 2005. *Bury the Chains.* Boston.
HOPKINS, K., 1978. *Conquerors and Slaves.* Cambridge.
JONES, A. H. M., 1956. 'Slavery in the Ancient World', *Economic History Review,* 9: 185–99; repr. in M. I. Finley (ed.), *Slavery in Classical Antiquity* (Cambridge, 1960; repr. 1968), 1–15.
JONGMANN, W., 2003. 'Slavery and the Growth of Rome', in C. Edwards and G. Woolf (eds.), *Rome the Cosmopolis.* Cambridge, 100–22.
KLEINER, D. E. E., 1977. *Roman Group Portraiture.* New York.
—— 1992. *Roman Sculpture.* New Haven.
LÉVY-BRUHL, H., 1934. 'Théorie de l'esclavage', in *Quelques problèmes du trés ancien droit romain.* Paris, 15–33; repr. in M. I. Finley (ed.), *Slavery in Classical Antiquity* (Cambridge, 1960; repr. 1968), 151–69.
MATTHEWS, J. F., 1984. 'The Tax Law of Palmyra: Evidence for Economic History in a City of the Roman East', *JRS* 74: 157–80.
NOONAN, J. T. JR., 2005. *A Church That Can and Cannot Change.* Notre Dame, Ind.
OLIVER, J. H., 1966. 'A Roman Governor Visits Samothrace', *AJP* 87: 75–80 (cf. P. R. C. Weaver, 'A New Latin Word?', *AJP* 87 (1966), 457–8).
PARRISH, D., 1984. *Season Mosaics of Roman North Africa.* Rome.
PATTERSON, O., 1991. *Freedom.* London.
PETERSEN, L. H., 2006. *The Freedman in Roman Art and Art History.* Cambridge.
ROSTOVZEFF, M. I., 1957. *The Social and Economic History of the Roman Empire* (2nd edn. rev. P. M. Fraser). Oxford.
RYBERG, I. S., 1955. *Rites of the State Religion in Roman Art.* Rome.
SALZMAN, M. R., 1990. *On Roman Time.* Berkeley.
SCHEID, J., 1986. 'La Thiase du Metropolitan Museum', in *L'Association dionysiaque dans les sociétés anciennes,* Collection de l'École Française de Rome 89: 275–90.
SCHEIDEL, W., 2004. 'Human Mobility in Roman Italy, I: The Free Population', *JRS* 94: 1–26.
—— 2005. 'Human Mobility in Roman Italy, II: The Slave Population', *JRS* 95: 64–9.
SCHIAVONE, A., 2000. *The End of the Past.* Cambridge, Mass.
SHERWIN-WHITE, A. N., 1939. *The Roman Citizenship.* Oxford (2nd edn. 1973).
SMALLWOOD, E. M., 1966. *Documents Illustrating the Principates of Nerva, Trajan and Hadrian.* Cambridge.
SYME, R., 1958. *Tacitus.* Oxford.
SOLIN, H., 1996. *Die stadtrömischen Sklavennamen.* Stuttgart.
WALKER, B., 1952. *The Annals of Tacitus.* Manchester (repr. 1968).
WEISS, A., 2004. *Sklave der Stadt.* Stuttgart.
WIRSZUBSKI, CH., 1950. *Libertas as a Political Idea at Rome During the Late Republic and Early Principate.* Cambridge (repr. 1968).

CHAPTER 40

LAW

JILL HARRIES

Two-and-a-half millennia after the publication, in *c.*450 BCE, of Rome's first written law-code, the Twelve Tables, Roman law is at a crossroads. One route takes forwards the academic study of Roman law as a legal discipline. Between 529 and 534 CE the emperor Justinian's lawyers assembled and codified texts on Roman law in the *Corpus Iuris Civilis*, which consisted of the *Justinianic Code* (of imperial laws), the *Digest* (excerpted writings of the classical jurists from the first to the early fourth centuries CE) and the *Institutes*, based largely on Gaius' *Institutes*, written in the second century CE. The texts collected in the *Corpus*, and in particular the *Digest*, underlie legal systems in mainland Europe (Vinogradoff, 1968; Stein 1999), Scotland (Stein 1968), and beyond. To understand the history and principles of Law, the study of Roman law, as law, was a necessary prerequisite. The scholarly tradition of interpretation, based on a specialized discourse concerning legal relationships, status, and rights, continues to contribute to modern scholarship on Roman law, analysed as law, regardless of the social and cultural contexts in which the texts were created (e.g. Zimmermann 1996).

The second way forward for Roman law is to reinstate legal texts into their Roman social, cultural, and chronological setting. John Crook's pioneering study of *Law and Life of Rome* (1967) argued effectively for the importance of law, including a necessary grasp of legal technicalities, for the understanding of Roman social relations. His attention later (1995) turned to the role of advocates, and consequently the courts, in the evolution of law, observing also that advocates, jurists, and others involved in the making of law all shared the same elite, rhetorical education. Modern Roman historians and some Roman lawyers have exploited legal writing as sources for social and economic history on such topics as status and citizenship (Gardner 1993), the household, family, and gender (Gardner 1986, 1998; Treggiari 1991; Evans Grubbs 2002; Frier and McGinn 2004), prostitution and sexual relations (McGinn 1998), landlords and tenants (Frier 1980), and crime (Robinson 1995; Harries 2007).

But students of ancient Rome who use law as an historical source ignore questions of source criticism relating to law at their peril. Some have seen Roman law as a specialized discipline with its own terminology and traditions divorced from its social context; if they are right, this has important implications. In the view of a historian of Roman Republican law, 'there is no necessary correlation between law and the society in which it operates. Of course, there is some connection, but precisely what that is is not inevitable and may often be tenuous. Law is very much the culture of the lawmakers' (Watson 2007: 9). While Watson's view may be overstated, the question raised is crucial to the position of Roman law in Roman Studies. The interpretation of Roman law as evolved by the Roman legal experts, the jurists, had its own traditions, terminology, and frameworks of reference. Students of Roman history and society must appreciate 'the dense interweave of substantive rules with complex strata of conflicting ideas and purposes' (Frier 2000: 447) which characterizes the ancient legal writers. Moreover, law does not automatically evolve in parallel with changes in social attitudes; legal discourse has a tendency to conservatism, and the content of law will depend on the responsiveness of the lawmaker to social trends. The picture is further complicated by the diversity of stakeholders in the lawmaking process (see the two following sections below) and the processes through which the texts came into being. Thus the connection between the legal texts, their authors, and the society within which they wrote cannot be taken for granted.

Defining Law

Romans avoided committing themselves to definitions of 'law', its boundaries, or its functions. In his introduction to the basics of Roman law, the third-century jurist Ulpian related *ius* (law as right) to *iustitia*, justice, and borrowed from an earlier jurist the 'elegant' reflection that law was 'the art of the good and the fair' (*Digest* (*D*).1.1.1.1). Others, from Cicero onwards, deriving from Greek legal philosophy, proclaimed the educative purpose of law as the 'teacher of life' (e.g. *D* 1.3.2; *Theodosian Code* (*CT*) 1.1.5, 429). The moralizing tone, characteristic of Roman elite discourse in many other contexts, reveals an interest in social engineering on the part of the lawmakers, and the rhetoric of imperial legislation from the first century onwards provided moral justification for the lawgiver and imposed a moral duty on the subject to observe the law.

In anthropological terms, law is concerned with the formulation of the rules and conventions which underpin the social order, and the procedures by which those rules were implemented or enforced (Roberts 1979; Humphreys 1985; Gagarin 1986: 1–17); the moral language of the Roman emperor as lawgiver can be read as an assertion of his privileged understanding of what those rules were or ought to be. However, not all rules or conventions are laws, and the purposes for which the law is designed, such as the resolution of disputes or the correction of offenders, may be met through the use of alternative procedures (e.g. mediation or informal arbitration to settle disputes) or sanctions (e.g. social isolation). How, then, were the boundaries of law to be recognized, or its remit defined? These issues were addressed by such legal theorists as H. L. A. Hart (1961), arguing for a combination of 'primary rules' imposing obligations with 'secondary rules' enabling recognition and implementation of the 'primary rules'. However, rules and conventions are themselves in a state of flux, and the decisions of both legislators and the courts may be influenced by extra-legal factors. In the view of the present writer, societies probably respond to questions of the limits of the law in their own way, influenced by their own social structures, levels of literacy, past cultural as well as legal practice, and perceived present needs.

Roman civil law (*ius civile*) centred on the 'legal action' (*actio*), under which suit could be brought and remedies sought for alleged injuries. Legal actions *in rem* (or corporeal things and rights) and *in personam* (suing a person in breach of an obligation or guilty of delict) concerned the dealings of individuals with each other (Gaius, *Institutes* 4.1–3), although the wider community was involved through the adjudication exercised by the judges and the regulation of specific actions by public statutes (e.g. Gaius, *Inst.* 4.15 (*Lex Pinaria*), 19 (*Lex Silia Calpurnia*)). It was essential for success that a litigant choose the right action and the right court. The probable opening chapters of the Twelve Tables (I.1–3) prescribe how a plaintiff may initiate a case (*in ius ire*) and what he may do if the defendant refuses to appear with him before a magistrate or claims to be old or ill. *In ius ire*, 'to go to law', means literally 'to go to [i.e. in search of] legal right (*ius*)'; much of Roman law, therefore, was directed to explaining how a litigant could assert his rights and claim remedies against those who had wronged him (Greenidge 1901/1971: 5–6, cf. *D* 1.1.11). From early times, the connection of a legal action with ritual was revealed in the law's obsession with correct wording; one reason why the *legis actio* was replaced by the praetor's formula was that a man could lose a suit about the cutting down of vines by referring to 'vines' rather than *arbores*, 'trees', the word used in the relevant clause of the Twelve Tables (Gaius, *Inst.* 4.11).

Roman public law (*ius publicum*) was never clearly or formally defined but related to the interests of the community as a collective. Crimes against society (which could include offences against individuals) were clearly part of public law; statutes (*leges*) relating to the constitution not only of Rome itself but also of other communities, such as *municipia*, were also 'public'; so too were procedures relevant to the construction of the community as an assemblage of households—guardianship (*tutela*), some forms of adoption (*adrogatio*), wills, and responsibility for funerals. Public law can be identified through the presence of institutional backing for its promulgation, interpretation, or implementation through public assemblies (*comitia*), the Senate, public courts (*iudicia publica*), and, later, courts of investigation presided over by a magistrate (*quaestiones*). Jurisdiction in matters relating to the household often rested with the College of Pontiffs, and in particular the *pontifex maximus*, as family law had an impact on the transmission of family *sacra*. Thus the Romans' concept of their *res publica* involved the community and the gods in areas which modern legal thought might term 'private', but which Romans assimilated into the *ius civile*, the law as it applied to citizens.

The Republic

The unwritten law of early Rome evolved in the context of a small face-to-face society, highly militarized and at risk from surrounding communities, with a diverse population and strong family and household structures (*familia* meant both property and household, *D* 50.16.195), headed by the *pater familias*, whose power was, in theory, absolute. Traditions about the time of the seven kings, from Romulus to Tarquinius Superbus, ascribed to the monarchical *leges regiae* the foundation of sacred law and many early public institutions. After the overthrow of the kings in *c.*510 BCE the political situation in the new Republic was unstable, as the plebeians sought for more rights and protection from abuse. According to the tradition, the creation of the Twelve Tables, by a Board of Ten, was one outcome of this factional strife. The law-code does not survive, but can be partially reconstructed (although details are controversial) from citations included by later writers, often for the sake of its archaic vocabulary (see Crawford *et al.* 1996: 555–721). Although both text and meaning are often obscure, the surviving provisions reflect the concerns of an agricultural community, including boundaries (defined as five-foot strips of land, VII.2–5), the magicking and destruction of crops (VIII.1–6), and aspects of *familia* law, such as guardianship, succession (V.3–10), marriage, and the regulation of funerals (X.1–10). Most characteristic of a self-help society was the provision that a thief who came by night could be lawfully killed (I.17); the principle that killing in self-defence was lawful was never seriously challenged.

Also typical of small communities was the emphasis in early Roman legal practice on the speaking of words to establish agreements, along with ritual actions, such as the formal taking of oaths by both sides in a dispute (*legis actio sacramenti*) or the striking of scales with a coin (*per aes et libram*) as a demonstration that a contract of sale had been confirmed. Rules on agreements, *stipulationes*, aimed at avoidance of ambiguity, insisting that one party make a complete statement of the agreement, as reached, to which the other must answer with a simple yes or no (Gaius, *Inst.* 3.92–3). The evolution of such oral exchanges empowered the individual as a legal agent; his words were a form of action, determined events, and had consequences. The Twelve Tables also contained an early example of the Roman predilection for using one legal act to achieve another: a son could be ritually 'emancipated' from his father's legal power if he were sold, fictitiously, three times (wording at Gaius, *Inst.* 1.132).

As Roman society became richer, more cosmopolitan, and more literate, new forms of procedures emerged and the shape of lawmaking also changed. Cicero defined Roman law in terms of its component parts, as they might be cited by an advocate: statutes (*leges*) and plebiscites, both laws passed by the People, senatorial resolutions, decided cases (*res iudicatae*), the authority of the jurists, the edicts of magistrates, custom, and fairness (*Topica* 28); under the Empire Gaius (*Inst.* 1.2) added imperial constitutions to the list and omitted decided cases, custom, and fairness. From 287 BCE laws passed by the People (*populus*) in assembly were binding on the whole state. Senatorial resolutions (*senatus consulta*) were in theory advisory only, although their importance as 'law' increased under the Empire, after the legislative assemblies (*comitia*) ceased to function (cf. Gaius, *Inst.* 1.4, that SCs have the 'force of law'). Cicero's mention of decided cases is puzzling, given that Roman law did not operate formally in terms of legal precedent based on court cases. However, Cicero has much to say in his rhetorical work about arguments based on analogy, and it was in this context that verdicts, and the arguments by which the verdicts were reached, could be deployed (Harries 2006: 134–46). Both custom—the *mos maiorum*—and appeals to fairness (*aequitas*) were part of the jurist's and the advocate's stock in trade (Cicero, *De Inventione* 1.14; *De Legibus* 1.18b; *Topica* 9; 23), although Gaius did not see them as part of the legal identity (*iura*) of the Roman people.

Under the Republic the edictal process allowed magistrates to issue laws and instructions in their own name, which were valid only for their period of office. However, the praetorian edict acquired a special status, creating a new category of law, the *ius honorarium*. It contained the legal formulae, by which a praetor would define what legal actions were available to plaintiffs, and what legal question should be addressed in the subsequent legal hearing. This meant that a legal hearing might be heard in two stages (at least): in the first, the praetor defined and 'gave' the action, issued his formula and appointed a judge, who was, in theory, acceptable to both parties; in the second, the appointed judge (*iudex datus*), who could be the praetor himself, adjudicated on the facts, and some minor legal points as well. Praetors could also issue interdicts, preventing certain actions (Greenidge 1901/1971: 210–27); Cicero's defence of Caecina in 69 BCE revolved round the recently issued praetorian interdict 'on armed violence' (Frier 1985: 171–83), an illustration also of the overlap of civil with criminal jurisdiction (cf. the Lex Lutatia *de vi*, passed 78 BCE). As praetors were not, necessarily, legal experts, they preferred to use the text of their predecessors as their starting-point and then amend as they (and their legal advisers) saw fit; new provincial governors also exploited the edicts of their predecessors. Under the Empire the praetors continued to preside over their courts, including the criminal courts, in the Forum of Augustus (Bablitz 2007: 13–50) but, under Hadrian, the praetor's edict was revised and its content fixed (*Fontes Iuris Romani Anteiustiniani*, 2nd edn., vol. 1, 335–89); by the third century it was known as the Perpetual Edict, and jurists, when referring to its provisions, wrote of 'the praetor'.

The late Republic witnessed two further significant developments. One was the emergence of the independent legal consultant, or jurist, as an authoritative interpreter of civil law and custom (Schultz 1946; Frier 1985). The roots of Roman jurisprudence lie in the legal interpretative activity of the pontifical college. One of the most influential late Republican jurists, Q. Mucius Scaevola (d. 82 BCE), was a figure of transition, being both *pontifex maximus* and author of an eighteen-book treatise *On the Civil Law* (*De Iure Civili*), based on the Twelve Tables. His treatise, probably designed to educate the new Roman citizens enfranchised after the Social War, became a classic and the subject of further juristic commentaries *Ad Mucium* under the Empire. He was also the last of the pontifical jurists. Thereafter legal consultancy and commentary were engaged in by members of the Roman elite as part of their careers in the secular, political, or administrative world of the Roman Empire. In the first century CE the achievement of the conventional career rewards of office and prestige by any senator solely *qua* jurist was possible, especially with imperial support, but difficult; as Cicero had informed Servius in 63 BCE, jurisprudence was not recommended as a route to the consulship (Cicero, *Pro Murena* 28).

However, the vigorous interpretative activity of jurists and others in the late Republic established the foundations of Roman civil-law concepts, notably that of *bona fides*, good faith, and how legal problems with transactions based on trust could be resolved. They had also evolved the concept of delict, an offence such as theft, damage (drawing on the Twelve Tables, e.g. VIII.3 and 4, and the third-century BCE *Lex Aquilia*), or outrage, which might be classed as criminal but which could be dealt with through civil procedures granting penal damages (see *D* 9.2 for some occasionally bizarre possible cases). It was perhaps Republican jurists, rather than their Imperial successors, who saw delict in terms of breaches of the law of obligations, a moral as well as a legal concept (for legal details, Nicholas 1962: 207–24; Watson 1964; Zimmermann 1996: 914–18).

The second major procedural change was the creation of a number of standing criminal courts (*quaestiones*), which gradually replaced the ad hoc jurisdiction of the People's courts (*iudicia populi*). The first was set up under a *Lex Calpurnia de repetundis* in 149 BCE for purposes of achieving restitution of resources extorted from provincials by their governors (Richardson 1987), and its procedures were reformed in 122 by Gaius Gracchus, whose law, or one closely related to it, survives in epigraphic form (Crawford *et al.* 1976: 65–112). In the distinctively archaic and clumsily repetitive language of Roman statute, it lays out a set of procedural rules to be followed, from the initiation of prosecution and who were allowed to prosecute, to the formation of juries (excluding senators and their relatives), the public trial itself, and the enforcing of a guilty verdict. Part of the agenda of reformers of public law, which was reflected in the Gracchan rules, was to hold public officials and magistrates to account: further courts were introduced over the next decades to try the crimes of *maiestas* (treason, damage to the 'greatness' of the Roman People), electoral corruption, embezzlement, forgery, public violence, murder, kidnapping, and perhaps outrage (*iniuria*), although the last, if set up as a court at all, may not have lasted long (for context, Riggsby 1999). Finally, in 18 BCE Augustus extended public jurisdiction to adultery, hitherto an offence punished by the family, by setting up the last of the new courts under the *Lex Iulia* on adulteries. Following a similar exercise by Sulla in 80 BCE, he also systematized procedures over the whole *quaestio* system, under the *Lex Iulia* on public courts (Jones 1972: Bauman 1980; Harries 2007: 12–20).

The Early Empire

After a series of statutes promulgated by Augustus, emperors largely abandoned public laws as their means of legislation. Instead, for purposes of general legislation, they resorted to the edict, which as magistrates they were entitled to issue (Millar 1977: 252–9). However, as the emperor's *imperium* as a magistrate was for life, so his edicts too became permanent and were notionally applicable under his successors as well. Such was the emperor's authority as supreme lawmaker that other legal pronouncements issued by him or his administration also acquired the force of law. These included letters to officials and provincials, and rescripts sent as replies to legal queries, which evolved into a genre of imperial legal rulings concisely expressed and offering an opinion on the legal point, but not the facts of a referred case (Honoré 1994; Corcoran 2000: 43–75). Deference to imperial rulings as absolute law also extended to the subscript, a brief note conveying an imperial response to a petition, written on the text itself; although authored by subordinates (and only a fraction of those actually issued survive), the public fiction was maintained that the emperor concerned himself personally with the affairs of even his humbler subjects. The extant subscriptions are also atypical in that they survive through selection, as authoritative statements of legal principle; many subscriptions would have been routine (Turpin 1991).

With the demise of the popular assemblies after Augustus, the Senate acquired a new importance as legislator, through *senatus consulta*, and as a law-court for the hearing of special cases involving senators. While no senatorial resolution is likely to have passed without imperial sanction, senatorial legislation through *consulta* reflects the concerns of a propertied class with questions of status, succession, and property ownership. Two resolutions passed in the second century, for example, regulated the succession of mothers to children (the SC Tertullianum) and, in 178, granted freeborn children the first right to inherit from their mothers (the SC Orphitianum); in both cases, illegitimate children were also allowed to benefit (Gardner 1986: 196–200). The notorious SC Silanianum ruled that when a head of household was killed, the slaves in the house who had failed to protect him were all liable to execution; this was challenged after the murder of the city prefect by his slave at Rome in 61, but unsuccessfully (Tacitus, *Annals* 14.43–4, cf. *D* 29.5.1 pr.). The Senate also evolved under Tiberius into the court that heard serious charges against fellow senators, including treason (*maiestas*), adultery, magic (also to be construed as treason), and extortion, although the praetor was still allowed a technical role (Richardson 1997). The younger Pliny, who prosecuted governors of Africa (*Letters* 2.11) and Baetica (*Letters* 3.4 and 9) for extortion and defended two corrupt (or unlucky) former governors of Bithynia on the same charge, provides important evidence for the flexibility of senatorial decision-making on cases involving their own.

Ultimate control of all law lay with the emperor and his advisers. Jurists were to be found in the Senate (such as C. Cassius Longinus, suffect consul in 30) acting independently or as members of the emperor's *consilium*, where they could directly influence imperial judgements. Many pronouncements bearing the emperor's name would in fact have been the creation of his jurists. Senatorial legal consultants, such as Caelius Sabinus (consul 69), Iavolenus Priscus (consul 86), or P. Iuventius Celsus (consul 117), were powerful figures in their own right. However, as imperial control over government strengthened with the evolution of a separate equestrian bureaucracy, senatorial jurists began to give way to jurists who worked within the imperial administration, answering directly to the emperor. The great Severan jurists, Papinian, Paulus, and Ulpian (on the last, see Honoré 2002), were non-Roman, dependent on imperial patronage and active as imperial servants in the bureaux of the *libelli* (petitions) and, in the cases of Papinian and Ulpian, as praetorian prefects (both of whom died violently). By late antiquity few jurists can be identified by name, and those named *honoris causa* in the imperial law-codes as a rule lack individual identities.

The jurist was more than an imperial adviser or senatorial careerist. Some academic jurists have no known link with the political world. The legal historian Pomponius recorded in the second century his belief that the two law 'schools' active at Rome in his own day had a dynasty of teachers going back to the time of Augustus (*D* 1.2.2.47; Liebs 1976); his lists of the traditionalists and modernizers combine the names of senators, like Cassius, the supposed founder of one of the schools, with academic jurists, such as Masurius Sabinus, who was also known to the elder Pliny, but as an antiquarian (*D* 1.2.2.50; Pliny, *NH* 15.38.126, myrtle wreath of the *triumphator*; *NH* 15.40.135, the use of laurel for purposes of purification; see also *NH* 7.43.135). Moreover, many jurists, whether senatorial, administrative, or academic, gave personal legal advice to clients and engaged in public teaching and disputation (Gellius, *Noctes Atticae* 13.13.1–4; *D* 23.3.78.4, Tryphoninus). Their voluminous publications (Ulpian the most prolific, at about 300 books in eight years) were analysed by F. Schultz (1946); since then there has been no major study of the early imperial jurists and their legal science as a whole. Nor have the imperial jurists been analysed in the context of Latin prose writing (but for the Republic, see Rawson 1978) or the cultural conventions of the 'Second Sophistic'.

As the Roman citizenship expanded, so too more people in the Roman Empire became subject to Roman law. The Flavian municipal law for Baetica, preserved in several incomplete bronze copies, of which the most extensive is the Law of Irni (Gonzalez 1986), dated to 91 CE, shows the extent to which western communities were expected to adopt Roman laws and institutions, even when they were not citizens (*Lex Irnitana* 93; cf. 89 on *recuperatores*; 91 on the *Lex Iulia* 'recently' passed on *iudicia privata*). In the Eastern Empire too, disputes between citizens of different, and often long-established, Greek communities were expected, by the time of Hadrian, to resort to Roman law in cases of disputed jurisdictions (Reynolds 2000). At the same time, Romans had to adapt a legal system originally designed for one community to serve in a world empire. This they did by allocating many duties performed by Roman magistrates at Rome to governors and by adjusting Roman legal forms, such as types of ownership, to serve in the provinces as well. Provincial public land, for example, was in the formal ownership (*dominium*) of the Roman people but the provincials were granted its usufruct (Gaius, *Inst.* 1.6). Problems still remained, however, with how land which the provincials could not own could be classified as religious (which required that it be owned); here Gaius cheerfully admits that provincial land, though not technically capable of being religious or consecrated, was nonetheless regarded as such. Such were the small adjustments repeatedly made by the ruling power. In some provinces, such as Egypt, the prefect's decisions came themselves to form a collection of precedents (Katzoff 1982). Resourceful provincials responded to the Roman presence by resorting to manipulation of the legal process to achieve their ends in family disputes; the Babatha archive (deposited in the frontier lands of Arabia in *c.*132) shows a village woman vigorously threatening her rivals with the prefect's justice—and receiving similar warnings in her turn (Lewis 1989; Oudshoorn 2007). In Egypt, nearly ninety years after the *Constitutio Antoniniana*, female litigants proudly asserted their right, 'under the law of the Romans', as mothers of three children to represent themselves in court (*P. Berlin* Moeller 1, AD 300). Legal adjustments, in their own interests, by both rulers and ruled, which included the modification of the physical shape of documents (Meyer 2004), were an integral part of the process of acculturation known, not entirely accurately, as 'Romanization'.

Late Antiquity: Codification, Law, and History

The period from the accession of Diocletian in 284 to the promulgation of the *Corpus Iuris Civilis* by 534 saw the appearance of three legal codifications. The first, authored in two stages in 292 and 294 by two imperial officials, Gregorius and Hermogenian, was a collection of rescripts from the time of Hadrian (Corcoran 2000: 25–43). The starting-point coincided with Hadrian's taking over of the praetor's responsibility to revise the *ius honorarium*. Although some of its contents survive independently through private collections such as the *Fragmenta Vaticana*, most of its contents are preserved through its inclusion, with some revisions, in the *Codex Iustinianus*. Then, in 429, Theodosius II and his lawyers initiated a grander project, to collect, first, the imperial constitutions from the time of Constantine, and second, the writings of the jurists, to make two preliminary law-codes, which would then be amalgamated to form the ultimate statement of law (*CT* 1.1.5, March 429). In the event, only the first part of the project, the collection of imperial constitutions, emerged in 438, lightly revised and with superfluous verbiage removed. The revision was, however, erratic, and considerable rhetorical content remained, an unhelpful aspect in the views of those concerned primarily with its legal content. Although largely ignored by students of law, the Theodosian Code has provoked considerable interest among the historians of late antiquity in recent years (Honoré 1986; Harries and Wood 1993; Matthews 2000; review discussion by A. D. Lee, 2002). Study has focused on how the text (which is incomplete) was created, its historical context (the wedding of Valentinian III and Eudoxia), the archival sources (Constantinople or more far-flung provenances), the arrangement and editing of the text, and the often shadowy legal draftsmen responsible for the language (and often the content) of the laws (Honoré 1986, 1999). Another line of enquiry has been to ask how the texts, which were often, though not invariably, generated in response to proposals or queries from outside, should be used as sources for late Roman history (Harries 1999; Humfress 2007). The insight of Fergus Millar (1977) that emperors often legislated in response to external promptings, and that their laws may thus reflect the agendas of those who proposed a reform, or may answer a question on an existing situation rather than create a new one, reveals late Roman imperial constitutions to be the product of negotiation between the interested parties. This has major implications for such 'reformers' as

Constantine I, whose 'Christian' legislation requires re-examination in the light of the legal tradition, as his bureaucrats would have understood it, as well as contemporary ecclesiastical concerns.

These methods of historical enquiry must in turn also be applied to the Code of Justinian (529, second edition 534), which amalgamated the Codes of Gregorius and Hermogenian with that of Theodosius and subsequent imperial *novellae* (new laws). Justinian's achievement was to carry through the whole Theodosian project, with the help of his chief legal adviser, Tribonian (Honoré 1978), as a celebration of the imperial restoration of 'eternal peace' to the world. Of the three texts, which comprise the *Corpus Iuris Civilis*, the Collection of Civil Law, the *Digest* has proved the most influential. Justinian's immediate aim was twofold. One was to provide the means of legal education in the law-schools of the empire. The second, which applied in particular to the excerpted works of the jurists assembled in the *Digest*, was to assert control over the past while also imposing for the future an imperial monopoly on jurisprudence. As was the practice with all the imperial law-codes, material not included ceased to count as law at all, and henceforward, juristic, like praetorian, law would emanate solely from the emperor.

Future Directions

Roman historians have long used Roman legal texts, in the shape of the Twelve Tables, statutes, often preserved epigraphically, juristic writing, and the imperial codifications as sources for economic, social, and even political history. Far less attention has been paid to questions relating to legal history and, in the case of the legal writings preserved in the late Roman codifications, *how* the legal texts should be used as historical sources. This is partly the fault of the ancient Roman lawyers, whose sometimes impenetrably technical prose has (understandably) caused them to be isolated in a specialist ghetto. One avenue worth further exploration is the study of the Roman imperial jurists as (admittedly fragmentary) Latin writers, subject to the same rules and conventions as other compilers of specialist treatises, for example, on architecture, music, or mathematics. Moreover, the facts that legal writers shared an education in rhetoric with their peers and were often public men (and therefore public speakers as well) suggest that legal writing too will have been shaped by literary conventions and the school exercises in argument, often designed to test legal knowledge in imaginary forensic contexts.

Historians of Greek law have been quick to adopt the insights of anthropology on the role of law in pre-literate societies, the relationships of rules to conventions, or the role of the courts, especially in ancient Athens, not as a means of resolving disputes but as a way of continuing feuds by other means. Roman law fits well into the context of comparative legal studies, enabling both texts and contexts to be contrasted with those of the Greeks and the Jews (see Hezser 2003), perhaps Persia, the Chinese, and other more recent empires. Both legal specialists and historians are well placed to analyse the legal provisions and philosophies of diverse communities; in the case of Roman law, of particular interest might be the effect of its republican background and the concept of the citizen as a being with rights and obligations on the evolution of law under the imperial autocracy (as compared with, for example, the Chinese perspective under the Han and other imperial dynasties). Most importantly of all, the role of law in formulating the identity of the citizen in relation to the state; the rights of the individual as they relate to those of the community; and the threat to states which accept the rule of law from those who deny the legal assumptions on which citizenship and community rest, are all issues to which the study of Roman law in Roman society has an important contribution to make.

Further reading

For students deterred by the perceived unapproachability of Roman legal texts, the best starting-point is Gaius, *Institutes* (tr. W. M. Gordon and O. F. Robinson, London: Duckworth, 1988), which aimed to explain Roman law from first principles; a more recent, but on occasion opaque, introduction is Nicholas 1962. Recent short studies, which seek to build bridges between Roman law and classical studies, are O. Robinson, *The Sources of Roman Law: Problems and Methods for Ancient Historians* (London: Routledge, 1997); D. Johnston, *Roman Law in Context* (Cambridge: Cambridge University Press, 1999); and G. Mousourakis, *The Historical and Institutional Context of Roman Law* (Aldershot: Ashgate, 2003). Justinian's *Digest*, a wonderful work to dip into as a preliminary exercise, was translated by Alan Watson *et al.* (Pittsburgh: University of Pennsyvlania Press, 1985). An accessible textbook is J. A. Borkowski and P. Du Plessis, *A Textbook of Roman Law* (3rd edn., Oxford: Oxford University Press, 2005); a more formidable mine of legal information is W. W. Buckland, *A Textbook of Roman Law* (3rd edn., ed. P. Stein, Cambridge: Cambridge University Press, 1966).

References

Bablitz, L. (2007), *Actors and Audience in the Roman Courtroom*. London: Routledge.

Bauman, R. A. (1980), 'The *Leges Iudiciorum Publicorum* and their Interpretation in the Republic, Principate and Early Empire', *ANRW* II.13: 103–233.

Corcoran, S. (2000), *The Empire of the Tetrarchs: Imperial Pronouncements and Government,* AD *284–324*². Oxford: Clarendon Press.

CRAWFORD, M. et al. (eds.) (1996), *Roman Statutes*, 2 vols., BICS Supp. 64. London: Institute of Classical Studies.
CROOK, J. A. (1967), *Law and Life of Rome*. London: Thames & Hudson; Ithaca, NY: Cornell University Press.
—— (1995) *Legal Advocacy in the Roman World*. London: Duckworth.
EVANS GRUBBS, J. (2002), *Women and Law in the Roman Empire*. London: Routledge.
FRIER, B. (1980), *Landlords and Tenants in Imperial Rome*. Princeton: Princeton University Press.
—— (1985), *The Rise of the Roman Jurists: Studies in Cicero's Pro Caecina*. Princeton: Princeton University Press.
—— (2000), 'Roman Law's Descent into History', *Journal of Roman Archaeology*, 13/2: 446–8.
—— and MCGINN, T. A. J. (2004), *A Casebook on Roman Family Law*, American Philological Association. Oxford: Oxford University Press.
GAGARIN, M. (1986), *Early Greek Law*. Berkeley: University of California Press.
GARDNER, J. (1986), *Women and Law in Roman Society*. London: Routledge.
—— (1993), *Being a Roman Citizen*. London: Routledge.
—— (1998), *Family and* 'familia' *in Roman Law and Life*. Oxford: Oxford University Press.
GONZALEZ, J. (1996), 'The Lex Irnitana: A New Copy of the Flavian Municipal Law', *Journal of Roman Studies*, 76: 147–243.
GREENIDGE, A. H. J. (1901; repr. 1971), *The Legal Procedure of Cicero's Time*. Oxford: Oxford University Press.
HARRIES, J. (1999), *Law and Empire in Late Antiquity*. Cambridge: Cambridge University Press.
—— (2006), *Cicero and the Jurists*. London: Duckworth.
—— (2007), *Law and Crime in the Roman World*. Cambridge: Cambridge University Press.
—— and WOOD, I. N. (eds.) (1983), *The Theodosian Code: Studies in the Imperial Law of Late Antiquity*. London: Duckworth.
HART, H. L. A. (1961), *The Concept of Law*. Oxford: Oxford University Press.
HEZSER, C. (ed.) (2003), *Rabbinic Law in its Roman and Near Eastern Context*. Tübingen: Mohr Siebeck.
HONORÉ, T. (1978), *Tribonian*. London: Duckworth.
—— (1994), *Emperors and Lawyers with a Palingenesia of Third-Century Imperial Rescripts, 193–305 AD*². Oxford: Oxford University Press.
—— (1986), 'The Making of the Theodosian Code', *Zeitschrift der Savigny Stiftung, Römische Abteilung*, 104: 133–222.
—— (1999), *Law in the Crisis of Empire, 379–455 AD: The Theodosian Dynasty and its Quaestors*. Oxford: Oxford University Press.
—— (2002), *Ulpian, Pioneer of Human Rights*². Oxford: Oxford University Press.
HUMFRESS, C. (2007), *Orthodoxy and the Courts in Late Antiquity*. Oxford: Oxford University Press.
HUMPHREYS, S. (1985), 'Law as Discourse', *History and Archaeology*, 1: 241–64.
JONES, A. H. M. (1972), *The Criminal Courts of the Roman Republic and Principate*. Oxford: Oxford University Press.
KATZOFF, R. (1982), 'Sources of Law in Roman Egypt: The Role of the Prefect', *ANRW* II.13: 807–44.
LEE, A. D. (2002), 'Decoding Late Roman Law', *Journal of Roman Studies*, 92: 185–93.
LENEL, O. (1889), *Palingenesia Iuris Civilis*. Leipzig.

Lewis, N. (1989), *The Documents from the Bar Kochba Period in the Cave of Letters: Greek Papyri*. Jerusalem: Hebrew University of Jerusalem.

Liebs, D. (1976), 'Rechtsschulen und Rechtsunterricht im Prinzipat', *ANRW* II.15: 197–287.

McGinn, T. A. J. (1998), *Prostitution, Sexuality and the Law in Ancient Rome*. Oxford: Oxford University Press.

Matthews, J. (2000), *Laying Down the Law: A Study of the Theodosian Code*. New Haven: Yale University Press.

Meyer, E. (2004), *Law and Legitimacy in the Roman World: Tabulae in Roman Belief and Practice*. Cambridge: Cambridge University Press.

Millar, F. (1977), *The Emperor in the Roman World*. London: Duckworth.

Nicholas, B. (1962), *An Introduction to Roman Law*. Oxford: Clarendon Press.

Oudshoorn, J. G. (2007), *The Relationship Between Roman and Local Law in the Babatha and Salome Komaise Archives*. Leiden: Brill.

Rawson, E. (1978), 'The Introduction of Logical Organisation in Roman Prose Literature', *Papers of the British School at Rome*, 33: 12–34.

Reynolds, J. (2000), 'New Letters of Hadrian to Aphrodisias: Trails, Taxes, Gladiators and an Aqueduct', *Journal of Roman Archaeology*, 13/1: 5–20.

Riccobono, S. (ed.) (1968), *Fontes Iuris Romani Anteiustiniani*². Florence.

Richardson, J. S. (1987), 'The Purpose of the *Lex Calpurnia de repetundis*', *Journal of Roman Studies*, 77: 1–12.

—— (1997), 'The Senate, the Courts and the *SC de Pisone patre*', *Classical Quarterly*, 47/2: 510–18.

Riggsby, A. (1999), *Crime and Community in Ciceronian Rome*. Austin, Tex.: University of Texas Press.

Roberts, S. (1979), *Order and Dispute: An Introduction to Legal Anthropology*. Oxford: Martin Robertson.

Robinson, O. (1995), *The Criminal Law of Ancient Rome*. London: Duckworth.

Schultz, F. (1946), *History of Roman Legal Science*. Oxford: Oxford University Press.

Stein, P. (1968), *Roman Law in Scotland*. Milan: Giuffrè.

—— (1999), *Roman Law in European History*. Cambridge: Cambridge University Press.

Treggiari, S. (1991), *Roman Marriage:* Iusti Coniuges *from the Time of Cicero to the Time of Ulpian*. Oxford: Clarendon Press.

Turpin, W. (1991), 'Imperial Subscriptions and the Administration of Justice', *Journal of Roman Studies*, 81: 101–18.

Vinogradoff, P. (1968), *Roman Law in Mediaeval Europe*, ed. P. Stein. Cambridge: Cambridge University Press.

Watson, A. (1964), *The Law of Obligations in the Later Roman Republic*. Oxford: Clarendon Press.

—— (2007), 'Law and Society', in J. W. Cairns and P. Duplessis (eds.), *Beyond Dogmatics: Law and Society in the Roman World*. Edinburgh: Edinburgh University Press, 9–35.

Zimmermann, R. (1996), *The Law of Obligations: Roman Foundations of the Civilian Tradition*. Oxford: Oxford University Press.

CHAPTER 41

SPECTACLE

KATHLEEN M. COLEMAN*

INTRODUCTION

IN 57 CE, says Tacitus scornfully, 'there were few events worth recalling, unless anyone fancies filling volumes with admiration for the foundations and beams with which the emperor had constructed his hulking amphitheatre on the Field of Mars' (*Annals* 13.31.1); such matters, he goes on to say, are fit for the *Daily Gazette*, not for annalistic history. The textual record from antiquity, almost exclusively composed by the elite, therefore eschews the subject of arena spectacles, except for glancing references. The only tract on this topic to have survived was written by the zealous Christian Tertullian, denouncing them as pagan idolatry; a collection of epigrams by Martial in the first century CE, fraught with textual and interpretive problems, offers a series of tantalizing cameos in honour of 'Caesar' (Coleman 2006). Similarly, snobbery censors the literary record of circus racing, although not without some trace of hypocrisy: the younger Pliny ridicules the circus fans who pledge allegiance to the colours of the circus factions—'how much popularity and clout there is in one worthless tunic!', as he puts it (*Letters* 9.6.3)—and yet, in recounting how Tacitus encountered a spectator in the stands who asked whether he was Tacitus or Pliny, he does not take umbrage at the assumption that he might attend the races himself (9.23.2–3).

The spectacles of the arena and the circus, although beneath mention in sophisticated discourse, were a pervasive cultural force in Roman society. The

* I am indebted to Katherine Dunbabin and William Slater for generous assistance and expert advice.

ritual origins of the spectacles of the circus and the arena, combined with their expense and logistic complexity, meant that they were held infrequently, whether on predictable dates (the *ludi circenses* of religious festivals) or to mark singular occasions (gladiatorial spectacles celebrating the death of a prominent figure, or the emperor's birthday). More pervasive in the towns and cities of the Roman world, although still perhaps seasonally determined, were the informal entertainers—the animal-tamers, acrobats, tightrope-walkers, jugglers, conjurors, fire-eaters, strongmen, puppeteers, fortune-tellers, street-musicians, and other itinerant showmen of antiquity—whose ephemeral presence can be glimpsed intermittently in such unexpected places as a simile in an astronomical manual of the first century CE, comparing the constellation Delphinus to an acrobat jumping on a springboard or leaping through a flaming hoop (Manilius, *Astronomica* 5.438–45; Blümner 1918).

The spectacle par excellence and, requiring the subjugation of a foreign enemy as its *raison d'être*, the least predictable, was the triumphal procession, in which the flora and fauna of the defeated region, and even personifications of topographical features, were flaunted alongside actual prisoners, whose dispatch marked the culmination of both the route and the display. If the surviving descriptions of these occasions have little veracity as an historical record (Beard 2007), they nevertheless provide compelling evidence for the power of the triumphal spectacle to rouse the Roman literary and artistic imagination (Brilliant 1999); and the fierce competition among Republican generals to earn a triumph, and the jealous abrogation of this privilege by the emperors, reflects the prestige to be earned by the deployment of large-scale spectacle even outside the circumscribed context of a military victory. Indeed, our focus on the competitive performance in the circus and the amphitheatre tends to eclipse the ritual significance of the procession that both initiated the event and constituted an integral part of the spectacle.

The Circus Maximus, the legendary site of the 'rape of the Sabine women' whereby Romulus secured the future of his newly populated city (Livy 1.9), has a more 'historical' association with the *Ludi Romani* ('Roman Games'), for which it is said to have been first furnished with seating by Tarquinius Priscus, a member of the Etruscan dynasty that succeeded Romulus (Livy 1.35.8–9). The Circus originated as a cult-site for the worship of the deities Murcia, Consus, and Sol, whose identification with it persisted throughout antiquity, and the *ludi circenses* (circus games) celebrated there were part of the religious calendar. By virtue of their association with this calendar, the Roman emperors forged a close link between *ludi circenses* and their own person: in Augustus' reign alone, in addition to traditional religious festivals, circus games regularly accompanied the celebration of his birthday, they were celebrated in gratitude for his recovery from illness in 28 BCE, and they marked the dedication of buildings associated with his family—specifically, the dedication of the Aedes Divi Iulii (the temple of the Divine Julius Caesar) in 29 BCE and of the temple of Mars Ultor ('the Avenger') in 2 BCE.

An Etruscan connection has been posited also for gladiatorial combat. The literary evidence is tenuous, resting upon: (i) a claim by the Augustan author, Nicolaus of Damascus (reported by Athenaeus, *The Learned Banqueters* [*Deipnosophistae*] 4.153), that the Romans took the practice of gladiatorial combat from the Etruscans (by which he might mean not that the Etruscans invented it, but that they were the intermediary); (ii) the supposition that the figure of Dis Pater, in whose guise the Christian author Tertullian (*To the Heathen* [*Ad Nationes*] 1.10.47, *Apology* 15.5) tells us that the corpses of gladiators were accompanied out of the arena, is to be identified with the Etruscan god of the dead, Charun; and (iii) the claim by the late Roman etymologist Isidore of Seville (*Etymologies* 10.247) that the term *lanista* for the owner of a gladiatorial troupe is an Etruscan word. These scattered remarks have been taken together with a series of remarkable tomb-paintings from Tarquinia, in Etruria, dating from the second half of the sixth century BCE, depicting a figure labelled 'Phersu', who is holding a long thong wrapped around the ankle of a hooded victim, while a large animal (probably a hound) savages the victim's thigh. Despite some affinity with an aggravated form of the death-penalty at Rome, whereby low-status criminals were exposed to beasts (*damnatio ad bestias*), the 'Phersu' paintings bear no resemblance to gladiatorial spectacles in the form in which the Romans themselves believed they first appeared, as man-to-man combat to mark the demise of a prominent figure, the earliest instance being identified—with remarkable unanimity—as the funeral of M. Iunius Brutus Pera in 264 BCE (Livy, *Periochae* 16; Valerius Maximus, *Memorable Deeds and Sayings* 2.4.7; Servius, *Commentary on the* Aeneid 3.67). Single combat, boxing, and chariot-racing, presided over by an individual and witnessed by spectators (probably the bereaved), are, however, depicted on the walls of a series of Samnite tombs from Paestum in southern Italy, dating from the period 530–450 BCE; whether these images, and some comparable South Italian vase-paintings, depict funerary practices which, perhaps mediated by Etruscan influence, were ultimately adopted by the Romans, is an as yet unproven hypothesis (Ville 1981: 1–42). The potential of gladiatorial combat as a vote-catcher was first realized by Julius Caesar, who held a gladiatorial display to honour the memory of his daughter Julia, eight years after her death (Dio, *Roman History* 43.22.3). On the same occasion he sponsored beast-hunts, a combination that was to become standardized as the *munus legitimum* ('regular display').

Under the Republic, gladiatorial combat remained firmly tied to funerary celebration, an occasion associated also with other types of display; at the funeral of L. Aemilius Paulus in 160 BCE a production of Terence's play *Hecyra* lost its audience to a competing attraction on the programme, gladiatorial combat (Terence, *Hecyra* 39–41). Beast-hunts (*venationes*) dated back to a display of elephants captured from the Carthaginians in Sicily in 252 BCE, during the First Punic War (Pliny, *Natural History* 8.16–17). By the late Republic, their production was a liturgy incumbent upon the aediles, annual magistrates responsible for infrastructure in the city of Rome; the correspondence between an increasingly frantic Caelius (in Rome) and Cicero (in Cilicia) concerning the acquisition of big cats to boost Caelius' record as aedile in 51 BCE—the exact species is uncertain—illustrates the political capital at stake (Cicero, *Letters to Friends* 8.2, 4, 6, 8, 9, 11). The attraction of watching dangerous beasts displayed in the arena must have satisfied an appetite for risk as well as a lively curiosity about the natural world; the late Republic witnessed intense competition in introducing exotic beasts to Roman audiences, so that the appearance of the first hippopotamus (shown by M. Aemilius Scaurus in 58 BCE), the first rhinoceros (shown by Pompey in 55), and the first giraffe (shown by Caesar in 46) testified to the prestige of their captors, who could harness the resources of empire for the delectation of the metropolis.

Such disparate details can be pieced together; but a continuous history of Roman spectacle is impossible. The near-silence of the textual record on the spectacles of the circus and amphitheatre means that our understanding of them is more fragmentary, and more delicately constructed from random scraps of information in virtually every surviving medium, than almost any other institution of the Roman world. Yet we know more than we did a century ago, and the last twenty-five years have been especially rich in interpretive studies that have refined the routine verdict of spectacle as merely the opiate of the masses. A comprehensive survey would be impossible within the scope of a handbook; instead, I shall discuss select advances involving different media and approaches, to give a sense of the interdisciplinary nature of scholarship on spectacle, and hint at some of the challenges that remain. I shall structure my discussion around four groups fundamental to the enterprise: the participants, the sponsors, the support-staff, and the spectators. To highlight commonalities, as well as differences, I shall treat circus and amphitheatre together throughout; arena-spectacles, being more alien to modern experience than racing, raise greater problems of interpretation, and therefore receive more extended treatment in what follows.

PARTICIPANTS

The spectacular career of the charioteer C. Appuleius Diocles in the second century CE was documented in exhaustive detail in a massive inscription from the city of Rome, now lost (*CIL* 6.10048); nearly 400 years later, at Constantinople, the charioteer Porphyrius was honoured with a monument adorned with epigrams commemorating his prowess (Cameron 1973). Nothing comparable has yet been found for a gladiator, and even for charioteers these documents are exceptional; most of the surviving epitaphs for both categories of performer are brief and formulaic. Their formulaic nature might seem to be a disadvantage, reducing our knowledge to a mass of lifeless statistics, and yet their very conventionality is an important indication that occupations such as service as a gladiator are mentioned as frankly and confidently as occupations that we might count more respectable (Hope 2000). Nor does convention suffocate individuality: the corpora of gladiatorial inscriptions scrupulously assembled for East (Robert 1940; Roueché 1993; Bouley 2001) and West (*EAOR* 1988–) exhibit some startling expressions and sentiments, evidently formulated by persons who, despite insecure Greek or Latin, had a message to entrust to posterity. An epigraphic corpus relating to the circus would enable a comparable picture to emerge.

For a sustained narrative about life as a gladiator we have nowhere to turn other than the fanciful rhetorical exercise of the ninth 'major declamation' ascribed to Quintilian. The protagonist is evidently freeborn and hence serving as an *auctoratus* ('contract' gladiator), having taken the *auctoramentum*, the oath of obedience that assimilated him to the servile status of regular gladiators, analogous to (and perhaps derived from) the ritual whereby a recruit submitted to military discipline upon joining the army (Diliberto 1981). The exact terms under which *auctorati* served, although quoted confidently in some modern literature, have yet to be determined. Something of the atmosphere of the gladiatorial barracks can be recovered from scattered references in literary sources, and from careful study of the remains of such sites as the Caserma dei Gladiatori at Pompeii or the Ludus Magnus in Rome; the horrifying paradox whereby gladiators who had lived and trained together would have to face each other in public combat was apparently mitigated by a combination of fatalism and professional pride (Coleman 2005).

The prizes amassed by Diocles, Porphyrius, and others demonstrate that by skill, or luck, a charioteer could escape a high-speed accident that would almost inevitably prove fatal. The appetite of the spectators for such catastrophes may be suggested by the lurid detail with which they are depicted in the surviving repertoire of circus representations in a wide variety of media (Humphrey 1986: 176–254), although narrative technique and the representation of temporal sequence may also determine the components in such scenes (Bergmann 2008). It seems reasonable to suppose that the arena offered an even greater likelihood of injury, if not death. Survival rates are difficult to calculate from epigraphic evidence, which is in any case restricted to gladiators whose relatives or fellow combatants had the means to fund their commemoration. For the first century CE, survival-rates for a gladiator over the course of his career have been calculated at 9 : 1 (Ville 1981: 318–25); the decreasing odds in subsequent centuries match a corresponding increase in judicial savagery (MacMullen 1986). A recently excavated necropolis at Ephesus has been identified as a gladiatorial graveyard on the basis of grave stele indisputably commemorating gladiators. Skeletal remains from this site demonstrate a relatively high proportion of healed to unhealed (i.e. fatal) wounds, thereby confirming the investment represented by highly trained combatants, who were not readily expendable (Kanz and Grossschmidt 2005). This new discovery exponentially increases our knowledge of medical facilities in gladiatorial barracks, which was hitherto limited mainly to the testimony of Galen, who administered medical treatment to gladiators at Pergamon in the mid-second century CE (Scarborough 1971).

Every new find represents a gain in knowledge, either confirming or advancing what we know already; but some gains are achieved by new methods of research. Experimental archaeology has considerably refined our understanding of gladiatorial combat through re-enactments performed by combatants equipped with armour and weapons that have been meticulously reconstructed from surviving representations in painting, mosaic, and sculpture. Experiments of this nature demonstrate that the *scutum*, the heavy shield wielded by the gladiator known as a *murmillo*, performed both a defensive and an offensive function, its sharp edge being available to slice into the opponent, as well as warding off his blows (Junkelmann 2000: 146). Rules of combat, on the other hand, are hard to recover without documentary evidence, and the tone in an artistic representation can be difficult to judge, if it is torn from its context. Sometimes, however, a new tactic can be established: the recent find of a series of sculpted panels from the late first century BCE at Fiano Romano (ancient Lucus Feroniae, some 18 km north of Rome) includes graphic representation of a gladiator treading on the foot of his opponent, who appears to have put out his hand to steady himself as he tumbles to the ground (http://www.archaeology.org/0709/trenches/gladiators.html); the honorific purpose of a tomb-relief, guaranteeing that the deceased (or his survivors) should take pride in what is depicted on it, suggests that such a move was permitted.

Aspects of ancient civilization that qualify as 'sensational' are particularly prone to tenacious misconceptions. One such pertaining to Roman spectacle is the oft-repeated notion that women were set to fight dwarfs in the arena. Through careful philological analysis, this ghost has finally been laid to rest: female fighters were a novelty, but not a travesty; they fought not against men (whether stunted or not), but against one another, so that the odds were even and proper combat was possible (Brunet 2004). Other problems relating to female participants, however, persist, such as the remit of the ban that Septimius Severus apparently put upon female combat on the basis that this practice brought respectable women into disrepute as well (Dio, *Roman History* 76.16.1). This edict, which can be dated to 202 CE, has been adduced to limit the date of another epigraphic testimony to female combatants, on a funerary inscription from Ostia (*EAOR* vol. 4, no. 29); but if Severus' ban was limited in scope, either temporal or geographic, then it is an insecure yardstick for dating anything else.

If we are relatively well informed about the careers of charioteers and gladiators, we know almost nothing of the origins, status, and training of the men who fought beasts. Even the distribution of the nomenclature for these persons—*bestiarii*/*venatores*—is uncertain, despite careful analysis of the language of the arena in a recent study (Mosci Sassi 1992). Their animal quarry, and the horses that raced in the circus, are vividly portrayed on mosaics from Britain to Syria; the particularity of naming them is unsurprising for race-horses, but startling for the wild animals, destined for death, which starred so briefly in circus or amphitheatre, both well-attested venues for animal displays. For a minutely regulated society, the presence of wild animals in urban areas, and their potential for unruly behaviour, raised issues of legal definition and the assigning of responsibility (Lanata 1998): could a *fera bestia*, a wild beast, be a *res mancipi*, formal property? Should wild animals be dealt with according to their species or their individual degree of savagery? What if they had been tamed? Perhaps the unpredictability of animal behaviour is one reason why beast-fighters, charioteers, and race-horses are so frequently the target of curses, vivid and horrifying in their intensity, whereas curses directed at gladiators have yet to be found; or maybe this apparent lacuna is a mere accident of survival (Tremel 2004: 105–234).

Solo performers—gladiators in single combat, or charioteers driving a team of horses—attracted a following for their skill and bravery. Bravery, if not skill, was also admired in the stoicism with which individual criminals endured the spectacle of the aggravated death-penalties to which they had been sentenced: crucifixion (in itself lacking in spectacular appeal, unless combined with something more animated), burning, or *damnatio ad bestias*. On special occasions, an ingenious theatrical element might be added by staging executions as mythological enactments (Coleman 1990). The accounts of the deaths of early Christian martyrs are a vivid, if somewhat tendentious, record of these events, bearing witness both to the frustration of officials faced with intransigent cult-followers who refused to pass the test of sacrificing to the emperor, and to the state of stubborn ecstasy in which the martyrs faced a horrifying death. Massed spectacles called for a source of disposable manpower on a grand scale. Criminals and, especially, prisoners of war manned the craft deployed in the rare *naumachiae*, staged naval battles, in which thousands lost their lives (Coleman 1993; Berlan-Bajard 2006). One such occasion is the source of another persistent misconception, the so-called 'gladiatorial salute' ('we who are about to die salute you'), with which gladiators are supposed to have greeted the emperor before engaging in combat. The salute was actually uttered—in the third person—by the prisoners of war who were about to man the ships in the *naumachia* that Claudius staged on the Fucine Lake in Central Italy in 52 CE, before his futile attempt to drain it (Suetonius, *Claudius* 21.6): *have imperator, morituri te salutant*, 'Hail, emperor! Those who are about to die salute you'. There is no evidence that such a salutation was pronounced by gladiators, nor that it was employed on any other occasion (Leon 1939).

Sponsors

We have already seen that the Romans themselves believed that the spectacles of the arena originated in funerary commemoration. Even after the provision of certain games became a regular liturgy for which office-holders were eligible for municipal funding, private individuals continued to sponsor games of their own accord, sometimes, indeed, in a funerary context. These acts of altruism, which of course accrued to the glory of the individual sponsor and his family, reflect the concept of *liberalitas*, the capacity for generosity that was the prerogative of the man who was free (*liber*) and could therefore own—and dispose of—his own property. Such acts stand alongside other civic benefits, such as endowments to support regular feasts, or free distributions of oil at the baths, or the restoration of a public building in the community. Such 'do-gooding', *euergetism* (from Greek *eu-*, 'well', and ergon 'deed'), provided amenities for the local community, and all but guaranteed that the benefactor would be commemorated with a statue in the town square. The statues themselves have largely disappeared, but the inscriptions are a precious source of information for the status of spectacle in the hierarchy of benefits enjoyed by local communities. The frequent boast that a city-official had performed a liturgy 'at his own expense' (that is, without availing himself of any official subsidy available to him by virtue of his office) demonstrates the cachet that accompanied these demonstrations of civic loyalty. The fundamental importance of spectacle as an integral feature of a Roman community is reflected in the clauses making provision for it in the colonial charter for the Republican colony of Urso in Spain (Welch 1994: 61–2). The walls of Pompeii are host to dozens of painted signs advertising the sponsorship of forthcoming spectacles (Sabbatini Tumolesi 1980), as well as to graffiti replicating cartoon-like figures of gladiators labelled with their tally of victories and reprieves (Langner 2001: nos. 1003, 1007–8, 1010–11, 1023–6, 1032–3, 1040, 1046), and the distribution of gifts or tokens (*missilia*) among the spectators by a mechanism referred to poetically as the 'bountiful cable' (*linea dives*) is illustrated on two wall-paintings, one from the *tablinum* of the Casa della Caccia Antica and another of unrecorded provenance (Naples Museum, inv. no. 9624; Killeen 1959). It is worth noting that Pompeii, having no circus, exhibits neither advertisements for chariot-racing nor graffiti illustrating it.

Euergetism, subject to the combined pressures of moral obligation and a desire for glory, provided the means of negotiating the relationship between the elite and the non-elite of a local community. Modern charitable donations are a misleading model; the terms of a gift might be laid down, or at least endorsed, by the community itself, and the privilege of donation could be a source of fierce competition among its most prominent members (Zuiderhoek 2007). Some forms of euergetism apparently required imperial sanction, reminding us of the bureaucratic ties that bound the far-flung cities of the empire to the emperor in Rome, and suggesting also that public spectacle was an aspect of communal relations so important as to require close imperial attention. The construction of a circus, a theatre, or an amphitheatre required the emperor's permission (*Digest* 50.10.3). Foundations that were established for putting on games are regularly commemorated on coins in the Greek East; the legends and images advertise both the city's wealth, measured in terms of *munera* (gladiatorial displays) and *venationes* (beast-hunts), and also the emperor's favour, represented, it seems, by the imperial privilege granting the city the right to mount the spectacles (Nollé 1992–3). Plutarch repeats the Platonic objection to bestowing honours on rich men who court popular favour by putting on shows or distributing gifts of money—he specifically mentions gladiatorial shows, unknown to Plato (Plutarch, *Rules for Politicians* 29)—and the tight imperial oversight of the mounting of games in the provinces may be in part motivated by fear that provincial affections might be transferred from the emperor, evidently the motivation behind clauses in the *Theodosian Code* preventing governors from sponsoring lavish shows (*Codex Theodosianus* 15.5.1 Mommsen–Meyer).

Yet, the mounting of spectacles could strain resources as well as display them. There is no secure evidence that entrance-fees were regularly charged—sponsors advertise their altruism, not their enterprise—and tickets were probably distributed free through networks of patronage, at least to locals. The *sordida merces* ('base profit') for which Tacitus (*Annals* 4.62–3) pours scorn upon the freedman Atilius, who built an enormous wooden amphitheatre at Fidenae that collapsed to scandalous loss of life in 27 CE, probably refers to fees charged to spectators making the short excursion from Rome, 8 km away, rather than to the inhabitants of Fidenae itself (Chamberland 2007). The official liturgies incumbent upon priests, upon *Augustales* (officials supervising the imperial cult), and upon certain magistrates had an inflationary effect, and by the High Empire they even threatened to drain the pool of potential candidates, especially in the East. This may explain, for instance, the background to a letter of Hadrian to the city of Aphrodisias in Asia Minor in 125 CE, where nominees to the high priesthood complained that they could not afford the office. In the letter Hadrian ratifies a proposal from the city magistrates that the high priests should contribute funds to the construction of an aqueduct instead of providing gladiatorial shows. This may suggest, not that the priests found the contribution to the aqueduct more burdensome than the funding of gladiatorial shows (Reynolds 2000: 16–19), but that, rather, the contribution to the aqueduct was offered as an incentive to candidates to stand for office (Coleman 2008), a fixed contribution being perhaps preferable to the uncertain costs involved in providing gladiators, whose rental fee rose in proportion to the severity of their injuries (Gaius, *Institutes* 3.146). Half-a-century later, however, imperial intervention was necessary empire-wide: a transcript of senatorial proceedings late in the reign of Marcus Aurelius testifies both to the sliding-scale of price-caps on the cost of gladiators for games in different categories (Oliver and Palmer 1955) and to the grading-system by which the gladiators themselves were ranked (Carter 2003), and the relation between the two.

Support-staff

More was at stake than simply the filling of priesthoods. Spectacle was a significant cog in the machinery of the Roman economy. The proportion of people living within and beyond the frontiers of the empire whose livelihoods depended upon supplying or administering the spectacles may be impossible to calculate, not least because the supply of most of the performers and support-staff is indistinguishable from the overall operations of the slave-trade. Race-horses were bred and trained (Humphrey 1986: Index 4, s.v. 'horse breeding'). Catching animals for the arena was an important sideline for the army (Epplett 2001), and their transportation and survival was entrusted—often unsuccessfully—to experts who are intermittently visible in both the literary and the epigraphic record (Jennison 1937: 137–81, MacKinnon 2006). As with the minutely differentiated tasks in a slave-run household, so, too, in the circus and amphitheatre there was a plethora of specialized staff, down to the *ministri* who raked the sand in the arena (Martial 2.75.5–6). Musicians played at critical moments during gladiatorial combat (Ville 1981: 372–5; Junkelmann 2000: 132–3). There were corpses to be disposed of: the bodies of humans, at least at Rome, may have been deposited in the Tiber, for its waters to cleanse the city of ritual pollution; animal meat may have been distributed to the plebs for consumption (Kyle 1998: 184–241). Whether there was an administrative structure in the amphitheatre to parallel the circus factions is unknown; certainly, the two institutions shared many functions in common. The factions, often misleadingly identified with fan-clubs, were the racing-stables, each represented by a different colour. An object-lesson in the use of later sources has recently revealed that the tenth-century Byzantine compilation, *The Book of Ceremonies*, preserves a rich vein of detail pertaining to the administration and resources in the circus (Nelis-Clément 2002). Since no such source exists for the support-staff of the amphitheatre, our information, as so often, depends upon inscriptions (mainly epitaphs), iconographic representations (especially rich in the depiction of musicians), and stray details in literary sources (Ville 1981: 366–79).

Spectators

Gambling, well attested for the circus (Balsdon 1969: 321), can hardly have been absent from the amphitheatre; a rare hint is provided by Ovid's recommendation that the aspiring lover attending a gladiatorial show should consult the object of his affections as to the odds when placing his bet (*Art of Love* 1.165–70). Ovid's tip for a pick-up presupposes seating as yet unsegregated by gender. A famous passage in Suetonius (*Augustus* 44) describes Augustus' seating-arrangements (Rawson 1987): at all types of display everywhere, the front row was to be reserved for the local senatorial class; in Rome, embassies from 'free and allied peoples' were to be banned from sitting in the orchestra at the theatre, since some cities sent freedmen as ambassadors; the sexes were to be segregated at gladiatorial displays, which implies that they already sat apart in the theatre and the circus. The rest of Augustus' strictures furthered his vision of a properly ordered society, keeping slaves apart from free persons, upper classes from lower, adults from children, married men from bachelors, soldiers from civilians; whether these arrangements applied outside the city of Rome, or how long they survived, is unknown, although the temptation to generalize from them is seldom resisted. Epigraphic evidence for seating-arrangements at other times and places, such as inscriptions from the amphitheatres at Lyons and Nîmes (*EAOR*, vol. 5, nos. 43, 44, 78), suggests that seating-privileges were as jealously guarded throughout the empire as they were in Augustan Rome, but the specificity of some of the categories (for example, separate seating for boatmen on the Rhône and its tributaries) reminds us of the individual stamp that each community put upon the seal of Roman identity represented by their deployment of public spectacle.

If the evidence of the late antique regionary catalogues can be trusted, the Colosseum had a capacity of 87,000 *loca* ('places'), although modern estimates calculate a maximum of only 50,000, a figure that may betray modern sensitivities about personal space, as well as the size of the average physique nowadays. The Circus Maximus held 250,000 spectators, according to the elder Pliny (*Natural History* 36.102); 385,000 or 485,000 *loca*, according to the regionary catalogues; 150,000 spectators by modern calculations (Humphrey 1986: 126). Whatever the exact numbers, thousands of people require sophisticated amenities if they are to watch for hours without getting restless (Scobie 1988), not to mention getting in and out efficiently, a process that is proving hard to visualize, especially as we do not know whether spectacle buildings were always—or, indeed, ever—packed to capacity. Analysis of flow-patterns in the Colosseum, the Circus Maximus, and the Theatre of Marcellus based on mathematical calculations paints a picture of brisk and orderly egress (Rose 2005), whereas experiments with a three-dimensional computer-model in the Experiential Technologies Center at the University of California at Los Angeles suggest that access for the upper levels was compromised by passage through a corridor that was low, dark, and narrow (Gutierrez *et al.* 2007). The rigid stratification in Roman society that kept privilege jealously guarded for the upper classes extends to the latrines, available in the Colosseum on the lower levels reserved for more important citizens, where the forces of gravity and the social hierarchy happily coincide (Lombardi, in Gabucci 2001: 234–40).

If a Pliny or a Tacitus could despise the enthusiasms of the common man, Suetonius' *Lives* display ample evidence that the cannier emperors saw fit to share them. His comment that Titus displayed partisanship for the Thracian style of gladiator 'without any loss of dignity or fairness' (*Titus* 8.2) shows how delicate was the balancing-act between appealing to the crowd and retaining the respect of the upper classes; and comparison with his trenchant disapproval of similar partisanship displayed by Caligula towards the faction of the 'Greens' in the circus (*Caligula* 55.2) shows how the ambiguous status of spectacle in the Roman value-system could be manipulated to support moral judgements. Suetonius does not countenance the possibility that the emperor's favouritism was a calculated move to ensure that at least one powerful faction would support him in time of need, a strategy perfected by the early Byzantine emperors (Greatrex 1997: 65). The uninhibited behaviour of spectators at the rousing events in circus and amphitheatre is a source of anxiety to pagan philosophers and Christian apologists alike, fearing loss of self-control and independent judgement; even personal safety was believed to be at risk, if it is legitimate to extrapolate from the theatre, where the younger Seneca identifies the scramble for *missilia* as a particularly threatening moment (*Letters* 74.7).

Attempts to generalize about Roman attitudes towards the various categories of spectacle are fraught with danger, because our textual sources are so fragmentary and almost exclusively reflect the views of the upper classes. In general, the circus seems to have prompted less animus, and less special pleading, than the amphitheatre (Wistrand 1992). Cicero can condone the arena for giving unworthy persons a chance to demonstrate physical bravery (*Tusculan Disputations* 2.41); Petronius can use it to ridicule the preoccupations of the freedman class (*Satyrica* 45–6, 52, 71.6; Kleijwegt 1998). The sources are consistent in condemning participation by members of the elite, who suffered the legal disability of *infamia* for doing so for profit, becoming literally 'unspeakable' (*infamis*), an attitude that seems to lurk behind Septimius Severus' ban on female gladiators, mentioned above; the scandalous coercion whereby certain emperors forced members of the upper classes to perform in public cannot have subjected them to *infamia*, since presumably no fee was incurred. Especially intriguing are the tales of emperors appearing in public as charioteers and gladiators, an act that flagrantly transgressed social norms, not to mention exposing the emperor to real physical danger. It is frequently emphasized that spectacles were occasions on which the emperor came face to face with the people, who therefore used them to express their opinions and make political demands (Hopkins 1983: 14–20; Wiedemann 1992: 166–70); the Byzantine hippodrome frequently witnessed the acclamation of a rival emperor (Greatrex 1997: 63). Yet, the vision of a spectacle building as a truly democratic forum is belied by the architecture, effectively a giant trap for the unruly; Caligula, at least, did not hesitate to arrest the ringleaders at a demonstration in the circus (Josephus, *Jewish Antiquities* 19.25–6; cf. Dio, *Roman History* 59.13.4). Nevertheless, spectacles, and the venues to hold them, were an indispensable accompaniment to the emperor's progress around his empire: Dio complains that members of the upper class, forced to build 'hunting-theatres and race-courses' wherever Caracalla expected to spend the winter, received no imperial subsidy whatsoever (*Roman History* 78.7.9).

Political considerations aside, spectacles were also occasions on which the people witnessed the bravery of the participants, whether slave or free, commoner or emperor: Nero's determination when he was helped back in after falling out of a ten-horse chariot—monstrously difficult to manage—may justly have impressed his subjects, regardless of the fact that he ultimately failed to finish the race, and regardless also of the scorn of the ancient sources, who unanimously insinuate that the prize he won was testimony merely to the judges' sycophancy (Suetonius, *Nero* 24.2; Dio, *Roman History* 63.14.1; Champlin 2003: 59). In general, it is the 'populist' emperors who evince enthusiasm for spectacle. Others express philosophical disdain, like Marcus Aurelius, who was grateful that his childhood nurse had dissuaded him from becoming a partisan of the Greens or the Blues in the races, or of gladiators shielded by the small *parma* or the massive *scutum* (i.e. the types known as *thraeces* and *murmillones*: *Meditations* 1.5). Marcus nevertheless attended, bringing paperwork with him to the circus, which provoked heckling (Scriptores Historiae Augustae, *Marcus* 15.1). He took steps to mitigate the violence of arena displays (Dio, *Roman History* 71.29), although what he complains about is not their cruelty, but their monotony (*Meditations* 6.46). Ennui towards the arena was not, however, an attitude universally shared among the upper crust: Marcus' tutor, the senator Fronto, was a passionate circus fan (*Letters to Friends* 2.3). Attempts to categorize attitudes to spectacle on grounds of class cannot do justice to the variety of individual responses to be glimpsed in our patchy record.

The Function of Spectacle

Apart from fiction (chiefly Petronius and Apuleius), most of our literary references to spectacle relay tidbits about its deployment at Rome, where the emperors and their agents spared neither ingenuity nor expense. But epigraphy and material culture have the potential to redress this imbalance, documenting the civic pride of a municipal sponsor who is able to grace his community with the display of a few pairs of gladiators or half-a-dozen beasts, or revealing the ubiquity of four-horse chariots or gladiatorial pairs as decorative motifs on cheap terracotta lamps empire-wide. The collection and analysis of regional evidence not only reveals the view from the provinces; it also has the potential to reveal regional differences. Images of spectacle from Sicily and North Africa, for instance, show an overwhelming preference for beast-fights and horse-racing over gladiatorial combat: why? Because the classes who could afford to decorate their homes with lavish mosaics earned at least some of their wealth from the beast trade, as has been suggested for the owner of the late antique villa at Piazza Armerina in the heart of Sicily (Wilson 1983: 97–8)? How far is it legitimate to infer an autobiographical element in a householder's choice of decor? What are the distribution patterns for motifs on lamps? Does the purchase of a lamp sporting a chariot represent a conscious preference over a floral motif or an erotic scene, or is it just what happened to be available?

In one sense, images of spectacle on the walls and floors of villas and town-houses appear to 'privatize' a phenomenon that is quintessentially public, while frequently emphasizing the link with the recurring rituals of the Roman calendar (Kondoleon 1999). But did actual performances take place in private? The race-tracks and arenas attached to the imperial palaces of late antiquity manifest an urge to display dangerous spectacles to the emperor's favoured guests. Did wealthy citizens do this too? If the extravaganzas that Petronius imagines at Trimalchio's dinner-party cannot be taken entirely at face-value (Jones 1991: 185–91), neither can the testimony of the Augustan author Nicolaus of Damascus, alleging that the Romans—scarcely fit to share his civilized world—stage gladiatorial fights to the death as dinner-entertainment (quoted by Athenaeus, *The Learned Banqueters* 4.153); yet, to dismiss these testimonies out of hand would be to sacrifice whatever kernel of truth they enshrine. Perhaps our notion of a dinner-party as a small, private affair gets in the way. Privately sponsored public banquets, complete with such entertaining entr'actes as the dancing-girls and fencing-displays at Domitian's feast in the Colosseum (Statius, *Silvae* 1.6), may be closer to the ancient reality. Indeed, Roman dining regularly constituted a spectacle in itself, the rich host's display of wealth and taste paraded before the eyes of spectators of humbler status in a manner reminiscent of the intimate banquets staged to public view by the popes and monarchs of early modern Europe (D'Arms 1999).

Even the banquets of the rich could erupt into violent display, if we are to believe anecdotes such as those illustrating the cruelty of Caligula, who had the hands of a pilfering slave cut off and slung around his neck, and then ordered the man to be paraded among the guests, accompanied by a placard declaring his crime (Suetonius, *Caligula* 32.2). The impulse to violent spectacle at Rome, manifested in such a reaction, achieves its acme in gladiatorial combat. Why the Romans indulged this impulse, and how it influenced the national psyche, are irresistible questions resistant to answers. A link between the army and the arena is easy to see, but harder to interpret. The influence seems to go in both directions: gladiators expert in close combat might be borrowed for military training (Coulston 1998), whereas the shorthand that was used to identify casualties in both contexts presumably originated with the army (Watson 1952). Sometimes it is less clear which is the chicken and which the egg: Livy assumes that a military manoeuvre was copied from the circus (44.9.3–5), whereas it may have been the other way round (Slater

2002: 326). The two worlds coalesce in legionary camps on the borders of the empire that were furnished with amphitheatres, an expedient of obvious utility for cowing the barbarians across the border, as well as for entertaining the troops and stiffening their morale.

Conversely, it may plausibly be supposed that, as the frontiers of the empire expanded and the soldiers protecting them were stationed further and further from the centre, metropolitan audiences needed to be reminded of Rome's militant ethic. Whether such displays of violence in urban arenas were cathartic or inflammatory is debatable. The high spirits—and high expectations—at games and festivals created moments of tension that are sporadically reflected in our sources (Zuiderhoek 2007), although only one full-scale riot is attested in an amphitheatre, at Pompeii in 59 CE; the occasion is depicted in a wall-painting from a private house (Pompeii I.iii.23; Naples Museum, inv. no. 112222), and discussed cryptically by Tacitus (*Annals* 14.17). Riots in the hippodrome in eastern cities in the early Byzantine period, however, are a constant theme, usually starting as scuffles between the two major factions, the Blues and the Greens. The Nika riot in Constantinople under Justinian in 532 CE, called after the watchword employed by the circus factions on that occasion, was ultimately suppressed in an action that killed 30,000 people; its tragic course, lavishly documented in the (admittedly contradictory) sources, can be traced directly to a misunderstanding between a vacillating emperor and his people (Greatrex 1997).

Tertullian's portrait of the games as idolatry (mentioned in my Introduction) is more than a rhetorical caricature. The *ludi circenses* seem never to have lost their ritual associations—the appropriation by the emperor of the space and rituals of the circus, far from secularizing it, enhanced his religious dignity—and the shrines installed in the Circus Maximus and the images of the gods carried in procession (and then seated to 'watch' the spectacle) furnish Tertullian with ample ammunition (*On the Spectacles* 7–9). Ritual solemnity attended gladiatorial spectacles too: the worship of Nemesis—an incarnation of fate and revenge—is closely associated with the amphitheatre (Hornum 1993), and the association that Augustus forged between arena displays and the imperial cult is maintained across the empire until the games finally decline in late antiquity, victim to inflation and, perhaps, a gradual shift in taste. Yet, too little is known about the religious function of amphitheatre displays, and it is not clear that the average spectator under the empire perceived them as religious occasions. Tertullian himself claims that they have become thoroughly secularized, although he argues that they preserve the taint of idolatry stemming from their religious origins (*On the Spectacles* 12.3). To him, the contemporary arena represents *atrocitas* (atrocity), and the circus *insania* (madness). The bias in a view from outside Roman culture—if a Christianized African *c.*200 CE can be said to come from 'outside the culture'—is relatively easy to identify, and the external perspective can tell us something important about contemporary perceptions, if not about the Romans' own view of what they were doing, not least because outsiders find worthy of comment what insiders may take for granted: for instance, a Jewish comment on the *cena libera*, the gladiatorial banquet held the night before a display, is unique in explaining it as a ritual to 'sweeten' the gladiator's blood, that is, to make him a worthy sacrificial victim (Brettler and Poliakoff 1990).

The attractions of chariot-racing are perhaps more comprehensible in our motorized age than in any other period since antiquity, since charioteers, like racing-car drivers, must have responded to multiple stimuli: the competitive instinct and the thrill of risk, but also the challenge of coordinating brain, nerve, and muscle to master a complex skill. The staged hunts of the circus and the amphitheatre also held an appeal still recognizable today, although becoming more alien as the animal-rights movement spreads. Gladiatorial combat, however, although sometimes likened to boxing, does not have a proper analogy in the modern world. Contemporary scholars have postulated many theories to 'explain' the arena: as a demonstration of power (Hopkins 1983; Futrell 1997) or, specifically, power over death (Wiedemann 1992); a collective psychosis of despair (Barton 1993); a fascination with risk (Plass 1995); an apotropaic ritual by the shedding of blood, a distraction from political emasculation, an outlet for a political voice, a technique for maintaining social order, an impulse to see the socially marginalized redeem themselves by bravery (Brown 1995). The fragmentary nature of ancient sources forces historians to juxtapose evidence from widely disparate times and places. Yet, the development of arena spectacles is clear. Under the empire, an indissoluble link is forged between emperor and spectacle, especially—but not exclusively—the spectacles of the amphitheatre: by surrogates presenting gladiatorial shows 'on the emperor's behalf' as part of his cult; by the lavish spending of imperially sanctioned money; by the display of techniques and qualities identical to those deployed by the emperor's soldiers on the frontier; and by the emperor himself, micro-managing the conditions under which communities—whether in Rome itself or in the most distant corners of the empire—were permitted to put on displays, and parading his person whenever his physical presence in a community coincided with a show, no matter that he personally may have found spectacle repellent. Spectacle connected the empire to the emperor. It was very serious entertainment.

Further reading

The ubiquity of spectacle in Roman culture is vividly exemplified by the range of contributions in Bergmann and Kondoleon 1999. Lively introductory articles, covering *inter alia* circus and amphitheatre and translated into English, are contained in Köhne and Ewigleben 2000, including a distillation by Junkelmann of his pioneering book (Junkelmann 2000: in

German, without any index, but nevertheless invaluable for the images alone; now updated in Junkelmann 2008). On the circus, Cameron 1973 and 1976, Humphrey 1986, and Nelis-Clément 2002 are fundamental; many stimulating contributions—archaeological, artistic, and literary—are contained in Nelis-Clément and Roddaz 2008. On the amphitheatre, despite the author's untimely death before completion of the manuscript, Ville 1981 is the most comprehensive and reliable study. Much fascinating information, accompanied by stimulating—if occasionally idiosyncratic—interpretation, is supplied by Wiedemann 1992. The corpora of gladiatorial inscriptions provide a plethora of vivid detail, often very puzzling. Specialized aspects and approaches are covered in the references below.

References

Balsdon, J. P. V. D. (1969), *Life and Leisure in Ancient Rome*, London: Bodley Head.

Barton, C. (1993), *The Sorrows of the Ancient Romans: The Gladiator and the Monster*, Princeton: Princeton University Press.

Beard, M. (2007), *The Roman Triumph*, Cambridge, Mass.: The Belknap Press of Harvard University Press.

Bergmann, B. (2008), 'Pictorial Narratives of the Roman Circus', in Nelis-Clément and Roddaz 2008: 361–91.

—— and Kondoleon, C. (eds.) (1999), *The Art of Ancient Spectacle*, Washington, DC: National Gallery of Art/Yale University Press.

Berlan-Bajard, A. (2006), *Les Spectacles aquatiques romains*, Rome: École Française de Rome.

Blümner, H. (1918), *Fahrendes Volk im Altertum = Sitzungsberichte der Königlich Bayerischen Akademie der Wissenschaften. Philosophisch-philologische und historische Klasse*, Heft 6.

Bouley, E. (2001), *Jeux romains dans les provinces balkano-danubiennes*, Paris: Presses Universitaires Franc-Comtoises.

Brettler, M. Z. and Poliakoff, M. (1990), 'Rabbi Simeon ben Lakish at the Gladiator's Banquet: Rabbinic Observations on the Roman Arena', *Harvard Theological Review*, 83: 93–8.

Brilliant, R. (1999), '"Let the Trumpets Roar!" The Roman Triumph', in Bergmann and Kondoleon 1999: 221–9.

Brown, S. (1995), 'Explaining the Arena: Did the Romans "Need" Gladiators?', *Journal of Roman Archaeology*, 8: 376–84 (review of Wiedemann 1992).

Brunet, S. (2004), 'Female and Dwarf Gladiators', *Mouseion*, 3rd ser. 4: 145–70.

Cameron, A. (1973), *Porphyrius the Charioteer*, Oxford: Oxford University Press.

—— (1976), *Circus Factions: Blues and Greens at Rome and Byzantium*, Oxford: Oxford University Press.

Carter, M. (2003), 'Gladiatorial Ranking and the *SC de pretiis gladiatorum minuendis* (*CIL* II 6278 = *ILS* 5163)', *Phoenix*, 57: 83–114.

Chamberland, G. (2007), 'A Gladiatorial Show Produced *in mercedem sordidam* (Tacitus, *Ann.* 4.62)', *Phoenix*, 61: 136–49.

Champlin, E. (2003), *Nero*, Cambridge, Mass.: The Belknap Press of Harvard University Press.

Coleman, K. M. (1990), 'Fatal Charades: Roman Executions Staged as Mythological Enactments', *Journal of Roman Studies*, 80: 44–73.

—— (1993), 'Launching into History: Aquatic Displays in the Early Empire', *Journal of Roman Studies*, 83: 48–74.

Coleman, K. M. (2005), *Bonds of Danger: Communal Life in the Gladiatorial Barracks of Ancient Rome*, Sydney: Department of Classics and Ancient History, University of Sydney.
—— (2006), *Martial, Liber Spectaculorum: Text, Translation, and Commentary*, Oxford: Oxford University Press.
—— (2008), 'Exchanging Gladiators for an Aqueduct at Aphrodisias (*SEG* 50.1096)', *Acta Classica*, 51: 31–46.
Coulston, J. C. N. (1998), 'Gladiators and Soldiers: Personnel and Equipment in *Ludus* and *Castra*', *Journal of Roman Military Equipment Studies*, 9: 1–17.
D'Arms, J. H. (1999), 'Performing Culture: Roman Spectacle and the Banquets of the Powerful', in Bergmann and Kondoleon 1999: 301–19.
Diliberto, O. (1981), *Ricerche sull' 'Auctoramentum' e sulla condizione degli 'Auctorati'*, Milan: Giuffrè.
EAOR (1988–) = *Epigrafia anfiteatrale dell'Occidente romano*, 6 vols. so far, Rome: Edizioni Quasar.
Epplett, C. (2001), 'The Capture of Animals by the Roman Military', *Greece & Rome*, 2nd ser. 48: 210–22.
Futrell, A. (1997), *Blood in the Arena: The Spectacle of Roman Power*, Austin, Tex.: University of Texas Press.
Gabucci, A. (ed.) (2001), *The Colosseum*, tr. M. Becker, Los Angeles: J. Paul Getty Museum.
Greatrex, G. (1997), 'The Nika Riot: A Reappraisal', *Journal of Hellenic Studies*, 117: 60–86.
Gutierrez, D. *et al.* (2007), 'AI and Virtual Crowds: Populating the Colosseum', *Journal of Cultural Heritage*, 8/2: 176–85.
Hope, V. (2000), 'Fighting for Identity: The Funerary Commemoration of Italian Gladiators', in A. E. Cooley (ed.), *The Epigraphic Landscape of Roman Italy*, London: Institute of Classical Studies, 93–113.
Hopkins, K. (1983), 'Murderous Games', in *Death and Renewal*, Cambridge: Cambridge University Press, 1–30.
Hornum, M. B. (1993), *Nemesis, the Roman State, and the Games*, Leiden and New York: E. J. Brill.
Humphrey, J. H. (1986), *Roman Circuses: Arenas for Chariot Racing*, London: B. T. Batsford.
Jennison, G. (1937), *Animals for Show and Pleasure in Ancient Rome*, Manchester: Manchester University Press; repr. Philadelphia: University of Pennsylvania Press, 2005.
Jones, C. P. (1991), 'Dinner Theater', in W. J. Slater (ed.), *Dining in a Classical Context*, Ann Arbor, Mich.: University of Michigan Press, 185–98.
Junkelmann, M. (2000), *Das Spiel mit dem Tod: So kämpften Roms Gladiatoren*, Mainz am Rhein: Verlag Philipp von Zabern.
—— (2008), *Gladiatoren: Das Spiel mit dem Tod*, Mainz am Rhein: Verlag Philipp von Zabern.
Kanz, F. and Grossschmidt, K. (2005), 'Stand der anthropologischen Forschungen zum Gladiatorenfriedhof in Ephesos', *Jahreshefte des Österreichischen Archäologischen Institutes in Wien*, 74: 103–23.
Killeen, J. F. (1959), 'What Was the *Linea Dives* (Martial, VIII,78,7)?', *American Journal of Philology*, 80: 185–8.
Kleijwegt, M. (1998), 'The Social Dimensions of Gladiatorial Combat in Petronius' *Cena Trimalchionis*', in H. Hofmann and M. Zimmerman (eds.), *Groningen Colloquia on the Novel*, vol. 9, Groningen: Egbert Forsten Publishing, 75–97.

Köhne, E. and Ewigleben, C. (eds.) (2000), *Gladiators and Caesars*, London: British Museum.
Kondoleon, C. (1999), 'Timing Spectacles: Roman Domestic Art and Performance', in Bergmann and Kondoleon 1999: 321–41.
Kyle, D. G. (1998), *Spectacles of Death in Ancient Rome*, London and New York: Routledge.
Lanata, G. (1998), 'Les Animaux dans la jurisprudence romaine', in Liliane Bodson (ed.), *Les Animaux exotiques dans les relations internationales: espèces, fonctions, significations*, Liège: Université de Liège, 53–79.
Langner, M. (2001), *Antike Graffitizeichnungen. Motive, Gestaltung und Bedeutung*, Wiesbaden: Dr. Ludwig Reichert Verlag.
Leon, H. J. (1939), '*Morituri te salutamus*', *Transactions of the American Philological Association*, 70: 46–50.
MacKinnon, M. (2006), 'Supplying Exotic Animals for the Roman Amphitheatre Games: New Reconstructions Combining Archaeological, Ancient Textual, Historical and Ethnographic Data', *Mouseion*, 3rd ser. 6: 137–61.
MacMullen, R. (1986), 'Judicial Savagery in the Roman Empire', *Chiron*, 16: 147–66.
Mosci Sassi, M. G. (1992), *Il linguaggio gladiatorio*, Bologna: Pàtron editore.
Nelis-Clément, J. (2002), 'Les Métiers du cirque, de Rome à Byzance: entre texte et image', *Cahiers du Centre Gustave Glotz*, 13: 265–309.
—— and Roddaz, J.-M. (eds.) (2008), *Le Cirque romain et son image*, Bordeaux: Ausonius Éditions.
Nollé, J. (1992–3), 'Kaiserliche Privilegien für Gladiatorenmunera und Tierhetzen. Unbekannte und ungedeutete Zeugnisse auf städtischen Münzen des griechischen Ostens', *Jahrbuch für Numismatik und Geldgeschichte*, 42–3: 49–82.
Oliver, J. H. and Palmer, R. E. A. (1955), 'Minutes of an Act of the Roman Senate', *Hesperia*, 24: 320–49.
Plass, P. (1995), *The Game of Death in Ancient Rome: Arena Sport and Political Suicide*, Madison, Wisc.: University of Wisconsin Press.
Rawson, E. (1987), '*Discrimina ordinum*: The *Lex Julia theatralis*', *Papers of the British School at Rome*, ns 55: 83–114; repr. in *Roman Culture and Society: Collected Papers*, Oxford and New York: Oxford University Press, 1991: 508–45.
Reynolds, J. (2000), 'New Letters from Hadrian to Aphrodisias: Trials, Taxes, Gladiators and an Aqueduct', *Journal of Roman Archaeology*, 13: 5–20.
Robert, L. (1940), *Les Gladiateurs dans l'Orient grec*, Paris: E. Champion.
Rose, P. (2005), 'Spectators and Spectator Comfort in Roman Entertainment Buildings: A Study in Functional Design', *Papers of the British School at Rome*, ns 60: 99–130.
Roueché, C. (1993), *Performers and Partisans at Aphrodisias in the Roman and Late Roman Periods*, London: Society for the Promotion of Roman Studies.
Sabbatini Tumolesi, P. (1980), *Gladiatorum paria. Annunci di spettacoli gladiatorii a Pompei*, Rome: Edizioni di Storia e Letteratura.
Scarborough, J. (1971), 'Galen and the Gladiators', *Episteme*, 5: 98–111.
Scobie, A. (1988), 'Spectator Security and Comfort at Gladiatorial Games', *Nikephoros*, 1: 191–243.
Slater, W. J. (2002), 'Mime Problems: Cicero *Ad fam.* 7.1 and Martial 9.38', *Phoenix*, 56: 315–29.
Tremel, J. (2004), *Magica agonistica. Fluchtafeln im antiken Sport*, Hildesheim: Weidmann.
Ville, G. (1981), *La Gladiature en Occident des origines à la mort de Domitien*, Rome: École Française de Rome.

WATSON, G. R. (1952), 'Theta nigrum', *Journal of Roman Studies*, 42: 56–62.
WELCH, K. (1994), 'The Roman Arena in Late-Republican Italy: A New Interpretation', *Journal of Roman Archaeology*, 7: 59–80.
WIEDEMANN, T. (1992), *Emperors and Gladiators*, London and New York: Routledge.
WILSON, R. J. A. (1983), *Piazza Armerina*, St Albans: Granada Publishing.
WISTRAND, M. (1992), *Entertainment and Violence in Ancient Rome*, Göteborg: Acta Universitatis Gothoburgensis.
ZUIDERHOEK, A. (2007), 'The Ambiguity of Munificence', *Historia*, 56: 196–213.

CHAPTER 42

IMPERIAL ECUMENE AND POLYETHNICITY

PETER FIBIGER BANG

> Now there were dwelling in Jerusalem Jews, devout men from every nation under heaven. And at this sound the multitude came together, and they were bewildered, because each one was hearing them speak in his own language. And they were amazed and astonished, saying, 'Are not all these who are speaking Galileans? And how is it that we hear, each of us in his own native language? Parthians and Medes and Elamites and residents of Mesopotamia, Judea and Cappadocia, Pontus and Asia, Phrygia and Pamphylia, Egypt and the parts of Libya belonging to Cyrene, and visitors from Rome, both Jews and proselytes, Cretans and Arabians—we hear them telling in our own tongues the mighty works of God.' And all were amazed and perplexed, saying to one another, 'What does this mean?' But others mocking said, 'They are filled with new wine.'
>
> (Acts 2: 5–13)

THE ancient Mediterranean was a complex patchwork of diverse ethnic groups and cultures. For the early Christians it took nothing short of a miracle to explain how the Jesus sect had been able to break out of its local cultural setting. On the day of the Pentecost, the church celebrated its own foundational myth; it was the story of the miraculous transformation of a small isolated band of Jews—the followers of a crucified charismatic leader—into a community of believers with universal aspirations. The Holy Ghost, so it was told, had descended upon the apostles, given them 'tongues as of fire', and thus enabled them to communicate the gospel across the barriers of understanding erected among men by the many different languages and dialects current in their world. It was to become a matter of no little consequence that the early Church Fathers were also practical-minded men. Rather than putting their faith in the repeated assistance of divine miracle to spread 'the good tidings', they chose to graft their religious teachings onto a much more potent force of cultural integration: the Roman Empire. By committing their beliefs to writing in the two imperial languages, Greek and Latin, they ensured that the Christian message would not be 'circumscribed by place' (Musurillo 1972: 49; Justin Martyr, *Apol.* 1.24).

The Roman emperors presided over a realm of staggering proportions, today the home of more than a score of nation-states, and had to bridge extreme contrasts within their far-flung territories. Two examples will illustrate the range. At Dendur, in Upper Egypt, a small temple, now in the Metropolitan Museum of Art in New York, depicted the emperor Augustus performing sacrifices to the gods on the reliefs carved on its façade. But that is not at all clear to the undiscerning modern eye accustomed to the conventions of Greek and Roman art. The temple was built in time-honoured Egyptian style and Augustus was portrayed as pharaoh (Bagnall and Rathbone 2004: 247–8). At such temples, old Egyptian cosmological beliefs and cultural traditions were kept alive long after the political order of the pharaohs had been supplanted by outside conquerors. Of the several hundred manuscripts kept in the library of the temple in the village of Tebtunis during the heyday of Roman rule, the overwhelming majority were written in various Egyptian scripts (Ryholdt 2005). Almost at the other end of the empire, the southern Gallic villages of Lessoux and La Graufesenque developed extensive rural proto-industrial productions of ceramic tableware that were exported far and wide. Based on the emulation of Italian prototypes and stamped with Latin seals, this red-slip pottery has come to signify the Roman period to many an archaeologist. Yet, these most Roman of artefacts were produced by communities of potters who in their daily intercourse spoke a Gallic language (Adams 2003, ch. 7; Hingley 2005, ch. 5).

Gallic language, Egyptian customs, imperial power, and Roman culture: both examples display a complex mixture of local and global, but the emphasis is different. While the Gallic potters, or their masters, exploited the opportunities provided by the empire to reach out of their locality, the leaders of the Egyptian temple attempted to appropriate a foreign, metropolitan monarch to shore up their regional variety of religious power and ritual. These differences, however, represent alternative strategies of response. What the two examples have in common is that local or regional brands of knowledge, culture, and power had been subsumed under an imperial cultural and political umbrella of much wider geographical extent. In the ideological language of the period, the empire was described as universal. The Roman emperor prided himself on the unbounded reach of his rule and the great variety of peoples under his sway (Augustus, *Res*

Gestae 26–33; Plin. *Pan.* 12–17; Whittaker 1994: chs. 1–2). Roman government suffered from no illusions that it could do without the forms of locally based power represented by diverse ethnic groups and instead push to create a homogeneous 'national' identity for the imperial population at large. The size of the empire and the constraints pre-industrial technology imposed on the movement of men and the speed of communication made strongly centralized control of life in the empire impossible. What mattered from the imperial perspective was not uniformity but the ability to tap into the resources of local societies and mobilize some of their means for the purposes of central government.

Extensive empire meant the ability to command a vast range of diverse resources. Celebrating the advantages of Europe, the Augustan geographer Strabo observed: 'It is amply supplied with warriors, and also with men fitted for the labours of agriculture, and the life of the towns' (Strabo 2.5.26). But one should not be led astray by the harmonizing rhetoric. Imperial polyethnicity, however inclusive, was not exactly a multicultural idyll. There was plenty of ethnic prejudice and tension (Isaac 2004). Polyethnicity, after all, was not based on equality of rights; it was the product of conquest, an expression of imperial subjection and hierarchy. As Strabo continued on the subject of Europe, it was through the labours of the imperial government that the various groups, each with their own specialty, were brought together and employed to 'receive mutual advantages from each other, the one aiding by their arms, the other by their husbandry, arts, and institutions'. The Roman Empire ordered ethnic diversity for strategic consumption. (Cf. McNeill 1986: 17; Eusebius, *Vit. Const.* 4.7.1–2.)

This principle was embodied in the biggest and single most important organization in the empire, the Roman army; it consisted of a core of citizen legions but these were complemented by vast numbers of non-citizen, auxiliary soldiers recruited from provincial subject populations, client kingdoms, and sometimes, and increasingly so as time wore on, from allied tribal communities on the fringes of the empire (Josephus, *Jewish War* 3.64–9; Ammianus Marcellinus 31.4.1–5). Auxiliary units were generally organized on an ethnic basis, at least in origin, and frequently supplied a particular specialty to the army, as did the famed Numidian cavalry or the Palmyrene archers and camel riders (Livy 30.33–5; Caesar, *BG* 2.7; *CIL* 16.106; Pollard 2000: 121–9; Roymans 2004). In official architecture and processions, the unrivalled capacity of the empire to draw on a great diversity of resources was publicized in dazzling displays of rare forms and expensive materials brought from afar. Egyptian obelisks, precious types of coloured marble, and elephants formed part of a visual semantics of power that demonstrated the universal authority of the Roman emperor. Hadrian's famed palatial villa at Tivoli, with its combination of Nilotic scenery, delicate Hellenizing architecture, Roman monumentalism, and exquisite collections of art works, was a representation, in microcosm, of the glories and might of imperial diversity—the fruit of victory, the spoils of conquest (Beard and Henderson 2001, ch. 2; Schneider 1986).

Universalism: Hegemony, Hierarchy, and the Depth of Integration

The secret to governing the polyethnic conglomerate which was the Roman Empire lay in the establishment of universal institutions. In recent years, the notions of 'local knowledge' and 'thick description', both coined by the late Clifford Geertz, have gained considerable currency. They stress the all-important role of local social settings in shaping and determining the character of cultural phenomena. Truth is specific and circumscribed, never general, in this perspective. This is the basic teaching of anthropology. What is customary in one place represents outrageous behaviour in another (Geertz 2000; cf. Wallace-Hadrill 1997). Universal institutions, however, operate on the opposite principle; they depend on transcending the boundaries of local communities to enable transfer of resources and communication of knowledge. Not only did the Roman army draw on a diverse range of communities for recruitment, it was also able to deploy such regiments in 'foreign' theatres. Their loyalties were carefully redirected from that of their local societies to the imperial monarchy and the Roman Empire. A ceremonial calendar, found in the garrison-city of Dura Europus on the Tigris, belonging to a regiment of the previously mentioned Palmyrene auxiliaries, shows the religious life of the soldiers to be centred on the cult of the emperors and Roman public holidays (Fink, Hoey, and Snyder 1940: 40–9; Haynes 1999).

The development of cross-cultural identities and institutions gave the army, and more broadly speaking Roman power, a distinct advantage in the face of local resistance. It was able to outflank such opponents by bringing resources to bear on the conflict drawn from outside the immediate geographical locale (cf. Gellner 1983: ch. 2). At the same time, this meant that the imperial government did not necessarily have to penetrate individual communities very deeply (Garnsey and Saller 1987). It had no need to command the undivided loyalty of all the members of each community. Even with an army 300,000–400,000 strong, only a small fraction of the population had to serve in the military. But that was still sufficient to outnumber, by a wide margin, the strength of any potential local rebellion. The Roman army served to consolidate and guarantee imperial supremacy.

Imperial power was hegemonic power. It was maintained across the Mediterranean world for centuries by a web of universal institutions which significantly reshaped the parameters of life. The Roman army was only the most important of these (Le Bohec 1994). A network of highways which spanned the length and breadth of the provinces was gradually constructed to facilitate the movement of the legions (Chevalier 1976). Even more important was tax. 'For', as Tacitus reminds us, 'among the peoples no peace without arms, no arms without pay and no pay without taxes' (*Hist.* 4.74). Imperial tribute was imposed on the vast majority of subject communities. That was a momentous cultural change. For many peasants, particularly in the western parts of the empire, this would have been the first time they had to pay a land tax to a centralized state authority. The payment of a tribute was the one aspect of imperial rule which touched the daily lives of most people. Taxation represented the quintessence of imperial subjection, as is clear from the famous remark ascribed to Jesus when questioned on the legitimacy of Roman taxes: 'Render unto Caesar the things that are Caesar's' (Matt. 22: 21). Should anyone doubt the wisdom in this, he only needed to take a look at the coins, Jesus reminded his audience with impeccable logic. Most coins would have been impressed with the imperial portrait on the obverse. The Romans did not initially impose a single unified currency on all subjected territories. Nevertheless, across vast stretches of land the Roman silver denarius was introduced as the main coin. But in eastern parts of the empire several long-established coinages had existed prior to the conquest. The Roman government was satisfied to maintain these for a long time, since they served well its need to receive taxes and provide payment to soldiers. But as symbols of power the imagery had to change; the portrait of the reigning emperor came to be stamped on the coins (Howgego 1995: chs. 3–4; Burnett, Amandry, and Ripollés 1992: 38–40).

For the majority of subjects, in other words, Roman power was present as infrastructure. Imperial panegyrists, as has recently been observed, liked to measure Roman power against a set of cosmological constants such as eternity or the world (Woolf 2001). 'Empire without end I have given', are the famous words which Virgil put in the mouth of Jove to announce the chosen and privileged position of Rome in the order of things (*Aeneid* 1.279). Indeed, the imperial government asserted for itself a position as a force or principle of cosmic organization (cf. Statius, *Silvae* 4.1). Across the empire, the imperial reigns served as the basis for calendrical reckoning: 'the 16th year of our Lord Trajanus Caesar' (*P.Lond.* 1177). The emperor was not only the measure of time, he was also a sacred person. As such, he and his predecessors were worshipped in cults which were gradually established, with a few exceptions, throughout the provinces of the realm during the first century CE (Beard, North, and Price 1998: 348–63). Numerous statues of the emperors were put up in just about every city and town. They came to be regarded as places of sanctuary (e.g. Pliny, *Ep.* 10.74). For what it was worth, they served to make the distant emperor manifest and symbolized his claim to be the fountain of justice and guardian of the established order of life, in short of civilization, the *oikoumenē*, as the Greeks called it (e.g. Pliny, *Ep.* 10.52; Seneca, *Clem.*; Dio Chrysostomus, *Or.* 1; Aristeides, *Or.* 26)

Thinkers such as Foucault (1970, 1979) and Said (1978, 1993) have taught us to appreciate the force of these phenomena as constitutive of culture and society rather than symbolic paraphernalia. In this perspective, empire is not primarily an arrangement of military domination but rather a hegemonic system of knowledge, ideology, and culture reordering the world of the subjects. It is easy to see how the Roman Empire can be fitted into such a framework. With the passing of time, the imposition of a tribute eventually led to the taking of censuses wherein persons were registered and properties measured and recorded (Hopkins 1991; Nicolet 1991; Duncan-Jones 1994: ch. 4). The census in the province of Egypt followed a fourteen-year cycle. Whether in fact the government always managed to go through with a full reassessment is a different matter. Most provinces would, at any rate, have experienced the census at different frequencies and some lands never fell under the surveyors' purview. Nevertheless, even if registration was less than total, the census still allowed the Roman government a greater degree of control of its territory; it was far from a negligible instrument of state power and continued to provoke resistance down the ages (Eusebius, *EH* 10.8.12; Lactantius, *Mort. Pers.* 23; cf. Wickham 2005, ch. 3, esp. pp. 87–93).

The activities of the surveyors also produced a body of expert literature which has been passed on to us in a collection of small manuals on the principles and practical methods of how to measure and classify territory (Campbell 2000). By far the most important and famous body of specialist literature to have come down to us from the Roman Empire, however, is Roman law (Frier 1985; Crook 1995; Johnston 1999). The so-called 'classical' portion of it, surviving as a compilation of excerpts in the *Digest of Justinian*, developed as commentaries on specific points of law and discussion of cases. It was a powerful tool with the potential to reorder social relations. During the early decades of the second century CE, in the newly founded province of Arabia, we already find the widow Babatha attempting, by the use of the instruments provided by Roman law, to recover control of her son's fortune from his male legal guardians (*P. Yadin* 13–15; Cotton 1993: 102–7). In the North African provinces, introduction of the Roman law of property tilted the balance against the peasantry in favour of the landowning elite (Fentress 2006). A similar result is likely to have been the outcome of the grant of a civic constitution, based on Roman-law models, to the small Spanish community of Irni during the reign of Vespasian. Henceforth, the political leaders of the town were awarded the privileged status of Roman citizenship (*Lex Irnitana* chs. 21–3, in Gonzalez 1986). But one should beware of exaggerating the impact of Roman-law rules. The exegetical literature of the jurists was large and unwieldy. Attempts at codification did not occur until very late in antiquity. Nor was there a standard publication where new regulations and rulings were collected and presented. What people took to be Roman law must have varied considerably depending on the legal writings and precedents available in their respective areas. This was particularly so since many customs and pre-conquest laws continued to operate after the imposition of Roman hegemony and were allowed to coexist with the imperial law (e.g. Sherwin-White 1973).

There were very clear limits to how closely the Roman imperial state could aspire to monitor and reorganize the structure of knowledge and culture among its subject populations. In their work, Foucault and Said were particularly interested in the whole gamut of institutions developing with the rise of the modern state: formalized bureaucracy, scientific disciplines, statistical reasoning, nationalism, and, in the case of colonial empires, institutionalized racism. But Roman government did not generate these forms of knowledge and institutions. The imperial state had only a very rudimentary bureaucracy, and certainly not one capable of refashioning society on the basis of statistical information (Garnsey and Saller 1987: chs. 1–2; pace Nicolet 1991). Registration was primarily a question of accountancy and control (Finley 1985; Woolf 2000). Nor had Roman government officials received a formal training guaranteed by a concluding examination; they did not constitute a professional corps of administrators. The imperial government also did not develop a similar set of formalized scientific disciplines such as anthropology and the orientalist philologies to systematically collect information about 'the other', that is, the indigenous populations of imperial colonies. Roman imperial culture and discourse was organized on entirely different principles. It was centred on the court of the monarch, aristocratic and cosmopolitan, where the modern state was bourgeois and bureaucratic, nationalist and racist.

People flocked from near and far to the imperial court. Lacking the bureaucratic apparatus of the modern state, the emperor attempted to govern his empire by making his subjects come to him (Millar 1977). Lavish public displays and extravagant expenditure in the capital Rome, the biggest city by far in the Mediterranean, advertised to people of influence, ambition, and talent the potential attractions of serving the Roman ruler of the world. The splendid life around the imperial palace comprised a great variety of personalities: traditional Roman senators, Greek philosophers, and eastern potentates, all of these and many more could be found rubbing shoulders and vying for influence at the emperor's court. Titus, the son of the senator Vespasian—the later emperor—was brought up in the palace with Britannicus, the ill-fated heir of the emperor Claudius (Suet. *Titus* 2). Members of allied royal families idled away time amidst the luxurious pleasures of the palace while awaiting or hoping to be awarded a vacant throne in one of Rome's client-kingdoms (Augustus, *Res Gestae* 32; Philo, *Leg. Gai.* 179; Suetonius, *Tib.* 37, *Cal.* 22).

Competition among these various groups for the emperor's favour bred tension and rivalry. When Titus ascended the imperial throne after his father Vespasian, he had to sever his ties with his oriental mistress, the Hellenic queen Berenice, and send her away from Rome so as to appease the sentiments of a Roman senatorial aristocracy that was jealously guarding its privileges (Suet. *Titus* 7). Granted such concessions, the Roman emperor could not allow himself to be monopolized by any one ethnic aristocratic group. In that respect, he resembled and consciously emulated Alexander the Great who had had to transcend his role as Macedonian king to become a universal monarch—the ruler of all his far-flung dominions.

The dilemmas of that transition may be illustrated from the Greek geographer Strabo's discussion of Alexander's choice of advisers:

> after withholding praise from . . . those who advised Alexander to treat the Greeks as friends but the Barbarians as enemies, Eratosthenes goes on to say that it would be better to make such divisions according to good qualities and bad qualities; for not only are many of the Greeks bad, but many of the Barbarians refined . . . And this, he says, is the reason why

Alexander, disregarding his advisers, welcomed as many as he could of men of fair repute and did them favours. As if those [Strabo then continues, in an aside against his rival Eratosthenes] who have made such a division [in Greeks and Barbarians], placing some people in the category of censure, others in that of praise, did so for any other reason than that in some people there prevail the law-abiding and the political instinct, and the qualities associated with education and powers of speech, whereas in others the opposite prevail!

So that, Strabo goes on to assert, when Alexander did not accept a division of the world into Hellenes and Barbarians, but promoted men of honour from everywhere, he was, in fact, doing 'what was consistent with, not contrary to, their advice; for he had regard to the real intent of those who gave counsel' (1.4.9, tr. H. L. Jones). This attempt at reconciling what may appear to be opposite views is not a simple case of inconsistency, as Isaac has recently claimed (Isaac 2004: 300). The basic problem is that the ruler needed both to preserve support in his original peer-group and to attract new constituencies. The solution lay not in making all cultures equal but in widening the appeal of the conquering culture by defining it more in terms of the achievement of excellence than of birth. Given enough time, such a move could be welcomed by elites all over the empire, by conqueror and conquered alike. A culture stressing excellence, or *virtus* and *aretē* as it was called in Latin and Greek, over mere birth enabled aristocratic groups to distance themselves from the *hoi polloi* by emulating the exacting standards set by the imperial court in cultural achievement. The result was a cosmopolitan, urban aristocratic civilization unifying Mediterranean elites in a moral economy of 'honour' where aristocrats strove and competed for distinction (Lendon 1997; cf. Veyne 1991).

The Roman Ecumene

That process was already well under way in the eastern Mediterranean before the Roman conquest. When Alexander blazed his victorious trail through the region, he left Greek-oriented elites in control almost everywhere and spawned the creation of a number of Hellenistic monarchies. From their courts Hellenic culture was projected and further refined. Alexandria, capital of the Ptolemies, with its Museion and famed library, set the pace. Stoic philosophers developed and theorized the ideal of cosmopolitanism (Walbank 1981; Whitmarsh 2004). When the Romans arrived in the area they tried to appropriate this culture for themselves—much of the time quite literally, in the form of spoliation of artworks, not to mention enslavement of skilled artists and grammarians. 'Captive Greece took her rustic conqueror captive', is the famous tag under which the poet Horace, tongue in cheek, summarized the process whereby Rome adopted Hellenic culture (*Ep.* 2.1.156). Tongue in cheek, because unlike many other conquerors, such as the

Mongols in China, faced with a more elaborate high culture, the Roman victors had no intention of allowing themselves to be culturally colonized. They took up the challenge and entered the game of competitive emulation with the Greeks.

The complexities of that process can be glanced from one of the great texts of Roman culture, the *Aeneid*. Composed by Virgil during the first decade of the Augustan monarchy, it offered a cosmological interpretation of the imperial, monarchical order. To that end, the origins of Roman history were inscribed into the Homeric cycle of poems cherished by the Greeks as foundational myths. The hero is Aeneas, the Trojan prince. We follow him out of the burning ruins of Troy, as he embarks on a long journey to found a new home for himself. Like Odysseus, he wanders for many years, until he finally settles on the shores of Latium in Italy where he is destined to pave the way for the coming of Rome. But before that can happen he has to reverse the defeat of the Trojan War. In the second part of the *Aeneid* the poem enters its Illiadic phase. Native opposition to the arrival of the Trojans is defeated on the battlefield and Aeneas wins for himself a place within the royal line of Alba Longa from which Romulus and Remus, the founders of Rome, were thought to have descended. So far the poem could be read as just another offshoot on the complex tree of Homeric tales. But there is a significant difference: the poem was written in Latin. In this way, Virgil did not only leave literary critics of later ages to ponder the futile question whether he or Homer was indeed the greatest, he also made a crucial contribution to the creation of an independent canon of Latin works to rival that of the Greeks.

In the encounter with Hellenistic culture, the Romans were not satisfied merely with taking over what was already there. They energetically set about inventing a rival tradition to match that of the eastern Mediterranean elites. This already started during the Republican period, where key figures included Cato the Censor, the playwrights Plautus and Terence, and, not least, Cicero (Gruen 1993; Habinek 1998). The patronage of the emperor and leading nobles consolidated and intensified these efforts. The immortal fame of Maecenas, Virgil, Horace, Propertius, Ovid, and Livy is a mark of the unprecedented success achieved by the Augustan court in the field of literature. But the emperors did not restrict themselves to one sphere only. In addition to the various branches of literature and—let us not forget—military prowess, the court, followed by aristocracies all over the Roman Empire, strove for distinction within a whole range of fields: monumental building, public ritual and largesse, and lavish private consumption which took the arts of living, dining, and loving to new levels of refinement. From Rome a cultural revolution spread outwards like rings in water (Zanker 1988; Wallace-Hadrill 1994, 2008; Toner 1995; Woolf 1996; Habinek and Schiesaro 1997; Veyne 1988). During the first two centuries of our era a spate of city-foundations and urban embellishment projects changed the landscape of the Roman Empire. In the western provinces this happened under the auspices of Latin culture, whereas in the East the culture of empire remained Hellenic. But many developments were nevertheless shared (Millar 1993; Woolf 1997 and 1998). Aqueducts and public baths became common features of urban life. Horse chariot-racing, gladiatorial contests, and staged hunts rose as favoured forms of urban entertainment where the power of imperial culture over the forces of disorder and nature were triumphantly celebrated (Hopkins 1983: ch. 1; Futrell 1997; Beacham 1999).

Within this broad cosmopolitan civilization or ecumene, to use a Greek term, literature served a key role as a vehicle for the formation of collective identities and the development of a shared discourse among the elites of the empire (Schmitz 1997). Recently an attempt has been made to explain this process in terms of the German philosopher Jürgen Habermas's theories of communication; the rise of a shared discourse generated a dialogue that enabled the emperors to maintain provincial loyalties for centuries (Ando 2000). Habermas (1992) first presented his ideas to explain the emergence and functioning of a public sphere in European states during the Enlightenment. Cafés, learned societies, and newspapers and magazines generated a public debate centred on the continuous improvement of society. The public sphere became the place where society questioned traditional institutions and debated their improvement. Such reflexivity, as Giddens has termed it (1990: 1–54, 100–11), was in many respects the very opposite of the cosmopolitan discourse developing in the Roman Empire. The latter was staunchly traditionalist. Where the Enlightenment philosophers had tried to collect all available knowledge in the famous *Encyclopédie* to destabilize traditions and urge improvement, learned men in the empire treasured encyclopedic knowledge to fortify the established order of things.

An instructive example of this is the attempt to reinvent the Greek cultural tradition known as the Second Sophistic (Swain 1996; Whitmarsh 2001; Alcock 2001). By the turn of the first century CE a number of cultural currents had gathered strength around a cult of a sacred or classical canon of texts. The worship of Homer as the fountain of Hellenic culture and wisdom was taken to new heights; and a select group of authors were promoted as models of Hellenicity, writing as they had done mainly in the Attic dialect of the fifth and fourth centuries BCE when Greece had not yet been subject to foreign dominion. For a man really to count as cultured and a true Hellene he had to spend a long and arduous time purifying his language in order to shape his speech on these revered, centuries-old models. This was a programme of education, *paideia*, which prized the compilation of encyclopedic knowledge of arcane historical detail and obscure matters of vocabulary. To literary critics brought up on an aesthetic of Romantic originality this cultural movement has seemed bookish and barren. But what it lacked in originality it made up for in playful intertextuality, sophisticated allusion, and polished virtuoso performance. This was an art intended for connoisseurs, only appreciated by the best; and the best were the people with leisure and money enough to follow through with the exacting standards of education set by this movement, no matter where they had been born (cf. Lucian, *The Scythian*). As a group only the landed aristocracy had the resources to aspire to the ideals of the Second Sophistic.

One might be forgiven for seeing the cultivation of a Greek identity, predicated on an idealized pre-Roman past, as a sign of resistance to the order of empire. But nothing could be further from the facts. The cultivation of a strong classical Greek identity served to assert a position of privilege and prominence for the eastern aristocratic elites within the empire (cf. Rogers 1991). In one of the more remarkable products of this artistic movement, Philostratus sets out the life of Apollonius of Tyana. A Greek sage who was believed to have lived under Nero and the Flavian dynasty, Apollonius is portrayed as the embodiment of Hellenic *paideia*. This enables him to travel, in cosmopolitan fashion, wherever he wishes around the empire, and the Roman authorities seek his advice on urgent matters of government. Thus he is presented as having assisted in the events which led to the overthrow of Nero. Though normally seen as a Philhellenic emperor, Nero's passion for Greek art and education was of the wrong kind. Touring old Greece to claim victory in many of the competitions of the sacred festivals, such as the Olympic Games, and even meddling with the calendar to fit them into the imperial itinerary, was not the business of a good ruler. He should not have interfered with the ways of the Greeks, but rather respected their traditions, kept out of the contests lest he steal their thunder, and presided over the preservation of the reigning order (Philostratus, *Apollonius* 5.7–10 and 27–41). The role of a good Roman emperor was to lend recognition and give ear to the concerns of *hoi aristoi*, the best men of the realm.

The emperors responded by patronizing the Greek revival. Under Hadrian a Panhellenic league was founded, centred on Athens, which at the same time received a number of imposing monumental buildings that are still among the most prominent ruins in the city today (Spawforth and Walker 1985; Oliver 1970). By participating in the imperial ecumene, elites staked out a claim to privilege and position within the Roman order. This is well illustrated by the works of Lucian. Though a native of Syria, his mastery of Hellenic *paideia* gave him a basis for asserting membership among the privileged classes of the realm (*Double Indictment*). Likewise, the works of the Jewish aristocrats Philo of Alexandria and Josephus were written to demonstrate that Jewish ways could exist within a framework of Hellenic culture and Roman political loyalty. The Jewish leaders, therefore, deserved the respect and trust of their Roman masters (Philo, *Leg.* 156–7; 276–329; Josephus, *Jewish War* 1.1–16; 4.314–25; *Ant.* 1.1–17).

High literary culture, however, served as a powerful vehicle of cultural integration precisely because it functioned efficiently to demarcate the boundaries of elite society and exclude others from access to privilege. On several occasions rivalry erupted into open violence between Hellenized Jewish and pagan Hellenic elites in the cities of the eastern Mediterranean (e.g. Philo, *In Flaccum*; Kasher 1985). The theme of exclusivity runs prominently through both Greek and Latin literature and philosophy, which abound in expressions of contempt for the mass of people, the uneducated, idiot(e)s (Lucian, *The Lie* 1.3; Seneca, *Ep.* 7; 19; 88; Horace *Serm.* 1.4; 1.10.72–91). Urban imperial society was not for the common folk, the great majority of the population. At the end of antiquity we find Augustine noting how some peasant communities were not even conversant in Latin and that he needed to find priests to send to such places who knew how to speak Punic (*Ep.* 209.3; MacMullen 1966). Greek and Latin high culture, in other words, was in a hegemonic position, but it did not enjoy a cultural monopoly and did not even aspire to one. Other forms of knowledge and identity coexisted with it, even among urban-dwellers. Lucian was at his satirical best when he castigated magicians, astrologers, and prophets who appealed to more popular and less exacting notions of (religious) truth (*Death of Peregrinus*, *Alexander the False Prophet*). Few knowledge systems, however, were initially able to rival the geographical reach and splendid appeal of imperial, courtly culture. But the creation of an ecumene gradually changed that. In the interstices of elite society the need to acquire at least a modicum of literacy to deal successfully with the imperial masters eventually ushered in the development of rival, less exacting systems of belief and literature (Hopkins 1991). 'Among us therefore these things are heard and learned from those who do not even know the forms of the letters, who are uneducated and barbarous in speech', Justin Martyr defiantly proclaimed of *logos*, of divine truth (*Apol.* 1.60.10). Christianity, with which we started and to which we have now returned, was to become the most successful of these alternatives. This happened when the Roman emperor Constantine became convinced of its divine truths and adopted the church as an instrument of the state. Put to right use, Christian scripture could draw the Roman ecumene together in an 'imagined' universal, catholic, community of believers.

References

J. N. Adams, *Bilingualism and the Latin Language*, Cambridge, 2003.

Susan E. Alcock, 'The Reconfiguration of Memory in the Eastern Roman Empire', in Susan E. Alcock *et al.* (eds.), *Empires: Perspectives from Archaeology and History*, Cambridge, 2001: 323–50.

Benedict Anderson, *Imagined Communities*, rev. edn., London and New York 1991.

Clifford Ando, *Imperial Ideology and Provincial Loyalty in the Roman Empire*, Berkeley and Los Angeles, 2000.

Roger S. Bagnall and Dominic Rathbone (eds.), *Egypt From Alexander to the Copts: An Archaeological and Historical Guide*, London, 2004.

Richard C. Beacham, *Spectacle Entertainments of Imperial Rome*, New Haven, 1999.

Mary Beard and John Henderson, *Classical Art From Greece to Rome*, Oxford, 2001.

—— John North, and Simon Price, *Religions of Rome*, 2 vols., Cambridge, 1998.

Andrew Burnett, Michael Amandry, and Pere Pau Ripollés, *Roman Provincial Coinage*, vol. 1, London, 1992.

Brian Campbell, *Writings of the Roman Land Surveyors: Introduction, Text, Translation and Commentary*, London, 2000.

Raymond Chevalier, *Roman Roads*, London, 1976.
Hannah Cotton, 'Roman and Local Law in the Province of Arabia', *JRS* 83 (1993), 94–107.
John Crook, *Legal Advocacy in the Roman World*, London, 1995.
Richard Duncan-Jones, *Money and Government in the Roman Empire*, Cambridge, 1994.
Elizabeth Fentress, 'Romanizing the Berbers', *Past and Present*, 190 (2006), 3–33.
R. O. Fink, A. S. Hoey, and W. F. Snyder, 'Feriale Duranum', *Yale Classical Studies*, 5 (1940), 1–222.
M. I. Finley, *Ancient History: Evidence and Models*, London, 1985.
Bruce W. Frier, *The Rise of the Roman Jurists: Studies in Cicero's* Pro Caecina, Princeton, 1985.
Michel Foucault, *The Order of Things: An Archaeology of Human Sciences*, London, 1970.
—— *Discipline and Punish: The Birth of the Prison*, tr. A. Sheridan, Harmondsworth, 1979.
Alison Futrell, *Blood in the Arena: The Spectacle of Roman Power*, Austin, Tex., 1997.
Peter Garnsey and Richard Saller, *The Roman Empire: Economy, Society, Culture*, London, 1987.
Clifford Geertz, *Local Knowledge*[3], New York, 2000.
Ernest Gellner, *Nations and Nationalism*, Oxford, 1983.
Anthony Giddens, *The Consequences of Modernity*, Stanford, 1990.
Julián González, 'The Lex Irnitana: A New Copy of the Flavian Municipal Law', *JRS* 76 (1986), 147–243.
Erich S. Gruen, *Culture and National Identity in Republican Rome*, London, 1993.
Jürgen Habermas, *The Structural Transformation of the Public Sphere: An Inquiry into a Category of Bourgeois Society*, tr. Th. Burger with assistance of F. Lawrence, Cambridge, 1992.
Thomas N. Habinek, *The Politics of Latin Literature*, Princeton, 1998.
—— and Alessandro Schiesaro (eds.), *The Roman Cultural Revolution*, Cambridge, 1997.
Ian Haynes, 'Military Service and Cultural Identity in the *auxilia*', in A. Goldsworthy and Ian Haynes (eds.), *The Roman Army as a Community*, JRA Suppl. 34 (1999), 165–74.
Richard Hingley, *Globalizing Roman Culture: Unity, Diversity and Empire*, Abingdon, 2005.
Keith Hopkins, *Death and Renewal: Sociological Studies in Roman History*, Cambridge, 1983.
—— 'Conquest by Book', in Mary Beard *et al.* (eds.), *Literacy in the Roman World, JRA* Suppl. 3, Ann Arbor, Mich. 1991: 133–58.
Christopher Howgego, *Ancient History from Coins*, London, 1995.
Benjamin Isaac, *The Invention of Racism in Classical Antiquity*, Princeton, 2004.
David Johnston, *Roman Law in Context*, Cambridge, 1999.
A. Kasher, *The Jews in Hellenistic and Roman Egypt: The Struggle for Equal Rights*, Tübingen, 1985.
Yann Le Bohec, *The Imperial Roman Army*, tr. R. Bate, London, 1994.
John Lendon, *Empire of Honour*, Oxford, 1997.
Ramsay MacMullen, 'Provincial Languages in the Roman Empire', *Journal of American Philology*, 87/1 (1966), 1–17.
William H. McNeill, *Polyethnicity and National Unity in World History*, Toronto, 1986.
Fergus Millar, *The Emperor in the Roman World*, London, 1977.
—— *The Roman Near East, 31 BC–AD 337*, Cambridge, Mass., 1993.
Herbert Musurillo, *The Acts of the Christian Martyrs*, Oxford, 1972.

C. Nicolet, *Geography, Space and Politics in the Early Roman Empire*, Ann Arbor, Mich., 1991.

J. H. Oliver, *Marcus Aurelius: Aspects of Civic and Cultural Policy in the East*, Hesperia Suppl. 13, Princeton, 1970.

Nigel Pollard, *Soldiers, Cities and Civilians in Roman Syria*, Ann Arbor, Mich., 2000.

G. M. Rogers, *The Sacred Identity of Ephesos: Foundation Myths of a Roman City*, London, 1991.

Nico Roymans, *Ethnic Identity and Imperial Power: The Batavians in the Early Roman Empire*, Amsterdam, 2004.

Kim Ryholdt, 'On the Contents and Nature of the Tebtunis Temple Library: A Status Report', in Sandra Lippert and Maren Schentuleit (eds.), *Tebtynis und Soknopaiou Nesos. Leben im römerzeitlichen Fajum*, Wiesbaden, 2005: 141–70.

Edward W. Said, *Orientalism*, London and New York, 1978.

—— *Culture and Imperialism*, London, 1993.

Thomas Schmitz, *Bildung und Macht. Zur sozialen und politischen Funktion der zweiten Sophistik in der griechischen Welt der Kaiserzeit*, Munich, 1997.

Rolf Schneider, *Bunte Barbaren*, Munich, 1986.

A. N. Sherwin-White, 'The Tabula of Banasa and the Constitutio Antoniniana', *JRS* 63 (1973), 86–98.

A. J. Spawforth and S. Walker, 'The World of the Panhellenion: I. Athens and Eleusis', *JRS* 75 (1985), 78–104.

Simon Swain, *Hellenism and Empire: Language, Classicism, and Power in the Greek World, AD 50–250*, Oxford, 1996.

J. P. Toner, *Leisure and Ancient Rome*, Cambridge, 1995.

Paul Veyne, *Roman Erotic Elegy*, Chicago, 1988.

—— *Bread and Circuses*, Harmondsworth, 1991.

F. W. Walbank, *The Hellenistic World*, London, 1981.

Andrew Wallace-Hadrill, *Houses and Society in Pompeii and Herculaneum*, Princeton, 1994.

—— '*Mutatio morum:* The Idea of a Cultural Revolution', in Habinek and Schiesaro 1997: 3–22.

—— *Rome's Cultural Revolution*, Cambridge, 2008.

T. Whitmarsh, *Greek Literature and the Roman Empire*, Oxford, 2001.

—— *Ancient Greek Literature*, Cambridge, 2004.

C. Whittaker, *The Frontiers of the Roman Empire: A Social and Economic Study*, Baltimore and London, 1994.

Chris Wickham, *Framing the Early Middle Ages*, Oxford, 2005.

Greg Woolf, 'Monumental Writing', *JRS* 86 (1996), 22–39.

—— 'Becoming Roman, Staying Greek', *Proceedings of the Cambridge Philological Society*, 40 (1997), 116–43.

—— *Becoming Roman*, Cambridge, 1998.

—— 'Literacy', ch. 30 in A. Bowman, P. Garnsey, and D. Rathbone (eds.), *The Cambridge Ancient History*, 2nd edn., vol. 11: *The High Empire, AD 70–192*, Cambridge, 2000: 875–97.

—— 'Inventing Empire in Ancient Rome', in Susan E. Alcock *et al.* (eds.), *Empires: Perspectives from Archaeology and History*, Cambridge, 2001: 311–22.

Paul Zanker, *The Power of Images in the Age of Augustus*, tr. A. Shapiro, Ann Arbor, Mich., 1988.

CHAPTER 43

AFTER ANTIQUITY

CLIFFORD ANDO

The analysis and periodization of the events and changes that take us from the Roman Empire at its height to whatever came after it have long occupied a distinguished place in European historiography (Burke 1976; Herzog 1993). The fascination of the topic has traditionally lain in the supposed magnitude of Rome's fall on the one hand, and in the specific shape given to European life by the successor states that ultimately replaced it on the other (Demandt 1984; Pocock 2003, 2005). The topic attracted no little prestige, too, from its inherent complexity, for the collapse of the Roman state, however understood, issued in multiple polities, of greater and lesser stability, as well as multiple vernaculars in law and language.

The participants in this historiographic tradition are diverse, but three themes characterize much of its life. First, it was a European tradition, produced first in Latin and later in Romance and Germanic languages, and preoccupied with explaining a European past and present. The historical self-awareness of the post-Roman West thus exercised a decisive influence in defining its scope and ambition. So it was, for reasons largely of politics but also of language, that what might and perhaps should have been a historical field embracing all lands once Roman came instead to marginalize Byzantium and exclude Islam, for the former was conceived as a rival, and the latter an enemy, by the Christian successor states to Rome of the medieval West. Second, in the analysis of cause, much attention was focused on barbarism and religion, to use Gibbon's phrase (1994: 3. 1068), and in both cases there was a sharp divide in assessment: the rise of Christianity was described as having either subverted or preserved the best of classical culture, while the barbarians as a group were convicted of destroying the empire, even as distinct barbarian tribes were adopted as forebears by emergent European states desirous of ethnic and linguistic individuation. Third, however positively the emergence of Europe was esteemed, the fall of Rome and the changes consequent to it were construed as a decline, a falling-off from classical ideals in reason, classical aesthetics in literary and decorative arts, and classical standards of prosperity in urban and economic life.

This field has been enormously vibrant in the last half-century, particularly so over the last generation. It has witnessed significant developments from within, as new modes of analysis, exercised upon newly gathered and collated data, have buttressed or called into question earlier truths or, indeed, offered altogether new conclusions. It has also faced challenges from without, from voices self-consciously positioned either ideologically or disciplinarily outside the grand narrative of Decline and Fall and the institutional pulpits whence it has been pronounced.

It is my aim in this chapter to survey some of these developments and to draw out (and occasionally to critique) their theoretical postulates and intellectual affiliations. The survey is not comprehensive (a much fuller biography, in support of a quite different analysis, may be found in Ando 2007). What I hope to provide is not so much a guide to the field, but to how the field came to be, and where it might go from here.

Literatures of Decline and Fall

Perhaps the easiest way to clarify the nature of the problem before us is to ask, 'When did classical antiquity end?' Was it an event, like the sack of Rome in 410, or the battle of Tours, on 10 October 732, in which the Frankish leader Charles defeated 'Abdul Rahman Al Ghafiqi, the Ummayad governor of Spain, and decisively halted the progress of Islamic arms into western Europe, or perhaps the crowning of Charlemagne as Imperator Augustus on Christmas day, 800, when the mantle of Rome was reclaimed from the eastern Roman Empire for the West? Or was it a process not articulable by *l'histoire événementielle*, but rather one to be captured by a more qualitative assessment? When, for example, did the world cease to be ancient, or classical, or Roman? When did the polities and cultures of the Mediterranean cease to be influenced by Rome, or to identify themselves, and be recognized by others, as Roman? When did a Roman past become discontinuous with one or more European or Islamic presents?

Problems of Method

To these questions historians have offered many answers; to those, classicists have made a number of distinctive contributions. The continuities and ruptures in politics and culture of the early Middle Ages look rather different, after all, if one looks forward rather than back, so to speak. To come to grips with the methodological challenges presented by analysis of this kind, which is to say, analysis in support of periodization, some reflection on the politics and practice of scholarship is in order, in at least three respects.

First, to the question what changed, when, in the classical world such that it was no longer classical, it does little good to respond that the fourth-century empire was demonstrably different from that of the second. (It likewise strikes me as unhelpful, not to say naive, to suggest that late antiquity is more 'solid', the 'classical period' more 'surreal' or 'weightless', on the grounds that the former is more recent, the latter more distant, and that 'we' must pass through the later period to come to 'our own world', as though one ever got *back* to the classical period without the mediation of later antiquity: Bowersock, Brown, and Grabar 1999: p. x.) For 'demonstrably' and 'different' are both terms of art: 'demonstrably' being one among many common adverbs that express a qualitative judgement on matters that can often be framed in quantitative terms—how different? different enough to matter?—while difference, to be meaningful, must be assessed along some axes and not others. The axes that one brackets may be elsewhere analysed, or simply set aside through *ceteris paribus* assumptions, but it is by reference to them that difference, which historians call change, becomes intelligible. Wholesale difference, genuine rupture, is so unlikely that it would constitute an *explanandum* in its own right.

Second, what we choose as an end depends on—or, if chosen first, itself might determine—what we choose as a beginning. Put another way, the story we tell about the end of antiquity must have a beginning, too, and what we select for those termini—both what they are, and what sort of things they are—will in turn shape the literary form by which that story is unfolded. This is particularly a problem for classicists, but not only for them. For ancient historians and classicists alike view the Mediterranean world as a political and cultural unity, and so have tended to see the transition to the post-classical world as a process, a gradual falling-away, however esteemed and of whatever complexity. The questions that history once begged, but which often now are asked, are what was classical about the classical world. What populations within that world participated in the cultural forms we deem classical? What of the economic system that sustained it, or the urban infrastructure in which it was practised?

Within Classical Studies the attempt to identify the end of antiquity has thus led recursively to an interrogation of the discipline's own unarticulated assumptions about its canon, taste, and judgement. The historical exclusion of Christianity from Classical Studies, along with the Semitic tongues of the ancient Mediterranean, are but two examples of patterns in disciplinarity and historiographic practice that have been well and clearly revealed by contemporary attempts to verify their status as symptoms of decline and phenomena of a post-classical world. For the rise of Christianity, like that of Islam, and the corresponding rise to prominence, in very different ways and to very different effects, of Hebrew and Arabic (to say nothing of

Syriac and Coptic), turn out, upon closer inspection, to have distinctly ancient roots. That they were living languages but largely oral and documentary in usage in the classical period, and became literary only in later antiquity, can scarcely justify their neglect by scholars of Roman Studies (Millar 1968, 1987).

The traditional sundering of the history of Africa and the Near East from that of Europe in the aftermath of the Islamic conquests likewise rests upon interrelated prejudices of long standing. One is an ideological practice, which ultimately found disciplinary expression in the modern academy, that drew a sharp distinction between Islam on the one hand and Judaism and Christianity on the other. Up to a point, this accorded with contemporaneous trends in Islamic intellectual life, which in matters of ethical and religious deportment dissociated itself from its late ancient, Greco-Roman-Arabic context, even as it absorbed and appropriated conventions and generic forms from all those cultures (Sizgorich 2004, 2009). That said, it is important to recall that Islam also houses important strands of historical self-awareness that recognize its contingent roots in late antique Arabia and celebrate its roots in Jewish and Christian antiquity, and that these originate in the words of the Prophet himself.

The other prejudice urging the sundering of African, Near Eastern, and ultimately Anatolian history from that of Europe is the kindred effort, originating in fifth-century Greece and clearly visible already in Herodotus and the Hippocratic treatise *Airs, Waters, Places*, to essentialize, analyse, and racialize distinctions between Greece and Europe on the one hand, and 'Asia' on the other (Harrison 2002). This, combined with the haunting legacy of Rome's contingent unification of the Mediterranean, enabled a historical failure, across many literatures of early modern and modern Europe, to acknowledge the deep currents that united the Fertile Crescent and Iranian plateau with the eastern coast of the Mediterranean—a unification realized at the political level by the Achaemenid, Ummayad, and Ottoman empires, and long the ambition of the Parthians and Sassanians (Fowden 1993; Millar 1998).

In both cases—that of the development of the Semitic languages into languages of literature and governance on the one hand, and on the other of the extension of Islamic control over formerly Roman lands on the other—what has enabled their adoption as markers of the end of antiquity are systematic exclusions at the heart of Classics or, to put it another way, the errant belief on the part of classicists that their story is the whole story of the Mediterranean, and that history comes to an end, as it were, when that belief is no longer sustainable.

The Place of Religion

Attempts to indict Christianity as causal in the decline of the empire have foundered on a different theoretical level. Christianity had spread to most major parts of the Roman world already under the Julio-Claudians. For their part, ancient

Christians regarded the appearance of Christ late in the reign of Augustus as an act of Providence: the unification of the world under the empire was thereby interpreted as preparing the world for his arrival. In seeking to offer an alternate narrative, opponents of Christianity in the modern world, whether early modern sceptics or Romantic devotees of Hellenism, as well as historians of 'Oriental' religions, nevertheless all succumbed to the Providentialist view that Christianity, for good or ill, marked a turning-point in history. For what they posited instead were histories in which Christianity did transform the empire, but did so by conquering a culture already corrupt, or replacing religions already bankrupt, or through its cynical adoption by a governing class who recognized its tendency to social and political conservatism.

On any of these views, Christianity's presence in history well prior to any standard index of Decline posed a challenge, which was met on both sides by historiographic sleights-of-hand. These worked to sideline Christianity and its adherents as in one way or another not part of classical antiquity; it was regarded rather as an exogenous force that came to act upon the empire but was not of it. This was achieved by postulating Christianity as in some essential respect non-Roman, or by describing its adherents as insufficiently populous or influential until some moment when their fortunes change. In significant respects these versions of Christian history parroted claims voiced already in antiquity (Smith 1990). For even then, post-Constantinian ecclesiastical historians and officials of the Church claimed that the conversion of Constantine had marked a turning-point in not simply the legal status but also the popularity of the Christian Church. Indeed, in their tellings, the Christian community (meaning, often enough, some notional community of the orthodox) had been quite literally otherwordly, isolated through both its own discipline and the hostility of the outside world. After 312, however, so many followed the emperor into his new religion that they overwhelmed the pedagogical capacities of the institution, and the Church thereby admitted pagan customs along with pagan converts. The long absence in modern scholarship of the tools, and later the initiative, to model the likely size of the Christian population statistically helped to allow this ancient claim to be taken at face-value well into the twentieth century.

As a result of scholarship from the 1990s in particular, the certainties that had sustained histories of religion under the empire as histories of conflict, in which a decontextualized Christianity not only triumphed, but triumphed *over* something, have been largely swept away. In their place an edifice is now being constructed on different foundations. The importance of these elements are two. First, scholars have brought critical attention to bear upon the ideological commitments of ancient ecclesiastics and found in their writing ongoing commitments, well after Constantine, to construe the history of their community as that of a minority constantly threatened by the allure, as well as violence, of a pagan majority (Thelamon 1981; Brown 1993). Second, following the lead of John Scheid (1985), Jonathan Z. Smith (1990), and Richard Gorden (1990), scholars now have analytic tools with which to distinguish the doctrinal postulates and social-theoretical commitments of ancient cults in more helpful ways. For what now seems clear is that the local religious systems of ancient city-states, with their 'city-councilor gods', as the Christian apologist Tertullian derisively named them, were organized homologously with the social and political structures of their communities. They worked, in other words, to shore up the stability of the here-and-now. In Smith's terms, they were locative. The ideology of what once were called 'mystery' or 'oriental' cults, including Christianity, was focused on some other world, whether removed in time, space, or eschatologically. They were utopian. What such a taxonomy will hopefully permit is the gradual rewriting of the religious history of the empire, such that Christianity can claim its context, as a religion of its place and time, among other religions of its kind; and that their contest with the locative cults of the empire can be re-described not in Providential but in historical terms.

Process or Event?

To these developments in the history of religion we might compare attempts within the grand narrative of Decline and Fall to make the reign of Diocletian and his establishment of the Tetrarchy a turning-point, either in respect to public law or imperial ceremonial; in the former arena because Diocletian shared power, and in the latter because he imported Persian customs (Gibbon 1994: 1. 387–90). But neither innovation was as revolutionary as often described. On the contrary, modern inquiry has revealed Diocletian's measures to be rather incremental developments upon, or mere formalizations of, processes long in maturation (Alföldi 1934, 1935; but cf. Potter 2004: 280–90). They appeared innovatory largely because they were so depicted in antiquity, by historians and polemicists eager to indict the radicalism of his regime, or simply lacking the tools of modern historiography by which incremental social and institutional change might be assessed and described. Ancient narrative historians likewise display little interest in the history of law and administration, and so signally neglect the arenas within which Diocletian and the Tetrarchs really did revolutionize government, namely taxation, provincial administration, and, up to a point, the structures of civil and military authority (Jones 1964: 37–70; Corcoran 1996; Lo Cascio, in *CAH*[2] 12. 170–83).

What these examples in both government and religion reveal are, on the one hand, the sheer fragility of any attempt to identify a moment *ante quem*, when the world really did possess the transparency and weightlessness some would assign it, and on the other the impulse modern historians often share with their ancient sources to locate agency even in social-historical processes in individuals (Pocock 1996). In this way, process has often surrendered to event.

The choice of end-points presents a challenge to non-classicists for correlative reasons. For if the transition from ancient to medieval was not a process, because it is not to be understood by reference to the reception of classical culture and its transformation, forgetting, or fragmentation—if the cause of antiquity's end was not, in a word, endogenous—then it must have been exogenous. In which case, it is hard to see how it, too, was not an event.

But what sort of event? The question gestures to the third respect in which the politics of scholarship impinge upon our inquiry, namely, that the histories of the period are multiple and contested, and were so already in antiquity. Accept for a moment the identification of antiquity and empire. Even as a matter of politics, narrowly construed, the dissolution of the Roman Empire was not a single event. Different parts of the empire passed out of Roman control at different times, some through conquest, others in negotiated settlement, some through revolt: Britain was simply abandoned by the central authority after the usurper Constantine III left for the mainland in 407; parts of Gaul centred on the Garonne were ceded by treaty in 418 to the Visigothic king Wallia; the Vandals took Africa by force in 429; and so on. What is more, some regions were later recaptured by the eastern Roman Empire, only to be lost again.

But what do we mean by 'Roman?' For if one thing is uniformly true of many of the successor states in the West, it is that their rulers traced their legitimacy in part to their maintenance of Roman institutions, and that they largely acknowledged the superior claim to Romanness of the court of Constantinople. They did so, despite being by birth or descent non-Roman, and indeed many drew elaborate distinctions in law, policy, and rhetoric between their civilian, Roman subjects and themselves and their peers as rulers, soldiers, and Goths (the term is used purely *exempli gratia*) (Amory 1997). Three challenges at least arise from consideration of this complex history. First, how shall we understand the interplay of social practice and ideologies of ethnicity in this period? Second, what was the role of law and discourse in sustaining a classicizing social order on the one hand, and in reifying distinctions of race that both invoked and subverted that order's norms on the other? And third, can the ready fragmentation of the empire in the fifth century tell us anything about the geographic assumptions that inform traditional histories of the 'classical world'? To these questions I will return in closing.

The Rise and Function of Late Antiquity

The principal development in studies of the late Roman and post-Roman worlds across the last forty years has been the hiving off of late antiquity as a special field of study (Brown *et al.* 1997). This began as, and in some respects remains, an anglophone concern, though its practitioners owe complex debts to, and exhibit numerous anxieties of influence toward, the varied achievements of scholarship on the continent. It is above all intelligible as a complex effort to stand aside from the problematic legacy of the classicizing and Eurocentric narratives of decline explicated above.

Late antiquity as a period is variously defined as commencing in 150, 200, or 250 CE, and terminating some five centuries later (on the termini of late antiquity see Brown 1971, whose subtitle declares its subject to be the years 150–750 but whose text announces a concentration on 'the period from about A.D. 200 to about 700' (p. 7); see also Bowersock, Brown, and Grabar 1999: p. ix; Cameron and Garnsey, at *CAH*^{2} 13. pp. xiii–xv; and Cameron, Ward-Perkins, and Whitby at *CAH*^{2} 14. pp. xvii–xix, 972–81). The chronological bookends are to a point arbitrary, and deliberately so, in at least two respects that matter here. First, late antiquity as a field had at its inception and, indeed, long maintained a reasoned and ideological opposition to periodizations based on events in what its practitioners deemed the realms of politics and war. (That traumatic events like the Roman defeat at Adrianople or the sack of Rome might have been turning-points in the history of culture was not often in those days canvassed—on the importance of the former see Lenski 2003; on the aftermath of the latter see Courcelle 1964.) One way—not the only way, to be sure—to start a new field in historical analysis is to claim for it a distinct period, and late antiquity could not, therefore, commence or end at the conversion or death of Constantine (312 or 337), or upon his unification of the empire (324), nor at the sack of Rome (410), the deposition of Romulus Augustulus (476), or the deaths of Justinian or Maurice or Heraclius (565, 602, and 641), all of which had been used before and some since. That said, fields and periods may also be defined by seizing upon new objects of study. What is regarded as change—what is regarded as significant change—depends in historical inquiry on what index one chooses, as also on what one brackets. This points to the second factor contributing to the chronological ambiguity of late antiquity. Its early advocates established its termini by reference to the rise and fall of movements in culture and society that by their very nature lacked clear-cut chronologies. Even the so-called holy man, whose 'rise and function in late antiquity' Peter Brown charted in perhaps the field's seminal article (Brown 1971), lacks such definition, quite in spite of the *post-eventum* claims to novelty and specific attributions of authorship put forward on his behalf by Christian polemicists in ages after. This constitutes another arena in which the uncritical reading of ancient (Christian) sources has helped to sustain distorted and misleading pictures of the late ancient past.

Late antiquity as a field was thus shaped for a generation by moves made at its inception, both of inclusion and exclusion, which were disciplinary in expression even when intellectual in origin. No moment better illustrates the ideological work performed in this era than the summation offered by Peter Brown to his remarkable review of A. H. M. Jones's magisterial *The Later Roman Empire, 284–602: A*

Social, Economic and Administrative Survey: it was, in his judgement, 'not a complete social history of the Later Roman Empire, but the first, irreplaceable chapter in the history of the Byzantine state' (Brown 1967: 43 = 1972: 73). Thus were whole fields of historical inquiry, when directed at the chronological heart of late antiquity, nevertheless banished to another discipline altogether.

The effect of this political spadework was a long sundering of the field into two quite distinct camps: those studying the Later Roman Empire, who believed that it declined and fell, and that its fall mattered, and whose objects of study were social and economic institutions indexed to the viability of government writ large; and those studying late antiquity, who focused on social and cultural phenomena whose history they disaggregated from specific political formations and which often straddled precisely those barriers of regime, whether chronological or geographic, that determined and often overdetermined the scope of inquiry in the Later Roman Empire.

Let me say now that not all scholarship of the 1970s and 1980s can be understood within this framework, not even of the anglophone world, and that America in particular, by virtue of the size and heterogeneity of its academic establishment, fostered throughout this period voices that stood apart from this ideological divide. That said, the force of innovation in the maturing field of late antiquity has generally come from outside, most notably from fields that either read the same texts, namely Early Christian Studies, or from those that bookend it, namely Classics and the (new) Early Middle Ages—the last being itself a field? a period? discovered in England over the last generation, which, again like late antiquity, recently found its voice in a new journal (vol. 1 of *Early Medieval Europe* appeared in 1992; vol. 1 of the *Journal of Late Antiquity* appeared in 2007). That said, the politics of disciplinarity long played a decisive role in the field and the space it created for itself in institutional life, and it would be a mistake even now to forget this.

Perhaps the most important move made by scholars of late antiquity in setting aside the framework of decline was the rejection of the system of moral and aesthetic valuation that had long animated it. This was, to be sure, at times a local expression of currents widely operative in historical and humanistic study at the time, by which whole classes of individuals and aspects of life were then being redeemed for history: sexuality, slaves, household structure, poverty, dreams, and peasants, to name a few. But it found its most distinct and most revolutionary articulation in perhaps its least obtrusive usage, namely, the study of classicism.

The situation and valuation of the classical in relation to the late antique presents distinct and important challenges, and constitutes an indispensable and unavoidable index to the politics of scholarship. This is so because the cultures of the Later Roman Empire—more on their multiplicity in a moment—were in some obvious ways classical, and in some ways difficult to articulate, not. Three abiding challenges present themselves from this fact: two arise from the data itself, and the third from its paradigmatic interpretation.

There is first the problem that a sense of posteriority was itself an enduring theme of virtually all classical literature, one richly varied in its expression, in part because the conservatism that made it meaningful was itself deeply rooted and multiply justified. Second, explicit claims to novelty within these cultures were as ideologically motivated as was praise of tradition. Explicating a culture so given to explicit self-interpretation without merely parroting its claims in a modern idiom has proven difficult indeed (see e.g. Marrou 1958: 621–702). How to define the 'late' in 'late ancient', when literary historians under Tiberius already labelled the Augustan period a golden age?

The third challenge facing contemporary historians of classicism in late antiquity derives from the dominant position occupied by its single greatest modern exponent. For late antiquity as a field has more than most in Roman Studies a single touchstone, namely, Edward Gibbon's *History of the Decline and Fall of the Roman Empire* (Ando 2008). In Gibbon's argument, the classicism of late ancient culture was a fatal weakness. For him, posteriority was not a stance, or not simply one. The problem was rather belatedness: in his view, the rigidity of classical canons in the curriculum produced thinkers hopelessly out of step with their times, doomed endlessly to revive classical solutions to problems for which they were essentially inappropriate. Gibbon thus made classicism central to decline and fall, and decline, while necessary, had also been bad. Thus did aesthetic and historical analysis issue in moral valuation. In part as a consequence of modern scholarship's own sense of posteriority to Gibbon, his analysis, and even more his subject, have demanded similar acts of valuation from his heirs.

Seen in this light, the emergence of late antiquity as a specifically anglophone phenomenon makes more sense, and something of the distinctiveness, as well as the weakness, of its approach may now be clarified. For the conjoining of a number of its methodological postulates thus finds specific origin: the avoidance of the trope of decline; the shunning of the political and institutional; the privileging of culture; the celebration of the novel. At the same time, it may now be apparent why so much of what we accept as new in late antiquity arises in the domain of culture more generally, and specifically in that of religion; and why the form of cultural history practised in late antiquity has been so attenuated. For what scholars were long unwilling to confront were the politics that made such claims to novelty meaningful: both the knowledge-interests against which they reacted, and the social, economic, and institutional frameworks that those knowledge-interests articulated and sustained. As a consequence, within a cultural-historical practice so overdetermined, the tendentiousness (in the term's narrow sense) of much late ancient cultural self-positioning can receive no scrutiny. What is more, the model of society thus implicitly endorsed demands a theoretically unsustainable degree of autonomy for culture. But this situation cannot endure. Forms of self-expression, like frameworks of moral and aesthetic discrimination, are products of history, and must for full understanding be subjected to the most robust possible forms of historical contextualization. This work remains.

Going Forward

Happily, significant advances in this project are now being made in at least three areas: economics, theories of the Mediterranean, and ethnicity. I take these in turn.

First, Michael McCormick and Chris Wickham, historians of Byzantium and the Early Middle Ages respectively, have each recently offered monumental studies of the late ancient and early medieval economy, from quite distinct theoretical camps (McCormick 2001; Wickham 2005). These clarify the facts on the ground in at least one incontrovertible way: in the scope and scale of interregional and macro-regional trade, in degrees of urbanization, and as a matter of demographics, the fifth and sixth centuries were a period of decline; in some areas, disastrously so. At a more complex level, there is now no excuse for those committed to cultural history not to locate cultural practice within quite specific political economies. The work performed by post-Roman aristocracies to maintain the prestige value of Latin as a literary language and language of government, for example, may now be clarified as never before, as, recursively, may the role of literary education in shoring up aristocratic privilege and consolidating the Romanness of the post-Roman cultures of the West.

Second, the publication of Peregrine Horden's and Nicholas Purcell's brilliant and challenging *The Corrupting Sea* has provoked widespread examination of the theories, assumptions, and data that have underlain historiography of the Mediterranean world. The periodic fragmentation of the world, as well as the multiple forms of consolidation it has sustained over time, are now themselves significant objects of study. Where late antiquity is concerned, several trends that were once interpreted as signs of retreat, decay, or corruption, on the grounds that they represented a change from classical (Roman) antiquity, should now receive renewed attention. These include the fragmentation of trade networks between Spain and western North Africa and between the former Narbonensis and Tarraconensis; the retreat of centres of political power to northern Italy and east of the Antilebanon; and the dissolution of ties between Britain and Gaul on the one hand, and Central Gaul and the Mediterranean on the other. What is at issue is not, I would stress, whether those changes were produced in part by war or represented the dismantling of an economy of unprecedented size and integration. The question is rather how to understand the world that replaced it.

Finally, the last twenty years have seen significant advances in the study of barbarians, which is to say, the various Vandalic, Gothic, Germanic, and Hunnic peoples who impelled the fragmentation of the empire and, in some cases, shaped the life of its successor states. As in the history of religion, this took the form initially of investigations into the literary and ideological commitments of the historians who transmit the bulk of our knowledge. This work went hand-in-hand with research into the conceptualizations of ethnicity at play in both ancient and modern scholarship, as well as the role of discursive practice in shaping ethnic and political identity at the time (Pohl 1997 and Pohl and Reimitz 1998 represent well the fruits of this labour). The achievements in these arenas have enabled newly critical investigations of the politics of race and politicization of literary culture in the post-Roman West (see e.g. Amory 1997).

This is an exciting time for the field.

References

Alföldi, Andreas, 1934. 'Die Ausgestaltung des monarchischen Zeremoniells am römischen Kaiserhofe', *MDAI(R)* 49: 1–118. Repr. in Alföldi 1970.

—— 1935. 'Insignien und Tracht der römischen Kaiser', *MDAI(R)* 50: 1–171. Repr. in Alföldi 1970.

—— 1970. *Die monarchische Repräsentation im römischen Kaiserreiche.* Darmstadt: Wissenschaftliche Buchgesellschaft.

Amory, Patrick, 1997. *People and Identity in Ostrogothic Italy, 489–554.* Cambridge: Cambridge University Press.

Ando, Clifford, 2007. 'Decline, Fall and Transformation', *Journal of Late Antiquity*, 1: 30–60.

—— 2008. 'Narrating Decline and Fall', in Philip Rousseau (ed.), *The Blackwell Companion to Late Antiquity.* Oxford: Blackwell.

Bowersock, Glen, Peter Brown, and Oleg Grabar (eds.), 1999. *Late Antiquity: A Guide to the Postclassical World.* Cambridge, Mass.: Belknap.

Brown, Peter, 1967. Review of A. H. M. Jones 1964. *Economic History Review*, 56: 327–43.

—— 1971. *The World of Late Antiquity, A.D. 150–750.* London: Thames & Hudson.

—— 1972. *Religion and Society in the Age of Saint Augustine.* London: Faber & Faber.

—— 1993. 'The Problem of Christianization', *Proceedings of the British Academy*, 82: 89–106.

—— *et al.* 1997. 'The World of Late Antiquity Revisited', *Symbolae Osloenses*, 72: 5–80.

Burke, Peter, 1976. 'Tradition and Experience: The Idea of Decline from Bruni to Gibbon', *Daedalus*, 105/3: 137–52.

Corcoran, Simon, 1996. *The Empire of the Tetrarchs: Imperial Pronouncements and Government, A.D. 284–324.* Oxford: Oxford University Press.

Courcelle, Pierre Paul, 1964. *Histoire littéraire des grandes invasions germaniques*[3]. Paris: Études Augustiniennes.

Demandt, Alexander, 1984. *Der Fall Roms: die Auflösung des römischen Reiches im Urteil der Nachwelt.* Munich: C. H. Beck.

Fowden, Garth, 1993. *Empire to Commonwealth: Consequences of Monotheism in Late Antiquity.* Princeton: Princeton University Press.

Gibbon, Edward, 1994. *The History of the Decline and Fall of the Roman Empire*, ed. David Womersley. London: Allen Lane.

Gordon, R., 1990. 'Religion in the Roman Empire: The Civic Compromise and its Limits', in M. Beard and J. North (eds.), *Pagan Priests: Religion and Power in the ancient World.* Ithaca, NY: Cornell University Press, 235–55.

Harrison, Thomas (ed.), 2002. *Greeks and Barbarians.* New York: Routledge.

Herzog, Reinhart, 1993. 'Introduction à la littérature latine de l'antiquité tardive', in Reinhart Herzog (ed.), *Restauration et renouveau. La littérature latine de 284 à 374 après J.-C.* Translation produced under the direction of Gérard Nauroy. Turnhout: Brepols, 1–49.

Horden, Peregrine and Nicholas Purcell, 2000. *The Corrupting Sea: A Study of Mediterranean History.* Oxford: Blackwell.

Jones, A. H. M., 1964. *The Later Roman Empire: A Social, Economic and Administrative Survey.* Baltimore: Johns Hopkins University Press.

Lenski, Noel, 2003. *Failure of Empire: Valens and the Roman State in the Fourth Century A.D.* Berkeley: University of California Press.

McCormick, Michael, 2001. *Origins of the European Economy: Communication and Commerce, A.D. 300–900.* Cambridge: Cambridge University Press.

Marrou, Henri-Irénée, 1958. *Saint Augustin et la fin de la culture antique.* Paris: E. de Boccard.

Millar, Fergus, 1968. 'Local Cultures in the Roman Empire: Libyan, Punic and Latin in Roman Africa', *JRS* 58: 126–34.

——1987. 'Empire, Community, and Culture in the Roman Near East: Greeks, Syrians, Jews, and Arabs', *JJS* 38: 143–64.

——1998. 'Looking East from the Classical World: Colonialism, Culture and Trade from Alexander the Great to Shapur I', *IHR* 20: 507–31.

Pocock, J. G. A., 1996. 'Classical and Civil History: The Transformation of Humanism', *Cromohs*, 1: 1–34. http//www.unifi.it/riviste/cromohs/1_96/pocock.html.

——2003. *Barbarism and Religion.* Vol. 3: *The First Decline and Fall.* Cambridge: Cambridge University Press

——2005. *Barbarism and Religion.* Vol. 4: *Barbarians, Savages and Empires.* Cambridge: Cambridge University Press.

Pohl, Walter (ed.), 1997. *Kingdoms of the Empire: The Integration of Barbarians in Late Antiquity.* The Transformation of the Roman World, 1. Leiden: Brill.

——and Helmut Reimitz (eds.), 1998. *Strategies of Distinction: The Construction of Ethnic Communities, 300–800.* The Transformation of the Roman World, 2. Leiden: Brill.

Potter, David S., 2004. *The Roman Empire at Bay, A.D. 180–395.* New York: Routledge.

Scheid, John, 1985. *Religion et piété à Rome.* Paris: Decouverte.

Sizgorich, Thomas N., 2004. 'Narrative and Community in Islamic Late Antiquity', *Past & Present*, 185: 9–42.

——2009. *Violence and Belief in Late Antiquity: Militant Devotion in Christianity and Islam.* Philadelphia: University of Pennsylvania Press.

Smith, Jonathan Z., 1990. *Drudgery Divine: On the Comparison of Early Christianities and the Religions of Late Antiquity.* Chicago: University of Chicago Press.

Stark, Rodney, 1996. *The Rise of Christianity: A Sociologist Reconsiders History.* Princeton: Princeton University Press.

Thelamon, F., 1981. *Païens et Chrétiens au IVe siècle. L'apport de l'*Histoire ecclésiastique *de Rufin d'Aquilée.* Paris: Études Augustiniennes.

Wickham, Chris, 2005. *Framing the Early Middle Ages: Europe and the Mediterranean 400–800.* Oxford: Oxford University Press.

PART V

IDEAS

CHAPTER 44

PHILOSOPHY

DAVID SEDLEY

THERE are countless available angles for viewing the cultural phenomenon that is Roman philosophy. Was it a regular part of the broad Roman negotiation with Greek culture, or did it emerge under its own peculiar dynamic and play by its own rules? To what extent do its literary manifestations, above all in the surviving masterpieces of Lucretius, Cicero, and Seneca, form a seamless whole with contemporary developments in the Greek philosophical world? Did Roman philosophy aspire to become independent of its Greek origins, and, if so, how far did it succeed?

All these questions will be relevant to the present chapter. But its primary perspectives will lie elsewhere. In the period from Cicero's first philosophical writings in 51 BCE to the death of Seneca in 65 CE, the period in which philosophy truly entered the Roman intellectual bloodstream, we can watch Roman thought grappling with the complex relation between, on the one hand, the exalted authority which the tradition had already conferred on a series of philosophical demigods, and on the other, philosophy as a participatory mode of intellectual and moral life. This makes it appropriate to focus on Roman perceptions of the great intellectual breakthroughs on which philosophy is built, and the role—if any—of paradigmatic individuals in these. At the same time, we will be able to glimpse the process of philosophy's gradual Latinization.

We must start at the story's celebrated beginning, in 155 BCE, when philosophy burst spectacularly onto the Roman scene. The heads of three leading philosophical schools, sent by Athens on an embassy to Rome, successfully persuaded the Senate to reduce a crushing fine imposed on Athens for its sack of Oropus. The impact on the local intelligentsia of the public performances which these philosophers gave while off duty in Rome was, despite the dire warnings of Cato the Elder, the start of the great Roman love-affair with philosophy. It became fashionable for Romans to study in the Athenian schools, and Greek philosophers became an increasingly prominent presence close to the seat of Roman power. However, the Mithridatic War of 88–86 BCE was the event with the single greatest impact in this regard. Sulla's prolonged siege and subsequent sack of Athens caused it finally to lose its status as the Greco-Roman world's philosophical metropolis, and initiated an irreversible philosophical diaspora around the Mediterranean world. Some philosophers moved away from the newly emerging centre of power, heading for Alexandria, Rhodes, and the various cultural centres of Asia Minor. Many others, however, chose instead to gravitate towards the new centre, finding patrons and pupils at or within easy reach of Rome.

For the following century and more Rome could credibly claim to be the Greco-Roman world's true hub of philosophical activity. Editorial work done there by Andronicus and, a generation later, by Thrasyllus is widely believed to have had a decisive effect on the arrangement of, respectively, the Aristotelian and the Platonic corpus. Various of the major Greek thinkers of the day either moved to Rome or at any rate had extended stays there, where they often had the ear of prominent politicians.

Rome's unfamiliar new situation, of becoming the home to what was essentially a dislocated Greek cultural phenomenon, helps account for the feverish interest shown by leading Romans of Cicero's day in acquiring a philosophical education and allegiance. An educated Roman could be expected to speak and write Greek with ease, and we can assume Greek to have been the language in which—from 155 BCE onwards—Romans conversed with their Greek philosophical visitors. Similarly, the prevailing practice between Roman and Roman—Cicero's letters are testimony to this—was to deploy Greek technical terminology freely, albeit within the frame of Latin sentences.

The literary giants Lucretius, Cicero, and Seneca worked, each in his own way, to build a native mode of philosophical discourse. But Latin did not succeed in fully supplanting Greek as Rome's philosophical vernacular. Greek remained the language of choice for a range of Roman philosophical writers, from Cicero's close friend Brutus, known to have been the author of at least one Greek philosophical treatise alongside others in Latin, to the Stoic emperor Marcus Aurelius, whose use of Greek for recording his own private thoughts eloquently testifies that the philosophers' continued preference for it was no mere literary affectation. The reason, in what follows, for nevertheless concentrating on a selection of Latin philosophical texts lies more in the aims of the present volume: authors like Lucretius, Cicero, and Seneca stand at the very heart of the Roman cultural tradition, in a way that could never be matched by their compatriots who chose to write in Greek.

The age in which Cicero wrote was in an important sense a transitional one, as I have already indicated, and this too makes its testimony especially illuminating. Philosophy down to the late second century BCE had been a living tradition in the Athenian schools, traceable back without interruption to their august founders Plato, Aristotle, Epicurus, and Zeno, and even, via Plato, to that paragon of the philosophical life Socrates. To study in a school's Athenian headquarters was to insert yourself into its living tradition. In the diaspora which Cicero's own lifetime witnessed, on the other hand, that institutional continuity was irreparably ruptured. In their self-imposed intellectual exile, the philosophers had to rebuild their heritage, above all through minute study of the precious *texts* of their school founders. Cicero's age is a transitional one because it manifests both styles of philosophical self-positioning.

Thus many of Cicero's own entourage, Cicero himself included, can claim some direct link to the Athenian schools, having sat at the feet of a teacher who was himself in turn a product of the Athenian golden age of philosophy. Their debts to their Greek teachers, alongside their reverence for the foundational texts, are a vital part of their self-definition. This is nowhere more in evidence than in the proem to Book 5 of Cicero's *De Finibus*, where Cicero and friends, at Athens in 79 BCE, enjoy a nostalgic visit to the site of the Academy. The city's philosophical decline is not left in doubt, but they cling with fierce pride to their remaining toeholds in it. Three of them have attended the lectures of Antiochus, still active in Athens as self-proclaimed standard-bearer of Plato's Academy (and of the Aristotelian school, which he deems a mere branch of it). But it is to the canonical writings of Plato and Aristotle and their early followers that the highest respects are paid. And, in parallel to this, Cicero's close friend Atticus is a regular visitor to the Epicurean Garden, proclaiming his personal devotion to its current head Phaedrus, while also acknowledging the school's fervent commitment to the cult of its founder Epicurus. In this telling snapshot, both ancient authorities and contemporary teachers are accorded duly calculated shares and degrees of respect.

Reverence for founders usually means reverence for authoritative texts. Although Cicero is an emphatically non-partisan type of Platonist (more on this below), he sometimes insists on Plato's unsurpassed authority in matters philosophical. But such authority, whatever it may amount to, does not replace reasoned argument. For instance in Book 1 of the *Tusculan Disputations*, on the soul's immortality, a doctrine to which Cicero was especially strongly drawn in the wake of his beloved daughter's death, the limited credit he allots to Pythagoras for being the first to assert the immortality thesis is utterly eclipsed by his admiration for Plato, whose merit in his eyes was to back it with brilliant argument (*Tusc.* 1.38–9, 53–5). Indeed, the reported Pythagorean tradition of invoking the master's mere assertion ('ipse dixit') as sufficient to authorize a doctrine is dismissed as philosophically unworthy: authority thus used stifles rational judgement (*De Natura Deorum* 1.10). Nevertheless, Cicero understands the tug of this kind of authority well enough to add the counterfactual remark: 'Even if Plato adduced no argument—see what a tribute I'm paying him—he would crush me with his sheer authority. But in fact he has adduced so many arguments that you can see how, in seeking to persuade others, he undeniably has persuaded himself' (*Tusc.* 1.49).

In making this concession, however, Cicero is paying tribute to Plato not as the ultimate guide to truth, but as a truly worthy intellectual companion and source of inspiration: he would not mind being wrong, if it were in the company of Plato (*Tusc.* 1.39–40). Here it is vital to bear in mind that Cicero's own adherence to the Academy is not one that assigns its founder any *doctrinal* authority whatsoever. It is, on the contrary, the Socratic-Platonic *method* that Cicero repeatedly invokes, and this is precisely the method—first instilled in him by his Academic teacher Philo of Larissa—of treating no one as authoritative, keeping debates alive, and siding provisionally with what on each occasion strikes one as the 'truer' or 'more probable' among the competing positions. Plato's position on some issue may occasionally win the day, as indeed his belief in the soul's immortality does in *Tusculans* 1. At the other extreme it may be relegated to a mere mention in some list of irreconcilably competing views, none of which is deemed capable of beating off its rivals (e.g. *Academica* 2.118, 124). And more often than either extreme, it simply goes unmentioned. For Platonism, understood as a philosophical system based on a synoptic reading of Plato's dialogues, was at this date not yet one of the live options among which Roman would-be philosophers had to choose. Such a lack of contemporary relevance makes it all the more striking that Plato's *auctoritas* should, in Cicero's estimation, place him head and shoulders above all other philosophers.

In what sense, then, *is* Plato authoritative for Cicero? I have already mentioned Cicero's awe at Plato's deployment of argument, but this is in fact just one part of his reverence for Plato's *eloquentia* (e.g. *Orator* 10, 'Plato, the weightiest authority and master (*auctor et magister*) not only of understanding but also of speaking'; *Tusc.* 1.24; *Off.* 1.4). Plato's seminal and unsurpassed contribution to the eloquence of Greek philosophical discourse is an achievement that Cicero not only unconditionally admires, but also aspires to match by becoming the creator of its Roman counterpart. For Cicero repeatedly rejects the familiar radical separation of philosophy from rhetoric, even going so far as to nominate the Academy itself as the real source of his own oratorical prowess (*Orator* 12; cf. 13; *De Or.* 1.47). His ambition in his philosophical writings is, in effect, to become the Roman Plato—not a Roman Platonist, but the writer who opened up philosophy to the Latin-reading public as Plato had to its Greek counterpart. Such an ambition dates back to his first major philosophical works, the *De Republica* and *De Legibus*, written in 51 BCE as his own Roman counterparts to Plato's two great political treatises the *Republic* and *Laws.* And it remains operative throughout the corpus of philosophical works that he composed at astonishing speed in 46–44, very near the end of his life.

With the almost sole exception of the *De Officiis*, these works were dialogues. Even if Cicero's preference for the dialogue form as such is a key part of his Platonic heritage, ultimately placed at the service of keeping debates alive and philosophical questions open, his actual uses of it owe comparatively little to Plato. (He acknowledges some debt to Aristotle in this regard, and we may guess the recent and contemporary Academy to have exerted some influence too.) An intriguing example of his simultaneous adherence to and independence of Plato is his uncompleted translation of the *Timaeus*. This work of Plato's, although its celebrated main part is Timaeus' speech about the origin of the world, is in fact a dialogue. Cicero begins his translation of it just after the start of the speech, systematically eliminating its residual dialogical features. Although in doing so he may appear to renounce his allegiance to the Platonic dialogue form, what he is in reality doing is refashioning it for his own ends. For the Timaean monologue was—had the work been completed, at any rate—designed to be placed in the mouth of one speaker, the Roman Pythagorean Nigidius Figulus, apparently with a second speaker lined up to reply with an opposing monologue, defending the Peripatetic point of view—the issue dividing them perhaps being whether the world is created or eternal. Thus a component of a Platonic dialogue is isolated from its context, refashioned as a monologue, then reset within a Ciceronian dialogue. Plato had written the speech to resolve the big questions of cosmology so far as they could be settled; Cicero redeploys it, it seems, precisely in order to keep those questions open.

Plato is a god (*Ad Att.* 4.16.3, 'deus ille noster Plato'), and it is his eloquence that does most to make him divine in Cicero's eyes: Jupiter himself, if he spoke Greek, would speak it as Plato does (*Brutus* 120–1). The divinization of philosophers was no casual matter, and neither Aristotle nor any Stoic was deemed worthy of it. In late Republican Rome the honour seems to be bestowed on just two philosophers, namely Plato and Epicurus, and this I take to be a sign of their peculiarly inspirational role in Roman thought. It is to Epicurus that we may now turn.

Lucretius is likely to have written his great Epicurean poem *On the Nature of Things* (*De Rerum Natura*) in the early to mid-50s BCE, just a few years before Cicero's double Platonic tour de force, the *De Republica* and *De Legibus*. Among the poem's most prominent motifs is that Epicurus' uniquely inspirational legacy raises him to the ranks of the gods. Epicurus refused to be terrorized by the menaces of false religion, instead discovering for himself, and passing on to us in his teaching, the fundamental laws of physics (1.62–79). As a result, his philosophy can be said to be 'sprung from a divine mind' (3.15), and he himself is to be counted a god (5.7–12). Indeed, so great is our debt to him that it places his claim to divinity ahead of others deemed for relatively banal reasons to be divinized benefactors of mankind, such as Ceres, Bacchus, and Hercules: for instead of devising mere bodily comforts, or exterminating literal monsters, he has freed our minds of moral malaise, the one truly frightful monster that stalks them (5.8–54).

Lucretius cannot be assumed to be altogether typical of Roman Epicureans in his day. For one thing, he displays no awareness of the recent developments in Epicureanism of which we happen to know a good deal from the contemporary Greek Epicurean Philodemus. (Philodemus was consulted as an authority by Cicero, and his school near Naples has left us an extensive record of its work through the historical fluke of its library's burial by Vesuvius in 79 CE and subsequent retrieval.) The suspicion arises that he was not an active part of any Epicurean group or school. Nevertheless, in the matter of Epicurus' uniqueness his voice is recognizably in tune with contemporary Roman responses. For two of Cicero's major dialogues, the *De Finibus* and *De Natura Deorum*, open by giving the platform to an Epicurean spokesman, respectively Torquatus on ethics and Velleius on theology; and these Roman Epicureans' perception of Epicurus' pivotal place in their lives and value systems eloquently extends and complements what we find in Lucretius.

For a start, Velleius too ranks Epicurus as one of his gods (*ND* 1.43), just as Lucretius does, and echoes an existing tradition in the school of calling Epicurus' methodological treatise the *Canon* 'heaven-sent'. But more instructive are the indications of what Epicurus' godlike powers consisted in. Where Plato, at least for Cicero, displayed divine powers of exposition, Epicurus' godlike superiority lay above all in his powers of intellectual *vision*.

No passage of Lucretius sets his agenda better than the lines from his first proem (1.62–79) in which he launches his eulogy of a great Greek predecessor, reverentially left unnamed but instantly recognizable as Epicurus. This great man, compared here to a military leader, was the first to fight back against the crushing effects of false religious belief, and he did so by a progression from ocular to mental vision. First, using his own eyes, he could see human life to be everywhere oppressed by religion. He then dared to raise those eyes to the heavens, from which the menaces of religion were staring down, and to return their stare. This in turn gave him the courage, now by his sheer power of mind, to smash open nature's gates and issue forth into the measureless universe beyond our own world's boundary or 'flaming walls' (*flammantia moenia mundi*), the fiery heaven. By this extraordinary projection of thought he was enabled to traverse the entire infinity of space, returning in triumph to teach us the limits of the possible and the impossible. In his victory, religion is the vanquished foe, we ourselves the winners.

Epicurus was the peerless pioneer of this breakthrough. But Roman readers must be taught to follow him on that same voyage, for only by their own direct insight into the universe's true nature, and not on another's say-so, can they be liberated from fear of the unknown. Cicero's Epicurean spokesman Velleius explains what is at issue to his Stoic opponent Balbus (*ND* 1.53–4):

For the same man who taught us everything else taught us also that the world was made by nature without the need for craftsmanship, and that this thing which you call impossible

> without divine creativity is in fact so easy that nature will make, is making, and has made infinitely many worlds. Just because you do not see how nature can do this without a mind, unable to develop your plot's *dénouement* you copy the tragic poets and resort to a god. You would not be demanding this god's handiwork if you saw the measureless magnitude of space, endless in all directions, by projecting and focusing itself (*se iniciens... et intendens*) into which the mind travels far and wide, seeing as a result no boundary of its extremities at which it could call a halt. In this measureless stretch of widths, lengths, and heights there flies an infinite mass of countless atoms, which despite the presence of void between them stick together and by taking hold of each other form a continuous whole. And from these are made those shapes and formations of things which you think are impossible without bellows and anvil. With this thought you have placed as a yoke upon our necks a permanent overlord, for us to fear day and night.

Velleius thus brings out what we can achieve for ourselves if we follow Epicurus on his odyssey of the mind. The key to eliminating oppressive creator gods from our world-view is to appreciate the inevitability that mere atomic accident, operating as it must do on an infinite scale, will produce worlds like our own, without the need for divine craftsmanship. That in its turn requires us to *see*, by mental projection, what the universe's infinity really means, just as Lucretius has described Epicurus as having done before us. The thought experiments, arguments, and mental exercises by which this vision can be achieved are set out at length by Lucretius towards the end of his first book (1.951–1051). For example, we are invited to imagine going to some hypothetical boundary of the universe and throwing a spear past it (968–83).

A terminological detail here requires a brief digression. Velleius, in speaking of the mind 'projecting itself', *se iniciens*, into infinite space, is capturing an Epicurean technical term, *epibolē tēs dianoias*, 'focusing of the intellect', which Epicurus himself had made central to his methodology. Similarly Lucretius (2.1044–7), in introducing his argument that beyond our own world there are countless others, writes: 'For given the infinite amount of space beyond these walls of our world, the mind demands an account of what further things lie there for the intellect to aim to reach with its gaze, and to which the mind's projection (*animi iactus*, cf. 2.740) can free itself and fly.' A possible subtext underlying Velleius' words is that the method of discovery which Epicurus pioneered was one which he thereby earned the privilege of naming. Elsewhere, at any rate, Velleius makes a similar claim about the term *prolēpsis* (*ND* 1.43–4): Epicurus was uniquely able to explain the universal human 'preconception' of god, having himself discovered and named this basic criterion of truth, one whose Latinization is presented as a matter of pressing concern (*anticipatio*? *praenotio*?). But the concern with Latinization of the technical term, even if here placed in the mouth of the speaker Velleius, is characteristically Cicero's own. When it comes to the mind's self-projection, what matters most is not to flag up the Greek *or* Latin terminology chosen, but to make as vivid as possible the act itself.

The superior mental vision which led Epicurus to the truth is what Roman Epicureans characteristically consider the source of his unique contribution to human happiness (cf. the remarks of the Epicurean Torquatus at *De Finibus* 1.14). They cite his writings as directly inspiring the same liberating vision in themselves. According to his proem to Book 3, when Lucretius reads or hears Epicurus' golden words of divine wisdom the walls of the world part (*moenia mundi | discedunt*), and he can see for himself, spread out before him, the infinite universe, free from interfering gods, from a grim afterlife, and from other terrors (3.9–30)—a careful replication of Epicurus' own intellectual breakthrough as described in the proem to Book 1.

The inspirational role attributed by Lucretius to Epicurus' text also finds a parallel in Cicero's Epicureans, who like to quote in precise Latin translation the master's canonical sayings. Such reverence for the master's *ipsissima verba* seems symptomatic of the awed respect in which the divine Epicurus or the divine Plato can be held by Romans of the period. But we must be aware, once again, of the difference. In the case of Plato, his supreme eloquence and his power of argument provide the motivation; in the case of Epicurus, it is his encapsulation of focal truths.

That such Roman attitudes are shaped by the particular schools in which they are located is clear enough, not only from these differences in the kind of reverence provoked, but also from a contrast with the other philosophical movements. The Stoic representatives who feature prominently among Cicero's speakers pay little of the same reverential respect to their school's founder Zeno, or to any other Greek Stoic. The same applies—indeed, more so—to Seneca, writing nearly a century later. Probably the most important single influence on Roman Stoicism is the Greek Stoic Posidonius, whom Cicero heard and admired, but he comes nowhere near to being divinized or heroized. Indeed, the nearest thing to a hero for Roman Stoics is Cicero's contemporary Marcus Cato, whose principled suicide, accompanied by a reading of Plato's *Phaedo*, brought him closer to the ideal of the Stoic sage than Chrysippus, Posidonius, or any other Greek Stoic had managed. But here we are moving away from philosophical authority, and towards that great passion of Roman Stoicism, the moral exemplum.

Stoicism too, like Epicureanism, is deeply interested in intellectual breakthroughs, but a telling contrast can be made. For Epicureans, our thought starts out imprisoned by the misleading bounds of our own world, which beguile us into placing ourselves at the centre, under the watchful eye of divine masters. Liberation consists precisely in scorning those apparent boundaries and passing beyond them. For a Stoic, those celestial boundaries are, on the contrary, real and all-important limits. The world whose centre is occupied by the earth on which we live is the universe's only world, divinely governed throughout, and learning our place in its bounded system is the key to our own happiness. The all-important quantum leap is the one which enables us to glimpse our own place in the goodness of that whole.

This radical transition is described by both Cicero and Seneca, in terms of how the conception of the good is arrived at. Their task is to explain our ability, not (as is often assumed) to use the word 'good' significantly in ordinary discourse, but to grasp the substantive nature and content of true goodness as this is understood in Stoic ethical theory. From a synthesis of their twin accounts, the main components emerge as follows. First, analogy with bodily health and strength leads to appreciation that there must exist a mental equivalent to these; and that mental item, as yet unspecified, thereafter serves as a place-holder for the good. The content of this good is then filled out by further use of 'analogy'. It is after a process of cataloguing and comparing a range of correct and admirable human actions that the great quantum leap occurs: the mind becomes aware of something they all have in common, namely a mutual agreement of purpose which not only binds them together but also itself utterly transcends them in value. It is in the recognition of that agreement and of its incomparable intrinsic value that awareness of the good first shines out. I shall return shortly to the reason why this process too is technically called 'analogy'.

Cicero's and Seneca's portrayals of intellectual progression to this grasp of the good are separated by a full century, and the contrast between them reveals much about the very different contexts in which they were writing. Cicero's account, placed in the mouth of his Stoic spokesman Cato in the *De Finibus*, revels in technicality. Much exercised with the task of forging a native Latin philosophical vocabulary, the author's focus is constantly on how one might best convey the existing Greek term of art. In the course of this short exposition (*De Finibus* 3.21, 33–4) he takes the opportunity to unveil his translations for 'value' (Greek *axia*, Latin *aestimatio*), 'correct action' (Greek *kathēkon*, Latin *officium*), 'conception' (Greek *ennoia*, Latin *intellegentia* or *notio*), 'agreement' (Greek *homologia*, Latin *convenientia*), and 'benefit' (Greek *ōphelēma*, Latin *quod prodest*). And even where no original Greek term is formally indicated, one can again and again instantly recognize precisely what Greek terminology Cicero is seeking to render.

Seneca, by contrast, here as nearly always, shows little interest in capturing or representing the appropriate Greek technical terminology, or indeed in using it to think with, however sure we may be that he is thoroughly familiar with it. His account of discovering the good is couched far more in the characteristically Roman language of exemplarity. Thus, where Cicero's speaker Cato introduces the technical notion of 'agreement' (*homologia*), thereby alluding to the Stoic goal of life, 'living in agreement (*homologoumenōs*) with nature', Seneca (*Ep.* 124.11–12) amplifies his own reference to the intrinsic value of actions' mutual 'harmony' (*concordia*) by appealing to the image of the idealized wise man, utterly in tune with the world plan: 'He has never cursed his luck, never given chance events an unhappy reception, and in the belief that he is a citizen and soldier of the universe he has undergone his travails as if they had been ordained by authority.'

Seneca's reconstruction of conceiving the good by analogy is further built up with a series of specific moral exempla. Paradigmatic acts of heroism from Rome's rich historical legacy, such as Fabricius' rejection of Pyrrhus' gold and Horatius' defence of the bridge, are invoked alongside appeals to experience of human nature, as part of the same 'analogical' process of selection and idealization. Moral exempla are among the most distinctive features of Latin philosophical writing. The practice had been as well exhibited in Cicero's own philosophical writings, such as the *De Officiis* and the *Tusculans*, as in Seneca. But Cicero had denied himself exempla when most closely mimicking his Greek Stoic originals, which seem to have discounted them as a proper basis for ethical argument. Hence in the Stoic doxography in *De Finibus* 3, from which I have just been quoting, exempla are starkly absent, and Seneca's greater degree of liberation from Greek Stoicism shows through in his integration of exempla into his own equivalent account.

A yet more striking point of comparison lies in the notion of 'analogy', which underlies both accounts. Cicero does not in this case cite the Greek term *analogia*, but he nevertheless introduces some heavy-duty technicality in order to give meaning to his Latin rendition of it: 'The conceptions of things arise in our minds when something is known either by experience (*usus*), or by combination (*coniunctio*), or by resemblance (*similitudo*), or by analogy (*collatio rationis*), and it is by this fourth and last that the idea of good arises' (*De Finibus* 3.33). He has here run through a standard Stoic list of the various species of concept formation (Diogenes Laertius 7.53) in order to locate within the genus the precise species he has in mind.

Shortly after, he continues: 'But we are aware of this good in its own right, and call it good, not by addition, increase, or comparison with others, but thanks to its own force.' Here too a technical Stoic distinction is being condensed. Stoic 'analogy' can on occasion be the product of mere increase or intensification, that being, for example, how the conception of a giant is arrived at by starting from that of a human being (Diogenes Laertius 7.53). Against such a background, Cicero's point is that the analogical move from mere admirable actions to the concept of the good involves a far more radical shift than that. Now and only now does he set aside the technical schema and try to convey his point graphically: 'For just as honey, although very sweet, is perceived as sweet by its own kind of taste, not by comparison with other things, so too this good that we are discussing is of the highest value, but that value differs in kind, not in degree.'

Cicero's Stoic has here faced up to the problem of explaining how the good can on the one hand be in an utterly different class from other values, yet on the other be grasped analogically by building up from those lower values. He achieves this by ambitiously devising his own Latin set of Stoic technical distinctions, thus providing one among Cicero's numerous contributions to his projected creation of a full Latin philosophical vocabulary.

Seneca's approach is subtly different (*Ep.* 120.4): 'Some people say that we simply happened upon the idea [of good]. That is incredible—that the model of virtue should have befallen someone accidentally. Our own [i.e. the Stoics'] view is that it has been inferred by observation plus the comparison of frequent actions with each other. Our philosophers believe that it is by *analogia* that both the honourable and the good have been understood.' Uncharacteristically, it may at first appear, Seneca has resorted to an imported Greek philosophical term. But he immediately hastens to dispel any such impression: 'Since this word has been granted citizenship by the Latin grammarians, it should not be condemned, I think, but restored to its citizenship. I shall use it, therefore, not just as a word that has gained admittance, but as one that is in use. So let me explain what this *analogia* is...' That is, the fact that *analogia* is a technical term of Greek Stoicism is emphatically not a justification for its use in the writings of a Roman Stoic. Its legitimate presence in Latin discourse depends instead, in Seneca's eyes, on its having arrived by a quite different route, via grammarians such as Varro as a term in grammatical debate, and done so sufficiently long ago to have by now gone native.

The brief self-defence is eloquently symptomatic of Seneca's ambition to Latinize philosophy. Such a project, of cutting philosophy adrift from its Greek roots and fully appropriating it for Rome, had been Cicero's own from the start (see e.g. *Tusc.* 2.5). But it is in Seneca that it finds its highest realization.

Further reading

The surviving writings of nearly all the major pagan Roman philosophers are available with parallel translation in the Loeb Classical Library. A rare exception is Musonius Rufus, who is translated in Lutz 1947.

A convenient introduction to Roman philosophy down to Marcus Aurelius is Morford 2002. Philosophy's place within Roman culture is explored in greater depth in the seminal Rawson 1985, and in Griffin and Barnes 1989 and 1997. Key moral aspects of Roman Stoicism are illuminatingly discussed in Reydams-Schils 2005. Roman Platonism is meticulously surveyed in Gersh 1986.

Godwin 2004 is a succinct introduction to Lucretius. Lucretius' relation to his Greek background is explored in Clay 1983, Algra, Koenen, and Schrijvers 1997, and Sedley 1998.

For Cicero's philosophical writings MacKendrick 1989, although idiosyncratic, can serve as a helpful introduction. Key aspects are well explored, with varying degrees of accessibility to the non-specialist, in Powell 1995. Two more demanding studies, both of major significance, are Hirzel 1883 and Lévy 1992.

For Seneca, Griffin 1976 is an indispensable guide to his life and work, Inwood 2005 a set of close philosophical analyses, and Cooper and Procopé 1995 an exemplary presentation of some of his key ethical and political texts.

Although the above chapter has concentrated on Roman philosophers who wrote in Latin, it is impossible to exclude from the phenomenon of 'Roman philosophy' others who wrote in Greek. Epictetus, although culturally more Greek than Roman, sheds much light on the Roman philosophical milieu where he learnt his Stoicism. Long 2002 is an accessible and indispensable guide to his writings, while Dobbin 1991 provides close commentary on one book of his *Discourses*. For Epictetus' Roman Stoic teacher Musonius, see Lutz 1947. On the *Meditations* of the Stoic Roman emperor Marcus Aurelius there has been a wealth of valuable studies, including Brunt 1974, Rutherford 1989, and Hadot 1998.

References

Algra, K. A., M. H. Koenen, and P. H. Schrijvers (eds.) (1997), *Lucretius and his Intellectual Background*, Amsterdam, Oxford, New York, and Tokyo: Dutch Academy of Sciences, Arts and Letters.

Brunt, P. A. (1974), 'Marcus Aurelius in his *Meditations*', *Journal of Roman Studies*, 64: 1–20.

Clay, D. (1983), *Lucretius and Epicurus*, Ithaca and London: Cornell University Press.

Cooper, J. M. and J. F. Procopé (1995), *Seneca: Moral and Political Essays*, Cambridge: Cambridge University Press.

Dobbin, R. (1991), *Epictetus, Discourses Book 1*, translated with commentary, Oxford: Oxford University Press.

Gersh, S. (1986), *Middle Platonism and Neoplatonism: The Latin Tradition*, 2 vols., Notre Dame, Ind.: University of Notre Dame Press.

Godwin, J. (2004), *Lucretius*, Bristol: Bristol Classical Press.

Griffin, M. (1976), *Seneca: A Philosopher in Politics*, Oxford: Oxford University Press.

—— and J. Barnes (eds.) (1989), *Philosophia Togata*, I: *Essays on Philosophy and Roman Society*, Oxford: Oxford University Press.

—— —— (eds.) (1997), *Philosophia Togata*, II: *Plato and Aristotle at Rome*, Oxford: Oxford University Press.

Hadot, P. (1998), *The Inner Citadel: The Meditations of Marcus Aurelius*, tr., Cambridge, Mass., and London: Harvard University Press.

Hirzel, R. (1883), *Untersuchungen zu Ciceros philosophische Schriften*, 3 vols., Leipzig: Teubner.

Inwood, B. (2005), *Reading Seneca*, Oxford: Clarendon Press.

Lévy, C. (1992), *Cicero academicus*, Rome: Coll. École Française de Rome.

Long, A. A. (2002), *Epictetus: A Stoic and Socratic Guide to Life*, Oxford: Clarendon Press.

Lutz, C. (1947), *Musonius Rufus: The Roman Socrates*, New Haven: Yale University Press.

MacKendrick, P. (1989), *The Philosophical Books of Cicero*, London: Routledge.

Morford, M. (2002), *The Roman Philosophers*, London and New York: Routledge.

Powell, J. G. F. (ed.) (1995), *Cicero the Philosopher*, Oxford: Clarendon Press.

Rawson, E. (1985), *Intellectual Life in the Late Roman Republic*, Baltimore: Johns Hopkins University Press.

Reydams-Schils, G. (2005), *The Roman Stoics*, Chicago: University of Chicago Press.

Rutherford, R. B. (1989), *The Meditations of Marcus Aurelius*, Oxford: Oxford University Press.

Sedley, D. (1998), *Lucretius and the Transformation of Greek Wisdom*, Cambridge: Cambridge University Press.

CHAPTER 45

POLITICAL THEORY

JOY CONNOLLY

It is something of a miracle that Rome continues to exert influence on political thought in today's liberal egalitarian democracies. Roman political theory grew out of the experience of a traditionalist, militaristic oligarchy whose priorities may be fairly described as the acquisition of glory and riches and the domination of the ancillary populace. In the political system that evolved as the empire grew, a system Polybius treats as a model of the Aristotelian mixed constitution, a small number of wealthy noble families commanded the lion's share of authority and political initiative, while the People were legally empowered to elect magistrates and (without formal debate) approve or reject laws the magistrates proposed. The simple principle of 'one man, one vote' was not the custom at Rome. Voting on legislation was skewed by tribal affiliation, with the ballots of long-settled rural areas close to the city outweighing those of the poor urban masses. Voting in elections for the major offices was openly weighted by economic standing, with the votes of the rich *classes* (including senators and *equites*) counting in aggregate for far more than those of everyone else. Like jury service, office-holding was the domain of the very well off, and elected magistrates wielded executive power: they were not representatives of the people's will. Under the Caesars, though some of the trappings of republican popular politics persisted, power was increasingly centralized in the hands of the imperial household and its appointees. Under both republican and autocratic government, Roman politics institutionalized social and economic inequalities; its political culture enshrined aristocratic values, the cluster of dispositions and practices known as the *mos maiorum*, 'ancestral custom'.

The contrast with Athens is acute. There, the establishment of democratic government in the revolution of 508/7 BCE and the crucial reforms of the 460s guaranteed legal and political equality among all free adult Athenian-born men, regardless of economic standing. Every citizen was eligible to serve on juries and in the executive council known as the *boulē*, which was chosen by lot, and every citizen had the right to speak up in the legislative assembly. Beyond the practical consequences for decision-making, the lottery's equalization of *timē* (meaning both 'esteem' and 'office') played a significant ideological role in the formation of the Athenians' political self-definition (Morris 1996; Cartledge 1996). Many of the major concerns of ancient Greek political theory—the Old Oligarch's critique of popular rule; Plato's modelling in *Republic* and *Gorgias* of rational argument and a notion of truth that he explicitly contrasts with sophistic and democratic debate; Aristotle's arguments limiting citizenship to virtuous men of leisure; even, perhaps, the Cynics' radical refusal to obey social convention—may be understood as a response to the particular challenges raised by democracy (Ober 1998). Today Athens' egalitarian ideology, along with its emphasis on broad participation and public debate, has granted it renewed importance in the eyes of scholars of liberal democracy. Theorists of popular deliberation, free speech, the formation of collective identity, and civic education, in particular, seek inspiration in Athens (Ober and Hedrick 1996; Balot 2006).

Until recently, such a turn in Roman Studies was almost unimaginable. This chapter eschews the surveying of concepts and debates available in other handbooks in favour of sketching out the major directions in which the field is moving, especially its points of productive contact with contemporary political theory. It should also correct what mars some textbook accounts of Roman thought: overemphasis of the debt to Greek philosophy, the defence of property rights, and the dominance of aristocratic values at the expense of exploring the Romans' innovative thinking about the nature and purpose of the state, the constitution of political legitimacy, the significance of class, and the micropolitics of the individual and collective body politic.

The student of Roman political theory today faces an array of challenges and opportunities. Foremost is the absence of an easily defined canon and the correspondingly vast scope of non-philosophical potential sources. Politics pervades Roman culture and identity: through much of Republican history, territorial expansion ensured that through military service and imperial governance a majority of citizens were intensively subjected to the collective authority of the state, and social values and self-understanding evolved accordingly. The prologue to one of the earliest surviving prose works in Latin, the elder Cato's *On Agriculture*, admits no gap between the virtues of the good farmer and the good citizen-soldier. The arena where glory is achieved, the *civitas* is where the Roman's obligations lie (Cicero, *Off.* 1.71); excuses must be made for abandoning it, as Sallust does when he explains his decision to write history as simply a different mode of engagement with politics (*Jug.* 3.1–4).

The broad reach of the political in Roman life, along with the careful distance the Romans maintained from the Greek culture they mined so assiduously, explains why Roman writers did not embrace the field of political *theoria* as Greek thinkers had defined it. Instead, they generated a hybrid discourse in which Greek concepts and debates—the various types of constitutional regimes, the nature of the best state, the four canonical virtues of wisdom, justice, courage, and moderation, and so on—are woven into history, poetry, oratory, and educational treatises. Even Cicero, who conceived his dialogues *Republic* and *Laws* as reworkings of Plato and Aristotle, and who, with Seneca, produced the most philosophically conventional works in the Latin canon, diverges from his predecessors with his highly unphilosophical tendency to treat Roman particularities in universal terms: he assimilates Roman law and archaic custom, for instance, to natural law (*Laws* 2.23). His dialogues' characters also underscore the tension between contemplation and action, philosophical truth and political opinion—a tension he treats elsewhere as emblematic of the divide between Greece and Rome—by openly debating the utility of theoretical discourse. As Laelius, a figure in Cicero's *Republic*, says to a young interlocutor interested in unusual cosmic phenomena, the problem is not the two suns that have recently appeared over Rome, but the fact that the city has split into two Romes; their task as thinkers is to bring unity to the city, not the heavenly spheres (*Rep.* 1.31–2).

The dispersed and contested feel of Roman theorizing about politics resonates with contemporary movements in the field. Political theory today retains a certain historical and purposive coherence—it involves the diagnosis and critique of political thought and action; its main concerns are justice, the nature of the public good, the source and maintenance of legitimacy, the distribution of power, the ways in which citizens experience governmental authority—but it is riding the currents of a paradigm shift. Interdisciplinarity is a new watchword, prodding theorists into dialogue with ethics, feminist and critical theory, literary theory, rhetoric, history, cultural studies, and the law. As Sallust and Cicero had done, contemporary theorists are intensively interrogating their responsibilities to practical politics. After a half-century of marginalization by the empirical priorities of political science, work on the interrelationship of politics with social and moral experience is drawing not only on traditional sources in philosophy, history, and sociology (Hume, Smith, Gibbon, Rousseau, Kant, Durkheim) but on the resources of post-war thought, especially poststructuralism, psychoanalysis, discourse analysis, and deconstruction.

Within classical scholarship, the history of Roman political thought is also in transition due to important shifts in the methods and assumptions of political and cultural history. Two general points seem clear, mirroring recent developments in

Hellenic Studies (Manville 1994). First is the shift from static to dynamic models of political practice. Theodor Mommsen presented Rome in his 1887–8 *Staatsrecht* as an objectively defined, fixed constitutional order, organized around unchanging concepts of justice. Also privileging fixity, but replacing constitutional abstraction with *Realpolitik*, historians Barthold Georg Niebuhr and Matthias Gelzer argued that the Senate was the true government of Rome, regularly buffeted by popular protests but retaining its authority through the era of the civil wars, when the size and wealth of the empire transformed the factionalism of a traditionally competitive aristocracy into fatal struggles between leaders of great armies. Through this lens, Roman political thought was studied with a view toward understanding what we may call 'senatorial' ideology: the tradition of ancestral civic virtue that Rome's great governing families were supposed to sustain, and a set of conservative political values organized around the protection of property and the retention of authority in the hands of a few. As for the key Roman notions of the free state (*libera civitas*) and the free citizen, so important for Machiavelli, James Harrington, Montesquieu, and many theorists of the eighteenth century age of revolutions, the historian Ronald Syme was not alone in judging that 'Liberty and the laws are high-sounding words. They will often be rendered, on a cool estimate, as privilege and vested interest' (Syme 1939: 2). Reconsiderations of the popular element in Roman politics, and the development of sophisticated theoretical tools with which to conceive and represent power, have fundamentally altered the conditions for studying Roman political theory. While few may adhere strictly to Fergus Millar's provocative suggestion that Rome should be viewed as a 'democracy' (1998: 11), recent studies treat the formation of legitimacy and the consolidation of power as dynamic processes manifested through public speech and subject to contestation (Morstein-Marx 2004; Connolly 2007). Scholarly grasp of the textuality of the constitution and of acts of legislation—that is, the consequences arising from the relation of written to unwritten in our sources—has grown increasingly nuanced (Lintott 1999: 2–8).

Second is the assertion that Roman politics is primarily to be understood through institutions and institutionalized roles and actions. While the significance of formal aspects of politics such as Senate meetings, elections, public assemblies (especially the non-voting assembly called the *contio*) is undeniable, it is equally clear that for Roman intellectuals they were not the primary focus of attention. Our knowledge of electoral and legislative practices is piecemeal precisely because no Roman writer bears careful witness to it. What mainly preoccupied Roman political writers were the ethical formation of the citizen, his obligations to the political community, and the relation of the leading citizen to the masses, and here a wide range of questions regarding the nature of the self, the collective, ideology, reason, persuasion, and the body comes into play.

Roman texts thus constitute a transformative resource for contemporary political theorists. Roman politics illuminates practices of public communication and the role of the people in the formation of policy and political concepts in conditions where a highly educated elite plays a dominant role in setting the parameters for political debate and cultural production. Cicero's corpus—sometimes precisely because of the internal inconsistencies between his speeches and his theoretical arguments—along with historiography, drama, epic, and pedagogical texts prompt rethinking of current problems in citizenship theory, such as the nature of the civic community, the extent of civic obligations, and the role of civility and common cultural values: Philip Pettit's *Republicanism*, a major contribution to political philosophy in its own right, makes a suggestive model for Roman Studies. Hannah Arendt's discussion of Roman conceptions of time, tradition, authority, and public speech in *On Revolution* has proved rich ground for scholars of the republican tradition. The call by some theorists to abandon the Platonic paradigm of political theory, where philosophers contemplate a stable order of abstractions such as 'justice' or 'wisdom' in lieu of an active model of engagement, is anticipated in the Romans' transformative appropriation of Greek philosophy (Cavarero 2002). In the international context, Cicero and Seneca speak to contemporary debates over cosmopolitanism, the theory of just war (*bellum iustum*), the law of nations (*ius gentium*), natural law, and the origins of human rights (Bauman 2000; Nussbaum 2001). Finally, the nature of senatorial dominance in the Republic and the transformation of Republic to Empire under Augustus raises key questions about the relationship of power to authority, charisma, law, and violence, to date partially explored by Michel Serres's speculative readings of Livy and Giorgio Agamben's revisitation of Roman law.

Meanwhile, many of the concepts and problems central to earlier scholarship on Roman political thought have migrated to cultural studies, with Roman writing on the formation of character, especially in the ethical and rhetorical tradition, helping to revitalize our understanding of the construction of identity, especially as regards gender, class, and nation (e.g. Gleason 1995; Dench 2005). Work on all these fronts promises to shift conventional assessments of the political canon in the Republic, which may be broadly defined as the elder Cato, Sallust, Cicero, and Cornelius Nepos, and the Empire, including Valerius Maximus, Velleius Paterculus, Curtius Rufus, the younger Seneca, Pliny, Quintilian, Tacitus, and Greek imperial writers such as Plutarch, Dio Chrysostom, and Aelius Aristides. Let us examine some of the central issues in detail, focusing on a traditional starting-point: Cicero's treatment of the nature and the purpose of the state.

The State

There are two typical starting-points of discussion of Roman ideas about the political community or, to use the modern term, the state (*res publica*, *civitas*).

The first is the phrase *res publica*, glossed by Cicero as *res populi*, the people's affair or property, which evokes the obligations of Roman contract law (*Rep.* 1.39; Schofield 1995). The second is the Roman appropriation of Greek constitutional theory, especially in the first book of Cicero's *Republic*, which echoes Plato (*Rep.* 291d–292a), Aristotle (*Pol.* 3.7, 1279a22–b10), and, closer in time to Cicero, Polybius (6.3.5–8, 6.10.1–16). Polybius' history of Rome probes the dynamics of what he takes to be the empire's inevitable decline, though he claims that through the Second Punic War the characteristically Roman values of courage and honesty warded off the enervating effects of imperial affluence (6.57–8). His diagnosis shares the anxieties of empire manifested by Plautus, whose comedies reveal acute awareness of the social and political significance of economic inequities adumbrated in Greek New Comedy (Leigh 2004: 100). It anticipates the commentary of Sallust and Cicero on the corrupting effects of extreme wealth, the transmutation of aristocratic competition for honour into struggles over power and property, and the threat to the state from the popular perception of ill-treatment at the hands of the rich and powerful few (Sallust, *Cat.* 5–7, 10–12, *Jug.* 7, 41; Cicero, *Off.* 1.26).

Taking Greek constitution theory as representative of the Roman perspective, however, misreads Roman concerns. Implicit in constitution theory is the notion that political power, or sovereignty, rests in a single body (the one, the few, or the many). Sovereignty is conventionally defined in Aristotelian terms as that which the rulers possess and the ruled do not (as Lenin put it, 'who does what to whom'): the sign of the sovereign's rule is the making of law, particularly laws that temporarily abrogate law, such as the senatorial decree declaring a state of emergency (closely examined by Agamben 2005). As part of his critique of conventional terminology in modern political analysis, Michel Foucault argued that this definition of sovereignty is vitiated by its treatment of power as something possessed and contained, when in fact the conditions under which sovereignty is established are never free from the workings of power (Foucault 1983). He suggested that power be understood instead in terms of 'governmentality', a neologism combining government and rationality. Governmentality conveys how political associations harness the energies of the body (both individual and collective) and 'conduct its conduct' by regulating its moral values in a variety of extra-legal methods widely dispersed across cultural discourses—for example, through religion, education, medicine, and the law.

Foucault's account enables a finely tuned assessment of the treatment of power in Roman sources. Cicero is fully aware that while the legislator's aim is to sow good morals, these cannot always be written down (*Laws* 1.20); it is for this reason that the leading citizen must yield himself up as an authoritative model of virtue in action for the populace to emulate (*Rep.* 2.69). An orator by profession, Cicero sees ruling power flowing in a dialogic relation between the leading citizens and the citizen mass. Rome, which Cicero takes to be the best regime (*Rep.* 1.34), is a mixed constitution consisting of a monarchic, an aristocratic, and a popular element

(*Rep.* 1.45), where the statesman does not exercise power over subjects but advises and persuades them, appealing to communal values and making a harmony out of previously dissonant elements (*De Orat.* 1.218, 223, 2.185–6; *Rep.* 2.69). In his role as an elected magistrate, he 'acts as the face of the state' (*se gerere personam civitatis*, a precursor of early modern notions of electoral representation), upholding its honour and enforcing the law and all constitutional rights, a task he should look upon as a committed trust (*fides*, *Off.* 1.124). Here Cicero's term *fides*, 'faith' or 'trust', evokes economic and social obligations, especially those related to the social practice of patronage, as well as the tradition of civil law.

Properly arranged, the mixed republic's great virtue is its fairness (*aequabilitas*, *Rep.* 1.69), which amounts to a double guarantee: freedom from arbitrary interference to all citizens, and proper rewards to the leading men who devote their lives to guiding the state. According to his famous definition, which draws on Peripatetic and Stoic thought, the republic is 'the concern of the people (*res publica*). And a people is not just any gathering of humans that has come together in one way or another, but a gathering of a multitude allied by consensus on law and the sharing of benefits' (*Rep.* 1.39). As Elizabeth Asmis points out, Cicero's vision of the republic retains enormous disparity in the assessment of proper contributions and rewards among different social groups, but his emphasis throughout *Republic* is on unity and consensus (Asmis 2004, 2005). Key to Cicero's thinking is his Aristotelian argument that human communities come together not because of weakness or fear, which drive them to construct a basic social contract, but by the power of nature, which plants affection and sociability in the hearts of men (*Rep.* 1.41) and makes reason the fount of law (*Laws* 1.18–19).

Of course, Cicero is no liberal democrat. In a law-court speech delivered in 56 BCE that offers a uniquely broad definition of the *boni* or 'good men' on whom the prosperity of the state rests, Cicero also describes the Senate as the 'guardian, supervisor, and defender' of the republic, whose duty is 'to support the grandeur of the next lowest orders, and to protect and increase the liberty and well-being of the people' (*Sest.* 137). His notion of just rewards uncritically replicates Rome's traditional distribution of benefits to the wealthy few, and his account of justice places undue emphasis on the protection of property against tactics of economic redistribution such as taxes or land reform. His emphasis on consensus and justice, however, powerfully invokes notions of accountability and fairness, and it helps decouple power from modern assumptions of unity and totality. The criteria Cicero sets for the pursuit of glory, a topic that took centre-stage in his final years, culminating in a lost treatise, make another significant gesture toward the community's role. Cicero acknowledges that the contest for glory can lead to acts of injustice, such as those committed by Caesar and Antony (*Off.* 1.26). He argues that glory is only worth pursuing if it is useful to the community as well as the individual, and honourable—as proved by the affection, confidence, and admiration of the populace (*Off.* 2.38). As A. A. Long observes, if Cicero diverges from

Stoic orthodoxy here in his willingness to discuss the practical utility of virtue, his is a serious attempt to argue that justice is the precondition for gaining lasting glory in the eyes of the citizenry (Long 1995).

From Cicero's treatment of consensus and the role of the people, we may glimpse how Roman political thought defamiliarizes modern terms such as power, sovereignty, and domination. His notion of sovereignty is both divided and extra-legal—divided in the sense that it is a partnership (*societas*) between the Senate and the popular assembly, and extra-legal in the sense that the senatorial order exerts its will through modes of power that are uninstitutionalized. He does not represent republican political power as divided between individual citizens or between Senate and people; on the contrary, he sees power as travelling among these parties, not a matter of simple individual agency, but constituting a network of obligation, consent, and judgement (*Off.* 1.49–52). Only in the wake of autocracy's emergence and the evolution of the imperial decree, or *lex regia*, is sovereign power conceived as belonging to the emperor by delegation from the *populus*: under the Caesars, popular sovereignty and absolute rule coexist.

The point raises a methodological question for the historian of political thought: is it correct to view political ideology as a domain dominated by one or another order or class? Some consider ideology, and by extension, political philosophy, as the triumph of elite values: the sociologist Pierre Bourdieu, who uses the language of magic to describe the ways political associations come to be understood, argues that the governing order acquires 'symbolic power' by claiming to speak for the people, and that over time this manipulative claim establishes elite values and purposes as the language of politics. In his view, though the people have a role to play in the initial legitimization of the ruling order, their consent is quickly transformed into grounds for exploitation. Others defend a two-way or dialogic model for ideology, pointing out that in the absence of predatory tyranny on the part of the ruling order, the popular endorsement of authority makes for a strong legitimizing force that also has the effect of appropriating ruling discourse as the rightful property of the citizenry as a whole (Pocock 1984).

In part because of the way republican ideology evolved over time, most corresponding Roman values and concepts can be split down the middle, operating simultaneously as the repository of elite ideology and the seedbed of popular identity. The founding myth of the Roman republic as told by Livy offers a fine example of the double meaning of the key Roman notion of *libertas*, or freedom (Brunt 1988). It tells of the overthrow of tyrants by the people, whom a small number of noble families governs on the guarantee that popular liberties will be protected. For elite Romans, the myth enshrines notions of individual heroism and aristocratic leadership: Brutus, the instigator of the rebellion, is a relation of the king, and a fantastical exemplum of noble, disinterested glory. In the popular cultural imagination the myth is a reminder of political renewal, declaring not only that future tyrants may be overthrown in the same way, but that it is the duty of the citizenry to cleanse itself of tyranny. Evidence of the dynamic mutability of political myth-making is the 'popularization' of the patrician noble Brutus, whom a powerful plebeian family eventually claimed as their ancestor. Sallust, in *Jugurtha* and the fragmentary *Histories*, favourably represents tribunes who exhort the assembled people to recall the assertive claims on behalf of freedom and economic equity made by their ancestors (*Jug.* 30–2, *Hist.* 3.48.6).

It would be a serious mistake, however, to see consensus, justice, and dialogue as the sole regulators of the community in Roman political thought; equally significant in the community's constitution and evolution is the role of violent conflict. This, too, is a characteristically Roman preoccupation. In Plato or Aristotle law and reason are universals that necessarily lie outside time and its vicissitudes, including violence; but Roman writers see a constitutive relationship between violence and the establishment of political order. Sallust identifies competition as the engine of the early Republic (*Cat.* 10–11); the second book of Cicero's *Republic* and the first pentad of Livy's history carefully embed their accounts of the evolution of the electoral system and the Twelve Tables in a narrative of struggle between the patrician governing order and the plebeian masses. All these accounts grant profound significance to class and class-conflict. Historical accuracy aside (a matter taken up by Raaflaub 2005), the point, well understood by Machiavelli in his *Discourses on Livy*, is that both writers understand violent conflict as a key generative force. Cicero's (and Seneca's) stress on civic harmony is best judged as responding to the valorization of violence, not only in Rome's historical experience, but in its understanding of itself as a distinct political organization.

The cyclical nature of violence in the Roman founding myth points to another key topic: the purpose of the state. We have already seen that Cicero's republic is defined by its consensus about law. Since the source of law is reason, and reason enables men to discern the just course of action and pursue their self-interest without doing harm to others, the republic is a regime of virtue—a conclusion borne out by many passages where the good citizen is understood as a truly virtuous man and where virtue and the republic are seen as mutually interdependent (e.g. *Rep.* 4.3, 5.1), and by the concern with moral decline in Roman literature from Cato to Juvenal and beyond (Caplan 1944). Under conditions where virtue is both the sign and support of the republic, individual action is paramount.

To see the significance of individual virtue in republican thinkers, especially Cicero and Sallust, is not only to grasp their mingled sensibility of vast potential and mortal fear—the constant awareness of the proximity of virtue to vice, twinning courage and authority with the tyrannical desire to dominate—but also the way republican thinking makes the eternal imminence of moral failure an essential ingredient in the state's survival. By identifying the quest for 'the happy and honourable life' as the purpose of the state (*Rep.* 4.3), Cicero at once closes the gap between private and public interests and asserts that constant self-government is required to maintain the good government of all. The unrealizability of the project provides its own automatic forward thrust—a dynamic that may shed light on Virgil's decision to end the *Aeneid* with a moral dilemma with no obvious right answer. Understood as an open-ended process, the republic itself remains forever unrealized, an unrealizability that wards off its own dissolution (Butler 2000: 268–9). Consider the importance of the moral exemplum. Romans who write about exempla (most of the writers mentioned in this chapter) seek to make the exemplum the master term of their texts, that which governs their readers' perceptions of the past and its relationship to their current practice. But the exemplum also resists its own purpose. Should everyone be a Regulus? a Brutus? a Fabius? What are the costs of maintaining the conditions of violence and conflict that create these examples in the first place?

The Citizen

To Renaissance readers, the way Roman civic ethics pre-empted the private—captured in Cicero's declaration that the goal of the individual and the goal of the community must be identical—furnished the perfect corrective to the pious but politically passive model of life advocated by Christian thinkers from Augustine onward. The Roman preoccupation with individual virtue may be seen in the earliest works of Roman literature—Ennius' claim in his epic *Annals* that Rome rests on its men and Cato's *De Agricultura* are both political manifestos in their way—but the first serious engagements with Greek political theory emerge amid the stresses of late Republican and early Imperial politics. Roman political thought arises out of the visible failure of aristocratic ethics, where the agonistic operation of aristocratic authority comes to prevail over the ideology of commonwealth and a popular politics relying too heavily on the trope of synecdoche, where only a part of the citizenry can participate in politics. Especially in Sallust's and Tacitus' histories, the vision of a unified body politic is revealed as a fantasy by the revelatory force of corruption, but their desire for moral understanding and didactic prescription is accompanied by the suspicion of moralism's ultimate efficacy. The result is a discourse marked by nostalgia, fear, hope, and fantasy, which draws attention to the role of passion and the body in political theory and practice.

Nowhere is the interest in this issue more clear than in Roman writing about education, which should be seen as a mode of political theory. In Rome, education *is* education for citizenship. To combat the vices generated by the acquisition of empire, Cicero, followed most closely by Quintilian, designed a system of education that trains the student into a model of the ideal republic itself—a micro-model of persuasive, dialogic reason—the good orator. Cicero's good orator is only able to assume a role in government because he is able to govern himself, in a kind of rule that maps the political order directly onto the body. Just as government acts through the capacity of the governed body (in the individual and collective sense) to moderate its own behaviour, protecting the freedom of the citizenry, so the careful strategies of self-government offered by rhetorical education gain for the orator a measure of freedom. Embracing and integrating habits of both body and mind, training in eloquence teaches the student to perform himself, attaching him to his own identity, and schooling him in a regime of right opinion and authority which others will recognize and imitate (Foucault 1983: 212). Quintilian's detailed twelve-book *Institutio Oratoria*, in particular, explores the ways in which the good Roman may be created—not only as a politician or a pleader in the law-court, but as a reader, a physical body in space, a subject highly attuned to the look of his body and the message it broadcasts in the circuitries of social interaction. Again, we see the attention Roman writers lavish on the notion of power—including the disciplines of education—as generative, producing subjects rather than containing or repressing them. To take a page from the Marxist Louis Althusser, Roman ideology produces agents whose freedom is born out of and reproduced through practices of unfreedom; or to put it another way, their unfreedom is a function of the systems, dispositions, and practices that define their subjectivity (and did so even before they were born). The rhetoricians turn their readers' attention to the mutual constitution of the political state and its subjects: they show how political beliefs take worldly shape.

The Empire

Cicero's account of justice in *De Officiis* posits that it is contrary to nature for someone to increase his own good at the cost of another's. The bonds of human association (*societas*) unravel under the pressure of such an act, just as if a body part spontaneously decided to absorb the strength of the adjacent part (3.21–2). The analogy recalls the parable eloquently told by the patrician Menenius Agrippa to the plebeians who withdrew from Rome early in its history to protest oppressive debt laws, where the Senate, the belly of the body, demands nourishment so that it in turn can nourish the rest of the body (Livy 2.32). Cicero's point is that the law of nature, 'which is the law of nations' (*ius gentium*, by which he means universal law), and the laws of particular peoples condemn the violation of human fellowship for the sake of self-interest. Individual men live well when they obey reason, which incorporates this principle of justice (*Off.* 3.23). Understanding society as the aggregate of individual interests, Cicero suggests that everyone should identify his good with that of the communal good. But he does not conclude from this that goods should be distributed equally; on the contrary, the good he explicitly identifies as universally shared is the security of property. Before we read him as a modern libertarian or radical conservative, however, we should remember that when Cicero rails against the government interference with personal property that is involved with redistribution, he is not advocating total non-interference. On the contrary, he encourages strong social values of benevolence that act almost with the power of laws. Hence his approval of the private benevolence of Roman nobles in Rome's early history (*De Rep.* 2.26, 33, 38) and his powerful critique of the lust for wealth. If Cicero does not fully confront the threat unequal property distribution poses to the republic, unlike Sallust or Tacitus, who see this clearly (*Jug.* 7.6; *Ann.* 1.2), it is because his notion of *libertas* forecloses enforced benevolence. Gift-giving, he believes, entails payback, and when the receiver cannot pay back what he receives, he is left in a permanent condition of obligation which destroys his autonomy (*Off.* 1.42).

Yet Cicero takes pains to stress that those who claim the duties incurred by the obligation of justice apply only within national borders 'wreck the communal association of human kind' (*Off.* 3.28). His global perspective leads him to generate an influential theory of just war: war must be pursued only for the sake of avenging an injury or in self-defence; it must be undertaken only after redress has been diplomatically sought; it must be formally declared (*Rep.* 2.31, 3.35; *Off.* 1.36). Seneca develops this line of thinking further, declaring that the common bonds of humanity are measured not by borders but 'by the sun' (*De Otio*). Their appropriation of Stoic thinking is given new life in the high Empire, when Greek sophists like Aelius Aristides justify the success of the Roman Empire by representing it as making possible 'democracy for the whole world' (*On Rome* 60).

Conclusion

It is one of the ironies of the history of Roman political thought that what has most troubled modern thinkers about it was the very thing that tends first to inspire them—Roman civic virtue, or more precisely, the belief that the common good is guaranteed not by law alone but by the virtuous behaviour of citizens who consistently put the interests of the collective ahead of their own. In the economic and cultural efflorescence of early modern society, when the opportunities for achieving recognition and riches expanded well beyond traditional notions of public service, the Romans' close identification between citizen and collective began to look like a kind of slavery. What kind of freedom is this, theorists asked, when the citizen, viewing himself as property and guarantor of the state, must shape his character and aspirations accordingly? What of his private ends (Constant 1819/1988)? And how may a modern state institutionalize virtue without eviscerating civil rights? If men like John Adams and James Madison were roused by Roman republican thinkers to condemn monarchy as tyranny and to praise mixed government, they ended their lives lamenting the death of republicanism in the United States, where (they believed) private interests had definitively triumphed over collective virtue and the values of the *vir civilis*. 'The Spirit of Commerce, Madam, which even insinuates itself into Families,' John Adams wrote to Mercy Warren in 1776, 'is much to be feared is incompatible with that purity of Heart and Greatness of soul which is necessary for an happy Republic' (1917: 222–3). In France matters took a different, dangerous turn. As the revolutionaries exhorted the citizens to develop a sense of self (*égoïsme*) that would 'conjoin its happiness with the happiness of all, that attaches its own glory to that of the *patrie*', as Robespierre did in 1794, they fused the classical republican commitment to virtue into a new vision of permanent transformative revolution—transmuting Roman ideology into the moralizing justification for state terror (Baker 1985).

Yet political conditions in Rome—its habits of imperial exploitation, its simultaneous, contradictory espousal of liberty and toleration of severe economic inequity, its financial and psychological investment in war, and its longing, expressed in tones of both nostalgic melancholy and bitter satire, for an unachievable, unfinalizable state of virtue—prove the enduring relevance of its political ideas.

References

Adams, John (1917). *The Warren–Adams Letters: Being Chiefly a Correspondence Between John Adams, Samuel Adams, and James Warren*: Vol. 1. *1743–1777*. Boston: Massachusetts Historical Society.

Agamben, Giorgio (2005). *State of Exception*. Chicago: University of Chicago Press.

Arendt, Hannah (1991). *On Revolution*. New York: Penguin.

Asmis, Elizabeth (2004). 'The state as a partnership: Cicero's definition of *res publica* in his work on the state.' *History of Political Thought*, 25: 569–99.

—— (2005). 'A new kind of model: Cicero's Roman constitution in *De Republica*.' *American Journal of Philology*, 126: 377–416.

Baker, Keith (1985). 'Memory and practice: politics and the representation of the past in eighteenth-century France.' *Representations*, 11: 134–64.

Balot, Ryan (2006). *Greek Political Thought*. Oxford: Blackwell.

Bauman, Zygmunt (2000). *Liquid Modernity*. Cambridge: Polity Press.

Brown, Wendy (2006). 'Power after Foucault.' In John S. Dryzek, Bonnie Honig, and Anne Phillips (eds.), *The Oxford Handbook of Political Theory*, 65–84. Oxford: Oxford University Press.

Brunt, P. A. (1988). 'Libertas.' In *The Fall of the Roman Republic and Related Essays*. Oxford: Oxford University Press.

Butler, Judith (2000). 'Dynamic conclusions.' In Judith Butler, Ernesto Laclau, and Slavoj Zizek (eds.), *Contingency, Hegemony, Universality: Contemporary Dialogues on the Left*, 263–80. London: Verso.

Caplan, Harry (1944). 'The decay of eloquence at Rome in the first century.' In Herbert A. Wichlens (ed.), *Studies in Speech and Drama in Honor of Alexander M. Drummond*, 295–325. Ithaca, NY: Cornell University Press.

Cartledge, Paul (1996). 'Comparatively equal.' In Ober and Hedrick 1996: 175–85.

Cavarero, Adriana (2002). 'Politicizing theory.' *Political Theory*, 30: 506–32.

Connolly, Joy (2007). *The State of Speech: Rhetoric and Political Thought in Ancient Rome*. Princeton: Princeton University Press.

Constant, Benjamin (1819/1988). 'The liberty of the ancients compared with that of the moderns.' In *Political Writings*, ed. Biancamaria Fontana, 309–28. Cambridge: Cambridge University Press.

Dench, Emma (2005). *Romulus' Asylum: Roman Identities from the Age of Alexander to the Age of Hadrian*. Oxford: Oxford University Press.

Ferrary, Jean-Louis (1995). 'The statesman and the law in the political philosophy of Cicero.' In Laks and Schofield 1995: 48–73.

Foucault, Michel (1983). 'The subject and power.' In H. Dreyfus and P. Rabinow (eds.), *Beyond Structuralism and Hermeneutics*, 208–26. Chicago: University of Chicago Press.

Gelzer, Matthias (1912). *Die Nobilität der römischen Republik*. Revised edn. Stuttgart, 1983.

Gleason, Maud (1995). *Making Men: Sophists and Self-presentation in Ancient Rome*. Princeton: Princeton University Press.

Laks, André and Malcolm Schofield (eds.) (1995). *Justice and Generosity: Studies in Hellenistic Social and Political Philosophy*. Cambridge: Cambridge University Press.

Leigh, Matthew (2004). *Comedy and the Rise of Rome*. Oxford: Oxford University Press.

Lintott, Andrew (1999). *The Constitution of the Roman Republic*. Oxford: Oxford University Press.

Long, A. A. (1995). 'Cicero's politics in *De Officiis*.' In Laks and Schofield 1995: 213–40.

Manville, Philip Brook (1994). 'Toward a new paradigm of Athenian citizenship.' In A. Boegehold and A. Scafuro (eds.), *Athenian Identity and Civic Ideology*, 21–33. Baltimore: Johns Hopkins University Press.

Millar, Fergus (1998). *The Crowd in Rome in the Late Republic*. Ann Arbor, Mich.: University of Michigan Press.

Morris, Ian (1996). 'The strong principle of equality and the archaic origins of Greek democracy.' In Ober and Hedrick 1996: 19–48.

Morstein-Marx, Robert (2004). *Mass Oratory and Political Power in the Roman Republic*. Cambridge: Cambridge University Press.

Niebuhr, Barthold Georg (1812). *Römische Geschichte*. Berlin.

Nussbaum, Martha C. (2000). 'Duties of justice, duties of material aid: Cicero's problematic legacy.' *Journal of Political Philosophy*, 8/2: 176–206.

—— (2001). 'Duties of justice, duties of material aid: Cicero's problematic legacy.' *Journal of Political Philosophy*, 8: 176–202.

OBER, JOSIAH (1998). *Political Dissent in Democratic Athens: Intellectual Critics of Popular Rule*. Princeton: Princeton University Press.

—— and CHARLES HEDRICK (eds.) (1996). *Demokratia*. Princeton: Princeton University Press.

PATTON, PAUL (2006). 'After the linguistic turn: post-structuralist and liberal pragmatist political theory.' In John S. Dryzek, Bonnie Honig, and Anne Phillips (eds.), *The Oxford Handbook of Political Theory*. Oxford: Oxford University Press.

POCOCK, J. G. A. (1984). 'Verbalizing a Political Act: Toward a Politics of Speech.' In Michael J. Shapiro (ed.), *Language and Politics*, 25–43. New York: NYU Press.

RAAFLAUB, KURT (2005). 'The conflict of the orders in archaic Rome.' In id. (ed.), *Social Struggles in Archaic Rome*, 1–46. London: Blackwell.

SCHOFIELD, MALCOLM (1995). 'Cicero's definition of *res publica*.' In J. G. F. Powell (ed.), *Cicero the Philosopher*. Oxford: Oxford University Press.

SYME, RONALD (1939). *The Roman Revolution*. Oxford: Oxford University Press.

CHAPTER 46

HELLENISM

TIM WHITMARSH

THERE was never a time when Greece was not on Rome's horizon. Southern Italy and Sicily began to be colonized in the eighth century BCE, the period to which Varro famously dated the city's foundation. By the seventh century Greek influence was on Rome's very doorstep. The Etruscans, occupying the territory to the north of the city (and providing the earliest Roman kings and prophets), had partially assimilated Greek culture, to the extent of using a form of their script. The nascent Roman state was bathed in Greek influence: its language, religion, and mythology were fundamentally shaped by their neighbours across the Adriatic. The traffic of cultural awareness, however, mostly travelled in one direction. Certainly, there are hints in the earliest Greek poetry of a dim knowledge of Rome and its environs: Hesiod's (seventh-century?) *Theogony* identifies Latinus, ruler of the 'Tyrrhenians' (a loose designation), as one of the sons of Circe and Odysseus (1011–16). (The Latins (Romans) and the Etruscans have been conflated here. Line 1014 is an interpolation.) In these early days, however, the Mediterranean was dominated—militarily, politically, and culturally—by Greeks and Phoenicians; the infant state of Rome, by contrast, barely registered on the Greek radar. It was only the self-serving myth-making of later generations, seeking to explain Rome's rise to dominance, that made Italy a preferred retirement home for veterans of the Trojan War and the Argonautic adventures (Erskine 2001, and more generally Wiseman 2004: 16–24), and made Roman king Numa a pupil of the Greek philosopher Pythagoras (Gruen 1990: 158–70).

By the third century BCE, however, the situation was very different. In 279 the Romans were defeated by Pyrrhus of Epirus at Ausculum: but this victory—the famous Pyrrhic victory, which cost the Epirotes dearly—was the last Greek military success of note against the Romans. Over the next 150 years Rome gained a strong grip over the Mediterranean, with decisive wars against both the Punic civilization in the West (centred on Carthage) and the Hellenistic successor kingdoms in the East (notably the Macedonians and Seleucids). In 146 the Achaean confederacy, centred in mainland Greece, was smashed by the Roman consul Mummius, and the city of Corinth razed to the ground. This left the Ptolemies, based in Alexandria, as the last major Greek military power: the forces of their last queen, Cleopatra VII, were finally defeated by Octavian at Actium in 31 BCE. This ultimately led to the creation of a single province covering the entirety of the Greek mainland, which the Romans designated by the antique Greek name of Achaea. Over the final three centuries before the Common Era, Rome gained a military, political, and economic precedence over Greece that it retained throughout antiquity.

From the third century BCE onwards increasing numbers of Greeks appeared in Rome, either as slaves of war, refugees, or economic migrants. The tragic reversal of fortune must have struck the city's inhabitants forcibly. Greek influence and power was crumbling before their eyes; this once-dominant people was now being humbled before the new leaders of the Mediterranean. The response to this was, however, at first sight startling and paradoxical. Rather than consign their memory to oblivion—as they had done, for example, to the Carthaginians—Romans chose, albeit not in unison, to lard the Greeks' civilization with deferential prestige. This phenomenon is what we mean by the phrase 'Roman Hellenism': certain Romans, at certain points in history, felt it desirable or even necessary to articulate their identity as Romans by advertising their commitment to Greek values—that is, by 'Hellenizing'. This was a phenomenon that endured over centuries, and across the full demographic range of Rome: the popular audiences who went to see Greek plays in translation in the second century BCE; the Roman aristocrats who hired Greek educators, set up statues in the *atria* of their houses, and listened to recitations; and the second-century CE emperors Hadrian, Antoninus Pius, and Marcus Aurelius, who adopted Greek values—variously, beards, boyfriends, and philosophy—in a peaceful, prosperous era culminating in what one later historian called the golden age of Roman imperial rule (Cassius Dio 71.36.4). It is this tension between Rome's military and political dominance over Greece and her apparent cultural submission, particularly in the formative first three centuries BCE, that forms the subject of this chapter.

Hellenism and the Rise of Empire

In order to unpick the reasons for this phenomenon, we should consider how the Roman Empire functioned. The creation of a pan-Mediterranean Roman empire was not, apparently, planned strategically (Gruen 1984), but it was certainly artfully put into practice. Although the most decisive and impressive events were the military conquests, in fact most annexation occurred through the subtler arts of diplomacy. A network of unequal treaties and patron–client relationships consolidated Rome's dominance without the need for costly and dangerous armies. The threat of military muscle was always there, but the instinctual tactic of Roman imperialism was to try to co-opt local elites by offering incentives to individuals and protection to the state. In terms of Roman administration, the empire consisted of a series of provinces, each with its own governor (and often one or more legions). In local-political terms, however, many cities of the Greek East at any rate were allowed to run their own affairs as before, with the civic elites (often buoyed by Roman support) occupying the positions of authority.

The eastern Mediterranean and its hinterland was a more or less Hellenized world, the bequest of the conquests of Alexander the Great. Rome's imperial strategy of incorporating provinces rather than assimilating them meant that the regent apparatus of the Hellenistic kingdoms was taken over rather than dismantled: most notably, the Romans took over the Hellenistic practice of fostering the worship of living rulers (Price 1984), a phenomenon that would have been abhorrent in Rome itself. Rome also learned from the East the aesthetics of power: monumental building, statuary, and coinage were adopted during the first three centuries BCE, and came to play a central role in the Roman language of power (see especially Zanker 1988). As important as the visible, external discourse of power was Greece's bequest of the concept of benevolent empire, rooted in the thought of such theorists as the fourth-century Athenian Isocrates. As Romans like Cicero explicitly acknowledged, it was to Greece that they owed their own understanding of the imperial mission to spread *humanitas*, or 'liberal values', over the world (*To his Brother Quintus* 1.1.27; see Woolf 1994: 118–25).

Knowledge of the Greek language was important too, since Latin was rarely spoken in the East. Greek was used for official inscriptions and announcements. Greek-speakers resented Romans who did not speak their language. An episode in *Lucius, or the Ass*, a magic-realist novel attributed to the Greco-Syrian satirist Lucian (second century CE) and set in northern Greece, makes the point: a thuggish Roman soldier speaks to an uncomprehending gardener in Latin, and attacks him when he receives no reply (44). The same language problems beset Romans further up the political ladder. In Philostratus' *Life of Apollonius of Tyana*, composed in the third century CE but set in the first, the eponymous sage advises the emperor Vespasian to take care with provincial governors, 'so that Greek-speakers rule Greeks, and Latin-speakers rule those who share their language and outlook. I will tell you where I got this idea. At the time I was staying in the Peloponnese, Greece was ruled by a man ignorant of Greek customs, and the Greeks for their part did not understand him at all' (5.36.5; tr. C. P. Jones).

A ruler of Greeks who does not speak Greek, then, is likely to run into trouble. This, of course, is only one perspective, and Philostratus' agenda is far from neutral: his biography of the Greek holy man is a vehicle for his own ideas about the cultural importance of Greece. The need for Roman rulers to communicate in the East was, however, real enough. Indeed, in the vast territory governed by Rome from the first century BCE onwards, Greek-speakers vastly outnumbered Latin-speakers. The consequences of this are spelled out by Cicero, in a speech defending the Greek poet Archias against the charge that he does not deserve his Roman citizenship:

> if anyone thinks that the public glory won from Greek verse is less than that from Latin, he is entirely in the wrong. Greek literature is read in nearly every nation, but Latin only within its own boundaries, and those (we must grant) are narrow. Seeing, therefore, that the actions that we have perpetuated are delimited only by the regions of the whole earth, we ought to desire that wherever the missiles from our hands have entered, our glory and fame should also penetrate. (*In Defence of Archias the Poet* 23)

In Cicero's mind, only communication in Greek can truly express the achievements of Rome, because Greek is much closer than Latin to being the *lingua franca* of the empire. The extravagant metaphor of the final sentence cited above brings vividly to life the relationship that he envisages between the Greek language and Roman Empire. Roman interactions with the Greek East created a rich cultural dialogue, which transformed both sides as they worked to accommodate the other (Ferrary 1988).

Acquaintance with Greek and Greek culture, then, served Rome's pragmatic need to govern the empire. What is more, Greek intellectuals could be corralled into the service of the imperial project. Geographers and ethnographers could help with foreign campaigns; doctors could help both in the city and on campaign; technical experts could advise on engineering projects, hydraulics, and siege machinery.

The Civilizing Narrative

In one sense, then, the Roman fondness for Greek culture was rooted in a practical concern with managing a vast empire. Yet this does not in itself explain why Hellenism became attractive to Romans, rather than a mere necessity. The Romans themselves liked to explain their own receptivity in terms of what we might style the 'civilizing narrative': the original Romans, this runs, had been feral rustics, and only the conquest of the East brought civilization. This topos can be found throughout Roman literature. An early example comes from the second-century

BCE poet Porcius Licinus, who claims that during the Second Punic War 'the Muse with winged step came among the savage, warlike people of Romulus' (fr. 1). In the first century BCE Cicero writes that, 'in learning and every literary genre Greece used to surpass us—it was easy to beat us when we were not competing!' (*Tusculan Disputations* 1.3). In the early first century CE Ovid writes of the time when 'Greece had not yet transmitted her conquered arts to her victors' (*Fasti* 3.101–2).

From one perspective, indeed, the civilizing narrative has some truth to it. Rome's cultural climate changed radically over the course of the Republic. From the late fourth century BCE, numbers of Romans took Greek names (*cognomina*). By the third century the Sibylline Books, written in Greek, had become a central part of Roman religious culture, and the cult surrounding them was performed 'in the Greek tradition' (*graeco ritu*: Gruen 1993: 227–30; Scheid 1995). These Greek religious trappings were an almost entirely Roman invention, but nonetheless significant for that: the cult 'could be and later was presented as Greek' (Scheid 1995: 25–6, at 26). Minted coinage in the Greek fashion was also a third-century innovation. The visual arts too were transformed. The sack of the Sicilian city of Syracuse in 211 BCE by Claudius Marcellus led to the mass relocation of Greek statuary and paintings to Rome. Much myth surrounds this event (see further below), but the effects seem real enough. By the first century, Greek-style statuary (whether in the form of originals or copies) was *de rigueur* in public spaces and aristocratic households, and Roman nobles were commonly being portrayed in statues and busts. The style, which scholars call 'veristic' (i.e. 'realistic'), represents the subjects as grimly austere, as if the costs of investment in the Hellenizing discourse of portraiture—with all the attendant associations of luxury, which we shall discuss shortly—needed to be defrayed by the adoption of an unmistakeably Roman severity. Domestic and civic architecture were also transformed over the Republican period, as the distinctive Roman peristyle house, stone temples, and civic buildings were adapted from Greek models.

It is in the realm of literature, however, that the debates over the civilizing narrative can be best traced. In the mid-third century a Greek freedman from Tarentum called Livius Andronicus translated (or, more accurately, adapted into Latin) and produced certain originally Greek plays. Among other Hellenizing compositions, he also rendered Homer's *Odyssey* into Latin. Later Romans credited Livius with the 'invention' of Latin literature (see esp. Cicero, *Brutus* 72–3), a point to which we shall return. Within a century, Ennius (239–169 BCE) had composed his tragedies and *Annals* (the latter in Greek-style hexameters), and Plautus (d. 184), Terence (*c.*190–159), and others their comedies, creative adaptations from Greek New Comedy, but with their own powerful momentum carrying their influence as far afield as Shakespeare, Molière, and Frankie Howerd. Other Hellenizing poets include Naevius (*fl.* mid.-3rd cent. BCE), Pacuvius (220–?130), and Accius (b. 170). By the second century, moreover, numbers of Greek philosophers could be found at Rome educating the wealthy and their children: the most famous example is

Panaetius (*c.*185–109 BCE), the Rhodian Stoic who was feted by Scipio Aemilianus and later influential on Cicero. Dropping Greek phrases into Latin discussion (a phenomenon that linguists call 'code-switching') became a sign of sophistication (Swain 2002). By the end of the first century BCE the intellectual menu at Rome was arguably as rich and varied as anywhere in the world (Rawson 1985: esp. 3–18). Even a resident Greek could be amazed by the resources on offer (Diodorus of Sicily 1.4.3–4).

What Greek culture offered was not just cultural window-dressing for the rich (although, as we shall see presently, there was an element of that), but also a genuine set of cultural resources that ranged from sophistication—discernible in, for example, a close attention to sculptural form, music, metre, language, and literary self-reflexivity—to a ready-made visual, musical, and verbal language for both expressing and evaluating the human self. Ennius' tragedies, to take one example, provided Roman audiences with what we may assume to have been an entirely new way of conceptualizing the human person, although the loss of all pre-Ennian Latin dramatic text makes it impossible to calibrate such assumptions. It is a fair bet that no earlier Roman poet ever described the diminution of madness in terms like these: 'the feelings of my heart do not chime at all with those of my eyes' (Ennius, *Alcmaeon* fr. 37 Warmington). The sentence drips with Euripidean subtlety, a blend of the sophistic, the medical, and the psychological.

Not all of this Hellenizing was entirely reverential. Roman comedy and tragedy of this period is set among Greeks, a fact the significance of which is hard to gauge. Is it simply a residual reminder of the Greek provenance of the original material? A mark of respect for the 'civilizing' nation? Or perhaps a way of shielding the Roman audience from too close an identification with morally risqué content? In support of the last interpretation, we could certainly note that Greeks are closely associated in comedy with dodgy behaviour: 'playing the Greek' is always aligned with excess and debauchery (e.g. Plautus, *Bacchides* 742–3, 812–13; further references at Gruen 1993: 262). Nevertheless, Hellenism is also associated with cultural elitism: the use of Greek references and loan-words plays to at least part of the audience's sense of themselves as educated (Gruen 1993: 232). The Greek setting is best interpreted as contributing to what we might call, borrowing a phrase from Froma Zeitlin (1986), a 'theatre of the other', fostering the audience's self-consciousness as a group distinct from those they are watching, and also of the relevance of the material to their own interests.

The first century BCE saw further developments. In the field of philosophy, we find Lucretius (*c.*94–55) rendering Epicurean doctrine in polished Latin hexameters, a task he describes (with a mixture of humility and self-aggrandisement) as 'difficult . . . on account of the poverty of the language and the newness of my subject matter' (1.136–9). The most important figure, however, is Cicero (106–43), whose various works in the fields particularly of ethics and political philosophy occupied a central place in the philosophical canon until the late Renaissance (see in general Striker 1995, and esp. Powell ed. 1995). To one of these crucial works, the *Tusculan Disputations*, we shall return presently. Cicero also translated, in two sections, the Hellenistic Aratus' poem on astronomy (the first of four Latin translations that we know of).

The other major Hellenizing force, in the literary world at any rate, was the wave of poets whom scholars like to label, following the lead of Cicero (*Orator* 161; *Tusculan Disputations* 3.45), the 'new poets' or 'neoterics' (a Greek word, implying both innovation and subversion). These adopted an aesthetic stance rooted in Hellenistic Alexandria, emphasizing the small-scale and subtle over the grand and bombastic, for their intensely personal and intensely Roman poetry about adulterous love, sex, and drink. The earliest extant neoteric—notwithstanding Cicero himself, who in his youth wrote elegant Greek-style poems, albeit more conservative in theme (Clausen 1986)—was Catullus (87–?54). Catullus' Hellenism is evident in the frequent use of Greek allusions and models, sometimes extending to translation: Poem 51 is a version of Sappho's most famous love poem (unceremoniously known as fragment 31), while Poem 66 renders Callimachus' *Lock of Berenice*. His risqué subject-matter included references to, among other things, pederasty, often stereotyped elsewhere as Greek.

Later neoterics settled on the metrical form of the elegiac couplet, again a characteristically Greek, indeed Alexandrian, form. Gallus (b. *c.*69 BCE), whose output only survives in a single fragment, was an acquaintance of the Greek poet and polymath Parthenius, whose prose *Love Stories* (written in Greek) are explicitly designed for Gallus to versify. Better known are Propertius (b. *c.*50 BCE)—the self-styled 'Roman Callimachus' (4.1.64)—Tibullus (b. *c.*50 BCE), and Ovid (43 BCE–17 CE). Fascinatingly, we also have the work of a neoteric woman poet, Sulpicia (dates unknown), six of whose poems survive in the corpus of Tibullus. The names given to the poets' love-objects are also Greek: Catullus' Lesbia, Gallus' Lycoris, Propertius' Cynthia, Sulpicia's Cerinthus, Tibullus' Delia, Ovid's Corinna. The names may also have been shared with some of the poetry collections. Certainly, there is in many cases a close relationship between beloved and the poetic text itself: the most obvious example is Catullus' Lesbia, a clear allusion to Sappho of Lesbos (see further Wyke 2002: 11–77).

In the late first century BCE two of history's greatest poets fashioned their eminently Roman works in dialogue with Greek models. The poems of Horace (65–8 BCE) are all focused on Rome. Hellenism is omnipresent, if varying in intensity. In the *Satires* and *Epistles* Greek models are relatively suppressed, albeit not entirely. The *Epodes*, however, are more obviously modelled on the aggressive iambics of Archilochus of Paros and to a lesser extent Callimachus; Horace would later claim to have 'first displayed Parian iambi to Latium, following the metres and spirit of Archilochus' (*Epistle* 1.19.23–5). In his most famous poems, the *Odes*, he presents himself explicitly as an emulator of Greek prototypes. The first *Ode* in the collection refers programmatically to the 'Lesbian lyre' (1.1.34), an allusion to the famous Greek poets Alcaeus and Sappho (see also 1.26.9–12, 1.32.5, 3.30.13–14, 4.3.11–12, 4.6.35). The varied metres he adopts ('Sapphics', 'Alcaics', 'Asclepiadeans', etc.) are also markers of intertextuality with Greek poets. Pindar is another explicitly identified model (4.2.1–8).

The works of Virgil (70–19 BCE), a friend of Gallus, also engage directly with Greek text. His earliest work, the *Eclogues*, distils the diverse output of the third-century Alexandrian poet Theocritus into a coherent pastoralism, now relocated to contemporary Italy. The emphasis upon the local landscape also permeates his *Georgics*, which combines emulation of the agricultural section of the seventh-century *Works and Days* by Hesiod of Ascra (and his numerous Alexandrian imitators) with praise of the bounty of Italian soil. As the poet himself writes, 'I sing an Ascraean song through the towns of Rome' (2.176). The importance, meanwhile, of the Homeric corpus to Virgil's most famous poem, the *Aeneid*, scarcely needs stating. In transforming the Greek stories of victory over Trojans into a vision of a neo-Trojan 'empire without end' (1.279), Virgil is also combining the political message that Rome has usurped Greece's position as the dominant force in the Mediterranean with a poetic claim on Rome's behalf to have absorbed and refashioned the founding narrative of Greek culture.

For all that it had a firm grip on Roman thought, and indeed practice, however, the 'civilizing narrative' is fundamentally an ideological construction. Of course Hellenism changed things, and of course there were all sorts of technical innovations; but any suggestion, implicit or explicit, that Hellenism was coterminous with civilization is problematic. The idea that third-century Rome, a prosperous and expanding state with a high level of technical accomplishment, needed 'civilizing' is misleading. It is, moreover, highly unlikely that anyone of the third-century Hellenizers thought of their peers as a coarse, rustic population. If Rome had ever been 'uncivilized', the memory of that time was irrevocably lost among the legendary thickets of suckling she-wolves and hilltop asyla. Finally, we can quickly see that the civilizing narrative is actually founded upon a single repeated trope, the idea of a 'first introducer' of a cultural feature from Greece to Rome: Livius Andronicus brings literature, Marcellus art, Ennius the hexameter, Lucretius Epicureanism, Cicero Stoicism, Propertius Callimachus, Horace lyric poetry, and so forth. Each of these claims can be contradicted, in that awareness of the Greek form (and in some cases, for example 'literature' and 'art', indigenous equivalents) can be demonstrated for an earlier period.

Indeed, all civilizing narratives must have an ideological dimension, in that they justify the changes that have occurred as ineluctable progress towards a better end. They have a particular appeal to imperialist states, seeking to repackage rapacity and gain as a positive benefit for the conquered people. The Romans justified their own conquests of 'barbarian' tribes in terms of the spreading of peace and human values (*humanitas*) and the creation of monuments and amenities (Woolf 1998: 1–23). Victorian British imperialists justified their conquests by introducing into

India roads, railways, telegraph systems, education, and banking, and more generally by promising to introduce 'orientals' to modern European standards of life (Saïd 1995: 31–7). Similarly, the American invasion of Iraq was justified with the promise to the Iraqis of political freedom and democracy. What is extraordinary about Roman Hellenism, however, is the reversal of the usual practice: the Romans were not claiming to impose their own 'superior' culture on the uncivilized Greeks, but taking on board the culture of the conquered people. Why was this?

The Ambiguities of Hellenism

The first point to note is that Rome's civilizing narrative was not straightforwardly one of cultural progress. Let us recall that many of Rome's founding myths, to some of which we have already alluded, marked her people as semi-civilized: Romulus and Remus suckled by a she-wolf, the population of the early city with criminals rescued from a hilltop sanctuary, the rape of the Sabine women. Such myths nurtured Rome's self-image as a warrior state.

The idea of decline from a primordial state of virtue is tightly woven into Rome's national mythology. The preface to Livy's monumental history, composed under Augustus, describes the process that followed Rome's acquisition of an empire (*imperium*): 'the gradual collapse of discipline, a subsidence as it were of morals... then they slipped more and more, and then began to move with headlong impetus, until we have reached the present times, in which we can endure neither our vices nor their cure' (preface 9). Virgil associates primeval Italy with the golden age, via the tradition that Saturn was an Italian king (*Eclogue* 4.6; cf. *Georgics* 1.118–46, *Aeneid* 8.314–27). A large part of Augustus' rhetorical aim was to present himself as restoring this state of pristine piety: 'By new laws passed on my proposal I brought back into use many exemplary practices of our ancestors which were disappearing in our time' (*Achievements of the Divine Augustus* 8.5). The return of the golden age was one of the promises the founder of the Principate made to his subjects, particularly through the staging of the 'secular' (i.e. marking a new era) games of 17 BCE, celebrated in a famous poem of Horace's (see, however, the cautions of Barker 1996).

For some Romans it was particularly the conquest of Greece, and the consequent introduction of 'luxury', that impelled the decline. These ideas tend to cluster most around the discourse of art, and in particular the Roman habit of expropriating it after conquering Greek states (see Pollitt 1978; Beard and Henderson 2001: 89–91). The most significant events are Marcellus' expugnation of Syracuse in 211 BCE, Aemilius Paullus' victories against Perseus of Macedon in 168 BCE, Mummius' sack of Corinth in 146 BCE, and Sulla's campaigns in Greece and Asia Minor in the early first century BCE. One source tells us that the artistic spoils brought back by Aemilius Paullus were so numerous that a whole day was set aside for them to be paraded through the city, along with the prisoners: 250 wagons were called for, a single day was scarcely long enough (Plutarch, *Aemilius Paullus* 32). The moral critique of this process began early. In an extraordinary passage which is worth quoting at length, Polybius (*c.*200–115 BCE), a Greek historian based in Rome, delivers his judgement on Marcellus' actions in Syracuse:

> The Romans, then, decided to transfer these things to their own city and to leave nothing behind. Whether they were right in doing so, and consulted their true interests or the reverse, is a matter admitting of much discussion; but I think the balance of argument is in favour of believing it to have been wrong then, and wrong now. If such had been the works by which they had exalted their country, it is clear that there would have been some reason in transferring thither the things by which they had become great. But the fact was that, while leading lives of the greatest simplicity themselves, as far as possible removed from the luxury and extravagance which these things imply, they yet conquered the men who had always possessed them in the greatest abundance and of the finest quality. Could there have been a greater mistake than theirs? Surely it would be an incontestable error for a people to abandon the habits of the conquerors and adopt those of the conquered; and at the same time involve itself in that jealousy which is the most dangerous concomitant of excessive prosperity. For the looker-on never congratulates those who take what belongs to others, without a feeling of jealousy mingling with his pity for the losers.
>
> (9.10; tr. E. S. Shuckburgh)

Polybius' critique operates at a number of levels. Unlike later Greeks, who tend to focus upon the sacrilege done to cult sites and the affront to the Greek heritage, he assumes—on the surface at least—the perspective of the imperial power and focuses upon the damage done to Rome, in terms of both its national morality and its standing in the eyes of 'lookers-on' (presumably Rome's potential competitors and allies, as well as her imperial subjects). There are two points to underline. First, Polybius makes use of the now familiar Roman discourse of the city's moral decline from a state of primeval simplicity, hitching it to his account of artistic Hellenization. Second, he implicitly invokes the idea that imperial conquest should, normatively, create a hierarchy between victor and vanquished. In this case, that hierarchy has been upset: Rome's 'incontestable error' is to 'abandon the habits of the conquerors and adopt those of the conquered'. This is a point to which we shall return.

Subsequent Latin literature is full of such jeremiads over the deleterious effects of Greek art and culture (see e.g. Sallust, *Catiline* 11; Cicero, *Against Verres* 2.4). I want to turn now, however, to the most celebrated luxury-hating, anti-Hellene of the Republican period, namely Cato the Censor (234–149 BCE; Astin 1978). Cato's stance towards Greece in general was in fact rather inconsistent—his writings, notably, are saturated with Greek intellectual influence (see Gruen 1993: 52–83, with caution)—but he certainly became a figurehead for those who would link the

Roman adoption of Greek habits with their moral decline into luxury. According to Plutarch, he 'besmirched all Greek culture and learning', prophesying that 'Romans would destroy their state by gorging themselves with Greek letters', and warning his son away from doctors, who he believed were out to destroy all non-Greeks (*Cato* 23).

Cato's turbid fervour was not, of course, universally shared; indeed, his fame rested precisely upon his extremism. Older generations of scholars tended to see a division between Catonians on the one hand and Hellenophile 'connoisseurs' on the other, whom they sometimes liked to cluster around the figure of Scipio Aemilianus. This picture of two opposing camps of card-carrying pro- and anti-Hellenes is undeniably too simplistic: we should, rather, be thinking in terms of different strategies for managing essentially the same phenomenon, viz. Rome's imperial dominance over Greece (Gruen 1993: 52–83, 223–71).

Nevertheless, whatever his own motives, and whatever the complexities of second-century imperial politics, Cato did in time come to signify a conservative reaction to Hellenism, in opposition to which a counter-movement developed. The dominant literary expression of this comes in the love poetry of the first century BCE. 'Let us live and love,' writes Catullus, 'and value all the mutterings of the old grouches (*severi*) at one *as* [a low-value coin]' (5.1–3). The *severi*—an undefined group of Catoesque straw men—are a repeated target of the neoterics. 'Begone, far away, ye grouches!' proclaims Ovid, parodying a formula from mystic initiation rites (*Love Poems* 2.1.3; cf. also e.g. Propertius 2.34.23). Where others decried the 'softness' (*mollitia*) of the Greek lifestyle (e.g. Sallust, *Catiline* 11.5; Silius, *Punica* 12.31–2), the neoterics reclaim the term as a slogan, an example of the familiar process (compare the modern 'queer', 'nigger') whereby the 'reterritorialization of a term that has been used to abject a population can become the site of resistance, the possibility of an enabling social and political resignification' (Butler 1993: 231). The love-poet is constructed as the inverse of the Roman military ideal: manly, enduring, duty-bound (e.g. Wyke 2002: 168–9, 174–5). Equally eloquent is the hijacking of the language of normative Roman culture to describe sexual passion. Famously, the life of the lover-poet is both contrasted with a military career, and also—following the lead of the Greek poetess Sappho—imaged as a kind of campaign (see esp. Lyne 1980: 71–8). 'Every lover is a soldier,' Ovid famously writes, 'and Cupid occupies his own fort' (*Love Poems* 1.9.1). More outrageously still, the lover is routinely presented as the 'slave' of his girlfriend (e.g. Lyne 1980: 78–81; Wyke 2002: 166–73), a subversion of the standard Roman call for masterful men. These polar reversals of standard social expectations are often consciously routed through a Greek model, the prologue to Callimachus' *Aetia*, where the Alexandrian poet distinguishes his subtle verse from boorish peers who produce thundering epic verse about 'the deeds of kings, or heroes of old, in thousands of verses' (*Aetia* fr. 1.3–5).

The neoterics' stance was calculated to outrage, but they were not alone in it. From the first century BCE onwards, recuperating holidays and tours in

Greece—taking in both culture and pleasures—were a regular part of the life of an elite noble (Bowersock 1965: 73–84). From this perspective, the golden age promised in the rhetoric of Caesar Augustus could be cheekily rewritten as an embrace of wealth and luxury (which is the usual connotation of gold), rather than as a return to simple values (Ovid, *Art of Love* 2.277–8, with Barker 1996: 444–5). Conversely, primordial Rome might look less like a paradise of manly virtue, and more like Juvenal's (*c.*55–115 CE) satirical account of:

> the days of Saturn... when men were poorly housed in chilly caves, which under one common shelter enclosed hearth and household gods, herds and their owners; when the hill-bred wife spread her silvan bed with leaves and straw and the skins of her neighbours the wild beasts; a wife not like thee, O Cynthia, nor thee, Lesbia, whose bright eyes were clouded by a sparrow's death, but one whose breasts gave suck to lusty babes, often more unkempt herself than her acorn-belching husband.
>
> (*Satires* 6.1–10; tr. G. C. Ramsay)

The allusions to Cynthia (the name Propertius gives to his girlfriend) and Lesbia (ditto Catullus) make it clear that Juvenal is invoking the standard contrast between traditional Roman morality and the neoteric embrace of 'civilization'. What is less clear, however, is whether the poem's narrator feels any more sympathy for the acorn-belching primitives than the decadents who, according to the civilizing narrative, replaced them.

Imperial Hellenism

Is there any thread that binds together all these diverse stances? It is a well-known fact that 'Roman responses to Hellenism consisted of a complex and partly incoherent mixture of adoption, adaptation, imitation, rejection and prohibition, while the rhetorical poses repeatedly struck included assertions of admiration, of condemnation and of reconciliation' (Woolf 1994: 120; see more fully Petrochilos 1974). *Tot homines, quot sententiae*, says a character in Terence (*Phormio* 454). Varied responses are to be expected in a complex, sophisticated, stratified capital that (by Augustus' day) housed over 1 million people.

Yet there is also a unifying substrate underlying these different opinions, namely a concern with the proper management of power. Let us re-emphasize that the questions raised by Roman Hellenism are certainly not whether Greeks are better than Romans or whether Rome should properly exercise imperial rule over its subject states. No extant Roman, whatever his or her stance on Hellenism, questions Rome's rightful dominance over Greece. Nor do any of the art-plundering generals or neoterics think of themselves as any the less Roman for their Hellenism. The issue is, rather, what is the most appropriate way for an imperial Roman to behave in relation to subject states. Should one cleave to native traditions, avoiding contamination by conquered cultures? Or should one take pleasure in (what British imperialists called) the 'fruits of empire'?

The challenge posed by Hellenism, in the eyes of some traditionalists, was that it threatened to invert the natural hierarchy of imperialism, by exalting the subject people above the conquerors. We have already seen Polybius' claim that it would be an 'incontestable error for a people to abandon the habits of the conquerors and adopt those of the conquered'. The most famous expression of this point belongs to Horace:

> Greece, conquered Greece, her conqueror subdued,
> And Rome grew polished, who till then was rude.
>
> (*Epistles* 2.1.156–7; tr. J. Conington)

The clever, epigrammatic phrasing anticipates the assumption that Rome, the imperial master, should normally dominate Greece. Greece's dominance is not just a paradox, it is also a reversal of the proper imperial order. But how is it that a conquered people can conquer its conquerors? The fear is not so much loss of political and economic control, as of loss of self-control (although the latter, according to ancient beliefs, could quickly lead to the former). The psychological model that Roman theorists adopted from the Greeks, which was broadly Stoic (with roots in Platonism), viewed reason and passion as distinct parts of the soul. The relationship between the two was imagined on the analogy of political rule: properly, reason should rule over the passions. The analogy between soul and city was not simply metaphorical; the implicit (and sometimes explicit) assumption was that those who regulated their passions were best equipped to regulate their fellow citizens (hence, for example, Plato's ideal of the philosopher-king).

The association of Greece with lambent sexuality and sensuality played to this fear of loss of self-control. For many Romans, the Greek lands represented what Edward Saïd describes, with reference to nineteenth-century French representations of the 'Orient', as 'an exotic yet especially attractive reality...a locale sympathetic to their private myths, obsessions and requirements' (Saïd 1995: 170). This exoticism was deeply ambivalent: seductive otherness can simultaneously attract and repel. Much as cultured Romans might find it intoxicating to sojourn in the Greek world—Virgil's trip to Athens, for example, is famously commemorated by Horace (*Odes* 1.3)—the risk of corruption was ever-present. Sallust explains how Asia Minor corrupted Sulla's army: 'in order to secure the loyalty of the army that he led into Asia, he had allowed it a luxury and licence foreign to the manners of our forefathers; and in the intervals of leisure those charming and voluptuous lands had easily softened (*mollire*) the feral spirit of his soldiers' (*Catiline* 11.5–6). The associations with softness, pleasure, and luxury paint Greek Asia as a harlot bent on seducing the Roman male. This discourse is tied to a larger problematization of the morality of contemporary Greeks (sometimes distinguished from their nobler ancestors): Greeks, in many Roman eyes, 'flattered, they were insincere, their sexuality was unpredictable and perverse, their speech flowery, and they lacked *grauitas*, moral weight' (Woolf 1994: 121).

Ironically, this orientalist discourse is itself Greek in origin, rooted as it is in the classical Athenian presentation of Persia as luxurious, effeminate, and untrustworthy. The seductive risks of conquest were also well established in the Greek imaginary. Alexander the Great's supposed transformation into a despot was accredited by some to his conquest of Persia: it was then that he started wearing Persian dress and demanding obeisance (see e.g. Plutarch, *Alexander* 45.1). What Roman Hellenophobia did was, in effect, simply to shift the inherited axis of inversion westwards.

Precisely where it was located, however, remained an issue of debate. Asia Minor—where Sulla's men found their fleshpots, according to Sallust—was universally associated with oriental softness. Greece itself, however, was ambiguously positioned between East and West, facing simultaneously towards tough, manly Rome and the indulgent, effeminate East. This ambiguous geographical location also had symbolic ramifications—most notably in rhetoric, where Roman Hellenizers like Cicero distinguished the austere 'Attic' style (named after Attica, the territory of Athens) from florid 'Asianism'. By enforcing this distinction within Greek literary models, rhetorical theorists could legitimize their own Hellenizing activity by displacing, without challenging, the negative association of Greece with the Orient. Even Umbricius, the fervent xenophobe of Juvenal's Third Satire, seems partially to exempt 'true' Greeks from his venom: 'I cannot, citizens, bear a Greek Rome. And yet how much of that filth [i.e. Rome's 'Greek' population] is actually Achaean? For years now Syrian Orontes has poured its sewerage into the Tiber...' (3.60–2). 'Achaean', in this context, means from mainland Greece (i.e. the province designated Achaea since Augustus). Umbricius' attack on Greeks seems pointedly to exclude mainlanders, focusing instead upon easterners whose credentials rest on spurious claims to Hellenism.

Roman Hellenism invariably contains contradictions. A *prima facie* anti-Hellene like Umbricius thinks that Hellenized Syrians are the real culprits; similarly, as we saw earlier, the arch-primitivist Cato is prepared to exploit Greek literary resources. Conversely, Cicero, one of the primary apostles of Greek intellectual culture at Rome, is prepared in his *Brutus* and *Orator* to divide Greek rhetoric into good (Attic) and bad (Asian). What is more, the same author's *Tusculan Disputations*, where he discusses the value of philosophy for Romans, begins with an astonishing attack on the Greek intellectual tradition: 'I have always held the view that in their own innovations our Roman forebears showed greater wisdom than the Greek, while what they borrowed from the Greeks they improved on, at least in those areas which they had decided were worth taking trouble over' (1.1; tr. A. E. Douglas). Cicero's underlying message is that Greek philosophy is suitable for Roman politicians—but only when suitably appropriated and Romanized. His approach to the Greeks is fundamentally no more consistent than Cato's, containing elements of both admiration and outright hostility: his 'aggressive stance towards Greece obfuscates the fact that he looks to foreign aid in dealing with a domestic crisis' (Gildenhard 2007: 78).

Roman responses to Hellenism cannot, then, be split neatly into pro- and anti-camps. Cato and Cicero alike project both a positive image of the Greek heritage as a resource for intellectual inspiration, and a negative set of stereotypes centring on the portrait of the feckless, insubstantial oriental. The diverse stances are, rather, to do with different balance, emphasis, and context. What is more—and this is the essential point—all Roman responses to Hellenism are ultimately imperialist: the question being asked is whether it represents a useful technique of rule or a threat that itself requires ruling. More than this, however, the stances of individuals tend to be complex and partially incoherent (the most prominent examples being the brazen use of Greek models to express anti-Greek sentiments). These inconsistencies derive from the ideological burdens placed upon the discourse of Roman Hellenism: the colonial language of cultural difference, overburdened as it is with myths of 'natural' hierarchy, are bound to produce tensions and distortions. Ideology, as Marx reminds us, is but the illusion of coherence; and colonial discourse, as a more recent critic puts it, characteristically strives to maintain the illusion of sharp, self-evident differences between conqueror and conquered even as the evidence to the contrary multiplies (Bhabha 1994: 66–84).

The Aesthetics of Empire

I want to return finally to the question of the appeal of Hellenism, and consider further reasons why the allure of captive Greece became so captivating. This will involve putting issues of imperial domination into temporary abeyance, and focusing instead upon the structure of Roman elitism. The upper classes of Roman society were essentially fluid and competitive (Hopkins 1983: 107–16). Hellenism became a token in this game of upwardly mobile *ambitio*: particularly from the first century BCE onwards, learning and 'taste' became markers of social distinction. A noble's *atrium*—the semi-public hall in the front of the Roman house—might well contain statues plundered from Greek sanctuaries, either copies or originals, to impress upon visitors and clients the owner's cultivation. Similarly, Greek intellectuals might be engaged as clients to magnify the achievements of their patrons, whether directly or indirectly. We have already seen Cicero defending Archias, who was given Roman citizenship after commemorating in verse victories by Marius, Lucullus, and others. Similarly in the early first century BCE, Theophanes of Mytilene was likewise rewarded with the citizenship after writing an apparently celebratory account of Pompey's campaigns. A little later we find epigrams (now in the *Greek Anthology*) by Antipater of Thessalonica celebrating the achievements of Lucius Calpurnius Piso Frugi, and Crinagoras of Mytilene extolling Augustus and his family. The satirist Lucian, writing in the second century CE, warns his addressee, an intellectual looking for patronage, not to take a position in a Roman house:

He does not want you at all for that purpose [i.e. to instruct him]; but because you have a long beard and a serious appearance and you are dressed modestly in a Greek cloak and everyone knows that you are a grammarian, rhetorician or philosopher, it seems good to him for such a man to be mixed in with his retinue and escort. For this will make him seem a lover of Greek knowledge and altogether a man of taste when it comes to education. As a result, my friend, there is a danger that you have hired out your beard and cloak, rather than your splendid speeches. (*On Salaried Posts* 25)

Lucian's writings instinctively home in on paradoxical mismatches between appearance and reality. This generic impulse explains the satirist's ironical claim that the patron is more interested in the external tokens of philosophy ('your beard and your cloak') than its edifying content; in practice, of course, many Romans did take an active and long-standing interest in Greek literature and philosophy. What Lucian does accurately identify, however, is the root cause of Roman Hellenism, viz. the competitive desire for status in the eyes of others. By the time in which he was writing the aristocratic 'status wars' fought over the terrain of education had engulfed effectively the entire elite of the empire, eastern and western (Gleason 1995; Schmitz 1997; Whitmarsh 2005: 37–40).

There is a further sense in which Lucian's comments capture an aspect of Roman Hellenism (here we rejoin the larger issue of imperial discourse). The superficiality that he attributes to the patron represents a deliberate Roman strategy of dividing cultural labour between Greece and Rome. Roman and Greek were conceived of as a complementary dyad, the former representing military and political power, the latter civilization and culture. In arguably the most famous set of lines in Virgil's *Aeneid*, Aeneas' father Anchises opines to him in patriotic vein in the Underworld:

Others, for so I can well believe, shall hammer forth more delicately a breathing likeness out of bronze, coax living faces from the marble, plead causes with more skill, plot with their gauge the movements in the sky, and tell the rising of the constellations. But you, Roman, must remember that you have to guide the nations by your authority (*imperium*), for this is to be your skill, to graft tradition onto peace, to shew mercy to the conquered, and to wage war until the haughty are brought low. (*Aeneid* 6.847–53; tr. W. F. Jackson Knight)

To Romans is allotted *imperium*, to Greeks (implicitly) the arts of sculpture, oratory, and astronomy. The division is, of course, in one sense undermined by

Virgil's own *Aeneid*, an ambitious literary work explicitly positioned in a filial relationship to the Homeric epics: proof, if any were needed, that Romans could have high cultural ambitions. From our different cultural vantage, Virgil may appear to be playing the Greek, 'cultural' role in relation to his patrons Maecenas and (ultimately) the emperor Augustus; yet there is no sign in the text that his literary production was likely to be seen as un-Roman. Once again, we see the fundamental incoherence typical of imperial ideology.

The 'aestheticization' of Hellenism—its association with non-essential, adorning activities, and its separation from hard issues of politics and economics—is further underscored by its location in the realm of *otium* or 'leisure' (Toner 1995). The Roman discourse of leisure arose at the same time as Hellenism began to impact: it was through stories of Greek influence that Romans explained their interest in sculpture, music, gardens, poetry, philosophy. Conversely, and perhaps predictably, we find Cato inveighing against frivolous leisure activities: 'men of renown and greatness should place no less store by their leisure (*otium*) than their work (*negotium*)' (Cicero, *For Plancius* 66). The irreversible effect, however, was that for the elite time and space were redefined to create appropriate zones for leisurely cultural activities. An excellent example is Cicero's *Tusculan Disputations*, built around quasi-dialogues on Greek philosophy supposedly held in his villa in Tuscany, at the time 'when I was at last freed completely, or to a great extent, from the exacting role of defending counsel and from my duties in the Senate' (1.1). The rural setting is distinctive (this is the only one of Cicero's works to refer to a place in the title), and the emphasis upon the author's *otium* recurrent. Greek philosophy is carefully segregated spatio-temporally from the real business of Roman politics: sharp, symbolic borders are drawn around the separate spheres of (Greek) culture and (Roman) politics. As we have seen so frequently, however, these sharp, ideologically motivated distinctions cannot be maintained for long: Cicero's essential argument is that the lessons of philosophy are indeed essentially useful for Roman statecraft.

Roman Hellenism is a complex phenomenon, but central to any understanding of Republican and Imperial Rome. The strong reactions it provoked invite us to consider it as polarizing opinions between different camps: anti- and pro-, traditionalists and modernizers, moralists and connoisseurs. This appearance is true enough as far as ethics and aesthetics go: there certainly was a wide gulf between, for example, Cato and the first-century neoterics. Politically, however, Roman Hellenism in all its varieties was consonant with imperial values. As the city of Rome transformed itself into a cosmopolitan, imperial hub, the fruits of empire were made available to its citizens: the only debate, as we have seen, was over *how* it was to be inserted into an imperial framework. Greek culture, whether in the form of professionals, artefacts, or merely personal style, was one among a number of imports from across the empire, such as the medicine and foodstuffs required to sustain a city of around 1 million people in Augustus' day. What was particularly significant about the importing of Hellenism (as opposed, for example, to the import of Egyptian grain or Syrian dye) was that it became *the* primary focus for elite competition.

Further reading

On historical aspects of the Roman conquest of Greece, Gruen 1984 is fundamental; Alcock 1993 incorporates a useful historical survey (in addition to a ground-breaking analysis of the archaeological record of Roman Greece). On the cultural transformations wrought by Hellenism upon Republican Rome, see briefly Woolf 1994, and more fully Gruen 1993, with Petrochilos 1974 on the conflicting views expressed. Hellenism touched every aspect of Roman life: see esp. Feeney 2005, Habinek 1998, Goldberg 2005, and Hunter 2006 on literature; Rawson 1985 on intellectual life more generally; Wallace-Hadrill 1994 on domestic architecture; Adams, Janse, and Swain eds. 2002 and Adams 2003 on linguistic contacts (including with Greek); Howgego, Heuchert, and Burnett eds. 2005 on coinage; Zanker 1988 on art; Griffin and Barnes eds. 1989 and Barnes and Griffin eds. 1997 on philosophy. A particular feature of recent approaches to Roman Hellenization has been the emphasis upon competition between local Italian peoples: see esp. Zanker ed. 1976, Dench 1995, 2005, Feeney 2005, and Wallace-Hadrill 2008, the last of which appeared too late to integrate into the text of this chapter. The Greek counter-response to Roman conquest is explored by Swain 1996 and Whitmarsh 2001. Lucid accounts of postcolonial theory can be found at Hall 1992 and 1996.

References

Adams, J. N. (2003), *Bilingualism and the Latin language*, Cambridge.

—— Janse, M., and Swain, S. (eds.) (2002), *Bilingualism in ancient society*, Oxford.

Alcock, S. E. (1993), *Graecia capta: the landscapes of Roman Greece*, Cambridge.

Astin, A. E. (1978), *Cato the censor*, Oxford.

Barker, D. (1996), '"The golden race is proclaimed?" The *Carmen saeculare* and the renascence of the golden race', *Classical Quarterly*, 46: 434–46.

Barnes, J. and Griffin M. (1997), *Philosophia togata*, II: *Plato and Aristotle at Rome*, Oxford.

Beard, M. and Henderson, J. (2001), *Classical art: from Greece to Rome*, Oxford.

Bhabha, H. K. (1994), *The location of culture*, London.

Bowersock, G. W. (1965), *Augustus and the Greek world*, Oxford.

Butler, J. (1993), *Bodies that matter: on the discursive limits of 'sex'*, New York.

Clausen, W. (1986), 'Cicero and the new poetry'. *HSCPh* 90: 159–70.

Dench, E. (1995), *From barbarians to new men: Greek, Roman and modern perceptions of peoples from the Central Appenines*, Oxford.

——(2005), *Romulus' asylum: Roman identities from the age of Alexander to the age of Hadrian*, Oxford.

ERSKINE, A. (2001), *Troy between Greece and Rome: local tradition and imperial power*, Oxford.

FEENEY, D. C. (2005), 'The beginnings of a literature in Latin', *Journal of Roman Studies*, 95: 226–40.

FERRARY, J.-L. (1988), *Philhellénisme et impérialisme: aspects idéologiques de la conquête romaine du monde hellénistique, de la seconde guerre de Macédoine à la guerre contre Mithridate*, Rome.

GILDENHARD, I. (2007), *Paideia Romana: Cicero's* Tusculan Disputations, *Cambridge Classical Journal*, supplementary vol. 30. Cambridge.

GLEASON, M. W. (1995), *Making men: sophists and self-presentation in ancient Rome*, Princeton.

GOLDBERG, S. (2005), *Constructing literature in the Roman republic: poetry and its reception*, Cambridge.

GREEN, P. (1990), *Alexander to Actium: the historical evolution of the Hellenistic age*, Berkeley.

GRIFFIN, M. T. and BARNES, J. (eds.) (1989), *Philosophia togata*, I: *essays on philosophy and Roman society*, Oxford

GRUEN, E. S. (1984), *The Hellenistic world and the coming of Rome*, Berkeley.

—— (1990), *Studies in Greek culture and Roman policy*, Leiden.

—— (1993), *Culture and national identity in republican Rome*, London.

HABINEK, T. (1998), *The politics of Latin literature: writing, identity, and empire in ancient Rome*, Princeton.

HALL, S. (1992), 'The question of cultural identity', in S. Hall *et al.* (eds.), *Modernity and its futures*, Cambridge: 273–316.

—— (1996), 'Who needs "identity"?', in S. Hall and P. du Gay (eds.), *Questions of cultural identity*, London: 1–17.

HOWGEGO, C., HEUCHERT, V., and BURNETT, A. (eds.) (2005), *Coinage and identity in the Roman provinces*, Oxford.

HOPKINS, K. (1983), *Death and renewal*, Cambridge.

HUNTER, R. (2006), *The shadow of Callimachus: studies in the reception of Hellenistic poetry at Rome*, Cambridge.

LYNE, R. O. A. M. (1980), *The Latin love poets: from Catullus to Horace*, Oxford.

PETROCHILOS, N. K. (1974), 'Roman attitudes to the Greeks', dissertation, Athens.

POLLITT, J. J. (1978), 'The impact of Greek art on Rome', *Transactions of the American Philological Association*, 108: 155–74.

POWELL, J. G. E. (ed.) (1995), *Cicero the philosopher: twelve papers*, Oxford.

PRICE, S. R. F. (1984), *Rituals and power: the Roman imperial cult in Asia Minor*, Cambridge.

RAWSON, E. (1985), *Intellectual life in the late Roman republic*, London.

SAID, E. (1995), *Orientalism: western conceptions of the orient*, 2nd edn., Harmondsworth.

SCHEID, J. (1995), '*Graeco ritu*: a typically Roman way of honouring the gods', *Harvard Studies in Classical Philology*, 97: 15–31.

SCHMITZ, T. (1997), *Bildung und Macht: zur sozialen unde politischen Funktion der zweiten Sophistik in der griechischen Welt der Kaiserzeit*, Munich.

STRIKER, G. (1995), 'Cicero and Greek philosophy', *Harvard Studies in Classical Philology*, 97: 53–61.

SWAIN, S. C. R. (1996), *Hellenism and empire: language, classicism, and power in the Greek world, AD 50–250*, Oxford.

Swain, S. (2002), 'Bilingualism in Cicero? The evidence of code-switching', in J. N. Adams, M. Janse, and S. Swain (eds.), *Bilingualism in ancient society: language contact and the written text*, Oxford: 128–67.

Toner, J. (1995), *Leisure and ancient Rome*, Cambridge.

Wallace-Hadrill, A. (1988), 'Greek knowledge, Roman power', review of Rawson (1985), *Classical Philology*, 83: 224–33.

—— (1994), *Houses and society in Pompeii and Herculaneum*, Princeton.

—— (2008), *Rome's cultural revolution*, Cambridge.

Whitmarsh, T. (2001), *Greek literature and the Roman empire: the politics of imitation*, Oxford.

—— (2005), *The Second Sophistic*, Oxford.

Wiseman, T. P. (2004), *The myths of Rome*, Exeter.

Woolf, G. (1994), 'Becoming Roman, staying Greek: culture, identity and the civilizing process in the Roman East', *Proceedings of the Cambridge Philological Society*, 40: 116–43.

—— (1998), *Becoming Roman: the origins of provincial civilization in Gaul*, Cambridge.

Wyke, M. (2002), *The Roman mistress*, Oxford.

Zanker, P. 1988 *The power of images in the age of Augustus*, tr. A. Shapiro, Ann Arbor, Mich.

—— (ed.) (1976), *Hellenismus in Mittelitalien: Kolloquium in Göttingen vom 5. bis 9. Juni 1974*, 2 vols., Göttingen.

Zeitlin, F. I. (1986), 'Thebes: theater of self and other in Athenian drama', in P. Euben (ed.), *Greek tragedy and political theory*, Berkeley: 101–41; repr. in J. Winkler and F. Zeitlin (eds.), 1990, *Nothing to do with Dionysus? Athenian tragedy in its social context*, Princeton: 130–67.

CHAPTER 47

RELIGIOUS PLURALISM

JÖRG RÜPKE

The Problem

Conceptualizing the religious history of Rome and the Roman Empire seems to be easy. Looking back to that period, we usually differentiate Christianity, Judaism (each given a separate chapter in this handbook), and the rest, to which this chapter is dedicated. We are used to differentiating different 'religions', even if it is difficult to provide a precise term for those we mean to refer to by 'the rest'. The term 'polytheism' is frequently used, but it reflects the perspective of people who regard themselves as monotheists, starting from the Alexandrian Jewish philosopher Philo (F. Schmidt 1987). However, the same people thus called 'polytheists' would have differentiated themselves, together with the Jews, from Christian thinkers who they in turn saw as 'atheists'. The task of differentiating 'religions' from each other brings with it another problem: How are the boundary-lines drawn? How do you classify an individual praying to different gods in the course of a lifetime or within the same week? Do Episcopalians, Mormons, and the Children of God, do Sunnites, Shiites, and Babis belong to different religions? The discipline of Religious Studies has developed a terminology of 'cults' and 'denominations' to deal with these problems, but the terminological choice itself implies normative statements of 'inside' and 'outside'. It has been argued that it was Christianity (singular!)—with its stress on belief and its wish to drive out 'heretics'—that came to create 'religion' as something different from social life and 'religions' as the plurality of its illegitimate forms. Could this explain the religious conflicts within the Roman Empire?

This chapter will argue that the development of the notion of a plurality of religions represents a larger change in ancient concepts, of which Christian thinkers were only a part. Thus focused, the following pages will not describe the wide variety of religious practices, reflections, and organizations before and besides Jewish synagogues and Christian churches, covered by the books listed as 'further reading'. In tracing concepts by analysing the history of different (Latin) terms, it will, however, take into account the factual variety of religious practices as a background to the intellectual development.

Terms and Concepts: *Religio*

Despite the surface continuity of the term, the concept of 'religion' is not identical with the concept implied in the Latin word *religio* (Feil 1986: 16–82; J. Z. Smith 1998). To explore the conceptual differences, the meaning, and, if necessary, the history of the meanings of different terms that might pertain to our concept of religion will be analysed. The body of texts thus taken into account is concentrated on Latin texts, as this chapter is concerned with the main lines of thought that determined political and juridical and religious action on a larger scale.

Cicero

Of all the words that might denote something like 'religion', *religio*, obviously, had the most consequential history. The word (and hence *religiosus*) is attested from Plautus, that is, the early second century BCE, onwards (*Asinaria* 781, *Curculio* 350, *Mercator* 881), clearly implying what we would term religious language. The semantic range reaches from a direct relationship with a deity all the way to a rather generalized sort of scruple. The word is frequent in Cicero, in the speeches as well as in philosophical texts. It occurs with exceptional frequency in the speeches against Verres, the administrator of the province of Sicily, collector of statues, and, in Cicero's view, unrestrained violator of human and divine property. These texts use the term and its adjective more than one hundred times. The much shorter speeches *On his House* and *On the Answer of the Haruspices* show between fifty and sixty occurrences, and the philosophical treaties *On the Nature of the Gods* and *On Laws* (with its second book concentrated on what we term religion—already the selection demonstrates the conceptual link between *religio* and our concept of religion) manifest the term with similar frequency.

Still, differences are important. Surely, as Ernst Feil in his two-volume history of the term has shown, in Cicero *religio* is not at all our umbrella term. Yet, his analysis, mostly based on *On the Nature of the Gods*, fails to take into account the fact that Cicero's use of the term in the dialogue, that is to say, by different speakers, is strategic and part of the *prosopoieia*, the characterization of the participants. Thus, the triad of *pietas*, *sanctitas*, and *religio*—which seems to juxtapose piety and dealing with the gods with religion—is part of the introductory section only (1.3 and 1.14). As the academic Cotta's later rendering of the title of Epicure's treatise *Peri osiotetos* as *De sanctitate, de pietate adversus deos* (1.115) shows, *sanctitas* as the science of venerating the gods (1.116) is an attempt to translate a Greek concept. Whereas the introductory section uses *sanctitas* in forms of questions or very general statements (Dyck 2003: 60, without noting the implications), Cotta questions the possibility of such a 'science' within the Epicurean framework. When the Stoic Balbus generally talks of the growth of *deorum cultus religionumque sanctitates* (2.5) and shortly afterwards defines *religio* as cult of the gods (2.8) he seems to imply differentiated concepts. The general claim of the first instance is obviously characterized as obfuscating and hence undermined by the author Cicero. The relationship of *pietas* and *religio* seems to be rather simple. The first describes the relationship with a human or divine natural superior. *Religio*, then, is the particular consequence—cult—in the case of the gods. Hence, the existence of the gods is the precondition for any piety or religiosity towards them (1.118 f.; similarly Lactantius, *Divine Institutions* 5.14).

Despite its initial context in the triad *religio–pietas–sanctitas*, *religio* emerges as a central concept. It appears frequently, however, only in certain opening or summarizing parts of the argumentation. The distribution among the discussants is unequal. The Epicurean Velleius never uses *religio*. The Stoic Lucius Balbus only in a few instances, talking about attention to public omens (e.g. 2.8. 10. 11), apart from the passage already mentioned and a rejection of *superstitio* as opposed to *religio*. It is the Academic and pontifex Cotta who most frequently employs the term *religio*. He uses both the singular and the plural. The plural juxtaposes *religiones* to *caerimoniae* (1.161) or *sacra* and *caerimonia* (3.5), in the first instance qualifying the *religiones* as 'public'. It is the task of the pontifex to defend these. Juxtaposition is supplanted by superposition in a passage dominated by the singular: 'the religion (*religio*) of the Roman people in general has two separate aspects, its ritual (*sacra*) and the auspices (*auspicia*), to which a third element is added when, as a result of portents and prodigies, the interpreters of the Sibyl or the diviners offers prophetic advice' (3.5, tr. P. G. Walsh). *Religio* is not a vague feeling (as his opponents are criticized for holding) or an 'empty fear' like *superstitio* (1.117), but something resulting from the acceptance of the gods as part of one's social order, a human disposition, a habit, that finds its expression in corresponding rituals (*cultus deorum*, 1.117). Thus, the existence of gods is a precondition for it (ibid.), the unrestrained multiplying of gods could endanger it (3.60).

There is a last critical turn to Cotta and his Academic position. In the exchange preceding Cotta's lengthy refutation of the Stoic position, Cotta qualifies his definition quoted above as the view of the pontifex and adds: 'Since you are a philosopher, I must exact from you a rationale for religion, whereas I am to lend assent to our forebears even when no rationale is offered' (3.6). *Religio* is a social fact of the highest importance for the stability of the community (3.94), but it is not an argument and cannot be introduced as such into philosophical discourse (see 1.118). Rather, *religio* is to be tamed by *ratio*, and this is the purpose of the whole book, as the author declares in the very opening of the first book: 'I am dealing with the problem of the nature of the gods, a problem that is most beautiful for the intellect and its ability to know and a topic that is necessary for the steering of religion' (1.1). This is the philosophical agenda repeated in the subsequent treatise *On Divination*, too (2.148–9). In a hierarchy of descending generality, Cicero could list 'tradition (*mos*), religion (*religio*), teaching, augural law, authority of the college' (2.70).

For Cicero, singular and plural do not correspond to our notion of religion and religions. Religion in the singular denotes a necessary corollary of every theism and finds its expression in different religions. Expression and restraint. You can argue about theism—that is a theoretical problem and stance—but not about *religio*. But you can judge *religiones* by social standards of legitimacy and common sense. For instance, does a specific *religio* really refer to a deity? In the earlier books *On Laws*, Marcus (Tullius Cicero) had dealt with the problem by rigorously restricting cults in his fictitious lawgiving to the public and familiar ones, while new or foreign ones could legitimately enter the local cosmos only by public decision (2.19). It is noteworthy that Cicero already deals in this second paragraph of his religious laws with the problem of religious separatism ('nobody should have new or foreign gods of his own'). His attempt to list the gods—always seen as heavenly, consecrated due to merits, laudable virtues—points one by one to problems of such a qualification in terms of public acceptance and legitimacy (ibid.). In *On the Nature of the Gods* Cotta dealt with this problem by rigorously referring back to traditional practice—he evokes Numa (3.43)—and a *reductio ad absurdum* of every historical, mythological, or analogue reasoning. To abbreviate the lengthy argumentation based on the countless gods already venerated in practice: if all those are gods who are known to have altars in Greece (3.46), would the lack of any known cult be an argument against other candidates (3.45)?

We will have to follow up on the practical problems involved in these 'solutions' to interpreting religious plurality shortly, but must stay with the history of the term *religio* and its possible plurals for a moment more, in order to enlarge the field beyond Cicero before writers from the third century onwards will be addressed.

Until the beginning of the second century CE Cicero's usage remains representative for Roman thinking. Obviously, the different *religiones* attain to different deities. But such a one-to-one relationship is not usual. *Religiones* could multiply, different religious ideas and their differing cultic consequences could be addressed to one god, could be practised by the same people at the same time or by different people. Hence, Tacitus' expression *religione Herculis*—'the religion of Hercules' (*Annals* 12.13)—implying a one-to-one relationship, is rather unusual. When—within a passage of conduct in war—the same historian states that the *religio Veneris* ('religion of Venus') of the Aphrodisienses and the *religio Iovis et Triviae* ('religion of Jupiter and Trivia') of the Stratonicenses had been preserved (3.62), he modifies the concept of *religio* and points to another level of pluralizing. As the Romans had their public *religio* (in the singular), others had theirs (Cicero, *Pro Flacco* 69), and these might be compared (*On the Nature of the Gods* 2.8). Cicero, it is important to notice, does not employ a plural in his talk about comparison. 'Every community has its religion and we ours', in the speech for Flaccus, is an exclamation, a statement of radical differences, not of possible choice or meaningful coexistence. As in *On the Nature of the Gods*, *religio* confers the notion of a totality, but it is a local totality, justifying our talk of 'Roman' or 'Athenian religion', disregarding the problems indicated by the recent coining of 'religions of Rome' (Beard, North, and Price 1998). Cicero's 'we' and 'our' does not reflect the complex composition of the Roman population which was already the case by his time (see Noy 2000).

Religio in Texts of the Third and Fourth Centuries CE

Religio does not figure prominently in most later texts (Feil 1986: 78). That holds true from Christian apologetics to the laws of the fourth century. Minucius Felix from Cirta, writing in the 240s (Barnes 2001: 151), was an attentive reader of Cicero. In his dialogue *Octavius* both adversaries, the sceptic as well as the Christian, employ the term *religio* in the very last sentences of their perorations, paired with *superstitio* and *pietas* (13.5, 38.7). For the Christian, it is *vera religio*—'true religion' (in 1.5, too)—not another religion. In the body of the text the context of the term is always ritual. That holds true for the more frequent usage in the speech of the Christian-to-be, Octavius (6.2, 7.1, 9.1, 10.1) as well as for the two *nostra religio* ('our religion') in the Christian answer within the same dialogue (29.2, 38.1).

Tertullian, writing earlier, basically conforms to this usage (e.g. *Apologeticum* 24, 33.1). *Religio* is based on the knowledge of god or gods and results in cults of very different kinds. Freedom of *religio* is claimed as the choice of the deity (24.6, 25), true *religio* is the cult of the one and true god (e.g. *On Games* 1.4), Roman *religio* could be termed *Romanae religiones* ('Roman religions') minutes later

(*Apologeticum* 26.3). Outside of *vera religio*, singular and plural do not make a difference.

In the early fourth century Lactantius follows and transcends Tertullian. The term *religio* is not important for his arguments, but it is useful and, in some texts, frequently used. It is helpful to start with the rare occurrences in his treatise *On the Death of the Persecutors* from *c*.313/16. Nero started the first persecutions when he realized that 'a multitude defected from the cults of the images to a new religion' (2.5). Here, as in other places, *religio* designates Christianity (11.3 and 7); the same Christians could be described as 'enemies of the public cults (*religionum publicarum*)' in the same passage (11.6). The frequent usage in the earlier *Divine Institutions* offers the key to understanding. *Religio* is usually paired with cult and gods, it is cult based on the acceptance of the deity to which a particular cult is addressed. Thus, as it is the explicit aim of Book 2 to demonstrate, religion addressed to false gods, humans, idols, is 'vain'. A one-to-one relationship is the underlying model, hence the plural for the 'religions of the deities' (2.17.6). Usual, Roman religion is their 'own', opposed to *religiones communes*—'common religions' (1.20.1). Here, the reason for Lactantius' famous re-definition of religion is to be found: 'By a bond of piety we are bound to God and tied up (*religati*), whence religion itself took its name' (4.28.3). Thus, *religio* and *superstitio* are to be differentiated according to the god addressed, only (4.28.11). Christians are tied by the true god to his cult, others by demons to the cults of vain idols. Even in key passages, Lactantius refrains from employing the singular *falsa religio* ('false religion') to denote the latter. It is the necessary intellectual act to identify the one and true god and to see through the limits of the human condition and knowledge—*sapientia*—which encourages Lactantius to employ *religio* as a general concept: no true cultic piety (*religio*) without philosophy, no true philosophy that would not result in true cultic piety—the topic of Book 1 (1.1.25). In this sense, *religio* sets men apart from the animals (*Epitome Divinarum Institutionum* 32.4).

Writing in the 340s, Iulius Firmicus Maternus prefers in his long list of cults from all over the empire which he considers ridiculous the terms *sacra* and *superstitiones* to *religiones*, but he uses both terms synonymously. Interestingly enough, Firmicus uses *profana(e) religio(nes)* two times in passages referring to texts, not to ritual (*De errore profanarum religionum* [not an authentic title] 17.4; 21.1). Here, even if associated with the cult that must necessarily follow, *religiones* offered the advantage of being more general than *sacra* and *superstitiones*.

Ammianus Marcellinus, writing in the second half of the fourth century, wrote of the emperor Constantius II that he disturbed the *Christiana religio simplex* with empty *superstitio* and thus stirred up many verbal controversies (21.16.18). He could, however, generalize personal *religiones* with the singular. The reforms of Julian intended, *pace* Ammianus, that 'everybody could fearlessly serve his religious disposition' (22.5.3). It is important to note that for the historian, cult dominated the perception of religion and religious differences. Thus he could oppose *cultus Christianus* to *deorum cultores* (21.2.4), could observe that 'Christian *religio* venerated martyrs' (27.7.6), could encounter a *ritus Christiani sacrarium* (26.3.3), or run into a Christian festival (27.10.2)—the image of religion as a particular lifestyle rather than ritual, prominently professed by Octavius, belonged to the past. Christianity, however, had successfully established the image of a densely knit unit in contrast to a multitude of other religious practices, even for a critical writer like Ammianus (see Davies 2004), characterized by some as 'aggressively pagan' (Rilke 1987: 137).

What are our findings thus far? In contrast to terms like *cultus*, *sacra*, or *caerimoniae*, *religio* (and its plural) implied a reflected belief, an intellectual stance towards the deities addressed by the cult. Thus, already in Cicero, *religio* was used to reflect upon the relationship of philosophy, theological reflection, and religious practices. Some Latin Christian writers, Lactantius above all, used this relationship to polemicize against non-Christian cult within the framework of their own philosophical argumentation. Such a concept could hardly reflect the realities of the formation of groups employing religious symbols for their group identity. Within the religious framework of the ancient world, the cult of a specific deity would only occasionally correspond with or constitute group boundaries. Speaking about a city's or a person's religion was thus difficult. The singular could be used to describe one's own 'religion'—as Licinius did in his so-called Tolerance Edict from 13 June 313 (Lactantius, *On the Death of the Persecutors* 48), but the dichotomy implied between 'us' and 'the others' would not reflect clear boundaries and differences among 'the others'. How, against this backdrop, could a plurality of religions, could group boundaries in terms of religion be conceptualized?

How to Express a Plurality of Religious Groups?

I start with an example. When the proconsul Saturninus questioned a group of Christians at Scili at the end of the second century, he attempted to articulate the conflict using the term *religio*, which he quickly defined as an oath in the name of, and a prayer for, the emperor (*Acta Scilitanorum* 3). The offer of the accusated Speratus to discuss things religious led him to shift the accusation to terms like 'being of such a persuasion' or 'participant of insanity' (7–8). In the end the self-definition as *Christianus* was sufficient for the death sentence (10), as Tertullian—irritated—reported (*Apologeticum* 3). However, if we believe the accuracy of the text already formed to the purposes of communal reading, the final reason given by the proconsul was the confession 'to live *ritu Christiano*' and to refuse to return *ad Romanorum morem* (*Acta* 14). The conflict was not to be couched in terms of 'religion'.

How did Latin speakers deal with the problem outside of the court? Minucius Felix, Christian and Ciceronian, demonstrates the central option. Already in the prooemium, the notion of 'error' sets the tone (1.4; 3.1; finally taken up in 40.1). Accepting the Christian god is a matter of intellectual cognition, Christianity is a philosophical option. The Christians are the better philosophers (20.1 against 13.1). Regardless of the development of the arguments, this perspective is explicitly given to the critic, probably built on the holder of high offices in Cirta Q. Caecilius Q.f. Natalis (Barnes 2001: 151). He characterizes himself as somebody who is not a member of the same 'sect' (*secta*), and talks of 'your sect' and finally, rhetorically (Rüpke 2006) beaten by Octavius, of 'already my sect' (40.2).

Secta, obviously translating the Greek *hairesis*, was primarily used to differentiate the philosophical schools of the early Hellenistic age, but could be used for Jewish groups like Saducees or Pharisees too (e.g. in Acts 4: 17; Josephus, *Bellum Iudaicum* 2.8.1). The term is rare in Cicero, who used it more frequently for political (e.g *Letters to Brutus* 10.1) than philosophical groups (e.g. *Pro Caelio* 40; *Brutus* 120), but appears frequently from the first century CE onwards. Tertullian uses the term explicitly in this sense (*Apologeticum* 3.6, 40.7, 46.2). It implied a legitimate choice among comparable options. By the beginning of the fourth century, in Lactantius and Firmicus, the term is no longer used as a self-description in apologetic texts, but it is attested in the so-called Tolerance Edict of 311 (Lactantius, *On the Death of the Persecutors* 34). Here, Licinius looked back on his earlier attempt to bring the Christians back to their 'good senses', as they have left 'their parents' sect' (34.1). The term is very frequently used for the 'catholic sect' as well as heretical and all varieties of sects in the norms collected in the sixteenth book of the Codex Theodosianus (in particular 16.5; for the terminology of religious groups in the Codex, see Zinser 2002). It must be stressed, however, that the instances of 'catholic' or 'orthodox sect' remained rare.

Another term within the field of philosophical schools was *disciplina*. It could denote both intellectual content and a way of life. *Disciplina magorum, Etruscorum, Chaldaica, augurum*, and *rei publicae* are phrases from the first centuries BCE; Cato the Elder warns already in the second century BCE of 'foreign discipline' (1.4). Military discipline, directly or metaphorically, remained the main notion, but did not exclude other developments. Apuleius, for instance, made frequent use of the word (*Metamorphoses* 3.19.4, 4.18; *De Deo Socratis* 3). Tertullian used the term (which was nearly absent from Latin translations of the New Testament, except seven times in Paul) for new traits of the Christian way of life (*Against the Marcionites* 4.36; *On Fasting* 12). Terminological fixation is missing in Minucius Felix, but the idea of a new way of life is given prominence (e.g. 5.1) and *disciplina* hence applied even to traditional cults (6.1, 8.2, 30.3). For Christians, it is something to be developed (35.3). Firmicus could polemicize against the devil's *disciplina* (*De Errore Profanorum Religionum* 18.1).

In contrast to the usage of the term *religio*, the terminology of religious groups is simple. A plurality of comparable choices could be expressed in terms of different philosophical schools. This implied a body of knowledge as—and this is important—a special way of life. By the term *disciplina*, this could be applied to certain types of religious specialists—magicians, *haruspices*, even augurs—already by the late Republic. To my knowledge, in Latin texts that usage was not extended to a wider variety of religions before the Christian apologetics took it up from the end of the second century, and did not reach official texts before the fourth century.

Religious Plurality: Proliferation and Control

So far, this analysis has implicitly or explicitly located religious plurality in a plurality of groups of persons exercising different religious options. This has informed the selection of terms and passages analysed. Yet religious plurality could be measured by other parameters too. Starting anew from Cicero and his time, in a perspective informed by his concept of *religio* instead of our notion of 'religion', such alternative parameters gain in importance. Given the structure of the concept of *religio* between the philosophical problem of the existence of the gods and the veneration due to them, the first problem for a local community is the inflation in the number of gods. This formulation implies a modern semiotical perspective: The primary signs of religious communication were the gods. It was and had been too easy to multiply them, turning every ethical concept, even every abstract concept not only into an image, but into a deity (Cicero, *On the Nature of the Gods* 3.61), and offering every exceptional individual the prospect of divinization. Inflation of signs is devaluation of signs, producing something—to return to object language—that is not worthy (ibid.) of the real god(s). The academic and pontifex Cotta uses a large part of his speech to deplore this development (3.38–64), and, as shown above, that was a primary concern of Cicero's literary legislation. The solution imposing itself in his traditionalist society consisted in curbing further proliferation by falling back on tradition. However, already Cicero's generation realized that even that is inconsistent. The forefathers' temple-building for the deity 'Fever' is a stock example used in *On Laws* (2.28) and in *On the Nature of the Gods* (3.63). Varro adhered to the growing multitude out of civic discipline, not on the basis of a philosophical rationale (*Divine Antiquities* 1, fr. 12). His historical research and systematization produced an even larger multitude, offering material for generations of Christian apologetics to poke fun at (Rüpke 2005*a*, 2006).

How, then, could control—a concept to be used intensively in the following reflections—be achieved? The gods themselves could neither be controlled nor sanctioned. They could form the object of a philosophical attack, but not of political or military action. Neither could *religio* be an object of control. It was *cultus*, it was individual *sacra*, that could be banned or tolerated. In his books *On Laws* Cicero's idea was to implement control by means of public priests (*sacerdotes*). In the commentary on his own formulations (2.30 on 2.20–1), he stresses their competence even with regard to private religiosity. Without the priests' help the citizens could not ritually satisfy their own private *religio*. Even if Cicero could not offer a complete list of *sacra*, he produced a complete list of priests (thus I understand his formulation at 2.30). Several priesthoods that gained high importance under the later Augustus, such as the Fratres Arvales or Salii, are not mentioned, but that is in concord with the pre-Augustan concentration of competition for priesthoods on four of the public colleges (see Rüpke 2008), thus ensuring the effectiveness of aristocratic control.

Cicero's solution was incoherent by his own standards. On the one hand, and in good republican tradition, he is operating with a clear-cut division of public and private, regulated either by public decision, that is, by means of certain procedures and—if one considers the agents—ultimately by the nobility, or by family tradition. On the other hand, he suggests that the private requires public regulation. In order to understand this 'incoherence' one has to add that in terms of usage, pragmatically, so to speak, the dichotomy of public and private was not as strict as the property law suggests. From this perspective, public spaces intruded into private houses—the atrium, for example (Rüpke 2002)—and non-public groupings might occupy public space or could be perceived as a danger to public order—associations of artisans, for instance.

The nearly contemporary law of the Roman colony Urso in Hispania Baetica offered a different solution, stressing the dividing-line of public and private. Public cult was to be financed and organized by the council and its magistrates. Financing and the infrastructure necessary for large public rituals formed the means of control, thus shaping the actual contents of the *sacra publica* (see the law's sections 65, 69–72; 128; see Rüpke 2006*a* for the following). Priesthoods, expiation, burials, and ancestor cult were beyond the public realm. This side of life simply could not be allowed to interfere with political activities. The regulations concerning pontiffs and augurs—usually taken as a testimony for the export of Roman religion—just tried to transfer structural elements of public religion. At Urso these priesthoods were not an element of public control, but are themselves subordinated to magisterial power.

Geographical Expansion

So far, the frame of analysis has been deliberately restricted to Rome or a single place—following Cicero's unreflected 'we'. As has been quoted above, it was common knowledge that other communities had their own *religiones*. The antiquarians extensively reflected on earlier imports. According to them, basically, Rome was made up of Latin, Etruscan, and Sabine gods and cults. The Trojan ancestry, postulated by Greeks from the third century BCE onwards (Erskine 2001: esp. 224) was accepted, religious imports could be imagined in the Virgilian narrative of the *Aeneid* (Cancik 2006; see also Barchiesi 2006). But these contacts were seen as events of a distant past. For the more recent past, cultural contact with Greece and the Hellenic world (so present in southern Italy and Etrurian towns) had been very intensive—and controversial. It was not *religio* that was at the centre of such controversies, but rather clothing, luxury ornaments, philosophy, or rhetoric. Yet, boundaries between religion and the profane could easily shift. In the first half of the second century BCE Numa's books had been condemned as Pythagorean philosophy according to the earliest testimony by the annalist Cassius Hemina (Pliny, *Natural History* 13.86). A generation later, writers thought of these books as containing pontifical law. Stolen statues of Greek deities filled public and private space at Rome as works of art. Eventually, however, some of them had to be accommodated in new temples. Thus, the nine Muses from Ambracia were transferred to the new temple of 'Hercules of the Muses'.

Due to continuous contact since the early urban phases, Rome, the city on the margins of the Greek world, had no significant difficulty accommodating and acculturating influx from the Greeks, be it Mater Magna from Asia minor or Venus Erycina from Sicily. Thus, the testimony of Cicero's dialogue *On the Nature of the Gods* is ambivalent. In itself a witness to the Romans' attempt to come to grips with Greek thinking on religion (historical and philosophical, Rüpke 2005*a*), the polemical concentration on the influx of Greek mythology (and ultimately religion) presented by Cotta (3.38 ff.) is a demonstration of parochialism (even if parts of the argumentation were taken over from the Greek academic Carneades). Other cultural and religious areas remained exotic, neither dangerous nor adaptable, for example, Syrian fish gods and Egyptian animals (3.39, the latter again in 3.48) or an Indian variety of Jupiter (3.42, Belus, i.e. Baal; Walsh 1997: 199). The existence of Egyptian variants of divine genealogies was noted more frequently (3.54 ff.), but those were not accorded the status of dangerous knowledge. Such genealogies were perceived as distant local variants, gaining no importance beyond those localities. Hence, interest in Egyptian cults at Rome was limited in that generation. Cicero's Cotta did not take the trouble to comment upon the removal of shrines to Isis from the Capitol during the 50s, the last of these pertaining to the year 48 BCE (Cassius Dio 42.26; see

Mora 1990: 75–87), hardly more than three years before Cicero wrote the books (he finished the composition before the death of Caesar). Marcus Terentius Varro (116–27 BCE) is reported to have resented the cult of Isis and Serapis. The paraphrase in Servius' commentary on Virgil's *Aeneid* (8.698) indicates Varro's urban perspective: 'every community has its own religion.'

Change was imminent, stressing more and more boundaries within local society and approaching the image of religious plurality encountered in chapter 3. Stirred by a famous incident of sexual fraud, in 19 CE the Senate debated about the expulsion of 'Egyptian and Jewish cults' (Tacitus, *Annals* 2.85.5). Suetonius, in his account (*Tiberius* 36.1–2), refers to 'external ceremonies' and 'rites'. Obviously, the Senate thought they should fight a superstition and ruled to destroy cultic paraphernalia and expelled the followers by various means. The combination of measures and the wording of Suetonius suggest ethnic and hence political implications. Mora points to the journey of Germanicus (1990: 93), who entered Egypt in 19 CE and won local sympathies by the measures he undertook in the famine, but also thus produced a serious conflict with Tiberius. The religious dimension, however, must have been important; followers of the cult were expelled, regardless of their ethnic identity, or had to stop 'profane rites', as Tacitus formulates. This is confirmed by Seneca, who adduces the information that the expulsion of 'alien' cults was legitimized by its classification as *superstitio*, argued for (among other facts, not related by Seneca) on the basis of abstinence from certain animals (*Letters* 108.22). Similar conceptual choices are visible in a religious context that was not polemical at all. The Roman institution of the organized training of Etruscan diviners (*haruspices*) was seen as fighting economic misuse of religion—secularization, one might say—by Cicero (*On Divination* 1.92). For Tacitus (*Annals* 11.15.1), however, the fact that 'foreign superstitions' were gaining strength was one of the main reasons for a similar measure by Claudius.

Certain phrases of these writers from the early second century CE look similar to those frequent in much later texts analysed before. Yet, we are encountering a terminology *in statu nascendi* rather than coined phrases. It is dangerous to use later reports as evidence for earlier perceptions. Trends, however, are clearly discernible. Identifying external agents as the main problem—as opposed to Livy's image of a Bacchic infection of Roman youth, formulated at the end of the first century BCE—became a strategy of growing importance. In the fourth century CE, for Firmicus Maternus the strike against the Bacchanalia was a fight against 'foreign' *superstitiones* (6.9) by an intact society, whose infection started only later with the import of the cult of Ceres/Proserpina from Henna (7). Disregarding all the counter-measures taken by the Roman public, by the turn of the second to the third century CE Tertullian identifies the Romanization of Serapis and the 'Italization' of Bacchus as the decisive breach of tradition (*Apologeticum* 6.10; cf. Minucius Felix 22.1).

Already by the second half of the first century CE the differentiation had become very sharp in terms of the trend just indicated. Yet it is still dominated by a Romanocentric view. Juvenal's often-quoted 'the Syrian river Orontes has already flown into the Tiber for a long time' (*Sat.* 3.62), does not explicitly talk about religion, but about culture in general, music and prostitution in particular. Religion, however, is part of the senatorial speech of a C. Cassius, composed by Tacitus in his account of a discussion about the collective killing of slaves after the murder of the urban prefect Pedanius Secundus by one of his slaves. He observes that by his time the family of slaves is formed by entire 'nations', 'that have diverse rites, foreign cults or none at all'—an argument that leaves fear of sanctions as the only remaining means of coercion (*Annals* 14.44.3). The archaeology of suburban Roman villas confirms that, with numerous sanctuaries which might just as well have served a taste for the religious exotic on the part of the owner as the exotic traditions of his slaves and freedmen.

The influx of cults to Rome, their blossoming at Rome, and the frequent establishment of a Roman centre of cults originating in other places (Isis, Christianity), has been described in detail in modern research. Rome, the capital, captivates and captivated the interest of modern as ancient intellectuals. Everyone venerates his gods, and the Romans all of them, is the summary observation of Caecilius (Minucius Felix 6.1), laying his stress on cult (6.3–7.1). A Romanocentric view is, however, dangerous. The image of Rome as 'temple of the whole world' uses a phrase that the Hermetic *Asclepius* applies to Egypt. An extraordinary mobility, enabled by the structures, needs, and possibilities of the Roman Empire, modified the religious landscape everywhere, as is clearly seen by an observer with experiences of Rome and Northern Africa, Minucius Felix (20.6, 'before the globe was open to commerce and the peoples mixed their rites and behaviours').

Conceptual Consequences of an Imperial Perspective

The apologetic argument was not interested in specifying the different subjects of such cults. Mobility is not identical with immigration. The young males who also frequently died young, whom Walter Scheidel has identified as the largest group of immigrants (2004), are not the part of a population which would be credited with being the most knowledgeable messengers of religion. Long-distance traders, however, wished to bolster their economic position in society; military officers and administrative personnel had much travel experience and experience in leading rituals (Haensch 1997). People like these, and intellectuals, could develop the bird-eye's view of the Roman Empire used by Christian apologetics in order to win freedom and acceptance for their own religious practice. The observation credited to the sceptic Caecilius that empires, provinces, and cities have and venerate their own deities (Minucius Felix 6.1) could be seen in its argumentative function in the earlier *Apology* of Tertullian: why, then, cannot we have a religion of our own (24.9)? Here, the group referred to as 'we' and the group composed of those enjoying full citizenship did not directly correspond.

Occasionally, consequences of the emergence of a continuous cultural space by the military and administrative establishment of the Roman Empire had been formulated earlier. Varro made a start. He did not only research the identity of the images of the Samothracian deities, venerated on their island in the north-east of the Aegean Sea, but declared that he was going to explain this to those who should know it (*Divine Antiquities* 15, fr. 206). At least by intention, this opened a space for communication about religion that transcended one's own city. In his praise of Italy and Rome, Pliny the Elder describes the mitigation of rituals (*Nat. Hist.* 3.39) as one of the functions of the establishment of the ecumene. He implies a trans-local discourse that implied local changes. The Roman dealing with the Druids and human sacrifice might offer an example (Rives 1995). In the second century, Lucian not only presented an assembly of gods critical of newcomers, but also analysed the establishment of a new cult, an oracle, in his *Alexandros* (Elm 2006, Bendlin 2006). Greek novels stage-managed their plots within an ecumenical Mediterranean imbued with mutually compatible religious practices (Waldner 2006).

The positions assembled so far did not imply any hierarchical ordering of such cultic practices. Yet such positions existed by the turn from the second to the third century. Celsus, as Arnaldo Momigliano has pointed out, produced a theology of the Roman Empire during the last quarter of the second century:

> If it is accepted that all of nature—everything in the world—operates according to the will of God and that nothing works contrary to his purposes, then it must also be accepted that the angels, the demons, heroes—everything in the universe—are subject to the will of the great God who rules over all. Over each sphere there is a being charged with the task of governance and worthy to have power, at least the power allotted it for carrying out its task. This being the case, it would be appropriate for each man who worships God also to honor the being who exercises his allotted responsibilities at God's pleasure. (p. 115 in the reconstruction of Hoffmann 1987; see Momigliano 1986: 289–90)

Despite the concentration on the emperor, Celsus' suggested consequence is utterly traditionalistic. Everywhere the (seemingly contingent) cults are part of the order of things, and hence participation is necessary and not bad, as it is ultimately referring back to the 'great God'.

L. Claudius Cassius Dio Cocceianus, perhaps writing in the 220s, a Roman consul of Greek background, is much more radical. His opposition to imperial cult (52.35.3) is combined with a strong insistence on the 'traditional' form of

(Roman) religious practices everywhere (52.36.1). For purely economic reasons he opts for Rome to be a religious centre by monopolizing circus races and keeping extra-Roman festival expenses at a moderate level (52.30.4, 7). A more centralizing model is implicitly present in Minucius Felix's non-Christian Octavius. The city of Rome is not only one of many, but a superior place because it attracts and venerates every god (6.1). Such a doubling or transfer is said to ensure Roman superiority on the scale of an empire. That, however, leaves open the function of the ongoing local cults.

Such inconsistencies remained unsolved, due to the combination of an urbanocentric view with what I have called the bird's-eye view of travelling officers, administrators, and merchants on trans-local religious plurality. For the period analysed here, there is no idea of unification of the empire by religion (contrary: Buchheit 1998). In practice, the symbolic loading of the centre dominated (Ando 2002; Cancik, Schäfer, and Spickermann 2006). It was only by the decree of Decius in 249 that local cults and central authority were integrated in a common framework. Now, compliance with the worship of local deities was made a matter of central concern and regulation (Rives 1999: 152). Still, the centre itself—personal (the emperor), not geographical (Rome)—did not emerge as the subject of a proper theology.

All of this does not reflect anything like a theory of religious plurality, neither does the widespread phenomenon of *interpretatio Romana*, Roman names given to 'foreign' deities (Ando 2005), mostly practised by local elites, who thus integrated traditional local deities into the media offered by Mediterranean religion, statues, inscriptions, and temple architecture. Yet, these reflections and practices attest to a growing complexity and importance of religion. Cult was more than the natural consequence of a religious disposition towards a contingent deity. It was subjected to rational explanation. It was subjected to universal standards of humanity. It was a necessary part of one's way of life, to which the division between public and private could not be applied. It was an economic and political factor. It was a medium of a non-religious discourse. These elements were neither new nor consistent. They fitted together with terminological changes, with *ratio* and *fides* controlling *religio* (e.g. Isidor, *De Differentiis* 2.139), with an insistence on *vera religio*, 'true religion', with *disciplina*, lifestyle, and morality (see Veyne 2005: 454–5), and *secta*, a grouping which is neither public nor private. Christians detected the origins of games and claimed them to be religious events (Tertullian, *On the Games*; Lactantius, *Epitome* 58). In the western provinces, by its use of inscriptions and architecture, religion became one of the most important media of public communication.

Another factor accrued. The mobility of more densely organized 'venerators'—by far not of every deity, *religio* and *cultus*—posed the problem of trans-local recognizability. Stabilization was achieved by different means. The rather standardized cult image of Mithras, unusual rituals and Egyptian decoration in the case of Isis (in general: Turcan 1996: 24–8), exchange of letters and collections of narratives in the case of the Christians, were equivalents in that perspective (see Rüpke 2005*b*). Yet they had very different consequences for the phenomenology of the ensembles and their success. Narratives could be much more easily propagated, adapted, and rephrased than images (see Elsner 1998: 235; Av. Cameron 1991: 19, 38–43), as the spread of Judaism and Christianity demonstrated.

For such a loaded concept of 'religion' and the appearance of boundary-creating 'cults', the religious framework of the empire became a problem, which it had not been in Cicero's day, from whose letters—as should be stressed for the readers of his philosophical treatises and orations—religion is virtually absent (Veyne 2005: 505). How could that bundle of life-shaping practices and beliefs which is more than *religio* be related to the empire and the emperor? To put it in a nutshell: it was not the empire that was crying for its own religion ('Reichsreligion'), but the mobility of the empire (succinctly Scheidel 2004: 22–3) had led to an accrued concept of religion that posed the question of its political position more and more urgently. From Aurelian and Diocletian onwards, the Roman administration strove to give an answer, if necessary by violent persecutions and penal law.

Conclusion

Without a concept of religion that allowed the drawing of unsurpassable boundaries between unities thus addressed, within our period religions could not be thought of in the plural in the modern sense. Neither *secta* and *disciplina* nor *religiones* fully arrived at fulfilling this function. The problem of a plurality that goes beyond the dual of 'we' and 'the others' was, however, present. It was a multi-dimensional plural, including a plural of religious signs as well as of places. 'Cults and religions', as modern research has come to say, do not capture these dimensions. The most important change between the first century BCE and the fourth century CE was not a change in numbers. Within the empire, religion changed its place in society. Only as a consequence, I should like to claim, did the problem of numbers, differences, and groups occur. We should no longer indulge in explanations based on the idea of 'syncretism' and 'transgression of boundaries' between Jews and Hellenists, Christians and astrologers, without looking carefully at the specific conditions of place and time. Of course, *katà tà pátria*, 'according to the way of the ancestors', could stress ethnic differences in the medium of religion. But intermarriage and mobility confounded the notion of *patria* (now Latin). Our modern concepts of 'religions' and 'cults' suggest boundaries that could not be seen by ancient agents and hence could not explain their acting. Thus, the Roman

Empire invites us not to reflect about the plurality of religions, but the boundaries that created 'religions'.

Further reading

For the complex religious situation of the Roman Empire, exchanges and common religious traits, a complete history or analysis is lacking; Rives 2007 is an overview. The chapters in volumes 11 and 12 of the 2nd edition of the *Cambridge Ancient History* and in Rüpke 2007 offer much material and relevant analyses. Succinct regional analyses are offered, for instance, by Sartre 2005: 274–342 (Syria); Woolf 1998: 206–38 (Gaul); and Spickermann 2003/7 (Germania). The situation of the centre is dealt with by Edwards and Woolf 2003 and Cancik, Schäfer, and Spickermann 2006. The notion of a separate class of 'oriental cult' is dissolved by the contributions in Bonnet, Rüpke, and Scarpi 2006. A critical bibliography for Roman religion is found in Belayche, Bendlin *et al.* (2000, 2003, 2007, 2009) and Wallraff 2007 for late antiquity.

References

Ando, Clifford (2002), 'The Palladium and the Pentateuch: towards a sacred topography of the later Roman empire', *Phoenix*, 55/3–4: 369–410.

—— (2005), 'Interpretatio Romana', *Classical Philology*, 100: 41–51.

—— and Rüpke, Jörg (eds.) (2006), *Religion and law in classical and Christian Rome* (Potsdamer altertumswissenschaftliche Beiträge 15), Stuttgart: Steiner.

Barchiesi, Alessandro (2006), 'Mobilità e religione nell'*Eneide*: Diaspora, culto, spazio, identità locali', in Elm von der Osten, Rüpke, and Waldner 2006: 13–30.

Barnes, T. D. (2001), 'Monotheists all?', *Phoenix*, 55: 142–62.

Beard, Mary, North, John, and Price, Simon (1998), *Religions of Rome.* 1: *A history*; 2: *A sourcebook*, Cambridge: University Press.

Belayche, Nicole, Bendlin, Andreas *et al.* (2000, 2003, 2007, 2009), 'Römische Religion (1990–1999)', *Archiv für Religionsgeschichte*, 2 (2000), 283–345; 5 (2003), 297–371; 9 (2007), 297–404; 11 (2009), 301–411.

Bendlin, Andreas (2006), 'Vom Nutzen und Nachteil der Mantik: Orakel im Medium von Handlung und Literatur in der Zeit der Zweiten Sophistik', in Elm von der Osten, Rüpke, and Waldner 2006: 159–207.

Bonnet, Corinne, Rüpke, Jörg, and Scarpi, Paolo (eds.) (2006), *Religions orientales—culti misterici: Neue Perspektiven—nouvelle perspectives—prospettive nuove* (Potsdamer altertumswissenschaftliche Beiträge 16), Stuttgart: Steiner.

Buchheit, Vinzenz (1998), 'Einheit durch Religion in Antike und Christentum', in Ernst Dassmann (ed.), *Chartulae: Fetschrift für Wolfgang Speyer.* Jahrbuch für Antike und Christentum suppl. 28. Münster: Aschendorff. 36–43.

Cameron, Averil (1991), *Christianity and the rhetoric of empire: the development of Christian discourse.* Sather Classical Lectures 55, Berkeley: University of California Press.

Cancik, Hubert (2006), '"Götter einführen": Ein myth-historisches Modell für die Diffusion von Religion in Vergils Aeneis', in Elm von der Osten, Rüpke, and Waldner 2006: 31–40.

——Schäfer, Alfred, and Spickermann, Wolfgang (eds.) (2006), *Zentralität und Religion*. Studien zu Antike und Christentum 39, Tübingen: Mohr Siebeck.

Davies, Jason P. (2004), *Rome's religious history: Livy, Tacitus and Ammianus on their gods*, Cambridge: Cambridge University Press.

Dyck, Andrew R. (ed.) (2003), *Cicero, De natura deorum liber I*, Cambridge: Cambridge University Press.

Edwards, Catharine and Woolf, Greg (eds.) (2003), *Rome the cosmopolis*, Cambridge: Cambridge University Press.

Elm von der Osten, Dorothee (2006), 'Die Inszenierung des Betruges und seiner Entlarvung: Divination und ihre Kritiker in Lukians Schrift "Alexandros oder der Lügenprophet"', in: Elm von der Osten, Rüpke, and Waldner 2006: 141–57.

——Rüpke, Jörg, and Waldner, Katharina (eds.) (2006), *Texte als Medium und Reflexion von Religion im römischen Reich*. Potsdamer Altertumswissenschaftliche Beiträge 14, Stuttgart: Steiner.

Elsner, Jaś (1998), *Imperial Rome and Christian triumph: the art of the Roman Empire AD 100–450*, Oxford: Oxford University Press.

Erskine, Andrew (2001), *Troy between Greece and Rome: local tradition and Imperial Rome*, Oxford: Oxford University Press.

Feil, Ernst (1986), *Religio: Die Geschichte eines neuzeitlichen Grundbegriffs vom Frühchristentum bis zur Reformation*. Forschungen zur Kirchen- und Dogmengeschichte 36, Göttingen: Vandenhoeck & Ruprecht.

Haensch, Rudolf (1997), *Capita provinciarum: Statthaltersitze und Provinzialverwaltung in der römischen Kaiserzeit*. Kölner Forschungen 7, Mainz: Zabern.

Hoffmann, R. Joseph (1987), *Celsus, On the True Doctrine: a discourse against the Christians*, New York: Oxford University Press.

Momigliano, Arnaldo (1986), 'The disadvantages of monotheism for a universal state', *Classical Philology*, 81: 285–97.

Mora, Fabio (1990; 1990*a*), *Prosopografia Isiaca*. 1: *Corpus prosopographicum religionis Isiacae*; 2: *Prosopografia storica e statistica del culto Isiaco*. EPRO 113, Leiden: Brill.

Noy, David (2000), *Foreigners at Rome: citizens and strangers*, London: Duckworth.

Rilke, R. L. (1987), *Apex Omnium: religion in the Res gestae of Ammianus*, Berkeley: University of California Press.

Rives, J. (1995), 'Human sacrifice among pagans and Christians', *JRS* 85: 65–85.

——(1999), 'The decree of Decius and the religion of empire', *JRS* 89: 135–54.

——(2007), *Religion in the Roman Empire*, Oxford: Blackwell.

Rüpke, Jörg (2002), 'Collegia sacerdotum—religiöse Vereine in der Oberschicht', in Ulrike Egelhaaf-Gaiser and Alfred Schäfer (eds.), *Religiöse Vereine in der römischen Antike: Untersuchungen zu Organisation, Ritual und Raumordnung*. Studien und Texte zu Antike und Christentum 13, Tübingen: Mohr Siebeck. 41–67.

——(2005), *Fasti sacerdotum Prosopographie der stadtrömischen Priesterschaften römischer, griechischer, orientalischer und jüdisch-christlicher Kulte bis 499 n. Chr.* Potsdamer Altertumswissenschaftliche Beiträge 12/1–3, Stuttgart: Steiner. 3 vols.

——(2005*a*), 'Varro's tria genera theologiae: religious thinking in the late Republic', *Ordia prima*, 4: 107–29.

Rüpke, Jörg (2005*b*), 'Buchreligionen als Reichsreligionen? Lokale Grenzen überregionaler religiöser Kommunikation', *Mittellateinisches Jahrbuch*, 40: 197–207.
—— (2006), 'Literarische Darstellungen römischer Religion in christlicher Apologetik: Universal- und Lokalreligion bei Tertullian und Minucius Felix', in Elm von der Osten, Rüpke, and Waldner 2006: 209–23.
—— (2006*a*), 'Religion in the lex Ursonensis', in Ando and Rüpke 2006: 34–46.
—— (ed.) (2007), *The Blackwell companion to Roman religion*, Oxford: Blackwell.
—— (2008), *Fasti Sacerdotum*, Oxford: Oxford University Press.
Sartre, Maurice (2005), *The Middle East under Rome*. Cambridge, Mass.: Harvard University Press.
Scheidel, Walter (2004), 'Human mobility in Roman Italy, I: the free population', *JRS* 94: 1–26.
Schmidt, Francis (1987), 'Polytheism: degeneration or progress?', in F. Schmidt (ed.), *The inconceivable polytheism: studies in religious historiography*. History and anthropology 3, London: Harwood Academic Press. 1–9.
Smith, Jonathan Z. (1998), 'Religion, religions, religious', in Mark C. Taylor (ed.), *Critical terms for religious studies*. Chicago: University of Chicago Press. 269–84.
Spickermann, Wolfgang (2003/2007), *Germania superior/Germania inferior: Religionsgeschichte des römischen Germanien 1–2*. Religion der römischen Provinzen 2/1–2. Tübingen: Mohr Siebeck.
Tranoy, Laurence (2000), 'The living and the dead: a struggle for space—approaches to landscape around Lyons', in John Pearce, Martin Millett, and Manuela Struck (eds.), *Burial, society and context in the Roman world*, Oxford: Oxbow. 162–9.
Turcan, Robert (1996), *The cults of the Roman Empire*, tr. Antonia Nevill, Oxford: Blackwell.
Veyne, Paul (2005), *L'Empire Gréco-Romain*, Paris: Ed. du Seuil.
Wallraff, Martin (2007), *Religionsgeschichte der Spätantike = Verkündigung und Forschung* 52,2. Gütersloh: Kaiser.
Waldner, Katharina (2006), 'Die poetische Gerechtigkeit der Götter: Recht und Religion im griechischen Roman', in Elm von der Osten, Rüpke, and Waldner 2006: 101–23.
Walsh, Patrick G. (1997), *The nature of gods*, Oxford: Clarendon Press.
Woolf, Greg (1998), *Becoming Roman: the origins of provincial civilization in Gaul*, Cambridge: Cambridge University Press.
Zinser, Hartmut (2002), 'Religio, Secta, Haeresis in den Häresiegesetzen des Codex Theodosianus (16,5,1/66) von 438', in: Manfred Hutter (ed.), *Hairesis: Festschrift für Karl Hoheisel zum 65. Geburtstag*. Jahrbuch für Antike und Christentum suppl. 34, Münster: Aschendorff. 215–19.

CHAPTER 48

JUDAISM

SETH SCHWARTZ

The Demands of Judaism as Ideological System

We may begin with a set of questions: to what extent and in what ways were the Jews integrated in the Roman world? Why was their integration initially so fraught (there were three cataclysmic revolts between 66 and 135 CE), but subsequently so successful? What can the answers to these questions tell us not only about the Jews but about the Roman state? Without prejudging the complex question of the relation between Judaism as a religious ideology and the actual cultural practices of the Jews, it will be helpful to begin with a brief account of what is known about Roman-era Judaism.

Judaism was monistic: its god was unique, he had a single holy place, the temple of Jerusalem, and his nation, Israel, was bound to him by an apparently indissoluble contract, whose terms were set out in the Pentateuch (or, Torah)—the first five books of the Hebrew Bible (Schwartz 2001: 49–87). A hereditary priestly clan, regarded as descendants in the male line of Moses' brother Aaron, played a special mediating role between God and Israel, because it presided over the sacrificial cult at the Jerusalem temple and also had special authority over the interpretation of the Torah (Schürer 1973–87: 2. 237–308; Sanders 1992: 77–102). But the Torah's Israel was essentially egalitarian in that its obligations were incumbent on the nation as a whole, without class distinction. Unlike ancient Near Eastern law-codes, which it in some respects resembles, the Torah was a public document, to be studied and enacted by all (i.e. all adult males). Even the priests were not meant to be an aristocracy (they were not permitted to own land), but merely a class of enablers or retainers, poised between privilege and pauperdom; what would later be called a clergy (cf. Brown 2001). Related to this egalitarianism is the fact that the Torah disapproved of relationships of personal dependency between Israelites. Such institutions as friendship, clientele, and vassalage, and to a surprising extent even the family, were discouraged, hedged about with limitations, or passed over in silence; Israelites are required to support one another, but unconditionally, without reciprocation, ideally anonymously, not with gifts (which inescapably generate personal gratitude and favour) but through charity (Lev. 19: 18; 25; Deut. 15; Weinfeld 1995; Hamel 1990).

Judaism's monism had as its corollary exclusivism. The Torah demands that Israelites reject all gods but Yahweh, the God of Israel, and everything associated with them, including their followers. Though the Torah is somewhat vague on the point, other biblical books make it clear that, at a minimum, any human relationship which may lead to worship of foreign gods is to be avoided, a prohibition extended in the books of Ezra and Nehemiah to all marriages with non-Israelites (even, apparently, if they were not 'idolatrous'; see Cohen 1999: 241–62; Hayes 2002). Many of the Torah's regulations had the effect (whatever their intention) of making inter-ethnic socialization very difficult; Israelites were not only barred from participation in their neighbours' religious celebrations, but could not even eat their food; the obligation to refrain from labour, apparently including all public business, one day out of every seven made participation in civic life very difficult in an environment in which the week (let alone the weekend) was not yet common.

Judaism as ideology, with its insistence on unconditional corporate solidarity, egalitarianism, and exclusivism, was indubitably effective—it had a traceable impact on the way Jews lived—but it was also utopian, unrealizable as a national constitution (Schwartz 2001: 55–69; 2005). As early as the third century BCE some elements of the priesthood acquired the trappings of an aristocracy, most importantly ownership of estates (Stern 1974: 20–35). By the second century BCE the ideal of absolute corporate solidarity fell victim (if it had not done so long before) first to a cultural war between reformist priests and their traditionalist opponents (Schürer 1973–87: 1. 137–73) and then to the rise of religious sectarianism (Baumgarten 1997). Perhaps more significantly, neither the Torah's insistence on dependency-free redistribution, nor its demand of absolute separatism, could ever be fully enacted. Since there was no way of enforcing charity laws, social institutions which had comparable redistributive effects—formal friendship, clientele, and vassalage—could never really be eradicated; nor could the institution Greeks called *xenia*—foreign guest-friendship (Schwartz 2007). Like all the little states of the eastern Mediterranean, the Jews needed their foreign friends (Herman 1987), and the institution is in fact well attested for Judaea. If this was so for Jews living in Palestine, it was all the more true for the growing number of Jews who by the third century BCE at latest lived elsewhere in the Mediterranean world (and subsequently also in parts of the Roman Empire far from the sea).

Real Jewish life was thus characterized by systemic tension between the totalizing demands of Judaism, and the exigencies of life in a pre-modern economic and social regime, and so, where successfully realized, by systematic accommodation. But the details of this accommodation varied widely over time and from place to place, and it is demonstrably the fact that it was not always successful. The most striking cases of its failure—the revolts mentioned above—will form the topic of the next section of this chapter.

The Onset of Roman Rule

The century-long collapse of the Seleucids starting in 164 BCE favoured the rise of local dynasties throughout their kingdom. Among these were the Hasmoneans in Judaea, a family of obscure background who seized the high priesthood of Jerusalem in 152 BCE and, following a series of conquests (of Idumaea, Samaria, the Jezreel Valley, and Galilee) assumed the royal title in 104 BCE (Schürer 1973–87: 1. 174–218). Many Judaeans questioned their legitimacy as both priests and kings, but the Hasmoneans succeeded nonetheless, by maintaining strategic friendships with the leading men in the conquered districts and in neighbouring principalities, by successful manipulation of the Ptolemaic rulers of Egypt and of pretenders to the declining Seleucid kingdom, and by harsh suppression of disturbances in Judaea (Schwartz 2000). Though they were never accepted by all Palestinian Jews, their military successes enhanced their legitimacy.

By the time of Pompey's conquest of Syria in 63 BCE the Hasmoneans' kingdom included almost all of Palestine west of the Jordan and some territory on the east bank of the river. Their kingdom was mainly Jewish because the Hasmoneans had insisted that the inhabitants of all or most of the territory they conquered convert (there is some doubt about the Greek cities of the coast and the Decapolis), whatever precisely this entailed (Cohen 1999: 109–39; Weitzman 1999). By 63, though, the Hasmoneans were in the throes of a dynastic war, which Pompey and his successor Aulus Gabinius attempted to resolve through a set of political arrangements that in their radicalism demonstrated that the Romans' approach to imperialism was far more interventionist than that of their Persian and Macedonian predecessors had been (Gabba 1999). Radical but ephemeral: the outbreak of the Roman civil wars generated a revival of the Hasmonean civil war, and eventually the loss of all Syria to the Parthians (40 BCE). The Hasmonean civil war in its turn strengthened the position of the Hasmoneans' non-Judaean friends—well-connected landowners who could mobilize manpower. The most successful of these was the family of the Idumaean grandee Antipater, which had until the Parthian invasion been successfully managing the career of the pretender Hyrcanus II (Schalit 1969; Shaw 1993; Richardson 1996; Kokkinos 1998). But the Hyrcanians failed to win the favour of the Parthians, and when Herod, son of Antipater, fled to Rome, then in a brief period of calm, the Senate was convinced by Octavian and Antony to name him king (conditional, it went without saying, on his helping the Romans reconquer Palestine).

Herod's political mission was exceptionally complex (for what follows see Schwartz 2001: 42–8). Though in some respects Antony and then Augustus inherited their system of rule in the East from the Hellenistic kingdoms, they, like Pompey, were far more interventionist. Hellenistic emperors might recognize local rulers who lacked legitimacy, but they rarely installed illegitimate rulers by force, and in general their presence in vassal kingdoms was less intrusive. By contrast, Herod was under constant pressure to please his incomparably powerful Roman friends, but also had to struggle to be accepted by his subjects, who included Judaeans, non-Judaean Jews (whose interests were often opposed), citizens of Greek cities, and residents of un-urbanized pagan territories. That it is impossible to provide an unambiguous evaluation of Herod's reign indicates something about the complexity of his task, which in turn informs us of the difficulties inherent in Roman–Jewish relations.

Herod (r. 37–4 BCE) was an activist ruler who poured money into his kingdom. He built cities and fortresses as monuments to his friends (Caesarea, Sebaste, Agrippeion, Antonia), his relatives (Antipatris, Phasaelis, Mariamme), and himself (two fortresses named Herodion) (Schürer 1973–87: 1. 287–329). Though Caesarea was probably intended as the chief port of entry for the vastly expanded traffic of Jewish pilgrims to Jerusalem, it was a dramatically Roman city (Raban and Holum 1996). The first landmark visitors saw as they entered the harbour was the looming temple of Roma and Augustus (Richardson 1996; Roller 1998). Similarly, Herod was perhaps the first eastern king to build an amphitheatre—a specifically Roman type of building decorated in this case with reminders of Roman power—and fund gladiatorial games and *venationes*, and this apparently in the immediate vicinity of Jerusalem (Levine 2002; he also funded extensive building projects in Greek cities of the Eastern Empire and was a patron of the Olympic games). The gold eagle Herod had installed over the main gate to the Jerusalem temple has also been thought a symbol of Roman rule, but this is far less certain. Herod also intervened in the Jerusalem high priesthood, changing it from a dynastic to an appointed position, presumably to keep it from becoming competitive with himself. (The Hasmoneans had supplanted the legitimate dynasty over a century earlier.)

Concurrently, though, Herod cultivated a certain kind of Jewish piety: he massively rebuilt the Jerusalem temple, and celebrated the partial completion of the project around 20 BCE in splendid style; he also appears to have rebuilt other holy places, like the Judaeo-Idumaean Cave of the Machpelah (traditionally the burial-place of the biblical patriarchs, who were also the putative ancestors of the Idumaeans) in Hebron; he zealously supported the people of Jerusalem during a famine; he insisted that foreign princes who married into his family be circumcised, and, as we now know from the excavations of his palace at Herodion, south-east of Bethlehem, shared the Jewish aversion to figurative images (Schwartz 2009).

The historian Josephus (37–*c.*100 CE) provides two strikingly different evaluations of Herod. In the *Jewish War*, Book 1 (*c.*80), Herod is represented as having mediated between Roman and Jewish demands with some measure of success: the Jews appreciated his gifts to them and did not begrudge his gifts to Greek cities and acts of homage to powerful Romans, having apparently, for the time being, reconciled themselves to new political realities; opposition to Herod was restricted to a tiny minority. The Romans, for their part, appreciated Herod's friendship and actively supported his efforts to make the Jews wealthier and more powerful.

In the *Jewish Antiquities*, Books 14–17 (*c.*90), though the facts are largely the same, the evaluation is completely different. Here, the tensions are emphasized: in fact Josephus describes a fundamental cultural misfit between Jews and Romans which all too easily turned into political unrest. In a remarkably lucid analytical passage (not otherwise Josephus' *forte*), he observes that Herod had thoroughly internalized the Roman political norms of honour and reciprocity: he paid extravagant court to his Roman friends and expected his subjects to do the same for him; but his Jewish subjects in the first place resented him because they had to pay for his courtship of the Romans. But more importantly, the whole economy of honour as embodied in monumental construction was unacceptable to them because they were accustomed to value only piety toward God. Thus, though the Jews welcomed Herod's reconstruction of the Jerusalem temple, they expressed their gratitude to God, not the king; and they appreciated his famine-relief programme, but it could not counteract all his other misdeeds. Herod's Greek subjects got along better with the king, since they could participate in the exchange of honour (Schwartz 2009; cf. Shaw 1989).

Josephus exaggerated. Even by his own account, Jewish opposition to Herod was not as widespread as Josephus claimed, and Greek and Roman support not as univocal. Nevertheless, his analysis is partly correct. Examination of the archaeology and epigraphy of first-century Jerusalem (summarized in Levine 2002) shows that on the whole its inhabitants *did* opt out of the empire-wide economy of honour and euergetism, or at any rate practised a remarkably peculiar variant of it, in a way that could only make life difficult for anyone trying to mediate between the Jews and the Roman state. Furthermore, Herod's own policies made matters worse. His highly effective encouragement of pilgrimage, and of close relations with the Jews of the Diaspora, only increased the Jews' collective exposure to a value-system at odds with the Roman norm, or, as Josephus would have put it, their devotion to piety.

Herod's activities had other destabilizing effects, too. Jerusalem now became a massive silver magnet. While much of the silver flowing into the temple treasury was unproductive, the rest was used to fund what had become a huge establishment, and so enriched priests, provisioners, and maintenance and construction workers, and this apart from the trade and manufacture generated by the secular needs of pilgrims. As a result, Jews who contributed to but were not in the position to benefit materially from the temple economy were in the aggregate impoverished by the temple, while Jerusalem and its environs, now dominated by the temple and pilgrimage economies, were massively enriched. Judaea thus came to have a highly inflationary economy, and a correspondingly 'abnormal' social regime (structurally not unlike that of Central Italy in the same period, though on a *much* smaller scale). It was necessarily dominated by people enriched by the temple and pilgrimage, who, to be reductive about it, had excellent material reasons for strong devotion to Jewish piety. This probably explains why Josephus' account of first-century Judaea is so focused on the priests, and why he sometimes writes about the Jewish sects—by definition populated by men (almost never women) of unusually strong religious devotion—as if all Jewish men belonged to one: in Jerusalem and Judaea (but not in Galilee and elsewhere) a surprising number did. And the same factor also may explain the remarkably prominent role young upper-class Jerusalemite priests played in the early stages of the rebellion against Rome.

Conversely, rising wealth in Jerusalem generated rising land-prices in its Judaean hinterland, which eventually made traditional, low-profit, grain, olive, and grape farming impossible, and probably led to the concentration of landholding. Farmers reduced thereby to tenancy or pushed off their land altogether were probably among those populating the tumultuous crowd scenes that were typical of first-century Jerusalem, if we can believe Josephus and the Gospels (which we can only with reservations and qualifications). Such displaced farmers may also have been among the 18,000 labourers left unemployed when the construction of Herod's temple was finally complete in 64 CE (for the last two paragraphs, see Goodman 1987: 51–75; 2002; cf. 2007: 397–422; Schwartz 2001: 87–99).

In sum, the initial failure of the Jews' integration in the Roman state can be attributed to the convergence of many factors, not least of which were the paradoxical effects of the policies of the highly integrationist vassal king Herod and his successors. One may think, merely for the sake of illustrative comparison, of the effects in the Muslim world today of the complicated, simultaneously pro-western and zealously Islamist, politics of the Saudi kings. Similarly, it is worth noting the counter-cultural potential, from the perspective of the Roman state, of Judaism as a system of values. This lends plausibility to the view that the Romans' suppression of the Jewish revolt, culminating in the razing of the temple and city of Jerusalem, was meant not only as a solution to a political problem, and as part of the Flavian dynasty's bid for legitimacy, but also as a frontal attack on Judaism itself (Rives 2007: 193–6; Millar 2005).

The Successful Integration of the Jews

The fact that there were inherent tensions between Judaism and the Roman state does not mean that the Jews always and everywhere resisted integration, if only because the revolt of 66–70 and the two which followed it (the Diaspora Revolt of 115–17 and the Bar Kokhba Revolt of 132–5) demonstrated that the Romans were prepared to exact a very high price from Jewish resisters (Pucci 1981; Barclay 1996; Schäfer 2003; Goodman 2004 and 2007: 445–511). Another immediate consequence of the revolts, a sharp decrease in the number of Jews living in the Roman Empire, especially in Palestine and Egypt, probably also played a role in the Jews' successful integration (Schwartz 2006).

Post-Revolt Palestine: Rabbis

Surviving Jewish literature written during the first 150 years of Roman rule—especially the works of Josephus and Philo of Alexandria—provides excellent evidence for the views of integrationist elites, with all their inner tensions and ambivalences, while the surviving writing of the following four centuries can be collectively characterized as secessionist. This is paradoxical because both first-century writers lived to see the failure of their visions, while the authors of the later books, the Palestinian rabbis, lived and taught at times when tensions between Jews and Rome rarely assumed violent form.

The rabbis started as the tiny post-70 remnant of the sprawling pre-70 class of priests, judges, pietists, and scribes who had been important in the post-Herodian administration of the Jerusalem temple and of the law (Cohen 1984; Hezser 1997). Their collective writing consists of legal texts (the Mishnah, *c.*200 CE; Tosefta, *c.*250), legal commentaries (the Palestinian Talmud, *c.*380; the Babylonian Talmud, produced several centuries later under Sassanian or early Muslim rule, will not concern us here), biblical exegesis (Genesis and Leviticus Rabbah, *c.*400–50), and liturgical poetry (the *piyyut*, sixth–seventh centuries) (Strack and

Stemberger 1996). The earlier texts in some measure bear comparison with contemporary Greek writing of the 'Second Sophistic' because, like some of the latter, the rabbis constructed in their writing a world in which Romans are scarcely present: in these texts, both Jewish and Greek, resistance takes the form of obliviousness. The rabbis continued to imagine Palestine as a country in which un-Romanized Jewish farmers lived in complete conformity with biblical/Jewish legal, social, and cultural norms. But when the realities of Roman rule do surface in the Mishnah or, more frequently, in the Tosefta and Talmud, they are portrayed far less benignly than in the works of contemporaneous eastern provincials like Plutarch or Pausanias, or even the moderately resentful Libanius (cf. Swain 1996). Few rabbinic texts evince anything as subtle as ambivalence to Rome; as in some Christian texts of the period, hostility is expressed with complete openness. But the hostility was tempered by fear: like some Christians, rabbis counselled conformity and evasion, even as they glorified martyrdom. In practice, then, rabbis, like Church Fathers, stood for a wary and grudging integration, in which the demands of the state were minimally met, the imperatives of *romanitas* firmly rejected.

The rabbis retained the collective consciousness of a battered, reduced, and disenfranchised royal bureaucracy which never stopped hoping for its restoration, even though the texts themselves hint that some individual rabbis were far better adjusted than their collective literature indicates. They had the luxury of cultivating this attitude for several reasons. In the aftermath of the revolts small groups of Jewish secessionists ceased to interest the Roman state. Though the rabbis, as embodiments of uncompromising devotion to the Torah, always had friends, admirers, and supporters among non-rabbinic Jews, they did not acquire real power and influence until the Late Empire, at earliest; during the late first and second centuries the short-term cost to the state of ignoring them was minimal. By the third century the rabbis had come to enjoy the patronage and protection of a genuinely integrationist Jewish grandee, the so-called patriarch. The patriarchs were descended from a prominent family of first-century Jerusalem who later became leading rabbis; in the course of the third century they succeeded in transforming themselves again, this time into a dynasty—based in the Galilean city of Tiberias—with quasi-episcopal power over some aspects of Jewish religious life, though their *authority* as leaders was formally recognized only under the Christian emperors of the fourth century. The patriarchs always retained their ties to the rabbis, employing some of them as members of a judicial bureaucracy in the process of institutionalization, but they became increasingly Romanized as their power grew (Hezser 1997; Levine 1979, 1996; Jacobs 1995). They thus came to act as an effective buffer between the rabbis and the state, serving, like Herod before them, as integrationist patrons of Jewish separatism. (This revived separatism was, unlike its earlier manifestation, politically neutralized—see below.)

Post-Revolt Palestine: Others

Hostility and unwilling compliance were not the only responses to the violence that the Roman state repeatedly exercised against the Jews in the late first and early second centuries, though other responses must be rather speculatively reconstructed from archaeology and from scattered hints in literary texts. In sum, the 'normalcy' of much northern Palestinian archaeology, numismatics, and epigraphy in the context of the High Imperial East strongly suggests that many or most Jews responded in much the same way as other Roman subjects. The largely Jewish cities of northern Palestine, Tiberias and Sepphoris, in addition to partly Jewish cities like Lydda-Diospolis, Joppa, and Caesarea Maritima, were all dominated by thoroughly integrationist city councillors; their coins, public and private inscriptions, and other physical remains all show that these were standard cities of the Roman East, and that Greco-Roman paganism constituted their religious norm.

The rulers of these cities produced no extant literary texts, so it is impossible to say anything about their subjectivity: did they continue to regard themselves as Jews? Did their Jewishness assume the same tenuous form as, say, the 'Phoenicianness' of Philo of Byblos or the 'Syrianness' of Lucian of Samosata? These same cities were also the centres of the rabbinic movement and of the increasingly powerful patriarchate. Do Talmudic stories, almost all concerning the late third or fourth century, about competition between patriarchs, rabbis, and city councillors reflect earlier conditions, or was such competition in fact enabled by a third-century decline of the curial classes, or by the fourth-century Christian state's willingness to patronize religious officials (including Jewish religious officials, as we know from the extensive legislation preserved in *Codex Theodosianus* 16.8), even at the expense of traditional elites? And what about non-elite residents of the cities? Did they buy into the Romanizing ideology (if any) of the *curiales*, prefer the Judaism of the rabbis, or adhere (as I believe most likely) to some incoherent mixture of the two? (For the previous two paragraphs, which do not represent scholarly consensus, see Schwartz 2001: 103–202.)

The Diaspora

Whatever the answer to these questions may be, it does seem certain that the mass of the Jews in Palestine after 135 found some way of coping with the conflicting demands of Judaism and the Roman state, though surely some simply opted out of Judaism altogether. And it is important to recall that the Jews' compromise was enabled not only by their own agency, but also by the Romans' elimination of their ideological and political centre, by the death or flight of almost the entirety of their former ruling class, and by the simple brute fact that there were far fewer Jews in Palestine in 150 than there had been a century earlier, and they were now hemmed in by two Roman legions.

In some ways—for example, their decentralization and their relatively small numbers—the experience of the Jews in Palestine after 135 had come to resemble that of Jews living elsewhere in the Roman Empire, in the Diaspora (Millar 1992; Gruen 2002). But 'diaspora' is essentially a theological, not a socio-political or cultural, category, and we must be careful not to be misled by the utility of this freighted term into thinking of Roman Jewry as a single entity possessing a discrete history. In fact, the Jews in Egypt (Barclay 1996; Modrzejewski 1997) had a strikingly different history, one very closely tied to that of Palestine, from Jews in Asia Minor (Trebilco 1991; Ameling 2004) or Italy (Noy 1993; Rutgers 1995) (there was a very large and important Jewish settlement outside the Roman Empire, in central Mesopotamia, which will not concern us here).

Or so we suppose, for Egypt contained the only Jewish settlements whose history is even partly recoverable, thanks to the survival of a not-insubstantial corpus of documentary texts, mainly of Ptolemaic date (Tcherikover, Fuks, and Stern 1957–64), and to the survival of the works of the philosopher Philo (*c.*10 BCE–*c.*50 CE). Philo in particular attests to, and embodies, the last florition of Jewish integrationism in the very large Jewish community of Alexandria. It seems likely that Egyptian Jews had for centuries been acculturating to the privileged Greek minority in Egypt, in addition to the fact that, like other immigrant groups in the Ptolemaic period, they were legally classified as 'Hellenes'. Philo in effect provided the ideological foundation for such an identification by arguing, in a long series of philosophical/exegetical essays on Pentateuchal stories and laws, for the identity of the highest Greek philosophical ideals with the values of the Torah; for Philo this justified not only study and contemplation of the latter, but the practical observance of Jewish laws.

Philo was anticipated in much of his argument by a text of the Hellenistic period, the *Letter of Aristeas* (Honigman 2003). Yet, while the earlier text celebrated the alliance of the Jews and the Ptolemaic dynasty, Philo wrote nothing comparable about Rome. Indeed, his two treatises about Rome, *In Flaccum* and *Legatio ad Gaium*, describe the unravelling of relations between Alexandrian Jews and the Roman state, a process Philo himself sought unsuccessfully to halt. The reasons for this failure are highly controversial, but it seems certain that, as in Palestine, Roman interventionism played an important role, though in ways much harder to describe (Gruen 2002; Schäfer 1997). At any rate, in 41 CE Claudius brought a period of civil disturbances between Jews and Greeks at Alexandria to an end by declaring that the Egyptian Jews had the right to use their own laws but had no corporate eligibility for Alexandrian citizenship, thereby bringing to an end the centuries-long dominance of the integrationist view among Egyptian Jews. Though rather little is known about what then happened, it is certain that there were minor uprisings—some fomented by refugees from Palestine—in Egypt at the time of the Great Revolt of 66–70, and in 115 a major uprising spread from Egypt to Cyrenaica, Cyprus, and Crete, and ended in 117 with the near-destruction of the Jewish settlements in those provinces (Pucci 1981).

No other Diaspora community approximated that of Alexandria in its size or in its cultural and political aspirations. For reasons presently to be explored, historians have tended to produce accounts of Jewish life in the non-Egyptian Diaspora which is far too static and normative, one might say far too optimistic. In reality, it is overwhelmingly likely that in many periods it had (like most Jewish life in better-attested periods) a much more volatile and improvisatory character than the standard literature suggests.

Outside Palestine, and the exceptional diasporic environment of early Roman Alexandria, the Jews lived in scattered, small, and, one must suppose (since evidence for the non-Egyptian Diaspora is episodic and poor, we cannot claim to *know* anything about it), highly unstable groups. All Jewish communities necessarily experienced attrition: individuals, groups, or even entire communities lost all sense of separate identity and merged into their pagan environments (the opposite process is attested but was surely far less common: Barclay 1996: 310–19; Goodman 1994).

What this implies is that evidence for Diaspora Judaism misleadingly concerns the Jewish hard-core, the most strongly self-identified members of Jewish religious corporations or communities, and not Jews who failed to leave recognizable material evidence of their Jewishness, either because they lived outside communal frameworks, or were weakly self-identified, or practised varieties of Judaism we cannot easily recognize as such, or concealed their Jewishness, or abandoned it. Furthermore, scholars tend to conflate scattered evidence for diasporic Judaism. It is, for example, barely possible to produce a history of the Jews of Greco-Roman Asia Minor (e.g. Trebilco 1991); but the illusion of continuity created thereby elides the fact that for many communities we have only one or two items of evidence apiece, and so we cannot know whether their strategies of corporate survival were actually successful or not (Bohak 2002).

Nevertheless, some Jewish communities indubitably found successful ways of resolving the tensions implicit in preserving Jewish life under Roman rule. And *urban* Jewish communities—which probably contained the majority of Diaspora Jews outside Egypt, though some rural settlements are attested—all faced certain shared challenges, due to the fundamental similarity of Roman cities, and so developed a set of common responses. So, while rates of attrition were high, communities died out or disbanded, Jewish communities in the Roman world did sometimes survive, in a way that other immigrant ethnic corporations did not. Surely part of the reason for their limited success was that the Jews came in many places to constitute local religious communities. The Jews, like Isis- and Mithras-worshippers, drew on a portable religious ideology, but they differed from the latter, who drew their members from the standard inhabitants of Roman cities or army camps and never demanded their full religious separation from their environment, by simultaneously validating partial integration and enabling partial separatism.

Although we cannot pretend to know in every case precisely what the Jews' 'civic compromise' consisted of, a few not-unimportant general points may be regarded as basically established: especially before the fifth and sixth centuries, but to some extent even then, even the most strongly self-identified Jews—that is, the ones about whom we have some information—were fairly highly acculturated in their Roman environments. For example, all used Greek, and in some places Latin, not only for routine communication (this is admittedly a guess, since we have no records of routine communication) but also for liturgical and other religious purposes: until the fifth century there is almost no evidence for Hebrew prayer or Torah study. Inscriptions from Asia Minor, Italy, and elsewhere quote the Septuagint, not a different Greek translation. Almost all Jewish communities came to possess synagogues, where they worshipped God with prayer and Torah study rather than sacrifice, and all synagogue buildings so far discovered use decorative and design elements borrowed from their Roman environments (Levine 2005). Furthermore, by the fourth century at latest, many Jewish communities used language and practices derived from the widespread urban social institution modern scholars call euergetism (Rajak and Noy 1993).

This final point bears emphasis, because in some places the benefactors included well-to-do pagans (e.g. Trebilco 1991; Chaniotis 2002). Although all small religious communities in the Roman Empire including the Jews were to some extent expansionist, welcoming adherents from outside the community, the Jews seem to have especially sought gentile supporters, not adherents, especially distinguished ones, who probably in many places played important roles in easing the Jews' communal existence in cities in whose municipal religious life and public affairs professing Jews found it hard to participate. Even the highly separatist rabbis acknowledged the importance of pagan friends and supporters for the maintenance of Jewish communal life, advising Jews living in mixed cities to celebrate pagans' weddings, tend the pagan sick, and mourn the pagan dead, 'because of the ways of peace', that is, to win not converts but friends.

Christianization

The gradual Christianization of the empire in the fourth and fifth centuries eventually altered the terms of the Jews' civic compromise in drastic ways. Social and political integration underpinned by religious and cultural compromise, and aided by gentile supporters, eventually lost their effectiveness in a Christian environment. Unlike their pagan predecessors, Christian emperors, starting with Theodosius I at latest, regarded the Jews as Roman citizens but concurrently as constituting a licit but inferior religious community; they fully authorized the Jews' internal communal institutions (pagan emperors had regarded them with indifference or hostility), but at the cost of the Jews' social and political separation—though the latter in practice could never really be fully achieved. Jews who wished to remain integrated in their cities could do so, provided they converted to Christianity. A well-known though dubiously historical Latin text, the *Letter of Severus Bishop of Minorca on the Conversion of the Jews*, describes a small but distinguished Jewish community which, under intense pressure from local Christians, preserved its local social and political role by converting *en masse* to Christianity, in 418 (Bradbury 1996).

These new conditions of Jewish life continued in force—in the broadest possible terms—in Christian Europe until the 'emancipation' of the Jews in the course of the nineteenth century. They may help to explain why Jewish life in late antiquity came to have a distinctively medieval, inward-turning, feel. The synagogue and the local religious community were now ubiquitous, even in still heavily Jewish northern Palestine; though Greek was still in general liturgical use, Hebrew began to experience a revival; in some places rabbis—who would play a critical role in the governance of medieval Jewish communities—began to acquire more prominence, and possibly influence (Schwartz 2001: 179–289).

References

Ameling, W., 2004. *Inscriptiones Judaicae Orientis*, vol. 2: *Kleinasien*. Tübingen.

Barclay, J., 1996. *Jews in the Mediterranean Diaspora from Alexander to Trajan (323 BCE–117 CE)*. Edinburgh.

Baumgarten, A., 1997. *The Flourishing of Jewish Sects in the Maccabean Era: An Interpretation*. Leiden.

Bohak, G., 2002. 'Ethnic Continuity in the Jewish Diaspora in Antiquity', in J. Bartlett, ed., *Jews in the Hellenistic and Roman Cities*. London, 175–92.

Bradbury, S., 1996. *Severus of Minorca: Letter on the Conversion of the Jews*. Oxford.

Brown, P., 2001. *Poverty and Leadership in the Later Roman Empire*. Hanover, NH.

Chaniotis, A., 2002. 'The Jews of Aphrodisias: New Evidence and Old Problems'. *SCI* 21: 209–42.

Cohen, S., 1984. 'The Significance of Yavneh: Pharisees, Rabbis, and the End of Jewish Sectarianism'. *Hebrew Union College Annual*, 55: 27–53.

—— 1999. *The Beginnings of Jewishness: Boundaries, Varieties, Uncertainties*. Berkeley.

Gabba, E., 1999. 'The Social, Economic and Political History of Palestine 63 BCE–CE 70'. *CHJ* 3: 94–167.

Goodman, M., 1987. *The Ruling Class of Judaea: The Origins of the Jewish Revolt Against Rome, AD 66–70*. Cambridge.

——1994. *Mission and Conversion: Proselytizing in the Religious History of the Roman Empire*. Oxford.

——2002. 'Current Scholarship on the First Revolt', in A. Berlin and J. A. Overman, eds., *The First Jewish Revolt: Archaeology, History and Ideology*. London, 15–25.

——2004. 'Trajan and the Origins of Roman Hostility to the Jews'. *Past & Present* 182: 3–29.

——2007. *Rome and Jerusalem: The Clash of Ancient Civilizations*. London.

Gruen, E., 2002. *Diaspora: Jews Amidst Greeks and Romans*. Cambridge, Mass.

Hamel, G., 1990. *Poverty and Charity in Roman Palestine, First Three Centuries CE*. Berkeley.

Hayes, C., 2002. *Gentile Impurities and Jewish Identities: Intermarriage and Conversion from the Bible to the Talmud*. New York and Oxford.

Herman, G., 1987. *Ritualised Friendship and the Greek City*. Cambridge.

Hezser, C., 1997. *The Social Structure of the Rabbinic Movement in Roman Palestine*. Tübingen.

Honigman, S., 2003. *The Septuagint and Homeric Scholarship in Alexandria: A Study in the Narrative of the Letter of Aristeas*. London.

Jacobs, M., 1995. *Die Institution des jüdischen Patriarchen*. Tuebingen.

Kokkinos, N., 1998. *The Herodian Dynasty: Origins, Role in Society and Eclipse*. Sheffield.

Konstan, D., 1997. *Friendship in the Classical World*. Cambridge.

Levine, L. 1992. 'The Jewish Patriarch (Nasi) in Third-century Palestine', *ANRW* II. 19. 2: 649–88.

——1996. 'The Status of the Patriarch in the Third and Fourth Centuries: Sources and Methodology', *Journal of Jewish Studies*, 47: 1–32.

——2002. *Jerusalem: Portrait of the City in the Second Temple Period (538 BCE–70 CE)*. Philadelphia.

——2005. *The Ancient Synagogue: The First Thousand Years*[2]. New Haven.

Lüderitz, G. 1983. *Corpus jüdischer Zeugnisse aus der Cyrenaika*. Wiesbaden.

Millar, F., 1992. 'The Jews of the Graeco-Roman Diaspora Between Paganism and Christianity'. In J. Lieu, J. North, and T. Rajak, eds., *The Jews Among Pagans and Christians in the Roman Empire*. London, 97–123.

——2005. 'Last Year in Jerusalem: Monuments of the Jewish War in Rome'. In J. Edmondson, S. Mason, and J. Rives, eds., *Flavius Josephus and Flavian Rome*. Oxford, 101–28.

Modrzejewski, J., 1997. *The Jews of Egypt from Rameses II to Emperor Hadrian*. Princeton.

Noy, D., 1993. *Jewish Inscriptions of Western Europe*. 2 vols. Cambridge.

Pucci, M., 1981. *Rivolta ebraica al tempo di Traiano*. Pisa.

Raban, A. and Holum, K., eds., 1996. *Caesarea Maritima: A Retrospective after Two Millennia*. Leiden.

Rajak, T. and Noy, D., 1993. 'Archisynagogoi: Office, Title, and Social Status in the Greco-Jewish Synagogue'. *JRS* 83: 75–93.

Richardson, P., 1996. *Herod: King of the Jews and Friend of the Romans*. Columbia, SC.

Rives, J., 2007. *Religion in the Roman Empire*. Malden, Mass.

Roller, D., 1998. *The Building Program of Herod the Great*. Berkeley.

Rutgers, L., 1995. *The Jews in Late Ancient Rome: Evidence of Cultural Interaction in the Roman Diaspora*. Leiden.

Sanders, E. P., 1992. *Judaism: Practice and Belief, 63 BCE–66CE*. Philadelphia.

SCHÄFER, P., 1997. *Judaeophobia: Attitudes Toward the Jews in the Ancient World.* Cambridge, Mass.

—— 2003. *The Bar Kokhba War Reconsidered: New Perspectives on the Second Jewish Revolt Against Rome.* Tübingen.

SCHALIT, A., 1969. *König Herodes: der Mann und sein Werk.* Berlin.

SCHÜRER, E., 1973–87. *History of the Jewish People in the Age of Jesus Christ (175 BC–AD 135).* 3 vols., revised and edited by G. Vermes, F. Millar, *et al.* Edinburgh.

SCHWARTZ, S., 2000. 'Herod, Friend of the Jews'. In J. Schwartz, Z. Amar, and I. Ziffer, eds., *Jerusalem and Eretz Israel: Arie Kindler Volume.* Tel-Aviv, 67–77.

—— 2001. *Imperialism and Jewish Society from 200 BCE to 640 CE.* Princeton.

—— 2005. 'A God of Reciprocity: Torah and Social Relations in an Ancient Mediterranean Society'. In Zs. Varhelyi and J.-J. Auber, eds., *A Tall Order: Writing the Social History of the Ancient World. Essays in Honor of William V. Harris.* Munich, 3–37.

—— 2006. 'Political, Social, and Economic Life in the Land of Israel, 66–235 CE.' In S. Katz, ed., *The Cambridge History of Judaism.* Cambridge, 4. 23–52.

—— 2007. 'Conversion to Judaism in the Second Temple Period: A Functionalist Approach'. In S. Cohen and J. Schwartz, eds., *Studies in Josephus and the Varieties of Ancient Judaism: Louis H. Feldman Jubilee Volume.* Leiden, 223–36.

—— 2009. 'Euergetism in Josephus and the Epigraphical Culture of First Century Jerusalem'. In H. Cotton *et al.*, eds., *From Hellenism to Islam: Cultural and Linguistic Change in the Roman Near East.* Cambridge, 75–92.

SHAW, B., 1989. Review of Goodman 1987. *JRS* 79: 246–7.

—— 1993. 'Tyrants, Bandits and Kings: Personal Power in Josephus'. *Journal of Jewish Studies,* 44: 176–204.

STERN, M., 1974. Greek *and Latin Authors on Jews and Judaism,* vol. 1. Jerusalem.

STRACK, H. and STEMBERGER, G., 1996. *Introduction to the Talmud and Midrash.* Minneapolis.

SWAIN, S., 1996. *Hellenism and Empire: Language, Classicism, and Power in the Greek World, AD 50–250.* Oxford.

TCHERIKOVER, V., FUKS, A., and STERN, M., eds., 1957–64. *Corpus Papyrorum Judaicarum.* 3 vols. Cambridge, Mass.

TREBILCO, P., 1991. *Jewish Communities in Asia Minor.* Cambridge.

WEINFELD, M., 1995. *Social Justice in Ancient Israel and the Ancient Near East.* Minneapolis.

WEITZMAN, S., 1999. 'Forced Circumcision and the Shifting Role of Gentiles in Hasmonean Ideology'. *Harvard Theological Review,* 92: 37–59.

CHAPTER 49

CHRISTIANITY

HAGITH SIVAN

Introduction

The facts are few and controversial. A man by the name of Jesus (Yeshu), from the obscure region of the Galilee, clashed with the Jewish establishment in Judaean Jerusalem and was dispatched to his death on orders of the Roman governor, like thousands of others, by the gruesome method of crucifixion (*c.*30 CE). The Galilean preacher left behind a rich legacy of parables and miracles. His admirers, few but fiery, set out from Judaea to spread his message throughout major urban centres in the eastern provinces. Two even reached the imperial capital of Rome. The appeal of this Galilean creed seemed inexplicable yet irresistible. It successfully enlisted intellectuals who were able to process its embryonic ideology into a sophisticated theological system; it developed an organizational network (the Church) that ultimately came to rival that of the Roman state itself; and it managed to inspire believers with readiness to follow the sect's founder to death.

Imperial decrees notwithstanding, by the third mid-century Christianity was sufficiently prominent to elicit empire-wide persecution. By the early fourth century it scored its most spectacular achievement with the conversion of the emperor himself. The choice proved irreversible. The newly adopted imperial creed opened widely hitherto-unexplored vistas. Citizens of Christian persuasion could adopt new ways of life, both permanent and temporary. They could serve in the ranks of the ecclesiastical administration; they could elect to withdraw from active careers into the tranquillity of monastic life in any of the monasteries that sprouted throughout the provinces; or they could dislocate themselves by embarking on a pilgrimage to localities which boasted sanctity.

In late antiquity, in spite of continuous dogmatic disagreements which had dogged the history of Christian ideology from its very beginning, the new state religion proved an exceptional bonding matter. In an age that witnessed uncertainties and insecurities liturgies and ceremonies drew crowds on a regular basis to attend reassuring services, to marvel at the magnificent mosaics that decorated the walls and floors of the churches, and to listen to sermons that promised rewards to believers, if not on earth then certainly in heaven.

To the un-Roman, Christianity presented an instrument of 'becoming Roman'. Through imperial and ecclesiastical initiatives the ideology of Roman Christianity, in several distinct guises, was exported to the world beyond the Roman frontiers. North of the Danube and the Rhine Rome's barbarian neighbours opted for 'Arian' Christianity, a choice which prevented assimilation while proving detrimental to the soundness and longevity of the kingdoms which these tribal confederacies were to establish on Roman soil. Along Rome's eastern frontiers a Monophysite form of the creed appealed from the fifth century onward to the nomads enlisted to protect the provinces against Persia and to regulate the movements of other nomads. The transfer from paganism to Christianity among the barbarians in the fifth century proved as rapid as the one from Christianity to Islam among Rome's allies in the seventh. In the East, then, the attachment to Rome went hand in hand with the adoption of the imperial creed and hence was transferable to the faith of whoever was in a position to propose rewards. In the West, precisely because Christianity isolated rather than assimilated the converted barbarians into the Roman religious landscape, it survived without Rome.

Jesus

At its two ends the life of Jesus, as reported and/or constructed, intersected with the Roman imperial order established by Augustus. His birth was hailed by an imperial census allegedly ordered on the occasion of the annexation of Judaea to Rome (6 CE), an act that reminded provincial taxpayers of their duties towards their *princeps*. At his trial he was accused of aspiring to kingship, an ambition which, by Roman standards of a highly suspicious emperor like Tiberius, bore faint yet distinct resemblance to an act of usurpation and hence constituted a danger to public order suitably curtailed by the timely execution of the designated leader. In terms of his own religion, Judaism, Jesus appeared to assume a messianic mantle which in his Galilean provenance denoted a miracle-maker. In Judaea and its principle city of Jerusalem it meant a trouble-maker.

Of the numerous activities ascribed to Jesus in the Gospels, miraculous healing of the unhealed reflected the way in which his appearance, in itself hardly unique in the turbulent Galilee of the first century, was perceived as God-sent (= messianic). Besides administering physical remedies Jesus preached a vision that delineated a kingdom of heaven to which all Jews had access. His was a classless Judaism that skipped centuries of post-biblical Jewish history. Positioning himself in direct line with the biblical prophets of old, Jesus delivered a message which was construed as a challenging rebuke to the Judaism of his own time. While calling on a biblical-prophetic form of faith, vigorously shunning idolatry and gentiles, he offered a new type of freedom from religious restraints.

In the early decades of the first century, as in the preceding century that marked the end of the Republic, the region of Judaea emerged as a hotbed of religious experimentation. In the desert between Jerusalem and the Dead Sea, an area which had exerted perennial fascination over seekers of secession, groups and individuals pursued ideologies of pure religiosity and of life untainted by institutionalized temple cult. The sight of men like John (the Baptist), roaming in the desert clad in camel hair and licking honey, might not have been rare or repellent (Matt. 3: 1–6). While the now-famous Qumran sect might have cherished its privacy and exclusivity, figures like John readily conducted mass baptism in the Jordan.

In Jerusalem well-entrenched groups like the Pharisees and the Saducees engaged in rivalries unhampered by the presence of the Roman procurator, who exerted his judgement over the province from coastal Caesarea. By comparison with both Caesarea and Judaea the Galilee of Jesus, Augustus, and Tiberius was a rural backwater in a relatively marginal area controlled by a Roman ally. To judge by Jesus' activities, contemporary Galileans were in dire need not so much of theological redemption as of the most basic necessities, including physical nourishment and medical attention. Early death and disabilities were rampant. This was a land where a fig tree had to be cursed for its bareness, as though nature itself disagreed with life there.

Jesus' call to leave one's family and to join him provided a complete way of life in a fragmented society, as though starting from scratch made eminent sense. In a world dominated by the vagaries of nature and the ruthless exaction of government, the Jesus option opened horizons of equality not on the basis of wealth, family, class, or rank but on the basis of an ostensibly free choice. The projection of a new universality, dependent on God, Christ, and the Church alone, assumed an interdependence different from the conventional and therefore was potentially both subversive and powerfully attractive. The inherent appeal in this type of theology not just to Jews but also to gentiles seeking alternatives must have been considerable.

An ideology moulded on the welfare needs of the socially inferior and economically weak acted like a beacon for Jewish women and men for whom Jesus depicted stimulating visions of an egalitarian future, in heaven if not on earth. In the eyes of his followers the suspension of contemporary customs was read as a return to the purest form of personal piety, just like the faith that had guided the steps of biblical patriarchs and prophets. The support garnered in the Galilee emboldened Jesus to challenge the Jerusalemite temple order and the guardians of the standards of religious behaviour. He defied norms by advocating reforms that could be interpreted as flagrant violation of the most basic biblical precepts. Nor did he hesitate to predict the fall of the temple, as biblical prophets had done.

On the eve of Passover Jesus appeared with his devout disciples in the Temple in Jerusalem. Assuming an authority with which he had not been invested by either the great priest or a monarch, he provokingly proceeded to expel moneylenders from the temple precinct. Clash, perhaps preventable, became imminent when upon seizure, Jesus, when questioned about his messianic aspirations, refused to deny or confirm the dangerous allegation. Facing consequence knowingly, Jesus' last words transformed death, a moment marked by banality and commonality, into a purposeful undertaking. The sublimation of death into a defining moment of collective identity empowered subsequent clashes between Christians and the Roman authorities. In later years martyrdom, or 'dying for God', came to signify the ultimate acquisition of membership in a highly exclusive circle to which access was sealed by blood.

To understand why Jesus, of all the idealists and self-proclaimed reformers who crowded the landscape of the Galilee and Judaea in the early decades of the first century, was able to inspire the kind of following that remained intensely loyal beyond death is no mean task. His demand for exclusive loyalty to himself presented a huge novelty, as did his self-assumed authority regarding law and custom. While he himself was willing to die for such convictions his death was seen as a promise of life and redemption for others. Perhaps herein lies the crucial difference between, say, the call of separatist groups like the Dead Sea Scrolls community to assume a life of Jewish perfection apart from mainstream Judaism and Jesus' insistence on inclusion via a reformulation of what it meant to be a Jew.

From Sect to Religion

In the intertwining of Judaism, Christianity, and Rome during the era of the *pax romana* (i.e. the first two centuries of the common era) the two religions drifted in different directions. Some Jews chose a road of armed resistance, rebelling several times against Rome, twice within sixty years in Judaea (66 and 132), and once at least in the north African Diaspora (117). The Temple in Jerusalem, once the cynosure of biblical and post-biblical Judaism, burnt to ashes (70). Hadrian forbade the entry of Jews to Jerusalem (*c.*130). Alexandrinian Jewry, once the crown among Diaspora communities, was decimated.

Accommodation between Roman imperial polytheism and Judaism appeared impossible. In the aftermath of the tragic loss of the Temple and of Jerusalem Judaism was transformed from a cult into a religion of words. A communal structure, the synagogue, once eclipsed by the dazzling Temple, became the heart of each congregation.

By contrast with Jewish national traumas, Jesus' followers and disciples-turned-missionaries adopted a path of least resistance. Confrontation with Rome was, on the whole, not sought. The encounters between Jesus and the Jewish establishment suggested that the two theologies were not likely to see eye to eye. To transfer a ruralized version of Judaism, as preached and practised by Jesus, into the cosmopolitan context of Roman urbanism, Paul dramatically modified the faith. Sabbath, circumcision, and other external marks of Judaism became secondary or were removed altogether. The notion of the chosen people elected by the One God was transformed from a covenant of circumcision to an equal-opportunity association to repent, or to die. Moments of Christians facing lions in the arena engendered public delight yet often also admiration of audiences while ushering reflections on the earthly power that coped with a new creed through the exercise of arbitrary judgement.

Paul preached in Diaspora synagogues where his novel ideology apparently failed to impress. Turning to the Roman world, the Christianity which Paul offered emphasized the centrality of a text and of a Saviour, an aspect which in the context of imperial Rome stood in hostile competition with ruler-worship, the sole cult which amounted to a form of universal religion in the empire. Amidst a plethora of cults, rites, and sects which offered the believer a variety of ways to reach true happiness, Christianity provided a spiritual universe which had been ordained in a manner calculated to infuse self-esteem, legitimacy, and a form of meaningful opposition to Roman arbitrariness.

The Bible remained the guide par excellence. In a polytheistic empire the constant appeal to a sacred text already hallowed by a well-established religion heightened the sense of familiarity. Paul's biblical interpretation generated an accessible model of behaviour and a vehicle of transformation. Christian exegesis emphasized an all-inclusive reading of the Bible that translated the body of believers out of its ethnic status into collective spirituality. Coupled with concessions regarding basic tenets of the Torah, the mixture of Bible and salvation made gentiles comfortable with Christianity in a way they had never before been with Judaism.

Faced with hostility and antagonism during three centuries of infancy and incubation, the Church was able to turn adversities into victories. Would-be martyrs recorded with gory and minute detail their last minutes; witnesses registered the resignation with which Christians met death in public. Their narratives contested the right of Rome to persecute monotheism. Even when outlawed, Christianity fitted comfortably into a general religious symbiosis already engineered by mystery cults, Judaism, and other eastern imports which caught the heart and the imagination of Romans throughout the empire. Preaching in major urban centres like Ephesus, Corinth, and Rome, Paul's promotion of Christ created a new type of urban ideology which no longer subscribed to promotion of state cults. The invention of what it meant to be Christian crafted an urban essence based on new, and old, categories of affiliation. The loftiest of ambitions in a Christianized environment was not to become a member of an exclusive circle, like the *amici principis* ('friends of the emperor'), but a friend of God (*amicus Dei*: Augustine, *Confessions* 6.15).

All believers belonged to the Church, a universal if somewhat amorphous body that positioned itself as the sole negotiator of mercy and salvation. The Church possessed the truth which the death of Christ obscured. Its authority was based on a twofold revelation, the Sinaitic theophany which had shaped the True Israel, and the life of Jesus which enacted a new covenant. Only the Church held the keys to the correct knowledge, but unlike the knowledge acquired through Mysteries or higher learning this was an ideological totalitarianism which could be shared by everybody. Through the sacraments individuals embarked on a road of certainty, perhaps the only certainty that Roman citizens could possess in times of violent upheavals. Ingeniously, Christianity demarcated human life as a thread between two knots, the knot of sin and of grace. Because of Adam and the primordial sin the possibility of salvation was removed. Through Christ and the Church it was reinstituted.

As preached by Paul and expounded by the brilliant brains of later theologians who harnessed their pen to the service of the faith, Christianity was born in polemics and evolved in controversy. It clashed with Judaism and with polytheism in wars of words of which the other side, ostensibly defeated, has been occasionally preserved. Above all, it waged wars within itself over the correct or orthodox form of the faith. The fact that Christ also led a life on earth generated an ongoing and a crucial controversy regarding his nature and his relations with the God-father. From the very beginning the Jesus ideology provided an umbrella that embraced a variety of religious experiences, each claiming to be the true and the sole road to knowledge of the Divine. Perhaps the most astonishing aspect of the dogmatic controversies and the vast industry of mutual accusations of heresy that accompanied the development of Christianity is precisely the fact that it remained one religion.

Already by the early third century military outposts like Dura Europus, which froze for 1,700 years in 256, accommodated a credal plurality expressed in architectural juxtaposition of temples to various gods, with a Mithraeum, a synagogue, and a Christian baptistery. The discourse of religious variety, seemingly paradoxical within so small a space, shows how identities were learnt. The walls of the small baptistery displayed the Good Shepherd, an image both basic and familiar yet also specific within a context of value and of difference. A depiction of the Samaritan woman who recognized Jesus reminded viewers of his impartiality to socially and ethnically entrenched distinctions. The Dura Mithraeum depicted a noble hunt, a pursuit for the privileged few which must have found ready echoes in the heart of the soldiers stranded so far from home in a territory constantly threatened by Persia. Dura's synagogue, the most lavishly illustrated sanctuary in town, challenged biblical allegorical interpretation with realistic depictions of major biblical events. At the centre of the Torah niche a schematic representation of the temple forged a visual bond of the spiritual attachment of all Jews to Jerusalem and to the House of God in spite of their destruction. At Dura Europus Christianity gently vied with other convictions which likewise offered means of escaping the routine constraints of life on the frontier between Rome and Persia.

The story of Dura Europus' communities masks the stages by which Christianity matured from a harassed minority to an organization ready for combat. A product of centuries of gestation, subsequent Christian historiography cast this process as leading inexorably to victory. The opposition between paganism and Christianity re-created a version of origins which replaced the question of beginnings with that of what happened afterwards. Hence, the greatest difficulty facing historians of early Christianity is to give it its infancy. More than other communities, Christianity was out to endow itself with exemplary history. The idealization of Christian values projected an instructive voyage throughout time. Christians were ready to believe in a direct line from Christ to Constantine.

Constantinian Christianities

When Constantine experienced a vision of a cross, interpreted by himself as a call to conversion, he understood the God of the Christians to be a god of war who espoused the cause of those who adopted his regalia. With astonishing ease the creed that had thrived on opposition to Rome integrated its theology with state ideology. Aided by Christ, Constantine could contemplate a Christian commonwealth that a Galilean had confidently claimed on the basis of a reformulated Judaism. Ironically, ecclesiastical monotheism and late Roman monarchy emerged as a perfect match.

The legalization of Christianity meant that internal conflicts, not least over attitudes to Rome, became Rome's business. In other words, matters of dogma, of the 'right' way or orthodoxy, became the inherited responsibility not only of Church leaders but also of emperors. The exceptional intertwining of imperial and ecclesiastical interests was fully understood by Palestinians like Eusebius of Caesarea. The Roman Empire that Eusebius envisaged under the patronage of a Christian court was a theocratic entity managed in tandem, on God's behalf, by both secular and religious leaders.

Eusebius represented an intellectual milieu which found Christianity profoundly satisfying. His writings bridged the seemingly unbridgeable with a leap of faith not uncharacteristic of the well educated. Yet, for the vast majority of the emperor's subjects these intellectual enterprises remained wholly outside their experience. For them, the transition from paganism to Christianity was facilitated by the rise to phenomenal popularity of individuals who acquired saintly status because, like Jesus, they defied norms while dispensing assistance to those whom state and society failed. A pilgrimage to the locations hallowed by the presence or the souvenirs of such saints became a hallmark of a new type of piety that paid homage to an ideology of physical mobility. For those with limited literacy the Bible became a tour guide and the Holy Land a live map which invited a unique experience of virtual reality. Best of all, the respectability conferred on Christianity by Constantine and his successors meant that even the rich and the mighty could practise Christian idealism without the risk of losing either prestige or power.

Constantine inherited a body of believers imbued with a strong sense of affiliation with the Church and with equally potent dissenting views regarding just which was the right Church. The plurality of doctrines which the Church had faced from its infancy presented an emperor seeking universal uniformity with virtually insurmountable problems. In the North African provinces, for example, the behaviour of Christian leaders during the era of persecution became a deciding factor in their suitability, or lack of it, to serve as spiritual guides. Hard on the heels of Constantine's own conversion the so-called 'Arian' controversy threatened the newly established Church–State alliance. Constantine called for an ecumenical council, the first in a long series of episcopal gatherings meant to address and redress ideological rifts and disputes. He also embarked on a programme of imperial legislation which was meant to curtail if not to kill all religions but Christianity.

Christianity under Constantine did not present a startlingly novel concept. Rather, it appropriated, adapted, and reinforced existing trends, amassing wealth while dispensing charity, shunning heterodoxy (heresy) while embracing eccentric hermits, and extolling a façade of uniformity by condemning all but Christian forms of religiosity. Most remarkable, and possibly a key to the ineluctable hold that Christianity took over the minds and hearts of Rome's citizens from the fourth century onward, was the adoption of a strident moral tone. Trends of a morality which, like Christianity, called for renunciation of the sensual and the sexual had been in vogue long before Constantine's conversion. The spiritual barometer of the empire at the dawn of the fourth century must have intensified the search for stability which emperors failed to provide.

Inevitably, the legalization of Christianity further launched a shift in social ideologies. Recognizing the need to negotiate gender, class, and ethnic identities in terms of a distinct discourse, the environment that the Church set out to create was constructed on an ambivalence. The present required articulation in terms that reconciled imperial and ecclesiastical self-definition, yet such concepts relied on vocabularies which had been formulated while the two seemed irreconcilable. To mediate the two, the ecclesiastical establishment condoned forms of spiritual display predicated on the proven success of individuals, like 'saints' or 'holy men', who acted along a line that barely divided perversity from respectability.

In a cultural environment in which an overwhelming number of people could not read, the language of images provided a crucial key for the transmission of ideas. Already the sepulchral imagery of the third-century Roman catacombs and sarcophagi, like the images in the remote baptistery of Dura Europus, radiated a message of salvation and redemption overlaid with unified ideology and purpose. The emphasis was on the acceptance of the faith of Christ. The location highlighted the need for discretion while highlighting the singularity of the process by which the creed was inserted into the varied landscapes of the empire. A century after the conversion of Constantine, Christian iconography gained sufficient confidence to aspire to merge contrasting legacies, defiance and conformity, humility and triumphalism.

The cult of Mary and its dogmatic, architectural, and artistic expressions can serve as a guide to the complex history of Christian ideology in late antiquity. In the early fifth century, seemingly out of nowhere, Mary won a firm place in the dogmatic firmament of orthodoxy as God's mother. Among Mary's most ardent supporters was the Jerusalem church. Her maternity had been celebrated in a feast, the Memory of Mary, that drew believers to march from Jerusalem to Bethlehem along the road that had once borne the pregnant Galilean. It took place every year in the heat of mid-August, precisely when the Jews of Palestine commemorated the destruction of the Temple, an event that Mary's son had predicted. At the ecumenical Council of Ephesus (431) the assembled bishops acknowledged Mary's exceptional status as a perpetual virgin yet also a model mother. By 600 the Jerusalemite feast had been transformed into a universal celebration; not, however, of Mary's maternity but of her death, assumption, and reunification with her Son.

In the Holy Land churches devoted to the cult of Mary bore a distinct triumphalist tone. The *kathisma* church, built between Jerusalem and Bethlehem on the spot where Mary had rested, was designed along octagonal lines. This was the model, rare among late ancient church architecture, which Zeno used in 484 when he consecrated a church to Mary atop of Mount Gerizim, the holiest place of the Samaritans, after the brutal suppression of a Samaritan revolt. And this was the design chosen by Abd el Malik for the Dome of the Rock in Jerusalem, a few miles only from Mary's *kathisma*, in 691. The association of Mary with moments of triumphs over other creeds, and with victories in adversity, facilitated the adaptation of Marian architectural ideology into other religious contexts. The golden dome atop the Temple Mount in Jerusalem defiantly dominated the urban landscape, proclaiming the triumph of Islam in the city that had generated both Judaism and Christianity.

At Rome, seat of powerful and ambitious bishops, the mosaics of the church of Santa Maria Maggiore celebrated the sanctioning of Mary as a *Theotokos* in iconographical terms which echoed both the Ephesian dogma and the principles of Roman imperial art. A cycle of biblical scenes, all derived from the Hebrew Bible, displayed conviction in the power of the God of Israel and in the superiority of Christianity and Christ over the temporalities of Rome and its emperors. Completed barely a year after the Council of Ephesus the church exemplified the rapid bolstering of dogmas which were poised to win universal approbation. At Santa Maria Maggiore the statement of Marian victory bolstered the texts and rites which provided the founding principles of the cult.

Romanizing the un-Roman

The originality of the imperial Christian discourse which the equilibrium of Church and State generated can be fully appreciated when examined within the context of Roman–barbarian relations. The conversion of the non-Roman world, beginning with that of the Visigoths in the fourth century, became a major instrument of imperial foreign affairs. In 376, after a shattering defeat at the hands of the Huns, the Visigoths begged the emperor Valens to allow them to cross the Danube into the safety they believed was to be found on Roman territory. Valens acceded to the request. Among the conditions imposed on the Goths, at least according to some sources, was conversion to the imperial creed. Valens was an 'Arian', convinced of Trinitarian internal hierarchy. Nor was 'Arianism' new to the Goths. It had already been exported from Constantinople in the late 330s with Ulfila, a Gothic 'apostle' whose missionary activities in Gothia provoked persecution and caused his expulsion. When the Goths settled south of the Danube *en masse* in 376, ostensibly to become useful members of Roman society, they already had a Bible in their own language, the singular achievement of their apostle.

In the ranks of tribal leadership Christianity came to be identified with a pro-Roman stand, while the anti-Roman camp among the Goths held fast to traditional tribal rituals. Religion, never before an inseparable attachment of barbarian inner politics, became a bone of contention even in a society innocent of intricate exchange between State and Church. During the landless years of 376–418, when the Goths wandered from the East to the West in search of a permanent piece of territory, self-styled Gothic 'kings', such as Alaric (395–410), resorted to Christianity when attempting to recapture the sedentary society that the Goths had lost north of the Danube and hoped to regain on Roman soil. Alaric's career provides insights into changing patterns of association among the Goths themselves, between the East and the West Roman empires, and between Romans and barbarians. He lived through a period in which theologians forged the contours of orthodoxy at the expense of 'heresy' and intellectuals constructed 'Romanitas' as the antithesis of the non-Roman or the barbarian.

When in 402 a military encounter between the Roman army, led by Stilicho, and the Visigothic confederacy, led by Alaric, ended with a stalemate, the event, in itself of small significance in the series of Roman–barbarian battles, challenged contemporary historians of religion. The engagement at Pollentia, fought on Easter Day, presented irreconcilable ambiguities. It provided a stimulus for a traditional panegyric of 647 verses in which the battle itself occupies barely thirty-five (Claudian, *De Bello Gotico* 580–615). The poem narrates how, on the eve of the battle, Alaric, a former employee of the Roman government, consulted oracles that naturally promised victory but proved false. It glossed over the fact that Stilicho entrusted the conduct of the combat into the hands of a polytheist barbarian who had been suspected of treachery but who proved his probity by dying fighting for the emperor.

Barely two years after Pollentia another poetic version of the same events, Prudentius' *Contra Symmachum*, transferred the actual scene of war from an earthly site into a contest between piety and impiety, *Romanitas* and *barbaritas*, legitimacy and usurpation. In Prudentius' rendering of Pollentia Alaric becomes the *tyrannus Geticus* ('Gothic tyrant') sworn to destroy Italy, to burn its golden palaces, and to force Gothic garbs on its senators. Although Christian, Alaric is cast as a successor of the pagan Goths who had opposed Romanization under Valens. His rivals, the emperor Honorius and the emperor's father-in-law Stilicho, take the field 'united in Christ' (*deus unus Christus utrique*, 711–13), after attending services. Imbued with the right Nicene zeal, the Roman army wipes out the 'Pannonian tribe' that had menaced Roman existence for so long. In reality, the liturgical aspect of warfare belonged to the Gothic and not to the Roman side. Pollentia had taken place on Easter Day, one of the holiest days of the Christian calendar. The Roman army surprised the Goths in the course of their celebrations. Orosius, a near-contemporary, could barely conceal his indignation at the manner in which the Roman victory had been achieved. In what amounts to a brief homily, he castigates not the Visigoths but the Romans:

> I remain silent on the unfortunate events at Pollentia when the command of the battle had been entrusted to Saul, a barbarian and a pagan. Utterly contemptuous of the most sacred

days (of the Christian calendar), he violated even holy Easter, forcing into a fight the enemy who had withdrawn on account of their religiosity. However, God's own judgement quickly manifests its will. We won the battle then but although victorious we were overcome (by the enemy's piety).

The image of an invading group, led by a leader whose main concern is to celebrate a Christian holy day during a march in the heart of an alien territory, suggests that Christianity had a major role in shaping the terms and projections of Gothic identity to insiders and outsiders.

The history of Alaric's confederacy explains both the short-lived success and the ultimate failure of the barbarian settlements in the western provinces, where a ruling barbarian elite remained an Arian minority in a sea of Roman catholic settlements. The arrangement emphasized the irony of the late ancient Roman–barbarian clash in which Christian armies, a 'barbarian' professing Arianism, and a 'Roman' espousing orthodoxy, were fighting over Roman territory in order to preserve a court in Italy. The factor of religion further elucidates why the conversion of a shrewd Frankish monarch like Clovis took place when there was no longer an emperor on the western imperial throne. The new alliance between a Gallic church and a Frankish catholic state could proceed unhindered.

The cleavage between Chalcedonian orthodoxy, as first formulated at the ecumenical Council of Chalcedon in 451, and the Mono-Miaphysite form of Christianity posed problems of identity at all levels of interaction, from humble practitioners who studiously avoided churches where the 'other' was present, to episcopal dignitaries who strove to dethrone each other. In Palestine, at the instigation of Bishop Juvenal of Jerusalem, Samaritan troops decimated anti-Chalcedonian monks. Christian sources bitterly recalled the ruthlessness of the Samaritans, as well as the miraculous healing of a blind Samaritan who applied the blood of a martyred monk to his eyes, and subsequently converted to Christianity. The authorized involvement of Samaritans, an ethnic minority, in inner-Christian conflicts drew protests from Palestinian monkish circles. The combination of court and Samaritan ideologies, seemingly irreconcilable, united to stem the tide of 'heresy' among the Christian communities in Palestine. Irony is palpable—the imperial persecutors of Samaritanism who aspired to stem this non-Christian form of monotheism through laws did not hesitate to use Samaritans to persecute their own co-religionists.

Conclusion: Becoming Autochthone

The stories that explained the birth of Christianity revolved around conflicts which assured the community of a recognizable identity. The conflict with Judaism ensured that birth was not a criterion for exclusion. The equality of origin that Christianity extolled reversed the order of existing propositions. It suggested that Christians thought about 'citizenship' in terms that allowed citizens to speak for themselves, albeit in a restricted fashion. In the Christian *polis* only the crucial equivalence between creed and citizenship had the right to define the city. A citizen was one reborn in Christ, a formulation that dispensed with the specificity of parenthood. The Church became the metaphor for the family and the fatherland.

The conflict with paganism confronted Christianity with a religious panorama which had endowed cities with an uninterrupted past from time immemorial. To combat and supplant a legitimacy that had been long established and to dispossess the city of its own past it was necessary to dethrone civic divinities. Christianity managed to minimize the distance between the beliefs that Jesus articulated in the rural Galilee and the urban soil which became the belief's basis of operation. Christ was inscribed over a panoply of founding gods and goddesses. Christianity grafted its rituals over the celebration of mythic ancestors. Imaginative operations ensured the necessary integration of Christianity into the pagan city. After Constantine, Christianity was in the best position to confer unity on the mythic complexity that was the basis of Roman polytheism. Not, however, without complications.

Once in charge, orthodoxy had to be defined. It became the version that took on a mythic character, a construct that aimed at reconstituting what was at stake. Internal controversies took over. When the emperor Anastasius (491–518) proposed to appease the Monophysites by adding a Monophysite touch to the liturgy in Constantinople's Saint Sophia, riots ensued. The rioters set on fire several palaces and were ready to support an imperial substitute. Religious schism and urban violence became intimately associated. The conjunction of dogmatic disputes and violence highlights the ambivalence of the Christian discourse that set up sedition as a model.

Ultimately, church and city, myth and politics were reconciled. In Gaza, a prosperous metropolis in late antiquity, an uncompromising bishop went to war in order to destroy the city's main sanctuary, the venerable abode of Marnas, Gaza's tutelary divinity (400). On the ruins of the temple the bishop planted a church. The campaign of destruction and reconstruction, although described as a triumph of religious righteousness, was a statement that expressed dissent rather than consensus. 'Taking gypsum he [the church's architect] marked out the fashion of the holy church according to the form of the plan which was sent by the Augusta Eudoxia... When the most holy bishop had made a prayer and bending of the knee, he bade the people dig. And straightaway all with one mind and with the same zeal began to dig chanting: "Christ has conquered"' (Mark the Deacon, *Vita Porphyri* 78).

Over a century later a Christian rhetor paid homage to Gaza's bishop for building and restoring the city to its architectural heyday in terms that smoothly blended the barriers which had once existed between past myth and present politics:

The excellence of a city derives from the harmony and the blending of the airs which divide the year equally among themselves. The majesty of its buildings and its inhabitants' proper way of life. These, indeed, are the characteristics of your city, which the two kindred servants of life, earth and sea, treat delicately, each with its own gifts... Follow me, then, toward the eastern gate of the city. After descending from here and turning to the left, you will no longer need a guide for the way, since the church is clearly visible and sufficient by itself to guide you to it...

(Choricius, *Second Encomium to Marcian, Bishop of Gaza* 4.28, tr. F. Litsas)

Christianity implemented a spacial revolution of town life by advancing ideals of a new, specifically Christian universe, protected by saints and churches. Displacing local divinities, Christian ideologues recast their creed as autochthone, as though it had always been an integral element of the fabric of life.

Further reading

It would be impossible to do justice to the staggering number of publications which relate to practically every aspect of Christianity in the first five centuries. A useful point of departure is the numerous guides, like this one, which provide efficient overviews and bibliographies. S. A. Harvey and D. Hunter (eds.), *The Oxford Handbook of Early Christian Studies* (Oxford, 2008) is the most recent example. Electronic databases such as ATLA provide additional bibliographical pointers. The series *New Documents Illustrating Early Christianity*, edited by G. H. R. Horsely, contains inscriptions and papyri relevant to the study of early Christianity. The Liverpool series *Translated Texts for Historians*, edited by G. Clark and M. Whitby, provides translations and commentaries of many important texts of late antiquity which are germane to the development of late ancient Christianity. Many literary sources are now available online. Among recent comprehensive bibliographies, see the *Handbook of Early Christianity: Social Science Approaches*, edited by Anthony Blast, Jean Duhaime, and Paul-André Turcotte (Walnut Creek, Calif., 2002), which contains 108 pages of references.

References

Boyarin, D., *Dying for God: Martyrdom and the Making of Christianity* (Stanford, 1999).

Brown, P., *The Body and Society: Men, Women, and Sexual Renunciation in Early Christianity* (New York, 1988).

—— *Authority and the Sacred. Aspects of the Christianisation of the Roman World* (Cambridge, 1995).

Brown, P., *The Rise of Western Christendom: Triumph and Diversity AD 200–1000*, 2nd edn. (Oxford, 2003).

The Cambridge History of Christianity, vol. 1: *Origins to Constantine*, ed. M. M. Mitchell and F. M. Young (Cambridge, 2006); vol. 2: *Constantine to c. 600*, ed. A. Casiday and F. W. Norris (Cambridge, 2007).

Castelli, E. A., *Martyrdom and Memory: Early Christian Culture Making* (New York, 2004).

Clark, G., *Christianity and Roman Society* (Cambridge, 2004).

Dodds, E. R., *Pagan and Christian in an Age of Anxiety: Some Aspects of Religious Experience from Marcus Aurelius to Constantine* (Cambridge, 1965).

Drake, H., *Constantine and the Christian Empire* (London, 2004).

Fletcher, R., *The Barbarian Conversion: From Paganism to Christianity* (Berkeley, 1999).

Frend, W. H. C., *Martyrdom and Persecution in the Early Church* (Oxford, 1965).

Harris, W. V. (ed.), *The Spread of Christianity in the First Four Centuries: Essays in Explanation* (New York, 2005).

Hayes A. L., *Christianity and Society in Documents, 100–600 AD* (Toronto, 1995).

Lenski, N., *The Cambridge Companion to the Age of Constantine* (Cambridge, 2006).

Markus, R. A., *Christianity in the Roman World* (London, 1974).

Momigliano, A., *The Conflict Between Paganism and Christianity in the Fourth Century* (Oxford, 1963).

Novak, R. M., *Christianity and the Roman Empire: Background Texts* (Harrisburg, Pa., 2001).

Odahl, C. M., *Constantine and the Christian Empire* (London, 2004).

Rahner, H., *Church and State in Early Christianity* (San Francisco, 1992).

Sivan, H., *Palestine in Late Antiquity* (Oxford, 2008).

CHAPTER 50

SEXUALITY

REBECCA FLEMMING

ROMAN sexuality is only just emerging from the scholarly shadows. As the sexual domain became a valid, and increasingly vital, subject of historical enquiry, it was classical Greece that was selected (most influentially by Foucault: 1984/5) to speak for the ancient world, and to challenge modern assumptions about the constitution, organization, and valorization of sexual desire, activity, and identity; with considerable, though certainly not uncontested, success. In the pursuit of radical difference from the present, past divisions were elided, and Rome's sexual patterns were subsumed within a classical paradigm of distinctly Greek construction. They are now breaking free, however, and more recent scholarship (e.g. Hallett and Skinner eds. 1997; Williams 1999; Fredrick ed. 2002; Langlands, 2006) has been concerned, quite precisely, with demarcating and exploring definitively Roman sexual territories.

Indeed, a range of claims have now been made about the wealth and variety of evidence which survives from Rome, combined with (and related to) the rich complexities of Roman society and culture, that imply more than just a demand for recognition of, and respect for, Roman sexual specificities within the study of the classical world and the historiography of sexuality more generally. The suggestion is (in, for example, the introductions to Fredrick ed. 2002 and Langlands 2006) that Rome actually has more to offer than the clear-cut simplicities of classical Greece (at least as imagined by Michel Foucault): more as historical object and more as dialogic subject for modernity. The expansiveness of Rome's empire, its messy cosmopolitanism, the violent transition from Republic to Principate, each involving losses and gains, validations and contradictions, continuities and changes, in abundance; all this makes Rome a more appropriate and productive interlocutor for the present than, say, the more confined spaces of democratic Athens. Moreover, while the distribution of surviving (and studied) Roman material is predictably uneven and unequal, favouring rich and powerful men, those more centrally located in space, time, and tradition, it is by no means exclusive, or homogeneous. There are alternative voices to be heard, more dispersed and diverse sources to be found, in Rome and her dominions, and a richer understanding to follow.

This short chapter can do little more than hint at that diversity, gesture towards the riches on offer, as it tries to draw together and develop the most recurrent themes to emerge from the recent scholarship on Roman sexuality. The aim is to provide a rough sketch of the Roman sexual domain as currently construed by the majority of scholars in the field, which includes some indication of the gaps within it, the intriguing territories beyond, and, indeed, includes some indication of more analytical gaps and distortions in recent approaches too. This will be, then, a critical summary, with suggestions for further investigation and thinking; and it intends, like much other work in the area, to serve the present mainly by supporting, and encouraging, a fuller and more accurate comprehension of the past rather than through anything more particular. The dialogue it invites is thus a quite diffuse and general one, which allows for historical differences and similarities, change and persistence over time, often simultaneously, jostling together in the complex, varied, and contested patterns of both then and now.

Ancient and Modern: Similarities and Differences

The point about allowing for both historical differences and similarities, continuities and ruptures, is a particularly important one to make here, because questions over which is to be prioritized over the other have been highly divisive in the scholarship so far, but somewhat unnecessarily (though understandably) so. For it is certainly possible to reconcile some—though not all—of these competing claims; indeed it is essential to do so if a manifestly lopsided and incomplete picture of the Roman world is to be avoided, with all its damaging implications for the understanding of both that specific society, and social patterns more broadly. For more general questions, more general theories of sexuality, are always at stake in these discussions as much as any historical particulars.

The most vocal insistence on historical difference has come from those who have repeatedly (though not identically) asserted that the defining dichotomy of modern sexual discourse—that between normative heterosexuality and its non-normative, but inevitable, partner, homosexuality—as categories producing critical aspects of identity, and social status, is absent from antiquity. This view has been most systematically propounded in relation to the Roman world by Craig Williams (1999), though his book does much more than prove a negative. To be more precise, then, the argument is that ancient evidence offers no indication that individuals were in any sense existentially classified or evaluated according to their sexual desire for females or males, as either the same or other than themselves. Rather, men, at least, were assumed to desire both male and female bodies, as part of being a man, with the ideology of masculinity then demanding that they act along similar lines with both, consistently play the man in all sexual encounters, and threatening those who failed to do so with the loss of manhood and all the privileges that entailed. Insofar as issues of identity are implicated in classical constructions of sexuality, they are, therefore, issues of gender identity, not of a separable sexual identity, a distinct and definitional sexual orientation as contained in the terms heterosexual and homosexual (and, less comfortably, bisexual). Clinging on to these modern concepts, and the conceptual system that underlies them, thus erects an insurmountable barrier to a real understanding of the workings of the ancient world; and current political strategies and moral argumentation based, implicitly or explicitly, on the presumption of their trans-historical validity are also flawed.

Despite the way that the above arguments are sometimes presented, their polemical framing, few scholars (if any) have, in fact, directly asserted the opposite. Those who have deployed modern terminology and concepts in discussing ancient sexuality, and who have done so in a conscious and considered fashion rather than lazily and without thought, have all done so equivocally (e.g. Cantarella 1988/92; Richlin 1992 and 1993; Taylor 1997; Brooten 1996; and even Boswell 1980). That is, all accept that there are salient historical differences, that such usage is qualified and problematic, but worth it because of the various political and/or analytical gains to be made through a particular insistence on continuity.

A specific case in point is Amy Richlin's emphasis on the resemblance and recurrence of themes of denigration, hate, and oppression across time in these contexts. Looking beyond the figure of the desiring male subject who is very much the focus of work by Foucault and others, looking beyond the man who performs roughly as ideology demands in the formulations above, to women and unmanly males, things appear rather different, that is, rather more the same. Ancient Rome and the modern West have some important hierarchies in common: patriarchy has persisted, in whatever precise forms, and ideologies of femininity show some points of convergence through the ages. Moreover, just as the content of the invective aimed at women by Roman men still has some purchase in modern terms, partially resonates with current vocabularies of sexual and sexist abuse, so too, Richlin avers, with the negative construction of the sexually aberrant Roman male. Not, she stresses, that there was a Roman concept of sexual deviance homologous to the modern notion of homosexuality, but that the negativity, the insult and injury, directed at the Roman deviant can be described as 'homophobic': as partaking in shared tropes and with congruent results to present hate-speech (Richlin 1993: 530).

It is, however, hard to see how homophobia can exist without homosexuality: and, while the rhetorical purpose of putting the nastiness back into Roman sexual discourse has certainly been well served, there is a sense in which this, self-consciously forced, emphasis on continuity rather undermines the more obvious (but no less important) connections established. Which is to say that, if women are to be kept more fully in the picture throughout (as they must be), if their persistent subordination is to be acknowledged and explored, in any adequate study of sexuality in ancient Rome, then the gendered structure of Roman sexual discourse needs to be appreciated and analysed on its own terms. Because, keeping the discussion within antiquity for a moment, those for whom it matters most whether the abuse that a sexually aberrant Roman male suffers is directed at his failures *as a man* or his failures *of sexual orientation*—that is, his errors in respect to the sex of his partners—are, arguably, the women of Rome. Certainly they are implicated in this discursive web of denigration. If the worst insult that can be hurled at a Roman male is that he 'submits to the female role' (*passus muliebria*: e.g. Tacitus, *Annals* 11.36) in sexual intercourse, that must have some impact on those for whom that role is socially mandated. To speak more generally, also, this is to point to divergences within the history of women's position too, to variations in the form and content of ideologies of femininity, even if they are variations on, or around, more continuous themes.

So, then, if full justice is to be done to all the participants in the Roman sexual system, female and male, ideologically compliant and non-compliant alike, both historical continuities and disjunctions must be allowed for, explored, and analysed. Just as any more general theory of sexuality, of configurations of sex, gender, and desire, must keep these various combinations and recombinations in view. One further point needs to be made in this respect too, which brings the discussion back to Foucault. For the differences between ancient and modern which he is interested in describing concern the formation of the self as much as (if not more than) the construction of sexuality: the variable ways in which ethical subjects are produced, and operate, in relation to a set of sexual ideas, values, and rules, within a wider ensemble of understandings, commitments, and contingencies. In particular he stresses that the world of classical antiquity was basically 'ethics-' not 'code-oriented' (1985: 30): built around the work done by the individual in relation to himself, not on the elaboration, and external enforcement, of precise rules of behaviour. In Greece and Rome the point was to recognize, establish, and maintain oneself as a proper ethical subject, to conduct oneself appropriately on that account, not because of dependence on, or deferral to, a systematic set of prescriptions.

There are, again, issues of gender here which Foucault fails to address. He offers a series of generalizations that are in fact specific claims about men, without noticing—or at least without scrutinizing—the gap between the two. Still, the critical distinction he draws has been widely accepted as a valid and important one, and there is a sense in which Foucault's analytical weaknesses here usefully serve to draw attention to some fault-lines in the classical system itself. For, certainly in the Roman world, there is no question that women are represented as having moral agency, as ethical subjects of some sort, but that subjectivity rapidly becomes discursively incoherent, since the dominant male model is only ever partially invoked in relation to women in the surviving literature, and clearly cannot be applied in its entirety, but nothing is offered in its place, as alternative or gap-filler. Obviously, in the real world Roman women will just have got on with life, decision-making, and self-reflection regardless, as indeed they, and the rest of the Roman population, will have got on with much else that is not described or analysed, and may not even be mentioned, in the ancient evidence. Nonetheless, these omissions and inconcinnities in the ancient discourses on self and sexuality are part of what needs to be studied and understood.

So, having thus expanded the repertoire of historical similarities and differences that are in play here, and insisted on an inclusive approach to ancient sexuality, it is time to take a closer look at some of the features referred to so far, and to be more particularly Roman in approach. That is not to say, however, that Rome has nothing in common with Greece, or indeed, cannot be located within a wider ancient Mediterranean context, a shared sexual order, because it can, but in a specific and distinctive form nonetheless.

The Roman Sexual Order (and its Discontents?)

To summarize, and then substantiate, what has been alluded to so far: one key feature of the shared sexual architecture in which Rome participates is the combination of a sharp division, and clear double-standard, between men and women as sexual subjects, with an assumption of their rough equivalence (though not identity) as sexual objects. So, for a Roman man, the realm of erotic arousal and gratification encompassed both male and female, with the acceptability and valorization of the different possibilities within that determined by factors—such as social status and sexual role—which operated across physiologies. For a Roman woman, on the other hand, it was unclear whether she could ever properly attain the position of sexual subject at all; certainly her only socially sanctioned erotic activity was with her husband.

While it has been doubted whether the inclusive approach to sexual objects for men was a traditional Roman formation, with suggestion (Wilkinson 1978) that Roman males only learnt to desire other males from their Greek neighbours, and indeed, did not learn that well, more recent studies have emphasized that the presumption of such desire, at Rome, can be traced back as far as the evidence goes (Williams 1999). Thus, one of Plautus' clever slaves, Palinurus, famously tells his young master, in a play of around 200 BCE: 'As long as you abstain from wife (*nupta*) and widow (*vidua*) and maiden (*virgo*), | From freeborn youth (*iuventus*) and boys (*pueri*), love whom you wish' (*Curc.* 37–8). Both male and female are available to be loved, are desirable, it is assumed; though this advice is focused on the categories of both with whom sexual relationships are prohibited. The point is strengthened through these injunctions, however, as they are made on the same basis for both sexes: that is, on grounds of social and legal status, though this works out somewhat differently for female and male.

This warning-off could, indeed, have been expressed more symmetrically, for it is basically freeborn, citizen status that is at issue across the board. It is no accident, however, that this status is constructed in relation to matrimony for girls and women, while it is more plainly put for youths and boys. Roman males were not conceptually defined in relation to marriage (or fatherhood), either as Roman or men (McDonnell 2006: 168–73), while Roman females were. Being a female citizen was about matrimony and childbearing, about forming a *iustum matrimonium*, a proper marriage within Roman law, which would produce Roman heirs, children in *patria potestas*. It was about being a *virgo*, unmarried but marriageable, through youth, status, and virginity; a *nupta*, a chaste citizen wife; or a *vidua*, a respectable widow. All were prohibited to men not their husbands: the only proper sexual relationship with a free, citizen woman is a conjugal one. Freeborn, male citizens, on the other hand, were prohibited to men who shared that status, full-stop; marriage was irrelevant to either party, and the fact that Palinurus refers to boys and youths in this context speaks simply to presumptions of male desirability at Rome, associated as they were with ideals of adolescent physicality.

The other point to make is that, while the line Palinurus draws between acceptable and unacceptable sexual partners for his master is one that would have been enforced by informal (though powerful and legally entrenched) mechanisms of public censure and family punishment in Republican Rome, following the Augustan legislation on marriage and adultery these prohibitions had the force of criminal law (Treggiari 1991: 262–89; McGinn 1998: 140–215). There are, to be specific, two crimes that emerge from the Augustan enactments, and are further distinguished and elaborated in the subsequent (and very extensive) juristic discourse on the subject, which together cover the same ground as the admonitions of Plautus' slave. These are the crimes of *adulterium*, usually translated as 'adultery', though that is a rather problematic trans-historical term, and of *stuprum* which defies translation (suggestions range from 'debauchery' to 'illicit intercourse' and back again). A formulation offered in the *Institutes* of the third-century CE jurist Modestinus, and preserved in Justinian's *Digest*, clearly differentiates the two, and also demonstrates the continuities with Plautus, half-a-millennium earlier: '*Adulterium* is committed with a wife (*nupta*); *stuprum* is committed with a widow (*vidua*) or maiden (*virgo*) or boy (*puer*)' (*Dig.* 48.5.35.1).

The sexual double standard is thus made completely explicit and foundational. *Adulterium* is a crime perpetrated with wives, the conjugal status of the male adulterer is irrelevant, with his perspective being shared by the jurist and enshrined by Justinian. *Stuprum* is perpetrated with both male and female partners, who share a certain social status, even if it is delineated in different terms. Male sexual subjecthood is confirmed through the definition of these offences, which also leaves Roman men, married or unmarried, plenty of space for legitimate sexual activity, and even romance, beyond the prescribed categories: with those of both sexes lower down the social order, most especially their own slaves, and prostitutes (who might be freeborn, but by 'making a living with their body' had forfeited the integrity and virtue which *stuprum* despoils), but also the freed or foreign. These rules also proved to be quite pliable in certain circumstances. Poetic conventions operated somewhat distinctly, for instance, not challenging these categories of permissibility directly, but stretching and blurring the boundaries in various ways. So Juventius, the young male object of Catullus' desires (and others') is presented in his verses, composed in the mid-first century BCE, as the scion of a noble house, but one who retains his anonymity in the most compromising positions he puts himself in (Wiseman 1985: 130–1); and 'Lesbia', the most famous pseudonym in Latin poetry, perhaps hides a married woman of equally elevated lineage, or at least conjures that image through concealment (Wyke 2002).

Freeborn Roman women themselves, by contrast, have no licit options, no flexibility. If married, any other sexual relationship is adulterous; and if not yet, or no longer, married, any erotic activity is almost as bad, technically *stuprum* in the Imperial era, but often still collapsed into *adulterium*. Moreover, while there are plenty of allegations that adultery was a popular female pursuit at Rome, at least from the late Republic onwards, this is basically male reportage (e.g. Sallust, *Catiline* 23 and 26; Seneca, *Ben.* 3.16.2–4), often formulated in such a way as to call into question its accuracy as anything other than a symbolic evocation of the city's wider moral decline (Edwards 1993: 34–62). That women's sexual behaviour should be made to stand for collective failure in this way tells its own story, of course, and the differential treatment accorded to Catullus and his Lesbia, for example, following Apuleius' later revelation that Lesbia was Clodia (*Apology* 10), and modern arguments that this is the Clodia so viciously attacked for her loose and licentious lifestyle, her wickedness and scheming, by Cicero in his defence of Caelius in 56 BCE, serves to underline the basic inequities at work here (Dixon 2001: 133–56). Even without Catullus, indeed, Cicero's speech in this case graphically illustrates Rome's sexual double standard. Whether the widowed Clodia, who must at least have had an affair with the younger Caelius even if the rest is slander and invention, should be seen as in any sense challenging that double standard, or perhaps pursuing her family's political aims through variations on the dynastic marriage alliance, or both, is uncertain; though the former view might gain some support from a rare female voice still audible from antiquity. The surviving elegies of Sulpicia, apparently a young woman from a very distinguished Roman family, celebrate her love-affair with one 'Cerinthus', a daring move to make in Augustan Rome even if this liaison was a purely poetic one ([Tib.] 3.13–18; Hemelrijk 1999: 134–60).

Respectable women's legal restriction to sex within marriage also included (or excluded) relationships with each other, though the phallic assumptions of the Roman sexual order make such encounters conceptually challenging as much as criminal. Still, an adulterous scenario between two women is referred to in one of the elder Seneca's *controversiae*, his record of the most notable contributions made to the genre of the forensic rhetorical exercise in a lifetime that spanned the last days of the Republic and the opening of the Principate. The imaginary case (mentioned at *Contr.* 1.2.23) is one of a man who found his wife in bed with another woman and killed them both, the legality of which response is the point of contention in the declamation. Unfortunately it is cited only in passing, and for the dubious taste of its colours, not its substantial arguments or existential assumptions, so much remains unclear. A key aspect of this unclarity is how a sexual relationship between two women is to be understood in respect to the roles played within it: the other crucial element of the ancient conception, and construal, of sexual activity. The initial framing of the case refers to both women in the same terms, but that is contradicted by the presumption, expressed in rather over-the-top Greek by the two orators actually quoted, that this is an asymmetrical exchange: between wife and adulterer, in which the adulterer is conceived in male, or pseudo-male, terms. The husband is given the words: 'But I looked at the man (*anēr*) to see whether he was born that way (*eggenētai*) or sewn on (*proserraptai*)', by one speaker and his colleague talks of 'a false-male adulterer' (*phēlarrēn moichos*). Alternatively, a later epigram of Martial (1.90) has the wife take the 'manly' (*virum*) role of adulterer with other women.

It is not, it should be said, that this poet or these rhetorical performers struggled, particularly, with the practicalities of two women in bed with each other (at least in their own minds), or that they struggled to fit them into the framework of adultery: but that the presumption, not just of asymmetry but also inequality, as intrinsic to sexual activity and sexual desire, is fundamental in the ancient world. Any sexual transaction needs what is widely, but somewhat misleadingly, referred to as an 'active', or 'penetrating' participant, and a 'passive', 'penetrated' participant, to be fully intelligible in classical terms. The misguidance lies in the fact that the ancient sources themselves do not deploy this dichotomy as such, in the abstract, and that, in as far as it does emerge, more cumulatively and implicitly, from Roman terminology and usage, it does so in a symbolic, evaluative, rather than literal fashion. The totalizing quality of some such division, the foundational failure of reciprocity, in the Roman construction of sexuality is hard to overstate, however, at least in ideological terms.

So, the practices that modern commentators (see especially Parker 1997) put under the 'active' heading are, in the very distinctive, and distinctively specific, domain of Latin sexual vocabulary, most importantly those articulated by the verbs *futuere*, *pedicare*, and *irrumare*. That is, to penetrate, phallically, the vagina, anus, and mouth respectively. All of these sex acts have validity in the Roman system, validity for, and validating of, a proper Roman man, regardless of whether those he penetrates are male or female: indeed, most Latin terminology is, in itself, entirely indifferent in that respect.

Thus, for example, one of the many sexual themes in Martial's epigrams, which make particular play of both the specificity and transferability of the Latin language in these respects, is that of competition between boys and women as partners in anal sex: that is, as objects of the verb *pedicare*. The poet claims that buggering boys is better, on aesthetic grounds—just as Chian figs are preferable to the larger *marisca* (Mart. 12.96)—and jealous wives should thus understand why their offers in this department may be rebuffed (see also 11.43). This was, nonetheless, an expected conjugal service, Martial implies, allegedly and authoritatively provided by a range of notable *matrona* from Roman history: such as Cornelia, Julia (the wife of Pompey), and Porcia (11.104). Proffering fellatio, being the object of *irrumare*, on the other hand, is the department of the prostitute, not the wife, and probably not even the girlfriend (compare and contrast e.g. Mart. 9.43 with 9.40 and 9.67); but is most often referred to as forced from another male, usually as punishment. Thus Martial warns a certain Gallus off a particular adulterous liaison because the husband is not a '*pedico*', and so will not be susceptible to Gallus' famously smooth buttocks: but rather 'he fucks mouths (*irrumat*) or fucks cunts (*futuit*)' (2.47). There is, then, only one possibility confronting Gallus if he is caught, the most humiliating reprisal of coerced fellatio, of being raped in the mouth, by the wronged husband (on these informal, but traditional, punishments for adultery, see e.g. Richlin 1981; cf. Mart. 2.60).

It might be thought that these illustrations from Martial, which could all be multiplied from other sources too, rather prove the questioned point. What holds *futuere*, *pedicare*, and *irrumare* together, makes them roughly equivalent for their male subjects, across the variation in the sex of, and meaning for, the objects of these acts, is, pretty precisely, their penetrative and active qualities. This is what they share, and which constitutes their masculine validity. The problem here is rather more with the other side of the equation, and whether the variety of corresponding roles can be described as 'passive' except as demanded by the 'activity' of whatever else is going on. The Latin verbs concerned can, of course, be used in the passive voice: Gallus could be described, for example, as 'being fucked in the mouth' (*irrumari*), as having something done to him. Alternatively, he could he said to fellate (*fellare*) the husband, just as recipients of vaginal or anal penetration can be said to move appropriately: *crisare* and *cevere* respectively. That is, they all perform sexual actions of their own, and indeed, it might well be argued that, in practical terms, if effort is to be quantified as such, these 'passive' partners might have rather more to do than their 'active' counterparts. Certainly, in English the language of oral sex, and phrases like 'sucking off' or 'giving a blow-job' in particular, make it pretty clear who is doing the actual work, where the action lies in such situations; and it is not with the penetrator, the '*irrumator*'.

The other problem comes in respect to what has been omitted so far, and for which there is no dedicated Latin verb, that is, the performance of cunnilingus, usually referred to by combining *lingere* (to lick) and *cunnus* (cunt), with some variations. This lack of linguistic precision is symptomatic of wider unease and uncertainty about this practice, which, despite being 'active' and 'penetrative', was totally despised, deemed disgusting, polluting, and even 'unmanly'. Martial's vicious attack on Nanneius, once an insatiable *cunnilingus* (in Latin this denotes the actor not the action) but now fortunately disabled in that department, illustrates many of these points (11.61). Referred to as a lingual husband (*maritus*) and oral adulterer (*moechus*), Nanneius' 'fucking tongue' (*lingua fututrix*) penetrates women so deeply that he could determine the sex, hear the cries, of anything in their wombs; which is so disgraceful and defiling that even the lowest whore tries to shut their doors on him, and would indeed rather give him a blow-job than a kiss! No aspersions have, therefore, been cast on Nanneius' manly, active, penetrating role, except insofar as his excesses have now made him orally impotent, unable to get it up in the mouth: the essential problem comes, rather, from his misuse, his pollution, of that part of the body itself. On the other hand, the *tribas* Philaenis, who fucks (*pedico*) boys and takes girls like an overexcited husband (*maritus*), is attacked by Martial for not extending her rejection of fellatio as insufficiently manly also to cunnilingus (7.67). Though Philaenis' extreme assumption of the male sexual role, and indeed, her pretty parodic adoption of the male role in eating, drinking, and exercise, is the real issue here, the root cause of the trouble, she is further ridiculed for this failure of masculine conduct.

Oral sex involving the female genitalia thus emerges as a rather ambiguous erotic activity which does not easily fit the active/passive dichotomy. It appears to, and there is a conceptual need for it to be thus comprehensible. Thus the tongue formally imitates the penetrative male role with a penetrated, female object (hence, presumably, Philaenis' mistake, or not); but, it also brings a different set of prohibitions, negative valuations, into play, alongside the more generic, but always feminizing, issue of excess. For the mouth has a special status in the body, it acts as a guardian of purity, in terms of both what goes in and what comes out (especially speech); so, indeed, fellatio is also problematic. As already mentioned, being fucked in the mouth was particularly humiliating for a man, and not that straightforward for a woman either, even though the basic gender alignment is correct for her; for there is the extra burden of oral pollution to bear in all such transactions. There is, then, greater complexity at work here than the more simplistic classifications of Roman sexual behaviour allow. Not that oral sex contradicts the basic evaluative framework, but it does complicate matters; and, in many ways Martial's satire (and that of other Latin poets) revels in these subtleties and multiplicities as much as it more plainly reinforces the main rules of the game.

For these texts do contribute to the maintenance of the dominant sexual order, and it is worth emphasizing that, in contrast to the prohibition on certain categories of person, the non-availability of respectable women and freeborn males to the defining figure of the Roman man, the bar on certain types of sexual activity is enforced entirely informally. There are no laws involved, just social judgement and self-control. The value system is continually iterated, praise and blame are constantly enacted in speech, writing, and life; but that still leaves plenty for the individual to do, and, as already noted, there are areas of flexibility as well as rigidity, numerous complicating factors, in the ways things operate.

These complexities can be illustrated by returning to the case of Gallus, the smooth-buttocked potential adulterer: his adultery will not go unpunished, but the real interest of the poem lies in the means of punishment, the confounding of expectation to arrive at an even worse outcome, and in the overall placement of the male actors in relation to each other and the wider ideological framework. Gallus is aligned with the anonymous, but definitely reprehensible, woman in all this, as his susceptibility to her play for him and his bottom both indicate; but he will be forced still further down the scale of effeminacy and denigration by a husband whose sexual predilections are impeccable and whose manliness will only be reinforced by what he might do to Gallus. The masculine superiority of husband over adulterer is undercut only by the suspicion that he allows his wife to be actively and notoriously unfaithful in order to engineer such situations, when greater conjugal discipline—or divorce—would be the ideal, indeed was legislatively mandated by Augustus. Still, a neighbouring epigram demonstrates that the idea of using a wife as bait to bring in desirable male prey for the husband is one which Martial's poetic persona is happy to entertain (2.39): 'I will not take Telesina as my wife. Why? She is an adulteress/whore (*moecha*). | But Telesina gives herself to boys (*pueri*). I will!'

This is a bit naughty, but does not fundamentally threaten the speaker's male status, and makes even more sense in an epigrammatic world in which women are generally assumed to be of loose morals, the only real question being whether this benefits the male lover (or at least the author) or not. This perspective, it should be said, leaves women, in contrast to men, without any moral purchase on the verses, as subjects. They receive plenty of abuse, and little praise, but nothing which they can do anything with, for themselves, as both Telesina and the unnamed but infamous (*famosa*) adulteress involved with Gallus show. The former is simply a cipher around whom male wishes and desires are arranged, and while the charges against the latter imply her agency, and condemn her actions, this is largely incidental and goes nowhere.

Gallus, indeed, can be taken still further into the complexities, but also the givens, of the Roman system. For he might have been called a *cinaedus*, the main term for a failed Roman man, a male gender deviant, but one which, because, of its centrality to a sexual order in which many and various forms of manly failure were possible, and its utility in a society in which sexual abuse played such a vital role in public discourse, is hard to pin down more precisely, offers challenges with its capaciousness and pliability. Still, in liking both other men's wives and being anally penetrated, and in his somatic softness, Gallus broadly conforms to a cinaedic model, as found across Latin literature. All of these elements share a feminine touch, adultery perhaps most surprisingly to modern sensibilities, but as already indicated, the Roman view is different: adultery is not just morally wrong, it is morally weak, demonstrating a failure of masculine self-control, perhaps not catastrophic in itself, but which through repetition and association might become so (especially e.g. Catullus 57). Moreover, the feminine part of a *cinaedus*' sexual activity with other men comes from the role, not the men themselves, and it is expanded on in more general conduct and comportment, from curled hair to a mincing gait and unbelted tunic (e.g. Martial 7.58; Aulus Gellius 6.12.5). Sexual behaviour is only part of being a *cinaedus*, the failure to be a man is much more widespread, but also patchy, in that more or less any of these features, singly or together, courts the label, which is a ubiquitous facet of Roman invective, from Catullus (e.g. 16 and 25) to the walls of imperial Pompeii (e.g. *CIL* 4.1772, 1825, and 4082).

There is a sense, therefore, in which the category dissipates through its frequency and variety, becomes a generic term of abuse; and there is then an obvious question raised about the 'materiality of the *cinaedus*', as Richlin puts it (1993). That is, given that the word appears in only hostile sources, that hostility is one of its defining features, were there really any *cinaedi* in ancient Rome? Or was the *cinaedus* essentially a conceptual antitype, a figure constructed to capture a key set of unmanly activities, and through his denigration and disavowal powerfully warn against them? This latter may not be incompatible with cinaedic materiality, however, since the set of values, the wider ideological framework, from which the idea of the *cinaedus* emerges is real enough, and had considerable, but certainly not complete, coercive force. So there undoubtedly were male gender deviants in ancient Rome, and they would have been well aware that they risked being labelled *cinaedi*, whatever their precise relationship with any of the stereotypes involved. Without any surviving voices from such men, however, without any self-identification with the *cinaedus* or almost any of his parts, little but speculation follows.

There is the younger Seneca's mid-first century CE allegation (*Ben.* 4.3.3–5) that the gifted but dissolute orator Mamercus Scaurus used to retell with pride a dinner-party exchange in which he joked that he would like to be fucked—apparently in the mouth—by his fellow guest Pollio, and meant it. There are various indications that what some called effeminate behaviour others considered sophisticated (e.g. Gellius 1.5.2–3), that the boundary of manliness was debatable and mobile in certain respects. The figure of the *cinaedus* is not actually engaged with, either positively or negatively, in any such conversations, though he may be lurking in the background; and, perhaps more strikingly, this sense of separation also carries into the recorded responses of those who were publicly accused of being *cinaedi*: most notably Julius Caesar and Augustus (see e.g. Suetonius *Iul.* 49–53 and 73 with Cat. 57; and *Aug.* 68–9 and 71). Neither directly denies it, indeed Caesar invited his poetic abuser Catullus to dinner, and allowed his troops to sing songs celebrating his rampant adultery, whoring, and sexual submission to King Nicomedes at his triumphs. This should not be seen as embracing a cinaedic identity, however, but rather rendering the *cinaedus* an irrelevance to him. It is his conquests which are emphasized in all this, as well as his magnanimity in victory, and Caesar's massively successful military and political career make him a real Roman man regardless, regardless of the accusations and their partial accuracy. Augustus' approach to, position on, the matter is the same, even if the style is different.

Many, of course, were not so lucky, and might have felt the bite of such accusations more acutely, from a far less privileged social position, but this point in itself, the deep divisions in Roman society from which it emerges, and the way in which certain forms of status, of achievement, did not so much protect men from the effects of being called a *cinaedus* as actually prevented them from being one, shows what distinctive terrain is being traversed here. Similarly, it makes little sense to call a slave a *cinaedus*, little abuse is involved, since sexual submission to his master is just part of the package, and there are more precise terms for male slaves specifically kept as sex toys. Freedmen and clients too might be caught up in this pattern of power and sexual service, a pattern which, as already emphasized, goes to the heart of Roman ideas about sexual activity. The assumption is that the master (or patron) would take the penetrative role, as appropriate to, confirming of, his superior position, and any reversals in this proper ordering, as might be hinted at by the physiques of favoured slaves (or not, see e.g. Mart. 11.63), were demeaning and reprehensible. These intrinsic inequalities in the Roman social structure, bound up as they were with Roman sexual concepts and practices, certainly argue strongly against the possibility of any kind of cinaedic community or 'subculture' existing in ancient Rome (*pace* Taylor 1997, and Richlin 1993), whatever else the reality of the *cinaedus* might have been: however many men there were who, knowingly or otherwise, fit the image, might have acted the part.

Finally, the question of materiality is still more starkly posed in relation to the rather rarer female equivalent of the *cinaedus*—the *tribas*—and, indeed, putting female sexuality in the picture again is instructive more broadly. In general, it should be said, the sexual abuse hurled at Roman women is associated with adultery, but this is not about being unwomanly (moral weakness and error, a tendency to lasciviousness and excess, these are all female characteristics after all) but rather about being a bad woman, and, of course, is symbolic of a deeper political and social malaise. Indeed, this is also the main point of Seneca the Younger's diatribe invoking the contemporary loss of femininity, the abandonment of the female role, as an even more extreme signal of the moral degeneration of the age, which precepts alone cannot rectify. Women 'are born to be submissive' (*pati natae*), he states in one of his letters (95.20–1), but some now match men in their lusts (as well as their drinking and wrestling) and have devised 'so perverse a variety of unchastity (*impudicitia*) that they enter men'. As a result of all this they have lost the privileges of their sex and now suffer what were exclusively male diseases—gout and baldness—thus literally embodying the wider ills of society.

Seneca does not use the term *tribas* here, but he could be describing Martial's Philaenis (who is also '*tribas* of *tribades*' at 7.70). The image of the female gender deviant does seem a reasonably established one in imperial Rome, built according to the general rules of both symmetry and asymmetry. Thus the unwomanly *tribas* mirrors the unmanly *cinaedus*, takes the male sexual role—with males and females—as he takes the female; both are reciprocal in their lack of reciprocity, and she is competitive in respect to other breaches of appropriately gendered conduct too. But there are also differences, beyond that of relative frequency, and the total absence of the *tribas* from the kind of casually abusive context in which the *cinaedus* thrives; for, as Philaenis illustrates, there is something intrinsically incoherent about the subject position of the female gender deviant, the woman who is, after all, being attacked for wanting to move up the sexual hierarchy, to leave inferiority and submission behind. The humour of Martial's poem emerges from her failure to construct the identity she seeks, her inability to make the idea of the *tribas*—the woman who adopts the male role—work in practice. Philaenis is essentially mistaken in what she considers manly: not just in the case of cunnilingus, but also, and more fundamentally, in her failure to realize that restraint, mastery over self and others, is essential to Roman manhood. So, she is revealed as a woman just as she tries hardest to be a man, raising questions about whether the project is possible at all.

That may be the point, that while denigration is the main moralizing strategy in respect to men, a constant attack on everything unmanly is what enforces dominant ideologies of masculinity; incoherence and impossibility form an integral part of the regulatory armoury for women, alongside the emphatic denunciation of adultery. This does tend to dematerialize the *tribas*, however, in contrast to both the *cinaedus* and the adulterous wife, whose existence is exaggerated rather than undercut in the, more extensive and complex, discourses that surround them. Moreover, on a practical level women's ability to lead an unconventional lifestyle was severely limited in the Roman world, even if the inclination was there. Nonetheless, some women—both rich and poor—certainly did not behave as they were meant to in the sexual domain, and while most are described in the surviving sources as straying in a stereotypically female manner, in the context of curses and binding spells, for example, women do adopt a more active and aggressive, 'masculine' persona in respect to both male and female objects of desire (e.g. *PGM* 16 and *Suppl. Mag.* 1.42). This material is complex, and so far found outside Rome, but (*pace* Winkler 1990) broadly speaking, the female minority seeks to compel relationships in the same way as the male majority (Ogden 1999: 60–6).

Such discussions rapidly become very speculative, however, though more could undoubtedly be made of some of the complicating hints that do survive in the ancient evidential record. Still, it has to be admitted that there will be gaps in any account of Roman sexuality, and that, despite a certain playfulness, there have been no seriously dissenting voices so far. Few have spoken from outside the literary elite, and no real challenge has been issued to the dominant value system. So, a more radical salvo is offered in conclusion, though perhaps not as radical as is sometimes made out, and one which also combines marginality and centrality in terms of its socio-political positioning, coming as it does from a philosopher drawn from, and influential among, the Roman elite, but who was exiled by successive Roman emperors in the second half of the first century CE, that is, the Stoic teacher Musonius Rufus. What Musonius undoubtedly does show, however, is the ongoing debate that surrounded sexual conduct in the Roman Empire, and the rather problematic position of women, as sexual and ethical subjects, within it: within limits that were certainly breached, but beyond view.

An Austere Ending

Musonius is reported to have asserted that anyone who is not completely lost to luxury and evil must recognize 'that sex is justified only in marriage and for the purpose of generating children' (fr. 12 Lutz). Even in marriage, sex for pleasure is unjust and illegitimate, and adultery, sleeping with other males, prostitutes, or slave girls, is even worse. All these activities reveal a lack of control and restraint, so that, even if no one else is harmed (as the husband is, in adultery), the perpetrator wrongs himself, dishonours and degrades himself, through such conduct. He demonstrates, indeed, that he is less worthy, less able to discipline his desires, than a woman: that the ruler is thus inferior to the ruled. For this, more or less, is the behaviour demanded of women, they are not allowed to sleep with their slaves, and surely men ought to be able to do better than them!

There is, then, a mixture of the dominant and the subversive here, wrapped up in a carefully constructed rhetorical package. On the one hand, few would in fact have assented to what Musonius claims all but the most morally degenerate know; on the other hand, he shares the assumption of a male subject position, and wants to use male superiority in support of his argument. He is opposed to the sexual double standard not because it is unfair to women, but because it degrades men; though elsewhere he is committed to a basic equality of virtue between the sexes (frgs. 3 and 4 Lutz). Still, his teachings on sexual matters (*aphrodisia*) have nothing to say to women, they do not even get any credit for their model behaviour, its apparent superiority is, instead, a problem to be resolved; but what Musonius has to say to men is quite distinctive, seems to fly in the face of much that has been discussed so far.

Still, Musonius could be cast as an ultra-conservative as much as a radical, and if he were to rephrase his diatribe, moderate his invective somewhat, he might well have been able to achieve broad consent to his basic premise. For the Romans placed no positive moral valuation on sexual activity itself, nor, unlike some Greeks, did they idealize any form of sexual relationship; and though that does not entail the reverse, that there is any negative valence to sex, it does give Musonius' position a certain logic. Moreover, it might gain further support from the permanent Roman nostalgia for a more austere age. For the only sex necessary to living an exemplary Roman (or Stoic) life is that to produce legitimate children—the continuation of the line is an obligation owed by all—anything beyond that is then, strictly speaking, excessive. Now, most Roman men would be less strict, would push the boundaries of the excessive out beyond moderate, and properly conducted, sexual relations with slave girls and boys, male and female prostitutes, and other categories of the readily available. Indeed, they might consider the total denial of these pleasures to be, in itself, excessive, an immoderate exercise of self-control that would unbalance a good life. But that is not to valorize sex itself; rather, the focus is on a particular way of living, one of moderation, self-mastery, and the pursuit of Roman greatness, which implies a certain attitude to sex, as also food and drink, for example (Foucault 1985).

Musonius is, therefore, very much part of a wider collective conversation about correct conduct in relation to sex in the Roman world, and though he holds an extreme position within it, he does not provide any real rupture. Despite the formal similarity of his views with later Christian doctrines, for example, they are quite different in their assumptions and anchorage. Sex does not yet carry with it the burden of the Fall, nor is its regulation about obedience to god's law; rather, it is about doing right by being a human being, a right which is part of the structure of the cosmos, but also needs to be found, followed, and worked on by humans themselves, which is where philosophy, its teachings and discipline, comes in.

There is a sense, however, in which this work has already been done for women; philosophy may offer some assistance, but basically, external circumstances, existing mores, have the situation sorted, whereas men have it all to do, even more so because they have their superiority to maintain. This is Musonius' version of the ongoing conundrum concerning women, sexuality, and subjectivity: that despite their manifest moral weaknesses, their inferiority, they in fact have heavier demands placed on them in terms of their sexual behaviour. Except that, in ancient terms, this kind of externally imposed restriction may be heavy but it is not hard, it is appropriate for those lacking in judgement and control; while it is the complexities of masculine conduct, the choices to be made, the control exercised, when there are so many other possibilities, that requires real effort, is really worthwhile. This is self-mastery, not being mastered, which is women's lot. There is, therefore, a lot at stake in Roman sexuality, as also in the modern world, with its own visions of value and order: so there seems plenty to discuss.

References

Boswell, J. (1980). *Christianity, Social Tolerance and Homosexuality*, Chicago: University of Chicago Press.

Brooten, B. J. (1996). *Love Between Women: Early Christian Responses to Female Homoeroticism*, Chicago: University of Chicago Press.

Cantarella, E. (1992). *Bisexuality in the Ancient World*, trans. C. Ó Culleanáin, New Haven: Yale University Press. First published as *Secondo natura: la bisessualità nel mondo antico*, Rome: Editori Riuniti, 1988.

Dixon, S. (2001). *Reading Roman Women: Sources, Genres, and Real Life*, London: Duckworth.

Edwards, C. (1993). *The Politics of Immorality in Ancient Rome*, Cambridge: Cambridge University Press.

Foucault, M. (1985). *The History of Sexuality*, vol. 2: *The Use of Pleasure*, tr. R. Hurley, Harmondsworth: Penguin. First published as *Histoire de la sexualité*, II: *L'Usage des plaisirs*, Paris: Gallimard, 1984.

Fredrick, D., (ed.) (2002). *The Roman Gaze: Vision, Power, and the Body*, Baltimore: John Hopkins University Press.

Hallett, J. P. and Skinner, M. (eds.) (1997). *Roman Sexualities*, Princeton: Princeton University Press.

Hemelrijk, E. A. (1999). *Matrona Docta: Educated Women in the Roman Élite from Cornelia to Julia Domna*, London: Routledge.

Langlands, R. (2006). *Sexual Morality in Ancient Rome*, Cambridge: Cambridge University Press.

Lutz, C. E. (1942). *Musonius Rufus: The Roman Socrates*, New Haven: Yale University Press.

McDonnell, M. A., (2006). *Roman Manliness: Virtus and the Roman Republic*, Cambridge: Cambridge University Press.

McGinn, T. A. (1998). *Prostitution, Sexuality and the Law in Ancient Rome*, Oxford: Oxford University Press.

Ogden, D. (1999). 'Binding Spells: Curse Tablets and Voodoo Dolls in the Greek and Roman Worlds', in V. Flint, R. Gordon, G. Luck, and D. Ogden (eds.), *Witchcraft and Magic in Europe: Ancient Greece and Rome*, London: Athlone Press.

Parker, H. (1997). 'The Roman Teratogenic Grid', in J. P. Hallett and M. Skinner (eds.), *Roman Sexualities*, Princeton: Princeton University Press: 47–65.

Richlin, A. (1981). 'Approaches to the Sources on Adultery at Rome', in H. P. Foley (ed.), *Reflections of Women in Antiquity*, New York: Gordon & Breach: 379–404.

—— (1992), *The Garden of Priapus: Sexuality and Aggression in Roman Humour*, 2nd edn. New York: Oxford University Press.

—— (1993), 'Not Before Homosexuality: The Materiality of the *Cinaedus* and the Roman Law Against Love Between Men', *Journal of the History of Sexuality*, 3: 523–73.

Taylor, R. (1997). 'Two Pathic Subcultures in Ancient Rome', *Journal of the History of Sexuality*, 7: 319–71.

Treggiari, S. (1991). *Roman Marriage: Iusti Coniuges from the Time of Cicero to the Time of Ulpian*, Oxford: Oxford University Press.

Wilkinson, L. P. (1978). *Classical Attitudes to Modern Issues*, London: William Kimber.

Williams, C. A. (1999). *Roman Homosexuality: Ideologies of Masculinity in Classical Antiquity*, Oxford: Oxford University Press.

Winkler J. J. (1990). *The Constraints of Desire: The Anthropology of Sex and Gender in Ancient Greece*, New York: Routledge.

Wiseman T. P. (1985). *Catullus and his Word: A Reappraisal*, Cambridge: Cambridge University Press.

Wyke, M. (2002). *The Roman Mistress: Ancient and Modern Representations*, Oxford: Oxford University Press.

CHAPTER 51

WOMEN

KRISTINA MILNOR

WHAT, after all, *is* a woman? Contemporary feminist theory has found this to be a provocative and difficult question (see e.g. Moi 1999). Is 'women' most appropriately a category of biology? Of society or culture? Of language? Is naming oneself a woman a right? A responsibility? A burden? These questions are difficult enough to address when we are speaking of the modern day, but become even more so when we look back to antiquity. Not only are we challenged by the gulf of time and culture between us and them, but we must also face the real problems in the surviving evidence: due to the patriarchal prejudice of ancient cultures in the first instance and of modern scholars in the second, classical studies has long been biased toward men and the story of their public, political, and military sphere. The lives of women, it is true, first began to be studied by classical scholars in the nineteenth century, but these analyses tended to reproduce either their authors' own assumptions about women and gender or those of their ancient sources. It was not until the 1970s that critics began systematically to challenge the 'silence' which had been imposed on ancient women and to question whether something could be done about it (most notably in Pomeroy 1975, but cf. Finley 1965). We are indebted to these pioneering studies for filling in some of the spaces which had been left in our picture of the ancient world—for pointing out what could actually be said about the lives of biologically female adult human beings in antiquity. But it is also true that they were forced to assume that what we mean when we say 'woman' today is the same as what the Romans meant when they said *femina*, or *mulier*, or *matrona*, or even *puella* (for a discussion of the different terms, see Treggiari 1991: 6–7). Such problems of vocabulary and translation are not, of course, confined to the study of ancient gender roles, but they do underscore the problem: if we're not sure what a woman is *now*, how can we be sure we know what one was *then*?

In answer to these questions, many scholars who study women in antiquity would probably adopt the position of Justice Stewart on obscenity: that while we may not be able to define exactly what a woman is or was, 'I know [her] when I see [her]'. This is perfectly fair, and necessary on some level if we are ever going to get anywhere. But for the purposes of this chapter I would like to press the issue somewhat, and consider how and in what contexts the category 'woman' had meaning for ancient Romans. In fact, I will argue, the Romans too had many different approaches to the question with which I began, approaches which do not converge on a single definition but nevertheless have certain attitudes, opinions, and assumptions in common. Yet perhaps more interesting than a definitive answer to the question is to see in what contexts it became important, that is, under what circumstances did the Romans think they needed to be able to identify 'women' as a distinct category? When and where does the taken-for-granted distinction between male and female become the site of cultural anxiety? Why, and how, did the Romans need to ask what a woman was?

Before I approach these questions, though, let me say a few words about what this chapter is not. I have not attempted here to provide a comprehensive account of women's role(s) in Roman society, history, and literature, since to do so would require a great deal more space and knowledge than I currently have. The books and articles cited in Further Reading and the References will provide more detailed information on the topics over which I pass below. This is not to say, however, that there is no theory behind what I say here. In recent years there has developed something of a rift, or perhaps simply a strong difference of opinion, between those who would prioritize the historical investigation of women's lived experience in antiquity and those who are more interested in the ways that 'woman' and femininity as ideas were constructed in ancient social discourses (see e.g. Gold 2004). It will be seen that my approach is closer to the second than the first of these, but I also believe (along with others) that the dichotomy between 'lived reality' and 'discursive representation' is a false one. To my mind, human lives are framed by a constant dialogue between social ideals and social experience, a dialogue between what people think they know of the world and what they live. So while I would never make the mistake of believing that words are the same as things, I also think that an authentic picture of ancient women's experience has to take into account the cultural truths about what it meant to be a woman with which both they and the men around them lived every day. It is these truths which I have tried to outline below.

That said, let us begin at the beginnings. One way in which scholars have approached the question of what a woman was for the ancient Greeks is to look at myths of origin, in particular the creation of the first woman, Pandora, as it is narrated in Hesiod's *Theogony* and *Works and Days* (e.g. Loraux 1993: 10, 72–110).

According to Hesiod, Pandora was created in the likenesses of the goddesses as a punishment for man following Prometheus' theft of fire; moulded from earth and water, she is 'a beautiful evil' (*kalon kakon*) who founds 'the race of women' (*genos gunaikon*) which will be a continuous drain on man's hard-earned goods and happiness for the rest of history. The idea that 'woman is an afterthought, created as a secondary category following the emergence of man' (Zeitlin, 1996: 53) is not by any means unique to the Greeks—the story of Pandora's creation has been compared, for instance, with that of Eve in Genesis. It is in certain senses curious, therefore, that one finds no similar stories amongst the Romans. Indeed, it is worth noting that there is a passage at the beginning of Ovid's *Metamorphoses* (1.80–8) which is clearly influenced by Hesiod's description of Pandora's 'birth'. Ovid too imagines a person created out of earth and water in the form of the gods, but for him that figure is humankind generally rather than 'woman' in particular, and instead of seeing the new creation as the origin of unhappiness in the world, Ovid sets it down in earth's first 'golden age' (*aurea... aetas, Met.* 1.89).

This is not to say that the Romans thought men and women were exactly equal, but it does suggest that they had less interest in a myth which articulates woman's profound otherness to the point of assigning her to an altogether different species. Similarly, in contrast with classical Greek medical texts which see women as profoundly different from and inferior to men in every aspect of their bodies, the author of the one treatise on gynaecology from the Roman period (Soranus: early 2nd cent. CE) explicitly denies that there is any difference between the sexes excepting the reproductive organs (*Gynecology* 3.5). Similarly, Galen, a doctor in Rome during the mid- and late second century CE, rather famously championed the idea that women's reproductive organs are simply the male ones retained inside the body because of the lesser heat in women's natures (*On the Usefulness of the Parts of the Body* 14.6). Again, although men and women may not be the *same* in the Roman-period texts, they are represented as *similar* in ways that contrast with the earlier Greek medical works (Dean-Jones 1994). Correspondingly, Roman originary myths do not tend to focus on woman as an-other creation. When we do get a description of male and female origins, we find femininity not as a kind of biological pathology, but as the natural result of the fundamental structure of society. In this vein, the agricultural writer Columella (12.1.1), quoting Cicero's translation of Xenophon's *Oeconomicus*, offers the story that when the god created human beings he determined that they should live together in a partnership. This *societas* would produce children but also provide help (*adiutoria*) and protection (*propugnacula*) to mortals in old age. But since human life has two sides, the 'outside' tasks of hunting and harvesting and the 'inside' ones of protecting and nurturing, the god created two sexes, one for each set of tasks, and formed male and female natures accordingly. This passage in Columella does, of course, ultimately derive from a Greek source, so it would be a mistake to put too much pressure on it as a uniquely Roman perspective. But it does suggest a counterpoint to the story of Pandora: whereas there society is structured as it is because women are different from men, the story of creation found in Columella has women be different because human society needs to be structured in a certain way.

The idea that the definition of 'woman' cannot be separated from the definition of her social role is not, as I said, unique to the Romans, but it is one which is frequently repeated and strongly emphasized in their myths and history. One of the most popular and enduring myths of early Rome is the story of the rape of the Sabine women, in which the early male settlers of the city stole the daughters and sisters of neighbouring tribes in order to take them as wives. Different authors offer different explanations for why this was necessary, but there is general agreement that it was motivated in part by the Romans' desire to create alliances with the peoples around them. Unfortunately, the Sabines did not take kindly to the theft of the women and declared war on their new neighbours; the women, however, had in the interim become reconciled to their Roman captors and interceded between the two armies, begging them not to force a choice between their family of birth and that of marriage. The story is obviously an important one—we have extended textual versions from Livy, Cicero, Ovid, Dionysius of Halicarnassus, and Plutarch, as well as a number of artistic representations—and clearly articulates the role which women could and did play in Roman society as a binding link between families (Miles 1995). Born into one, they could marry into another, and create a next generation which was (to quote Livy's Sabine women themselves) *nepotum illi, hi liberum* ('grandchildren on the one side, children on the other', Livy 1.13.2).

In other words, one thing which Roman women were was 'related to men', in the role(s) of mothers, aunts, wives, sisters, daughters, and granddaughters. This is a deeply patriarchal perspective and one which is famously enshrined in Roman naming practices. Where men had three names, praenomen, nomen, and cognomen, women were simply called by the feminine version of the family name, e.g. Julia of the Julii (Dixon 2001: pp. x–xi). Thus, every woman in a family technically had the same name. A wife retained her natal family name, although she could additionally be identified with the genitive of her husband's name ('Terentia Ciceronis', or 'Cicero's Terentia': Treggiari 1991: 414). In addition, with a few exceptions, all Roman women were formally required to have a male 'tutor' to oversee their legal and business dealings; only Vestal Virgins and, after the Augustan social legislation of 18–17 BCE, certain women who had born three children were free to act on their own behalf. Still, the majority of women must have been formally subject on some level to male control (Gardner 1986: 5–29).

Of course, there is clearly a difference between the laws and social customs which govern people's lives and the how they actually live them. *Tutela mulierum perpetua*—the principle in Roman law that all women required a male guardian to oversee business for them—is a case in point. The argument has been persuasively made (Dixon 2001*b*) that the principle originated as a means to protect family property which, in contrast with classical Greek practices, could pass in Rome to female heirs. By establishing a male tutor who was from her family of birth, unless the woman had been formally given over to another family through marriage *cum manu*, her agnatic relatives could rest assured that her property would remain within their control. As time moved on, however, both marriage and inheritance practices changed, and we find tutela defended (by Cicero among others) as a means of protecting women from their own *infirmitas consilii* ('weakness of judgement', *Pro Murena* 27). Yet late Republican and Imperial Roman history is full of women who acted on their own behalf where their own money was concerned (e.g. Caerellia, from whom Cicero himself borrowed money: *Ad Att.* 12.51.3; 15.26.4). By the time of Gaius (middle of the 2nd cent. CE), the jurist could speak of the idea that tutela was necessary because women were flighty of judgement as *magis speciosa... quam vera* ('more specious... than true': *Inst.* 1.189), albeit something which was popularly believed. In other words, the idea that women were creatures who needed men to care for them seems to have originated in this instance as a popular explanation for a system actually born from patriarchy's desire to care for itself, a circumstance which resulted in certain contradictions between social ideals and social practice.

Indeed, the fact that Roman women could possess property—inherited or otherwise—seems to have been an important aspect of their role in the Roman social imagination. It is not surprising, for instance, that one of the few places in the *Digest of Roman Law* where we find an actual definition of 'women' is in the context of inheritance: Ulpian quotes Pomponius, a jurist of the early second century CE, who wrote that when a bequest consisted of all of a woman's clothing, that which she wore as a child (*infans*), as an adolescent (*puella*), and as a young woman (*virgo*) should also be included, *mulieres enim omnes dici, quaecumque sexus feminini sunt* ('since all those are called women who are [members] of the female sex': *D* 34.2.25.9). On the surface, this comment might seem like an answer to my opening question. But the context indicates that Ulpian was seeking a broad definition of 'woman' in order to construe the inheritance as liberally as possible; he is similarly generous in the next sentence, where a woman's *mundus* ('adornment') is defined as anything which makes her more attractive (*mundior*). Elsewhere he notes, *mulieris appellatione etiam virgo viripotens continetur* ('a girl ready to have sex with a man is also included in the term "woman"': *D* 50.16.13 pr), which would seem to imply that the term *mulier* was generally restricted to adults. Clearly in ancient Roman law, as today, what constituted a woman was fluid and context-specific, but it seems to have been particularly urgent to find a stable, and broad, definition in the context of inheritance.

The idea that women could possess and transmit property by no means appears in our Roman sources as an unproblematically good thing: in addition to Cicero's memorable negative portraits of the wealthy matrons Clodia in the *Pro Caelio* and Sassia in the *Pro Cluentio*, the rich wife appears as a difficult figure from Plautus (see e.g. *Mostellaria* 702–3) to Horace (*Carm.* 3.24.17–20) to Juvenal (*Sat.* 6.136) (for a discussion see Saller 1984: 204). Yet Roman history also preserves the stories of instances when women were able and willing to contribute their private money to the well-being of the state: in 387 BCE, when the Gauls demanded a ransom payment after capturing the city (Livy 5.50) and during the Second Punic War in 214 (Livy 24.18), Roman women came forward and volunteered their personal wealth to assist the public treasury. In the speech which he put into the mouth of the tribune Lucius Valerius supporting the repeal of the *Lex Oppia* in 195 BCE, Livy has him use these incidents to support his contention the gold used for women's jewellery should be considered not wasted on luxury, but *praesidium … ad privatos et ad publicos usus* ('a protection … for both private and public ends', 34.7.4). It is against this background that we should imagine a famous speech given by Hortensia in the Forum in which she opposed the attempt by the triumvirs in 42 BCE to support the war against the assassins of Caesar with a tax on the wealthiest Roman women. Although we do not know what she actually said, Appian's version of the speech plausibly has her state that while the women would be happy to fund a war against a foreign enemy, they have no intention of giving money for their countrymen to fight each other (*BC* 4.33).

Hortensia's speech, both as a historical event and as it is depicted by Appian, makes a usefully representative moment for examining what it meant to be a Roman woman. On the one hand, the triumvirs seem to have recognized, correctly, that elite women's property was a significant untapped resource on which they would have liked to draw, as they had the wealth of elite men. On the other hand, their attempt was ultimately unsuccessful, perhaps in part because of the argument which Appian has Hortensia marshal against them in her speech: women, and therefore their property, are exempted by their nature (*phusis*) from the business of men. As she puts it, after listing the various offences of which the triumvirs have accused their enemies, 'why are we to share in the punishments, we who did not take part in the crimes?' (*BC* 4.32). Her point is that for the triumvirs to use their public authority to seize female property is for them to violate the boundary which exists between the world of women and that of men, a boundary which she, like Columella, sees as 'naturally' ordained. It is not at all surprising to discover that the Romans, like almost every other ancient Mediterranean society, were invested in the idea that women's 'correct' place was the home and her most important tasks were the domestic ones she performed there. Hortensia's point is thus not itself especially noteworthy; what is more curious is that it is made in a speech before a group of magistrates, in the Forum, the heart of Roman civic life. Hortensia is using the language of traditional domestic virtue in a public arena to make a statement about Roman politics.

In this sense, Hortensia is one in a long line of 'great Roman matrons' who stretch back to Hersilia, wife of Romulus and leader of the captured group of Sabine women, and forward to the powerful women of the imperial household such as Galla Placidia. These women were remarkable in that they were able to make a place for themselves in public life by stretching the boundaries of the traditional 'good' domestic roles of mother, sister, or wife. Other noteworthy examples include Cornelia, mother of the revolutionary Gracchi brothers; Servilia, half-sister to the Republican leader Cato and mother of Brutus the tyrannicide; and Fulvia, wife of the triumvir Mark Antony. Under the early Empire, with the rise of the powerful women of the *domus Caesarum*—mothers, sisters, wives, and daughters to emperors—the paradox began even to be expressed in the very landscape of the city of Rome: imperial women became patrons of large public building projects, such as the porticus and shrine to Concordia dedicated by Augustus' wife Livia which celebrates the traditional 'fellowship' between husband and wife (Flory 1984). Yet concordia was also a civic virtue, so that the shrine additionally emphasized the peace and domestic tranquillity which the Julio-Claudian house had brought to Rome. Because of the importance of the family in Roman culture, 'private' relationships between men and women not only had an impact on civic life generally, they also created literal spaces for virtuous femininity in the urban environment.

Of course, not all Roman women were virtuous, in reality or ideological representation. If one Roman answer to the question 'what is a woman?' would be 'a (good) wife' or 'a (good) mother', another one would certainly be 'a (perfidious) mistress' or 'a (sexually depraved) prostitute'; if there were virtues and virtuous roles which were understood to be distinctly feminine, there were also vices and negative stereotypes which were particularly associated with women. Because of the importance of morality in Roman thought and the close relationship between (imagined) chastity and social respectability, it is not surprising to find the dichotomy between good women and bad ones being expressed in terms of sexual purity, between the matron and the whore. It seems to have been important in Rome, however, that these moral categories should not only exist but be visible in the clothing that a woman wore. Respectable matrons wore the *stola* (a long dress), *palla* (mantle), and bound their hair with *vittae* (fillets); prostitutes, on the other hand, wore the toga, the same garment as adult male citizens. In the *Lex Julia de adulteriis*, part of the Augustan social legislation of 18–17 BCE, one of the penalties for adultery was that a guilty woman had to don the toga in place of her stola. This emphasizes two things: first, that Roman society could only imagine two kinds of women, the respectable matrona and the prostitute, and that failure to maintain your status as the former meant automatic identification with the latter; second, that there was a certain amount of cultural anxiety about being able to tell the difference between the categories, so that an external marker was required to allow society at large to 'read' the nature of the woman underneath the clothes (McGinn 1998: 156–71).

In the same way, however, that we can find in Rome both implicit and explicit challenges to the boundaries established for 'good' women and their domestic roles, we also find instances of dissent to the definitions established for what made a Roman woman 'bad'. One place in which these vices and stereotypes are famously explored, exploited, and—to a certain extent—resisted is in Latin elegy, where we find the overbearing, often sexually promiscuous *domina* as the desired object of the poet. It has been argued that we should see in these elegiac women, who are so different from those held up to be admired in other genres and history, a kind of 'counter-cultural feminism'—an attempt to create a 'new, more meaningful set of values' (Hallett 1984: 247) for the poem's audience. On the other hand, there is clearly no easy or uncomplicated relationship between the world of elegy's 'demi-monde', populated by pathetic, lovelorn poets and their domineering mistresses, and mainstream Roman culture, which celebrated 'traditional' military and civic roles for men and domestic ones for women. It has be noted, for instance, that, within the literary discourse of elegy, the domineering *puella* is represented not as a 'real' woman, but rather as a construct of the text, material to be made and manipulated in the same way that the mythical artist Pygmalion sculpted the beautiful statue with which he fell in love (Sharrock 1991). Thus, the 'power' of elegiac women actually redounds to the authority of the poet: 'by identifying with the slave in his role as lover, and by using the mistress to characterize his poetic voice, the author gains the "advantages" he sees in these objectified figures, but also maintains his mastery and masculinity by asserting his control over them' (McCarthy 1998: 178).

In this sense, we might say that 'what a woman is' in the context of elegy (and other male-authored literary genres) is actually a man—that is, the female figures which appear in the works of Catullus, Propertius, Virgil, Ovid, and so on are simply figments of the male author's imagination and serve merely to support the male figures in the text. This is one reason why so much attention has been given to the few, very few, female-authored works which have come down to us—important work, to be sure, but unfortunately limited by the quantity of surviving material. For this and other reasons, I would also argue that it is necessary to consider seriously the implications of statements like that which Ovid makes at the beginning of the third book of the *Ars Amatoria*: defending his decision to address a book to women and thus 'arm the Amazons', he notes *ipsa quoque et cultu est et nomine femina Virtus*: '(manly) virtue herself is by dress and name a woman' (*AA* 3.23). It is, of course, a joke, which Ovid underscores by the juxtapositioning of *femina* and *vir-tus* at the end of the line: this most masculine character trait—whose very name is based on the word for man (*vir*)—is not only conventionally represented as a woman, but the word itself is grammatically feminine. But it is also, I would argue, a productive exposure of a paradox, namely the extent to which women generally, and perhaps especially Roman women, seem always to exceed attempts to confine and define them. As much as Roman patriarchy would have liked to imagine a world in which women were marginal, its own history, cultural practices, and even language worked against it.

Perhaps this is an overly 'optimistic' fallacy (Richlin 1993). But I'd like to defend it with one more example which, I think, illustrates some of the possibilities, not just of 'reading resistantly' (as recommended in Joplin 1984) but of seeing the ways in which texts may actually resist themselves. The fifth book of the *Aeneid* is rather famously patriarchal (Nugent 1992): it begins as Aeneas and his crew sail away from Carthage, back on track towards the imperial glory that will be Rome, about to be foretold explicitly in the Underworld visit of Book 6; much of the book is taken up with the funeral games in honour of Aeneas' father Anchises, in which both Trojan fathers and sons participate in exhibitions of battle-skills; this celebration of masculine military prowess is explicitly set against the temperament and behaviour of the women, who, tired of wandering the sea, burn the Trojan ships in an attempt to force the group to stay in Sicily. Although these women at first seem to represent genuine female dissent to the masculine thrust of the narrative, they are never given a real place in the text, as their single voice (*vox omnibus una*: 5.616) is provided by Iris, sent by Juno to stir them to action. Finally, Book 5 is set against the background of Dido's suicide and funeral pyre, the glow of which the fleet witnesses as it sails away in the first lines of the book. In these opening lines Virgil notes that, although they did not know specifically what fire they were witnessing, the crew nevertheless had a sense that things were amiss: *quae tantum accenderit ignem | causa latet; duri magno sed amore dolores | polluto, notumque furens quid femina possit, | triste per augurium Teucrorum pectora ducunt*: 'what circumstance had lit up so great a fire they did not know; but the hard suffering brought on by a great love violated, and the knowledge of what a frenzied woman could do, led the hearts of the Trojans through unhappy foreboding' (5.4–7).

On one level, this seems like an appropriately male-centred introduction to a male-centred book: the Trojans are not sure what has happened to Dido but they are aware of the sort of things that unhappy women are wont to do; ignorant of the actual events of the text, they are able to fall back on what they do know (*notum*) about women's unstable and passionate natures (*furens quid femina possit*). This brings them little comfort, which it shouldn't: we as readers know that not only has Dido killed herself, but she has cursed Aeneas, his men, and their descendants with unending war (*pugnent ipsique nepotesque*, 4.629). On one level, then, the foreboding which the Trojans feel about what 'an enraged woman' might have done is well founded. But on another level we are confronted in these lines with the limits of the sailors' 'knowledge': they actually have no idea how bad the situation is; indeed, it will be many generations hence, perhaps not until Virgil writes the *Aeneid*, that the full implications of Dido's curse will be recognized. Moreover, although we are told here that the Trojans have knowledge of 'what an enraged woman can do', we will see later in the book exactly how unprepared they are for the anger of the Trojan women and the burning of the ships, an action which Ascanius describes as *furor* (5.670, echoing *furens* above), and which leaves Aeneas 'thunderstruck by the harsh disaster' (*casu concussus acerbo*, 5.700). What exactly is it that these men know about women?

In fact, I would argue, what is dramatized at the beginning of *Aeneid* 5 is exactly the kind of anxiety around women and their 'possibilities' which we see elsewhere in Roman history and literature. Although, on the one hand, Roman culture seems to have refused the ideological construction of women which would see them as entirely other—members of a wholly different species from men—on the other hand it clearly found their presence unsettling, perhaps precisely because it could not imagine how society would function without them. As Augustus himself is supposed to have said, quoting to the assembly a famous speech by Metellus Numidicus, 'nature has made it that we can't live with them [*sc.* women] particularly comfortably, but we can't live without them at all' (*ita natura tradidit, ut nec cum illis satis commode, nec sine illis uno modo vivi possit*: Aulus Gellius, *NA* 1.6.2). But this was not simply a concern about the necessities of biological reproduction; rather, it seems to have had to do with the importance which Romans accorded domestic, especially family, life and women within it. This becomes particularly clear with the advent and development of imperial rule, when the *domus Caesarum* became the central political unit in the Roman state, but it was true even before then, as can be seen in the myth of the Sabine women and the role which women increasingly held under the Republic as possessors and transmitters of family wealth. Although in various instances Roman men may have enjoyed the fantasy that they could stabilize, delineate, and confine the women in their midst, those efforts could never be entirely successful due to the conflicting ideals and ideologies which also existed in Roman culture. It is in exposing and exploring these conflicts that we may not only learn more about the conditions under which Roman women lived, but see how 'knowledge' about gender was an important touchstone in almost every aspect of Roman life.

Further reading

I have not tried here to write a history of the modern study of ancient Roman women and/or to trace the development and influence of first-, second-, third-, and fourth-wave feminism in Roman Studies. Such essays can be very valuable, however, and readers seeking a more historical or theoretical overview are encouraged to consult the essays in Rabinowitz and Richlin 1993, especially the Introduction; Dixon 2001*a*; McClure 2002; and the older but still valuable essay by Blok 1987. Generally speaking, feminist classical scholarship in the 1970s and early 1980s tended to focus—as did much work in women's history at that time—on recovering the facts and material circumstances of ancient women's lives, in an attempt to compensate for the centuries of male bias in historical studies. This can be seen in Pomeroy 1975; Cantarella 1987; and the first publication of Lefkowitz and Fant (the still-standard collection of primary sources) in 1975. Much of this early scholarship was focused on Greece over Rome, although some noteworthy exceptions are Herrmann 1964, Gardner 1986, and Kampen 1981. The last is especially important, as it focuses not just on Roman women, but on working women, a topic still rarely addressed. On the other end of the social spectrum, Purcell 1986 is still indispensable reading for anyone interested in the role which imperial women played in (re)defining Roman gender roles. Since the 1990s began there has been more interest expressed in Roman women generally (e.g. Hemelrijk 1999), but also and especially in the ways that representations of women function in Roman texts and visual arts: for example, Joshel and Richlin (on Livy and Ovid respectively) in Richlin 1992; Bergmann 1996 on women in Roman wall-painting; Keith 2000 on women in Roman epic; the essays by Wyke, collected in her 2002 volume, on the elegiac mistress; and Ginsburg 2006 on Agrippina the Younger. Recent years have seen a turn away from studies of 'women' in particular to 'gender' more generally (noteworthy exceptions are the essays in McHardy and Marshall 2004 and Schultz 2006) and have also tended to become incorporated into work on, for instance, sexuality, the family, and early imperial history (for the last, see Milnor 2005).

References

Bergmann, B. (1996), 'The Pregnant Moment: Tragic Wives in the Roman Interior', in N. Kampen (ed.), *Sexuality in Ancient Art.* Cambridge and New York: Cambridge University Press. 199–218.

Blok, J. (1987), 'Sexual Asymmetry: A Historiographical Essay', in J. Blok and P. Mason (eds.), *Sexual Assymmetry: Studies in Ancient Society.* Amsterdam: J. C. Gieben. 1–57.

Cantarella, E. (1983), *Ambiguo malanno: condizione e immagine della donna nell'antichità greca e romana.* Rome: Editori Riuniti.

——(1987), *Pandora's Daughters: The Role and Status of Women in Greek and Roman Society,* tr. M. B. Fant. Baltimore: Johns Hopkins University Press.

Dean-Jones, L. (1994), 'Excursus: Medicine: The "Proof" of Anatomy', in E. Fantham *et al.* (eds.), *Women in the Classical World.* Oxford and New York: Oxford University Press. 183–205.

Dixon, S. (2001), *Reading Roman Women.* London: Duckworth.

——(2001*a*), 'Re-readings: A Partial Survey of Scholarship' in Dixon 2001: 3–15.

——(2001*b*), 'Womanly Weakness in Roman Law' in Dixon 2001: 73–88.

Finley, M. I. (1965), 'The Silent Women of Rome', *Horizon,* 7: 57–64.

Flory, M. B. (1984), '*Sic exempla parantur*: Livia's Shrine to Concordia and the Porticus Liviae', *Historia,* 33: 309–30.

Gardner, J. F. (1986), *Women in Roman Law and Society.* London: Croom Helm.

Ginsburg, J. (2006), *Representing Agrippina: Constructions of Female Power in the Early Roman Empire.* Oxford and New York: Oxford University Press.

Gold, B. (2004), 'My Sister's Words Are Swallowed by the Next Wave', in M. B. Skinner (ed.), *Gender and Diversity in Place: Proceedings of the Fourth Conference on Feminism and Classics,* http://www.stoa.org/diotima/essays/fc04/.

Hallett, J. P. (1984), 'The Role of Women in Roman Elegy: Counter-Cultural Feminism', in J. Peradotto and J. P. Sullivan (eds.), *Women in the Ancient World.* Albany, NY: SUNY Press. 241–62.

Hemelrijk, E. A. (1999), *Matrona Docta: Educated Women in the Roman Élite from Cornelia to Julia Domna.* London and New York: Routledge.

Herrmann, C. (1964), *Le Rôle judiciaire et politique des femmes sous la République romaine,* Collection Latomus 67. Brussels: Latomus.

Joplin, P. (1984), 'The Voice of the Shuttle is Ours', *Stanford Literature Review*, 1/1: 25–53.

Kampen, N. B. (1981), *Image and Status: Roman Working Women in Ostia.* Berlin: G. Mann.

Keith, A. M. (2000), *Engendering Rome: Women in Latin Epic.* Cambridge and New York: Cambridge University Press.

Lefkowitz, M. and M. Fant (2005), *Women's Life in Greece and Rome: A Source Book in Translation*, 3rd edn. Baltimore: Johns Hopkins.

Loraux, N. (1993), *The Children of Athena: Athenian Ideas About Citizenship and the Division Between the Sexes*, tr. C. Levine. Princeton: Princeton University Press.

McCarthy, K. (1998), 'Servitium Amoris: Amor Servitii', in S. R. Joshel and S. Murnagham (eds.), *Women and Slaves in Greco-Roman Culture.* London and New York: Routledge. 174–92.

McClure, L. K. (2002), 'Editor's Introduction', in *Sexuality and Gender in the Classical World: Readings and Sources.* Oxford: Blackwell. 1–15.

McGinn, T. A. J. (1998), *Prostitution, Sexuality, and the Law in Ancient Rome.* Oxford: Oxford University Press.

McHardy, F. and E. Marshall (2004), *Women's Influence on Classical Civilization.* London and New York: Routledge.

Miles, G. B. (1995), 'The First Roman Marriage and the Theft of the Sabine Women', in *Livy: Reconstructing Early Rome.* Ithaca and London: Cornell University Press. 179–219.

Milnor, K. (2005), *Gender, Domesticity, and the Age of Augustus.* Oxford and New York: Oxford University Press.

Moi, T. (1999), 'What is a Woman?', in *What is a Woman? and Other Essays.* Oxford and New York: Oxford University Press.

Nugent, S. G. (1992), '*Aeneid* V and Virgil's Voice of the Women', *Arethusa*, 25: 255–92.

Pomeroy, S. B. (1975), *Goddesses, Whores, Wives, and Slaves: Women in Classical Antiquity.* New York: Schocken Books.

Purcell, N. (1986), 'Livia and the Womanhood of Rome', *PCPS* 32: 78–105.

Rabinowitz, N. S. and A. Richlin (eds.) (1993), *Feminist Theory and the Classics.* London and New York: Routledge.

Richlin, A. (1992), *Pornography and Representation in Greece and Rome.* Oxford and New York: Oxford University Press.

—— (1993), 'The Ethnographer's Dilemma and the Dream of a Lost Golden Age', in Rabinowitz and Richlin 1993: 272–303.

Saller, R. (1984), 'Roman Dowry and the Devolution of Property in the Principate', *CQ* 34/1: 195–205.

Schultz, C. E. (2006), *Women's Religious Activity in the Roman Republic.* Chapel Hill, NC: University of North Carolina Press.

Sharrock, A. R. (1991), 'Womanufacture', *JRS* 81: 36–49.

Treggiari, S. (1991), *Roman Marriage.* Oxford: Clarendon Press.

Wyke, M. (2002), *The Roman Mistress: Ancient and Modern Representations.* Oxford and New York: Oxford University Press.

Zeitlin, F. I. (1996), 'Signifying Difference: The Case of Hesiod's Pandora', in *Playing the Other.* Chicago: University of Chicago Press. 53–86.

CHAPTER 52

SPACE AND GEOGRAPHY

KAI BRODERSEN

> From writing my mind positively recoils. For the *Geographika*, upon which I had settled, is a serious undertaking. So severely is Eratosthenes, whom I had proposed as my model, criticized by Serapio and Hipparchus; what, do you think, will be the case if Tyrannio is added to the critics? And, by Hercules, the subject is difficult of explanation and monotonous (*homoeideis*), and does not seem to admit of as much embellishment (*antherographeistai*) as it seemed.
>
> (Cicero, *Ad Atticus* 2.6.1)

By the time Cicero wrote about his writer's block on geography to his friend Atticus in 59 BCE, Rome had conquered a substantial part of the *oikoumene*, the 'inhabited world'. Rome's success in opening up new space for Roman rule had engendered, in educated circles, a lively interest in conceptualizing space, in *geo-graphein*—an interest shared by recent research (beginning with Harley and Woodward 1987 and Nicolet 1988) which supports this chapter's attempt to explore the relationship of space and geography, and the relevance of this relationship for Roman Studies.

For any observer, ancient and modern, small spaces—a plot of land, a neighbourhood, a field-system—are easiest to comprehend. By crisscrossing space, a 'mental image' develops (cf. Brodersen 2003) and allows for a perception and presentation of space in suitably easy formats, which can be used, for example, to establish ownership of, or obligations on, the land. In the Roman world there was a well-established method to present small spaces in lists or sometimes graphic formats. The skills of the *gromatici* (surveyors; cf. Lewis 2001) made it possible to designate and record plots of lands in texts or plans (*formae*). One such plan was discovered in Lacimurga (*AE* 1990, 529; Sáez Fernández 1990), and shows that the *forma* supports, rather than replaces, a text, with individual plots of land drawn as rectangles of widely differing sizes, depending on other features drawn within them, while the text inscribed in all of them individually declares that all rectangles represent the same size of plot. The land outside these plots is simply represented as empty space; it was irrelevant for the surveying's purposes. Similarly, the large group of drawings with inscriptions from Arausio which form the so-called 'Orange Cadastre' (*CIL* XII 1244; cf. Piganiol 1962) only represent the field-system itself, are not drawn to scale nor to a uniform orientation. It is the text written into the individual rectangles which describes each plot of land. However useful *formae* were for their immediate purposes, they never allowed for combining such representations of space to produce a wider-ranging *geo-graphia.*

For traders, soldiers, messengers, pilgrims, or other travellers traversing larger spaces there was an ancient way of conceptualizing space in a linear mode (Janni 1984) and of presenting it in an easily reproduced everyday format: simple lists of stations along coastlines (a so-called *periplus*) or roads (an *itinerarium*; cf. Adams and Laurence 2001). These lists often detail the distances, but not the orientation of routes, between stations, and are preserved through many inscriptions, especially the so-called milestones and *stakeholder*, but also in private lists (cf. Matthews 2006), souvenirs (e.g. decorative cups from Hadrian's Wall, *AE* 1950, 56 [Amiens], *CIL* VII 1291 = *RIB* II 2, 2415.53 [Rudge], *Britannia* 2004, 344 [Moorlands], or silver goblets from Vicarello *CIL* XI 3281–4) as well as in transmitted 'official' texts from the late antique world like the *Itinerarium Provinciarum Antonini Augusti* (cf. Löhberg 2006). While *periplus* and *itinerarium* are indeed usually 'monotonous' and devoid of the chance of 'embellishment', there occasionally were more elaborate versions of such presentations in *itineraria picta* (Vegetius 3.6) which allowed for illustrations; the itinerary of Matthew Paris (Lewis 1987) may represent a later version of such a document. They could also enable the display not only of one line, but of a network of lines, providing—like a modern diagram for underground or suburban railways—a representation of the 'topological' relationships between the lines (like stations allowing access to more than one route, cf. Brodersen 2003), while often massively distorting the 'geographical' realities which a modern map with a uniform scale would present. The so-called Peutinger Table, a twelfth-century image probably based on a late antique diagram (Talbert 2004, 2010; *contra* Albu 2005), presents the space under Roman rule (lands beyond it hardly feature at all) in such a diagram measuring 34 cm by 6.75 m!

Of course, *itineraria* cannot be produced for, and used in, 'uncharted' territory, where the only reliable routes would run along coastlines or riverbanks, with no stations as yet being known. So when, for instance, Caesar was 'stumbling through

Gaul' (Bertrand 1997), or when Augustus' generals tried to penetrate Germany, they had to rely on natural routes like rivers along whose banks they would be able to march into, and return from, a land for which no *itinerarium* as yet existed (Brodersen 2001). Soon they began to build stations along the newly found river routes, and only then started to construct the roads which were to shape the actual landscape of conquered space ever since. At the same time, these new routes and their representation in the familiar format of the *itinerarium* enabled the conceptualizing of the newly won space: a recently discovered massive monument at Patara (Isik 2001) celebrates the inclusion of Lycia into the Roman Empire in 43 CE by presenting lists of stations and their distances along the routes which were to open up the new province.

Neither the surveyor's text or *forma* nor the *periplus* and *itinerarium* enabled an understanding and a description of *all* the earth, *geo-graphein*. So when an educated Roman like Cicero tried to get to grips with geography, he would not resort to these ultimately practical genres, but rather access models which had been developed by Hellenistic scientific theory. Thus, Cicero had asked his friend Atticus for a copy of the geographical work by Serapion, a Greek scientist—'of which,' however, as Cicero soon admitted to Atticus (2.4.1), 'between you and me, I scarcely understood a thousandth part'. Other geographies appeared to be easier to comprehend: in his *De Republica* Cicero stated that 'nearly all of the Peloponnesus is in the sea, and apart from the people of Phlius there are none whose territory does not touch the sea' (2.4.8), and when criticized for this statement (which contradicts travellers' experiences, of course), defended it in a letter to Atticus (6.2.3): 'For the fact that all cities on the Peloponnesus are maritime I have relied on the *tabulae* of a man who is not useless, but—also according to your judgement—proven, Dicaearchus... and have therefore transferred that passage verbatim from Dicaearchus.' Cicero, then, took geography seriously enough to attempt to read scientific works, however misleading they proved to be when applied to real space.

How typical is this difference between 'space' and 'geography', between the perception and presentation of space in, on the one hand, an everyday format (any *itinerarium* of the Peloponnesus would have made it obvious that Phlius is not the only non-maritime city on the Peloponnesus) and, on the other, in the *tabulae* of scientific geography (which Cicero follows)? And how relevant is this difference for Roman Studies today?

While the genres of *periplus* and *itinerarium* are well attested, both through authentic documents from the ancient world (inscriptions, papyri) and through ancient texts copied in the Middle Ages, many works of Hellenistic theorists—Dikaiarchos, Eratosthenes, Hipparchos, Tyrannion, Serapion, and others—and many 'minor' Greek and Latin geographies have been lost but for fragments. We do, however, have in Greek most of the seventeen books of *Geographika* by Tyrannion's pupil Strabon (Radt 2002–), who wrote a generation after Cicero, just before Augustus is said to have advised his successors to keep the empire within the *termini* reached by his time (Tacitus, *Annals* 1.11). We also have the didactic poem on geography, translated and expanded by later authors, by Dionysios of Alexandria ('the Periegete'), written under Hadrian, when the empire had reached its largest size (Amato 2005), as well as the *Geographika* of the Alexandrinian scholar Claudius Ptolemaeus, who compiled his work a generation later (Stückelberger 2006). In Latin, we have the three books which Pomponius Mela wrote on the eve of Britain becoming a Roman province in 43 CE (in 3.49 he writes about Britain *quippe tamdiu clausam aperit ecce principum maximus*, 'which was so long closed but is now being opened up by the greatest of the leaders', which must refer to Claudius' conquest; cf. Romer 1998), the four geographic books of the massive *Naturalis Historia* (3–6) which Pliny the Elder wrote a generation later (cf. Murphy 2004), and Solinus' influential *Collectanea*, as well as several other late antique geographical works mainly based on Pliny's work which, in turn, is partly based on Pomponius Mela.

For a study the relationship of 'space' and 'geography' in Rome, this earliest surviving and remarkably influential Latin geographical work will thus be a suitable guide, not least because he is 'a minor writer, a popularizer, not a first-class geographer' (Romer 1998: 27) with theories of his own. Pomponius Mela starts his work on *orbis situs*, the 'lie of the land', as the English phrase has it, or rather the lie of the world (the traditional title *De Chorographia*, 'lands' description', is probably a later version) with these words, echoing Cicero's lament about the difficulties of the task and the lack of chances for embellishment:

The lie of the world (*orbis situs*) is what I set out to give, a difficult task and one hardly suited to eloquence—for it consists chiefly in names of peoples and places and in their rather puzzling arrangement; to trace this completely is a time-consuming rather than a welcome subject. Nevertheless it is a very worthwhile task to consider and understand, and one which—if not by the talent of the present author—at least through the act of contemplation repays the effort of those who give it their attention. I shall say more elsewhere and more exactly; now let me address the things which are most clear and most unambiguous. First then I shall present what the *forma* of the whole is, what its greatest parts are, how its individual parts are, and how they are inhabited. Then again shall be recorded the coastlines and shores as they exist inward and outward, and how the sea enters them and surrounds them, adding to this the nature of the regions, and their inhabitants. To make that easier to know and accept, the *summa* will first be revisited in a little more depth. (1.1–2)

Pomponius Mela promises to present the *orbis situs* in two stages: first the *forma* of the whole and its parts, with references to the inhabitants in the tradition of Greek geography and ethnography, then a more detailed description of the coastlines and shores in the tradition of the *periplus*. Before this, however, a *summa* of what his readership could be expected to know about geography:

So 'all' (*omne*) is that to which we have given the name of world (*mundus*) and sky; it is one (*unum*) and embraces itself and everything with a single ambit. It differs in its parts: where the sun rises it is given the name of east or sunrise; where it sinks, as west or sunset; where it begins its descent, south; opposite to that north. In the middle of this the lofty earth (*terra*) is encircled on all sides by the sea, and also divided into two sides (*latera*) which one calls *hemisphaeria* from east to west, and it is differentiated by five horizontal zones: the middle zone is plagued by heat, the outer ones by cold. The remaining two habitable zones have the same annual seasons, but not at the same time. The *antichthones* inhabit one, we the other. The lie (*situs*) of the former zone is unknown because of the heat of the intervening zone, and that of the latter is now to be described. (1.3–4)

In reminding his audience of what they already know, Pomponius Mela starts with the universe and the four cardinal points, progresses to the earth, which he describes as encircled by water and as divided into two hemispheres and five zones, of which three are uninhabitable, while of the two remaining temperate ones only one is known and inhabited. These views, including the one that the world is a globe, are owed to Hellenistic theory, of course, and demonstrate that the *summa* of such theoretical speculation could be expected to be well enough known by a first-century Roman readership for an author to only summarize rather than expound these theories. The consequences for Roman Studies are evident, in that when the Roman propaganda aimed at ruling the world it was clear to contemporaries that this referred to only one of the two *oikoumenai*, inhabited zones; the other *oikoumene* was not part of Rome's assumed mission. We happen to know how widely such 'general knowledge' of the rudiments of Hellenistic geographic theories ranged: when, under Caligula and again under Claudius, Roman soldiers were ordered to cross the Channel for a conquest of Britain, they dared to refuse because this would lead the army beyond the one known inhabited zone, the *oikoumene* (Cassius Dio 60.19.2; cf. 62.4.2).

This zone stretches from east to west and, because it is situated this way, is somewhat longer than it is wide at its widest point. It is entirely surrounded by Ocean, and from it receives four seas: one from the north, from the south two, a fourth from the west. Those other seas will be recounted in their own places, this last one, at first narrow and not more than ten miles wide, opens up the land mass and penetrates it. Then, spreading in length and width, it pushes back the shores, which recede widely, but when the same shores almost come together at the opposite end, the sea is reduced to a space so constricted that the opening is less than a mile wide. From there it spreads out again, but very moderately, and again it proceeds into a space even more constricted than the previous one. After the sea is received by this space, its size increases greatly again, and it is connected to a huge swamp, but only by a tiny aperture. The whole sea, both where it comes in and as far as it reaches, is called by a single name *Nostrum Mare*, 'our sea'. (1.5–6)

The *oikoumene* then is an oblong entity encircled by water; this water penetrates into the *terra* at four places, from the north once, from the south twice, and once from the west. It is the latter sea which Mela next describes in highly schematic detail: a passage of 10 miles is followed by an expanse of great length and width, ending in a passage of less than 1 mile; then follow a moderate expanse, a yet smaller passage, a greater expanse, a tiny passage, and a huge swamp. No directions other than 'the west', where the sea begins to penetrate the land, are given, and the reader is invited to imagine it a succession of straits and wide seas. If one were to attempt a pictorial representation of what is described here (a task not envisaged by Pomponius Mela), it would have to be a very schematic diagram, resembling pearls of different sizes on a string stretching from west to east. This is important to realize, because modern readers, familiar with maps of the Mediterranean, cannot avoid to use their own 'mental map', but if they assume the same kind of map for an ancient reader they are likely to arrive at conclusions which a Roman would not, and indeed could not, have thought of. Ancient readers, for instance, had no difficulty with Kolaios' claim that he had been blown by a steady eastern wind from the sea by Libya right across to the waters beyond the Straits of Gibraltar (Herodotus 4.152). Also, this world-view explains the priority attributed to the completion of the conquest of all regions adjacent to *Nostrum Mare* before tackling parts of the *oikoumene* further inland.

The schematism of Pomponius Mela's description continues. After naming the parts of *Nostrum Mare*—in modern terminology these are the main basin (which is presented as one unit), the Sea of Marmara, the Black Sea, and the Sea of Azov—he explains the division of the *oikoumene* into three continents:

> By this sea and by two famous rivers, the Tanais [Don] and the Nile, the whole (*universa*) it is divided into three parts. The Tanais, descending from north to south, flows down almost into the middle of Maeotis (Sea of Azov), and from the opposite direction the Nile flows down into the sea. Those lands that lie from the Strait to those rivers, on the one side we call Africa, on the other Europe. Whatever is beyond those rivers is Asia. (1.8)

Again, there is no indication of direction other than a line from north to south for the Don, and from south to north for the Nile, both flowing into our sea, and there is no indication that the mouths of these rivers are situated anything but 'opposite' each other. Later texts based on this idea led to the schematic image of 'our' world as a T inside an O (the so-called T-O schema) which was to become a powerful image for world and world rule in the Middle Ages (von den Brincken 1986).

This *summa* of the schematic view is further developed in a refined, but still very schematic, presentation of the three continents:

> Asia is being touched by the Ocean, differing by name as by position, from three directions: the *Eous* (eastern) from the east, from the south the Indian, from the north the Scythian. Asia itself, reaching eastward with a huge and continuous coastline, stretches itself on this end over a coast as wide as Europe, Africa, and the sea that extends between them. Then, after its coastline has advanced uninterrupted for some distance, it lets in the Arabian and the Persian Seas from what we call the Indian Ocean, and from the Scythian the Caspian. Therefore, being narrower where it lets them in, Asia expands again and becomes as wide as it had been. Then as soon as it arrives at its own limit and the boundaries it shares with other lands, the middle is met by our waters; the rest of it goes by one horn to the Nile, by the other to the Tanais. (1.9)

Thus the schematic T-O description of the earth is developed further. Starting in the east, Asia is described as a wide expanse which is narrowed where the outer ocean penetrates it in the Red ('Arabian') and Persian as well as Caspian Sea (which is also presented as a gulf); as before, no details are given for the direction or extent of these gulfs, suggesting, like the description which follows, a symmetry of the lie of land. In a similarly schematic way Europe and Africa are described and the peoples living on these land masses are named, before Pomponius Mela concludes the first part of his work with the words: 'This is the full extent of our earth (*noster orbis*), these are its largest parts and the shapes and the peoples of the parts' (1.24).

The schematic view of *Noster Orbis* of which Pomponius Mela only has to remind his audience, as he expects their familiarity with it, has several further implications for Roman Studies. According to this view, the whole of our *oikoumene* is situated north of the hot equatorial zone, with what we today refer to as southern Africa assumed to be a different, if unreachable, *oikoumene* beyond that zone (and hence not part of Rome's imperial mission). It was therefore considered feasible to circumnavigate Africa (and thus to reach Asia, notably India) already in the Roman world, if not before (witness reports on such a circumnavigation under Necho II in Herodotus 4.42, or of Hanno's *periplus* of Africa and Eudoxos' voyage referred to by Pomponius Mela 3.90), and explorations of the 'outer' ocean were repeatedly attempted (Roller 2006). Also, if the Nile divided the continent and flows into 'our' sea, it was likely to be somehow connected to the ocean encircling the earth. Accordingly, several missions tried to establish this connection under Augustus (cf. the boastful inscription by Aelius Gallus, *CIL* III 14147 = *ILS* 8995 and Strabo 17.1.54) and Nero in 66 CE (Seneca, *Quaestiones Naturales* 6.8.3).

> Now I shall describe its coastlines and regions with greater preciseness, and so it is most convenient to begin from the point where Our Sea enters into the land mass; and preferably to begin with these lands that are on the right side of inflow, then to line up (*stringere*) the shores in the order in which they lie, and, when all the places which touch that sea have been traversed, to collect (*legere*) also those places, which the Ocean girds, until the course of the work which is now begun, has sailed around both the inside and the outside of the *orbis* and returns to where it began. (1.24)

What follows as the second and by far the largest part of Pomponius Mela's work is a detailed *periplus* describing, first, all major stations along the shores of the Mediterranean Sea in all its parts, from the Straits of Gibraltar along African and Asian through the Propontis, Black Sea, and Sea of Azov to the mouth of the River Tanais (Don) and thence onward along the European coastlines back to the Straits. The major islands in the Sea of Azov, the Black Sea, and the Mediterranean, which could not be accommodated in the *periplus* as this simply follows one coastline, appear in a separate section, after the description of the stations on the sea-coast is finished (2.97–126). Incidentally, there is some evidence that Pomponius Mela is not alone in such an arrangement of the islands: the (figurative) representations of, first, regions along the sea, and then of islands separately, is also known from the celebration of the Roman Empire in the *Sebasteion* at Aphrodisias (Smith 1998). In Pomponius Mela's work a second *periplus* starts again from there and circumnavigates the earth along the outside shores of Europe, Asia, and Africa. In it, Pomponius Mela lists nearly 2,000 toponyms. Unlike in the schematic geography with which Pomponius Mela began his work, the Nile is not now regarded as a dividing-line; rather, the whole of Egypt is considered to be a part of Asia, with the Catabathmus at the westernmost part of Egypt marking the terminal point of Africa against Asia. And the Nile, for which Pomponius Mela reports, with an explicit reference to the schematic theories with which he begins his work, the view that it, 'originating in the lands of the *antichthones*, emerges again in ours, after it has penetrated beneath the ocean in an unseen channel' (1.54), is referred to in the *periplus* part of the work as originating in western Africa (3.96), without any reference to the discrepancy between the theoretical and the *periplus* views.

Lest it be thought that Pomponius Mela is alone in dividing the schematic *geographia* as developed by Hellenistic theory from the everyday format of perceiving and presenting space in the format of a *periplus*, a brief look at other Roman geographers will be helpful. The first two of the seventeen books of *Geographika* by Strabo, for example, refer to the history of the subject and, after a 'second beginning' (2.5.1), to theoretical geography, before beginning, in Book 3, with a very detailed *periplus* of the *oikoumene* starting in the westernmost part of Spain. Also in this work there are contradictions between the schemata of theory and the *periplus*; Africa, for example, is a trapezoid in the theoretical books (2.5.33), but a triangle in the *periplus* part (17.3.1)—a difference which a map would have brought out immediately but which goes unnoticed in Strabo's text. Pliny the Elder deals with cosmology in the book preceding the four *periplus* books (*NH* 3–6) on the *partes* of the earth, at the end of which he adds 'yet another instance of ingenious invention by the Greeks, and indeed of the most exquisite subtlety, so that nothing may be wanting to our view of the *situs* of the earth and its various regions' (6.211), quite separate from what had been said before. Dionysius the Periegete uses the Nile as the border between Africa and Asia when he explains form of the world schematically (18), but defines a region farther east as the border, apparently to avoid a division of the *periplus* of Egypt (178). Thus, also for these and other ancient writers, the scientific *geographia* (so favoured by the likes of Cicero) presented quite different models of the world from the *periplus* and *itinerarium*.

The linear perception and presentation of space on the one hand, and the theory-based *geo-graphia* on the other, seem to have existed side by side in different circles. It did not occur to Cicero to check an *itinerarium* of the Peloponnesus when he needed information about maritime cities there as long as he had access to the *tabulae* of Dikaiarchos, and it made no sense for imperial propaganda to put up a scientific *tabula* of the newly conquered space in Lycia when an *itinerarium* was the concept most easily understood by the people who were to be impressed. It is tempting, however, for modern historians to assume that the 'practical' Romans 'must have' combined the linear and the theory-based approaches of conceptualizing space, and expect evidence for this view to emerge. It is thus certainly no coincidence that discoveries of 'maps' are greeted with much publicity. In 2005 an inscribed pottery shard from southern Italy, often called the 'Soleto Map', was celebrated as 'western world's oldest map' (*Daily Telegraph*, 19. 11. 2005), and in 2006 the 'Papiro di Artemidoro', which presents, *inter alia*, a short text on the geography of Iberia and an unfinished map-like diagram, was acquired for 2.75 million Euro for the Egyptian Museum in Turin and put on display for the first time during the Winter Olympics (Gallazzi, Kramer, and Settis 2008) as the earliest surviving classical map. For both artefacts the authenticity is still being debated (Yntema 2006; Brodersen and Elsner 2009 with bibliography). However, even if authentic, neither find would prove an understanding of the implications of the linear and the theory-based approaches of conceptualizing space in the Roman world: about the Turin papyurs Mary Beard said: 'It seems pretty clear that it was a rather dull route-plan of some area of Spain (which area is not entirely certain), marking major roads and rivers, places along them and the distances between. It is not, in other words, what people have called the "missing link" in ancient cartography, the start of map-making in the modern sense' (Beard 2006).

More specifically, there is no evidence whatsoever that Ptolemy's *geographia* was created for, or used by, imperial propaganda, let alone in teaching. It is therefore highly misleading to present a map, based on Ptolemy's instructions, in a modern historical atlas as the 'Worldview of the Roman Empire' (Stier *et al.* 1958: 34), and it is even more misleading to assume that Roman geography would allow for such concepts as the one attributed by Sir Ronald Syme to Augustus, who explained the attempts to conquer Germany and Bohemia with the emperor's insight that it 'would provide a shorter frontier and a shorter line of communication, substituting for the line Cologne–Bâle–Vienna the line Hamburg–Leipzig–Prague–Vienna' (Syme 1934: 353, 'and elsewhere' according to Syme 1978: 52, n. 5).

In sum, any pursuit of Roman Studies which includes an attempt to understand the Roman thought-world will do well in realizing that there are specific ways in which space was conceptualized. While *geo-graphia* provided the educated with (too) difficult theories about 'all' the world, demonstrating how much more there is to the globe than the *oikoumene*, the modes of perceiving and presenting space in the more widespread and familiar *periplus* and *itinerarium* formats enabled not only a military, but also a mental conquest of space, but did not allow for a *geographia*.

It was only in the early modern Age of Discovery that both modes of conceptualization of space were seen as a unity, and it was again Pomponius Mela's work which mattered for that. The *periplus* part of his work had proved to be a fairly reliable guide to the *oikoumene*'s coastlines along the Mediterranean and the

Ocean, including the west coast of Africa. It was the *summa* of the geographic theories, however, which fascinated the early modern discoverers, as Pomponius Mela was an accessible work in Latin which also stated that there *is* another temperate zone beyond the equator, and another hemisphere. So a heavily annotated copy of a 1498 printed edition of his work (which survives in the Huntingdon Library, San Marino, Calif., as acc. 87547; cf. Brodersen 1994, 20–1) was among the few books which Pedro Alvares Cabral had with him when he was on a voyage along the west coast of Africa and found himself blown westwards—until he landed in the other, the *antichthones' oikoumene* on the other hemisphere, which he 'knew' from Pomponius Mela, and thus discovered Brazil, in 1500 CE.

References

Adams, C. and Laurence, R. (eds.), *Travel and Geography in the Roman World.* London and New York: Routledge, 2001.

Albu, E. 'Imperial Geography and the Medieval Peutinger Map', *Imago Mundi*, 57 (2005), 36–148.

Amato, E. (ed.), *Dionisio di Alessandria, Descrizione della Terra abiata.* Milan: Bompiani, 2005.

Beard, M., 'The Artists of Antiquity', *Times Literary Supplement*, 8 Mar. 2006, pp. 1–3.

Bertrand, A., 'Stumbling Through Gaul: Maps, Intelligence, and Caesar's *Bellum Gallicum*', *Ancient History Bulletin*, 11 (1997), 107–22.

Brodersen, K. *Pomponius Mela, Kreuzfahrt durch die Alte Welt.* Darmstadt: WBG, 1994.

—— *Terra Cognita: Studien zur römischen Raumerfassung.* 2nd rev. edn. (Spudasmata 59) Hildesheim: Olms, 2003.

—— 'Wir wären römisch geworden!' in St. Krimm and U. Triller (eds.), *Europäische Begegnungen.* Munich: BSV/Oldenbourg, 2001: 9–28.

—— and Elsner, J. (eds.), *Images and Texts on the 'Artemidorus Papyrus'.* Stuttgart: Steiner, 2009.

Gallazzi, C., Kramer, B., and Settis, S. (eds.), *IL Papiro di Artemidoro (P. Artemid.).* 2 vols. Milan: LED, 2008.

Harley, J. B. and Woodward, D. (eds.), *The History of Cartography*, I: *Cartography in Prehistoric, Ancient, and Medieval Europe and the Mediterranean.* Chicago and London: University of Chicago Press, 1987.

Isik F., *et al.*, *Miliarium Lyciae.* (Lykia 4 for 1998/9). Ankara: Anadolu akdeniz kültürleri, 2001.

Janni, P., *La mappa e il periplo.* Rome: Giorgio Bretschneider, 1984.

Lewis, M. J. T., *Surveying Instruments of Greece and Rome.* Cambridge: Cambridge University Press, 2001.

Lewis, S., *The Art of Matthew Paris in the Chronica Majora* (California Studies in the History of Art 21). Berkeley: Univ. of California Press, 1987.

Löhberg, B., *Das Itinerarium provinciarum Antonini Augusti.* 2 vols. Berlin: Franke & Thimme, 2006.

MATTHEWS, J., *The Journey of Theophanes*. New Haven: Yale University Press, 2006.
MURPHY, T., *Pliny the Elder's 'Natural History'.* Oxford: Oxford University Press, 2004.
NICOLET, C., *L'Inventaire du monde: géographie et politique aux origines de l'empire romain.* Paris: Fayard, 1988.
PIGANIOL, A., *Les Documents cadastraux de la colonie romaine d'Orange.* Gallia Suppl. 16. Paris: CNRS, 1962.
RADT, ST. (ed.), *Strabons Geographika*, 10 vols., Göttingen: V&R, 2002–.
ROLLER, D. W., *Through the Pillars of Herakles: Greco-Roman Exploration of the Atlantic.* London: Routledge, 2006.
ROMER, F. E., *Pomponius Mela's Description of the World.* Ann Arbor, Mich.: University of Michigan Press, 1998.
SÁEZ FERNÁNDEZ, P., 'Estudio sobre una inscripción catastral colindante con Lacimurga.' *Habis*, 21 (1990), 205–27.
SMITH, R. R. R., '"Simulacra Gentium": The "ethne" from the Sebasteion at Aphrodisias.' *Journal of Roman Studies*, 78 (1987), 50–77 and pls. 1–9.
STIER, H.-E., *et al.* (eds.), *Großer Atlas zur Weltgeschichte.* Braunschweig: Westermann, 1958 (and reprints).
STÜCKELBERGER, A., *et al.* (eds.), *Ptolemaios, Handbuch der Geographie*, 2 vols. Basle: Schwabe, 2006.
SYME, R., *History in Ovid.* Oxford: Oxford University Press, 1978.
—— 'The Northern Frontiers Under Augustus.' *Cambridge Ancient History*, vol. 10. Cambridge: Cambridge University Press, 1934: 340–81.
TALBERT, R. J. A.: 'Cartography and Taste in Peutinger's Roman Map', in R. Talbert and K. Brodersen (eds.), *Space in the Roman World: Its Perception and Presentation* (Antike Kultur und Geschichte 5). Münster: Lit, 2004: 113–41.
—— *Rome's World: The Peutinger Map Reconsidered.* Cambridge: Cambridge University Press, 2010.
VON DEN BRINCKEN, A.-D., 'TO–Karte'. In I. Kretschmer *et al.* (eds.), *Lexikon zur Geschichte der Kartographie*, 2 vols. Vienna: Deuticke, 1986: 2. 812–15.
YNTEMA, D. G., 'Ontdekking "oudste kaart" een grap?', *Geschiedenis Magazine (Spiegel historiael)*, 41 (2006), 5.

CHAPTER 53

ARCHITECTURE

EDMUND THOMAS

I. Studying Roman Buildings

> The buildings of savages, considered on their own merit, have no place in this book. We are concerned with architecture, that is the 'monumental building' of craftsmen conscious of the beauty of certain forms and eager to heighten and perpetuate them.
>
> (Plommer 1956: 1)

The opening to the first volume of *Simpson's History of Architectural Development* exposes the fundamental place commonly given to Roman buildings in the civilizing process of European culture. Behind this view, so alien to today's postcolonial world, lies a more lasting problem. Perhaps more than other aspect of Roman culture, the study of architecture is affected by two preconceptions, the first resulting from its durability, the second from later attitudes. First, because buildings appear as a solid and visible legacy of Roman culture, it is assumed that Romans themselves clearly recognized the meaning of 'architecture'. Yet, within a short time-span two ancient writers, Varro and Vitruvius, presented different views. Vitruvius, the more fortunate in transmission, was ambivalent about the definition of 'architecture', calling it first a compound of aesthetic concepts—organization, layout, good rhythm, symmetry, correctness, and allocation (*De Arch.* 1.2.1), but, a chapter later (1.3.1), a combination of scientific domains—building, mechanics, and orology. As he treats these unevenly, his original conception of 'architecture' plausibly embraced only 'building', in six books—specifically, planning, materials, columnar design, and public and private structures—and was revised to include the other two sciences in the final ten (Pellati 1947–9). For Varro, architecture was one of nine 'disciplines'; his lost treatise can hardly have contained such technicalities or defined 'architecture' so comfortably within the parameters of the modern academic subject. Roman architecture defies typologies and taxonomies (Gros 1996–2001: 1. 17). It is unsettling that we do not know more clearly the boundaries of the science practised by the *architecti* of Rome.

As the themes of Vitruvius' first six books proved more compelling to the text's Renaissance interpreters and their patrons, and skills in his other two sciences declined, 'building' naturally came to dominate modern conceptions of 'architecture'. But there are other, less narrow ways of defining the field. The areas of concern to ancient architects also included the design of siege-engines, military arsenals, and bridges; the building activities of emperors and senators embraced roadworks, temporary theatres and amphitheatres, even ships; the triumphal arches, amphitheatre, and funerary structure shown on the contractor Haterius' tomb and the villas and painted stage-like structures on Campanian murals are omitted or peremptorily dismissed by Vitruvius, as are the geometrical and cosmological interests of the mathematician Archimedes and the philosopher Thales, whom Lucian ranks alongside the architect Hippias; and Daedalus, designer of the Minoan labyrinth and symbolic precursor of ancient architects, reportedly extended his work, like Leonardo, to flying-machines. The gap between the shifting reality of the ancient discipline and our own limited conception of 'Roman architecture' is remarkable.

The second preconception is more serious. Unlike other varieties of their art, the Romans' architecture is held to show 'excellence and originality' (Kampen 2003: 375). Despite modern technological advances, scholars still highlight its 'staggering difficulty, great expense, and organizational intricacy' (Taylor 2003: 5), inviting students to contemplate how such awe-inspiring buildings were completed and specialists to provide answers to these seemingly unanswerable questions or to evaluate Roman buildings as the highest achievements of the science. To many engaged in the discipline, questions of language, meaning, and ideas appear otiose, as if it were impossible today to fathom the minds that conceived these 'superhuman' projects. The priority of most researchers is to understand 'how it was done', rather than why. Comparison of architecture with any of the other realms of the Roman imagination explored in this book highlights the conceptual gap today between students of those areas and those who study the architecture of the Romans. It is as if our understanding of Roman epic were limited to metrical analysis or lexical computation, or studies of political theory addressed only constitutional issues.

Certainly, several scholars of the last twenty years have emphasized not the unequalled achievement of Roman builders, but the imperfections of their works. The Pantheon is now regarded as a botched compromise (Davies, Hemsoll, and

Wilson Jones 1987) and for all the romantic associations with Hadrian may have been rebuilt under Trajan instead (Hetland 2007; Grasshoff *et al.* 2009); the Baths of Caracalla are seen as flawed in the execution of their design (DeLaine 1997: 64–5); the Oppian wing of Nero's Golden House is noted for its awkward planning, the main hall of the Trajan's Markets derided as 'grossly clumsy' (Ball 2003: 56–61, 272); even the Colosseum is studied not only for its 'technical perfection' (Gros 1996–2001: 1. 328), but also for its experimentation (Lancaster 2005*a*). Now it is not only classicists who study such buildings; a wide range of other specialists bring fresh perspectives, including architects, engineers, geologists, and art historians

Yet, for all the varied skills applied to Roman buildings and the sophistication of the tools and techniques used to study them, the basic aims of the discipline have changed little since the days of the Italians Giuseppe Lugli and Luigi Crema or the Germans Richard Delbrück and Hans Kähler. True, we know more about several important areas: the modular design of the columnar orders (Wilson Jones 2000); the practicalities and real costs of large-scale construction projects in terms of materials and manpower (DeLaine 1997); the techniques used to assemble structures of ambitious conception (Giuliani 1990; Lancaster 2005*a*); the planning in the workshop (Haselberger 1994); and the sources of materials or logistics of their transportation (Herz and Waelkens 1988). The depth and variety of these investigations, added to the modern techniques of digital photography and computer-aided design, mean that the student of ancient Roman architecture in the early twenty-first century is immeasurably better equipped than her predecessor fifty years ago. But in overall scope these studies echo the concerns of Lugli, Crema, and others in foregrounding matters of process and leaving unexplored what these structures meant to those who conceived or used them.

This focus of modern scholars on pragmatic issues is partly a response to the excesses of some of their forebears. Those studying Roman buildings in today's post-ironic world feel liberated from the desire for overarching explanations, which marked the responses of earlier scholars to the question of meaning in Roman architecture. Grand theories are now unfashionable. The arguments of the symbolists—Hans Peter L'Orange (1953), Earl Baldwin Smith (1956), and Karl Lehmann (1945), who saw domes, arched lintels, and ornamental column displays as reflecting ideas of political or cosmic hierarchy, associated with the imperial cult (Yegül 1982)—have been discredited. Considerations of the symbolic or metaphorical role of architecture (Drerup 1966; Demandt 1982) occupy a marginal place within the discipline; scepticism is expressed about the occurrence and significance of such forms (Joyce 1990). Following Richard Krautheimer's warning that 'symbolic significance . . . merely accompanied the particular form . . . chosen for the structure . . . as a more or less uncertain connotation which was only dimly visible and whose specific interpretation was not necessarily agreed upon' (1942: 9), attempts to decipher that significance have waned. Down-to-earth motives for urban design are preferred (Burrell 2006). But, if earlier *post festum* interpretations of architectural symbolism are distrusted, one may still seek in Roman buildings, as in medieval cathedrals, 'truths ramified, disruptive and multi-layered' (Crossley 1988: 121).

The triumph of the pragmatists began in Germany, where Delbrück (1907–12) challenged a prevailing tendency to stereotype Roman architecture as, typically, a thought-world of arches and vaults presented in self-conscious opposition to the rectilinear buildings of 'the Greeks'. His insistence on archaeological realities and avoidance of theorizing was followed by others such as Wolf-Dieter Heilmeyer (1970), for whom techniques of Roman construction or formal variations in ornament were positivistic data indicating relative chronology rather than visual expression. If Heilmeyer retained something of the older, romantic search for the genius architect in attributing Hadrian's Pantheon to the Syrian Apollodorus (Heilmeyer 1975), that hypothesis was rooted in formalistic analysis, if also retaining something of the Hegelian impulse to see conceptions of space as reflections of the spirit. In Italy Lugli (1957) emphasized materials and techniques, focusing on Rome, while Crema (1959) highlighted type and typology, providing for the first time a global and historically nuanced view of Roman architecture. John Ward-Perkins refashioned the subject for British students, revising older works (Anderson and Spiers 1907; Robertson 1943) to stress 'the essentially practical nature' of Roman approaches to 'problems of construction' (Ward-Perkins 1973: 51). By contrast with his predecessors, Ward-Perkins emphasized the architecture of the provinces, albeit without the chronological nuances applied to the capital. His general account with Axel Boëthius (1970), later revised and published separately (1981), remains the most authoritative overall treatment of the subject in English today. Yet a reader of Ward-Perkins's book might be forgiven for thinking that there were no patrons of provincial Roman buildings and that few ideas were communicated by these agglomerations of materials spread across the different European regions.

The sheer range and complexity of Roman architecture create special problems for its historians, who must decide how to divide their topic: whether chronologically to emphasize general formal or stylistic developments (Anderson and Spiers 1907); by geographical area to highlight regional difference (Ward-Perkins 1981); or by building type to stress the architectural changes that accompanied specific social uses (Gros 1996–2001: 1. 18–21). None of these arrangements is without prejudice. Chronological approaches overlook not just regional or functional variations, but similarities in meaning between buildings distant in date, and are vulnerable to the fallacy of linear progression from the simple to the complex; a regionalist focus cannot easily account for developments across the whole empire; and typological divisions seem too crude to explain buildings whose forms were only loosely linked to functions, with labels like 'atria' and 'porticoes' applied to very different functional realities; for more diversified buildings like tomb monuments, typologies have little value at all (Gros 1996–2001: 2. 380).

Against the mainstream accent on the application of form to function, some voices have attempted to renegotiate the boundaries of the discipline. In France Gilles Sauron has emphasized the 'constant relation between decoration and its patrons', interpreting the late Republic through an 'archaeology of looking' (1994: 13–15). In England John Onians (1988) explains ancient architecture in terms of rhetoric and psychology rather than structure and design. Such re-branding of buildings as objects of experience or media for ideas, rather than solutions to practical problems, has opened challenging new vistas for students of Roman architecture, which may mirror more closely the ways in which contemporaries perceived their built environment. But, because their hypotheses are rejected on empirical grounds and their approaches perceived as detached from traditional methods, few so far have followed their examples.

On the continent, by contrast, more speculative approaches to meaning in architecture are securely anchored in formalistic presumptions and procedures. Prominent here are the German archaeologists Paul Zanker and Henner von Hesberg, and, in France, especially Pierre Gros (1996–2001). For Hesberg (1990), architectural ornament is not only a means of dating archaeological monuments, but a 'leading cultural form' (*kulturelles Leitform*) expressive of its time. The argument has obvious circularity and some common ground with earlier searches for a *Zeitgeist* in ancient architecture. But more concerning is that Hesberg's argument depends on detailed, perhaps subjective, stylistic analysis of architectural fragments and takes little account of ancient views on architecture or its decoration. Gros recognizes rhetorical and symbolic uses of architecture, presenting Roman buildings in a historically nuanced social context. But one seeks in vain an approach like that of the philosopher Robert Hahn (2001) to archaic Greek temples, who highlights their relation to pre-Socratic thought, showing how architecture acted as a dynamic idea in ancient culture, not merely an adjunct or reflection of it.

In the land of Frank Lloyd Wright, for whom architecture was 'the scientific art of making structure express ideas' (Wright 1941: 141), the search for architectural meaning has sometimes taken a more abstract direction. Frank Brown revitalized the discipline with his uniquely penetrating interpretations of meaning. If his analyses of the basic spatial notions of Roman temples or fora (Brown 1961) may seem as dated today as modernist skyscrapers in our cities, his brilliant lateral reasoning in recognizing the 'pumpkins' of Hadrian despised by Apollodorus in the gored domes of Tivoli and Baiae (Brown 1964) will long stand as a model for how architectural remains may be imaginatively and constructively related to ancient literary sources. Brown's disciple William MacDonald, in his first book on Roman architecture, highlighted the conceptual implications of the Roman architectural 'revolution' between Nero and Hadrian. Although he stressed that his emphasis was on direct evidence of standing remains, MacDonald's originality was to consider them in terms of communication of ideas and human personalities. 'Masterpieces such as the Pantheon', he wrote, with barely a hint of Hegelianism, 'were above all expressions of immanent cultural forces, and technology, though important, was a secondary factor in their creation' (MacDonald 1982: 5).

In his even more innovative second volume (1986), MacDonald discussed characteristics of urban architecture across the Roman Empire with a fresh vision, replacing dry typology with evaluations of aesthetic or social meaning. His identification of 'urban armatures' and analysis of 'cardinal themes' are so far removed from the historical context of Roman buildings that this book remains today an art-historical essay, rather than a true cultural analysis, but his suggestions of common formal properties and modes of design across the empire need serious contextualization. Others have focused on mathematical or cosmological aspects of design, especially for the Pantheon itself (Loerke 1990; Sperling 1997; Martines 2000), or analysed the geometry of individual buildings or even whole cities (Watts and Watts 1992); yet MacDonald's general proposition (1986: 246) that a shift from geometric to arithmetic conceptions informed the use of un-classical and proto-baroque forms in urban space, invites further investigation. The contribution of ancient mathematics to reconceptualizing architectural space and its role in wider cultural change are still to be addressed.

Nevertheless, the last twenty-five years have seen more growth in the study of Roman architecture than any other similar period, whether measured in terms of empirical additions to knowledge, expansion into new fields, or adoption of new methodologies. The material evidence has increased through excavation and topographical research at cities such as Verona (Frova and Cavalieri Manasse 2005), Carthage (Hurst, Fulford, and Peacock 1994), and Caesarea Maritima (Holum and Raban 1996). Aided by new, computer-based techniques, students of architecture attempt serious answers to questions similar to those asked by other cultural historians: Geographic Information Systems show how the social character of towns like Pompeii (Laurence 1994) or Empúries in Spain (Kaiser 2000) is mapped by changes in urban space (Jones and Bon 1997); artefactual analysis highlights how the decoration and use of individual rooms in Roman houses reflected social realities (Allison 2004); scholars are sensitive to the role of ideologies (Trillmich and Zanker 1990) in shaping the built environment of antiquity, from the Augustan transformation of the Athenian Agora 'down to the wheel-ruts in the paving stones' at Pompeii (Wallace-Hadrill 1995). Regional and chronological variations of civic assembly buildings are not only considered matters of style or typology, but related to larger, political issues of urban layout (Balty 1991). The architecture of whole regions from the Levant to Spain is now better understood. The analysis of architectural ornament has advanced so far in methodology that it is studied no longer only for stylistic change or variation (Strong 1953; Léon 1970), but in terms of ideal planning (Wilson Jones 2000) or visual 'semantics' (Gros 1989). Ancient architectural terminology is no longer straightforwardly applied to archaeological remains, but scrutinized and questioned (Callebat 1995; Leach 1997).

Changes in approach to Vitruvius are symptomatic of the shift in method in Roman architectural history in general. Many past shortcomings of the subject can be attributed to the peculiarity of what one might call 'the Vitruvius problem'. In a field extending geographically from Britain to Arabia and from the Caucasus to the Atlas Mountains, and chronologically from the putative Palatine wall of Romulus to Justinian's Santa Sophia, an anomaly is that the observations and concerns of this military engineer have remained central to modern constructions of the idea of Roman architecture. Vitruvius grew up in northern Italy, served in the Roman state service under Julius Caesar in North Africa, and was probably an example of that parochial, professional middle-class grouping, the *apparitores* (Purcell 1983). His only known public commission is the colonial basilica he describes at Fanum. Modern scholars stress the narrowness and conservatism of his treatise, its essentially rhetorical purpose, and its omissions or limitations (*Le Projet de Vitruve*, 1994). The absence of amphitheatres from his treatise and minimal discussion of bath-buildings illustrate the work's limited value for explaining archaeological data. The *De Architectura* is no longer naively invoked as an authority for constructions of all historical periods and in all areas of the empire, but examined for its methods and sources within the narrow cultural context of the late Hellenistic age. Considered more relevant to second-century BCE Asia Minor than first-century Rome (Ciotta 2003), its precepts are studied as ideological statements (McEwen 2003). If the 'Vitruvian' triad of beauty, stability, and utility reappears in later contexts (Lucian, *Hippias* 4) and Vitruvius' own reputation lasted into the fourth century (Wilson Jones 2000: 35), this may be merely evidence of the proliferation and resilience of architectural cliché in contemporary culture rather than a confirmation of his influence on design.

Although modern scholars are not as tied to Vitruvius' words as their predecessors, it will always be tempting, while his work remains the sole surviving ancient treatise on architecture, to highlight his precepts, from methods of making Roman concrete (Oleson *et al.* 2006: 30–41) to designs of surviving structures (Ros 1997). But the text overshadows the conception and scope of the discipline more generally. Questions asked of construction or technique, the privileged status of the columnar orders, the critical analysis of buildings as diverse as public baths, private houses, and civic basilicas, and the very labelling of archaeological remains—all owe their conception to the weight given to such topics in Vitruvius' own treatise. For all the discrepancies between the work's insularity and modern methodologies, or between its ideas and most extant material culture, the *De Architectura* is still heralded as 'an essential companion' for enquiries about Roman design (Wilson Jones 2000: 33).

Yet the questions that architectural writers ask today are different. Thomas Markus (1993), for example, discusses sociological rather than aesthetic or technological issues. He sees buildings primarily as social objects, not structural achievements, their forms as evidence of human identity, power relations, and cultural order, not simply processes of construction or design. Buildings have social meaning, from their materials and ornamentation to their functions, uses, and spatial structure. The design and imagination of the built environment can liberate or confine human lives. In comparison with such wider socio-cultural issues, many studies of Roman architectural history look rather limited.

To understand Roman architecture properly as a cultural system, we must rethink the questions traditionally asked of the subject and ask new ones. The second part of this chapter therefore reflects on the framing of scholarly debates on Roman architecture in recent decades. The discipline is dominated by several conceptual oppositions. Ten of these are presented below. Many are modern, some subject to long-standing controversy, causing issues to be sharply polarized; all must be redefined to explain subtleties and nuances in the evidence. Then five alternative oppositions drawn from ancient thinking are presented which can help shape future research, not to re-polarize debate, but to introduce new fields of enquiry. Their dialectic reflects the equivocal status of architecture in Roman culture and throws light on that essential, overriding duality in any period or style of architecture, the relation between form and meaning. There is no space here to discuss all fully; but they offer valid thematic paradigms for seeing Roman architecture in its cultural context and assessing past studies or planning future ones.

II. Rethinking Polarities

A. Past Debates on Roman Architecture

1. *Archaeology or Architectural History*

Just as the subject area of Roman architecture is diverse and elusive, so the nature of the modern discipline is hard to pin down, contested on one side by classical archaeologists and on the other by art or architectural historians (Kampen 2003: 373). For the former, Roman buildings are one aspect of a variegated material culture requiring interpretation or explanation; for the latter, what demands attention is the process of design itself. The methodologies of the two approaches are reconcilable. Without drawings, logbooks, financial records, or, usually, even architects' names, Roman architectural history is necessarily focused on archaeological evidence; architects are considered of little interest when few are known to be connected with more than one building (Lyttelton 1974: 16). Processes of design or construction are inferred from material remains (DeLaine 1997).

Yet the ultimate goals of archaeologists and architectural historians seem opposed. While the former explain extraneous processes through architectural evidence, the latter invoke evidence from beyond the material world to understand structural remains in their proper historical and social context. The relation between the two disciplines becomes fluid when scholars shift their focus between the buildings and the cultures or societies that conceived them. Architectural meaning, both a matter of physical form and a feature of society, lies inevitably in the nexus between these two domains. Neither archaeologists nor architectural historians see their principal aim as understanding the meaning or symbolic significance of Roman buildings for contemporaries. Those with such interests must adapt methodologically like chameleons, acting now in one role and now in the other. Without constant disciplinary adjustment and interaction with literary or epigraphic sources, the traditional focus of philologists or historians, the question of meaning may disappear. At present, it is often buried in the fertile borderland between archaeology and architectural history.

2. *Form and Function*

Roman buildings hardly fit the modernist ideal of a perfect match between form and function. Notions of *decor* corresponded not to this, but to the expected correlation between architecture and social rank or religious status: according to this moral criterion, buildings were approved for suiting the status and image of their owners or communities; for propriety or moderation in materials, rather than excess. Even Cicero's famous explanation of the overhanging eaves of the Capitoline Temple (Cic. *De Or.* 3.180) reflects rhetorical special pleading and cannot be taken seriously as a design principle. Because architectural terminology failed to keep pace with physical changes, understanding building types from archaeological remains is constantly challenging. The semicircular blocks of seating found across the Eastern Empire served multiple functions: as not only theatres, but performance halls, council chambers, and meeeting-places for other assemblies; in the West, the seats of local government, *curiae*, are hard to identify by form alone without their once-typical feature, banks of wooden seats (Balty 1991); and the many porticoes throughout the empire are not reducible to typologies, but form an ill-defined category loosely grouped by a common label, which, since its origin from Greek stoas, had varied applications, from temple porches to street-side colonnades, not easily reconcilable with a single concept. The modernist ideal is a dubious basis for the questions asked of Roman architecture.

3. *Utility and Ornament*

That principle is often justified by citing the Romans' own concerns: Vitruvius preached the virtues of stability, attractiveness, and utility; Cato saw orientation towards practical needs as preventing moral degeneration. The Roman aptitude for utilitarian structures is interpreted as a reaction against ornate 'Greek' architecture. But distinctions between the ornamental and functional significance of buildings are more rhetorical than real. With Roman aqueducts, for example: 'the opposition...has been drawn too starkly; aqueducts served both purposes, and the symbolic value of public fountains...was derived both from their appearance and from their value as fountains that people actually used' (Wilson 1998: 93).

The temple of Hadrian at Cyzicus was not only 'the biggest and most beautiful of all temples' (Cassius Dio 70.3.4), but had invented 'devices and supports, which...did not previously exist in human society' (Aelius Aristides 26.21). Dio Chrysostom insisted on the utility of his new public building project at Prusa, despite opponents' claims that it failed to meet popular needs (47.13–15).

Just as the rhetorician 'pseudo-Longinus' advocated a literary grandeur that 'no longer falls outside utility and benefit', public buildings surpassed the monumentality of Nature by their practical value. Structures of daily use were celebrated as visual adornments and for their potential durability. Even non-structural columns were not purely decorative: as *ornamenta* they had a semantic function, to communicate social distinctions (*discrimina*) (Gros 1989).

4. *Public Architecture and Private Building*

The division of the most recent and thorough handbook on Roman architecture into separate volumes on public and private architecture (Gros 1996–2001) reflects a long-standing demarcation of the subject, if one hardly stressed by Vitruvius. But it overlooks the close links that existed since Republican times between the design of public temples and that of private domestic buildings. The identification (Boyancé 1940) of 'Catulus's temple' with the round 'Temple B' of the Largo Argentina in Rome—the temple of *Fortuna huiusce Diei* founded by Q. Lutatius Catulus (consul 102 BCE)—suggests its influence on the aviary of Varro's villa at Casinum (Coarelli 1983: 201–11; Sauron 1994: 135–67). More generally, when 'public buildings' were almost always results of private patronage, built on private land, financed with private money, and designed, surely, to the wishes of private individuals, how valid is the conventional distinction between 'public buildings' and 'private' ones? The interests of Roman patrons are recognized in notable cases like Pompey's Theatre or the Forum Augustum, yet virtually ignored in discussions of provincial architecture. If Cicero and Pliny's letters attest to personal taste in domestic architecture, why are we less ready to explain similarly the forms of 'public buildings'? Where literature or inscriptions illuminate the process of establishing municipal buildings, the influence of individual patrons on public decision-making is loudly attested. Archaeological evidence of uncompleted projects, typically explained in economic or societal terms, may sometimes be the residue of personal conflicts.

5. *West and East/Greek and Roman*

The division of the architecture of the Roman Empire into 'western' and 'eastern' factors is one of the most long-standing oppositions applied to the subject. It overshadows the analysis of theatres (Sear 2006: 24–5), civic squares (Balty 1991), even domestic buildings. Geographically based distinctions have some validity. But one might think of a cultural 'regionalism' underlying architectural patronage, rather than purely formal distinctions. Regional, social, religious, and cultural differences were all reflected in architecture. Medieval and later buildings are seen in such terms (Clarke and Crossley 2000; Lefaivre and Tzonis 2003).

The assumed contrast between 'West' and 'East' is rooted in an older polarization between 'Greek' and 'Roman' architecture. Airy Greek temples are often implicitly contrasted with bulky Roman structures. For Franz Wickhoff (1900), the architecture of the Roman East derived from western designers; conversely, Josef Strzygowski (1901) observed the insidious influence of 'eastern' style on the 'purity' of 'western' forms. Later scholars disputed the direction of influence between 'East' and 'West' (Ward-Perkins 1965), identifying competition between 'traditional', eastern architects and Roman builders seeking to break the mould. Within this polarity lurks the phantom of originality. The arch and vault, once hailed as Etruscan or Roman 'inventions', are now attributed either to Macedonian architects learning from the 'East' (Boyd 1978; Gossel 1980) or inventive Greek designers, even the philosopher Democritus (Dornisch 1992: 233). Conversely, eastern churches are believed to originate in Roman civic basilicas. But obsessions with retrospective aetiologies can obfuscate the contemporary significance of such forms. In other areas of ancient cultural studies, scholars now think more constructively of 'Hellenization' and 'Romanization' not as absolute formal shifts, but as varieties of 'code switching' within Roman culture itself (Wallace-Hadrill 1998).

6. *Centre and Periphery*

The opposition between 'metropolitan' and 'provincial' architecture remains prominent within the agenda of Roman architectural studies. It has especially dogged discussions of architectural ornament. Donald Strong (1953) saw the influence of 'provincial' workshops on the architectural decoration of the capital, but Volker Strocka (1988) argued that such influence was in the reverse direction. Distinctions between 'metropolitan' and 'regional' styles still dominate work on materials and design. Ward-Perkins established the orthodoxy that provincial buildings were poorer versions of those in Rome, with inferior materials or artists and a 'time lag' following the introduction of similar forms at Rome. That is now questionable. If vaulted buildings appear later in Asia Minor and Syria than Rome, and with inferior materials to Roman concrete (Dodge 1990), the long urban traditions of these regions ensured that other innovations in design such as the 'arcuated lintel' arrived here soonest. An offshoot of the revelations that the Porticus Aemilia at Rome is not the barrel-vaulted structure formerly assumed to bear that name (Cozza and Tucci 2006) is that Rome actually lagged behind other Italian cities in the development of concrete architecture (Lancaster 2005*a*: 5). Even during the Empire, it was often Italy that learned from other regions, rather than the reverse.

Provincial buildings were no mere 'replications' of Roman archetypes (MacMullen 2000: 126), like the American embassies that President Truman wanted built across the world as exact reproductions of the White House (Crossley 1988: 116). Architectural form was a blend of 'Roman' and 'provincial' elements. The duality of centre and periphery was not a polar opposition, but an area of interchange (Champion 1995).

7. *Republic and Empire*

For provincial architecture the Augustan period is commonly regarded as one of decisive change. Ward-Perkins saw 'very little that was Roman, in the narrower, Italian sense of the word', in earlier western municipal architecture (1970: 18). The existence of Vitruvius' treatise and his omission of many forms of Imperial architecture have encouraged the recognition of a dichotomy between Republican buildings and those of the Empire. But there is no simple contrast in Roman concrete construction between 'experimental' forms in the late Republic and structurally more 'advanced' works of the early Empire, nor any linear development in architectural technology. The early terraced sanctuaries of Latium are more 'developed' in their uses of concrete and spatial forms than most buildings in first-century Italy. If the 'standardization' of the Corinthian order under Augustus established a model for later temples (Gros 1996–2001: 2. 470–503), it relied on substantial development of the form during the previous century (Wilson Jones 2000). Its variant, the composite capital, might have had ideological uses for Augustus (Onians 1988: 42–8), but it arose as a formalization of earlier Italic forms.

In the provinces, the emergence of a distinctive ornamental language for civic buildings was already under way a generation before the Principate (Hesberg 1990). In Rome, Pompey's Theatre was more progressive in design and ideology than most buildings of Augustus' reign. As Vitruvius attests, the minds of Augustan architects looked backwards, not ahead. The forms of tomb monuments, one of the most creative areas in the history of architecture, hardly changed between the first century BCE and the second century CE (Gros 1996–2001: 2. 380–467). No neat line can be drawn at 27 BCE to distinguish 'Republican' and 'Imperial' architecture, as conveniently demarcated in the Pelican History of Art (Boëthius and Ward-Perkins 1970).

8. *Conservatism and Innovation*

It is problematic to label Vitruvius a 'conservative', whether due to his attachment to Hellenistic ideas, especially the Ionic style of Hermogenes (Gros 1973), or because of his limited discussion of concrete. Such features of his work may be a truer reflection of its didactic genre than of his practice as an architect.

But should an architect be regarded as an 'innovator' only if he privileges those areas of architecture which we today regard as advances? Contemporaries perhaps more readily understood other aspects of building as innovation. The conception of an *aedis augusta* in the civic basilica at Fanum or the creation of basilicas in the Roman forum (Welch 2003) could, for example, have been seen as a particularly bold step. The whole question of innovation in architectural design needs careful consideration.

9. *The Column and the Arch*

The combination of vaulted forms with columnar architecture is one instance of this. The use of columnar arcades as a symbolic icon—most famously in the 'Tabularium' and Colosseum—or later of arcuated lintels in Imperial buildings, the 'temple of Hadrian' at Ephesus or the reservoir of Hadrian at Athens—signals that in the wider culture of the Roman world the columnar order and the arch were considered sufficiently opposed to be brought together in such blended solutions. That supposition is confirmed by evidence of tensions among building-workers at Miletus (Buckler 1923: 34–6). But, rather than indicating a broad cultural clash between Greek and Roman architectural languages, the uses of the column and the arch in provincial buildings witness a continuing dialectic within Greco-Roman architectural thinking.

10. *Interior and Exterior*

To many, the greatest legacy of Roman architecture is the increased attention to interior, rather than exterior space. The Constantinian basilica at Trier stood out with its contrast of bleak exterior and internal grandeur; the Baths of Caracalla show exuberant interior ornament but external sparseness; and the temple tombs around Rome were designed as decorative interiors within plainer shells. Yet notions of interior and exterior space were subtler in Roman antiquity than for modern architecture. Sometimes the shift was evident in changes in materials or decoration; but differences were not always clearly stated. Many open spaces were comparable to interiors in ornamental features. Should the show façades of

Antonine Ephesus or Side or Plancia Magna's gate court at Perge be regarded as exterior or interior space? Should the covered hemicycles of the Fora of Trajan and Augustus and the Pantheon rotunda be regarded as interiors of analogous character, as the common pattern of their marble pavements suggests? That Agrippa's Pantheon probably had a similar pavement, but was not completely roofed, makes the issue even more contentious.

B. New Polarities for Thinking about Roman Architecture

1. *'Architecture' or 'Building'?*

The ancient Roman conceptual opposition between 'architecture' (*architectura*) and 'building' (*aedificatio*) is altogether less subjective than Nikolaus Pevsner's famous distinction between Lincoln Cathedral and a bicycle shed (Pevsner 1942: 7), but no less tendentious. It is, of course, a false division, since, for Vitruvius at least, the two terms were not alternative formulations, but intrinsically related, the latter being a subdivision of the former. Yet evidence for Romans' thinking about their built environment is dominated by the contrasting positions represented by these two terms. The difference reflects not so much a distinction between utility and aesthetics as opposing perspectives on buildings: as the outcome of a social process, *aedificatio* (literally 'house-creation'), or as a product of a technical procedure, *architectura*. Both words are related to analogous Greek words, *oikodomia* and *architektosunē*, but in each case a substantive difference in meaning between the Greek and Latin words has significant implications for the perception of the activity it describes. Whereas *architektosunē* (*technē*) is both the science of architecture and a broader social virtue of public service, *architectura* is restricted to the technical 'art' of architecture per se. By contrast, while in the Greek world *oikodomia* was an activity of those in the building trade, the Latin term *aedificatio*, despite its superficial similarity in form, was the achievement of a patron.

2. *Designer and Patron*

There were striking differences between what a building meant to its *architectus* and what it meant to its *aedificator*. Neither was solely concerned with the building's ability to serve a practical purpose. While some architects also engaged with morality or cosmological issues, patrons looked to present reputation or future immortality. Vitruvius is *not* 'the only authentic... insight into the workings of a Roman architect's mind' (Wilson Jones 2000: 30). We also have the views of the Pergamene architect Nicon, father of Galen, albeit through a series of enigmatic fragments (Thomas 2007: 92–100, 256–8).

The meaning of a building is usually connected with the intention of its 'author'; and, being the object of contracts and commissions for particular purposes, buildings may be thought unaffected by any 'fallacy of intention'. But their ultimate

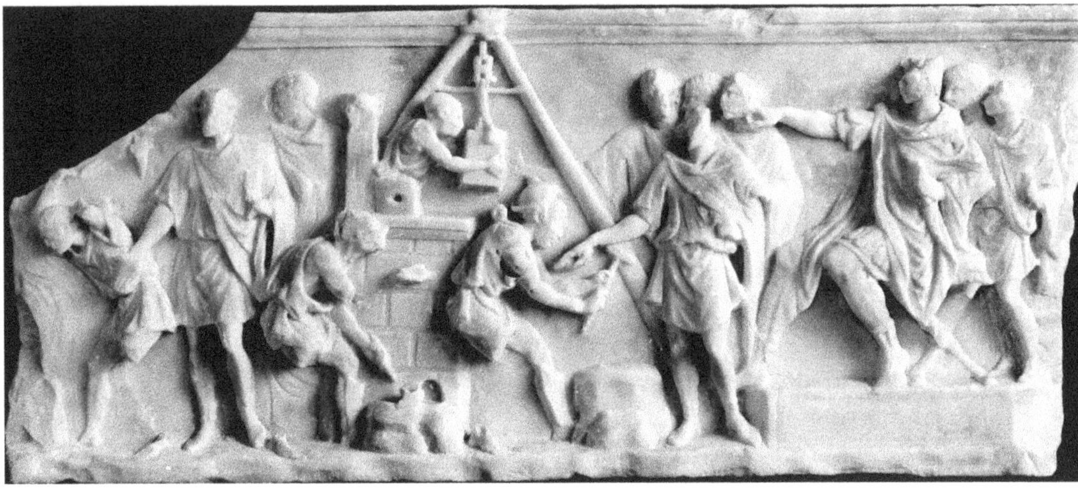

Fig. 53.1. Marble relief from Terracina (Rome, Museo Nazionale)

authorship is ambiguous. Some Roman architects claimed responsibility for the buildings they designed, but credit was more often taken by the patrons who commissioned them, or even by distant emperors.

The different perspectives of individuals involved in building projects are well illustrated on the Terracina relief (Rome, Museo delle Terme, inv. 231008; fig. 53.1). The scene depicted apparently relates to harbour structures built at Terracina in the 30s BCE (Coarelli 1996). To the left, the architect—possibly the naval engineer Lucius Cocceius Auctus, who helped create the Portus Iulius at Avernus—wears a tunic and mantle, holds a scroll of drawings in his left hand, and points downwards in a gesture of authority over the manual work of construction. To his right, the contractor (*redemptor*)—perhaps the architect Caius Postumius Pollio (Anderson 1997: 44–8)—similarly attired and also holding a scroll, gestures at a slightly higher angle, suggesting a greater authority in managing the project. Above them both, further right, sits their patron—plausibly Marcus Agrippa, Prefect of the Fleet in 36 BCE—raised on a platform and seated on a curule chair. In his left hand he holds his rod of office, while his right arm is extended on a higher plane still, indicating overall control and a larger perspective.

The viewer's impression of the main personalities within this project is simplified by the limited size of the relief. In reality, the question of authorship was more uncertain: the period of a building's construction often extended to more than one patron, contractor, or designer. Public buildings begun by one individual might be completed by another, sometimes years later. The gap between intention and result was complicated when the actual workforce had an input into the design (Buckler 1923). Even when complete, a building's meaning could be further redefined by its maintenance, restoration, or changed use.

Because we know so little about the individuals involved at each stage of a building's construction, the question of its meaning is far from straightforward. What we do know of the relations between architects and patrons suggests that, from its initial conception onwards, the responsibility for a building was constantly disputed. The key to understanding Roman architecture is to recognize not only the social and economic relationships involving financing patrons and designing architects, but also the tensions between them and the contested nature of design.

3. *Building and Audience*

Academic studies of Roman buildings usually analyse them in isolation. Yet at their height they were not the deserted ruins we see today, but used spaces, often packed with crowds. At times of celebration and other public occasions their meanings were dramatically altered. They were not passive backdrops, but interacted with 'the viewer'. The use of bodies, eyes, ears, and even noses to judge buildings ensured a continuous dialectic between Romans and their architectural environment.

The experience of architecture is starting to receive more attention. Private houses (Bek 1976; Wallace-Hadrill 1994) and cityscapes (Bek 1985) are analysed for underlying aesthetic principles; street space is studied as a potential visual experience (Yegül 1994; Favro 1994, 1996); movement through Roman architectural space was an ideological act (Corbeill 2002). Urban areas of the Roman Empire demanded multiple responses of seeing, reading, and listening.

4. *The Built and the Written*

One way into ancient architectural experience is through analysis of texts. But, despite extensive recent literary studies on descriptions of works of art and architecture (*ekphraseis*), the study of architecture has yet to profit from this attention. When archaeologists tackle written sources on architectural themes, it is to illuminate attitudes to existing buildings or reconstruct others presumed to exist. Little due is paid to architectural descriptions in themselves as a strategy that elucidates ancient discourse on architecture in general or to the potential impact of the genre on built form. The duality between real architecture and the verbal architecture that is the product of literary imagination needs consideration. How did the relation between written descriptions and standing buildings differ from that between the *trompe l'oeil* architecture of Oplontis or Boscoreale and the three-dimensional structures of Herculaneum and Pompeii?

5. *The Monumental and the Ephemeral*

Similarly under-explored is the relation between buildings designed to last and temporary structures. The built culture of Republican Rome did not consist solely of 'permanent' monuments of tufa, travertine, or concrete attested by archaeological remains. Urban space was often defined by temporary buildings marking particular occasions: banqueting pavilions; theatres; pyres and ritualized settings for funerals; altars; arches and trophies. Ceremonial occasions like triumphs gave even permanent buildings added meaning (Favro 1994). As historians increasingly emphasize the social and religious rituals framing such structures, it is necessary to study more closely the structures themselves. Works of limited duration, such as the costly theatres erected in Republican Rome (Sear 2006: 54–7), were in their own time as socially significant as more lasting buildings.

Roman architectural studies have come a long way. But there is still far to go. As new material continues to be uncovered, its study demands a conceptual sophistication that matches the sophistication in techniques. Many important cultural themes discussed for later periods have so far been barely approached for Roman architecture: monumentality, identity, and regionalism are all fertile fields for exploration in the diverse cultures of the Roman Empire. The potential responses of users to Roman buildings are rarely considered in their own right; aesthetics is seldom explored; relations between durability and ephemerality and between building and text receive little discussion. Only by tackling such wider issues more fully can we begin to penetrate the profundity of the idea that was Roman architecture.

References

Allison, P. M. 2004. *Pompeian Households: An Analysis of Material Culture* (Los Angeles).

Anderson, J. C. 1997. *Roman Architecture and Society* (Baltimore).

Anderson, W. J. and Spiers, R. P. 1907. *The Architecture of Greece and Rome: A Sketch of its Historic Development*, 2nd edn. (London).

Ball, L. F. 2003. *The Domus Aurea and the Roman Architectural Revolution* (Cambridge).

Balty, J.-C. 1991. *Curia Ordinis. Recherches d'architecture et d'urbanisme antiques sur les curies provinciales du monde romain* (Brussels).

Bek, L. 1976. 'Antithesis: a Roman attitude and its changes as reflected in the concept of architecture from Vitruvius to Pliny the Younger', in *Studia Romana in honorem Petri Krarup* (Odense), 154–66.

—— 1985. '*Venusta species*: a Hellenistic rhetorical concept as the aesthetic principle in Roman townscape', *Analecta Romana Instituti Danici*, 14: 139–48.

Boëthius, A. and Ward-Perkins, J. B. 1970. *Etruscan and Roman Architecture* (Harmondsworth).

Boyancé, P. 1940. '*Aedes Catuli*', *MEFRA* 57: 64–71.

Boyd, T. D. 1978. 'The arch and the vault in Greek architecture', *AJA* 82: 85–100.

Brown, F. E. 1961. *Roman Architecture* (New York).

—— 1964. 'Hadrianic architecture', in L. F. Sandler (ed.), *Essays in Memory of Karl Lehmann* (New York), 55–9.

Buckler, W. H. 1923. 'Labour disputes in the province of Asia', in W. H. Buckler and W. M. Calder (eds.), *Anatolian Studies Presented to Sir William Mitchell Ramsay* (Manchester), 27–50.

Burrell, B. 2006. 'False fronts: separating the aedicular façade from the imperial cult in Roman Asia Minor', *AJA* 110: 437–69.

Callebat, L. 1995. 'Dénominations métaphoriques dans le vocabulaire de l'architecture', in L. Callebat (ed.), *Latin vulgaire, latin tardif. IV. Actes du 4e colloque international sur le latin vulgaire et tardif. Caen, 1994* (Hildesheim), 633–42.

Champion T. C. (ed.), 1995. *Centre and Periphery: Comparative Studies in Archaeology* (London).

Ciotta, G. (ed.), 2003. *Vitruvio nella cultura architettonica antica, medievale e moderna. Atti del convegno internazionale di Genova, 5–8 novembre 2001* (Genoa).

Clarke, G. and Crossley, P. 2000. *Architecture and Language* (Cambridge).

Coarelli, F. 1983. 'Architettura sacra e architettura privata nella tarda Repubblica', in *Architecture et société de l'archaïsme grec à la fin de la République romaine* (Rome), 191–217.

—— 1996. 'La costruzione del porto di Terracina in un rilievo storico tardo-repubblicano', in *Revixit ars. Arte e ideologia in Roma dai modelli ellenistici alla tradizione repubblicana* (Rome), 434–54.

Corbeill, A. 2002. 'Political movement: walking and ideology in Republican Rome', in D. Fredrick (ed.), *The Roman Gaze: Vision, Power, and the Body* (Baltimore), 182–215.

Cozza, L. and Tucci, P. 2006. '*Navalia*', *Archeologia Classica*, 57: 175–202.

Crema, L. 1959. *L'architettura romana* (*Enciclopedia Classica*, 3.12) (Turin).

Crossley, P. 1988. 'Medieval architecture and meaning: the limits of iconography', *Burlington Magazine*, 139, no. 1019 (Feb.), 116–21.

Davies, P., Hemsoll, D., and Wilson Jones, M. 1987. 'The Pantheon: triumph of Rome or triumph of compromise?' *Art History*, 10: 133–53.

DeLaine, J. 1997. *The Baths of Caracalla: A Study in the Design, Construction, and Economics of Large-scale Building Projects in Imperial Rome*, *JRA*, suppl. 25 (Portsmouth, RI).

Delbrück, R. 1907–12. *Hellenistische Bauten in Latium* (Strassburg).

Demandt, A. 1982. 'Symbolfunktionen antiker Baukunst', in D. Papenfuss and V. M. Strocka (eds.), *Palast und Hütte. Beiträge zum Bauen und Wohnen im Altertum von Archäologen, Vor- und Frühgeschichtlern* (Mainz), 49–62.

Dodge, H. 1990. 'The architectural impact of Rome in the East', in M. Henig (ed.), *Architecture and Architectural Sculpture in the Roman Empire* (Oxford), 108–20.

Dornisch, K. 1992. *Die griechischen Bogentore: zur Entstehung und Verbreitung des griechischen Keilsteingewölbes* (Frankfurt am Main).

Drerup, H. 1966. 'Architektur als Symbol. Zur zeitgenössischen Bewertung der römischen Architektur', *Gymnasium*, 73: 181–200.

Favro, D. G. 1994. 'The street triumphant: the urban impact of Roman triumphal parades', in Z. Çelik, D. Favro, and R. Ingersoll (eds.), *Streets: Critical Perspectives on Public Space* (Berkeley), 151–64.

—— 1996. *The Urban Image of Augustan Rome* (Cambridge).

Frova, A. and Cavalieri Manasse, G. 2005. 'La basilica forense di Verona alla luce dei nuovi scavi', in X. Lafon and G. Sauron (eds.), *Théorie et pratique de l'architecture romaine: la norme et l'expérimentation. Études offertes à Pierre Gros* (Aix-en-Provence), 179–201.

Giuliani, C. F. 1990. *L'edilizia nell'antichità* (Rome).

Gossel, B. 1980. *Makedonische Kammergräber* (Berlin).

Grasshoff, G., Heinzelmann, M., and Wäfler, M. 2009. *The Pantheon in Rome* (Bern).
Gros, P. 1989. 'L'*auctoritas* chez Vitruve. Contribution à l'étude de la sémantique des ordres dans le *De Architectura*', in H. Geertman and J. J. de Jong (eds.) *Munus non ingratum: Proceedings of the International Symposium on Vitruvius' De Architectura and Hellenistic and Republican Architecture. Leiden 20–23 January 1987* (Leiden), 126–33.
——1996–2001. *L'Architecture romaine du début du IIIe siècle avant J.-C. à la fin du haut empire*, 1. *Les monuments publics*; 2. *Maisons, palais, villas et tombeaux* (Paris).
Hahn, R. 2001. *Anaximander and the Architects: The Contributions of Egyptian and Greek Architectural Technologies to the Origins of Greek Philosophy* (Albany, NY).
Haselberger, L. 1994. 'Ein Giebelriß der Vorhalle des Pantheon. Die Werkrisse vor dem Augustusmausoleum', *MDAI(R)* 101: 279–308.
Heilmeyer, W.-D. 1970. *Korinthische Normalkapitelle. Studien zur Geschichte der römischen Architekturdekoration* (Heidelberg).
——1975. 'Apollodorus von Damascus—der Architekt des Pantheon', *JDAI* 90: 317–47.
Herz, N. and Waelkens, M. (eds.), 1988. *Classical Marble: Geochemistry, Technology, Trade* (Dordrecht).
von Hesberg, H. 1990. 'Bauornament als kulturelle Leitform', in Trillmich and Zanker 1990: 341–66.
Hetland, L. 2007. 'Dating the Pantheon', *JRA* 20: 95–112.
Holum, K. G. and Raban, A. (eds.), 1996. *Caesarea Maritima: A Retrospective After Two Millennia* (Leiden).
Hurst, H. R., Fulford, M. G., and Peacock, D. P. S. 1994. *Excavations at Carthage: The British Mission.* 2: *The Circular Harbour, North Side* (Oxford).
Jones, R. and Bon, S. (eds.), 1997. *Sequence and Space in Pompeii* (Oxford).
Joyce, H. 1990. 'Hadrian's Villa and the "Dome of Heaven"', *MDAI(R)* 97: 347–81.
Kaiser, A. 2000. *The Urban Dialogue: An Analysis of the Use of Space in the Roman City of Empúries*, BAR international series 901 (Oxford).
Kampen, N. B. 2003. 'On writing histories of Roman art', *AB* 85: 371–86.
Krautheimer, R. 1942. 'Introduction to an "Iconography of Medieval Architecture"', *JWCI* 5: 1–33. Repr. in R. Krautheimer, *Studies in Early Christian, Medieval, and Renaissance Art* (London, 1971), 115–50.
Lancaster, L. C. 2005. *Concrete Vaulted Construction in Imperial Rome* (Cambridge).
——2005a. 'The process of building the Colosseum: the site, materials, and construction techniques', *JRA* 18: 57–82.
Laurence, R. 1994. *Roman Pompeii: Space and Society* (London and New York).
Leach, E. W. 1997. 'Oecus on Ibycus: investigating the vocabulary of the Roman house', in Jones and Bon 1997: 50–72.
Lefaivre, L. and Tzonis, A. 2003. *Critical Regionalism: Architecture and Identity in a Globalized World* (Munich and London).
Lehmann, K. 1945. 'The Dome of Heaven', *AB* 27: 1–27. Repr. in W. E. Kleinbauer (ed.), *Modern Perspectives in Western Art History: An Anthology of Twentieth-century Writings on the Visual Arts* (New York, 1971), 227–70.
Léon, P. 1970. *Die Bauornamentik des Trajansforums und ihre Stellung in der früh- und mittelkaiserzeitlichen Architekturdekoration Roms* (Vienna).
Loerke, W. C. 1990. 'A re-reading of the interior elevation of Hadrian's Rotunda', *JSAH* 49: 22–43.
L'Orange, H. P. 1953. *Studies on the Iconography of Cosmic Kingship in the Ancient World* (London and Oslo).

Lugli, G. 1957. *La tecnica edilizia romana: con particolare riguardo a Roma e Lazio* (Rome).

Lyttelton, M. 1974. *Baroque Architecture in Classical Antiquity* (London).

MacDonald, W. L. 1982–6. *The Architecture of the Roman Empire*, vol. 1: *An Introductory Study*, 2nd edn.; vol. 2. *An Urban Appraisal* (New Haven).

McEwen, I. K. 2003. *Vitruvius: Writing the Body of Architecture* (Cambridge, Mass.).

MacMullen, R. 2000. *Romanization in the Time of Augustus* (New Haven).

Markus, T. 1993. *Buildings and Power: Freedom and Control in the Origin of Modern Building Types* (London).

Martines, G. 2000. 'The relationship between architecture and mathematics in the Pantheon', *Nexus Network Journal*, 2/3: 57–61, online at http://www.nexusjournal.com/Martines.html.

Oleson, J. P., Bottalico, L., Brandon, C., Cucitore, R., Gotti, E., and Hohlfelder, R. L. 2006. 'Reproducing a Roman maritime structure with Vitruvian pozzolanic concrete', *JRA* 19: 29–52.

Onians, J. 1988. *Bearers of Meaning: The Classical Orders in Antiquity, the Middle Ages, and the Renaissance* (Princeton).

Pellati, F. 1947–9. 'La Basilica di Fano e la formazione del trattato di Vitruvio', *RPAA* 33–4: 153–74.

Pevsner, N. 1942. *An Outline of European Architecture* (Harmondsworth).

Plommer, W. H. 1956. *Ancient and Classical Architecture* (London).

Le Projet de Vitruve [1994]*: objet, destinataires et réception du De architectura* (Rome).

Purcell, N. 1983. 'The *apparitores*: a study in social mobility', *PBSR* 38: 125–73.

Robertson, D. S. 1943. *A Handbook of Greek and Roman Architecture*, 2nd edn. (Cambridge).

Ros, K. E. 1997. 'Vitruvius and the design of the Carthage theater', *L'Africa Romana*, 11/2: 897–910.

Sauron, G. 1994. *Quis Deum. L'expression plastique des idéologies politiques et religieuses à Rome à la fin de la République et au début du principat* (Rome).

Sear, F. B. 2006. *Roman Theatres: An Architectural Study* (Oxford).

Smith, E. B. 1956. *Architectural Symbolism of Imperial Rome and the Middle Ages* (Princeton).

Sperling, G. 1997. *Das Pantheon in Rom: Abbild und Mass des Kosmos* (Neuried).

Strocka, V. M. 1988. 'Wechselwirkungen der stadtrömischen und kleinasiatischen Architektur unter Trajan und Hadrian', *MDAI(I)* 38: 291–307.

Strong, D. E. 1953. 'Late Hadrianic architectural ornament at Rome', *PBSR* 21: 118–51.

Strzygowski, J. 1901. *Orient oder Rom: Beiträge zur Geschichte der spätantiken und früchristlichen Kunst* (Leipzig).

Taylor, R. 2003. *Roman Builders: A Study in Architectural Process* (Cambridge).

Thomas, E. V. 2007. *Monumentality and the Roman Empire: Architecture in the Antonine Age* (Oxford).

Trillmich, W. and Zanker, P. (eds.), 1990. *Stadtbild und Ideologie. Die Monumentalisierung hispanischer Städte zwischen Republik und Kaiserzeit* (Munich).

Wallace-Hadrill, A. 1994. *Houses and Society in Pompeii and Herculaneum* (Princeton).

—— 1995. 'Public honour and private shame: the urban texture of Pompeii', in T. J. Cornell and K. Lomas (eds.), *Urban Society in Roman Italy* (London), 39–62.

—— 1998. 'To be Roman, go Greek: thoughts on Hellenization at Rome', in *Modus operandi: Essays in Honour of Geoffrey Rickman* (London), 79–91.

Ward-Perkins, J. B. 1965. 'The Roman West and the Parthian East', *PBA* 51: 175–99.
—— 1970. 'From Republic to Empire: reflections on the early provincial architecture of the Roman West', *JRS* 60: 1–19.
—— 1973. 'The cryptoportico: a practical solution to certain problems of Roman urban design', in *Les Cryptoportiques dans l'architecture romaine* (Rome), 51–6.
—— 1981. *Roman Imperial Architecture* (Harmondsworth).
Watts, C. M. and Watts, D. J. 1992. 'The role of monuments in the geometrical ordering of the Roman master plan of Gerasa', *JSAH* 51: 306–14.
Welch, K. 2003. 'A new view of the origins of the Basilica: the Atrium Regium, Graecostasis, and Roman diplomacy', *JRA* 16: 5–34.
Wickhoff, F. 1900. *Roman Art* (London).
Wilson, A. I. 1998. 'Water supply in ancient Carthage', in J. T. Peña *et al.*, *Carthage Papers*, *JRA* Suppl. 28 (Portsmouth, RI), 65–102.
Wilson Jones, M. 2000. *Principles of Roman Architecture* (New Haven and London).
Wright, F. L. 1941. *Frank Lloyd Wright on Architecture: Selected Writings 1894–1940*, ed. F. Gutheim (New York).
Yegül, F. K. 1982. 'A study in architectural iconography: *Kaisersaal* and the imperial cult', *AB* 64: 7–31.
—— 1994. 'The street experience of ancient Ephesus', in Z. Çelik, D. Favro, and R. Ingersoll (eds.), *Streets: Critical Perspectives on Public Space* (Berkeley), 95–111.

CHAPTER 54

SCIENCE

PAUL T. KEYSER

It is most peculiar that there should be any such thing as Roman science, if by ancient science we mean the sort of thing Greeks did. Every human culture has ways of arranging its knowledge of the natural and human worlds into some system, and putting that system to use. Cultures continually assimilate and reject imported knowledge and its uses—rejecting what contravenes tradition and assimilating the useful. The genius of Greek science is precisely its weak binding to specifically Greek tradition—making it more readily assimilated by other cultures. There is, however, almost no ancient analogue for assimilators of Greek science who created works of science in a language other than Greek. The genius of the Roman assimilators of Greek science stands on their desire to bring home and master the cultural products of their captives.

Greek science was based on argument in public discourse, the desire to confute opponents, and the rhetoric of a market-place of ideas (Lloyd 1996: 20–46), arising in and among numerous city-states sharing broad cultural values (language, politics, religion, etc.), linked through active travel and trade networks, but lacking a stable central hegemony. Moreover, its practitioners shared a belief in the interpretability of the natural world (the Greek philosophers who denied that produced no science). Greek science depended only weakly on specifics of Greek culture, eschewing accounts alleging immediate divine causation, thus offering a formal compatibility with any cultural system, insofar as that system did not *demand* unmediated divine causation for most or all natural phenomena.

Every age is transitional between its own past and present, and at the time Romans began to encounter it Greek science was no longer producing new syntheses, but exploring the existing syntheses and the gaps within and between them. The former multiplicity of city-states had become an oligopoly of kingdoms, each offering patronage of various sorts to scientists, engineers, and doctors. Stoics began to collect *paradoxa*, a kind of logic of refutation based on the accumulation of anomalies, while Epicureans gathered alternate explanations, all equally tenable so long as none were divine (Asmis 1984: 321–30). Doctors and engineers especially, but also astronomers and mathematicians, provided ever-richer descriptions of phenomena, results, and theories. Finally, some practitioners absorbed data and theories from cultures such as Egypt and Babylon, creating the disciplines of alchemy and astrology (Keyser and Irby-Massie 2006).

Babylonians, Carthaginians, Copts, Jews, and others who chose to participate in this project and discourse did so in Greek, so far as we can discover. For example, the following composed in Greek: Bērossos on Babylonian cosmology and history (Burstein 1978); Hanno the Carthaginian on the geography of West Africa (Ramin 1976; Blomqvist 1979); and Dōsitheos on mathematics and astronomy, despite probably being Jewish (Netz 1998). However, in each case their native traditions continued, little affected by Greek ideas. Similarly, Egyptians who went down to Alexandria often published under Greek names (though contrast Manethōn), whereas Coptic and Demotic mathematical texts are invariably anonymous (Depuydt 1998; Hoffmann 2000). Lack of evidence may mislead (although late Babylonian cuneiform tablets and Coptic or Demotic papyri are not rare), and counterfactuals are slippery to think with, but such evidence would suggest that Roman science, like Roman literature as a whole (Feeney 2005: 229), might never have happened.

Romans too had their own native science, isolated traces of which appear in extant works from Virgil to Pliny, but strongly represented perhaps only in Cato, *De Agricultura*. But even Cato tended instead to assimilate and present Greek science. Roman wisdom, whether scientific or not, was based on personal *auctoritas*, itself based upon publicly validated accomplishment, per se leaving few openings for assimilation of foreign ideas. Such openings were, however, provided by Rome's geographical and political position as a successful hill-fort at the boundary of several regions. Geography alone does not determine outcomes, but sets the stage for possible outcomes. Rome mediated between hill and plain, between Etruria and Latium, and profited from its location as the nexus of many polyglot interactions (Torelli 1989; Momigliano 1989; Cornell 1995: 163–8; Adams 2003: 112–44). Economic motives encouraged Rome to welcome foreign goods—and ideas (an early example being the numeral system and alphabet: Keyser 1988; Bonfante and Bonfante 2002: 52–6, 94–8). But foreign practices could not be adopted without reservation or limit, for the proper observance of custom maintained the integrity and continuity of the Roman people and state, as Ennius notes: *moribus antiquis res stat Romana uirisque* ('ancient rules and men sustain the state of Rome', *Annales*, Book 5, fr. 156 Sk., from Augustine, *De Civitate Dei* 2, 21).

Thus the question for us depends on whether we consider the problem from the inside outward—'why ever did the Romans adopt *Greek* science, and not (say)

Etruscan, Carthaginian, or Egyptian systems?'—or instead from outside inward—'why alone of cultures encountering the Greeks did the *Romans* start practising Greek science in their own language?' Any account that dwells on detail risks descending into mere antiquarianism, what Aristotle might have called the morass of contingency. But any account that attempts to weave a pattern risks being carried aloft into mere *eisegesis* or retrojection.

The tradition of scholarship from Roman times until now presents serious obstacles to comprehension of ancient science. The Greek science that Romans first assimilated became, precisely because of subsequent Roman influence, the least well preserved. Moreover, textbooks, handbooks, and popular works, in every era and field of knowledge, will tend to survive through generations of copyists and fluctuations of fashion in preference to the more profound or transgressive efforts of research. Since the Renaissance classical scholars have exacerbated this defect by focusing their attention primarily on two well-documented eras, namely the fifth to fourth centuries BCE in Athens and the first century BCE to the first century CE in Rome. In addition, the available works of Roman science are rarely viewed synoptically, and a relatively large proportion of them are hardly studied at all. Finally, scholarship has tended to accept narratives that in effect presume a Roman outlook, that is, emphasizing founders, authorities, centres, utility, and boundaries.

Roman culture manifests practices that may fairly be termed ancestor-worship (Rawson 1985: 98–9; 322), seen in the religious sphere as the reverence due to the Lares and Penates, and in the ancestor-masks worn at funerals, but, more relevantly for our purpose, shown in the deference, almost awe, granted to the *mos maiorum* ('the ways of the ancestors'). The attitude per se is not unique, and can be paralleled among Egyptians (Parkinson 1997: 13–17, 203–11), Chinese (Lloyd 1996: 167, 193), and even the Inca, not to mention Hesiod, in his praise for the lost Golden Age.

But Rome expelled the kings, and either never developed or else abolished the 'palace economy' so typical of ancestor-worshipping cultures, which indeed persisted in Egyptian, Chinese, and Incan cultures. Instead, each Roman *pater familias* and *imperator* appears to have organized the economy of his 'household' as a 'palace' economy, that is, all goods were owed to him, but also all dependants were owed a distribution. Thus, there was no single central locus of authority and practice, no king and court, but rather many 'big men' competed for resources and authority.

Such a complex of concepts leads in several relevant directions. Since the ancestors are the persisting authority for action, and the eldest is seen as wisest, *ex officio*, a conservative or even archaizing outlook may be expected. Moreover, for any practice, one expects an early authoritative founder, analogous to the *prōtos heurētēs* of early Greek thought (Zhmud 2006). There will also emerge the desire for an authoritative answer to any valid question, as if in a courtroom; debate can only be conducted with explicit deference to *auctoritas*. Thinkers in such a milieu may be expected to privilege textbooks and syntheses over disputatious and endless research. Then again, and famously Roman, they will prefer pragmatic and prescriptive answers that lead to successful undertakings, rather than possibly lengthy investigations that might lead to understanding. Throughout there will be a longing for unity—one system, one synthesis, within which all answers are found.

No culture is omniscient, and no wise man knows everything, and so, unless all cultures are utterly static, every culture will from time to time encounter external novelty. Assimilation and rejection were organic elements of Roman culture from the beginning, manifested as they encountered their Italian neighbours (and active also in their encounter with Greek science). Both are means of mastery, and the man of *auctoritas*, the 'big man' whether *pater familias* or *imperator*, must be a master of wisdom as well. But the wise head knows when to delegate and to whom, and thus Roman patronage will extend to science, in which the client will provide practical service.

Turning in another direction, let us note that all cultures begin as xenophobic: the foreigner is a threat and a competitor for resources. As populations grow, all other things being equal, the cultures that succeed in assimilating neighbours (rather than destroying or evicting them) will grow faster, and thus more greatly expand and prosper. Thus, enduring cultures tend, to an ever greater degree as time passes, to be those that have assimilated foreign elements. The hill-fort on the Tiber did not grow along a mighty river (unlike Egypt, Mesopotamia, and China), but by alliance and war among relatively dissimilar cultures, and by the exertion of *auctoritas*. However, Rome provided an explicit path to citizenship, allowing for a more organic assimilation (analogous to that employed by the three fluvial societies). Cultures often assimilate neighbours by enslaving the women and raising their children as natives (the sons sometimes can become citizens, as happened with the Sabines); rarely do cultures allow subjected adult males such hope. Rome systematically, albeit often reluctantly, and not universally until 212 CE, extended citizenship to male subjects and allies.

Xenophobia will privilege native wisdom above foreign arts and devices. One thus expects that Roman authorities will prefer native wisdom, and only deploy or exploit foreign science when it has been somehow safely assimilated. This too leads in the direction of patronage, but one in which the foreign client composes works for the patron, in his honour and ostensibly for his use.

Auctoritas and native wisdom, assimilation and rejection, patronage and *praxis*, are all organic elements of Roman culture from its beginning, and all active later in their encounter with Greek science. The earliest stages are scarcely known, but, for example, it seems that the Greek hero and god Asklēpios (Aesculapius), in response to a plague, was naturalized in Rome (291 BCE), on the liminal Tiber Isle (Livy 10.47; Scarborough 1993: 23; Beard, North, and Price 1998: 1.12–13, 69–70), and soon thereafter the *Lex Aquilia* (286 BCE) records medical practitioners (who clearly had long existed). Evidence also suggests that in early Rome medical care—and presumably the requisite wisdom—was provided by the *pater familias* or, in the field, the *imperator* (Polybius 3.66.9; Cato, *Agr.* 70–3, 122–3, 126–7, 157–60). If indeed the head man was expected to be the wise man (as also for the Greek 'Seven Wise Men'), such knowledge was likely to be learned through some apprenticeship system, as Cicero attests for oratory and the law (Wallace-Hadrill 1988: 232).

Native wisdom was also deployed in the arena of 'civil engineering', being primarily responsible for the Cloaca Maxima (6th cent. BCE?—Livy 1.38.6, 1.56.2; Dionysius of Halicarnassus, *AR* 3.67.5, 4.44.1; Richardson 1992: 91–2; and H. Bauer in Steinby 1996: 1.288–90), as well as the Via Appia under the *auctoritas* of Ap. Claudius Caecus (312 BCE) and the Anio Vetus aqueduct (272 BCE: see Morel 1989: 482 on both), and here too the wisdom was likely passed on from master to apprentice. Similarly, town-planning by early Romans does not follow Greek models but native Roman layouts, as for example at Cosa and Paestum (273 BCE: Morel 1989: 483, 487–91).

In all these fields the wise men were men with *auctoritas*, an aristocratic predominance in native science that established intellectual conservatism. The foregoing sketch sufficiently displays the particularly Roman genius for both assimilation and rejection of foreign wisdom and practice. That particular and contingent genius compounded with the particular and contingent Greek scientific spirit produced in time what we call Roman science—perhaps a better term would be Romanized Greek science.

The Turning-point

No one event marks the first Roman assimilation of Greek science; rather, it begins among the repeated encounters with South Italian Greeks, in Campania and then on the Gulf of Taras, throughout the third century BCE. Whether any native science—aqueducts, medicine, roads, or town-planning—was published in any sense in this period, as the *fasti* were by Cn. Flavius (300 BCE: *HLL* §108.3, 111.3), is possible in principle but dubious in practice, and no evidence exists. More likely, Romans sought to master Hellenic culture and bring it, like its practitioners, under their sway, and only in doing so were written works produced. For example, Greek legends about Aeneas and other west-faring heroes were deployed for political effect in the third and second centuries BCE (Gruen 1990: 12–15), and importations of Greek divinities (Venus Erycina, 217–215 BCE; Magna Mater, 204 BCE) managed for state purposes. Even more so, Greek science, so readily transmissible to new hosts, represented for the Roman elite a risk of diluting their power through its potential to erode their *auctoritas* in technical *praxis* (agronomy, architecture, medicine, war, etc.), and must also be managed, both at home and abroad.

But risk comes at a turning-point, as in Greek *krisis* (or Chinese *weiji*), and the opportunities outweighed the dangers by *c.*220–200 BCE. We see the authorities, either as particular 'big men' or else acting through the Senate, balancing assimilation and rejection to optimize control. The ruling class asserted its control of the cultural tradition—Greek wisdom could not be allowed to determine Roman ways; rather, Roman ways must remain superior to foreign ways (Gruen 1990: 158–70).

The Roman Senate in 219 BCE first tested the idea of hiring a Greek doctor at state expense, Archagathos of Lakonia (to whom they also granted citizenship), whose practice in the centrally sited 'Crossroads of Acilius', at first successful, then fell out of favour (Pliny 29.12–13, based in whole or part on Cassius Hemina). Evidently there were some who believed that Greek medicine had proven itself in the two generations since Aesculapius had taken up residence on Tiber Isle (Nutton 2004: 157–70)—and others, traditionalists like Cato, who wished to reject what they saw as excessive Greek influx (Pliny 29.14; Gruen 1992: 52–83).

Cato and his lifetime stand at the centre of the turn (Astin 1978); he operates as a man of *auctoritas* and master of wisdom, both native and Greek. Cato's military service included duty at Syracuse as *tribunus militum* under Marcellus (Cic. *Senec.* 10; Astin 1978: 6–7), where he doubtless was as impressed as his *imperator* by the power of Archimedes' technical skill in defence (214–212 BCE). Presumably, besides the booty paraded through Rome, the machines, their builders, and perhaps Archimedes' writings were confiscated for the good of Rome. Cato himself composed a lost work on the military art (Astin 1978: 184–5, 204–5), and as *censor* sponsored the construction of the Basilica Porcia, a public Roman building in the style of a Greek *stoa* (184 BCE: Livy 39.44.6–7; Plutarch, *Cato* 19.2; Richardson 1992: 56; Steinby 1996: 1.187), as well as improving the Cloaca Maxima (Astin 1978: 84).

Cato's own work on agronomy and agriculture emphasized the central controlling role of the *pater familias* (2, 3, 143) and preference for native Roman remedies and methods (135, 139, 146, 149, 160), as most stridently expressed in his (earlier?) advice to his son (*apud* Pliny, *Nat. Hist.* 29.14; Astin 1978: 189–203; *HLL* §162, esp. B.3). He records the name of Minius Percennius of Nola (contrast his practice in the *Origines*), for an accomplishment in sowing the seed of the Tarentine cypress (151; *cf.* 152; Speranza 1971: 11–13)—that is, he promotes Italian wisdom explicitly. Although Cato does not make it explicit, his own claims and practices are indebted to Greek works (Boscherini 1970; Richter 1973; Pasquazi 1989); the clearest example being the encomium of cabbage (156–7), which is based upon a Greek source evident in (and may be identical to) Mnēsitheos of Kuzikos (*apud* Oreibasios, *Coll.* 4.4 [*CMG* 6.1.1, p. 100], *cf.* Pliny, *Nat. Hist.* 20.80–1; Grant 1997: 300–302). Greek recipes (24, 80, 82, 102, 105, 112, 158.2) and Greek plants (8, 27, 35, 37, 40, 133) are recommended.

Cato in his youth must have observed the political advantages gained by the incorporation of the worship of Venus Erycina in 217–215 BCE (Livy 22.9–10, 23.30–1; Beard, North, and Price 1998: 1.83; Schilling 1982: 233–66), as well as the Magna Mater from Ida via Pergamon in 204 BCE (Livy 29.11, 14; Ovid, *Fasti* 4.247–348; Beard, North, and

Price 1998: 1.96–8). On the other hand, he also saw the effect of the edict of 213 BCE (Livy 25.1.9–11) expelling foreign superstition and confiscating books of prophecy. In all cases the goal seems to have been the same: balancing assimilation and rejection to optimize control. If Cato indeed passed time in philosophic discourse with the Pythagorean Nearchos of Taras (204 BCE: Cicero, *Senec.* 39, 41; Plutarch, *Cato* 2.3; accepted by Mele 1981: 69–77; doubted by Gruen 1992: 66–7), it is clear that he accepted only doctrines that reinforced Roman mores (Roman and Roman 1994: 77–90).

Cato thus oversaw or participated in the partial assimilation of useful Greek science (military, medical, agricultural). Other forms of Greek science were less useful and more troubling, whether or not acquired as booty (like Archimedes' works), but they too were mastered in one way or another. It was on Cato's authority that his slightly older contemporary Ennius was brought to Rome in 204 BCE (Nepos, *Cato* 1.4), when Cato served as quaestor under Scipio Africanus. Ennius, among other lost works, composed the *Euhemerus* (explaining the Greek gods on the reductionist principle that they were all, like Herakles and Asklepios, divinized humans), and the *Epicharmus* (explaining the Greek gods on the old allegorical principle that they represented the elements composing the world), making Greek philosophy available in Latin, probably for the first time, and showing both how disputatious it was, and how iconoclastic (*HLL* §117, esp. C.d.2–3). This may be analogous to the presentation of Greeks in Plautine comedy, which served to relax and redirect social tensions, thus conserving structures of power (Gruen 1990: 155). Soon after Cato's censorship the same goal is visible in the Senatorial decree for the destruction of forged Pythagorean books purportedly connecting Numa to Pythagoras (181 BCE: Livy 40.29; Pliny, *Nat. Hist.* 13.84–8; etc.), who, though an aristocrat, promoted secret societies. Cato's contemporary, M. Fulvius Nobilior, *cos.* 189 BCE, *cens.* 179 BCE, built the temple of 'Hercules of the Muses' at Rome wherein he placed his commentary on the *fasti*, which besides folk etymologies of the month names (Varro, *LL* 6.33; Censorinus 20.2–4, 22.9; Macrobius Theodosius, *Sat.* 1.12.16, 1.13.21), advocated astral studies as a means to comprehend the divine (Iōannēs 'Lydus', *Ost.* 16 [p. 47 W.]; Boyancé 1955; *HLL* §190.3), thus placing Greek speculations about the sky under the aegis of civil religion. C. Sulpicius Gallus, *cos.* 166 BCE, also knew how to employ Greek astronomy as a means to power: he is said to have calmed a Roman army faced with a lunar eclipse of 168 BCE (Pliny, *Nat. Hist.* 2.9), and wrote a volume on Greek astronomy (Varro *apud* Pliny, *Nat. Hist.* 2.53), in which he described the planetary spheres (Cicero, *Rep.* 1.23; Gruen 1992: 244; Evans 1998: 80, 82, 455, n. 9; *HLL* §189.2).

As Rome's *auctoritas* spread over ever-greater swathes of Greek territory, ever-greater amounts of Greek science became available in Rome and to Romans, requiring ever-greater care and effort to manage. The library of Perseus of Macedon could be assimilated as booty; but the influx of numerous Greek scholars (Polybius, Book 31, fr. 24.6–7; Pliny, *Nat. Hist.* 35.135; Plutarch, *Aem. Paul.* 6.4–5, 28.11; Gruen 1992: 247–8), and the arrival of Kratēs of Mallos, librarian of Pergamon, as ambassador and professor (Suetonius, *Gramm.* 2; Kaster 1995: 58–60; Broggiato 2001: p. xviii) brought challenges to native wisdom and thus to Rome's *auctoritas.* Assimilation must be limited, and excess rejected—and so the philosophers were expelled (161 BCE: Suetonius, *Gramm.* 25.2; Gellius 15.11.1; Kaster 1995: 272–3), an expulsion in which Cato may have actively participated (Pliny, *Nat. Hist.* 7.113; Gruen 1990: 171–4; 1992: 259–60; *HLL* 189.1.c). The Roman embassy of the three scholarchs, Academic, Stoic, Peripatetic, in 155 BCE provided another opportunity for assimilation and rejection (*HLL* §189.1.d). The lectures of Carneades the Academic were immensely popular, but Cato objected to their tendency to reduce respect for, and obedience to, the ancestral laws of Rome (Cicero, *Rep.*, Book 3, fr. 9; Cicero, *ND* 3.43–4; Pliny, *Nat. Hist.* 7.112; Plutarch, *Cato* 22.3–5; Diogenes Laertius 4.62–6; Astin 1978: 174–6; Long and Sedley 1987: §§68–70), and thus sought to hurry their business and their departure. Epicurean philosophers, probably also viewed as subversive, were also driven out (154 BCE: Athenaeus, *Deipn.* 12 [547A]; *HLL* §189.1.c), and the Senate expelled three groups of sectarians whose practices offered alien insights: adherents of Jupiter 'Sabazius' (an Eastern god with orgiastic rites), some Jewish sect, and astrologers (139 BCE: Valerius Maximus 1.3.2; Cramer 1951: 14–17; Smallwood 1981: 128–30; Lane 1979; cf. Johnson 1984).

Medical science and military science could be accepted; other sciences must be rejected. The looting of Carthage (146 BCE) provided another opportunity to assimilate useful science, the agricultural work of Mago, which was translated, by the Greek Dionusios, a.k.a. Cassius, for the benefit of Rome (Speranza 1971: 75–119; *HLL* §196.2). Either these stimuli, or simply the accumulating effects of all that had gone before, resulted in a steadily increasing number and kind of texts of Roman science, all now fragmentary, but showing a mix of wisdoms, native and assimilated Greek. Iunius Silanus (146 BCE), and the father and son Hostilius Saserna (*c.*125 BCE), wrote on agriculture and exploited Hipparchos' theories (*HLL* §196.3); Trebius Niger (*c.*140 BCE) wrote on biology, or anyway *paradoxa* of the animal world, very much in the Stoic manner (Pliny, *Nat. Hist.* 9.80, 89–93, 10.40, 32.15); and C. Acilius, writing Roman history in Greek as had many others, now introduced geography to his narrative (*c.*142 BCE; *FGrHist* 813; *HLL* §160.2). As Strabōn the Greek would later remark, territory to be ruled must be known.

VARRO AND COEVALS

The works of M. Terentius Varro and M. Tullius Cicero, both extant and lost, more deeply assimilate and synthesize Greek science. Six authors will primarily concern us, whose birth-dates follow in sequence: Varro (116 BCE), Cicero (106 BCE), Caesar

(100 BCE), Lucretius (*c.*95 BCE), Nigidius (*c.*90 BCE), and Vitruvius (*c.*85 BCE). Several of Varro's many works were dedicated to his friend and patron Sex. Pompeius Magnus (106–48 BCE), for example, the *Ephemeris Navalis*, a kind of nautical guide, as well as the *Origin of Latin*; Pompey was also patron to Theophanēs of Mytilēnē the geographer (Cicero, *Pro Arch.* 24; Rawson 1985: 105–9). Patronage was crucial in Rome, as always and everywhere, but Pompey's practice was partly modelled on the Greek king he emulated, Alexander the Great (Plutarch, *Pomp.* 34.5, 46.1, cf. also 35.3–4, 38.2; Appian, *Mithr.* 116–17), and he honoured Poseidōnios of Apamea as a second Aristotle (Strabōn 2.3.8, 11.1.6; Pliny, *Nat. Hist.* 7.112; Plutarch, *Pomp.* 42.5). Pompey also sponsored the work of his freedman Pompeius Lenaeus in translating Mithridates' pharmacy (Pliny, *Nat. Hist.* 25.5; Speranza 1971: 63–5). In contrast, the patronage of T. Pomponius Atticus (100–32 BCE) in support of Cicero and others is comparable to Hellenistic *leitourgoi* by 'benefactors' (*euergetai*: Robert 1935; Veyne 1976: 228–71; Gruen 1993: 348–51; Ma 1999: 182–214). That is, a wealthy and well-connected private citizen disbursed resources to promote culture, including the composition of scientific works (Rawson 1985: 100–4). Atticus tried to get Cicero to write geography (Cicero, *Ad Att.* 2.4, 2.6, 2.7), and encouraged Cicero's philosophic efforts, especially as his publisher; he seems also to have encouraged Cornelius Nepos, who did write geography.

Varro, who outlived the other five save Vitruvius, wrote more than all of them, but only a few percent of his work survives, so that Rome's greatest scholar, and his scientific work, are poorly known (Rawson 1985: *passim*; Cardauns 2001). He studied under L. Aelius Stilo in Rome and then in Athens under the Academic Antiochos of Askalon; after military and political service with Pompey the Great he turned to writing by 81 BCE, producing dozens of works over the next fifty-four years. The one scientific of his two extant works, the *Res Rusticae*, presents as a dialogue among prominent landowners all that the elite needed to know about estate-management. His *Disciplinae* was an encyclopedia of the liberal arts in nine volumes: first grammar, rhetoric, and dialectic; then arithmetic, geometry, astronomy, and music, plus medicine and architecture. This division of science endured, becoming the later Neoplatonist *trivium* (contents of Books 1–3) and *quadrivium* (contents of Books 4–7), although medicine and architecture were also long regarded as suitably 'liberal'. The arts of what became the *trivium* were easy for the Roman oligarchy to assimilate to their own native traditions. The other arts covered by Varro may in some ways have been more socially disruptive, regarded either as banausic (arithmetic for merchants, geometry for surveyors: Rawson 1985: 156–69), or else potentially subversive—music (as Plato had warned in *Republic* 3 (411ab), 4 (424bc), or cf. Aristophanes, *Clouds* 964–72) and astronomy/astrology (insofar as it removed from the oligarchy the locus of control for predicting political events: Wallace-Hadrill 1988: 233). Medicine was disruptive to the traditional role of the *pater familias* or the *imperator* (still valid in the late Republic:

Cicero, *Tusc.* 2.16.38; Plutarch, *Crass.* 25.5, 25.11; Rawson 1985: 84–6). Architecture was perhaps similarly ambiguous (walls, roads, and aqueducts having long been the province of the elite: Rawson 1985: 86–8, 191; Gruen 1992: 132–3). Agriculture Varro covered in the separate, and extant, work *Res Rusticae*; geography seems to have been largely subsumed into history, geometry, or astronomy, although Varro did compose a *periplous* of the Mediterranean, *Ora Maritima*, and a treatise on tides, *De Aestuariis*. Some of his seventy-six *logistorici* covered science, such as the *Tubero: De Origine Humana* on foetal formation, but we perceive only the tip of an iceberg whose hidden masses largely populate later extant works such as Vitruvius, Pliny, Macrobius Theodosius, Augustine, and Martianus Capella.

Cicero survived well, but is primarily received by scholars as a politician and orator; nonetheless, his role in rendering Greek, especially Stoic, science into Latin is crucial, and not separable from his work on other aspects of Greek philosophy (cf. *Tusc.* 2.5), to which he turned late in life, as consolation for the death of politics, and encouraged by T. Pomponius Atticus. His work *On the Republic* (of the late 50s BCE) followed Plato's lead in wedding politics to astronomy, and he produced translations of Aratos' *Phainomena* and of (part of) Plato's *Timaeus*. The geocentric spherical-earth cosmology at the close of his *Republic* elicited a commentary from Macrobius Theodosius, thus influencing medieval cosmology. His *On the Nature of the Gods*, *On Divination*, and *On Fate*, a trilogy, treat contemporary theology, especially Stoic, as well as the physics and logic of causation.

C. Iulius Caesar produced, besides the geography of the *Gallic War* (Rawson 1985: 259–63), a lost Greek work on the stars (Pliny, *Nat. Hist.* 18.212; Macrobius, *Sat.* 1.16.39), and sponsored the reconfiguration of the Roman calendar by Sōsigenēs (Rawson 1985: 109–14). He planned a public library (later created by Asinius Pollio, with Varro as first librarian: Pliny, *Nat. Hist.* 35.10, 35.26, 36.33), granted citizenship to doctors (Suetonius, *Iul.* 42.1), took an interest in nautical technology (*BG* 5.1), and may have planned a geographical survey of his empire, eventually accomplished by M. Vipsanius Agrippa. From the time of Ptolemy I, Hellenistic kings had sought to show themselves masters of the intellectual as well as political realm (perhaps harking back to the 'Seven Wise Men' of Greece), and Caesar sought to glorify Rome in the same way (cf. his remark on the playwright Menander versus P. Terentius Afer, in Suetonius, *Ter.* 5, or his praise of Cicero's works as glories of Rome, in the preface of his own work *On Analogy*: Cicero, *Brutus* 252–3; Pliny, *Nat. Hist.* 7.117).

T. Lucretius Carus undertook to Romanize the least Latin of the Greek schools, that of Epikouros (Epicurus), in his *De Rerum Natura*. Notably, his inspiration was Empedoklēs (Empedocles; 1.704–41), and his source Epicurus, and not more recent atomists, like his contemporary Philodēmos (Furley 1978: 4–5; Sedley 1998: 71–91, 166–85), or the Latin Epicureans such as C. Amafinius and Rabirius mentioned by Cicero (*Acad.* 1.5–6, *Tusc.* 1.6, 2.7–8, 4.6–7; Howe 1951; *HLL* §189.1.e). He writes frankly as an advocate or evangelist, promoting atomism as a liberating doctrine, in the era of the conflicts with L. Sergius Catilina and Sex. Pompeius, and having seen the troubles of the Marian and Sullan era—eschewing politics is rational when political activity is violent chaos. Lucretius sought to explain atomism in a memorable way, to ground all of science in it (optics, biology, etc.), and to validate it as a doctrine with a worthy tradition, and no threat to Romans (Roman and Roman 1994: 238–48). He rose to the challenge of the poverty of Latin vocabulary to express alien concepts (1.139–45), a recurrent theme in Roman science.

Pythagorean books had been publicly burned, astrologers banished as a foreign superstition—now the diligent scholar Nigidius Figulus renewed the teaching of Pythagoras (Cicero, *Timaeus* 1) and Latinized astrology. This erudite, versatile, and wide-ranging scholar (comparable to Varro, cf. Gellius 19.14.3) composed works on the winds (like Theophrastos), the nature of human beings (like Hippocrates), zoology (like Aristotle), and astrology/astronomy (like many Greeks). Though his works survived his death in exile to be used by authors as late as Augustine and Macrobius Theodosius, now only scraps remain (Swoboda 1889/1964; Della Casa 1962).

Vitruvius' work on architecture was written for Augustus, although Vitruvius' intellectual formation was entirely Republican. He was a trained engineer, pensioned by Octavian for service, whose technical handbook has literary pretensions, and seems to have been in part aimed at Roman senators and equestrians who directed building projects (Gros, Corso, and Romano 1997; Rowland and Howe 1999). His plan is in part Pythagorean, aiming at ten volumes despite his material (McEwen 2003). He begins with theoretical principles, town-planning, and surveying, then (Book 2) covers building materials, then (Books 3–4) the proportional principles of temples and columns; Book 5 treats public buildings (plus music theory), Book 6 private buildings, Book 7 non-structural aspects of buildings, Book 8 the nature of water, its natural and artificial distribution; then Book 9 covers astronomy (including sundials and water-clocks), and finally (Book 10) mechanical devices of all kinds (cranes and levers, water-wheels and pumps, pneumatic organs, catapults and other siege engines: Fleury 1993) are described. The material on siege-craft (10.13–15) closely parallels chapters in his contemporary Athēnaios Mechanikos (pp. 9.4–10.4), their common source likely being Agēsistratos (7.*pr.*14); his sources are otherwise hard to detect, although Hermogenēs of Alabanda is often suspected (*c.*200–150 BCE). Many sections of Vitruvius' work begin with an Aristotelian doxographical survey of prior work; some of the items recorded are unique (e.g. Archimēdēs' discovery of specific gravity, 9.*pr.*9–12). Likewise, he gives two explanations of lunar phases, both of the early third century BCE: Aristarchos of Samos thought moonlight was reflected sunlight, the phases being explained by geometry, whereas his contemporary Berossos of Babylon claimed the luminous lunar hemisphere is attracted by sunlight which rotates the moon (9.2). Vitruvius' cosmos is described in mechanical terms: the heavens rotate about the earth on pin-like poles beyond the stars, round which wheel-rims roll as on a lathe (*tornus*: 9.1.2); the seven planets 'wander' from west to east, one above another, 'as if on a staircase' (9.1.5). For the planets outside the sun, Vitruvius gives the most accurate ancient solar periods—Mars 683 days (four days less than the modern value), Jupiter 11 years, 313 days (two days less), and Saturn 29 years, 160 days (seven days less)—and explains their apparent retrogradations through an alleged greater attraction by solar rays at greater distances (9.1.10–13). For Mercury and Venus, Vitruvius offers a heliocentric model in which the sun's rays serve as a centre which those planets 'crown', their varying speeds being explained by their varying distance from the attractive sun (9.1.6–9).

Some authors of this period (*c*.100–40 BCE) who did not remain in fashion through ages of copyists nonetheless serve to round out the picture even through their exiguous fragments. Other Romans than Vitruvius and Varro wrote on architecture, such as Fuficius and P. Septimius (Vitr. 7.*pr*.14: the former the first Roman to have written a monograph on architecture). Egnatius, like Lucretius, wrote a *De Rerum Natura* in at least three volumes (two brief fragments in Macrobius, *Sat.* 6.5.2, 12). Pompeius Lenaeus' work of pharmacy has been mentioned; probably the biological (or paradoxographical) work of Sornatius belongs to this era as well (Pliny, *Nat Hist.* 1.*ind*.31–2, 32.68; Münzer 1927).

Work for the *Princeps*

Vitruvius then stands for the transition to works composed in some way for the *princeps*, a genre sometimes practised by Greeks (e.g. Dioklēs' medical epistle; Dikaiarchos' surveys; Xēnagoras to King Philip: Plutarch, *Aemil.* 15.9–11; or the pseudo-Aristotelian *On Kosmos* to some King Alexander), and familiar to Chinese (Lloyd 1996: 39–43). Patronage continued—for example, Aelius Gallus supported the geographer Strabōn (Syme 1995: 243, 322, 360). The patron of all patrons, however, was the *princeps*, to whom Aelius dedicated his own work on antidotes (Galen, *Antid.* 2.1, 17 [14.114–15, 203 K.]), and whose personal doctor was the pharmacist Antonius Musa, whose recipes survive in Galen (Michler 1993). Moreover, assimilation and synthesis of Greek science informed the works of Roman scientific writers, who are rarely credited with innovations, and hesitate to engage in theoretical disputes. Those three features are on display in the authors who will now primarily concern us: the philosophers Sextius and Seneca, Manilius on astrology, Mela on geography, Celsus and Scribonius in medicine, Frontinus in architecture, and Pliny the Elder in everything.

Q. Sextius renounced his political offices to pursue philosophy, including natural philosophy, under Tiberius and Caligula (Seneca, *QN* 7.32.2; von Arnim 1923). He adapted Stoicism and Pythagoreanism to a Roman outlook, for example arguing for vegetarianism not on the basis of metempsychosis, but on the basis of hygiene and ethics (avoidance of cruelty). The school did not survive its founder's demise, but its character is indicative of the way Greek science was assimilated by Romans.

L. Annaeus Seneca, a well-connected Italian born in Spain, rose to philosophical and political prominence under Claudius, and became Nero's tutor and later advisor. He studied both under Stoics and under Q. Sextius. The natural philosophy of his *Natural Questions*, like his tragedies, is fundamentally ethical; the topics covered are those of the ancient field of *meteorologika*, that is, comets, meteors, winds and other allegedly atmospheric phenomena, and even rivers, earthquakes, and volcanoes. Seneca seeks to assimilate the Stoic natural philosophy of Poseidōnios (d. 50 BCE), but shows pervasive originality in canvassing the doxography of the various questions he considers, often suggesting novel or at least compromise solutions (Inwood 2005).

Manilius composed five volumes on astrology, some under Augustus, the fourth under Tiberius; he sought to refute Lucretius by finding the operation of universal divine fate as manifested in the stars (Goold 1977). His work is not a handbook for the casting of nativities, but an explanation of determinism in the *kosmos*; he therefore opened with a cosmogony and anthropology (1.1–254), assimilating Stoic works (especially Chrysippos, d. 205 BCE). He described the heavens, fixed stars, planets, and circles, much as had Aratos (d. *c.*240 BCE); his treatment of the planets was quite brief (1.532–8, 805–8, and probably in the 4-folio lacuna at 5.709), doubtless because his sources were pre-Hipparchan, when astrology did not yet make much use of the planets (cf. Nechepso-Petosiris, *c.*150 BCE). He describes varieties of comets at greater length (1.809–926), again reflecting early astrology. Most of the work treats the powers of the zodiacal signs (when rising or occupied by sun or moon); he treats also zodiacal geography (4.585–817).

Pomponius Mela was born in a small town in southern Spain (2.6.96), and composed his geographical survey for Claudius in 43 CE (3.6.49). He assimilates and organizes the world as known to Eratosthenēs (d. *c.*195 BCE) for the purposes of Roman rule, although his depiction of the western Mediterranean is more contemporary, based partly on autopsy (and partly on someone like Artemidōros of Ephesos, *fl.* 104 BCE, or Poseidōnios). His data on northern Europe are almost unique, and may reflect some recent writer such as Philēmōn (Pliny, *Nat. Hist.* 4.95, 37.33, 37.36; Ptolemy, *Geog.* 1.11). Starting from the Pillars of Hēraklēs, he proceeds coastwise like an early Greek *periplous*, but in a direction opposite the usual—that is, he first covers the Mediterranean's African coast (rather than European), then the Palestinian coast, then around by the Black Sea and the European coast back to the Pillars, and so out around the *oikoumenē* along its Oceanic coast, northern

Europe, Asia, India, and Africa, and finally back to the Pillars (Romer 1998). Some of what he reports is very ancient indeed—he is both the best and latest witness to the actual text of a fragment of Xenophanēs (Keyser 1992).

A. Cornelius Celsus, active under Tiberius, composed an encyclopedia devoting eight volumes to medicine, seven to rhetoric, six to philosophy, five to agriculture, and some to military science (perhaps including mechanics); only the medical books survive (Schulze 2001). He covers regimen in four books, pharmacy and surgery in two each, thus covering only therapy, and omitting anatomy and etiology; his approach is clearly Empiricist, but moderate, and he cites numerous recipes from earlier pharmacists (mostly Greeks), because they work. He had read widely, and assimilates works from the Hippocratic corpus up through Asklēpiadēs of Bithynia (d. 90 BCE). More likely a wealthy scholar than a practising physician (he mentions no patron), he may nevertheless have had some medical experience; evidently he sought to update Varro.

Scribonius Largus of Sicily, active under Caligula and Claudius, and client of Iulius 'Kallistos', composed in both Greek and Latin; his only extant work is a single scroll of pharmacy (Sconocchia 1993). A practising physician with experience on gladiators, he travelled with the court to Britain in 43 CE. His manual, addressed to his patron, claims to be of practical benefit, and engages in no theory; his recipes are derived from numerous Greek and some Latin sources, both ancient (Hippocratic corpus, Hērophilos) and recent (Zopyros and Tryphōn, both of Gortyn, plus Antonius Musa and Iulius Bassus). He praises the practical efficacy of remedies employed not by professionals but *pagani*.

Sex. Iulius Frontinus, of the senatorial order and successful in politics both under Vespasian and again under Nerva and Trajan, was appointed *curator aquarum* probably in 95 CE. He wrote a work on military science (lost but probably treating both tactics and engineering), and a surviving *Strategems*, in addition to his *On the Water-system of Rome*, giving history, law, and science (Grimal 1944/2003; Peachin 2004). His methods are pragmatic and precise; he is adept at manipulating the integers and fractions of his calculations.

C. Plinius Secundus was born in northern Italy (Como), and educated at Rome under Tiberius and Caligula; a member of the equestrian order, he served as an officer in the Rhine legions during the reigns of Claudius and Nero (Keyser 1999; Murphy 2004). His literary output was initially based on his military experience, but under Nero he kept a low profile, writing on law and language, and practising law. The sister's son whom he adopted as C. Plinius Secundus, Iunior, has recorded his uncle's work habits and output (*Epist.* 3.5). Having befriended the elder son of T. Flavius Vespasianus, during their military service, Pliny's career advanced rapidly after 70 CE, culminating in his appointment as admiral of the western Roman fleet, stationed at Misenum. The old soldier died on duty, rescuing victims of, and observing, the eruption of Vesuvius in 79 CE. His lost work on Germany probably informed most of Tacitus' reports, and thus influenced the post-medieval myth of the 'noble savage' (cf. also *Nat. Hist.* 16.2–6). But the work for which he is now mostly known, his *Natural History*, is a massive, thirty-six-volume encyclopedia, dedicated to the emperor Titus, and prefixed with a one-volume preface and table of contents; its subject is Nature—life itself (*pr.*13). Pliny regarded life as *vigilia* (*pr.*18), that is, being on watch and on duty; to assist one's fellow mortals was the highest duty and a divine path (2.18, 25.2–3). This work aims to benefit Rome and her folk (the rulers of all the world that mattered), by providing secure knowledge, the sole reliable guide for ethical activity. He writes as an informed layman, and devout adherent of Stoicism, which he sees as supporting traditional and 'natural' Roman ways (cf. 27.1–3). He collects marvels of Nature to demonstrate the transcendent wisdom and power of the pervasive cosmic *pneuma* (cf. 2.207–8, etc.), and to serve as limit-cases, tracing the boundaries of knowledge. The encyclopedia represents the natural world ordered as if by a quartermaster, facts on parade, treasures in a triumph (cf. *pr.*17), in a relentlessly anthropomorphic system—for example, the one-plus-four books on humans and animals (7 and 8–11) are balanced by the five books on useful extracts (28–32), surrounding the pair of octets on plants (12–19) and their uses (20–7). Pliny sticks close to the facts, as he sees them (*pr.*17), that is, observations informed by the Stoic theory of *sympatheia* (e.g. 20.1–2). His imagery is often baroque (36.101) and even pathetic (5.54, 5.97–8, 6.1–2); he addresses the Latin-vocabulary problem not via erudite calques but by transliteration and the use of banausic diction (*pr.*13, 32). Pliny's encyclopedia survived because of its enduring popularity, exploited extensively by Gargilius, Serenus, Solinus, Capella, and Isidore.

L. Iunius Moderatus Columella of Gades, an acquaintance of Seneca, composed a systematic survey of agriculture in an epic dozen books, probably during Nero's reign, assimilating not only a long list of Greek writers, but more directly (it seems) Cato, Celsus, and Vergil (Noè 2002). He engages with predecessors, values practical experience, especially his own, and offers an almost capitalist approach to agriculture; his work was exploited by Gargilius and Palladius Aemilianus.

Some writers, obscure now, formed equally significant threads of the tapestry of Roman assimilation and synthesis in the long first century of the Roman Empire. Probably before Manilius there was Attius, whose *Praxidica* Pliny cites (1.*ind.*18, 18.200) for the doctrine that sowing is best when the moon is in masculine signs; the title refers to the Orphic exactors of justice (Pausanias 9.33.3). The agronomist Oppius is probably also Augustan; he wrote *On Woodland Trees*, which survived to be used by Macrobius Theodosius (Speranza 1971: 69–72). M. Vipsanius Agrippa, son-in-law and admiral to Augustus, completed a survey of the lands ruled by the emperor, which was posthumously engraved as a map in the Porticus Pollae; Agrippa's first wife had been the daughter of Cicero's friend Atticus; his two sons by his third wife, Iulia, were adopted by Augustus in 17 BCE; Agrippa died five years later (Grilli 1990; Nicolet 1991: 95–122). Cornelius Bocchus, probably the historian whose chronicle ended in 49 CE (*PIR2* C-1333), is cited by Pliny for minerals from

Spain (*Nat. Hist.* 16.216; 37.24, 97, and 127). And the emperor Titus himself is credited with a poem on the comet of 76 CE (Pliny, *Nat. Hist.* 2.89), and with a recipe for a plaster by the pharmacist Asklēpiadēs in Galen, *Comp. Med. sec. Locos* 10.3 (13.360 K.).

Twilight and Reconfiguration

Greek science of the second-century CE operated at a remarkable level of synthesis and comprehension (Galen and Ptolemy); Roman science of the same period is poorly represented, being mostly *agrimensores* or metrologists such as the various Hygini, as well as Balbus, Iunius Nipsus, Siculus Flaccus, and Volusius Maecianus (Campbell 2000). Such works owed little to Greek and much to Latin traditions. Likewise the Quintilii composed an agricultural manual now lost (*PIR2* Q-21, 27), and Iulius Titianus wrote a lost description (*chorographia*) of the provinces of the Roman Empire, cited by Servius, *In Aen.* 4.22, 11.651, and by Gregorius of Tours, on Aetna. Moreover, the Latin historian and geographer Tacitus similarly exploited Latin traditions, Pliny on Germany and recent Romans on Britain, to compose his geographies. The Platonist polymath Apuleius not only translated the pseudo-Aristotelian *On the Kosmos*, but also the neo-Pythagorean number theory of Nikomachos of Gerasa (*c.*120 CE); he also wrote a lost *Quaestiones Naturales* in Greek, a work on fish (*Apol.* 36), as well as *De Arboribus* and *De Medicinalibus*, a work on astronomy and *meteorologika*, and a handbook on music theory (Cassiodorus, *Inst. Div.* 2.5.10).

Synthesis more than assimilation marks the few works of Roman science to survive the long and chaotic third century: Ampelius, Censorinus, Gargilius, the *Medicinae Plinii*, Nemesianus, and Solinus. Ampelius was the tutor of the emperor Macrinus, and his epitome of the world, cosmology, geography, and all, barely survived (Arnaud-Linder 1993). Solinus digested Pliny and Mela for ready use, highlighting the marvels; around the same time the remedies recorded by Pliny were extracted in a physician's *vademecum* now anonymous, the *Medicinae Plinii* (Önnerfors 1964). Gargilius too extracted Pliny, plus Celsus, Columella, and Dioskoridēs (*c.*60 CE), to produce his medical and agricultural works (Maire 2002). Censorinus, another Platonist, among other, lost, works, composed a monograph for his patron in 238 CE on the Roman concept of the birthday, representing Varro and Suetonius (Rapisarda 1991), deploying numerology, astrology, and cosmology, much of it Greek, and most of it very archaic (some names are found only here). Nemesianus (*c.*284 CE) wrote didactic poems on hunting and fishing—of which only part of the *Cynegetica* survives, drawing on Virgil, and perhaps Grattius (*c.*10 BCE).

Early in the third century Caracalla had extended the definition of Roman citizen, already greatly widened, to include every free adult male. Romans, whether old urban citizens or newly enfranchised *pagani* and foreigners, continued to accept Roman traditions as authoritative, and presumably expected the legal, political, and cultural system to endure. Certainly the synthesis and representation of Latin science reinforces the perception that tradition increasingly privileged the wisdom of the *maiores*. When Greeks were cited, or even assimilated, the older the better.

History threw a surprise into that stream—Neoplatonism as created by Plotinos the Egyptian and Porphyry the Syrian, both working in Greek, transformed the philosophy, religion, and science of the empire. Within two generations (*c*.260–*c*.320 CE), the consensus world-view became more unified than it had been for centuries, and *daimones*—faceless nameless agents of transcendent divinity—were found everywhere. The very old Roman *numina* had returned, with a twist. Lactantius (*c*.295 CE), who composed a poem on the phoenix, and later argued that the spherical-earth theory was absurd and ill-founded (*Divine Institutes* 3.24), as well as Iulius Firmicus Maternus (*c*.345 CE), who composed an astrological handbook heavily dependent on old works such as Manilius (Monat 1992–7), stand for the transition. Moreover, both were converts to Christian monotheism, the eastern religion whose influence and power in the empire grew rapidly in the same era (the state religion by the end of the fourth century). Christians of this era, although suspicious of science that could not be forced into harmony with their cosmology, were rarely antagonistic towards science per se, and of the writers who will now primarily concern us, some were Christian.

The twin new paradigms, Christianity and Neoplatonism, were assimilated, and scientific learning was reconfigured, across the same range of topics, medicine being the best-represented among surviving works (*c*.340–*c*.480 CE). The Christian Calcidius (*c*.375 CE) translated and commented on Plato's *Timaeus* (Moreschini *et al.* 2003), from which he extracts a Neoplatonist cosmology (assimilating predecessors, e.g., Adrastos, *c*.125 CE, and Porphyry). Avienius, aristocrat and poet, translated Aratos and the geographical poem by Dionusios Periēgētēs (*c*.135 CE); his *Ora Maritima* is in the style of an archaic Greek *periplous*, and incorporates very ancient Greek sources, most over 700 years old. Remmius Favinus the metrologist is credited in some manuscripts with the extant poem *On Weights*, giving the Archimedean specific-gravity procedure (Grimaudo 1990). An anonymous innovator (*c*.370 CE) offered a plan to reform the Roman army and its technical corps; his devices, such as ox-powered paddle-boats and scythe-wheeled chariots, were probably never built (Giardina 1989). Palladius Aemilianus (*c*.425 CE) exploited the work of the Greek agronomist Vindonius Anatolios to produce a work in fourteen volumes, most of which assimilates Columella, Gargilius, and Cetius Fauentinus' third-century epitome of Vitruvius (Vera 1995).

Four Latin medical writers from this era survive *in extenso* to provide a more detailed view of medical science among late Romans. Greek medical writers continued to debate etiologies and offer remedies, and Galen's works had become standard. Yet the Christian Marcellus of Bordeaux (*c.*400) offers thirty-six chapters of remedies easy to prepare and based on traditions independent of Galen, primarily from Scribonius and the *Medicinae Plinii*, as well as more recent Latin works (Meid 1996). Similarly, Theodorus Priscianus' work is a collection of practical recipes based mainly on his own experience, plus Scribonius, Pliny, and Gargilius (Fraisse 2003). He was a student of the imperial physician Vindicianus, and probably the author of a Greek text on epilepsy (Alex. Trall. 1.559 Puschm.). Caelius Aurelianus (*c.*450 CE) translated and updated the work of the three-centuries-old pre-Galenic figure Soranos (*c.*120 CE), in two works, one on chronic and one on acute diseases (Mudry 1999; van der Eijk 1999). Vegetius, also around mid-century, compiled three technical treatises: the *Epitoma Rei Militaris* in four volumes, the *Digesta Artis Mulomedicinalis* in three, and the *De Curis Boum Epitoma* in one. The first he says is based on Cato, Celsus, and Frontinus; the hippiatrics derive from Pelagonius (*c.*375 CE) and other Latin works, and the third work exploits Columella. Pelagonius himself used Celsus and Columela, as well as the Greek Apsurtos (*c.*250 CE?).

Three Neoplatonists writing comprehensive works show the range and power of the new synthesis: Mallius Theodorus (*c.*390 CE), Macrobius Theodosius (*c.*430 CE), and Martianus Capella (perhaps *c.*430 CE). The earliest, a Christian, during a mid-life retirement from politics composed a philosophical treatise (entirely lost), which according to Claudian, *Panegyric on Theodorus* 67–112, illuminated the Greek cosmology of Kleanthēs, Chrysippos, Dēmokritos, Pythagoras, and others, all of the third century BCE or earlier, explaining their theories on elements, the motions of the stars and planets, the lunar cause of tides, and meteorology including comets. Macrobius Theodosius composed a commentary on the myth at the end of Cicero's *Republic*, Book 6, the 'Dream of Scipio', interpreting it using Neoplatonism to extrapolate selectively from the text, working primarily from Porphyry, probably via some now-lost Latin intermediary; excurses cover arithmetic, astronomy, music theory, and geography (including an apparently unique tidal theory). His *Saturnalia* is a dialogue centred around Virgil as a repository of arcane lore, with excerpts from Lucretius, Serenus Sammonicus (*c.*210 CE), and others, and includes a discussion on medicine and physiology (7.4–9). Martianus Capella imagined the *Marriage of Philology and Mercury*, a curious allegory in which Books 3–9 cover the three literary disciplines (the 'trivium') and the four mathematical arts, geometry, arithmetic, astronomy, and music theory (in that order). Capella fused Varronian encyclopedism with the Neoplatonic doctrine of salvation via mathematical knowledge. His geometry depends on Euclid, but includes geography from Pliny and Solinus; his arithmetic assimilates Nikomachos (via Apuleius?); and his music theory largely reproduces Aristeidēs (*c.* 3rd cent. CE).

The book on astronomy appears more original, including the same semi-heliocentric system found in Vitruvius (Bovey 2003).

It becomes increasingly hard to speak of Roman science after the fifth-century collapse of the Western Empire and of Rome herself, but some Latin writers saw themselves as working in the old Roman tradition, now deeply Christianized. But not absolutely—Boethius (*c.*520 CE) composed Neoplatonic works on philosophy, arithmetic, music theory (and apparently astronomy and geometry), and intended a full Varronian or even Ciceronian set. He sought to revive Roman assimilation of Greek science under Theodoric; it was he who coined *quadrivium* to refer to the Neoplatonist reception of mathematical sciences (Guillaumin 1995). The Christian Cassiodorus Senator achieved the full range of works in his astonishingly long life (b. 485, d. 585), though most is lost. His *Variae* (*c.*545) include epideictic digressions on mathematics, astronomy, music theory, surveying, and biology, intended to demonstrate Ostrogothic acceptance of Roman traditions; he made use of recent Latin writers, especially Boethius (Halporn and Vessey 2004). His *Institutes* were a pedagogic outline of a Christian education, including the *quadrivium* (2.4–7), with references to numerous Latin authors old and recent, as well as Greeks, mostly very old (Gaudentius and Basil of Caesarea are two relatively recent citations). Agnellus practised and taught in Ravenna around 580 CE, working within the Alexandrian tradition of Galenic exegesis and commentary, propounding his own clinical results within the commentaries (Palmieri 2005). The Christian Gildas, himself barely Roman, composed a geographical sketch of his native Britain (*c.*545 CE), quoted from Orosius (*Hist.* 1.2.76–7) who followed Ptolemy (*Geography* 2.1–2), with new details by Gildas on the southern lowlands (Higham 1994).

We end where we began, in a Roman province—now a 'barbarian' kingdom—with a non-native speaker of Latin: Isidore, Bishop of Seville (*c.*630 CE), who, as if Pliny had changed his Stoic for a Christian straitjacket, surveys his world of marvels and summarizes what can be known in twenty volumes (Barney *et al.* 2006). Such men, then, determined how science survived and was practised in the West until Europe rediscovered the Greeks and their manifold ways. A borderland hill-fort had led the way in assimilation, but their culture of ancestor-worship and reverence for tradition eventually mummified what was received, and little weight or honour was ever given to innovation and debate.

Further reading

The entries on the major Roman scientists in Keyser and Irby-Massie 2008 should be consulted both for content and further bibliography, some of which is reproduced in the bibliography here (see also Keyser 1999 on Pliny); overviews of Roman science are mostly lacking, but see Rawson 1985 on scholarship, Wallace-Hadrill 1988 and Gruen 1990, 1992 on

Roman reception of Greek ideas, Scarborough 1993 on Roman medicine, and Feeney 2005 for wise words on early Roman literature. Jacobs 1992 provides a framework for understanding how Greek science was received and transformed by Romans.

References

Adams, J. N. *Bilingualism and the Latin Language* (Cambridge, 2003).

Arnaud-Linder, M.-P. *Aide-mémoire (Liber memorialis)* (CUF, 1993).

Asmis, E. *Epicurus' Scientific Method* (Ithaca, NY, 1984).

Astin, A. E. *Cato the Censor* (Oxford, 1978).

Barney, S. A., Lewis, W. J., Beach, J. A., and Berghof, O. *The Etymologies of Isidore of Seville* (Cambridge, 2006).

Beard, M., North, J., and Price, S. *Religions of Rome*, 2 vols. (Cambridge, 1998).

Blomqvist, J. *The Date and Origin of the Greek Version of Hanno's Periplus* (Lund, 1979).

Bonfante, L. and Bonfante, G. *The Etruscan Language*, 2nd edn. (Manchester, 2002).

Boscherini, S. *Lingua e scienza greca nel de Agri Cultura di Catone* (Rome, 1970).

Bovey, M. *Disciplinae cyclicae: l'organisation du savoir dans l'oeuvre de Martianus Capella* (Trieste, 2003).

Boyancé, P. 'Fulvius Nobilior et le dieu ineffable', *Revue de Philologie* 3/29 (1955), 172–92.

Broggiato, M. (ed.), *Cratete di Mallo: i frammenti* (La Spezia, 2001).

Burstein, S. M. *The Babyloniaca of Berossus* (Malibu, Calif., 1978).

Campbell, B. *The Writings of the Roman Land Surveyors* (London, 2000).

Camporeale, G. 'Ai primordi di Roma: Ancora sull' apporto degli Etruschi', in L. Aigner-Foresti, *Die Integration der Etrusker* (Vienna, 1998), 149–64.

Cardauns, B. *Marcus Terentius Varro* (Heidelberg, 2001).

Cornell, T. *Beginnings of Rome* (Routledge, 1995).

Cramer, F. H. 'Expulsion of Astrologers from Ancient Rome', *Classica et Medievalia* 12 (1951), 9–50.

Della Casa, A. *Nigidio Figulo* (Rome, 1962).

Depuydt, L. 'The Demotic Mathematical Astronomical Papyrus Carlsberg 9 Reinterpreted', in *W. Clarysse et al.* (eds.), *Egyptian Religion: The Last Thousand Years* (Leuven 1998), 1277–97.

Evans, J. S. *The History and Practice of Ancient Astronomy* (Oxford, 1998).

Feeney, D. 'The Beginnings of Literature in Latin', *Journal of Roman Studies*, 95 (2005), 226–40.

Fleury, P. *La Méchanique di Vitruve* (Caen 1993).

Fraisse, A. 'Médecine rationelle et irrationelle dans le livre I des *Euporista* de Théodore Priscien', in Nicoletta Palmieri (ed.), *Rationnel et irrationnel dans la médecine ancienne et médiévale* (Saint-Étienne 2003), 183–92.

Furley, D. J. 'Lucretius the Epicurean: On the History of Man', in Olof Gigon (ed.), *Lucrèce: huit exposés, suivis de discussions = Entretiens sur l'Antiquité Classique* 24 (Geneva 1978), 1–27.

Giardina, A. *Le cose della guerra: De rebus bellicis* (Milan, 1989).

Goold, G. P. *Manilius Astronomica* (LCL, Cambridge, Mass., 1977).

Grant, R. M. *Dieting for an Emperor* (Leiden, 1997).

Grilli, A. 'La geografia di Agrippa', in A. Ceresa Gastaldo and M. Grant (eds.), *Bimillenario di Agrippa* (Genova, 1990).

GRIMAL, P. *Les Aqueducs de la ville de Rome* (CUF, 1944; repr. 2003).
GRIMAUDO, S. 'Metrologia e poesia nel tardoantico: struttura e cronologia del *Carmen de ponderibus et mensuris*', *Pan*, 10 (1990), 87–110.
GROS, P., CORSO, A. and ROMANO, E. *Vitruvio, De Architectura* (Turin, 1997).
GRUEN, E. *Studies in Greek Culture and Roman Policy* (Brill, 1990).
—— *Culture and National Identity in Republican Rome* (Ithaca, NY, 1992).
—— 'The Polis in the Hellenistic World', in *Nomodeiktes: Greek Studies in Honor of Martin Ostwald* (Ann Arbor, Mich., 1993), 339–54.
GUILLAUMIN, J.-Y. *Institution arithmétique: Boèce* (CUF, 1995).
HALPORN J. W. and VESSEY, M. *Cassiodorus: Institutions of Divine and Secular Learning* (Liverpool, 2004).
HARRISON, S. J. *Apuleius: A Latin Sophist* (Oxford, 2000).
HIGHAM, N. J. *The English Conquest* (Manchester, 1994).
HOFFMANN, F. *Ägypten: Kultur und Lebenswelt in griechisch-römischer Zeit; Eine Darstellung nach den demotischen Quellen* (Berlin, 2000), 103–37, 271–7.
HORSTER, M. and REITZ, CH. (eds.), *Antike Fachschriftsteller* (Wiesbaden, 2003).
HOWE, H. M. 'Amafinius, Lucretius, and Cicero', *American Journal of Philology*, 72 (1951), 57–62.
INWOOD, B. *Reading Seneca* (Oxford 2005).
JACOBS, J. *Systems of Survival: A Dialogue on the Moral Foundations of Commerce and Politics* (New York, 1992).
JOHNSON, S. E. 'The Present State of Sabazius Research', *ANRW* II.17.3 (1984), 1583–1613.
KASTER, R. A. (ed.), *C. Suetonius Tranquillus: De Grammaticis et Rhetoribus* (Oxford, 1995).
KEYSER, P. T. 'The Origin of the Latin Numerals, 1 to 1000', *American Journal of Archaeology*, 92 (1988), 529–46.
—— 'Xenophanes' Sun on Trojan Ida', *Mnemosyne*, 45 (1992), 299–311.
—— 'C. Plinius Secundus', *Dictionary of Literary Biography*, vol. 211, *Ancient Roman Writers*, ed. W. W. Briggs (Bruccoli Clark Layman, 1999), 235–42.
—— and IRBY-MASSIE, G. L. *Encyclopedia of Ancient Natural Scientists* (London, 2008).
—— —— 'Science, Medicine and Technology', in Glenn R. Bugh (ed.), *The Cambridge Companion to the Hellenistic World* (Cambridge, 2006), 241–64.
LANE, E. N. 'Sabazius and the Jews in Valerius Maximus: A Re-Examination', *Journal of Roman Studies*, 69 (1979), 35–8.
LLOYD, G. E. R. *Adversaries and Authorities* (Cambridge, 1996).
LONG, A. A. and SEDLEY, D. *The Hellenistic Philosophers*, 2 vols. (Cambridge, 1987).
MA, J. *Antiochos III and the Cities of Western Asia Minor* (Oxford, 1999).
MAIRE, B. *Les Remèdes tirés des légumes et des fruits: Gargilius Martialis* (CUF, 2002).
MCEWEN, I. K. *Vitruvius: Writing the Body of Architecture* (Cambridge, Mass., 2003).
MEID, W. *Heilpflanzen und Heilsprüche* (Innsbruck, 1996).
MELE, A. 'Il pitagorismo e le popolazioni anelleniche d'Italia', *Annali dell' Istituto universitario Orientale di Napoli. Seminario di studi del mondo classico. Sezione di archeologia e storia antica*, 3 (1981), 61–96.
MICHLER, M. 'Principis medicus: Antonius Musa', *ANRW* II.37.1 (1993), 757–85.
MOMIGLIANO, A. 'The Origins of Rome', *The Cambridge Ancient History*, vol. 7/2, 2nd edn. (Cambridge, 1989), 52–112.
MONAT, P. (ed.), *Firmicus Maternus: Mathesis*, 3 vols. (CUF, 1992, 1994, 1997).
MOREL, J.-P. 'The Transformation of Italy, 300–133 B.C.: The Evidence of Archaeology', *The Cambridge Ancient History*, vol. 8, 2nd edn. (Cambridge, 1989), 477–516.

Moreschini, C. *et al.*, *Calcidio: Commentario al Timeo di Platone* (Milan, 2003).
Mudry, Ph. (ed.), *Traité des Maladies aiguës et des Maladies chroniques de Caelius Aurelianus* (Nantes, 1999).
Münzer, Fr. 'Sornatius', *RE* 3A.1 (1927), 1137–8.
Murphy, T. *Pliny the Elder's Natural History* (Oxford, 2004).
Netz, R. 'The First Jewish Scientist?', *Scripta Classica Israelica*, 17 (1998), 27–33.
Nicolet, C. *Space, Geography, and Politics in the Early Roman Empire* (Ann Arbor, Mich., 1991).
Noè, E. *Il progetto di Columella* (Como, 2002).
North, J. A. 'Religious Toleration in Republican Rome', *Proc.Cambr.Philol.Soc.* 25 (1979), 85–103.
Nutton, V. *Ancient Medicine* (London, 2004).
Önnerfors, A. *Plinii Secundi Iunioris qui feruntur De medicina libri tres* (Berlin, 1964) = *CML* 3.
Pailler, J.-M. 'Caton et les bacchanales', *Proceedings of the British School at Rome* 54 (1986), 29–39.
Palmieri, N. *Agnellus de Ravenne. Lectures galéniques: le 'De pulsibus ad tirones'* (Saint-Étienne, 2005).
Parkinson, R. B. *The Tale of Sinuhe* (Oxford, 1997).
Pasquazi, A. 'Sopra alcuni nomi di piante nel "De Agri Cultura" di Catone', *Giornale Italiano di Filologia* 41 (1989), 29–37.
Peachin, M. *Frontinus and the curae of the curator aquarum* (Heidelberg, 2004).
Ramin, J. *Le Périple d'Hannon/The Periplus of Hanno* (Oxford, 1976).
Rapisarda, C. A. *De die natali ad Q. Caerellium* (Bologna, 1991).
Rawson, E. *Intellectual Life in the Late Roman Republic* (London, 1985).
Richardson, L. jr., *New Topographical Dictionary of Ancient Rome* (Baltimore, 1992).
Richter, W. Review of Boscherini 1970, in *Gnomon*, 45 (1973), 757–62.
Robert, L. 'Notes d'épigraphie hellénistique. XLI', *Bulletin de Correspondence Hellénique* 59 (1935), 421–5 (library at Kos, *c.*200–180 bce).
Roman, D. and Roman, Y. *Rome, l'identité romaine et la culture hellenistique* (Paris, 1994).
Romer, F. E. *Pomponius Mela's Description of the World* (Ann Arbor, Mich., 1998).
Rowland, I. and Howe, T. N. *Vitruvius, Ten Books on Architecture* (Cambridge, 1999).
Scarborough, J. 'Roman Medicine to Galen', *ANRW* II.37.1 (1993), 3–48.
Schilling, R. *La Religion romaine de Venus*, 2nd edn. (Paris, 1982).
Schulze, C. *Celsus* (Hildesheim, 2001).
Sconocchia, S. 'L'opera di Scribonio Largo e la letteratura medica del 1 sec. D.C', in *ANRW* II.37.1 (1993), 843–922.
Sedley, D. *Lucretius and the Transformation of Greek Wisdom* (Cambridge, 1998).
Smallwood, E. M. *The Jews Under Roman Rule*, 2nd edn. (Leiden, 1981).
Speranza, F. *Scriptorum Romanorum De Re Rustica Reliquiae* (Messina, 1971).
Steinby, E. M. (ed.), *Lexicon Topographicum Urbis Romae*, 6 vols. (Rome, 1993–2000; vol. 1, 1996).
Swoboda, A. *P. Nigidii Figuli operum reliquiae* (Vienna and Prague 1889; repr. Amsterdam, 1964).
Syme, R. *Anatolica: Studies in Strabo* (Oxford, 1995).
Torelli, M. 'Archaic Rome Between Latium and Etruria', *The Cambridge Ancient History*, vol. 7/2, 2nd edn. (Cambridge, 1989), 30–51.
van der Eijk, Ph. (ed.), *Ancient Histories of Medicine* (Leiden, 1999), 397–452.

Vera, D. 'Dalla "villa perfecta" alla villa di Palladio', *Athenaeum*, 83 (1995), 189–211, 331–56.
Veyne, P. *Le Pain et le cirque* (Paris, 1976).
von Arnim, H. 'Sextius', in *RE* 2A.2 (1923), 2040–1.
Wallace-Hadrill, A. Review Article: 'Greek Knowledge, Roman Power', *Classical Philology*, 83 (1988), 224–33.
Wiseman, T. P. 'Roman Legend and Oral Tradition', *Journal of Roman Studies*, 79 (1989), 129–37.
Zhmud, L. *The Origin of the History of Science in Classical Antiquity. Peripatoi*, 19 (Berlin and New York, 2006).

CHAPTER 55

TIME AND CALENDAR

DENIS FEENEY

THE earliest documentable traces of a recognizably Roman culture already bear the signs of a society that is deeply invested in the semiotics and regulation of time. The Romans' work on time remains one of the most distinctive features of their civilization throughout its duration, and its influence lives on palpably today, in the form of the reformed Julian calendar which all the readers of this book inhabit. The centre of the city was from an early period the venue for marking and commemorating both recurrent and elapsed past time, and the festival calendar was a crucial part of the city's religious and political life. As the power of Rome spread, the state needed to interact with the very different time systems of other states. The growth of a historiographical tradition within the city enforced the codification of past Roman time and its correlation with other historical time schemes, while the transformation of the city from a Republic to an autocracy entailed the complete transformation of time's regulation and presentation. At any period of Roman history one enters, the organization of time will be found to be integral to the way the Romans represented to themselves their religion, their past, and their identity as a culture.

The Romans themselves believed that their calendar was devised by their second king, Numa Pompilius, whose traditional years of rule are 715–673 BCE. These dates are certainly far too early for the developed calendar we know from the historical period, but most scholars agree that the pre-Julian calendar is a document with roots in the time of the kings: the calendar preserves a role for the 'king' (*rex*) on 24 March and 24 May, while the major festivals do not include the crucial Republican cult of Jupiter Optimus Maximus, which must, on this hypothesis, have been introduced after the establishment of the primary festivals during the monarchy (Cornell 1995: 104–5). There are clear indications that the calendar was originally lunar, like the Muslim calendar, with each month notionally corresponding to the period between one new moon and the next. There is evidence for this view in the elaborate ancient customs for announcing the key days of the month, preserved in Varro (*De Lingua Latina* 6.27) and Macrobius (*Saturnalia* 1.15.9–13). According to these sources, on the first day of each month, the Kalends, the priests announced on the Capitoline Hill when the Nones would come, either on the fifth or the seventh day, while on the Ides a sheep was sacrificed to Jupiter on the Capitoline by Jupiter's priest, the *Flamen Dialis.* As pointed out by Michels (1967: 21), these ceremonies make a lot of sense in a lunar calendar, with the Kalends as 'the day after the evening on which the crescent had been first sighted', the Nones as 'the day when the moon was at the first quarter', varying in its distance from the Kalends depending on 'how soon after the actual conjunction the crescent moon became visible', and the Ides as 'the day of the full moon'. Despite these origins, however, the Republican calendar as we know it is clearly not lunar, since the months have fixed lengths, and the overall scheme actually aims at keeping some kind of track of the *solar* year, by intercalating in February every other year in order to average out a 365-day year over a four-year period. Even this fairly rough approximation of the original designer was not realized in practice, especially during periods of military crisis and political chaos, when intercalation was not regularly performed (Blackburn and Holford-Strevens 1999: 670).

It was actually of no practical consequence that the notionally lunisolar Republican calendar was neither really lunar nor solar. In use, the calendar was a device for regulating ritual and civil affairs so that Roman citizens could organize their religious, political, legal, and business activities. The fact that the calendar did not necessarily track the natural year in more than a rough and ready fashion did not make it unfit for these purposes, any more than it detracted from the calendar's symbolic power as a religious instrument (North 1989: 602–3) or from its immense social significance as a device used by kings, aristocrats, and priests to stage the community's identity as a civic unit (Laurence and Smith 1995–6: 141–2). Our modern assumptions about what calendars are for are profoundly conditioned by our upbringing within a Julian calendar. As a result of this familiarity with Caesar's revolutionary calendar we take it for granted that a calendar is there precisely to *measure time*, to create an ideal synthesis of natural and socially or humanly organized time and in the process to capture a 'time' which is out there, waiting to be measured. In virtually all societies throughout human history, however, this is not what calendars have been for, since time is not something waiting to be measured, but the product of the operation of measurement. The important study of time and calendar in ancient Judaism by Stern (2003: 59–60) makes the issues clear: 'The calendar should not be perceived, necessarily, as a time-measuring scheme. Its primary purpose, in any society, is to facilitate the co-ordination of events and activities, and to measure the duration of activities and processes... for instance, to determine the dates of festivals, establish the length of contracts and agreements, etc. The calendar is fully purposeful without any underlying notion of the time-dimension.' The fact that all calendars operate in conjunction with either the sun or the moon or both likewise predisposes us to feel that they are attempting to measure time, on the post-Julian assumption that the relationship between the movements of earth and sun somehow *is* what time is. Yet this is not the case, as Stern again makes clear: 'The reason why the moon and sun are employed in the construction of calendars is that their courses are universally knowable, and reasonably regular and predictable... The courses of the moon and sun do not have, however, intrinsic time-measuring properties.'

When observing ancient societies it is natural for a modern person to feel frustration that they did not have more 'accurate' or 'useful' calendars, yet it is the result ultimately of a post-Caesarian frame of mind to assume that what counts in a calendar is 'accuracy' and that what calendars are for is to be 'useful' in a sense that corresponds to a modern sense of utility. One need only look at the situation in Athens to see that a sophisticated imperial power could work quite happily with two different and unreconcilable calendars in operation (Dunn 1988): the archon's calendar of twelve lunar months regulated the festival cycle, while much civil life was controlled by the council's prytany calendar, which divided the year into ten units, one for each presidency of the council held by each of the ten tribes.

The Republican calendar, then, despite its lack of precise fit with natural patterns, served the needs of the Roman state for some five centuries. It laid down the cycles of recurring rituals, with all of their symbolic significance for the community, and it came to mark the distinctive characters of days for legal and political purposes, signifying when it was possible to conduct public business such as convening assemblies or holding law-courts: from this origin, supposedly, came the calendar's title, *fasti*, denoting the *dies fasti*, the days on which the presiding magistrate could legitimately speak (*fari*). Quite when the calendar in this form was made public as a written document is a controversial topic. It is possible that at first the publicly available calendar listed only the festivals together with the Kalends, Nones, and Ides, so that everyone had to rely on oral pronouncements from the priests as to the legal character of the days in the coming month; a properly regular pattern will have only been established in written form in public as late as the end of the fourth century BCE, when Cn. Flavius is said to have displayed written versions of the calendar in the Forum during his term as aedile in 304 BCE (Michels 1967: 106–18; Rüpke 1995*a*: 245–74; Oakley 2005: 610–13).

An originally oral scheme of public announcements would fit with the evidence we discussed above for the priests' announcement of the key days of the month, Nones and Ides. It would also fit well with other important ceremonies of public announcement of time which we can reconstruct from the archaic and mid-Republican Roman state, where crucial phases of the city's time were announced by the city's officers in symbolically organized space at the heart of the city's civic area, the Forum. The Comitium, at the north-west end of the Roman Forum, mediated between the Senate-house and the open ground of the Forum, providing a space for the assemblies to meet and vote: it was aligned north–south and east–west so as to provide lines of sight to mark the passage of the sun (Coarelli 1992: 1.140). It was here that the consul's functionary took his stand to call out the hours that marked the beginning, middle, and end of the day for the purposes of law and business: he called noon when from the Senate-house he saw the sun between the Rostra and the Graecostasis, and the last hour when the sun sloped from the Maenian Column to the Prison (Pliny, *Natural History* 7.212; Coarelli 1992: 2.22–7; Laurence and Smith 1995–6: 140). As attractively suggested by Gratwick (1979: 319), 'if he had a relay of deputies in hailing-distance of one another, they could take up his cry, or blow horns... to proclaim "Roman standard time" to a wider area than that of the forum'.

In 263 BCE the Comitium was the location chosen by M.' Valerius Messalla for the sundial he had looted from Catania in Sicily, which he placed on a column near the Rostra (Gratwick 1979: 319–20). It may well not have been the first sundial set up in Rome, for there are accounts of earlier ones by the temple of Quirinus, or on the Capitoline hill, or else by the temple of Diana on the Aventine (Censorinus, *On the Birthday* 23.6). But Valerius' was certainly the first in the Forum, and it remained in use for a century. The sundial was moved just over four degrees of latitude north from its original location halfway down the east coast of Sicily. This means that it would still have marked noon precisely and the hours around noon pretty accurately (a midsummer hour at Rome is less than two-and-a-half minutes longer than at Catania), but it would no longer have been able properly to mark the equinox and the solstices. Considering the divergence between the calendar and the seasons with which the Romans normally lived anyhow, it is not surprising that no one should have been concerned at the failure of the sundial to correspond with the seasons, and its only job in its new home at Rome will have been to mark the hours. It is striking that the use of sundials in Rome generated a normal Latin use of the Greek loan-word *hora*, 'hour', in the sense commonly used in modern English ('he was here an hour ago', etc.), whereas in Greek *hora* continued to mean 'season' and did not develop this extended use (Gratwick 1979: 320–1). The mid-Republican city of Rome was evidently a place where the organization of days and the demarcation of time within the day had a pervasive impact on the citizen's life.

This symbol-laden north-west corner of the Forum was the spot chosen for a shrine to Concord by the same Cn. Flavius who had first made the *fasti* public. Fifty metres from the Comitium, at the bottom of the Capitoline hill, the new shrine displayed another striking measurement of Roman time. Flavius had made the recurrent annual time of the city available to the people in written form when he published the *fasti*, and now he established a mark in the onward movement of the city's time, counting down from a crucial benchmark in the past. Flavius fixed the time of his dedication with an inscription declaring that the shrine had been dedicated in the 204th year *post Capitolinam aedem dedicatam*, 'the 204th year after the dedication of the Capitoline temple [of Jupiter]' (Pliny, *Natural History* 33.19). Flavius' method of dating attests to the powerful temporal significance of the temple of Jupiter, which was the centre of a complex time machine on the Capitoline hill (Purcell 2003: 26–32; Hölkeskamp 2004: 139–42, 144–6). The temple of Jupiter was persistently associated with the expulsion of the last king and the foundation of the Republic, and is thus coextensive in time with the Republic itself, standing as a visible embodiment of the duration and durability of the Republic. Each year the chief magistrates of the Republic, the consuls, sacrificed to Jupiter at the beginning of their term of office, and each year they drove a nail into the temple's doorposts on the god's feast day, the Ides of September. The consuls gave their name to the year, so that the time of the Republic's past was marked by ranks of paired names. This catalogue of names was given the same title of *fasti* as the annual calendar, with the result that the Romans' developed calendrical system, making it possible to fix both a day and a year in time, comprises two items both labelled *fasti* (Mommsen 1859: 200–1; Hanell 1946: 69). Near to the temple of Jupiter, on another peak of the Capitoline hill, stood the temple of Juno Moneta, 'Remembrancer'. Here were stored lists of magistrates on linen rolls together with standard weights and measures, and here the Republic's coins were minted: Juno Moneta, then, 'is the goddess who acts as guarantor both of historical memory and of standards of measurement and coinage, and who also guards against falsifications of either' (Meadows and Williams 2001: 48).

This entire Republican system—communal festival calendar, paired *fasti*, eponymous annual magistrates—was completely remade by Caesar's calendrical reform and by the revolutions in Roman time set in motion by his adopted son, Augustus. Before we look at the transformations entailed in the transition from Republican to Imperial time, we need to consider the other frameworks of time which the Romans had to engage with in the course of their city's expansion from being a mid-Italian city to the ruler of a Mediterranean empire.

From the very beginning the Roman state will have been accustomed to dealing with the variety of local time systems endemic in the ancient world. Each city had its own calendar, as it had its own weights and measures, currency, and religion; each city also had its own way of recording past time, often based, like the Roman system, on the Greek practice of identifying a given year with the name of a magistrate. People in the ancient world no more thought of using one calendar or time system than they thought of using one currency. Our own familiarity with the universally used Christian-based era of BC/AD or BCE/CE makes it extremely difficult to imagine what it was like to manoeuvre around past time when it involved—as for the Romans it inevitably and increasingly did—the past time of more than one society. Without a universally accepted dating scheme, the societies of the ancient world had to chart past time by a complex system of correlation, lining up significant events in the distinct time-columns of different cities, each of which had its own calendar, dating system, and eras. The historians of Greece had perfected a Panhellenic framework of cross-reference by the time the Romans came onto the stage of Mediterranean history. For Rome to become a world empire it was essential that the Romans become part of the time schemes of the Greeks, and the work that went on to make this happen was collaborative work, conducted by both Romans and Greeks. The project of synchronization was a technical challenge of a high order for them, and it provides us with a demanding test case in the history of Roman Hellenization, as the Romans and Greeks made sense of the contours of the Roman past and present through media that had been devised for Greek cities and empires.

There was a great deal at stake in every stage of this synchronizing process (Feeney 2007: 7–67). Fundamentally, any 'date' is a correlation between two or more events, for there is no such thing as an absolute date, however much it may feel to inhabitants of the BCE/CE grid as if '2010' is somehow an absolute. For the most part, we simply cannot help thinking of ancient writers as working with dates, which to us are numbers. But they are not connecting numbers, they are connecting significant events and people. In so doing they are not placing events within a pre-existing time frame, they are constructing a time frame within which the events have meaning (Wilcox 1987). The Romans' time horizons are not plotted out with numbered milestones in a series but dotted with clusters of people in significant relationships with each other through memorable events. In order to fix a point in time which would hold good outside one individual city, the Romans and Greeks had to decide at any given moment which people and events were to be correlated, and from which 'columns' of time. It was highly significant, for example, that Cicero's friend Atticus should organize his book of years (*Liber Annalis*) around Roman consuls and Athenian archons, with Athens and Rome becoming counterparts in the construction of a shared Greek and Roman past. This perspective, which may also be glimpsed in the contemporary chronological works of Cornelius Nepos and Varro, reveals the progress that Romans had made in putting themselves on the *oecumene*'s map of time, making themselves partners in culture as well as in chronology.

The example of the date for the foundation of the city shows how much could depend on the apparently neutral question of where an event is to be plotted in time (Feeney 2007: 86–100). At first, the Greeks were content to say that Rome had been founded in the immediate aftermath of the Trojan War, one or two generations after the fall of Troy. It was almost certainly the Greek historian Timaeus of Tauromenium who first brought the foundation out of this mythical time and closer to the beginnings of historical time, in what we call 814/13 BCE. Crucially, he also put the foundation of Carthage, the other great non-Greek power of the

Western Mediterranean, in this same year, so that his synchronism symbolically aligns the two future adversaries with each other at the same starting-point 550 years before the outbreak of their first war in 264 BCE. Yet it was not until two generations later, towards the end of the war with Hannibal, that someone placed the foundation of Rome in the zone of time that later became canonical, when Fabius Pictor, almost certainly following the Greek historian Diocles of Peparethus, said that Rome had been founded in the first year of the eighth Olympiad (what we call 748/7 BCE). Since the first Olympiad (776 BCE) had only recently been established by Eratosthenes as some kind of demarcation line between the 'historical' and the non-historical, Fabius (and Diocles?) are now going one step further than Timaeus and claiming that Rome's beginnings belong within the grid of Panhellenic time.

For the Greek-writing Roman senator Fabius, this is an important part of his objective of showing that Rome is not a barbarian outsider but an equal participant in the Greek cultural world of Italy, Sicily, and Greece 'proper'. Such a move would be a reaction against the snobbery displayed by, for example, the third-century BCE Alexandrian scholar Eratosthenes, whose *Chronographiae* included no date for the foundation of Rome. According to the kind of approach one can detect in Eratosthenes and his follower in the next century, Apollodorus, Rome only becomes implicated in significant chronology when it is involved in the time schemes of mainland Greece, which only happens when Greek and Roman events start interpenetrating at the moment of the Greek king Pyrrhus' invasion of Italy in 280 BCE. 'Barbarian' peoples like the Samnites and the Opici never get to have their origins dignified with a mark in Hellenic time, so that they remain stuck in what Fabian (1983), in a study of anthropologists' constructions of time, calls an 'allochrony', an 'other-time', a temporal space that is qualitatively unlike 'ours', in being static, early, undeveloped. Fabius Pictor, then, would be reacting against a Greek view which tried to keep representing the Roman past as isolated and unintegrated, not involved with Greece's past, and not participating in the movement of progressive historical time.

The period of the late Republic and early Principate sees a number of universal histories being produced, impelled by the Romans' virtually complete dominance of the Mediterranean and its hinterlands (Feeney 2007: 65–7). Such histories tend inevitably to plot the rise of the Roman hegemony against the backdrop of a succession of former empires, which have passed the inheritance of empire on from one to another in a pattern which modern scholars often refer to as the *translatio imperii*. This succession of empire is an important way of apprehending patterns in past history, with Rome taking over dominion from Alexander's successors just as Alexander had taken over dominion from Persia. Crucially, this way of thinking about past time has important implications for the future, since contemplating the eventual collapse of all past hegemonies is liable to lead to imagining the future collapse of one's own. A well-read Roman general, Scipio

Africanus Minor, could weep and quote Homer as he watched Carthage burning to the ground in 146 BCE: 'A day will come when holy Troy will be destroyed, and Priam, and his people' (*Iliad* 4.164–5 = 6.448–9). As he explained to the patiently enquiring Polybius, standing beside him, he was struck by the mutability of fortune, reflecting that some time a similar fate would overtake Rome (Polybius 38.21–2).

Having sketched the implications of Rome's rise to world power in terms of the rewriting of the *oecumene*'s time charts by the period of the early Principate, we may return to the question of what effect the new institutions of the Principate had on the Roman conceptualizing and representing of time. The key moment here is clearly 1 January, 45 BCE, when Julius Caesar's reform of the Republican calendar took effect—though 'reform' is a misleading word for what he did, since 'Caesar did not reform the Roman calendar, but abandoned it and instituted the solar calendar of 365¼ days which was stable and agreed with the seasons' (Bickerman 1980: 47). Only after this date was it for the first time feasible in the Mediterranean world to have the civil and natural years in harmony under the same standard of representation. Caesar's initiative here was part of a large-scale process of systematizing and personal control in many departments of Roman life, by which his name and presence were made indispensably central. Plutarch preserves a splendid joke by Cicero which brings out the realization of the power of both the calendar and its author. When someone remarked that the constellation of the Lyre would be rising the next day, Cicero said 'Yes, by decree' (Plutarch, *Caesar* 59.3). Here the power of Caesar is seen as controlling the celestial movements themselves, and since the Lyre rises on the fifth day of January according to Caesar (Ovid, *Fasti* 1.315–16), Cicero was making his epochal observation when the new calendar was not yet four days old. Contemporaries immediately saw the point that the new calendar made it possible for precise dates to be assigned to natural processes such as seasons, equinoxes, solstices, and solar passage from constellation to constellation, processes which hitherto could not be plotted onto any civil calendar and could only be described in meteorological terms, such as the rising and setting of particular stars. It is also clear that the new calendar enforced a deepened apprehension of the already powerful Roman cult of the anniversary: the birthday in particular becomes a newly compelling focus of interest, with the new form of the birthday poem coming into vogue at just this time (Feeney 2007: 156–66).

The personal power of the dictator received formal attention in the very appearance of the *fasti*, since public festivals (*feriae publicae*) were added to commemorate half-a-dozen of Caesar's victories. The Republican *fasti* had been a beautifully clean and austere document, one that embodied the idealized corporatism of the Republic. The name of no human being appears on our only surviving exemplar of the Republican *fasti*, the Fasti Antiates Maiores, and they contain only two references to historical events, ones absolutely crucial to the city's existence: the foundation of the city on 21 April, and its near destruction by the Gauls with the battle of the Allia on 18 July. Caesar's innovations heralded an avalanche of new imperial commemorations under Augustus, whose name and deeds, together with those of his family, are spread all over the numerous *fasti* that survive from the early Principate. The revolutionary Julian calendar, with its new use in constructing the Principate's part in Roman practice, played a profoundly important role in the integration of the regime into the changing religious and ideological patterns of post-Republican life. In adding all these meanings to the dense semiotic displays of the Roman year, the new *fasti* progressively redefined the meaning of what living as a Roman now meant, capitalizing on the *fasti*'s age-old function as a vehicle for representing Roman ideology and identity (Beard 1987). The period of Augustus' rule was when the greatest part of this work on the *fasti* was done; Rüpke (1995*a*: 416) well points out that much of the impetus for addition and elaboration died away as the regime consolidated itself and the reign of Augustus became itself a foundational period in its own right. By the time of Claudius the revolutionary momentum was more or less played out, even though the calendars clearly continued in use. All of our surviving monumental inscribed Imperial *fasti* come from the reigns of Augustus and Tiberius, although additions are occasionally registered on them up to Claudius' reign.

Augustus reworked not only the calendrical *fasti* but also the consular *fasti*, making the list of magistrates of the Republic into a kind of 'prequel' to his own and his family's quasi-regal power. The past time of Rome is commemorated in Augustus' so-called 'Capitoline Fasti', named from their present site in the Capitoline museum; originally they were associated with the temple of his father at the eastern end of the Forum. The monument exhibits the parade of annually elected magistrates—usually consuls, or else *tribuni militum* during the years in the early Republic when they were the eponymous magistrates. Starting in the year 23 BCE, however, a major change may be seen, as Augustus' assumption of *tribunicia potestas* is commemorated. By the time the monument is marking the year 1 CE we see a new formula firmly in place. Each year leads off with Augustus' name and the year of his tenure of *tribunicia potestas*, and only after this line of information are the two consuls of the year inscribed. In 5 CE and subsequent years his name is joined by that of a colleague in *tribunicia potestas*, his designated heir Tiberius, with the consuls likewise tucked in underneath. The effect is bizarre, following on from the consuls of the Republic. Every year there appears the same name, with a power that is not consular, and not Republican; this name is accompanied by a sequentially numbered office that has a dating power independent of the consuls' eponymity, so that the *fasti* of the Roman people start to look like a king-list. The consuls continue to give their name to the year for dating purposes until 537 CE, but the measurement of Roman time has been changed for ever by the addition of a new and quasi-monarchical way of counting off the years of the emperor's tenure of power.

The new regime likewise enforces a change in historiographical ways of recording time, for the traditional Roman mode of history-writing cannot survive unscathed under the new dispensation. The distinctive Roman form of history since Fabius Pictor had been 'annalistic', organized around the Republican format of the successive pairs of annually elected consuls, and giving a year-by-year account of the life of the city and its empire. Ideally, the subject-matter and the format are mutually determining, 'due to the structure of the state', which is based precisely on 'annually elected magistrates who actually ran the state' (Verbrugghe 1989: 222). The consuls not only provide a backbone for the city's dating system together with an organizing principle for the events of a given year; they also generate the action which is the material for the historian. We are not dealing with a mere dating system, but with a way of organizing and apprehending events which is inextricably embedded in the ideology of the society: 'the annalistic tradition . . . spoke for the endurance of an aristocratic ideal that was the essence of the Republic' (Frier 1999: 205). Accordingly, the period before the foundation of the Republic was marked as somehow falling out of 'proper' Roman time, since the kings' reigns were not susceptible to the normative rhythms of the city. This is why Livy groups all of Roman experience before the expulsion of the kings into one self-contained introductory book, after which the norms of Roman politics, narrative, and time all begin from the same first tick of the Republican clock at the beginning of Book 2 (*annuos magistratos*, 'annual magistrates', 2.1.1). The work of Tacitus, especially in the *Annals*, shows how radically this inherited historiographical mode has been deformed by the new autocracy (Ginsburg 1981). Tacitus systematically reduces the consuls' role in the narrative from that of actors to ciphers, mirroring their relegation in public life from chief executive officers to honorific place-holders. Instead of leading off the year in the nominative and being projected into actually doing something, as regularly in Livy, Tacitus' consuls are cited in the ablative absolute construction as a mere date.

The time systems of the new monarchy were, then, extremely powerful and pervasive. But it is indicative of the Romans' characteristic preferences and also of ancient conditions of life that the reach of the new calendar should not be universal. First of all, the new calendar by no means supplanted the traditional *parapegmata*, books or else inscribed stones with a moveable peg, which made it possible to track cycles which were not in the calendar. Since the solar year was so successfully measured by Caesar's calendar, Italian parapegmata concentrated on other rhythms—local nundinal cycles, the 29- or 30-day lunar cycle, and eventually the cycle of the seven-day week (Lehoux 2007). Virgil's *Georgics*, for example, captures a rhythm of country life which is quite independent of the city's *fasti*, and which is based entirely on meteorological patterns and lunar parapegmata. Time is organized and signalled in the georgic world by the constellations, the seasons, the forces of wind and rain, sun and moon. There is not a single date in the *Georgics*, nor the name of a month or a festival.

Further, the Romans made no effort to impose the calendar on their empire, and in this regard they are very unlike some other empires, such as the Chinese, whose ancient term for incorporating some new region into the empire was to say that its inhabitants had 'received the calendar' (Gell 1992: 313). In the originally less urbanized Latin West the Roman calendar rapidly became normative, but especially in the long-established civic culture of the predominantly Greek East local calendars in all their discrepant variety continued in use. Partly this is a reflection of the Romans' general administrative preference for laissez-faire and subsidiarity, and their lack of interest in imposing the calendar is related to a wide range of similar policies in other spheres, such as religion, where they made no effort to systematize empire-wide religious practice. Partly, however, this hands-off tendency reflected the way that the Roman calendar itself continued to be a distinctive marker of Romanness. Its reach was not universal: it was not meant to be a unifying grid for all the peoples of the empire, but retained its specific power for Roman citizens as a context for apprehending and exploring Roman identity (Laurence and Smith 1995–6: 148). Hence the crucial role of the calendar in the army, where it discharged an important acculturating function as it massaged the diverse recruits into an empire-wide unit through shared anniversaries and festivals. Where the army went, the calendar went too.

The special importance of the calendar in the Romans' work on their identity is nowhere more clearly visible than in the outsider's view provided by Plutarch in his so-called 'Roman Questions'. Plutarch composed two sets of *Aetia* ('Origins' or 'Causes'), one Greek, one Roman, commonly called the 'Greek and the Roman Questions' after their Latin titles, *Quaestiones Graecae et Romanae.* A dozen of Plutarch's 113 Roman *aetia* concern calendrical questions, such as: 'Why do they adopt the month of January as the beginning of the new year?' (*Moralia* 267F). Plutarch has fifty-nine Greek Questions, and only one of them refers to a calendar (292D).

The disparity is partly due to the fact that the Greeks did not have a single calendar for all Greeks, in the way that the Roman calendar can embrace all Roman citizens. Plutarch could, one imagines, have posed more than one question about individual Greek calendars, but the Roman calendar provides more of a unifying focus for enquiry. Still, the disparity goes much further. The exercise in comparison brings out how deeply Roman culture is implicated in the temporal and calendrical. For Plutarch, it is not possible to talk about Roman culture without engaging with their representations of time. What was true for Plutarch remains true for us.

Further reading

Laurence and Smith 1995–6 give an invaluable brief overview of the cultural meanings of the *fasti*; Samuel 1972 is the standard handbook on Greek and Roman chronology (much thinner on Roman). Hannah 2005 is an excellent introduction to the workings of Greek and Roman calendars, while Lehoux 2007 is now the last word on parapegmata. Blackburn and Holford-Strevens 1999 is a priceless resource; good discussions of the Roman calendar are to be found in Bickerman 1980; Brind'Amour 1986; Michels 1967; Rüpke 1995*a*. On synchronism and historiography, the overlooked work of Wilcox 1987 is fundamental; on time in historiography, see also Mazzarino 1966: 2.2.412–61; Momigliano 1977. On the problems of Roman chronography, see Cornell 1995: 399–402. On annalistic history, see Oakley 1997: 21–108. Zerubavel 2003 offers much rich comparative material on the organization of time. I discuss Roman representations of time in general in Feeney 2007.

References

Beard, Mary (1987), 'A complex of times: no more sheep on Romulus' birthday', *Proceedings of the Cambridge Philological Society*, 33: 1–15.

Bickerman, E. J. (1980), *Chronology of the Ancient World*², London: Thames & Hudson.

Blackburn, Bonnie and Holford-Strevens, Leofranc (1999), *The Oxford Companion to the Year: An Exploration of Calendar Customs and Time-Reckoning*, Oxford: Oxford University Press.

Brind'Amour, Pierre (1986), *Le Calendrier romain: recherches chronologiques*, Ottawa: University of Ottawa Press.

Coarelli, F. (1992), *Il foro romano*. Vol. 1: *periodo arcaico*³; Vol. 2: *periodo repubblicano e augusteo*², Rome: Edizioni Quasar.

Cornell, T. J. (1995), *The Beginnings of Rome: Italy and Rome from the Bronze Age to the Punic Wars (c. 1000–264 BC)*, London and New York: Routledge.

Dunn, F. M. (1988), 'The uses of time in fifth-century Athens', *Ancient World*, 29: 377–52.

Fabian, J. (1983), *Time and the Other*, New York: Columbia University Press.

Feeney, Denis (2007), *Caesar's Calendar: Ancient Time and the Beginnings of History*, Berkeley: University of California Press.

Frier, Bruce W. (1999), *Libri Annales Pontificum Maximorum: The Origins of the Annalistic Tradition*², Ann Arbor, Mich.: University of Michigan Press.

Gell, Alfred (1992), *The Anthropology of Time: Cultural Constructions of Temporal Maps and Images*, Oxford and Washington, DC: Berg.

Ginsburg, J. (1981), *Tradition and Theme in the* Annals *of Tacitus*, New York: Arno Press.

Gratwick, A. S. (1979), 'Sundials, prostitutes, and girls from Boeotia', *Classical Quarterly*, 29: 308–23.

Hanell, K. (1946), *Das altrömische eponyme Amt*, Lund: Gleerup.

Hannah, Robert (2005), *Greek and Roman Calendars: Constructions of Time in the Classical World*, London: Duckworth.

Hölkeskamp, K.-J. (2004), *Senatus Populusque Romanus: Die politische Kultur der Republik—Dimensionen und Deutungen*, Stuttgart: Franz Steiner.

Laurence, Ray and Smith, Christopher (1995–6), 'Ritual, time and power in ancient Rome', *Accordia Research Journal*, 6: 133–51.

Lehoux, Daryn (2007), *Astronomy, Weather, and Calendars in the Ancient World: Parapegmata and Related Texts in Classical and Near-Eastern Societies*, Cambridge: Cambridge University Press.

Mazzarino, Santo (1966), *Il pensiero storico classico*, Bari: Laterza.
Meadows, Andrew and Williams, Jonathan (2001), 'Moneta and the monuments: coinage and politics in Republican Rome', *Journal of Roman Studies*, 91: 27–49.
Michels, Agnes Kirsopp (1967), *The Calendar of the Roman Republic*, Princeton: Princeton University Press.
Momigliano, A. (1977), 'Time in ancient historiography', in *Essays in Ancient and Modern Historiography*, Oxford: Blackwell: 179–204.
Mommsen, T. (1859), *Die römische Chronologie*², Berlin: Weidmann.
North, J. A. (1989), 'Religion in Republican Rome', *The Cambridge Ancient History*², 7/2, Cambridge: Cambridge University Press: 573–624.
Oakley, S. P. (1997), *A Commentary on Livy Books VI–X*. Vol. I, Oxford: Clarendon Press.
—— (2005), *A Commentary on Livy Books VI–X*. Vol. III, Oxford: Clarendon Press.
Purcell, Nicholas (2003), 'Becoming historical: the Roman case', in D. Braund and C. Gill (eds.), *Myth, History, and Culture in Republican Rome: Studies in Honour of T. P. Wiseman*, Exeter: Exeter University Press: 12–40.
Rüpke, Jörg (1995*a*), *Kalendar und Öffentlichkeit: Die Geschichte der Repräsentation und religiösen Qualifikation von Zeit in Rom*, Berlin and New York: De Gruyter.
—— (1995*b*), '*Fasti*: Quellen oder Produkte römischer Geschichtsschreibung?', *Klio*, 77: 184–202
Samuel, Alan E. (1972), *Greek and Roman Chronology: Calendars and Years in Classical Antiquity*, Munich: C. H. Beck.
Stern, Sacha (2003), *Time and Process in Ancient Judaism*, Oxford: Littman Library.
Verbrugghe, G. P. (1989), 'On the meaning of *Annales*, on the meaning of Annalist', *Philologus*, 133: 192–230.
Wilcox, Donald J. (1987), *The Measure of Times Past: Pre-Newtonian Chronologies and the Rhetoric of Relative Time*, Chicago: University of Chicago Press.
Zerubavel, Eviatar (2003), *Time Maps: Collective Memory and the Social Shape of the Past*, Chicago: University of Chicago Press.

Name Index

Includes all referenced authors.

Subject Index

Illustrations are indicated by bold entries.

Ingram Content Group UK Ltd.
Milton Keynes UK
UKHW030646070723
424710UK00002B/2

9 780198 856009